INTELLIGENCE

INTELLIGENCE

THE SECRET WORLD OF SPIES
An Anthology

Third Edition

Edited with Introductions by

Loch K. Johnson
UNIVERSITY OF GEORGIA
SCHOOL OF PUBLIC AND INTERNATIONAL AFFAIRS

James J. Wirtz
NAVAL POSTGRADUATE SCHOOL

NEW YORK   OXFORD
OXFORD UNIVERSITY PRESS
2011

Oxford University Press, Inc., publishes works that further Oxford University's
objective of excellence in research, scholarship, and education.

Oxford   New York
Auckland   Cape Town   Dar es Salaam   Hong Kong   Karachi
Kuala Lumpur   Madrid   Melbourne   Mexico City   Nairobi
New Delhi   Shanghai   Taipei   Toronto

With offices in
Argentina   Austria   Brazil   Chile   Czech Republic   France   Greece
Guatemala   Hungary   Italy   Japan   Poland   Portugal   Singapore
South Korea   Switzerland   Thailand   Turkey   Ukraine   Vietnam

Published by Oxford University Press, Inc.
198 Madison Avenue, New York, New York 10016
http://www.oup.com

Oxford is a registered trademark of Oxford University Press

Library of Congress Cataloging-in-Publication Data
Intelligence: the secret world of spies: an anthology / [edited by] Loch K. Johnson,
    James J. Wirtz.—3rd ed.
        p. cm.
    Rev. ed. of: Intelligence and national security. c2008.
    ISBN 978-0-19-973367-5
    1. United States. Central Intelligence Agency. 2. Intelligence service. 3. Intelligence service—
        United States. 4. National security. 5. National security—Government policy—United States.
        6. Spies.   I. Johnson, Loch K., 1942–   II. Wirtz, James J., 1958–
        III. Intelligence and national security.
    JK468.I6I467 2011
    327.12—dc22   2010021364

Printing number: 9 8 7 6 5 4 3

Printed in the United States of America
on acid-free paper

This book is dedicated to the memories of
Michael Handel, Naval War College,
and H. Bradford Westerfield, Yale University,
early leaders in the field of intelligence studies.

ABOUT THIS BOOK

The **Third Edition** of *Intelligence: The Secret World of Spies (An Anthology)* provides a comprehensive set of readings in the field of intelligence studies. Loch K. Johnson and James J. Wirtz's anthology spans a wide range of topics, from how the United States gathers and interprets information collected around the world to comparisons of the American intelligence system with the secret agencies of other nations. The readings are written by renowned experts, and each article is prefaced by a brief, framing introduction written by the editors.

The text addresses a wide range of material including: the meaning of strategic intelligence; methods of intelligence collection; intelligence analysis; the danger of intelligence politicization; relationships between intelligence officers and the policymakers they serve; covert action; counterintelligence; accountability and civil liberties; the implications of the major intelligence failures in 2001 and 2002 regarding, respectively, the terrorist attacks against the United States and the faulty estimates about weapons of mass destruction in Iraq; and intelligence as practiced in other nations.

This edition also contains valuable pedagogical features, including: 39 articles on intelligence by leading experts (24 of which are new to this edition); 10 thorough, chapter-length introductory essays by Johnson and Wirtz, which serve as "road maps" for the reader; brief synopses of each article; author profiles; charts and figures on intelligence organization and leadership; discussion questions following each chapter; a select bibliography; and a new Epilogue.

BRIEF CONTENTS

CONTENTS

---

*   New in the Third Edition.

producers of intelligence, outlined in this chapter.

PREFACE

As the references at the end of this anthology indicate, several fine texts on intelligence have been published in the past few years. Missing, though, has been a set of readings to accompany them. We have tried to fill that gap with this collection of outstanding articles on intelligence. To help orient those who use this book, we have added essays of our own to introduce each set of readings. Selecting the pieces for this anthology proved difficult, because space limitations forced us to exclude many first-rate articles. We believe, however, that the articles included in this volume will provide the reader with a good introduction to the breadth of this fascinating and relatively new field of scholarly inquiry.

NEW TO THIS EDITION

More than half of the selections are new to this edition, filling previous gaps and taking into account the latest events and research findings in the field. For example, insights are presented into the intelligence failures associated with the 9/11 attacks against the United States. Fresh evidence on the faulty estimates about weapons of mass destruction in Iraq in 2002 is also included. Each section introduction has been updated and, further, a new epilogue is provided along with added attention to homeland security issues.

The book covers a wide range of topics, from the history of intelligence in the United States to how the nation gathers and interprets information collected around the world. It also includes comparisons of the American intelligence system with the secret agencies of other nations.

Among the specific subjects examined in the anthology are the meaning of national security intelligence; methods of intelligence collection; intelligence analysis; the danger of intelligence politicization; relationships between intelligence officers and the policymakers they serve; covert action; counterintelligence; accountability and civil liberties; the implications of major intelligence failures in 2001 and 2003 regarding, respectively, the terrorist attacks against the United States and the prediction that Iraq possessed unconventional weaponry; and intelligence as practiced in other nations.

ACKNOWLEDGMENTS

The editors take this opportunity to thank the authors and publishers whose work we reprint for allowing us to showcase their outstanding research in these pages. We express our appreciation, as well, to the reviewers who gave the draft of the third edition a thorough critique and offered many useful suggestions. They include H. L. Goodall, Jr. (Arizona State University), Mark M. Lowenthal (Johns Hopkins University), William M. Nolte (University of Maryland), and William H. Parrish (Virginia Commonwealth University). We also thank the Freedom House and the U.S. Senate for allowing us to draw on our earlier writings for them in the preparation of a couple of the introductory essays in this volume. We acknowledge our debt to Rebecca Eversole and Scott Oney for proofreading; to William J. Daugherty (Armstrong Atlantic State University), Allen Dupont (Young Harris College), Bruce Farcau (Valencia Community College), Gardel Feurtado (The Citadel), George C. Fidas (The George Washington University),

Glenn Hastedt (James Madison University), Ann Marie Kinnell (University of Southern Mississippi), Ken Kitts (Marion University), David Lorenzo (Virginia Wesleyan College), Pete Peterson (University of San Diego), Edward Schatz (Southern Illinois University), J. David Singer (University of Michigan), Stephan Sloan (University of Oklahoma), Frank J. Smist, Jr. (Rockhurst University), John D. Stempl (University of Kentucky), and Michael Turner (Alliant International University) for their guidance on article selection; to Leena S. Johnson for editorial suggestions; and to Lawrence J. Lamanna and Marie Milward, Ph.D. candidates in International Affairs at the University of Georgia, for their research assistance; to Angela Riley, Senior Production Editor, for production assistance; to Maegan Sherlock, Editorial Assistant, for editorial assistance; to India Gray for copyediting; and to Jennifer Carpenter, Acquisitions Editor, for her steady encouragement and enthusiasm for the project.

Loch K. Johnson
James J. Wirtz

ABOUT THE EDITORS

Loch K. Johnson is Regents Professor of Public and International Affairs at the University of Georgia, senior editor of the international journal *Intelligence and National Security*, and author of several books on U.S. American foreign policy and national security, including most recently *the Threat on the Horizon: An Inside Account of Intelligence Reform between the End of the Cold War and 9/11* (Oxford, 2010). He has won the Certificate of Distinction from the National Intelligence Study Center; the *Studies in Intelligence* Award from the Center for the Study of Intelligence; and the V.O. Key Prize from the Southern Political Science Association. He has served as secretary of the American Political Science Association and president of the International Studies Association, South. Johnson was special assistant to the chair of the Senate Select Committee on Intelligence in 1975–76; staff director of the House Subcommittee on Intelligence Oversight in 1977–79; and special assistant to Les Aspin, chair of the Aspin-Brown Commission on Intelligence, in 1995.

Born in Auckland, New Zealand, Professor Johnson received his Ph.D. in political science from the University of California, Riverside. At the University of Georgia, he has won the Josiah Meigs Prize, the university's highest teaching honor, as well as the Owens Award, its highest research honor. He also led the founding of the new School of Public and International Affairs at the University in 2001. Professor Johnson has been a Visiting Fellow at Oxford University (2003) and at Yale University (2005). In 2009, he was named a Phi Beta Kappa Visiting Scholar.

James J. Wirtz is Dean of the School of International Graduate Studies at the Naval Postgraduate School, Monterey, California. He is the author of *The Tet Offensive: Intelligence Failure in War* (Cornell University Press, 1991, 1994) and has co-edited several books, including *Strategic Denial and Deception* (Transaction, 2002) and *Balance of Power: Theory and Practice in the 21st Century* (Stanford, 2004). He is section chair of the Intelligence Studies Section of the International Studies Association and the President of the International Security and Arms Control Section of the American Political Science Association. He is general editor of the book series *Initiatives in Strategic Studies: Issues and Policies*, published by Palgrave MacMillan.

A native of New Jersey, Professor Wirtz earned his degrees in Political Science from Columbia University (M.Phil. 1987, Ph.D. 1989), and the University of Delaware (M.A. 1983, B.A. 1980). He was a John M. Olin Fellow at the Center for International Affairs, Harvard University, and a Visiting Professor at the Center for International Security and Cooperation, Stanford University.

ABOUT THE CONTRIBUTORS

James A. Barry served as deputy director of the CIA's Center for the Study of Intelligence.

Bruce D. Berkowitz, a former fellow at the Hoover Institute, is the author of several books and articles on U.S. intelligence.

Richard A. Best, Jr., is a Specialist in National Defense with the Foreign Affairs, Defense, and Trade Division of the Congressional Research Service, Library of Congress, Washington, D.C.

Richard K. Betts is Leo A. Shifrin Professor of War and Peace Studies in the Department of Political Science at Columbia University and author of *Soldiers, Statesmen, and Cold War Crises* (1991).

Robert D. Blackwill served as Special Assistant to the President and Senior Director for European and Soviet Affairs on the National Security Council staff from 1989–90 and, more recently, as adviser to President George W. Bush on Iraq.

James Burch is an officer in the U.S. Navy currently assigned to U.S. Northern Command, and has served with the National Security Agency.

Conrad Burns, a third-term Republican U.S. senator from Montana, is a senior member of the Defense Appropriations Subcommittee and a former Marine.

Frank Church, Democrat of Idaho, led the 1975–76 Senate inquiry into allegations of CIA abuses and served as chairman of the Senate Foreign Relations Committee.

Percy Cradock served as chairman of the British Joint Intelligence Committee from 1985 to 1992.

Jack Davis, a former CIA analyst, is currently with the CIA's Sherman Kent Center.

Alan Dershowitz is Felix Frankfurter Professor of Law at Harvard University and author most recently of *Preemption: A Knife That Cuts Both Ways.*

John J. Donohue is Leighton Homer Surbeck Professor of Law at Yale University.

Glenn Hastedt received his Ph.D. in political science from Indiana University, is chair of the Justice Studies Department at James Madison University, and is the author of *American Foreign Policy: Past, Present, Future,* 6th ed. (Prentice Hall).

Frederick P. Hitz, inspector general of the CIA from 1990 to 1998, is a lecturer at the University of Virginia School of Law.

Arthur S. Hulnick is Associate Professor of International Relations at Boston University, a veteran of U.S. Air Force Intelligence and the CIA, and author of *Keeping Us Safe* (Praeger, 2004).

Rhodri Jeffreys-Jones is Professor of American History at the University of Edinburgh and the author of several books on intelligence history.

Robert Jervis is Adlai E. Stevenson Professor of International Politics at Columbia University, former president of the American Political Science Association, and the author of many books and articles on international relations and intelligence.

Jennifer D. Kibbe is Assistant Professor of Government at Franklin and Marshall College and has been a postdoctoral fellow at the Brookings Institution.

Mark M. Lowenthal author of *Intelligence: From Secrets to Policy*, 4th ed. (2009), has served as deputy assistant secretary for functional analysis in the State Department's Bureau of Intelligence Research, as staff director of the House Permanent Select Committee on Intelligence, and assistant director of Central Intelligence for analysis and production.

Frederic F. Manget is with the Office of Legal Affairs at the CIA.

Phyllis Provost McNeil is a former CIA intelligence officer, U.S. Naval officer, and director of the Federal Executive Programs at the Kennedy School of Government, Harvard University, who served on the staff of the Aspin-Brown Commission in 1995–96 and wrote the intelligence history section of its final report.

Stephen C. Mercado is an analyst in the CIA's Directorate of Science and Technology.

William Nolte, a career intelligence officer with the National Security Agency, has also served as Deputy Assistant Director of Central Intelligence for Analysis and Production.

Alexander Orlov was head of Soviet intelligence in Spain during the Spanish Civil War when he defected to the West.

Paul R. Pillar is on the faculty of the Security Studies Program at Georgetown University. Concluding a long career in the CIA, he served as National Intelligence Officer for the Near East and South Asia from 2000 to 2005.

Paul J. Redmond is the former Chief of Counterintelligence at the CIA.

Jeffrey T. Richelson is author of *The Wizards of Langley, The U.S. Intelligence Community, A Century of Spies,* and *America's Eyes in Space.*

David B. Rivkin, Jr., is a partner in the Washington, D.C., office of Baker-Hostetler, and has served in legal and policy positions in the Reagan and George H. W. Bush Administrations.

Dakota Rudesill is a recent graduate of Yale University School of Law and severed in the U.S. Senate as a national security aide from 1995 to 2003.

Daniel Snow received an M.B.A. degree from the Marriott School of Management at Brigham Young University and has published on economic espionage.

Stan A. Taylor, a professor of political science at Brigham Young University, has served as a staff member of the Senate Select Committee on Intelligence (1976–79) and has co-authored *America the Vincible: U.S. Foreign Policy for the Twenty-First Century* (1994).

Gregory F. Treverton served on the staff of the Church Committee and as vice chairman of the National Intelligence Council, and is currently with RAND in Santa Monica, California School of Law.

Admiral Stansfield Turner served as Director of Central Intelligence from 1977 to 1981 and, previously, as the commander of the U.S. Second Fleet and the NATO Striking Fleet Atlantic, as well as the commander in chief of NATO's Southern Flank.

Stephen A. Vaden is a graduate of the Yale University School of Law.

Michael Warner serves as chief historian for the Office of the Director of National Intelligence.

Amy B. Zegart is Associate Professor of Public Policy at the School of Public Affairs at the University of California, Los Angeles.

INTELLIGENCE

I

INTELLIGENCE IN THE UNITED STATES

AN INTRODUCTION

Hamlet: "...we defy augury. There is a special providence in the fall of a sparrow. If it be now, 'tis not to come—if it be not to come, it will be now—if it be not now, yet it will come—the readiness is all..."

—SHAKESPEARE, *Hamlet*, 5.2.217–219

Americans have mixed attitudes when it comes to intelligence and intelligence agencies. Some are fascinated with the image of the secret agent, spy, or covert operator who moves easily across international boundaries, uses the latest high-tech gadgetry, frequents only the trendiest resorts, and spends his or her time with glamorous members of the opposite sex. Intelligence professionals happily cultivate this image. A Central Intelligence Agency (CIA) identification card and a well-crafted story about secret operations has gotten more than one Agency mail clerk off the hook for speeding in some country village. Some see intelligence agencies as rogue elephants, giant bureaucracies beyond public scrutiny or the control of elected officials. From this perspective, intelligence agencies are threats to democratic institutions because they can be hijacked by conspiratorially minded politicians to undertake some nefarious scheme.

Given that public accountability is central to democracy, some wonder whether intelligence organizations that undertake secret operations, deal with secret information, and produce restricted reports are compatible with government based on democratic principles. Others never think at all about intelligence organizations or prefer to believe that intelligence agencies possess unlimited information about all significant threats to national security. Every so often, however, a tragic event shatters the complacency of this third group, which of course includes its share of government officials, leading to much recrimination and a hunt for those responsible for the latest intelligence failure.

Today we live in the Information Age, in a world undergoing an information revolution. The Internet and desktop computers allow millions of people to access and manipulate unlimited amounts of data and to transmit information to a global audience at

1

virtually no cost. This type of capability was available only to large government organizations (for example, the CIA) just a few short decades ago. As the Al Qaeda terrorist attacks against the United States in September 2001 demonstrate, we also live in an age when intelligence, the ability to make sense out of this endless stream of data, is at a premium. The information revolution is affecting everyone, including intelligence analysts and the way they gather, analyze, and disseminate intelligence reports and estimates. But the full impact of the Information Age on intelligence agencies remains a matter of debate. With more state and nonstate actors acquiring the communications, transportation, and weaponry needed to influence world events, intelligence agencies face the challenge of trying to stay ahead of these actors before they can wreak havoc on U.S. interests. The Information Age has actually placed even greater pressure on the U.S. intelligence community to sift through this torrent of information to detect new threats to the United States and its interests.

DEFINING INTELLIGENCE

So what exactly is intelligence? Scores of definitions are available. Some are simple; Thomas F. Troy, for instance, defines intelligence as "knowledge of the enemy" (Troy 1991–92, 433). And some definitions, like the one offered by *The Economist*, are a bit more convoluted. According to this respected periodical, intelligence is

> the painstaking collection and analysis of fact, the exercise of judgment, and clear and quick presentation. It is not simply what serious journalists would do if they had time; it is something more rigorous, continuous, and above all operational…that is to say related to something that somebody wants to do or may be forced to do. (quoted in Troy 1991–92, 442)

Many definitions of intelligence begin with Sherman Kent's description of the concept. Kent, an early theorist and practitioner of intelligence, defined it as *knowledge*, as *organization*, and as an *activity*. This definition allowed him to describe the way intelligence services collect and analyze information, the finished intelligence product that agencies provide to policymakers, and the way intelligence services are organized (Kent 1949). Mark Lowenthal, a contemporary intelligence theorist and practitioner, borrowed a page from Kent's work when he devised

this succinct description of the three dimensions of intelligence:

> Intelligence as process: Intelligence can be thought of as the means by which certain types of information are required and requested, collected, analyzed, and disseminated, and as the way in which certain types of covert action are conceived and conducted.

> Intelligence as product: Intelligence can be thought of as the product of these processes, that is, as the analyses and intelligence operations themselves.

> Intelligence as organization: Intelligence can be thought of as the units that carry out its various functions. (Lowenthal 2006, 9)

We add a twist to Lowenthal's definition by adding the phrase *national security* to the term *intelligence* to suggest that the readings we have collected focus on issues of great importance, the stuff of national policy debate. *National security intelligence* contributes to the processes, products, and organizations used by senior officials to create and implement national foreign and defense policies. National security intelligence thus provides warning of immediate threats to vital national security interests and assesses long-term trends of interest to senior government officials. National security intelligence is of political importance because it can shape the course and conduct of U.S. policy.

INTERDISCIPLINARY APPROACH

In the essays that follow, our contributors address intelligence in the three ways described by Kent and Lowenthal. Sometimes they address intelligence as a process: Parts II and III, for example, address key facets of the "intelligence cycle," a commonly accepted way to divide the process of producing intelligence. Sometimes they write about intelligence as a product. References abound, for instance, to finished intelligence (research reports and analysis) and current intelligence (daily news summaries such as the *National Intelligence Daily*). The contributors also discuss the impact of organization on intelligence—that is, the way the structure of national intelligence and the relationship between and within intelligence organizations shapes intelligence processes and products.

Three academic disciplines have focused on the study of intelligence, and essays from each of these schools are contained in this volume. *Political scientists* are primarily interested in intelligence as a process. Drawing on the fields of psychology, organizational theory, security studies, and international relations, they explore the challenges inherent in developing accurate and timely estimates of current and future events. *Historians* provide compelling accounts of intelligence failures, explaining how the road to surprise, paved with what in hindsight appears to be clear indications of trouble, was missed or misinterpreted by analysts or ignored by policymakers. *Scholars of public policy* focus on the management and oversight of secret organizations in a democratic setting. They are particularly interested in striking a balance between the need for secrecy in intelligence matters to preserve and enhance national security and the need for citizens in a democracy to know about the activities of their government.

Because each of these schools borrows freely from the others, they generally use the same concepts, terminology, and history in their research. Their work also is cumulative in the sense that it incorporates earlier findings and reflects points of consensus in the literature on intelligence. The essays we have chosen suggest that despite different approaches and formal training, those writing about intelligence are forming a distinct and relatively coherent field of scholarly endeavor, a true interdisciplinary approach to the study of intelligence.

The essays we have selected reflect the way scholars organize their research in the field of intelligence studies. Part I offers an overview of the evolution of the U.S. intelligence community, as well as a look at the current literature on intelligence and a wide-ranging conversation on key intelligence issues. Parts II and III contain readings that address critical functions of the intelligence cycle (collection and analysis), which inevitably leads to a discussion of intelligence failures and surprise. Parts IV and V deal with intelligence dissemination (another critical aspect of the intelligence cycle), the general relationship between the intelligence community and policymakers and intelligence politicization, and the deliberate or inadvertent corruption of intelligence estimates. Parts VI and VII discuss the paramilitary (covert action) and security (counterintelligence) operations conducted by the U.S. intelligence community, activities of increasing importance to policymakers in the aftermath of the September 11 terrorist attacks on the Pentagon and the World Trade Center. The essays in Part VIII probe into the issue of intelligence oversight and the

problems that arise when secret organizations are maintained in a democracy. Part IX looks at the circumstances surrounding the major intelligence failures associated with the terrorist attacks of 9/11 in the United States, along with the faulty intelligence analysis in 2002 that concluded Iraq probably possessed weapons of mass destruction. Part X offers a brief look at intelligence organizations in other countries. Finally, the Epilogue sums up the major intelligence challenges that lie ahead for the United States and other democracies.

THE U.S. INTELLIGENCE COMMUNITY

Although some intelligence agents live in foreign capitals, work the diplomatic cocktail circuit, undertake daring operations, and are known to most of the world by an assumed name, most intelligence managers and analysts spend their careers at a desk, becoming experts on a few subjects. Their job is to scrutinize and make sense of the deluge of information provided by national collection systems—everything from agent reports to pictures taken by spy satellites. Some analysts work with information collected from people who know or have access to sensitive information. This human source intelligence is known as *humint*. The Central Intelligence Agency and the Defense Humint Service, which is part of the Defense Intelligence Agency, are the organizations within the U.S. intelligence community that collect the majority of humint. Analysts also work with signals intelligence (*sigint*), which is information obtained from intercepted communications, radar emissions, or data transmissions. The National Security Agency is the primary collector of sigint. Geospatial intelligence (geoint—formerly known as imagery or imint) is information gathered chiefly by the National Geospatial-Intelligence Agency, through the use of spy satellites and reconnaissance aircraft. Geoint sometimes offers realtime electro-optical, radar, or infrared images of specific areas of interest. Measurement and signature intelligence (*masint*) consists of data that describe distinctive physical characteristics of a specific event, such as measuring the contents of a rocket plume or the size of a nuclear explosion. The Defense Intelligence Agency and the armed forces collect masint. Analysts also participate in the inter-agency process, the way mid-level officials from across the U.S. government make and implement policy. They are members of specific expert communities who have a professional or academic interest in a given area of study.

Most intelligence work has little to do with physical exertion and everything to do with mental activity.

Once information is collected, it is disseminated to a variety of organizations to produce "all-source" finished intelligence. These analyses are at the heart of the "data fusion process" because they are intended to combine all relevant information to provide a coherent and accurate depiction of the topic at hand. All-source analyses of long-term interest are generally referred to as "intelligence estimates," although the intelligence community also provides all-source intelligence on topics of immediate concern.

Three civilian organizations provide the majority of strategic all-source intelligence estimates to national policymakers. The National Intelligence Council (NIC) consists of about 20 National Intelligence Officers who are experts on specific issues or regions. Working for the Director of Central Intelligence, they supervise the production of major intelligence reports, often referred to as National Intelligence Estimates (NIEs). The National Foreign Intelligence Board, which is made up of senior representatives drawn from across the intelligence community, approves the estimates produced by the NIC, thereby generating a "community-wide" position on a particular subject. The Directorate of Intelligence (DI) is where the majority of all-source analysis is conducted within the CIA. Organized into offices that cover geographic regions and specific political, military, or economic issues, analysts produce current intelligence and undertake long-term research efforts, such as NIEs. The third organization that produces all-source intelligence is the State Department's Bureau of Intelligence and Research (INR). It is organized into bureaus covering regional and issue areas, and its analysts supply finished intelligence to the Secretary of State and other Department of State officials. It produces the *Morning Summary*, which is provided daily to the Secretary of State.

The Department of Defense also maintains a vast network of organizations that produce finished intelligence, which deals mostly with foreign militaries. The DIA provides finished intelligence on military issues to the Secretary of Defense, the Office of the Secretary of Defense, and the Joint Chiefs of Staff. Additionally, each of the military services maintains specialized intelligence capabilities. The U.S. Army runs the National Ground Intelligence Center. It produces all-source analysis on foreign armies and security forces. The Intelligence Center of the Office of Naval Intelligence gathers information about foreign surface ships, submarines, and undersea weapons and monitors the capabilities of foreign sensor systems and ocean surveillance systems. The National Air Intelligence Center is the Air Force's analytical organization that monitors foreign air forces and space programs. The Marine Corps Intelligence Activity provides finished intelligence to guide acquisition decisions for the Marines and to plan military operations. Each of the unified commands (such as the U.S. Central Command, or CENTCOM) runs a Joint Intelligence Center that produces intelligence directly related to military activities in the unified command's area of responsibility.

Other government departments and agencies operate specialized intelligence bureaus. The Department of Energy's Office of Intelligence, for instance, collects open-source information and produces classified and unclassified estimates dealing with foreign energy and technology programs. The DOE is especially concerned with monitoring international programs that could lead to the further proliferation of nuclear weapons. The Treasury Department also maintains a small intelligence bureau that monitors international economic, financial, and security affairs.

Domestic counterintelligence activities are primarily the responsibility of the Federal Bureau of Investigation's National Security Division. The FBI investigates and monitors foreign efforts to spy against the U.S. government and industry. It also conducts operations against hostile intelligence services operating within the United States. Recently, the bureau has been under pressure to place less emphasis on investigating terrorist activities within the United States with an eye toward criminal prosecution and to take more direct action to capture or interdict terrorists before they can strike.

THE READINGS

In our first essay, a prominent intelligence historian, Michael Warner, examines the difficulties of studying intelligence. He explores various research methods and promising sources of information to enhance our understanding of how secret agencies fit into the framework of democratic governments. The second essay is drawn from the final report of the Aspin-Brown Commission (1996). Prepared by

Commission staff member Phyllis Provost McNeil, the essay offers an overview of the U.S. intelligence community's evolution. A former Director of Central Intelligence, Admiral Stansfield Turner, adds to the history lessons with a look at how U.S. intelligence functioned during the turbulent presidency of George W. Bush. Finally, a well-known scholar of intelligence based in Scotland, Rhodri Jeffreys-Jones, brings the story of U.S. intelligence up-to-date with his analysis of the CIA's decline in recent years.

1. SOURCES AND METHODS FOR THE STUDY OF INTELLIGENCE

MICHAEL WARNER

This essay, written by the historian for the Office of the Director of National Intelligence, charts the demanding terrain faced by scholars in the field of intelligence studies. Warner examines the challenges that accompany the selection of appropriate research methods to mine the voluminous archives on espionage now available in the United States and Europe.

Intelligence can be thought of as that which states do in secret to support their efforts to mitigate, influence, or merely understand other nations (or various enemies) that could harm them. By its nature as an activity that could involve the loss of fragile sources or means of understanding and influence—not to mention the lives of troops, subjects, and even leaders—intelligence is treated by its practitioners as sensitive and confidential. Even the accidental disclosure of some analytical, informational, or operational advantage over a rival or an enemy is presumed to be tantamount to the loss of that advantage while it is still potentially useful. Thus the penalties for disclosure have always been severe— and those for espionage even harsher. Nations have sought thereby to terrify disloyalty and also to protect the advantages that secret means seem to bring to decisionmaking. Wherever such life-and-death stakes obtain, intelligence is conducted with some full or partial cloak of secrecy, and the evidence of it is typically unavailable to onlookers.

Intelligence thus by definition resists scholarship. As a result, the study of intelligence is not one field but two. Intelligence studies have been conducted one way on the "outside," with no official access to original records, and another way on the "inside," where a few scholars have intermittently enjoyed sanctioned (if not always complete) access to the extant documentation. The differing natures of the source materials available to scholars on the inside and the outside, naturally, have caused academic researchers and students of intelligence to work differently from official historians and investigators in the employ of the state.

The sources and methods of both the "outside" and the "inside" scholars, interestingly enough, can bring their practitioners quite close to genuine historical understanding. Over the last 60 years, a handful of governments have episodically sought to understand the experiences of their various intelligence services. The results have been uneven, across and within governments, but they have been real, and in places they have laid a solid foundation for historical and even theoretical work on intelligence on the outside. Intelligence studies in academia, on the other hand, have quickened over the last two decades in the fields of history and political science as more scholars of the diplomatic and military arts grasp the importance of intelligence for their own disciplines, and gain familiarity with the relevant documentation. In so doing, they have begun to create a community of intelligence scholars and have helped to reclaim the study of intelligence from those who would have us believe in the omniscience or the omnipotence of the discipline's practitioners.

Both inside and outside scholars, however, labor under differing strains imposed by the nature of intelligence as a secret enterprise. These strains need not be debilitating, but they impose significant impacts on the quality of the final products. What follows is not a bibliographical or archival guide to records-holdings in any particular country. It is not possible in one article to survey the literature and collections around the world that hold documents of possible interest to researchers in the intelligence field. Even for researchers of intelligence in the United States, such a survey would have the ironic disadvantages of being both lengthy and vague. It would also be quickly out of date as new files are released. This chapter is rather a set of field notes for using the sources that are available and are likely to emerge over the foreseeable future. It is also a reflection on the burdens that must be shouldered by researchers on both sides of the wall of secrecy that surrounds intelligence.

WHAT ARE THE SOURCES?

In describing the sources used in the historical study of intelligence, it is easier to start on the inside and work outward. That is, by examining first the way in which intelligence activities appear to those holding access to the official records, and then how they appear to the much larger set of scholars who do not enjoy such access. Historians in the employ of their governments work primarily from the office and operational files, from cable traffic and budget data, and from interviews, artifacts, and other sources, to identify and assemble the clues to what happened and what it meant.

The first place for the official historian to look is always "the file." Like virtually all governmental organizations from the late nineteenth century onward, intelligence agencies are hierarchies, and their officers at multiple levels have created and preserved files on their activities. The growing professionalism and rationalism of the various agencies gradually supplanted the work of the amateurs, the friends of royalty, and the charlatans who had dominated espionage since ancient times. Efficient paperwork and good filing systems were keys to this evolutionary triumph. The sort of files that got saved—and eventually made their way to official historians—have tended to be archived by office first, by subject next, and then sometimes by operation or activity, according to the records protocols governing the larger department or organization in which they are embedded. Even the independent intelligence agencies of the United States adapted this classification scheme from the filing systems of the State and War Departments, without much change. Indeed, filing systems in their fundamental outlines seem so similar across organizations and eras that they would seem to be following almost a law of nature.

A mature organization will follow protocols governing how and when files are opened, maintained, archived, or purged. The extent to which such protocols are set and followed is an indicator of the quality of the organization's leadership—or at least of its administrative acumen. The researcher typically checks all the extant and relevant files he or she can locate, which means reading those from all the organization's levels of approval and review. Activities or subjects enduring over several years will have multiple files, some of them running for multiple volumes. Smaller and simpler activities or operations (which is not to say less successful or important ones) will obviously have thinner files. Files kept overseas are typically abbreviated; those at headquarters in the capital are longer, because there is more time to keep them, more clerical staff to do so, and usually more storage space.

One rule of thumb for the official researcher is that the more expensive the activity or topic, the more places one finds files on it. Costly activities and projects ordinarily require more personnel and logistical expenses, hence more accounting and security controls, and therefore more legal counsel, and thus more files. The agency's legal, financial, logistical, and security offices can be expected to keep their own files on larger activities. The director of the agency may have a file on it, if it demands his attention or a briefing for higher authorities. Something really important will merit files in other agencies, and in the executive branch's archives as well. These can be quite valuable for the researcher because they provide a different (if not always more objective) perspective on the activity.

Not all important incidents, projects, issues, or events are well documented. The converse is also true: events or topics with scanty documentation are not always insignificant. Here is a quandary in intelligence research: what to infer from a situation in which there are few or no files? That can happen in at least two circumstances. First is when events are happening too quickly for everything to be documented by the people on the spot. In such cases the documentation will typically come in the form of summary cables and after-action reports, which are good to have, but not always as accurate and complete as a researcher might wish. The second case is when the head of the agency or one of its units was specifically ordered to keep the "paper trail" as short as possible—possibly by destroying it. Such instances would seem to be rare, even in secret services, but there are exceptions that prove the rule (like the CIA's "Track II" in Chile in 1970), for reasons that should be obvious.[1] It is difficult to do anything in a bureaucracy without authorizations and funds, and difficult to show such authorization if it is not written down somewhere. More typical is that some extraordinary aspect will be added to an operation already under way, as with the abortive assassination plotting in the CIA's Guatemala coup operation in 1954.[2] Such operational annexes will most likely have been authorized orally.

Various officials for reasons of their own will sometimes keep "private" files. As these files are by definition maintained outside of the office's records management protocols, they are naturally structured in whatever way that keeps them useful and convenient for the individuals who created them. The saintly and conscientious intelligence officer who deliberately seeks to keep future historians well informed, however, is another rarity. Indeed, a savvy official historian immediately (if silently) questions the motives of anyone who keeps such a file, and wonders what axe he or she is grinding. The first such collection this author ever encountered was surely started because the compiler of it thought he should have been kept on as head of an office that had been assigned to the care of a younger rival. Simply put, he saved the items that made him look prescient, and hoped someone would notice someday. The more common private files to be saved, however, are compiled willy-nilly over the course of a career, as the official runs across something he thinks is interesting or amusing or otherwise worth squirreling away. Eventually he leaves or retires, and either "wills" his collection of miscellany to some colleague, or leaves it behind in a desk or safe to be found months or even years later by successors who might or might not take the trouble to save its contents.

The next place to look for records, especially if the activity took place overseas, is in the cable traffic. Intelligence agencies (even domestic ones) live by their official communications channels, and the messages sent along them are meticulously preserved and organized. Cable files are rigidly chronological, and cables themselves are supposed to be drafted so as to be economical and clear in their prose. They have to be, for the safety and success of the operation and the people involved, not to mention the expense of sending them.

Cables can be a wonderful source for historians, even when misleading, trivial, or turgid—or sometimes all at once. Indeed, when compared with staff memoranda produced at a leisurely pace in the home offices, cables generally seem terse, articulate, and definitive. Cables are the residue of a dying technology, however, and thus in reading them it is vital for the contemporary researcher to understand how cable traffic differs from modern messaging over computerized, global networks. Cables could take many hours to reach their recipients, especially if there were significant time-zone differences between the end points of the messages. In the days of hand encoding and decoding, moreover, a long cable usually meant late hours in the coderoom for some poor junior officer. Not a few cabled instructions had been overtaken by events by the time their addressee finally read them.

It almost goes without saying that telephone conversations are usually lost. Senior officials have always had their aides or secretaries keep office diaries and phone logs, and perhaps to paraphrase important calls as well. Prime ministers or presidents may even have had their conversations taped. The era is long past, however, and it did not last long to begin with, when senior *intelligence* officials would tape phone calls. By the 1960s important intelligence telephone calls were supposed to be placed on secure phones, the use of which has increased steadily over time as the secure phone networks expanded. Sometimes phone calls have presumably been recorded by foreign adversaries, but such third parties are rarely so kind as to release the transcripts to scholars.

A third key source for insider researchers is budget data. Budgets are sure indicators of the priorities of an organization, and to that organization's priority in the larger scheme of policy implementation. They are also an index for comparison in looking at operations themselves; they indicate the relative size of the operation, giving a rough indication of whether the project in question represents a barn, a table, or a thimble.

Agency-wide budgets serve another purpose— that of giving the researcher a benchmark for the quality of and challenges facing the organization's leadership. Declining budgets are a severe test of a leader's ability. Indeed, sometimes it can be high praise indeed to say that a agency head was only able to hold his ground; that he preserved the organization's core mission and staff and even maintained its operational tempo while his budgetary base eroded. Tough decisions are forced on a leader in such times; he or she has to trim somewhere to preserve other priorities, and such choices generally result in disagreements and even bitterness among the managers whose projects and offices lose out.

On the other hand, growing budgets force a different set of challenges on a leader. Budget hikes allow him to throw money at problems, and many directors are tempted to do just that, often with meager and short-lived results. In a situation of sharply increasing resources, merely maintaining previous levels of staff and activities is a sign of poor or challenged leadership.

Another help on the inside, sometimes, is the personnel file of someone involved in an activity. This is helpful especially when living memory is deficient. If it contains performance evaluations for the time in question, or names of other people involved, such a file gives a researcher important reference points. It also provides clues to the orientation of the officer in question—his professional training and background—that may have had a bearing on the decisions or operation in question. A roster of the personnel involved also helps in surmounting the difficulties posed for intelligence scholarship that are caused by secrecy and compartmentation. One cannot assume that an event that was prior in time helped to cause a later one, or a prior report caused a subsequent decision, since the personnel involved may have had no access to such information. Sometimes it is possible to show that someone involved in an earlier operation was—or could not have been—in a position of responsibility to have had a role in a later one. The converse is true as well—sometimes two things that looked similar were really independent, with no common personnel.

Lastly, for intelligence agencies after the mid-1980s, internal electronic mail records can be important, or even vital. American governmental agencies began putting crude computers on the desktops of their officials in the 1980s; the employees using these early hub-and-spoke systems could sometimes communicate with one another via simple messaging programs. It took another decade, and the decisive victory of the IBM-clone personal computer, for such technology to become ubiquitous in the government and its intelligence bureaus. After about 1995, the internal e-mail becomes an indispensable source.

These various forms of e-mail present several problems to the researcher. They might not exist for certain offices or periods, given the archiving requirements and habits of the agencies and the officials manning them. They may not reflect the views of all the important officers involved in a decision or an operation. The most important officials in any organization typically have the least time to write them, and thus an agency head will typically leave behind a thin collection of e-mails. E-mails collectively carry a huge amount of information—and more importantly, circumstance—but it is often highly fragmented and elliptical. They cannot substitute for traditional sources, both oral and documentary, because even in the age of e-mail, many decisions still get made face-to-face, or over the telephone.

Inside scholars use published secondary materials as much as they can get them, but generally for establishing context for narratives that are based primarily on still-classified files. It can be tough to square the outside histories with the inside information, and the insiders always worry that something produced on the outside is incomplete. Official researchers can rarely call a colleague on the outside to ask if she checked collections X and Y in preparing her latest book—in part because security considerations can preclude such contacts. This is the signature weakness of inside scholarship—it can never be placed fully in the context of the literature written on the outside and reviewed by all the people in the various scholarly disciplines who might be able to explain or expand upon its findings.

This lengthy discussion of sources for official research in intelligence must seem quite elementary to any historian working in the documentary record of twentieth-century military or diplomatic history. That is no coincidence, for military and diplomatic history is precisely what historical research in intelligence is. Intelligence is not some privileged realm where the usual dynamics of organizational and group behavior do not apply; intelligence agencies are bureaucracies, and thus no exception to the rules of historical scholarship. In studying them, the scholar gathers the records and facts and arranges them according to the time-honored ways of archival practice and scholarship. An intelligence service will possess more secrets, and sometimes more colorful characters, but its job is to assist the making and the implementing of a nation's strategic decisions. Its records therefore exist in the same milieu and the same patterns as the diplomatic and military ministries that intelligence serves.

SOURCES ON THE OUTSIDE

Scholarly work on the inside is often dedicated to the production of uncomplicated organizational or operational narratives. In contrast, writing intelligence history from academia or private life—that is, without access to the official, classified documentation—is in some ways more interesting because it is more difficult, depending on the availability of declassified documentation. Where there are files to work from, the outside researcher will use them in ways quite similar to that of his or her counterparts on the inside who have access to the complete official record. On the other hand, where few records have been released, the researcher has to appraise his or her sources in the knowledge that they are surely fragmentary. He has to word his judgments accordingly, erring always on the side of caution, and building to generalizations only on stable bases of fact.

Such a labor has traditionally resembled the writing of ancient history, with the advantage (sometimes) of having living participants to interview. Like ancient history, much of the best work is heavily literary in character, rather than historical in the Rankean sense of depicting events *wie es eigentlich gewesen war* ("as they actually happened"). This is not meant as a criticism or a pejorative. Livy, Tacitus, and Thucydides, to name but three ancient historians, sought by the portrayal of fascinating but flawed characters against the backdrop of grand narratives to illustrate the larger themes of nature, society, and Man himself.[3] Where histories of intelligence aspire to be more Rankean than literary, they tend to resemble in some ways the works of modern historians writing about ancient times. They have to rely on fragments, not files. Their chronologies are sometimes hazy. Physical evidence is sparse, and mostly monumental (i.e. on the scale of ruined public works). There are few surviving pictures to consult. Rumor and myth are everywhere, often so intertwined with fact that, in some cases just beyond the reach of living memory, truth and fiction can no longer be separated. The one obvious advantage that intelligence historians have over ancient historians is in the opportunity to interview their subjects—if they will talk.

A careful researcher first tracks down any and all official documents, studies, reports, and histories that might be available on his or her topic. In Western countries these documents are usually well-intended attempts at explaining their subjects. Such official releases have their distinct limitations: they are restricted by the scope of their charters (sometimes lamentably narrow), by the rigors of the declassification process (sometimes exhaustive), and by the objectivity, aptitude, and curiosity of their authors (sometimes curiously lacking). Nonetheless, they provide an important touchstone of accepted fact that the researcher can use as a platform for further inquiry, or at least a landmark along the way.

Such official products can be crucial. Indeed, the quality of the work done on the inside can eventually determine the prospects that outside scholars have for getting a story right (that should be a sobering thought for official historians). The multi-volume history of British intelligence in World War II produced under the supervision of Sir F.H. Hinsley in the 1980s remains a seminal work and a guide to scholarship not only in British but in Allied and Axis activities as well. The big break for scholars of the US Intelligence Community was the publication of the *Final Report* of the US Senate's special committee that met under the leadership of Sen. Frank Church in 1975–76. The so-called Church Committee's seven volumes mark the watershed in forming public knowledge of American intelligence. The Committee's survey of the history of the Central Intelligence Agency from its founding to the mid-1970s is not comprehensive but it is still particularly valuable, in being balanced, insightful, and reliable (in large part because it was based on the still-classified histories produced or held in the CIA's History Staff). The Church Committee volumes laid the bedrock for academic work on the Intelligence Community.

The researcher next looks for the declassified documents themselves, beginning with the most authoritative. The availability of such records depends on the country and the time period in question. For the years before World War II, many Western nations have made military and diplomatic files related to intelligence available to scholars, although often not the files of the actual intelligence bureaus. Many researchers in intelligence are interested in the period of the Cold War and its aftermath, however, and declassifications for them are typically piecemeal and incomplete. In some countries few if any records have been declassified. The bulk of those released in the United States represent finished intelligence products.[4] Few policy or administrative documents, and even fewer operational records, are available. Complete files are rarer still.

Integrating the inside and the outside is another parallel with ancient history. When real documents begin turning up in public archives, it can be tricky to match them up with the accreted legends that both informed and were themselves formed by an earlier body of literature written without any access to the sources. Ancient historians have to do a similar thing in trying to square the tangible discoveries of modern archeology with the epics of Homer, for instance, or the writings of Herodotus. Indeed, here is the capital shortcoming of intelligence scholarship on the outside: the lack of reliable data, and the consequent inability to determine when all the important records have been consulted.

News reports that are roughly contemporaneous with the activity under scrutiny are useful for both inside and outside research. They are fragmentary and often wrong, but they have a certain vitality and immediacy, and they not infrequently touch on ground truth (sometimes better than reporters know). Some intelligence operations show up in garbled form in the newspapers not long after they take place. The trouble for any outside observer is that of determining which of the myriad press reports accurately reflect real activities. This can be all but impossible to do, even for friendly intelligence officers reading in the newspapers about contemporary operations that security compartmentation gives them no formal access to. For adversaries it can be even tougher.

Memoirs of intelligence professionals, and of decisionmakers who relied on them, are often useful, especially if one bears in mind the adage that no memoirist loses an argument in his own memorandum-for-the-record. There are few "inside" memoirs, produced by an officer given access to the classified files and written as part of his official duties. Occasionally, a senior official will be given limited access to selected files some years after her retirement, and her manuscript will be sanitized to remove any classified information before it is published. More typical is the memoir produced with no access at all. A handful of memoirs are themselves small-scale intelligence operations—witness Kim Philby's *My Silent War*, produced while Philby was a pet of the KGB in Moscow.[5] His subtle mockery of CIA counterintelligence chief James Angleton—to name but one example—must be viewed according to how it may have served the KGB's interests to embarrass a pillar of its Main Enemy's defenses.

Oral histories should be viewed in a similar light. There are a surprising number of former intelligence officers at large who can be (but usually have not been) interviewed. Indeed, at the time of this writing, there are still several hundred living intelligence veterans of World War II, a handful of them actually working with US intelligence organizations today, six decades removed from the end of the war. This (sometimes) allows researchers to have their drafts commented on by participants in the historical events, or at least by people who knew "how it felt" to do intelligence work in 1944, or 1964, or 1984. Oral history, however, falls in the same historiographical genre as the memoir literature and has to be judged by basically the same rules (indeed, when the subject of an oral history has died, the transcript of his or her interview is for all intents and purposes an informal memoir). The advantages and pitfalls of oral history are well known, and need not be reviewed here. Researchers on the outside probably make better use of oral history than their counterparts on the inside, in part because for the former, memories may be their only sources.

RESEARCH METHODS

Intelligence emerged as a professional discipline before and during World War I, first in Britain, and soon afterward in the other belligerents. It developed from three prior disciplines: diplomacy, reconnaissance, and internal security, and the dividing lines between it and these fields have remained ambiguous, and porous. The scholar of it must know something of each of these fields—particularly how states defend themselves and employ their "levers of national power"—to understand intelligence. Just as the sources for intelligence history are often the same as those used by military and diplomatic historians, the methods are similar as well.

The sources largely determine the methods, in the sense that one must work with what one has. Over the last three decades we have seen rapid progress in the methods of historical inquiry in intelligence. The key to this development has been scholarly access to (and use of) declassified intelligence files from several of the combatants in World War II. That war was a conflict so vast and revolutionary (for some aspects of intelligence) that a familiarity with its details affords insights into the functioning of all twentieth-century intelligence disciplines and many of the organizations that undertook them. The benefits of this heightened understanding have particularly enriched scholarship among academic and private researchers in intelligence, but its independent impact on official historians in the intelligence agencies should not be overlooked. It affords them detailed knowledge of the personnel and precedents of Cold War agencies, and provides bases for comparison across agencies, disciplines, and even national intelligence systems. The resulting progress in methodology, both inside and outside the intelligence agencies, has at last raised intelligence scholarship in many instances to the level of quality achieved by diplomatic and military historians a generation or more earlier.

The key method for inside researchers—and their chief methodological advantage—is the drafting of a reliable chronology for the activity or organization under scrutiny. It is easier to write a coherent narrative when one can say what happened first, next, and last. Where chronology is not, or cannot be, established, the conclusions drawn from the evidence must be regarded as tentative or even as suspect. Chronology is a vital clue in sorting causes and effects, and more than one "urban legend" circulated among intelligence officials (and even among scholars) has been debunked by the simple method of carefully charting events along a reliable time sequence.

Chronology is vital in another way as well. Knowing not only the sequence of activities and events but also the timing of the production and subsequent release of (both internal and public) information about them helps one judge the value of secondary reference materials (and even of some primary sources). It is crucial to understand how much material was and was not available to the author of a history or the drafter of a memo. This is an obvious factor to consider in reading the work of historians on the outside. Anything written about strategic intelligence and military campaigns against Germany in World War II, for instance, must be read with particular care if it was published before the revelation of the ULTRA secret in 1974. Similarly with works on certain Cold War espionage cases in the United States, if published before the public release in 1995 of the "Venona" cables (the decryptions of Soviet intelligence telegrams sent to and from foreign posts, mostly during World War II). It is a factor to consider when reading histories written by government historians as well. Several early official histories of US intelligence, for example, were written without access to the mysteries of signals intelligence or "humint" operations. This reality does not falsify the arguments or discredit the facts cited in works published before these key releases, but it does make them incomplete in important ways.

Inside researchers also have an advantage in being able to establish reliable organizational charts. They can determine the degrees and channels of command and control. It is crucial to chart the hierarchy of organizations, sub-units, and personnel; accurate knowledge can hardly be overstated in its importance to understanding activities that take place in secret for the benefit of a handful of decisionmakers. This can also be done by outside researchers, when enough files are available; witness the labors of Philip H.J. Davies in charting the early history of Britain's MI6.[6] Determining subordination can be tricky for an observer of intelligence agencies, however, even when the individual under scrutiny held military rank. Not a few intelligence officers in the past have held deceptively insignificant ranks or titles, yet wielded considerable influence in their own agencies, and even over rival or allied organizations working in the same locale (Sir William Wiseman of MI6 during World War I comes to mind in this context).[7]

Another avenue into what intelligence was doing in a particular capital or operation is to undertake a careful reading of the political, diplomatic, and military events that provided the backdrop for the intelligence activities in question. Understanding what a president, premier, or commander had in mind (and what was far from his mind) provides a vital clue to a researcher. It allows later observers to speculate as to what those decisionmakers might have asked their intelligence operatives to obtain, to do, or to prevent. Whether one finds documentation of such "requirements" that way will obviously depend on whether the requirements were levied or not—on whether the leader actually asked for such results from his intelligence services, and whether the operatives in those agencies had the will and the capability to meet his needs.

The researcher should also read what the target of the intelligence activities has to say about the subject operation (or the agency that mounted it). That is, if a target says anything at all—in some instances an adversary never notices his pocket was picked. But ordinarily the adversary discovers the operation or activity at some point, and reacts. The scope and sharpness of that reaction can reveal how effective the operation might have been. Indeed, this gets close to another "method" for understanding intelligence activities: that of gauging the impact of an operation on the enemy. What if anything did it make him do, or what options did it deny him? If it seemingly did nothing, why not? These are vital questions to ask, and to answer, although they entail a significant risk. More than one researcher (and practitioner) has become captivated by the action-reaction-deception nature of the clandestine world and consequently been lost in the "wilderness of mirrors" that some critics take all intelligence work to be.

CONCLUSION

Guarding against such wandering among the mirrors of spy legends can be a difficult task, given the paucity of sources, but it is ultimately a worthwhile one. The researcher has three principal defenses, or rather three standards that transcend the seemingly closed world of secret activities. These are comparison, objectivity, and impact. All are tough to achieve, but consistently aspiring to achieve them has the beneficial effect of keeping intelligence scholarship from wandering into partisanship or irrelevance.

Both inside and outside scholars have sought to compare and contrast intelligence disciplines and organizations across multiple national experiences and time periods. Unfortunately, this is not yet possible to do in a systematic manner. Among large nations, only the United States has declassified almost all of its intelligence files from before 1941, and US intelligence before World War II still lacked certain operational components that several other countries had already developed. Undeterred, several scholars—Glenn Hastedt, Kevin O'Connell, and the late Adda Bozeman, among them—have done promising work in this field, drawing what seem to be valid generalizations from the secondary literature.[8] But even these pioneers of comparative intelligence systems would readily concede that their judgments must be tentative ones for the time being.

Objectivity is vital in intelligence scholarship. Partisan or bureaucratic biases have always afflicted writings about recent and contemporary events, of course, but they are easy to spot and probably do not do permanent harm. Many authors, of many persuasions, have managed to set such biases aside and write valuable works on intelligence. What is more debilitating in the long run is the subtler (and less conscious) bias that seeps in from the researcher's basic approach to writing intelligence history. One should remember that a bias can be for something or someone as well as against it. In the present case, one may be forgiven for concluding that academic historians will tend to favor "complexity" in their explanations; that journalists like to tell a good story, and that official historians will give their own agency the benefit of the doubt when narrating

disputes with other agencies. All researchers, moreover, can tend to privilege the views of the people who talked to them or were thoughtful enough to write things down and save their files. The historian must bear in mind the adage that "the man who saves his files tells the story"—but that man's piece of the story may not always be the most interesting or important part. Bias is admittedly a hazard for scholars working in the records of any organization, and not just for intelligence historians. It probably is a more serious one for intelligence scholars, however, given the paucity of reliable source material. Therefore the obligation to adhere to objective standards and judgments is all the heavier.

What these methods collectively point to is a constant need to search for the impact that intelligence made on events. The researcher, both inside and outside the organization, must constantly ask what it was that an intelligence agency actually accomplished with the mission, resources, and authorities allotted to it. How well did it serve decisionmakers in their deliberations and the conduct of their offices? These are tricky questions to answer even with full access. Determining how well an agency worked with what it had to work with is the intelligence scholars' contribution to achieving the ultimate goal of all intelligence scholarship: learning how intelligence made a difference. Did it make policy more effective, or less, and why? That in turn is a question that ultimately has to be answered by a community of intelligence scholars, both those on the inside and those on the outside, who can compare their respective sources and methods and reach consensus on the best ones to apply to various historical issues and questions. It is also a question that must be addressed by scholars of national and international affairs writ large, who must bring their techniques to bear alongside the findings of the intelligence scholars in crafting a fuller understanding of the past.

Patient and sometimes brilliant scholarship, both inside and outside the spy agencies, has taught us much about the history and the nature of intelligence. Such progress has been accomplished despite the problems faced by both "inside" and "outside" researchers. Those on the outside lack access to the full official record, while those on inside have a subtler but still serious impairment: their inability to have their findings reviewed by the optimum range of scholarly peers, and thus to consider the fullest possible context for their conclusions. Nonetheless, one can be encouraged by the growing tendency of official, academic, and private researchers alike to conclude from their studies that intelligence is, in the most charitable sense of the term, subordinate. By definition, it does not make decisions, negotiate treaties, win wars, or settle disputes; those functions are performed by policymakers, diplomats, judges, commanders, and their staffs. It is neither an omniscient conspiracy, nor an omnipotent panacea. Intelligence is a support function, sometimes usefully informing and implementing decisions. Its contribution assists (or hampers) national leaders in the conduct of their duties, but it cannot perform said duties for them. Beware any piece of scholarship that says it has.

QUESTIONS FOR FURTHER DISCUSSION

1. What sources and methods would you find most useful, were you to undertake research into the organization and activities of intelligence agencies?
2. What differences exist between "outside" and "inside" intelligence scholars?
3. Until recently, why have intelligence studies been ignored by mainstream academic organizations such as the American Political Science Association?
4. How would you characterize the sources and methods used by the author who prepared the first essay in this volume?

ENDNOTES

1. The Chilean campaign is discussed in detail by Kristian C. Gustafson in "CIA Machinations in Chile in 1970," *Studies in Intelligence* 47 (2003).

2. See Gerald Haines' addendum on this plot in Nicholas Cullather, *Secret History: The CIA's Classified Account of its Operations in Guatemala, 1952–1954* (Palo Alto, CA: Stanford University Press, 1999).
3. "My purpose is not to relate at length every motion, but only such as were conspicuous for excellence or notorious for infamy. This I regard as history's highest function, to let no worthy action be uncommemorated, and to hold out the reprobation of posterity as a terror to evil words and deeds." Tacitus, *Annals*, III:65.
4. James Van Hook of the Department of State observes that the most authoritative varieties of finished intelligence—such as the American "National Intelligence Estimates"—are truly committee products produced under tightly controlled conditions. In that way, and others, they may represent prime specimens for the application of textual "deconstruction" and other critical methods.
5. Kim Philby, *My Silent War* (New York: Grove, 1968).
6. Philip H.J. Davies, *MI6 and the Machinery of Spying: Structure and Process in Britain's Secret Intelligence* (London: Frank Cass, 2004).
7. Richard B. Spence, "Englishmen in New York: The SIS American Station, 1915–21," *Intelligence and National Security* 19/3 (2005).
8. Glenn P. Hastedt, "Towards the Comparative Study of Intelligence," *Conflict Quarterly*, 11/3 (Summer 1991). Kevin O'Connell, "Thinking About Intelligence Comparatively," *Brown Journal of World Affairs*, Vol. 11/1 (Summer/Fall 2004). Adda Bozeman, "Political Intelligence in Non-Western Societies: Suggestions for Comparative Research," in Roy Godson, ed., *Comparing Foreign Intelligence: The US, the USSR, the UK, and the Third World* (Washington, DC: Pergamon-Brassey's, 1988).

From Michael Warner, "Sources and Methods for the Study of Intelligence," in Loch K. Johnson, ed., *Handbook of Intelligence Studies* (New York: Routledge, 2007), pp. 17–27. Reproduced by permission of Taylor and Francis Books UK.

2. THE EVOLUTION OF THE U.S. INTELLIGENCE COMMUNITY—AN HISTORICAL OVERVIEW

PHYLLIS PROVOST McNEIL

Written by an Aspin-Brown Commission staff member, this essay reviews the long and colorful history of successes, failures, scandals, and reforms that have shaped America's secret agencies.

The function of intelligence as an activity of the U.S. Government is often regarded as a product of the Cold War. Indeed, much of what is known today as the Intelligence Community was created and developed during the Cold War period. But intelligence has been a function of the Government since the founding of the Republic. While it has had various incarnations over time, intelligence has historically played a key role in providing support to U.S. military forces and in shaping the policies of the United States toward other countries.

THE EARLY YEARS OF THE REPUBLIC

During the Revolutionary War, General George Washington was an avid user of intelligence as well as a consummate practitioner of the intelligence craft. Records show that shortly after taking command of the Continental Army in 1775, Washington paid an unidentified agent to live in Boston and surreptitiously report by use of "secret correspondence" on the movements of British forces. Indeed, Washington recruited and ran a number of agents, set up spy rings, devised secret methods of reporting, analyzed the raw intelligence gathered by his agents, and mounted an extensive campaign to deceive the British armies. Historians cite these activities as having played a major role in the victory at Yorktown and in the ability of the Continental Army to evade the British during the winters at Valley Forge.

In a letter to one of his officers written in 1777, Washington wrote that secrecy was key to the success of intelligence activities:

The necessity of procuring good intelligence is apparent and need not be further urged—All that remains for me to add is, that you keep the whole matter as secret as possible. For upon Secrecy, success depends in most Enterprises of the kind, & for want of it, they are generally defeated, however, well planned....[letter to Colonel Elias Dayton, 26 July 1777]

Washington was not the only one to recognize the importance of intelligence to the colonials' cause. In November of 1775, the Continental Congress created the Committee of Secret Correspondence to gather foreign intelligence from people in England, Ireland, and elsewhere on the European continent to help in the prosecution of the war.

Washington's keen interest in intelligence carried over to his presidency. In the first State of the Union address in January 1790, Washington asked the Congress for funds to finance intelligence operations. In July of that year the Congress responded by establishing the Contingent Fund of Foreign Intercourse (also known as the Secret Service Fund) and authorizing $40,000 for this purpose. Within three years, the fund had grown to $1 million, about 12 percent of the Government's budget at the time. While the Congress required the President to certify the amounts spent, it also allowed him to conceal the purposes and recipients of the funds. (In 1846, this latter provision was challenged by the House of Representatives, but President Polk, citing national security grounds of protection of sources, refused to turn over more specific information on the use of the Fund to the Congress.) Judging by the paucity of the historical record, interest in intelligence as a tool of the Executive appears to have waned in succeeding Administrations, although occasional lapses in performance sometimes produced controversy. During the War of 1812, for example, military intelligence failed to discover that British troops were advancing on Washington until they were 16 miles from the Capital. The Secretary of War had refused to believe that the British would invade Washington, and military intelligence reported from this perspective.

Intelligence regained prominence during the Civil War. Both the Union and Confederate leadership valued intelligence information, established their own spy networks, and often railed at the press for providing intelligence to the other side. The Confederate forces established the Signal and Secret Service Bureau with the primary charter of obtaining northern newspapers. On the Union side, the Departments of the Navy, State, and War each maintained an intelligence service. Union codebreakers decoded Confederate messages and learned that the plates for Confederate currency were being manufactured in New York. In June of 1861, the first electronic transmission of information was sent from an aerial reconnaissance platform—in this case, a balloon—directly to President Lincoln on the ground. Two months later, Union forces established a Balloon Corps. Although disbanded after two years, it succeeded in detecting a large concentration of Confederate troops preparing to attack at Fair Oaks, Virginia.

In 1863, the first professional intelligence organization was established by the Union forces, the Bureau of Military Intelligence. Headed by the Commander of the Army of the Potomac, General Joseph Hooker, the Bureau prepared evaluations of the Confederate Army's strength and activities based on sources that included infiltrations of the Confederacy's War and Navy Departments. It was considered the best run intelligence operation of the Civil War. Yet, Hooker's ineffective use of intelligence (reportedly he was inundated with information) was largely responsible for the Confederate victory at Chancellorsville. Similarly, it has been suggested that Lee's defeat at Gettysburg was partially attributable to his lack of intelligence on the strength and deployment of Union forces.

The Bureau of Military Intelligence was disestablished at the end of the war. A byproduct of its dissolution was the Secret Service, established in 1865 to combat counterfeiting.

A PEACETIME ROLE FOR INTELLIGENCE

Prior to the 1880s, intelligence activities were devoted almost exclusively to support of military operations, either to support deployed forces or to obtain information on the views or participation of other countries in a particular conflict. In March 1882, however, the first permanent intelligence organization—the Office of Naval Intelligence—was created within the Department of the Navy to collect intelligence on foreign navies in peacetime and in war. Three years later, a similar organization—the Military Intelligence Division—was created within the Army to collect foreign and domestic military data for the War Department and the Army.

The Administration of Theodore Roosevelt saw perhaps the most active use of intelligence for foreign policy purposes by any President until that time. Historians note that Roosevelt used intelligence operatives to incite a revolution in Panama to justify annexing the Panama Canal. In 1907, the President also relied on intelligence that showed the military build-up of the Japanese as justification to launch the worldwide cruise of the "Great White Fleet" as a display of U.S. naval force.

For the most part, however, the early part of the twentieth century was marked not by an expanded use of intelligence for foreign policy purposes, but by an expansion of domestic intelligence capabilities. The Justice Department's Bureau of Investigation (the forerunner of the FBI) was established in 1908 out of concern that Secret Service agents were spying on members of Congress. By 1916, the Bureau had grown from 34 agents focusing primarily on banking issues to 300 agents with an expanded charter that included internal security, Mexican border smuggling activities, neutrality violations in the Mexican revolution, and Central American unrest. After war broke out in Europe, but before the United States joined the Allied cause, the Bureau turned its attention to activities of German and British nationals within our borders.

WORLD WAR I

At the time the United States entered the war, it lacked a coordinated intelligence effort. As a champion of open diplomacy, President Woodrow Wilson had disdained the use of spies and was generally suspicious of intelligence. His views on the subject appeared to change, however, as a result of a close association developed with the British intelligence chief in Washington.

In fact, British intelligence played a major role in bringing the United States into World War I. Public revelations of German intelligence attempts to prevent U.S. industry and the financial sector from assisting Great Britain greatly angered the American public. Subsequently, British intelligence presented Wilson with the decryption of German diplomatic and naval traffic showing a German effort to entice the Mexican government into joining Germany against the United States in return for Texas, Arizona, and New Mexico if Germany won the war. Later declassified and disclosed to the public, this intercepted communication, known as the "Zimmerman Telegram," infuriated Wilson and added support to his address before a joint session of Congress in 1917 urging that the U.S. declare war on Germany.

In June of 1917, the first U.S. signals intelligence agency was formed within the Army. Known as "MI-8," the agency was charged with decoding military communications and providing codes for use by the U.S. military. In 1919, at the end of the war, the agency was transferred to the State Department. Known as the "Black Chamber," it focused on diplomatic rather than military communications. In 1921, the Black Chamber celebrated perhaps its most significant success by decrypting certain Japanese diplomatic traffic. The intelligence gained from this feat was used to support U.S. negotiators at a Washington conference on naval disarmament. Yet, despite such successes, President Hoover decided that the State Department's interception of diplomatic cables and correspondence could not be tolerated. Apparently agreeing with the alleged, yet oft-quoted statement of his Secretary of State, Henry Stimson, that "Gentlemen do not read each other's mail," Hoover returned the agency to a military orientation under the Army Signal Corps.

Other intelligence entities remained in existence after the end of WWI but saw their resources cut substantially. An exception to this general trend was the Justice Department's Bureau of Investigation, which saw a marked expansion of its mission and workforce. In 1924, J. Edgar Hoover was named director of the Bureau [renamed the Federal Bureau of Investigation (FBI) in 1935]. The FBI's charter was broadened particularly in the years leading to World War II, when concerns for U.S. internal security were mounting in the face of German aggression in Europe. The FBI was made responsible for investigating espionage, counterespionage, sabotage, and violations of the neutrality laws. It was also during this period that the first effort was made to coordinate the activities of the various intelligence elements of the Government. An Interdepartmental Intelligence Coordinating Committee was created for this purpose, but because the Committee lacked a permanent chair and participating agencies were reluctant to share information, it had limited impact.

WORLD WAR II AND ITS AFTERMATH

The years immediately before the United States entered World War II saw American interest in developments in Europe and the Pacific intensify dramatically, prompting both formal and informal efforts to gather and analyze information. President Franklin Roosevelt relied heavily on American and British friends traveling abroad to provide him with intelligence on the intentions of other leaders. One such friend was William J. Donovan, an aficionado of intelligence and a veteran of World War I, whom Roosevelt sent to Europe in 1940 to gather information on the stability of Britain and again in the spring of 1941 to gather information on Italian Dictator Mussolini, among other matters. Upon his return, Donovan lobbied hard for the creation of a centralized, civilian intelligence apparatus to complement that of the military.

In July 1941, in response to Donovan's urging, Roosevelt appointed Donovan as Coordinator of Information (COI) to form a non-military intelligence organization. The Coordinator of Information was to "collect and analyze all information and data which may bear upon the national security" for the President and those he designated. The Coordinator was given the authority, "with the approval of the President," to request data from other agencies and departments, but was specifically admonished not to interfere with the duties and responsibilities of the President's military and naval advisers. FBI Director J. Edgar Hoover, fearing a loss of authority to the new Coordinator, secured the President's commitment that the Bureau's primacy in South America would not change.

Borrowing heavily from the British intelligence model, Donovan created a special staff to pull together and analyze all national security information and empaneled an eight-member review board, drawn from academia, to review analysis and test its conclusions. In concert with the Librarian of

Congress, COI Donovan organized the Division of Special Information at the Library, to work with Donovan's analytical staff and to coordinate scholarship within the Library and in academia. In theory, the Division was to provide unclassified information to Donovan's staff, who would combine it with classified information to produce an analysis that would be reviewed by the special board before presentation to the President. Although in practice the process did not operate precisely as planned, the concept of centralized analysis was established.

The surprise attack on Pearl Harbor by the Japanese on December 7, 1941, brought America into the war and revealed a significant failure on the part of the U.S. intelligence apparatus. As subsequent investigations found, intelligence had been handled in a casual, uncoordinated manner, and there had been insufficient attention to certain collection requirements. The lack of coordination among agencies, principally the Army and the Navy, resulted in a failure to provide timely dissemination of relevant information to key decisionmakers. Moreover, intelligence analysts had grossly underestimated Japanese capabilities and intentions, revealing a tendency to misunderstand Japanese actions by looking at them with American cultural biases. After the war, the resolve of America's leaders "never again" to permit another Pearl Harbor largely prompted the establishment of a centralized intelligence structure.

America's entrance into World War II created an immediate need for intelligence to support the warfighter. While the Army and the Navy maintained their own intelligence capabilities, none were prepared to provide the kind of support needed.[1] To bolster this effort, the Office of Strategic Services (OSS) was created in June 1942, under the recently established Joint Chiefs of Staff to succeed the Coordinator of Information. William Donovan remained in charge of the reorganized unit. In addition to assuming the analytical role of its predecessor, the OSS was chartered to carry out clandestine operations against the Axis powers on a worldwide scale. It was not, however, readily accepted by the Joint Chiefs of Staff (JCS), who remained skeptical of the value of OSS activities, and the new unit faced strong competition from the FBI and the Army's intelligence organization.

Usually glamorized as the dashing operations arm of the U.S. Army (with its well-known espionage exploits with the Resistance in Europe), the OSS's contribution to intelligence production has gone largely unnoticed. It was, however, one of the seven major intelligence producers and was an important training ground for a generation of intelligence analysts, as well as operatives. Decidedly different than the British system, the OSS established the tradition of putting analysts and operatives in the same organization. The difficulties, however, that the OSS had in establishing itself within the JCS structure reaffirmed Donovan's belief that the peacetime successor to the OSS should be a civilian organization directly responsible to the President. In 1944, Donovan started campaigning for this model.

In the meantime, substantial intelligence capabilities were created in the military services to support the war effort. Army intelligence operations were supervised by the Military Intelligence Division of the Army General Staff. Its operating arm, the Military Intelligence Service (MIS), was created in 1942 and carried out collection activities around the world, including agent operations, signals interception, and photo reconnaissance. MIS also provided intelligence analysis to U.S. and allied commands. At the same time, intelligence elements were assigned directly to operating forces in the field. These intelligence units collected and analyzed tactical signals intelligence, interpreted photos, and performed ground reconnaissance missions. Aerial reconnaissance missions were run by the Army Air Corps. To provide counterintelligence support, including the debriefing of prisoners and defectors, the Army Counterintelligence Corps was established in 1942 with both domestic and overseas missions.

Army signals intelligence analysts succeeded in breaking and exploiting the code systems used by the Imperial Japanese Army, producing intelligence which many believe shortened the war in the Pacific. In England, after the U.S. joined the war, Army teams participated in the work begun by the Polish and continued by the British to decode German military communications encrypted with the Enigma cipher machines. The intelligence produced by this effort, codenamed "ULTRA," gave the Allies unparalleled insight into the workings of the German military and shortened the war in Europe.

Within three days of the devastating and embarrassing attack on Pearl Harbor, the Navy's Combat Intelligence Unit at Pearl Harbor was busy trying to crack the Japanese Fleet code, JN25. By April 1942, enough information was known to allow the American Pacific Fleet to deal the first blow without visual sighting of the Japanese Fleet at the Battle of Coral Sea. By May 1942, Navy cryptanalysts succeeded in cracking the Japanese code. This significant naval intelligence capability, on par with the British and Polish decryption of the German code, allowed the Americans to defeat the Japanese at the Battle of Midway and to countermeasure the Japanese during the rest of the war in the Pacific.

Also in the Pacific theater, an Allied Translator and Interpreter Section, composed of 2,000 American Nisei soldiers, interrogated Japanese prisoners and exploited captured documents. Since the OSS did not operate in the South Pacific Theater, special human source intelligence capabilities were established, using Australian and Philippine guerrilla forces as well as a special Army long-distance reconnaissance team known as the Alamo Scouts.

Similarly, the Marine Corps developed and deployed the Navajo Code Talker Program in May 1942. By 1945, operating in both theaters of the War, 400 Native American Navajo members of the Corps were encoding, transmitting, and decoding English messages in the complex language of the Navajo Indians. The Code Talkers have been credited with playing a significant role in the Marine Corps victory on Iwo Jima. So successful was this method of encryption and communication that it was employed in the Korean and Vietnam conflicts.

Toward the end of the war, the Administration was left to decide what to do with these intelligence capabilities. A vigorous and heated debate ensued between those who favored the Donovan idea of an independent, civilian intelligence organization reporting directly to the President and those who favored retention and control of intelligence by the military. The State Department, among others, weighed in heavily against the Donovan approach.

In September 1945, while the debate continued, President Truman, acting on a recommendation from his Budget Director, abolished the OSS by Executive Order and divided its functions between the War and State Departments. State received the research and analysis function, combining it with the existing analytical office to form the Interim Research and Intelligence Service (IRIS). The War Department formed the Strategic Services Unit (SSU) out of the clandestine side of the OSS. President Truman had unrealized hopes that the State Department would take over the coordination of intelligence for the Government.

At about the time the OSS was being disbanded, a study commissioned by Navy Secretary James Forrestal and chaired by private businessman Ferdinand Eberstadt was published. While the report dealt principally with the issue of military unification, it also recommended coordination of the intelligence function through the establishment of a National Security Council (NSC) and a Central Intelligence Agency (CIA). The NSC would coordinate the civilian and military national security policy for the President. The CIA, under the auspices of the NSC, would serve "to coordinate national security intelligence." While the military generally supported the recommendation calling for centralized coordination of "national security" intelligence, it was unwilling to give up its own collection programs and analytical capabilities.

THE CENTRAL INTELLIGENCE GROUP

While the recommendations of the Eberstadt study were to influence significantly the content of what eventually became the National Security Act of 1947, they were not immediately implemented. However, President Truman decided to settle the question of whether there should be a centralized civilian intelligence organization.

Reflecting his dissatisfaction with what he perceived to be the haphazard nature of intelligence collection, his desire to have one authoritative source for intelligence advice, and, above all, his desire to avoid another Pearl Harbor, President Truman issued an executive directive on 22 January 1946 establishing a National Intelligence Authority, a Central Intelligence Group (CIG) "under the direction of a Director of Central Intelligence" (DCI), and an Intelligence Advisory Board. The latter body comprised civilian and military heads of intelligence agencies who were to advise the DCI. The National Intelligence Authority, comprising the Secretaries of War, State, Navy, and the President's personal representative, was charged with planning, developing, and coordinating the intelligence effort. Finally, the CIG (a small interdepartmental group—not an independent agency) was responsible for coordinating, planning, evaluating, and disseminating intelligence and overtly collected information. Funding and staffing of the CIG were provided by other departments and agencies which retained control over their own intelligence efforts.

The first DCI, Rear Admiral Sidney Souers (who wrote the intelligence section of the Eberstadt study), reluctantly accepted the appointment and stayed in the position only six months. Under his tenure, the

CIG played a limited analytical role due to Souers' reluctance to challenge the analytical product of the State Department's IRIS. But the IRIS was soon decimated by congressional budget cutting, and most of its positions were dispersed throughout the Department and to other agencies. In all, 600 positions were transferred from the IRIS to the National Intelligence Authority, the CIG, and the military services. This left the Department with a skeleton analytic group, thus limiting its mission to providing intelligence support only to the policymakers within the Department of State.[2]

The second DCI, Lieutenant General Hoyt Vandenberg, proved more aggressive than his predecessor, gaining authority for the CIG to hire personnel and acquire its own administrative support, as well as expanding clandestine collection, research and analysis, and the overall size of the organization. At the behest of the President, the first national estimate, on Soviet intentions and capabilities, was produced in 1946 during Vandenberg's tenure.

At the time Vandenberg became DCI, in June of 1946, legislation was being drafted in the Congress and in concert with the Truman Administration to provide for the unification of the military establishment under a Secretary of Defense. Inasmuch as the CIG would need an annual appropriation to continue in existence, Vandenberg saw an opportunity to incorporate legislative language creating an independent central intelligence agency with several features modeled on the existing charter of the CIG. Within a month of assuming the duties of DCI, Vandenberg submitted a proposal describing this new entity, with the support of the Truman Administration, which consisted basically of the pertinent language from the 1946 presidential directive and language that had been previously published in the Federal Register.

THE NATIONAL SECURITY ACT OF 1947

In the ensuing congressional debate on the Vandenberg proposal, several issues emerged about the role of the DCI.

One was whether the DCI should be a civilian or military officer. Some argued that if the DCI were an active duty military officer, he would be subject to the control of his parent service. On the other hand, the military was recognized as the principal consumer of intelligence and controlled most of the resources devoted to it. The legislation ultimately provided that the President could appoint either a civilian or a military officer as the DCI, but if a military officer were appointed, he would be removed from the control of his parent service.

Another issue was whether the DCI should be a member of the National Security Council that was being established by the bill as the White House focal point for national security matters. Navy Secretary James Forrestal argued strongly against this proposal saying that the Council would be too large to accomplish its business and that the new DCI would have ready access without formal membership. His argument was persuasive and the DCI's proposed membership on the NSC was dropped.

A third issue was the relationship of the DCI to other agencies, in particular, the FBI. The draft proposal provided that the new Central Intelligence Agency would serve as the focal point within the Government where intelligence would be gathered and evaluated. As such, the CIA would necessarily require access to information collected by other agencies. The military agreed to this coordinating role for the CIA so long as the military was able to maintain its own collection and analytical capabilities to support military operations. The FBI, however, insisted on limiting the CIA's access to FBI files only if written notice was given first and only if access was "essential to the national security."

On July 27, 1947, President Truman signed into law the National Security Act of 1947, creating a postwar national security framework. A National Security Council was created to coordinate national security policy. The Act created the position of Secretary of Defense and unified the separate military departments (the Army, the Navy, and the newly created Air Force) under this position. The Act also established the Joint Chiefs of Staff to serve as the principal military advisers to the President and the Secretary of Defense. Finally, a Central Intelligence Agency was established with the Director of Central Intelligence as its head. At the time of its creation, the CIA was the only agency charged with a "national" intelligence mission.

The statutory language regarding the authorities and functions of the new Central Intelligence Agency was left intentionally vague. In part this reflected the bureaucratic sensitivities involved in specifying in the law the DCI's roles and missions in regard to other agencies, and, in part, the desire to avoid wording that other governments might find offensive. Thus, there was no mention of "espionage" or "spying" in the statute, nor was there any wording to suggest that covert actions (i.e., secret operations to influence political conditions in other countries) were part of the new agency's charter. Rather, the CIA was authorized to perform "services of common concern" to other intelligence agencies as may be determined by the National Security Council and to perform "such other functions and duties related to intelligence affecting the national security as the National Security Council may from time-to-time direct." (The NSC did, in fact, issue directives in 1947 and 1948, providing specific authority for CIA's operational and analytical functions.)

The 1947 Act also included an express prohibition on the CIA's having any "police, subpoena, law-enforcement powers, or internal security functions," reflecting the congressional and public desire to ensure that they were not creating a U.S. "Gestapo" and to preserve the FBI's primacy in domestic matters. The law also made the DCI responsible for "protecting intelligence sources and methods from unauthorized disclosure."

THE EARLY YEARS OF THE CIA

The early years of the CIA appear to have been difficult ones as the Agency attempted to establish itself within the Government, amid growing concern about Communist gains in Eastern Europe and Soviet expansionism.

Rear Admiral Roscoe Hillenkoetter was DCI at the time the CIA was created. He organized the Agency into two principal divisions: one dealing with intelligence operations and the other with analysis. The analytical arm, in response to policymaker interest, prepared and disseminated short-term intelligence pieces. DCI Hillenkoetter found it difficult, however, to force other agencies to participate in the development of longer papers despite the language of the 1947 Act. The emphasis on producing short-term pieces, on the other hand, was often seen as intruding on the role of other producers such as the State Department, the military departments, and the FBI. There was also conflict on the operational side. The Government considered initiating psychological warfare operations overseas to counter Soviet expansionism, but the NSC preferred that the State Department, rather than the CIA, be responsible for them. It was only when the Secretary of State vigorously objected to this role for the Department that it was assigned to the CIA.

In January 1948, less than a year after the CIA was created, the National Security Council, exercising its oversight role under its Executive Secretary Sidney Souers,[3] asked three private citizens to examine comprehensively CIA's "structure, administration, activities, and interagency relations." Allen Dulles, William Jackson and Matthias Correa, three New York lawyers with experience in intelligence, submitted their highly critical report in January 1949. Although the NSC found the criticism of DCI Hillenkoetter and the CIA "too sweeping," it nevertheless accepted the report's basic findings: CIA was not coordinating intelligence activities in the Government; the correlation and evaluation functions were not well organized, and other members of the fledgling Intelligence Community were not fully included in the estimates process; and the DCI lacked sufficient day-to-day contact with the work of CIA. The Dulles-Jackson-Correa report called upon the DCI to exert "forthright leadership," and to actively use existing coordination bodies, such as the Intelligence Advisory Committee (IAC) comprising the leaders of the military and civilian intelligence agencies. For example, the report urged that the final coordination of intelligence estimates be done through IAC, to establish estimates as "the most authoritative statement[s] available to policymakers."

The Dulles-Jackson-Correa report also made the point that coordination and planning could only be effective with a strong DCI and CIA. It therefore recommended that the DCI reorganize his office to include on his immediate staff the heads of CIA's main components. The report also stated that the CIA would benefit from civilian leadership and recommended that if another military DCI was appointed, he should resign his military commission "to free him from all service ties and from rotations that would preclude the continuity needed for good intelligence work."[4]

Also during 1948, the Congress established "The Commission on Organization of the Executive Branch of the Government." Chaired by former President Herbert Hoover, the Commission established a sub-group to look at national security organizations, including CIA. This group, headed by New York businessman Ferdinand Eberstadt,[5] concluded that the basic organizational arrangements for national security were sound, but there were problems in carrying out the function. The CIA was specifically criticized for not being properly organized to assimilate all information concerning scientific developments abroad, to estimate the significance of these developments, and to give direction to collectors. Concern was also expressed that the CIA was not being given access to all available information within the Government. The fear that other countries might develop nuclear weapons led the Eberstadt group, with some urgency, to state:

> Failure properly to appraise the extent of scientific developments in enemy countries may have more immediate and catastrophic consequences than failure in any other field of intelligence.

In its November 1948 report, the Hoover Commission mission called for "vigorous efforts" to improve CIA's internal structure and the quality of its product, especially in scientific and medical intelligence. A senior-level "evaluation board or section" within CIA was proposed to work solely on intelligence evaluations. Finally, the Commission urged positive efforts to foster "relations of mutual confidence" between CIA and its consumers.[6]

Lieutenant General Walter Bedell Smith, who succeeded Hillenkoetter as DCI soon after the outbreak of the Korean War, took the initial steps to implement the recommendations of the Hoover and the Dulles-Jackson-Correa reports. Among his first steps was to recruit Allen Dulles, an OSS veteran, as Deputy Director for Plans, and to establish a Board of National Estimates chaired by William Langer of Harvard University.

In 1949, Congress enacted additional legislation for the CIA providing its Director with certain administrative authorities necessary for the conduct of clandestine intelligence activities that were not available to government agencies generally. In particular, the new law permitted the DCI to expend appropriated funds for procuring goods and services to carry out the Agency's functions without having to comply with the cumbersome procurement rules applicable to other government agencies. It also permitted the Agency to expend appropriated funds based solely on a voucher signed by the DCI.

1950S AND 1960S: THE DEVELOPMENT OF THE INTELLIGENCE COMMUNITY

The decades of the 1950s and 1960s saw an expansion and an intensification of the Cold War as well as an expansion in the size and responsibilities of U.S. intelligence agencies to cope with its challenges.

THE 1950S

Acting on the recommendations of a commission of senior officials headed by George Brownell,

President Truman, by classified memorandum, established the National Security Agency (NSA) in October 1952 in recognition of the need for a single entity to be responsible for the signals intelligence mission of the United States. Placed within the Department of Defense, NSA assumed the responsibilities of the former Armed Forces Security Agency as well as the signals intelligence responsibilities of the CIA and other military elements. In 1958, the National Security Council issued directives that detailed NSA's mission and authority under the Secretary of Defense.

CIA meanwhile made important strides. Its analytical efforts during the Korean War established the Agency as a key player in the defense and foreign policy areas. On the operational side, the National Security Council reissued its 1948 directive on covert action to achieve peacetime foreign policy objectives in 1955, reemphasizing that implementation responsibility was with the CIA. In 1954, President Eisenhower approved the concept of a high-flying reconnaissance aircraft to fly above the Soviet air defense systems. Due largely to CIA's special procurement authorities and ability to carry out the mission in secret, the President established the effort as a joint CIA-Air Force program. The ability of the program to develop and field the U-2 (by 1955) earlier than planned and below the original cost estimate was a clear success for the participants. Before the end of the decade photos provided by the U-2 figured prominently in defense planning.

In 1954, Congress once again sought to examine the organization and efficiency of the Executive Branch and revived "The Commission on Organization of the Executive Branch of the Government." With former President Hoover again at the helm, the "Second Hoover Commission" formed a sub-group headed by General Mark Clark to study the agencies of the Intelligence Community.[7]

The Clark task force recommended that the CIA be reorganized internally to focus better on its primary missions, and that the DCI appoint a "Chief of Staff" or executive officer to run the day-to-day operations.[8] It also called for a permanent "watchdog" commission to oversee the CIA, comprising members of the House and Senate and distinguished private citizens appointed by the President.[9] A year later, in 1956, President Eisenhower established the Presidential Board of Consultants on Foreign Intelligence Activities (later renamed the President's Foreign Intelligence Advisory Board by President Kennedy). Shortly after it was formed, the Board issued a critical review of the DCI's management of the Intelligence Community. Later, in 1957, on the Board's recommendation, President Eisenhower established the United States Intelligence Board as the single forum for all intelligence chiefs to provide advice to the DCI on intelligence activities.

In 1957, spurred by the Soviet launch of Sputnik, the CIA and the Air Force began planning for the first photo reconnaissance satellite. Publicly referred to as "the Discoverer Weather System" and recently declassified as "CORONA," the system was successfully operational by 1962.

THE 1960S

The decade of the 1960s was marked by significant technological advances, further expansion of the Intelligence Community, and the first tentative efforts of a DCI to exert control over it. But, as far as the public was concerned, it started with the notable failure of the CIA at the Bay of Pigs. An invasion of Cuban expatriates, trained by the CIA, launched an invasion of Cuba in the spring of 1961 with the intent of ousting the Castro regime. Without U.S. military assistance, the invasion crumbled. The reputation of the Agency suffered significantly.

In August of the same year, Secretary of Defense McNamara created the Defense Intelligence Agency (DIA) to consolidate and to coordinate the production of intelligence analysis by each of the military services and to serve as the principal source of intelligence support to the Secretary and his staff, as well as to the Joint Chiefs of Staff and the unified commands. DIA opened a new production center in 1963, but the military departments continued to maintain their own analytical capabilities. In 1965, DIA was given responsibility for administering the newly-created Defense Attache system, consisting of uniformed military personnel serving in embassies and collecting, by overt means, information useful to the military.

In the meantime, there were substantial advances in U.S. technical collection capabilities. Photographs taken by the U-2 were a large factor in the successful resolution of the Cuban missile crisis in 1962. The first photo reconnaissance satellite was launched the same year. The first high altitude, high speed reconnaissance aircraft, the SR-71, was built and tested by the CIA a short while later. While these technical collection efforts had been ongoing for several years in both CIA and the Air Force, they were formally consolidated, pursuant to a national security directive,

in 1961 within the National Reconnaissance Office (NRO).

While the fact of its existence remained classified, the NRO was designated a separate operating agency of the Department of Defense, reporting to the Secretary of Defense albeit with the DCI retaining a role in selecting key personnel as well as substantial control over the budget, requirements, and priorities of the organization. Using the special procurement authorities of the DCI, the NRO was able expeditiously to procure and to operate satellite collection systems for the Intelligence Community.

In addition to the NSA, DIA, and NRO, each of the military services maintained substantial intelligence organizations, both at the departmental level and at the tactical level. These organizations typically collected information and provided analysis regarding the weapons systems, tactics, and capabilities of foreign counterpart forces. This information and analysis were used to support the weapons acquisition process in each service, to support force development and contingency planning, and were incorporated into training programs.

The growth of intelligence efforts within the Department of Defense served to accentuate the relative lack of the DCI's role over the rest of the Community. In July 1961, the President's Foreign Intelligence Advisory Board proposed to the President that the DCI be separated from the CIA and head-up an Office of Coordination in the White House. President Kennedy did not endorse the recommendation but in January 1962 issued a letter to his new DCI John McCone stating:

> As head of the Central Intelligence Agency, while you will continue to have overall responsibility for the Agency, I shall expect you to delegate to your principal deputy, as you may deem necessary, so much of the detailed operation of the Agency as may be required to permit you to carry out your primary task as Director of Central Intelligence.

In 1963, DCI McCone established a National Intelligence Programs Evaluation Staff to review and evaluate Community programs and cost-effectiveness. Later in the decade, DCI Helms set up a National Intelligence Resources Board to review all community programs and budgets, and to referee community disputes.[10]

But the burgeoning U.S. military involvement in the Vietnam War, the efforts to block Communist expansion in Laos and to deal with conflicts in the Middle East (notably the Arab-Israeli Six-Day War of 1967), effectively precluded serious efforts by the DCIs to assert greater control over the Intelligence Community.

THE 1970S; THE DECADE OF TURMOIL AND REFORM

The decade of the 1970s began with serious efforts to institute DCI control over the Intelligence Community, but they were eventually undermined by a series of sensational disclosures in the media, followed by unprecedented investigations of the Intelligence Community within the Executive Branch and by the Congress. During the latter half of the decade, new reforms were adopted and new oversight mechanisms put into place. While the intelligence functions of the Government continued, Congress began to take a much more active role in determining their cost and overseeing their execution.

In December 1970, President Nixon directed Deputy Director of the Office of Management and Budget James Schlesinger to recommend how the organizational structure of the Intelligence Community should be changed to bring about greater efficiency and effectiveness. The Schlesinger report, completed in March 1971, found, among other things, that intelligence functions were fragmented and disorganized; collection activities were unnecessarily competitive and redundant; intelligence suffered from unplanned and unguided growth; intelligence activities were too costly; and, because analytical products were provided on such a broad range of topics, they often suffered in quality. The report called for basic reform of the management structure with a strong DCI who could bring intelligence costs under control and improve analytic quality and responsiveness. Among other things, the study recommended that the DCI put together a consolidated budget for the Intelligence Community and oversee its execution.

Following-up on the recommendations in November 1971, President Nixon issued a directive calling for improvement in the intelligence product and for more efficient use of resources. The DCI was made responsible for "planning, reviewing, and evaluating all intelligence programs and activities and in the production of national intelligence." The Nixon directive reconstituted the United States Intelligence Board to assist the DCI, and set up the Intelligence Committee[11] of the NSC to coordinate and to review intelligence activities. It also established an Intelligence Resources

Advisory Committee, comprising representatives from the State and Defense Departments and OMB, to advise the DCI on the consolidated intelligence budget. In March 1972, DCI Helms created a special "Intelligence Community Staff" to assist him in the daily execution of his Community responsibilities.

None of these changes had a substantial impact at the time, however, because the Government became largely preoccupied with the Watergate affair in 1973 and 1974. There was only tangential involvement by the CIA in Watergate primarily through the activities of former employees, and in the preparation of a psychological profile of Daniel Ellsberg.[12] The press, however, motivated to some extent by the distrust generated by Watergate, increasingly began to report critically on intelligence activities. Press articles covered allegations of collection efforts undertaken against U.S. citizens during the Vietnam era, attempts to assassinate foreign leaders or destabilize communist regimes, and efforts to raise the remains of a Soviet submarine off the floor of the Pacific.

In December 1974, in reaction to reports of CIA's support to the non-Communist resistance forces in Angola, Congress passed an amendment to the Foreign Assistance Act, known as the "Hughes-Ryan amendment," which for the first time required that the President report any covert CIA operations in a foreign country (other than for intelligence collection) to the relevant congressional committees (which, at that time, included the armed services committees, foreign relations committees, and appropriations committees in each house of Congress).

The various media revelations also led to official investigations in both the Executive branch and the Congress:

A. THE ROCKEFELLER COMMISSION

The Commission on CIA Activities Within the United States, chaired by Vice President Rockefeller, was created by President Ford on 4 January 1975, to determine whether CIA employees had engaged in illegal activities in the United States. The inquiry was later expanded to include the CIA's foreign intelligence charter and to make suggestions for operational guidelines. In June 1975, the Commission issued its report which, among other things, confirmed the existence of a CIA domestic mail opening operation; found that in the late 1960s and early 1970s the Agency had kept files on 300,000 U.S. citizens and organizations relating to domestic dissident activities; found that President Nixon tried to use CIA records for political ends; and concluded that the CIA had no involvement in President Kennedy's assassination. The Commission also found "that the great majority of the CIA's domestic activities comply with its statutory authority." In looking to the future, the Commission called for a joint congressional oversight committee and a stronger executive oversight mechanism; consideration by the Congress to disclose "to some extent" CIA's budget; and appointment of two confirmed deputy directors, one to manage the CIA and one to advise the DCI on military matters. The Commission further recommended that the DCI serve no more than 10 years.

B. THE CHURCH COMMITTEE

Twenty-three days after the Rockefeller Commission was empaneled, the Senate announced its own investigatory body, the Committee to Study Government Operations with Respect to Intelligence Activities (also known as the Church Committee after its Chairman). Handling one of the largest investigations ever undertaken by the Senate, the Church Committee was charged with looking at CIA domestic activities; covert activity abroad, including alleged assassinations of foreign leaders; alleged abuses by the Internal Revenue Service and the FBI; alleged domestic spying by the military; and the alleged interceptions of the conversations of U.S. citizens by the National Security Agency. The Committee's inquiry lasted for almost a year, resulting in a six-volume report, released in April 1976. The Committee recommended, among other things, that the President consider separating the DCI from the CIA; that the authorities of the DCI over elements of the Intelligence Community be enhanced; that statutory charters be established for CIA, DIA, and NSA; that the National Foreign Intelligence Budget be published; and that clandestine support to repressive regimes that disregarded human rights be prohibited by law. The Committee lauded several reforms (including a ban on assassination) already implemented by President Ford.

C. THE PIKE COMMITTEE

The House counterpart to the Church Committee was the Select Committee on Intelligence to Investigate Allegations of Illegal or Improper Activities of Federal Intelligence Agencies. Impanelled in February 1975, the committee was also known by the name of its Chairman, Congressman Otis Pike.

The Pike Committee's report was voted down by the House in January 1976, and was never officially issued. Portions, however, were leaked to a New York newspaper, the *Village Voice*.

D. THE MURPHY COMMISSION

In June 1975, around the time that the Rockefeller Commission was completing its inquiry into intelligence improprieties, another congressional commission, the Commission on the Organization of the Government for the Conduct of Foreign Policy, was culminating a three-year study which included an examination of the organization and performance of the Intelligence Community. Headed by veteran diplomat Robert Murphy,[13] the Commission recommended that the DCI be given greater status in the White House and the Intelligence Community; that the DCI delegate his responsibility for running the CIA to a deputy; that the DCI occupy an office geographically closer to the White House to better enable him to carry out his role as presidential adviser; and that the CIA change its name to the Foreign Intelligence Agency.[14] The Commission also recommended that covert action should be employed only where it is clearly essential to vital U.S. purposes and only after a careful process of high level review. It further urged that the NSC's Committee on Intelligence be actively used as the principal forum to resolve the differing perspectives of intelligence consumers and producers, and "should meet frequently for that purpose."

REFORM AND OVERSIGHT

Even as the Church and Pike Committees were continuing their investigations, the Executive branch undertook extensive efforts to bring about reform.[15]

In the summer of 1975, President Ford ordered the implementation of 20 of the 30 recommendations of the Rockefeller Commission, to include measures to provide improved internal supervision of CIA activities; additional restrictions on CIA's domestic activities; a ban on mail openings; and an end to wiretaps, abuse of tax information, and the testing of drugs on unsuspecting persons. Ford did not agree to public disclosure of the intelligence budget, however, nor did he readily agree to a separate congressional oversight committee.

President Ford issued the first Executive Order on intelligence on 18 February 1976 (E.O. 11905),[16] before either the Church or Pike investigating committees had reported. For the first time, a description of the Intelligence Community and the authorities and responsibilities of the DCI and the heads of other intelligence agencies, were specified in a public presidential document. The order also set up a Committee on Foreign Intelligence as part of the National Security Council, chaired by the DCI and reporting directly to the President, as the focal point for policy and resource allocation on intelligence.[17] A number of restrictions on intelligence agencies were also instituted, including a ban on assassinations as an instrument of U.S. policy. To monitor compliance with the Order, a new Intelligence Oversight Board was established within the Executive Office of the President.

Both congressional investigating committees recommended in their final reports that permanent follow-on committees be created to provide oversight of the intelligence function and to consider further legislative actions as might be necessary.

The Senate acted first in May 1976, creating the Select Committee on Intelligence. The House followed suit a little over a year later, creating the Permanent Select Committee on Intelligence. Both committees were made responsible for authorizing expenditures for intelligence activities (although the Senate was limited to "national" intelligence, whereas the House mandate included both "national" and "tactical" intelligence activities), and for conducting necessary oversight. The resolutions creating both committees recognized that they would be kept "fully and currently informed" of intelligence activities under their purview. Both committees were added to the list of those to receive notice of covert actions under the Hughes-Ryan amendment. The Senate committee also was given responsibility for handling the confirmation proceedings when the DCI and the Deputy DCI were nominated by the President.

While efforts were made in succeeding months to let emotions over intelligence activities subside and to establish more "normal" relationships between the Legislative and Executive branches, the hiatus was relatively short-lived. In 1977, the Senate Committee reexamined the question whether the aggregate intelligence budget should be released publicly. This issue would continue to be debated for the next two decades. The statement of newly-appointed DCI Turner that he had no problem with the release of this figure aroused protests from those who believed disclosure could assist hostile

intelligence services in deciphering U.S. intelligence activity.

In August 1977, DCI Turner prompted a more substantial controversy by announcing his intention to reduce the CIA's Directorate of Operations by 800 people. The first reductions occurred on 31 October 1977 (called the "Halloween Massacre" within CIA) when 200 officers were fired. Critics of the DCI charged that he was destroying the CIA's human source collection capability in favor of technical collection programs run by the Department of Defense. (Some in Defense, on the other hand, perceived Turner as attempting to take over those programs.)

On 24 January 1978, President Carter issued a new Executive Order on intelligence which reaffirmed the DCI's Community-wide authority over priorities, tasking, and the budget; contained additional restrictions on collection techniques, participation in domestic activities, and human experimentation; and reiterated the ban on assassinations. Intelligence agencies were specifically required to promulgate procedures to govern the collection of information on U.S. citizens and persons admitted to the U.S. for permanent residence.

Notwithstanding the new presidential order, both congressional committees proceeded to consider bills in 1978 which would have dramatically overhauled the Intelligence Community. Following the suggestions of the Church Committee as well as incorporating various aspects of the Executive branch reforms, the Senate committee developed a comprehensive bill entitled the "National Intelligence Reorganization and Reform Act of 1978." The bill called for the creation of a "Director of National Intelligence" with broader powers than the DCI to serve as head of the Intelligence Community. The Director of National Intelligence would have retained leadership of CIA[18] with the authority to delegate this responsibility to a Deputy or Assistant Director at the President's discretion. The bill also contained a long list of restricted or banned activities, provided specific missions and functions for each element of the Intelligence Community, stipulated rigorous review and notification procedures for covert action and clandestine collection, and instituted numerous requirements for reporting to Congress.

While the Carter Administration initially supported the attempt to draft "charter" legislation, it ultimately withdrew its support in the face of growing concern that the intelligence function would be hamstrung by having too much detailed regulation in statute. After extended negotiations with the two intelligence committees, the Administration agreed to a measure limited to establishing the ground rules for congressional oversight. The Intelligence Oversight Act of 1980 provided that the heads of intelligence agencies would keep the oversight committees "fully and currently informed" of their activities including "any significant anticipated intelligence activity." Detailed ground rules were established for reporting covert actions to the Congress, in return for the number of congressional committees receiving notice of covert actions being limited to the two oversight committees.

Congress also passed, with the support of the Carter Administration, the Foreign Intelligence Surveillance Act of 1978, providing for a special court order procedure to authorize electronic surveillance for intelligence purposes, activities that had previously been conducted based upon a claim of constitutional authority of the President.

Finally, in response to continued criticism from the congressional committees over the usefulness of national intelligence estimates, a new mechanism for the development of estimates was established. DCI Colby, in 1973, had established the National Intelligence Officer system in lieu of the Board of Estimates. He had appointed the first six NIOs in an effort to make intelligence more responsive to policymaking. By the end of the decade, DCI Turner formed the NIOs into the National Intelligence Council. Reporting to the DCI, the Council comprised a Chairman and eight National Intelligence Officers, who were considered the senior analysts of the Intelligence Community within their respective areas of expertise. As such, they would supervise the preparation of estimates, ensure quality control, and present the results of their work to policymakers as required.

1980S: A DECADE OF GROWTH AND SCANDAL

The beginning of the decade saw the election of a President, Ronald Reagan, who had made the revitalization of intelligence part of his campaign. Intelligence budgets were increased, and new personnel were hired. The vast majority of rules and guidelines adopted during the Ford and Carter Administrations remained in place. However, by the middle of the decade, the U.S. experienced a series of spy scandals, and the first serious breach of the

oversight arrangements with the Congress. While the organization of the Intelligence Community remained stable during the decade, it was a period of burgeoning growth and activity.

During the 1980 presidential election, intelligence became a targeted campaign issue. The Republican Party platform contained a plank asserting that the Democrats had impaired the efficiency of the Intelligence Community and had underestimated the Soviet's military strength. President Reagan came into office promising to improve intelligence capabilities by upgrading technical systems and strengthening counterintelligence.

To make good on these promises, Reagan appointed William Casey, a veteran of the OSS, as DCI, and announced that the DCI, for the first time, would hold cabinet rank. With this presidential mandate, Casey sought and received higher budgets for intelligence and instituted an unprecedented period of personnel growth across the Intelligence Community.

On 4 December 1981, almost a year into his Administration, President Reagan issued his Executive Order on intelligence (E.O. 12333). It generally reaffirmed the functions of intelligence agencies (as outlined in the previous order) and continued most of the previous restrictions, but it set a more positive tone than its predecessor, and gave the CIA greater latitude to gather foreign intelligence within the United States and to provide assistance to law enforcement. The Executive Order also provided a new NSC structure for reviewing intelligence activities, including covert actions.[19]

Meanwhile, the congressional intelligence committees demonstrated a willingness to provide legislative authority sought by the Intelligence Community. In 1980, the Classified Information Procedures Act was passed to protect classified information used in criminal trials. In 1982, following the public revelation of the names of certain CIA officers that appeared to result in the murder of one officer, the Congress passed a new law making it a crime to reveal the names of covert intelligence personnel. In October 1984, Congress exempted certain operational files of the CIA from disclosure under the Freedom of Information Act. However, legislative proposals offered in 1984 calling for a fixed term for the DCI and Deputy DCI and requiring that they be career intelligence officers, were not passed.

The 1986 Goldwater-Nichols Act, which reorganized the Department of Defense and shifted authority from the military departments to the Joint Chiefs and theater commands, also had an impact on intelligence. The Defense Intelligence Agency and Defense Mapping Agency were specifically designated as combat support agencies, and the Secretary of Defense, in consultation with the DCI, was directed to establish policies and procedures to assist the National Security Agency in fulfilling its combat support functions. The Act also required that the President submit annually to Congress a report on U.S. national security strategy, including an assessment of the adequacy of the intelligence capability to carry out the strategy.

1985: THE YEAR OF THE SPY

Beginning in 1985, the Intelligence Community experienced an unprecedented rash of spy cases that led to numerous recommendations for change.

The defection of former CIA officer Edward Lee Howard in the spring of 1985 was followed by the arrests of John A. Walker, Jr. and Jerry A. Whitworth, Navy personnel with access to highly sensitive information; CIA employees, Sharon Scranage and Larry Wu-Tai Chin; former NSA employee, Ronald W. Pelton; FBI agent, Richard Miller; and an employee of Naval intelligence, Jonathan J. Pollard. The Walker-Whitworth, Pelton, and Howard cases dealt especially serious blows to U.S. intelligence. As the year drew to a close, a Marine guard at the U.S. Embassy in Moscow confessed to having passed information to the Soviets and was charged with allowing Soviet personnel to enter the chancery building. It was further disclosed that the U.S. had determined its new chancery in Moscow had been thoroughly bugged during its construction. Coming in close succession, these disclosures shocked the public and the Congress.

Various efforts were taken within the Executive branch to identify and correct shortcomings in counterintelligence and security. The Secretary of Defense commissioned a special inquiry into Defense policy and practice. The Secretary of State commissioned a review of embassy security, including the vulnerability of U.S. diplomatic establishments to electronic penetration. The CIA undertook an internal review of counterintelligence and its procedures for handling defectors.

The congressional intelligence committees also investigated these problems and prepared lengthy reports recommending change. In 1988, the Senate committee asked a group of distinguished private citizens, led by New York businessman Eli Jacobs,

to review the progress that had been made in counterintelligence and to provide recommendations for further improvements. Their report was provided in 1989, but did not result in any legislation being enacted at the time. This was due in part to the fall of the Berlin Wall, and dramatic changes taking place in the Soviet Union, which lessened the intensity of focusing on problems with spies.

THE IRAN-CONTRA AFFAIR AND ITS AFTERMATH

In November 1986, Congress learned that representatives of the Reagan Administration, contrary to the announced policies of the Government, had sold arms to the Government of Iran in return for its assistance in securing the release of U.S. hostages held in Lebanon. Initiated by members of the NSC staff, the operation was accomplished with the assistance of some officers of the CIA and the Defense Department pursuant to a retroactive covert action "finding" signed by President Reagan in January 1986, which had never been reported to the Congress. It was also disclosed that the NSC staff members involved in the sales had overcharged the Iranians for the weapons and had used the proceeds to support the anti-Communist rebels, the "Contras," in Nicaragua at a time when such assistance was prohibited by law. The veracity of public statements made by the President and other senior officials with knowledge of the episode appeared in doubt. CIA and other intelligence agencies were quickly drawn into the controversy, which collectively became known as the Iran-Contra affair.

A special prosecutor was appointed to look into possible criminal activity, and investigations ensued in both the Executive branch and the Congress. In December 1986, the President commissioned a Special Review Board, chaired by former Senator John Tower. Three months later, the Tower Board found that the Iran and Contra operations were conducted outside of regularly established channels and that intelligence oversight requirements had been ignored. The Board also faulted President Reagan's management style. While not recommending organizational changes *per se,* the Board urged that a better set of guidelines be developed for approving and reporting covert action. The Board also recommended that Congress consider merging the two intelligence committees into a single joint committee.

In early 1987, the House and Senate formed separate investigating committees, but later agreed to form a Joint Committee for purposes of interviewing witnesses and holding hearings. After months of intense public hearings, a majority of the Committee issued a lengthy account of its work in the fall of 1987. It recommended, among other things, that a statutory Inspector General be created at the CIA and that the legal requirements for reporting covert actions to the congressional oversight committees be tightened.

Lawrence Walsh, the special prosecutor appointed in January 1987, carried on his investigation of the Iran-Contra affair for almost seven years, and brought criminal prosecutions against the key NSC figures involved, some CIA employees, and a former Secretary of Defense. President Bush later issued pardons to six of those charged.

Legislation creating a statutory Inspector General for the CIA was enacted in 1989. Although the Inspector General reported to the DCI, he could be removed only by the President. Among other things, the law required that the Inspector General submit semi-annual reports to the congressional intelligence committees, summarizing problems that had been identified and corrective actions taken.

Legislative efforts to tighten the covert action reporting requirements did not succeed for several more years. In 1988, with the election of President George Bush, a former DCI, Congress received assurances that the experience of Iran-Contra would not be repeated and that appropriate consultations would occur on future covert actions. These assurances did not put the matter to rest as far as the committees were concerned, but did serve to dampen congressional fervor to legislate precise time requirements for reporting.

1990–1995: THE END OF THE COLD WAR AND RETRENCHMENT

The three years following the election of President Bush saw profound changes in the world that had enormous impacts on the Intelligence Community. In the fall of 1989, the Berlin Wall came down and Germany began the process of reunification. The Communist regimes of Eastern Europe gave way to democratic rule. In August 1990, Iraq invaded Kuwait. Shortly thereafter, the Soviet Union began to break apart with many former Soviet Republics declaring independence. In early 1991, the U.S. together with NATO allies (and the agreement of the Soviet Union) invaded Kuwait to oust the occupying Iraqi forces with a fearsome display of modern weaponry. Later in the year, Communist rule ended in Russia.

Some began to question whether an intelligence capability was needed any longer; others urged significant retrenchment. Leaders within the Intelligence Community began streamlining their agencies and reorienting toward new missions, with a greater focus on transnational threats. Congress pushed them along by proposing a new Intelligence Community structure, and mandating across-the-board reductions in personnel.

The period ended with a shocking new spy case at the CIA and renewed calls for reform.

THE GULF WAR

The Gulf War of 1991, brief though it was, had profound repercussions for U.S. intelligence. Never had so much information been conveyed so quickly from intelligence systems to warfighters with such devastating effect. The accuracy of U.S. precision guided weapons astounded the world. The war also highlighted the need for the United States to expand its own efforts to link intelligence systems with combat systems and to train military personnel to use these systems effectively. The U.S. recognized that the future of warfare was apt to be battles fought at a distance between opposing forces, placing a premium on the availability of intelligence on the nature and disposition of hostile forces.

Yet the Gulf War also demonstrated problems with intelligence. Initially, the Intelligence Community was not well prepared to support military operations in this locale, but given time in the fall and winter of 1990 to put together a capability, the job was done. The Joint Intelligence Center was established during the war with representation from the key intelligence agencies and provided a model of providing crisis support to military operations. Indeed, a permanent National Military Joint Intelligence Center was established shortly after the conflict at the Pentagon and later at all unified commands. Still, the war illuminated problems in disseminating imagery to the field as well as the limitations of U.S. human intelligence capabilities. In addition, a substantial problem arose with competing CIA and military assessments of the damage caused by allied bombing.

THE GATES TASK FORCES

In 1991, after a wrenching confirmation process which provided the first public examination of the analytical process at the CIA, DCI Robert Gates undertook a comprehensive reexamination of the post-Cold War Intelligence Community. The recommendations of 14 separate task forces produced significant change: analysis would be made more responsive to decisionmakers; a formalized requirements process would be established for human source intelligence collection; new offices were created at the CIA to coordinate the use of publicly available ("open source") information and to improve CIA support to the military. The staff of the DCI, which supported him in his Community role, was strengthened. And, after much negotiating about which entities to include, a new Central Imagery Office, under the joint control of the DCI and the Secretary of Defense, was established to coordinate imagery collection and to establish uniform standards for the interpretation and dissemination of imagery to the field.

BOREN-McCURDY LEGISLATION

While the Gates task forces were at work, legislation was introduced by the respective Chairmen of the Senate and House intelligence committees to restructure the Intelligence Community. The bills called for the creation of a Director of National Intelligence with authority over the intelligence budget as well as authority to transfer personnel temporarily from one intelligence agency to another. The DNI would continue to establish requirements and priorities for intelligence collection and serve as the President's intelligence adviser. In this regard, the analytical element of the CIA would be transferred under the control of the DNI, leaving the remainder of the CIA to be administered by a separate agency director. The legislation also proposed a National Imagery Agency to coordinate imagery tasking, collection, processing, and dissemination.

Given the actions taken by DCI Gates to implement the results of his task forces, however, the committees did not push for enactment of their alternative proposals. Instead they opted to codify and to clarify the existing statutory framework that had been largely unchanged since 1947. The Intelligence Organization Act of 1992 (enacted as part of the Intelligence Authorization Act for 1993) for the first time defined the Intelligence Community by law, enunciated the three roles of the DCI, set forth the authorities and responsibilities of the DCI in relation to other elements of the Intelligence Community, and articulated the responsibilities of the Secretary of Defense for the execution of national intelligence programs. Among other things, the Secretary was required to consult with the DCI prior to appointing the Directors of the NSA, the NRO,[20] and the DIA.

Congress continued to debate whether the intelligence budget should be declassified. In 1991 and 1992, Congress passed non-binding "Sense of Congress" resolutions urging the President to make public the aggregate funding for intelligence. President Bush declined to do so, as did President Clinton in 1993.

THE VICE PRESIDENT'S NATIONAL PERFORMANCE REVIEW

In 1993, as part of the Clinton Administration's overall effort to "reinvent" government, a team from the Vice President's National Performance Review looked at the Intelligence Community and suggested that several actions be taken to consolidate activities and build a sense of Community in order to be more efficient and to better serve customers. The review found that the Community was too often drawn apart by the competition for new programs and budget allocations and recommended rotational assignments among agencies as a means of promoting a broader, more collegial perspective. The review's recommendation that the Intelligence Oversight Board be merged into the President's Foreign Intelligence Advisory Board was accomplished by Executive Order in September 1993.

THE AMES SPY CASE

In February 1994, Aldrich H. Ames, a CIA employee with almost 30 years' experience in operations, was charged with spying for the Soviet Union since at least 1985. During this period, he was alleged to have disclosed virtually all of the CIAs active Soviet agents, many of whom were later executed or imprisoned. In May, Ames and his wife pled guilty and were sent to prison.

The ensuing investigations by the CIA Inspector General and by the congressional intelligence committees reported that Ames had exhibited serious personal problems and a penchant for exorbitant spending which should have brought him under security scrutiny. The investigations also highlighted problems in coordinating counterintelligence cases between the FBI and the CIA. Notwithstanding the seriousness of Ames' disclosures and the numerous shortcomings on the part of CIA officers, DCI Woolsey meted out what were perceived as relatively mild disciplinary measures. The confidence of the public and the Congress in the CIA appeared considerably eroded.

In the fall of 1994, new legislation was enacted to improve counterintelligence and security practices across the Intelligence Community, and, in particular, to improve the coordination between the FBI and CIA. In addition, the President created a new bureaucratic framework for handling counterintelligence matters, to include the placement of FBI counterintelligence specialists within the CIA.

THE CREATION OF A NEW COMMISSION

Even before the Ames case provided the immediate impetus, the congressional intelligence committees anticipated that the Executive branch would conduct a comprehensive review of the Intelligence Community. When this failed to materialize, the Senate committee, and, in particular, its Vice Chairman, Senator John Warner, developed legislation to establish a commission to study the roles and capabilities of intelligence agencies in the post-Cold War era, and to make recommendations for change. The legislation was approved in October 1994, as part of the Intelligence Authorization Act for 1995.

QUESTIONS FOR FURTHER DISCUSSION

1. Which do you think was a more important factor leading to the establishment of the CIA in 1947: the Pearl Harbor attack, President Truman's management style, or the rising threat of the Soviet Union? Why?
2. When did the CIA become a "key player" in the U.S. government, according to the author?
3. What were the most important developments in the evolution of U.S. intelligence since World War II?
4. What were the CIA's most important successes and failures prior to the creation of the Aspin-Brown Commission in 1994?

ENDNOTES

1. Former Secretary of State Dean Rusk recalled the 1941 state of the U.S.'s intelligence effort in testimony before a Senate subcommittee: "When I was assigned to G-2 in 1941, well over a year after the war had started in Europe, I was asked to take charge of a new section that had been organized to cover everything from Afghanistan right through southern Asia, southeast Asia, Australia, and the Pacific. Because we had no intelligence organization that had been giving attention to that area up to that time, the materials available to me when I reported for duty consisted of a tourist handbook on India and Ceylon, a 1924 military attache's report from London on the Indian Army, and a drawer full of clippings from the *New York Times* that had gathered since World War One. That was literally the resources of the G-2 on that vast part of the world a year after the war in Europe started."

2. In 1957, this group was renamed the Bureau of Intelligence and Research.

3. The same Sidney Souers who had been appointed the first DCI by President Truman in January 1946. Souers served as Executive Secretary of the NSC from 1947 to 1950.

4. Although NSC 50 was issued to implement the report's recommendations, DCI Hillenkoetter did not take follow-up action on its numerous recommendations.

5. The same person who proposed the creation of the National Security Council and the CIA in a 1945 report to Navy Secretary Forrestal.

6. The depth and importance of this problem was revealed when President Truman announced that the Soviets had detonated a nuclear device in September 1949. The CIA's only coordinated estimate on the urgent question of when the Soviets would have a nuclear weapon gave three incorrect predictions: 1958, 1955 and 1950–1953, and none of the predictions was accepted by all departments.

7. In its 1955 report, the Second Hoover Commission recognized for the first time the existence of an "intelligence community" within the Government, naming the NSC, CIA, NSA, FBI, Department of State, Army, Navy, Air Force, and the Atomic Energy Commission as its members.

8. Allen Dulles, who had been elevated to DCI in 1953, did not appoint a Chief of Staff, due to his active interest in the operation of the CIA. Instead, he appointed General Lucien Truscott as his deputy to resolve jurisdictional disputes between CIA and the military services, in an attempt to increase his community coordination capabilities.

9. In 1956, the House and Senate Armed Services Committees, and the Senate Appropriations Committee established intelligence subcommittees, and the House Appropriations Committee formed a "special group" under its chairman.

10. The United States Intelligence Board, previously established in the 1950s to serve as the DCI's primary advisory body, was used unevenly by DCIs depending on their interests in Community management.

11. The Intelligence Committee, chaired by the National Security Advisor, consisted of the Attorney General,

the Under Secretary of State, the Deputy Secretary of Defense, the Chairman of the Joint Chiefs of Staff, and the DCI.

12. CIA officials refused the White House request that the CIA be used to cover-up the Watergate affair.

13. In 1976, Murphy was appointed by President Ford as the first chairman of the newly-formed Intelligence Oversight Board, and as a member of PFIAB.

14. The principal author of these conclusions was reportedly William Casey, later to become DCI.

15. It should also be noted that DCI Colby appointed a study group within CIA, headed by James Taylor, which issued an internal report in October 1975: "American Intelligence: A Framework for the Future." The Taylor study asserted that intelligence needed to become more efficient and effective, and more compatible with our democracy. The study suggested refining the current intelligence system and focused on the role of the DCI, including the relationship with the Secretary of Defense and the Intelligence Community, arguing that the DCI needed more influence over both substantive judgments and resource management. The report noted that the DCI's responsibilities, but not his authorities, had grown considerably since 1947. The study recommended separating the DCI from CIA (which would be run by its own director),

and appropriating funds to the DCI who would allocate them to program managers.

16. This order and succeeding orders issued by President Carter (E.O. 12036,1978) and President Reagan (E.O. 12333,1981) listed the following members of the Intelligence Community: CIA, NSA, DIA, DOD reconnaissance offices, INR/State, intelligence elements of Army, Navy, Air Force, Marines, FBI, Treasury, and DOE (then known as the Energy Research & Development Administration). Staff elements of the DCI were added in the Carter and Reagan orders.

17. The other members of the CFI were the Deputy Secretary of Defense for Intelligence and the Deputy Assistant to the President for National Security Affairs. The CFI reported directly to the NSC.

18. Those who thought the DNI must retain a direct management role over the CIA argued that separating the DNI from the CIA would deprive the Director of a strong institutional base and would subject him to more pressure from the policymakers.

19. Neither President Bush nor President Clinton issued executive orders on intelligence that supersede E.O. 12333. It remains in effect.

20. In 1992, as the legislation was under consideration, the President declassified the fact of the NRO's existence.

From Phyllis Provost McNeil, Aspin-Brown Commission, "The Evolution of the U.S. Intelligence Community—An Historical Perspective," Preparing for the 21st Century: An Appraisal of U.S. Intelligence, Appendix A, *Report of the Commission on the Roles and Capabilities of the United States Intelligence Community* (March 1, 1996).

3. INTELLIGENCE AND THE SECOND BUSH ADMINISTRATION

ADMIRAL STANSFIELD TURNER

The Director of Central Intelligence from the Carter Administration evaluates the uses of intelligence by the George W. Bush Administration—a period during which the United States suffered two of its most unfortunate intelligence failures: the 9/11 attacks in 2001 and the faulty prediction that Iraq possessed weapons of mass destruction in 2002.

When he became president, George W. Bush inherited George Tenet as his DCI. He opted to try him out even though Tenet came with a long history of association with Democrats. There is no hard evidence to confirm it, but it is easy to speculate that the new president's father may have influenced him to give Tenet a try in the name of reducing turnover in the job of DCI and of keeping the position apolitical. How well Tenet performed and how well he was supported by George W. Bush are questions it is too early to attempt to answer fairly. What we can do, though, is look at how they dealt with intelligence and consider what additional lessons their experiences give us for shaping American intelligence for the future.

In May 2001, Bush appointed Brent Scowcroft to head a commission to review the state of our intelligence. The commission produced a study the following December. It reportedly recommended both separating the DCI from the CIA and transferring three collection agencies housed in the DOD to the management control of the DCI (NSA for electronic spying, NGA for photographic spying, and NRO for the operation of spying satellites). This was the most radical solution yet proposed for empowering the DCI. For some reason the study remains classified and is inaccessible. It seems likely that the solution proposed by the commission was not supported by the Bush administration, particularly Secretary of Defense Donald Rumsfeld, the then and still "owner" of those three agencies. In his view, "There may be ways we can strengthen intelligence, but centralization is not one."[1] From remarks George Tenet has made on intelligence reform, it seems likely he would have been in opposition as well.[2] His view is, "I don't think you should separate the leader of this country's intelligence from a line agency."[3] In short, the report was dead on arrival.

On August 6, 2001, Tenet submitted to the president a President's Daily Brief with an article titled "Bin Laden Determined to Strike in U.S."[4] From what we can learn, the president must have assumed that his departmental and agency heads would do what they should to anticipate and blunt such a strike and did not pursue it further. From August 6 until September 11, though, Tenet continued to sound a shrill alarm, even antagonizing some people by his persistence. He told the Intelligence Community, "We are at war."[5] The Community paid so little attention to the DCI that some intelligence agency heads never even saw Tenet's warning and none took any direct or specific action. This clearly demonstrates the indifference of those agency heads to direction from the DCI. It also bespeaks Tenet's lack of interest in the activities of the Community in that he did not seek to find out what they were doing in response to his warning. Overall he is reported to have given Community matters very little attention.

When the attacks of 9/11 occurred, Tenet was the first member of the Bush national security team to respond with a plan of action. It was not a Community plan. Rather, Tenet proposed using CIA operatives to guide the military into Afghanistan. Within the CIA he had worked to get the espionage and covert action people ready for such an eventuality. They were ready and performed superbly in helping guide the military to a quick victory over the Taliban. His performance with this aggressive, action-oriented plan must have appealed to the president and confirmed the wisdom of keeping Tenet on.

The Taliban had not yet been driven out of Afghanistan when the administration began considering an invasion of Iraq. According to Bob Woodward, on December 21, 2002, the president questioned Tenet about whether the intelligence indicating that Iraq had weapons of mass destruction (WMD) was solid enough. Tenet's reply was that it was a "slam dunk."[6] It is difficult to guess what drove him to this unequivocal response, because the estimates of his and other agencies following the problem were hardly that clear. Was this because he is a decisive person? Was it because he wanted to please Bush? Was it because he was listening to those in the CIA who believed Iraq had WMD and discounting the naysayers? Was it because he ignored what other agencies were saying, particularly the State Department's Bureau of Intelligence and Research?

Beyond Tenet's personal role, it is clear that something was terribly amiss within the CIA's analytic branch if it let the DCI get that far off track. The Agency reportedly acknowledged in a classified report in late 2004 that its estimate of chemical weapons in Iraq before our invasion was wide of the mark. This, if true, would be an unprecedented move of acknowledgment that a major estimate was in serious error. Surely Agency people have found over the years that some of their products missed the mark. Here, they apparently felt they were so far off the mark as to require a confession. It is reported that there will be further, similar retractions on biological and nuclear weapons. It is likely that the "slam dunk" blunder (assuming Tenet said it, and that seems likely since he has not publicly refuted Woodward) was a very large factor leading to Tenet's resignation. Whether he was eased out by the president or had just had enough we may never know. He left on July 11, 2004. He will be remembered as the DCI who brought stability to the CIA after the turnover of three DCIs between late 1991 and his arrival in 1997; and who improved the morale of an organization battered by public and congressional scrutiny since 1986.

However, Tenet and most of the Intelligence Community failed to recognize that Saddam Hussein or the United Nations had in one way or another disposed of Iraq's chemical and biological weapons and its program for developing nuclear weapons. It took a long time to establish authoritatively that there had been no WMD in Iraq at the time of our invasion. In the meantime, national attention shifted back to the intelligence failure of 9/11. On November 27, 2002, Congress created the National Commission on Terrorist Attacks upon the United States, known as the 9/11 Commission. It was composed of ten members, half appointed by the president and half by Congress, with equal representation by each political party. The commission released its public report on July 22, 2004. When it was published by the Government Printing Office (as well as in an authorized paperback edition from W. W. Norton & Company), it instantly became a best-seller. This is rather unusual for a government document, but it reflects an intense national interest. One finding of this report was that there were "pervasive problems of managing and sharing information across a large and unwieldy government that had been built in a different era to confront different dangers."[7]

Congress used the commission's report as a basis for drafting a statute on intelligence reform. On December 17, 2004, the president signed the Intelligence Reform and Terrorism Prevention Act into law. There had been intense debate over just how much added authority should be given the DCI in this legislation. The Senate wanted a strong leadership role. The House, influenced by pressure from the DOD, favored a much lesser one. The end result was, of course, a series of compromises. Where genuine compromise was not possible, there is ambiguity. On balance the law provides for a leader for the Intelligence Community who is weaker than what was recommended by the 9/11 Commission. One still unanswered question is whether the Intelligence Reform and Terrorism Prevention Act of 2004 prepares us to deal more confidently and effectively with terrorism. Another and even more important unanswered question is whether we could and should be doing even more and, if so, what?

In my judgment the answer to the first question is a qualified "yes." Depending on just how the ambiguities in the legislation are resolved, we are probably going to be better prepared. My answer to the second question is that we definitely can, and must, do more because these congressional changes to our intelligence organization are only halfway measures. Congress needs to remove some of the ambiguities in the Intelligence Reform Act.

Alternatively, the president could supplement the law through an executive order or by instructions to his national security team for dealing with those ambiguities. Either of these solutions would not, of course, be as permanent or as binding as a change in the law.

The new law made one highly significant change that went beyond what was possible with presidential prerogatives alone: to separate the role of DCI from that of head of the CIA. As we have seen, several presidents have suggested that DCIs delegate responsibility for managing the CIA to their deputies, but now there actually is a divorce.[8] Beyond that, though, the law confuses what should be done as a matter of management by the executive and what needs to be enshrined in statute. For instance, with whom and how much the new director of national intelligence (DNI) should consult when preparing budgets is normally a matter of executive choice and style. Prescribing it in law, as the Intelligence Reform Act does, was just an attempt to give the DOD more say. Also, the requirement of the law that money appropriated by Congress must pass through the DOD en route to the individual DOD intelligence agencies dilutes the budgeting authority that the act gives the DNI. These are the kinds of issues that make the Intelligence Reform Act less than clear-cut.

The big question, then, is whether President Bush will line up with the presidents since FDR who have favored giving more authority to the DCI or whether he will give in to the DOD's persistent efforts to keep the DCI's authority limited. For instance, whenever you create a new bureaucratic entity, as the 1947 National Security Act did with the DCI, whatever authorities the new position is assigned, unless they are completely new, must be taken from other entities that already have them. In the case of the 1947 act, those transferred authorities were primarily from the bureaus of intelligence of the Army, Navy, and State Departments. Even though those departments themselves were willing in 1947 to have a centralized intelligence organization in addition to their own intelligence bureaus, they were not willing to relinquish control over any of their intelligence activities. The most powerful writ the new DCI received in the 1947 act was "to make recommendations to the NSC for the coordination of…intelligence activities."[9] In short, it was a coordinator that was created, not someone with the authority to exercise real control over our intelligence apparatus.

Beyond entrenched parochialism, I surmise that much of the resistance to empowering a DCI to control all intelligence activities of the government comes from a concern that a powerful secret organization could be a danger to our democracy. This may have been a factor with both FDR and Harry Truman, who lived through the era of such a muscular, and ultimately destructive, organization as the Gestapo. We saw how FDR, in a desire to have more centralized intelligence, first created the Coordinator of Information and later the OSS, but never gave either access to one of the most valuable sources of intelligence: signals intercepts. Donovan complained about this enough that it could not have been an oversight. What we do not know is why Roosevelt was consciously and deliberately keeping his intelligence coordinator weak.

Truman was even more apprehensive. He wanted to know what his "spooks" were doing. In the first month after World War II ended, he wrapped up the OSS. Yet over time, the responsibilities of the new global position of the United States forced him to support the National Security Act of 1947, which created a DCI. Later he even agreed to expand the DCI's authorities into espionage and covert action, as well as into analysis. So it is very hard to draw lines when assigning responsibilities in tasking intelligence agencies. Giving too much authority to any one agency risks creating a monster; too little and you risk having a toothless, ineffective organization.

When Eisenhower became president, a great opportunity to strengthen the role of the DCI was missed. Ike understood the military's needs for intelligence as well as anyone. He saw an overriding need for greater central control. He wrote, "I concur in the need for strong centralized direction of the intelligence effort of the United States through the NSC and the DCI."[10] In fact, though, there was no significant strengthening of the DCI during Eisenhower's tenure simply because Ike's DCI, Allen Dulles, was not interested in managing the Intelligence Community. The irony here is that Truman, perforce, left the position of the director of central intelligence stronger than when he took office, even though he did not want a strong DCI; but Ike, who wanted a strong DCI, was thwarted in that desire by the indifference of his DCI to the larger Community dimensions of his job.

John Kennedy, despite being burned at the Bay of Pigs by the CIA's ineptness, moved further toward empowering the DCI than had his predecessors. A year after taking office, he became the first president to endorse in a written directive the concept of separating the roles of DCI and head of the CIA. He clearly signaled that being DCI was the primary duty: "As head of the CIA, while you will continue to have over-all responsibility for the Agency, I shall expect you to delegate to your principal deputy, as you may deem necessary, so much of the direction of the detailed operation of the Agency [CIA] as may be required to permit you to carry out your primary task as DCI."[11] At the same time, Kennedy did not ask Congress to change that portion of the National Security Act that required the same person to be both DCI and head of the CIA.

Lyndon Johnson was so suspicious of and indifferent to his intelligence apparatus that he drove John McCone to resign. While Johnson worked better with Richard Helms as DCI, the position itself was not changed significantly during his tenure.

Richard Nixon was even more mistrusting of the CIA. He did, though, commission James Schlesinger to review the state of our intelligence. When Schlesinger reported that the DCI lacked authority, Nixon gave that office more control over the preparation of the intelligence budget.

Gerald Ford's perspective on empowering the DCI was shaped by a concern that Congress not use the Church Committee report as a way of hobbling the CIA. To preempt Congress, he issued the first presidential executive order on intelligence. It emphasized what should not be done more than what should, constraining the DCI rather than empowering him or her.

Jimmy Carter sympathized with Ford's constraints and even added a few of his own. The logic, though, of his wanting a single person to be responsible for getting the intelligence he needed to him led to the greatest strengthening of the DCI ever. This included both "full and exclusive" responsibility for submitting the budget for all intelligence agencies and for control of collection operations. But resistance from the military to the DCI's having these authorities was growing well before Carter left office.

That led to Ronald Reagan's reissuing the presidential executive order on intelligence in a weaker form than Carter's, despite his having campaigned on a pledge to revitalize the CIA. For example, rather than giving the DCI "full and exclusive" responsibility for the intelligence budget, the DCI was to do this "with the advice of the program managers and departments and agencies concerned."[12] This Reagan order persisted through the presidency of George H. W. Bush. That is

surprising to me, since, as a former DCI, George H. W. Bush might well have had ideas of his own on the best role for the DCI. The Reagan executive order also remained in force during the presidency of Bill Clinton, whose indifference on intelligence meant that there were few changes in authorities during his tenure.

Under George W. Bush, the ink was hardly dry on the Intelligence Reform and Terrorism Prevention Act of 2004 before there was talk about the need to amend it because of the number of compromises in the new DNI's authorities. Still, I believe a key portion of the Intelligence Reform Act, the separation of the jobs of managing the Intelligence Community and running the CIA, is highly desirable. In my experience, the two jobs were just too much for one person to do well on top of being the president's intelligence advisor. As a result, most DCIs have neglected their responsibility to manage the Intelligence Community, even when they have been given sufficient support from presidents to exercise effective management.

Additionally, the two positions inherently conflict. The more attention a DCI pays to running the CIA, the more he is suspect by the Community of favoring the CIA above the other intelligence agencies. And, indeed, DCIs have almost always found that the CIA provided them, by far, the best finished intelligence, and so it was natural to lean on the CIA more than on the others. Over the years, this has resulted in an unhealthy jealousy of the CIA, especially among the intelligence agencies housed in DOD, and this mitigates significantly against true interagency cooperation and sharing. On the other side of that coin, the more time the DCI spends as Intelligence Community director, the less the CIA people see him as looking out for their interests. So the DCI has to walk a tightrope, which prevents his being a forceful advocate for either the Community or the CIA.

Most people in the DOD have opposed the creation of a DNI out of concern that the DNI's powers might intrude into the military's role in intelligence. Yet the actual authorities established for the DNI in the Intelligence Reform Act are less than those that President Carter gave me in his executive order on intelligence and are considerably less than those Brent Scowcroft's commission reportedly recommended.

CIA people have opposed the separation of the head of the Agency and the DCI, I believe, because it demotes the head of their agency down from being someone who reports directly to the president to someone on the second tier.

Opponents from both the DOD and CIA regularly adduce the oversimplistic argument that creating a DNI would simply be adding another layer of bureaucracy. This is nothing more than pandering to the pejorative connotation of "bureaucracy." All bureaucracies are not bad. We need to judge each proposal to add to existing bureaucracies by whether the functions to be performed are sufficiently important to warrant emplacing more bureaucrats. In this instance, the void in what needs to be done to coordinate budgets, collection, and analysis calls for some corrective action, I believe. In addition, a sizable bureaucracy for coordination already exists in the DCI's Community staff and may not have to be enlarged very much.

The debate on a DNI, then, has been not only intense, but often misleading. For instance, the chairman of the House Armed Services Committee warned that a DNI might not invest in new technical systems needed for collecting military intelligence, and that a DNI might somehow interfere with the flow of intelligence within the military's chain of command. Both assertions were based on questionable assumptions: one, that a DNI would necessarily neglect the military's interests, and two, that military interests always come before any others.

Another is that of the chairman of the Joint Chiefs of Staff. During the debate on the Intelligence Reform Act, he wrote a letter to a congressman insisting that the money for all intelligence agencies under military control had to flow from the Office of Management and Budget to those agencies through the DOD, not directly from the DNI; and that the agencies' recommendations for what they needed in their budgets had to pass to the DNI through the DOD. In short, the DOD would always be astride the flow of dollars between the DNI and the agencies. The power the DNI would get from holding the purse strings would be considerably diminished. As noted earlier, the chairman's proviso was written into the Intelligence Reform Act, giving the DOD a more influential position in the budget process than any of the other departments; that is, State, Homeland Security, Justice, Treasury, and Energy. In this age of combating terrorism by many means other than military power, that may not be desirable.

The question, then, is will insertions like the chairman's proviso, and how it is interpreted and put into action, leave the new DNI with adequate authority? Or will he or she be only a figurehead—another drug czar giving speeches? Historically, despite the exhortations of a number of presidents, DCIs have lacked authority over the disparate elements of the Community. Still, with the CIA as a base of power, DCIs have always had CIA people moving about within the Intelligence Community, keeping them informed about what was going on. And, being head of the CIA gave the DCI leverage within the Community. For instance, let's assume the DCI wanted an estimate written on some topic that the military considered sensitive, because it might affect their appropriations from Congress. The DCI would try to persuade the Defense Intelligence Agency to participate in the project. The DIA might resist, though it could do so only up to a point. That would be when the DCI, playing his role as head of the CIA, would direct the CIA to do the study on its own. The DIA could protect its interests only by joining in. Today, the new DNI might or might not be able to persuade the CIA to do that study on its own. The CIA director's loyalty might be more with his peer in the DIA than with his superior, the DNI. The DNI's hand, then, is weaker than was the DCI's. That, ironically, is the result of legislation that came from the 9/11 Commission's report that recommended empowering the new DNI. This should not be surprising, though. Throughout this book we have repeatedly seen failed attempts to empower a centralized head of intelligence, going all the way back to Franklin Roosevelt, who established the COI/OSS, but did not give it access to signals intercepts.

Today we have the same result from still another commission investigating the state of our intelligence. This one was cochaired by a senior judge, Laurence H. Silberman, and a former U.S. senator, Charles S. Robb. President Bush tasked it in February 2004 to study our intelligence as it related to weapons of mass destruction. It reported out on March 31, 2005, and its conclusions are harshly critical of our intelligence process as presently constituted. It describes the Intelligence Community as "fragmented, loosely managed, and poorly coordinated" and as being in "a closed world."[13]

The report's primary conclusion is that we need "an empowered DNI."[14] Beyond that it also concludes that the Intelligence Community has "an almost perfect record of resisting external recommendations."[15] The report then goes on to enumerate seventy-four specific recommendations. The irony is that these neither "empower" the DNI any more than does the existing law of December 17, 2004, nor do they suggest ways to overcome the Intelligence Community's inherent resistance to change the report as described. These recommendations, though, have considerable merit. Some suggest ways to organize the Intelligence Community better: for example, by mission rather than function, and with "a management structure that allows him [the DNI] to see deep into the Intelligence Community's component agencies."[16] The recommendations also suggest a number of improvements in operational procedures, such as more outside oversight and more innovative human intelligence techniques.

What the report does not suggest is how the new DNI should go about imposing such organizational and procedural changes on the Intelligence Community's fifteen agencies, those with the "almost perfect record of resisting external recommendations." It specifically notes that the law of December 2004 gives the new DNI powers that are only somewhat broader than before. It appears that the commission expected the DNI to be sufficiently persuasive to convince the agencies to reach agreement by consensus. I do not understand why the commission did not recommend empowering the DNI more when its report includes the statement, "They [the intelligence agencies] are some of the government's most headstrong agencies. Sooner or later, they will try to run around—or over—the DNI."[17]

The resistance to change we are seeing in this latest report, and what we have seen in the history of U.S. intelligence since FDR, is the product of two factors. The first is that the secrecy that is so essential to good intelligence makes the intelligence professionals feel that outsiders just cannot fully understand their work. They discount criticism as uninformed, as much of it is. They sincerely believe that outsiders simply cannot be well enough informed to be able to criticize meaningfully.

The second factor leading to resistance to change is that our present system of intelligence is a heritage of the Cold War. Back then, our security depended on being able to deter or defeat a military assault from the Soviet Union or its proxies. Under that circumstance, military needs for intelligence received number-one priority. That was particularly the case when the military was in combat, as with the conflicts in Korea and Vietnam. The military also played a dominant role in intelligence during the Cold War because the DOD has always had a huge

budget—today, it's more than $400 billion a year. Consequently, it has been by far the most powerful bureaucracy in the government, readily garnering allies from industry and within Congress—the military-industrial-congressional complex. With the amounts of money and the number of jobs involved, the wishes of this group, each member of which has a separate agenda, cannot be disregarded by either Congress or the president. But should such a group have as dominant an influence on intelligence today when the threat to the country is terrorism, not war, and the military is not the dominant player in our response to terrorism?

I can imagine cases in which even the intelligence normally required for full military combat might have to take second place to the kinds of intelligence-gathering necessary to prevent another 9/11 or to uncover the proliferation of WMD. I cannot imagine someone in the DOD voluntarily putting military intelligence needs behind such requirements. It might even be unfair to ask them to do so. When I discuss such possibilities with military colleagues, they simply cannot overcome their conviction that the intelligence needed on the battlefield must always have number-one priority. This stems from their core belief that not just lives but the fate of our very society might be at stake in war. Yet 9/11 severely impacted our society and cost nearly three thousand lives. A nuclear 9/11 would make September 2001 seem like child's play. Decisions on how to employ our intelligence assets must, in my view, rest in the hands of someone who can make balanced judgments about what comes first for the nation.

There has not been much public discussion of the possibility that under some circumstances nonmilitary requirements for intelligence might take priority over military. That, though, must be a good part of what the 9/11 and Scowcroft Commission had in mind when attempting to promote a stronger role for the leader of the Intelligence Community. With the Scowcroft report sidelined and the 9/11 Commission report's key recommendations not fully implemented, there is not much hope today, in my view, that even the most urgent nonmilitary requirements could take precedence over military ones. The case cited earlier of our failure to detect the 1998 Indian nuclear tests in advance shows that always according top priority to the military can be costly to the country. The Intelligence Reform Act makes several attempts to strengthen the hand of the DNI for such exigencies. One way is to give him or her veto power over any of the secretary of defense's nominees for head of NRO, NSA, or NGA. While this is an improvement over the past situation, it does not go far enough. The loyalty of the heads of those agencies will always be with the secretary of defense, who nominates, feeds, and promotes them, not with the DNI simply because he or she did not veto them.

What would it take to have a DNI with the authority to assign and enforce priorities for national needs over the military's requirements? It would be (1) "full and exclusive" responsibility for preparing the consolidated intelligence budget—in other words, the final say before the budgets are sent to the president, and (2) transfer of management control of NSA, NRO, and NGA from the secretary of defense to the DNI, as reportedly recommended by the Scowcroft report. This second point goes further than Carter's executive order by assigning NSA, NRO, and NGA to the DNI for management, as well as operations. I had only operational control. Because I did not have management control—for example, pay, assignments, and promotions—how effectively I could exercise operational control depended very much on personalities and my ability to elicit their cooperation. Some were extremely responsive. Some were extremely resistant.

Under the Scowcroft concept of having the three technical collection agencies, NSA, NRO and NGA, managed by the DNI, it would be logical and efficient to co-locate the CIA's human intelligence branch, the Directorate of Operations, with them. That would bring all forms of collection together under one coordinator. It would allow the DNI to orchestrate intelligence collection based on the needs of the country at that time; and to ensure that the development of new collection capabilities was done in a balanced and reinforcing way. However, it would also mean breaking up the CIA.

If the DO migrated to a new organization for all collection under the DNI's direct control, so should another branch of the CIA, the Directorate of Science and Technology, which provides technical support to collection operations. The analytic branch, the Directorate of Intelligence, would be all that was left of the CIA. Can we afford to break up this venerable institution that has, indeed, done much to keep our country secure? My opinion is that there would be much more gained than lost from doing so. It would be better not only for the nation but for the professionals in the CIA as well.

To begin with, the CIA's reputation in the country is at a nadir today. For its first twenty-nine years, the Agency was a mysterious government entity shrouded in secrecy, but presumed by the public to be doing something very good for the security of the country. Then came the Church Committee report of 1976, which exposed a number of improprieties and illegalities in the CIA's past. This drove the Agency's reputation way down. During my tenure as DCI, the national media were persistently criticizing the Agency for misdeeds of the past, and few colleges permitted CIA recruiters on their campuses. The CIA had been dragged out from under its cloak of secrecy, and in a very unpleasant way. From then until now, the Agency's standing with the public has waxed and waned with events. When I was DCI, our failure to understand Islamic fundamentalism sufficiently to anticipate the fall of the shah of Iran hurt the CIA's reputation badly. In later years, the Agency was battered by a failure to forecast the collapse of the Soviet Union very far in advance and by several almost inexcusable lapses of internal security such that it had Soviet spies in its midst.

The point is that the CIA today is an institution about which the public is reasonably informed. The recent failures over 9/11 and WMD in Iraq have once again seriously eroded the CIA's standing. The various commissions that have studied these failures, especially that of Silberman-Robb, have focused public attention on CIA shortcomings. It is going to be difficult to restore both the standing of the CIA with the public and the morale of its people. Splitting the CIA into organizationally separate bureaus of collection and analysis would allow each, in a sense, to start over. The new managers of each entity could define their new missions and begin to establish their own reputations without carrying as much liability from the past. Additionally, the managers of the new entities would have a better opportunity to break with unhealthy habits and procedures of the past, such as the fierce resistance to change that the Silberman-Robb report identified. Interestingly, one of the great icons of the CIA's DO, Ted Shackley, wrote in his memoir just prior to his death in 2002, that the appointment of a DNI "would be a good time to get rid of a set of initials that are carrying a heavy load of opprobrium and suspicion, however unjustified." And that then "the CIA would in effect disappear."[18]

Shackley, unfortunately, was right. The organizational name CIA has become more of a liability than an asset. The dissolution of the CIA would especially reduce the unhealthy rivalry between that Agency and the DOD intelligence elements. That has been, and is, one of the greatest weaknesses with our intelligence system.

What we could have, then, would be a deputy to the DNI for collection who would have full management control of the CIA's Directorate of Operations, the NSA, the NRO, and the NGA; and a second deputy to the DNI who would have authority to coordinate what was the CIA's analytic arm, plus similar elements throughout the Intelligence Community, but not dictate the results of their analyses. There are those who would, quite reasonably, argue that there are advantages to keeping collectors and analysts close to one another, rather than under separate management structures. A past recurring problem has been the failure of collectors to appreciate just what the analysts needed to know. Some DCIs have even reorganized to bring the two elements closer. Such actions, however, have been only palliatives, not solutions, because while they have brought CIA analysts closer to CIA human intelligence operatives, they have not brought the CIA analysts closer to DOD's human and technical collectors nor DOD analysts closer to CIA human intelligence operators. What we need today is to organize in ways that will increase the amount of discourse between all collectors, human and technical, and all analysts wherever they are in the Community.

There would, of course, be risks of placing considerably greater authority in the hands of the new DNI. The primary one is that a single decision-maker can be too certain of himself or herself and head in a wrong direction. A few DCIs, in my opinion, have had rather narrow perspectives. Offsetting this risk is the existing diversity and independence among the fifteen intelligence agencies and the fact that there is always the resort of appealing to the president. Secretaries of state and defense are not usually bashful people.

Another risk is that if we remove NSA, NRO, and NGA from the DOD, the military will simply re-create their own versions of them based on the excuse that they need them for tactical intelligence. This, indeed, could happen. If it does, we would waste money duplicating such functions.

Finally, there are risks that any system wherein the DNI has meaningful control over the intelligence branches of major departments like Defense and State simply will not work because it requires crossing territorial boundaries. The departments concerned might just stymie the DNI one way or another, through bureaucratic inertia, for instance. That would be unfortunate, but would not place us in a significantly different position from the one we are in today.

Are the stakes high enough to warrant such a realignment? The undue weight of military influence over intelligence collection and analysis in an era when we are combating a global and amorphous enemy, terrorists, is just one factor. Another is that the present system of decision-making is one of consensus. With the right combination of highly cooperative personalities, decision-making by consensus can be fine. With the wrong combination it can be a disaster. Committees do tend to offer answers that represent the least common denominator. Much more important, though, are the risks that consensus will not come rapidly enough or be sufficiently decisive to deter terrorists. Our terrorist opponents are imaginative, resourceful, and decisive. We cannot afford to be less. We have been fortunate not to have had another 9/11. However, the unfortunate result of that is an unhealthy complacency has set in. This is reflected in solutions that satisfy most people, and sound good, but in reality are weak responses to the problem. A true transformation to meet the challenge of terrorism cannot be a series of half-measures, such as those in the Intelligence Reform Act.

Now that we have gone through a spirited debate on the Intelligence Reform Act, my two-part recommendation—including giving full budget authority and management control of NSA, NRO, and NGA to the DNI—may seem more idealistic than realistic. That it is. At the same time, I believe it is important that we think through what the ideal solution to our intelligence problem is. Without the high goal in mind we may miss it altogether. Moreover, if a president, some influential groups in Congress, or a vocal segment of the public understands where we should be going, we might find a way to move more dramatically and effectively than we have.

On balance, I believe government leaders owe it to all Americans to push forward a bold transformation in this vital area, rather than be cowed by turf barons, bureaucrats, or timid souls. We just cannot afford to wait to learn by more failures like 9/11 and going to war in Iraq on the flawed assumption that WMD were there. Congress has left us in the difficult position of having created a much needed CEO for our $40 billion intelligence apparatus, but not having given that CEO adequate authority to do the job. This could be the worst of all worlds; that is, a DNI without direct control of the CIA and not enough control of the Intelligence Community to compensate.

At the same time, although the military's role in national security is less critical than it was during World War II and the Cold War, it is still very important. Perhaps even more to the point, we cannot ignore the power of the military-industrial-congressional complex. We should explore such compromise solutions as:

- Providing that in time of war control of the collection and analytic systems would shift to the Department of Defense on order of the president; and that from time to time in peacetime we would actually do such a transfer every so often to ensure it will work smoothly.
- Recognizing that directing electronic intercept and photographic systems to military problems can occasionally be time-urgent, the secretary of defense could be given a trump card, which only he or she personally could play, to override the DNI in situations of urgent military concern. Each time this was done the secretary would be required to notify the president, together with making a recommendation as to whether it was appropriate to shift control of all collection to the secretary of defense.
- On less time-urgent decisions on collection, priorities for analysis, and budget line items, it should be adequate protection for the military if there are committees established to debate these issues, with ultimate resort to appeal to the president.
- On budget issues where the secretary of defense believes that the DNI is not allocating sufficient resources to some area, it should be permissible for the secretary to add to the DNI's allocation from other funds available to DOD. This would be applicable particularly to tactical intelligence.

Even with these concessions to the military, we could have a DNI who would be a much stronger CEO for the Intelligence Community than at present. We need to be wary, however, of several good-intentioned but faulty proposals to strengthen the DNI further. One is to give the position a fixed term in office; ten years is often suggested. The objective would be to reduce the concern of a DNI that he or she might be fired for not acceding to political pressures to slant the intelligence. Balanced against

that is the possibility that a DNI who carried over from one president to the next—and that would be inevitable—would simply be incompatible with the new president. I cannot, for instance, imagine a Bill Casey and a Jimmy Carter being able to work together. DNIs are utterly dependent on support from the president to have a productive directorship. We have seen how the lack of rapport between Truman and Hillenkoetter, Johnson and McCone, Ford and Colby, and Clinton and Woolsey resulted in little being accomplished. Beyond that, a fixed term could be a disaster for the country if a president made a poor choice for DNI and the nation was saddled with that person for a set number of years.

Another faulty proposal is to give the DNI cabinet status. Casey and Tenet are the only DCIs to have had it. It would be nice if the DNI could speak from the same level as the cabinet secretaries with whom he or she is dealing, but that is more a matter of pride than of effectiveness. The downside of cabinet status for the DNI is overriding: It gives the appearance of the DNI's being on the president's politically partisan team.

There is still one more faulty idea being discussed. That is that we should rely less on cooperation with foreign intelligence services. Surely there are hazards in foreign liaison. Many foreign intelligence services cannot keep secrets. Many have quite different agendas from ours. Yet for us to have our own agents in every remote area of the world where terrorists may plot and train is unrealistic. Moving into an antiterrorism mode has forced us to rely more, not less, on tapping into foreign intelligence networks.

Beyond proposals that would make life more difficult for a DNI, there are those who are opposed to empowering the DCI/DNI on the grounds that changes in organizational wiring diagrams and in bureaucratic alignments will not improve our intelligence. What is needed, they contend, is better analysis, collection, and information exchange. These skeptics are both right and wrong. Elevating and empowering the DNI will not in itself solve problems.

We need, though, to look at some of the ways an empowered DNI could ensure better performance. To start with analysis, the new DNI should be the chief analyst for the Intelligence Community. He or she should be the person who challenges the products of analysis, demanding justification for the deductions made and the conclusions reached. He or she is the best person to show the analysts what decision-makers like the president would want to know about a particular situation and to inject special insights from his or her contacts with the president, cabinet officers, and chiefs of foreign intelligence services. He or she needs to set standards as to how confident an intelligence estimate should sound, insisting on the use of probabilities to do so. What if the CIA's analysts had been required to place a percentage on their confidence that Iraq had WMD in 2003? Would they have called it 70 percent? 90 percent? or a slam dunk? And the Intelligence Reform Act specifically requires that the DNI ensure that there is competitive analysis among the various analytic agencies. That would have meant that in 2003 the lesser probability assigned to WMD by the State Department's intelligence bureau would have been given more weight than it was. Who but someone outside and above the chiefs of the analytic bureaus, like a DNI, could require the use of probabilities and insist on competition? The more clear it is that the DNI truly is the CEO of the Intelligence Community, the more likely it is that he or she will be able to guide analysis in such directions. Finally, as chief analyst the DNI should present to the president orally or in writing the President's Daily Brief, National Intelligence Estimates, and other significant intelligence products. The president needs to know where his chief advisor on intelligence stands on all intelligence products that reach him. Additionally, the DNI needs to know what comments, if any, the president has on them.

Another area of analysis where an empowered DNI could play an important role is in personnel recruitment and training. The Bush administration is committed to a 50 percent increase in the number of analysts in the CIA. Doing so in a way that will have an impact in the short term, as well as the long, will be a challenge. It will mean recruiting academics, businesspeople, and retired military officers for mid-level to senior positions, as well as bringing in lots of brand-new people at the bottom. The prestige and broad perspective of the DNI could help a great deal in inducing more experienced people to shift careers or, at least, to take a sabbatical from their normal work. Special incentive pay from Congress would also be a big help in getting the personnel buildup rolling. A DNI speaking from the perspective of the Community as a whole would be much better positioned to persuade Congress to do this than would individual agency heads.

It is also important that the Community not rely only on infusions of talent from outside to improve its analytic products. A DNI with real authority could mandate the temporary interchange of analysts between agencies as a way for the strongest in the Community to help the weakest. Even two highly capable analytic organizations could benefit from cross fertilization. Again, it would take the authority of a DNI to effect such exchanges.

With regard to collection, the strong hand of a DNI is also badly needed today. The standard response to the clear shortcomings in information collection against terrorism is that there is too little human intelligence. The administration is committed to a 50 percent increase in the CIA's human intelligence operatives. The FBI and the DOD are also increasing emphasis on human intelligence. But contending that our problems with intelligence stem largely from insufficient human intelligence resources is a misleading and superficial diagnosis. It misses the point of how important it is to have balance and coordination between the various systems for collecting information. Whether human intelligence is under-represented can be judged only by looking at the total picture. To begin with, are we doing the best possible with what we have? Are clues from one system of collection being passed to others to cue them onto targets? Is the information we most need likely to come from human sources, electronic, or photographic? And what are the chances of getting a human agent in the right place?

Terrorists are a difficult target for human intelligence. In August 1990, our intelligence failed to predict Iraq's forthcoming invasion of Kuwait, and the failure was quickly blamed on a lack of human intelligence. I asked a friend who was a retired CIA human intelligence operative what the chances were that the CIA could have inserted an agent close enough to Saddam Hussein to learn that he was contemplating an attack on Kuwait. My friend instantly formed a zero with his thumb and forefinger. I am sure he did not mean we should not have tried. He certainly knew that when we were both active in the CIA, the human intelligence team had been able to insert an agent into a Middle Eastern terrorist group, and doing so had saved a lot of lives. It is just not easy. For instance, we almost inserted a second agent into a second terrorist group when I was DCI. The last rite of passage, however, was that this agent had to assassinate a particular government official in order to prove his *bona fides*. When they asked whether I would authorize the assassination in the interest of saving more lives, I said no. This is not to say that

I was right or wrong. It is just another example of the always challenging, and sometimes insuperable, problems involved in infiltrating human agents. It is especially difficult with terrorist groups that are small, closely knit, and rather homogeneous. In addition, our human intelligence operations have heretofore been targeted primarily against nations. And with nations a substantial amount of the CIA's success has been with "walk-ins" who volunteered to help us, not recruitments. Other, perhaps, than experience with attempts to penetrate drug rings, trying to get inside terrorist groups will take entirely new skills, techniques, and procedures. For instance, it appears from the outside that the Directorate of Operations still insists that its operatives must be U.S. citizens without close familial ties abroad. When we expected sources to come to us, that may have been acceptable. In recruiting a terrorist to play traitor to his group, though, it is making the task unnecessarily difficult.

The administration's recent decision to increase CIA human intelligence operatives by 50 percent will compound the learning problem. This is not to say we should not pay more attention to collection by human intelligence, but we should not be overly expectant, especially in the near term. What is truly needed most is to find just where each type of spying fits into our overall collection effort. Only someone looking at the entire picture, like a DNI, can do that objectively.

Further, there is the issue of inadequate exchange of information among intelligence agencies, something very evident in the failure to forecast the events of 9/11. A strong DNI could be effective here because the Intelligence Reform Act gives him or her a mandate to "establish uniform security standards and procedures."[19] Misuse of the security classification system has for decades been a principal device intelligence agencies have employed to keep some of their most sensitive information to themselves. Today, the head of any intelligence agency can create any number of "codewords." Access to such codeword information is limited to people that agency has approved. The purpose is noble—to limit the risk of leaks of highly sensitive information. The application is, however, often maliciously parochial. It gives that agency an advantageous position within the Community of knowing something others do not. Knowledge is often power. Now, under the Intelligence Reform Act, the DNI can take control of all codewords and supervise their use.

In sum, it is easy, but misleading, to say that changing the DNI's position on the wiring diagram and enhancing his or her authorities is not going to be productive. It is an unacceptably parochial argument to claim that a DNI will likely neglect the military's interests. It is being alarmist to say that a more powerful DNI may steer our intelligence in wrong directions. The contending interests of agencies in our intelligence system today have prevented real reform for fifty-eight years. Such resistance is not going to disappear overnight. A key point here is how much more important the position of DCI/DNI has become since 9/11. Intelligence is truly our first line of defense against terrorists. We do not want to have to pick up the pieces after another terrorist attack like 9/11, or worse. We must anticipate the terrorists and cut them off before they can act. President Bush has labeled terrorism the number-one threat we face. In that case, it would be irresponsible not to give the person who manages that first line of defense the tools to do it as well as possible.

It is important, as never before, that the American public, not just politicians and bureaucrats, understand the issues at stake in how we organize and operate our nation's intelligence activities. Each of us has an interest in whether our intelligence apparatus is operating on as sound a footing as possible. Determining that will not be a one-time event—for example, the passing of a law or the signing of a presidential executive order. We will be remiss as a nation if we, the public, do not constantly examine and reexamine whether we are doing everything we can to enable our intelligence system to provide us with the warning we need to forestall terrorists.

Finally, a strong DNI could be the needed focal point for liaison with foreign intelligence services. None of them want to deal with the CIA today, the DIA tomorrow, and so on. In addition, we need one U.S. authority to determine just what of our intelligence we are willing to share with other countries in exchange for their information. Liaison relationships have become of increasing importance as the priority for our intelligence has shifted from the Cold War to terrorism. We cannot hope to have sources in every backwater where terrorists may plot and train, as they have in places like Thailand, Indonesia, and Somalia. We need clues from local intelligence services. A good example of why such liaison can be important is the four bombings in London on July 7, 2005. This was a case in which

British-born Muslims of Pakistani extraction went to Pakistan for education in madrassas. Had there been good intelligence liaison between Great Britain and Pakistan, the Pakistanis might have been alert to this and informed British intelligence about it. That in itself would not necessarily have prevented the bombings, but adding such a clue would have made it more likely.

It is a moment for the president, Congress, and we, the people, to stand up and say, "Yes, we really do want to make defeating terrorists the country's top priority, and empowering a strong director of national intelligence would be a big step in that direction."

QUESTIONS FOR FURTHER DISCUSSION

1. Do you agree with Secretary of Defense Donald Rumsfeld that "centralization" would be a mistake for U.S. intelligence? Why or why not?
2. Why did DCI Tenet's "slam dunk" comment become so controversial?
3. Why does Admiral Turner believe that the new Office of DNI is largely a "figurehead"?
4. What could be done to strengthen the Office of the DNI along the lines Admiral Turner would prefer? Would this be wise?

ENDNOTES

1. Scot J. Paltrow and David S: Cloud, "Reports on 9/11 Say Clinton, Bush Missed Chances in Terrorism," *Wall Street Journal*, March 24, 2004, 1.
2. Clearly Tenet had a change of heart from his days as staff director of the Senate Select Committee on Intelligence, when he drafted legislation and held hearings in 1992 to create a Director of national intelligence and a separate director of the CIA (S. 2198).
3. Walter Pincus, "Tenet Criticizes Intelligence Bill," *Washington Post,* December 2 ,2004.
4. David C. Morrison, "U.S. Intelligence Reform," in *Great Decision,* 2005 ed., Foreign Policy Association, New York, 11.
5. Ibid., p. 16.
6. Bob Woodward *Plan of Attack* (New York: Simon & Schuster, 2004), 249.
7. Morrison "U.S. Intelligence Reform," 10.
8. The new law establishes the position of Director of National Intelligence (DNI) in lieu of the DCI as overall coordinator of national intelligence operations.
9. The National Security Act of 1947 as cited in *Central Intelligence: Origin and Evolution* (Washington, D.C.: CIA History Staff, Center for the Study of Intelligence, Central Intelligence Agency), 29.
10. Memorandum for the Statutory Members of the National Security Council and the Director of Central Intelligence as cited in "Central Intelligence," 50.
11. "Central Intelligence," 67.
12. Executive Order 12333, December 4, 1981, as cited in "Central Intelligence," 131.
13. Report of the Commission on the Intelligence Capabilities of the United States Regarding Weapons of Mass Destruction, Overview of the Report, 5.
14. Ibid., 17.
15. Ibid., 6.
16. Ibid., 18.
17. Ibid., 6.
18. Ted Shackley with Richard A. Finney, *Spymaster: My Life in the CIA* (Dulles, Va: Potomac Books, 2005).
19. H.R. 10, The 9/11 Recommendations Implementation Act, Section 1012,17.

4. THE RISE AND FALL OF THE CIA

RHODRI JEFFREYS-JONES

In the aftermath of the 9/11 and Iraqi WMD failures, the CIA bore the brunt of the blame for the intelligence mistakes that were made—even though it is only one of the sixteen secret agencies in the United States. This essay examines the dramatic rise and fall of America's premier espionage organization.

1. AN AGENCY THAT ROSE AND FELL

The rise of the Central Intelligence Agency (CIA) stemmed from the adoption of a doctrine of central intelligence. That led to the foundation of the CIA in 1947. Once established, the agency achieved ascendancy in the intelligence community, developed an effective U.S. analytical capability, and acquired a reputation for successful covert actions. All this gave the CIA a high standing in government circles, and increased the likelihood that policymakers would pay heed to its findings. The agency became an icon of American culture, its acronym a source of worldwide fascination, its business the business of the world's greatest power. It made a significant contribution to America's national security and to world peace.

But by the early years of the twenty-first century the CIA had lost its former high standing. Its fall may be traced to a number of earlier setbacks and difficulties. The Bay of Pigs disaster of 1961 was a failed attempt to liberate Cuba from communism, and an unmistakable intimation of frailty. Then in the mid-1970s, the agency came under attack from both ends of the political spectrum. Disclosures about its assassinations policy and other malpractices alienated those on the left of the spectrum. Disclosures about its alleged manipulation of intelligence for political reasons enraged right-wingers. The CIA recovered some of its standing in the 1980s, but by the 1990s improved relations between Moscow and Washington threatened the very existence of an agency that seemed to have become synonymous with the Cold War. Subsequently the CIA took some of the blame for not predicting the 9/11 attack, and

much of the blame for inventing the "weapons of mass destruction" scare that led to the Iraq war of 2003. At the end of 2004, an intelligence reform act ended the primacy of the CIA in the American intelligence community.

The rise and fall of the CIA is not, however, a matter of simple chronological progression. The seeds of decay were apparent from the beginning, and the agency continued to do some excellent work even as its star waned. Moreover, the history of the CIA is about more than its rise and fall. It has spawned a variety of thought-provoking and often controversial debates.

2. DISCUSSION POINTS

Some of the debates have been about democratic principles. Devotees of American democracy were glad to see the CIA, a civilian agency, take center stage in an intelligence community heavily populated by the military. But others of equally democratic inclination worried that the CIA was elitist, and dominated by male, white, Ivy League types. In the knowledge that effective democracy depended on open government, a powerful cadre of reformers demanded congressional oversight of the secret agency. Fears of excessive secrecy fuelled complaints about the politicization of intelligence. What complicated these controversies was that liberals and conservatives played alternating roles—the CIA started life as the creation of liberals, and later became the darling of the Right.

Other debates have been about the effectiveness of the agency. From the beginning, there were those who doubted whether the conduct and administration of covert operations belonged in a civilian intelligence agency. Some critics argued that covert operations would be counterproductive whoever undertook them, as even when they succeeded they made America unpopular. Debate on the agency's intelligence analyses has been endless. Inevitably the CIA made mistakes, and critics pounced on these. The agency's inability to predict certain surprise attacks led to especially strong opprobrium. Still another kind of debate focuses on the authorship of failure—was it always the fault of the agency, or did the CIA director sometimes act as the fall guy for the president? Clearly, any account of the rise and fall of the CIA must take into account a variety of issues.

3. THE FOUNDING OF THE CIA

With the creation of the CIA in 1947, the United States for the first time had a permanent peacetime intelligence capability. America had previously engaged in *wartime* intelligence activities, but on a temporary basis. While George Washington, for example, had been a proficient spymaster, his intelligence activities were responses to short-lived crises. Many years later in World War I, the State Department established a more thoroughly organized intelligence system known as U-1, but by 1927 it had been entirely dissolved (Jeffreys-Jones 2002, 11–23, 60–79).

In September 1939, war once again broke out in Europe. By March 1941, Federal Bureau of Investigation (FBI) Director J. Edgar Hoover suspected that America might soon join that war, and that this would once again require a boost to the nation's intelligence apparatus. British intelligence had a high reputation in the United States and by this time was on a war footing, so Hoover sent two officials to find out how it worked. These officials, Hugh G. Clegg and Lawrence Hince, sent back a critical evaluation, and Hoover used this as the basis of a report he submitted to President Franklin D. Roosevelt. One matter upon which he commented was the feeling within the British intelligence community that there might be an advantage to combining MI-5 and MI-6, respectively Britain's domestic and foreign intelligence agencies (Charles 2005, 232).

President Roosevelt and his advisers now sent the New York attorney William J. Donovan on a fact-finding mission to London. Donovan studied the covert operations the wartime Special Operations

Executive (SOE), as well as the more established MI-5 and MI-6. Although MI-5 and MI-6 never did merge, Donovan returned home convinced of the virtue of a centralized intelligence system. In July 1941, Roosevelt established the Office of Coordinator of Information (COI), and put Donovan in charge. In December, Japan attacked Pearl Harbor, and America was at war. Roosevelt and his war cabinet steadily ratcheted up the nation's intelligence capability. In June 1942, the president issued an executive order that replaced the COI arrangement with a larger agency, the Office of Strategic Services (OSS). This agency had a foreign remit that included covert operations, and its agents operated with some distinction behind enemy lines. Donovan was once again in charge.

Toward the war's end, Donovan recommended that there should be a *peacetime* central intelligence agency with a substantial capability. Donovan's admirers have hailed him as the father of the CIA—for example, Thomas F. Troy, an official CIA historian, in his book about the CIA's origins (1981). Others, such as CIA veteran David F. Rudgers, argue that while Donovan was significant, he was just one of several persuasive advocates of peacetime central intelligence (Rudgers 2000, 3). For by the war's end in 1945, there was an extensive lobby for a peacetime organization. After Roosevelt's death the new president, Harry Truman, disbanded the OSS, but in 1946 set up an interim replacement unit, the Central Intelligence Group (CIG). This became the CIA the following year.

President Truman supported the idea of central intelligence as a means of countering the Soviet Union. The Soviets were an adversary to be feared because their victory over Germany had empowered and emboldened them, and, above all, because of their alien communist ideology. CIG's very first tasking directive identified an "urgent need" for intelligence on the Soviets. However, Capitol Hill supported legislation setting up the CIA for a different reason. Senators and Congressmen remembered the Japanese attack at Pearl Harbor. They vowed that America should never again be caught by surprise, and supported a central intelligence agency that would better protect America in the future (Jeffreys-Jones 1997, 23, 25–26).

There were other reasons, too, for the establishment of the CIA. One was the feeling that the British had bossed the international context in which the United States had operated, partly through the operations of its vaunted secret services. America now needed its own capability not just to protect its sovereignty, but also because it had become a great power with worldwide responsibilities. Another factor was that in the depression years of the 1930s and then in the course of World War II, the nation had become accustomed to setting up federal agencies to cope with grievous problems. With the carnage of the recent war fresh in Americans' minds, there was support for the idea that the latest new agency should be civilian in character. Later on, there were other reasons why people supported the work of the CIA, for example its ability to promote U.S. technological, scientific, and economic ascendancy.

Others opposed the CIA, sometimes arguing that its creation and rise to prominence were the result of an elitist conspiracy. In fact, conspiracy fears shaped the CIA from the very beginning. From the moment when the *Chicago Tribune* learned of Donovan's plans for a peacetime agency there was a campaign in the press against any super-agency on lines reminiscent of Germany's hated secret police. Both Donovan and Hoover fell under suspicion for allegedly wanting to preside over an "American Gestapo." What sealed the fate of both men was the fact that President Truman was ill disposed toward them—he regarded Donovan as a boastful prima donna, and disliked Hoover's FBI because he believed it had a poor record on civil liberties. The outcome of all these suspicions was a divide-and-weaken policy. The National Security Act of 1947 gave the director of the CIA the further title of Director of Central Intelligence (DCI), with responsibility to coordinate the work of the entire intelligence community. However, it banned the CIA itself from operating domestically, and prohibited the FBI from doing foreign work. Given the rivalries between the two institutions, the result was decades of poor coordination, to the ultimate detriment of national security (Jeffreys-Jones 2007,137–48).

Although the CIA lacked the authorization to spy at home, it did receive the go-ahead to expand in another way. It could not just spy abroad, but also conduct covert operations. This meant, for example, that it could secretly undermine or support a foreign government. Its extensive covert-action programs would later be controversial (Prados 2006; Weiner 2007).

Some critics attributed those programs' excesses to the weakness of congressional oversight in the first seventeen years of the agency's existence. Though the CIA was the world's first democratically sanctioned foreign intelligence agency and Congress had the right and duty to oversee the expenditure of every dollar of taxpayers' money, until the mid-1970s legislators rarely interfered with the day-to-day running of the agency. Their inaction was not an indication of weakness. It reflected the fact that congressional leaders generally approved of the CIA's activities, including its covert actions. In the early Cold War years, they also operated on the principle that this was a secret agency, and that imprudently asked questions might give rise to damaging leaks (Barrett 2005, 45S–60).

4. THE GOLDEN YEARS OF INTELLIGENCE

In 1949, the Soviet Union shocked the world's democracies by exploding a prototype atomic bomb. The earlier than-expected timing of this technical breakthrough stemmed partly from atomic espionage against the United States. Clearly there was a need for the CIA and FBI to overcome the rivalries that divided them, and to concentrate on counterintelligence. Equally, it was evident that America would need to compete in the realm of offensive espionage. America resorted to scientific espionage of its own. The CIA's Berlin office used seductive women as one method of extracting secrets from eastern scientists, and sometimes to persuade them to defect. This program did not weaken communist technology as much as its originators hoped, but it did yield a scientific dividend for the United States (Maddrell 2006, 1, 79, 198).

Advances in Soviet military technology were alarming because they posed a threat to American security, because the Soviet Union used its totalitarian apparatus to hide its technology, and because the resulting obfuscation lent itself to opportunistic distortion by what President Dwight D. Eisenhower would blisteringly label the American "military-industrial complex." The challenge for the CIA was not only to steal Soviet secrets, but also to evaluate the Soviet arsenal in a more objective manner, and to assess what the Kremlin intended to do with it. It was a secret agency with the mission of opening up the secrets of America's potential adversary.

Another question was this: the Soviets may have had the technology, but was their economy strong enough to challenge America's military ascendancy? How quickly could they produce nuclear warheads and the means to deliver them, planes and intercontinental ballistic missiles (ICBMs)? President Eisenhower had military experience and took an informed interest in such matters. More than most presidents, he drove the intelligence agenda (Andrew 1995, 4, 199, 223). Allen Dulles, his pick as CIA director (1953–61), had a matching interest in economic analysis. He faced a daunting problem. In a command economy such as the Soviet Union's, the national currency is no guide to value, and it was no easy task to compare the cost of a missile component with that of a glass of vodka. But by 1955 the CIA's Office of Research Reports had five hundred experts working on economic analysis, a greater number than all the other analysts combined. They were able to show, in defiance of Air Force contentions, that the Soviet economy was too weak to sustain a threatening level of bomber production (Zelikow 1997,166–68).

Unable to send in spies at ground level, the CIA operated both below and above the terrestrial surface. It helped British colleagues drill a tunnel right under the heavily patrolled border into the communist sector of Berlin. The 450-yard excavation was so situated that, prior to the East German authorities' exposure of its existence in 1956, technicians were able to listen advantageously to Soviet electronic communications (Stafford 2003, 2). Aerial reconnaissance was a further source of information. With Richard Bissell in charge, the CIA sponsored the U-2 plane, which overflew Soviet test sites at altitudes beyond the reach of ground-to-air missiles or fighter aircraft.

Equipped with high-technology cameras and operational from 1956, the U-2s produced images in which President Eisenhower showed a personal interest. These images ultimately showed that 1CBM development was less advanced than the Kremlin boasted. The "missile gap" of which the American military had warned was just as much of a myth as the preceding "bomber gap." This knowledge soothed American nerves, and helped to save the world from a nuclear holocaust. And by the time the Russians had developed a new missile and shot down a U-2 plane in 1960, America had in place a spy satellite program (yet another Eisenhower/ CIA initiative) promising ever-more-sophisticated images of military developments behind the iron curtain.

In tandem with its intelligence activities, the CIA ran covert operations. It had an extensive program of secret propaganda, with activities ranging from the secret subsidization of pro-American radio programs in Central Europe to buying up all the ink in France to hamper the printing of communist literature at the time of the 1948 election. The agency passed dollars under the table to anti-communist magazines like Britain's *Encounter*. It operated anti-communist networks through private American groups—students, organized labor, émigrés, intellectuals, women, Catholics, African Americans, businessmen, and journalists. Some of these citizens knew where the money was coming from, others did not. Most shared the anti-communist goal of the CIA, though not all of them were happy about being subsidized by a secret government agency (Wilford 2008, 8).

The CIA also ran covert-action programs. Some of the agency's covert actions were outright failures—its attempt (in collaboration with the British) to overthrow the communist government of Albania in 1949, its futile encouragement of uprisings in East Berlin (1953) and Hungary (1956), and its effort to support a coup in Indonesia in 1958. So effective was the CIA's publicity and news-control machine, and so united was opinion against the Soviet Union at the height of the Cold War, that these failures did little harm to the agency's reputation.

Meanwhile, the CIA's leaders were able to boast of a string of successes. The communists fell short at the polls in France and Italy. There was also success in the Philippines, where the CIA's Edward Lansdale developed a counterinsurgency doctrine. Lansdale said it was better to educate than to bomb the natives. Rather than send in the marines when a nation was threatened by communism, America should help the locals to build and defend their own nation (Blaufarb 1977, 39–40). By 1953, the Filipino communist insurrection was over.

The CIA supported foreign politicians who professed hostility to communism even if those politicians were themselves undemocratic. In 1953, it encouraged a coup against the democratically elected government of Iran, installing in power the shah, a monarch who ensured that his nation would be a reliable source not just of anti-communism, but of oil, too. In 1954, with President Eisenhower in active support, the CIA helped to overthrow the democratically fleeted government of Guatemala. Critics complained that the Guatemalan coup favored the interests of the U.S.-based multinational, the United Fruit Company, and that it inflicted another right-wing dictator on a foreign nation (Schlesinger and Kinzer 1983, 220–21). But the trail was murky, and the CIA's reputation as an operational miracle-worker continued to blossom. Though the 1950s had been a decade of brilliant intelligence achievements, instead they entered CIA mythology as the golden age of operations.

5. THE TROUBLED 1960S

In January 1961, General Lansdale submitted to incoming president John F. Kennedy an intelligence assessment of the situation in South Vietnam. He warned that the communist insurgency was gathering pace, and recommended that the United States should identify first-class local leadership and give them the means to overcome the danger (Prados 2006, 337–38). Lansdale would remain opposed to U.S. military intervention, advocating "de-Americanization" and an effort to win the "hearts and minds" of the Vietnamese people. Kennedy and his successor, President Lyndon B. Johnson, ignored this advice by attempting to pursue counterinsurgency and military tactics simultaneously.

Kennedy and his CIA similarly ignored the principle of indigeneity when planning for an agency-led invasion to land at Cuba's Bay of Pigs in April 1961. Cuban fighters repelled the invasion, and it failed to topple the Fidel Castro regime. In preparing for the operation, the CIA had made no attempt to assess whether the Cuban people would support it, and in the event they did not. Another factor contributing to the humiliating defeat was the fact that Castro's air force had been expecting the attack and strafed the landing force—the CIA's secrecy procedures had kept only the American people in the dark.

In firing Dulles and Bissell for the Bay of Pigs disaster, Kennedy admitted that he was equally to blame. But he explained to Dulles that under the American constitutional system the president could only be replaced once every four years, so it was the CIA director who had to be the scapegoat and resign. The punitive removal of its top officials dulled the CIA's pristine sheen, and the agency received another blow at the end of the year—for in December 1961, the Defense Intelligence Agency (DIA) came into existence. The DIA was not a direct response to the Bay of Pigs, having been in gestation for a number of years as the army, navy, and air force tried to sink their rivalries and speak with a united and more powerful voice. But the Bay of Pigs postmortem had identified military inexperience as a factor contributing to the Cuban failure, and CIA pessimists had reason to dread that in the years to come policymakers would listen to the agency with one ear cupped in the direction of the Pentagon's DIA (Mescall 1991, 159, 194–97).

In spite of being in some ways an intelligence disaster, the Cuban Missile Crisis of the following year gave the CIA an opportunity to restore its standing. President Kennedy had authorized the placement of forty-five Jupiter missiles in Italy and Turkey. These were nuclear-tipped and within range of Soviet targets. Some analysts had warned that Moscow would consider this a serious threat to the balance of power, but Kennedy did not ask the CIA to assess possible Soviet reactions until after he had taken the decision and was committed to deployment (Nash 1997, 3, 97). The Soviet premier Nikita Khrushchev now reacted with an attempt secretly to install in Cuba an equivalent array of SS-4 and SS-5 missiles—apparently he, too, neglected to call for an intelligence assessment of the likely adversarial reaction (Fursenko and Naftali 1998, 64, 71). American intelligence theorists at this time generally argued that in order to avoid the politicization of estimates, decision-making and analytical processes should be kept apart. However, in the lead-up to the missile crisis political-intelligence communications seemed to have broken down altogether (Betts 2003, 60).

Nevertheless, the CIA emerged from the affair with credit. John A. McCone had by now succeeded Dulles as director. He offended some of the old guard by moving the agency away from its Ivy League orientation, and in the direction of technical rather than human intelligence. Yet he still revealed a rare bit of individual human intuition in guessing that the Soviets would place missiles in Cuba. McCone persuaded President Kennedy and his advisors to consider the implications in a meeting on August 23, 1962 (May and Zelikow 1997, 35). On October 14, a U-2 photographic overflight confirmed the existence of Soviet missile sites in Cuba. For a few days, the superpowers squared up to each other and the world teetered on the brink of nuclear war. But Kennedy had been given the time to prepare his options, and was able to negotiate a compromise. Both the Jupiters and the SS 4/5s were withdrawn, and the most dangerous moment in modern history had passed.

In the Vietnamese new year holiday (Tet) at the end of January 1968, communist forces launched a spectacular surprise attack on American positions and those of their South Vietnamese allies. The Tet attack failed to inspire a general uprising, and the American counteroffensive was so effective that well over half of the 84,000 communist attack force ended up as casualties. But the Tet initiative was nevertheless effective in that it destroyed the credibility of Lyndon B. Johnson's administration's claim that the war was going well. General William C. Westmoreland, the commander of the U.S. military forces in Vietnam, had fueled the optimism by insisting that his war of attrition against the enemy was succeeding. The sheer scale of the Tet campaign made him look foolish, and damaged U.S. morale.

Tet had the effect of discrediting the military's intelligence estimates compared with those of the CIA. Back in 1966, CIA analyst Sam Adams had put enemy strength at closer to 600,000 than the 270,000 figure that formed the basis of military attrition claims. His larger estimate seemed to explain the enemy's eventual ability to mount an offensive (Adams 1975, 62, 64). In June 1971, leaked documents on American decision-making on Vietnam—the Pentagon Papers—seemed to throw the CIA in a good light, and Adams published his account of events in 1975, adding to the impression that the CIA had shown a wise skepticism about a disastrous war. It was all too easy to overlook the facts that military analysts, too, had had their doubt about the Vietnam strategy, and that the post-McCone CIA leadership, whatever reservations it may have had, held back from telling Presidents Johnson and Richard Nixon that the war was going badly—instead, the CIA's leaders had delivered "intelligence to please."

Meantime, trouble was brewing for the covert operators. In spite of his best efforts, Lansdale was unable to persuade the White House and the military command to give counterinsurgency a chance, and to stop bombing the people whose hearts and minds they were trying to woo. Then in Operation Phoenix, an effort to counter the terrorist tactics of the enemy, the CIA itself ignored the principles of counterinsurgency, and operated an assassination campaign against suspected communist activists. Such operations were problems in themselves, rather than solutions.

6. REVELATIONS AND REFORM

If but slowly at first, the problems came home to roost. In a book published at the start of 1967, the journalist Thomas B. Morgan argued that the CIA's foreign "interventionism" was the prime cause of America's unpopularity in the world—he meant *all* the agency's covert actions, not just the crimes and the failures (Morgan 1967, 9–10). But what really upset Americans were revelations about the CIA's *domestic* operations in violation of the agency's charter. Just after Morgan's study appeared, the Californian Catholic magazine *Ramparts* exposed the agency's use of U.S. voluntary groups like the National Students Association to conduct clandestine propaganda

around the globe. The national media made a fuss, the affair was a profound shock to the intelligentsia, and the CIA's operators beat an ignominious—though limited—retreat from a cherished range of activities (Wilford 2008, 4–5).

Then in 1974–75, in the wake of the demoralizing Watergate scandal that had forced President Nixon to resign, there was a flood of revelations. Americans were shocked to read about Phoenix, about another assassination program aimed at foreign leaders like Castro, about the CIA's part in the recent overthrow of the elected government in Latin America's oldest democracy, Chile, about the agency's illegal espionage activities against Vietnam War protestors, and about a whole range of other controversial activities. The Senate and the House of Representatives launched the biggest investigation in American history.

Though the chairman of the Senate committee, Frank Church, at first claimed that the CIA was a "rogue elephant out of control," he soon changed his mind (Johnson 1985, 119). Secretary of State Henry Kissinger told the House intelligence inquiry that the president had personally authorized every covert action of recent years (Olmsted 1996, 142). No longer seen as the prime culprit, the CIA survived. But from now on it had to answer to more powerful congressional oversight by committees set up in both the Senate and the House.

Since the 1970s, this oversight has varied in quality and intensity. Critics have variously suggested that congressional vigilance collapses at times of crisis and heightened patriotism, that over time oversight committee members become too friendly with CIA officials, and that legislators only address intelligence inadequacies in the wake of some shocking incident that has focused the attention of the press—and thus the voters—on the need for scrutiny (Ransom 1984, 225; Smist 1990, 20–22; Johnson 2007, 344). Nevertheless, since the 1970s any president thinking of using the CIA for nefarious purposes has run the danger of a day of reckoning with Congress.

President from 1977 to 1981, Jimmy Carter wound down the covert-action capabilities of the CIA. This, however, did not save him from his own day of reckoning. In 1979, disaster struck for his administration when Islamic leaders in Iran overthrew the shah. The CIA had for years been warning about political repression in Iran and in 1978 produced an assessment called "Iran after the Shah." But not until 1979 did the agency begin to issue urgent alerts. With the DIA too closely aligned with the shah's military and Washington's leadership turning deaf ears to the CIA, the revolution caught America by surprise (Donovan 1997, 159–60). What made matters worse was that the mullah-led Teheran government held hostage fifty-two U.S. embassy staffers, and used captured documents to show that many of them had been working for the CIA. The agency now disappointed the luckless Carter by bungling a rescue attempt. When Ronald Reagan ran on the Republican ticket for president in 1980, he prospered from the failings of Carter's CIA.

7. VICTORY IN THE COLD WAR

President Reagan lived up to his promise to "unleash" the CIA. William Casey, his choice as director, rebuilt the agency's covert capabilities. As before, this became evident in Latin America. In Nicaragua, a group known as the Sandinistas had recently overthrown an invidious right-wing dictatorship. The CIA now trained and paid a terrorist counterrevolutionary group known as the Contras, and tried to ruin the new government by mining Nicaragua's Corinto harbor, an action that violated international law.

The CIA also broke its own country's laws regarding both Nicaragua and Iran. Congress had got wind of the CIA's help to the Contras, and legislated against it. There was other legislation that made it illegal to export arms to Iran. But with Israeli help the agency brokered a deal whereby the Iranians illegally received American tactical missiles in exchange for illegally routing CIA money to the Contras. In the event, the whole exercise proved to have been unnecessary, as the citizens of Nicaragua voted out the Sandinistas of their own accord in a free election in 1990. Leaks about the Iran-Contra operation by this time caused a scandal in Reagan's second term as president (1985–89). But the national mood had changed. Most Americans did not just forgive Reagan and his CIA, they adored them.

While President Reagan had an endearing personality, it was his administration's apparent "victory" in the Cold War that really impressed his admirers. The debate about that victory came to center on the politicization of intelligence, a process that had already loomed large in the 1970s.

When Henry Kissinger was national security advisor in the Nixon administration, he manipulated the intelligence product of the CIA. He exaggerated the Soviet nuclear threat in order to persuade Congress to appropriate funds for an antiballistic missile (ABM) system that would potentially have given America a strategic advantage over its Cold War adversary. With this card in hand, Kissinger was in a stronger position in negotiations, and induced Moscow to agree to the strategic arms-limitation treaties (SALT) of 1971–72. When CIA analysts showed there was a history of Soviet infractions of such agreements, Kissinger suppressed the evidence in order to bolster confidence in his diplomacy and win congressional approval of the treaties. A safer world was the end that justified his duplicitous means, but when the story inevitably leaked out, it meant that people were less likely to trust the CIA and the intelligence process in the future.

At a time when President Carter was negotiating a further round of arms reductions, SALT II, a group of anti-Kissinger conservatives challenged the CIA's interpretation of Soviet data (Cahn 1998, 186). To placate its critics and try to win Senate approval for its diplomacy, the government set up a system of "competitive estimates." Team A, the usual CIA analysts, looked at Moscow's aggressive declarations and saw them as "exhortative" (Freedman 1997, 138). But a more hawkish Team B, non-CIA experts who looked at the same evidence on a confidential basis, dismissed the idea that the communists were bluffing, insisting that they meant what they said and constituted a real danger to American national security. The Senate failed to ratify SALT II.

President Reagan's administration called for a Strategic Defense Initiative, popularly known as "Star Wars" after the 1977 movie of that title. Whereas the ABM system would have been ground-based, this time satellite-controlled laser beams would destroy incoming enemy missiles. Once again, Congress agreed to fund an expensive program that was justified by exaggerated intelligence estimates of Soviet capabilities. Critics alleged that the agency's Soviet expert Robert Gates (a future director of the CIA) delivered politicized intelligence to please. The CIA played another role, too, in the Reagan administration's effort to win the Cold War and free Europe from communism. It ran economic sabotage operations against the Soviet oil industry, and secretly subsidized the anti-communist movement in the pivotal state of Poland.

By 1989 the Cold War was over, and in 1991 the Soviet Union dissolved. Having been in decline in the 1970s, the CIA now appeared to have climbed to new heights. Its supporters argued that it had contributed to the collapse of European communism.

Some of them claimed that the Star Wars program that the CIA's intelligence had underpinned had been an effort to induce emulative Soviet expenditure, a profoundly clever ploy that broke the communist economies (Diamond 2008, 8).

8. SEARCHING FOR A NEW MISSION

However, the CIA was to be the victim of its own success. It had been a Cold War agency. By the very act of winning the Cold War, it seemed to remove the reason for its own existence. Victory had another unwanted consequence. With the elimination of the imminent communist danger, one could find fault with the CIA without being unpatriotic. Critics now charged that the CIA had believed its own hyperbole about the Soviet threat. They alleged that this had resulted in a rigid mindset, and a failure to realize that the Soviet economy was in bad shape. Thus, the fall of European communism had caught America by surprise, leaving it without a game plan for the post-communist world.

Senator Daniel P. Moynihan (D-Mass.), a respected figure in American politics, called for the abolition of the CIA. Under fire from Moynihan and others, the agency now experienced a damaging setback, the Aldrich Ames affair. Prior to his arrest in 1993, Ames had worked for the agency as a counterintelligence officer, but from 1985 he spied on a commercial basis for the Soviets and then, in the post-communist era, for Russia. His treason damaged the American defense effort and led to the betrayal of U.S. secret agents and the execution of several of them. The discovery that Ames had operated with impunity in spite of leaving a trail of indiscretions damaged the CIA's reputation for counterintelligence.

The agency went through a difficult time, shedding a quarter of its staff in 1993–94 and going through five directors between 1991 and 1997. It undertook reforms. George Bush, Sr., president from 1989 to 1993 and a former director of the CIA, initiated a "Glass Ceiling Study" that encouraged the recruitment of more women. The CIA additionally tried to reach out to a broader ethnic spectrum, and in 1995 President Bill Clinton issued an executive order ending its ban on the recruitment of homosexuals. The agency also made an effort to be more open about its activities. Such changes pleased some of its critics, yet annoyed others who thought it was putting "political correctness" above national security. But at least the survival of the agency was assured. Under the chairmanship first of Les Aspin and then of Harold Brown, a presidential commission undertook America's biggest-ever single inquiry into secret intelligence. In 1996, it recommended that the CIA should continue to function as an independent agency. It also recommended against the idea that the DCI should give way to a more powerful "intelligence tsar" who would preside in his stead over the entire intelligence community.

One way in which the agency sought to survive was to search for new, post-Cold War roles. By the end of the 1990s, it had identified an Islamist terrorist group, Al Qaeda, as a danger to American safety. Al Qaeda was nevertheless able to strike a devastating blow against America in the first year of the administration of President George Bush, Jr. The inquest into why America had been unable to prevent the 9/11 attack was long and bitter. Politicians, scholars, and journalists identified causes for the failure, and fixed the responsibility on a number of individuals and institutions. The main official inquiry into the event listed five occasions in the twenty months leading up to September 2000 when the CIA failed to pass on information about Al Qaeda suspects to its rival institution, the FBI (9/11 2004, 355). However, the CIA did not bear the brunt of the criticism, and even benefited from the fiasco—on the premise that intelligence failure had resulted from intelligence underfunding, the nation's leaders increased the budget of the CIA in line with that of the entire intelligence community.

9. THE END OF ASCENDANCY

More trouble lay ahead, however. When America invaded Iraq in 2003, the Bush administration justified the action on the grounds that Iraq had been helping Al Qaeda, and that its undemocratic regime was planning to produce chemical and nuclear weapons of mass destruction (WMDs). Subsequent investigations proved that both assertions were false, that the nuclear WMD charge had been supported by a forged document, and that the CIA had delivered intelligence to please instead of challenging the administration's assumptions about Iraq. CIA director George Tenet had been close to President Bush and had given his imprimatur to the WMD claims, and he now had to resign.

The Intelligence Reform and Terrorism Prevention Act of 2004 addressed America's security problems in ways that affected the CIA. It established what the Aspin-Brown commission had rejected, a new post of director of national intelligence (DNI). Unlike the now-defunct DCI, the holder of this post would not be director of the CIA, and the hope was that the new arrangement would give the DNI an authority to command the whole of the intelligence community that the DCI had never managed to exert. The law aimed to end CIA-FBI bickering and was an affirmation of the principle of centralized intelligence. Its admirers saw it as part of the blueprint for a safer America (Lynch and Singh 2008, 116). For the CIA, though, it meant a lower standing. Its intelligence findings would be less likely to challenge the military's in the future, and the agency was expected to redouble its covert-operational activities.

These activities were certainly in evidence. When captured in various parts of the world, Al Qaeda and other terrorist suspects were tortured in order to obtain information on their plans and colleagues. From 2002, the U.S. base at Guantanamo Bay, Cuba, housed a prison for terrorist suspects, and other suspects were held in compliant nations like Poland. The illegally kidnapped suspects were described as having been "tendered" to locations convenient for their interrogation. For several years, the press carried stories about the CIA's prominent role in these operations.

The agency's reputation sank to a new low. The titles of books being written about the agency carried words like "failure," "decline," and "fall" and complained about the phenomena of intelligence to please and politicization (Diamond 2008, 13; Goodman 2008, 147).

Not all of these books were reliable. Take, for example, *Legacy of Ashes*, a book by a *New York Times* journalist that concentrated on the CIA's failings and won popular plaudits. Tim Weiner, the author, concentrated on the spicy side of history and failed to consult scholarship in the field that might have led him to more balanced conclusions (Weiner 2007; Johnson and Jeffreys-Jones 2008, 882, 886–87).

In spite of the bad press, the CIA was still capable of good work, for example in the case of its contribution to efforts to prevent the proliferation of nuclear-weapon technology. In 2003, CIA intelligence led to the seizure of a ship carrying nuclear-weapon materials to Libya, and in the following year it uncovered a black market in nuclear weapons technology involving Iran and North Korea, as well. Furthermore, critics were startlingly unaware that the CIA's errors were not always of its own making. As Senator Church had discovered in 1975, the CIA is a creature of the executive.

Criticism was less evidence of the CIA's decline than a symptom of it. For the true nature of that decline rested in the agency's loss of standing. It had relinquished its ascendancy over and to a degree its independence within the intelligence community, and much of its *reputation* for objective analysis. Its capabilities remained, but it was a fallen agency in the sense that its analyses now fell on deaf or unsympathetic ears.

QUESTIONS FOR FURTHER DISCUSSION

1. How did the CIA become America's leading intelligence organization?
2. What were the CIA's highest and lowest historical points before the 9/11 attacks in 2001?
3. Were the 9/11 and Iraqi WMD intelligence failures exclusively a CIA responsibility?
4. Does the U.S. intelligence community need a "central" intelligence agency, or can the Office of the DNI play that coordinative and integrative role?

REFERENCES

Adams, S. 1975. Vietnam Cover-Up: Playing with Numbers. *Harper's* (May): 41–44, 62–73.

Andrew, C. 1995. *For the President's Eyes Only: Secret Intelligence and the American Presidency from Washington to Bush.* London: HarperCollins.

Barrett, D. M. 2005. *The CIA and Congress: The Untold Story from Truman to Kennedy.* Lawrence: University Press of Kansas.

Betts, R. K. 2003. Politicization of Intelligence: Costs and Benefits. In *Paradoxes of Strategic Intelligence: Essays in Honor of Michael. Handel,* ed. R. K. Betts and T.G. Mahnken. London: Frank Cass.

Blaufarb, D. S. 1977. *The Counter-Insurgency Era: U.S. Doctrine and Performance, 1950 to the Present.* New York: Free Press.

Cahn, A. H. 1998. *Killing Detente: The Right Attacks the CIA.* University Park: Pennsylvania State University Press.

Charles, D. M. 2005. "Before the Colonel Arrived": Hoover, Donovan, Roosevelt, and the Origins of American Central Intelligence. *Intelligence and National Security,* 20, no. 2:225–37.

Diamond, J. 2008. *The CIA and the Culture of Failure: U.S. intelligence from the End of the Cold War to the Invasion of Iraq.* Stanford, Calif.: Stanford University Press.

Donovan, M. P. 1997. Intelligence and the Iranian Revolution. In *Eternal Vigilance? 50 Years of the CIA,* ed. R. Jeffreys-Jones and C. Andrew. London: Frank Cass.

Freedman, L. 1997. The CIA and the Soviet Threat: The Politicizaiion of Estimates, 1966–1997. In *Eternal Vigilance? 50 Years of the CIA*, ed. R. Jeffreys-Jones and C. Andrew. London: Frank Cass.

Fursenko, A., and T. Naftali. 1998. Soviet Intelligence and the Cuban Missile Crisis. In *Intelligence and the Cuban Missile Crisis*, ed. J. G. Blight and D. A. Welch. London: Frank Cass.

Goodman, M. A. 2008. *Failure of Intelligence: The Decline and Fall of the CIA*. Lanham, Md., Rowman and Littlefield.

Jeffreys-Jones, R. 1997. Why Was the CIA Established in 1947? In *Eternal Vigilance? 50 Years of the CIA*, ed. R. Jeffreys-Jones and C. Andrew. London: Frank Cass.

———. 2002. *Cloak and Dollar: A History of American Secret Intelligence*. New Haven: Yale University Press.

———. 2007. *The FBI: A History*. New Haven: Yale University Press.

Johnson, L. K. 1985. *A Season of Inquiry: The Senate Intelligence Investigation*. Lexington: University Press of Kentucky.

———. 2007. A Shock Theory of Congressional Accountability for Intelligence. In *Handbook of Intelligence Studies*, ed. L. K. Johnson. London: Routledge.

Johnson, L. K., and R. Jeffreys-Jones. 2008. Review Roundtable: Tim Weiner's *Legacy of Ashes: The History of the CIA. Intelligence and National Security* 22, no. 6:878–891.

Lynch, T.J., and R.S. Singh, *After Bush: The Case for Continuity in American Foreign Policy* (Cambridge: Cambridge University Press, 2008).

Maddrell, P. 2006. *Spying on Science: Western Intelligence in Divided Germany 1945–1967*. Oxford: Oxford University Press.

May, E. R., and P. D. Zelikow. 1997. *The Kennedy Tapes: Inside the White House during the Cuban Missile Crisis*. Cambridge, Mass.: Belknap/Harvard University Press.

Mescall, P. 1991. The Birth of the Defense Intelligence Agency. In *North American Spies: New Revisionist Essays*, ed. R. Jeffreys-Jones and A. Lownie. Lawrence. University of Kansas Press.

Morgan, T. B. 1967. *The Anti-Americans*. London: Michael Joseph.

Nash, P. 1997. *The Other Missiles of October: Eisenhower, Kennedy and the Jupiters, 1957–1963*. Chapel Hill: University of North Carolina Press.

9/11. 2004. *The 9/11 Commission Report: Final Report of the National Commission on Terrorist Attacks upon the United States*. New York: Norton.

Olmsted, K. S. 1996. *Challenging the Secret Government: The Post-Watergate Investigations of the CIA and FBI*. Chapel Hill: University of North Carolina Press.

Prados. J. 2006. *Safe for Democracy: The Secret Wars of the CIA*. Chicago: Ivan R. Dee.

Ransom, H. R. 1984. Secret Intelligence in the United States, 1947–1982: The CIA's Search for Legitimacy. In *The Missing Dimension: Governments and Intelligence Communities in the Twentieth Century*, ed. C. Andrew and D. Dilks. London: Macmillan.

Rudgers, D. F. 2000. *Creating the Secret State: The Origins of the Central Intelligence Agency, 1943–1947*. Lawrence: University Press of Kansas.

Schlesinger, S., and S. Kinzer. 1983. *Bitter Fruit: The Untold Story of the American Coup in Guatemala*. Garden City, N.Y.: Anchor Books/Doubleday.

Smist, F. J. 1990. *Congress Oversees the United States Intelligence Community, 1947–1989*. Knoxville: University of Tennessee Press.

Stafford, D. 200.1. *Spies Beneath Berlin*. New York: Overlook.

Troy, T. F. 1981. *Donovan and Berlin CIA: A History of the Establishment of the Central the Intelligence Agency*. Frederick, Md.: Aletheia/University Publications of America, 1981.

Werner, T. 2007. *Legacy of Ashes: The History of the CIA*. London: Allen Lane.

Wilford, H. 2008. *The Mighty Wurlitzer: How the CIA Played America*. Cambridge, Mass.: Harvard University Press.

Zelikow, P. 1997. American Economic Intelligence: Past Practice and Future Principles. In *Eternal Vigilance? 50 Years of the CIA*, ed. R. Jeffreys-Jones and C.Andrew. London: Frank Cass.

Reprinted with permission from Rhodri Jeffreys-Jones, "The Rise and Fall of the CIA," in Loch K. Johnson, ed., *The Oxford Handbook of National Security Intelligence* (New York: Oxford University Press, 2010), 122–137.

INTELLIGENCE COLLECTION

Hamlet: "If thou art privy to thy country's fate
Which happily foreknowing may avoid
O, speak!"

—SHAKESPEARE, *Hamlet*, 1.1.134–136

Professional intelligence officers often think of their primary mission of information collection and analysis in terms of an "intelligence cycle" (see Figure II.1). The CIA defines the cycle as "the process by which information is acquired, converted into intelligence, and made available to policymakers" (CIA 1983, 17). The first phase in the cycle is planning and direction—that is, the identification of what kinds of information need to be collected ("requirements"), which agencies will do the collecting, and what means ("tradecraft" or modus operandi) will be used. These are questions for senior management, and the top senior manager in the U.S. intelligence community is the Director of Central Intelligence (DCI), whose office is located at CIA Headquarters in Virginia.

Once these decisions about planning and direction are made—and they are driven chiefly by a sense of threats to the United States—the collection of information begins by way of machines (surveillance satellites, for example) and human agents. Then the acquired information is processed. This processing step can involve the translation of materials into English if originally in a foreign tongue or, say, the enlargement of photographs taken by satellite or U-2 cameras. Once the material is in a format an analyst can work with, the job is to make sense of the information, bringing insight to "raw" data—what we mean by *analysis* (or what the British call *assessment*). Finally, the evaluated information must be disseminated in a timely manner to policy officials in the White House and elsewhere. It must be accurate and relevant to the current issues of the day, as well as free of bias.

The purpose of the intelligence cycle is to provide policymakers with useful knowledge to assist them in weighing decision options. As the CIA puts it, "Intelligence is knowledge and foreknowledge of the world around us—the prelude to Presidential decision and action" (CIA 1983, 17). The seemingly simple sweep of the cycle, as depicted in Figure II.1, is in fact a complicated series of interactions among, on the one hand, intelligence officers and their organizations (the producers of information) and, on the other hand, policymakers (the consumers of information). As information moves from aerial

FIGURE II.1 A depiction of the intelligence cycle. *Source*: From *Fact Book on Intelligence*, Office of Public Affairs, Central Intelligence Agency (October 1993): 14.

surveillance platforms or agents ("assets") in the field back to the CIA and other intelligence agencies in the United States and then on to policy councils, many things can go wrong. As discussed in the articles of this part of the book, the collection phase alone is replete with challenges, beginning with decisions about which nations or groups the United States wishes to target for gathering information.

TARGETING

From the vantage point of an astronaut in space, the world may seem small, and it is indeed becoming smaller, in a sense, as advancing technology brings about a decrease in communications and travel time between continents. Yet from the vantage point of an intelligence agency, the world remains vast, with nearly 200 sovereign nations and a wide galaxy of groups, factions, and cells spread across the globe—a fragmentation greatly accentuated by the end of the Cold War and the splintering of the bipolar world of that era. No nation—not even one with the affluence enjoyed by the United States—can hope for perfect transparency into all these nations and factions. Priorities must be set. So nations and groups with intelligence organizations engage in "threat assessment" calculations, establishing a list of places and people that are especially threatening or that present an opportunity to advance the national interests. These targets are ranked from high to low priority—say, from the high of the Al Qaeda terrorist organization to the low of Japanese fishing boats off America's shores suspected of harvesting

illegal quotas of salmon. This assessment—which can lead to heated debate among policymakers and intelligence managers—is important, for it becomes a blueprint for spending priorities with respect to intelligence collection.

During the Cold War (1945–1991), the United States had one preeminent intelligence target: the Soviet Union and its communist allies. This target accounted for upward of 70 percent of the U.S. intelligence budget (which tends to run at about 10 percent of the overall defense budget in any given year). The intelligence budget reached a high point of some $30 billion during the Reagan Administration, when the president declared the U.S.S.R. an "evil empire" and directed the intelligence agencies to ratchet up a covert war against global communism (especially in Nicaragua and Afghanistan). Today, the world has grown more complex, and intelligence targeting is more diffuse—and even more expensive: more than $44 billion, according to newspaper accounts. As President Bill Clinton's first DCI, R. James Woolsey, observed, the Soviet dragon had been slain, but "we live now in a jungle filled with a bewildering variety of poisonous snakes" (Woolsey 1993).

Throughout the Clinton years, Target No. 1 was not a single nation or group but a more generic global threat: the proliferation of weapons of mass destruction (WMD), or so-called NBC weapons (nuclear, biological, chemical) that could destroy thousands—even millions—of people in a brief interlude of horror. The events of September 11, 2001 had a profound effect on reassessing America's threat status, as the perpetrators of the catastrophic attacks against New York City and the Pentagon catapulted their organization, Al Qaeda (and its patron, the Taliban regime in Afghanistan), to Intelligence Priority No. 1. Stunning events of violence can quickly change America's sense of threat, leading to a rapid reorientation of intelligence resources toward new requirements and "tasking."

Often such events seem to come out of the blue, as with the Japanese attack against Pearl Harbor or the September 11 attacks—although in both of these instances there were early warnings that were missed, ignored, or lost in the labyrinths of the intelligence bureaucracy. Sometimes the failure to anticipate danger is not so much related to mistakes in intelligence collection as it is to the inability or unwillingness of policymakers to take action on the information they have been provided. In 1995, the CIA warned the Clinton Administration of "aerial terrorism" in which airplanes might be used by terrorists to destroy skyscrapers in the United States or abroad, but policymakers did little to enhance airport security (Johnson 2002).

As they examine collected information, intelligence officials and policymakers can also suffer a failure of imagination as to what it means. "The danger is not that we shall read the signals and indicators with too little skill," Thomas C. Schelling (1962) noted, looking back at the Pearl Harbor attack. "The danger," he continued, "is in a poverty of expectations—a routine obsession with a few dangers that may be familiar rather than likely"—in sum, a "great national failure to anticipate."

Rwanda provides a memorable example of how unanticipated disasters can leap quickly from the bottom to the top of America's international threat assessment priorities. In 1993, a genocidal civil war suddenly erupted in this African nation. "When I became Secretary of Defense [in 1993], I served several months without ever giving Rwanda a thought," recalled Les Aspin of the Clinton Administration. "Then for several weeks, that's all I thought about. After that, it fell abruptly off the screen again and I never again thought about Rwanda" (quoted in Johnson 2002, 20). The list of "shooting stars" or "flavors of the month," as intelligence professionals sometimes refer to these sudden crises, has included such places in recent decades as Grenada, Panama, Yugoslavia, and Somalia. All too often, the United States has had inadequate information about these locations, having focused its intelligence resources on more obvious threats from "rogue nations" such as North Korea and Iraq.

TYPES OF INTELLIGENCE

SUBSTANTIVE INTELLIGENCE

Policymakers and intelligence professionals must decide, too, what substantive types of intelligence should be collected: military, political, economic, or cultural. Respectively, *military intelligence* might involve a concentration on the worldwide flow of weapons of mass destruction or, more narrowly, on the efficiencies of North Korean missile fuel. *Political intelligence* can run the gamut from gathering information on presidential candidates in a French national election to sorting out the plethora of party factions in the Russian *duma*. For *economic intelligence*, U.S. officials may want to have information on the likely strategies of the Organization of Petroleum Exporting Countries (OPEC) or on the degree to which Afghanistan in the wake of the

Taliban regime has a chance of building a viable economic infrastructure. Regarding *cultural intelligence*, officials may want to know the extent to which high vodka consumption is ravaging Russian society, or the destabilizing effects of the AIDS epidemic on the leadership in countries (such as Zaire) that are heavily afflicted by this global pandemic.

From among these choices, the military dimension has been in the forefront of considerations about the funding of intelligence collection. In the United States, about 85 percent of the intelligence dollar is spent on the military intelligence agencies (although these agencies do collect some information relevant to the other substantive areas). Critics of intelligence collection in the United States have complained that the tasking is tilted too much toward Support to Military Operations (SMO, in Pentagonese)—especially protecting the war fighter in the foxhole or at sea, or the pilot in the cockpit of a fighter plane—at the expense of Support to Diplomatic Operations (SDO), that is, gathering "diplomatic intelligence" (political, economic, and cultural information) that might help prevent the outbreak of war in the first place.

"The traditional idea of intelligence is the spy who provides the enemy's war plans," noted a CIA memorandum written during the Cold War. Yet, as the memo correctly argued, despite the pressures toward SMO:

> …intelligence is concerned not only with war plans, but with all the external concerns of our government. It must deal with the pricing debates of OPEC and the size of this year's Soviet crop.... It is concerned with Soviet strength along the Sino-Soviet boarder, with the intricacies of Chinese politics, with the water supply in the Middle East, with the quality of Soviet computers and its impact on our own export controls, with the narcotics trade in Southeast Asia, even with the struggle for control of Portuguese Timor. (Senior CIA analyst, declassified by the Church Committee, 1975a)

CURRENT AND RESEARCH INTELLIGENCE

Officials must decide as well whether they seek information about what happened yesterday and what is likely to happen today and tomorrow (*current intelligence*), such as answers to the questions, "Where is Osama bin Laden?" "Where will Al Qaeda strike next?" or information of a deeper kind that provides a longer perspective and more nuanced understanding of world affairs (*research intelligence*, addressing such questions as, "How has Al Qaeda been able to attract so many young recruits to its anti-American cause?" "To what extent will Muslim extremists rally in Iraq to drive out U.S. troops?"). Most officials desire current intelligence, and they want precision—not vague warnings about a possible attack somewhere, sometime. This kind of information can be hard to obtain and can often be wrong. Research intelligence poses its own set of difficulties inherent to any deep probe into a topic, including the costs of time and money required to carry out the research. Further, research intelligence is often unread by busy policymakers who shun lengthy, footnoted tomes. Yet in-depth intelligence is vital for a more meaningful understanding of world events. Unfortunately, though, it is being given short shrift, as increasingly resources are directed toward current intelligence, anticipating and trying to answer questions that flare up in the daily in-boxes of harried policymakers.

SECRETS AND MYSTERIES

An added dimension of intelligence collection is the distinction made by intelligence professionals between secrets and mysteries. *Secrets* are empirical facts that, with luck and perseverance, the United States might be able to acquire—steal, if necessary—such as information about the number of Chinese nuclear submarines, their range, and the location of their docking sites. *Mysteries* are the more imponderable questions faced by intelligence officers and policymakers, such as the likely longevity of the current Chinese leadership, or whether democracy will take root in Iraq in the aftermath of the U.S. invasion to overthrow the regime of dictator Saddam Hussein. No one really knows the answers to mysteries; their importance, though, warrants grappling with possible outcomes regardless, and a well-trained analyst can often come up with helpful insights for policymakers to consider as they contemplate the future. The collection phase of the intelligence cycle concentrates on unearthing secrets, leaving the sifting of tea leaves about mysteries to analysts steeped in the history and culture of foreign lands.

COLLECTION METHODS

After deciding what kind of information are required to assist foreign policy decision making, officials ask the intelligence agencies to gather the desired data. Here we enter the domain of the "ints"—that is, the various intelligence methods used for collecting information around the world (Berkowitz and Goodman 2000; Lowenthal 2003; Shulsky and Schmitt 1993).

OSINT

The most mundane of the ints, though in some ways the most important, is simply tapping into public sources of information—open-source intelligence, or *osint*. Authorities report that about 80 percent of all the information found in intelligence reports during the Cold War was based on data acquired by traditional library research, such as digging through Soviet and Chinese newspapers. Today the osint figure is even higher, approaching 95 percent, as Russian, Chinese, and other formerly closed societies have become more open, as the Internet takes on importance as a wellspring of information, and as television and radio stations (along with periodicals and newspapers) proliferate around the globe. Ironically, in spite of these burgeoning open sources, intelligence analysts often eschew publicly available data in favor of the more titillating and exotic information that comes to their desks from overseas clandestine sources—even though they are trained to search open sources first, then turn to clandestine sources to fill in the missing pieces of the puzzle.

On the clandestine side of intelligence collection, the ints (as introduced in the Introduction to Part I) include geoint, sigint, masint, and, last but not least, humint. These acronyms, widely used by intelligence professionals, stand for imagery intelligence, signals intelligence, measurement and signals intelligence, and human intelligence.

GEOINT

Imagery, or geospatial intelligence (geoint), refers to photography, the snapshots taken by reconnaissance airplanes such as the U-2 or unmanned drones such as the Predator, as well as by surveillance satellites that revolve around the earth at altitudes ranging from a few hundred miles to over 200,000 miles in deep space (either in polar orbit, sweeping around the earth, or geosynchronous orbit, hovering over a particular country or region). Today, the photographs from satellites do not even have to be developed; they are sent digitally to U.S. ground stations and fed quickly to policymakers and warriors who need the information in as close to real time as possible. The picture resolution is impressive, capable of distinguishing a football from a jackrabbit.

Geoint (until recently known as "imint" or imagery intelligence) is much sought and appreciated by policymakers when it can display irrefutable evidence about an adversary's hostile actions against the United States, as when the U.S. ambassador to the United Nations, Adlai E. Stevenson, was able during the 1962 Cuban missile crisis to convince American and world opinion of Soviet provocation in the Western Hemisphere by laying on the table clear U-2 photos of Russian missiles in Cuba. More recently, in 2003 Secretary of State Colin Powell used satellite photographs to argue the U.S. case that Iraq still possessed chemical weapons capabilities and had permitted the establishment of a terrorist training camp within its nation—although in this instance (unlike Cuba) confirmation of the intelligence reports proved elusive.

Imagery is hardly a panacea, even though it attracts the lion's share of the U.S. intelligence budget. (Just the launching of a Greyhound-bus-sized intelligence satellite can cost $1 billion.) For starters, half the world is covered with clouds at any moment and, naturally, darkness is a hindrance as well (although the United States has made great strides in developing cameras that can overcome these obstacles to some extent). More difficult to deal with has been the tidal wave of images flowing back to the United States, cloudy weather and nocturnal conditions notwithstanding—some 400 images a day. A shortage of photo interpreters means that only a small fraction of these pictures are carefully studied.

Further, adversaries have grown skilled at hiding their activities, as demonstrated by the surprise nuclear tests in India during 1994 (Johnson 2001). Indian officials had determined exactly when U.S. satellite cameras would be passing over their nuclear testing facility near Pokharan in the Rajasthan Desert. In synchrony with these flights (every three days), Indian nuclear scientists camouflaged their activities. Ironically, U.S. officials had explicitly informed the Indian government about the timing of U.S. satellite coverage for South Asia, in hopes of impressing on them the futility of trying to conceal test activity. Even without this unintended assistance, though, the Indians could have calculated the cycles for themselves, as even amateur astronomers can track the orbits of spy satellites.

The Indians also adroitly used deception techniques to fool intelligence photo interpreters. For instance, ground cables normally moved into place for a nuclear test were nowhere to be seen in U.S.

satellite photographs of the site; the Indians had devised less-visible ignition techniques. The Indians also stepped up activities at their far-removed missile testing site, in an attempt to draw the attention of spy cameras away from the nuclear testing site.

In 2002, when U.S. troops first entered eastern Afghanistan's rugged Shah-i-Kot Valley as part of Operation Anaconda in search of Al Qaeda terrorists and their Taliban hosts, the military command had at its disposal the best geoint platforms available: satellites, reconnaissance airplanes, Predator drones. Nonetheless, "despite these high-tech systems, the intelligence estimate failed to accurately portray the enemy's size, location, principal weapons and course of action," notes *New York Times* reporter Sean Naylor (2003, A13).

Geoint has other liabilities. Satellite and U-2 cameras are unable to see through roofs into buildings or basements where chemical and biological weapons may be manufactured. Even large-scale nuclear weapons programs can be hidden from the prying cameras, as the North Koreans have managed to demonstrate by locating their nuclear weapons operations in deep underground caverns. Moreover, while the spy cameras can provide some idea of an adversary's military capabilities, they have nothing to say about the intentions of these adversaries.

SIGINT

To supplement imagery, nations also rely on the gathering of signals intelligence, especially the electronic communications that travel between telephones and personal computers. At the United Nations in 2003, Secretary Powell also played the transcripts of confidential telephone conversations between Iraqi officials to demonstrate further that they were trying to deceive U.N. inspectors and world public opinion. Once again, though, we run into the problem of information overload, as a firehose of sigint transcripts from around the world overwhelms the ability of U.S. translators and analysts to keep up with the torrent. According to a recent estimate (Millis 1998), only about 10 percent of all sigint transcripts are examined by analysts. An intercepted September 10, 2001 telephone conversation between Al Qaeda terrorists indicating that a major attack would occur against the United States the next day ("Tomorrow is zero hour") was not translated until September 12, the day after the attacks.

In addition, adversaries have learned to use deception against sigint just as they do against geoint.

Reportedly, in 2002 Bin Laden handed his cell phone to his bodyguard and had him travel away from where the Al Qaeda leader was heading in his escape from Afghanistan, thereby drawing U.S. intelligence officers in the wrong direction. People tell lies over the telephone, too; intercepts cannot be taken at face value but rather are sometimes a source of disinformation. Further, the current switch in technologies from airwave transmissions of telephone conversations to underground optic fibers ("light pipes") has significantly complicated the science of intercepting telephone conversations. Still, sigint has had its moments of success and is highly valued by policymakers, as when intercepted communications in an African nation recently saved the lives of a U.S. ambassador and his family on their way to a local airport by tipping them off to a planned ambush by an indigenous rebel faction. The ambassador altered his travel route, and he and his family escaped the trap.

MASINT

Weapons systems, such as ballistic missiles and nuclear warheads, give off emissions as they are being tested, and factories produce gases and waste products. Measurement and signatures intelligence can provide information about these and other forms of weapons systems and can add significantly to America's understanding of an adversary's military preparedness. Or they can reveal what is being made inside a factory: normal pharmaceuticals or lethal chemical or biological substances.

HUMINT

The oldest form of spying (and some say the world's second oldest profession) is the use of human intelligence—the cloak and dagger agents of James Bond fame. These spies are not Americans but rather local assets recruited by U.S. intelligence officers, who then serve as their "case officers." To avoid the kinds of concealment and deception against geoint and sigint as practiced by the Indians and the North Koreans, the United States would like to have an asset inside the Indian test bunkers or within the North Korean caverns. A well-placed asset might also be able to ascertain whether a suspicious factory is making aspirin or serin (a chemical nerve agent)—a distinction that distant satellites and U-2s are unable to make. Particularly helpful in today's world would be having an asset in attendance at Al Qaeda strategy sessions in a cave somewhere in the mountains of northern Pakistan, perhaps sitting on

the dirt floor next to Bin Laden himself. Afterward the spy could secretly transmit, by using rapid electronic communications from a palm-held computer to a satellite and down to his CIA case officer in Kabul, the plans for the next Al Qaeda operations in the jihad against the United States.

These wishes are difficult to fulfill, since access to North Korean caverns or Al Qaeda strategy sessions in the rugged mountains of Afghanistan is, to say the least, difficult. North Korea has sophisticated security systems, and Al Qaeda painstakingly vets its recruits—especially those given proximity to Bin Laden. Beyond questions of access, spies can be highly unreliable. Sometimes they fabricate reports just to justify their stipend from the CIA. Of 200 asset reports on missile sightings in Cuba during the crisis of 1962, only six proved accurate (Powers 1979, 447). Sobering, too, is the fact that all of America's assets in Cuba and in East Germany during the Cold War turned out to be double agents, loyal not to their CIA case officers but to their own communist governments.

Spies are often the most venal individuals in a society, with dubious histories of human rights abuses—perhaps even with criminal records as murderers. Though sometimes necessary for America's security, assets are unlikely to be boy scouts or nuns (as realists like to chide those squeamish about the business of espionage). The employment of unsavory characters by the United States raises serious ethical questions, however, about the extent to which the United States should be in alliance with drug dealers, liars, thieves, and assassins—even if they can occasionally provide useful information.

Despite the controversies and drawbacks associated with the use of human assets, the United States has had some notable humint successes. Prior to the missile crisis, for example, the Soviet military intelligence officer Col. Oleg Vladimirovich Penkoski provided valuable information about Soviet military bases and missile sites. These data, including drawings of missile bases in the U.S.S.R., helped CIA analysts discern the presence of Soviet ballistic missiles in Cuba.

ALL-SOURCE FUSION

None of these collection methods is perfect. At best, each may provide some pieces for the puzzle that the intelligence agencies have been asked to solve. The objective is to use them all and hope for a synergism among them—an "all-source fusion," in intelligence lingo—that will provide policymakers with a more comprehensive understanding of the world and especially of our adversaries. As the United States has become more sophisticated in its techint capabilities, the nation's collection successes have continued to improve, and the country is generally regarded as the most effective gatherer of intelligence in the world—even in the face of a rising ability of nations and groups to evade surveillance, and despite the striking failure of the intelligence agencies to warn the American people of the September 11 attacks.

The weakest link in the collection chain has been humint, and, in the aftermath of the 9/11 tragedy and the mistakes about WMDs in Iraq in 2002, the United States is now engaged in a crash program to improve this part of the equation by hiring new case officers, assets, analysts, managers, and translators who understand the language and culture of places like Afghanistan, Iraq, and Pakistan, a part of the world largely ignored throughout most of the Cold War. Another weakness has been the lack of adequate sharing of information among the intelligence agencies and with policy officials—a defect that will require significant organizational and cultural changes throughout the government, further complicated by the creation in 2003 of a poorly defined Department of Homeland Security that has been plagued in its early days with management and organizational confusion.

THE READINGS

The articles that follow describe the process of intelligence collection. Arthur S. Hulnick, an accomplished practitioner and student of intelligence, begins this section with a discussion of how reality deviates from the idealized description of intelligence production depicted by the intelligence cycle. Instead of a cycle, Hulnick suggests that the production of finished intelligence occurs along two ongoing and parallel processes involving collection and analysis, and that structured collaboration between policymakers and analysts is rare. Intelligence support to ongoing law enforcement, counterterrorism and counterintelligence operations is characterized by other patterns of interaction that have little to do with a "cycle." Hulnick suggests that it is time to develop new concepts to describe the process of creating finished intelligence.

Jeffrey Richelson describes the array of new technologies that have fueled the competition between hiders and finders when it comes to collection. He describes how the emergence of various types of sensors and platforms, usually operated at some distance from their target, are used to collect information. Richelson notes that these technical systems have revolutionized intelligence collection, but that it is wrong to treat them as a panacea. Adept opponents can still hide their activities from eyes and ears in the sky and use denial and deception to spoof sensors and mislead analysts. Questions also remain unanswered about how to bring this advanced technology to bear against various non-state actors that are adept at hiding in plain site.

Our third essay describes human source intelligence—the stuff of spy novels and movies—placing it in strategic context over the last half century. As Frederick Hitz notes, the nature and effectiveness of humint is not only influenced by the target environment where agents must operate, but by changing political attitudes toward espionage and covert action. The domestic and international setting is not always conducive to the conduct of human source intelligence, and collection shortcomings are often punctuated by some notable foreign policy failures and lapses in national security. Hitz highlights the latest challenge facing intelligence managers: penetrating the new threat posed by non-state actors.

Although open-source information is sometimes dismissed by intelligence professionals, who point to espionage or technical intelligence as the best way to pry into another society, Stephen Mercado highlights the important role played by open-source information. Data gathered from open sources can be used to target more precise collection activities or to place information gathered using clandestine means in a broader context. Mercado warns his audience, however, that the skills required to be an accomplished open-source analyst need to be cultivated. Without language skills and an understanding of other cultures, it is difficult to exploit the wealth of data made available by the information revolution.

Our final essay, written by James Wirtz, offers a comparison of the intelligence failures surrounding the Japanese attack on Pearl Harbor and the September 11, 2001, Al Qaeda attack on the United States. Wirtz demonstrates that despite popular perceptions, collection failures cannot be blamed for the surprises suffered by the United States, and that there is always accurate information in "the intelligence pipeline." Bolt out of the blue attacks are more of a myth than a reality.

5. THE INTELLIGENCE CYCLE

ARTHUR S. HULNICK

Although just about every book on intelligence offers the intelligence cycle as a model for the production of finished intelligence, insiders know that the model is at best a stylized version of reality. It captures the functions that more or less have to occur to produce intelligence, but it has little to do with how policymakers, intelligence managers, and analysts go about accomplishing those tasks. In this chapter, a scholar with an insider's perspective suggests that the notion of a "cycle" is misleading when it comes to describing how intelligence is actually produced.

No concept is more deeply enshrined in the literature than that of the "intelligence cycle." I studied the intelligence cycle as an undergraduate in Sherman Kent's book on strategic intelligence and then later when I attended the U.S. Air Force Intelligence School in 1957.[1] In 1965, in the training courses required by the Central Intelligence Agency (CIA), I studied it yet again. When it came time to start writing about intelligence, a practice I began in my later years in the CIA, I realized that there were serious problems with the intelligence cycle.[2] It is really not a very good description of the ways in which the intelligence process works. Additionally, it ignores two main parts of intelligence work, counterintelligence and covert action. There is an alternative view.

THE FIRST STEP

Let us start at the beginning and look at what is wrong. The notion that policy makers, or intelligence consumers, as they are sometimes called, provide guidance to intelligence managers to begin the intelligence process is incorrect. Policy consumers do sometimes indicate their main concerns to intelligence managers, but often they assume that the intelligence system will alert them to problems, or provide judgments about the future. Consumers will sometimes tell intelligence managers what they are worried about, or the direction in which they intend to take policy—but not always.

Still, it is usually not too difficult for intelligence managers to learn what policy makers are up to,

but the managers often have to take the initiative to obtain the information. If intelligence managers at various levels are in touch with their policy counterparts, this sharing of information may work quite well. Over the years, intelligence managers have tried to systematize this process by asking policy officials to provide specifics on their concerns. In the Carter administration, for example, a system of National Intelligence Topics (NITs) was created as a way of soliciting guidance for intelligence. Later, they were called Key Intelligence Questions (KIQs). In some cases, when policy consumers failed to submit NITs or KIQs, managers had to resort to sending policy officials a list of topics, asking them to cross out the ones they thought were not necessary, or adding those they wanted to add to the list. Even then, the lists were sometimes ignored.

In the end, intelligence managers have to make decisions about the subjects that ought to be covered. Often, this is driven by world events. But, none of this provides guidance for intelligence collection. The guidance comes from within the system. Secretary of Defense Donald Rumsfeld, in the George W. Bush administration, is reported to have once said that "we don't know what we don't know," but that is usually not the case. Intelligence managers often know what gaps exist in the intelligence data base, derived from intelligence collectors, and analysts. Filling the gaps is what drives the intelligence collection process, not guidance from policy makers. Thus, the first step in the intelligence cycle is incorrect in reality.

THE SECOND STEP

The second step is equally incorrect. Collection managers cannot wait for guidance in regard to gaps in the intelligence data base to begin the collection process. The gaps will be filled once the collection process is under way. For example, in running espionage operations, commonly called HUMINT (for human intelligence), it may take months or years to find a person who has access to the information needed and is willing to be recruited as a spy. The same may be true for technical collection sensors. Satellites in space, which make up many of the sensor platforms, are not nearly as flexible as managers would wish. Thus, anticipating the intended targets cannot be overlooked. For example, during the British confrontation with Argentina over the Falkland Islands, the United States could not help the British with space imagery because the satellite, programmed to observe the Soviet Union at that time, only passed over the Falklands at night.

Of course, with the use of unmanned aerial vehicles, imagery collection has become more easily refocused on targets of opportunity, but the unmanned aircraft may still not be in the right place when they are needed. Even open source intelligence (OSINT), which has been given new life in recent years because of the proliferation of information on the Internet, requires planning to ensure access to needed material. Intelligence managers need sophisticated software to mine the data because there is so much of it.

THE REAL DRIVERS

For all these reasons, intelligence managers, and not policy officials, are the real drivers of the intelligence collection process. Clearly, intelligence moves from collection to analysis, as the intelligence cycle holds, but analysts do not always need new intelligence material to understand world events. The data base is already so large that a competent analyst could write about most events without any more than open sources to spur the process. The incremental addition of new intelligence from human sources or technical sensors may modify the analytic process but rarely drives it.

The job of the analyst is, in part, to evaluate raw material and put it in perspective. The analyst receives intelligence material from a variety of sources, including media reports, official reports from other government agencies, as well as reports from the intelligence collection process. In my experience as a practicing analyst in the military and in the CIA, raw reports from human sources or technical sensors are sometimes fragmentary, biased, contradictory, or just plain wrong. In order to analyze the data, the analyst compares the new material with the existing data base and previous analysis. Hanging a finished product—whether it is current reporting or a longer range estimate—on one source usually does not work well. This is apparently what happened in the case of the estimate on weapons of mass destruction (WMD) in Iraq that helped trigger the invasion of that country. The estimate was based, in part, on the reporting of one rather poor and unreliable source. The estimate turned out to be quite wrong, as we now know.[3]

OPERATING IN PARALLEL

A better way of looking at the relationship of intelligence collection and intelligence analysis is to think of the two processes as operating in parallel rather than sequentially. The two processes are co-equal in terms of utility. It is important to note as well that raw reporting from the collection process, set up into standardized formats, usually goes to policy officials as well as to analysts at about the same time. Though this may not always be true in other intelligence systems, it is certainly true in the United States. Whereas senior policy officials may not see a great deal of the raw reporting, there are usually watch centers at the various policy agencies that screen the raw reporting and send forward the most interesting ones.

Unfortunately, as I have already noted, some of this raw intelligence may be incomplete, contradictory, or just wrong. Policy officials sometimes take the reporting as having been judged and evaluated. Thus, I have heard officials say that the CIA has reported an event, when in fact what the officials have seen is an unevaluated agent report passed along to them by their watch centers. It is not possible to stop this flow of raw reporting. As Bob Gates, the former Director of the CIA once noted to me, once the spigot is opened, it is not possible to close it, even though allowing consumers to have raw reporting at about the same time as the analysts receive them creates some serious problems for the analysts. Collection managers often take a different view. They believe they are doing a great service to the policy community by providing this raw reporting. If the intelligence cycle really worked, the circulation of raw reports to policy officials would not happen.

A MAJOR PROBLEM

Since intelligence collection and intelligence analysis operate in parallel and should be co-equal, one would expect that there would be a great deal of information sharing between the two. Regrettably, this is not always the case. Because of restrictions of information sharing, psychological barriers, fears of compromising sources, and security concerns, the intelligence collection process and the intelligence analytic process not only operate in parallel, they are sometimes quite independent of each other. This is a major problem.

When I first joined the CIA, I was assigned on a temporary basis to an office in the Directorate of Plans (DDP), later renamed the Directorate of Operations (DO), and in 2005, renamed yet again as the National Clandestine Service (NCS). My job was to deal with incoming reports from the field. When an interesting report came in one day, I asked my boss if we should alert the relevant analyst about it. He rejected the idea, saying that our job was to send reports like it to the White House, and not to the Directorate of Intelligence, since analysts were not worth the attention. I was shocked. Later, when I became an analyst, I did my best to establish good relations with my operational colleagues, but there were issues.

BARRIERS TO COMMUNICATION

In those days there were physical barriers, manned by armed guards, to prevent analysts and operations officers from visiting each other's offices. Later, the physical barriers were removed, but the psychological ones remained. Operations people feared that somehow analysts would mishandle reports from the field and reveal the identity of clandestine sources. Analysts mistrusted operations officers because they were thought to be devious and untrustworthy. This mistrust was kindled in part because analysts in those days tended to be introverts who found the extroverted personality of the typical operations officers to be abrasive. Operations people tended to think that the introverted analysts were "wimps."

Over the years these stereotypes have largely been overcome, but recent efforts to increase communication between analysts and operators by colocating them have not always been successful. Agency managers have pushed analysts to take tours overseas with field stations, but it is more difficult for an operations officer to serve a tour as an analyst. Similar issues may not arise in other intelligence agencies unless they have co-equal collection and analysis components.

The Defense Intelligence Agency (DIA), for example, was immune to this sort of "stovepipe" problem because it was mostly an analytic rather than collection agency. As Defense HUMINT grows, perhaps the same problem will arise. The National Security Agency (NSA) and the National Geospatial Intelligence Agencies (NGIA) are devoted mostly to collection, but they tend to be tightly compartmentalized, creating a different kind of "stovepipe" problem. In theory, all the intelligence agencies should share raw data and coordinate analysis, but for a variety of reasons they do not always do so. This was one of the main critiques of both the 9/11 Commission and the commission investigating the intelligence failure surrounding the estimate on WMD.

A MIXED BAG

There is a tendency among intelligence agencies to hold back the most sensitive and exciting reports until the agency's leaders have been able to deliver the reports to senior policy officials, thus highlighting the skill and cleverness of their people and "scoring points" with the officials. One effort to spur interagency communications has been the establishment of centers, where all the agencies have representation and where their representatives can easily talk with their counterparts, even informally, to discuss events and incoming intelligence. The establishment of these centers has been something of a mixed bag. We know from the 9/11 investigations that the then-existing counterterrorism center (CTC) was not a place where all information was shared.[4]

Now, efforts at intelligence reform have "morphed" the CTC into a National Counterterrorism Center (NCTC), controlled by the new Director of National Intelligence (DNI). Will that spur the agencies into more easily sharing their best and most sensitive data? It would be nice to think so, but experience shows that this does not always happen, even at the highest level.

THE FINAL STAGES

In the final stages of the intelligence cycle finished intelligence, broken down into a variety of products, emerges from the analytic process. It is supposed to be delivered to policy officials—the literature refers to this delivery as dissemination—and then policy officials either make decisions or create further requirements and the cycle starts over again. This, too, is a distortion of what really happens. Much of this depends on the kind of intelligence product that is being delivered. These products include warning intelligence, in which consumers are alerted to "breaking news," current intelligence to update consumers on world events on which they already have some knowledge, in-depth studies on particular situations or issues, and forecasts of the future, the estimate. All products are received and used in a different way, but none of them really drive the policy process.

Warning intelligence is supposed to alert policy officials to breaking world situations, especially those for which they may have to take action. Both intelligence managers and policy consumers hate surprise. It is embarrassing for intelligence when the system misses an event about which it should have had information. For example, the CIA failed to detect the fact that the Indian government planned to conduct a nuclear test in 1998. Later investigations revealed that this was both a collection and an analysis failure. The CIA had no assets it could tap in India at that time, and the Indian analyst at the CIA had somehow missed the fact that the Indian prime minister had declared his intention to hold the tests. Despite the fact that there was little the U.S. government could do to stop the tests, policy officials were nonetheless outraged at this failure.[5]

Even greater outrage was directed at the entire intelligence community for its failure to detect the 9/11 terrorist attack on the United States. This has been exhaustively examined and has led to the restructuring of the intelligence system. Yet, there is considerable evidence that there was little that might have been done to avert the disaster. But, it illustrates the point that policy officials expect the intelligence system to be all-knowing, all-seeing, and always correct. As Richard Betts pointed out many years ago, intelligence failure is probably inevitable.[6]

Warning of crisis should come early enough so that policy officials can have time to develop some kind of considered response. Unfortunately, the warning may come so late that it is really an alert that the crisis has already begun. Using a system that is composed of warning centers at major military commands, tied in to warning centers at all the intelligence agencies and in policy departments in Washington, and taking advantage of the proliferation of twenty-four-hour TV and Internet outlets,

the warning network rarely misses the start of a crisis, and it is then able to reach out to decision makers quite rapidly. When the decision makers ask intelligence officers how they should respond to the crisis, typically intelligence officers decline to provide advice, thus staying clear of the policy process.

THE MOST USEFUL PRODUCT

Current or daily intelligence is the most ubiquitous of all types of intelligence products, delivered at all levels and usually first thing in the morning. It is designed to supplement the media, based on the assumption that policy officials have already gotten their media inputs from newspapers or television news. It is the most popular of all intelligence products because current intelligence is an "easy read," short, and to the point. For those policy officials who only have ten or fifteen minutes a day to absorb intelligence products—and consumer surveys consistently show that this is about all the time policy officials have for such things—current intelligence is rated as the most useful product from the intelligence community. The idea of this product is to summarize events, explain how they fit into some context, and suggest what might happen next. It is a very journalistic methodology.

Unlike warning intelligence that may lead to policy action, as the intelligence cycle suggests, current intelligence hardly ever leads to policy decisions—and it is not meant to do so. Instead, it gives generalists at senior levels a chance to find out about events outside their main areas of responsibility. Specialists often complain that the daily intelligence flow does not provide the level of detail they would need to make policy, but the current intelligence products are not designed for specialists. In fact, it would be quite likely that specialists would have seen a great deal of the raw intelligence data that lay behind the current intelligence product anyway.

During the 9/11 investigation, much was made of the fact that one daily publication, the *President's Daily Brief* (PDB), had on August 6, 2001, reported the possibility that terrorists might use commercial aircraft as cruise missiles to attack commercial or government buildings within the United States.[7] Critics of the president took this to have been a warning the president and his senior staff had missed, but normally the PDB would not have been the kind of intelligence product used for warning.

The warning would have been delivered in a much more specific document devoted entirely to the subject. Intelligence managers have never expected the PDB or similar publications to be more than educational in nature. Certainly, these publications do not drive the intelligence process.

IN-DEPTH STUDIES

The same might be said for the myriad in-depth intelligence studies churned out by the analytic components. These studies have proliferated in recent years, although they were rarely attempted at the beginning of the Cold War. These studies are designed to provide in-depth analysis on specific subjects and are meant more for policy officials at working levels rather than senior decision makers, who rarely have the time to read them. These studies help in forcing analysts to come to grips with a specific subject, provide useful information to consumers within the intelligence system, and support policy makers as they design policy initiatives.

The production of these studies grew over the years as a way of giving analysts a vehicle for attacking a problem in more depth than was possible in a daily or weekly publication, and without the fuss and bureaucracy involved in producing the more formal national estimate. Policy officials sometimes request these in-depth studies, along the lines suggested by some versions of the intelligence cycle, but in many cases, the studies are produced because analysts are directed by intelligence managers to write them, or analysts themselves believe they should be written. When Robert M. Gates took over the Directorate of Intelligence (DI) at the CIA during the early days of the Reagan administration, he decreed that analysts should produce at least two of these in-depth studies every year. Gates was fond of pointing out that the DI produced about 5,000 of these studies one year. It was not clear, however, how many of them were actually read.

In recent years, these studies have been more carefully tailored to the needs of policy officials. The same might be said for the Defense Intelligence Agency products, which are geared to military needs, or those coming from the State Department's intelligence and research unit, which has always focused its analysis on foreign policy issues. The fourth category of product, the estimate, is the one most likely to drive the policy process, at least in theory. But the reality is often different.

THE REALITY OF ESTIMATES

The estimate is a creature of the Cold War, but has its roots in World War II. It is supposed to be a forecast of the future that decision makers can use to build policy, just as the intelligence cycle proposes. The estimate is supposed to be drawn by analysts from all the producing agencies, coordinated by the analysts among themselves to reach an agreed forecast, with dissenting views included. Then, it is blessed by the agency leaders; is signed off at the top; is sent to the president, the National Security Council, and staffs; and serves as the basis for policy discussions. There are actually cases where this has happened, where decision makers have waited for the intelligence community's views as embodied in the estimate, but these cases are rare.

The reality is that policy officials often know what they want to do even before they receive the estimate and hope that this product will confirm in some way the wisdom of the path they have already chosen. When the estimate conflicts with their views, policy consumers may dismiss it as uninformed, useless, or even obstructionist. When it agrees with what they think they already know, then they may see it as confirming, irrelevant, or again useless. Although one would think that policy makers would want to know when they were heading in the wrong direction, this is not usually the case. Policy consumers do not welcome intelligence that is nonconfirming, perhaps because the large egos that brought them into positions of power do not permit admissions of ignorance.

THE WMD CASE

There is no better example of what can go wrong in the estimates process than the recent experience with the problems related to Iraq and Saddam Hussein's alleged possession of weapons of mass destruction. We now know how the intelligence system politicized the estimate to meet the needs of the George W. Bush administration. The estimate on WMD was flawed from the beginning. It was based on the reporting of only a few unreliable sources. Then, analysts made several faulty assumptions about the weapons Saddam Hussein had had or used before the first Gulf War. Finally, policy officials used the estimate to convince both Americans and other nations that Saddam was about to develop nuclear weapons. All of this was wrong.[8]

According to James Risen, intelligence officials in both the collection and analysis arms of the CIA, as well as those in other agencies, knew the sources were poor and the conclusions wrong, but they could not fight senior managers who wanted to satisfy the political needs of the White House. Even more corrupting, it appears that Secretary of Defense Rumsfeld, fearing that the estimate would not support the already planned invasion of Iraq, sent his own officials, neither of them intelligence officers, to find the "correct" information.[9] All these steps were perversions of the estimates process. One can only hope that such antics will not take place in the future.

For all the reasons cited, it seems clear to me that trying to learn how intelligence works by using the intelligence cycle model will lead to misunderstandings about what really happens in the intelligence world. Collection and analysis are really parallel processes. The key to their effective functioning lies in the extent to which there is good communication between the two processes. There needs to be, as well, good communication between intelligence managers and policy consumers throughout the intelligence process. At the same time, however, intelligence managers must stand up to policy officials when they seek to make the intelligence judgments conform to political needs.

INTELLIGENCE AND POLICY

In the early days of the Cold War, the founders of the CIA debated the extent to which intelligence should be close to policy. Sherman Kent, a Yale professor who went on to establish the national estimates system in the CIA, and one of the early thinkers about the intelligence process, believed as did "Wild Bill" Donovan and others, that if intelligence became enmeshed in the policy process, it would lose its value. Kent argued that the best way to avoid politicization of intelligence was to remain distant and aloof. Later, Roger Hilsman, one of the intelligence chiefs at the State Department, took a different view. Hilsman thought that intelligence had to be close to policy to remain relevant.[10] The experiences of the Bush era suggest that Kent may have been right all along.

Nonetheless, other studies have shown that there must be good communication between policy consumers and intelligence managers if intelligence is to be on target and meet the needs of decision makers. At the same time, intelligence managers have to stand up to efforts by policy officials to skew intelligence judgments when the conclusions are at variance with the political

proclivities of partisan officials. No one said this would be easy. It is a constant challenge to provide "truth to power." Intelligence must deliver the unvarnished bottom line. Policy officials can go elsewhere for politicized information if they wish, but at their own peril.

LOOKING AT COUNTERINTELLIGENCE

Leaving aside the collection and analysis processes in intelligence, one cannot understand the entire intelligence system without looking at counterintelligence. Counterintelligence is largely defensive in nature, and it is not part of the traditional intelligence cycle—although some writers have tried to adapt the cycle into a counterintelligence model.[11] In my view, counterintelligence follows an entirely different and unique path, with a model of its own. It is certainly worth studying because counterintelligence is a major function of intelligence, consists of both active and passive components, and has become as controversial as any aspect of the intelligence function in government.

In its earliest forms, counterintelligence usually meant counterespionage, stopping enemy, adversary, or even friendly spies from stealing a country's own secrets. Of course, the target country might very well be carrying out espionage against the enemies, adversaries, or friends at the same time as it tries to defend against similar sorts of spying. Thus, stealing secrets for one's country is good and necessary; having one's secrets stolen is dangerous and despicable. U.S. intelligence officers, for example, are rewarded for their successes in gathering information from their targets, even though some of what they do may be illegal in the countries they target. At the same time, other U.S. intelligence officers are heralded for their ability to root out foreign spies and are castigated when they fail to do so. After all, espionage is illegal in the United States and must be stopped.

MORE DIVERSE

Today, counterintelligence has become much more diverse than just stopping spies. It now means countering terrorism, narcotics flows, global organized crime, and subversion. Whatever the threat, however, the patterns of intelligence activity in fighting all of them are similar. It has nothing to do with the intelligence cycle. Instead, there is a counterintelligence methodology that is unique.

First, in countering national security threats, counterintelligence units must identify and locate the evil-doers. This might be foreign intelligence operatives working for a hostile intelligence service, a terrorist cell, a unit of a crime "army," or a group of narcotics pushers. There are several proven intelligence methods for identifying the "bad guys," including the use of: penetrations, or "moles," to get on the inside of the groups or services; surveillance, either physical or technical; informants; and intelligence derived from captured or detained individuals. All have both positive and negative aspects.

Based on the Cold War experience, we know that it is possible to recruit officials of a foreign intelligence service to turn coat and betray some of the activities of their operatives. There are several known cases where the United States was able to place a mole inside a foreign service, and there were a number of U.S. intelligence officers— such as Aldrich Ames, John Walker, and Robert Hanssen—who gave away U.S. secrets to the Soviets. The FBI seemed quite capable of recruiting penetrations of crime groups such as the Sicilian Mafia. Penetrating a terrorist cell is far more difficult and dangerous. Terrorist cells are usually made up of a handful of people, all of whom may be bonded by family or religious ties. Even if a terrorist cell member wanted to become a "double agent," the first hint of disloyalty to the cell could result in death.

Physical or electronic surveillance is another proven method of identifying counterintelligence targets. Overseas, this kind of surveillance can be mounted against potential targets as a result of decisions by intelligence managers. In the United States, however, the rules are more strict. Counterintelligence officials would, in most circumstances, be required to go through a legal process and obtain a warrant before employing surveillance against a U.S. citizen, a resident alien, or a U.S. person. This issue became frontpage news early in 2006 when the *New York Times* revealed that President George W. Bush had authorized surveillance of communications without warrant, arguing that Congress had given the president the authority to do so.[12] The issue may not be resolved until a court case is brought, or new legislation is passed defining the parameters of surveillance use domestically.

USING INFORMANTS

Informants can be very useful in identifying counterintelligence targets. Informants are not recruited agents, but rather people who see something amiss and report their suspicions to authorities. In hostage situations, informants may be able to point out where unusual activity is taking place. For example, prior to 9/11, flight school managers reported to the Federal Bureau of Investigation (FBI) their concerns about Middle Eastern men seeking flight training only to steer aircraft, rather than learn to take off and land. Unfortunately, FBI senior officials refused to grant field agents permission to interview the informants, claiming that there was no probable cause to do so.[13]

Informants can also cause a lot of wasted effort. During the sniper crisis in Washington, DC, in 2002, in which two men were able to terrorize the area by random attacks on innocent targets, requests for information resulted in more than 100,000 inputs, of which 40,000 were worth investigating.[14] People who have experience in fielding informant reports note that often the reports are used to denounce spouses, parents, or unpleasant neighbors, and provide no useful intelligence. Nonetheless, informants can prove to be helpful in identifying bad guys.

INTELLIGENCE FROM INTERROGATION

After 9/11 a good deal of controversy arose over the use of intelligence gained from the interrogation of detainees, either overseas or here at home. In the wake of 9/11 some men of Middle Eastern Muslim extraction, who were not U.S. citizens, were required to register with the federal government. Some of these people had irregularities in their visas, had overstayed their stay in the United States, or were in the United States illegally. They were detained in somewhat harsh conditions and in some cases, badly mistreated. It did not appear, however, that much effort was made to find out if any of them had ties to terrorism.

At the same time, as the United States geared up to take down the Taliban government in Afghanistan, some Taliban fighters or people associated with Al Qaeda were captured, turned in by informants, or sold to the United States, by Afghan warlords. These people, dubbed "enemy combatants" by the Bush administration, were shipped to the Guantanamo Naval Base in Cuba, where U.S. authorities said U.S. legal rules did not apply to them. These people were interrogated using what some described as harsh methods, or even torture, according to press reports.

After the United States invaded Iraq in 2003, more detainees were captured on the battlefield.

These fighters were imprisoned in Iraq at some of Saddam Hussein's former prisons, including the infamous one at Abu Ghraib. It was at this location that the worst abuses took place. Apparently, unschooled, unscreened, untrained guards were turned loose to abuse the prisoners in the mistaken belief that this would "soften them up" for interrogation. All of these situations involving detainees were handled badly.

Long experience has taught that there are effective ways to interrogate prisoners, using methods that do no harm to the subjects while producing useful intelligence. Unfortunately, those lessons were not applied effectively in the post-9/11 situations. The literature on interrogation methods, on training interrogators, on handling subjects should have been readily available to anyone involved in trying to extract intelligence from detainees. Anyone who has been involved in intelligence style interrogations knows that torture is ineffective and counterproductive, as well as abhorrent and illegal. Since those experiences, the rules have been changed to exclude such behavior by U.S. officials.

A good interrogation may yield only bits and pieces of information, but if intelligence collectors are careful, they may be able to piece together a broader picture from a series of subjects. The main aim, of course, is to try to learn something about the cells, or units, that the subjects have come from, especially about their plans for future operations.

STOPPING THE BAD GUYS

After the "bad guys" have been identified, then a decision has to be made about the kinds of operations that will be mounted to stop whatever kind of plan or activity might be under way against U.S. interests. This creates a dilemma. Usually, intelligence officers will press to extend or broaden the collection effort to make sure that all the bad guys have been identified and located. At the same time, law enforcement officials are eager to bring the bad guys to justice. This creates a serious problem, often described as the "cops and spies" dilemma.[15]

The divisions between law enforcement and intelligence in the United States have deep roots. Unlike many other industrialized countries, the United States does not have a domestic intelligence service, such as the MI-5 in Great Britain, or the DST in France. Instead, the United States has relied for many years on the FBI—which is really a law enforcement organization—to gather counterintelligence and then act to bring lawbreakers to justice. In

other countries, the domestic intelligence services collect and analyze counterintelligence in parallel with counterpart foreign intelligence organizations, which work beyond the country's borders. When suspected criminal behavior is uncovered, the domestic intelligence services may turn to national police organizations to carry out law enforcement operations against the suspects.

INTELLIGENCE VERSUS LAW ENFORCEMENT

In the United States, however, where no domestic intelligence service has existed, there have been both legal and procedural barriers between the national intelligence services, whose focus has been almost exclusively abroad, and the FBI, which has always had a role in domestic counterintelligence. Traditionally, counterintelligence collected abroad was passed to the FBI, which then determined, usually in consultation with the Justice Department, whether there was probable cause to open a criminal investigation. This would be used to gather evidence that could be brought if a court case arose. This was different from the gathering and analysis of intelligence data, which traditionally was not treated or handled as evidence.

Because of cover considerations and the need to protect the identity of intelligence officers, intelligence managers did not want their people to have to appear in court, and wanted as well to protect the sources and methods used to collect intelligence. The FBI was under no such strictures, but the evidence they gathered had to be backed by appropriate warrants and protected according to legal standards. The Aldrich Ames case is a perfect example of how this system used to work.

A joint CIA and FBI team was able to track down Ames and identify him as a Soviet mole in the CIA. Then, the FBI obtained a warrant under the Foreign Intelligence Surveillance Act (FISA) to be certain that they had the right target. Once that was done, a second FBI team, with a criminal warrant, took over the investigation and gathered evidence that might be used to prosecute Ames. In the end, Ames agreed to a plea bargain and the case never came to court, but it illustrates how a firewall was in place to separate the counterintelligence investigation from the criminal one.[16]

TAKING DOWN BARRIERS

Since 9/11 some of the barriers between intelligence and law enforcement have been weakened, but the cops and spies dilemma still exists. Under the new rules, the FBI may levy requirements on the U.S. intelligence services to collect information specific to their domestic needs. It is not yet clear if such intelligence would be used as evidence in court cases. More likely, the FBI would ask that intelligence be gathered to support its newly created National Security Branch, which combines the FBI's older counterterrorism and counterintelligence units with its newer intelligence bureau, created after 9/11.

At the same time, the CIA and the FBI have drawn more closely together with a strong push from Congress. FBI agents have been assigned to the CIA for counterintelligence purposes for many years, and more recently, to fight terrorism. CIA officers are reportedly working closely with FBI field offices where antiterrorism task forces have been created. While this may break down traditional barriers between the two agencies, there is still some resentment among CIA officers about the growing role of FBI attachés serving abroad, and FBI concerns about the reluctance of CIA officers to share information.

THE COUNTERINTELLIGENCE MODEL

So, when one looks at the pattern of counterintelligence functions, it does not look at all like the intelligence cycle. Instead, it may be seen as follows:

IDENTIFICATION
PENETRATION
EXPLOITATION
INTERDICTION
CLAIM SUCCESS

In this pattern, exploitation is the process of learning as much as possible about the bad guys before moving against them. Interdiction means either arresting the law breakers or pre-empting their operations. Though political leaders often talk about bringing the enemy to justice, suggesting that they would be arrested and taken to trial, convicted, and punished in the fight against terrorism, pre-emption may be the preferred course of action, especially overseas. In one case, for example, a U.S. *Predator* with a missile on board was reportedly used to strike a terrorist leader in Yemen, killing him and his associates while they were driving in the desert.[17] One might argue that this was punishment before trial, or alternatively, that this was necessary

to prevent the terrorist from leading a strike against the United States.

The downside of pre-emption is that sometimes innocent victims are slain along, with the intended targets. That was apparently what happened when the Bush administration launched a missile from a drone aircraft against Ayman alZawahiri, Osama bin Laden's deputy, early in 2006. The missile killed 17 people, according to press reports, but not the intended target, who later broadcast an attack on Mr. Bush, equating him with Adolf Hitler. Despite the failure to kill Zawahiri, the Bush administration later said that the attack had indeed killed an important terrorist leader and was worth the cost.[18]

EXPLOITATION BEFORE INTERDICTION

In the counterintelligence model, exploitation comes before interdiction, meaning that as much intelligence should be gathered before the case or operation is turned over to law enforcement. Of course, in cases in which there is pressure to stop the enemy or adversary, exploitation may come before the intelligence is fully gathered. For example, in the case of the "Lackawanna Six," exploitation was cut short because of the need for political leaders to show that they were cracking down on terrorism. The Six were Yemeni immigrants living outside Buffalo, New York, who went to Afghanistan before 9/11 in the misguided belief that training with the Taliban fighters was going to be something of a lark.[19]

When they discovered that the Taliban were really training terrorists, the Yemeni immigrants returned to the United States. After 9/11, they turned themselves in to authorities to explain what they had done. They were quickly arrested, and eventually jailed. No one at the time seemed to realize that at least one or two of them might have been sent back to Afghanistan as double agents to penetrate Al Qaeda. Even an effort to learn more about their experiences was cut short by the pressure to achieve quick convictions to show that the government was moving swiftly against terrorism.

CLAIMING SUCCESS

Finally, in the last step of the counterintelligence process, authorities often make public claims of success, a rare step in intelligence work. Normally, intelligence managers try very hard to keep successes secret so that they might be repeated. An oft-quoted CIA saying is, "The secret of our success is the secret of our success."[20] In cases in which intelligence has been gathered successfully, it is critical to protect sources and methods. In counterintelligence, however, the claim of success, made when the case has ended, could be used to convince the public that the government is ever watchful and actually doing something with the billions of dollars spent on intelligence. During his tenure as FBI director, J. Edgar Hoover made a fine art out of going public with counterintelligence success. His senior agents all received training in public relations and the FBI was made to look good, even when serious mistakes had been made.[21]

Whereas intelligence is usually carefully hidden (except for the counterintelligence cases), intelligence failure quickly becomes public. This is a serious problem for intelligence managers. In the early days of the CIA there was no public affairs function even to deal with the public or the media. When Admiral Turner became director, however, he instituted a Public Affairs Office, much to the chagrin of many old-timers. Since then, the CIA has had to wrestle with the appropriate response when media queries arise. This is especially true when a spy case, such as the capture of Aldrich Ames, becomes public knowledge, or when a covert action surfaces.

More forthcoming CIA directors, such as George Tenet, have had the Public Affairs Office respond generously to media questions. Under the successor regime of Porter Goss as CIA director, however, the CIA seemed to return to a more conservative approach. In such cases, it would not be uncommon for the media to receive the standard answer to questions about intelligence. This says that the CIA "can neither confirm nor deny allegations of intelligence activity," which is little more forthcoming than "no comment." Nonetheless, enterprising reporters, such as Bill Gertz of the *Washington Times* and James Risen of the *New York Times*, seem to be quite successful in learning about inside stories at the CIA and other intelligence agencies.

DEFENSIVE COUNTERINTELLIGENCE

There are defensive measures in counterintelligence that do not fit into either the traditional intelligence cycle or the model just described. These measures are often lumped together as various aspects of security. They include careful background checks on prospective employees, including the use of polygraph interviews to verify the information candidates submit on their applications, and continuing monitoring of employees throughout their careers. Facilities used for intelligence and other governmental functions are extensively guarded and patrolled, monitored with alarm and surveillance devices, and protected by barrier entry devices to keep out unwanted visitors.

Some facilities have protective systems in roadways and parking areas that can be activated to stop suicidal vehicle bombers. Buildings may be shielded electronically to prevent an adversary's use of listening devices or electronic surveillance to intercept and steal secrets. Most important, employees are trained in security awareness, so that they can report anything that seems to be a threat. They are taught to protect the secrets with which they have been entrusted, and this responsibility lasts even after they leave their employment.

For example, those of us who were once inside the system and signed secret agreements are obligated to submit their published materials, including this Chapter, to their agencies for review before they are given to their editors and publishers. This is not censorship, but rather a of this system to ensure that no secret information is inadvertently released. Some CIA authors have taken advantage of this system to include blacked-out passages in their books, demonstrating that they really were prepared to release sensitive information but were stopped by the review process. This tends to sell more books and can be a clever marketing ploy.

THE COVERT ACTION FUNCTION

The last function of intelligence—and again one not included in the intelligence cycle—is that of covert action, or special operations. This activity is not really intelligence in its traditional role of gathering and analyzing information, but rather the use of intelligence resources to carry out the national security policy of the state using surreptitious methods. Intelligence agencies around the globe carry out such operations because they have the necessary secret facilities and personnel. All through the Cold War, it was covert action that drew most of the attention and most of the criticism of American intelligence.

General Jimmy Doolittle, one of the notable heroes of World War II, after taking a hard look at intelligence in the immediate postwar period, concluded that the United States would have to be more clever, more tricky, and more devious than our Communist adversaries if we were to overcome their bid for world domination. He stated that Americans would just have to accept this "repugnant" policy.[22] When the CIA became involved in trying to overthrow governments in Guatemala, Iran, Indonesia, and Cuba, and was severely criticized in some quarters for having done so, it became clear that there were limits to what the American people were prepared to accept.

Much has been written about the nature and limits of covert action, and there seems no need to repeat that here.[23] Though covert action does not fit into the intelligence cycle, there is a pattern to this function worth outlining. This pattern is similar to other aspects of policy development and implementation, except that covert action is supposed to be secret and to disguise the role of the United States.

POLICY FORMULATION

The pattern of policy formulation looks a bit like the intelligence cycle, but in reality it is quite different. In the first step of the policy process policy officials within the national security bureaucracy recognize and identify a problem they must address. Theoretically, the identification of the problem comes from intelligence, but in reality policy officials often see this at about the same time as intelligence officials because both receive the incoming data at about the same time, as explained earlier.

In the next step policy officials begin to seek options for dealing with the problem, assuming some role for the United States is necessary. At this point, one of the options might well be a covert action. We know from long experience with covert action that it only makes sense as an adjunct to policy and should not be the policy itself.[24] Thus, the choice of using covert action remains with decision makers and is not chosen by intelligence. The conventional wisdom in some circles during the Cold War was that intelligence managers decided to mount covert actions independent of policy officials. (This notion that the CIA was a "rogue elephant" running amok was debunked during the famous investigations of intelligence held by Senator Frank Church in the 1970s. Church learned that all CIA covert actions had been directed in some way by the White House and funded in secret by members of Congress.[25])

Finally, decision makers at the top choose the option they desire and direct its implementation. In the case of covert action, this requires that the president issue a written finding that the covert action is needed. Then the appropriate intelligence official must brief the Intelligence Oversight Committees of Congress, in secret, about the policy "on a timely basis." Congress has often pressed presidents to issue the findings before the option is implemented, but presidents have usually chosen to ignore this, claiming that it infringes on their freedom of action.[26]

The pattern looks like this:

PROBLEM RECOGNITION
OPTION CREATION
OPTION SELECTION
IMPLEMENTATION

Intelligence analysis should feed into the process at all stages, but we know that the options that policy officials choose are driven by many things. Intelligence is not always at the top of the list.

CONSEQUENCES OF COVERT ACTION

Covert action has both short- and long-term consequences. This is true of all kinds of policy choices, but because covert action is kept secret, the normal debate about policy choices takes place among a relatively small group of people. The result is that short-term solutions, which may seem attractive at the time they are chosen, may prove to have unintended consequences in the long run. There are too many examples to cover here, and the literature on covert action is voluminous. It is sufficient to say that U.S. governments rarely think about the long-term consequences of policy choices and, in that regard, covert action is no different from more open kinds of policies.

There is a long tradition in intelligence that intelligence officers do not offer policy recommendations to decision makers. Though this may be true for the delivery of finished intelligence products, it is not so in regard to covert action. As Dr. James Steiner, a former CIA officer, has pointed out, in covert action, especially in war on terrorism, the attempt to be policy-neutral does not apply.[27] For many years, a senior CIA officer has been assigned to the White House staff to help work out the details of covert action when policy makers decide to have such operations.

This officer's role is to make sure that requested covert actions are feasible and supportable. Thus, the officer is as much a policy maker as an intelligence official.[28]

It is argued elsewhere in this chapter that one way to address the short-term versus the long-term consequences of covert action is to set up a center, much like other interagency centers in U.S. intelligence. This center, however, should include both intelligence and policy officials. Its goal would be to analyze how a covert action might work and what its impact would be. The intelligence officers assigned to such a center should come from both the analytic and the operational units of the CIA. Traditionally, covert action has been kept compartmentalized within operations units, without the benefit of analytic inputs.

It seems pretty clear that presidents will always want to have the option of using some form of covert action against enemies and adversaries. No presidents in living memory, even those who were suspicious of covert action, have ever said that they would not use it. Therefore, the intelligence agencies that might be involved in such operations—primarily the CIA in the present U.S. intelligence community—must be prepared to be tasked to carry out covert action, and must maintain the capability to do so.

A FLAWED VISION

I suspect that, despite my preaching about alternatives to the traditional intelligence cycle, it will continue to be taught both inside government and elsewhere. Nonetheless, it would be encouraging to think that those so deeply wedded to the flawed concept of the intelligence cycle would, in the course of studying this volume, realize that there is an alternative to the traditional view of how intelligence works. Perhaps they might even consider it for discussion. Yet we know that people tend to look for confirming rather than disconfirming data. They will seek to defend the intelligence cycle, rather than consider the alternatives. Nonetheless, the intelligence cycle is a flawed vision, and thus poor theory. One need only ask those who have toiled in the fields of intelligence.

QUESTIONS FOR FURTHER DISCUSSION

1. What is the greatest shortcoming in using the notion of a "cycle" to describe the production of finished intelligence?
2. If intelligence production actually consists of a series of parallel processes, at what point do those processes meet to produce analysis of interest to policymakers?
3. Do you think that operational intelligence breaks down any meaningful distinction between intelligence producers and consumers?
4. Can you devise a better model to capture what really goes on in the production of finished intelligence?

ENDNOTES

1. Sherman Kent, *Strategic Intelligence for American World Policy* (Princeton: Princeton University Press, 1966). I studied an earlier version published in 1948.
2. See, for example, Arthur S. Hulnick, "The Intelligence Producer-Policy Consumer Linkage: A Theoretical Approach," *Intelligence and National Security* 1 (May 1986).
3. James Risen, *State of War: The Secret History of the CIA and the Bush Administration* (New York: Free Press, 2006).
4. The 9/11 Commission Report (New York: W.W. Norton, 2003), pp. 339–60.
5. Arthur S. Hulnick, *Fixing the Spy Machine: Preparing American Intelligence for the 21st Century* (Westport, CT: Praeger, 1999), p. 59.
6. Richard K. Betts, "Analysis, War, and Decision: Why Intelligence Failures Are Inevitable," *World Politics* 31 (1978).
7. Arthur S. Hulnick, *Keeping Us Safe: Secret Intelligence and Homeland Security* (Westport, CT: Praeger, 2004), p. 16.
8. Risen, *State of War.*
9. Hulnick, *Keeping Us Safe,* pp. 85–86.
10. Roger Hilsman, *Strategic Intelligence and National Decision* (Glencoe, IL: Free Press, 1956).
11. "CSIS and the Security Intelligence Cycle," available at http://www.csis-scrs.gc.ca (accessed 1 April 2004).
12. Risen, *State of War,* pp. 39–60.
13. 9/11 Report.
14. Arthur S. Hulnick, "Indications and Warning for Homeland Security: Seeking a New Paradigm," *International Journal of Intelligence and CounterIntelligence* 18 (Winter 2005–6).
15. Hulnick, *Keeping Us Safe,* pp. 103–18.
16. See, for example, Pete Earley, *Confessions of a Spy: The Real Story of Aldrich Ames* (New York: G.P. Putnam's Sons, 1997).
17. Hulnick, *Keeping Us Safe,* p. 72.
18. Craig Whitlock and Walter Pincus, "Qaeda Deputy Mocks Bush," *Washington Post,* 31 January 2006.
19. Hulnick, *Keeping Us Safe,* pp. 126–27.
20. Hulnick, *Fixing the Spy Machine,* p. 81.

21. Ronald Kessler, *The Bureau: The Secret History of the FBI* (New York: St. Martin's Press, 2002).

22. Harold M. Greenberg, "The Doolittle Commission of 1954," *Intelligence and National Security* 20 (December 2005), pp. 687–94.

23. See, for example, Abram Shulsky and Gary Schmitt, *Silent Warfare* (Washington, DC: Brassey's, 2002).

24. James E. Steiner, "Restoring the Red Line Between Intelligence and Policy on Covert Action." *International Journal of Intelligence and CounterIntelligence* 19 (Spring, 2006), pp. 156–65.

25. See, for example, Rhodri Jeffreys-Jones, *The CIA and American Democracy*, 3rd ed. (New Haven, CT: Yale University Press, 2003).

26. Christopher Andrew, *For the President's Eyes Only* (New York: Harper Collins, 1995).

27. Steiner, op. cit.

28. Hulnick, *Fixing the Spy Machine*, pp. 82–83.

6. THE TECHNICAL COLLECTION OF INTELLIGENCE

JEFFREY T. RICHELSON

This essay reviews the new technologies that have been harnessed in the collection of information and how they have been incorporated into the production of intelligence. When introduced, each of these technologies provided a significant advantage to collectors but, as Richelson explains, each of them is subject to countermeasures that limit their effectiveness.

INTRODUCTION

For much of mankind's history, the collection of intelligence was conducted largely through the efforts of spies—who observed enemy activities and purloined documents. Intelligence was occasionally acquired when coded messages were stolen and decoded. Only in the last hundred years have technological advances allowed intelligence to be collected by a vast array of mechanical systems, often operated at a considerable distance from the target, an activity referred to as "technical collection."[1]

There are six key aspects to technical collection activities. One is the sensors—such as photographic equipment—used to gather data. A second is the platforms that carry the sensors, which with the sensors constitute a technical collection system. The targets of the collection effort—including missile fields, nuclear reactors, and terrorist training camps—constitute a third component. Fourth is the product of the collection effort—such as the images of the missile fields, reactors, and training camps, or intercepted communications between the chief of a weapons of mass destruction production facility and a senior government official. In addition, there is question of the value of technical collection operations—which is determined by the uses to which the intelligence obtained can be put—such as supporting diplomacy, guiding weapons acquisition, planning and carrying out military operations, treaty verification, and warning of upcoming attacks or other events that a nation might wish to forestall.

A final, but important, consideration is the limitations of technical collection. While such systems may produce a wealth of data, they do not guarantee that all key intelligence desired will be obtained. The plans of a foreign government or terrorist group, for example, may be unobtainable by technical means if the target government or group are sufficiently vigilant in the safeguarding of their plans.

IMAGERY SENSORS, PLATFORMS, AND TARGETS

The value of observing foreign activities, particularly military-related activities, from overhead has been apparent to military and intelligence officials for at least as long as there have been the means for obtaining an overhead vantage point. According to Chinese and Japanese folklore, spotters ascended in baskets suspended from giant kites or were strapped directly onto them. In April 1794, French forces were reported to have kept a balloon aloft for nine hours, with its passenger, Colonel Jean-Marie Joseph Coutelle, making continuous observations during the battle at Fleurus, Belgium. Balloons were used to carry observers and, less frequently, cameras, during the American Civil War.[2]

As a result of the Wright Brothers' invention of the airplane in 1903, a key intelligence resource in World War I were reconnaissance aircraft—planes equipped with cameras that could photograph enemy fortifications, troop deployments, and the battlefield. During, and in the years leading up to, World War II photographic reconnaissance aircraft played an even greater role. Britain managed to conduct covert flights over Germany, while German aircraft brought back photographs of Soviet territory prior to the German invasion of the Soviet Union in June 1941. During the war, British and American planes photographed German military and industrial installations and areas on a regular basis—to aid in targeting and damage assessment.[3]

The advent of the Cold War ensured that overhead reconnaissance retained its importance, particularly for the United States, as it sought to pierce the veil of secrecy established about almost every aspect of Soviet life—especially its military capabilities. The possibility that a satellite could be outfitted with a camera to take pictures of any place on earth that it passed over was noted by the RAND Corporation as early as 1946. In August 1960 that vision was realized when the United States orbited a camera-carrying satellite codenamed Corona.

A satellite such as Corona, in a polar orbit that took it over all of the earth from pole to pole, could photograph Soviet military activities in the northern reaches of the Soviet Union, air-fields in the Middle East, and battles in sub-Saharan Africa. In the decades since the first Corona orbited the earth, the capabilities of such satellites have increased dramatically—as has the number of nations that operate such satellites.

The photographic reconnaissance satellite has become the imagery satellite—for capturing the visible light reflected by an object is not the sole means of obtaining an image of a target. The infrared radiation (heat) reflected by an object can also be used to produce an image during daylight, and in the absence of cloud cover (which blocks the reflected radiation). The heat independently generated by an object can also be used to form an image, even in darkness. That second type of infrared imagery can provide data on developments taking place at night that ordinary visible light sensors cannot.

A third means of obtaining imagery from a satellite is through the use of radar (radio detection and ranging). Radar imagery is produced by bouncing radio waves off an area or an object and using the reflected returns to produce an image of the target. Since radio waves are not blocked by clouds, radar imagery can be obtained not only day or night but even when clouds block the view of a satellite's visible-light and infrared imagery sensors.

Imagery satellite capabilities have also advanced in a number of other ways. The most important is the development of real-time capabilities. The Corona satellites and several other US and Soviet spy satellite systems operated in the 1960s, 70s, 80s were "film-return" satellites. An image was formed on film, just as an image would be formed on a conventional camera. When the film supply carried by the satellite was exhausted, part of the satellite (in the case of the United States, a capsule) carrying the film would be returned to earth and recovered.

Today, almost all imagery satellites are digital and operate in near real-time—the optical systems rely on charged couple devices which translate the varying visible-light levels of the object viewed into numbers, which are immediately relayed back to earth (via a relay satellite) and reconstructed into an image. Infrared and radar imagery are also transmitted in real-time.

Even before the advent of real-time satellites, whose lifetimes are not limited by film supply, the lifetimes of film-return satellites grew from the single day of early Corona missions to weeks, and, for some satellites, many months. But real-time imagery satellites can operate for between five and ten years. Satellites today also have far greater resolution than the first photo-graphic reconnaissance satellites—that is they can detect far smaller objects than the first satellites. While it is incorrect to claim that a satellite can read a license plate, they can certainly detect a white object of similar dimensions laid on a dark surface.

As noted, there has also been a growth in the number of nations operating high-resolution imagery satellites. For the first decade of space reconnaissance the United States and Soviet Union were duopolists. In 1975, China launched its first photographic reconnaissance satellite. It would not be until 1995 that another nation would join the space reconnaissance club—when France launched a spacecraft designated Helios into orbit from a site at Kourou in French Guiana. Israel and Japan followed. Israel has launched several Ofeq (Horizon) satellites into orbits that focus primarily on the Middle East. Japan has launched a pair of reconnaissance satellites, one radar imagery satellite (Radar-l) and one visible-light satellite (Optical-1). And there is the prospect that a number of other nations, including Germany and Italy, will deploy imagery satellites for military intelligence purposes.

Today, the United States operates a constellation of about six imagery satellites, all of which provide real-time imagery. The constellation includes three advanced versions of the first real-time imagery satellites, the KH-11, which can produce both visible-light and infrared imagery. It also includes two radar imagery satellites (codenamed Onyx) and one stealth satellite (originally designated Misty) which was intended to be difficult for target nations to detect.

Russia, faced with resource constraints, operates a less extensive military space program than did the Soviet Union but still operates real-time imagery satellites. France has continued to launch Helios satellites, the latest being Helios 2A, which was launched in December 2004 and is reported to carry both visible-light and infrared sensors. Meanwhile, Japan has plans to add radar and optical satellites to its present constellation.[4]

The targets for those satellites are determined by the national security concerns of each nation, as well as by their intelligence alliances. United States satellites, reflecting their owners' global interests, have been targeted on nuclear facilities in North Korea, Iran, Pakistan and other nations; construction of underground weapons of mass destruction production or command and control facilities in Libya and Russia; refugee movements in Africa; and terrorist training camps in Afghanistan and elsewhere.

Other nations' targets will often be a subset of those of the United States. Russian satellites undoubtedly photograph terrorist facilities in Chechnya, nuclear facilities in Iran, and missile sites in China. Israeli satellites are focused on the Middle East—particularly terrorist and weapons of mass destruction facilities, as well as airbases and other military facilities in the region. Japan's spy satellite program owes it existence to North Korea's 1998 launch of a ballistic missile that passed over its territory. North Korean missile and nuclear facilities and activities are among the primary targets of Japan's imagery satellites, along with Chinese missile sites and airfields. French military, diplomatic, and commercial interests in the Middle East, Asia, Europe, and Africa provide its satellites with a large array of potential targets—including military developments in the Balkans, Iran's construction of nuclear facilities at Arak and Natanz, and the territory surrounding France's space launch facility at Kourou.

The initial development and improving capabilities of imagery satellites has not made other forms of overhead imagery collection obsolete. During the early days of the Cold War, United States Air Force pilots flew modified bombers, equipped with cameras, along the periphery of the Soviet Union and China to obtain imagery of airfields, ports, and other facilities that could be photographed from outside those nations' borders. Occasionally, those modified bombers were sent into Soviet airspace to obtain imagery of targets farther inland.

Then in 1956, the CIA pilots began flying deep into the Soviet territory employing a specially designed plane, the U-2, which flew at over 65,000 feet and which the CIA believed, incorrectly, would not be detected by Soviet radar. It carried a special long-focal-length camera capable of photographing objects as small as a man, and bringing back images of roads, railroads, industrial plants, nuclear facilities, aircraft, and missile sites within a strip 200 miles wide by 2,500 miles long.[5]

Overflights of the Soviet Union ceased after Francis Gary Powers and his U-2 were shot down on May 1, 1960. But the US still continues to operate U-2s, and has employed a variety of additional spy planes, particularly the Mach 3 SR-71, in the decades after the US mastered the art of conducting reconnaissance from space—even after the quality of satellite photos equaled or surpassed that of the lower-flying aircraft.

Some countries were restricted to employing aerial reconnaissance until they developed satellite imagery capabilities—for example, Israel and France. The United States continued their use because, while satellites could provide far more extensive coverage and were immune to being shot down like aircraft, planes still could play an important role.

They can supplement satellite coverage—a single plane costs far less than an additional satellite. They can provide a quick reaction capability since an aircraft can head directly for a target, while a satellite cannot photograph a target until its orbit and the rotation of the earth place the target in view—a process which can take several days. Those same constraints mean that a satellite cannot arbitrarily cover any stretch of territory desired—but aircraft can cover the territory between any two points, for example, the movement of an invading army toward its objective or the movement of refugees toward a border.

Another type of overhead imagery system has some of the virtues of satellites and aircraft, and some of its own advantages. Unmanned aerial vehicles (UAVs) equipped with electro-optical systems or infrared sensors are operated without a pilot by remote control—thus the political risks and risk to life involved in manned reconnaissance operations are eliminated. And unlike satellites or aircraft, UAVs can remain over a target, at high altitudes, for extended periods of time (e.g. 20 hours), keeping watch on a particular target or area—such as a terrorist training camp or nuclear test site.

While the US began operating drones (pilotless aircraft that could not be maneuvered) and UAVs during the Cold War, it is in the post-Cold War that UAVs have become a more significant component of US reconnaissance activities. The CIA began flying Predator UAVs over Bosnia in 1994. After the initiation of military operations in Afghanistan the US began equipping Predators with Hellfire missiles so that immediate action could be taken if imagery indicated the presence of a terrorist target. Even more recently, the US has been deploying the Global Hawk UAV—capable of operating at over 60,000 feet for 20 hours and carrying electro-optical, infrared, or radar-imaging sensors.

SIGNALS INTELLIGENCE SENSORS, PLATFORMS, AND TARGETS

Traditionally, signals intelligence (SIGINT) is treated as one of the most important and sensitive forms of intelligence. The interception of foreign signals can provide data on diplomatic, military, scientific, and economic plans or events as well as on the characteristics of radars, spacecraft, and weapons systems.

SIGINT can be broken down into two basic subcategories: communications intelligence (COMINT) and electronics intelligence (ELINT). As its name indicates, COMINT is intelligence obtained through the interception, processing, and analysis of the electronic communications of foreign governments, organizations, or individuals, excluding radio and television broadcasts. The communications intercepted may be transmitted in a variety of ways—including conventional telephones, walkie-talkies, cell phones, the Internet, and computer networks.

ELINT encompasses electronic non-communications signals, including the electronic emanations of radar systems and foreign instrumentation signals—the signals transmitted during the operation of space, aerial, terrestrial, and sea-based systems. The signals from radar systems can be used to identify their existence as well as determine their characteristics, such as pulse repetition frequency and pulse duration. Intelligence about pulse repetition and pulse duration can be used in designing electronic countermeasures to neutralize the radars in the event of combat.

One category of foreign instrumentation signals intelligence (FISINT) is telemetry intelligence (TELINT)—obtained from intercepting the signals transmitted during missile tests to those conducting the tests, permitting them to evaluate the missile's performance. Interception of those signals by a foreign intelligence organization makes it possible for analysts to determine many of the capabilities of foreign missile systems—including the number of warheads carried, payload and range, warhead accuracy, and warhead size (which can be used to estimate yield).

Collection of signals intelligence is accomplished by a multitude of systems, from satellites in outer space to submarines under the seas. The proliferation of satellite reconnaissance systems with imaging missions to a variety of different nations has not yet been matched by an equivalent proliferation of SIGINT satellite systems, and the US remains, by a large margin, the foremost user of such systems.

Several types of satellites are used to collect signals intelligence—including geosynchronous and low-earth orbiting satellites. Geosynchronous satellites operate about 22,000 miles above the earth's equator, with their rotation around the earth matching the rotation of the earth below, so they, in effect, hover over the same point on the equator. In that orbit the same portion of the earth (about 1/3) remains in their electronic view constantly—which is important in being able to continuously monitor a communications link or insuring that a satellite is in the right place when infrequent missile tests take place. The United States pioneered the use of such satellites for communications intelligence purposes in 1968 with the launch of a satellite designated CANYON. Presently, the US operates two separate constellations of geosynchronous signals intelligence satellites, which can intercept communications transmitted on UHF and VHF frequencies, as well as telemetry from missile tests.[6] The Soviet Union has been the only other nation to operate geosynchronous signals intelligence satellites.

ELINT satellites operate in lower orbits. Both the US and Soviet Union/Russia have operated ocean surveillance satellites, orbiting the earth at about 600 miles altitude, which intercept the electronic signals from ships at sea as a means of detecting the presence of the ships and tracking their movements. The US, Russia, and China have also operated satellites in about 500-mile orbits which targeted the electronic emissions from radar systems—including ballistic missile warning radars as well as aircraft-detection radars. France has placed experimental SIGINT packages on satellites with other primary missions, possibly as a prelude to developing its own signals intelligence satellite. In the US, in the 1990s, the two systems were combined into one system that targeted both ships at sea and radars on land.

Britain aborted plans in the 1980s to build its own geosynchronous SIGINT satellite, codenamed ZIRCON, for budgetary reasons. A willingness to devote considerable financial resources to a SIGINT satellite program is only one challenge facing a nation with such ambitions. There is also the technological challenge involved in developing and operating the satellites as well as the requirement for ground stations, often on foreign territory, to operate the satellites as well as receive their data in a timely fashion.

One of the advantages satellites have over signals intelligence aircraft is that they can intercept signals from across a much wider territory than aircraft. Thus, the first US ELINT satellite, GRAB, first launched in 1960, could intercept signals from territory 3,790 miles in diameter, while the P2V Neptune, an ELINT aircraft that operated in the same era could only target signals within a 460 mile diameter.[7]

In addition, such aircraft, and their crews, may be targets for hostile forces. Over one hundred US airmen were lost in the early days of the Cold War on ELINT missions that flew into or near Soviet territory. In 1968, North Korea shot down a US EC-121 on a signals intelligence mission, while in 2001 a Chinese aircraft forced a US Navy EP-3 to land on Hainan Island.

But given the economics involved, many more nations are involved in other forms of signals intelligence collection. The US conducted the first aerial missions during World War II, which were targeted on Japanese radars in the Pacific. Today, not only the United States, but China, Israel, Britain, France, Italy, Germany, Russia are among the nations that use aircraft to intercept signals—both communication signals as well as radar emanations. And such aircraft, in addition to being far more financially viable than satellite systems for many nations, can get much closer to the source of the targeted communications or electronic signals than a satellite— thereby improving the ability to capture the signals of interest, some of which satellites may not be able to intercept.

Ground-based signals intelligence systems are also deployed extensively throughout the world. During the Cold War the United States operated a series of circular antenna arrays in Europe and Asia targeted on the high-frequency communications of the Soviet Union, China, and other communist countries. Unlike the VHF and UHF signals that leaked out into space, making them vulnerable to space collection, high-frequency signals bounce off the atmosphere and return to earth where they can be intercepted—often thousands of miles away. Not surprisingly, the Soviet Union also operated an extensive network of ground stations, with stations in widely dispered locations—including the Soviet Union, Vietnam, and Cuba.

While the collapse of the Soviet Union led to the closure of many of the sites where such arrays were operated—in Augsburg, Germany and San Vito, Italy for example—another type of ground-based SIGINT collection is flourishing due to the growth of communications satellites.

In the 1960s, the United States military and private corporations began placing satellites into geosynchronous orbit to relay communications between widely distant spots on earth. The Soviet Union followed with its own constellations of military and civilian communications satellites. The signals sent to and/or from those satellites can be intercepted by satellite dishes stationed in any areas that either receives the signals from the satellite or can access the signals sent to the satellite.

The US first targeted Soviet military communications satellites, such as the Molniya satellites which operated in highly elliptical orbits, using intercept equipment located in Great Britain, Japan, and elsewhere. In the 1970s it began improving its ability to intercept civilian satellite communications. One outshoot of that effort was the ECHELON program—an ability to do keyword searches of the communications traffic (particularly written communications such as faxes) intercepted at ground stations operated by the US and key SIGINT allies (including the United Kingdom and Australia). But the United States and those allies are not alone in this practice. The signals intelligence organizations of a number of nations—including China, Switzerland, Germany, and France—also maintain one or more satellite dishes allowing them to intercept the traffic being relayed through communications satellites.

Another often-used platform for intercepting foreign signals are embassy or consular rooftops. The United States and Soviet Union made extensive use of their embassies and consulates to intercept communications in foreign capitals and other key cities during the Cold War. That practice continues today, with internal military, police, political, and economic communications all being targets.

Using ships outfitted with intercept equipment to monitor communications or intercept other electronic signals was not uncommon during the Cold War. The Soviet Union maintained a large fleet of antenna-laden ships, know in US terminology as AGIs (for Auxilliary General—Intelligence), that operated near US submarine facilities in the United States and abroad, as well as near US space launch facilities such as Vandenberg Air Force Base in California. For a time the United States maintained a set of ships dedicated to the SIGINT collection. The risks involved in such activities were illustrated when Israel bombed a US ship collecting SIGINT during the June 1967 Six-Day War and the following year North Korea seized a similar ship. While the US stopped using such unarmed ships, it did outfit others with intercept equipment and continues to conduct such operations today.

While most other nations are not able to, and have no need to, deploy fleets of SIGINT collection ships, they do operate some. Britain, France, Germany, and Italy are European nations with such ships. Thus, in May 2000, the French newspaper *Le Monde* reported that the French ship, the *Bougainville*, was headed for a secret destination on a signals intelligence mission. Five years earlier, it had been reported that China was operating eight SIGINT ships—including the *Xiangyang Hong 09*, which was used to monitor US-South Korean Team Spirit exercises in the Sea of Japan and Yellow Sea.[8]

Submarines have also been used for signals intelligence collection. During the Cold War a US attack submarine might be instructed to locate itself in the White Sea, close enough to the Soviet coast to allow it to intercept the telemetry signals associated with the test of a submarine-launched ballistic missile. Other submarine missions involved transporting frogmen to locations in the Barents Sea and Sea of Okhotsk so they could place taps on Soviet cables carrying military communications. Many such SIGINT missions were conducted under a joint program involving both US and British submarines. In 2006, a new US attack submarine was sent to operate off the coast of Latin America, with a signals intelligence mission.

Collectively, signals intelligence systems can be used to gather intelligence about a wide variety of foreign activities—the negotiating strategies of foreign nations; diplomatic exchanges between a foreign ministry and its embassies or between countries;

the details of military exercises; the capabilities and performance characteristics of missile, space, aerial, and other military systems; the intentions of foreign governments and terrorist groups, and the plans and technical secrets of foreign corporations.

MEASUREMENT AND SIGNATURE INTELLIGENCE, SENSORS, AND TARGETS

Photographic and communications intelligence can trace their identities as major collection disciplines back to the early twentieth century. The broader imagery intelligence (IMINT) and signals intelligence disciplines were clearly established between 1940 and 1965. In contrast the concept of "measurement and signature intelligence" (MASINT) as a discipline encompassing a number of distinct collection and analysis activities is far more recent, first being coined by the Defense Intelligence Agency in the 1970s. As will become clear, in many ways, MASINT is, essentially, "all other technical collection." MASINT categories include radar, geophysical, infrared and optical, nuclear radiation, materials, and multi- and hyper-spectral imagery.

As noted above, radar can be used to obtain images of targets. But the use of non-imaging radar for intelligence collection is the more traditional use. The US has used ground-based and sea-based radars—such as COBRA DANE on Shemya Island and COBRA JUDY aboard the USNS *Observation Island*—to detect and track missile launches and to gather data on missile characteristics. In the 1970s, an official historian of the COBRA DANE program described it as providing the "primary source" of data on the Soviet missile tests that terminated on Kamchatka.[9] Smaller radars, in aircraft, may be used to produce instantaneous intelligence on whether an approaching aircraft is hostile. A radar on the F-15E aircraft, when focused head-on another aircraft can determine the number of blades in the opposing aircraft's engine fan or compressor. The blade count helps determine the type of engine, and assesses if the plane is hostile. The shooting down of two Iraqi EXOCET-equipped Mirage F-1s during the first Persian Gulf War has been attributed to such collection and analysis.

Three sensors fall into the geophysical category: acoustic, seismic, and magnetic. Acoustic sensors detect sound waves. In the 1960s the US employed ground stations with acoustic sensors to detect the sound waves generated by atmospheric nuclear tests. Since the 1950s, the United States has operated the

Sound Surveillance System (SOSUS)—a network of undersea hydrophones that can detect the acoustic signals produced by submarines. The data collected by SOSUS allows far more than simple detection of submarines. The distinct noises made by a submarines engine, cooling system, and movement of its propellers can be translated into a recognition signal. And in 1995 and 1996, SOSUS hydrophones off California picked up the sound of French nuclear weapons being exploded under the atolls in the South Pacific.[10]

Seismic sensors have been used by the United States and a multitude of other nations to detect the signals generated by nuclear tests. Such detection relies on the fact that nuclear detonations, as do earthquakes, generate waves that travel long distances either by passing deep through the earth (body waves) or by traveling along the earth's surface (surface waves). Body and surface waves can be recorded by seismometers or seismic arrays at significant distances (over 1,200 miles) from the point of detonation. Exploitation of the data involves distinguishing between earthquakes (which originate from two bodies of rock slipping past each other) and detonations (a point source), filtering out background and instrument noise, and converting the seismic signal into an estimate of explosive yield when appropriate.

Magnetic sensors are often used on anti-submarine aircraft such as the P-3C Orion, which the US employs and has sold to a variety of other nations in Europe and Asia. The plane's Magnetic Anomaly Detector (MAD) is used in concert with its Submarine Anomaly Detector to determine whether known submarine magnetic profiles are present. To get a good MAD reading, the plane must fly as low as 200 to 300 feet above the water.

Infrared and optical sensors that are considered MASINT sensors are ones which produce data without imagery. Both the United States and the Soviet Union/Russia have operated satellite systems—the Defense Support Program (DSP) in the case of the United States—which detect missile launches by the infrared (heat) signature generated by their missile plumes. Beyond providing warning or notification of missile launches DSP's non-imaging infrared sensor has proven capable of providing several types of intelligence information. In addition to being able to identify specific missile types, by the uniqueness of their plume's infrared signature, DSP satellites have proven useful, due to their ability to detect a variety of heat sources, in monitoring the movement of aircraft flying on afterburner, the movements of spacecraft, large detonations (including exploding ammunition dumps and plane crashes), and certain industrial processes.

Optical sensors, known as bhangmeters, have been placed on a variety of US (and probably Soviet/Russian) satellites to detect the bright flashes of light associated with the fireball from an atmospheric nuclear explosion. In September 1979, a US VELA satellite appeared to detect a double flash of light somewhere in the South Atlantic, which had uniformly been associated with nuclear tests. That apparent detection set off a controversy, that persists to this day, as to whether some nation had attempted to covertly set off a low-yield nuclear device.[11]

Nuclear radiation sensors, largely placed on satellites, including the DSP, VELA, and Global Positioning System (GPS) satellites, detect such phenomenon as the X-rays and gamma rays associated with a nuclear explosion. Such information, along with other nuclear detonation signatures, can help estimate the yield, location, and altitude of the detonation.

Materials sampling—the gathering and analysis of effluents, debris, and particulates—associated with weapons of mass destruction programs has been a significant element of the intelligence activities of the United States, the Soviet Union/Russia, the United Kingdom, and other nations for many decades. In World War II the United States obtained samples of water from the River Rhine, in order to search for any signs that the Germans were operating a plutonium-producing nuclear reactor in the vicinity.

Another aspect of these activities has been the use of aircraft and ground stations to gather the debris from nuclear detonations—either atmospheric detonations, or underground detonations that have vented debris into the atmosphere. Such debris can be crucial for determining, among other things, whether the device employed plutonium or enriched uranium, and whether it was a nuclear or thermonuclear device. The US first determined that the Soviet Union had detonated an atomic bomb by the analysis of debris obtained by a US weather reconnaissance aircraft. After the examination of the debris collected after China's first test, in October 1964, US analysts concluded, to their great surprise, that China's first atomic bomb had relied on highly enriched uranium rather than the expected plutonium.

More recently, during William J. Clinton's presidency, the US analysis of soil collected from the vicinity of a Sudanese pharmaceutical factory led to the identification of EMPTA—a precursor chemical in the production of chemical weapons. That identification led to the targeting of the factory in retaliation for the 1998 al-Qaeda attacks on two US embassies in Africa.[12]

Conventional visible-light, infrared, and radar systems produce imagery whose content can be mined for intelligence by looking at its size and shape—e.g. does the image show a missile, and if so, what are its dimensions? Or, does the image show a nuclear testing ground, a nuclear reactor, or an airfield? In contrast, intelligence is extracted from multi-spectral and hyper-spectral imagery, which can be obtained from satellites (such as LANDSAT) or aircraft, on the basis of detecting and understanding the spectral signatures of the targets, available from the image.

Multi-spectral imagery is produced from the collection of multiple, discrete bands of electro-optical imagery collected simultaneously. Hyper-spectral imagery employs at least sixty narrow contiguous spectral bands, including the visible light, infrared, thermal infrared, ultraviolet, and radio wave segments of the electromagnetic spectrum. The data produced by examining those bands allows analysts to detect an object's shape, density, temperature, movement, and chemical composition.

The primary missions to which such imagery is expected to contribute are: support to military operations; non-proliferation; counternarcotics; mapping, charting, geodesy; technical intelligence; and civil applications (for example, urban planning). Specific applications may include the determination of beach composition; the location of amphibious obstacles; battle damage assessment; support of special operations; countering camouflage, concealment, and deception; analysis of the terrain; and vegetative cover and stress determination.

Identification and classification of targets such as operational nuclear facilities can be achieved by the exploitation of multi-spectral data—since such data yields "false color" images in which hot water discharges from a reactor would appear in red and orange in the image. Likewise, the reflectivity of healthy vegetation differs from that of dead vegetation (as well as vegetation which overgrows an earth-covered object such as a bunker) for wavelengths beyond visible light. Thus, examination of multi-spectral photography can lead to visual identification of such camouflaged sites by their distinct colors.

The utility of multi-spectral imagery (MSI) was demonstrated during Operation Desert Storm in 1991. Ground forces found the multi-spectral data useful in identifying disturbances in the terrain (indicating possible passage of Iraqi forces), as well as detecting wet areas that could slow down an advance. In addition, the "planning and execution of ground maneuvers, including the 'Left Hook,' were highly dependent on multispectral imagery." Naval forces employed it to identify shallow areas near coastlines for operational planning, to determine water depths, and to plan amphibious operations. Air Force planners used MSI data in conjunction with terrain elevation data to display attack routes and targets as they would appear. Subsequently, MSI data was used in support of operations in Haiti, Bosnia, and elsewhere.[13]

THE VALUE AND LIMITATION OF TECHNICAL COLLECTION

That technical collection operations can provide intelligence of significant value was demonstrated throughout the twentieth century. During World War I, photographic reconniassance provided intelligence on enemy troop movements. Communications intelligence allowed the British, as a result of their interception and decoding of a telegram from the German foreign minister to his envoy in Mexico, to accelerate US entry into World War I—for the telegram offered Mexico the chance to regain lost territory in the American southwest if it entered the war on Germany's side and attacked the United States.

In World War II, all sides conducted extensive photographic reconnaissance operations to identify targets and assess the impact of bombing runs—particularly important in an era where precision bombing was only a dream. The ability of British codebreakers to penetrate the Germany Enigma machine proved of enormous value—both in fighting the land war and in the Battle of the Atlantic. America's ability to break Japanese codes was crucial in winning the Battle of Midway, the battle which turned the war in America's favor.

World War II also saw the birth of two other forms of technical collection. As noted earlier, the US conducted the first ELINT mission—to gather the emissions from Japanese radar systems—during that war. The collection of water from the River Rhine to determine if any nuclear reactors were in operation represented one form of what would come to be known as measurement and signature intelligence. Another US operation, the flights of bombers equipped to detect a gas associated with the production of plutonium was yet another early example of MASINT.

During the Cold War satellite imagery and the telemetry intelligence branch of ELINT were of primary importance for the United States in assessing the capabilities of Soviet strategic forces. Imagery was vital in determining the numbers of intercontinental ballistic missiles (ICBM) and submarine-launched ballistic missiles and the locations of ICBMs fields. Telemetry intelligence, whether obtained through space or other systems, allowed the US to determine the specific characteristics of Soviet missiles, including the number of warheads each carried.

Soviet photographic reconnaissance satellites allowed the Kremlin's rulers to be confident that they had a good understanding of US strategic capabilities. Collectively, the existence of overhead reconnaissance and other technical collection capabilities allowed the negotiation of arms control agreements, since each side had an independent means of monitoring compliance, and providing reassurance that the other side was not in the process of preparing for a surprise attack.

Today the international environment is significantly different from what it was two decades ago—with the collapse of the Soviet Union, the concern over rogue state acquisition of nuclear weapons, the threat from fundamentalist Islamic forces, and the global reach of international terrorist organizations such as al-Qaeda.

Despite those developments technical collection capabilities remain a significant factor in the ability to gather intelligence. Imagery can still identify the dispersal of strategic and conventional military forces, from missile silos to airbases, the presence of above-ground nuclear facilities, and suspicious construction activities. It remains important to treaty verification, and can provide warning of events that a nation's senior officials and diplomats would seek to forestall with advance knowledge—as when, in 1995, the US was able to persuade India to forego conducting a planned nuclear test after imagery indicated that preparations were underway.

It also remains vital in providing support to military planners and combat commanders when diplomacy fails. Imagery continues to help identify potential targets, particular points in such targets to attack, and in assessing the damage done from such attacks. And with real-time capabilities, properly equipped commanders in the field have the ability to look over the horizon and see the enemy—his numbers, deployments, and movements—without delay.

SIGINT as well as MASINT continues to be of relevance. Intelligence about the radar systems of nations that might be the subject of air attacks is of great value to the potential attacker. Intelligence about Iraqi radar systems was of importance to US and British air forces during both wars with Iraq—allowing aircraft whose mission was to jam Iraqi radars to do their job before attack aircraft arrived.

Telemetry intelligence also remains important to a number of nations—especially the United States, whose senior officials are concerned with the development of new missile systems not only in traditional countries of interest—Russia and China—but in Iran, North Korea, India, and Pakistan.

Communications intelligence, in the form of intercepted and deciphered diplomatic communications, ordinary telephone communications, cell phone traffic, e-mails, and Internet traffic, continues to be a significant activity of large and medium powers, as well as smaller nations. Collectively the world's signals intelligence organizations are looking for diplomatic secrets, plans for military or terrorist actions, violations of arms and commercial agreements, and industrial secrets.

The increased concern with the development of weapons of mass destruction by rogue states, and the possible acquisition of such weapons by terrorist groups has only heightened the pre-existing concern about the proliferation of weapons of mass destruction. The potential ability of a variety of MASINT systems and techniques—such as material sampling of soil and water and collection of gases emitted by plutonium production—to provide warning that the production of weapons of mass destruction is underway provides an incentive for nations to develop and operate such systems.

Of course, the fact that technical collection systems can produce significant intelligence does not necessarily imply that they are not without their limitations or that they are, in relative terms, as valuable as they were in an earlier era. Thus, key documents that may shed light on diplomatic or military intentions or capabilities—unless foolishly transmitted by fax in an insecure manner—are immune from technical collection systems. At times, such documents can be obtained via a human source.

Technical collection systems can be subject to denial and deception. A nation which knows or suspects that some activity—for example, preparations for a nuclear test or WMD production—would be of interest to another nation's reconnaissance satellites may take care to eliminate or minimize the chance that those satellites will detect the preparations. Measures that might be taken include operating at night, not operating when a foreign reconnaissance satellite is estimated to be in range, and conducting test preparations under cover of another, more innocuous activity. A significant factor in India's ability to surprise the US with its 1998 nuclear test was the precautions taken to avoid detection by US spy satellites—including operating at night.

As both terrorist groups and some nations have learned, one means of avoiding having one's plans or activities detected through foreign communications intercept operations is to either communicate by means that are either not subject to remote interception, sufficiently cryptic to provide no crucial information, or are transmitted in a manner unlikely to be detected. Use of a courier, a phone conversation in which one terrorist alerts another that "tomorrow is the day" without providing further information, and a covert message accessible only through an obscure Internet site are respective examples.

Nations interested in hiding their weapons of mass destruction activities can also take actions to prevent other nations' MASINT collection from revealing those activities. During the Cold War the US actively sought to suppress the emissions of the krypton-85 gas associated with plutonium production. Other nations closely guard their WMD facilities, which can prevent foreign intelligence assets from collecting soil or other samples that can be used to shed more light on what is going on inside those facilities.

The international environment may also conspire to reduce the value of technical collection. The Soviet Union was a nation that did not try to hide the fact that it had a nuclear weapons program, engaged in extensive testing of its missile systems, and built a variety of naval vessels in its well-known shipyards. In contrast, some nations have small nuclear programs, make an enormous effort to conduct such activities covertly, and may engage in minimal or no testing of any nuclear devices they develop. Further, terrorist groups do not have the infrastructure that allows accumulation of intelligence from monitoring a large number of facilities, and are adept at covert communications.

The response from those seeking to detect such activities may include more intensive use of resources. Wider satellite reconnaissance operations can reduce the ability of a target nation to conduct operations in secret. Further, the distribution among the types of reconnaissance might be altered—for example, relying more extensively on radar imagery. Attempts may also be made to emplace technical collection devices—such as video cameras and eavesdropping antennae—near a target to obtain continuous coverage, rather than relying on intermittent coverage from satellites and aircraft.

Technical collection may also be conducted in different ways. Different types of sensors might be used, which focus on different parts of the electromagnetic spectrum or collect information in entirely new ways—just as the first ventures to collect debris from a nuclear explosion, or the gases emitted during plutonium production represent new ways to uncover other nations' nuclear secrets.

One can expect that the value of technical collection will continue to be significant, but to also rise and fall, reflecting the continued contest between hiders and finders—with the developers of technical collection systems seeking to overcome the tactics that their targets employ to evade their collection systems.

QUESTIONS FOR FURTHER DISCUSSION

1. What types of technical intelligence are readily accessible to average college students today?
2. What types of technical intelligence would be most useful in combating terrorism?
3. Is technical intelligence inherently more credible than information gathered from human sources?
4. Can technical collection ever be used to discover another actor's intentions?

ENDNOTES

1. Technical collection is often incorrectly referred to as technical intelligence—this term, however; means the intelligence concerning technical details of objects such as weapons systems, space systems, and nuclear facilities.
2. William E. Burrows, *Deep Black: Space Espionage and National Security* (New York: Random House, 1986), pp. 28–29.
3. Jeffrey T. Richelson,—*A Century of Spies: Intelligence in the Twentieth Century* (New York: Oxford, 1995), pp. 33–37; 157–172.

4. Jeffrey T. Richelson, "The Whole World is Watching," *Bulletin of the Atomic Scientists*, January–February 2006, pp. 26–35.

5. On the history of the U-2, see: Chris Pocock, *The U-2 Spyplane: Toward the Unknown* (Atglen, PA: Schiffer Military History, 2000).

6. There are two types of geosynchronous satellites. One type, of which CANYON is an example, trace figure-eights about the equator, rising to about 10 degrees above and below the equator. In doing so their altitude above the earth varies from 19,000 to 24,000 miles. A second type is a subclass of geosynchronous satellite— the geostationary satellite. Such satellites stay above the same point on the equator, at an altitude of 22,300 miles, without tracing significant figure-eights.

7. Dwayne A. Day, "Listening from Above: The First Signals Intelligence Satellite," *Spaceflight*, August 1999, pp. 339–347.

8. Desmond Ball, "Signals Intelligence in China," *Jane's Intelligence Review*, 7,8 (August 1995), pp. 365–370.

9. Dr Michael E. del Papa, *Meeting the Challenge: ESD and the Cobra Dane Construction Effort on Shemya Island* (Bedford, MA: Electronic Systems Division, Air Force Systems Command, 1979), pp. 2–3.

10. Science Applications International Corporation, *Fifty Year Commemorative History of Long Range Detection: The Creation, Development, and Operation of the United States Atomic Energy Detection System* (Patrick AFB, FL: Air Force Technical Application Center, 1997), p. 114; WilliamJ. Broad, "Anti-Sub Seabed Grid Thrown Open to Eavesdropping," *New York* Times, July 2,1996, pp. C1, C7.

11. Jeffrey T. Richelson, *Spying on the Bomb: American Nuclear Intelligence from Nazi Germany to Iran and North Korea* (New York: W.W. Norton, 2006), pp. 283–316.

12. Daniel Benjamin and Steven Simon, *The Age of Sacred Terror* (New York: Random House, 2002), pp. 259, 355–356.

13. James R. Asker, "US Navy's Haiti Maps Merge Satellite Data," *Aviation Week & Space Technology*, October 17,1994, p. 49; Ben Ianotta and Steve Weber, "Space-Based Data Found Useful in Haiti," *Space News* September 26–October 2, 1994, p. 6.

From Jeffrey T. Richelson, "The Technical Collection of Intelligence," in Loch K. Johnson, ed. *Handbook of Intelligence Studies* (London: Routledge, 2007), pp. 105–117. Reproduced by permission of Taylor and Francis Books UK.

7. HUMAN SOURCE INTELLIGENCE

FREDERICK P. HITZ

Human source intellengence—espionage and covert action—is the most controversial mission undertaken by the intelligence community. In this outstanding overview, Frederick Hitz describes the controversies, successes, failures, and personalities that shaped the practice of human intelligence over the last sixty years. As the threat of transnational terrorism continues to loom on the strategic horizon, HUMINT will continue to be in high demand within the law enforcement and intelligence communities.

When President Truman signed The National Security Act of 1947 into law, creating the Central Intelligence Agency (CIA), he believed not that he was creating a new espionage organization for the United States, but rather that he was greatly improving the manner in which important national intelligence would find its way to his desk. Earlier he had disestablished the Office of Strategic Services (OSS), the wartime foreign intelligence collection and analytical entity, declaring that he did not want an American Gestapo in peacetime. By 1947, he had changed his mind on the need for a civilian intelligence organization for three principal reasons. First, and most important, the lessons of the 1941 Pearl Harbor attack strongly suggested the need for greater early warning of a future surprise attack on the United States. Second, he needed a centralizing intelligence organization that would gather and analyze all the intelligence reports headed for the Oval Office and attempt to make something coherent out of them so he would not have to do it himself. It is not clear that he wanted the new organization to go out and collect intelligence information on its own, as this had been tasked primarily to the Armed Services and to the Federal Bureau of Investigation (FBI). Third, he was convinced by Secretary of the Navy James Forrestal and others in his Cabinet that the U.S.S.R. would become a problem now that the Nazis were defeated, and that he needed a window into Stalin's thinking and imperial ambitions, especially in Western Europe. The Cold War was beginning.

The CIA got off to a slow start. Its early directors were military men who had a limited idea of the coordinating role the CIA was intended to play and were aware of the bureaucratic sharks circling them, representing the parochial interests of the military departments, the FBI, and the State Department, all of which wanted to maintain their direct access to the president on intelligence matters. Two events conspired to change this modest approach. George F. Kennan penned his famous "Long Telegram" from Moscow, alerting Washington in 1946 to Stalin's imperialist designs on that part of Europe not already under Soviet control, and recommending a policy of "containment" by the United States. At the very least, this would require affirmative action by the United States in funding democratic political parties, labor unions, student groups, and cultural organizations in Italy, France, and Western Germany to oppose the Communist elements seeking to dominate these entities. In addition, to be most effective, the hand of the United States should remain hidden. The military were not the appropriate weapon to oppose clandestine Soviet infiltration and the State Department rejected the assignment, so the fledgling CIA got the job. Luckily, there was language in the 1947 Act creating the CIA that directed it to perform, with the authorization of the president, vice-president, and secretaries of defense and state acting as the National Security Council, "such other functions and duties related to intelligence affecting the national security as the National Security Council may from time to time direct." Thus was created the covert action responsibility of the CIA that grew enormously from 1948 to 1952 under the leadership of Frank Wisner. Wisner's so-called Office of Policy Coordination (OPC) was lodged ostensibly in the Department of State, but in reality it was an operational element of the CIA.

The second major development was the arrival on the scene of two savvy Directors of Central Intelligence (DCI). Air Force Lieutenant General Hoyt S. Vandenberg and retired Army General Walter Bedell Smith (who had been Eisenhower's wartime chief of staff) knew what the organization required to move up to the big leagues and were prepared to fight for it. Vandenberg was responsible for securing for future DCIs the requisites to do their job. The National Security Acts of 1947 and 1949 that he had lobbied for (and that had also shown the handiwork of an outside commission appointed by President Truman in 1949 that included Allen Dulles) gave the DCI unparalleled authority in Washington. They gave Vandenberg and his successors as DCI the power to: hire and fire his subordinates; spend money on their own say-so without further justification; short-circuit the federal government's cumbersome procurement authorities in order to perform the intelligence mission; and act across the range of intelligence collection, analysis, and dissemination responsibilities. The scope of authority was to include activities from classic espionage, to special operations (covert action), to all-source analysis, to briefing the president's National Security Council. In short, Vandenberg got the CIA, and the DCI especially, off to a running start before he returned to the Air Force. Bedell Smith took the new organization the rest of the way.

Bedell resuscitated the CIA's estimative intelligence, a function that had earned its stripes during the wartime OSS period but had lain dormant upon the OSS's demise. Estimative intelligence looks out to the future, attempting to foresee problems of concern to the president that may be coming down the line. With Truman's go-ahead, Bedell created a Board of National Estimate reporting to the DCI, led by the same Harvard history professor, William Langer, who had put it together for General Donovan during World War II. Professor Langer managed to convince a number of wise men from the nation's best universities to work for him and Bedell, tasking them with tracking the future course of the Cold War rivalry with the U.S.S.R.

DCI Smith also made it clear that covert action and special operations existed in a chain of command extending from the DCI, and in coordination with the other espionage capability that the DCI oversaw for the president, the Office of Special Operations (OSO). He thus contrived to bring Wisner's OPC into the CIA in fact.

The OSO's responsibility was to gather foreign intelligence information by secret means (i.e., classic espionage). It was often stumbling over or wandering into operations conducted by the OPC, because the foreign actors who stole the secrets were often the same ones who could manage the propaganda or organize the political meetings for the OPC. This is an important historical point. If the CIA did not take the field to secretly oppose Soviet propaganda, backdoor election-eering, and subversion in Western Europe, several of the United States' most important allies might have been in jeopardy. Furthermore, intelligence activity that connoted "action" was very much in the American character. It drew many adherents in the early CIA both because there was a perceived need (as the constant stream of national security directives from the president and National Security Council attested) and because, if successful, you could see the results. At the same time, the slow, painstaking process of recruiting spies to report on happenings behind the Iron Curtain and in the Soviet Union itself had to be undertaken. In the late 1940s and 1950s this was difficult and dangerous work, new to Americans of whom very few spoke the relevant languages, Russian, Polish, Czech, and Hungarian. It required a patience and professionalism in terms of tradecraft that the OPCers sometimes overlooked or made fun of. The spy recruiters and handlers (of whom DCI-to-be Richard Helms was a prominent representative) were dubbed "the prudent professionals" and were not as esteemed or promoted as quickly as the OPC "action" types. Bedell tried to end all that by making of the OSO and OPC one clandestine service, directed by one chief, Allen Dulles, who reported to him. Over time it worked. The two skill sets became a little more interchangeable, although DCI Smith noted in his farewell remarks to President Truman that he thought the CIA was expending far too little effort with too meager results in acquiring intelligence penetrations of the Soviet Union.

Bedell was, of course, succeeded by DCI Allen Dulles, who jumped on the Eisenhower administration's desire to contain the Soviet Union by mounting covert action programs rather than confronting it with U.S. military force. As Supreme Commander, Allied Forces, Europe, in World War II, General

Eisenhower had been a consumer of Britain's ENIGMA German code-breaking successes and knew both the role and the limitations of intelligence. As president, he believed strongly that the Soviet worldwide advance had to be stopped, if not rolled back, and covert action operations seemed a cheap and relatively low-risk way to do it. Enamored of early successes in overthrowing regimes in Iran (1953) and Guatemala (1954), the president and his advisors at the CIA grew accustomed to pushing the envelope in operations, overlooking close shaves and longer term backlash.

However, this extraordinary progress in spying on the U.S.S.R. and containing its influence during the Eisenhower years encountered several highly public setbacks as well. The revelation in May 1960, initially denied by President Eisenhower, that the Soviets had shot down a U-2 surveillance aircraft flying over Soviet territory, disrupted the Paris summit. The plan to secretly train Cuban exiles to land on Cuban soil to overthrow the Castro regime—later adopted by President Kennedy, and put into practice half-heartedly in an indefensible location at the Bay of Pigs—abruptly ended a run of successes by the CIA. Kennan's X article had alerted Washington to the bitter adversities ahead in confronting as politically hardened a foe as the Soviets; so it was naturally only a matter of time before a handful of poorly conceived or blighted operations gave the CIA an enduring notoriety and taint abroad, and dispelled the aura of the Agency's infallibility around Washington. The Bay of Pigs disaster triggered the replacement of Allen Dulles by John McCone, whose signal innovation as DCI was to put the analytical consensus within his own Agency under intense personal scrutiny.

The tattered doctrine of plausible deniability, however, still held an occasionally disproportionate allure for Kennedy and later presidents. After a national wake-up on the shores of Cuba's Bay of Pigs, JFK raised CIA's operational arm from the ashes, only to shoot for the moon all over again in *Operation Mongoose*, which saw the Agency embark on a rash of sometimes frantic missions to overthrow a now-entrenched Fidel Castro.

Despite the evident hazards of the profession, presidents relied substantially on CIA spies in Berlin to counter Soviet pressure there. The Eisenhower Kennedy years were the beginning of the era of America's greatest technical intelligence successes as well, with spies and electronics working hand-in-glove in Berlin and elsewhere; with

the construction of the U-2 high-altitude photo-reconnaissance aircraft; and with the refinement beginning in the 1960s of overhead satellite surveillance, eventually able to communicate images and intercepted electronic signals to Washington in real time. Nonetheless, it was on Cuba, in the October missile crisis in 1962, that U.S. intelligence showed that it had arrived at a position of sufficient maturity in its collection systems to be able to support President Kennedy with intelligence from all three principal collectiori branches: SIGINT, IMINT, and HUMINT. The U-2 flyovers were the first to supply photographs of Soviet medium and intermediate-range ballistic missiles being transported to, unloaded, and installed in Cuba. Signals intercepts pointed to a heavy buzz of communications around the part of the island where the missiles were being installed, and human sources witnessed the transfer of mysterious long tubes on highways too small to accommodate them. Although there were many details that human sources were unable to provide, our principal spy, Oleg Penkovsky, from his vantage point at the pinnacle of Soviet military intelligence, reported on the ranges and characteristics of the IRBMs and MRBMs which were being installed. He also revealed that General Secretary Khrushchev was way out in front of his Politburo in thus challenging the United States so close to its home territory.

The fact that President Kennedy had Penkovsky's insights into Khrushchev's overexposure, confirming the observations of his own former ambassador to the U.S.S.R. Llewelyn Thompson, meant that JFK was prepared to give up the strategic advantage of a surprise attack on the installation and, in a masterstroke of statecraft, give General Secretary Khrushchev an opportunity to escape from the corner into which he had painted himself. In my view, this was the apex of U.S. intelligence support to the president during the Cold War.

After October 1962 prosecution of the Vietnam War became the overriding national security concern of Presidents Kennedy, Johnson, and Nixon. The CIA built up its presence in South Vietnam and collected useful human intelligence, from captured Vietcong and North Vietnamese prisoners especially, that permitted it to report consistently that the Government of South Vietnam (GOSVN) was unlikely to prevail in the war unless it took a more active role in the fighting and was able to win over greater support in the Vietnamese countryside. The CIA's rejection of the validity of high body counts that were held by American millitary intelligence to signal attrition in the North Vietnamese capacity to wage the war is reminiscent of today's intelligence controversy about the import of the nonexistence of weapons of mass destruction (WMD) in Iraq.

In the case of Vietnam, the CIA more or less stuck to its guns that North Vietnam was not being defeated in 1968 despite its loss of manpower, whereas it was "dead wrong" in its assessment of the existence of chemical and biological weapons stores in Iraq in 2003, according to the Silberman-Robb Presidential Commission Report. In both cases the requirement of good, on-the-ground, contemporaneous human source reporting was critical to CIA intelligence judgments. In Vietnam we had it, whereas in Iraq we did not. Silberman-Robb found that the critical National Intelligence Estimate of October 2002 on Iraqi WMD was based on unilateral spy reporting that dated from 1991 and UN weapons inspection reporting that dated to 1998. There was no direct, on-the-ground HUMINT after that before the outbreak of the war. Over the decades, the NIE process had taken on its share of taxing intelligence puzzles, but it was clearly compromised and out of date in this one.

It is ironic that, as today, the great blows to the quality and competence of CIA human source reporting in the 1970s were delivered during a Republican presidency, on the watch of a national security establishment that valued and to some extent depended on good intelligence for its activist foreign and defense policy. Although Richard Nixon privately disparaged the Ivy Leaguers at Langley whom he believed had favored his opponent in the 1960 presidential race against JFK, he needed good intelligence on Vietnam to support the Paris peace talks Secretary of State Henry Kissinger was conducting with the North Vietnamese, and also his overtures to China. Indeed, when it looked as if an unabashed Marxist, Salvador Allende, was poised to win the Chilean presidential election of 1970, it was to the CIA that President Nixon turned, improperly bypassing the rest of his foreign policy establishment and the U.S. Congress to mount a coup against a democratically elected Latin American leader.

Watergate and the Nixon resignation turned the tide against this manifestation of executive imperialism, while the CIA caught a fair measure of popular and congressional backlash. Investigative reporter Seymour Hersh wrote a series of articles in the *New York Times* in December 1974 setting forth the ways in which the CIA (and the FBI) had illegally spied on American anti-Vietnam War protesters, opened

people's mail, tested hallucinogenic substances on unwitting subjects, and otherwise acted outside the bounds of an already broadly demarcated charter without the knowledge of Congress or the American people.[1]

Congressional reaction was swift and severe. The U.S. Senate and House of Representatives each convened investigating committees to hold extensive public hearings on CIA abuses. Senator Frank Church, a Democrat from Idaho who was running for president, tried to lock then-DCI William Colby into admissions that the Agency had attempted to assassinate several world leaders such as Fidel Castro, Patrice Lumumba of the Congo, Rafael Trujillo of the Dominican Republic, and Salvador Allende, without a president's authorization, claiming that the CIA was a "Rogue Elephant." In the end, the Church Committee was unable to substantiate these allegations. There was some assassination plotting at the CIA, directed by presidents, but none was shown to have been carried out successfully.

However, the Senate's inquiry caused President Ford to create a blue ribbon panel headed by Vice-President Rockefeller to look into the matter and to preempt Congress's certain desire to legislate restrictions on U.S. intelligence activity. Thus was born the effort to establish greater executive and legislative branch oversight of the intelligence community. President Ford promulgated Executive Order 11905 in February 1976, which banned assassination of foreign political leaders by U.S. intelligence operatives or their surrogates, among other restrictions. The order contained a number of additional dos and don'ts that were binding on the intelligence community, and it was reissued by Ford's successors, Carter and Reagan, in substantially the same form. After several years of trying to pass legislation establishing more comprehensive and binding charters for intelligence community agencies such as the FBI, CIA, NSA, and NRO, real-world dangers posed to the United States by the Soviet Union caused the public and Congress to regain some equilibrium on the subject of further restraining U.S. intelligent gathering capabilities, and the effort was dropped. Congress settled for one paragraph in the Intelligence Authorization Act of 1980. It required the DCI and the president to keep Congress "fully and currently informed" of all intelligence activities, including covert action, consistent with the president's constitutional authorities and the DCI's duty to protect "sources and methods from unauthorized disclosure."

Congress believed it could settle for this paragraph instead of the several-hundred-page charter bill, because it had established in 1975 and 1976 permanent oversight committees of the House and Senate to review intelligence community programs and operations, just as every other department and agency in the executive branch is reviewed.

Some argue that since the creation of the House Permanent Select Committee on Intelligence (HPSCI) and the Senate Select Committee on Intelligence (SSCI), with rotating memberships after seven years service, the CIA has never been the same aggressive collector of human intelligence that it was during the height of the Cold War. I disagree. The world had changed by 1975. Although the Soviets still maintained a nuclear arsenal pointed at America's heartland, it was on the downhill side of the slope economically and politically. It had an aging leadership and an increasing inability to provide for the needs and wants of its people. The United States was receiving more volunteers as spies from the Soviet Union, as its high-ranking cadres became increasingly gloomy about the country's future prospects. In the United States Vietnam had exploded the postwar consensus surrounding U.S. foreign policy, and a stronger demand for oversight and accountability for all of America's overseas activities had emerged.

When this era of intelligence reform ended, the full-time housecleaners who worked at Langley and the FBI had managed to stay out of the headlines for the most part. Spying against private citizens clearly violated the 1947 Act but made for no more than a sideshow when compared to spy-hunting inside the U.S. government. Light almost never shines on this most sensitive area of surveillance, counterespionage, but in this domain of intelligence work especially, tumult has been virtually inseparable from tradecraft. Penetrations and double-crosses can be expected in the competition among major intelligence services, but the integrity of intelligence operations rests on how well very fragmentary and circumstantial clues about possible security breaches can be read. Moles were often uncovered only years after their work got started. Indeed, when the Cold War did end abruptly, counterespionage work was not ready to wind down but was putting itself in high gear, as Americans were making inroads into the former Warsaw Pact services, shedding light on turncoats here at home.

American intelligence contended with a number of notorious penetrations in the Cold War, and most spectacular of these was the early discovery that the Soviets had recruited the top British liaison official in America, Kim Philby. Philby had until then been regarded as one of MI6's best men—a man in line to be its next director, a brilliant and affable character, and a mentor to many of Langley's rising stars. The United States had depended heavily on him personally for many of our early postwar efforts in Europe. Philby had been in a position to alert Moscow to many of the biggest and most sensitive intelligence exploits under way: the development of the atomic bomb and the VENONA project, through which the NSA was attempting to break encrypted communications from the Soviet embassy and the New York consulate during World War II. But he could not prevent the NSA from discovering an old codename, Homer, referring to a British mole in the U.K. embassy in Washington. Homer was one member of the entire Cambridge Five spy ring, another of whom was quickly tied to Philby, as a friend boarding at Philby's home. In 1951, Philby's official career effectively ended. But it took another decade's worth of revelations for his career as a double-agent to be sufficiently understood to put him in criminal jeopardy, whereupon he defected.

James Jesus Angleton, the CIA's master spy-hunter, was one among many of Philby's former friends on whom his treachery left a lasting impression. Angleton's occupation at the CIA was actually not widely known. He was simply, "the Ghost of Langley," the man who showed up unannounced at the DCI's office for an immediate, private audience with the boss. A classics major and poet at Yale who moved in the same circles as T.S. Eliot and Ezra Pound, Angleton was picked toward the beginning of his career to run the counterintelligence operation in Rome, during the crucial 1947 elections that kept the Italian Communist Party out of power. Angleton's early career also solidified CIA liaison operations with other services, including those of Britain and Israel. And he worked alongside the Mafia during his Rome posting. The Mafia had operated on behalf of the OSS in wartime Italy, and had helped to perfect some of the more lethal aspects of the CIA's tradecraft.

Angleton's cunning instincts came to the attention of Allen Dulles, who asked him in 1954 to head the CIA's counterspy operations. By 1959, Angleton had unearthed Jack Dunlap as a mole in the NSA who had reached high-level "no inspection" clearances. But in retrospect, though the Philby affair had ignited Angleton's imagination, it had not furnished the CIA with the kind of tradecraft lessons that would shed a much clearer light on future penetration controversies. In 1961 Angleton seemed to be nearing more breakthroughs, having been given personal charge of debriefing a defecting KGB major, Yuri Golitsyn, but Golitsyn became increasing problematic for the CIA over time. In addition to the key information he did betray, he was willing to speculate endlessly about other penetrations of U.S. intelligence, and spun out theories that Angleton showed himself ready to embrace. Among the most troubling questions he raised was the identity of the mole Sasha, a codename that sparked the most tortuous inquisition that the Agency would ever launch: These investigations had such disproportionate impact on work at the Agency that their records remain completely restricted to this day. And Golitsyn insisted with some vehemence to CIA officers, after each subsequent defector surfaced, that anyone to follow him would almost certainly be a plant, blunting the CIA Counterintelligence Staff's instincts. The name of one of those subsequent defectors, Yuri Nosenko, was much later cleared of being a Soviet double agent, but Nosenko fell afoul of his own glaring penchant for fabrication, and at first cast the most severe suspicions upon himself. Working on Angleton's behalf, J. Edgar Hoover's FBI went to extremes to try to extract a confession from Nosenko but were ultimately unsuccessful. Meanwhile, Nosenko had languished in solitary confinement for three years. In the aftermath, Hoover judged Angleton poisonously misguided, and the debacle helped to drive a permanent wedge between the FBI and CIA, from which neither agency extricated itself until after September 11.

Angleton put at least fifty intelligence officers under surveillance during his career, and removed at least sixteen from the service. Problems at the CIA became more severe as his views darkened into clinical paranoia over the course of the 1960s. The only personal trust Angleton was ultimately able to sustain was in his closest circle. Meanwhile he elaborated plots with Golitsyn's help. As facts became hunches, and his hunches increasingly bordered on the absurd, he came into permanent conflict with the Agency's leadership. Finally, he could not find a distinction between political loyalty and personal allegiance to his theories. He was barred from direct contact with Golitsyn in 1968 by DCI Dick Helms, and ushered into retirement in 1974 by DCI Bill Colby, while the Hersh revelations of domestic spying

were in the headlines. His Counterintelligence Staff was diminished from 300 to 80.

The counterespionage underworld that defends against other powerful foreign intelligence agencies is a reality in which things remain extraordinarily indeterminate. A myriad of conceivable avenues might lead to operational betrayal. Angleton's version of reality was to adopt the premise that the most successful Soviet campaigns were those of knowingly false information—disinformation—that could operate at a great remove from the Agency's headquarters. Penetrations were less important than the false tracks onto which the CIA could be lured. But in truth the kinds of judgment calls are immensely difficult that spy-hunters must make to arrive at breakthroughs in cases of penetration. Major revelations might never come down the road. And surveillance might fail to turn up any mole at all. Moreover, in the life-or-death stakes of the Cold War, there was always the potential that too broad or intrusive a mole-hunt would leave more self-inflicted damage to CIA operations than unearthing a mole would stanch. Nevertheless, crucial countermeasures still had to be taken, and in counterespionage it was often the effort to run down trails of minor lifestyle and procedural misconduct that kept operations secure.

Philby was the result of a relatively spectacular breakthrough, but the Aldrich Ames and Robert Hanssen penetrations during the 1980s and 1990s remained almost entirely invisible for years after the investigations got rolling. Ames and Hanssen did their damage over a period of time when CIA attitudes about lifestyle and procedural misconduct had remained too lax for too long. The Agency lost the distinction between operations in the outside world and the life of discipline required inside. Most espionage operations are carried out in the gray areas of administrative procedure; but over the years, these moles built microcosms of that mission right in the offices that they ran at the CIA and FBI. Like all other skilled professions, intelligence officers have to accept a high level of personal autonomy in those they rely upon; but the basics of tradecraft, on-time reporting, and drug and alcohol-free behavior are important too. Over the long haul, the maintenance of strict operational routine and personal integrity goes a fair ways toward assuring the success of the intelligence community in its operational mission.

Within the CIA, the chaos that followed Operation CHAOS (the controversial CIA domestic mail-opening program revealed in 1974) lasted well into the Carter presidency and the tenure of DCI Stansfield Turner. President Carter put the CIA back on the offensive in his changing attitude to the Sandinistas in Nicaragua, and the covert action he instigated to oppose the Soviet take-over of Afghanistan in 1979. Still, it remained for Ronald Reagan to initiate an across-the-board revitalization of both U.S. defense and intelligence resources that would reverse the post–Vietnam War drawdown and counter ongoing outbreaks of Soviet aggression. President Reagan authorized a covert action to train and reinforce the *contra* resistance to the Marxist Sandinista revolution of 1979 in Nicaragua, and a second covert program to build up the *mujahedeen* factions opposing the Soviet-controlled government in Afghanistan. At the same time, he initiated a research program to intercept incoming missiles in space. The Kremlin began to believe the United States was trying for a first-strike capability against the U.S.S.R. and initiated a worldwide intelligence alert called Project Ryan to report on indicators confirming such an effort. At the same time, old age and sickness were removing Soviet premiers at a record rate. In March 1985 a completely new figure ascended to power in the Kremlin, Mikhail Gorbachev, who was focused on curtailing Soviet commitments to defend communism everywhere (the Brezhnev Doctrine) and reforming the economy to provide a better response to the needs of the Soviet people. Meanwhile the Reagan administration was having a difficult time keeping the U.S. Congress on board for the operation to support the *contras*. After the second amendment curtailing CIA support for the *contras* passed Congress—and was signed into law by the president because it was attached to an omnibus and year-end appropriations bill—some members of the administration on the National Security staff and in the CIA concocted a scheme to sell embargoed weaponry to Iran in exchange for information about terrorists who had abducted Americans in the Middle East, using the proceeds from the sales to supply weapons illegally to the *contras*. The Iran-Contra scheme finally blew up in the press in fall 1986, sending the Reagan White House and William Casey's CIA into a tailspin.

It took die appointment in 1987 of Judge William Webster as DCI, a former Director of the FBI and U.S. Court of Appeals judge, to restore legitimacy and integrity to CIA operations after the Iran-contra fiasco. Meanwhile, CIA covert operators got congressional approval to supply Stinger missiles to the Afghans *mujahedeen*, a policy that proved pivotal to driving the Soviets out of Afghanistan. As unintentionally transparent as the Nicaraguan covert action was to the world, so the cooperation by the CIA with the Pakistani intelligence service to supply armaments to Afghani and Arab guerillas in Afghanistan was painted as a state secret within the boundaries of "plausible deniability." The Soviets knew where the weaponry, especially the Stingers, was coming from, but they were in no position to do much about it, despite the concerns of Pakistan's nervous chief of state, Mohammed Zia-ul-Haq.

To date, the Afghan covert action has been the last big successful clandestine political operation mounted by the CIA in which the U.S. hand did not show to an impermissible degree. By and large, the CIA officers involved kept their promise to Pakistan's rulers that they would physically stay out of Afghanistan and work through the Pakistani intelligence service, the ISI. The advent of both round-the-clock cable news programming and instant worldwide communications via the Internet have successfully impinged upon the United States's ability to maintain the necessary secrecy of a major covert political operation. This was made manifest in the administration of President George H.W. Bush, when the president, despite his tour of duty as DCI and his appreciation for the role of intelligence, turned instead to the American military to deal with both Manuel Noriega in Panama in 1989 and Saddam Hussein in the first Gulf War in 1991. When President Clinton sought to make use of covert action in overthrowing Saddam in the mid-1990s, he found it was impossible. Congress had gained an appetite for micromanaging an operation that could have high domestic stakes, and the CIA had too few covert assets to bring it off.

By the same token, viewed in retrospect, in the mid-1980s it would turn out that the United States had suffered unprecedented high-level penetrations of its intelligence services, through die handiwork of Aldrich Ames in the CIA and Robert Hanssen in the FBI. Ames began his espionage for Soviet handlers in March 1985 in order to get $50,000 to buy himself out of debt. He was a thirty-year spy in the CIA's operations directorate who had specialized in Soviet matters, arriving at a senior level even though he had a mediocre record—which included numerous episodes of alcohol abuse, security violations, and a chronic inability to get his financial accountings and contact reports about meetings with Soviet officials in on time. In short, Ames probably should never have been permitted to be on the front line, meeting and assessing Soviet officials one-on-one. But he was. And he used his position and his knowledge of how both the Soviet and U.S. intelligence systems operated to betray, over a period of nine years, every agent working for the United States against the U.S.S.R.; details of numerous U.S. operations against the Soviets; and the names of his colleagues who were engaged in the effort. Ames's betrayal led to the certain execution of ten U.S. spies and probably more, along with die compromise of hundreds of U.S. intelligence operations. The arrest of Aldrich Ames in 1994 provoked a wave of disillusionment and dismay in the American public, and among the congressional oversight committees, that such a sloppy and seemingly inept spy could betray so much over such a long period, not only without being caught, but without the CIA having mounted a serious effort to track him. The damage to the Agency's reputation was nothing short of devastating.

For the FBI, no less damaging was the tale of Robert Hanssen, a dour misfit who had used his superior information technology skills to eventually burrow into the deepest corners of the Bureau's counterintelligence operations against the U.S.S.R. Hanssen managed to turn over vast amounts of operational detail and names of U.S. agents to the Soviets in an on again–off again career of espionage that began in the late 1970s and continued until his arrest in February 2001. Hanssen's case was a tougher one to crack than Ames's because Hanssen had been careful never to meet with his Soviet handler, conducting all his business with the Soviets through dead drops in a park near his home in Northern Virginia. Furthermore, Hanssen had compromised many of the same spies named by Ames or by Edward Lee Howard, another CIA turncoat of the period; so it took an analysis of operations that had gone sour that could not have been compromised by Ames or Howard, and also the help of a Soviet source, before Hanssen's own activities could be distinguished and an arrest finally made.

At the same time that these spy wars were taking place between the Soviet and U.S. intelligence services, the CIA was beginning to enjoy real success in running Soviet and Bloc volunteer spies who were supplying vast amounts of useful intelligence information about Soviet and Warsaw Pact war-fighting plans in Europe, and Soviet military research and development (R&D). In the former case, Ryszard Kuklinski, a high-ranking member of the Polish General Staff, passed the CIA all of the Warsaw Pact plans that crossed his desk from 1972 until his defection in 1981; and in the second case, Adolph Tolkachev provided his U.S. case officer with the latest Soviet military R&D on stealth technology and air defense missilery from the late 1970s until 1985, saving the U.S. taxpayer millions of dollars in unnecessary defense expenditure. These successful Soviet spy volunteer recruitments at the end of the Cold War, and others like them, proved the value of a vigorous human source collection program at the time that the Soviet regime was under severe internal stress.

The need for espionage did not disappear with the dismantling of the Berlin Wall in 1989 and the dismemberment of the U.S.S.R. in 1991. The successor Russian government kept its intelligence officers in the field and the West at bay on a number of important issues. Yet, over time, the threats targeted by American intelligence agencies began to shift. As authoritarian regimes calcified or collapsed over the decade of the 1990s—frequently ex–Cold War client governments—the new threats would become proliferating weapons of mass destruction and emerging nonstate terrorist factions, exemplified by Osama bin Laden and Al Qaeda.

In a series of bold and ever more sophisticated attacks, beginning with that on the Khobar Towers, a U.S Air Force billet in Saudi Arabia in 1997; followed by the bombings of U.S. embassies in Dar es Salaam and Nairobi in 1998; and the attack on the U.S.S. Cole in 2000, this affluent Saudi veteran of the mujahedeen effort against the Soviets in Afghanistan, Osama bin Laden, showed he was capable and desirous of inflicting unacceptable damage on the United States in order to drive it out of the Muslim holy places of the Middle East. His organization, known as Al Qaeda, or the Franchise, had in 1991 volunteered to lead the Islamic effort to force Saddam Hussein to leave Kuwait, but his offer was overlooked by the Saudi royals. Subsequently in exile in the Sudan, and after 1995 in Afghanistan as a guest of the Taliban regime, Osama preached Islamic unity and defiance in opposing the West's continued military basing in the region and the support it was giving to autocratic and selfish rulers in Saudi Arabia, Egypt, and the Gulf who were doing nothing to provide for their populations. The CIA, in particular in the U.S. intelligence community, became alarmed at the growing strength, sophistication, and appeal of Osama's rhetoric against the United

States' role in the Middle East, which targeted it as the "far enemy." After President Clinton's weak and ineffective response to the African embassy bombings, the CIA established a task force to track Osama and Al Qaeda, but it was never able to deliver the knockout punch on his compound in Afghanistan or stop his continuing deadly momentum during the Clinton years, even though then-DCI George Tenet "declared war" on Al Qaeda in an attempt to bring focus to American intelligence's counterterrorist strategy.

In 2001 the CIA began receiving heightened liaison reporting from U.S. allies in Europe and the Middle East that Al Qaeda was planning something big. But where—in the region or against a U.S. installation overseas—was unknown. This was becoming Osama's trademark: long months of preparation and then a sudden strike. But just like the U.S. government's previous experience with a massive surprise attack on U.S. territory at Pearl Harbor, we were not prepared nor really expecting an attack in the continental United States. September 11, 2001, was an unforeseen and life-shattering wake-up call on the capacity of nonstate, religious-inspired terrorism to threaten stable societies like the United States and our European allies. It took President George W. Bush minutes to declare that the United States was involved in a war against terror and that all the military and intelligence resources of the United States would be deployed to win it.

What were those intelligence resources? In late 2001, in what condition did the intelligence community find itself to take on Osama bin Laden, Al Qaeda, and the challenge of religious-based international terror? With the passing of the Cold War, the CIA had been downsized and had in addition witnessed the dramatic departure of large numbers of expert spy handlers and analysts whose skills had been shaped by the challenge of the Soviet Union, and who did not have much interest in and familiarity with the milieu of terrorism, drugs, crime, and weapons proliferation, issues which would be the meat and potatoes of Presidential Decision Directive 35 that set the blueprint for intelligence community targeting after the Cold War ended. So they retired, and took with them their knowledge of spy tradecraft and of foreign languages. On top of that, as the 9/11 post-mortems would show, the intelligence agencies had grown into mature bureaucracies without much initiative, imagination, or creativity. They faced a target that operated in the shadows of nation-states but wasn't one; that had

low overhead and a tight network of collaborators that it deployed with iron-handed discipline; and that possessed one unassailable attribute: Many of its adherents were willing to commit suicide for the cause, and would strap on a bomb just to take civilian bystanders with them.

Other problems beset the intelligence agencies in 2001 as well. A division between domestic and international spheres of terrorism no longer existed. A plot that could begin in a Hamburg mosque or a Madrid suburb could be planned for immediate execution in New York or Washington. The divided responsibilities between the FBI and CIA that historical accident and concern about domestic civil liberties had spawned in the aftermath of World War II were hindrances in the 21st century to the kind of instant information sharing and teamwork that cell phones and Internet access in the hands of our terrorist attackers demanded, Compartmentalization and "need to know" take on sinister meanings when the effect is to deny intelligence to a sister agency equally charged with the responsibility to pre-empt a terrorist act.

Some of the more egregious barriers to intelligence sharing and teamwork between the intelligence agencies were struck down in the USA-PATRIOT Act passed in October 2002, and in the Intelligence Reform Bill, passed in December 2004. Now, wiretap permissions, when granted, run to the individual who is the target of the surveillance, not the instrument by which he intends to communicate. Grand jury testimony in terrorist cases can be shared among the law enforcement and intelligence entities having an interest in the matter. The Foreign Intelligence Surveillance Act (FISA) has been amended to include among the parties against whom the U.S. government may seek authorization for electronic surveillance from the special Foreign Intelligence Surveillance Court not just spies but terrorists as well; and the standard for authorizing surveillance has been broadened to encompass those as to whom terrorism is "a principal purpose" of their activity and not "the" purpose. There are additional sections in the 2001 Act that beef up the anti–money laundering provisions of federal statute and enhance the "sneak and peek" possibilities open to law enforcement, as well as enable more Internet intrusion of suspected terrorists. It is possible that some of the more aggressive portions of the USA-PATRIOT Act may be modified somewhat to include a greater measure of accountability.

The intended changes included in the Intelligence Reform Act of 2004 date back to the Church Committee era but trespassed on more turf, and would only see the light of day three years after September 11, with some of the most intense bureaucratic lobbying of any intelligence bill. In the Act, there has been a concerted effort to remedy one of the principal perceived deficiencies in the performance of the intelligence agencies prior to 9/11, namely the absence of "an attending physician" who could treat the patient as a whole and be responsible for the work of all the specialists racing around performing tests on the patient on their own. That metaphor, used by the 9/11 Commission to sway Congress and the president, was the premise behind creating the new position of Director of National Intelligence (DNI). The DNI was intended to be the intelligence czar, a Cabinet officer holding both managerial and budgetary authority over the entire intelligence community. He would also be the president's principal intelligence adviser.

When the dust settled after passage of the Act, the DNI's lines of command were not as clear as the Commission hoped for. The Defense Secretary and the Department of Defense (DOD) continue to share many of the DNI's management and budgetary authorities relating to the intelligence agencies under the command of the DOD. The DOD intelligence agencies—NRO, NSA, DIA, and NGA—account for 80 percent of the intelligence budget. There is also the matter of information sharing, which the Act seeks to encourage by requiring the DNI to have a subordinate responsible for creating an information sharing environment in the intelligence community.

The 2004 Act also treats the intelligence community's self-inflicted wounds reprented by the failures to warn of the 9/11 attacks and to accurately account for the weapons of mass destruction stockpiled by Saddam Hussein since 1991—believed ready for dispersal to terrorists by Saddam at some point if the UN embargo of Iraq was not lifted. The existence of Iraqi WMD was one of the principal reasons cited by the Bush administration for preparing to go to war against Iraq. A seemingly authoritative National Intelligence Estimate (NIE) circulated by the CIA in October 2002 detailed the supposed holdings of chemical and biological weapons by the Iraqi Ba'athist regime, and the efforts of the regime to make nuclear weaponry advances. Furthermore, United Nations testimony drawn from the NIE by Secretary of State Colin Powell in February 2003, on the eve of the Iraq War, was used to sweep aside Allied opposition to the invasion. It has become painfully clear since that Saddam suspended his WMD programs after 1991 to get out from under the UN-sponsored embargo. There were no WMD stockpiled in Iraq prior to the war, as Saddam had destroyed them.

What made the U.S. intelligence community's views on Iraqi WMD so objectionable was not that they held such preconceptions (most other knowledgeable intelligence services held identical views—the UK, Russia, Germany, France, and Israel), but that the NIE sought to justify the weapons' existence on outdated and unconfirmed reporting. The proprietary data dated from 1991; reports from UN inspectors stopped in 1998; and assessments rested heavily on unilateral sources like "Curveball" whose credibility was in question. The analytical tradecraft employed by the CIA on the critical NIE was fatally deficient.

At the same time, the president's decision to spread the war from Afghanistan to Iraq sounded alarm bells for quite a few veteran intelligence officers within the ranks. A number of these in-house critics believed the move into Iraq would instantly squander goodwill that the American government had gained in the Islamic world as a result of the September 11 attacks. Some intelligence officers subscribed to the view, later corroborated in the post-invasion Iraq Survey Group's two reports, that the inspections broken off in 1998 and the sanctions in place after had already boxed in Saddam.

Moreover, although DCI George Tenet had gained the confidence of the hawks on the president's war cabinet, both Vice President Cheney and Defense Secretary Donald Rumsfeld made it known in the press that they harbored deep distrust of the CIA's analysis of Iraq. The Defense Secretary had steered the 1998 Rumsfeld Commission that took the CIA to task to sharpen its poor nonproliferation reporting, against a backdrop of two missed calls at the Agency in five years—Saddam Hussein's startling WMD advances up to the 1990 Gulf War, and India's clandestine nuclear tests in 1996. The vice-president possessed quite the opposite disposition, misappropriating even dubious raw intelligence leads to hype the imminent threat from the Ba'athist regime. Analysts at Langley found themselves frozen out of most White House planning. The war cabinet opened a small ad hoc shop within the Defense Department to cherry-pick intelligence reporting from across the community, to be seeded in the media to reinforce two bogus claims: (1) that Iraq's Ba'athists had entered into an active pact with bin Laden's network, and that (2) the Ba'athists were on the verge of going nuclear. The Secretary was known to scorn the DIA's Iraq analysis as well, and he overruled pointed warnings issued by the Army Chief of Staff that the U.S. military could not occupy the country without a contingent of 300,000 soldiers. Amidst rising tensions and mounting controversy over Saddam's alleged possession of nuclear weaponry, Tenet balked too, sending a formal request to the Department of Justice to begin a criminal investigation to identify the source of a leak of a CIA operative's identity (a career officer who was unwittingly dragged into the dispute over the war's strained *casus belli*) even though it was sufficiently clear that the leaker would have to have been a senior White House official.

As the war wore the military down until it was an occupation in disarray, disgruntlement surfaced publicly. First, Richard Clarke, the former counterterrorism czar at the National Security Council made searing statements against the administration at the 9/11 Commission hearings, and then the departing National Intelligence Officer for the Middle East, Paul Pillar spoke out:

> If the entire body of official intelligence analysis on Iraq had a policy implication, it was to avoid war—or, if war was going to be launched, to prepare for a messy aftermath. What is most remarkable about prewar U.S. intelligence on Iraq is not that it got things wrong and thereby misled policymakers; it is that it played so small a role in one of the most important U.S. policy decisions in recent decades.[2]

The overlord at the D1A for Iraq planning, Spider Marks, told a reporter at the *Times* that prewar misjudgments had been made in many quarters, not just in the Cabinet leadership. "We lost our finger on the pulse of the Iraqi people and built intelligence assessments from a distance."[3] Out in Langley, the CIA has been under a pall.

The blunt consensus in the 9/11 Commission report and on Capitol Hill in the Intelligence Reform Act of 2004 to downgrade the CIA was probably not ill-advised. The Agency now has the leeway to be loyal at arm's length during domestic imbroglios, and in principle it has a new referee in the DNI. This has hardly been an auspicious time, however, to watch the demoralization at the CIA, with constant leaking of sensitive intelligence information and the hemorrhaging of experienced intelligence officers into lucrative private-sector security jobs or

retirement. Where does that now leave the CIA and the intelligence community, who bear the preponderant responsibility to inform the president about terrorists and their targets *before* these attacks occur? Future performance alone will provide the answer. The intelligence community has weathered its share of crises in the past. Yet there are some systemic reasons to be concerned.

To start with, the intelligence agencies allowed their capabilities to attenuate markedly during that ten-year period between the disintegration of the Soviet Union and September 11, 2001. There are still too few intelligence officers who have studied and understand Arabic civilizations or who have lived in the Middle East at some point in their careers. Moreover, many of the collection techniques of the Cold War have been rendered obsolete by cell phones, the Internet, and other aspects of changing technology. The CIA cannot continue to operate as it did in the pre-Iraq period, largely excluded from the hard targets that the United States is up against. Where it has no physical presence, the Agency has historically relied for HUMINT primarily on defectors, detainees, legal travelers, opposition groups, and foreign government liaison services, but these sources divulge their secrets at some distance in time and space from the ongoing developments inside the target they are reporting on. Getting inside the adversary's organization is thus a higher priority than it was even in the Cold War. Yet even though the Directorate of Operations budget is now more than double its pre-September 11 levels, an estimated 80–90 percent of intelligence information about Al Qaeda still comes in as S1GINT.[4] The whereabouts, goals, and tactics of terrorists are thus available only imprecisely and intermittently.

In the HUMINT area, American intelligence is still behind other services in having linguists who speak the hard languages of the Middle East, Central Asia, or Southeast Asia. In addition, this assignment is becoming less appealing to spy runners from the standpoint of safety and quality of life. Increasingly, CIA operatives will bring back key intelligence only by acting with the flexibility, the skills, and the cover it takes to run operations unlinked with an official installation—under nonofficial cover. Consequently, the problems spies face conducting espionage will be more dangerous. Families, too, will be divided, as many overseas tours in areas of prime concern to the intelligence agencies are not safe for young children.

Furthermore, there has been an especially rocky post-Tenet transition for the current Director of the Central Intelligence Agency (DCIA), former Congressman Porter Goss. Mr. Goss has been criticized for bringing a number of hostile and inexperienced congressional staffers with him to Langley, making for even more precipitous erosion from the ranks among senior officers with substantial field experience. This will hinder the CIA's ability to take full advantage of the uptick in personnel recruitment, because so many experienced officers appear to be leaving. Goss announced that rebuilding the operations directorate would be the overriding priority of his tenure, but an irony thus far has been the number of critics comparing the present impasse to DCI Stansfield Turner's first year, marked by some of the most severe confrontations and mishandled purges the Directorate had ever experienced. By the end of 2005, Goss had lost one Directorate of Operations head, two deputy directors, and more than a dozen department, division, and station heads.[5]

An equally fundamental point is that Americans are not the "good guys" any more in many areas of the Middle East. This sounds simplistic, yet much of U.S. intelligence success during the mature stages of the Cold War occurred because Soviet and Soviet Bloc officials volunteered to work for the American or British intelligence services as a way to oppose the corruption and misery of their own lives behind the Iron Curtain. That motivation appears less prevalent in the Middle East today. The United States is perceived as a threatening, non-Islamic outside force, only interested in the region's petroleum resources. Perhaps President Bush's hard push for democratic governments in the region will alter this attitude. It will be a hard sell.

The upshot of pervasive suspicions in the region about American aims is that, to be successful, the CIA and the other intelligence community HUMINT collectors will have to work indirectly, and multilaterally, through the good offices of friendly intelligence services, the operational channels called intelligence liaison. Since September 11 the CIA has been doing that in a major way, trading superior resources and technology for on-the-ground intelligence information about terrorist threats. The CIA has built a formalized network of over two dozen liaison offices, and DOD has gotten into the game as well, with less formal and even lower profile liaison and reconnaissance missions for the special forces. These DOD operations do not fill the need

for nonofficial cover and penetrations, but they do have a tactical yield.

The difficulty liaison relationships present, however, is that we are no longer in complete control of the spy operation. Our liaison intermediaries will influence both whom we target and how we manage the take. The result is bound in many cases to be a dilution of the product and a diminished timeliness. But the most worrisome deficiency will be a lack of confidence that one is getting the full picture, with the ongoing potential to leave the United States vulnerable and the region unstable. It is worth remembering the lessons of the Pakistani lSI's control over our access to the *mujahedeen* during the 1980s and 1990s in Afghanistan, or the heavily slanted read of the opposition that the Shah's SAVAK presented the CIA in Iran's prerevolutionary decades. Nevertheless, liaison operations account so far for nearly all of the 3,000 suspected terrorists who have been captured or killed outside the Iraq theater.[6]

Disruptions in these liaison relationships comes with the territory, but the CIA's experiences in Latin American counternarcotics operations have provided a number of relatively useful lessons for working with less corruptible, more trustworthy elite units in the more questionable partnerships with foreign services. Porter Goss has rightly pronounced himself wary of leaning too far toward liaison operations. There are, however, elements of liaison operations that cannot be replaced by CIA HUMINT work. The first of these is legal access: To carry out targeted killings in a foreign country, it becomes prudent to give and receive assurances from other sovereign governments. Kidnapping also is best avoided wherever the local service is willing to kick down the door for us. And shutting down nearly endlessly reroutable financing pipelines to terrorists requires a willingness to do so on the part of many sovereign partners simultaneously.

The intelligence community's technical collection programs may not be in much better shape than its HUMINT. Signals intelligence gathering is hindered by inadequate translation capabilities, while a wary target will be more willing to communicate by word of mouth, cleft stick, and carrier pigeon, than by telephone or more modern means. From an operational standpoint, the fallout from the brouhaha over warrantless surveillance by the NSA of communications from potential terrorists abroad with individuals in the United States that arose in early 2006 may further limit the gathering of useful intelligence. Actually, it appears that most Al Qaeda instructions are moving through Arabic websites on the Internet, which intelligence services worldwide are not yet recovering or translating in a comprehensive or timely fashion.

When all is said and done, counterterrorism and counterproliferation intelligence gathering follows a new paradigm. It is less about classic espionage than persistent tracking of terrorists and their potential weapons by good detective work and perceptive mining of reams of open sources. This is no longer back-alley skulking in a trench coat. It is down-and-dirty police investigative work, tracing radicals and their bomb-making materials, and recruiting informants to watch mosques and radical meeting sites. That is why in the United States it is so importacant for the CIA to work well with the FBI, with Customs, with Immigration and Naturalization, and with local police first responders. Intelligence gathering in the 21st century is now less about James Bond or George Smiley than it is a Frankenstein composite of law enforcement, spies and forensics.

QUESTIONS FOR FURTHER DISCUSSION

1. Have legislative initiatives overly constrained the U.S. practice of human source intelligence?
2. Should the United States abandon covert operations?
3. Should human intelligence play a greater role in Homeland Security?
4. Is human intelligence just a conduit for deceptive information?

ENDNOTES

1. Seymour Hersh, "Huge CIA Operation Reported in U.S. Against Antiwar Forces. Other Dissidents During Nixon Years," *New York Times.* December 22, 1974; Hersh, "President Tells Colby to Speed Report on CIA," *New York Times,* December 24, 1974; Hersh, "3 More Aides Quit in CIA Shake-Up," *New York Times,* December 30, 1974.
2. Paul R. Pillar, "Intelligence, Policy, and the War in Iraq," *Foreign Affairs* 85 (March/April 2006), pp. 15–27, at 16.
3. Michael R. Gordon, "Catastrophic Success: Poor Intelligence Misled Troops About Risk of Drawn-Out War," *New York Times,* October 20, 2004.
4. Dana Priest, "Foreign Network at Front of CIA's Terror Fight," *Washington Post,* November 18, 2005.
5. Dafna Linzer, "A Year Later, Goss's CIA Is Still in Turmoil," *Washington Post,* October 19, 2005.
6. Ibid.

8. OPEN-SOURCE INTELLIGENCE

STEPHEN C. MERCADO

Open-source intelligence is a hot-button issue inside the intelligence community; many intelligence professionals do not believe it constitutes real intelligence. In the view of this intelligence professional, however, data gleaned from open sources can place other types of information in context. And as readers of the *Chicago Tribune* know, passing references to the most treasured state secrets are sometimes made in the open press.

Our age's increasingly voluminous open-source intelligence (OSINT) sheds light on issues of the day for all-source analysts, covert collectors, and policymakers, but have we done enough to exploit its potential? My short answer is "No," and here's why I think so.

Collecting intelligence these days is at times less a matter of stealing through dark alleys in a foreign land to meet some secret agent than one of surfing the Internet under the fluorescent lights of an office cubicle to find some open source. The world is changing with the advance of commerce and technology. Mouse clicks and online dictionaries today often prove more useful than stylish cloaks and shiny daggers in gathering intelligence required to help analysts and officials understand the world. Combined with stolen secrets, diplomatic reports, and technical collection, open sources constitute what one former deputy director of intelligence termed the "intricate mosaic" of intelligence.[1]

Today's commercial and technical advances are only the latest developments in a collection discipline whose pioneers began developing the field in the late 1930s. Building on early work at Princeton University to monitor foreign short-wave radio, the Foreign Broadcast Intelligence Service (FBIS) in 1941 began to turn radio into a primary intelligence source during World War II.[2] The government did not neglect the printed word either. The Interdepartmental Committee for the Acquisition of Foreign Periodicals (IDC) gathered Axis publications through a global collection network.

The men and women who labored in the OSINT fields of the day produced products that compared well in quantity and quality to those of other agencies that stamped their documents "SECRET." Dr. Charles B. Fah, writing in mid-1942 as chief of the Far Eastern Section, Office of Strategic Services (OSS), praised the output of FBIS as "indispensable in our work" and "the most extensive single source available" on developments in Japan and occupied Asia. The OSS itself fared less well, failing to establish an agent network in Japan and reporting the fabrications of an Italian "con man" in Rome as its most valuable source on developments in Tokyo.

Publications also held up well against classified reports. John King Fairbank, the Harvard sinologist who led his field in the postwar era, recounted how, after reading an inaccurate and "unintelligent" British report on Japanese shipbuilding, he advised Col. William Donovan that better intelligence on the issue would be found in "scrutinizing the Japanese press." The OSS director evidently found Dr. Fairbank's brief compelling, for he sent the young academic, literate in Chinese and Japanese, to China to help organize a publications procurement program.[3]

NAVIGATING COLD WAR WATERS

After the guns of the Second World War fell silent, intelligence officers expert in open sources continued to help analysts and officials navigate the murky waters of the Cold War. For example, analysts in FBIS, whose acronym by then stood for the Foreign Broadcast *Information Service*, and the Foreign Document Division (FDD) led the CIA in detecting the developing estrangement between Moscow and

Beijing. FBIS and FDD officers began discerning signs of the Sino-Soviet split from their readings of propaganda material in the early 1950s. In contrast, some CIA officers from the covert side of the house erred, along with many observers elsewhere, in dismissing as disinformation the open evidence well into the next decade.[4]

Throughout the Cold War, in fact, OSINT constituted a major part of all intelligence on the Soviet Union, China, and other adversaries. OSINT on the Soviet Union, for example, grew from modest beginnings to become the leading source. In the closing years of World War II, intelligence officers searched German, Japanese, and Russian documents in the Army's Special Documents Section and the joint Army-Navy Washington Document Center for clues to Soviet technical capabilities. By the late 1950s, the CIA and Air Force had discovered a "wealth of information" in the increasing flow of books and periodicals from the Soviet Union.[5] By the early 1960s, one insider wrote that "In aggregate, open sources probably furnish the greater part of all information used in the production of military intelligence on the Soviet Union."[6] By the decade's end, another wrote of the "tidal wave of publicly printed paper" that both supported and threatened "to swamp" the Intelligence Community. He also offered an example of OSINT's value: "Intense scrutiny of the North Vietnamese press and radio has been an essential intelligence element in support of [the] US effort" in the Indochina conflict.[7]

It is worth noting in passing that all powers exploited OSINT during World War II and the Cold War. Indeed, our adversaries used technical information from open sources in the United States and other advanced industrial nations to monitor foreign developments and to save time and money on their own projects. The US aerospace publication *Aviation Week*, dubbed "Aviation Leak" for its scoops, was a perennial favorite. The journal was among the US technical periodicals that East German intelligence, among others, translated to monitor current developments in aerospace.[8]

By the Cold War's end, commercial and technical changes had made evident the value of OSINT. Radio, the cutting edge in the 1930s, remained a key source in the Second World War and the years thereafter. When Soviet tanks rolled into Budapest in 1956, for example, intelligence officers in Washington kept current through radio reports. One veteran of the CIA's Directorate of Operations (DO), referring to Moscow's suppression of the Hungarian

uprising, wrote: "It is a well-known phenomenon in the field of intelligence that there often comes a time when public political activity proceeds at such a rapid and fulminating pace that secret intelligence, the work of agents, is overtaken by events publicly recorded."[9] Some 30 years later, intelligence officers at Langley and government leaders across the Potomac watched, glued to their television sets, as CNN broadcast the fall of the Berlin Wall.[10]

The world today abounds in open information to an extent unimaginable to intelligence officers of the Cold War. When the Soviet Union sent the first man into space in 1961, secretive officials revealed little and lied even about the location of the launch site. In contrast, television reports, Internet sites, and newspaper articles heralded China's first manned flight into orbit in 2003. Even intelligence services have emerged from the shadows to some extent. Two journalists caused a stir in 1964 by writing a landmark book on the US Intelligence Community. Today, former case officers recount their clandestine careers.[11]

OSINT, OSINT EVERYWHERE . . .

The revolution in information technology, commerce, and politics since the Cold War's end is only making open sources more accessible, ubiquitous, and valuable. Simply put, one can gather more open intelligence with greater ease and at less cost than ever before. The explosion in OSINT is transforming the intelligence world with the emergence of open versions of the covert arts of human intelligence (HUMINT), overhead imagery (IMINT), and signals intelligence (SIGINT).

The Intelligence Community has seen open sources grow increasingly easier and cheaper to acquire in recent years. The Internet's development and commercial innovation has given us Web sites, "amazon.com," and countless other vendors. During the Second World War, Dr. Fairbank traveled far and at great expense to gather Japanese publications in China and send them to Washington. Today, anyone, anywhere, can order Japanese media with a click of the mouse from amazon.co.jp or other online merchants and receive the orders by express air shipment. In the "old days," not so long ago, academics and analysts made the pilgrimage to Maryland to browse the shelves of Victor Kamkin's unmatched store for Soviet publications. In the present, one can go online from the comfort of home to www.kamkin.com to buy from the half-million Russian titles in stock or to place a custom order.

Moreover, the IT revolution extends beyond the printed word. More and more local radio and television broadcasts, for example, are found on the World Wide Web. Monitors no longer need to sit close to the broadcast source. Nor do they always need an expensive infrastructure of antennas and other equipment to listen to radio or watch television.

Beyond the usual public media, OSINT is expanding into the areas of HUMINT, IMINT, and SIGINT. In the words of one advocate with experience in both the government and private sector, "OSINT now pervades all of the collection disciplines." He notes that one can gather intelligence today by overtly tasking collectors to elicit information, ordering commercial satellite imagery, and using software to conduct traffic analysis.[12]

IMINT, for example, is becoming such a commercial commodity as to be in danger, in the view of one intelligence expert, of ceasing to be an "INT." Japan offers a fine demonstration of media exploitation of commercial IMINT. A major magazine known for its focus on North Korea, for example, prominently and frequently displays commercial imagery of such sites as the nuclear facilities at Yongbyon and the alleged residences of leader Kim Chong-il. Journalists combine the IMINT with published defector information, leaks, and other sources to analyze issues. As an example of open IMINT closer to home, the Federation of American Scientists (FAS) used Space Imaging photographs of a DPRK missile site to argue in 2000 that P'yongyang's missile threat was far less than Washington had claimed. Whatever the merits of the FAS argument, the case underscores the opening of the covert INTs.[13]

Even so, OSINT is no replacement for covert collection. Rather, open sources increasingly enhance secret collection programs. The CIA, NGA, NSA, and other actors on the classified side all benefit from the growing volume of open data serving them as collateral information. Too, OSINT allows covert collectors to marshal limited resources for the most intractable problems. Digital Globe and Space Imaging will never replace NGA, for example, but government acquisition of their commercial imagery for basic requirements can relieve NGA of mundane tasks and permit it focus on higher priorities.

In addition to their influence on collection disciplines, open sources have long played a major role in covert action. Imperial Japan, for example, employed the German, Alexander von Siebold, to influence foreign opinion in Tokyo's favor. The agent launched the journal *Ostasien* (East Asia) in 1899 with Japanese backing, contributed favorable articles to the European media, and otherwise worked to shape views on Japan. He also monitored the media, submitting his "Baron von Siebold's Report on the Press" to inform the Japanese of foreign developments and opinion.[14] In the Cold War, covert organs of the major powers disseminated news and views through front organizations to win hearts and minds. Open sources still constitute the core of political covert action today, except that overt organizations are often conducting the campaigns.[15]

SURROUNDING TARGETS HARD AND SOFT

Not only are open sources increasingly accessible, ubiquitous, and valuable, but they can shine in particular against the hardest of hard targets. OSINT is at times the "INT" of first resort, last resort, and every resort in between.

To some, this assertion may represent an overselling of OSINT. Arthur Hulnick, a former CIA officer who went on to teach at Boston University has written about OSINT's importance: "Neither glamorous nor adventurous, open sources are nonetheless the basic building block for secret intelligence." He has also noted how OSINT, whether conveyed via FBIS or CNN, provides early warning. He has even estimated that open sources may account for "as much as 80 percent" of the intelligence database in general. Nevertheless, Hulnick has suggested that OSINT would probably be far less useful against such tough cases as North Korea.[16]

However, open sources may often be more useful in penetrating closed borders than open societies. Because OSINT is intelligence derived from open sources, fewer sources mean greater coverage is possible with a limited number of monitors. Take the two Koreas, for example. The Democratic People's Republic of Korea (DPRK), with perhaps the world's most authoritarian government, is a relatively easy OSINT target. North Korea has only two major daily newspapers: *Nodong Sinmun* and *Minju Choson*, the newspapers of the ruling party and the government, respectively. There is no opposition newspaper in the capital and no lively provincial media to offer competing opinions or expose wrongdoing. The Republic of Korea (ROK), on the other hand, has a boisterous press, comprising over a dozen newspapers centered in Seoul, with views spanning the full spectrum of political opinion. Each day brings a flood of government statements, corporate press releases, editorials, scoops, and scandals. In relative terms, monitoring P'yongyang's media is like sipping through a straw; following Seoul's open sources is like drinking from a fire hose.

P'yongyang media, while controlled, constitute a valuable resource to anyone seeking to understand the DPRK. More than mere propaganda, as Dr. Wayne Kiyosaki, an expert literate in Korean and well-versed in the media, argued in his study of DPRK foreign relations, P'yongyang's communications are a tool of mass indoctrination. As such, they provide "a barometer of priorities."[17] Dr. Adrian Buzo, a former Australian diplomat with the rare experience of residing in P'yongyang, has seconded the value of DPRK media as a "continuing record of the regime's priorities, of its ideological concerns, and of key personnel changes." Warning readers against the common trap in the West of dismissing the media "out of hand," he has advised that "Sustained exposure to the DPRK media is an essential requirement for the would-be analyst, both in itself and as an essential check on the reportage of the DPRK's adversaries."[18]

Finally, continuing with the DPRK as an example, US analysts and policymakers often have little beyond OSINT upon which to base their judgments. The State Department has no embassy in P'yongyang. Few foreigners reside in the capital; even fewer live in the provinces. Opportunities to make contact with the rare North Koreans who reside or travel abroad have been poor. Only the trusted few may make an international telephone call, send a fax, exchange e-mails, or surf the Internet. Such restrictions reduce covert collection opportunities. The open record for HUMINT is telling. Ambassador Donald Gregg, an "Asia hand" whose DO career included a stint in Seoul, has described the DPRK as "one of the longest-running intelligence failures in the history of US espionage."[19]

Other nations fare no better. One would expect the Japanese, former colonial overlords of Korea for more than 30 years, to accomplish more covert collection against their neighbors than their writings suggest. Tsukamoto Katsuichi, a retired army general with experience as defense attaché in Seoul, has confessed: "No country is as opaque as the DPRK (North Korea). Almost no information leaks out of there. Therefore, we have no choice but to make our judgments based on the little announced in the official newspaper *(Nodong Sinmun)* and radio broadcasts (Korea Central News Agency), as well as a limited

number of visitor accounts."[20] A former officer of the Public Security Intelligence Agency (PSIA), Japan's equivalent to the FBI, has also written that analysis of "published materials" is "central" to analyzing the DPRK, given the absence of nearly all else. Such OSINT, he has written, is "more important and indispensable than is generally imagined."[21]

. . . BUT FEW TO SAIL THE SEA

Today, open source has expanded well beyond "frosting" and comprises a large part of the cake itself. It has become indispensable to the production of authoritative analysis.

—*John Gannon, former Chairman, National Intelligence Council*[22]

With open sources so accessible, ubiquitous, and valuable, one would expect to see OSINT occupying a commensurately large space within the Intelligence Community. This is not the case. Too many people still reject OSINT as intelligence. Worse, too few are able to gather and exploit open sources. Worst of all, the Intelligence Community assigns only a handful of those capable people to the task.

Too many people still mistake secrets for intelligence. The enduring popularity of the fictional James Bond bears much of the blame, perhaps, for the misperception outside of the Intelligence Community that a tuxedo, pistol, and charm are the main tools of intelligence gathering. Even some insiders err in believing intelligence to be identical with covert sources and methods. The following opinion of a retired DO officer is typical: "Despite frequent references to 'open source intelligence,' within the CIA this term is somewhat of an oxymoron. By definition, intelligence is clandestinely acquired information—stolen, to put it bluntly. Information from a magazine, a television broadcast, or someone's newsletter may be valuable, but it is not intelligence."[23]

More than 40 years after Sherman Kent, the CIA's father of intelligence analysis, persuasively argued that intelligence is knowledge, some still confuse the method with the product. Sadly, such confusion is widespread. As one DPRK watcher noted: "Much of the best political intelligence comes from careful culling of public sources, like reading reports in the North Korean media, but within the intelligence community this source is not considered as reliable as more esoteric technical means, like satellite photography and communications intercepts, or spies."[24] However, as a staff director of the House Permanent

Select Committee on Intelligence (HPSCI) once explained to a deputy director of operations, "We don't give you brownie points for collecting intelligence by the hardest means possible."[25]

A few examples should suffice to support Kent's definition of intelligence:

- An intelligence officer would likely have received high marks for stealing a map of the Khabarovsk area of the Soviet Far East in 1988. Drawn at a scale of 1:10,000 and running to 80 pages, the map of the General Staff's Military Topographic Headquarters would have taken a classified stamp and stayed within a secure vault, available only to those with a need to know. The map, published in 1998 and advertised as the first of this scale declassified in Russia, is for sale today.[26]
- Stanislav Levchenko, a KGB officer working under cover as a reporter in Japan, defected to the United States in 1979. In 1983, a Japanese journalist conducted more than 20 hours of interviews with him, during which the former operative named agents and discussed tradecraft. The resulting book and Levchenko's press conferences were, according to a US intelligence officer, more revealing than his CIA debriefing.[27]
- On 7 June 1942, the day after the US "miracle" at Midway due to the top-secret breaking of Japanese communications, the *Chicago Tribune* trumpeted on its front page that the US Navy had known of Japanese plans "several days before the battle began." A Japanese officer reading that newspaper probably would have grasped that the naval codes were insecure.[28]

Information openly acquired, whether open from the start (say, a telephone book), declassified, or leaked, is intelligence when assessed and disseminated appropriately.[29] History abounds with examples of OSINT collection by intelligence officers:

- Military attachés have long attached magazine photographs of aircraft, ships, and tanks to their classified reports.
- Japan's Kempeitai in wartime Shanghai gathered the writings of Agnes Smedley and Edgar Snow in the course of collecting intelligence on the Chinese Communist Party.[30]
- Various services culled intelligence from the pages of the Soviet military daily *Krasnaya Zvezda* (Red Star), including the wartime Imperial Japanese Army's Harbin Special Services Agency and the postwar US Intelligence Community.[31]

Beyond the persistent dismissal of open sources as intelligence, the US Intelligence Community suffers from America's general indifference to foreign languages and ideas. Any intelligence agency reflects the society from which it comes. Americans, living in a vast country and speaking a language that has become the world's *lingua franca*, show little interest in learning other languages or, indeed, knowing what those outside their borders think. The result is an Intelligence Community recruiting officers from among a relatively small pool of Americans who, through immigration or education, possess the expertise in foreign languages and area studies required for collecting open sources.

Knowing foreign languages is the key to exploiting OSINT. An account with LexisNexis and a subscription to the *Wall Street Journal* are hardly sufficient. English is declining from the world's dominant language to merely "first among equals."[32] Even the Internet fails the monolingual American. Chinese is slated to surpass English as the Internet's leading language in the near future.[33] Domain names, once issued only in English or other languages with Roman letters, increasingly appear in Arabic, Chinese, Farsi, Korean, and other non-alphabet languages. Put simply, English is best for monitoring nations where English is used. But what intelligence challenges confront the United States in Australia, Britain, Canada, Ireland, or New Zealand? On the contrary, languages with which Americans are least familiar are precisely those of countries of greatest concern: Arabic (Iraq), Chinese (China), Farsi (Iran), Korean (DPRK), and Pashto (Afghanistan), to name only some examples.

Although facing such challenges, the United States lacks the education base upon which to develop tomorrow's intelligence officers. Relatively few Americans pursue a foreign language from secondary school through the university level. Worse, most university language students still study the Romance tongues or German in courses designed chiefly to produce professors of literature. The Intelligence Community must then compete with the private sector for the handful of competent linguists graduating from university. The bleak alternative is to start adults on crash courses at the Defense Language Institute (DLI) or elsewhere on some of the world's most difficult languages.

On a related issue, an indifference to foreign languages and even foreign sources in translation diminishes the OSINT value of the US mass media. American journalists on the whole have been ignorant of the countries on which they have reported. Most who have covered the nuclear dispute between P'yongyang and Washington, for example, cannot read a Korean restaurant menu, let alone the pages of *Nodong Sinmun*. Worse, as one observer noted of an earlier period of crisis: "Reporters did not routinely read translations of the North Korean news by the Foreign Broadcast Information Service. Nor did they avail themselves of information circulating among outside experts by e-mail and fax."[34] The resulting level of reporting has been so poor that one prominent academic who can read Korean wrote recently of having to turn to Pyongyang's "tightly controlled press" for information on Washington-P'yongyang relations.[35]

The reluctance of US publishers to introduce foreign books in translation further lessens the flow of open sources available to Americans. For example, ROK movie star Ch'oe Un-hui and her former husband, the director Sin Sang-ok, gained extraordinary access to Kim Chong-il after he kidnapped them in 1978 in a bid to upgrade P'yongyang's film industry; they worked for him until their escape in 1986. Their account of the Dear Leader, complete with photographs, appeared in 1988 in Seoul and Tokyo. They were for years the only outsiders who had known Kim and written of their experience, but no American publisher saw fit to issue the book in translation. The same is true of numerous books in recent years, from other insiders, including the architect of DPRK ideology and Kim's private sushi chef.[36]

An example closer to home is that of Dr. Emmanuel Todd's *After the Empire: The Breakdown of the American Order*. Published originally in 2003 in French, the book appeared the same year in various languages, including German, Italian, Japanese, Korean, and Spanish. The belated appearance a year later of the American edition of a book regarding what a prominent academic—who had forecast in 1976 the eventual fall of the Soviet Union—sees as Washington's futile struggle to maintain a global hegemony stands as an indictment of the US publishing industry.[37]

Compounding the problem of insufficient foreign information reaching the United States, the decline of area studies since the Cold War's end has reduced the pool of able applicants prepared to exploit foreign information in the vernacular. Russian studies, for example, have suffered grievously in funding and enrollment. Many graduates have found that US businesses prefer to send monolingual accountants to Moscow to teaching a Russian expert accounting.

Area experts seeking university tenure find positions going to political scientists churning out papers on "rational choice" regarding countries they know hardly at all. Students attending courses of area studies today are more often seeking their ethnic roots than preparing to join the Intelligence Community. For example, a German professor teaching Korean political economy at a time of high military tension between Washington and P'yongyang found that around three quarters of his students at Columbia University were Asians or Asian-Americans. He wrote, "I was astonished by the relative lack of interest in Korea among American students, especially in such a tense situation as at present, when only deep knowledge about modern Korea can help prevent potentially disastrous policy decisions."[38]

All of this would be bad enough, but even worse is the fact that only a handful of capable officers with language and area skills are casting their nets into the global sea of open sources for intelligence. The results have been catastrophic. In the words of one former DO officer who has argued that "covert collectors should not be blamed" for missing Usama Bin Laden: "It is virtually impossible to penetrate a revolutionary terrorist organization, particularly one structured and manned the way al-Qa'ida is. The responsibility falls on the intelligence community's overt collectors and analysts." He suggests that the information was out there, but that analysts were simply not reading the relevant foreign media. The same lack of OSINT exploitation, he asserts, was also behind Washington's failure to comprehend the rise to power of Ayatollah Khomeini in Iran a quarter century ago.[39] Two senior CIA officers warn that things are likely to grow worse. They note how "knowledge of culture, history, and language will be even more critical as the amount of open-source material increases." They also admit that, "Inadequate American foreign language skills are a mismatch for the exponential growth in foreign language materials."[40]

BUILDING A NEW "CRAFT" OF INTELLIGENCE

"The collection of foreign intelligence is accomplished in a variety of ways, not all of them either mysterious or secret. This is particularly true of overt intelligence, which is information derived from newspapers, books, learned and technical publications, official reports of government proceedings, radio and television. Even a novel or play may contain useful information about the state of a nation."

—*Allen Dulles, The Craft of Intelligence* [41]

The words of the former director of central intelligence (DCI) seem even more true today than when he published them over 40 years ago, but the Intelligence Community needs to build a better ship to sail the sea of open sources. FBIS, the largest and best equipped of the disorganized collection of offices engaged in OSINT, is too small a craft with too few hands to navigate the waters and harvest the catch. Analysts, by and large, lack the knowledge of foreign languages, media expertise, and time to do their own fishing.

WHAT IS TO BE DONE?

First, the DCI should increase the number of language officers at FBIS. Officers with knowledge of foreign languages, countries, and media are necessary to gather and analyze open sources, as photo interpreters are required to make sense of satellite imagery. The sea of open sources is arguably as large as that of covert communications, so one could argue that there should be as many open source officers surfing the Web as there are signals intelligence officers breaking secure communications. Required are college scholarships for students literate in Chinese and other innovative means of enlarging the pool of future OSINT officers.

Second, the Intelligence Community should take steps to turn the motley group of OSINT units into an organized fleet, with FBIS as the flagship. At a minimum, the Intelligence Community would do well to designate FBIS as the coordinator for OSINT. An enhanced FBIS could build on its expertise, its databases, and its longstanding role of serving the entire Intelligence Community by coordinating the output from the various embassy press translation units, military gray literature collectors, and such. An alternate, and more ambitious, plan would be to build a central agency for open intelligence based on FBIS. The new organization would be for OSINT what the DO is for HUMINT, National Reconnaissance Office is for IMINT, and the National Security Agency is for SIGINT.[42]

Third, the Intelligence Community must organize its own technical resources and tap those of the private sector to exploit the latest information technology for OSINT collection, analysis, production, and dissemination. OSINT collectors, all-source analysts, and others would benefit from smarter

search engines, enhanced machine-assisted translation software, and better tools for incorporating audio and video streams into intelligence reports.

Above all, the Intelligence Community requires a sustained approach to open sources. As with other collection disciplines, one cannot conjure OSINT programs out of thin air. Assembling a substantial number of officers competent in Arabic, Chinese, Farsi, Korean, and other languages and expert in fishing in the OSINT seas, then giving them the sources and methods to do their work, would be no small feat.

QUESTIONS FOR FURTHER DISCUSSION

1. Is open-source intelligence a lost art that is only now being rediscovered by the intelligence community?
2. Why are some intelligence professionals resistant to the idea of open-source intelligence?
3. What skills are needed to become a practitioner of open-source intelligence?
4. Is the information revolution making open-source information more valuable?

ENDNOTES

1. Russell Jack Smith, *The Unknown CIA: My Three Decades with the Agency* (Washington, DC: Pergamon-Brassey's, 1989), 195.
2. Information on the Princeton Listening Center, launched in 1939, is available at http://libweb.princeton.edu:2003/libraries/firestone/rbsc/finding_aide/plc.html. For a history of FBIS during the Second World War, see Stephen C. Mercado, "FBIS Against the Axis, 1941–1945," *Studies in Intelligence,* Unclassified Edition no. 11 (Fall-Winter 2001): 33–43.
3. For Dr. Fah's comment, see Mercado, 41. On the Italian "confidence trickster" who fooled James Jesus Angleton and other OSS officers, see David Alvarez, *Spies in the Vatican: Espionage and Intrigue from Napoleon to the Holocaust* (Lawrence: University Press of Kansas, 2002), 248–53. Regarding Dr. Fairbank's role in OSS, see John King Fairbank, *Chinabound: A Fifty-Year Memoir* (New York: Harper Colophon, 1983), 174–75.
4. The downgrading of the "I" in FBIS from "Intelligence" to "Information" reflects the mistaken notion that only stolen secrets count as intelligence. CIA counterintelligence officers, under the leadership of James Jesus Angleton, were among those in Washington who continued to dismiss the growing evidence of the Sino-Soviet split well into the 1960s. On how OSINT officers led the way in understanding the breakup of

"monolithic communism," see Harold P. Ford, "Calling the Sino-Soviet Split," *Studies in Intelligence*, Winter 1998–99, Unclassified Edition: 57–71. On Angleton, see also Harold P. Ford, "Why CIA Analysts Were So Doubtful About Vietnam," *Studies in Intelligence*, Unclassified Edition No.

5. J. J. Bagnall, "The Exploitation of Russian Scientific Literature for Intelligence Purposes," *Studies in Intelligence* (Summer 1958): 45–49. Declassified article.

6. Davis W. Moore, "Open Sources on Soviet Military Affairs," *Studies in Intelligence* (Summer 1963-declassified article): 101.

7. Herman L. Croom, "The Exploitation of Foreign Open Sources," *Studies in Intelligence* (Summer 1969-declassified article): 129–30.

8. Joseph Becker, "Comparative Survey of Soviet and US Access to Published Information," *Studies in Intelligence* (Fall 1957-declassified article): 43; John O. Koehler, *Stasi: The Untold Story of the East German Secret Police* (Boulder, CO: Westview Press, 1999), 110. Becker's article includes a reference to Soviet reading of *Aviation Week*.

9. Peer de Silva, *Sub Rosa: The CIA and the Uses of Intelligence* (New York: Times Books, 1978), 120.

10. Antonio J. Mendez, with Malcolm McConnell, *The Master of Disguise: My Secret Life in the CIA* (New York: William Morrow & Co., 1999), 337. On the monitoring of television in the Cold War, see Maureen Cote, "Veni, Vidi, Vid-Int," *Studies in Intelligence*, Fall 1990. Unclassified.

11. See David Wise and Thomas B. Ross, *The Invisible Government* (New York: Random House, 1964). Notable insider accounts of recent years include Duane "Dewey" Clarridge, *A Spy for All Seasons* (New York: Simon & Schuster, 1997) and Robert Baer, *See No Evil* (New York: Crown, 2002).

12. Mark M. Lowenthal, "OSINT: The State of the Art, the Artless State," *Studies in Intelligence* 45, no. 3 (2001): 62.

13. On IMINT ceasing to be an "INT," see Gregory F. Treverton, *Reshaping National Intelligence for an Age of Information* (New York: Cambridge University Press, 2001), 87. A Japanese magazine notable for its prominent use of commercial IMINT on DPRK pol-mil issues is *SAPIO*, which advertises itself as an "international intelligence magazine." See *SAPIO*, 8 January 2003, for example, for use of Digital Globe imagery of alleged residences of Kim Chong-il. Regarding the FAS dispute, see *New York Times*, 11 January 2000.

14. Foreign Ministry Diplomatic Records Office and Nihon Gaikoshi Jiten Editorial Committee, eds., *Nihon Gaikoshi Jiten* [Dictionary of Japanese Diplomatic History] (Tokyo: Yamakawa Shuppansha, 1992), 361. A British historian of Japanese diplomatic history has also written of "indications" that Von Siebold went beyond OSINT for the Japanese Foreign Ministry and Army. Ian Nish, "Japanese Intelligence and the Approach of the Russo-Japanese War," in Christopher Andrew and David Dilks, eds., *The Missing Dimension: Governments and Intelligence Communities in the Twentieth Century* (Urbana: University of Illinois Press, 1984), 19.

15. Frederick L. Wettering, "(C)overt Action: The Disappearing 'C,'" *International Journal of Intelligence and Counterlntelligence* (Winter 2003–2004), 566–67.

16. Arthur S. Hulnick, *Fixing the Spy Machine: Preparing American Intelligence for the Twenty-First Century* (Westport, CT: Praeger, 1999), 8, 40–41.

17. Wayne S. Kiyosaki, *North Korea's Foreign Relations: The Politics of Accommodation, 1945–75* (New York, Praeger, 1976), x–xi. Dr. Kiyosaki, a graduate in Korean of the Defense Language Institute who later honed his media insights at FBIS, knew of what he wrote.

18. Adrian Buzo, *The Guerrilla Dynasty: Politics and Leadership in North Korea* (Boulder, CO: Westview Press, 1999), 284–85. On the value of DPRK media in charting personnel changes in P'yongyang, it is worth noting that the standard reference works, such as the annual *North Korea Directory* of Japan's impressive Radiopress and the online biographic compilations of the ROK's National Intelligence Service (www.nis.go.kr) are based on media monitoring. For one journalist's recognition of the value of following P'yongyang's media, see Gordon Fairclough, "To See North Korea, Keep Your Eyes Peeled On the Official Press," *Wall Street Journal*, 19 February 2004:1.

19. Donald P. Gregg, "A Long Road to P'yongyang," *The Korea Society Quarterly*, Spring 2002: 7.

20. Tsukamoto Katsuichi, "Kitachosen josei to Higashi Ajia no anzen hosho," *Securitarian*, July 1995: 22. General Tsukamoto, who began his career as a commissioned officer of the Imperial Japanese Army and finished it as commander of the Ground Self-Defense Force's Western Army, has written several books on Korean security issues.

21. Noda Hironari (pseud.), *CIA supai kenshu: Am Koan Chosakan no taikenki* [CIA Spy Training: One PSIA Officer's Account] (Tokyo: Gendai Shokan, 2000): 169–170. It is interesting to note that PSIA changed its English name, but not its acronym, in 2003, replacing "Investigation" with "Intelligence."

22. John Gannon, "The Strategic Use of Open-Source Information," *Studies in Intelligence* 45, no. 3 (2001): 67.

23. Thomas Patrick Carroll, "The Case Against Intelligence Openness," *International Journal of Intelligence and Counterintelligence* (Winter 2001–2002): 561.

24. Leon V. Sigal, *Disarming Strangers: Nuclear Diplomacy With North Korea* (Princeton, NJ: Princeton University Press, 1998), 234.

25. Sherman Kent, *Strategic Intelligence for American World Policy* (Princeton, NJ: Princeton University Press, 1949). There is no more succinct definition of intelligence than the title of Part I: "Intelligence Is Knowledge." For the HPSCI staff director's remark, see Mark M. Lowenthal, "Open Source Intelligence: New Myths, New Realities," *Defense Daily Online*, reprinted in The Intelligencer (Winter 1999): 7.

26. This and many other declassified Russian maps have been advertised on line at East View Information Services of Minneapolis, MN (www.eastview.com).

27. Levchenko's interviews, which appeared in abbreviated form in a series running in the Japanese weekly magazine *Shukan Bunshun* over five weeks in mid-1983, were issued later that year as a book. Shukan Bunshun, ed. *Refuchenko wa shogen suru* [Levchenko Testifies] (Tokyo: Bungei Shunju, 1983). Haruna Mikio, a former Washington bureau chief of Japan's Kyodo News Agency with extensive contacts in the US Intelligence Community, wrote that an unidentified CIA officer was "surprised" at how much more detailed he found Levchenko's public revelations. See Haruna Mikio, *Himitsu no fairu: CIA no tainichi kosaku* [Secret Files: The CIA's Operations Against Japan] (Tokyo: Shinchosha Bunko, 2003), volume 2, 483. Whatever the accuracy of Haruna's purported source, Levchenko's Japanese book is more revealing than the one he published in the United States: *On the Wrong Side: My Life in the KGB* [Washington: Pergamon-Brassey's, 1988).

28. "Navy Had Word of Jap Plan to Strike at Sea," *Chicago Tribune*, 7 June 1942. On the "miraculous" character of the victory, see Gordon Prange *et al., Miracle at Midway* (New York: McGraw-Hill, 1982).

29. Intelligence officers have long worried about the damage done through the leaks of classified intelligence and even the gathering of published information by adversaries. Leaks are an old problem. See, for example, Allen Dulles, *The Craft of Intelligence* (New York: Harper&Row, 1963), 241–43. On leaks today, see James B. Bruce, "The Consequences of Permissive Neglect," *Studies in Intelligence* 47, no. 3 (2003,

Unclassified). Becker, "Comparative Survey," 35, noted in 1957 Soviet exploitation of US open sources and the repeated failures of the US Government from the 1940s to find a solution to the problem.

30. Tsukamoto Makoto, *Arujoho shoko no shuki* [Memoirs of an Intelligence Officer] (Tokyo: Chuo Bunko, 1998), 195. Agnes Smedley (*China's Red Army Marches*, 1934) and Edgar Snow (*Red Star Over China*, 1938) were prolific American writers with extraordinary access to Chinese communists.

31. Nakano Koyukai, ed., *Rikugun Nakano* Gakko [Army Nakano School] (Tokyo: Nakano Koyukai, 1978), 176, and Moore, "Open Sources," 104.

32. David Graddol, "The Future of Language," *Science* 303 (27 February 2004): 1329–31.

33. The prediction on Chinese Internet was made at a conference of the World Intellectual Property Organization, according to the *Financial Times*, 7 December 2001.

34. Sigal, *Disarming Strangers*, 221.

35. Bruce Cumings, *North Korea: Another Country* (New York: New Press, 2004), 47–48.

36. The architect of North Korea's Chuch'e philosophy, Hwang Chang-yop, has written a number of books, including *Na nun yoksa ui chilli rulpoatta: Hwang Chang-yop hoegorok* [I Saw the Truth of History: Memoirs of Hwang Chang-yop] (Seoul: Hanul, 1999). A Japanese sushi chef in Kim's service, publishing under the pseudonym Kenji Fujimoto, wrote *Kin Seinichi no ryorinin* (Tokyo: Shinchosha, 2003). These are two of many insider accounts likely never to see the light of day in the United States.

37. Emmanuel Todd, *After the Empire: The Breakdown of the American Order* (New York: Columbia University Press, 2004), *Après I'empire: Essai sur la décomposition du système américain* (Paris: Gallimard, 2003) and *La Chute finale: Essai sur la décomposition de la sphère soviétique* (Paris: Robert Laffont, 1976).

38. Constantine Pleshakov, "Russian Studies: A Sinking Academic Atlantis," *Japan Times*, 15 March 1995:17. Dr. Ruediger Frank of Humboldt-Universität zu Berlin noted the general lack of interest in "An Interview with a Visiting Lecturer," *Annual Report 2002–2003*, Weatherhead East Asian Institute, Columbia University, 21.

39. Robert D. Chapman, "The Muslim Crusade." *International Journal of Intelligence and Counterintelligence* (Winter 2002–2003): 613–14.

40. Aris A. Pappas and James M. Simon, Jr., "The Intelligence Community: 2001–2015," *Studies in Intelligence* 46, no. 1 (2002): 45. For a view of how deficiencies in foreign languages hurt covert collection, see

Matthew M. Aid, "All Glory Is Fleeting: SIGINT and the Fight Against International Terrorism," *Intelligence and National Security* 18, no. 4 (Winter 2003): 100–102.

41. Allen Dulles, *The Craft of Intelligence* (New York: Harper&Row, 1963), 55. For a similar view, see Robert D. Steele, *The New Craft of Intelligence: Personal, Public, Political* (Oaktoh, VA: OSS International Press, 2002). For those interested in a concrete example of literature serving as a guide to intelligence, see how poems in the DPRK literary journal *Choson Munhak* [Korean Literature] signaled the preparation of Kim Chong-il to succeed his father. Morgan E. Clippinger, "Kim Chong-il in the North Korean Mass Media: A Study of Semi-Esoteric Communication," *Asian Survey* (March 1981): 291.

42. Creating a central OSINT agency is far from a novel idea. The proposal surfaced, for example, in *Studies in Intelligence* in 1969. See Croom, "Exploitation," 135.

9. PEARL HARBOR AND 9/11

JAMES J. WIRTZ

Although there is a popular perception that surprise attacks come with little forewarning, collection failures rarely are responsible for the success of strategic surprise attacks. Investigations undertaken in the aftermath of disaster always reveal accurate information in the intelligence pipeline. Reforms to prevent a "bolt out of the blue attack" thus do little to reduce the prospects of future intelligence failure.

During my first trip to Hawaii, I made my way to a place considered sacred by most US citizens, the USS *Arizona* memorial at Pearl Harbor. Survivors often greet visitors to the memorial, amswering questions and retelling their memories of the day that the Japanese attacked the US Pacific Fleet. When it came my turn, I asked what the weather was like that fateful morning. The answer was "like today." A few putty clouds dotted the blue Hawaiian skies, a light breeze pushed ripples across the turquoise water of the harbor, stirring the warm tropical air to create one of the most idyllic anchorages on earth. September 11 also dawned clear and blue over New York City, the kind of late summer day that highlights perfectly the United States' front door, the spectacular edifice of promise and prosperity that is lower Manhattan. Given the setting, it is no wonder that the events of both Pearl Harbor and September 11 came as a complete shock to eyewitnesses. Neither could have happened on a more pleasant morning.

We now know, however, that initial eyewitness interpretations of both of these surprise attacks, as bolts out of the blue, were incorrect. Indications of what was about to happen were available before the Japanese attack on Pearl Harbor. In fact, one of the accepted tenets of the literature on surprise attacks is that in all cases of so-called intelligence failure, accurate information concerning what is about to transpire can be found in the intelligence system after the fact. It is thus to be expected that revelations will continue about the signals that were in the intelligence pipeline prior to the terrorist attacks of September 11. And as in the afternath of Pearl Harbor, the US government will hold a series of investigations to discover how organizational shortcomings or mistakes made by specific officials were responsible for the intelligence failure that paved the way for the destruction of the World Trade Center and the attack on the Pentagon.

It is not surprising that similarities exist between the attack on Pearl Harbor and the terrorist attacks of September 11 because both events are examples of a more general international phenomenon—the surprise attack. Despite the fact that they occurred over 50 years apart and involve different kinds of international actors with highly different motivations, a pattern exists in the events leading up to surprise and its consequences. Exploring these similarities can help cast the tragedy of September 11 in a broader context, an important initial step in reducing the likelihood of mass-casualty terrorism in the future.

WARNING SIGNS

Although Pearl Harbor and the September 11 attacks are sometimes depicted as totally unanticipated events, both incidents were preceded by clear indications that the United States faced an imminent threat. Prior to Pearl Harbor, US-Japanese relations had reached a nadir. By the summer of 1941, the administration of US President Franklin Roosevelt had placed economic sanctions on the Japanese to force them to end their war against China. These sanctions were the proximate cause of the Japanese attack. Japanese officials believed that the US embargo against them would ruin their economy, while destruction of the

US fleet would provide them with some maneuvering room. They intended to quickly seize resource-rich lands in the Far East, fortify their newly conquered lands, and then reach some sort of negotiated settlement with the United States.

The Roosevelt administration recognized that it faced a crisis with Japan, although senior officials in Washington did not realize that Oahu was in danger until it was too late. In their minds, it made no sense for the Japanese to attack the United States because they simply lacked the economic resources or military capability to defeat the US military in a long war. In an ironic twist, the Roosevelt administration was ultimately proven correct in this estimate. The Japanese attack on Pearl Harbor eliminated the possibility of US acquiescence to the creation of a Japanese empire in the Pacific as well as the eventual peace arrangement Japan hoped to achieve.

The situation that faced the United States was even more clear cut, if not quite as grave, prior to September 11. Various studies and commissions (such as the government's Gilmore commission) described the ongoing struggle against terrorism and predicted that a significant terrorist attack on the continental United States was a virtual certainty. The United States was actually engaged in a war with Al Qaeda, an international network of terrorist groups throughout the 1990s. Al Qaeda may have been loosely linked to the militias that battled US Ranger units in Somalia in 1993. Al Qaeda also was involved in the bombing of the office of the program manager for the Saudi Arabian National Guard in Riyadh in November 1995 and in the attack on the Khobar Towers complex in Dahran in July 1996.

These attacks on US interests in 1995 and 1996 changed the way forward deployed US forces operated within the Arabian Peninsula. New "force protection" regulations were promolgated to protect US military personnel, requiring commanders to observe stringent requirements to ensure their safety. In Saudi Arabia, US operational units were consolidated at Prince Sultan Air Base and advisory components were moved to Eskan Village, a housing complex south of Riyadh. Intelligence collection efforts also concentrated on the new threat, providing forces throughout the region with improved tactical and operational warning. At times, US forces were placed at "Threateon Delta" in expectation of an immediate attack. The hardening of the "target" on the Arabian Peninsula forced Al Qaeda to look for vulnerabilities elsewhere.

Any lingering doubts about the ongoing threat were dispelled by Al Qaeda's bombing of the US embassies in Kenya and Tanzania in August 1998 and the attack against the USS *Cole* in October 2000. The United States even returned fire following the 1998 embassy attacks by launching cruise missile strikes against suspected terrorist training camps in Afghanistan and a pharmaceutical plant in Sudan that was believed to have links to Al Qaeda. US government agencies had a clear idea that Osama bin Laden was committed to attacking US interests globally. Bin Laden's 1998 *fatwa* represented a declaration of war on the United States and called upon supporters to kill US officials, soldiers, and civilians everywhere around the world. This assessment of bin Laden's intentions was reflected in a variety of publicly available sources. The US Congressional Research Service published a compelling warning about bin Laden's campaign of terror entitled "Terrorism: Near Eastern Groups and State Sponsors" on September 10, 2001. A compelling description of bin Laden's alliance with the Taliban and his political agenda was even published in *Foreign Affairs* in 1999.

Pearl Harbor and the terrorist attacks on September 11 were not bolts out of the blue. But because they were generally perceived to have occurred without warning, they both have changed attitudes and produced policies that have reduced the likelihood and consequences of surprise attack. Pearl Harbor focused strategists' attention on the need to avoid the consequences of surprise attack, especially when it came to US nuclear deterrent threats. The fear of a surprise attack made the nuclear balance of terror appear delicate. As a result, enormous efforts were undertaken to guarantee that US strategic forces could survive a Soviet nuclear attack and still be able to assure destruction of the Soviet Union. Today, the administration of US President George Bush is trying to minimize the effects or a potential terrorist incident by improving homeland defenses and consequence management, spending US$35 billion on homeland defense programs. US military forces also are pre-empting attacks by taking the battle to the terrorists and by training foreign militaries to deal with the threat.

STRUCTURAL VULNERABILITIES

Despite common misperceptions, it was the US Army, and not the US Navy, that was responsible for the defense of Pearl Harbor in December 1941.

This division of responsibilities helped to create the conditions for surprise. When Washington issued a war warning to its forces in Hawaii, Army officers took steps to safeguard against sabotage, locking up ammunition and concentrating aircraft on the center of runways so they could be more easily guarded. In contrast, Navy officers thought that the war warning would prompt a vigorous effort on the part of the Army to use long-range aircraft to patrol the waters around Oahu. Army officers thought that Naval intelligence had been keeping tabs on the whereabouts of the Japanese fleet; they did not realize that Navy analysts had lost track of Japanese aircraft carriers in the weeks leading up to Pearl Harbor. Further, the Army and Navy staffs on Oahu never confirmed their expectations about what each other was doing to safeguard the islands from attack. Even perfect liaison between the services, however, might not have been enough to prevent disaster because no mechanism existed to collect and disseminate all-source intelligence to the operational commanders who could put it to good use. There is little evidence to suggest that the Japanese knew about these organizational weaknesses in Hawaii's defenses, but organizational shortcomings facilitated their effort to catch the US fleet unprepared.

Al Qaeda might have understood the organizational weakness that reduced the likelihood that its operatives would be detected before they struck. While there was a unified command structure in the Persian Gulf to address the local terrorist threat, organizational responsibilities in the US government largely diverged at the water's edge. The Department of Defense and the Central Intelligence Agency (CIA) focus on foreign threats and intelligence collection, while the Federal Bureau of Investigation focuses on internal security and investigating crime.

Local and State police forces operate in their own jurisdictions and US airport security, until recently, was largely the responsibility of private firms. Additionally, the definition of terrorism was not without organizational consequences. Was it a form of war or a type of natural disaster that would fall under the jurisdiction of the Federal Emergency Management Agency? Was it a homegrown threat involving high explosives (e.g. the destruction of the Alfred P. Murrah Federal Building in April 1995) or a new type of threat involving weapons of mass destruction (e.g. the Aum Shinrikyo attack on the Tokyo subway in March 1995)? And as this debate about the likelihood and form of mass-casualty terrorism unfolded in the years leading up to September 11, front-line government agencies in the war against domestic terrorism were allowed to atrophy. US Customs and Immigration agents now find themselves unprepared for their new role in combating domestic terrorism.

US citizens tend to focus on technological solutions to problems, often forgetting that organization shapes the ability to respond to emerging challenges. Strong organization—the ability to orchestrate the efforts of a vast array of individuals and bureaucratic actors—is imperative if the United States is to effectively spend its resources in the war on terrorism. Despite inter-service rivalry and bureaucratic preferences, the organizational shortcomings that existed prior to Pearl Harbor were relatively easy to minimize compared to the bureaucratic and legal challenge created by today's war. After Pearl Harbor, clearer lines of responsibility were drawn between the services. By contrast, legal questions and scores of jurisdictional issues presently complicate official efforts to create the governmental structures and relationships needed to generate a comprehensive response to terrorism.

TECHNOLOGICAL SURPRISE

The ability to utilize technology creatively played an important role in both the Japanese attack on Pearl Harbor and the terrorist attacks or September 11. When historians write about technical surprise, they focus on the unexpected introduction of hardware or weapons that cannot be quickly countered by an opponent. The attack on Pearl Harbor, for example, was made possible when the Japanese developed an aerial torpedo that could function in the shallow waters of Pearl Harbor. But the Japanese success at Pearl Harbor was made possible by a broader integration of technology with a new concept of operations that brought the full capability of carrier aviation to bear in a decisive way. This demonstration of professional military prowess combined new technology, tactics, and strategy in a surprisingly devastating way. Carrier aviation itself was not a secret, but the Japanese exploited this new technology with so much daring and skill that it was impossible even for those who understood the threat posed by Japan to recognize that they faced such grave and immediate danger.

Al Qaeda also achieved a technological surprise on September 11. Again, there was nothing particularly novel about the use of aircraft to conduct a suicide mission—ironically it was the Japanese who introduced the kamikaze during the October 1944 US invasion of the Philippines. But by using a host of modern technologies produced by the information revolution and globalization. Al Qaeda operatives were able to plan, orchestrate, and execute a major "special operations" attack without the hardware, training, or infrastructure generally associated with conducting a precision strike at intercontinental ranges. Al Qaeda used the Internet, satellite telephones, and cell phones to coordinate their international operations, especially to communicate with operatives in the United States. They also used the international banking system to fund cells in the United States without drawing undue attention. Al Qaeda operatives rode the rails of the information revolution, harnessing international communication and financial networks to carry out their nefarious scheme.

In both instances of surprise, the opponent used technology in an innovative way to launch a devastating over-the-horizon attack. And prior to both attacks, the technology employed was actually well known to US officials and officers. Indeed, in the case of the September 11 attacks, US citizens, as the major beneficiaries and supporters of globalization, were probably the world's leading experts when it came to harnessing new instruments of communication and commerce. However, they lacked a keen awareness of the desperation and creativity of their enemies, leading them to underestimate opponents' willingness to find ways to circumvent defenses to gain the element of surprise.

THE INTEREST–THREAT MISMATCH

During the 1990s, the debate about the United States' role in world affairs revolved around concerns about the interest-threat mismatch. In the aftermath of the Cold War, low-level, nagging threats—ethnic violence, terrorism, or just instability and unrest—permeated parts of the world. Some observers suggested that these threats had little effect on US national interests. People who suggested that the United States become involved in places like Rwanda or even Kosovo, for instance, were really thinking with their hearts and not their heads. The issue was not whether the United States should work to stop genocide. Instead, the concern was that intervention meant an open-ended US commitment to social engineering that realistically had little prospect of success. Intervention was an option available to the United States, but it was

not without opportunity costs and significant risks. Intervening in far away places like Afghanistan to stop Taliban human rights abuses or to deny Al Qaeda a secure base of operations was never even considered. Bush ran his 2000 presidential campaign on reducing the United States' international "over-commitments" abroad. The United States "casualty aversion" seemed to be a major factor in limiting US intervention to stop ethnic violence and other forms of carnage. Anti-democratic and anti-market forces, specifically a fundamentalist backlash against the way globalization spreads Western culture, was not deemed of sufficient strength to pose a significant security threat.

In the late 1930s, the US intelligence community also perceived a mismatch between US interests and the desirability of responding to the threats that were emerging across the globe. This perception is difficult to explain in hindsight, given the genocidal and aggressive policies of the Nazi regime and Japan's imperial ambitions. On the eve of Pearl Harbor, the Nazis had overrun virtually all of Europe and Japan had been engaged in a war in China for nearly a decade. Still, the United States seemed to believe that they could somehow escape the wave of fascism and violence that was sweeping the globe.

Both Al Qaeda and Imperial Japan attacked the United States in an effort to limit US influence and to stop the spread of free markets, democracy, and liberal ideas into the Middle East and East Asia. Japan believed that US officials would not have the will to challenge their initiatives in Asia; Japanese leaders felt US "casualty aversion" would lead to a negotiated settlement in Asia. Bin Laden apparently expected a relatively ineffectual US military response (again driven by US concerns about casualties) that would in the end spark a revolution in moderate Arab regimes, if not a full blown clash of civilizations between Islam and the West. Bin Laden and the Japanese, however, underestimated how surprise attacks would alter the political balance within the United States and the way US citizens perceived foreign threats. Both also failed to recognize how quickly US military power could lie brought to bear against them.

AFTERSHOCK

Many more points of comparison are possible between Pearl Harbor and September 11. At Pearl Harbor, the US military stopped about 8 percent of the attacking force from either reaching its target or returning home. On September 11, airline passengers actually stopped 25 percent of the attacking force from reaching its target, saving a US landmark from severe damage or total destruction. US intelligence analysts issued a war warning before the Pearl Harbor attack, and the US military managed to engage the enemy. On September 11, intelligence reports of possible terrorist threats had not yet been translated into a compelling warning, and the US military failed to interfere with Al Qaeda's suicide mission.

It also is too early to make a full comparison between the two events. Japan's experience after Pearl Harbor was so unpleasant that the war inoculated Japan's leaders and public alike against aggression and armed conflict. By contrast, Al Qaeda faces extermination. Pearl Harbor had a generation effect on young people in the United States, serving as a warning that the possibility of aggression and surprise can never be eliminated in international relations. However, it remains unclear what lessons the young will draw from witnessing die destruction of the World Trade Center on live television.

Pearl Harbor and September 11 are similar in at least one more important respect. Both surprise attacks renewed US interest in world affairs, creating a popular conviction that suffering and oppression in distant places can only be ignored at the expense of US security. Both attacks halted a creeping isolationism and both prompted changes in US government and a renewed commitment to the defense of democracy and economic liberty. The origins of the Department of Defense, the CIA, and a host of intelligence agencies and programs can be tied to that fateful morning over 60 years ago. One can only wonder how the United States will change as the effects of September 11 begin to ripple across governmental institutions and popular culture. We can hope that these changes will not only reduce US vulnerability to mass-casualty terrorist attacks but also eliminate the incentives for others to carry out terrorist acts in the future.

QUESTIONS FOR FURTHER DISCUSSION

1. Why do analysts and policymakers alike seem insensitive to deteriorating political conditions when assessing the possibility of attack?
2. Can you think of other similarities or differences in the two instances of surprise considered here?
3. Do national leaders and intelligence analysts have a tendency to underestimate their opponents?
4. Do you think these surprise attacks were successful because of technical or operational innovation on the part of the side seeking surprise?

From James J. Wirtz, "Déja Vu? Comparing Pearl Harbor and September 11," *Harvard International Review* Vol. 24 (Fall 2002): pp. 73–77. Reproduced with permission.

INTELLIGENCE ANALYSIS

Hamlet: "There are more things in heaven and earth Horatio,
Than are dreamt in your philosophy!"
—SHAKESPEARE, *Hamlet*, 1.5.167–169

The hardest and most unforgiving task in the intelligence cycle is analysis. It is difficult because the fundamental problem facing intelligence analysts is that all information is inherently ambiguous. Most raw data about the world around us reaches us without any indication about its importance, its inherent meaning, or what it portends for the future. It is up to analysts to place this information in its historical context, in the context of current events, or in an appropriate analytical framework to uncover its meaning and significance so that policymakers or senior military officers can respond appropriately. Yet analysts sometimes lack the appropriate theoretical or historical framework to identify signals, lack accurate information about what is about to happen, and must deal with noise—misleading or superfluous information about coming events (Wohlstetter 1962). In fact, the dominant view among observers is that failures of intelligence are inevitable and that when they occur, important signals are always found in the intelligence pipeline that embarrass analysts and lead to much acrimony about the latest intelligence failure.

To avoid surprise, intelligence analysts often have to use old information to predict the future.

Information about ship movements or what happened at some clandestine meeting, for example, might reach them hours or even weeks after actual events, but analysts have to use this rather dated information to gain insight into an even more distant future. In a sense, they are in a race to use old information to predict what is about to unfold, before events catch them by surprise. The target of intelligence analysts always has a head start in the race, and sometimes analysts fail to close the information gap before it is too late. The history of surprise is in fact replete with warnings that were *almost* issued in time: A message warning of the possibility of hostile Japanese action, for instance, reached the U.S. Navy commander at Pearl Harbor just as the attackers headed for home. Intelligence analysts thus face a deadline, but they can never be quite sure how much time they have left before their effort to develop an accurate estimate of the future is literally overtaken by events.

On the rare occasions when they obtain clear indications of what is about to happen, analysts also have to be wary. Opponents often use denial (efforts to hide their true intentions or operations) and deception (inaccurate information about current operations and intentions) to mislead analysts. Denial and deception can take many forms. Sometimes it is best to hide information from the prying eyes of reconnaissance satellites or agents on the ground so that accurate information fails to reach analysts. Sometimes intelligence targets will try to blend into their surroundings to try to make themselves appear innocuous. This is a good way to hide, because intelligence agencies lack the resources to monitor people, organizations, or states that appear to be engaged in routine and nonthreatening kinds of activities. Deception can also take the form of exaggerating one's capabilities in the effort to ward off attack or coerce opponents who might alter their policies because they mistakenly believe that they are in a weak military or diplomatic position. Denial and deception thus create a host of problems for analysts. When things sound too good to be true, analysts should suspect deception, because they face an opponent who would like to do nothing more than put their minds at ease while carrying out some nefarious scheme. When things become too quiet, analysts should suspect that collection systems might be failing to alert them to potential problems. For intelligence analysts, no news, or the fact that events seem to be going according to plan, is not necessarily good news.

Analysts also have to deal with the fact that the actions of some opponents might defy logic or be fundamentally irrational in that they fail to further the known objectives of the state or nonstate actor in question. Governments, militaries, bureaucracies, and terrorist syndicates have multiple decision centers, factions, and interests, and it is often difficult to harness all these individuals and organizations into unified and purposive behavior. Analysts might be correct in predicting what action an opponent should take, but they might turn out to be wrong when the opponent lacks the organizational or political wherewithal to carry out the predicted action. In other words, even if analysts discover what another state or nonstate actor intends to do, they cannot say categorically that it will occur, because the other party might not be able to implement its plan.

States or nonstate actors who seek to surprise their opponents often do so out of desperation. They generally lack the military, diplomatic, or economic resources to achieve their objectives without the force multiplier offered by surprise. They want to present their opponents with a *fait accompli*, then

hope they will reach a negotiated settlement before their opponents rally to reverse the gains obtained from using surprise. The fact that state and nonstate actors can launch what amounts to a reckless gamble creates real problems for intelligence analysts. States and nonstate actors wishing to achieve surprise are engaged in an extraordinarily risky enterprise, which often, with good reason, looks implausible to intelligence analysts. Prior to the Cuban Missile Crisis, for example, analysts at the CIA predicted that the Soviet Union would not place offensive missiles in Cuba, because such an action would prompt a strong reaction from the United States and prove to be counterproductive. In effect, analysts recognized the possibility that the Soviets might place offensive missiles in Cuba, but they dismissed this course of action as implausible because it entailed too much risk from the Soviet perspective (Wirtz 1998).

The risk inherent in the effort to gain the element of surprise, according to Michael Handel, creates a paradox that works against intelligence analysts: "The greater the risk, the less likely it seems, and the less risky it becomes. In fact, the greater the risk, the smaller it becomes" (Handel 1977, 468). So even when intelligence analysts detect signals of what is about to happen, they often dismiss these signals as too fantastic to be credible. Or even worse, they find it impossible to convince senior officials that the opponent is about to launch what appears to be a hare-brained operation. It might be impossible to improve on the Bard, but this might be a good way to think about the challenge of intelligence analysis: There are, in fact, more things in life than we can dream of; the opponent is likely to pick one of them and to try to hide it from us, and analysts will have extraordinary difficulty convincing senior officials that something bad is about to happen.

IMPEDIMENTS TO ACCURATE ANALYSIS

Only the most creative and diligent minds can succeed as analysts. Good analysts have to be able to step outside the conventional military, diplomatic, and bureaucratic wisdom of their day to see vulnerabilities and opportunities that others might be tempted to exploit. They also face real-time constraints when it comes to generating their analysis. Estimates have to be accurate and delivered to officials or military officers in time to be used effectively.

Over the years, scholars and intelligence professionals have worked hard to understand general challenges in the process of intelligence analysis and the specific kinds of problems that can trip up analysts. Often, these studies come in the aftermath of spectacular events, and they tend to focus on the problems that seem to have contributed to the latest failure of intelligence. After Pearl Harbor, for instance, it appeared that a lack of "all-source" intelligence might have contributed to intelligence failure, so the Central Intelligence Agency was created to guarantee that at least one organization would have access to all of the data collected by the U.S. intelligence community. Despite the episodic attention that intelligence analysis receives, scholars and practitioners seem most concerned about problems that are idiosyncratic to intelligence analysis and about the constraints created by the limits of human cognition and organizational pathologies.

IDIOSYNCRATIC CHALLENGES

Although intelligence analysis shares many similarities with journalism or academic research, several aspects of turning raw data into finished intelligence are unique and create special problems for analysts. A host of these idiosyncratic challenges exist. Probably the best-known challenge is the "cry wolf" syndrome. Analysts have to be careful about repeatedly issuing warnings that fail to materialize, because policymakers are likely to stop heeding alerts if they turn out to be false alarms. Responding to warnings also is not without costs. Forcing an opponent to respond repeatedly to false alarms is a good way to create operational, financial, and political strains that soften it up for the real initiative. The "ultra" syndrome, named after the intelligence obtained from decrypted Nazi radio communications in World War II, occurs when analysts become overly dependent on highly valuable intelligence gained from a credible and reliable source. At a critical moment, however, the source might fail to produce important information for any number of reasons, and analysts might be caught without other sources or methods to track important developments. Alternatively, analysts might take the absence of information from a credible source as evidence that nothing important is going on, a judgment that can lull them into a false sense of security even when other indicators suggest that trouble is brewing (Kam 1988).

Because developing estimates of what is going to happen in the future is so difficult and unforgiving, analysts and the intelligence production process can fall into routines that are reassuring but that in the end prove to be highly counterproductive. Intelligence reports that are supposed to provide insight into future events can sometimes become reports on what has happened in the recent past or compilations of reports about past activities. Instead of offering a glimpse into the future, finished intelligence can take on a historical quality by summarizing events over the last few days or weeks. This "historical intelligence" often carries greater weight than more speculative intelligence about the future, because it is grounded in real evidence about past events. Information about what *has* happened is far more credible to the reader than information about what *might* happen.

A similar type of problem emerges when intelligence estimates become a matter of routine, involving the repeated assertion of key analytical judgments without recognition of either the passage of time or changing circumstances. Intelligence estimates having to do with the development of weapons systems often fall into this trap. For instance, in the years immediately following World War II, it was widely assumed that the Soviet Union would need about five years to acquire an atomic bomb. This estimate was repeated in 1946, 1947, 1948, and 1949—the year that the Soviets actually detonated their first nuclear device. Apparently, analysts lost track of the fact that the five-year window at the heart of their analysis was not a moving target but was instead pegged to 1945. The "five-year window" actually is rather common in intelligence estimates—especially in predictions of how long it might take for a state or nonstate actor to develop chemical, biological, or nuclear weapons and associated delivery systems—because it allows analysts to draw attention to a problem without setting in motion difficult political, economic, or military actions to deal with it. By predicting something that might happen in the relatively distant future, one can still claim that a warning was given, without forcing policymakers to act immediately to solve the problem.

THE LIMITS OF HUMAN COGNITION

Humans everywhere share one thing that transcends culture, history, and politics: human cognition and psychology. Whether they are leaders or led, highly educated or poorly educated, world travelers or stay-at-home country bumpkins, they all share the same cognitive biases and patterns of perception. Analysts, however, must struggle to overcome their own psychological presets if they are going to avoid cognitive pitfalls that often bedevil the analytic process.

First, people generally do not realize that their initial perception of the world occurs without much conscious awareness. Although cognitive psychologists might cringe at this explanation, our minds use what amounts to a pattern recognition program to help order the world around us and to bring a reality we recognize to our conscious mind (Heuer 1999). Without this precognition, we would be condemned to forever revisit first principles, to spend all our time just interpreting our sensory perceptions. If this situation were to occur, it would be extraordinarily difficult for us to learn or to generalize across various experiences and events. But because this precognition is extremely powerful, it can be dangerous from the analyst's perspective. If his or her mind places incoming data into the wrong pattern, the analyst will find it difficult to reinterpret the data in a more useful way or in a way that better corresponds to reality.

Second, how we interpret events or others' actions is often shaped by a series of cognitive biases. When others do something that has a negative effect on us, we tend to see them as evil people who intended to harm us, but when we do something that has a negative impact on others, we tend to see ourselves as having no choice in the matter, as being boxed in by circumstances. This thinking pattern is known as the *fundamental attribution error.* Similarly, people tend to take too much credit for the good things that happen and take too little blame when bad things happen. These biases complicate analytical work, because they prevent analysts from recognizing weaknesses that can be exploited by opponents or ways their own country is contributing to a deteriorating international situation. People also tend to interpret information in terms of what is on their mind when they receive the information or what comes to mind when they hear the information. Individuals interpret the world around them not based on the collected wisdom of humankind but in terms of living memory and experience, especially the vivid events that happen in their lives. This phenomenon is known as the *availability principle.* Thus, the life experiences and educational background of analysts is critical to the process of producing finished intelligence, because analysts have to compare incoming information with the historical and theoretical knowledge they possess to generate a useful estimate.

The key point to remember about the impact of human cognition on intelligence analysis is that the human mind tends to fill in the missing pieces of information, sometimes in ways that are difficult for analysts to recognize. For instance, *mirror imaging* often is a problem for analysts. That is, it generally is difficult for them to see the world from another person's perspective, especially when their differences with the person are created by a lack of shared cultural or historical perspective. But in the absence of clear information about what motivates others, analysts will "mirror image" by projecting their own values and motivations onto others in an effort to interpret these others' behavior. Analysis based on mirror imaging rarely is productive, because it tends to place data in a wrong analytical framework, which easily produces misleading estimates.

ORGANIZATIONAL PATHOLOGIES

Because most intelligence analysis takes place in an institutional setting, bureaucracy itself can have a negative impact on the process of creating finished intelligence. Analysts can become preoccupied with defending institutional turf by keeping analysts from other organizations from undertaking work that replicates or contradicts their estimates. Organizations have a keen interest in preventing others from encroaching on their mission and issue domain, because they are interested in preserving their slice of the budgetary pie. Defending an organization's past positions on a given issue can also get in the way of honest estimates of a developing situation; it is difficult to admit that past estimates might have been inaccurate, because such an admission would call into question the usefulness of current intelligence products.

Organizations also have to create the proper working atmosphere to encourage analysts to take risks and to think "outside the box," to use a popular phrase. Although a full discussion of the issue of intelligence politicization must wait for Part IV, we should mention here that organizations must send a message to their rank and file that those who make bold predictions will not suffer negative consequences if their estimates fail to materialize. Intelligence organizations must cultivate independent thinkers, even if they sometimes ignore bureaucratic decorum to make their opinions known. Indeed, if signals can always be found somewhere in the intelligence production process in the aftermath of an analytic failure, more often than not an "intelligence dissenter" can be found in the organization, someone who bucked the conventional wisdom and predicted accurately what was about to happen. An organization that can empower these dissenters so that their views obtain a fair hearing can greatly improve its performance. Of course, too much free thinking can produce disorder, acrimony, and a failure to reach a conclusion or consensus that policymakers might put to good use (Odom 2003). Striking a balance between consensus and healthy debate is a never-ending struggle for those who manage the production of finished intelligence.

Intelligence organizations are also prone to specific bureaucratic problems related to the process of intelligence production. Secrecy and compartmentalization lie at the heart of intelligence analysis; after all, this is what distinguishes secret organizations from other organizations (newspapers, television networks, Internet sites) that disseminate information to government officials, military officers, and the general public. Secrecy can impede analysis, because as information becomes increasingly sensitive, the number of analysts who have the necessary clearances to view the information diminishes. Moreover, finished intelligence based on highly sensitive sources often is distributed only to a limited number of individuals; these restrictions can have negative consequences if the people who can put the information to good use are not given access to finished intelligence.

Compartmentalization also is an effort to restrict the dissemination of information within intelligence organizations. If a hostile agent penetrates an organization by becoming a trusted agent or operative, compartmentalization prevents that person from gaining access to all the secrets kept by an agency. But compartmentalization impedes the efforts of analysts to develop a comprehensive intelligence estimate. If various analysts are allowed to look at only a small piece of the intelligence puzzle, will they know who else holds the other critical pieces, or will they ever be able to figure out the whole picture from just a few pieces of information?

THE READINGS

The articles that follow provide a sense of the difficult challenges faced by intelligence analysts. Few articles shape an entire intellectual endeavor, but "Analysis, War, and Decision," by Richard Betts of Columbia University, made that type of contribution to the field of intelligence analysis. The careful reader will detect that many of the themes raised in this opening essay are expressed forcefully and

clearly in Betts' analysis. In describing the cognitive, idiosyncratic, and bureaucratic challenges faced by analysts, Betts states that it is not possible to use organizational reforms to overcome all of these problems simultaneously, because making progress in resolving one type of problem only makes other problems worse. Eliminating false alarms, for example, only makes it more likely that analysts will fail to respond to signals of real danger. Betts' article is probably best known for his bold judgment, made at the outset of the piece, that intelligence failures are inevitable and that despite the resources invested and the reforms undertaken, it is realistic to expect only marginal improvements in the performance of intelligence organizations. But his article also offers an outstanding overview of the problems that can creep up as analysts try to place raw intelligence in some useful context and convince policymakers that they should act on their estimates.

In a candid description of not only what life is like for a senior policymaker but also how intelligence can contribute to policymaking itself, Ambassador Robert D. Blackwill explains how analysts from the Office of European Analysis (EURA) supported him as he represented U.S. interests in various forums. Blackwill's description of 18-hour workdays and an inability to pay attention to anything not related to the immediate problem in his in-box should change the minds of those who think the life of a senior official is glamorous. "A Policymakers's Perspective on Intelligence Analysis" also describes how Blackwill found finished intelligence directed toward a general audience of no particular value and how he cultivated personal and professional relationships to obtain outstanding staff and analytical support from EURA. Blackwill tells a rare story in the literature on the nexus between intelligence and policy, a story of an outstanding intelligence success. Even though it appears mundane, it really is no small accomplishment. Blackwill describes the bureaucratic obstacles that had to be overcome and the personal sacrifices that had to be made by analysts to create a useful exchange between intelligence professionals and policymakers.

In "The Challenges of Intelligence Analysis," William Nolte describes how the changing strategic and technological setting has forced intelligence organizations to come to terms with a deluge of information. The information revolution has led to the creation of a large, complex, and technologically sophisticated intelligence community, but old work habits and organizational cultures persist.

Nevertheless, Nolte also describes how new information technologies and analytic tools are breaking down the traditional distinction between analysts and policymakers and collectors and analysts, producing "collaborative" work spaces where all concerned can work on a specific issue or project. Nolte does an outstanding job at describing how the information revolution is transforming the intelligence community.

Richard Best summarizes various views on the role played by intelligence in shaping the decisions of the George W. Bush administration on the eve of the Second Gulf War. He outlines the tensions that exist between analysts, who want to provide nuanced and qualified estimates to policymakers, and policymakers who want definitive judgments to build political support for their policies. Best suggests that it is wrong to lay the blame for perceived strategic or political failure on the doorstep of intelligence analysts: "Intelligence analysis can inform policymaking, but it does not substitute for it."

10. ANALYSIS, WAR, AND DECISION: WHY INTELLIGENCE FAILURES ARE INEVITABLE

RICHARD K. BETTS

The history of diplomatic and military affairs is riddled with instances when intelligence analysts failed to provide timely warning of what was about to unfold. Betts presents a strong explanation of why intelligence failures are inevitable, as well as insights into the myriad challenges that analysts must overcome to offer useful estimates of future events. In arguing that the nature of intelligence analysis prevents all but modest improvements in the performance of intelligence organizations, Betts offers a compelling argument that continues to serve as the conventional wisdom on the limits of intelligence reform and analysis.

Military disasters befall some states, no matter how informed their leaders are, because their capabilities are deficient. Weakness, not choice, is their primary problem. Powerful nations are not immune to calamity either, because their leaders may misperceive threats or miscalculate responses. Information, understanding, and judgment are a larger part of the strategic challenge for countries such as the United States. Optimal decisions in defense policy therefore depend on the use of strategic intelligence: the acquisition, analysis, and appreciation of relevant data. In the best-known cases of intelligence failure, the most crucial mistakes have seldom been made by collectors of raw information, occasionally by professionals who produce finished analyses, but most often by the decision makers who consume the products of intelligence services. Policy premises constrict perception, and administrative workloads constrain reflection. Intelligence failure is political and psychological more often than organizational.

Observers who see notorious intelligence failures as egregious often infer that disasters can be avoided by perfecting norms and procedures for analysis and argumentation. This belief is illusory. Intelligence can be improved marginally, but not radically, by altering the analytic system. The illusion is also dangerous if it abets overconfidence that systemic reforms will increase the predictability of threats. The use of intelligence depends less on the bureaucracy than on the intellects and inclinations of the authorities above it. To clarify the tangled relationship of analysis and policy, this essay explores conceptual approaches to intelligence failure, differentiation of intelligence problems, insurmountable obstacles to accurate assessment, and limitations of solutions proposed by critics.

I. APPROACHES TO THEORY

Case studies of intelligence failures abound, yet scholars lament the lack of a theory of intelligence.[1] It is more accurate to say that we lack a positive or normative theory of intelligence. Negative or descriptive theory—the empirical understanding of how intelligence systems make mistakes—is well developed. The distinction is significant because there is little evidence that either scholars or practitioners have succeeded in translating such knowledge into reforms that measurably reduce failure. Development of a normative theory of intelligence has been inhibited because the lessons of hindsight do not guarantee improvement in foresight, and hypothetical solutions to failure only occasionally produce improvement in practice. The problem of intelligence failure can be conceptualized in three overlapping ways. The first is the most reassuring; the second is the most common; and the third is the most important.

1. FAILURE IN PERSPECTIVE

There is an axiom that a pessimist sees a glass of water as half empty and an optimist sees it as half full. In this sense, the estimative system is a glass half full. Mistakes can happen in any activity. Particular failures are accorded disproportionate significance if they are considered in isolation rather than in terms of the general ratio of failures to successes; the record of success is less striking because observers tend not to notice disasters that do not happen. Any academician who used a model that predicted outcomes correctly in four out of five cases would be happy; intelligence analysts must use models of their own and should not be blamed for missing occasionally. One problem with this benign view is that there are no clear indicators of what the ratio of failure to success in intelligence is, or whether many successes on minor issues should be reassuring in the face of a smaller number of failures on more critical problems.[2] In the thermonuclear age, just *one* mistake could have apocalyptic consequences.

2. PATHOLOGIES OF COMMUNICATION

The most frequently noted sources of breakdowns in intelligence lie in the process of amassing timely data, communicating them to decision makers, and impressing the latter with the validity or relevance of the information. This view of the problem leaves room for optimism because it implies that procedural curatives can eliminate the dynamics of error. For this reason, official post mortems of intelligence blunders inevitably produce recommendations for reorganization and changes in operating norms.

3. PARADOXES OF PERCEPTION

Most pessimistic is the view that the roots of failure lie in unresolvable trade-offs and dilemmas. Curing some pathologies with organizational reforms often creates new pathologies or resurrects old ones;[3] perfecting intelligence production does not necessarily lead to perfecting intelligence consumption; making warning systems more sensitive reduces the risk of surprise, but increases the number of false alarms, which in turn reduces sensitivity; the principles of optimal analytic procedure are in many respects incompatible with the imperatives of the decision process; avoiding intelligence failure requires the elimination of strategic preconceptions, but leaders cannot operate purposefully without some preconceptions. In devising measures to improve the

intelligence process, policy makers are damned if they do and damned if they don't.

It is useful to disaggregate the problem of strategic intelligence failures in order to elicit clues about which paradoxes and pathologies are pervasive and therefore most in need of attention. The crucial problems of linkage between analysis and strategic decision can be subsumed under the following categories:

1. ATTACK WARNING

The problem in this area is timely prediction of an enemy's immediate intentions, and the "selling" of such predictions to responsible authorities. Major insights into intelligence failure have emerged from catastrophic surprises: Pearl Harbor, the Nazi invasion of the U.S.S.R., the North Korean attack and Chinese intervention of 1950, and the 1973 war in the Middle East. Two salient phenomena characterize these cases. First, evidence of impending attack was available, but did not flow efficiently up the chain of command. Second, the fragmentary indicators of alarm that did reach decision makers were dismissed because they contradicted strategic estimates or assumptions. In several cases hesitancy in communication and disbelief on the part of leaders were reinforced by deceptive enemy maneuvers that cast doubt on the data.[4]

2. OPERATIONAL EVALUATION

In wartime, the essential problem lies in judging the results (and their significance) of interacting capabilities. Once hostilities are under way, informed decision making requires assessments of tactical effectiveness—"how we are doing"—in order to adapt strategy and options. In this dimension, the most interesting insights have come from Vietnam-era memoirs of low-level officials and from journalistic muckraking. Again there are two fundamental points. First, within the context of a glut of ambiguous data, intelligence officials linked to operational agencies (primarily military) tend to indulge a propensity for justifying service performance by issuing optimistic assessments, while analysts in autonomous non-operational units (primarily in the Central Intelligence Agency and the late Office of National Estimates) tend to produce more pessimistic evaluations. Second, in contrast to cases of attack warning, fragmentary tactical indicators of *success* tend to override more general and cautious strategic estimates. Confronted by differing analyses, a leader mortgaged to his policy tends to resent or dismiss the critical ones, even when they represent the majority view of the intelligence community, and to cling to the data that support continued commitment.[5] Lyndon Johnson railed at his Director of Central Intelligence (DCI) at a White House dinner:

> Policy making is like milking a fat cow. You see the milk coming out, you press more and the milk bubbles and flows, and just as the bucket is full, the cow with its tail whips the bucket and all is spilled. That's what CIA does to policy making.[6]

From the consensus-seeking politician, this was criticism; to a pure analyst, it would have been flattery. But it is the perspective of the former, not the latter, that is central in decision making.

3. DEFENSE PLANNING

The basic task in using intelligence to develop doctrines and forces for deterrence and defense is to estimate threats posed by adversaries, in terms of both capabilities and intentions, over a period of several years. Here the separability of intelligence and policy, analysis and advocacy, is least clear. In dealing with the issue of "how much is enough" for security, debates over data merge murkily into debates over options and programs. As in operational evaluation, the problem lies more in data mongering than in data collecting. To the extent that stark generalizations are possible, the basic points in this category are the reverse of those in the previous one.

First, the justification of a mission (in this case, preparedness for future contingencies as opposed to demonstration of current success on the battlefield) prompts pessimistic estimates by operational military analysts; autonomous analysts without budgetary axes to grind, but with biases similar to those prevalent in the intellectual community, tend toward less alarmed predictions.[7] Military intelligence inclines toward "worst-case" analysis in planning, and toward "best-case" analysis in operational evaluation. (Military intelligence officials such as Lieutenant General Daniel Graham were castigated by liberals for *under*estimating the Vietcong's strength in the 1960's but for *over*estimating Soviet strength in the 1970's.) Air Force intelligence overestimated Soviet air deployments in the "bomber gap" controversy of the 1950s, and CIA-dominated National Intelligence Estimates (NIE's) underestimated Soviet ICBM deployments throughout the 1960's (overreacting, critics say, to the mistaken prediction of a "missile gap" in 1960).[8]

Second, in the context of peacetime, with competing domestic claims on resources, political leaders have a natural interest in at least partially rejecting military estimates and embracing those of other analysts who justify limiting allocations to defense programs. If the President had accepted pessimistic CIA operational evaluations in the mid-1960's, he might have withdrawn from Vietnam; if he had accepted pessimistic military analyses of the Soviet threat in the mid-1970's, he might have added massive increases to the defense budget.

Some chronic sources of error are unique to each of these three general categories of intelligence problems, and thus do not clearly suggest reforms that would be advisable across the board. To compensate for the danger in conventional attack warning, reliance on worst-case analysis might seem the safest rule, but in making estimates for defense planning, worst-case analysis would mandate severe and often unnecessary economic sacrifices. Removing checks on the influence of CIA analysts and "community" staffs[9] might seem justified by the record of operational evaluation in Vietnam, but would not be warranted by the record of estimates on Soviet ICBM deployments. It would be risky to alter the balance of power systematically among competing analytic components, giving the "better" analysts more status. Rather, decision makers should be encouraged to be more and less skeptical of certain agencies' estimates, *depending on the category of analysis involved.*

Some problems, however, cut across all three categories and offer a more general basis for considering changes in the system. But these general problems are not very susceptible to cure by formal changes in process, because it is usually impossible to disentangle intelligence failures from policy failures. Separation of intelligence and policy making has long been a normative concern of officials and theorists, who have seen both costs and benefits in minimizing the intimacy between intelligence professionals and operational authorities. But, although the personnel can be segregated, the functions cannot, unless intelligence is defined narrowly as the collection of data, and analytic responsibility is reserved to decision makers. Analysis and decision are interactive rather than sequential processes. By the narrower definition of intelligence, there have actually been few major failures. In most cases of mistakes in predicting attacks or in assessing operations, the inadequacy of critical data or their submergence in a viscous bureaucracy were at best the proximate causes of failure. The ultimate causes of error in most cases have been wishful thinking, cavalier disregard of professional analysts, and, above all, the premises and preconceptions of policy makers. Fewer fiascoes have occurred in the stages of acquisition and presentation of facts than in the stages of interpretation and response. Producers of intelligence have been culprits less often than consumers. Policy perspectives tend to constrain objectivity, and authorities often fail to use intelligence properly. As former State Department intelligence director Ray Cline testified, defending his analysts' performance in October 1973 and criticizing Secretary Kissinger for ignoring them:

> Unless something is totally conclusive, you must make an inconclusive report…by the time you are sure it is always very close to the event. So I don't think the analysts did such a lousy job. What I think was the lousy job was in bosses not insisting on a new preparation at the end of that week [before war broke out]…the reason the system wasn't working very well is that people were not asking it to work and not listening when it did work.[10]

II. BASIC BARRIERS TO ANALYTIC ACCURACY

Many constraints on the optimal processing of information lie in the structure of authority and the allocation of time and resources. Harold Wilensky argues persuasively that the intelligence function is hindered most by the structural characteristics of hierarchy, centralization, and specialization.[11] Yet it is precisely these characteristics that are the essence of any government. A related problem is the dominance of operational authorities over intelligence specialists, and the trade-off between objectivity and influence. Operators have more influence in decision making but are less capable of unbiased interpretation of evidence because they have a vested interest in the success of their operations; autonomous analysts are more disinterested and usually more objective, but lack influence. Senior generalists at the policy level often distrust or discount the judgments of analytic professionals and place more weight on reports from operational sources.[12] In response to this phenomenon, the suggestion has been made to *legislate* the requirement that decision makers consider analyses by the CIA's Intelligence Directorate (now the National Foreign Assessment Center) before establishing policy.[13] Such a requirement would offer no more than wishful formalism. Statutory fiat cannot force human beings to value

one source above another. "No power has yet been found," DCI Richard Helms has testified, "to force Presidents of the United States to pay attention on a continuing basis to people and papers when confidence has been lost in the originator."[14] Moreover, principals tend to believe that they have a wider point of view than middle-level analysts and are better able to draw conclusions from raw data. That point of view underlies their fascination with current intelligence and their impatience with the reflective interpretations in "finished" intelligence.[15]

The dynamics of decision are also not conducive to analytic refinement. In a crisis, both data and policy outpace analysis, the ideal process of staffing and consultation falls behind the press of events, and careful estimates cannot be digested in time. As Winston Churchill recalled of the hectic days of spring 1940,

> The Defence Committee of the War Cabinet sat almost every day to discuss the reports of the Military Coordination Committee and those of the Chiefs of Staff; and their conclusions or divergences were again referred to frequent Cabinets. All had to be explained or reexplained; and by the time this process was completed, the whole scene had often changed.[16]

Where there is ample time for decision, on the other hand, the previously mentioned bureaucratic impediments gain momentum.[17] Just as information processing is frustrated by constraints on the time that harried principals can spend scrutinizing analytic papers, it is constrained by the funds that a government can spend. To which priorities should scarce resources be allocated? The Schlesinger Report of 1971, which led to President Nixon's reorganization of U.S. intelligence, noted that criticisms of analytic products were often translated into demands for more extensive collection of data, but "Seldom does anyone ask if a further reduction in uncertainty, however small, is worth its cost."[18] Authorities do not always know, however, which issues require the greatest attention and which uncertainties harbor the fewest potential threats. Beyond the barriers that authority, organization, and scarcity pose to intelligence lie more fundamental and less remediable intellectual sources of error.

1. AMBIGUITY OF EVIDENCE

Intelligence veterans have noted that "estimating is what you do when you do not know,"[19] but "it is inherent in a great many situations that after reading the estimate, you will still not know."[20] These observations highlight an obvious but most important obstacle to accuracy in analysis. It is the role of intelligence to extract certainty from uncertainty and to facilitate coherent decision in an incoherent environment. (In a certain and coherent environment there is less need for intelligence.) To the degree they reduce uncertainty by extrapolating from evidence riddled with ambiguities, analysts risk oversimplifying reality and desensitizing the consumers of intelligence to the dangers that lurk within the ambiguities; to the degree they do not resolve ambiguities, analysts risk being dismissed by annoyed consumers who see them as not having done their job. Uncertainty reflects inadequacy of data, which is usually assumed to mean *lack* of information. But ambiguity can also be aggravated by an *excess* of data. In attack warning, there is the problem of "noise" and deception; in operational evaluation (particularly in a war such as Vietnam), there is the problem of overload from the high volume of finished analyses, battlefield statistics, reports, bulletins, reconnaissance, and communications intercepts flowing upward through multiple channels at a rate exceeding the capacity of officials to absorb or scrutinize them judiciously. (From the CIA alone, the White House received current intelligence dailies, Weekly Reports, daily Intelligence Information Cables, occasional Special Reports and specific memoranda, and analyses from the CIA Vietnam Working Group.) Similarly, in estimates for defense planning, there is the problem of innumerable and endlessly refined indices of the strategic balance, and the dependence of assessments of capabilities on complex and variable assumptions about the doctrine, scenarios, and intentions that would govern their use.

Because it is the job of decision makers to decide, they cannot react to ambiguity by deferring judgment.[21] When the problem is an environment that lacks clarity, an overload of conflicting data, and lack of time for rigorous assessment of sources and validity, ambiguity abets instinct and allows intuition to drive analysis. Intelligence can fail because the data are too permissive for policy judgment rather than too constraining. When a welter of fragmentary evidence offers support to various interpretations, ambiguity is exploited by wishfulness. The greater the ambiguity, the greater the impact of preconceptions.[22] (This point should be distinguished from the theory of cognitive dissonance, which became popular with political scientists at the time it was being rejected by psychologists.)[23] There is

some inverse relation between the importance of an assessment (when uncertainty is high) and the likelihood that it will be accurate. Lyndon Johnson could reject pessimistic NIE's on Vietnam by inferring more optimistic conclusions from the reports that came through command channels on pacification, interdiction, enemy casualties, and defections. Observers who assume Soviet malevolence focus on analyses of strategic forces that emphasize missile throw weight and gross megatonnage (Soviet advantages); those who assume more benign Soviet intentions focus on analyses that emphasize missile accuracy and numbers of warheads (U.S. advantages). In assessing the naval balance, Secretary of Defense Rumsfeld focused on numbers of ships (Soviet lead), and Congressman Les Aspin, a critic of the Pentagon, focused on total tonnage (U.S. lead).

2. AMBIVALENCE OF JUDGMENT

Where there are ambiguous and conflicting indicators (the context of most failures of intelligence), the imperatives of honesty and accuracy leave a careful analyst no alternative but ambivalence. There is usually *some* evidence to support any prediction. For instance, the CIA reported in June 1964 that a Chinese instructor (deemed not "particularly qualified to make this remark") had told troops in a course in guerrilla warfare, "We will have the atom bomb in a matter of months."[24] Several months later the Chinese did perform their first nuclear test. If the report had been the only evidence, should analysts have predicted the event? If they are not to make a leap of faith and ignore the data that do not mesh, analysts will issue estimates that waffle. In trying to elicit nuances of probability from the various possibilities not foreclosed by the data, cautious estimates may reduce ambivalence, but they may become Delphic or generalized to the point that they are not useful guides to decision. (A complaint I have heard in conversations with several U.S. officials is that many past estimates of Soviet objectives could substitute the name of any other great power in history—Imperial Rome, 16th-century Spain, Napoleonic France—and sound equally valid.) Hedging is the legitimate intellectual response to ambiguity, but it can be politically counterproductive, if the value of intelligence is to shock consumers out of wishfulness and cognitive insensitivity. A wishful decision maker can fasten onto that half of an ambivalent analysis that supports his predisposition.[25] A more objective official may escape this temptation, but may consider the estimate useless because it does not provide "the answer."

3. ATROPHY OF REFORMS

Disasters always stimulate organizational changes designed to avert the same failures in the future. In some cases these changes work. In many instances, however, the changes persist formally but erode substantively. Standard procedures are constant. Dramatic failures occur only intermittently. If the reforms in procedure they have provoked do not fulfill day-to-day organizational needs—or if, as often happens, they complicate operations and strain the organization's resources—they fall into disuse or become token practices. After the postmortem of North Korea's downing of a U.S. EC-121 monitoring aircraft in 1969, there was, for several months, a great emphasis on risk assessments for intelligence collection missions. Generals and admirals personally oversaw the implementation of new procedures for making the assessments. Six months later, majors and captains were doing the checking. "Within a year the paperwork was spot-checked by a major and the entire community slid back to its old way of making a 'quick and dirty' rundown of the JCS criteria when sending in reconnaissance mission proposals."[26] The downing of the U-2 over the Soviet Union in 1960 and the capture of the intelligence ship *Pueblo* in 1968 had been due in part to the fact that the process of risk assessment for specific collection missions, primarily the responsibility of overworked middle-level officers, had become ponderous, sloppy, or ritualized.[27] At a higher level, a National Security Council Intelligence Committee was established in 1971 to improve responsiveness of intelligence staff to the needs of policy makers. But since the subcabinet-level consumers who made up the committee were pressed by other responsibilities, it lapsed in importance and was eventually abolished.[28] A comparable NSC committee that *did* serve tangible day-to-day needs of consumers to integrate intelligence and policy—the Verification Panel, which dealt with SALT—was more effective, but it was issue-oriented rather than designed to oversee the intelligence process itself. Organizational innovations will not improve the role of intelligence in policy unless they flow from the decision makers' views of their own needs and unless they provide frequent practical benefits.

None of these three barriers are accidents of structure or process. They are inherent in the nature of intelligence and the dynamics of work. As such, they constitute severe constraints on the efficacy of structural reform.

III. THE ELUSIVENESS OF SOLUTIONS

If they do not atrophy, most solutions proposed to obviate intelligence dysfunctions have two edges: in reducing one vulnerability, they increase another. After the seizure of the *Pueblo*, the Defense Intelligence Agency (DIA) was reprimanded for misplacing a message that could have prevented the incident. The colonel responsible developed a careful microfilming operation in the message center to ensure a record of transmittal of cables to authorities in the Pentagon. Implementing this check, however, created a three-to-four hour delay—another potential source of failure—in getting cables to desk analysts whose job was to keep reporting current.[29] Thus, procedural solutions often constitute two steps forward and one step back; organizational fixes cannot transcend the basic barriers. The lessons of Pearl Harbor led to the establishment of a Watch Committee and National Indications Center in Washington. Although this solution eliminated a barrier in the communication system, it did not prevent the failure of timely alert to the Chinese intervention in Korea or the 1973 October War, because it did not eliminate the ambiguity barrier. (Since then, the Watch Committee has been replaced by the DCI's Strategic Warning Staff.) DIA was reorganized four times within its first ten years; yet it continued to leave most observers dissatisfied. The Agranat Commission's review of Israel's 1973 intelligence failure produced proposals for institutional reform that are striking because they amount to copying the American system of the same time—which had failed in exactly the same way as the Israeli system.[30] Reform is not hopeless, but hopes placed in solutions most often proposed—such as the following—should be circumscribed.

1. ASSUME THE WORST

A common reaction to traumatic surprise is the recommendation to cope with ambiguity and ambivalence by acting on the most threatening possible interpretations. If there is *any* evidence of threat, assume it is valid, even if the *apparent* weight of contrary indicators is greater. In retrospect, when the point of reference is an actual disaster attributable to a mistaken calculation of probabilities, this response is always justifiable, but it is impractical as a guide to standard procedure. Operationalizing worst-case analysis requires extraordinary expense, it risks being counterproductive if it is effective (by provoking enemy countermeasures or pre-emption), and it is likely to be ineffective because routinization will discredit it. Many Israeli observers deduced from the 1973 surprise that defense planning could only rest on the assumption that no attack warning will be available, and that precautionary mobilization should always be undertaken even when there is only dubious evidence of impending Arab action.[31] Similarly, American hawks argue that if the Soviets' intentions are uncertain, the only prudent course is to assume they are seeking the capability to win nuclear war.

In either case, the norm of assuming the worst poses high financial costs. Frequent mobilizations strain the already taut Israeli economy. Moreover, countermobilization can defeat itself. Between 1971 and 1973, the Egyptians three times undertook exercises similar to those that led to the October attack; Israel mobilized in response, and nothing happened. It was the paradox of self-negating prophecy.[32] The Israeli Chief of Staff was sharply criticized for the unnecessary cost.[33] The danger of hypersensitivity appeared in 1977, when General Gur believed Sadat's offer to come to Jerusalem to be a camouflage for an Egyptian attack; he began Israeli maneuvers in the Sinai, which led Egypt to begin maneuvers of its own, heightening the risk of accidental war.[34] To estimate the requirements for deterrence and defense, worst case assumptions present an open-ended criterion. The procurement of all the hedges possible for nuclear war-fighting—large increments in offensive forces, alert status, hardening of command-control-and-communications, active and passive defenses—would add billions to the U.S. defense budget. Moreover, prudent hedging in policy should be distinguished from net judgment of probabilities in estimates.[35]

Alternatively, precautionary escalation or procurement may act as self-fulfilling prophecies, either through a catalytic spiral of mobilization (à la World War I) or an arms race that heightens tension, or doctrinal hedges that make the prospect of nuclear war more "thinkable." Since evidence for the "action-reaction" hypothesis of U.S. and Soviet nuclear policies is meager, and arms races can sometimes be stabilizing rather than dangerous, the last point is debatable. Still, a large unilateral increase in strategic forces by either the United States or the Soviet Union would, at the least, destroy the possibility of gains desired from SALT. A surprise attack or defeat makes the costs of *under*estimates obvious and dramatic; the unnecessary defense costs due to *over*estimates can only be surmised, since the minimum needed for deterrence is uncertain. Worst-case analysis as a standard norm would also exacerbate the "cry wolf" syndrome. *Unambiguous* threat is not an intelligence problem; rather, the challenge lies in the response to fragmentary, contradictory, and dubious indicators. Most such indicators turn out to be false alarms. Analysts who reflexively warn of disaster are soon derided as hysterical. General William Westmoreland recalled that the warnings that had been issued before the 1968 Tet Offensive were ignored. U.S. headquarters in Saigon had each year predicted a winter-spring offensive, "and every year it had come off without any dire results.... Was not the new offensive to be more of the same?"[36]

Given the experience of intelligence professionals that most peace-time indicators of suspicious enemy activity lead to nothing, what Colonel who has the watch some night will risk "lighting up the board" in the White House simply on the basis of weak apprehension? How many staffers will risk waking a tired President, especially if they have done so before and found the action to be needless? How many distracting false alarms will an overworked President tolerate before he makes it clear that aides should exercise discretion in bothering him? Even if worst-case analysis is promulgated in principle, it will be compromised in practice. Routinization corrodes sensitivity. Every day that an expected threat does not materialize dulls receptivity to the reality of danger. As Roberta Wohlstetter wrote of pre-Pearl Harbor vigilance, "We are constantly confronted by the paradox of pessimistic realism of phrase coupled with loose optimism in practice."[37] Seeking to cover all contingencies, worst-case analysis loses focus and salience; by providing a theoretical guide for everything, it provides a practical guide for very little.

2. MULTIPLE ADVOCACY

Blunders are often attributed to decisionmakers' inattention to unpopular viewpoints or to a lack of access to higher levels of authority by dissident analysts. To reduce the chances of such mistakes, Alexander George proposes institutionalizing a balanced, open, and managed process of debate, so that no relevant assessments will be submerged by unchallenged premises or the bureaucratic strength of opposing officials.[38] The goal is unobjectionable, and formalized multiple advocacy certainly would help, not hinder. But confidence that it will help systematically and substantially should be tentative. In a loose sense, there has usually been multiple advocacy in the U.S. policy process, but it has not prevented mistakes in deliberation or decision. Lyndon Johnson did not decide for limited bombing and gradual troop commitment in Vietnam in 1965 because he was not presented with extensive and vigorous counterarguments. He considered seriously (indeed solicited) Under Secretary of State George Ball's analysis, which drew on NIE's and lower-level officials' pessimistic assessments that any escalation would be a mistake. Johnson was also well aware of the arguments by DCI John McCone and the Air Force from the other extreme—that massive escalation in the air war was necessary because gradualism would be ineffective.[39] The President simply chose to accept the views of the middle-of-the-road opponents of *both* Ball and McCone.

To the extent that multiple advocacy works, and succeeds in maximizing the number of views promulgated and in supporting the argumentive resources of all contending analysts, it may simply highlight ambiguity rather than resolve it. In George's ideal situation, the process would winnow out unsubstantiated premises and assumptions about ends-means linkages. But in the context of data overload, uncertainty, and time constraints, multiple advocacy may in effect give all of the various viewpoints an aura of empirical respectability and allow a leader to choose whichever accords with his predisposition.[40]

The efficacy of multiple advocacy (which is greatest under conditions of manageable data and low ambiguity) may vary inversely with the potential for intelligence failure (which is greatest under conditions of confusing data and high uncertainty). The process could, of course, bring to the surface ambiguities where false certainty had prevailed; in these cases, it would be as valuable as George believes. But if multiple advocacy increases ambivalence and leaders do *not* indulge their instincts, it risks promoting conservatism or paralysis. Dean Acheson saw danger in presidential indecisiveness aggravated by debate: " 'I know your theory,' he grumbled to Neustadt. 'You think Presidents should be warned. You're wrong. Presidents should be given confidence.' "[41]

Even Clausewitz argued that deference to intelligence can frustrate bold initiative and squander crucial opportunities. Critics charged Henry Kissinger with crippling U.S. intelligence by refusing to keep analysts informed of his intimate conversations with foreign leaders.[42] To do so, however, would have created the possibility of leaks and might thereby have crippled his diplomatic maneuvers. It is doubtful that Nixon's initiative to China could have survived prior debate, dissent, and analysis by the bureaucracy.

It is unclear that managed multiple advocacy would yield markedly greater benefits than the redundancy and competitiveness that have long existed. (At best it would perfect the "market" of ideas in the manner that John Stuart Mill believed made liberalism conducive to the emergence of truth.) The first major reorganization of the American intelligence community in 1946-1947 emphasized centralization in order to avert future Pearl Harbors caused by fragmentation of authority; the latest reorganization (Carter's 1977 extension of authority of the Director of Central Intelligence over military intelligence programs) emphasized centralization to improve efficiency and coherence. Yet decentralization has always persisted in the overlapping division of labor between several separate agencies. Recent theorists of bureaucracy see such duplication as beneficial because competition exposes disagreement and presents policy makers with a wider range of views. Redundancy inhibits consensus, impedes the herd instinct in the decision process, and thus reduces the likelihood of failure due to unchallenged premises or cognitive errors. To ensure that redundancy works in this way, critics oppose a process that yields coordinated estimates—negotiated to the least common denominator, and cleared by all agencies before they are passed to the principals. George's "custodian" of multiple advocacy could ensure that this does not happen. There are, of course, trade-off costs for redundancy. Maximization of competition limits specialization. In explaining the failure of intelligence to predict the 1974 coup in Portugal, William Hyland pointed out, "if each of the major analytical components stretch their resources over the same range, there is the risk that areas of less priority will be superficially covered."[43]

The problem with arguing that the principals themselves should scrutinize numerous contrasting estimates in their integrity is that they are constantly overwhelmed by administrative responsibilities and "action items"; they lack the time to read, ponder, and digest that large an amount of material. Most intelligence products, even NIE's, are never read by policy makers; at best, they are used by second-level staffers as background material for briefing their seniors.[44] Consumers want previously coordinated analyses in order to save time and effort. In this respect, the practical imperatives of day-to-day decisions contradict the theoretical logic of ideal intelligence.

3. CONSOLIDATION

According to the logic of estimative redundancy, more analysis is better than less. Along this line of reasoning, Senate investigators noted critically that, as of fiscal year 1975, the U.S. intelligence community still allocated 72 percent of its budget for collection of information, 19 percent for processing technical data, and less than 9 percent for production of finished analyses. On the other hand, according to the logic of those who focus on the time constraints of leaders and the confusion that results from innumerable publications, quantity counteracts quality. The size of the CIA's intelligence directorate and the complexity of the production process "precluded close association between policy makers and analysts, between the intelligence product and policy informed by intelligence analysis."[45] For the sake of clarity and acuity, the intelligence bureaucracy should be streamlined.

This view is consistent with the development of the Office of National Estimates (ONE), which was established in 1950 and designed to coordinate the contributions of the various organs in the intelligence community for the Director of Central Intelligence. DCI Walter Bedell Smith envisioned an operation of about a thousand people. But William L. Langer, the scholar Smith imported to organize ONE, wanted a tight group of excellent analysts and a personnel ceiling of fifty. Langer prevailed, and though the number of staff members in ONE crept upwards, it probably never exceeded a hundred in its two decades of existence.[46] Yet ONE could not eliminate the complexity of the intelligence process; it could only coordinate and integrate it for the production of National Intelligence Estimates. Other sources found conduits to decision makers (to Cabinet members, through their own agencies, or to the President through the National Security Council). And some policy makers, though they might dislike the cacophony of multiple intelligence agencies, were suspicious of the consolidated NIE's, knowing that there was pressure to compromise views in order to gain agreement. Over time, the dynamics of bureaucracy also blunted the original

objectives of ONE'S founder. From a cosmopolitan elite corps, it evolved into an insular unit of senior careerists from the CIA. The National Intelligence Officer system that replaced ONE reduced the number of personnel responsible for coordinating NIE's, but has been criticized on other grounds such as greater vulnerability to departmental pressures. Bureaucratic realities have frustrated other attempts to consolidate the intelligence structure. The Defense Intelligence Agency was created in 1961 to unify Pentagon intelligence and reduce duplicative activities of the three service intelligence agencies, but these agencies regenerated themselves; in less than a decade they were larger than they had been before DIA's inception.[47]

The numerous attempts to simplify the organization of the analytic process thus have not solved the major problems. Either the streamlining exercises were short-lived, and bureaucratization crept back, or the changes had to be moderated to avoid the new dangers they entailed. Contraction is inconsistent with the desire to minimize failure by "plugging holes" in intelligence, since compensating for an inadequacy usually requires *adding* personnel and mechanisms; pruning the structure that contributes to procedural sluggishness or complexity may create lacunae in substantive coverage.

4. DEVIL'S ADVOCACY

Multiple advocacy ensures that all views held by individuals within the analytic system will be granted serious attention. Some views that should receive attention, however, may not be held by anyone within the system. Virtually no analysts in Israel or the United States believed the Arabs would be "foolish" enough to attack in 1973. Many observers have recommended institutionalizing dissent by assigning to someone the job of articulating apparently ridiculous interpretations to ensure that they are forced into consideration. Establishing an official devil's advocate would probably do no harm (although some argue that it may perversely facilitate consensus-building by domesticating true dissenters or providing the illusory comfort that all views have been carefully examined;[48] worse, it might delude decision makers into believing that *uncertainties* have been resolved). But in any case, the role is likely to atrophy into a superfluous or artificial ritual. By the definition of the job, the devil's advocate is likely to be dismissed by decision makers as a sophist who only makes an argument because he is supposed to, not because of its real merits. Institutionalizing dev-il's advocacy is likely to be perceived in practice as institutionalizing the "cry wolf" problem; "There are limits to the utility of a 'devil's advocate' who is not a true devil."[49] He becomes someone to be indulged and disregarded. Given its rather sterile definition, the role is not likely to be filled by a prestigious offi-cial (who will prefer more "genuine" responsibility); it will therefore be easier for policy makers to dismiss the arguments. In order to avert intelligence failures, an analyst is needed who tells decision makers what they don't want to hear, dampening the penchant for wishful thinking. But since it is the job of the devil's advocate to do this habitually, and since he is most often wrong (as would be inevitable, since otherwise the conventional wisdom would eventually change), he digs his own grave. If the role is routinized and thus ritualized, it loses impact; but if it is not routin-ized, there can be no assurance that it will be operat-ing when it is needed.

Despite the last point, which is more important in attack warning than in operational evaluation or defense planning, there is a compromise that offers more realistic benefits: *ad hoc* utilization of "real devils." This selective or biased form of multiple advocacy may be achieved by periodically giving a platform within the intelligence process to minority views that can be argued more persuasively by pres-tigious analysts outside the bureaucracy. This is what the President's Foreign Intelligence Advisory Board and DCI George Bush did in 1976 by commission-ing the "Team B" critique of NFE's on Soviet strate-gic objectives and capabilities. Dissenters within the intelligence community who were skeptical of Soviet intentions were reinforced by a panel of sympathetic scholars, with a mandate to produce an analysis of their own.[50] This controversial exercise, even if it erred in many of its own ways (as dovish critics con-tend), had a major impact in promoting the reex-amination of premises and methodology in U.S. strategic estimates. The problem with this option is that it depends on the political biases of the authori-ties who commission it. If it were balanced by a com-parable "Team C" of analysts at the opposite extreme (more optimistic about Soviet intentions than the intelligence community consensus), the exercise would approach regular multiple advocacy, with the attendant limitations of that solution. Another variant would be intermittent designation of devil's advocates in periods of crisis, when the possibility of disaster is greater than usual. Since the role would then be fresh each time, rather than ritualized, the

advocate might receive a more serious hearing. The problem here is that receptivity of decision makers to information that contradicts preconceptions var-ies inversely with their personal commitments, and commitments grow as crisis progresses.[51]

5. SANCTIONS AND INCENTIVES

Some critics tribute intelligence failures to dishonest reporting or the intellectual mediocrity of analysts. Suggested remedies include threats of punishment for the former, and inducements to attract talent to replace the latter. Other critics emphasize that, will or ability aside, analytic integrity is often submerged by the policy makers' demands for intelligence that suits them; "the NIE sought to be responsive to the evidence, not the policy maker."[52] Holders of this point of view would institutionalize the analysts' autonomy. Unobjectionable in principle (though if analysts are totally unresponsive to the consumer, he will ignore them), these implications cannot eas-ily be operationalized without creating as many problems as they solve.

Self-serving operational evaluations from mili-tary sources, such as optimistic reports on progress in the field in Vietnam or pessimistic strategic esti-mates, might indeed be obviated if analysts in DIA, the service intelligence agencies, and command staffs were credibly threatened with sanctions (fir-ing, nonpromotion, reprimand, or disgrace). Such threats theoretically could be a countervailing pres-sure to the career incentives analysts have to promote the interests of their services. But, except in the most egregious cases, it is difficult to apply such standards without arbitrariness and bias, given the problem of ambiguity; it simply encourages an alternative bias or greater ambivalence. Moreover, military profes-sionals would be in an untenable position, pulled in opposite directions by two sets of authorities. To apply the sanctions, civil authorities would have to violate the most hallowed military canon by having civilian intelligence officials interfere in the chain of command. In view of these dilemmas, it is easier to rely on the limited effectiveness of redundancy or multiple advocacy to counteract biased estimates.

Critics concerned with attracting better talent into the analytic bureaucracy propose to raise sal-aries and to provide more high-ranking positions (supergrades) to which analysts can aspire. Yet American government salaries are already very high by academic standards. Those who attribute DIA's mediocrity (compared to CIA), to an insufficient allocation of supergrades and a consequent inability to retain equivalent personnel are also mistaken; as of 1975 the difference in the grade structures of DIA and CIA had been negligible.[53] And the fact that CIA analysts cannot rise to a supergrade position (GS-16 to 18) without becoming administrators is not convincing evidence that good analysts are underpaid; GS-15 salaries are higher than the maximum for most tenured professors.

Non-military analysts, or high-ranking soldiers with no promotions to look forward to, have fewer professional crosspressures to contend with than military intelligence officers. But an analyst's autonomy varies inversely with his influence, and hortatory injunctions to be steadfast and intellectually honest cannot ensure that he will be; they cannot transcend political realities or the idiosyncrasies of leaders. Richard Helms notes that "there is no way to insulate the DCI from unpopularity at the hands of Presidents or policy makers if he is making assessments which run counter to administrative policy. That is a built in hazard of the job. Sensible Presidents understand this. On the other hand they are human too." Integrity untinged by political sensitivity courts professional suicide. If the analyst insists on perpetually bearing bad news, he is likely to be beheaded. Helms himself succumbed to policy makers' pressures in compromising estimates of the MIRV capabilities of the Soviet SS-9 missile in 1969, and the prospects for Cambodia in 1970.[54] The same practical psychological constraints are reflected in an incident in which Chief of Naval Operations Elmo Zumwalt, who had already infuriated Nixon and Kissinger several times with his strategic estimates, was determined to present yet another unwelcome analysis; Secretary of Defense Schlesinger dissuaded him with the warning, "To give a briefing like that in the White House these days would be just like shooting yourself in the foot."[55]

6. COGNITIVE REHABILITATION AND METHODOLOGICAL CONSCIOUSNESS

The intertwining of analysis and decision and the record of intelligence failures due to mistaken preconceptions and unexamined assumptions suggest the need to reform the intelligence consumers' attitudes, awareness, and modes of perception. If leaders were made self-conscious and self-critical about their own psychologies, they might be less vulnerable to cognitive pathologies. This approach to preventing intelligence failure is the most basic and

metaphysical. If policy makers focused on the methodologies of competing intelligence producers, they would be more sensitive to the biases and leaps of faith in the analyses passed to them.

> In official fact-finding…the problem is not merely to open up a wide range of policy alternatives but to create incentives for persistent criticism of evidentiary value.[56]

Improvement would flow from mechanisms that force decision makers to make explicit rather than unconscious choices, to exercise judgment rather than engage in automatic perception, and to enhance their awareness of their own preconceptions.[57]

Unlike organizational structure, however, cognition cannot be altered by legislation. Intelligence consumers are political men who have risen by being more decisive than reflective, more aggressive than introspective, and confident as much as cautious. Few busy activists who have achieved success by thinking the way that they do will change their way of thinking because some theorist tells them to. Even if they could be forced to confront scholarly evidence of the dynamics of misperception it is uncertain that they could consistently internalize it. Preconception cannot be abolished; it is in one sense just another word for "model" or "paradigm"—a construct used to simplify reality, which any thinker needs in order to cope with complexity. There is a grain of truth in the otherwise pernicious maxim that an open mind is an empty mind. Moreover, the line between *perception* and *judgment* is very thin, and consumers cannot carefully scrutinize, compare, and evaluate the methodologies of competing analyses, for the same prosaic reason (the problem of expertise aside) that impedes many proposed reforms: they do not have the *time* to do so. Solutions that require principals to invest more attention than they already do are conceptually valid but operationally weak. Ideally, perhaps, each principal should have a Special Assistant for Rigor Enforcement.

Although most notable intelligence failures occur more often at the consuming rather than the producing end, it is impractical to place the burden for correcting those faults on the consumers. The most realistic strategy for improvement would be to have intelligence professionals anticipate the cognitive barriers to decision makers' utilization of their products. Ideally, the Director of Central Intelligence should have a theoretical temperament and personal skills in forcing unusual analyses to the attention of principals; he might act as George's "custodian" of the argumentation process. To fulfill this function, the DCI should be not only a professional analyst and an intellectual (of the twelve DCI's since 1946, only James Schlesinger met those criteria, and he served for only three months), but also a skilled bureaucratic politician. These qualifications seldom coincide. The DCI's coordinating staff and National Intelligence Officers should be adept at detecting, making explicit, and exposing to consumers the idiosyncrasies in the assessments of various agencies—the *reasons* that the focus and conclusions of the State Department's Bureau of Intelligence and Research differ from those of DIA, or of naval intelligence, or of the CIA. For such a procedure to work, the consumers would have to favor it (as opposed to negotiated consensual estimates that would save them more time). There is always a latent tension between what facilitates timely decision and what promotes thoroughness and accuracy in assessment. The fact that there is no guaranteed prophylaxis against intelligence failures, however, does not negate the value of incremental improvements. The key is to see the problem of reform as one of modest refinements rather than as a systematic breakthrough.

IV. LIVING WITH FATALISM

Organizational solutions to intelligence failure are hampered by three basic problems: most procedural reforms that address specific pathologies introduce or accent other pathologies; changes in analytic processes can never fully transcend the constraints of ambiguity and ambivalence; and more rationalized information systems cannot fully compensate for the predispositions, perceptual idiosyncrasies, and time constraints of political consumers. Solutions that address the psychology and analytic style of decision makers are limited by the difficulty of changing human thought processes and day-to-day habits of judgment by normative injunction. Most theorists have thus resigned themselves to the hope of marginal progress, "to improve the 'batting average'—say from .275 to .301—rather than to do away altogether with surprise."[58]

There is some convergence in the implications of all three ways of conceptualizing intelligence failures. Mistakes should be expected because the *paradoxes* are not resolvable; minor improvements are possible by reorganizing to correct *pathologies*, and despair is unwarranted because, seen *in perspective*, the record could be worse. Marginal improvements

have, in fact, been steadily instituted since World War II. Although many have indeed raised new problems, most have yielded a net increase in the rationalization of the system. The diversification of sources of estimates of adversaries' military power has grown consistently, obviating the necessity to rely exclusively on military staffs. The resources and influence of civilian analysts of military data (principally in the CIA's Office of Strategic Research but also in its Directorate of Science and Technology) are unparalleled in any other nation's intelligence system. At the same time, the DCI's mechanism for coordinating the activities of all agencies—the Intelligence Community Staff—has grown and become more diverse and representative, and less an extension of the CIA, as more staffers have been added from the outside. In 1972, a separate Product Review Division was established within the staff to appraise the "objectivity, balance, and responsiveness" of intelligence studies on a regular basis. It has conducted postmortems of intelligence failures since then (the Yom Kippur War, the Cyprus crisis of 1974, the Indian nuclear test, and the seizure of the *Mayaguez*).[59] (Previously, postmortems had been conducted by the analysts who had failed, a procedure that hardly guaranteed objectivity.)

Within the Pentagon, capabilities for estimates relevant to planning were enhanced with the establishment of an office for Net Assessment, which analyzes the significance of foreign capabilities in comparison with U.S. forces. (CIA, DIA, and NIE's only estimate foreign capabilities.) Civilian direction of military intelligence was reinforced by an Assistant Secretary of Defense for Intelligence after the 1970 recommendation of the Fitzhugh Commission, and an Under Secretary for Policy in 1978. Experiments in improving communication between producers and consumers have been undertaken (such as, for example, the testing of a Defense Intelligence Board in late 1976). The dominance of operators within the intelligence community has also waned—especially since the phasing out of paramilitary operations in Southeast Asia and the severe reductions in size and status of CIA's covert action branch that began in 1973. Dysfunctions in the military communications system, which contributed to crises involving intelligence collection missions in the 1960's (the Israeli attack on the U.S.S. *Liberty* and North Korea's seizure of the *Pueblo*) were alleviated (though not cured) by new routing procedures and by instituting an "optimal scanning system" in the Pentagon.[60] Statistical analyses of strategic power have become progressively more rigorous and comprehensive; as staffs outside the executive branch—such as the Congressional Budget Office—have become involved in the process, they have also become more competitive.[61]

Few of the changes in structure and process have generated more costs than benefits. (Some critics believe, however, that the abolition of the Office and Board of National Estimates and their replacement with National Intelligence Officers was a net loss.) But it is difficult to prove that they have significantly reduced the incidence of intelligence failure. In the area of warning, for instance, new sophisticated coordination mechanisms have recently been introduced, and since the institution at the time of the 1974 Cyprus crisis of DCI "alert memoranda"—"brief notices in a form which cannot be overlooked"[62]—no major warning failure has occurred. But the period of testing is as yet too brief to demonstrate that these adaptations are more effective than previous procedures. In the area of operational evaluation, it is clear that there was greater consciousness of the limitations and cost-ineffectiveness of aerial bombardment during the Vietnam War than there had been in Korea, due largely to the assessments made by the offices of Systems Analysis and International Security Affairs in the Pentagon and Secretary of Defense McNamara's utilization of CIA estimates and contract studies by external analytic organizations.[63] Yet this greater consciousness did not prevail until late in the war because it was not consensus; Air Force and naval assessments of bombing effectiveness contradicted those of the critical civilian analysts. Nor has the elaboration and diversification of analytical resources for strategic estimates clearly reduced the potential for erroneous planning decisions. Determination of the salience and proper weight of conflicting indicators of strategic power and objectives or of the comparative significance of quantitative and qualitative factors is inextricable from the political debate over foreign policy: uncertainties always remain, leaving the individual's visceral fears or hopes as the elements that tilt the balance of judgment.

Although marginal reforms may reduce the probability of error, the unresolvable paradoxes and barriers to analytic and decisional accuracy will make some incidence of failure inevitable. Concern with intelligence failure then coincides with concern about how policy can hedge against the consequences of analytic inadequacy. Covering every hypothetical vulnerability would lead to bankruptcy, and hedging against one threat may aggravate a different one. The problem is thus one of priorities, and hedging against uncertainty is hardly easier than resolving it. Any measures that clarify the cost-benefit trade-off's in policy hedges are measures that mitigate the danger of intelligence failure.

One reasonable rule in principle would be to survey the hypothetical outcomes excluded by strategic premises as improbable but not impossible, identify those that would be disastrous if they *were* to occur, and then pay the price to hedge against them. This is no more practicable, however, than the pure form of worst-case analysis, because it requires willingness to bear and inflict severe costs for dubious reasons. Escalation in Vietnam, after all, was a hedge against allowing China to be tempted to "devour" the rest of Southeast Asia. The interaction of analytic uncertainty and decisional prudence is a vicious circle that makes the segregation of empirical intelligence and normative policy an unattainable Platonic ideal.

In the simplest situation, the intelligence system can avert policy failure by presenting relevant and undisputed facts to non-expert principals who might otherwise make decisions in ignorance. But these simple situations are not those in which major intelligence failures occur. Failures occur when ambiguity aggravates ambivalence. In these more important situations—Acheson and Clausewitz to the contrary—the intelligence officer may perform most usefully by *not* offering the *answers* sought by authorities, but by offering *questions*, acting as a Socratic agnostic, nagging decision makers into awareness of the full range of uncertainty, and making the authorities' calculations harder rather than easier. Sensitive leaders will reluctantly accept and appreciate this function. Most leaders will not; they will make mistakes, and will continue to bear the prime responsibility for "intelligence" failures. Two general values (which sound wistful in the context of the preceding fatalism) remain to guide the choice of marginal reforms: anything that facilitates dissent and access to authorities by intelligence producers, and anything that facilitates skepticism and scrutiny by consumers. The values are synergistically linked; one will not improve the use of intelligence without the other. (A third value, but one nearly impossible to achieve, would be anything that increases the time available to principals for reading and reflection.)

Intelligence failures are not only inevitable, they are natural. Some are even benign (if a success would not have changed policy). Scholars cannot legitimately view intelligence mistakes as bizarre, because they are no more common and no less excusable than academic errors. They are less forgivable only because they are more consequential. Error in scholarship is resolved dialectically, as deceptive data are exposed and regnant theories are challenged, refined, and replaced by new research. If decision makers had but world enough and time, they could rely on this process to solve their intelligence problems. But the press of events precludes the luxury of letting theories sort themselves out over a period of years, as in academia. My survey of the intractability of the inadequacy of intelligence, and its inseparability from mistakes in decision, suggests one final conclusion that is perhaps most outrageously fatalistic of all: tolerance for disaster.

QUESTIONS FOR FURTHER DISCUSSION

1. Why is it so difficult to strike the correct balance in undertaking intelligence reforms?
2. Why is it impossible to overcome many of the problems faced by intelligence analysts?
3. Who in the intelligence community should play the role of "devil's advocate"?
4. How might net assessment contribute to better intelligence analysis?

ENDNOTES

1. For example, Klaus Knorr, "Failures in National Intelligence Estimates: The Case of the Cuban Missiles," *World Politics*, XVI (April 1964), 455, 465–66; Harry Howe Ransom, "Strategic Intelligence and Foreign Policy," *World Politics*, XXVII (October 1974), 145.

2. "As that ancient retiree from the Research Department of the British Foreign Office reputedly said, after serving from 1903–50: 'Year after year the worriers and fretters would come to me with awful predictions of the outbreak of war. I denied it each time. I was only wrong twice.'" Thomas L. Hughes, *The Fate of Facts in a World of Men—Foreign Policy and Intelligence Making* (New York: Foreign Policy Association, Headline Series No. 133, December 1976), 48. Paradoxically, "successes may be indistinguishable from failures." If analysts predict war and the attacker cancels his plans because surprise has been lost, "success of the intelligence services would have been expressed in the falsification of its predictions," which would discredit the analysis. Avi Shlaim, "Failures in National Intelligence Estimates: The Case of the Yom Kippur War," *World Politics*, XXVIII (April 1976), 378.

3. Compare the prescriptions in Peter Szanton and Graham Allison, "Intelligence: Seizing the Opportunity," with George Carver's critique, both in *Foreign Policy*, No. 22 (Spring 1976).

4. Roberta Wohlstetter, *Pearl Harbor: Warning and Decision* (Stanford: Stanford University Press 1962); Barton Whaley, *Codeword Barbarossa* (Cambridge: The M.I.T. Press 1973); Harvey De Weerd, "Strategic Surprise in the Korean War," *Orbis*, VI (Fall 1961); Alan Whiting, *China Crosses the Yalu* (New York: C1 Macmillan 1960); James F. Schnabel, *Policy and Direction: The First Year* (Washington, D.C.: Department of the Army 1972), 61–65, 83–85, 274–78; Michael I. Handel, *Perception, Deception, and Surprise: The Case of the Yom Kippur War* (Jerusalem: Leonard Davis Institute of International Relations, Jerusalem Paper No. 19, 1976); Shlaim (fn. 2); Abraham Ben-Zvi, "Hindsight and Foresight: A Conceptual Framework for the Analysis of Surprise Attacks," *World Politics*, XXVIII. (April 1976); Amos Perlmutter, "Israel's Fourth War, October 1973: Political and Military Misperceptions," *Orbis*, XIX (Summer 1975); U.S. Congress, House, Select Committee on Intelligence (hereafter cited as HSCI], *Hearings, U.S. Intelligence Agencies and Activities: The Performance of the Intelligence Community*, 94th Cong., 1st sess., 1975; Draft Report of the House Select Committee on Intelligence, published in *The Village Voice*, February 16, 1976, pp. 76–81.

5. David Halberstam, *The Best and the Brightest* (New York: Random House 1972); Morris Blachman, "The Stupidity of Intelligence," in Charles Peters and Timothy J. Adams, eds., *Inside the System* (New York: Praeger 1970); Patrick J. McGarvey, "DIA: Intelligence to Please," in Morton Halperin and Arnold Kanter, eds., *Readings in American Foreign Policy: A Bureaucratic Perspective* (Boston: Little, Brown 1973); Chester Cooper, "The CIA and Decision-Making," *Foreign Affairs*, Vol. 50 (January 1972); Sam Adams, "Vietnam Cover-Up: Playing War With Numbers," *Harper's*, Vol. 251 (June 1975); Don Oberdorfer, *Tet!* (Garden City, N.Y.: Doubleday 1971). For a more detailed review, see Richard K. Belts, *Soldiers, Statesmen, and Cold War Crises* (Cambridge: Harvard University Press 1977), chap. 10.

6. Quoted in Henry Brandon, *The Retreat of American Power* (Garden City, N.Y.: Doubleday 1973), 103.

7. Betts (fn. 5), 160–61, 192–95. On bias within CIA, see James Schlesinger's comments in U.S., Congress, Senate, Select Committee to Study Governmental Operations with Respect to Intelligence Activities [hereafter cited as SSCI], *Final Report, Foreign and Military Intelligence*, Book I, 94th Cong., 2d sess., 1976, 76–77.

8. *Ibid.*, Book IV, 56–59; William T. Lee, *Understanding the Soviet Military Threat: How CIA Estimates Went Astray* (New York; National Strategy Information Center, Agenda Paper No. 6. 1977), 24–37; Albert Wohlstetter: "Is There a Strategic Arms Race?" *Foreign Policy*, No. 15 (Summer 1974); Wohlstetter, "Rivals, But No Race," *Foreign Policy*, No. 16 (Fall 1974); Wohlstetter, "Optimal Ways to Confuse Ourselves," *Foreign Policy*, No. 20 (Fall 1975). There are exceptions to this pattern of military and civilian bias: see *ibid.*, 185–188; Lieutenant General Daniel Graham, USA (Ret.), "The Intelligence Mythology of Washington," *Strategic Review*, IV (Summer 1976), 61–62, 64; Victor Marchetti and John Marks, *The CIA and the Cult of Intelligence* (New York: Knopf 1974), 309.

9. The U.S. intelligence *community* includes the CIA, Defense Intelligence Agency (DIA), National Security Agency, the intelligence branches of each military service, the State Department Bureau of Intelligence and Research, the intelligence units of the Treasury and Energy Departments, and the FBI. Before 1973, coordination for national estimates was done through the Office of National Estimates, and since then, through the National Intelligence Officers. The Intelligence Community Staff assists the Director of Central Intelligence in managing allocation of resources and reviewing the agencies' performance.

10. HSCI, Hearings (fn. 4), 656–57.

11. Wilensky, *Organizational Intelligence* (New York: Basic Books 1967), 42–62, 126.

12. *Ibid., passim* The counterpoint of Cooper (fn. 5) and McGarvey (fn. 5) presents a perfect illustration.

13. Graham Allison and Peter Szanton, *Remaking Foreign Policy: The Organizational Connection* (New York: Basic Books 1976), 204.

14. Quoted in SSCI, *Final Report* (fn. 7), I, 82.

15. *Ibid.*, 267, 376; SSCI, *Staff Report, Covert Action in Chile 1963–1973*, 94th Cong., 1st sess., 1975, 48–49. The Senate Committee deplored the tendency of decision makers to focus on the latest raw data rather than on refined analyses, a practice that contributed to the intelligence failure in the 1974 Cyprus crisis. SSCI, *Final Report* (fn. 7), I, 443. But the failure in the October War was largely due to the *reverse* phenomenon: disregarding warning indicators because they contradicted finished intelligence that minimized the possibility of war. HSCI Draft Report (fn. 4), 78; Ben-Zvi (fn. 4), 386, 394; Perlmutter (fn. 4), 453.

16. Churchill, *The Gathering Storm* (Boston: Houghton Mifflin 1948), 587–88.

17. "Where the end is knowledge, as in the scientific community, time serves intelligence; where the end is something else—as in practically every organization but those devoted entirely to scholarship—time subverts intelligence, since in the long run, the central institutionalized structures and aims (the maintenance of authority, the accommodation of departmental rivalries, the service or established doctrine) will prevail." Wilensky (fn. 11), 77.

18. Quoted in SSCI, *Final Report* (fn. 7), I, 274.

19. Sherman Kent, "Estimates and Influence," *Foreign Service Journal* XLVI (April 1969), 17.

20. Hughes (fn. 2), 43.

21. "The textbooks agree, of course, that we should only believe reliable intelligence, and should never cease to be suspicious, but what is the use of such feeble maxims? They belong to that wisdom which for wane of anything better scribblers of systems and compendia resort to when they run out of ideas." Carl von Clausewitz, *On War*, ed. and trans. by Michael Howard and Peter Paret (Princeton: Princeton University Press 1976), 117.

22. Robert Jervis, *The Logic of Images in International Relations* (Princeton: Princeton University Press 1970), 132; Jervis, *Perception and Misperception in International Politics* (Princeton: Princeton University Press 1976), chap, 4; Floyd Allport, *Theories of Perception and the Concept of Structure* cited in Shlaim (fn. 2), 358. Cognitive theory suggests that uncertainty provokes decision makers to separate rather than integrate their values, to deny that inconsistencies between values exist, and even to see contradictory values as mutually supportive. John Steinbruner, *The Cybernetic Theory of Decision* (Princeton: Princeton University Press 1974), 105–8.

23. See William J. McGuire, "Selective Exposure: A Summing Up," in R. P. Abelson and others, eds., *Theories of Cognitive Consistency* (Chicago: Rand McNally 1968), and Irving L. Janis and Leon Mann, *Decision Making: A. Psychological Analysis of Conflict, Choice, and Commitment* (New York: Free Press 1977), 213–14.

24. CIA Intelligence Information Cable, "Remarks of the Chief of the Ranking Military Academy and Other Chinese Leaders on the Situation in South Vietnam," June 25, 1964, in Lyndon B. Johnson Library National Security Files, Vietnam Country File [hereafter cited as LBJL/NSF-VNCF], Vol. XII, item 55.

25. See for example, U.S. Department of Defense, *The Senator Gravel Edition: The Pentagon Papers* (Boston: Beacon Press 1971) [hereafter cited as Pentagon

Papers],Vol. II, 99; Frances Fitzgerald, *Fire in the Lake* (Boston: Atlantic-Little, Brown 1972), 364; Special National Intelligence Estimate 53–64, "Chances for a Stable Government in South Vietnam," September 18, 1964, and McGeorge Bundy's covering letter to the President, in LBJL/NSF-VNCF, Vol. XIII, item 48.

26. Patrick J. McGarvey, *CIA: The Myth and the Madness* (Baltimore: Penguin 1974), 16.

27. David Wise and Thomas B. Ross, *The U-2 Affair* (New York: Random House 1962), 56, 176, 180; Trevor Armbrister, *A Matter of Accountability* (New York: Coward-McCann 1970), 116–18,141–45, 159,187–95; U.S. Congress, House, Committee on Armed Services, *Report, Inquiry Into the U.S.S. Pueblo and EC-121 Plane Incidents* [hereafter cited as *Pueblo and EC-121 Report*], 91st Cong., 1st sess., 1969,1622–24,1650–51; U.S. Congress, House, Committee on Armed Services, *Hearings, Inquiry Into the U.S.S. Pueblo and EC-121 Plane Incidents* [hereafter cited as *Pueblo and EC-121 Hearings*], 91st Cong., 1st sess., 1969, 693–94, 699–700, 703–7, 714, 722, 734, 760, 773–78, 815–16.

28. SSCI, *Final Report* (fn. 7), I, 61–62; HSCI Draft Report (fn. 4), 82.

29. McGarvey (fn. 26), 16.

30. Shlaim (fn. 2), 375–77. The proposals follow, with their U.S. analogues noted in parentheses: appoint a special intelligence adviser to the Prime Minister (Director of Central Intelligence) to supplement the military chief of intelligence; reinforce the Foreign Ministry's research department (Bureau of Intelligence and Research); more autonomy for non-military intelligence (CIA); amend rules for transmitting raw intelligence to research agencies, the Defense Minister, and the Prime Minister (routing of signals intelligence from the National Security Agency); restructure military intelligence (creation of DIA in 1961); establish a central evaluation unit (Office of National Estimates). On the U.S. intelligence failure in 1973, see the HSCI Draft Report (fn. 4) 78–79.

31. Shlaim (fn. 2), 379; Handel (fn. 4), 62–63.

32. *Ibid.*, 55.

33. Shlaim (fn. 2), 358–59. The Israeli command estimated a higher probability of attack in May 1973 than it did in October. Having been proved wrong in May, Chief of Staff Elazar lost credibility in challenging intelligence officers, complained that he could no longer argue effectively against them, and consequently was unable to influence his colleagues when he was right. Personal communication from Michael Handel, November 15, 1977.

34. *Washington Post*, November 27, 1977, p. A17.

35. Raymond Garthoff, "On Estimating and Imputing Intentions," *International Security*, II (Winter 1978), 22.

36. Westmoreland, *A Soldier Reports* (Garden City, N.Y.: Doubleday 1976), 316. See the postmortem by the President's Foreign Intelligence Advisory Board, quoted in Herbert Y. Schandler, *The Unmaking of a President* (Princeton: Princeton University Press 1977), 70, 76, 79–80.

37. Wohlstetter (fn. 4), 69.

38. George, "The Case for Multiple Advocacy in Making Foreign Policy," *American Political Science Review*, Vol. 66 (September 1972). My usage of the term multiple advocacy is looser than George's.

39. Henry F. Graff, *The Tuesday Cabinet* (Englewood Cliffs, N.J.: Prentice-Hall 1970), 68–71; Leslie H. Gelb with Richard K. Berts, *The Irony of Vietnam: The System Worked* (Washington, D.C.: Brookings, forthcoming), chap. 4; Ball memorandum of October 5, 1964, reprinted as "Top Secret; The Prophecy the President Rejected," *Atlantic Monthly*, Vol. 230 (July 1972); McCone, memorandum of April 2,1965, in LBJL/NSF-VNCF, Troop Decision Folder, item 14b.

40. Betts (fn. 5), 199–202; Schandler (fn. 36), 177. George (fn. 38), 759, stipulates that multiple advocacy requires "no major maldistribution" of power, influence, competence, information, analytic resources, and bargaining skills. But, except for resources and the right to representation, the foregoing are subjective factors that can rarely be equalized by design. If they are equalized, in the context of imperfect data and time pressure, erroneous arguments as well as accurate ones will be reinforced. Non-expert principals have difficulty arbitrating intellectually between experts who disagree.

41. Quoted in Steinbruner (fn. 22), 332.

42. Clausewitz (fn. 21), 117–18; HSCI, *Hearings* (fn. 4), 634–36; William J. Barnds, "Intelligence and Policy-making in an Institutional Context," in U.S. Commission on the Organization of the Government for the Conduct of Foreign Policy [hereafter cited as Murphy Commission], *Appendices* (Washington, D.C.: G.P.O., June 1975), Vol. VII, 32.

43. HSCI, *Hearings* (fn. 4), 778.

44. SSCI, *Final Report* (fn. 7), IV, 57; Roger Hilsman, *Strategic Intelligence and National Decisions* (Glencoe, Ill.: Free Press 1956),40. During brief service as just a low-level staff member of the National Security Council, even I never had time to read all the intelligence analyses relevant to my work.

45. SSCI, *Final Report* (fn. 7), I, 344, and IV, 95 (emphasis deleted).

46. Ray S. Cline, *Secrets, Spies, and Scholars* (Washington, D.C.: Acropolis 1976), 20.

47. Gilbert W. Fitzhugh and others, *Report to the President and the Secretary of Defense on the Department of Defense, By the Blue Ribbon Defense Panel* (Washington D.C.; G.P.O., July 1970), 45–46.

48. Alexander George, "The Devil's Advocate: Uses and Limitations," Murphy Commission, *Appendices* (fn. 42), II, 84–85; Jervis, *Perception and Misperception* (fn. II),417.

49. *Ibid.*, 416.

50. U.S. Congress, Senate, Select Committee on Intelligence, Report, *The National Intelligence Estimates A-B Team Episode Concerning Soviet Capability and Objectives*, 95th Cong., 2d sess., 1978; *New York Times*, December 36, 1976, pp. 1, 14; *Washington Post*, January 2, 1977, pp. A1, A4.

51. George H. Poteal, "The Intelligence Gap: Hypotheses on the Process of Surprise," *International Studies Notes*, III (Fall 1976), 15.

52. Cline (fn.46), 140.

53. SSCI, *Final Report* (fn. 7), I, 352. A valid criticism is that military personnel systems and promotion standards penalized intelligence officers, thus encouraging competent officers to avoid intelligence assignments. This situation was rectified in the service intelligence agencies by the early 1970's, but not within DIA. *Ibid.* Betts (fn. 5), 196–97.

54. SSCI, *Final Report* (fn. 7), 1, 77–81. See also U.S., Congress, Senate, Committee on Foreign Relations, *Hearings, National Security Act Amendment*, 92d Cong., 2d sess. 1972, 14–24.

55. Zumwalt, *On Watch* (New York: Quadrangle 1976), 459.

56. Wilensky (fn. 11), 164.

57. Jervis, *Perception and Misperception* (fn. 22), 181–87.

58. Knorr (fn. I), 460.

59. SSCI, *Final Report* (fn. 7), I, 276, and IV, 85; U.S., Congress, House, Committee on Appropriations, *Hearings, Supplemental Appropriations for Fiscal Year 1977*, 95th Cong., 2d sess., 1977, 515–621; *Washington Post*, February 15, 1977, p. A6; Paul W. Blackstock, "The Intelligence Community Under the Nixon Administration," *Armed Forces and Society*, I (February 1975), 238.

60. Joseph C. Goulden, *Truth Is the First Casualty* (Chicago: Rand McNally 1969), 101–4; Phil G. Goulding, *Confirm or Deny* (New York: Harper &. Row 1970), 130–33, 269; *Pueblo and EC-I21 Hearings* (fn. 27), 646–47, 665–73, 743–44, 780–82, 802–3, 865–67, 875, 880, 897–99; *Pueblo and EC-121 Report* (fn. 27), 1654–1656, 1662–67; Armbrister (fn. 27), 196ff, 395; U.S. Congress, House, Committee on Armed Services, Report, *Review of Department of Defense Worldwide Communications: Phase I*, 92d Cong., 1st sess., 1971, and *Phase II*, 2d sess., 1972.

61. See, for example, James Blaker and Andrew Hamilton, *Assessing the NATO/Warsaw Pact Military Balance* (Washington, D.C.: Congressional Budget Office, December 1977).

62. SSCI, *Final Report* (fn. 7), I, 61; Thomas G. Belden, "Indications, Warning, and Crisis Operations," *International Studies Quarterly*, XXI (March 1977), 192–93.

63. *Pentagon Papers*, IV, 111–12, 115–24, 217–32. CIA critiques of bombing results begin even before the Tonkin Gulf crisis. CIA/OCI, Current Intelligence Memorandum, "Effectiveness of T-28 Strikes in Laos," June 26, 1964; CIA/DDI, Intelligence Memorandum, "Communist Reaction to Barrel Roll Missions," December 29, 1964. But ambivalence remained even within the CIA, which occasionally issued more sanguine evaluations—e.g., CIA Memorandum for National Security Council, "The Situation in Vietnam," June 28, 1965 (which McGeorge Bundy called directly to the President's attention), and CIA/OCI, Intelligence Memorandum, "Interdiction of Communist Infiltration Routes in Vietnam," June 24, 1965. (All memoranda are in LBJL/NSF-VNCF, Vol. I, item 5, Vol. III, items 28, 28a, 28b, Vol. VI A, items 4, 5, 8.) See also *Pentagon Papers*, IV, 71–74. See also the opposing assessments of the CIA, the civilian analysis in the Pentagon, and the Joint Chiefs in NSSM-I (the Nixon Administration's initial review of Vietnam policy), reprinted in the *Congressional Record*, Vol. 118, part 13, 92d Cong., 2d sess., May 10, 1972, pp. 16749–836.

From Betts, Richard K., Analysis, War and Decision: Why Intelligence Failures Are Inevitable. *World Politics* 31:1 (1978), 61–89. Reprinted with the permission of Cambridge University Press.

11. A POLICYMAKER'S PERSPECTIVE ON INTELLIGENCE ANALYSIS

ROBERT D. BLACKWILL AND JACK DAVIS

As Robert D. Blackwill reveals in this interview with CIA analyst Jack Davis, the life of a senior policy official in the U.S. government—in this case, an ambassador—can be overwhelming. Policymakers must focus on the pressing issues of the day, leaving little time to study broad-gauged intelligence reports. What officials need, and what Blackwill sought out, was a team of analysts who were willing to respond directly to his requests for information. Blackwill offers the reader a glimpse into the lives of policymakers and analysts as they interact.

Sherman Kent, in *Strategic Intelligence for American World Policy*, his path-breaking effort to join intelligence doctrine and practice for post-World War II America, concluded that:

> There is no phase of the intelligence business which is more important than the proper relationship between intelligence itself and the people who use its products. Oddly enough, this relationship, which one would expect to establish itself automatically, does not do this. It is established as a result of a great deal of conscious effort...[1]

Despite guidance from Kent and numerous subsequent authors, the terms of engagement between intelligence analyst and policymaker are still ill-defined doctrinally and thus practiced as much to suit the immediate preferences of the players on both sides of the relationship as to meet the fundamental demands of sound policymaking. The quest to join sage principle—*what should work*—to solid practice —what does—is more important than ever in post-Cold War America, as resources for intelligence support of policymaking are cut back more rapidly than responsibilities.

The original pillar of Ambassador Blackwill's doctrinal views on intelligence and policy was self-interest—his effort to make the relationship work for him personally under trying conditions. He served as Special Assistant to the President and Senior Director for European and Soviet Affairs,

National Security Council Staff, during 1989–90, a tumultuous period that witnessed the collapse of the Soviet Union and the reshaping of Europe. The more lasting pillar is his concern for the national interest—a belief that the United States can ill afford prevailing patterns of ineffective ties between experts on events overseas and policymakers in Washington.

SOME KEY POINTS

The Ambassador's framework for defining the requirements for sound intelligence-policy relations consists of four key points:

- Roughly 90 percent of what passes for national security analysis in the US Government, including structured study of events overseas, is done by intelligence analysts.
- The national interest requires that this effort be effectively joined to the policymaking process.
- The officials who carry most of the day-to-day burden of policymaking on key issues are so besieged by time-consuming responsibilities that decisions on how much to stay informed on events overseas and in what way are narrowly based on self-interest in managing the pressures and getting the job done.
- Intelligence professionals have to carry nearly all the burden to convince each key policy official that they are committed to servicing his or her analytic needs via customized expert support.

Thus, to meet their responsibilities in promoting the national interest, intelligence professionals have to become expert not only on substantive issues but also on serving the self-interest of policy professionals by providing specialized analytic support.

A SHAKY START

I first met the Ambassador in November 1987, when he was teaching in the CIA-funded Kennedy School Seminar on Intelligence and Policy. He seized the attention of the class of some 30 Directorate of Intelligence (DI) division chiefs and managers from elsewhere in the Intelligence Community by asserting that as a policy official he never read DI analytic papers. Why? "Because they were nonadhesive." As Blackwill explained, they were written by people who did not know what he was trying to do and, so, could not help him get it done:

> When I was working at State on European affairs, for example, on certain issues I was the Secretary of State. DI analysts did not know that—that I was one of a handful of key decision-makers on some very important matters. Why bother to read what they write for a general audience of people who have no real responsibility on the issue.

More charitably, he now characterizes his early periods of service at the NSC Staff and in State Department bureaus as ones of "mutual ignorance":

> DI analysts did not have the foggiest notion of what I did; and I did not have a clue as to what they could or should do.

An unpromising start. Yet during his 1989–90 NSC Staff tour, Ambassador Blackwill—by the lights of DI analysts working with him on European affairs—raised analyst-policy relations to an exemplary level. Time after time, the DI's Office of European Analysis (EURA) provided much-needed intelligence support under stringent time constraints. In a tribute with resonance in the hometown of the Washington Redskins, Blackwill called the EURA crew his "analytic hogs," opening up holes in the line for him to run through. At least one EURA analyst considers this period "the most exciting and meaningful" of his career.

The balance of this article consists of the Ambassador's replies to my questions.

FROM MUTUAL IGNORANCE TO MUTUAL BENEFIT

Q: What caused your apparent change of mind about the utility of DI analysis?

A: I had started to rethink my position even before our 1987 classroom encounter. As chief negotiator for the MBFR talks,[2] I worked closely for the first time with Agency analysts—those assigned to the US delegation. They regularly came up with information and interpretations that helped me sharpen my approach to the individual negotiating issues. When I gave them a special task, they delivered to suit my schedule, even if it meant considerable inconvenience to them.

One more matter important to negotiators, and to heavily engaged policymakers generally. Unlike other intelligence people I had worked with in the past, including those from State, my informal talks about possible US tactical initiatives with CIA analysts from the Arms Control Intelligence Staff did not end up in the *Washington Post*.

My understanding of the role of intelligence was also broadened by my work at Kennedy School. In addition to the CIA seminar, I collaborated with Professors Ernest May and Richard Neustadt on a course called "Assessing Other Governments." Here, the importance of country expertise, of language skills, of perspective and a sense of history were underscored by well-documented case studies. Then there was the survival factor. I knew soon after [President] Bush's election in November 1988 that I was to be selected for the NSC Staff job on both Europe and the USSR. This meant longer hours and more pressures for me than ever before. Frankly, I was concerned about forgetting what my 10-year-old daughter looked like. So I sat down in Cambridge and planned how I was going to interact with Executive Branch colleagues, with Congress, with the press—and with intelligence. I decided that in my own self-interest I had to arrange to get as much support as practical from Agency analysts.

Q: Why Agency analysts?

A: You mean besides the fact there are many more of them in my areas of responsibility than in the other intelligence outfits? My experience at State convinced me that INR [Bureau of Intelligence and Research] works for the Secretary. I suppose it is the same at Defense. I judged that Agency analysts would be much more likely to provide close and continuous support to an NSC Staff director.

Back to State. From my White House perspective, the State Department almost never met a deadline it could not miss. Then there is also the confidentiality factor. As I said earlier, your musings about possible policy initiatives are not leaked to the press by the DCI to shoot down your policy.

The most important consideration is that Agency analysts are better informed about individual countries than anyone else in the [US] Government. And I judged they had the wit—the historical perspective I spoke of—to interpret this information for my benefit and the President's benefit. I just had to determine whether they had the professional interest and enterprise to be responsive to my overtures.

Let me expand on one point. Intelligence analysts—essentially DI analysts—do 90 percent of the analysis by the USG on foreign affairs. Policy officials, even those with academic backgrounds, are too busy with more pressing matters.

In some administrations, the most heavily engaged and influential policy officials on any given issue spend 90 percent of their time assessing their policy competitors in Washington. I am talking here about getting ready to leverage competing Administration officials, not just Congress. Busy decision-makers concentrate what little time they have for foreign policy analysis on narrowly focused aspects of key agenda issues—often how to deal effectively with their foreign counterparts. Let me tell you any policy official who can do his own research on all aspects of an issue, cannot be very important—because he is not fully engaged in the coalition-building and power-leverage games essential for getting serious policy work done in Washington.

And there is no second team. If Agency analysts do not do the work of keeping up with developments overseas that the decisionmakers need to know about, it does not get done. It was in my self-interest to see if I could get those analysts working for me, to help me keep up with a broad range of developments I could not possibly follow on my own.

WHAT WORKS, AND WHAT DOES NOT

Q: You have mentioned self-interest a couple of times.

A: Let me explain. The policymakers who count the most—those five to 10 on any issue who have the most power for getting anything done, decided, implemented—work much harder than intelligence analysts. During 1989-90, I was often at my desk from 7 in the morning till 10 at night. Others at the NSC Staff, Brent Scowcroft and Bob Gates for instance, started even earlier.[3] Unlike analysts we had no evening tennis games. No weekends.

Even with these hours, as I indicated, I needed help to stay informed. But it had to be the right kind of help. I could not afford to read intelligence papers because this or that intelligence agency was entitled to produce them. It did not matter to me how much work the Agency had put into its products, or how polished they were in scholarly terms. In fact, I could not afford the time to read intelligence papers written by personal friends and colleagues. I could only read intelligence products tailored to help me get through my substantive schedule. There was no other rational choice.

Q: The old issue of "adhesive analysis."

A: You asked, so let me unload here. During my [1989–90] NSC tour, the Agency was still putting out gobs of analytic products that I never read. During the two years I did not read a single [National Intelligence] estimate. Not one. And except for Gates, I do not know of anyone at the NSC who did. The reason, at least for me, is simple. There was no penalty to be paid for not reading an NIE. It did not cost you anything in terms of getting done the most important policy things you had to get done.

The same goes for your other general audience papers. I got them, but I did not read them. I am sure somebody did or you would not bother to put them out. Let me grant without hesitation that there is a lot you put out for good reason that has nothing to do with policymakers at my level. I think however that you ought to consider the cost-benefit ratios of producing papers that are read mostly by specialists at the desk level at State and Defense, or by policy officials with general interest but no direct say on an issue.

Q: What about the NID [*National Intelligence Daily*]? I've heard a number of NSC Staff members praise its utility over the years.

A: Of course, I was interested in the PDB [*President's Daily Brief*] because President Bush read it. As for the NID, I would spend, literally, 60 seconds a day on it. This was a defensive move. I wanted to know in advance what would likely be leaked to the press by readers in Congress. Other than that, there was, again, no cost to me, no penalty, from not having read the NID.

Q: What did you read, aside from what you commissioned directly from DI analysts?

A: Despite what you hear about policymakers not having time to read, I read a lot. Much of it was press. You have to know how issues are coming across politically to get your job done. Also, cables from overseas for preparing agendas for meetings and sending and receiving messages from my counterparts in foreign governments. Countless versions of policy drafts from those competing for the President's blessing. And dozens of phone calls. Many are a waste of time but have to be answered, again, for policy and political reasons.

Q: Let's turn to what you commissioned from DI analysts.

A: One more minute, please, on what I did not find useful. This is important. My job description called for me to help prepare the President for making policy decisions, including at meetings with foreign counterparts and other officials. One thing the Agency regularly did was send me memos on the strategic and tactical agendas of foreign officials; in effect, what they wanted from the United States. Do you think that after I have spent long weeks shaping the agenda, I have to be told a day or two before the German foreign minister visits Washington why he is coming?

O.K. What did I want from analysts? I want their reading of what is going on in the domestic affairs of country "X" or "Y"—countries the President is planning to visit to advance foreign policy or countries from which we are going to receive important visitors to discuss problems and bilateral strategy, or countries on which, for one reason or another, we feel a need to get US policy into better shape.

What is going on domestically in these countries that could have an impact on how the President's counterparts and my counterparts will behave? What pressures are they under at home?

Although I knew the national security issues cold, I could not become expert on all important issues affecting Germany or France or Italy at the national level, much less at the provincial or state levels. DI analysts knew this, and they helped me bone up on what I needed to understand to nuance and sharpen the US approach.

You also have to consider that President Bush, as a political animal, was naturally interested in the domestic politics of other leaders, even when there was no pressing bilateral business on the table.

Q: We variously call this "opportunity analysis," or "value-added analysis." Sometimes we call it "targeted tactical analysis."

A: I never put a label on it. Your terms are all good ones. Incidentally, the MacEachin metaphor you told me, about scouts and coaches, is also useful.[4] Yes, intelligence analysts should help key policymakers make the best game plan by telling them what they do not know or appreciate sufficiently. Regarding my own needs, this was mostly, as I said, on the domestic politics of the countries I was dealing with.

Whatever label you put on it, the service I got on Europe from EURA was superb and invaluable. As you know, when I traveled to Europe, EURA analysts prepared a daily cable for me on key developments. They got it to me first thing in the morning European time, which means they worked late into the night in Washington to get it done. I appreciated that immensely. Once a senior State Department colleague joined me for breakfast in Brussels as I was reading my very own newsletter. He studied it with great interest and asked me where it came from. I chose not to give him a clear answer.

EURA people met without exception whatever deadlines I set for informal memos while I was in Washington. They also were responsive and quick with some major projects I laid on with little advance notice. My only problem with their written work is sometimes the text had gone through too many levels of review and began to read like a NID article. If I wanted a NID article, I could read one. What I wanted was the analyst's unvarnished response to my questions. After I made this point, the incidence of overpolished papers diminished.

Q: What about briefings?

A: Yes, because you get a chance to ask questions, briefings can be more helpful than memos. Here, too, I got first-rate customized service. Whenever I asked for briefings in my office, the analysts who came were both informed and responsive. Really terrific people.

Again, I was mostly interested in domestic affairs in this and that country. From time to time, though, I would ask the analysts in my office what the response of a European government would be to the policy initiatives the President was considering or that I was thinking of recommending to the President. Their unrehearsed responses here were also useful. I always hesitated to put such requests into writing for fear of leaks to the press. I learned you can trust DI analysts. They were well informed. Ready to help. And they kept their traps shut.

Q: That sounds like a good advertisement for DI analysts.

A: You bet. They were expert on their subjects. They were responsive to my needs. And they did not leak my confidences to the press.

POLITICIZATION NOT AN ISSUE

Q: Did your NSC Staff colleagues resent your close ties to DI analysts?

A: Not that I was aware of. The people who worked for me, rather than being resentful, made use of EURA support on their own.

Q: What about this kind of closeness pushing analysts across the line into policymaking?

A: Again, I saw no problem with EURA analysts. When I asked, they provided advice on tactics to support an established policy. They were good at that too. But the EURA people did not get into policy prescription. And where it did happen on occasion with others, when intelligence people started recommending policy, I pushed them back.

Q: What about telling you what you wanted to hear, or avoiding bad news?

A: Not a problem. I wanted their help in avoiding setbacks as well as for advancing policy goals. If there were negative developments I had to know about, they let me know. We had trust going both ways.

I would like to continue with this for a minute. I know during the Gates confirmation hearings [for DCI during 1991] the media were full of charges of analysts writing to please policymakers. My experience was different. I would argue that at least in my experience close professional relationships encouraged frankness—not politicization. But I know it does not always turn out that way.

Just as top policy aides have got to deliver bad news to the President when called for, intelligence people have got to have the intellectual courage to tell key policy officials that something is not working, or is not going to work. It is tough, really tough, to stop a policy failure based on ignorance of the ground truth. Intelligence analysts have got to rise to this challenge. I am not talking about shouting it from the rooftops. NSC directors are especially resentful when Congress is told bad news before they have a chance to think about it. But limited distribution memos should work. Private briefings might be even better, since that gives the policy official a chance to ask questions.

Often it is important to decisionmakers to know how to get to the least bad outcome, to limit the damage. I think options papers work very well here, especially if they are delivered after bad news forces key policymakers to focus on an issue. Somalia is a good example. The analysts could table a paper or lay on a briefing outlining three possible outcomes six months down the road, and what opportunities, leverage, and so forth the United States has to influence the outcome.

INTELLIGENCE AND POLICY TRIBES

Q: Why do not more overworked policy officials lean on Agency analysis the way you did?

A: I guess some do, though I do not personally know of any case quite like mine with EURA. The absence of a pattern of effective relations probably reflects a combination of professional differences and mutual ignorance about what really makes the relationship work.

I am not the only policy official who decided that too many intelligence products still are nonadhesive. They are, or were when I last served, too long and complex. Analysts love words and complexities; it is one of their strengths. Good policymakers are driven by the need to take action. They need problems broken down, simplified. You and I have been through this before, and you can probably make a better list of tribal differences than I can. The key still is getting close enough to the individual policymaker to find out what he needs.

Policymakers do not as a rule know what intelligence analysts can do for them. They read Estimates, think pieces, the NID, and say, in effect, "What does this have to do with *my* problems"? They do not see it as their job to teach analysts how to be helpful. Besides, they would not have the time.

Q: How did your counterpart NSC Staff senior directors stay informed, and, for that matter, others in the Bush administration who were the kinds of key hands-on policy officials you think the Agency should cultivate?

A: The only honest answer is, I do not really know. I was too busy with my own affairs. But I seriously doubt that any of them [during 1989–90] received the kind of customized support from the Agency that I am talking about.

Q: This seems to bother you.

A: Yes. As a citizen and taxpayer it sure does. I am talking here about the national interest. Let's go back to my statement that the Intelligence Community does 90 percent of foreign affairs analysis in the USG.

Policy choices are made and policy actions are taken whether or not the expertise of analysts is brought to bear. But how can anyone argue that we should pay for this expertise and not make use of it?

I do not mean to say it is all the analysts' fault, but I am fully prepared to argue that if an analyst's work does not have an impact on policymaking as a process, including in the long run, he or she is taking pay under false pretenses. A lot that you do is useful to someone. You have to make it more useful to those who count.

Let me say this: the Agency's understanding of the world is probably needed more today than ever. The world and the challenges the United States faces are changing so rapidly. Also, the new [Clinton] administration does not seem to have yet defined its policy approach. The costs of tribal tensions between analysts and policymakers—mutual ignorance, really—may be rising.

AT A LOWER LEVEL

Q: Much of what you have had to say relates to officials at your level, the NSC senior director and departmental assistant secretaries and above. What about one level down—deputy assistant secretaries, office directors?

A: I would say, much the same. Find out who counts—the five or 10 midlevel officials who have the most influence on more senior decisionmakers—and cultivate close relations with them. Trade customized support for access to the real agenda, and so forth.

A PROGRAM FOR THE DI

Q: How would you combine your various recommendations for Agency analysts into a program? If you were advising the DCI or DDI, what measures would you propose to enhance the effectiveness of relations between analysts and policy decisionmakers?[5]

A: Thank you for letting me know in advance this question was coming. It is a good question, and I have given it considerable thought. Let's see if the seven measures I have sketched out add up to a program.

1. Identify the 30 or so senior policy officials who count—those who really carry weight with administration Cabinet officers on key foreign policy issues. These officials, usually assistant secretaries in policy departments or special assistants to the President on the NSC Staff, regularly set the thinking of NSC principals on major policy decisions. As a rule, these are the assessors of foreign governments, or the analysts of last resort. To contribute to sounder policymaking, intelligence analysts have to reach this group. Remember, the list of policy notables has to be carefully worked out and kept up to date, because office titles do not always reflect real policy weight.

2. Approach the policy officials who count as if they were motivated solely by self-interest. Their self-interest has to be worked on because they are just too busy to allow either institutional considerations or personal friendships to determine their attitude toward intelligence analysts.

3. Learn as much as you can about each senior official. Study them as carefully as you do foreign leaders. For example, read everything they have written on the subjects in their policy portfolios. Check them out through mutual contacts.

4. Take the initiative to establish ties. This is an essential obligation of intelligence managers, because policy officials will rarely seek them out.

- For new appointees, send a letter asking for an appointment and spelling out your areas of expertise and the services you are ready to extend.
- For serving officials, anticipate a major pending visit or event and offer to send over your analysts for a briefing on any one of several related aspects. For example, if the prime minister from Denmark is to visit the President, the DI manager should signal that he will bring over his Denmark analyst to fill the policymaker in on any gaps in understanding in time for the latter to prepare briefing memos for his or her principal, be it the Secretary of State or the President.
- Whenever DI managers know of travel plans by a key policy official, offer to send over country analysts who can fill in the official's knowledge on areas of his choice.
- Have the DCI set up luncheon meetings in town (CIA Headquarters is just too inconvenient), at which analysts and their managers can establish their credentials as entrepreneurial experts.

5. Customize intelligence papers and briefings to solidify the relationship. Many policy officials, overwhelmed by the volume both of their activities and of seemingly important information, will welcome specialized newsletters. They will welcome even one-page summaries of key events overseas that provide the kind of information and analysis they want at the time of day or week they prefer to set aside for keeping up with developments. For the same reason—fear of being overwhelmed—many will welcome customized briefings and memos relating to their policymaking responsibilities on matters on which the DI country analyst is much better informed than they can be or than anyone else in the government. Give them something they will really miss if they do not get it.

6. Place the best and most promising analysts on tours in the policy world. The Agency could offer, free of charge, 50 first-rate people to policy officials around town. Intelligence officers can learn something about how to use intelligence resources effectively by reading about policymaking. You can learn some more by periodic visits to a policymaker's office. But the best way to learn about a

different bureaucracy is just the same as the best way to learn about any alien tribe—go live with them for a couple of years.

7. Reward those managers and analysts who are successful in gaining and maintaining access. As a rule, once a win-win relationship takes hold, momentum will keep it going. Once the policy official knows the intelligence unit can and will deliver support when it is needed, he will provide in exchange access to the real policy agenda. But policy officials come and go, and the Agency has to take care of those with talent at starting over again with newcomers who, as almost always will be the case, will not seek you out.

FINAL THOUGHTS

Q: How do you stay informed on events overseas these days, while working again at Kennedy School?

A: My main current interest is Russian politics and military affairs. I have been spending one week per month in Russia, dealing directly with the General Staff. While at Harvard, I spend a couple of hours each morning on the Internet. It is amazing how much good information and worthwhile commentary is out there for those with the interest and the time. While at the NSC, I had the interest but not the time.

Internet, CNN, increasing visits by all sorts of Americans. The competition for the DI analyst is becoming much stronger. This means you are going to have to work much harder to find a comparative advantage. How do you get more expertise—living there, of course, language, and history?

I worry a bit about this. Just as you cannot rely on quality alone to get your job of informing policy done, you cannot rely only on access. In fact, marketing without a quality product to deliver is worse than passivity.

Q: Final question. At the end of a long day, which is it, working for more expertise, or for more access?

A: The answer, I suppose, is more efficiency. I imagine a textbook breakdown would have the analysts spending 40 percent of their time on collection and other activities for building expertise, 30 percent on analysis and writing—putting things together, and 30 percent on assuring impact on the policymaking process. I never managed an analytic unit, and this is just a guess. I do not think you are anywhere near the last 30 percent.

One final thought occurs to me. Managers in particular should spend enough time establishing and keeping up effective links to the policy-making world that they begin to feel guilty about not having enough time for their other duties. It is that important.

QUESTIONS FOR FURTHER DISCUSSION

1. Why are policymakers often dissatisfied with the analysis they receive from the intelligence community?
2. Why is it difficult for policymakers to obtain useful analysis and information from intelligence analysts?
3. Should policymakers view the intelligence community as an extension of their own staff?
4. Will the "information revolution" help analysts build constructive relationships with policymakers?

ENDNOTES

1. Princeton University Press (1949), p. 180.
2. Mutual and Balanced Force Reduction negotiations between NATO and the Warsaw Pact.
3. Scowcroft was Special Assistant to the President for National Security Affairs. Robert M Gates, subsequently Director of Central Intelligence, was then Deputy Special Assistant.
4. Douglas A. MacEachin, currently CIA's Deputy Director for Intelligence, uses the scout-coach metaphor for analyst-policymaker relations to underscore that it is the scout's responsibility to help the coach prepare to win the game and not to predict the outcome of the game before it is played.
5. This question was communicated in a letter sent in October 1991 and answered in an interview in November 1991. The DI has been moving in the recommended direction for several years. When the interviewer showed an outline of Blackwill's program to DDI Douglas MacEachin (October 1993) he said, "I guess Bob [Blackwill] and I agree."

Reprinted with permission from Jack Davis, "A Policymaker's Perspective on Intelligence Analysis," *Studies in Intelligence* 38 (1995): 7–15.

12. THE CHALLENGES OF INTELLIGENCE ANALYSIS

WILLIAM M. NOLTE

It should come as no surprise that the information revolution is transforming the intelligence community. Nevertheless, this ongoing transformation is not well understood by intelligence professionals. Intelligence transformation is an evolutionary process, not the product of some well-thought-out plan. William Nolte describes how the information revolution is changing the way today's intelligence professionals go about their business, creating new collaborative work spaces that are breaking down traditional procedures used to organize the production of finished intelligence.

---

1. INTRODUCTION

A decade ago, a chapter summarizing intelligence analysis, let alone offering an assessment of the literature on the subject, would have had few resources to draw on. The section on the literature would have been, if nothing else, very brief. A few journals, including the *International Journal of Intelligence and Counterintelligence* and *Intelligence and National Security*, published articles on analysis. (As did CIA's *Studies in Intelligence*, but with relatively little of its work unclassified or declassified at that time.) Analysis appeared, however sporadically, in histories of intelligence, or of the CIA, or of particular events, but for the most part the emphasis in this literature was on espionage or covert action. In intelligence fiction as well, the emphasis was largely on the very real human drama of clandestine collection, rather than on the less dramatic work of intelligence analysis. Tom Clancy's decision to base much of his work on the Jack Ryan character, that is, the analyst turned man of action, provided an often-ironic touch, however improbable, to his early works.

This emphasis in the literature mirrored, at least to some degree, the emphasis within the intelligence services. Here I am speaking primarily about the services of the United States, though I suspect it is largely true of other services as well. For most of the history of modern American intelligence, the training and education of the analytic workforce largely came with them to the job. That is to say, most of their formal education took place in colleges or universities before they entered government service. Analytic training within the services for many years consisted of relatively short courses on an agency's "writing style" or the formats governing analysis and reporting in a given agency. But there was little or nothing to match the intense initial training provided to officers selected for the CIA's clandestine service, to cite one example. Analysts could pursue advanced degrees on their own, or perhaps take short courses on a new geographical or topical area to which they had been assigned. But much analytic "training" remained the on-the-job variety. Only in the late 1990s did the CIA's intelligence directorate begin to offer an extensive (and, in pre-9/11 budgets, expensive) program of analytic training interspersed with on-the-job analytic assignments. At roughly the same time (1999), Richards Heuer's *The Psychology of Intelligence Analysis* appeared (Heuer 2006).[1]

2. THE VOLATILE ENVIRONMENT

In retrospect, the 1990s were an important period in the development of intelligence analysis, complicated to some degree (as will be noted later) by a relatively austere budget climate, certainly in the case of the American services. This development will permit this chapter to avoid repetition of basics covered in such works as Heuer's, Mark Lowenthal's

Intelligence: From Secrets to Policy (2008), and the very fine *Analyzing Intelligence*, edited by Roger George and James Bruce (2008), among other recent work (see reference list).

Overriding such developments internal to the craft of intelligence, however, the 1990s transformed the environment in which analysts operated. That decade brought the end of one important environmental factor confronting intelligence and the intensification of another. In the first instance, the end of the Cold War removed a large part—the dominant part—of the raison d'etre of Western intelligence.[2] For decades intelligence agencies and their staffs had been able to rely on the constant presence of the Soviet Union occupying the greater part of both their budgets and their attention. This target environment was never completely static, of course, but relative to the first years of the twenty-first century, it looks remarkably stable. Even when other actors drew the attention of the Western national security instruments, including intelligence, they came, in the case of China, North Vietnam, Cuba, or the authoritarian states of the Nasserite Middle East, with significant reflections of Soviet ideology, views toward the United States and the West, and even equipment, doctrine, and technology. A Soviet-built T-72 tank remained a T-72 tank, at the tactical level, whatever flag it flew and whether it was painted for European or desert conditions. For decades, the overriding objective of Western intelligence was to assess the capabilities and intentions of the Soviet Union, its allies, and its surrogates. And then it was gone.

The loss of the Soviet Union, along with the "peace dividend" that followed, created major problems for Western intelligence services. At one level, bureaucratic and structural realities associated with modern civil services made it at least difficult for the intelligence services to react with agility (a favored term, in wish if not in practice) in adjusting to the new post–Cold War environment. More importantly, no new environmental metaphor emerged to replace that of the Cold War in defining national security for the United States and its allies. For the decade after the collapse of the Soviet Union, events moved to the fore several candidates for this conceptual design, starting with the "New World Order" associated with the First Gulf War. Since 2001, of course, we have dealt with the "Global War on Terrorism" as a proposed metaphor. To an unfortunately great extent,

however, the national security instruments of the United States continue to reflect a "post–Cold War" sense of mission, purpose, and structure (Arquilla 2008; Robb 2007).

To be thinking, even implicitly, in "post–Cold War" terms in 2008 or 2009 is extraordinary. Who, by way of comparison, thought of the national security environment of 1964 or 1965 in "post–World War II" terms?

If the collapse of the Soviet Union ended one defining element of the national security environment, the information revolution (and all it has wrought, including, to a great degree, globalization) preceded that event, continued through it, and will remain a driving force in national security affairs for years, if not decades, to come. The duration of this transforming change, its pervasive impact, and its two-edged implications make this the center of any effort to renew twenty-first-century analysis and analytic methodology.

In attempting to confront the national security challenges presented by changes in information technology (and information behavior, a related but different issue), many of the leading military thinkers and planners of the 1990s thought in terms of a "revolution in military affairs" (RMA) (Owens 2000). Some in the intelligence professions, including this author, even began to think and write about an analogous "revolution in intelligence affairs" (Barger 2005; Nolte 2005). Partly this was a recognition that momentous changes in defense and military affairs cannot fail to have an impact on the intelligence professions, support to the military being a primary function of intelligence.

In more recent years, several critics, drawing on the experiences in Iraq, Afghanistan, and in the war on terror in general, have pointed to the shortcomings of the RMA literature (Shachtman 2007). Without question, some of the statements and projections of the RMA visionaries (especially the thought that information technology would "eliminate the fog of war") were excessive. But it would be hard to deny that information and related technologies have had a profound effect on the way recent wars have been fought and future wars will be fought. In what we now call second- and third-generation warfare, or industrial warfare, the line infantry soldier was something of lowest-common-denominator cannon fodder. This is a harsh term, to be sure, and is in no way intended to dishonor those who served in those roles. But compare the investment in an infantryman anywhere from the Napoleonic Period through Vietnam to the investment in front-line personnel in the first decade of the twenty-first century and a dramatic difference emerges. Leave aside for the moment that these personnel are human beings and fellow citizens, no commander in the twenty-first century will expend these resources—and the investment they represent—in ways accepted as inevitable only a generation or two ago.

In many respects, intelligence, especially intelligence analysis, had its own counterpart to second- and third-generation industrial warfare. The relatively small group of highly skilled analysts and researchers in the Research and Analysis branch of the World War II Office of Strategic Services were gradually replaced, in many agencies, by thousands and thousands of analysts largely engaged in "production," that is, the nearly industrial process of extracting from the voluminous collection of both technical and human intelligence agencies information of value for transmission to a set of largely anonymous "customers." In many instances, the industrial nature of this effort was reinforced by a process that did not involve the direct involvement of living, breathing customers, but of bureaucratized (even industrialized) "requirements lists," produced at some level and renewed at some level by the customers, but too often the belated and often outdated perceptions of staffs built solely for the purpose of producing such lists.

In the information environment of the Cold War, the relatively (and only relatively) small volume of material involved and the relatively static nature of the adversary permitted this often-creaky system to function, although never with great agility or efficiency. Nevertheless, it worked, creakily and inefficiently in many respects, but no more inefficiently (and ponderously) than the major adversaries it was deployed against.

3. THE ONGOING INFORMATION REVOLUTION

If the end of the Cold War (and the subsequent loss of target focus) marks one component of the environmental shift that has transformed national security in the last two decades, the information revolution, in all its consequences is the factor that did not end but which intensified. It is important to note at the start that the emphasis here is not on information technology per se, though the information revolution clearly begins at the technological level. The information and communications technology of the twenty-first century is, literally, the carrier for a far broader range of effects, wonderfully described over a decade ago by Frances Cairncross as "the death of distance" (1997).

The implications of this truly revolutionary change in information need not be elaborated here.[3] One implication on intelligence, however, must be addressed. Until the twentieth century, as Michael Herman has long noted, intelligence equaled information. Whether it came from clandestine or "open" sources rarely mattered (Herman 1996). The historical reality was that political and military leaders (especially the latter) generally operated in an environment in which accurate "intelligence" generally meant little more than they could observe with their own eyes. Any—repeat, any—information that spoke to the health of a political rival or the state of the roads on an army's line of march, was precious because information on such matters was generally both scarce and painfully (sometimes tragically) unreliable.

In this environment, information scarcity was the norm not the exception. In the twentieth century, with the rise of totalitarian regimes whose first (or nearly so) order of business was information control in service of state security, even the flows of information formerly available, especially in the period from the Congress of Vienna to the First World War, when the Great Powers operated with a high degree of openness and comity, were closed off. The Red Army did not exactly welcome officers to observe its operations or maneuvers. In the case of both Nazi Germany and the Soviet Union, such outside observers as did obtain access to military equipment and bases, for example, were likely to be treated to deception operations far more sophisticated than those generally experienced a generation or two before.

This development forced responses even from democratic states. One important and direct consequence was the development of larger and more complex intelligence organizations to collect, evaluate, and analyze information. The other, slightly more indirect, was a steady increase in the emphasis on clandestinely acquired information, with the resulting devaluation of information openly acquired. This development, already underway in the Second World War, accelerated in the Cold War, especially in what became a "golden age of technical intelligence." For the first time in history, keeping a commander informed of what was over the next hill could be, at least in many circumstances, as easy as showing the commander a picture (or image) of the reverse slope. Moreover, the satellites producing those images were also capable of providing information from other sensors, including signals and measurement intelligence.

Technology has nevertheless proven at the very least a "dual-use" factor. Within a generation, the satellite imagery that was one of America's most jealously guarded secrets of the Cold War became a commercial product. And encryption, once reserved for communication of the most sensitive secrets of state, became ubiquitous. All the while, of course, the volume of information increased at exponential rates. The characteristic information condition of intelligence, that is, information scarcity, almost overnight became an environment of information overload. Roberta Wohlstetter's use of the signal to noise ratio in intelligence and warning remains valid (Wohlstetter 1962). It's just that the imbalance between noise and signal has increased dramatically.

This is not to say that only the "noise" has increased. So has the signal, if by that we mean the amount of information being produced in a global environment on issues affecting national security. In the Cold War, it was easy to say that the placement and readiness of Soviet forces in the western Soviet Union or Eastern Europe was high-priority national security information. Information on a potential transmission of virus from an animal to humans may have been important, but not critically or immediately as a national security issue.

As the first decade of the twenty-first century has made clear, the military and political intentions and capabilities of rival states, whether peer rivals, near peers, or regional peers, continue to represent a significant measure of what we may call the "standing requirements" for intelligence services. Other traditional issues for intelligence collection and analysis, including economics and trade, also show no sign of disappearing from the agendas of intelligence recipients. At the same time, however, terrorism, international public health, food safety, climate change, large-scale human rights abuses and other issues, that at one time may have been peripheral to national security concerns, or tangential to great-power interactions of confrontations, have assumed greater (and greatly volatile) significance in national security affairs. The reality of such a varied and volatile environment will shape the intelligence future, including the future of intelligence analysis.

4. BEYOND PRODUCTION: THE ANALYTIC FUTURE

At least in the American intelligence services, generations of new employees have been introduced to the "intelligence production cycle." For readers who slept through that briefing or never received it: the recipients of intelligence have information needs, which they transmit to intelligence producers, who then transform information needs into intelligence requirements. For the most part, this means looking at the respective sources of intelligence (or "ints," as in humint, sigint, etc.) and asking which "int" can support which need. Leaving aside the all-too-human and all-too-bureaucratic tendency for these sessions to deteriorate into a frenzy of every int responding to every need (except for some politically or bureaucratically unattractive ones) with "We can, we can!" this process then leads to the assignment of collection requirements to the various int-specific agencies. Who then collect against that requirement, using their respective sources and methods, process the collection by various means, and convert it into a format (or product) that is then conveyed to the requestor. Who, in the final stage of the cycle, then provides feedback that can then be incorporated into another round of requirements setting, setting in motion another production cycle.

Mild sarcasm notwithstanding, the darned thing worked. In an industrial age, in an otherwise industrial selling, against a relatively fixed and finite set of targets, this not only worked (with less than full efficiency, to be sure); it even has value for the future (Krizan 1999). Some intelligence problems will almost certainly lend themselves to this process for many years to come. Such assurances notwithstanding, the production cycle, even modernized to resemble a "production process," will be inadequate to meet the needs of the intelligence future, especially but not exclusively the analytic future.

In part, this reflects the limits of the very idea of production, let alone its collection component. For years, experienced analysts in several agencies could joke about the younger analyst who, asked where his or her "traffic" came from, would respond by mentioning the room or office where they picked up the day's collection "take." Over time, the room may have disappeared, replaced by electronic delivery of newly collected material, but the process varied little beyond the format. To a greater degree in "single-source" agencies (the National Security Agency, the National Geospatial-Intelligence Agency and its predecessors, for example), but still to a lesser degree in the "all-source" world, analysis was a byproduct of collection. It would be only a slight exaggeration to say that the Cold War American intelligence apparatus ultimately became a heavily capitalized data-collection industry, with renewal of the industry and its capital investment as a major—if not the major—interest of the community's leadership. Estimates may vary of the ratio of spending on collection versus analysis, but whether that ratio was 8:1 or 16:1, the emphasis was clear.

Moreover, most of this collection expenditure was on clandestine collection, especially technical collection, for in truth, the Cold War represents, at least from the Cuban Missile Crisis, a golden age for technical intelligence.[4] Working against a denied target in the Soviet Union (or a set of denied targets, including Soviet allies and surrogates), this was an occurrence of consequence for the United States and its allies. The Soviets, emblematic of twentieth-century totalitarian states, placed information control at the center of state security efforts, and they were by and large very good at these efforts. For the United States and its allies, experiencing a golden age in technical intelligence during the Cold War was an enormous and fortunate achievement, although the use of the word fortunate should not be taken to minimize the innovation, imagination, and effort that made such good fortune possible.

If there is to be an "intelligence process cycle" for the twenty-first century with an equally successful outcome, collection seems an inadequate description of the component bearing responsibility for gathering, assembling, and *creating* information. First of all, the range of national security issues and the nature of the actors engaged in those issues will little resemble the powerful but ponderous totalitarians of the last century. Denied targets and closed societies will remain, as in North Korea, but these will be exceptions. Dangerous exceptions to be sure, but exceptions nonetheless (Glionna 2008). A more characteristic issue will be the closed or secure project within a relatively (to one degree or another) open environment. Iran's nuclear establishments, and certainly its plans for its nuclear effort, will be closed and treated as state secrets. But Iran itself is a significantly open society, as an hour or two on the web will attest, and open-source information and expertise will gain in importance even as Iran

continues its "secret" programs and resembles, in certain areas, an at-least-partially closed state.[5] Non-state issues in national security (that is to say issues that exist largely apart from the interests of intent of a single government) will be even more "open," though the policies of states in encouraging, discouraging, or otherwise dealing with a given development will remain, to varying degrees, state secrets.

This is certainly true of such issues as climate change. It is almost certainly truer of such issues as demographic change and international public health. At first instance, the intelligence analyst's challenge in dealing with public health will not be to task clandestine collection resources, but to know as much about this issue, or some component of it, as his or her counterpart at the Public Health Service, the Centers for Disease Control, or in one of several schools and departments at the nearest state university.

This raises, as it must, the issue of open-source information, which the author prefers to describe as an issue of both open-source information and open-source expertise. The bank robber Willie Sutton famously said he robbed banks "because that's where the money is." Twenty-first-century analysts will truly need to rely first on "collection," but to a greater degree research and communication with open sources and experts for the simple reason "that's where the information is."

The American intelligence community has been under pressure to rely more on open-source information for over a decade. And it has taken steps to respond to this pressure. But it has not made the conceptual change from acting because the Intelligence Reform Act mandates it or because Congress keeps bringing it up to acting because it fully acknowledges that the twenty-first-century operating environment demands the change. It must make the fundamental shift of believing that in the twenty-first-century intelligence will be about information, not about secrets. Some part of the information will be secret or otherwise classified of course, either because it reflects sources and methods or because it reflects the confidentiality of advice provided to the president and other decision makers. The fact remains, however, that an age of intelligence, golden or not, is over.

This is not to suggest that the United States should retire its clandestine collection capabilities. It does mean that the balance, first of all in investment, but more importantly in focus, must shift toward "where the information is." As noted above, the Intelligence Reform and Terrorism Prevention Act mandated greater use of open source information. In the early days of the "DNI era," implementation of this seemed to offer great promise. Without question, progress in both open source and its intimate companion, information sharing, have been made. But the reality remains that open source, however it may now be described at the DNI level as "the source of first resort," remains a stepchild in US intelligence. Add to that the truly unfortunate decision to relegate, and there can be no gentler word, open-source issues to the "collection" directorate of the office of the DNI, and then to sublet open source operations to a renamed Foreign Broadcast Information Service, itself long a stepchild within CIA, and the outcome was predictable. Whatever progress the DNI has achieved has been inadequate to keep pace with the emerging information environment. In other words, progress at pace .2X, in an environment moving at pace X, ultimately translates into "falling behind" or even failure. The late Peter Drucker once noted that inside an organization there are only costs; the benefits are felt outside. And subordinating open source to "collectors" would have been like IBM leaving the decision on personal computers to executives schooled in mainframes. In fact, to a great degree that happened, with similar and predictable consequences for IBM.[6]

Accepting open-source information and expertise as the source of first resort means nothing without a shift in the power balance within the US intelligence community. This means empowering analysts to be researchers, and it means finally achieving the long-stated goal of creating an analyst-driven rather than collection-driven intelligence system. This means empowering analysts to fill "collection gaps" not by simply tasking collection components (although this must remain part of the strategy for filling what should be called "analytic gaps" or "knowledge gaps"), but by empowering them to commission research, build their own networks of outside experts, and to do so without begging permission from collectors and security officers. Empowered analysts will not just "process" collected information or data; they will be intimately involved in the creation of new information, in collaboration, it should be emphasized, with "collectors" and others, including security and counterintelligence officers.

This is a critical point. Much has been made of former DNI McConnell's decision to update the "need-to-know" principle in American intelligence

to one premised on "responsibility to provide."[7] But this remains little more than a goal in an operating environment in which the potential benefits of sharing information, building networks, and so on, are not weighted equally with security concerns.

5. ANALYST AND CLIENT: A FIDUCIARY RELATIONSHIP

Empowering the analyst means empowering the analyst's role as fiduciary agent for the recipient of that analysis. Here again, the industrial model of intelligence production shows its age. The idea that the "customer" provides information needs, which are then converted into intelligence requirements, which are in turn parceled out to the various agencies, which in turn collected and processed information, which was then analyzed and turned into "product" of various forms, which is then provided to customers, who on digesting the product create a revised set of needs, provided a certain rough transparency to an otherwise obscure process.

On the other hand, it rarely ever operated that way. Too often, needs were bureaucratized into requirements lists, which may or may not have reflected the needs of the current set of "customers." Over time, of course, as the flow of information and intelligence increased exponentially in volume, so did the production of product, all of which ended up in the in baskets of customers far too busy to update their requirements. From time to time, agencies accused of "collecting for collection sake," would come up with questionnaires and other devices for measuring "customer satisfaction," often to the puzzlement of "customers" who could not figure out who these people were who were submitting this call for data or why those people, whomever they were, thought the customer had time to fill out some questionnaire.

Too often, the production cycle became the production conveyer, with the end of the line being the burn bag or, in a more recent time, the delete key. Two factors contributed to this. The first was a desire, laudable on its own terms, to keep the customer out of the production process itself. This was laudable, first of all, to avoid politicization; secondly because, as noted, the customers were busy.

The second factor was a tendency to see the analyst as the marketing representative for the collector. That is, the analyst represented his or her collection "int." In almost a decade coordinating national intelligence estimates, I cannot recall a CIA analyst announcing "you're on your own on this one, gang. The humint on this is terrible." Or an NSA analyst saying "the only material we have on this is from a foreign service that is the dumping ground for every incompetent in the ruling class." One might notice a certain reticence on the part of an agency representative, a preoccupation with shuffling his or her papers when called on, but rarely a willingness to support a judgment that seemed at odds with the information coming from that agency's collection.

This is not as craven as it may sound. Group think is at least as dangerous as a failure to integrate analysis, and there is a certain wisdom—almost in Madisonian terms—of having agency analysts defend their agency's collection.[8] Excessive integration (and the "group think" likely to emerge from such excess) of the American intelligence establishment remains as much a threat to an effective intelligence effort as does inadequate integration. It may be, however, that we are now at a point where some shift in the sense of "who the analyst works for" is required. This may entail supplanting the view of the recipient of intelligence from customer to client, with the analyst's fiduciary responsibility toward that client superseding his or her responsibility to an individual agency.

Fiduciary relationships, as opposed to commercial relationships, have at their core the belief that the professional's primary responsibility is to the achievement of the client's interests, not the professional's. A car salesman may see a personal ethical responsibility in suggesting that a car is larger than I need. He or she does not have a professional responsibility to do so. My financial advisor has, on the other hand, a fiduciary responsibility to advise me against a sale or purchase he considers unwise. In the end, if I insist, the advisor should put through the sale. Unless, of course, he or she believes that to do so would undermine his or her status as a professional. I can, along the same lines, decline my physician's advice that bungee jumping is not exactly what my aging retinas need. He can, in turn, suggest that if I ignore his advice I should seek another specialist.

All of this suggests a more interactive replacement for the traditional production cycle. When CIA launched its first Galileo project in 2005,[9] the judges were astonished by the number of entrants urging the intelligence community to pursue wiki and blog technologies. Many thought this was simply unacceptable, but within a very short time intellipedia was born, and one gathers that something approaching routine blogging now takes place not only among analysts but with clients as well.

It is right to look with some concern at such interaction between analysts and clients, as well, one might suggest, as between collectors and clients. But here we are. This is the information environment we are in, for better or for worse. The most likely outcome, of course, is that it will be "for better *and* for worse." Healthy institutions, almost by virtue of their health and alertness to their operational environments, tend to maximize the value of such developments while minimizing their downsides. The Army's response to companycommander.com is an extraordinary case of institutional health. Faced with an uncontrolled—along with unencrypted and unauthorized—exchange of information from company and platoon officers in Iraq, on personal-computer email, the Army faced an obvious decision: shut this down and punish the violators. Instead, the Army took on companycommander.com (now part of Army Knowledge Online), providing ground rules and security.

This is what healthy institutions do. They align with their environment, they embrace change, and, in the national security professions, they do so with the result of enhancing the odds on mission success, and perhaps saving lives. A fresh look at the intelligence process and the roles therein can achieve that result for American intelligence. At the center of this effort must be an analytic workforce empowered to act as the fiduciary agents of the clients they serve. If one of the concerns with such a development is that of potential "clientitis," we need to look at our last issue, the ethics of analysis.

6. EMPOWERING THE ANALYST: RESEARCH AND ANALYTIC DEVELOPMENT

One consequence of the information environment of the last twenty years or so has been the phenomenon known as "volume, velocity, variety." With seemingly staggering speed, and with no prospect the phenomenon will slow or disappear, information scarcity, the characteristic intelligence environment since it became the world's second oldest profession has given way to chronic, systemic information overload.

To a degree, the information environment that has produced this result has also provided tools for coping with it, part of the ongoing "dual-edged" impact of most information processes. Information technology in various forms continues to be employed in ever-expanding ways to support the analytic effort. In the American case, the surge of investment since September 2001 has brought a dramatic increase in both human and technical resources. Less certain is whether growth (or "increased production") can ever keep pace with an information environment exploding at Moore's Law pace. It is even less certain that growth can serve as the strategy for dealing with an operational environment in which the target is expanding across multiple (volume, variety, velocity) dimensions. Finally, it is doubtful, again citing the American example, that the budget surge of the post-9/11 era will continue. One consequence of the release of the top figure for America's National Intelligence Program will be that both Congress and the public will weigh future increases of a budget pushing past $50 billion per year severely against other, competing needs.[10]

A final consideration in coping with this explosion is that the client community is unlikely to expand apace with the growth of collection. In other words, growth at the front end of the process does not guarantee commensurate growth in processing and analytic resources. Nor does it promise any relief for the user confronting extraordinary "in-box" demands.

What is to be done? One option would be to insist that growth remains a strategy and that intelligence occupies a privileged call on public resources. This could be described as "the way we've always done it—but more!" strategy. An alternative would be to seek qualitative rather than quantitative strategies for dealing with the challenges ahead. For the analyst this means a direct confrontation with the demand for increased production. One chronic qualitative concern, often expressed (internally but also by external commissions and oversight bodies) but never fully acted on, is the tendency for current or short-term analysis to drive out strategic or long-term analysis.

Perhaps the time has come to reverse that trend, with the explicit stipulation that this is not a problem that can be "grown out of." Adding an additional 10 or 15 percent to the analytic workforce (unlikely in the budget environments of the next several years) with no changes in strategy and leadership discipline will only add to the glut. As an alternative, intelligence leaders need to take a cue (actually more than one) from their military colleagues.

The first change should involve commitment to a "staffing ratio" that commits a percentage of the analytic workforce to long-term or strategic work.

Whether that involves 5 percent, 10 percent, or some other number is less important than a commitment to "fence off" this investment from deflection to current issues.

Such an arrangement would also require the development of structures to support the long-term research effort. Again, the military provides an important instructive model, in the research centers located at all of the major service war and staff colleges. Intelligence researchers would use similar facilities not only to conduct their own studies, but to extend their analytic and research networks, and to support teaching and other mentoring of less-senior analysts. Simply stated, many of the truly important innovations in the American military since the 1970s have come from a commitment to such long-term research and (human) development efforts. The Center for Army Lessons Learned and the lessons-learned culture it and similar efforts elsewhere in the military have built and strengthened, radical (in terms of the military status quo) efforts such as Colonel Douglas MacGregor's *Breaking the Phalanx,* and even the recent field manuals on counterinsurgency and stability operations would simply not have been possible without policies and structures that balance the short-term against the longer term (MacGregor 1997). If intelligence (and with it the State Department and homeland security) are to carry their weight, with the military, in the twenty-first-century national security establishment, they must have both a leadership commitment to such efforts and the resources to make those efforts meaningful and successful.

7. THE ETHICS OF TWENTY-FIRST-CENTURY ANALYSIS

For most analysts, the controversy over the role of intelligence in failing to warn of the 9/11 attacks (connecting the dots, and so on), however severe, paled in comparison to many of the accusations raised over the role of intelligence analysis in the period preceding the 2003 invasion of Iraq. It is one thing, even in the most severe of circumstances (Pearl Harbor or 9/11), to be found wanting in skill or methodology. It is quite another to be thought of as complicit in a plot to politicize intelligence as part of a concerted effort with policymakers to mislead a country (or countries, in this case) debating whether to go to war.

However tragic the costs of a failure to warn or analyze correctly, analytic failures are, in the intelligence profession, a cost of doing business. This cost, in the most extreme cases, of course, is measured in human lives, a burden that cannot be ignored or understated. But physicians lose patients, and any medical student who cannot cope with that reality should consider other career options. The same is true for intelligence professions.

"Cooking the books" remains, nevertheless, a far deeper and more corrosive infraction. This is especially true for intelligence officers serving in open and democratic societies that have made the decision to permit the creation of powerful and secret institutions of state in the common defense. Historically, professions had been identified by their commitment to a code of ethics, in part because of fiduciary responsibilities of the sort described above.

In larger measure, an ethical sense is essential to public service (where all actions are taken with the public's money and in the public's name) and most centrally in those public services that authorize its members to perform actions enjoined from the public at large. Police officers and judges can use lethal force or incarcerate their fellow citizens, the military are authorized the privilege of conducting societally approved violence. Intelligence officers are permitted to lie, deceive, and eavesdrop on other persons, and to do so under a veil of secrecy.

In the American case, the intelligence services operated in this environment without meaningful supervision for the first three decades of their modern existence, a situation reversed after the 1970s. In other countries, even democratic ones, the ratio of intelligence history to overseen intelligence history is even more dramatic. That notwithstanding, the reality of external (usually legislative or parliamentary) oversight, in some cases augmented by judicial review, is now almost universally understood if not fully practiced.

The first ethical principle for intelligence analysts, then, is one they share with their colleagues in other aspects of the intelligence establishments. That is, they must understand that the days of intelligence as a secret service operating under no restraint but reasons of state or "the wishes of the crown" are over. In the democracies, intelligence will operate under law and within the values of their larger, sponsoring society. They must understand, as must their publics, that they operate at times on the edges of that value system, and that many of their fellow citizens would prefer not to do the things intelligence officers (or police officers, for example) do in their name. But the basic principle remains:

the limits of conduct permitted for an intelligence service's conduct will be set and must be set external to that service.

For analysts, much of the discussion that follows springs from the desire to put into practice the long-espoused sense that the purpose of intelligence is "to bring truth to power." Before proceeding, we must stipulate that no amount of expertise, no level of exposure to information—openly or clandestinely acquired—gives intelligence a monopoly on truth. The supply rooms of intelligence agencies do not list crystal balls as standard office equipment. We need to consider this reality when we think of the role of the recipient of intelligence, and his or her responsibility to choose to accept the judgments of intelligence, to reject them in favor of other sources (including past experience, personal knowledge, or even "gut" instinct), or to accept selective portions of the intelligence presented.

That last option may appear problematic, at least within near memory of a period in which the "cherry picking" of intelligence was described and was frequently and loudly denounced as both unusual and unusually venal. In reality, of course, decision makers, civilian and military, have always used intelligence selectively, and they always will. Sometimes successfully and to their credit; at other times, less successfully. The reality is that intelligence will never be the only "source" with which decision makers can and must deal. Many years ago, a president of the American Historical Association gave as his presidential address something called "Every Man His Own Historian," (Becker 1931) and to a great degree, every decision maker in the twenty-first century will be his or her own intelligence collector and intelligence analyst. This has always been the case, and intelligence has often found itself overruled by decision makers on grounds of prior experience, alternative (and private or even personal) sources of information available to the decision maker, or an unwillingness to reconsider long held beliefs. We should not, to be sure, eliminate total folly as an element in the decision-making process.

It will always be so. In an age where the decision maker can turn to his or her laptop and either e-mail a private network of experts or "Google" the subject under discussion, the role of the decision maker in selecting from various assessments (or using those assessments selectively) grows ever larger. The analyst has a responsibility to bring truth to power; there is no corollary responsibility on the part of the decision maker to accept that version of the truth, though it is to be hoped that its rejection is based on something more than its inconvenience to a decision or policy.

One of the reforms of the Intelligence Reform and Terrorism Prevention Act was the establishment of an analytic integrity officer within the office of the Director of National Intelligence. In the first phase of that program, the analytic integrity officer has made significant progress in establishing doctrine, to use a military term not altogether popular in "civilian" intelligence services, governing analytic standards.[11] One can argue that much of their work (e.g., properly describing the quality and reliability of sources, distinguishing between intelligence fact and analytic judgment, maintaining analytic consistency or highlighting changes in analysis) reflects "standards" that should have been implicit in analysis from all time and for all time.

There is, however, the virtue of making such standards explicit and indoctrinating (another often unpopular term) analysts to understand that they have a professional responsibility to those standards that must at least require them to resist such factors as "the way we've always done it," or "this is the way my supervisor wants it," or "this is what my agency's collection says." It may be too early to say whether these standards become imbedded in the professional identity of American intelligence analysts, but their promulgation nevertheless represents a large step toward the declaration that the analyst is more than an end stage to a production process, one in which the interest of the producer can challenge if not supersede the interest of the client.

Failures and missteps notwithstanding, the creation and operation of large-scale, secret, and powerful intelligence organizations within the world's democracies is one of the significant achievements in twentieth-century governance. These organizations did not emerge full-grown or fully developed, but changed over time and with changing times. Late in the century, the democracies adjusted to the demands to bring these most "secret services" under increased measures of legal regulation and legislative or parliamentary oversight. For analysts as for other professionals within the intelligence services, an understanding of their responsibilities within these frameworks is a final, critical ethical consideration. As twenty-first-century analysts grapple with all the challenges outlined above (and more than a few not mentioned here), they need remember that

they operate on license from societies that permit their intelligence services to operate in ways not permitted most citizens. As police officers and military personnel are warranted to use lethal force on society's behalf and under rules created not by the services themselves but by leadership external to those services, so intelligence officers (including but not limited to analysts) must operate within similar frameworks.[12] The late-twentieth-century development that places even the most secret of a democratic society's secret services under legal, legislative, and even judicial oversight represents an extraordinary chapter in the history of intelligence. It remains yet another part of the complex, uncertain, and often volatile operating environment facing twenty-first-century intelligence professionals, including analysts.

QUESTIONS FOR FURTHER DISCUSSION

1. How is the information revolution changing the way analysts go about their business?
2. Do you think generational change will produce a revolution in intelligence production?
3. What problems are likely to follow in the wake of new ways of producing intelligence?
4. Can intelligence professionals "manage" the information revolution? Or are they just along for the ride?

ENDNOTES

1. One development external to the Intelligence Community should also be noted here, and that is the growth of intelligence studies as an academic discipline, including programs at undergraduate and graduate levels focused on intelligence analysis.
2. This is especially true for the United States, which, at least since the 1970s, had placed a far smaller portion of its "intelligence" efforts into counterintelligence or state security efforts than most nations.
3. Not, it must be noted, the first such revolution. And almost certainly not the most important (Eisenstein 1979).
4. The reference here to "a" golden age rather than "the" golden age is purposeful. Institutions, like civilizations, may have more than one golden age, depending on such factors as leadership, creativity, and success in dealing with changing environments.
5. It is worth keeping in mind, in Iran and in other states, even "technical" programs, such as those involving weapons development, are never *just* technical

programs. For the impact of political decisions on such programs, see DeVilliers et al. (1993).

6. More than a decade ago, Ruth David, then the deputy director for science and technology at the CIA, spoke frequently of the need for an "agile intelligence enterprise," with the thought that such an enterprise would emphasize "speed, flexibility, and capacity through collaborative operations." Although one can point to progress in making American intelligence more collaborative if not more agile, the question remains of measuring progress not by the internal metric of "how far we've come," but by the external metric of what the external environment demands (David 1997).

7. This is an important initiative on the part of the DNI. Nevertheless, American intelligence continues to operate in an environment in which the value of protecting information, including sources and methods, remains something to be balanced against the value of sharing that information. Without question, over time this had evolved toward a situation in which risk management or cost/benefit analysis of whether and how to expose information could become merely a "cost analysis" or even a "potential cost analysis," with little reference to real or potential benefits. That said, a serious research and investment effort in twenty-first-century intelligence requires inclusion of counterintelligence and security in such an effort. Perhaps the outcome is primacy for "responsibility to share" with a renewed understanding of the validity of "need to know."

8. It was commonplace during the 1970s for journalists to applaud the leadership on the Senate Watergate committee of Senator Sam Ervin of North Carolina, then to lament that for some reason this visionary leader continued to vote for tobacco subsidies. In the best Madison terms, of course Senator Ervin voted for such subsidies, confident he could represent the economic interests of his constituents, permit his reelection, and be assured that senators from other states would outvote him.

9. Galileo, now under the sponsorship of the DNI, is a project in which intelligence officers submit papers, produced on their own time, on some aspect of innovation as applied to the intelligence process.

10. Even within the national security, intelligence will face pressure from military forces requiring significant reinvestment after extended wartime deployments, state and local homeland security agencies seeking federal funding to compensate for depressed local budgets, and even a possible desire to place more investment on diplomatic and international development instruments of national security.

11. Under the leadership of first professor Nancy Tucker of Georgetown and then professor Richard Immerman of Temple University.

12. See Hehir (2002) for a review of the just-war tradition, one possible frame of reference for intelligence officers. A question this author puts to his University of Maryland students is whether one can substitute "intelligence" for "war" in Fr. Hehir's discussion of just-war tradition and find that tradition applicable. The volume edited by Jan Goldman (2006) is also useful. James Olson's work (2006) has the advantage beyond utility of also being fun, with the inclusion of fifty or so ethically challenging scenarios for intelligence action, along with comments from academics, former intelligence officials, clergy, and students, among others.

REFERENCES

Arquilla, J. 2008. *Worst Enemy: The Reluctant Transformation of the American Military.* Chicago: Ivan Dee.

Barger, D. 2005. *Toward a Revolution in Intelligence Affairs.* Santa Monica: RAND Corporation.

Becker, C. 1931. *Everyman His Own Historian.* Presidential Address, American Historical Association.

Cairncross, F. 1997. *The Death of Distance.* Boston: Harvard University Business School Press.

David, R. A. 1997. *The Agile Intelligence Enterprise: Enhancing Speed, Flexibility, and Capacity through Collaborative Operations.* Draft in possession of the author.

DeVilliers, J. W., R. Jardine, and M. Reiss. 1993. Why South Africa Gave Up the Bomb. *Foreign Affairs* (Nov./Dec.).

Eisenstein, E. 1979. *The Printing Press as an Agent of Change.* Cambridge: Cambridge University Press.

George, R. Z., and J. B. Bruce, eds. 2008. *Analyzing Intelligence.* Washington, D.C.: Georgetown University Press.

Glionna, J. M. 2008. The Information Fortress Known as North Korea. *Los Angeles Times* (November 14).

Goldman, J., ed. 2006. *The Ethics of Spying.* Lanham, Md.: Scarecrow Press.

Hehir, B. 2002. International Politics, Ethics, and the Use of Force. *Georgetown Journal of International Affairs* (Summer/Fall).

Herman, M. 1996. *Intelligence Power in Peace and War.* Cambridge: Cambridge University Press.

Heuer Jr., R. J. 2006. *The Psychology of Intelligence Analysis.* New York: Novinka Books.

Krizan, L. 1999. Intelligence Essentials for Everyone. Washington, D.C.: Joint Military Intelligence College, 1999.

Lowenthal, M. M. 2008. *Intelligence from Secrets to Policy.* 4th ed. Washington, D.C.: Congressional Quarterly.

Macgregor, D. A. 1997. *Breaking the Phalanx: A New Design for Landpower in the 21st Century.* Westport, Conn.: Praeger.

Moore, D. T. 2006. *Critical Thinking and Intelligence Analysis.* Washington, D.C.: Joint Military Intelligence College.

Nolte, W.M. 2005. Rethinking War and Intelligence. In *Rethinking the Principles of War; ed.* A. McIvor. Annapolis: Naval Institute Press.

Olson, J. M. 2006. *Fair Play: The Moral Dilemmas of Spying.* Washington, D.C.: Potomac Books.

Owens, W. A. 2000. *Lifting the Fog of War.* New York: Farrar, Strauss, Giroux.

Robb, J. 2007. *Brave New War: The Next Stage of Terrorism and the End of Globalization.* Hoboken: John Wiley and Sons.

Shachtman, N. 2007. How Technology Almost Lost the War: In Iraq, the Critical Networks Are Social—Not Electronic. *Wired* 15, no. 12.

Wohlstetter, R. 1962. *Pearl Harbor: Warning and Decision.* Palo Alto: Stanford University Press.

Reprinted with permission from William M. Nolte, "Intelligence Analysis in an Uncertain Environment," in Loch K. Johnson, ed., *The Oxford Handbook of Intelligence Studies* (New York: Oxford University Press, 2010): 404–421.

13. INTELLIGENCE AND THE WAR IN IRAQ

RICHARD A. BEST, JR.

When only a rudimentary capability to produce weapons of mass destruction was discovered in Iraq following America's invasion of Iraq in 2003, many commentators saw this as evidence of intelligence failure. As a Congressional Research Service analyst notes, however, it is wrong to lay the blame for strategic or political failure at the doorstep of the intelligence community.

SUMMARY

A continuing issue for Congress is the question of whether the U.S. Intelligence Community failed to provide accurate information about Iraqi capabilities to develop and use weapons of mass destruction (WMD) and whether the Bush Administration systematically misused intelligence to garner support for launching Operation Iraqi Freedom in March 2003 and for continuing military operations in Iraq. The Senate Intelligence Committee submitted a report on the Intelligence Community's performance in July 2004 (S.Rept. 108-301), but a follow-on assessment of the use of intelligence has not been prepared and has become the source of controversy that led to a rare closed session of the Senate on November 1, 2005. This report explores in general terms the relationship between the production of intelligence and the making of policy as reflected in the period prior to the war against Iraq in March 2003 and the implications for Congress.

BACKGROUND

Intelligence has an important but not conclusive role in support of the policymaking process. Intelligence agencies collect information, process, and analyze it; they then disseminate analytical products to officials throughout the federal government. Policymakers, however, base their decisions on a wide variety of factors, including available intelligence, but also on their own assessment of the costs and benefits of a course of action (or inaction), considerations of geopolitical objectives, ideology, available resources, diplomatic (and domestic

political) risks—a variety of factors well beyond the purview of intelligence agencies. Even when official justifications for a chosen course of action highlight the conclusions of intelligence estimates, there are usually multiple factors involved. Intelligence may be good or bad and policies may be good or bad, but in the real world good policy may be made in the absence of perfect intelligence and sound intelligence may not preclude making poor policy. This is not to say that intelligence is irrelevant to policymaking, but that it is almost invariably imperfect because hostile foreign countries and groups work hard to mask their capabilities and intentions, and many factors are inherently unforeseeable. In addition, intelligence agencies do not always perform at maximum effectiveness.

Subsequent to the Persian Gulf War of 1991, the U.S. Intelligence Community supplied vast quantities of information and analysis on Iraq to policymakers, including Congress. Much of the intelligence derived from U.S. national collection systems—satellites, intercepted signals, agent reports, and the like. Some derived from liaison relationships with the intelligence services of the United Kingdom and other countries. Whereas the mass of documentation was large, the quality of the collected data and the analysis based on it has been criticized, with many pointing to the absence of direct reporting on Saddam Hussein's close advisers and his weapons acquisition offices. Postwar assessments have in general concluded that available human intelligence (humint) failed to provide reliable information on decisions made within Saddam Hussein's inner circle and, most notably, on Iraqi capabilities for producing and delivering weapons of mass destruction (WMD) and the extent of Iraqi WMD stockpiles.[1]

Despite the importance of intelligence, the evidence collected and analyzed by U.S. intelligence agencies in recent years may not have been the central factor in framing U.S. policies towards Iraq. The concerns that the U.S. and other countries had in regard to Iraq were not under dispute—Hussein had used WMD against Iran and against his own people; he had pursued aggressive attacks on neighboring states; he had failed to comply with U.N. demands in regard to WMD restrictions. Some senior policymakers in the Bush Administration had come into office with a deep conviction that Saddam Hussein's government presented an ongoing threat to U.S. and Western interests in the Middle East.[2] These views may not have been directly influenced by subsequent intelligence reporting; senior officials may even have discounted some analysts' conclusions because they recalled that intelligence agencies were caught by surprise when the extent of Iraq's nuclear programs in the late 1980s was revealed after the Persian Gulf War.

Even with widespread agreement on the nature of the Iraqi regime and the general parameters of its policies, there were differing viewpoints on the most appropriate response, both at the U.N. and in the U.S. However, because much of the Bush Administration's explanation of its case, especially beginning in the summer of 2002, included references to intelligence judgments, especially about Iraqi WMDs, the wide-ranging debate about Iraq in the U.S. came to focus on intelligence judgments. This was the case in 2002–2003 and, given postwar assessments of prewar intelligence, has remained so. In particular, the prewar intelligence estimate that Iraq was reconstituting an extensive nuclear program was in large measure discredited.[3] The absence of evidence of pervasive and operational ties between Iraq and Al Qaeda has also brought prewar assessments into question.

The Senate Intelligence Committee's July 2004 report set forth the limitations of prewar intelligence at considerable length.[4] Although the report was unanimous, there have been sharp disagreements over the question of whether the committee should also address the use of pre-war intelligence by the Administration and by Members of Congress. At one point, Chairman Roberts argues that, "The threshold question for the committee should be whether our intelligence agencies produced reasonable and accurate analysis, not how that intelligence was used by policymakers."[5] Vice Chairman Rockefeller, on the other hand, cited Section 14(a)(1) of S.Res. 400, which serves as a charter for the Select Intelligence Committee and includes "use" of information as a matter of committee oversight. He maintained that, "the committee's Republican chairman has refused to look at the whole picture, excluding from the inquiry the subject of how intelligence was used, or potentially misused, and whether policymakers in any way shaped the intelligence they received."[6] An agreement was announced in February 2004 that the terms of reference of the committee's investigation would address the issue of whether public statements by U.S. officials were substantiated by intelligence information.[7] S.Rept. 108-301 provided the committee's treatment of prewar intelligence assessments in July 2004; it served as phase I of the committee's work.

The preparation of phase II, which is to include the committee's assessment of the use of intelligence by government officials, has been the source of continued differences of opinion among Members. Senator Roberts indicated that preparation of the phase II report was "very close," but Senator Rockefeller maintained that "only token work, at best, has been done."[8] The persistence of the disagreement was cited by Senator Reid, the Minority Leader, in his call for an unusual closed session of the Senate on November 1, 2005, to discuss the status of phase II. Discussions on phase II have since been undertaken by members of the Senate Intelligence Committee, but no schedule has been published for completion; media reports suggest that differences remain.[9]

EXECUTIVE BRANCH COMMENTS ON INTELLIGENCE ON IRAQ PRIOR TO MILITARY OPERATIONS

A brief review of the Bush Administration's public statements provides some insights into the Intelligence Community's contribution to the Administration policymaking on Iraq. The lack of definitive intelligence was a recurring theme even as the determination to confront Iraq hardened in the months after the defeat of the Taliban regime in Afghanistan. In an August 2002 speech, Vice President Cheney warned about the threat from

Iraq and addressed the availability of intelligence: "Many of us are convinced that Saddam will acquire nuclear weapons fairly soon. Just how soon, we cannot really gauge. Intelligence is an uncertain business, even in the best of circumstances."[10]

The Vice President articulated reasons for forcing regime change, basing his argument on a comprehensive assessment of Iraq's record before and after the Persian Gulf War of 1991, especially U.N. Security Council resolutions that Iraq accepted and then evaded. Mr. Cheney's remarks indicated a certain skepticism about intelligence agencies also alluded to by other Administration officials. He recalled "Prior to the Gulf War, America's top intelligence analysts would come to my office in the Defense Department and tell me that Saddam Hussein was at least five or perhaps even 10 years away from having a nuclear weapon. After the war we learned that he had been much closer than that, perhaps within a year of acquiring such a weapon."[11]

In a major address to the United Nations on September 12, 2002, President Bush also discussed the absence of intelligence. He noted that, "Today, Iraq continues to withhold important information about its nuclear program—weapons design, procurement logs, experiment data, an accounting of nuclear materials and documentation of foreign assistance." He cited intelligence that has since been called into question by Administration critics. "Iraq employs capable nuclear scientists and technicians. It retains physical infrastructure needed to build a nuclear weapon. Iraq has made several attempts to buy high-strength aluminum tubes used to enrich uranium for a nuclear weapon. Should Iraq acquire fissile material, it would be able to build a nuclear weapon within a year." He concluded that "The first time we may be completely certain he has nuclear weapons is when, God forbid, he uses one."[12]

Later, the President expressed views about intelligence not unlike Mr. Cheney's:

Many people have asked how close Saddam Hussein is to developing a nuclear weapon. Well, we don't know exactly, and that's the problem. Before the Gulf War, the best intelligence indicated that Iraq was eight to ten years away from developing a nuclear weapon. After the war, international inspectors learned that the regime has been much closer—the regime in Iraq would likely have possessed a nuclear weapon no later than 1993. The inspectors discovered that Iraq had an advanced nuclear weapons development program, had a design for a workable nuclear weapon, and was

pursuing several different methods of enriching uranium for a bomb.[13]

The 2003 State of the Union speech, delivered on January 28, also contained a number of references to intelligence reports and judgments concerning Iraq. "Our intelligence officials estimate that Saddam Hussein had the material to produce as much as 500 tons of sarin, mustard and VX nerve agent." "U.S. intelligence indicates that Saddam Hussein had upwards of 30,000 munitions capable of delivering chemical agents." "From three Iraqi defectors we know that Iraq, in the late 1990s, had several mobile biological weapons labs." In a portion of the speech that became controversial, the President described Iraq's potential nuclear capabilities:

The International Atomic Energy Agency confirmed in the 1990s that Saddam Hussein had an advanced nuclear weapons development program, had a design for a nuclear weapon and was working on five different methods of enriching uranium for a bomb. The British government has learned that Saddam Hussein recently sought significant quantities of uranium from Africa. Our intelligence sources tell us that he has attempted to purchase high-strength aluminum tubes suitable for nuclear weapons production. Saddam Hussein has not credibly explained these activities.

Secretary of State Colin Powell, in a February 2003 address to the U.N., stated that "every statement that I make today is backed up by sources, solid sources. These are not assertions. What we are giving you are facts and conclusions based on solid intelligence." Notably, Director of Central Intelligence (DCI) George Tenet was sitting immediately behind Powell as he spoke. In a wide-ranging discussion of Iraq's activities, Secretary Powell acknowledged disagreements among analysts regarding intended uses of the aluminum tubes (arguably a key component of a nuclear weapons program), but he argued that "Iraq had no business buying them for any purpose. They are banned for Iraq."[14]

PREPARING PUBLIC STATEMENTS BASED ON INTELLIGENCE

This use of intelligence has been a source of considerable debate. Speeches given by senior Administration leaders did not describe in detail the disparate sources or the complex analytical reasoning that lay behind the intelligence judgments that were cited. Some observers believe that intelligence was simplified to the point of distortion in order to shape the public debate. A former National Intelligence Officer, Paul Pillar, argues that the "Administration used intelligence not to inform decision-making, but to justify a decision already made." He further criticizes the Administration for "aggressively using intelligence to win public support for its decision to go to war."[15]

One problem might be that the process by which White House speeches are drafted is less sensitive to the complexities of intelligence analysis than the policy-making processes of the National Security Council. According to one media account, public discussion of the rationale for attacking Iraq was coordinated beginning in August 2002 in the White House by a group of Administration officials described as the White House Iraq Group (WHIG), consisting largely of communications specialists.[16] According to the account, "a 'strategic communications' task force under the WHIG began to plan speeches and white papers." The WHIG, according to the account, "wanted gripping images and stories not available in the hedged and austere language of intelligence." While intelligence analysts expressed greatest concern about Iraq's chemical and biological warfare efforts, speech writers focused on nuclear issues. According to the account, "For a speech writer, uranium was valuable because anyone could see its connection to an atomic bomb. Despite warnings from intelligence analysts, the uranium would return again and again, including the January 28 State of the Union address and three other Bush administration statements that month."[17]

As Iraqi nuclear capabilities became a major source of postwar controversy, Deputy National Security Adviser Stephen Hadley acknowledged that the reference in the State of the Union speech to British reports that Iraq had attempted to obtain significant quantities of uranium in Africa should not have been included, given doubts among U.S. analysts about the veracity of the British report. But he maintained that other intelligence sources, too sensitive to describe in a public address, did indicate other Iraqi efforts to acquire uranium from Africa.[18]

IMPLICATIONS OF THE PROCESS FOR CONGRESS

Intelligence estimates are normally written by analysts, who attempt to portray all attendant ambiguities to provide policymakers with context. Rarely are matters described in terms of black or white but more often are portrayed using a kaleidoscope of grays. Unclassified summaries may further blur analytical judgments to protect intelligence sources and methods. Some critics charge that summaries may be edited to avoid political difficulties. Nevertheless, the question of how well the Intelligence Community performs remains extremely important in view of uncertainties over the possession and possible use of WMDs by Iran, North Korea, and terrorist groups. Congressional oversight can help ensure effective performance by the Intelligence Community by evaluating collection capabilities and analytical standards and by holding intelligence officials accountable. Ultimately, however, policies will be judged on their results. Intelligence analysis can inform policymaking, but it does not substitute for it.

QUESTIONS FOR FURTHER DISCUSSION

1. Was the war against Iraq successful because it prevented Saddam Hussein from acquiring a nuclear weapon?
2. If policymakers waited until matters were cut and dried, if they waited for definitive proof of clandestine weapons production, would it be too late to act?
3. Do you think that when intelligence analysts actually make a contribution to the formation of policy, charges of politicization and manipulation are sure to follow?
4. Do you think the debate over intelligence and the Second Gulf War betrays a fundamental misunderstanding of the role of analysts in the making of foreign and defense policy?

ENDNOTES

1. In addition to the assessment of the Senate Intelligence Committee (S.Rept. 108-301) discussed below, see U.S., Commission on the Intelligence Capabilities of the United States Regarding Weapons of Mass Destruction [the WMD Commission], Mar. 31, 2005. The Commission was headed by Laurence H. Silberman and former Senator Charles S. Robb.
2. See the highly critical letters of Donald Rumsfeld and Paul Wolfowitz of Clinton Administration policies towards Iraq in 1998 (website of the Project for the New American Century [http://www.newamericancentury.org]). Rumsfeld was later appointed Secretary of Defense and Wolfowitz, Deputy Secretary of Defense in first months of the Bush Administration. In early 2006, Paul Pillar, a former senior intelligence official who

has written critically of Administration policies, stated that "intelligence on Iraqi weapons systems did not drive its decision to go to war." Rather, the "decision to topple Saddam was driven by other factors—namely, the desire to shake up the sclerotic power structures of the Middle East and hasten the spread of more liberal politics and economics in the region." Paul R. Pillar, "Intelligence, Policy, and the War in Iraq," *Foreign Affairs*, March/April 2006.

3. See *Statement by David Kay on the Interim Progress Report on the Activities of the Iraq Survey Group (ISG)*, Oct. 2, 2003, [http://www.odci.gov/cia/public_affairs/speeches/2003/david_kay_10022003.html]. The Report adds, however, that "We have discovered dozens of WMD-related program activities and significant amounts of equipment that Iraq concealed from the United Nations during the inspections that began in late 2002."

4. U.S. Congress, 108th Congress, 2d session, Senate, Select Committee on Intelligence, *U.S. Intelligence Community's Prewar Intelligence Assessments on Iraq*, S.Rept. 108–301, July 9, 2004.

5. Pat Roberts, "A Panel Above Politics," *Washington Post*, Nov. 13, 2003, p. 31.

6. John D. Rockefeller IV, "Avoiding a Critical Inquiry," *Washington Post*, Nov. 18, 2003, p. 25.

7. Senate Select Committee on Intelligence, "Chairman Roberts and Vice Chairman Rockefeller Issue Statement on Intelligence Committee's Review of Pre War Intelligence in Iraq," Press Release, Feb. 12, 2004.

8. *Congressional Record*, Nov. 1, 2005, pp. 12103–12104.

9. See "Schedule Drafted for Intelligence Probe," *Washington Post*, Nov. 17, 2005, p. A8.

10. Vice President Speaks at VFW 103rd National Convention, Aug. 26, 2002, available online at [http://www.whitehouse.gov/news/releases/2002/08/20020826.html].

11. Ibid. Whether the Intelligence Community undertook a rigorous "lessons learned" exercise after the Persian Gulf War to assess the inability to detect Iraqi nuclear efforts is unknown. There was such an effort after the Indian nuclear tests of 1998; see CRS Report 98-672, *U.S. Intelligence and India's Nuclear Tests: Lessons Learned*, by Richard A. Best, Jr., Aug. 11, 1998.

12. Remarks by the President in Address to the United Nations General Assembly, Sept. 12, 2002, [http://www.whitehouse.gov/news/releases/2002/09/20020912-l.html].

13. Remarks by the President on Iraq, Cincinnati (OH) Museum Center, Cincinnati Union Terminal, Oct. 7, 2002, [http://www.whitehouse.gov/news/releases/2002/10/20021007-8.html].

14. Secretary Colin L. Powell, Remarks to the United Nations Security Council, Feb. 5, 2003. In 2005 Powell expressed regret about incorrect intelligence on which the U.N. speech was based. ABC News Transcripts, 20/20 Interview, Sept. 9, 2005.

15. "Intelligence, Policy, and the War in Iraq."

16. Barton Gellman and Walter Pincus, "Depiction of Threat Outgrew Supporting Evidence," *Washington Post*, Aug. 10, 2003, p. A1. Responsibilities for presidential communications are described in Martha Joynt Kumar, "The Contemporary Presidency: Communications Operations in the White House of President George W. Bush: Making News on His Terms." *Presidential Studies Quarterly*, June 2003.

17. Gellman and Pincus, "Depiction of Threat."

18. Press briefing on Iraq WMD and SOTU speech, July 22, 2003, [http://www.whitehouse.gov/news/releases/2003/07/20030722-12.html]; it also provides a useful description of White House speech preparation procedures.

From Richard A. Best, Jr., "U.S. Intelligence and Policymaking: The Iraq Experience," *CRS Report for Congress* (Order Code RS21696, updated December 2, 2005).

IV

THE DANGER OF INTELLIGENCE POLITICIZATION

Hamlet: "Do you see yonder cloud that's almost in shape of a camel?"

Polonius: "By th' mass and 'tis, like a camel indeed."

Hamlet: "Methinks it is like a weasel."

Polonius: "It is backed like a weasel."

Hamlet: "Or, like a whale?"

Polonius: "Very like a whale."

—SHAKESPEARE, *Hamlet*, 3.2.378–384

Intelligence politicization is a complex phenomenon. The literature on intelligence suggests that politicization occurs when intelligence analysis is either deliberately or inadvertently skewed to give policymakers the results they want, not the unvarnished truth about the situation at hand. For intelligence analysts and managers, politicization is considered a mortal sin, a fundamental violation of their commitment to provide policymakers with honest answers and estimates. The U.S. intelligence community is supposed to be isolated from the political fray so that analysts and managers can tell policymakers the truth without fear of recrimination, no matter how unpleasant or politically damaging the truth might be to policymakers. The grand bargain within the intelligence community is that analysts will not meddle in politics and policy, and policymakers will not ask or force analysts to "cook the books" to guarantee that analysis supports their policy or political preferences.

Sherman Kent is the intelligence professional best known for championing this separation of intelligence analysis from policy. In his writings, published in the immediate postwar period, Kent, a historian who was in charge of the CIA's Office of National Estimates, warned that it would be a mistake for analysts to get too close to policymakers, because their analysis would inevitably be influenced by policymakers' political agendas. Above all, Kent (1949) argued that analysts have to maintain their objectivity if their estimates are to have any value. Intelligence professionals often champion Kent's view of the importance of analytical objectivity, because it empowers them to pursue their intellectual and analytical interests to their logical—and sometimes even illogical—conclusions. Much in the same way that academic freedom empowers intellectuals to champion unpopular causes or to offer unpleasant observations about contemporary society, isolating analysts from policymakers allows intelligence professionals to set their own research agendas. From the viewpoint of intelligence professionals, Kent's emphasis on objectivity and analytical detachment makes perfect sense. After all, who is better able to set research agendas than analysts themselves?

Too much analytical detachment or too little interaction between analysts and policymakers, however, virtually guarantees that finished intelligence will fail to address the issues that fill policymakers' in-boxes. Forced to focus on issues of immediate importance, policymakers simply ignore "academic" analyses—i.e., anything that fails to address the problems that preoccupy them. Repeated complaints that intelligence lacks relevance has led to calls for the production of "actionable" intelligence, estimates that policymakers will find useful in developing and executing current policy. This view is most closely associated with Robert Gates, a former Director of Central Intelligence. Gates and his supporters believe that relevance, not just objectivity, should govern intelligence production and that intelligence managers should shape finished intelligence so that it meets the needs of policymakers. According to those who embrace this perspective, intelligence managers, by interacting closely with policymakers and with a view of all intelligence assets, can create relevant finished intelligence from a variety of sources. The intelligence manager, not the analyst, would create the questions addressed in finished intelligence and sometimes even shape the answers. In a speech to analysts at the CIA in 1992, Gates explained what amounted to a revolutionary vision of the future of intelligence production:

> Unwarranted concerns about politicization can arise when analysts themselves fail to understand their role in the process. We do produce a corporate product. If the policymaker wants the opinion of a single individual, he can (and frequently does) consult any of a dozen outside experts on any given issue. Your work, on the other hand, counts because it represents the well-considered view of an entire directorate and, in the case of National Estimates, the entire intelligence community. Analysts ... must discard the academic mindset that says their work is their own. (quoted in Betts 2002, 64)

It appeared to many analysts that Gates' vision of actionable intelligence guaranteed that intelligence would be politicized. If intelligence managers tailored intelligence analysis to meet policymakers' agendas, managers could be expected to generate a series of leading questions that would produce answers that would support existing political or policy preferences.

What is the correct balance between objective and actionable intelligence? How detached or engaged should analysts be in the policymaking process? These questions are generating much debate among academics, elected officials, and intelligence professionals. Although the most effective balance between these two positions depends on the issues at stake, the personalities involved, and the bureaucratic and political climate, it does appear that the debate itself becomes most acute at times of policy failure or when the intelligence community is out of step with changing political realities.

SOURCES OF POLITICIZATION

Although politicization can take a variety of forms, scholars focus on three ways in which the production of finished intelligence can be corrupted by undue policy or political influence. First, analysts can be directly pressured to emphasize findings that support the policies and preferences of officials or to ignore issues that could cause political or personal embarrassment. Sometimes this pressure comes in direct requests to support existing policy. Because they are viewed by most observers as inherently credible and not influenced by the wishes of officials, intelligence findings can be used to terminate political debate or to gain political support. Thus, this type of politicization is best viewed as corruption of the intelligence process, because intelligence analysts are considered politically detached observers and are supposed to stand above the political fray and provide honest estimates. By contrast, other sources of politicization are produced by human frailty or organizational pathologies, not the direct manipulation of the intelligence process for political gain.

Charges that the intelligence production has been subjected to direct manipulation for political reasons emerged in the immediate aftermath of Gulf War II, when conclusive evidence supporting administration claims that Saddam Hussein had an active program to produce weapons of mass destruction (WMD) and a large stockpile of these weapons failed to materialize. Critics of the Bush Administration claimed that "worst case thinking," if not outright manipulation, dominated the interpretation of every scrap of evidence collected about Iraqi weapons programs and that most of this spin was concocted by administration officials looking to justify military actions against the kleptocracy that ruled in Iraq. Although some members of the intelligence community have suggested that the intelligence picture was far less conclusive than many administration officials suggested, most seem to stand by their general assessments of Iraq's overall desire to acquire and possess chemical, biological, and nuclear weapons. It is up to future historians to tell us whether the cup was really "half full," "half empty," or "completely drained" in terms of Iraq's chemical, biological, or nuclear capability and exactly who was responsible for "overselling" the Iraqi WMD threat.

Second, senior officials and officers sometimes give subtle and not-so-subtle cues to intelligence managers and analysts about the kinds of analyses they welcome or abhor. If intelligence consumers fawn over or reward analysts who provide them with encouraging reports but dismiss, berate, or punish analysts who bring them disconcerting news, they will send a powerful signal to analysts everywhere. Analysts will line up to provide consumers with positive estimates but shrink from the prospect of reporting bad news. Given the nature of senior leadership—only the most intractable problems and disputes are resolved at the top of the bureaucratic hierarchy—it takes an exceptional official to welcome the receipt of another negative report and to thank the bearer of bad news. Exceptional leaders cultivate a reputation for demanding the unvarnished truth from their staffs, and they make sure that not just the bearers of good news are recognized for outstanding efforts.

An interesting example of this second type of politicization occurred during the Vietnam war. General William C. Westmoreland, commander of U.S. Military Assistance Command, Vietnam (MACV), had asked his command historian to produce a study of sieges throughout history to generate some insights into the North Vietnamese effort to overwhelm the U.S. Marine firebase at Khe Sanh, which was located just below the demilitarized zone that separated North from South Vietnam. The command historian was asked to study the matter and to deliver a briefing to the MACV staff. After describing various battles that had occurred throughout history, the historian concluded that the news was not good for the Marines: Most besieged fortresses fell because the attacker retained mobility. Needless to say, the news shocked the officers present at the briefing. When it concluded, Westmoreland thanked the historian for his report and turned to the staff, saying that now that they had heard the worst-case assessment, he would no longer tolerate anyone thinking, planning, or acting as if the siege of Khe Sanh would end in defeat. Whatever his motives, Westmoreland virtually guaranteed that whoever was in that room that day would think twice before bringing the boss bad news in the future.

Third, analysts can skew their estimates to advance their professional interests, attack their personal or professional rivals, or simply advance their careers. They can ignore negative trends or mistakes, especially if they are about to transfer into another organization or receive a promotion. It is better to leave one's position on a high note than to draw negative attention to problems that can jeopardize an otherwise positive record, especially at critical times. No news is always good news to those in charge of running a large organization; deciding not to rock the bureaucratic boat rarely damages one's career prospects. Politicization in this sense is really a form of careerism: Analysts or intelligence managers place a greater emphasis on enhancing their job prospects than on fulfilling their responsibilities. Sometimes conflict between professional responsibilities and personal interests occurs when analysts' findings call into question the performance or policies of their home organization or institution. Making senior officials aware of analyses that undermine the preferences or priorities of one's home institution is fraught with professional danger, and few people will persevere in the face of opposition from virtually everyone they encounter in the workplace.

John McCone's performance as director of the Central Intelligence Agency in the months leading up to the Cuban Missile Crisis provides an outstanding example of someone who did not allow concerns about his interests and reputation to get in the way of his responsibilities. During the summer of 1962, a consensus emerged among CIA analysts that it was unlikely that the Soviets would place offensive missiles in Cuba, and this finding was reported officially to policymakers in Special National Intelligence Estimate (SNIE) 85-3-62, "The Military Buildup in Cuba." McCone, however, became increasingly concerned about the possibility that the United States might suffer some sort of intelligence failure related to Cuba, as the Soviets attempted to shroud their activities on the island in secrecy. Despite the CIA's official estimate, an estimate that was reported to the most senior officials in the Kennedy administration, McCone pushed agency analysts to repeatedly reassess their judgments about Soviet activities in Cuba. McCone was less concerned about his reputation or his agency's track record for being correct and more interested in preventing the president from being caught by surprise by some nefarious scheme (Usowski 1988).

INTELLIGENCE AS POLITICS?

Politicization is a charge often leveled when intelligence estimates actually support one political position over another. In other words, when analysts "hit their mark" and produce timely finished intelligence that addresses matters of national importance and debate, charges are sometimes raised that someone has unduly influenced the intelligence process or that analysts are following their own policy or political agenda at the expense of objectivity. According to Richard Betts:

> For issues of high import and controversy, any relevant analysis is perforce politically charged, because it points to a policy conclusion. Various disputes—about which elements of information are correct, ambiguous, or false; which of them are important, incidental, or irrelevant; in which context they should be understood; and against which varieties of information pointing in a different direction they should assess—are in effect, if not in intent, disputes about which policy conclusion stands or falls. (Betts 2002, 60)

Because intelligence estimates are inherently credible, individuals who oppose findings that are adverse to their political position have to attack the objectivity of the intelligence process, not the inherent validity of the analysis. After all, few people have access to the classified materials used to develop intelligence estimates, so it is difficult for most observers to validate the intelligence community's findings through independent analysis. Ironically, when intelligence estimates have a political impact and help shape policy—the very goal of the intelligence community—some people interpret

that effect as evidence that the process must have been corrupted to serve political ends.

A variation of this phenomenon occurs when analysts themselves cry foul when their estimates are ignored by policymakers. This situation usually occurs when analysts warn policymakers of impending policy failure or indicate that past estimates were inaccurate and in need of significant revision. There are a variety of reasons, however, that policymakers might choose not to act on specific estimates. They might have information from other sources that provides different perspectives on current issues, or they might believe the effort to utilize the intelligence by changing policy might create more problems than are solved. In this sense, analysts break the grand bargain inherent in the relationship between the intelligence community and policymakers by going public in an effort to use estimates to shape policy.

THE READINGS

In the selections that follow, the authors explore politicization in its various forms. In the first selection, James Wirtz describes the tensions and pressures that shape relationships between intelligence professionals and policymakers. He describes the normative theories that influence discussions of the intelligence-policy nexus, focusing on the "ideal" types of relationships depicted by these theories and their prescriptions for avoiding politiciziation. Wirtz also describes how the information revolution is creating new challenges for existing theory, breaking down barriers between analysts and officials, and creating competing sources of information and analysis that threaten to overshadow finished intelligence products.

In the second selection, Glenn Hastedt explores the controversial terrain of unauthorized disclosure of classified information. Using the second Iraq war as a case study, he describes the variety of ways secret information becomes a matter of public discourse through leaks and examines the motives of policymakers for using leaks to advance policy positions. Hastedt also identifies the circumstances—increased media coverage, institutional rivalry, and foreign policy debate—that lead policymakers to use intelligence leaks as a powerful tool to influence political discourse in Washington, D.C.

14. THE INTELLIGENCE-POLICY NEXUS

JAMES J. WIRTZ

Although there is no consensus on how intelligence professionals and policymakers can avoid the risks of politicization, there are competing ideas about the proper intelligence-policy nexus at the heart of government. One approach strives to maintain distance between analysts and the officials they serve, while the other strives to make analysis relevant to current policy concerns. As the information revolution continues to transform the ways policymakers and analysts interact, however, new challenges and opportunities are beginning to characterize the intelligence-policy nexus.

INTRODUCTION

The intelligence-policy nexus is a critical part of modern government. Policy makers rely on intelligence professionals for data about broad international trends and their potential consequences, information about the intentions and capabilities of friends and foes alike, and specific warnings needed to avert disaster. Intelligence managers and analysts look to the policy establishment for their raison d'être. The intelligence community exists solely to provide policy makers with the information and analysis needed to formulate effective public policies. Few relationships in government are as symbiotic as the intelligence-policy nexus. One might thus expect that it would be relatively easy for intelligence professionals and policy makers to maintain smooth and productive working relations. Yet, few relationships are as challenging or produce as much controversy as the interaction between policy makers and intelligence professionals. The modus vivendi that governs their work is fragile, and disagreements that originate deep within the bureaucracy can easily find their way into tomorrow's headlines. The accusation that the Bush administration manipulated finished intelligence to support the decision to launch a preventive war against Iraq in 2003, for example, is the latest contentious issue in the history of the intelligence-policy nexus in the United States.

A variety of problems can emerge to bedevil relations between the intelligence and policy-making communities. The best-known pathology, politicization, occurs when policy makers place overt or subtle pressure on intelligence analysts and managers to produce intelligence estimates that support current political preferences or policies. Other issues, however, have received far less attention in the literature on intelligence. For example, there is no consensus about what constitutes best practices when it comes to intelligence-policy interaction, which can lead to acrimony as intelligence managers attempt to institute reforms. The information revolution also is creating new points of friction as intelligence analysts and policy makers interact using informal channels of communication, creating new challenges for those charged with monitoring the contents of finished intelligence—formal written reports that reflect a deliberate judgment made by analysts.

This chapter explores the tensions and pressures that shape interaction between intelligence professionals and policy makers as they go about the business of informing, making, and executing foreign and defense policy. The first section describes the two normative theories that offer competing explanations of how relations between intelligence professionals and policy makers should be organized. It also explores the intelligence pathologies that can emerge if either of these theories is applied with too much stringency. The second section explores the origins and consequences of politicization. The third section examines how the information revolution is transforming the relationship between analysts and officials, producing benefits as well as unintended consequences. Although technology has always shaped the intelligence cycle—setting intelligence requirements, collecting data, analyzing information and producing finished intelligence, and communicating information to people who can put it to good use—the information revolution might actually be altering the intelligence-policy nexus, creating an entirely new dynamic in relations between the intelligence and policy-making communities.

A THEORY OF THE INTELLIGENCE-POLICY NEXUS?

Two normative theories animate the debate about best practices in the intelligence-policy nexus. One, most closely associated with the work of Sherman Kent, focuses on ensuring the independence of intelligence analysts when it comes to providing information to policy makers.[1] Kent's thinking, which shaped the formation and early evolution of the U.S. intelligence community, identifies the importance of political and policy detachment when it comes to producing relevant and effective finished intelligence. The other operational framework, most closely associated with the reforms instituted in the mid-1980s by then Director of Central Intelligence Robert M. Gates, focuses on providing "actionable" intelligence, information of immediate and direct use to policy makers.[2] To produce actionable intelligence, analysts have to maintain close working relationships with policy makers, literally looking into officials' inboxes to make sure finished intelligence addresses important policy issues of the day. These frameworks appeal to different groups within the government, produce specific benefits, and exhibit unique intelligence pathologies.

THE KENT APPROACH

Sherman Kent's approach to the intelligence-policy nexus is based on the premise that effective intelligence is independent intelligence. Analysts must maintain their distance from current policy and policy makers to prevent their reports from being shaped by their customers' preferences. In Kent's view, intelligence managers and analysts should be free to set intelligence requirements and production plans for finished intelligence products, deciding which projects best support policy makers. This approach guards against politicization because it creates real procedural and even physical barriers that prevent policy makers from influencing the questions addressed and answers presented in finished intelligence. Analysts often champion this model of the intelligence-policy nexus because it

provides them with the intellectual freedom to pursue their interests within the relatively broad guidelines created by intelligence managers.

At the core of the Kent approach is a grand bargain between policy makers and intelligence professionals. The intelligence community is master of its own house, but analysts and intelligence managers must avoid becoming embroiled in political decisions or commenting publicly or even privately on current policy or political issues. This division of responsibility is especially important because it gives intelligence analysts a special cachet in the U.S. political system, where the intelligence community is often seen as an objective source of information that is beyond the reach of partisan influence. Intelligence professionals take this bargain seriously. The organizational culture of the Central Intelligence Agency (CIA), for instance, reinforces this bargain through formal and informal norms and rules against political or policy commentary in the products produced by the Agency. Finished intelligence analysis also is scrubbed clean of policy content or obvious political bias that might have inadvertently crept into the work of analysts.

The strength of Kent's approach is that it preserves the independence of analysts by separating the intelligence community from the overt pressure or organizational and interpersonal incentives that can shape intelligence to conform to current policy or the personal and political biases of policy makers. Yet, by creating a strong barrier against politicization, Kent's prescriptions can separate intelligence too completely from policy makers, leading to other problems. For instance, policy makers are "inbox driven": They only have the time and energy to deal with their areas of responsibility or issues of immediate importance. Thus, weighty research papers offering reviews of broad issue areas or regions are likely to be ignored by policy makers. Those who are not responsible for the issues or regions covered will not read the paper, while those with a professional interest in the topic will seek more detailed analyses. Similarly, in-depth reports are likely to be ignored by most policy makers who have no responsibility for the issue surveyed. Without a good understanding of the issues that preoccupy specific policy makers, high-quality finished intelligence might be viewed as useless by intelligence consumers because it covers the wrong topics, arrives too late to be of use, lacks the proper level of detail, or addresses the wrong facet of the problem at hand. In fact, without some sort of collaboration between analysts and policy makers, the arrival of timely, relevant, and useful finished intelligence would depend on luck.

Organizational pathologies also can emerge if intelligence managers and analysts become too detached from the needs of policy makers. Analysis can take on a life of its own as the personal or bureaucratic agendas of intelligence professionals begin to take precedence over the needs of their consumers. For instance, critics charged that the CIA's Office of Soviet Analysis (SOVA), especially its division specializing in the study of the Soviet economy, became increasingly scholastic as the Cold War progressed. Because the command economies of the Communist bloc had little in common with those of the capitalist West, the CIA was forced to create an entirely new academic discipline to understand Soviet economic performance and capability.[3] Promising academics were recruited from the best graduate schools and given specialized training, journals were founded to cultivate new methodologies and to provide a forum for theoretical debate, and analysts worked hard to gain insights into Soviet economic performance, a state secret of the Communist regime in Moscow. As analysts sought to sharpen their methodological skills and improve the sophistication of their theories, however, they began to lose sight of the big picture, especially the fundamental question that suggested itself to policy makers in the early 1980s. Could the Soviet command economy compete over the short term with the capitalist economies of the West, or was the regime in Moscow built upon an economic house of cards?

ACTIONABLE INTELLIGENCE

When Robert Gates, then Deputy Director for Analysis at the CIA, became frustrated with the unwillingness of CIA analysts to provide intelligence to meet the specific requirements of administration officials, actionable intelligence was born. Under Gates's system, analysts might have been asked, for example, when—not if—the Soviet economy would collapse. Intelligence professionals cried foul, noting that by posing specific and pointed questions, Gates was attempting to shape the analysis to suit the expectations of policy makers. In response, Gates suggested that he was trying to make analysts less academic so that they would produce relevant and timely finished intelligence that responded to the needs of administration officials.

The core assumption behind actionable intelligence is that analysts must be aware of the needs of

policy makers and that intelligence managers have an obligation to task analysts so that they produce useful intelligence for their clientele. According to Gates:

> My view has been all along from the very beginning of my career—and perhaps due to the fact that I have served on the National Security Council—that the Intelligence community has to be right next to the policymaker, that [the analyst] has to be at his elbow—that he has to understand what is on his mind. He has to understand what his future concerns are. He has to understand what his agenda is. He has to understand some of the initiatives that he is thinking about taking. He has to be willing to ask the policymaker what he's working on, or what came of his last conversation with a world leader so that the intelligence can be made relevant; so that the Director, or the office director, or what can go back and give guidance to the analysts.[4]

From this perspective, policy makers already have a reasonable idea of what they need—information to help them implement their policies. Most of the support they require from the intelligence community is largely technical in nature: demographic, geographic, political, economic, and military data about the issue at hand and how allies and adversaries are responding to U.S. policies. Some observers have even noted that as crises emerge, policy makers should communicate with analysts directly to increase the flow of information and the timeliness of analysis. Under these circumstances, analytic debates within the intelligence community are counterproductive and actually reduce the confidence policy makers have in finished intelligence. When the chips are down, officials want information they can use to solve problems, not competitive analysis designed to highlight various theoretical or methodological approaches to the issues of the day.[5] In fact, some policy makers have discovered that the intelligence community can actually serve as an extension of their office staff, providing a ready source of analysis and information tailored to meet their personal interests and agendas.[6]

In reality, much of the finished intelligence produced by analysts takes the form of actionable intelligence: The information supplied to policy makers often is matter-of-fact data about what is occurring in a specific part of the world, the state of a foreign economy or industry, or the capability of a weapons system. Moreover, elected officials usually enter office with a pre-existing worldview and policy agenda; they look to the intelligence community to help them implement their policies. If intelligence professionals fail to recognize this political and policy reality, they risk becoming irrelevant.

Nevertheless, following the Gates model too closely can create its own set of problems. There is a possibility that policy makers will pose biased questions to the intelligence community to guarantee that analysis favorable to their positions will emerge, or that they will fail to pose the correct questions, leading to an incomplete understanding of the challenges they face. If analysts also concentrated only on actionable intelligence, they might lack the time to conduct the independent, in-depth research needed to uncover threats and trends not on current policy agendas. When they initially took office, for instance, members of the Bush administration had not placed Al Qaeda on the top of their foreign and defense policy agendas. Instead, they were more concerned with improving Russian-American relations, deploying a U.S. missile defense system, and reducing U.S. military commitments overseas. It was up to the intelligence community to increase the salience of the terrorist threat to the United States among senior officials.

Normative theory and practice thus highlight the competing priorities that animate the intelligence-policy nexus. Analysts need some leeway, unconstrained by the preference of policy makers or even intelligence managers, to pursue their hunches and interests, regardless of current political or policy preferences. Without this freedom, policy makers would lack independent information and insight into current and emerging international issues. For their analysis to be relevant and timely, however, intelligence professionals must possess a keen awareness of policy makers' current interests and responsibilities. What policy makers require is information and finished intelligence reports that address the issues found in their inboxes. They also would benefit from long-term research that highlights emerging problems before they become crises or sources of embarrassment.

POLITICIZATION

Politicization, the effort of policy makers to shape intelligence to conform to their policy or political preferences, can emerge in both overt and subtle ways. Although the term suggests that intelligence analysts are victims when policy makers manipulate intelligence to suit their needs, intelligence professionals can themselves politicize intelligence when they allow bureaucratic or personal incentives to influence their estimates and reports. Intelligence managers and analysts can "pander" to policy makers by presenting them with information and analysis that meets their expectations and confirms their chosen policies. Intelligence estimates also can appear to be politicized when they are effective, that is, when they actually have a policy or political impact.

Overt politicization occurs when policy makers deliberately pressure analysts to produce estimates that support their policies or to shape the intelligence cycle to confirm current policy or political preferences. The act of deliberately shaping intelligence estimates would have to be driven by expediency or desperation because policy makers run a grave risk by preventing accurate, if unpleasant, information and finished intelligence from informing national policy. In extreme cases of politicization, senior officers or policy makers can even retaliate against analysts for providing them with information that contradicts their existing beliefs or plans. In the days leading up to Operation Market Garden, the Allied airborne-armor operation to seize the Rhine River crossings in September 1944, Major Brian Urquhart, Chief of Intelligence for the British I Airborne Corps, detected signs that Nazi armored divisions were actually bivouacked in Arnhem, that last objective of the Allied advance. When Urquhart relayed to his superiors this information, which called into question the feasibility of the entire operation, he was visited by a senior medical officer who placed him on sick leave.[7]

Overt politicization, however, is difficult to keep concealed, because analysts and intelligence managers will go to great lengths to resist what they believe are illegitimate efforts to influence their finished intelligence reports. In the aftermath of the Vietnam War, for instance, Samuel Adams, a former CIA analyst who helped develop estimates of enemy troop strength during the war, charged that senior intelligence officials and military officers deliberately suppressed his findings because they gave the Viet Cong greater strength than had been reported in previous intelligence estimates. The controversy over the incident only increased in the aftermath of the conflict, and became the subject of a CBS news documentary and libel litigation between General William C. Westmoreland (retired), who was the former head of the Military Assistance Command in Vietnam and CBS.[8] Some controversies boil over even more quickly. Following the second Gulf War, accusations emerged that the members of the George W. Bush administration had tried to undermine the credibility of Ambassador Joseph Wilson, who investigated reports that Iraqi agents had attempted to purchase yellowcake, a nuclear material, from Niger. Wilson had turned in a memo to intelligence officials in February 2002, explaining why the alleged Iraqi activity was probably a hoax. When the president claimed in his 2003 State of the Union Address that Iraq had sought uranium in Africa, Wilson went public in a July 6, 2003, editorial in the *New York Times*, stating that the Bush administration knowingly lied about the status of Iraq's nuclear program. In retaliation, Bush administration officials allegedly "outed" Valerie Plame, Wilson's wife, effectively ending her career as a clandestine CIA officer.[9]

Although they make headlines, charges that policy makers deliberately engage in politicization are relatively rare. Instead, policy makers and intelligence managers can shape analysis in more subtle, and sometimes even inadvertent, ways. Those who bring positive news can be rewarded with praise in front of colleagues, whereas those who bring unwelcome information can be chastised or criticized in front of their coworkers. "Positive" estimates are more likely to be rewarded with promotions, increases in pay, or sublime inducements important to bureaucrats—a larger office, new furniture, travel. "Negative" estimates are unlikely to be rewarded; in fact those with an eye for finding potential trouble in a generally positive situation are often avoided by policy makers whose workday is often spent responding to a never-ending series of crises, problems, or complaints. Loss of access to policy makers can take the form of *bureaucratic death*, a situation in which intelligence officials are no longer invited to important meetings because of their history of providing contradictory or discouraging reports.[10] Only the smartest and toughest policy makers encourage their staffs to take steps to avoid sending inadvertent signals to subordinates and intelligence managers to prevent analysis from being shaped to meet their expectations or to emphasize the positive aspects of every situation. Indeed, some observers have noted that the ability to literally pressure subordinates to provide honest assessments is a key to success in politics and war.[11]

Without knowing it, however, efforts to encourage analysts to provide their honest opinion can have unintended consequences. During the Vietnam War, for example, General Westmoreland was provided with a negative assessment of his command's ability to hold the marine position at Khe Sanh, the findings of an estimate that he had personally requested. After hearing the report, which was delivered to his entire staff, he thanked the analysts for their best estimate and then stated that he would no longer tolerate gloomy evaluations of the marine's prospects at Khe Sanh. Years later, Westmoreland's chief of intelligence, Major General Philip Davidson (retired) remarked that he had never heard a negative prediction for the outcome at Khe Sanh. In what was an apparent effort to bolster morale, Westmoreland had told his command that he no longer wanted negative reports about the situation at Khe Sanh. It is not surprising that his staff complied.[12]

When intelligence has an effect on important foreign and defense policy debates, charges of politicization often emerge. Ironically, when intelligence analysts offer timely and relevant estimates to policy makers, they are sometimes accused of meddling in political affairs because their reports have an impact, favoring one side in a political dispute over another. As issues become increasingly a matter of heated partisan politics or less focused on technical issues, the role played by intelligence analysts as neutral purveyors of information and analysis increases. Moreover, if the finished intelligence in question was not backed by a clear analytical consensus, there always will be intelligence "dissenters" ready to take their case to elected officials or the media. As Richard Betts has noted, this is exactly the situation that emerged in the controversy over enemy strength during the Vietnam War: The effort to shape an analytical consensus spilled over into acrimony that lasted for years and became a matter of public and political debate.[13]

THE INFORMATION REVOLUTION AND THE INTELLIGENCE POLICY NEXUS

The information revolution has broken down barriers of space and time by virtually eliminating the costs of communication, even at intercontinental distances. The computer and the Internet have provided individuals with an ability to organize and analyze information that was unheard of only a few decades ago. The Internet itself is a positive-sum institution: The more people who have access to the Internet and this virtually free means of communication, the more powerful the tool becomes for all concerned.[14] The real power of new computing and communication architectures is that they can potentially allow people everywhere and anywhere to find and interact with each other in real time.

As with any technology, the information revolution contains its own embedded ideology, so to speak: People will find that it should be employed in a particular way, regardless of the intentions of its designers. In fact, the inventor of a machine is often unaware of the logic inherent in the technology he or she is creating. Gutenberg was a Catholic, but his printing press made the Protestant reformation possible because printing facilitated the dissemination of competing ideas (i.e., heresy).[15] The automobile transformed America—dispersing extended families and building suburbs and new American cultures.[16] The automobile's effects, however, were perceived only when the transformation of society was well under way.

The information revolution also is transforming society. It is an egalitarian technology that breaks down social, economic, political, and bureaucratic barriers and allows people direct access to each other's very personal "inboxes," for the most part facilitating frank communication even across hierarchical organizations. At the same time, the information revolution also documents human interaction as it channels not just formal, but informal, communication into what amounts to official or corporate records. In a sense, people have to convert private interactions into a public record to participate in the information revolution, but they seem to accept this as the price of entry for using the new technology.

Because we use information revolution technologies on a daily basis, we often overlook the subtle and even not so subtle changes it is bringing to everyday life or well-understood bureaucratic practices. In terms of the intelligence-policy nexus, for example, the information revolution has reframed the opportunities for interaction between intelligence analysts and policy makers in ways that are not well captured by either the Gates or Kent frameworks. The barriers to interaction assumed by the Kent model, which are supplied by intelligence managers or by the process of crafting formal intelligence estimates, are completely broken down by the information revolution. Policy makers and their staffs can now easily communicate on a daily basis directly with analysts. It is increasingly difficult for analysts to stand above the fray of politics or policy if they are bombarded with a barrage of questions about current policy, calls for data, or requests for commentary or supplemental information about media coverage of some international event. Moreover, as the volume of this informal interaction between policy makers and analysts increases, it can begin to drown out the message carried by the formal estimates offered by intelligence organizations. Because of the sheer volume of interaction between analysts and policy makers, it also might be nearly impossible for intelligence managers to monitor this informal communication, and any effort to restrict analysts' access to this communication technology would be resisted on both personal and professional grounds. The information revolution has created a new medium for interaction between analysts and policy makers that, by its very nature, flies in the face of the norms suggested by Kent's framework.

Policy makers' access to analysts is so great that it can overwhelm them, degrading their ability to provide significant actionable intelligence called for by the Gates model. It might be difficult for individuals outside of government or the military to understand, but as members of a "service industry," intelligence analysts must place the immediate needs of administration officials ahead of other important professional or organizational objectives. Questions or requests for information, no matter how trivial, must receive a prompt and complete response. Additionally, because service is part of the ethos of the intelligence community, performance metrics are focused on measuring responsiveness to policy makers' demands, not the quality or thoroughness of the response given or the opportunity costs created by setting aside long-term research projects. Because everyone within the policy-making and intelligence communities is virtually free to task analysts, intelligence managers are no longer able to set production priorities or timelines. In fact, because managers are judged by the same production metric as analysts, they have little incentive to intervene in informal communications to protect analysts from being endlessly besieged with questions by policy makers.

The information revolution offers more opportunities for intelligence analysts to interact with officials while making it increasingly difficult for analysts to hold their attention. Because policy makers have ready access to nongovernmental sources of information provided by twenty-four-hour cable television and Internet news services, intelligence analysts have to hold the attention of policy makers by providing catchy titles to reports that exaggerate the importance or the certainty underlying estimates. The Silberman-Robb Commission, which investigated the intelligence community's account of Iraq's weapons of mass destruction program prior to the second Gulf War, found that the *President's Daily Brief* (PDB)—a tightly held piece of finished intelligence that is read by a few select senior officials on a daily basis—suffered from various flaws and created several problems.[17] PDBs tended to contain bold statements and judgments that were probably intended to engage the reader but failed to convey a sense of the qualifications, judgments, or assumptions that were embedded in the analysis. Commissioners were concerned that a daily exposure to PDB briefings might "create, over time, a greater perception of certainty about their judgments than is warranted." Questions posed to PDB briefers are answered in future PDBs or in a Senior Executive Memorandum, which are distributed to all those who receive the PDB. Commissioners believed that the volume of reporting that could be produced by a question of clarification, for example, could create a false impression among PDB recipients that the president was intensely interested in a subject, thereby shaping priorities and policy.[18]

The commissioners also searched in vain for evidence of politicization in the intelligence community's reporting on Iraqi weapons of mass destruction programs. What they uncovered, however, was evidence of the impact of the information revolution—especially the breakdown of hierarchy. The CIA Ombudsman for Politicization told the commissioners, for example, that analysts on Iraqi issues worked under more "pressure" than any other analysts in the history of the CIA. For months they were required to provide enormous amounts of both formal and informal reporting directly to the highest officials in the U.S. government. These officials also questioned analysts directly about their work to explore the assumptions and data that were used. Policy makers are justified in asking these types of questions, regardless of their motivations, but the fact that senior officials apparently scrutinized analysts directly probably affected subsequent analysis. Analysts also were under pressure "to answer the mail quickly," which in itself can be detrimental to calm contemplation of complicated issues.[19] Cutting and pasting is not a measured reassessment of first principles or even secondary assumptions, and it unfortunately occurs when timeliness takes precedence over depth in the information age.

CONCLUSION

Intelligence reform is cyclical. Sometimes scholars and other observers warn that analysts are too detached from policy makers' concerns and are producing finished intelligence that is dated or irrelevant. At other times, concerns about politicization emerge; observers worry that intelligence analysts and managers are no longer serving as an independent source of information for policy makers and that the intelligence cycle has been corrupted by all sorts of political or bureaucratic considerations. Since the early 1980s, the pendulum has been swinging in favor of producing "actionable" intelligence, but in the aftermath of a series of intelligence setbacks leading up to and following the September 11, 2001, terror attacks, observers have had second thoughts about the status of the U.S. intelligence community. Intelligence reform, based on organizational change, is the order of the day.

It is extraordinarily difficult to strike a balance between detachment and responsiveness in the intelligence-policy nexus. As Betts noted, fixing one type of intelligence problem only exacerbates other types of problems.[20] For instance, providing all available information to analysts would overwhelm them; by contrast, restricting the flow of information creates the risk that they will not receive critical bits of information needed to make sense of emerging threats. Because the correct balance of detachment and responsiveness depends upon the specific issue or problem confronting intelligence analysts and policy makers, it is virtually impossible ex ante to fine-tune the intelligence-policy nexus.

In a sense, those interested in intelligence reform are addressing a moving target. The proper balance in the relationship between intelligence professionals and policy makers is shaped by external and internal factors. Externally, the changing threat environment and issue agenda create different types of challenges for the intelligence community. Reporting on developments within nation states requires different collection and analytical capabilities than does reporting on terrorist networks or superempowered individuals. Internally, new communication and information processing capabilities—combined with the way analysts and policy makers actually use these novel capabilities—are creating new modes of interaction within the intelligence-policy nexus. It might be too early to sound the death knell for the Kent and Gates models, but in the future it will probably become increasingly difficult to capture the reality of the intelligence-policy nexus within these competing theoretical frameworks.

QUESTIONS FOR FURTHER DISCUSSION

1. What factors drive intelligence analysts and policymakers to collaborate?
2. Should intelligence reforms strive to maintain distance between analysts and the officials they serve, or make analysis relevant to current policy concerns?
3. How is the information revolution changing the relationship between analysts and policymakers?
4. Will the information revolution increase the risks of politicization of intelligence?

ENDNOTES

1. Sherman Kent, *Strategic Intelligence for American World Policy* (Princeton: Princeton University Press, 1946).
2. H. Bradfor Westerfield, "Inside Ivory Bunkers: CIA Analysts Resist Managers' 'Panderin'—Part II," *International Journal of Intelligence and Counterintelligence* 10 (Spring 1997), pp. 19–54; Richard K. Betts, "Politicization of Intelligence: Costs and Benefits," *Paradoxes of Strategic Intelligence*, eds. Richard K. Betts and Thomas Mahnken (London: Frank Cass, 2003), pp. 59–79.
3. David M. Kennedy, *Sunshine and Shadow: The CIA and the Soviet Economy* (Cambridge: Harvard University, JFK Case Program, 1991).
4. Gates quoted in Westerfield, "Inside Ivory Bunkers."
5. William Odom, *Fixing Intelligence: For a More Secure America* (New Haven, CT: Yale University Press, 2003).
6. Jack Davis, "A Policymaker's Perspective on Intelligence Analysis," *Studies in Intelligence* 39 (1995), pp. 7–15.
7. Sir Brian Urquhart, who was Under-Secretary-General of the United Nations (UN) from 1974 to 1986, played a leading part in the development of UN peacekeeping operations throughout the Cold War. Urquhart was eventually knighted for his service to the United Nations.
8. James J. Wirtz, "Intelligence to Please? The Order of Battle Controversy During the Vietnam War," *Political Science Quarterly* 106 (Summer 1991), pp. 239–63.
9. "Then & Now: Joseph Wilson," CNN, 19 June 2005, available at http://www.cnn.com/2005/US/03/07/CNN25.tan.wilson/index.html.
10. Mark Lowenthal, *Intelligence: From Secrets to Policy* (Washington, DC: CQ Press, 2003), p. 148.
11. Eliot Cohen, *Supreme Command* (New York: Free Press, 2002).
12. Phillip Davidson, Interview II by Ted Gittinger, June 30, 1982, Oral History Collection, LBJ Library, Austin, Texas, pp. 23–24; and William C. Westmoreland, A *Soldier Reports* (Garden City, NY: Doubleday, 1976), p. 338.
13. Betts, pp. 73–74.
14. Bill Gates, *The Road Ahead* (New York: Penguin, 1996).
15. Printing increased literacy because it provided common people with something to read. Without printing, Martin Luther could not have encouraged people to read the Bible themselves.
16. George F. Kennan, *Around the Cragged Hill* (New York: W.W. Norton, 1994).
17. Commission on the Intelligence Capabilities of the United States Regarding Weapons of Mass Destruction, "Report to the President of the United States," 31 March 2005.
18. Ibid., pp. 160–81.
19. Ibid., pp. 187–89.
20. Richard Betts, "Analysis, War, and Decision: Why Intelligence Failures Are Inevitable," *World Politics*, 21 (October 1968), pp. 61–89.

From James J. Wirtz, "The Intelligence Policy Nexis" in Loch K. Johnson, ed., *Strategic Intelligence: Understanding the Hidden Side of Government Vol. 1:* (Westport, Connecticut: Praeger, 2007): pp. 139–150. Copyright © 2007. Reproduced with permission of ABC-CLIO, LLC.

15. PUBLIC INTELLIGENCE

GLENN HASTEDT

In this discussion of the controversial issue of intelligence "leaks," Glenn Hastedt explores why policymakers go public with classified information. Moving beyond the often-voiced complaint that leaks have a fleeting effect but can seriously compromise intelligence "sources and methods," Hastedt provides an analysis of circumstances that turn policymakers toward "public intelligence." He finds that there is no single motive or objective behind the effort to use classified information to bolster policy positions. By identifying a new realm of interaction among the intelligence community and policymakers, Hastedt suggests that leaks of classified information are an increasingly common form of intelligence politicization.

"We were almost all wrong." This was the conclusion reached by David Kay about the assertion that Iraq possessed weapons of mass destruction.[1] Kay was the United States' top weapons inspector in the period leading up to the Iraq War and his admission pointed to the presence of a serious intelligence failure on the part of the US intelligence community. Intelligence analysis by governments is conducted in secret. This is true regardless of whether the sources used are open or restricted and whether the analysis is competitive or consensual. Our thinking about intelligence takes this context of secrecy as its foundational reference point. Yet intelligence does not always remain secret. On occasion it becomes public. A review of instances where intelligence has become public shows that it does so in a variety of ways. The two key dimensions are whether it is contested or not and whether it is sustained over time or an isolated occurrence. Four patterns emerge: promotional, orchestrated, warring, and entrepreneurial. This stands in sharp contrast to the almost universal tendency to combine all such instances under the single heading of "leaks." Doing so obscures the underlying dynamics of public intelligence, the forces that give rise to it, and the potential consequences that public intelligence has for secret intelligence. The need for systematic attention to public intelligence is seen both in past examples of its occurrence and most recently by the manner in which intelligence was used during the buildup to the Iraq war.

PUBLIC INTELLIGENCE

Conventional accounts of intelligence failures focus on the dynamics of the intelligence process and the inherent difficulty of anticipating events in world politics.[2] These explanations are inadequate because the world of "secret" intelligence coexists with the world of "public" intelligence. Its internal dynamics contribute both to the occurrence of specific intelligence failures and, if unchecked, to cumulative degradation of the overall quality of intelligence.

Public intelligence is not a new phenomenon but it is one that has risen in prominence due to several reinforcing changes in the complexion of American politics. By public intelligence we refer to secret intelligence that has become part of the societal debate over the conduct of American foreign policy. One is the change in the nature of legislative-executive relations in foreign policy. The period of bipartisanship, to the extent that it existed, has long since ended. So too has the notion of two presidencies in which the president was de facto granted far greater powers to deal with foreign policy issues than he was to deal with domestic policy problems. In their place we find presidents and legislators suspicious of each other's agenda and in competition to control the direction of American foreign policy. These conflicts are most pronounced in periods of divided government but are present even when one party is in control of both branches. Contributing to this institutional competition is the lack of a foreign policy consensus among the public at large or elites. The broad areas of agreement on the content and conduct of American foreign policy that existed prior to the Vietnam War have yet to be reconstructed. If anything the passage of time and repeated controversies over the use of force have deepened the dividing lines on foreign policy and made them more evident. Finally, there is the changed nature of media coverage of foreign policy events. The advent of 24 hour per day/seven days per week news programming with its heavy emphasis on breaking news, visual images, and instant (and conflicting) expert opinion places great obstacles in the way of an administration's efforts to demonstrate that it is on top of a situation, present its foreign policy in a positive light, speak with one voice, and avoid the appearance of engaging in ad hoc policy making.

These three features, institutional rivalry, lack of foreign policy consensus, and increased media coverage, combine to create a foreign policy making environment that accentuates the normal advantage held by immediate policy questions and current intelligence over long-range issues. It also favors the politics of confrontation and competition over that of problem solving. Placed in this setting secret intelligence becomes a tantalizing resource not simply for its ability to shed light on a situation but for its ability to alter the political logic by which decisions are made in the broader political arena. But in order to do so, it must stop being secret and become public.

Secret intelligence becomes public intelligence through unauthorized leaking of secret intelligence, the sanitized release of secret material, or public references to sources and analyses. It does not become public in a uniform manner. We can distinguish between four different patterns depending upon whether the leaked intelligence emerges in a sustained or episodic fashion and whether or not it is contested. The four patterns are presented in Table 15.1.

When secret intelligence is leaked in an episodic manner and is uncontested then public intelligence is promotional intelligence. Here we have secret intelligence being made public largely on a "one-shot"

basis and under circumstances where it is not countered by the leaking of contrary secret intelligence. The essential purpose of public intelligence under these circumstances is either to draw attention to oneself or to a policy problem, or to defend or distance oneself from a policy failure. President Dwight Eisenhower made intelligence public in this fashion in the aftermath of the failed Paris Summit meeting with Nikita Khrushchev. In a nationally televised address from the Oval Office he showed a U-2 photograph of the North Island Naval Air Station in San Diego. Trying to build support for his open skies program he noted: "I show you this photograph as an example of what could be accomplished through United Nations aerial surveillance." In releasing this photo he rejected calls from his advisors that he make public actual U-2 photographs of the Soviet Union. Nevertheless, releasing even these photos made public a secret intelligence capability.[3]

On 14 April 1969 a North Korean MIG fighter shot down a US navy aircraft in international airspace. Intelligence concluded that the attack was a command and control accident. The Nixon administration adopted a different position. It held the North Korean attack to be calculated and premeditated. In a news conference a few days after the attack Nixon asserted the North Koreans knew what they were doing "because we know what their radar showed. We, incidentally, know what the Russian radar showed." This was the first public revelation of American capabilities to read North Korean and Russia radar systems.[4]

Another example of promotional public intelligence comes from late in the Ford administration. The B Team report on Soviet strategic capabilities was completed on 2 December 1976. This report was highly critical of the intelligence community's established view of the Soviet threat. Within a few weeks its conclusions were leaked to the press.[5] The incoming Carter administration engineered its own promotional leak of intelligence. On 18 April 1977 Carter delivered a nationwide address in which he stressed the seriousness of the energy crisis facing the United States. To support his cause he released a declassified 18-page CIA report, "The International Energy Situation: Outlook to 1985" The Senate Select Committee on Intelligence publicly challenged the conclusions of the report but it did say the episode had "understandably given rise to questions about his [Carter's] use of intelligence."[6]

President Reagan engaged in promotional public intelligence in trying to garner support for his "Star

TABLE 15.1 PATTERNS OF PUBLIC INTELLIGENCE

		Time Frame	
		Episodic	Sustained
Contested	*Uncontested*	Promotional	Orchestrated
	Contested	Entrepreneurial	Warring

Wars" initiative. In a nationally televised March 1983 speech he denounced the Soviet Union as an "evil empire." Two weeks later he went on television and put forward his strategic defense initiative. In the course of his presentation he made public a wide range of imagery intelligence that included photos of a large Soviet Sigint station in Cuba, Soviet arms shipments to Cuba and Nicaragua, and the construction of an airfield on Grenada.[7]

More recently promotional public intelligence surfaced in 1998. The United States and North Korea were engaged in a complex diplomatic enterprise as the Agreed Framework began to come undone. The *New York Times* ran a prominent story asserting that "U.S. intelligence agencies had detected a huge secret underground complex in North Korea that they believed to be the centerpiece of an effort to revive the country's frozen nuclear weapons program, according to officials who have been briefed on the intelligence information."[8] The origins of the story have been linked to the head of the Defense Intelligence Agency who regularly gave information to Republican congressmen. Two days after it appeared the Pentagon said the site was a large hole in the ground and said it had no evidence that North Korea was not abiding by the Agreed Framework.

When secret intelligence is contested and episodic in public then it becomes entrepreneurial intelligence. As with promotional public intelligence, entrepreneurial intelligence involves a burst of leaked intelligence focused on a specific issue. This time, however, more is involved here than drawing attention to a situation. Public intelligence is entrepreneurial in the sense that it is being used in a competitive environment. The opponent, so to speak, is not inertia or a policy stream that appears to be set in motion without opposition. Here, public intelligence is used in a competitive environment in which both sides to a dispute are using intelligence to advance or block a policy. The objective is to convince consumers (policy makers) that their position is superior politically or strategically to that being offered by a competitor. A prime example comes from the Carter administration and the "discovery" of a Russian combat brigade in Cuba by the National Security Agency.

The Central Intelligence Agency (CIA) gave an ominous interpretation to this revelation. When briefed on the situation Senator Frank Church, who was in a difficult and ultimately unsuccessful reelection campaign, went public with the story. Church was a highly visible and outspoken opponent of

US foreign policy in Vietnam and the Third World. In 1975 he was named chair of the Senate Select Committee to Study Governmental Operations with Respect to Intelligence Activities. It investigated allegations of CIA abuses of power and assassination plots. Now Church was on the political defensive. He was accused of being soft on communism for meeting with Fidel Castro. Church went public with this intelligence as a means of reestablishing his foreign policy credentials. He then demanded that Strategic Arms Limitation Talks (SALT II) be cancelled unless the brigade left immediately. President Carter responded by going on television and stating "we have concluded, as the consequences of intensified intelligence efforts, that a Soviet combat brigade is currently stationed in Cuba…it is not an assault force… its purpose is not clear…this status quo is not acceptable." Not surprisingly his statement did not effectively counter Church's charges. In fact, the reality was that Kennedy had agreed in 1963 that a Soviet brigade could remain in Cuba. Carter refused to admit that his administration and the intelligence community had forgotten this. Instead twice more Carter would go on television referencing intelligence in an attempt to establish that his administration was on top of matters and that the situation did not present a security threat. One time he declared: "American intelligence has obtained persuasive evidence that…it presents no threat to us." The other time he spoke of increasing American intelligence capabilities.[9]

A third situation emerges when leaked intelligence is carried out on a sustained basis and is uncontested. In this instance public intelligence is orchestrated intelligence. Secret intelligence is being leaked on a systematic basis in order to advance a policy position. More often than not orchestrated public intelligence will emanate from the executive branch. It has greater access to the products of the intelligence community and it is responsible for the selection and execution of foreign policy. In situations where public intelligence is orchestrated no significant amount of countering public intelligence or assertions relating to intelligence capabilities or analysis are aired to challenge the position being advanced although the position itself may be challenged by Congress or other political actors.

One example of orchestrated public intelligence occurred during the missile gap controversy in the late 1950s over the relative strengths of the US and Soviet nuclear forces. Beginning in the mid 1950s the Air Force began providing a "steady stream of sensitive information" to sympathetic members of Congress. Foremost among them were Senators Henry "Scoop" Jackson and Stuart Symington who frequently aired alarmist interpretations of the situation.[10] Symington often referred to information in National Intelligence Estimates (NIEs) that contradicted the Eisenhower administration's less alarmist position on the issue. One such instance was in 1958 when in rejecting the administration's estimates of Soviet missile strength he publicly asserted that he had "other" intelligence on the matter.

Intelligence also made its way to the press. Joseph and Stuart Alsop repeatedly referred to intelligence reports and capabilities in their articles and columns. In 1956 they wrote that "it could positively be stated that no Soviet Inter-Continental Ballistic Missile (ICBM) test had not yet occurred" but that American intelligence routinely underestimated Soviet nuclear developments by two years and that current American intelligence estimates predicted a test in 1958. In 1957 Stuart Alsop followed with a column in which he stated that the United States possessed "convincing evidence" that the Soviet Union had tested an experimental version of a very long range ballistic missile. The story was confirmed a few days later by the *New York Times*. In 1958 one of their columns leaked the projected range of the Soviet ICBMs contained in intelligence estimates. In 1957 *Newsweek* ran a story on DCI Allen Dulles and an NIE prediction that the Soviet Union would have an operational ICBM capability by the end of 1959.

The Kennedy administration engaged in the practice of orchestrated public intelligence during the Cuban missile crisis. The first public showing of intelligence came in Great Britain on 23 October 1962. Prime Minister Harold Macmillan had requested that the BBC be permitted to show photos of missile sites in order to build support for the American position in the British public. American intelligence officials had convinced Secretary of Defense Robert McNamara not to release these pictures for fear of giving the Soviet Union information they might lack on the state of American photo reconnaissance capabilities. Yet the Kennedy administration soon used photo intelligence to build its case at the United Nations with great effect. On 25 October Adlai Stevenson, the American ambassador to the United Nations, displayed a series of U-2 photographs documenting the construction of Soviet missile sites at San Cristobal and Guanajay.[11]

Another example of orchestrated intelligence comes from the Reagan administration. It involved the North Korean attack on a South Korean jet liner, KAL 007, on 1 September 1983. The plane had veered off course into Soviet airspace when it was shot down. The Reagan administration was first to go public with the announcement. Secretary of State George Shultz stated there was no doubt that the pilot of the North Korean MIG knew he was attacking a civilian airliner because Russian radar had tracked KAL 007 for two hours and the pilot had reported the shoot-down to authorities on the ground. Soon after Shultz's statement it became increasingly clear to American intelligence officials that the attack actually may have been an accident. The administration, however, pressed ahead with its case. On 4 September President Reagan played Sigint recordings of conversations between the pilot and authorities detailing his actions leading up to firing his missile and his reaction to destroying KAL 007. Reagan made these excerpts public the next day. Jeanne Kirkpatrick then used a longer excerpt from the Sigint intercepts in making the American case at the United Nations.

Finally, secret intelligence may become public intelligence when it is leaked on a sustained and contested basis. The result is warring intelligence. The competition need not be equal but the overall effect of having contending accounts of a situation emerge from secret intelligence over a protracted period of time is to preclude the emergence of a clear end point to the policy debate. Rather than pursuing a "sale" and moving on to other policy issues, here the opposing sides are involved in a siege in which the objective is to wear challengers down to the point where their opposition is no longer politically significant. Warring intelligence is not inevitable even where a policy debate exists. Secrecy may hold in parts of the national security establishment and its oversight system even when intelligence is becoming public from other parts.

One long running episode of warring intelligence centered on the state of the US-Soviet strategic balance in the late 1960s. By the late 1960s the focus of this policy debate had shifted from the performance capabilities of the Soviet Anti-Ballistic Missile (ABM) system to the need for an American ABM system and the capabilities of the Soviet SS-9. The technical issue here was whether or not the SS-9 had multiple warheads or multiple independently targeted warheads. The political issue was whether or not to fund the Safeguard ABM system requested by the Nixon administration. Much testimony was presented to Congress including assertions by

Secretary of Defense Melvin Laird as to the need for the Safeguard system. After listening to the conflicting testimony Senator Albert Gore publicly asserted that the "National Intelligence Estimate does not concur with the statements made by Dr. Foster [Director of Defense, Research and Engineering at the Pentagon] and by Mr. Laird." Laird was publicly on record as having asserted that the Soviet Union was undertaking an arms buildup that would give it a first strike capability against the United States. Shortly after Gore's statement information on the contents of a new estimate were leaked to the press revealing CIA disagreements with the Pentagon over the extent of the SS-9's capabilities.

In a June 1969 press conference Nixon sought to build public support for the Safeguard system by publicly referencing secret intelligence. He asserted:

> in recommending Safeguard, I did so based on intelligence information at that time. Since that time new intelligence information with regard to the Soviet success in testing multiple entry vehicles…has convinced me that Safeguard is even more important…there isn't any question that it [SS-9] has a multiple weapon and that its footprints indicate that it just happens to fall in somewhat the precise area in which our Minuteman silos are located.[12]

Laird went on the offensive in March 1970 when he charged that "for some time, the Soviet forces which became operational in a given year have often exceeded the previous intelligence projections for that year." To support his case Laird released the national estimate projections for 1966–70.[13] Later that year, Laird showed reporters film of Soviet multiple warhead tests to bolster his case.[14]

Warring intelligence also surfaced during the Reagan administration. It came into office determined to change the direction of American foreign policy toward Central America from one emphasizing human rights to one centered on halting the spread of communism through the region. El Salvador was the first target for this reversal in policy. In 1981 the State Department released a White Paper citing documents considered to be authoritative as indicating that in late 1980 the Soviet Union and Cuba agreed to deliver weapons to the Marxist guerrillas operating in that country. Secretary of State Alexander Haig stated that this was an example of unprecedented risk taking on the part of the Soviet Union and a challenge to the future of American-Soviet relations. Instead of galvanizing

American support for a policy change the White Paper provoked great debate. Soon after its release *New York Times* columnist Flora Lewis wrote of the existence of a 29-page dissenting paper within the intelligence community. Among the arguments it made was that intelligence not supporting the administration's desired change in policy was suppressed. Later news stories questioned the translation of various materials cited and Haig's allegations that the intelligence available pointed to unprecedented Soviet risk taking. In March 1982, as the El Salvadoran elections neared, the Reagan administration released some previously classified intelligence reports to bolster its position. In congressional testimony Haig described the intelligence as providing "overwhelming and unrefutable" evidence that the Salvadoran guerrillas were under foreign control. To further its case the State Department publicly presented an alleged Nicaraguan rebel leader operating in El Salvador. Much to the embarrassment of the State Department he recanted his story. Next the administration released intelligence photos showing a military buildup in Nicaragua. The photos were from an SR 71A spy plane rather than a satellite to try and protect its true capabilities. The potential benefits of this revelation were quickly negated by a *Washington Post* story that the administration had secretly authorized the spending of $19 million to train a 500-person paramilitary force to attack Nicaraguan power plants and bridges as well as disrupt the flow of weapons to El Salvador. There was further damaging news for the administration in November when *Newsweek* ran a story revealing the existence of a covert war to overthrow the Nicaraguan government and the US involvement in training and organizing the Contra rebel forces in Honduras. The culmination of this political conflict in which warring intelligence played a central part was the passage of the Boland Amendment that barred the use of US funds to overthrow the Nicaraguan government.

CHARACTERISTICS AND CONSEQUENCES OF PUBLIC INTELLIGENCE

Regardless of which of these four forms public intelligence takes, it has a set of common characteristics. First, public intelligence is incomplete intelligence. It is intelligence out of context. The purpose of public intelligence is not to tell the whole story but to highlight a certain aspect of a policy problem. Second, public intelligence is action prompting.

Good intelligence needs to be policy relevant but it does not dictate policy. Public intelligence takes on an oracle quality in which it appears to be revealing some divine truth that theretofore has been hidden from view. It gives the impression that great dangers await unless some now self-evident action is taken. Third, public intelligence is accusatory. The guilty party changes. It may be a policy maker who has failed to take appropriate action, another country that has not lived up to its word, or an intelligence agency that has not performed up to standard. Fourth, public intelligence lacks nuance. Under the best of circumstances it is difficult to express the level of certainty that exists in intelligence analysis and to highlight those aspects of a situation that are known and those that are unknown. Public intelligence is presented with an aura of certainty and conviction. All of the uncertainty that surrounds the analytic process is absorbed leaving an absolutist quality. Finally, there is little, if any, penalty for being wrong. Public intelligence achieves its desired impact not through the qualities of good "secret" intelligence presented earlier but through the ability to move the public debate and the range of acceptable policy options. In this respect the reach and staying power of bad news far exceeds that of good news. It becomes the intelligence of choice regardless of its insightfulness.

Beyond distorting the analytic process and the intelligence product that emerges from it, these characteristics of public intelligence contribute to intelligence failures in other ways. Public intelligence makes achieving consensus more difficult because it raises the stakes for organizations and individuals by calling into question their competence and integrity. This is most notably the case where leaks are systematic and lead to blame laying and scapegoating. The challenge to consensus building exists at multiple levels. Not only does it affect the ability of highly visible policymakers to work out policy agreements, it also complicates the efforts of those working anonymously within the intelligence community to forge a consensus on how to interpret the information they have. Beyond making the achievement of consensus more difficult, public intelligence has the potential for reducing viable policy options. It does so both by presenting a problem in stark black and white terms and in ways that lend themselves to first case thinking. This creates the potential for masking a policy failure under the guise of an intelligence failure. Finally, another consequence is the loss of credibility for intelligence products. The cumulative

effect of making intelligence public over time and across policy arenas is to call into question the value of future intelligence and produce calls for the reform and restructuring of the intelligence community. The danger is that the organizational reforms will not address (and cannot address) all the factors that contributed to the intelligence failure. As a consequence not only will there be the inevitable future intelligence failure but there may also occur a spiraling public distrust of intelligence.

PUBLIC INTELLIGENCE AND THE IRAQ WAR: A CASE STUDY

The George W. Bush administration engaged in a campaign of orchestrated public intelligence in the lead-up to the Iraq War that was part of the administration's broader campaign to build support for the war. It was not an entirely one-sided campaign as doubts were expressed about the quality of the intelligence being cited by the administration. The challenges did not, however, take the form of leaked secret intelligence or the release of sanitized secret intelligence. They either were public rebuttals based on conclusions reached by others who examined the same data or secret doubts raised by intelligence agencies. In the case study that follows both the intelligence made public by the administration and commentary about its accuracy are presented.

The campaign to build support for the war began in August 2002 with two comments made by Vice President Cheney. The first came on 7 August. Responding to a question at the Commonwealth Club in San Francisco, Cheney said "it is the judgment of many of us that in the not too-distant future he [Saddam Hussein] will acquire nuclear weapons." In a speech to the National Convention of the Veterans of Foreign Wars on 26 August which referenced intelligence in highlighting the threat posed by Saddam Hussein, Cheney stated "there is no doubt that Saddam Hussein has weapons of mass destruction." He continued, "we now know that Saddam has resumed his efforts to acquire nuclear weapons. Among other sources we've gotten this from firsthand testimony from defectors, including Saddam's own son-in law, who was subsequently murdered at Saddam's direction." Hussein Kamel, Saddam's son-in-law, managed Iraq's special weapons program until he defected to Jordan in 1995. He was killed in February 1996. The actual information he gave contradicted Cheney's public interpretation of it. Kamel stated Iraq's uranium enrichment program had not been restarted after the 1991 Persian Gulf War.[15]

Also in August 2002 under the direction of Chief of Staff Andrew Card the Bush administration set up a White House Iraq Group (WHIG) to ensure that the various parts of the White House were working in harmony on Iraq.[16] The group met weekly. Its members were Karl Rove, the president's senior political advisor; Karen Hughes, Mary Matlin, and James Wilkinson, communications strategists; Nicholas Calio, legislative liaison; Condoleezza Rice, national security advisor and her deputy Stephen Hadley; and I. Lewis Libby, Cheney's chief of staff. In a 6 September interview with the *New York Times* Card hinted that the purpose of the unit was to sell the war. He observed, "from a marketing point of view, you don't introduce new products in August."[17]

WHIG formed a strategic communications task force to work on speeches and white papers dealing with Iraq. The first White Paper produced, "A Grave and Gathering Danger: Saddam Hussein's Quest for Nuclear Weapons," went through at least five drafts but was never published. Working with administration officials beyond those in WHIG the document brought together intelligence reports and press clippings. It contained the claim that Iraq "sought uranium oxide, an essential ingredient in the enrichment process from Africa." It claimed that a satellite photograph shows "many signs of the reconstruction and acceleration of the Iraqi nuclear program." And it stated that "since the beginning of the nineties, Saddam Hussein has launched a crash program to divert nuclear fuel for…nuclear weapons." None of these assertions was accurate but all would appear in later administration statements. The claim that Iraq sought uranium from Africa was false. The second claim left out a statement by United Nations Chief Weapons Inspector Hans Blix that "you don't know what's under them [the buildings in the photos]." The third claim was presented as if referring to the current situation rather than the early 1990s as was actually the case.

President Bush and British Prime Minister Tony Blair met at Camp David on 7 September and each made public pronouncements regarding the seriousness of the threat. Blair cited a report from the International Atomic Energy Agency (IAEA) showing "what's been going on at the former weapons sites" and Bush said an IAEA report placed Iraq "six months away from developing a [nuclear] weapon. I don't know what more evidence we need." Neither reference was to a contemporary IAEA report. In Blair's case he was referencing news reports. President Bush was citing an IAEA report written in 1996 and updated in 1998 and 1999. It stated that

> based on all credible information to date, the IAEA has found no indication of Iraq having achieved its program goal of producing nuclear weapons or of Iraq having retained a physical capacity for the production of weapon usable nuclear material or having clandestinely obtained such material.

The report did say that before the Gulf War Iraq was six months to a year away from having a nuclear capacity.

The following day the *New York Times* quoted anonymous administration officials on Iraq's possession of aluminum tubes whose specifications made them ideally suited as component parts of a centrifuge. That morning Rice, Cheney, Rumsfeld, and Secretary of State Colin Powell made appearances on TV talk shows. Rice stated on CNNs "Late Edition" that "we do know that there have been shipments going…into Iraq, for instance of aluminum tubes that really are only suited to…nuclear weapons programs, centrifuge programs." She noted that "there will always be some uncertainty about how quickly he can acquire nuclear weapons…but we don't want the smoking gun to be a mushroom cloud." Cheney on NBC's "Meet the Press" in speaking of the Iraqi nuclear program said "increasingly we believe the United States will become the target." Rumsfeld on CBS's "Face the Nation" asked viewers to imagine an 11 September with weapons of mass destruction.[18]

Next to speak for the administration was President Bush. At the United Nations on 12 September he repeated the charge that Iraq "has made several attempts to buy high strength aluminum tubes used to enrich uranium for a nuclear weapon. Should Iraq acquire missile material, it would be able to build a nuclear weapon within a year." Seized shipments were cited as proof. To buttress its case, the same day that Bush addressed the UN the administration released a background paper, "A Decade of Deception and Defiance: Saddam Hussein's Defiance of the United Nations." Included in the section on "the Development of Weapons of Mass Destruction" were already public references to a 2001 Iraqi defector who said he visited 20 chemical, biological, and nuclear weapons facilities there and a public report by the International Institute for Strategic Studies purporting to show that Saddam Hussein could build a bomb in months if he were able to obtain the necessary missile material.

One week after Bush spoke to the UN, Rumsfeld told the Senate Armed Services Committee that "at this moment" Iraq was trying to obtain the material needed to complete a nuclear weapon. On 26 September President Bush continued this theme of certainty stating "the Iraq regime possesses biological and chemical weapons. The Iraq regime is building the facilities necessary to make more biological and chemical weapons." The president's comments came around the same time a classified Defense Intelligence Agency document concluded that "no reliable information on whether Iraq is producing or stockpiling chemical weapons or whether Iraq has or will establish its chemical agent facilities."[19]

The charge that Iraq sought aluminum tubes in order to produce nuclear material originated within the US government with a CIA engineer-turned-analyst.[20] It was presented to UN nuclear inspectors in January 2002. His interpretation was not uniformly accepted by the intelligence community. Centrifuge scientists working for the Department of Energy were among those who rejected it. Controversy within the intelligence community over how to interpret the purpose of the aluminum tubes continued until September 2002 when it became necessary to take a position in the NIE that was about to be released. When put to a vote the Energy Department and State Department's Bureau of Intelligence and Research said no. The four other intelligence agencies participating in the deliberations, the Defense Intelligence Agency, the National Image and Mapping Agency, the National Security Agency, and the CIA, said "yes." The NIE was released affirming the interpretation stating that "most analysts" believed the aluminum tubes were intended for a centrifuge.

The validity of these allegations was quickly challenged. The Institute for Science and International Security (ISIS) in a report cited by the *Washington Post* asserted that "by themselves, these attempted procurements are not evidence that Iraq is in possession of, or even close to possessing nuclear weapons....They do not provide evidence that Iraq has an operating centrifuge plant."[21] The IAEA report also charged, and the administration acknowledged, that not all in the intelligence community agreed with the administration's public assessment of the situation.

In early March 2003, prior to the beginning of the war, Mohamed El Baradei, director general of the

IAEA, rejected the Bush administration's assertion that Iraq had sought to purchase aluminum tubes in order to produce nuclear-grade material. The IAEA undertook an intensive investigation into the aluminum tubes allegation after it returned to Iraq in November. Its preliminary conclusion, reached in January 2003, was that the aluminum tubes were "not directly suitable" for centrifuges. More likely they were to be used in the production of conventional artillery rockets. In its March report the IAEA noted that Iraq had tried unsuccessfully for 14 years to make these 81 mm tubes that would resist corrosion and perform well. In the course of these failures they had progressively raised the technical standards of the tubes they sought. Additionally, the ISIS concluded that the presence of "vanodized" features in the tubes that Powell would report to the UN in February 2003 actually increased the likelihood that they were for rockets and not centrifuges. The Institute reported that Powell's staff was briefed on this point prior to the address.[22]

The assertion that Iraq was trying to obtain "significant quantities of uranium from Africa" emerged in a 50-page intelligence report released by British Prime Minister Tony Blair on 24 September.[23] The report also indicated that Iraq could deploy nerve gas and anthrax weapons within 45 minutes of being ordered to do so by Saddam Hussein. On the question of Iraq's ability to build a nuclear weapon the report put forward a one to two year time frame should UN sanctions be lifted. President Bush said Iraq could do so within one year. The report became the center of controversy after David Kelly, a senior British weapons expert, committed suicide on 18 July 2003 following his testimony to a parliamentary committee investigating a BBC report that Blair's government had "sexed up" the report by exaggerating the claim that Iraq could deploy chemical or biological weapons in 45 minutes. Kelly was the suspected source of this allegation. Evidence revealed that Kelly had made a more subtle argument, similar to one that American intelligence officials would make regarding the accuracy of the Bush administration's caricature of Iraq's weapons of mass destruction capability. He told another BBC reporter that "it was a statement that was made and it just got all out of proportion.... In the end it was just a flurry of activity and it was very difficult to get comments in because people at the top of the ladder didn't want to hear some of the things." Memos revealed that the phrase "may be able to deploy" became "are able to deploy".[24] Kelly concluded that he did not think

Blair's staff was being "willfully dishonest" but that they had changed the wording for "public consumption," "to put things into words that the public will understand."[25]

On 2 October, between President Bush's address to the United Nations and his speech in Cincinnati on 7 October in which he stated "the evidence indicates Iraq is reconstituting its nuclear weapons program" and that "satellite photographs reveal that Iraq is rebuilding facilities at sites that have been part of its nuclear program in the past," the administration released a White Paper based on the classified NIE it had just produced. Entitled, "Iraq's Weapons of Mass Destruction Program," its lead "key judgment" was that "if left unchecked it [Iraq] probably will have a nuclear weapon during this decade." In the body of the text it stated:

> Baghdad could produce a nuclear weapon within a year if it were able to procure weapons-grade missile material abroad. Baghdad may have acquired uranium enrichment capabilities that could shorten substantially the amount of time necessary to make a nuclear weapon.[26]

The White Paper repeated the conclusion expressed by Bush on 26 September that Baghdad "has chemical and biological weapons" and that it "has begun renewed production of chemical warfare agents." The White Paper also contained maps and aerial photographs and made the case that new construction facilities were related to Iraq's nuclear program. One month before the war began personnel on the ground were able to verify that this interpretation was inaccurate.

In Bush's 7 October speech the president stated: "we have discovered through intelligence that Iraq has a growing fleet" of unmanned aircraft and worried they might be targeted on the United States. He also asserted that in 1998 "information from a high-ranking Iraqi nuclear engineer who had defected revealed that despite his public promises, Saddam Hussein had ordered his nuclear program to continue." This could, Bush continued, provide weapons of mass destruction to terrorist groups or allow Iraq to attack the United States. Left unsaid in these intelligence revelations was the fact that the defector, Khidhir Hamza, while he defected in 1998, had not worked in Iraq's nuclear program since 1991 and the conclusion that Iraq could attack the United States was counter to secret congressional testimony provided by the CIA. This testimony was declassified after Bush's speech. In it the CIA rated as "low"

the possibility that Iraq would initiate a chemical or biological attack on the United States but might take the "extreme step" of assisting terrorist groups if provoked.[27]

The next major salvo involving the orchestrated use of public intelligence came in President Bush's 28 January 2003 State of the Union Address. In it he stated: "the British government has learned that Saddam Hussein recently sought significant quantities of uranium from Africa." Shortly after the 11 September 2001 terrorist attacks the CIA received information from Italy's Military Intelligence and Security Service that in February 1999 Iraq's ambassador to the Vatican had openly traveled to Niger and a few other African states. No particular importance was attached to the trip at the time. Now Italy's intelligence service raised the possibility that the purpose of the mission was to purchase uranium ore, Niger's major export.

The report was not met with widespread credence within the intelligence community for a number of reasons, including the absence of corroborating documentation. The report was, however, stovepiped to high ranking administration officials including Vice President Cheney who would engage in a "year long tug of war" with the agency over the truthfulness of the Italian theory. By early 2002 public references to Iraq's attempted purchase of uranium were appearing. The CIA stated "Baghdad may be attempting to acquire materials that could aid in reconstituting its nuclear weapons program" in a declassified report given to Congress shortly after the president's State of the Union address. Powell told the House International Affairs Committee that "with respect to the nuclear program, there is no doubt that the Iraqis are pursuing it."

In an effort to resolve questions over the report's authenticity the CIA arranged for retired Ambassador John Wilson to fly to Niger to investigate the matter in February 2002. The trip lasted eight days and Wilson concluded the allegations were without merit. He could find no evidence that a document arranging for such a sale was signed and concluded that there was not any uranium available for export since all of it had been pre-sold. The first press accounts of Wilson's trip surfaced 15 months after his trip and the affair quickly became entangled in revelations from the White House that Wilson's wife was a CIA employee. The allegations were first publicly refuted just prior to the beginning of the Iraq War when IAEA Director Mohamed El Baradei declared key documents that had been given to the

IAEA in February 2003 by the CIA to be forgeries. The CIA had come into possession of these documents in October 2002 when an Italian journalist turned them over to the American embassy in Rome. It considered the documents to be of "dubious authenticity" and little value since they contained no new information.[28]

After the war had ended, in July 2003, it was revealed that on two occasions in October 2002 the CIA raised strong doubts about the Niger-Iraq uranium connection. The CIA warned in memos that the allegation that Iraq had tried to acquire 500 tons of uranium from Niger rested on weak evidence and was not particularly significant. It also came to light that DCI George Tenet called Steven Hadley, Condoleezza Rice's assistant, the day before President Bush's 7 October Cincinnati speech and got him to agree to remove this reference ("The regime has been caught attempting to purchase substantial amounts of uranium oxide from sources in Africa") from that speech.[29]

Still, this same reference appeared in Bush's State of the Union address in slightly altered form. A few days before the speech Robert Joseph, a presidential assistant for nonproliferation, asked the CIA if the reference to Iraq's attempted purchase of 500 tons of uranium from Niger could be included in the State of the Union address. Alan Foley, the CIA official contacted, objected to mentioning Niger and the specific amount. Joseph agreed but countered by suggesting that more general language could be used, noting the British intelligence report's less precise language. Foley responded that the CIA had objected to this formulation too but the British went ahead with it using their own sources.[30]

Public intelligence was at the heart of Secretary of State Powell's 5 February 2003 address to the UN Security Council. A few days before the speech, he cautioned observers that he would not present a "smoking gun." In making his case, however, he affirmed that "every statement I make today is backed up by sources, solid sources.... These are not assertions. What we are giving you are facts and conclusions based on solid intelligence." Powell was accompanied by DCI George Tenet in a move intended to symbolize the certainty of the information that he presented in his 90-minute multimedia presentation that included photographs, intercepted phone conversations, and charts linking Iraq to al-Qaeda.

Powell stated: "We know from sources that a missile brigade outside Baghdad was dispersing rocket launchers and warheads containing biological agents to various locations." UN weapons inspector David Kay would later report that he found no evidence that "any chemical weapons were present on the battlefield, even in small numbers." Powell also asserted that the United States has "satellite photos that indicate banned materials have recently been moved from a number of Iraqi weapons of mass destruction facilities." The material Powell identified was used for hazardous material transfers. Missiles identified in the photos were later destroyed by UN weapons inspectors. Powell also affirmed that "we have first hand descriptions of biological weapons factories on wheels and rails." President Bush would later cite the capture of two of these facilities as proof that Iraq had weapons of mass destruction.[31] UN weapons inspectors concluded that they were not suitable for this purpose and the CIA also had its doubts. He claimed that "We know Iraq has embedded key portions of its illicit chemical weapons infrastructure within its legitimate civilian industry." Kay reported that evidence indicates Iraq did not have a large centrally controlled chemical weapons program after 1991 and that all remaining stocks were destroyed after 1995. Finally, Powell stated: "We have detected one of Iraq's newest UAVs [unmanned aerial vehicles] in a test flight that went 500 kilometers...Iraq could use these small UAVs...to deliver biological agents to its neighbors or if transported to other countries, including the United States." Iraq did have a large UAV program. It was used for surveillance. Kay stated that it did not have a deployment capability and had not successfully been mounted with a chemical sprayer.

President Bush would publicly reference intelligence at least twice more before the war began. In his 8 February 2003 radio address to the nation he stated: "We have sources that tell us that Saddam Hussein recently authorized Iraqi field commanders to use chemical weapons." Then, in delivering his final ultimatum to Iraq on 17 March, the president told the nation that "intelligence gathered by this and other governments leaves no doubt that the Iraq regime continues to possess and conceal some of the most lethal weapons ever devised."[32]

IRAQ WAR PUBLIC INTELLIGENCE POST MORTEM

The characteristics and consequences of public intelligence identified earlier were on display in the buildup to the Iraq War and the postwar debate. The incompleteness of the public intelligence was evident in the outdated nature of much of the information on Iraq's weapons of mass destruction program and the controversial nature of the interpretations given to it. After the war Paul Wolfowitz acknowledged there had been a tendency to emphasize weapons of mass destruction because of differences in the administration over the strength of other charges such as its ties to al-Qaeda.[33] The public intelligence was action-prompting. It was used to paint a picture of grave and imminent threat. Additional on-site weapons inspections would take too much time. Congressional authorization of military actions could not wait until after the November elections but had to be given before then.

The public intelligence was accusatory. Saddam Hussein was the villain. It was his actions that public intelligence documented. He had created the foreign policy problem facing the United States. Moreover, since he had demonstrated a ruthless willingness to use military force, repeatedly broken his word and engaged in deception there could only be one interpretation of his actions. On 2 December 2003 White House press secretary Ari Fleischer observed that "Saddam Hussein would be misleading the world" by denying that he had weapons of mass destruction. "You've heard the president say repeatedly that he has chemical and biological weapons."[34] Public intelligence was presented in absolute terms. Intelligence analysts noted that they were not responsible for the manner in which it was presented to the public. One senior official stated that "the president's speechwriters took 'literacy license' with intelligence."[35] Another said "we were careful about language, and it's not fair to accuse the analysts for what others say about our material."[36] After the war the administration took two different positions on the strength of the intelligence it used. Wolfowitz expressed both views. On one occasion he asserted "there was no oversell."[37] On another he commented "If there's a problem with intelligence...it doesn't mean anybody misled anybody. It means that intelligence is an art and not a science."[38] Finally, public intelligence such as that concerning the aluminum tubes or the attempted purchase of uranium from Niger continued to be aired even as support for these interpretations from the intelligence community disappeared. They continued to be good stories even though they were based on bad intelligence.

Turning to the broader consequences of public intelligence, evidence of scapegoating was easy to find. For three weeks in July 2002 a battle raged over who was responsible for the "16 words" in Bush's 2003 State of the Union address that referenced Iraq's attempt to buy uranium from Africa. Initially President Bush and national security advisor Condoleezza Rice blamed the CIA. DCI Tenet accepted responsibility for the statement. The laying of blame on the CIA did not end the controversy. By the end of the month Bush accepted "personal responsibility" for the matter. In February 2004 Tenet made a public speech at Georgetown University in which he defended the CIA's analysis of information before the war and rejected charges that political considerations had affected the intelligence product. Never, he said, did the intelligence community say "there was an imminent threat" and that "no intelligence agency thought that Iraq's efforts had progressed to the point of building an enrichment facility or making missile material. We said such activities were a few years away."[39]

Public intelligence also limited options. In February 2004, Colin Powell commented that he did not know if he would have recommended an invasion of Iraq had he known that it did not possess a stockpile of banned weapons.[40] Powell is speaking to the accuracy of the intelligence but, in part, this misses the point. Public intelligence directs our attention not to its accuracy but the manner in which intelligence is used. What made changing direction difficult is the way in which public intelligence raises the stakes of a decision and casts problems in simple terms. Here, public intelligence was being used—and being used by the president—to justify war. And, as Walter Pincus noted in his *Washington Post* article on the allegation that Iraq tried to buy uranium in Africa, Bush kept repeating the charge because by the time he gave his 2002 State of the Union address "almost all other evidence had either been undercut or disproved by UN inspectors in Iraq."[41] It was all he had left. If intelligence was preventing a shift in policy it was not secret intelligence that was doing so but public intelligence.

Loss of confidence in the intelligence community was not long in coming. Congressional investigations were launched into the quality of the intelligence available to the Bush administration in the period leading up to the war and how intelligence was used by the White House.[42] Overseas, the Polish government expressed concern that it had been misled by prewar intelligence claims. Perhaps most telling, the accuracy of the intelligence community's prewar assessments became part of a larger questioning of its abilities in the 9–11 Commission's public hearings into that day's tragedies.

CONCLUSION

The surprise Japanese attack of 7 December 1941 on Pearl Harbor cemented in the minds of policy makers the importance of information for the conduct of American foreign policy. Yet for many years little scholarly attention was given to intelligence. It was a largely unexamined area of American national security policy. In one sense we are far removed from this state of neglect. Memoir accounts by intelligence professionals and policy makers have provided us with great insight into the role played by intelligence and intelligence organizations in the making of American foreign policy. Congressional hearings and investigations have provided still another entry point into the practice of intelligence. Case studies of surprise have generated concepts and frameworks that permit comparisons across time and space. As a consequence we are now able to move beyond identifying and debating the elements of intelligence and begin to explore creating theories of intelligence.[43] At the same time there are still gaps in our understanding of intelligence. One of these is the political reality that not all intelligence remains secret. Sometimes it becomes public intelligence. The framework presented here demonstrates that there is no single pattern to the process by which secret intelligence becomes public intelligence. It is not enough to simply refer to it as leaked intelligence. Further development of theories of intelligence must incorporate this public dimension of intelligence into its analysis if our understanding of the interplay of intelligence and policy is to move forward. The case study of orchestrated intelligence in the lead-up to the Iraq War presented here highlights one pattern of public intelligence. It reveals the underlying characteristics of public intelligence and demonstrates the negative consequences it has for the intelligence function and the ability of intelligence agencies to provide credible and timely advice to policy makers.

QUESTIONS FOR FURTHER DISCUSSION

1. What is promotional intelligence?
2. Under what circumstances should policymakers release classified information to the public?
3. Did policymakers deliberately mislead the public about alleged Iraqi activities in Niger, or did their statements accurately reflect intelligence estimates?
4. Is there a single process whereby secret intelligence becomes public?

ENDNOTES

1. "Kay: 'We were almost all wrong,'" *Washington-post.com*, 28 January 2004, 12:50 pm.
2. See Mark Lowenthal, *Intelligence: From Secrets to Policy*, 2nd edn. (Washington, DC: Congressional Quarterly Press, 2003), pp. 108–10; Shlomo Gazit, "Intelligence Estimates and the Decision Maker," *Intelligence and National Security*, 3 (1988), pp. 261–7; and Alfred Maurer et al. (eds.), *Intelligence: Policy and Process* (Boulder: Westview Press, 1985).
3. Christopher Andrew, *For the President's Eyes Only: Secret Intelligence and the American Presidency from Washington to [H.W.] Bush* (New York: Harper Collins 1995), p. 249.
4. Ibid., p. 357.
5. Ibid., p. 424.
6. Ibid., p. 432.
7. Ibid., p. 471.
8. Chalmers Johnson, *Blowback: The Costs and Consequences of American Empire* (New York: Owl Books 2000), p. 134.
9. Andrew, *For the President's Eyes Only* (note 3), p. 445.
10. John Prados, *The Soviet Estimate* (Princeton, NJ: Princeton University Press 1986), p. 59.
11. Andrew, *For the President's Eyes Only* (note 3), pp. 295–8.
12. Ibid., pp. 357–8.
13. Prados, *The Soviet Estimate* (note 10), p. 193.
14. Ibid., p. l95.
15. "Sounding the Drums of War," *The Washington Post*, 10 August 2003, p. A9.
16. Barton Gellman and Walter Pincus, "Depiction of Threat Outgrew Supporting Evidence," *The Washington Post*, 10 August 2003, p. Al.
17. Ibid.
18. "Sounding the Drums of War," *The Washington Post*, 10 August 2003, p. A9.
19. Dana Priest and Walter Pincus, "Bush Certainty on Iraq Arms Went Beyond Analysts' Views," *The Washington Post*, 7 June 2003, p. Al.
20. Gellman and Pincus, "Depiction of Threat Outgrew Supporting Evidence" (note 16).
21. Joby Warrick, "Evidence on Iraq Challenged," *The Washington Post*, 19 September 2003.
22. Joby Warrick, "Some Evidence on Iraq Called Fake," *The Washington Post*, 3 March 2003.

23. Glenn Frankel, "Blair: Iraq Can Deploy Quickly," *The Washington Post*, 25 September 2002.

24. Glenn Frankel, "Blair Aides Shaped Iraq Dossier," *The Washington Post*, 23 August 2003, p. A14.

25. "British Court Hears Arms Expert on Tape," *The Washington Post*, 14 August 2003, p. A12.

26. Iraq's Weapons of Mass Destruction Programs, October 2002. <www.cia.gov/cia/reports/iraq>.

27. Dana Milbank, "For Bush, Facts Are Malleable," *The Washington Post*, 22 October 2002.

28. Walter Pincus and Dana Priest, "U.S. Had Uranium Papers Earlier," *The Washington Post*, 18 July 2003, p. A1.

29. Walter Pincus and Mike Allen, "CIA Got Uranium Mention Cut in Oct," *The Washington Post*, 13 July 2003, p. Al; Dana Milbank and Walter Pincus, "Bush Aides Disclose Warning From CIA," *The Washington Post*, 23 July 2003, p. Al; and Walter Pincus, "Bush Team Kept Airing Iraq Allegation," *The Washington Post*, 8 August 2003, p. A10.

30. Pincus and Priest, "U.S. Had Uranium Papers Earlier" (note 28).

31. Mike Allen, "Bush: 'We Found Banned Weapons'," *The Washington Post*, 31 May 2003.

32. Dana Milbank, "Bush Remarks Confirm Shift in Justification for War," *The Washington Post*, p. Al. 1 June 2003, p. A18.

33. Karen DeYoung and Walter Pincus, "U.S. Hedges on Finding Iraqi Weapons," *The Washington Post*, 29 May 2003, p. Al.

34. Milbank, "Bush Remarks Confirm Shift in Justification for War" (note 32).

35. Gellman and Pincus, "Depiction of Threat Outgrew Supporting Evidence" (note 16).

36. "Transcript: CIA Director Defends Iraq Intelligence," *Washingtonpost.com*, 5 February 2004.

37. DeYoung and Pincus, "U.S. Hedges on Finding Iraqi Weapons" (note 33).

38. Walter Pincus and Dana Priest, "Lawmakers Begin Iraq Intelligence Hearings," *The Washington. Post*, 19 June 2003, p. Al6.

39. A transcript of his comments is available at <washington post.com>: "Tenet: Analysts Never Claimed Imminent Threat Before War."

40. Glenn Kessler, "Powell Says New Data May Have Affected War Decision," *The Washington Post*, 3 February 2004, p. Al.

41. Walter Pincus, "Bush Faced Dwindling Data on Iraq Nuclear Bid," *The Washington Post*, 16 July 2003, p. Al.

42. Dana Priest, "House Probers Conclude Iraq War Data Was Weak," *The Washington Post*, 28 September 2003, p. Al; and Walter Pincus, "Intelligence Weaknesses Are Cited," *The Washington Post*, 29 November 3002, p. A18.

43. See, for example, Loch Johnson, "Preface to a Theory of Strategic Intelligence," *International Journal of Intelligence and Counterintelligence*, 16 (2003), pp. 638–63; and David Kahn, "An Historical Theory of Intelligence," *Intelligence and National Security*, 16 (2001), pp. 79–92.

From Glenn Hastedt, "Public Intelligence: Leaks as Policy Instruments—The Case of the Iraq War," *Intelligence and National Security* 20 (September 2005): 419–439. Reprinted by permission of the publisher (Taylor & Francis Ltd, http://www.informaworld.com).

V

INTELLIGENCE AND THE POLICYMAKER

Barnado: "Sit down awhile
And let us once again assail your ears,
That are so fortified against our story."
—SHAKESPEARE, *Hamlet*, 1.1.31–33

Policymakers—elected officials, career civil servants, and senior military officers—have an extraordinarily important part to play in the intelligence cycle. They are the individuals who must develop or change policy in response to the estimates and reporting produced by the intelligence community. Without effective communication among policymakers and intelligence analysts and managers, there is simply no way to put intelligence to good use in making and conducting foreign or defense policy.

LINES OF COMMUNICATION

Although the September 11 tragedy is reshaping the lines of communication between the intelligence community and policymakers, intelligence managers and analysts direct most of their efforts toward five clients within the U.S. government. First and foremost is the president and his immediate staff. The relationship with this client is crucial

and is often handled personally by the Director of National Intelligence (DNI). Occasionally, when the issues are important or the topics under consideration are complex or highly technical, the DNI (or, prior to 2005, the DCI) will bring analysts to the White House or the old Executive Office Building to brief the president or members of his staff. In the past, some DCIs were not particularly welcome at the White House, but most have served as the Chief Intelligence Officer to the president.

Second, the intelligence community maintains close links with the National Security Council (NSC), which supports the president in his conduct of U.S. foreign and defense policy. The NSC is staffed by military officers, political appointees, career civil servants, and intelligence professionals who are experts on various issues and regions. The intelligence community supports the NSC as it works to coordinate foreign and defense policy across a variety of government agencies and the military services and as it monitors policy implementation.

Third, intelligence managers and analysts have traditionally forged relationships with political appointees and senior career civil servants throughout the Defense and State departments. In the Defense Department, the intelligence community focuses on providing information to the civilians within the Office of the Secretary of Defense and the military officers who fill the ranks of the Joint Staff. These contacts within cabinet departments and with the Joint Staff are important, because these individuals make recommendations that are used by top staffers directly supporting the president in the formulation of national policy. These officials also make sure their own organizations work faithfully to implement policy generated by senior members of the administration. In the aftermath of September 11, interaction is also increasing with the Departments of Justice, Commerce, Treasury, Agriculture, and Homeland Security, under the guidance of the DNI.

Fourth, the intelligence community interacts with individual members of Congress, Congressional committees, and their staffs. In this role, intelligence managers provide not only finished intelligence to elected officials but also information related to Congressional oversight of the activities of the intelligence community (Lowenthal 2006).

The intelligence community also is a great contributor to the *interagency process*, a system of consultations between mid-level officials over the formulation and conduct of foreign and defense policy. All organizations with a vested interest in the policy at hand are asked to arrive at a consensus that they can support. The interagency process can be cumbersome because it must accommodate multiple players with a variety of interests and because it gives tremendous power to holdouts—organizations that demand specific concessions to move forward with policy. The interagency process thus affects the intelligence community in two ways: (1) by the policies that flow from the interagency process, and (2) by contributing intelligence materials that influence the nature of the interagency debate. Because they share the same long-term perspective on policy, career civil servants and intelligence professionals often have more common positions with each other in interagency debates than they do with the political appointees who face severe time constraints in terms of achieving their objectives.

THE ROLE OF POLICYMAKERS

Policymakers obviously need to use intelligence to advance national objectives, but they also play an important part in other functions of the intelligence cycle. Policymakers often have a great deal to say when it comes to setting intelligence requirements—that is, identifying topics that should be of interest to the intelligence community when it comes to collecting data and producing finished intelligence. Policymakers generally leave the technical and often arcane process of collecting information to intelligence professionals, although they sometimes intervene if intelligence operations pose grave political or military risks. The U-2 reconnaissance program attracted the attention of senior officials because of the risks of using aircraft to overfly Soviet or Cuban territory in the late 1950s and early 1960s. Policymakers can also turn to the intelligence community with specific requests for information that help them devise policy or political positions, a process that can lead to frustration if policymakers hold unrealistic expectations about intelligence capabilities. Policymakers tend to think that experts and information on just about everything reside somewhere within the intelligence community, an expectation that ignores budgetary and bureaucratic reality (Lowenthal 2006). The risk of intelligence politicization also looms large if policymakers begin to see intelligence as simply another weapon in partisan politics.

The intelligence community would not exist if it were not for policymakers' need to make foreign and defense policy. But intelligence managers sometimes are wary of policymakers and worry about sharing too much sensitive intelligence. There is always a risk that officials will leak classified information to the media. Officials "leak" for a variety of reasons (see Glenn Hastedt's chapter on "public intelligence" in this volume). Sometimes they leak classified information to score political points by bolstering their position or damaging the position of their opponents. Sometimes they leak information to focus government or public attention on a problem they believe is being overlooked. Sometimes they leak information because they like to feel important; journalists might even be expected to return a favor by putting a positive news spin on one's pet policy or by writing a favorable story about one's performance in office. Most of the time, the information that is leaked is of transient importance. However, some leaked information can cause grave damage to national security or destroy the effectiveness of intelligence programs created at enormous expense. A September 1971 *Washington Post* article written by Jack Anderson is a case in point. Anderson wrote that U.S. intelligence organizations, in Operation

GUPPY, were intercepting telephone calls made by Politburo members from their limousines as they drove around Moscow (Anderson 1973). Soon after the report, the transmissions ceased. What is maddening from the perspective of the intelligence community is the fact is that these "leakers" are rarely if ever identified, reprimanded, or prosecuted for releasing classified information. Most intelligence officials probably would wish that Anderson had not written the story, but they are most critical of the government official (who of course might have been a member of the intelligence community) who gave Anderson the piece of information in the first place.

Occasionally, the president and his closest advisers decide to reveal classified information as part of a deliberate effort to build public and international support for national policy. Today, the public has almost come to expect that U.S. administrations will present their case using classified information—radio intercepts, pictures taken from reconnaissance satellites, or even agent reports. Although the president is within his rights to authorize the use of classified material in a public forum to support national policy, members of the intelligence community consider this type of action to be a mixed blessing. They recognize the enormous impact that classified information can have on public opinion, but they worry that using current intelligence in this way can compromise sources and methods. In other words, revealing classified information provides clear indications to opponents about how the intelligence community collects and analyzes data. Even though it might seem unlikely that publicly revealing a reconnaissance photo can do lasting damage, revelations of classified data can have a cumulative effect. Over time, those targeted by the intelligence community can build a good picture of how information is gathered and analyzed, allowing them to identify and rectify vulnerabilities that were being exploited for the purposes of intelligence collection. Intelligence managers and analysts focus on these long-term consequences when classified data are made public. They tend to worry that their future ability to collect and analyze information is being mortgaged to meet today's political demands.

INTELLIGENCE FOR THE POLICYMAKER

The relationship between the intelligence community and policymakers also varies in terms of the nature of the information supplied to senior officials. *Warning intelligence* informs policymakers about direct and immediate threats to national security or the impending failure of foreign policy. To produce warning intelligence, however, someone has to designate exactly what needs to be monitored. Intelligence analysts would prefer for policymakers to give them a list of people, places, or things that should be watched closely, while policymakers would rather deliver blanket orders to the intelligence community to take all necessary steps to avoid being surprised. If a warning needs to be delivered, analysts then face the problem of getting busy policymakers to pay attention to what at first glance might appear to be some minor disturbance (after all, warnings of potential disasters always appear less threatening than actual disastrous events). Sometimes, analysts face the opposite problem: They have to communicate to policymakers that signs of impending danger are overblown. Analysts have to place alarming news or diplomatic reporting in an analytical or historical context, and sometimes they have to convince policymakers not to overreact to events that appear threatening. Warning intelligence also works best when standard procedures are in place to communicate quickly and credibly to senior officials. Given the difficulty of getting people to pay attention to disturbing information, it also helps to have some sort of feedback mechanism in place so that analysts can be assured that their warnings have been received and understood.

Policymakers also rely on the intelligence community for *current intelligence*. Compared with other finished intelligence products, current intelligence—the *National Intelligence Daily* (NID) and *President's Daily Brief* (PDB)—resembles newspaper reporting. Working on the NID is a lot like working as a journalist at a major newspaper or television network. The NID and PDB are best thought of as classified newspapers, with feature articles and shorter "news stories" about important current and upcoming events. Analysts involved in the production of this current intelligence face many challenges, especially those created by competing news organizations. Given the advent of global news networks, Internet communications, and satellite television phones, current intelligence can be easily "scooped" by global media outlets, much to the chagrin of intelligence analysts. Instead of trying to beat the news cycle (an impossible task given the fact that cable news networks are monitored in offices throughout the government), intelligence analysts comment on the veracity of media stories or provide additional insights based on classified information. Current intelligence is unlikely to tell policy experts new information about their specific fields of expertise, but it does provide them with a body of knowledge about events that are affecting other parts of the government.

Analysts also conduct *basic research*—major research products that can take months to complete. They undertake these "term papers" to gain expertise or to respond to specific questions raised by policymakers. Basic research helps analysts place current events in their correct historical or political context and provides them with the background needed to identify and trace the impact of obscure issues that can undermine well-crafted policies. Unless policymakers ask for these basic research reports directly, however, they are unlikely to read them and often respond negatively to in-boxes that seem to be filled with an endless stream of detailed intelligence reports. When it comes to intelligence, policymakers value brevity and relevance. The challenge for intelligence managers is to make sure that basic research is delivered to policymakers who would be interested in the report—i.e., individuals who already are experts in the field addressed by the research.

Intelligence estimates—the National Intelligence Estimates (NIEs), for example—are formal intelligence reports produced by the entire intelligence community to support key policy decisions. These estimates require close coordination with policy agendas because they attempt to single out and explore the key issues on which some policy hinges. To be useful, these estimates have to be closely coordinated with policy agendas, a situation that requires policymakers to provide the intelligence community with the lead time necessary to perform the analysis. Accusations about politicization of the intelligence process are most likely to emerge with intelligence estimates, because they are directly linked to issues of political or policy importance.

Finally, policymakers, to the consternation of intelligence professionals, sometimes request raw intelligence—agent reports, reconnaissance photographs, or intercepted communications—so that they can evaluate these materials themselves. Dissemination of this kind of information is risky from the perspective of intelligence managers, because it can easily compromise the sources or methods used to collect and analyze raw intelligence. But it is the timing of these requests that is especially disconcerting to intelligence professionals; the requests usually occur in moments of crisis, when information flows increase and critical decisions have to be made on short notice. When it matters most, policymakers or senior military commanders want to serve as their own chief intelligence analyst; they want to view raw data to make up their own minds about its meaning. But policymakers rarely have the expertise or knowledge to place raw intelligence in its proper context or to judge the authenticity or accuracy of the information, and a crisis is a poor time to attempt to develop that skill set. The best policymakers and senior officers resist the urge to serve as their own chief intelligence analyst and instead bombard analysts and managers with a series of questions to assess the degree to which they are confident in their assessments (Hulnick 1986).

GETTING OVER THE ROUGH SPOTS

One important perspective that separates career intelligence officers from policymakers who are political appointees is a different perception of the time available to accomplish the tasks before them. Political appointees are under pressure to show results quickly, or at least to demonstrate some progress on vexing issues before the next election. Intelligence professionals tend to see policy cycles in a longer perspective. In the rush to gain results, policymakers want support from the rest of the "career bureaucracy" to gain their policy objectives quickly. By contrast, intelligence analysts are less interested in the success of a specific policy per se and more interested in preserving the long-term effectiveness of the relationship between the intelligence and policy communities; they are likely to cry foul if they are pressured to supply intelligence to be used as ammunition in the political fray.

This difference in perspectives about time constraints and objectives creates several rough spots in the relations between elected officials and intelligence professionals. Policymakers want clear recommendations from the intelligence community and complain when finished intelligence tends to survey the range of possible future contingencies and policy outcomes. When intelligence analysts hedge their bets, policymakers suspect some sort of bias, especially when the reservations voiced by analysts conflict with policymakers' preferences. Policymakers, especially those with minimal government experience, often know little about how intelligence estimates are developed. Without knowing the individuals responsible for the analysis, they are sometimes not sure of how seriously to take various finished intelligence reports. As a result, they are reluctant to accept intelligence judgments that conflict with their preferences, which are of course the very findings that should enter into the policy formulation process. The intelligence community sometimes exacerbates this problem by carefully choosing the language used in estimates to suggest subtle differences in the confidence it has in key findings. These subtle variations are often lost on policymakers who know little of the distinctions that are being made. Additionally, policymakers are unlikely to wade through stacks of current intelligence reports and research papers in search of relevant material and often become frustrated by the need to cull through mountains of paperwork to get to a few useful nuggets of information (Hulnick 1986).

When dealing with policymakers, analysts also encounter their own problems. It is difficult to monitor the twists and turns in the debate over policy to guarantee that intelligence reports and estimates are relevant. Standardized intelligence products do little to address the concerns or needs of individual policymakers and are often ignored. Policymakers will also ignore information if it fails to address the issue that is filling their in-box at a given moment. If left to their own devices, policymakers tend to ask for opinions about policy options, advice which is beyond the purview of intelligence managers and analysts (Hulnick 1986).

THE READINGS

In the selections that follow, our contributors shed light on the relationship between policymakers and the intelligence community. Jack Davis addresses the sources of tension in relations between intelligence analysts and policymakers and various criticisms voiced by both parties about the behavior of their counterparts. In response to this criticism, Davis develops a series of best practices for both policymakers and analysts that can help steer them away from many of the pitfalls that can complicate their relationship and the development of effective policy.

In "Tribal Tongues: Intelligence Consumers, Intelligence Producers," Mark Lowenthal, a former senior official in the U.S. intelligence community, suggests that even though policymakers and intelligence professionals are on the same team, they do not always follow the same play book. Lowenthal describes how different organizational pressures and bureaucratic cultures shape the way policymakers and intelligence professionals view their roles and relationships, creating a gap that is often difficult to bridge in practice. Lowenthal also makes the key observation that policymakers can greatly influence the quality and timeliness of the intelligence they receive, even though they are often unaware of the way they shape intelligence inputs into the policymaking process.

The final selection consists of an extract from the final report of the Aspin-Brown Commission (1996). It underscores the necessity for policymakers to provide guidance to intelligence officers with respect to the informational needs of those holding high office. The report underscores that "intelligence agencies cannot operate in a vacuum."

16. INTELLIGENCE ANALYSTS AND POLICYMAKERS

JACK DAVIS

In this thoughtful overview of the tensions that complicate the relationship between intelligence analysts and policymakers, Jack Davis notes that at the heart of most problems is a shared judgment: criticism is politically motivated. His list of best practices is intended to steer the interaction between officials and analysts onto more productive paths.

This chapter is occasioned by public interest in reported tensions between Central Intelligence Agency (CIA) analysts and policy-making officials of the administration of President George W. Bush regarding the significance of ties between the Saddam Hussein regime and Al Qaeda terrorists, an important factor in the U.S. decision to invade Iraq in 2003. No evaluation of the latter case is provided. The chapter addresses, instead, general patterns of tensions between intelligence analysts and policy officials, in order to provide a context for public assessment of the Iraq-Al Qaeda incident when the public record is more complete as well as provide enhanced understanding of similar future instances of tension.

Over the years, most of the tens of thousands of written and oral assessments produced by CIA analysts in an effort to support the policy-making process have been received by policy officials with either appreciation or silence. Many of the assessments are in response to policy-maker tasking, usually a sign of expectation of useful insights. Many consist of briefings and exchanges via telephone or teleconferencing, where the fact that policy officials invest the time to elicit and discuss analysts' assessment of an important national security issue is testimony to the value the officials expect to receive. Many assessments, as to be expected considering the volume of production, miss the mark for the targeted officials in terms of relevancy, timing, or fresh insights, and thus evoke no reaction.

That said, tensions in the relationship between CIA intelligence analysts and administration policy makers are a common occurrence—an essentially normal by-product of the two camps' distinctive professional missions. The analyst's professional commitment is to assess national security issues without bias for or against the outcomes sought by the incumbent presidential administration; the policy maker's professional commitment is to articulate, advocate, and advance the administration's national security agenda.

Often, the resultant tension in the relationship helps both camps to deal more effectively with the challenges of analytic and policy-making uncertainty that usually attend complex national security issues. Under policy-maker criticism or questioning of judgments, analysts tend to revisit their initial views of the soundness of assumptions about what drives the issue and the implications of incomplete, ambiguous, and contradictory evidence. In response, policy officials often are moved to recalculate the elements of their own assessments of threats to and opportunities for advancing U.S. interests.

At times, though, tensions take a turn that does not serve well sound analysis effective policy making, or the national interest; charges of *politicization*, or analytic distortion to support or undermine a policy initiative, issue forth from one or both camps. These cases usually arise when policy officials repeatedly reject the analysts' studied interpretative judgments on the status of or outlook for a complex national security issue, especially when such judgments are seen to complicate policy initiatives that are politically important to an administration.

If tensions are a normal occurrence, and their elimination both impractical and unwise, recommendations of ground rules to enhance benefits and curb dangers would seem called for. But first one should make a closer assessment of the roots and branches of the tensions.

Tensions in analyst–policy maker relations in the United States can be traced back at least to the establishment in 1941, under the auspices of the Office of Strategic Services (OSS), of the first bureaucratically independent cadre of intelligence analysts. Sherman Kent, who later played a major role in setting professional standards for CIA analysis, came away from his World War II experience in the OSS with the conviction that relations between producers and consumers of intelligence assessments are not naturally harmonious, despite the common goal of advancing U.S. national security interests. Kent did not much change his views about inherent strains in the relationship during his years of analytic service with the CIA (1951–67).

Why not harmonious? The character of the policy issue at stake, personalities in both camps, the degree of contention about policy direction among administration leaders, and the role of Congress as a third party to the policy-making process from time to time have contributed to the onset and intensity of analysts' policy maker tensions. The underlying constant, though, is the aforementioned difference in perspective on professional mission between the producers of intelligence analysis and their policy-making clients.

THE ANALYSTS' PERSPECTIVE

CIA analysts are concentrated in the Directorate of Intelligence (DI), which takes pride in its organizational independence from the President, the Secretaries of State and Defense, and the other policy makers its intelligence assessments are intended to serve. The conceit that DI assessments are free of policy and political influence or bias comes across in the slogans by which the analysts and their leaders usually define their professional mission: *objective analysis, carrying truth to power, telling it like it is.*

Over the decades, on many critical and controversial national security issues—for example, Soviet strategic arms, the Vietnam War, Central American insurgencies—considerable substantive expertise, much sweat equity, and tough-minded assessment of assumptions and evidence have gone into the analysts' Interpretation of past and ongoing events. The usual bureaucratic result was and is a readiness among analysts to defend key judgments against criticism, even though they are aware of gaps and other flaws in their information.

Regarding prediction of future developments, where unexpected intermediate events can throw seemingly sound forecasts off course, analysts also have confidence in their expertise and work ethic, and they take pride in their belief in the independence of their judgments from policy and political influences.

Concerted public criticism of flawed analytic performance on major national security issues spawns intervals of analytic humility for the DI as an organization, its leaders, and usually the analysts directly involved. But for the most part, confidence, even overconfidence, in substantive judgments is a staple of the analyst's environment. Especially the more experienced DI analysts tend to see themselves as the best informed on the issues they follow as well as the most objective national security professionals in the U.S. government. Over the decades, on many issues they probably have been.

Analysts vary in their experiences with and attitudes toward policy officials. That said, a common first reaction to criticism of their assessments by policy officials is to suspect that either politics or the critics' lack of requisite substantive expertise is at work. Digging in at the heels in defense of the original assessment at times follows. Probably more often, the analysts undertake a reappraisal of their assumptions, evidence, and argumentation, though a substantial change in judgments does not necessarily result.

THE POLICY MAKER'S PERSPECTIVE

Policy officials, for their part, also vary in their experiences with and attitudes toward CIA analysts. A good number of career policy officials over the decades have considered the DI analysts on their accounts not only the best informed among the governmental community of intelligence analysts, but also the quickest to respond to requests for analytic assistance. This subset of policy officials also appreciates that CIA assessments, unlike those issued by analysts in policy-making departments, are rarely skewed to support a party to the bureaucratic politics that usually colors the policy-analysis process on national security issues.

The tendency among officials closest to the president runs differently. These essentially political appointees, because of their own partisan cast, can be quick to attribute partisan motivation to

CIA analysts. Especially when a political party has been out of power for some years, newly appointed Republican officials tend to see the Agency as dominated by holdover liberal Democrats, whereas new Democratic officials tend to see the strong influence of Republican conservatives. Many top-level appointees have served in previous presidential administrations and have requisite confidence in their own analytic skills and substantive knowledge of the issues. Some carry over from previous service critical views of the competence of Agency analysts as well as of their perceived propensity to an antiadministration bias.

Regarding professional mission, both career officials and political appointees see themselves as action officers as well as policy analysts. Their job is to get accomplished their vision of the president's national security agenda—the goals, strategies, and tactics that emerge from policy analysis.

Unlike intelligence professionals, policy officials are little pained by a merger of an administration's interests in domestic U.S. politics and foreign policy goals. As a rule, to policy officials, especially presidential appointees, government is politics as well as policy. The merger of policy and political advocacy at times requires building a "yes case" or a "no case" amidst inconclusive evidence of the soundness of a policy initiative and the uncertain implications for policy success of daily developments involving, for example, U.S. diplomatic or military campaigns.

This does not mean administration officials are ready to ignore CIA assessments that, say, would give political opponents in Congress ammunition to criticize policy. Often policy officials will ask analysts to "unpack" their assessment, revealing what is fact and what is opinion, or they will call for a briefing and an exchange of views either to enlighten or to leverage analysts.

In sum, at root, tensions, when they occur, represent a collision between the analyst's mission-driven belief that policy-maker criticism of carefully crafted assesments reflects politics or limited substantive command of issues and the policy official's mission-driven belief that CIA assessments that complicate a well-deliberated initiative reflect antiadministration bias or poor analysis.

THE ANALYTIC BRANCHES OF TENSION: OPINIONS, FACTS, EVIDENCE

Though difficult to untangle in actual cases of analyst–policy maker tensions, separating the varieties of analytic production into three branches—opinions, facts, and evidence—serves to clarify both the character of strains in the relationship and potential ground rules for managing tensions.

Regarding estimative judgments or opinions on issues of high uncertainty (for example, multiyear projections of political developments in unstable foreign countries, or prediction of the outcome of protracted U.S. military and diplomatic engagements in violence-prone regions), even well-informed policy makers at times gain insights from intelligence analysts' well-argued estimative judgments.

But when analysts' bottom-line judgments are seen as implicit criticism of and potentially harmful to policy agendas, administration officials are prone to dismiss them as "opinions."

Secretary of Defense Donald Rumsfeld, in an October 24, 2002, press briefing, went to great lengths to define the limits of the analysts' opinions in such circumstances: "If you think about it, what comes out of intelligence is not fixed, firm conclusions. What comes out are a speculation, an analysis, probabilities, possibilities, estimates. Best guesses."[1] Further, policy officials claim, often with justification, that the opinions regarding future developments spawned by policy analysis are sounder than analysts' opinions, if only because they are able to take fuller account of the weight of carrots and sticks the United States may be ready to deploy.

More than once, policy officials have let it be known, in particular, that they are little interested in whether analysts think U.S. initiatives will succeed. The analyst's main job, according to critics, is to provide assessments that enable policy analysts to reach sound judgments about what actions to take to implement policy, despite the uncertainty that fogs complex world events. The analyst's focus should be on strengths and weaknesses of foreign players, their tendencies, motivations, and risk calculations that would help policy officials identify potential dangers and U.S. leverage points.

Regarding facts, tensions are infrequent and usually involve competing methods of determining facts. Here a fact is defined as something concrete and reliably detected and measured: what a foreign adversary said in a recorded speech or intercepted conversation, as opposed to what he or she meant or actually intends to do.

A prominent official once observed, regarding facts, that policy makers are like surgeons. "They don't last long if they ignore what they see once they cut the patient open."[2]

When policy officials are hesitant to accept as fact a condition or development reported by analysts that could complicate political goals or policy implementation, they tend to challenge the sources and methods the analysts relied on in their determination of facts. During military engagements, for example, military officials have preferred to determine battlefield damage to the enemy as recorded in post-flight reports by U.S. pilots, and to dismiss the analyst's usually more modest calculations of damage that were based on, say, overhead imagery.

The most noteworthy tensions between CIA analysts and policy officials usually are over differences about the meaning of available evidence—that is, differences over what to conclude about something knowable but not conclusively known to either intelligence or policy professionals.

On the issues that give rise to major tensions, first, there are gaps in information because of secrecy and collection limitations. Second, the available evidence reflects a body of reporting parts of which are of questionable reliability and are contradictory and ambiguous. Concerning, for example, the dispute between CIA analysts and prominent administration officials over Saddam Hussein's regime's connection to the U.S. war on terror: What will history show the burden of the evidence to have been regarding the nature of Iraq's prewar ties to Al Qaeda terrorists—a minor or major threat to U.S. interests?

Regarding the meaning of inconclusive evidence, former CIA Director and Cabinet member William Casey (1981–87), in a dispute with analysts over the Soviet role in International terrorism, set forth his standard for keeping a policy-sensitive issue on the table: "Absence of evidence is not evidence of absence."[3] In effect, if a development or relationship is plausible, analysts cannot prove a negative to the satisfaction of officials with minds and agendas of their own.

In disputes with analysts about the meaning of inconclusive evidence, policy makers can insist on raising as well as lowering the bar of proof regarding judgments that could have a negative impact on their agendas. Once, when an analyst averred that reliable evidence had become available that indicated a suspected development that undermined an administration policy initiative was "almost certainly taking place," a policy critic retorted that the analyst "couldn't get a murder-one conviction in an American court with [his] evidence."[4]

THE CRITIC'S CHALLENGES TO DI TRADECRAFT

Policy officials have been generous in spelling out the elements of their criticism of Agency analysis. In doing so, the officials at times were motivated principally to improve the quality of support they receive for the demanding task of policy analysis and implementation. At times, the motivation also included an effort to defang or discredit politcally unhelpful assessments. And at times the objective was to shape an intelligence deliverable into a tool that would lend political support to administration policy.

It is worth noting that policy officials who have been generally complimentary of the analyst's performance as well as those long dissatisfied with performance table similar criticisms.

Part of the analyst–policy maker tension in evaluating evidence reflects a difference in professional attitude toward odds. To an analyst, the judgment that the evidence indicates that a development favorable to U.S. interests is unlikely usually means the odds against the existence or emergence of the development at issue are roughly 4 to 1. Given such odds, the busy analyst as a rule is ready to go forward with his or her assessment and move on to the next assignment.

In contrast to a policy maker with an agenda to advance, the same starting odds of roughly 1 in 5 can make it promising as well as politically necessary to stay on the case. Moreover, on politically important issues the official will not overlook the prospect that the analyst's pessimistic judgment could be off base because, first, they are insufficiently informed about the current state and potential fluidity of foreign forces at play, and, second, because do not appreciate the impact on developments of U.S. carrots and sticks, if a policy initiative gathers backing.

The reluctance of critical policy officials to rely on what they see as unhelpful assessments on issues important to an administration goes beyond professionally necessary "positive thinking" on their part. Critics also point out what they see as systemic weaknesses in the analyst's tradecraft (i.e., analytic methodologies).

First, since cognitive bias is pervasive, analysts, like all observers, tend to see more quickly and vividly what they expect to see and, conversely, tend not to see and properly credit information that would undermine their prior judgments. Critics contend that analysts delude themselves if they think they are exempt from this so-called confirmation bias because of their claims to "objectivity."

Critics have made this point over the decades in defending requests that analysts take another look at their interpretation of the evidence regarding the rate of success of the strategic hamlet program in Vietnam (1960s), the seriousness of Soviet plans for winning a nuclear war (1970s), the battlefield successes of U.S.-backed insurgents in Nicaragua (1980s), and after September 11, 2001, the significance of Iraqi-Al Qaeda connections to the war on terror.

The analyst's phrase "we have no evidence that X exists" is judged particularly unhelpful by those officials dedicated to either blunting the threat or seizing the policy opportunity in question. The critics note that analysts rarely admit they have no evidence that X does not exist. Besides, one critic averred, "policymaking is not [done] in a court of law."[5] A similar criticism is that analysts are too tied to the specific reports that reach their "inbox" and do not take sufficient account of the inherent aggressiveness, ruthlessness, and duplicity of U.S. adversaries.

Policy-making critics also complain that analyst training and incentives place too much emphasis on "straight line, single outcome" analysis on complex and uncertain issues. Critics say this "make the call" approach is both unhelpful to sound decision making and prone to error.

Former Deputy Secretary of Defense Paul Wolfowitz, long a critic of Agency analysts, observed in an interview conducted in 1994 that analysts' assertiveness in the face of uncertainty can turn an Agency assessment on complex issues into a weapon for one policy-making camp to use against another. In contrast, by tabling alternative interpretations, analysts would provide a tool useful to all participants in policy debates and decision making.

Further, the critics aver that, especially when policy stakes are high, analysts should expend much more effort evaluating what they don't know and why they don't know it before issuing estimative judgments downplaying dangers on which policy officials are focused. For example, could gaps in information that lead analysts to discount the likelihood of potentially harmful developments of concern to U.S. officials be caused by denial and deception (D&D) operations, or inadequate U.S. collection, or flawed assumptions about which pathways and relationships an adversary is pursuing to effect the feared development?

The 1999 report of a commission chaired by the former Secretary of Defense Donald Rumsfeld, after noting past intelligence failures on timely detection of foreign ballistic missile developments, cautioned analysts not to be quick to conclude that absence of evidence indicated absence of vigorous weapons programs by potentially hostile countries. The report, instead, charged analysts with pursuing alternative plausible explanations for "particular gaps in a list of [program] indicators."[6]

In truth, policy officials may prize the analyst who can come quickly to a crisp conclusion on issues surrounded by uncertainty that supports their agenda. But policy officials who see CIA judgments as obstacles to their agenda are themselves quick to connect the make-the-call culture to the analyst's record of analytic failures from the Cuban missile crisis to the Iraqi invasion of Kuwait.

Perhaps most important, according to the critics, it is the duty of responsible policy officials to ask probing questions; to insist on critical review of the evidence; to send analysts back to the drawing board for another look; in effect, to pull any loose thread in an unhelpful intelligence assessment.

Secretary of Defense Rumsfeld in his October 24, 2002, press briefing referred to the importance of engagement and criticism: "to the extent there's no feedback coming from…a user of intelligence, then one ought not expect that the level of competence…on the part of people supplying the intelligence will be as good…as if there's an effective interaction."[7] Granted, political overtones often color these criticisms. But in tradecraft terms they represent reasonable standards for policy officials to levy on analysts charged with providing distinctive value added to U.S. policy-making efforts.

DEFINING PROFESSIONAL AND UNPROFESSIONAL ANALYSIS

The doctrinal basis for a response to criticism by administration officials should reflect definitions of professional and unprofessional standards for intelligence analysts as agents both of the national interest and of the policy-making process. Thus, a definition of analytic professionalism should posit as equally important standards both *objectivity* (defined as tough-minded evaluation of evidence and other sound analytic practices) and *utility* (defined as distinctive data and insights policy officials find useful for managing threats to and opportunities for advancing U.S. interests).

Neither objectivity without utility, nor utility without objectivity, would meet the test of the author's following definition: The mission of intelligence analysts is to apply in-depth substantive expertise, all-source information, and tough-minded tradecraft to produce assessments that provide distinctive value-added to policy clients' efforts to protect and advance U.S. security interests. The analyst's long-held standard of analytic objectivity has helped to promote an institutional ethic of pursing independence from all biases, including policy and political influences, in making judgments in the face of substantive uncertainty. But studies, including those commissioned by the Agency, indicate that *substantive biases* (experience-based mindsets) are all but essential for effectiveness in an environment of high-volume production and tight deadlines. In such circumstances, the effect on production of an "open mind" is akin to the burden of an "empty mind." In addition, *cognitive biases* (especially seeking confirmation for experience-based assumptions amidst inconclusive evidence) in effect are hardwired mental traits.

Pursuit of the defined mission regarding objectivity, then, comes down to an effort to minimize bias by critical review of the assumptions driving the analyst's mindset and of the adequacy of the available evidence to draw any meaningful judgment, and, if so, the content of the judgment.

Also to fulfill the defined professional mission, analytic deliverables must be seen by policy officials to have utility as they define their professional agenda, which, as previously indicated, is to posit and enact an administration's politically colored policy agenda. The analysts who would produce an assessment with high potential for utility to the policy-making process can no more ignore the political context in which their clients operate than they can ignore where the latter are on their learning curves (e.g., how much background information is needed) and decision-making cycles (e.g., planning stage or implementation stage).

To take account of the politics of policy making is not a license for intelligence professionals, as analysts, to become policy makers, or their speechwriters or spear carriers. But if an analyst is not close enough to the process to feel the political pressures affecting policy making, he or she probably is not close enough to produce professionally crafted deliverables that provide distinctive value added.

Thus, there will always be a danger that analysts, in constructing their written assessments and oral commentary, will introduce a policy or political slant—either deliberately or through disregard of analytic standards. Analysts have done so in the past, and likely will do so from time to time in the future.

A politicized and therefore unprofessional assessment can be defined as an analytic deliverable that reflects either (1) the analyst's motivated effort to skew building-block assumptions, evaluation of the evidence, and bottom-line judgments to support—or oppose—a specific policy, political entity, or general ideology, or (2) a conspicuous disregard for analytic standards that produces unmotivated but similarly distorted outputs that could affect the policy-making process.

From the policy makers' agenda-oriented perspective it makes little difference whether what they see as analytic bias is motivated or unmotivated. One senior official, for example, complained that every assessment that indicated or implied that an administration initiative was flawed constituted analytic policy making, because it provided ammunition for Congress to oppose funding the initiative.

As long as policy-makers' criticism of the objectivity, soundness, or utility of analysis reflects a legitimate tradecraft concern, they are not necessarily putting pressure on analysts to engage in unprofessional behavior. Policy officials have the license to change the intelligence question in search of insights in addition to those embedded in the analyst's initial assessment, to ask that assumptions and evidence be examined more thoroughly, and to request customized follow-on assessments. That is part of their job description, whether they are seeking fresh insights or analytic support for their established views.

Thus, it is not unprofessional behavior for analysts, on their own or when requested, to provide assessments that set out to make the case for an alternative view to their unit's agreed interpretations of ambiguous evidence of ongoing developments and estimative projections of complex trends. The only professional requirements are that such efforts at, say, devil's advocacy, be clearly labeled and vested with appropriate analytic standards for crafting a challenge to the mainline views on an issue embedded with substantive uncertainty.

Additionally, it is not unprofessional behavior for an analyst, when requested to address matters clarifying tactical policy options for dealing with specific threats to and opportunities for an established general policy. The key to sound "action" or "implementation" analysis is for the analyst to identify plausible initiatives and evaluate them in cost-benefit terms, and for the policy makers to choose what course to pursue and bear responsibility for their decisions.

Finally, for a manager to tighten tradecraft standards on a politically sensitive policy issue before an analyst's assessment goes forward under a corporate DI seal is not necessarily a signal of unprofessional behavior. Painful to the analyst, yes. Politicization of his assessment, no.

Analysts and their managers and leaders must be vigilant in identifying, deterring, and decrying unprofessional assessments as herein defined; when engaged in analysis, they are and must remain intelligence professionals, not policy or political aides—or critics. If an analytic cadre is to deserve its vaunted organizational independence, it must be ready to hold its ground, in the name of the national interest, against pressures for politicization, no matter the source, the intensity, or the circumstances.

But analysts must also take seriously the "cry wolf" danger of levying charges of politicization whenever their authority to control the key judgments of an assessment is abridged.

More to the point, if ever teamwork must prevail over turf warfare and over the individual analyst's sense of entitlement to determine what "call" to make on a matter of substantive uncertainty, it is when the analytic corps is constructing assessments on politically contentious policy issues. Over the decades, many analysts who have made adjustments to initial assessments that maintained objectivity while enhancing utility have felt the sting of colleagues' unreasonable charges of politicization.

THE ANALYST'S RESPONSE TO POLICY-MAKER CRITICISM: BEST PRACTICES

The challenge for analysts, then, is to turn tensions to professional advantage by maintaining rigorous analytic tradecraft standards while enhancing the utility of their assessments to policy makers. Despite a popular reputation for flawed performance, CIA analysts regularly meet this demanding standard. To turn on its head an observation on policy success and failure attributed to President Kennedy after the 1961 Bay of Pigs debacle: Analytic failures draw a thousand critics; analytic successes are orphans.[8]

Call them "ground rules," call them "best practices," lessons can be learned from both failures and successes, and recommendations made for how analysts should respond to policy-maker criticism. The underlying concept behind the recommendations that follow is that analysts carry the heavier burden of managing tensions in policy-maker relations in a manner that advances the national interest. The main reason is that the policy-making camp is the more powerful of the two. Policy officials have many alternative sources to Agency analysts for information and insight, including their own staffs and departmental analytic organizations; the academic, research, and business communities; the media and the Internet. In contrast, Agency analysts have no comparable alternative market that would justify the large size of their cadre and high volume of production of assessments. Congress demands and receives a steady stream of oral briefings from Agency analysts but is rarely seen as an equal to administration officials as a client for written assessments.

The central theme of the recommendations is that analysts are professionally required to take the tradecraft elements of policy-maker criticism seriously, no matter how much they may perceive that the politics of policy advocacy also are at play. Analysts, thus, should respond to criticism with a reassessment not only of the argumentation and judgments of the original assessment but also of whether it provided utility or distinctive value for the policy-making community. The goal is to take tradecraft issues off the table, so to speak, in an effort to isolate and then defuse any politically motivated elements of policy-maker criticism.

First, become expert on the policy maker's world. Analysts should commit to learning as much about the U.S. policy-making process and their key policy-making clients as, say, a national security correspondent for a major newspaper or other media outlet is expected to command. Analysts, starting from year one, have to spend quality time analyzing how Washington works, warts and all, even if this slows down the pace of grasping how Baghdad, Beijing, or Buenos Aires work. In particular, analysts should understand their client's role as action officer as well as policy analyst. This investment will enable analysts to role-play the policy clients who have criticized an assessment, not to mortgage analytic integrity but to evaluate tradecraft performance through a different set of eyes.

Second, become accomplished at understanding and managing substantive uncertainty. Analysts are taught and are generally aware that their judgments on complex issues are based on thoughtful but fallible assumptions that in turn color their evaluation of fragmentary, contradictory, ambiguous, and otherwise inconclusive evidence. They have been cautioned about mindset and confirmation bias. Yet the norm is to rely on these powerful but vulnerable mental processes to get their assessments out under tight deadlines, and with a confident judgment.

Usually the resultant assessment holds up well against both the expectations of policy-making clients and the subsequent course of events. Usually, But what to do when a policy official conveys doubts or outright criticism?

Here, without being too quick to jettison original argumentation and judgment, the analysts should move from passive to active awareness of the limitations of their analytic craft. More active attention to the perils of analysis amidst substantive uncertainty entails taking a more thorough accounting of plausible alternative explanations and outcomes that were discarded or downplayed during the crafting of the assessment that drew criticism.

Casual re-examination of an assessment by its author and production unit to take the measure of alternatives at times is helpful, but the process of "talking about alternatives" is prone toward defense rather than critical evaluation of the original argumentation. More structured and externalized challenges to the assessment hold greater promise of fresh insights that either strengthen confidence in, or point to useful modifications of, the assessment that drew criticism.

Tested approaches to alternative or challenge analysis include devil's advocacy, key assumptions check, quality of information review, and argument mapping. A more experimental technique, known as analysis of competing hypotheses, tests which of several plausible explanations for a complex event or trend stands up best against a battery of relevant information.

Third, become adept at role-playing. At times, as indicated, analysts will be well positioned to prepare a professional response to criticism by undertaking an open-minded assessment of the *policy critic's paradigm* (i.e., mental model) on a contentious issue. However colored by political considerations it may at first seem to the analysts, deconstruction will help identify the critic's assumptions, evaluation of evidence, and calculations of likelihood. Once this information is at hand, the analysts may see a path toward revision of their own assessment that both protects objectivity and enhances utility.

Fourth, lean forward professionally with action analysis. Analysts should not hesitate to respond to

criticism about unhelpful analysis by changing the question from the one they initially believed should be addressed to one policy critics call for—again a posssible path to both objectivity and utility. Often the shift, as previously indicated, is from what is the most likely interpretation of an event or relationship or the most likely future path of development, to depiction of the direct and indirect leverage the United States has to reduce dangers and seize opportunities.

In most cases, analysts can be professionally comforted by assuming savvy administration officials, despite a politically required public optimism, know their policy initiative is facing heavy obstacles, even before the CIA assessment elaborated the point. What is now in demand are intelligence insights for doing something about the obstacles.

An analyst once tabled an assessment that placed emphasis on the general political dynamics in country Z, including both domestic reform tendencies promoted by the United States and a deliberate show of independence from Washington on certain international issues. The word came back that the high-level U.S. official who had asked for the assessment "wanted to leverage the president of country Z, not love him."[9]

Fifth, master techniques for evaluating inconclusive evidence. More deliberate analyst attention to evaluating evidence on contentious policy issues is another promising avenue for stripping tradecraft complaints from policy-maker criticism of analytic performance. Careful consideration of alternative meanings of gaps in information, especially regarding suspected programs to develop weapons of mass destruction (WMD), can help build credibility with critics.

Analysts can organize and asssess what is known and unknown to determine, for existance, whether the gaps in expected indicators more likely represent limited U.S. collection and substantial D&D, an innovative approach to WMD development, or nonexistence of a concerted development effort. The aforementioned analysis of competing hypotheses is well suited to provide an externally structured (that is, minimally subjective) competition to see which explanation is the most and least compatible with available related information.

Sixth, use estimative terminology carefully. Analysts have a professional obligation in maintaining integrity while supporting the policy-making process to avoid compounding substantive uncertainty with linguistic confusion. This is essential to managing tensions on sensitive issues. To deter both misunderstanding and manipulation of judgments, analysts should avoid vague estimative phrases such as "real possibility" and "good chance." Though not without risk of an exaggerated precision, analysts should aim to set boundaries to key judgments (e.g., "we judge the likelihood of *development Z* to be low—on the order of 10 to 20 percent"). On controversial issues analysts should also avoid nonfalsifiable judgments such as "it is possible," "suggests that," and "according to reports." They should provide instead an evaluation of the authenticity, adequacy in terms of completeness and consistency, and significance of the evidence. And when no confident judgment can be made, analysts should say so directly.

As previously indicated, policy officials tend to stick to initiatives even against long odds. An assessment that calculates an estimated probability of a development at, say, roughly 80 percent is making transparent a roughly 1-in-5 prospect of being wrong. An assessment that develops the longshot case using plausible alternative assumptions and evaluations of the evidence, as well as the analyst's preferred 4-in-5 prospect can serve professionally to provide distinctive value added to policy-maker criticis without sacrifice of analytic integrity.

Seventh, be responsive to criticism but not at the cost of objectivity. As long as an analytic unit believes it has done its homework in evaluating evidence and in considering alternative explanations and projections, it should stand by its estimative judgments even if policy-maker criticism persists or intensifies. But the unit should also work to ensure continued access to and credibility with critical clients by varying the focus and perceived utility of its deliverables. Analysts should consider the following "1-3-1" approach to an issue of critical policy import on which they are engaged in producing nearly daily assessments.

- Once a week, issue an assessment that features a net judgment, whether or not the one favored by policy officials. Include a credible accounting of the impact of recent developments and reports.
- Several times a week, put the net judgment approach aside and employ action analysis to address tactical dangers and policy opportunities on which direct and indirect U.S. leverage could be applied.
- Once a week, change the question via the tradecraft of alternative analysis, in order for both analysts and policy makers to examine the issue

from another angle, for example: *what-if analysis* (what policy makers would see, if the likelihood of development X increased), *risk-benefit analysis* (the adversary's estimated calculations affecting its motivation for and ability to engage in development X), and *if-then analysis* (implications of the advent of the high-impact, low-probability development regarding X).

Finally, what of the danger that analysts' efforts to curb their own substantive and cognitive biases will generate deliverables that provide unwarranted support to the clients' biases and political agenda while weakening respect for the production unit's professional judgment?

There may be no win-win answer to the vulnerability of unintended consequences of attempts at professional accommodation of the tensions attending policy-maker criticism of analysis. Policy makers, for example, have been known to tear off the cover page (literally and figuratively) explaining the main view of the analysts and the context for presenting an alternative view—and then citing the latter as the Agency's judgment.

But avoidance of the initiatives recommended above for professional accommodation of criticism and instead countering policy-maker exaggeration of certitude with analyst exaggeration will help neither camp. As a rule, a blending of deliverables that indicates an openness toward alternative interpretations with regular affirmation of what analysts believe to be sound, if vulnerable, judgments will protect analytic professionalism, maintain credibility with and access to the policy clients, and best serve the national interest.

Analysts and production units unsure of how to proceed when confronted with policy-maker criticism with political overtones should engage the Agency's Ombudsman for Politicization and other detached veteran practitioners for help in identifying the best professional response. Agency training courses that include case studies on managing tensions would also help prepare analysts and managers for their initial exposure to friction with their policy-maker clients.

Largely as a result of internal as well as external reviews of flawed analytic performance regarding judgments about Iraqi WMD arsenals and programs under the Saddam Hussein regime, many recommendations for dealing with criticism of analysis by policy officials similar to those outlined above have been adopted or reinforced as tradecraft doctrine by

CIA's senior leadership. As this chapter was written (March 2006) the difficult tranformation from doctrine to practice was under way.

POLICY MAKER PREROGATIVES—AND THEIR LIMITS

The preceding two sections of the chapter addressed: (1) analysts' professional prerogative to stick to their best judgment after testing it for soundness, no matter the intensity of policy-maker criticism; (2) their obligation to mitigate tensions via alternative means of support to policy clients, such as action analysis; and (3) the breach of professionalism entailed in both deliberate and unintentional politicization of analysis.

What about the rights and wrongs of the admittedly more powerful policy-making camp? The national interest is best served when the two camps work together to combine sound intelligence analysis with sound policy analysis. That said when the two camps clash, what are the prerogatives of policy officials and what actions should be considered a breach of their professional obligations?

The questions and answers that follow are an attempt by the author, long an observer of the relationship but a member of the analytic camp, to set ground rules for policy officials that would enhance the benefits and temper the dangers of tensions in analyst-policy maker relations.

1. *Are policy makers entitled professionally to reach, publicize, and act upon estimative judgments that diverge from intelligence assessments on a national security issue?*

Yes. As indicated throughout this chapter, intelligence analysis, especially inherently fallible interpretative and predictive analysis, is an input to and not a substitute for policy analysis. Policy makers as analysts take account of other providers of information and judgment, and also bring their own, often considerable, experience, insights, and biases to the difficult tasks of policy formulation and implementation, for which they must take ultimate responsibility.

2. *Are policy officials professionally entitled to ask intelligence analysts to take another look at their estimative judgments (e.g., to review assumptions, evidence, and argumentation)?*

Yes. Policy makers are commissioned to devise, promote, and enact the president's national security

agenda. They know when a policy consensus is taking shape and the time for action is approaching on issues, despite intelligence assessments that sound a caution. Yet officials, especially those with an appreciation for the distinctive role of intelligence analysis, hesitate to ignore intelligence findings and estimative judgments that call into question the underpinnings for U.S. initiatives. One response in these circumstances is to ask analysts to go back to the drawing board. Furthermore, from the point of view of the national interest, well-articulated criticism of analysis is much preferable to inadequate guidance for the execution of intelligence deliverables and scant attention to the assessments once delivered.

3. *Are policy makers professionally entitled to urge analysts to review and revise their confidence levels in analytic judgments?*

Yes. For the same, usually healthy, reasons, one analyst or intelligence agency challenges another's conclusions on whether a shrouded current relationship or indeterminate future development is *nearly certain, probable,* or *unlikely,* policy makers may ask analysts to rethink their degree of confidence in a judgment. Once again, the answer assumes estimative judgments are inherently subject to error and that policy makers' criticism of analysis is more useful to sound performance than their ignoring of analysis. Needless to say, intelligence analysts are professionally bound to stick to judgments on probability that survive their critical review; and intelligence professionals must take care not to allow the pressure of a process of repeated requests for revision to move the bottom line further toward one supportive of policy than the analysts' tradecraft would justify.

4. *Are policy makers professionally entitled to ask analysts to provide well-argued alternatives to their studied bottom-line judgments (e.g., devil's advocacy)?*

Yes. Policy officials are at least as wary of the consequences of policy failure as analysts are of intelligence failure. They are professionally entitled to task analysts to use their skills and resources to present for consideration alternative or multiple views of a complex and uncertain issue. At times a call for, say, devil's advocacy may be a caution against the perils of groupthink, especially in cases in which policy makers agree with the analysts' judgments. At times the policy maker's motive will be to move Agency analysis to closer alignment with his or her own thinking. As long as rigorous analytic tradecraft norms are adhered to for whatever form of alternative analysis is solicited, and the analyst's preferred bottom-line judgment is firmly attached to the deliverable, intelligence professionals should welcome the opportunity for customized service to their policy making counterparts.

5. *Are policy makers professionally entitled to ask analysts to change the question they address (say, from whether a development is likely, to how it might occur)?*

Yes. Once an administration adopts an initiative, policy makers tend to move forcefully into their action-officer mode and have limited interest in analysts' views, based on the latter's reading of the evidence, on whether the policy is likely to succeed, much less whether the policy was wise to undertake. Policy officials have a job to do—to make the policy work. They are professionally entitled to ask intelligence analysts to provide action or implementation analysis—that is, expert assessment of opportunities for moving the policy forward and of specific dangers to be avoided, taking account of insights into the adversary's strengths, weaknesses, and "game plan."

6. *Are policy makers professionally entitled to seek analytic judgments from sources other than CIA and other U.S. professional intelligence organizations?*

Yes. No matter how strongly intelligence professionals would prefer otherwise, policy officials, in pursuit of their policy-making and political goals, have a right to rely on whatever sources of information and insight they choose, either to supplement or to substitute for the support they get from intelligence professionals. This includes use of business, academic, and other nongovernmental sources; their own staffs, whether configured as a policy-making or intelligence unit; and also, as has happened, foreign intelligence services. Policy makers, in short, are entitled to reap the benefits of as complete and varied a set of substantive inputs as they can command as they undertake the arduous task of managing an uncertain and often perilous national security issue. If policy makers use different sources of analytic support simply because they want more cordial answers than those provided by intelligence professionals, then the policy officials must bear the burdens of self-deception, policy failure, and political censure when such outcomes prove to be the case.

7. *Are policy makers professionally entitled to attribute to intelligence analysts judgments that overstate or understate analysts' confidence levels?*

No. Once a studied, clear, and (if challenged) revisited statement of likelihood regarding a development, relationship, threat, or opportunity is established by Agency analysts, policy officials can attribute it to intelligence in order to buttress their own views, or reject it in favor of their own alternative statement of likelihood. But they do not have the authority to attribute to intelligence professionals an estimative judgment the latter do not hold.

8. *Are policy makers professionally entitled to force analysts to alter their best estimative judgments?*

No. As already acknowledged, policy officials are entitled professionally to reject intelligence assessments and reach and promote their own estimative judgments (Question 1, above), and are also entitled to urge analysts to rethink and recast Agency intelligence judgments (Question 3, above). That clarified, under no circumstances are policy officials professionally entitled to force intelligence analysts to change estimative judgments. Obviously, there are risks to treating as inviolate intelligence judgments that are contrary to policy preferences. Events may prove the analysts to be wrong. Congressmen may complicate the funding and execution of an administration's strategy and tactics by using intelligence findings and estimative judgments to block or modify policy initiatives. Unauthorized leaks to the media of intelligence positions may create an untimely public debate over policy. These circumstances can cause a run-up in immediate costs ranging from embarrassment of the administration to the thwarting of what history may judge to have been a sound policy initiative. But the long-term costs to the integrity and morale of intelligence professionals of forcing them to change their judgments will likely cause much greater harm to the national interest by weakening a vital arm of the national security establishment.

9. *Are policy officials professionally entitled to use the media to criticize intelligence analysts' competence, in an effort to protect an administration from congressional and public criticism of a policy initiative?*

No. As argued in this chapter, policy officials are entitled, indeed encouraged, to criticize through government channels either a specific body of analysis or intelligence tradecraft generally. Furthermore, as policy professionals, they are entitled to raise publicly their criticism of analysis as long as it is couched in analytic terms and is not, in effect, a politically motivated *ad hominem* attack. That is, as policy professionals, they are not entitled to criticize publicly a careful body of intelligence work and the credentials of the analysts who produced it merely to relieve themselves of the burden of credible defense of their own contrary judgments. In principle, nearly all parties to the uniquely American system for making national security policy proclaim the value of maintaining the integrity of intelligence analysis. A practice of trying to leverage a congressional vote or public debate on a policy initiative by criticizing the credentials of analysts who produce uncongenial analysis undermines the principle.

10. *Are policy officials professionally entitled to apply pressure on Agency leaders to remove from a production unit a manager or analyst responsible for assessments with judgments policy makers see as biased, wrong, or otherwise unhelpful?*

No. Analysts and their managers should be judged by Agency leaders solely in terms of professional credentials and adherence to analytic tradecraft norms, including good-faith efforts to respond to tradecraft criticisms by policy officials through the various means outlined earlier in this chapter (e.g., key assumptions check, devil's advocacy). The challenge of reaching sound analytic judgments amidst the perils generated by substantive complexity and uncertainty should not be compounded by a requirement for "political correctness" or fears about job security.

11. *Are policy officials professionally entitled to request Agency analysts to engage in policy advocacy, for example, to produce a "white paper" that is released as an intelligence product?*

No. Agency analysts may assist by providing information for the production of a white paper, but this and other formats of policy advocacy must be issued under the seal of a policy-making department or staff. The role of Agency analysts is to provide analytic support to policy planning and implementation by administration officials—and not to make, advocate, or criticize policy. Again, the long-term importance to the national interest for Agency analysis to be and be seen as a source of substantive objectivity as well as policy utility far outweighs any short-term political advantage gained from using an adulterated form of intelligence analysis to gain public or congressional support for a policy initiative.

CONCLUDING THOUGHTS

What about enforcement of these or any other set of ground rules aimed at moderating tensions in analyst–policy maker relations? U.S. experience has shown that presidents and their inner circles from time to time will play by their own rules. Agreed prerogatives and constraints and authoritative calls of "foul" might nonetheless serve well over the long haul, if only to evoke second thoughts about ignoring a transparent set of rules for improving both intelligence analysis and national security policy making.

Presidential administrations already have an instrument in place for monitoring the adequacy and quality of intelligence analysis, along with all other intelligence functions. The President's Foreign Intelligence Advisory Board (PFIAB) is well situated, both to help shape the ground rules and to monitor for analyst compliance. Over the decades, PFIAB members—former administration officials, members of Congress, and military and business leaders—collectively have commanded formidable knowledge about analysts and policy makers. And as a rule, PFIAB staff reports on analytic performance have been noted for both independence and insight.

For the Agency, the Ombudsman for Politicization has served since the early 1990s to educate new analysts about professional standards, to monitor for politicization, and to counsel analysts about the concerns they raise on the issue. Over the years, the Ombudsman, selected by and serving at the pleasure of the Director for Intelligence, has been a highly qualified former intelligence manager serving part-time as an independent contractor.

The following recommended changes relating to the Ombudsman are intended to strengthen both the educational and protection functions, including by participation in shaping ground rules and more active monitoring for compliance on the part of policy officials as well as intelligence professionals.

- Change the position name to Ombudsman for Analytic Professionalism (OAP). The professional obligations for analysts in the management of tensions involve more than the avoidance of policy or political bias.
- Provide the OAP with a small staff. The rise in importance to U.S. national security of countering weapons proliferation and terrorism—issues on which conclusive evidence will be a rarity—is likely to increase tensions over the meaning of

available information and thus the demands on the OAP.

- To ensure the independence of and enhance analyst confidence in the OAP, have the newly instituted Director of National Intelligence nominate and Congress confirm the title holder to serve a fixed term of five years.
- To help hold policy makers as well as analysts accountable in their management of tensions, require the OAP to provide the intelligence oversight committees of Congress with periodic reports on the compliance of both camps with agreed ground rules.

This chapter, by design, has mentioned Congress only briefly, although it is the third side of the triangle that constitutes the U.S. system for making and implementing national security policy. Yet for any set of ground rules for governing analyst–policy maker relations to have a lasting impact, Congress, on its own or in response to public demand, must take action to promote and monitor such an initiative. The goal, one last time, would be to ensure that the inevitable tensions between Agency analysts and administration officials are managed to the benefit of the national interest.

QUESTIONS FOR FURTHER DISCUSSION

1. Given their professional missions, why is there acrimony between analysts and policymakers?
2. Does a policymaker have the right to question analysts about their findings?
3. Should analysts ever make their estimates public to force policymakers to accept them?
4. Should policymakers have the right to alter questions put to analysts after receiving a discouraging estimate?

ENDNOTES

All statements of fact, opinion, or analysis expressed are those of the author and do not reflect the official positions or views of the CIA or any other U.S. government agency. Nothing in the contents should be construed as asserting or implying U.S. government authentication of information or Agency endorsement of the author's views. The material has been reviewed by the CIA to prevent the disclosure of classified information.

1. Quoted in "Rumsfeld on New DoD Intelligence Team," *Early Bird* (newsletter), Department of Defense (October 25, 2002), available at http://www.defenselink.mil/news/Oct2002/t10242002_t1024sd.htm

2. Author's interview with Paul Wolfowitz, "Paul Wolfowitz on Intelligence-Policy Relations," *Studies in Intelligence* 39 (Langley, VA: Central Intelligence Agency, 1996).
3. Author's interview with CIA analysts present when the remark was made at CIA Headquarters, Langley, VA, in 1982, cited in Jack Davis, *Tensions in Analyst-Policymaker Relations: Opinions, Facts, and Evidence*, Occasional Papers, CIA, Kent Center 2 (2003), p. 3.
4. Comment made to the author in April 1980, CIA Headquarters, Langley, VA, cited in Davis, "Tensions," p. 3.
5. Author's interview with Paul Wolfowitz, "Paul Wolfowitz."
6. Intelligence Side Letter [to Congress and the Director of Central Intelligence], Report of the Commission to Assess the Ballistic Missile Threat to the United States (March 18, 1999).
7. Quoted in "Rumsfeld on New DoD Intelligence Team," *Early Bird*.
8. *Editor's note:* After the Bay of Pigs failure in 1961, President Kennedy observed, "There is an old saying that victory has a hundred fathers and defeat is an orphan," cited in Arthur M. Schlesinger, Jr., *A Thousand Days: John F. Kennedy in the White House* (Boston: Houghton Mifflin, 1965), p. 289.
9. Author's recollection of a 1973 incident, cited in Davis, "Tensions," p. 6.

NOTE ON SOURCES

The views on and of policy officials are based on remarks made at press conferences and in unclassified statements in reports by governmental commissions, media interviews, and discussion forums. Note, for example, the following publications that are available on the CIA website (http://www.cia.gov). Note also, the unclassified source cited for the evaluation of and recommendations for analysts by the Missile Commission, chaired by Donald Rumsfeld.

BIBLIOGRAPHY

Armstrong, Fulton T. "Ways to Make Analysis Relevant But Not Prescriptive," *Studies in Intelligence* 46 (2002).

Davis, Jack. "[Ambassador Robert Blackwill] A Policymaker's Perspective on Intelligence Analysis," *Studies in Intelligence* 38 (1995).

———. "Paul Wolfowitz on Intelligence-Policy Relations," *Studies in Intelligence* 39 (1996).

Report of the Commission to Assess the Ballistic Missile Threat to the United States: Intelligence Side Letter [to Congress and the DCI], March 18, 1999.

The views on and of intelligence analysts and on the analyst-policy maker relationship generally are based on the following unclassified publications that, unless otherwise indicated, are available on the CIA website (http://www.cia.gov).

BIBLIOGRAPHY

Davis, Jack. *Analytic Professionalism and the Policymaking Process: Q&A on a Challenging Relationship*, Occasional Papers, CIA, Kent Center, Volume 2, No. 4 (2003).
———. "Combating Mindset," *Studies in Intelligence* 36 (1992).
———. *Improving CIA Analytic Performance: Analysts and the Policymaking Process*, Occasional Papers, CIA, Kent Center, Volume 1, No. 2 (2002).
———. *Improving CIA Analytic Performance: DI Analytic Priorities*, Occasional Papers, CIA, Kent Center. Volume 1, No. 3 (2002).
———. *Sherman Kent's Final Thoughts on Analyst–Policymaker Relations*, Occasional Papers, CIA, Kent Center, Volume 2, No. 3 (2003).
———. *Tensions in Analyst-Policymaker Relations: Opinions, Facts, and Evidence*, Occasional Papers, CIA, Kent Center, Volume 2, No. 2 (2003).
———. "Facts, Findings, Forecasts, and Fortune-telling." In *Intelligence and the National Security Strategist: Enduring Issues and Challenges*, ed. Roger Z. George and Robert D. Kline (Washington, DC: CIA, 2004).
Heuer, Richards J., *Psychology of Intelligence Analysis*. (Washington, DC: CIA, 1999).

17. TRIBAL TONGUES: INTELLIGENCE CONSUMERS, INTELLIGENCE PRODUCERS

MARK M. LOWENTHAL

Lowenthal suggests that the bureaucratic cultures of the policymaking and intelligence communities often form a significant barrier when it comes to the relationship between the consumers and producers of intelligence. Both policymakers and intelligence professionals are preoccupied with the demands of their own positions and tend to believe that their motivations and objectives are shared by everyone. "Tribal Tongues" offers many insights into the way policymakers and intelligence professionals view the real world around them.

In the Aftermath of the Cold War and the Gulf War there has been much soul-searching in the executive and Congress concerning the organization and role of the intelligence community: How should it be organized? Which issues should it be covering? What are the emerging issues that should be addressed now? These are of course important questions. But they tend to by-pass more fundamental issues within the intelligence community that are of a more permanent—and thus, perhaps—more important nature because they deal with how the community functions and fulfills its role on a daily basis. One of these is the relationship between the intelligence consumers and the intelligence producers.

Most analyses of the U.S. intelligence process pay lip service to the consumer-producer relationship. Although occasional serious forays on the subject exist, such as Thomas Hughes's *The Fate of Facts in the World of Men*,[1] most either ignore or downplay the importance of this relationship as a significant shaper of intelligence *throughout* the so-called intelligence process, starting with collection and ending with its final consumption.

A major problem is that the consumer-producer relationship resembles that of two closely related tribes that believe, mistakenly, that they speak the same language and work in the same manner for agreed outcomes. Reality, when viewed from either perspective, suggests something wholly different. Indeed, one is often reminded of George Bernard Shaw's quip about Britons and Americans being divided by a common tongue.

WE ALL WANT THE SAME THING

Most policymakers (i.e., consumers) work on the assumption of basic support throughout the government for their various policy initiatives, including support by the intelligence community. The first problem lies in the very word *support*. For policymakers, this means a shared and active interest and, if necessary, advocacy. This runs counter, however, to the intelligence community's long-standing position not to advocate any policy. Rather, the intelligence community tends to see itself, correctly or not, as a value-free service agency, although at its upper levels the line begins to blur.

Second, the intelligence community, like all other parts of the permanent government bureaucracy, has a "we/they" view of its political masters. The intelligence community is part of the *permanent* government; those making policy are politically driven *transients*, even when nominated from within the professional ranks of agencies. Indeed, with the exception of the uniformed military, nowhere else in the entire foreign policy and defense apparatus can there be found as many career officials at such senior levels as in the intelligence community. They can sometimes be found at the level equivalent to deputy secretary and clearly predominate at and below the level equivalent to assistant secretary.

Compounding this professional versus political, "we/they" conflict is the fact that consumers can and do advocate policy initiatives that run athwart intelligence community preferences. For example, the political demands for visibly intrusive arms-control monitoring methods, regardless of their minimal contribution to verification, pose real dangers for counterintelligence. The need to go public with information in order to justify policy initiatives or to brief foreign officials in order to build international support for policies often poses dangers to intelligence sources and methods. Such confrontations must often be resolved at the cabinet level and, although there will be some cutting and pasting to accommodate intelligence concerns, the overall policy will generally prevail. This is as it should be within the U.S. system of government. At the same time, it deepens the "we/they" syndrome.

Finally, the two groups have very different interests at stake. A successful policy is what the consumers were hired to create and execute. The intelligence community's reputation however, rests less on the success of any policy than on its ability to assist in the formation of that policy and to predict potential outcomes—both good and bad. The producers are only vulnerable if the policy is perceived as failing because the intelligence support was in some way lacking. Ironically, the intelligence community is rarely given credit if the policy succeeds. In part, this is a self-fulfilling outcome given the distance the producers cultivate from the process; in part, it is the natural bureaucratic phenomenon of scrambling for honors.

THE VALUE OF A FREE COMMODITY: PRICELESS OR WORTHLESS?

Intelligence products arrive in the consumers' limousines, pouches, and in boxes every morning and evening. They are part of the established routine. These products are, for their readers, basically cost-free subscriptions that were never ordered and never have to be paid for, perks of the job. High-level policy consumers have no real sense of either budgetary or mission/manpower cost to their departments or agencies for the very existence of these products, even if some of the products come from entities that they control. Thus, the secretary of defense will rarely be faced with a significant trade-off between required intelligence programs for the Defense Intelligence Agency and the National Security Agency versus next year's weapons procurement, nor will the secretary of state have to juggle the Bureau of Intelligence and Research's budget against prospective embassy closings.

Intelligence production, for the consumers, exists somewhere beyond their ken, as if unseen gnomes labor to produce the papers that magically arrive. If the analyses are good, all the better; if they are not, consumers are unlikely to advocate redirecting some of their resources to improving them.

Moreover, the very regularity with which these products appear has a lulling effect. The standard items—the *National Intelligence Daily,* the *Secretary's Morning Summary*—are essentially newspapers. Anyone who has read yesterday's edition or watched last night's 11:00 p.m. news can predict what is likely to be covered in this morning's edition. Indeed, while these publications are all lumped together as part of the "current intelligence" emphasis of the intelligence community, in reality they represent items that can safely be given to customers the next day. They are not urgent warnings or long-awaited breakthroughs, items that scream "read me now." Rather, they are part of the daily routine.

To break through this lulling effect, intelligence has to be able to prove to its consumers that it brings "value added" to the steady drone of information, analysis, and opinion that comes from both within and beyond the intelligence community. But one bureau or agency's memo looks much like another's, unless you bother to read them and assess them. How do you assure that, if only one will be read, it's yours? In reality, the unstated value added that intelligence producers bring is their sources. But, for very good reasons, raw intelligence is rarely presented to consumers. The intelligence is given context and comment, analysis that again makes it look like everyone else's.

How does the producer break out of this trap? One way is simply packaging, designing products that *do* scream for attention when there is a truly important piece of intelligence or a fastbreaking event about which the producers know first. The second is establishing a track record, although this still depends on whether the consumer reads intelligence analyses and remembers who was right and who was wrong.

In the end, consumers incur no real and regular penalty for ignoring this daily flow of information. In managing their day, high-level consumers establish methods to cut down on reading extraneous material. At the very highest levels, a large portion of daily intelligence products probably falls into this category. These consumers assume that their subordinates will read what they must within their areas of responsibility and that truly urgent items will come to their attention.

CONSUMER BEHAVIORS THAT MATTER

In reality, the intelligence consumer does more than just consume. He or she is not some eager, expectant eye and mind waiting at the end of the intelligence process. The consumer helps set the agenda, from intelligence priorities, to collection, to format.

AGENDA

Consumers have their own sets of priorities and preferences, issues in which they are deeply interested, those in which they must take an interest by their nature, and those they would just as soon ignore. If they bother to communicate these preferences to the intelligence producers (a rare enough occurrence), and the producers respond accordingly, then the entire intelligence process has already been influenced. Although producers will not cease to try to cover all the issues that *they* believe are important, only those intelligence officers with a taste for abuse and a desire to be ignored will try to force these on an unwilling consumer. This can put producers in an awkward position, especially if the subject in question is one they feel quite strongly deserves attention. It can also run athwart the intelligence community's "warning function," namely, the requirement that it look ahead for issues—especially sleepers—that have the potential to become grave concerns.

COLLECTION

The most senior consumer, the president, can also determine what gets collected and what does not for reasons of policy beyond the preferences of the intelligence producers. The U.S. policy in the shah's Iran of having no contact with the mullahs,[2] or President Jimmy Carter's termination of U-2 flights over Cuba, both come to mind.

"WHAT DON'T I KNOW"?

To the producer, the ideal consumer is one who knows what he doesn't know. Unfortunately, this quality can be hard to come by. It is understandable that senior officials dislike admitting areas of ignorance within their fields of responsibility. Those who do, however, have a clear advantage, especially if they are willing to take steps, among them

requested analyses and briefings, to remedy the situation. Similarly, it is important for the consumers to distinguish between what they must know, what they'd like to know, and what is simply enjoyable but unnecessary. Failure to do this well, and continually, can lead to one of two traps—either consuming too much time on some subjects or too little on others. Given the primacy of time management, this should be a crucial skill for the harried consumer. Once this skill is acquired, and its results communicated to the producers, it again establishes priorities and agendas.

DEALING WITH UNCERTAINTY

Neither producers nor consumers like intelligence gaps. At best they are annoying; at worst they can be both crucial and frightening. They do exist, however, and are often responsible for uncertainties in estimates and analyses. As strange as it may seem, such uncertainties appear to be very difficult to convey, at least in English. "If/then" constructions can become long laundry lists covering all the possibilities, without regard to likelihood; "on the one hand/on the other hand" often creates octopuses of sentences—too many hands spoil the analyses. The absence of an easily used subjunctive really hurts.

Unfortunately, consumers often interpret these very real problems of limited sources and uncertain outcomes as pusillanimity on the part of producers. "They have a best guess," consumers suppose, "they're just hedging so they won't be wrong." The inability on the part of producers to convey adequately the cause and nature of uncertainty and ambiguity tends to alienate a largely dubious audience.

"SHOOTING THE MESSENGER"

This consumer behavior is as old as recorded history—if the messenger brings bad news, kill him. Unfortunately, it still happens. The messenger is not killed; he is first berated and then, on subsequent occasions, ignored. In part this consumer behavior stems from the darker side of the "we all want the same thing" syndrome. Once consumers have figured out that they and their intelligence people do *not* all necessarily want the same thing, they become suspicious of the producers. Do they have their own agenda for their own dark reasons? If they are not actively supporting me are they working against me? Unfortunately, the delivery of "bad news," usually some piece of intelligence or an analysis that questions preferred or ongoing policies, fits this more paranoid view all too well.[3]

What, however, is the producer's alternative? Suppress the intelligence and risk having the consumer blindsided or even badly embarrassed, a sure blow to credibility? Better to err on the side of caution and risk opprobrium, knowing full well that this, too, can harm credibility. Either way, the outcome largely rests on the intelligence's reception by the consumers, on their maturity, experience, and willingness to be challenged by people who are not a threat to their policies.

THE CONSUMER AS ANALYST

Consumers are, by and large, a self-confident group. They have achieved fairly exalted and responsible positions through either the trial by fire of long professional careers or through the hurly-burly of private enterprise or partisan politics. No matter the route, they assume that it is not just connections and luck that have brought them to their current positions. This self assurance is all to the good, although it can lead to some aberrant behavior.

The first such behavior has to do with issues of long standing regarding which the consumer believes that he or she knows as much, if not more, than the intelligence analysts. Certainly, assistant secretaries of state for Europe, the Near East, and so on, are likely to have spent a large portion of their professional careers on these issues, and they probably know some of the key players in the region on a personal basis. Interestingly, the same perception eventually takes hold of senior officials dealing with Soviet issues, regardless of their previous experience. At least two factors are at work here. First, the long-standing nature of the U.S. rivalry with the Soviets lends an air of familiarity, whether deserved or not. Second, after about two years in office, the average secretary of state has met with his Soviet counterpart more than half a dozen times and probably feels he has greater insight into Soviet thinking than do "ivory tower" analysts who have only seen the Soviet Union from 150 miles up.[4] The recent upheaval in the Soviet Union and Eastern Europe may have tempered the first attitude, now that the familiar signposts of relations have gone. This probably results, however, in increased emphasis on the second attitude, the value of high-level, face-to-face contacts over analysis by those more remote from events.

For this type of reaction the "value-added" question becomes paramount. What can the producer bring to the issue that is new, insightful, and useful? Here, the natural inclination, if not necessity, to hedge analyses works against the producer and only serves to reinforce the prejudice of the consumer.

The second "consumer-as-analyst" behavior manifests itself during those periods of intense activity usually misnamed crises. Suddenly, the premium for current intelligence rises dramatically; consumers will often cry out for the "raw intelligence." There is the sudden assumption that at moments like these, trained intelligence analysts will somehow get in the way, that they will, perhaps inadvertently, distort the incoming information. Ideally, the intelligence officers should resist, offering to come back in several minutes with some sort of analysis or context along with the raw intelligence. Quite simply, consumers are probably less well suited at these moments to serve as their own analysts. Their ability to assess objectively and dispassionately what is happening is usually inverse to the importance of the issue, its intensity, and the amount of time they have been dealing with it. This is not to say that consumers have nothing of analytical value to bring to the process, including during crises. They should not, however, act to cut off the contributions of professional expertise. At worst, they will get an alternative point of view that they are always free to reject.[5]

THE ASSUMPTION OF OMNISCIENCE

For the United States as a global power, it is difficult to find many issues or regions that are not of at least some minimal interest. For the consumer this translates into the erroneous assumption that somewhere in the labyrinths of the intelligence community there is at least one analyst capable of covering each issue that comes along.

The source of this assumption is most likely a conceit derived from the expectation that U.S. interests must be matched by U.S. capabilities, that intelligence managers must know that *all* bases should be covered. Interestingly, this runs counter to the often heard criticism (and accepted folk wisdom) that the intelligence community has traditionally spent too much time and effort on the Soviet target, to the disadvantage of less sexy albeit no less important issues.

Unfortunately, there is no safe way for the producers to correct the assumption of omniscience. The intelligence community is loath to admit that it is not true and is fearful of the criticism that will ensue if this is discovered. Yet, in a world of unlimited issues and limited intelligence resources gaps are unavoidable. How resources are allotted either to close or to allow gaps remains a murky process based on past experience and known or—more likely—perceived consumer interest. Too often this process degenerates into a debate over the size of the intelligence budget, raising the suspicion among consumers (and congressional overseers) that cries of insufficient coverage are in reality pleas for more resources that will be redirected to areas that the intelligence community sees fit. Were the producers, however, to address the issue forthrightly and ask consumers, say down to the assistant secretary level, for a list of issues that had to be covered and those that could be given shorter shrift, it is unlikely that they would get consensus. Here again the "free commodity" issue is at work, only now consumers would be asked to give up something that they had always received, even if they had never had any great use for it.

Inevitably, one of the issues that has long been considered below the threshold will suddenly require attention. With a little luck there may be an analyst somewhere who has at least passing familiarity with it. This is the moment when the producers hope to shine, to prove the "value added" they bring to the process. If they succeed, however, they also reinforce the omniscience assumption, which sooner or later will be found, painfully, to be false.

THE ABSENCE OF FEEDBACK

Intelligence consumers have neither the time nor the inclination to offer much feedback on what they are getting or not getting. This stems from several sources. First, the throwing of bouquets is not a habit in government nor should it be expected.[6] Second, there is rarely enough time. As soon as one problem is solved or crisis ended, it is time to move on to the next. But the absence of feedback enforces the producers' image of top consumers as "black holes," into which intelligence is drawn without any sense of the reception or effect. The result is to deny the producers any guidance as to how they are doing.

At the same time, it must be admitted that, despite calls on their part for feedback, many in the intelligence community are quite content with the status quo. They do not favor "report cards"; they fear that they will only hear the negative and not receive any praise; they are concerned lest feedback becomes a means by which consumers would try to affect the content of intelligence to elicit greater

support for policies. None of this needs to happen if the feedback process is honest and regularized.

There also would be genuine benefits. The intelligence community is made up of analysts who largely enjoy their work and who believe, as individuals, that the issues they cover are worthy of attention. At the working level, however, they exist in relative isolation, without any reference point as to how well their work fulfills its purported purposes among the consumers. Analysts will continue to work on what they believe to be relevant and important unless or until consumers offer guidance as to preferences, needs, and style. In short, producers need to be told how best to shape their products and focus for the consumers, but the initiative for doing so remains with the consumers.[7]

Feedback is also an area where Congress, in its oversight role, can be helpful. Congress has, in the past, reviewed important policy issues for which intelligence was a major factor and has offered objective assessments of the quality of intelligence and the uses to which it was put by consumers. The Senate Select Committee on Intelligence, for example, offered a critique of the famous Team A-Team B competitive Soviet analysis and called the exercise worthwhile but flawed in its execution. This same committee also found that President Jimmy Carter's release of Central Intelligence Agency analysis of Soviet oil prospects was largely driven by his own political needs.[8] Similarly, the House Permanent Select Committee on Intelligence offered a scathing review of intelligence on Iran prior to the fall of the shah. The same committee's review of intelligence prior to the Mariel exodus from Cuba concluded that U.S. surprise on that occasion was not due to lack of intelligence warnings.[9]

Such a service is quite useful and can be done by Congress objectively and without partisan rancor. However, the two Select Committees on Intelligence also have limits on their time and cannot provide this sort of review regularly. Congress is an intelligence consumer as well, although it is not privy to the full extent of the analyses that flow to policymakers in the executive. Thus, Congress can supplement feedback from consumers but cannot fully substitute for it.

PRODUCER BEHAVIORS THAT MATTER

Just as the consumer does more than consume, the producers do more than simply collect, analyze, and produce. Their behavior also affects the product and the perceptions held by the consumers.

CURRENT VERSUS LONG-TERM INTELLIGENCE

All intelligence agencies, managers, and analysts are constantly tugged between the need for current intelligence and the desire to write longterm intelligence. Thomas Hughes portrayed the struggle as one of "intelligence butchers" (current intelligence, done in short, sharp chops of material) versus "intelligence bakers" (long-term intelligence, done in prolonged melding and blending). As cute as Hughes's model is, it gives the mistaken impression that the choice of which type of intelligence to emphasize lies with the producers. This tends not to be so. Rather, it is the very nature of how foreign and defense policy is handled by consumers that drives the choice. Intelligence producers claim not to be bothered by this consumer preference for current intelligence, but this too is not entirely correct.

Current intelligence (i.e., tonight, tomorrow, this week) will always dominate. That is the very nature of the U.S. policy process. It is very "now" oriented, creating a series of difficult choices among issues all crying for attention. Indeed, there is very little sense of completion, because each issue laid to rest has too many successors waiting for attention as well. The drive of current events even tends to distort the notion of "long-term" analysis, which becomes the next ministerial meeting, the next arms-control round, the next summit, next year's budget process at best.

Much lip service is given by both producers and consumers to the need for long-term intelligence. Yet nothing in their daily lives indicates what use they would make of such intelligence if it existed. For consumers it would represent luxury items, things to be read when or if the press of current business allowed. For producers it would mean just a chance to be more wrong at a greater distance from the events—a constant concern.

Some will argue that the intelligence community already produces long-term analyses in the form of the National Intelligence Estimates (NIEs). But what is the function of the NIEs? In theory they represent the best judgment of the entire intelligence community on major issues, as conveyed by the director of central intelligence to the president. Some NIEs are done at the request of consumers, most often a fast-track or Special NIE (SNIE, pronounced "snee"). Other NIEs are done at the suggestion of an intelligence organization or are initiated by national intelligence officers, who perceive a need among consumers.

But beyond their impressive name and theoretical status, do NIEs really influence long-term policies? Or are they, in the scathing words of the House Permanent Select Committee on Intelligence, "not worth fighting for"?[10] It is difficult to find many NIEs that have substantially influenced ongoing policy debates. Various intelligence agencies participate earnestly in the NIE game largely to keep track of their brethren and to preserve their own points of view. NIEs are important simply because they exist and not because of any great value that they regularly add to the process. More often they serve either as data bases for budget justifications (in the case of the annual NIE on Soviet programs) or as the source of self-serving and often misleading quotations for use by consumers during policy debates.

Although both producers and consumers constantly cry out for more long-term and less current intelligence, it remains unclear that the outcry has any substance beyond a general and unsubstantiated belief that, if it were produced, long-term intelligence would give greater coherence to policy.

PORTRAYING UNCERTAINTY

One of the most difficult problems that producers face on a daily basis is the need to portray uncertainty. Every issue that is analyzed has gaps, unknown areas, competing plausible outcomes. As much as producers would like to be able to predict with finality, they both know that it is rarely possible and tend to write so as to cover, at least minimally, less likely outcomes so as not to be entirely wrong.

Portraying this in writing can be difficult. In the absence of a widely used subjunctive tense, producers use other techniques: "perhaps, although, however, on the one hand/on the other hand, maybe." There is nothing intrinsically wrong with any of these, although their net effect can be harmful for several reasons.

First, their use becomes habitual, creating written safety nets that allow the producers to keep all their bets covered. Second, and perhaps more important, they strike the consumer, especially with repetition, as "weasel words," efforts by the producers to avoid coming down on one side or another of any issue.

Producers do not spend enough time or effort explaining why these uncertainties remain. Consumers, being thus uninformed, tend to revert to their omniscience syndrome and see pusillanimity instead.

THE PERCEIVED PENALTY FOR CHANGING ESTIMATES

Producers do not like to be wrong, but they realize they are fallible. They also, however, do not like having to make changes in estimates, fearful of the cost to their credibility with the consumers. Wide swings are especially anathema; better to adjust one's estimates gradually, to bring the consumers along slowly to the new view. Thus, if for years the estimate has said "T is most likely," and producers now believe that "Z is most likely," few will want to jump directly from T to Z. Instead, they would rather move slowly through U, V, W, X and Y, preparing the consumer for the idea that Z is now correct.

In this case, the perception may be worse than the reality. Most consumers, if properly prepared as to why there is a change (new data, new sources, new models, and so on), are likely to accept it unless changes become so regular a phenomenon as to raise serious questions.[11] Again, it is largely an issue of communications, of adequately explaining the uncertainties inherent in any estimate and the factors that have led to the change. Unfortunately, the outcome is so dreaded that the process rarely takes place.

MIRACLES VERSUS SAINTS

One of the necessary premiums put on all intelligence writing (with the exception of some NIEs) is brevity. Less is more when dealing with overly busy readers. Unfortunately, this runs counter to the desire burning within nearly every analyst to tell as much of the story as possible, to give the reader background, context and, in part, to show off. (For example: "You can't really understand the FMLN insurgency in El Salvador unless you go back to the Spanish land grants of the sixteenth century." A plausible point, but not an analysis that any busy reader is likely to read.)

Analysts tend not to err on the side of brevity. It becomes, therefore, the task of the intelligence production managers to edit material down to a suitable length. Analysts must be admonished to "just tell the miracles, and not the lives of all the saints involved in making them happen."

The miracles versus saints problem, however, also poses a difficult managerial decision. Analysts cannot write about the miracles with any facility until they have mastered the lives of the saints. Managers therefore have to be flexible enough to allow their analysts the time to study, and even to write about the saints, if only for use in background papers sent to other analysts. But this time must not be allowed to conflict with ongoing demands for written products, including those about the very miracles in question. It's a tough call, but one that has a payoff later on.

JADED VERSUS NAIVE

Given a choice between appearing jaded or naive on a given subject, the average intelligence professional will choose to appear jaded at least nine times out of ten. No one wants to appear to be the new kid on the block. Instead, analysts act as though they have seen it all and done it all before. This is especially troublesome in group meetings with peers, where appearances matter.

What this means, in terms of analysis, is that few situations are treated as being truly new, regardless of their nature. But some situations *are* new or different and do require analysis that has not been done before. A nuclear power plant blows up catastrophically; the Chinese sell intermediate-range ballistic missiles; or the Soviet Union allows its East European satellites to remove their Communist governments. By taking the jaded approach analysts force themselves, first of all, to play catch-up to situations that are ongoing, having initially wasted time playing them down. Moreover, they allow themselves to appear less than perspicacious before their consumers and now must spend time explaining away their previous stance, for which there may be little justification beyond mind-set.

The fix here is apparently simple—approach issues with a more open mind. But how can this be implemented? It cannot be institutionalized or even easily taught. It largely depends on production managers who continually ask skeptical questions, forcing their analysts to rethink. It is not easy, but it is achievable.

"COVERING THE WORLD"

This is the producers' version of the agenda issue. At most times there will be more issues crying out for attention than resources available to cover them all adequately. Producers, however, do not want to let any one of these issues slip, in part out of concern that they will choose the wrong ones and not be ready if they become more important or if consumer interest is suddenly piqued. Interestingly, this behavior on the part of producers only reinforces the consumers' belief in the intelligence community's omniscience. Feedback from consumers is an essential ingredient in making choices. If this is absent, however, then the intelligence producers must decide, knowing they cannot cover everything. They must also be able to distinguish, which they sometimes do not, between issues genuinely requiring serious attention and those that do not. They may also find as noted earlier, that there are important issues that consumers do not want to address. Here, the producers are torn, their professional responsibilities and best judgment at odds with the political realities. Overall, producers tend to side with covering more than less.

REPORTING "NO CHANGE"

Although the intelligence community cannot cover everything, it does keep track of more issues than most of its consumers can or want to deal with. Because of the limits on space in written products and the consumers' time, much goes unreported. But a second filtering process also takes place. On issues that are not "front burner" but are still of some interest, analysts will choose not to report developments or, more significantly, the lack of developments. The absence of activity is taken to mean the absence of any need to report.

There is value, however, to reporting periodically (admittedly at long intervals) on these issues and nondevelopments. If the analysts or managers know that the Rumanian nuclear program is of interest but that nothing new has happened in the last six months, there is nothing wrong with reporting that to consumers. What is the effect of such a report? First, it shows the consumer that the producers are alert, that they are tracking areas of interest beyond the self-evident. Second, it allows consumers to check off that issue on their mental lists. They can assume, probably correctly, that the producers will alert them to any change. For the moment, they need not worry about it. There is, however, a cost to such reporting, in that it tends to reinforce the consumers' omniscience assumption. Still, the net effect remains a positive one, albeit infrequent.

THE ABSENCE OF SELF-ANALYSIS

This is the flip side of the absence of consumer feedback. Like everyone else in the government, intelligence analysts and officials are busy people. As soon as one crisis ends they move on to the next with very little reflection on what worked and what did not. Nor do they spend much time trying to sort out

why certain analyses in certain situations work well and others do not, why warnings and indicators flag proper attention in some cases but not others, why the synergism of collection resources works for this topic or region and not for that.

Admittedly, genuine critical self-examination is difficult. The payoff for having it done more regularly, not by "outside" reviewers in the intelligence community but by the analysts and their supervisors themselves, is a much clearer insight into their institutional behaviors and processes that can greatly improve their work and their ability to serve the consumers.

CONCLUSION

The production and use or disuse of intelligence as part of the policy process is the net result of several types of mind-sets and behavior within and between two groups that are more disparate than most observers realize. Moreover, the disparity is more likely to be appreciated by one group, the intelligence producers, than it is by the intelligence consumers. As argued here, the consumers play a much greater role *throughout* the intelligence process and at all stages in that process than is customarily realized. Certain aspects of the gap between these two groups will never be bridged. Other aspects, like the issue of supporting policy, *should* never be bridged. Nonetheless, there remains much that can be done—even within current structures and processes—to improve communications between the two groups. The views expressed in this article are the author's and not attributable to any government agency.

QUESTIONS FOR FURTHER DISCUSSION

1. What accounts for the differences in perspectives between the permanent government and the political government?
2. What is the "value-added" problem faced by intelligence analysts and managers?
3. Why is it so difficult to correct a mistaken estimate?
4. How should the intelligence community report on "non-developments"?

ENDNOTES

1. Thomas Hughes, *The Fate of Facts in the World of Men* (New York: Foreign Policy Association, 1976).
2. See Gary Sick, *All Fall Down* (New York: Penguin Books, 1985), pp. 36, 64, 91, 104–105.

3. Needless to say, not all paranoia is unjustified. There have undoubtedly been instances in which intelligence analysts have tried to work against policies with which they disagreed. Most analysts, however, and certainly their senior supervisors know the severe penalty for being caught in such a compromising position and would most often prefer to avoid it, even at the risk that the policy will go forward. Most often, the cost to future credibility far outweighs the value of stopping one specific policy initiative.

4. During the first U.S.-Soviet ministerial meeting of the Bush administration, the deputy national security adviser, Robert Gates, who has spent a considerable part of his intelligence career as a Soviet analyst, was in Moscow for the first time. President Mikhail Gorbachev reportedly kidded Gates, asking him if the Soviet Union looked different from the ground than it did from satellites.

5. There is evidence that President George Bush, perhaps reflecting his past tenure as director of central intelligence, has a predilection for "raw traffic" and that he liked to sort out differences among reporting on his own without a sifting by lower-level analysts. See Andrew Rosenthal, "White House Aims to Sharpen Role in Panama Plots," *New York Times*, October 13, 1989, p. A-8; and Maureen Dowd, "2-Summit Plan Reflects Bush Style: Intense (Relaxed) Personal Diplomacy," *New York Times*, November 6, 1989, p. A-14.

6. Feedback is so rare that, when it occurs, the effect can often be comical. When one senior official noted his pleasure over a piece of intelligence analysis, the initial reaction among those responsible was, first, elation, quickly followed by doubts. Was this memo so good, they wondered, or was it that all of the others that received no such notice were so bad?

7. The President's Foreign Intelligence Advisory Board (PFIAB), a group of outside experts that reviews both intelligence analysis and operations, provides such guidance. It was PFIAB, for example, that suggested the Team A-Team B competitive analysis. However, PFIAB meets infrequently, reportedly once a month, and remains somewhat removed from the daily needs of producers. It cannot substitute entirely for direct producer feedback.

8. See Senate Select Committee on Intelligence, *The National Intelligence Estimates AB Team Episode Concerning Soviet Strategic Capability and Objectives and The Soviet Oil Situation: An Evaluation of CIA Analyses of Soviet Oil Production*, 95th Cong., 2d sess. 1978.

9. See House Permanent Select Committee on Intelligence, *Iran: Evaluation of U.S. Intelligence Performance Prior to November 1978*, 96th Cong., 1st sess., 1979, and *Cuban Emigres: Was There a U. S. Intelligence Failure?* 96th Cong., 2d sess., 1980.

10. See House Permanent Select Committee on Intelligence, *Iran*.

11. There have been cases, however, in which wide swings did hurt credibility. In the mid-1970s U.S. intelligence estimates of the portion of Soviet gross national product devoted to defense went from 6 to 7 percent in the mid-1970s to 10 to 15 percent, leading some consumers to question the validity of the new estimates as well. Critics in Congress suspected that the change was created to support the Ford administration's larger defense budget. See John W. Finney, "Soviet Arms Outlay May Be Bigger Slice of Pie Than Once Thought," *New York Times*, February 23, 1976, p. 13, and "U.S. Challenged on Arms Estimate," *New York Times*, March 8, 1976, p. 11. When the intelligence community repeated its estimate a year later, this threatened to discomfit the plans of the new Carter administration, which was in the midst of its review of Presidential Review Memorandum #10 on U.S. strategy. In drawing up PRM-10, Carter administration officials purposely excluded some of the premises that they saw driving the new estimates. See Hedrick Smith, "Carter Study Takes More Hopeful View of Strategy of U.S.," *New York Times*, July 8, 1977, p. A–1.

From: Mark M. Lowenthal, "Tribal Tongues: Intelligence Consumers, Intelligence Producers," *Washington Quarterly* 15 (Winter 1992): 157–168. Reprinted by permission of the publisher (Taylor & Francis Ltd, http://www.informaworld.com).

18. THE NEED FOR POLICY GUIDANCE

ASPIN-BROWN COMMISSION

It is said that policymakers get the intelligence they deserve. Without specific requests from senior policy officials, the intelligence community is left to its own devices when it comes to selecting intelligence requirements and targets. As the Aspin-Brown Commission noted, the intelligence community is sometimes left without any guidance. This is especially the case when the National Security Council reconstitutes itself with the change of administrations; during this period, senior officials are diverted from their normal duties of conducting routine oversight and helping to establish desired intelligence requirements and targets. The Commission recommended dedicated committees, lodged in the NSC, to set long-term intelligence needs and to evaluate intelligence priorities periodically in the face of a changing strategic landscape.

Intelligence agencies cannot operate in a vacuum. Like any other service organization, intelligence agencies must have guidance from the people they serve. They exist as a tool of government to gather and assess information, and if they do not receive direction, chances are greater that resources will be misdirected and wasted. Intelligence agencies need to know what information to collect and when it is needed. They need to know if their products are useful and how they might be improved to better serve policymakers. Guidance must come from the top. Policymaker direction should be both the foundation and the catalyst for the work of the Intelligence Community.

The drafters of the National Security Act of 1947 understood the importance of such guidance in creating the National Security Council (NSC).[1] The NSC was created to coordinate the policies and functions of the departments and agencies of the Government relating to all aspects of national security, including the intelligence function.

Since then, each Administration has created its own structure and procedures to meet the policy objectives and management styles of the President and his senior advisers responsible for national security. Historically, intelligence information has made significant contributions to the substantive work of the NSC, whatever its structure; but where top-level guidance for intelligence requirements and policies is concerned, the role of the NSC and its staff has varied.

In some Administrations, formal NSC committees composed of cabinet-level officials have been established to provide guidance on intelligence matters. Such committees have been supported by a small professional staff within the NSC. In other Administrations, the national security advisor has delegated most intelligence issues to a senior member of the NSC staff. In some Administrations, the NSC principals and/or staff have taken an active and consequential role in providing guidance on intelligence matters; in others, they have served principally to coordinate the intelligence response during times of crises.

INTELLIGENCE AS AN NSC FUNCTION FROM THE NIXON ADMINISTRATION TO THE PRESENT

President Richard M. Nixon took office in 1969 and created an NSC structure shortly thereafter. Not until 1971, however, did his Administration create an "Intelligence Committee," one of the four top committees within the NSC responsible for providing policy guidance on national security issues. In addition, the NSC structure during the Nixon Administration contained a separate committee to approve and coordinate covert actions (the 40 Committee).

In 1975, the blue-ribbon "Commission on the Organization of the Government For the Conduct of Foreign Policy" (the Murphy Commission) reviewed this structure and found it largely ineffective. The Murphy Commission recommended that the NSC Intelligence Committee "should be actively used as the principal forum for the resolution, short of the President, of the differing perspectives of intelligence consumers and producers, and should meet frequently for that purpose."

In 1976, almost two years into his presidency, President Gerald R. Ford issued a new Executive Order on intelligence, abolishing the existing NSC structure on intelligence and creating in its place a "Committee on Foreign Intelligence" (CFI). This new Committee was composed of the Director of Central Intelligence, the Deputy Secretary of Defense for Intelligence, and the Deputy Assistant to the President for National Security Affairs. The Administration directed this committee to "control budget preparation and resource allocation" for national intelligence, as well as to establish priorities for collection and production. The Executive Order spelled out several specific tasks the CFI should accomplish, among them giving direction on the relationship between tactical and national intelligence and providing "continuing guidance to the Intelligence Community in order to ensure compliance with policy direction of the NSC."

This structure proved short-lived. President Ford remained in office less than a year thereafter, and his successor, President Jimmy Carter, immediately replaced the existing NSC apparatus with a two-committee structure consisting of a Policy Review Committee (PRC) and a Special Coordinating Committee (SCC). Depending upon the subject matter under consideration, the PRC would be chaired by, and composed of, different Administration officials, including the DCI when it addressed intelligence issues. The SCC was chaired by the National Security Advisor, and addressed the review and policy considerations of special activities, including covert action.

In 1978, President Carter provided more specific guidance on intelligence matters and issued a separate Executive Order on intelligence. It stipulated that the PRC, when dealing with intelligence matters, would be responsible for the establishment of requirements and priorities for national foreign intelligence, review of the intelligence budget, and the periodic review and evaluation of intelligence products. It was also charged with submitting an annual report on its activities to the NSC.

Three years later when he assumed office, President Ronald Reagan abolished the Carter NSC structure without creating a separate standing committee on intelligence, relying instead on a separate element on the NSC staff. He also signed Executive Order 12333, a broad statement of intelligence responsibilities and policies, which provided that the NSC "shall act as the highest Executive Branch entity that provides review of, guidance for, and direction to the conduct of all national foreign intelligence, counterintelligence, and special activities, and attendant policies and programs."

Later, as part of a reorganization of the NSC staff, a series of "Senior Interagency Groups" (SIGs) were created, one of which dealt with intelligence. Chaired by the DCI, the "SIG-I" was chartered to establish requirements and priorities for national foreign intelligence and review the program and budget for national intelligence as well as proposals for sensitive operations.

In 1989, President George Bush eliminated the Reagan NSC structure, and returned to a two-Committee structure, consisting of a "Principals Committee" and a "Deputies Committee." The Principals Committee was chaired by the National Security Advisor; the Deputies Committee, by his Deputy. A separate staff office coordinated intelligence programs.

Two years into the Administration, the NSC conducted the first in-depth review of intelligence requirements. The document that instituted the review, known as "National Security Review-29," noted that "senior policy makers traditionally have neglected their critical role in setting intelligence priorities and requirements." It produced a lengthy list of government-wide intelligence requirements, but it failed to assign priorities in a way that usefully guided collection efforts or the allocation of resources.

In 1993, President Bill Clinton took office. He retained the "Principals Committee/ Deputies Committee" structure to coordinate major foreign policy issues and created a system of "Interagency Working Groups" to handle more routine issues. A separate staff office coordinated intelligence activities. In April, 1995, a new presidential directive was issued which, for the first time, stated in priority order what a President considered to be his intelligence requirements and established a working group of mid-level policy officials to review more regularly intelligence policies and requirements.

SHORTCOMINGS OF THE PAST

The Commission sees several shortcomings in the historical process described above. The institutional role played by the NSC in providing guidance and direction for intelligence activities has varied widely. Often substantial lapses occur at the change of Administrations when there is no guidance at all. As a result, a consistent level of guidance concerning appropriate roles for intelligence, as well as the guidance establishing requirements and priorities for collection and analysis, has, all too often, been missing.

In practice, the NSC's structures created to perform such functions often have foundered. Senior officials, such as cabinet secretaries or their deputies, who represent their respective departments and agencies at NSC-level meetings, usually have little or no background in intelligence and are inundated by the press of other duties. Intelligence is too often viewed as a support function that is "someone else's responsibility." Subordinates are increasingly sent to meetings in place of principals, and meetings become progressively less frequent. As a result, a true "consumer driven" intelligence process has never fully evolved within the NSC, regardless of the Administration in office.

The Commission believes the NSC as an institution should provide clearer guidance for intelligence, through regular tasking and a better organizational framework for handling intelligence issues. Several close allies visited by the Commission during its inquiry have effective mechanisms at the senior levels of governments to ensure that their intelligence agencies receive timely, ongoing guidance from the political level. In Great Britain, for example, a Cabinet-level office known as the Joint Intelligence Committee (JIC) brings together senior British policymakers and intelligence officials on a weekly basis. The JIC, functioning since 1936, is responsible for setting intelligence priorities on an ongoing basis, and for producing a weekly intelligence summary. Members include the principal producers and consumers of intelligence. While clearly the work and value of structures such as the JIC are facilitated where the government is considerably smaller than the U.S. Government and principally staffed by career civil servants, the Commission believes the concept embodied in the JIC can also be made to work in the United States.

WHAT NEEDS TO BE DONE

The Commission recognizes that every President must be free to use and structure the National Security Council as he or she sees fit, including the performance of its statutory role to provide direction to the Intelligence Community. From the Commission's standpoint, however, the particular structure decided upon by a president is less important than a clear and consistent understanding and implementation of the roles it should perform. Even when Administrations change, the functions of the NSC should not. Top-level direction to intelligence agencies would be greatly strengthened by a more institutionalized role for the NSC, one that is not rewritten every two or four years. The more the role of the NSC varies, the more difficult it is to develop and sustain working relationships that provide clear, frequent direction for intelligence and guidance for its collection and analytic efforts.

In the view of the Commission, the institutional role played by the NSC structure should include setting the policy guidelines for intelligence activities, stating what the intelligence agencies are expected to do and what they should not do. The NSC structure should clarify, for example, whether intelligence agencies should collect economic intelligence or analyze intelligence on the environment, whether they perform analysis of publicly-available information, and what rules should govern intelligence-gathering where allied and friendly governments are concerned.

The institutional role of the NSC also should include providing guidance for ongoing intelligence collection and analysis, to say what is needed and when, clarifying what is helpful and not helpful. What are the issues on the "front burner" for the President and other policymakers? What information would fill a void? On what subjects is intelligence adding little of value? Where does intelligence have access to information that would be of considerable value, but is not being collected?

It should also be the institutional role of the NSC (but not the NSC staff by itself) to assess, from time to time, the performance of the Intelligence Community in satisfying their substantive needs as policymakers, reporting its conclusions, as appropriate, to the President.

In the section that follows, the Commission proposes a two-tier NSC structure for carrying out these roles. It is intended as a model for this and future Administrations.

Whatever NSC structure may be adopted for intelligence, however, it must not interfere with the direct reporting relationship between the President and the Director of Central Intelligence, which must be preserved. The importance to the intelligence function of having a strong relationship between the President and the DCI cannot be overemphasized. The Commission was consistently told by former DCIs that where their relationship was strong, it had repercussions across the entire Government, including the Congress, giving vitality and purpose to the whole enterprise. Conversely, where the relationship was weak, it took a heavy toll on the esprit and influence of the Intelligence Community.

3-1. The Commission recommends the establishment within the National Security Council of a "Committee on Foreign Intelligence" (CFI), chaired by the Assistant to the President for National Security Affairs and including the Director of Central Intelligence, the Deputy Secretary of State and the Deputy Secretary of Defense. The Chair should invite other senior officials to attend as may be appropriate given the meeting agenda.

The CFI should meet at least semi-annually and provide guidance to the DCI for the conduct of intelligence activities, to include establishing overall requirements and priorities for collection and analysis. Appropriate NSC staff should formulate the agendas and supporting materials for these meetings, with NSC members and their staffs providing such assistance as may be required. The CFI should report annually to the President on its activities.

3-2. The Commission recommends that a "Consumers Committee" be established as a subordinate element of the CFI. This Committee should be chaired by the Deputy Assistant to the President for National Security Affairs and should include senior representatives at the Undersecretary level of the parent CFI members as well as senior representatives of other principal intelligence producers and consumers within the Government, e.g. the Secretaries of Commerce and Treasury, the U.S. Trade Representative. The Consumers Committee should meet at least monthly and provide continuous, ongoing guidance with respect to the priorities for intelligence collection and analysis to meet the needs of the Government. The Consumers Committee should monitor and periodically report to the CFI with respect to how well the Intelligence Community is meeting the needs of consumers, identifying gaps and shortcomings where appropriate. The NSC staff

should be responsible for formulating the agendas and supporting materials for each meeting, with NSC members and their staffs providing such assistance as may be required.

The Commission opted for this bifurcated approach for several reasons. The Commission believes that the major overarching issues in the intelligence area are best left to a small group, consisting of the principal cabinet officers who are responsible for, and the users of, intelligence. The Commission believes such a group should be chaired by the National Security Advisor because he can approach the issues from the viewpoint of the President and has responsibility for coordinating national security matters on his behalf.

However, it is unrealistic to expect such a senior group to play an active role in setting ongoing requirements and priorities for intelligence-gathering and analysis. This function necessarily requires more frequent meetings and must be carried out at a lower level of representation. Membership should be at a high enough level so that the participant can represent the policies of his or her agency or department, but also at a level where the participant can be a regular attendee at the monthly meetings. Whoever may be designated, however, should have or be able to obtain a grasp of the overall intelligence requirements and priorities of the department or agency they represent.

The Commission believes that a forum outside the Intelligence Community (but including a representative of the Intelligence Community) should evaluate the substantive contributions made by the intelligence agencies. Hence, this role is suggested for the Consumers Committee. This is a function that the NSC has not performed in the past but is needed for the effective operation of the Intelligence Community.

Finally, the Commission does not contemplate that either the CFI or its subordinate Consumers Committee would perform oversight or management functions. The DCI would continue to report to the President and not to either of these committees. The function of both bodies would be to provide guidance to the Director of Central Intelligence and, through him, to the Intelligence Community as a whole. If disagreements arose which could not be resolved inside the NSC structure, each cabinet-level official would retain the right to appeal to the President.

THE PRESIDENT'S FOREIGN INTELLIGENCE ADVISORY BOARD

While not a part of the NSC structure, the President has another body at his disposal to provide advice on intelligence matters—the President's Foreign Intelligence Advisory Board (PFIAB). First created by Executive Order in 1961, the PFIAB is charged with advising the President with respect to the quality, quantity, and adequacy of intelligence collection, analysis, counterintelligence, and other activities.[2] The PFIAB is also authorized to assess the adequacy of management, personnel and organizational arrangements in the intelligence agencies. Composed of private citizens, usually with some government experience, the number of PFIAB members has varied from one Administration to another.[3]

Historically, the PFIAB often has produced insightful and critical reports. Early boards were instrumental in analyzing and promoting the technical developments of the 1960s which revolutionized intelligence gathering. In the last several years, the PFIAB has looked at issues such as personnel practices within intelligence agencies and intelligence-sharing with multinational organizations.

The Commission supports the continuation of the PFIAB but believes that its role would be enhanced and its contributions more significant if it sought to perform functions that are not being performed elsewhere, either by the NSC or within the Intelligence Community itself. The Commission has noted in the course of its inquiry that very little thought is given by the Intelligence Community to the future, to finding creative technical or managerial solutions to the problems of intelligence or focusing on long-term issues and trends. By virtue of its membership, the PFIAB appears uniquely positioned to serve this function by bringing to bear the experience and expertise of the private sector and respected former government officials. Presidents must ensure that persons appointed to the Board have the qualifications necessary to perform this role and an adequate staff capability to support them.

QUESTIONS FOR FUTHER DISCUSSION

1. What are the problems that have troubled the National Security Council's effort to guide the intelligence community?
2. Do you think that the National Security Council should be the government organization charged with evaluating the intelligence community's support to policymakers? If not, who should?
3. What might account for the conclusion that intelligence managers rarely focus on the long-term trends and issues facing the intelligence community?
4. Do you think the risks of politicization will increase if the policymakers spend more time evaluating the usefulness of intelligence?

ENDNOTES

1. The statutory members of the NSC are the President, the Vice President, the Secretary of State, and the Secretary of Defense. Secretaries and Deputy Secretaries of other Executive departments may also serve on the NSC at the pleasure of the President. The present NSC includes the Secretary of the Treasury, the U.S. Ambassador to the United Nations, the U.S. Trade Representative, the Assistant to the President for National Security Affairs, the Assistant to the President for Economic Policy, and the Chief of Staff to the President.

   The Chairman of the Joint Chiefs is principal military adviser to the NSC and may attend and participate in NSC meetings. The Director of Central Intelligence also may attend and participate.

   The NSC is served by a staff headed by the Assistant to the President for National Security Affairs (who is often referred to as the National Security Advisor). The composition and organization of the NSC staff are left to the discretion of the President.
2. The PFIAB replaced an earlier "President's Board of Consultants on Foreign Intelligence Activities" that had been created by President Eisenhower in 1956. The PFIAB was disbanded in 1977 by President Carter but reconstituted by President Reagan in 1981.
3. The current Executive Order governing the PFIAB, E.O. 12863 (Sept. 13, 1993), limits membership to 16 individuals.

Reprinted from the Commission on the Roles and Capabilities of the United States Intelligence Community (the Aspin-Brown Commission), *Preparing for the 21st Century: An Appraisal of U.S. Intelligence* (Washington, D.C.: U.S. Government Printing Office, March 1, 1996):29–35.

VI

COVERT ACTION

Hamlet: "… And there put on him
What forgeries you please…"
—SHAKESPEARE, *Hamlet*, 2.1.19–20

Covert action (CA) may be defined as those activities carried out by national governments or other organizations, such as terrorist groups, to secretly influence and manipulate events abroad. The emphasis is on indirect, nonattribution, clandestine operations; the role of the government or other entity engaged in covert action is neither apparent nor publicly acknowledged (Godson 1996; Prados 1986; Treverton 1987). This approach to advancing one's interests is also sometimes referred to as the "Third Option"—between sending in the Marines on the one hand and relying on the diplomatic corps to achieve one's goals on the other hand. The use of military force is "noisy" and likely to draw a quick reaction from adversaries, as well as stir up criticism at home, while diplomacy can be notoriously slow and often ineffectual. Thus, covert action has a special appeal to some policy officials; with this tool, they can move rapidly and in relative quiet, avoiding lengthy debate over tactics and broader objectives (hence, another euphemism for CA: the "quiet option"). Covert action has the added advantage of usually costing less than a major military buildup.

THE EVOLUTION OF COVERT ACTION IN THE UNITED STATES

The use of covert action is older in the United States than the nation itself, having been used extensively by the colonial insurgents during the Revolutionary War (Knott 1996). The revolutionaries secretly urged France to aid the war effort by providing the colonial rebels with covert arms, and General George Washington initiated a campaign of propaganda against his British military adversaries. Soon after the founding of the new nation, President Thomas Jefferson secretly supplied arms to insurgents in Tripoli as a means for fermenting a coup against the unfriendly throne of the Bashaw, and President James Madison authorized paramilitary operations against the Spanish in Florida. During the Civil War, the North and the South both used covert actions for spreading propaganda and supplying arms to sympathizers.

Not until World War II, though, did the United States begin to carry out covert actions in a more concerted manner. President Franklin D. Roosevelt established an Office of Strategic Services (OSS) to engage not only in espionage but also in the sabotage of bridges and railroad tracks in Germany, the dissemination of propaganda, and the support of resistance groups. Although the OSS was disbanded after the war, President Harry S. Truman understood the importance of intelligence—Pearl Harbor had taught him—and he created the Central Intelligence Agency (CIA, or "the Agency") in 1947. The statutory language of the National Security Act of that year left open the possibility that the new Agency might be called on to engage in operations beyond the collection of intelligence. Without mentioning covert action explicitly, the law stated that the CIA had authority to "perform such other functions and duties related to intelligence affecting the national security as the National Security Council may from time-to-time direct."

The immediate challenge of the Soviet Union and its avowed intent to spread communism far and wide turned the Truman Administration toward this ambiguous phrase in the National Security Act. The administration interpreted the language broadly as an invitation to unleash the CIA to fight against Soviet expansion and the activities of other communist countries and movements. In the late 1940s and early 1950s, secret funding went to pro-Western labor unions, political parties, and publishers in Europe; anticommunist dictators in Latin America; and pro-Western factions in Asia, Africa, and the Middle East. By the end of the 1960s, the Agency had hundreds of operations under way around the world. During the major overt wars in Korea (1950–53) and Vietnam (1964–75), the budgets grew for CIA paramilitary or secret warlike operations in those nations.

When the United States withdrew from the unpopular war in Vietnam, funding for covert action began a downward slide, accelerated by the attempted misuse of the CIA by the Nixon Administration during the Watergate affair in 1973–74 and by investigative disclosures in 1975 that the Agency had spied on American citizens and tried to subvert the democratically elected president of Chile (Salvador Allende). When President Jimmy Carter entered office in 1977, the CIA's covert action budget had fallen to less than 5 percent of the Agency's funding (in contrast to over 50 percent during the Vietnam war). President Carter kept the budget at that level initially, but following the Soviet invasion of Afghanistan in 1979, he increased the funding for covert action sixfold.

When the Reagan Administration came into power, this secret instrument of foreign policy entered its heyday. The Reagan Doctrine, a term coined by the media, entailed an all-out covert struggle led by the CIA against communist partisans around the world—especially in Nicaragua and Afghanistan but also in El Salvador, Angola, Cambodia, and Eastern Europe, and against the Soviet Union itself.

The Iran-*contra* scandal (1987), in which the Reagan Administration resorted to covert actions in Iran and Nicaragua without proper reporting to Congress and in defiance of a law (the Boland Amendment) strictly prohibiting such operations in Nicaragua, discredited the CIA generally and covert action in particular. The budget for CA dropped to its lowest levels since the opening months of the Cold War: less than 1 percent of the Agency's annual budget (Johnson 1996). The funding remained at this level throughout the first Bush Administration and rose modestly when the Clinton Administration turned to the CIA for help with its foreign policy woes in Haiti, Africa, and the Balkans.

It would take the terrorist attacks against the United States on September 11, 2001, to really stimulate the covert action budget, which began a rapid rise in the name of combating world terrorism. The use of CIA paramilitary operations against the Taliban regime in Afghanistan, in tandem with overt military operations by the indigenous Northern Alliance and U.S. bombing missions, opened a new chapter in America's reliance on covert action. Events in Afghanistan in 2001–02 pointed to a successful triple-threat formula for the accomplishment of U.S. foreign policy objectives: a combination of pinpoint bombing, local allied insurgents, and paramilitary operations conducted by the CIA and Pentagon Special Forces. This formula was applied in Iraq in 2003, although in the context of a much larger overt U.S. invasion force in this second Persian Gulf War.

THE METHODS OF COVERT ACTION

Covert action takes four forms, often used in conjunction with one another: propaganda (psychological warfare operations, or "psy ops"), political operations, economic operations, and paramilitary (PM) operations—with the last including assassination as a subset. These activities are estimated to have accounted for 40, 30, 10, and 20 percent, respectively, of the total number of covert actions during the Cold War (Johnson 1989). Paramilitary operations were, however—and continue to be—by far the most expensive and controversial form of CA.

PROPAGANDA

During the Cold War, the open instrument of U.S. propaganda was the United States Information Agency (USIA), which released, through American embassies abroad, a vast amount of information about the United States and its objectives. As a supplement to this overt flow of information, the CIA (following presidential directives) inserted comparable, often identical, themes into secret media channels around the world. As with the USIA releases, the CIA's propaganda was in almost all cases (98 percent) accurate, if partial to the policies of the United States; about 2 percent of the propaganda was false ("black").

Indigenous agents ("media assets") secretly working for the CIA in foreign countries—journalists, radio and television commentators, op-ed and magazine writers, book authors—expressed "their" views through local media channels, although the material was often written verbatim for them in their native tongues by propaganda specialists in the Operations Directorate at CIA Headquarters in Langley, Virginia. Local audiences understandably looked on these seemingly homegrown sources of information—their own newspapers—as far more credible than USIA press releases. In return for these services, the media assets would receive cash payments and travel stipends from their local CIA "case officer," who normally operated out of the American embassy in the nation's capital. During the height of the Cold War, the CIA made 70 to 80 insertions into various media outlets each day—a great tidal wave of information flowing secretly from Agency headquarters into hundreds of hidden channels around the globe.

In tightly controlled totalitarian regimes where it was difficult (if not impossible) to recruit local media assets, the CIA relied on infiltrating propaganda. Such efforts could be quite primitive, including the lofting of air balloons to carry speeches, magazines, books, and transistor radios into forbidden territories where—thanks to these airborne deliveries—a deprived citizenry might have the opportunity to read about the outside world. Most of the balloons aimed at the U.S.S.R. crashlanded in that empire's vast expanse, with unknown but probably negligible effects. The CIA also dispatched airplanes to drop leaflets over isolated regimes or transmitted radio broadcasts (sometimes from makeshift stations in remote jungles). Most successful were the radio transmissions directed toward the Soviet Union and other adversaries, especially those conducted by

Radio Free Europe (RFE) and Radio Liberty (RL), operating in Munich initially under the auspices of the CIA, until their secret ties with intelligence were leaked to the press in the early 1970s, at which point the U.S. government provided overt funding for the radio stations. Supporters credit these stations with having helped to sustain hope behind the Iron Curtain among dissident groups and slowly, but steadily, abetting the erosion of support for the Communist party in Moscow and Eastern Europe. Critics are less sure that they contributed much to the fall of the Soviet Union.

Although the CIAs secret propaganda operations against the Soviet Union and China during the Cold War have been praised by some in the United States and Europe, its operations in the developing world have been subjected to widespread criticism. The best known and most controversial example is Chile during the 1960s (Treverton 1987). In the Chilean presidential election of 1964, the CIA spent $3 million to mar the reputation of Salvador Allende, the Socialist candidate with suspected ties to Moscow. On a per capita basis, this amount was equivalent to the expenditure of $60 million in a U.S. presidential election at the time, a staggering level of funding likely to decide the outcome of a presidential election whether in Chile or the United States. The CIA managed to thwart Allende's election in 1964, but he persevered and in 1970 won the presidency in a free and open election.

The CIA then turned to a range of propaganda and other covert actions designed to destroy Allende's regime. The Agency poured $3 million into the country to support anti-Allende secret propaganda between 1970 and 1973, in the form of press releases, radio commentary, films, pamphlets, posters, leaflets, direct mailings, paper streamers, and vivid wall paintings conjuring images of Communist tanks and firing squads that would supposedly soon become a part of life in Chile. Printing hundreds of thousands of copies, the CIA blanketed the country, which is predominantly Catholic, with an anti-Communist pastoral letter written many years earlier by Pope Pius XI. The effect was to substantially weaken the Allende government.

Another successful CIA propaganda operation took place in Central America in 1954. The Agency set up a radio station in the mountains of Guatemala. Local media assets began to broadcast the fiction that a revolution had erupted and that the people of Guatemala were joining the movement in large numbers; meanwhile, other CIA recruits began a march against the pro-Communist dictator Jacobo Arbenz. With a speed that surprised even the CIA instigators, the reports became something of a self-fulfilling prophecy, and the hapless Arbenz, panicked by the mythical prospect of the masses storming his palace, resigned before a shot was fired. This bloodless coup was a heady experience for covert action advocates, coming only seven years after the establishment of the CIA and on the heels of a similar victory in Iran (though one that relied on clandestine political maneuvering as well as propaganda). It began to seem as though the world could be transformed toward a pro-Western orientation by Madison Avenue public relations techniques, secretly applied.

Despite these early successes, the CIA's use of propaganda has had its share of critics. Early in the Cold War, the CIA funded the National Student Association inside the United States as part of its propaganda operations. The purpose was to encourage young Americans to travel abroad and counter Soviet efforts at manipulating international student conferences. Critics were enraged, though, by this trespassing of the CIA into the activities of groups within the United States, an activity strictly prohibited by the Agency's founding statute. The specter of influencing American audiences, not just foreign countries, arose again when it became public that the CIA was sponsoring the publication of anti-Communist books written by Soviet defectors as well as U.S. authors. The idea of American students and writers on the payroll of a secret intelligence agency struck civil libertarians as beyond the pale. So did the revelation that the CIA had journalists on its payroll. The estimates ranged from three dozen, conceded by the Agency, to over 400 alleged by investigative reporters. Furthermore, it came to light that the CIA had secretly encouraged its U.S. media assets to write negative reviews of books published by American authors critical of the Agency. Some of George Orwell's worst fears appeared to have come true in the United States.

Troublesome, too, was the notion of "blowback" or "replay": the insertion of propaganda abroad only to have it waft back to U.S. audiences by way of American correspondents innocently reading CIA media plants in foreign newspapers and reporting this information to American readers. Critics raised doubts as well about the propriety of placing secret propaganda into the media outlets of fellow democracies. The U.S.S.R. and Communist China, yes, because their citizens had no access to accurate information about the world, their masters had no compunction about manipulating their own media, and the regimes were hostile toward the United States. But Denmark, France, and Germany seemed a different story—at least for critics, if not for the CIA's Operations Directorate.

Sometimes the Agency's propaganda operations looked as though they had been crafted by an imaginative descendent of Franz Kafka. As a means for discrediting Fidel Castro of Cuba, one CIA plan (according to the public testimony of an intelligence officer before a U.S. Senate investigating committee in 1975) consisted of

> spreading the word that the Second Coming of Christ was imminent and that Christ was against Castro [who] was anti-Christ. And you would spread this word around Cuba, and then on whatever date it was, that there would be a manifestation of the thing. And at that time—this is absolutely true—and at that time just over the horizon there would be an American submarine which would surface off of Cuba and send up some star-shells. And this would be the manifestation of the Second Coming and Castro would be overthrown. (Church Committee 1975b)

The CIA called this operation "Elimination by Illumination." Fortunately, someone in the higher reaches of the Agency had the good sense to cancel this absurd exercise before it was attempted.

POLITICAL COVERT ACTION

Governments also carry out covert actions—or "special activities," as the United States likes to clothe the concept in its official and (rare) public references to the subject—of a political nature. Secret payments to friendly foreign politicians and bureaucrats are one example. Critics scorn this method as nothing less than bribery to advance America's national interests around the world. Advocates, however, prefer a more sanguine interpretation: not bribery, but rather stipends for the advancement of global democracy—what British intelligence officers in Her Majesty's Secret Service refer to affectionately as "King George's cavalry."

According to the public record, during the Cold War the CIA's political sponsorships included political parties, individual politicians, or dictators in (from a longer, mostly classified list) Italy, Jordan, Iran, Ecuador, El Salvador, Angola, Chile, West Germany, Greece, Egypt, Sudan, Suriname,

Mauritius, and the Philippines. The secret funds were used to win the favor of influential government officials, to help win elections for pro-Western factions (Italy was a heated electoral battleground in the early days of the Cold War), to recruit and build parties and regimes opposed to communism, and to strengthen labor unions in opposition to Communist party takeovers (again, Italy and the rest of Europe were pivotal).

Propaganda and political covert action are meant to work hand-in-glove, and sometimes both are subsumed under the "political" label. Some offices in the CIA's Operations Directorate take on the attributes of a political campaign headquarters, with intelligence officers engaged in the mass production of brochures, speeches, placards, campaign buttons, and bumper stickers (never mind that campaign buttons look a little out of place on tribal warlords or that some of the developing countries where the bumper stickers are sent may have only a few automobiles). Their common purpose during the Cold War was to persuade important foreign officials to turn a favorable eye toward the United States and away from the Soviet Union—or, more recently, away from adversaries such as Saddam Hussein in Iraq or the global network of Al Qaeda terrorist organizations. In this sense, the Cold War and the era since may be thought of as a subterranean political struggle between the United States and its enemies abroad, in which intelligence organizations have waged a clandestine war to win the hearts and minds of people around the world and to place into government positions men and women of an ideological persuasion compatible with America's interests.

ECONOMIC COVERT ACTION

A further weapon in a nation's arsenal of clandestine operations is the use of subversion against an adversary's means of economic production. During its campaign to ruin Allende, the CIA provided financial support to factions within Chile for the purposes of encouraging strikes—especially against the trucking industry—that would roil the regime in commercial chaos. Earlier, during the Kennedy Administration, the CIA planned to undermine Soviet-Cuban relations by lacing 14,125 bags of sugar bound from Havana to Moscow with an unpalatable (though harmless) chemical substance. At the eleventh hour, a White House aide learned of the proposal and, deeming it excessive, put a stop to it (Wicker 1966).

In the conduct of economic covert action, foreign currencies may be counterfeited, the world price of trading commodities depressed (especially harmful to one-crop economies, as in the case of Cuba's reliance on sugarcane), harbors mined to discourage commercial shipping (carried out by the Johnson and Nixon Administrations against North Vietnam and by the Reagan Administration against the Marxist regime in Nicaragua), electrical power lines and oil-storage tankers dynamited (again, North Vietnam and Nicaragua), oil supplies contaminated (North Vietnam), and even clouds seeded in an effort to disrupt weather patterns over the enemy's territory (in North Vietnam, to no effect).

Today, a prime target of economic dislocation is an adversary's computer systems. With skillful hacking ("cyberwarfare"), a nation's or group's financial transactions can be left in disarray, its bank assets stolen, its communications hopelessly tangled, and its military command-and-control capabilities frozen—an electronic assault that could be at least as dislocating as a military attack.

PARAMILITARY COVERT ACTION

While some of the covert actions we've mentioned earlier can be quite devastating (such as the mining of harbors), paramilitary or warlike operations are usually the most extreme and controversial forms of a nation's secret foreign policy. They can involve large-scale "secret" warfare—something of an oxymoron, since the extensive use of military force against an adversary does not stay secret for long, as the "quiet option" soon becomes noisy (an overt-covert action). The CIA's Special Operations Group (SOG), a subsidiary of its Operations Directorate, sponsored many guerrilla wars during the Cold War. From 1963 to 1973, the Agency backed the Hmong (Meo) tribes of North Laos in a war against the Communist Pathet Lao, who served as puppets of North Vietnam. The two sides fought to a draw, before the United States finally withdrew from the struggle. From the public record alone, it is clear that the CIA has also supported pro-Western insurgents in Ukraine, Poland, Albania, Hungary, Indonesia, China, Oman, Malaysia, Iraq, the Dominican Republic, Venezuela, North Korea, Bolivia, Thailand, Haiti, Guatemala, Cuba, Greece, Turkey, Vietnam, Afghanistan, Angola, and Nicaragua.

In these operations, the CIA's main role was to provide advice and weaponry. Anti-Communist dissidents during the early stages of the Cold War became the beneficiaries of a wide range of arms shipments from the United States, compliments of the CIA, including high-powered rifles, suitcase bombs, fragmentation grenades, rapid-fire machine guns, 64-mm antitank rockets, .38-caliber pistols, .30-caliber M-l carbines, .45-caliber submachine guns, tear-gas grenades, and supplies of ammunition. When the Reagan Administration came into office, it funneled through the CIA a reported $3 billion worth of weaponry to anti-Soviet fighters in Afghanistan (the *mujahideen,* or "soldiers of god"). Among the weapons were sophisticated shoulder-held Stinger and Blowpipe missiles capable of bringing down Soviet bombers. This "secret" supply of armaments to the *mujahideen* is said to have been an important consideration in Moscow's decision to withdraw from its losing "Vietnam" war in Afghanistan.

Since the end of the Cold War, the CIA has provided substantial amounts of arms and financial support to a new list of pro-U.S. factions, especially in the Middle East, the Balkans, and South Asia. Recipients have included the Iraqi National Congress, an umbrella group of insurgents opposed to Saddam Hussein's regime; opponents of Serbian expansion in Bosnia and Kosovo; and the Northern Alliance, along with other anti-Taliban factions, following the 2001 terrorist attacks against the United States that were widely thought to have been masterminded by Al Qaeda cells based in Afghanistan. In the 2002–03 war to root out Al Qaeda and Taliban forces from Afghanistan, the CIA introduced the use of unmanned aerial vehicles (UAVs) such as the Predator, equipped with cameras and Hellfire missiles to spot and quickly eliminate enemy forces—the newest, and highly lethal, approach to paramilitary operations.

As part of its paramilitary operations, the CIA is extensively involved in the training of foreign soldiers to fight on behalf of U.S. interests. These programs have entailed the training of foreign soldiers for guerrilla warfare, as well as counterterrorism. The CIA's military advisers for such purposes are often borrowed from the Department of Defense (DoD) and given nonofficial battlefield gear, a conversion known by insiders as "sheepdipping." The CIA's paramilitary program includes support to the Department of Defense in the development of the Pentagon's own unconventional warfare capability, known as Special Operations (or "Special Ops" for short) and carried out by elite Special Forces. For example, the CIA has provided armaments to the DoD for covert sales abroad. Some of the weapons sold to Iran by the Defense Department in the notorious arms-sale scandal of 1986–87 (the Iran-*contra* affair) had their origin in the CIA's paramilitary arsenal.

Moreover, the CIA provides training for military and police units in the developing world, particularly security personnel responsible for the protection of their nation's leaders. Among the skills taught at Camp Perry, the Agency's training facility in Virginia, are lessons in how to protect communications channels and the techniques of "executive driving" (designed to impart spin-away steering skills for maneuvering an automobile through terrorist roadblocks).

During those rare moments when the United States is not involved in the support of paramilitary wars in one place or another (as in the early years of the Carter Administration), the CIA's Special Operations Group bides its time by carrying out training operations for its own personnel and by maintaining its military hardware (including a small navy and air force). Above all, SOG is kept busy in its added responsibility to provide support for intelligence collection operations, especially in remote regions like the mountains of Afghanistan and Pakistan, where U.S. paramilitary officers have recently developed geographic expertise and contacts with local warlords.

ASSASSINATION PLOTS

A special category within the realm of paramilitary operations is the assassination of individual foreigners—needless to say a subject fraught with controversy. This option has gone by a number of euphemisms, used in hushed tones within the government of the United States: "executive action," "terminate with extreme prejudice," or "neutralize." At one time during the Cold War, proposals for assassination were screened by a special unit within the CIA called the "Health Alteration Committee." (Its counterpart in the Soviet Union was the KGB's "Department of Wet Affairs.")

Fidel Castro was America's prime target for death during the Kennedy Administration, although none of the plots against him succeeded. Another target for "health alteration" during the Kennedy years was Patrice Lumumba, the Congolese leader. Members of a rival Congolese faction beat the CIA to the punch, however, and murdered Lumumba for their own political reasons related to an internal power struggle. In 2003, the CIA launched a Hellfire missile from an Unmanned Aerial Vehicle (UAV)—a drone—called a Predator. Hovering at 10,000 feet above the deserts of Yemen, it destroyed an automobile filled with suspected Al Qaeda members. The occupants, including one who turned out to be an American citizen, died a fiery death. The Predator and its larger version, the Reaper, have become the most lethal instruments of CIA paramilitary covert action.

A BALANCE SHEET

Since the outbreak of the Cold War and the establishment of the CIA in 1947, covert action has exercised a fascination on most presidential administrations. But what have been the results? This question may be answered according to practical outcomes and ethical considerations. With respect to practicalities, a further distinction must be made between the short-term and long-term consequences of covert action.

The practical results have been mixed. Sometimes covert action has led to stunning successes for the United States, at least over the short term. In Europe in the immediate aftermath of World War II (particularly in Greece and Italy), in Iran (1953), in Guatemala (1954), and less spectacularly throughout Latin America in the 1950s, covert action played a major role in thwarting Communist and Marxist political leaders and movements—often sponsored openly or covertly by the U.S.S.R. Over the short run, the CIA also chalked up notable successes in Laos (1963–73), Afghanistan (1982–88), Panama (1989, toppling the corrupt dictator General Manuel Antonio Noriega), and Afghanistan and Iraq (2001–03).

Yet, the lasting value of some of these "victories"—the long-term consequence—has been questionable. Iran is hardly a close friend of the United States today; Guatemala and Panama are as poor and repressive as ever; the first Afghanistan intervention brought the Taliban regime to power, which in turn supported the Al Qaeda terrorist organization; and the second Afghanistan and Iraq interventions are unlikely to have brought global terrorism to a halt (although in Afghanistan it took a useful step in that direction). Earlier there were the Bay of Pigs fiasco, the madcap plots to dispatch Fidel Castro (exploding cigars, secret powders designed to make his

charismatic beard fall out), the pouring of millions of dollars into the sinkhole of the Angolan civil war, and the Iran-*contra* scandal and its dismissal of the Constitution. Along the way came the CIA's abandonment of temporary allies in a string of anti-Communist paramilitary operations, including the freedom fighters in Hungary and at the Bay of Pigs, the South Vietnamese who aided the CIA and ended up buried in cemeteries throughout Saigon as the United States fled Indochina, the Meo tribesmen in Laos, the Khambas in Tibet, the Nationalist Chinese in Burma, and the ever-suffering Kurds.

On practical grounds, perhaps the best conclusion one can draw based on the empirical record is that covert action (like overt economic sanctions or aerial bombing) sometimes succeeds and sometimes fails. Its chances seem best when the objectives are limited, when strong opposition groups already exist within a target nation or group, and, in the case of paramilitary operations, when it is aided and abetted by overt precision bombing and elite DoD Special Forces on the ground.

THE READINGS

In the first article of this section, Former Senator Frank Church (D, Idaho), who in 1975 led a searing investigation into legal violations of the intelligence agencies, argues in the next selection that the covert action instruments of the CIA during the Cold War were "put to the service of reactionary and repressive regimes that can never, for long, escape or withstand the volcanic forces of change." A strong critic of most covert actions during the Cold War, Senator Church nonetheless saw a potential role for this approach, say, if a timely clandestine intervention were able to avert a nuclear holocaust or if covert action might aid the people of another nation in their struggle against an unpopular Marxist regime.

James A. Barry, a former CIA officer, likewise addresses the pros and cons of covert action. Applying just-war theory to the study of covert action, Barry establishes a checklist of safeguards to ensure that clandestine interventions abroad comport with some degree of ethical standards. High on his list: The covert action has to be "approved by the president, after due deliberation within the Executive Branch, and with the full knowledge and concurrence of appropriate members of the Congress." No more Iran-*contra* affairs.

19. COVERT ACTION: SWAMPLAND OF AMERICAN FOREIGN POLICY

SENATOR FRANK CHURCH

The chairman of the Senate Intelligence Committee that investigated intelligence abuses in 1975–76 finds in the excesses of the CIA abroad the symptoms of an illusion of American omnipotence that entrapped and enthralled the nation's presidents throughout the Cold War. Writing in the middle of the Cold War, the Senator saw no place for bribery, blackmail, abduction, or assassination in America's relations with the rest of the world.

Two hundred years ago, at the founding of this nation, Thomas Paine observed that "Not a place upon earth might be so happy as America. Her situation is remote from all the wrangling world." I still believe America remains the best place on Earth, but it has long since ceased to be "remote from all the wrangling world."

On the contrary, even our internal economy now depends on events far beyond our shores. The energy crisis, which exposed our vulnerable dependence upon foreign oil, made the point vividly.

It is also tragic but true that our own people can no longer be made safe from savage destruction hurled down upon them from the most hidden and remote regions on Earth. Soviet submarines silently traverse the ocean floors carrying transcontinental missiles with the capacity to strike at our heartland. The nuclear arms race threatens to continue its deadly spiral toward Armageddon.

In this dangerous setting, it is imperative for the United States to maintain a strong and effective intelligence service. On this proposition we can ill-afford to be of two minds. We have no choice other than to gather, analyze, and assess—to the best of our abilities—vital information on the intent and prowess of foreign adversaries, present or potential. Without an adequate intelligence-gathering apparatus, we would be unable to gauge with confidence our defense requirements; unable to conduct an informed foreign policy; unable to control, through satellite surveillance, a runaway nuclear arms race.

"The winds and waves are always on the side of the ablest navigators," wrote Gibbon. Those nations without a skillful intelligence service must navigate beneath a clouded sky.

With this truth in mind, the United States established, by the National Security Act of 1947, a Central Intelligence Agency to collect and evaluate intelligence, and provide for its proper dissemination within the government. The CIA was to be a clearing house for other U.S. intelligence agencies, including those of the State Department and the various military services. It was to be an independent, civilian intelligence agency whose duty it was, in the words of Allen Dulles, CIA Director from 1953–1961:

> To weigh facts, and to draw conclusions from those facts, without having either the facts or the conclusions warped by the inevitable and even proper prejudices of the men whose duty it is to determine policy and who, having once determined a policy, are too likely to be blind to any facts which might lend to prove the policy to be faulty.

"The Central Intelligence Agency," concluded Dulles, "should have nothing to do with policy." In this way, neither the President nor the Congress would be left with any of the frequently self-interested intelligence assessments afforded by the Pentagon and the State Department to rely upon.

In its efforts to get at the hard facts, the CIA has performed unevenly. It has had its successes and its failures. The CIA has detected the important new

Soviet weapons systems early on; but it has often over-estimated the growth of the Russian ICBM forces. The CIA has successfully monitored Soviet adherence to arms control agreements, and given us the confidence to take steps toward further limitations; but it has been unable to predict the imminence of several international conflicts, such as the 1973 Arab-Israeli War. In a word, though it deserves passing marks for its intelligence work, the CIA has certainly not been infallible.

While one may debate the quality of the agency's performance, there has never been any question about the propriety and necessity of its involvement in the process of gathering and evaluating foreign intelligence. Nor have serious questions been raised about the means used to acquire such information, whether from overt sources, technical devices, or by clandestine methods.

What has become controversial is quite unrelated to intelligence, but has to do instead with the so-called covert operations of the CIA, those secret efforts to manipulate events within foreign countries in ways presumed to serve the interests of the United States. Nowhere are such activities vouchsafed in the statutory language which created the Agency in 1947, "No indication was given in the statute that the CIA would become a vehicle for foreign political action or clandestine political warfare," notes Harry Howe Ransom, a scholar who has written widely and thought deeply about the problems of intelligence in modern society. Ransom concludes that "probably no other organization of the federal government has taken such liberties in interpreting its legally assigned functions as has the CIA."

The legal basis for this political action arm of the CIA is very much open to question. Certainly the legislative history of the 1947 Act fails to indicate that Congress anticipated the CIA would ever engage in covert political warfare abroad.

The CIA points to a catch-all phrase contained in the 1947 Act as a rationalization for its operational prerogatives. A clause in the statute permits the Agency "to perform such other functions and duties related to intelligence affecting the national security as the National Security Council may, from time to time, direct." These vague and seemingly innocuous words have been seized upon as the green light for CIA intervention around the world.

MALIGNANT PLOTS

Moreover, these interventions into the political affairs of foreign countries soon came to overshadow the Agency's original purpose of gathering and evaluating information. Just consider how far afield we strayed.

For example:

- We deposed the government of Guatemala when its leftist leanings displeased us.
- We attempted to ignite a civil war against Sukarno in Indonesia.
- We intervened to restore the Shah to his throne in Iran, after Mossadegh broke the monopoly grip of British Petroleum over Iranian oil.
- We attempted to launch a counter-revolution in Cuba through the abortive landing of an army of exiles at the Bay of Pigs.
- We even conducted a secret war in Laos, paying Meo tribesmen and Thai mercenaries to do our fighting there.

All these engagements were initiated without the knowledge or consent of Congress. No country was too small, no foreign leader too trifling, to escape our attention.

- We sent a deadly toxin to the Congo with the purpose of injecting Lumumba with a fatal disease.
- We armed local dissidents in the Dominican Republic, knowing their purpose to be the assassination of Trujillo.
- We participated in a military coup overturning the very government we were pledged to defend in South Vietnam; and when Premier Diem resisted, he and his brother were murdered by the very generals to whom we gave money and support.
- We attempted for years to assassinate Fidel Castro and other Cuban leaders. The various plots spanned three Administrations, and involved an extended collaboration between the CIA and the Mafia.

Whatever led the United States to such extremes? Assassination is nothing less than an act of war, and our targets were leaders of small, weak countries that could not possibly threaten the United States. Only once did Castro become an accessory to a threat, by permitting the Soviets to install missiles on Cuban soil within range of the United States. And this was the one time when the CIA called off all attempts against his life.

The roots of these malignant plots grew out of the obsessions of the Cold War. When the CIA succeeded the Office of Strategic Services of World War II, Stalin replaced Hitler as the Devil Incarnate.

Wartime methods were routinely adopted for peace-time use.

In those myopic years, the world was seen as up for grabs between the United States and the Soviet Union. Castro's Cuba raised the specter of a Soviet outpost at America's doorstep. Events in the Dominican Republic appeared to offer an additional opportunity for the Soviets and their allies. The Congo, freed from Belgian rule, occupied the strategic center of the African continent, and the prospect of Soviet penetration there was viewed as a threat to U.S. interests in emerging Africa. There was a great concern that a communist takeover in Indochina would have a "domino effect" throughout Asia. Even the lawful election in 1970 of a Marxist president in Chile was still seen by some as the equivalent of Castro's conquest of Cuba.

In the words of a former Secretary of State, "A desperate struggle [was] going on in the back alleys of world politics." Every upheaval, wherever it occurred, was likened to a pawn on a global chessboard, to be moved this way or that, by the two principal players. This led the CIA to plunge into a full range of covert activities designed to counteract the competitive efforts of the Soviet KGB. Thus, the United States came to adopt the methods and accept the value system of the "enemy." In the secret world of covert action, we threw off all restraints. Not content merely to discreetly subsidize foreign political parties, labor unions, and newspapers, the Central Intelligence Agency soon began to directly manipulate the internal politics of other countries. Spending many millions of dollars annually, the CIA filled its bag with dirty tricks, ranging from bribery and false propaganda to schemes to "alter the health" of unfriendly foreign leaders and undermine their regimes.

Nowhere is this imitation of KGB tactics better demonstrated than in the directives sent to CIA agents in the Congo in 1960. Instructions to kill the African leader Lumumba were sent via diplomatic pouch, along with rubber gloves, a mask, syringe, and a lethal biological material. The poison was to be injected into some substance that Lumumba would ingest, whether food or toothpaste. Before this plan was implemented, Lumumba was killed by Congolese rivals. Nevertheless, our actions had fulfilled the prophesy of George Williams, an eminent theologian at the Harvard Divinity School, who once warned, "Be cautious when you choose your enemy, for you will grow more like him."

ALLENDE "UNACCEPTABLE"

The imperial view from the White House reached its arrogant summits during the Administration of Richard Nixon. On September 15, 1970, following the election of Allende to be President of Chile, Richard Nixon summoned Henry Kissinger, Richard Helms, and John Mitchell to the White House. The topic was Chile. Allende, Nixon stated, was unacceptable to the President of the United States.

In his handwritten notes for this meeting, Nixon indicated that he was "not concerned" with the risks involved. As CIA Director Helms recalled in testimony before the Senate Committee, "The President came down very hard that he wanted something done, and he didn't care how." To Helms, the order had been all-inclusive. "If I ever carried a marshal's baton in my knapsack out of the Oval Office," he recalled, "it was that day." Thus, the President of the United States had given orders to the CIA to prevent the popularly elected President of Chile from entering office.

To bar Allende from the Presidency, a military coup was organized, with the CIA playing a direct role in the planning. One of the major obstacles to the success of the mission was the strong opposition to a coup by the Commander-in-Chief of the Chilean Army, General Rene Schneider, who insisted that Chile's constitution be upheld. As a result of his stand, the removal of General Schneider became a necessary ingredient in the coup plans. Unable to get General Schneider to resign, conspirators in Chile decided to kidnap him. Machine guns and ammunition were passed by the CIA to a group of kidnappers on October 22, 1970. That same day General Schneider was mortally wounded on his way to work in an attempted kidnap, apparently by a group affiliated with the one provided weapons by the CIA.

The plot to kidnap General Schneider was but one of many efforts to subvert the Allende regime. The United States sought also to bring the Chilean economy under Allende to its knees. In a situation report to Dr. Kissinger, our Ambassador wrote that:

> Not a nut or bolt will be allowed to reach Chile under Allende. Once Allende comes to power we shall do all within our power to condemn Chile and the Chileans to utmost deprivation and poverty, a policy designed for a long time to come to accelerate the hard features of a Communist society in Chile.

The ultimate outcome, as you know, of these and other efforts to destroy the Allende government was a bloodbath which included the death of Allende and the installation, in his place, of a repressive military dictatorship.

Why Chile? What can possibly explain or justify such an intrusion upon the right of the Chilean people to self-determination? The country itself was no threat to us. It has been aptly characterized as a "dagger pointed straight at the heart of Antarctica."

Was it to protect American owned big business? We now know that I.T.T. offered the CIA a million dollars to prevent the ratification of Allende's election by the Chilean Congress. Quite properly, this offer was rejected. But the CIA then spent much more on its own, in an effort to accomplish the same general objective.

Yet, if our purpose was to save the properties of large U.S. corporations, that cause had already been lost. The nationalization of the mines was decided well before Allende's election; and the question of compensation was tempered by insurance against confiscatory losses issued to the companies by the U.S. government itself.

No, the only plausible explanation for our intervention in Chile is the persistence of the myth that communism is a single, hydraheaded serpent, and that it remains our duty to cut off each ugly head, wherever and however it may appear.

Ever since the end of World War II, we have justified our mindless meddling in the affairs of others on the ground that since the Soviets do it, we must do it, too. The time is at hand to re-examine that thesis.

Before Chile, we insisted that communism had never been freely chosen by any people, but forced upon them against their will. The communists countered that they resorted to revolution because the United States would never permit the establishment of a communist regime by peaceful means.

In Chile, President Nixon confirmed the communist thesis. Like Caesar peering into the colonies from distant Rome, Nixon said the choice of government by the Chileans was unacceptable to the President of the United States.

The attitude in the White House seemed to be: If—in the wake of Vietnam—I can no longer send the Marines, then I will send in the CIA.

WHAT HAVE WE GAINED?

But what have we gained by our policy of consummate intervention, compared to what we have lost?

- A "friendly" Iran and Indonesia, members of the OPEC cartel, which imposes extortionate prices on the Western World for indispensable oil?
- A hostile Laos that preferred the indigenous forces of communism to control imposed by Westerners, which smacked of the hated colonialism against which they had fought so long to overthrow?
- A fascist Chile, with thousands of political prisoners languishing in their jails, mocking the professed ideals of the United States throughout the hemisphere?

If we have gained little, what then have we lost? I suggest we have lost—or grievously impaired—the good name and reputation of the United States from which we once drew a unique capacity to exercise matchless moral leadership. Where once we were admired, now we are resented. Where once we were welcome, now we are tolerated, at best. In the eyes of millions of once friendly foreign people, the United States is today regarded with grave suspicion and distrust.

What else can account for the startling decline in American prestige? Certainly not the collapse of our military strength, for our firepower has grown immensely since the end of World War II.

I must lay the blame, in large measure, to the fantasy that it lay within our power to control other countries through the covert manipulation of their affairs. It formed part of a greater illusion that entrapped and enthralled our Presidents: the illusion of American omnipotence.

Nevertheless, I do not draw the conclusion of those who now argue that all U.S. covert operations must be banned in the future. I can conceive of a dire emergency when timely clandestine action on our part might avert a nuclear holocaust and save an entire civilization.

I can also conceive of circumstances, such as those existing in Portugal today, where our discreet help to democratic political parties might avert a forcible take-over by a communist minority, heavily subsidized by the Soviets. In Portugal, such a bitterly-unwanted, Marxist regime is being resisted courageously by a people who earlier voted 84 percent against it.

But these are covert operations consistent either with the imperative of national survival or with our traditional belief in free government. If our hand were exposed helping a foreign people in their struggle to be free, we could scorn the cynical doctrine of "plausible denial," and say openly, "Yes, we were there—and proud of it."

We were there in Western Europe, helping to restore democratic governments in the aftermath of World War II. It was only after our faith gave way to fear that we began to act as a self-appointed-sentinel of the status quo.

Then it was that all the dark arts of secret intervention—bribery, blackmail, abduction, assassination—were put to the service of reactionary and repressive regimes that can never, for long, escape or withstand the volcanic forces of change.

And the United States, as a result, became ever more identified with the claims of the old order, instead of the aspirations of the new.

The remedy is clear. American foreign policy, whether openly or secretly pursued, must be made to conform once more to our historic ideals, the same fundamental belief in freedom and popular government that once made us a beacon of hope for the downtrodden and oppressed throughout the world.

QUESTIONS FOR FURTHER DISCUSSION

1. Why is Senator Frank Church so critical of U.S. covert actions?
2. Does he see any need for covert action at all in the conduct of American foreign policy?
3. Against what kinds of nations was covert action directed by the United States, according to Senator Chruch?
4. What kinds of covert action, if any, do you think are morally acceptable for the United States, and under what conditions?

20. COVERT ACTION CAN BE JUST

JAMES A. BARRY

Exploring the use of covert action from the point of view of just-war theory, Barry establishes benchmarks for judging the morality of this controversial form of secret foreign policy. He eschews the use of highly invasive clandestine operations but advances an ethical justification for certain forms of covert action.

In 1954, President Dwight Eisenhower appointed a panel to make recommendations regarding covert political action as an instrument of foreign policy. The panel, headed by General Jimmy Doolittle, included the following statement in its report:

> It is now clear that we are facing an implacable enemy whose avowed objective is world domination by whatever means and at whatever cost. There are no rules in such a game. Hitherto acceptable norms of human conduct do not apply. If the United States is to survive, long standing American concepts of "fair play" must be reconsidered. We must develop effective espionage and counterespionage services and must learn to subvert, sabotage and destroy our enemies by more clever, more sophisticated means than those used against us. It may become necessary that the American people be made acquainted with, understand and support this fundamentally repugnant philosophy.[1]

Today, this conclusion of the Doolittle report appears exaggerated—even its authors were uncomfortable with the "repugnant philosophy" they deemed necessary—and fortunately America did not abandon its moral traditions much less "acceptable norms of human conduct." Nevertheless, covert political action did become an important tool of U.S. policy, and the threat of international communism was so compelling a rationale that most covert action operations needed no more specific justification. This objective was used to justify covert coups, assassination attempts, and other activities that in hindsight appear reprehensible. These actions—pursued under a crusading variant of *Realpolitik*—seem to many today to be questionable in their objectives and disproportionate to the threat.

The cold war justification for covert action began to draw fire, in part because of the late 1960s opposition to the Vietnam War and in part because of the revelation of abuses by the Central Intelligence Agency (CIA) such as assassination plots against foreign leaders. As a result of those revelations, greater attention was paid to managing covert actions. But, until recently, the adequacy of the Soviet threat to justify covert action was not seriously doubted in Washington.

COVERT ACTION AND THE NEW WORLD ORDER

Since the dismantling of the Berlin Wall, the abortive coup in the Soviet Union, and the dissolution of the Soviet empire, this once compelling anticommunist rationale for covert action has lost all validity. But this is not to say that the United States should eschew the method of covert action. The Gulf War shows that aggression by hostile states remains a threat. And other challenges—such as terrorism, narcotics trafficking, and the proliferation of weapons of mass destruction—are likely to require the United States to consider covert responses.

What, then, would replace the cold war justification that has shaped covert action policy since the founding of the Central Intelligence Agency?

One approach to assessing the justification for intervention overseas, an approach that has received renewed attention in recent years, derives from the natural law tradition and those rules regarding the use of force by states that fall under the rubric of "just-war theory." Just-war theory was used extensively by the Bush administration to explain its decision to go to war, under United Nations auspices, against Iraq.[2] More recently, a symposium of jurists, philosophers, theologians, government officials, and military officers affirmed that just-war theory is useful in evaluating low-intensity conflict.[3]

JUST-WAR THEORY: TRADITIONAL AND MODERN FORMULATIONS

Just-war doctrine can be traced to Saint Augustine in the fourth century A.D., and especially to Saint Thomas Aquinas, who codified it in the thirteenth century. Just-war theory is a set of moral guidelines for going to war (the so-called *jus ad bellum*), and a set of moral guidelines for the conduct of hostilities (*jus in bello*).[4] Though associated with Catholic scholars, just-war theory is not a religious teaching but rather part of a moral tradition, dating from Aristotle, a tradition that emphasizes ethical consideration in decision making.

According to Thomas, the act of going to war must have the following three characteristics if it is to be a moral act: the action must be ordered by proper authority; the cause must be just; and there must be an intention of promoting good or avoiding evil.[5] Later authorities added three further criteria: the action must be a last resort and peaceful alternatives (negotiations, sanctions, and so forth) must be exhausted or judged ineffective; there must be a reasonable probability of success anticipated; and the damage which the war entails must be expected to be proportionate to the injury or the injustice which occasions it.[6]

Once these conditions are met, according to this formulation of just-war theory, the belligerent is subject to two further constraints in his conduct of the war: his actions must be discriminate, that is, directed against the opponent not against innocent people; and the means of combat must be proportionate to the just ends envisioned and under the control of a competent authority.[7]

The first of these constraints has been further refined, under the so-called "principle of double effect," to encompass situations in which injury to innocent parties is unavoidable. Under this principle, a belligerent may permit incident evil effects. However, the action taken must not be evil in itself; the good effect and not the evil effect, must be intended; and the good effect must not arise out of the evil effect, but both must arise simultaneously from the action taken.[8]

Modern political theorists in the just-war tradition have focused primarily on the criterion of just cause. The majority favors the view that the only justifiable cause for war is to repel aggression. Traditionally, however, there were two others: to retake something wrongfully taken and to punish wrongdoing.[9] Another area of debate has been whether forcible intervention could be justified in order to reform a state's political system, for example, in the case of flagrant human rights abuses.[10]

JUST-WAR THEORY AND COVERT ACTION

One former intelligence practitioner, William Colby, has argued that "a standard for selection of covert actions that are just can be developed by analogy with the long-standing effort to differentiate just from unjust wars."[11] And former Director of Central Intelligence (DCI) William Webster has noted that in its deliberations the CIA's Covert Action Review Group explores three key questions regarding a proposed covert action: "Is it entirely consistent with our laws? Is it consistent with American values as we understand them? And will it make sense to the American people?"[12]

With respect to the latter two considerations, a reformulation of the just-war criteria in common sense terms would probably appeal to the American people. It seems fair to conclude that the people would support a covert action if:

> The action is approved by the president, after due deliberation within the Executive Branch, and with the full knowledge and concurrence of appropriate members of the Congress;
>
> The intentions and objectives are clearly spelled out, reasonable, and just;
>
> Other means of achieving the objectives would not be effective;
>
> There is a reasonable probability of success; and
>
> The methods envisioned are commensurate with the objectives.

Further, it is reasonable to presume that the American people would approve of methods that minimize injury (physical, economic, or psychological) to innocent people, are proportionate to the threat, and under firm U.S. control.[13]

Those who advocate or approve such covert actions, however, bear the additional burden of demonstrating why they must be conducted secretly. As ethicist Sissela Bok has pointed out, every state requires a measure of secrecy to defend itself, but when secrecy is invoked citizens lose the ordinary democratic checks on those matters that can affect them most strongly.[14] In addition, as Charles Beitz has argued, a special problem of operational control can arise when intermediaries (especially foreign agents) are employed—because their aims may differ from ours, and because the chain of command may be ambiguous or unreliable.[15] Finally, most covert actions will necessarily lack the public legitimacy and legal status under international law of a declared, justifiable war. This makes it incumbent on those advocating such actions to take into account the consequences of possible public misunderstanding and international opprobrium.

JUST WAR AND THE CHILE CASE OF 1964

Reverend John P. Langan, S.J., of the Kennedy Center for Ethics and Public Policy, Georgetown University, notes that just-war theory has both material and formal aspects, and that the formal aspects, such as just intention and proportionality are applicable to a broad range of situations where one has to do harm to another, including punishment, surgery, and—by extension—political or economic intervention.[16] It would appear that the framework of just-war theory could be useful for making choices regarding covert actions, since they can cause suffering or moral damage, as war causes physical destruction. To explore this, consider how the guidelines would have applied to covert U.S. interventions in Chile in 1964 and 1970.[17]

BACKGROUND

As part of its worldwide buildup of covert action capabilities in the early 1950s, the CIA established a capacity to conduct covert propaganda and political influence operations in Chile. In 1961, President John Kennedy established the Alliance for Progress to promote growth of democratic institutions. He also became convinced that the Chilean Christian Democratic Party shared his belief in democratic social reform and had the organizational competence to achieve this goal, but lacked the resources to compete with parties of the Left and Right.

U.S. INTENTIONS

During 1961, the CIA established relationships with key political parties in Chile, as well as propaganda and organizational mechanisms. In 1962, the Special Group (the interagency body charged with reviewing covert actions) approved two CIA proposals to provide support to the Christian Democrats. The program was intended to strengthen democratic forces against the Socialist challenge from Salvador Allende Gossens, who was supported by the Soviet Union and Cuba. When President Lyndon Johnson succeeded Kennedy, he continued the covert subsidies, with the objective of making Chile a model of democracy, and preventing nationalization of Chilean branches of American corporations.

The Chilean presidential election of 1964 was a battle between Allende and Eduardo Frei Montalva, a liberal Christian Democrat. The election was viewed with great alarm in Washington. The *New York Times* compared it to the Italian election of 1948, when the communists had threatened covertly to support democratic parties. Similarly, in 1964, the Johnson administration intervened in Chile, according to the Church Committee Report, to prevent or minimize the influence of Marxists in the government that would emerge from the election. Cord Meyer, a former CIA covert action manager, argued that the intervention was intended to preserve Chile's constitutional order.

POLICY APPROVAL

In considering the 1964 election operation, the Johnson administration used the established mechanism, the interagency Special Group. By 1963, according to Treverton, the Special Group had developed criteria for evaluating covert action proposals. All expenditures of covert funds for the 1964 operation (some $3 million in all) were approved by the Group. (There is no indication that the Congress approved these expenditures or was even informed in detail of the operation.) In addition, an interagency committee was set up in Washington to manage the operation and was paralleled by a group in the U.S. embassy in Santiago. Meyer contends that covert intervention on behalf of Christian Democratic candidates had very wide support in the administration, and the Church Committee confirms that the covert action was decided upon at the highest levels of government.

OTHER U.S. ACTIVITIES

Covert action by the CIA was an important element, but not the only aspect of U.S. policy. Chile was chosen to become a showcase of economic development programs under the Alliance for Progress. Between 1964 and 1969, Chile received well over a billion dollars in direct, overt U.S. aid—more per capita than any other country in the hemisphere. Moreover, funding to support the Frei candidacy was funnelled overtly through the Agency for International Development, as well as secretly through the CIA. Frei also received covert aid from a group of American corporations known as the Business Group for Latin America.

PROBABILITY OF SUCCESS

That the 1964 covert action had a reasonable probability of success is evident from the outcome—Frei won a clear majority of the vote, 56 percent. According to Church Committee records, a CIA postmortem concluded that the covert campaign had a decisive impact. It is not clear from available records whether a calculation of the likelihood of success was part of the decision-making process. According to Treverton, the CIA was required under Special Group procedures to make such an estimate, and it is likely that their view would have been optimistic, since they had penetrated all significant elements of the Chilean political system.

METHODS EMPLOYED

In the 1964 election operation the CIA employed virtually its entire arsenal of non-lethal methods:

> Funds were passed through intermediaries to the Christian Democrats.

> The CIA provided a consultant to assist the Christian Democrats in running an American-style campaign, which included polling, voter registration, and get-out-the-vote drives.

> Political action operations, including polls and grass roots organizing, were conducted among important voting blocs, including slum dwellers, peasants, organized labor, and dissident Socialists.

> CIA-controlled assets placed propaganda in major Chilean newspapers, and on radio and television; erected wall posters; passed out political leaflets; and organized demonstrations. Some of this propaganda employed "scare tactics" to link Allende to Soviet and Cuban atrocities.

> Other assets manufactured "black propaganda"— that is, material falsely attributed to Allende's supporters and intended to discredit them.[18]

CONSTRAINTS IMPOSED

Significant constraints were imposed, however. Paramilitary and other lethal methods were not employed. The CIA rejected a proposal from the Chilean Defense Council to carry out a coup if Allende won. The Department of State turned down a similar proposal from a Chilean Air Force officer. Moreover, the Special Group turned down an offer from American Businessmen to provide funds for covert disbursement. According to the Church Committee, the Group considered this "neither secure nor an honorable way of doing business."

COVERT ACTION AND THE 1970 ELECTION

Under Chilean law, Frei could not serve two consecutive terms as president. As the 1970 elections approached, therefore, the United States faced a dilemma. The Christian Democrats had drifted to the left, and were out of step with the view of President Richard Nixon's administration. The conservative candidate, Jorge Alessandri, was not attractive, but there was even greater concern about an Allende victory.

The CIA began to warn policy makers early in 1969 that an Allende victory was likely. In March 1970, the 303 Committee (successor to the Special Group) decided that the United States would not support any particular candidate, but would conduct a "spoiling operation" aimed at discrediting Allende through propaganda. The effort failed when Allende won a slim plurality in the September 4 election. Since no candidate won a clear majority, the election was referred to a joint session of Congress, which in the past had always endorsed the candidate who had received the highest popular vote. The joint session was set for October 24, 1970.

U.S. INTENTIONS

Senior U.S. officials maintained that their preoccupation with Allende was defensive and aimed at allaying fears of a communist victory both abroad and at home. Henry Kissinger, then assistant to the president for national security affairs, later noted that what worried the United States was Allende's proclaimed hostility and his perceived intention to create "another Cuba." Nixon stated in a *New York*

Times interview:

> There was a great deal of concern expressed in 1964 and again in 1970 by neighboring South America countries that if Mr. Allende were elected president, Chile would quickly become haven for Communist operatives who would infiltrate and undermine independent governments throughout South America.[19]

The intelligence community, however, offered a more subtle analysis of the threat. According to an assessment by the CIA's Directorate of Intelligence:

Regarding threats to U.S. interests, we conclude that:

1. The U.S. has no vital national interests in Chile. There would, however, be tangible economic losses.
2. The world balance of power would not be significantly altered by an Allende government.
3. An Allende victory would, however, create considerable political and psychological costs:
   a. Hemispheric cohesion would be threatened by the challenge that an Allende government would pose to the OAS, and by the reactions that it would create in other countries. We do not see, however, any likely threat to the peace of the region.
   b. An Allende victory would represent a definite psychological setback to the U.S. and a definite psychological advance for the Marxist idea.[20]

When Allende won a plurality of the popular vote, the thrust of U.S. covert action shifted to preventing his accession to the presidency by manipulating the congressional vote, by another political gambit, or by support for a military coup.

POLICY APPROVAL

Until the middle of September, management of the covert action against Allende was entrusted to the 40 Committee (a new name for the 303 Committee), which Kissinger headed. After the popular vote, the committee asked Edward Korry, the U.S. ambassador in Santiago, for a "cold-blooded assessment" of the likelihood of mounting a coup and organizing an effective opposition to Allende. With negative evaluations from both Korry and the CIA, the committee explored a so-called "Rube Goldberg" gambit in which Alessandri would be elected by the Congress, then resign allowing Frei to run in a second election. The ploy was turned down.

By this time, Nixon had taken a personal role. On September 15, Donald Kendall, chief executive officer of Pepsi Cola, and Augustine Edwards, an influential Chilean publisher who had supported Frei during the 1964 election, communicated their alarm at the prospect of an Allende victory to the Nixon administration. According to Kissinger, Nixon was alarmed by their views and decided that more direct action was necessary. He called in DCI Richard Helms and ordered the CIA to play a direct role in organizing a military coup. Further, Helms was told not to coordinate CIA activities with the Departments of State and Defense and not to inform Ambassador Korry. The 40 Committee was not informed, nor was the Congress. This activity was called "Track II," to distinguish it from the 40 Committee program, "Track I."[21]

OTHER U.S. ACTIVITIES IN CHILE

Track II was a carefully guarded secret, but U.S. displeasure with the prospect of an Allende victory was not. According to Kissinger, all agencies were working to prevent the election. The Chilean government was threatened with economic reprisals, and steps were taken to inform the Chilean armed forces that military aid would be cut off. Separately from the CIA's efforts, several large American companies had financed Alessandri's campaign. One company, ITT, offered the CIA $1 million, but Helms turned it down.

PROBABILITY OF SUCCESS

When Helms left the Oval Office on September 15, he had a page of handwritten notes. The first entry read "less than one in ten chance of success." His pessimistic assessment was echoed by Ambassador Korry. According to his correspondence with the Church Committee, Korry consistently warned the Nixon administration that the Chilean military was no policy alternative. From Santiago, according to Church Committee documents, the CIA reported: "Military action is impossible; the military is incapable and unwilling to seize power. We have no capability to motivate or instigate a coup." (This view apparently was based on an evaluation of the military's political will; in 1973 the armed forces showed their capability by removing Allende from power.)

The CIA's view was shared by the managers of Track II. According to David Phillips, chief of the CIA's Chile Task Force, both he and his supervisor were convinced that Track II was unworkable. The

Deputy Director for Plans, Thomas Karamessines, was adamant that the Agency could not refuse the assignment, but briefed Nixon several times on the progress of the operation, always pessimistically.[22]

METHODS EMPLOYED

Although both Track I and Track II were intended to prevent Allende's taking power, they employed different methods. Track I included funding to bribe Chilean congressmen, propaganda and economic activities, and contacts with Frei and elements of the military to foster opposition to Allende. Track II was more direct, stressing active CIA involvement in, and support for, a coup—without Frei's knowledge. The CIA specifically offered encouragement to dissident Chilean military officers who opposed Allende but who recognized that General Rene Schneider, the Chilean Chief of Staff would not support a coup. These dissidents developed a plan to kidnap Schneider and take over the government, and this became known to CIA officials. Two unsuccessful kidnap attempts were made; on the third attempt, on October 22 1970, General Schneider was shot and subsequently died. Both the Church Committee and the Chilean inquiry concluded that the weapons used were not supplied by the United States, and that American officials did not desire or encourage Schneider's death. Neither, however, did they prevent it.

CONSTRAINTS IMPOSED

Unlike the 1964 effort, the 1970 covert operation did not involve extensive public opinion polling, grass roots organizing, or direct funding of any candidate. Moreover, Helms made clear that the assassination of Allende was neither feasible nor politically acceptable, and when a right-wing Chilean fanatic, General Arturo Marshall, offered to help prevent Allende's confirmation, the CIA declined because of his earlier involvement in bombings in Santiago.

EVALUATING THE 1964 AND 1970 CHILE OPERATIONS

A just-war theorist reviewing the two covert operations would likely reach two conclusions. First, the 1964 operation was more justifiable than the 1970 activity. And, second, both operations would have benefited from a more rigorous application of the *jus ad bellum* and *jus in bello* criteria.

U.S. authorities probably would have considered that their covert intervention in the 1964 election was generally consistent with the *jus ad bellum*. It had

clear objectives, which the administration would have likely considered akin to repelling aggression (preservation of an important democratic force in Chile and defense against the establishment of another communist stronghold in the Western hemisphere). These were set by President Kennedy based on his assessment of the commonality of U.S. and Chilean interests. While not a last resort, it was conducted in the context of an overall overt policy (the Alliance for Progress). It was likely to be successful; was limited in scope and used political methods generally proportionate to the perceived threat in that they were essentially the same as those used by the USSR. It was approved in accordance with the established procedures. In retrospect, the process would have been morally strengthened if Congress had been consulted, even though there might have been an increased risk of causing the operation to fail owing to leaks.

Some doubts can be raised regarding consistency with the *jus in bello*. The need for "scare tactics" and "black propaganda" is not obvious. (If indeed Allende's affinities to the USSR and Cuba were on the public record, promulgation of this truthful information should have been adequate.) As Bok notes, lying and deception carry a "negative weight" and require explanation and justification.[23] If not clearly necessary to respond to Cuban or Soviet activities, such deceptive actions would not meet the test of proportionality.

The 1970 "Track II" operation, in contrast, violated virtually all of the just-war guidelines. Its objective was clear (prevent Allende's confirmation), but little thought apparently was given to the consequences for the Chilean people or political system. The normal process was bypassed, and Nixon made the fateful Track II decision in a state of high emotion.[24] No expert believed that success was likely. The methods chosen were initially inadequate (the "spoiling operation") and, subsequently, when support for coup-plotting took center stage, the intermediaries could not be controlled. Although injury to innocent parties was a foreseeable outcome of the coup, no advance provision was made to prevent or minimize it. In light of the intelligence assessment that the United States lacked vital interests in Chile, it is hard to rationalize support for a potentially violent military coup as a proportionate response.

In sum, the Chile case shows that just-war theory can provide a useful framework for evaluating political action by asking penetrating questions: Is the operation directed at a just cause, properly authorized, necessary, and proportionate? Is it likely to succeed, and how will it be controlled? Is it a last resort, a convenience, or merely an action taken in frustration? In the case of the 1964 operation, the answers to most of these questions were satisfactory; in 1970, they were not.

REFORMS SINCE THE 1970S

In the more than two decades since Track II, significant improvements have been made in controlling covert action. The doctrine of "plausible deniability," which allowed senior officials to disclaim responsibility for their actions, has been replaced by one intended to secure direct presidential accountability. Since the Hughes-Ryan Amendment of 1974, a series of laws has been enacted requiring the president personally to "find" that proposed covert actions are important to the national security, and to report such operations to Congress in a timely manner. (Debate has continued over what constitutes timely notification.) In the wake of the Iran/*contra* scandal more stringent procedures were implemented by the Executive Branch and then by Congress.

Under the current system, established by the Reagan administration in 1987 and refined by legislation in 1991, a written Finding must be signed before a covert action operation commences, except that in extreme circumstances an oral Finding may be made and then immediately documented in writing. A Memorandum of Notification (MON), also approved by the president, is required for a significant change in the means of implementation, level of resources, assets, operational conditions, cooperating foreign countries, or risks associated with a covert action. Each Finding or MON includes a statement of policy objectives; a description of the actions authorized, resources required, and participating organizations; a statement that indicates whether private individuals or organizations or foreign governments will be involved; and an assessment of risk. A Finding or MON is reviewed by a senior committee of the National Security Council (NSC), and by the NSC Legal Advisor and Counsel to the President. Copies of Findings and MONs are provided to the Congress at the time of notification, except in rare cases of extreme sensitivity.[25]

AN APPROACH FOR THE 1990S

These reforms are positive, because they provide for broader consultation, a legal review, presidential accountability, and Congressional involvement in covert action decisions. However, the content of Findings and MONs, as described above, leaves much to be desired from the perspective of just-war theory. The Chile case suggests that explicit attention to the key questions raised by just-war guidelines can strengthen the ethical content of covert actions. In short, the current system addresses the legality, feasibility and political sensitivity of proposed covert actions. It does not ensure that they are right according to an ethical standard.

The United States would be well-served by establishing a policy process modeled after the just-war criteria. To do this, the current procedures should be revised so that, at each stage in the covert action approval process, difficult questions are asked about the objectives, methods, and management of a proposed operation. It is equally important that they be answered in detail, with rigor, and in writing—even (perhaps especially) when time is of the essence. Covert operators are reluctant to commit sensitive details to paper, but this is essential if the United States is to meet high standards of accountability when the easy rationalization of fighting communism is no longer available.

A decision-making process structured explicitly around just-war criteria lines is, in many ways, simply a restatement of Webster's criteria of consistency with law, American values, and public mores. In that sense, just-war criteria merely reiterate the obvious and make explicit the goals that the United States has striven towards in its reforms of the covert action process since the mid-1970s. But there is value to building a more systematic framework for substantive debate, even if many of these questions are already considered in the CIA's Covert Action Review Group, the senior NSC groups or the oversight committees. The questions of concern include:

Just Cause: Exactly what are the objectives of the operation? Is it defensive—to repel an identifiable threat—or is it intended to redress a wrong, to punish wrongdoing, or to reform a foreign country?

Just Intention: What specific changes in the behavior or policy of the target country, group, or individual does Washington seek? What will be the likely result in the target countries and in other countries? How will the United States or the international community be better off?

Proper Authority: Who has reviewed the proposal? Are there dissents? What is the view of intelligence analysts on the problem being considered? Have senior government officials discussed the proposal in detail? Has the Congress been advised of all significant aspects of the covert activity? If notification has been restricted, what is the justification?

Last Resort: What overt options are being considered? What are their strengths and weaknesses? Why must the proposed activity be secret?

Probability of Success: What is the likelihood that the action will succeed? What evidence is available? Are there differing views of the probability of success?

Proportionality: Why are these methods necessary? Are they the same as those being used by the adversary, or are they potentially more damaging or disruptive? If so, what is the justification?

Discrimination and Control: What steps will be taken to safeguard the innocent against death, injury, economic hardship, or psychological damage? What will be done to protect political institutions and processes against disproportionate damage? If some damage is inevitable, what steps are being taken to minimize it? What controls does Washington exercise over the agents to be employed? What steps will be taken if they disregard our directions? What steps will be taken to protect the agents, and what are our obligations to them? How will the operation be terminated if its objectives are achieved? How will it be terminated if it fails?

Each of these questions should be investigated in the initial approval process, and in periodic reviews by the NSC and the oversight committees.

THE CASUISTRY OF COVERT ACTION

Critics of just-war theory note that, in the hands of advocates the criteria can deteriorate into mere rationalizations of intended actions. Scholars acknowledge that moral reasoning is especially complex and difficult in cases involving politics and international affairs.[26] Just-war theory, then, can be exceedingly useful as an organizing principle, but—in itself— does not necessarily provide clear answers.[27] How can this inherent uncertainty be minimized?

William Colby has suggested giving special attention to the criteria of just cause and proportionality.[28] With respect to just cause, a recent report by a panel of distinguished scholars has recommended that covert action should be undertaken only in support of a publicly articulated policy.[29] Open, public debate would go a long way toward determining whether a proposed course of action could be construed as a just cause. The need for such debate is so fundamental that, if secrecy or political fear prevents it, this in itself would seem to be grounds for rejection of any suggested operation.

Assessments of proportionality cannot have recourse to the same open scrutiny, because they involve secret methods. Nevertheless, proposed activities must pass strict tests of consistency with American values. Loch Johnson has attempted to rank-order various types of covert operations into a "ladder of escalation" and he introduces a useful concept of "thresholds" that involve different degrees of risk and interference in foreign countries.[30] Following Johnson, proposed covert activities could be arrayed for debate under thresholds of increasing ethical concern:

> Limited Concern would arise if the means would cause minimal damage to people or the political system: Examples might be the benign provision of truthful information; support to existing political forces; or intervention to keep elections honest.
>
> Significant Concern would arise from the use of methods that could cause psychological damage or disrupt the political system: Examples might be a manipulative use of information; the rigging of elections or other distortion of political processes; or the creation of new political forces or strengthening of existing ones out of proportion to their indigenous support.
>
> Serious Concern would result from lying or other techniques that could cause personal suffering or economic hardship: Examples might be the deceptive use of information; non-lethal sabotage; or economic disruption.
>
> Grave Concern would attend any operation involving loss of life or major change in a political system: Examples might be the use of lethal force; or forcible changes in government.

The greater the level of concern, the greater the obligation on the advocate of covert action to show why the proposed method is necessary.

POLICY IMPLICATIONS

The end of the cold war means that U.S. policy on covert action can no longer be based on sweeping generalities. Covert interventions abroad should be less frequent; each proposed action must be justified on a case-by-case basis, and on its own merits. Adopting a covert action management system that makes explicit use of the guidelines and thresholds above would move the process substantially in this direction.

Under these guidelines, the types of covert actions that involve the gravest moral risks—lethal force and forcible changes of government—would be reserved for the clearest threats to U.S. security of for redressing the most serious abuses of human rights. The bias would be towards the lower levels of intervention—primarily propaganda and political action programs that carry less risk of destruction and moral damage. This would mean that the United States would have less need for a standing capability for large-scale covert infrastructure of covert action programs to provide a base for mobilization if necessary.

Though the principle is not derived, strictly speaking, from just-war guidelines, it is equally important that the United States keep faith with its foreign agents. Indeed, a morally rigorous approach would strongly discourage any covert action in which the United States raises the hopes of its supporters overseas, only to abandon them when the political will to continue the operation is lost. U.S. officials would be required to level with their agents about the risks of an operation, the probability of success, and the steps that would be taken to safeguard their interests.

The just-war guidelines set a higher ethical standard than a policy based solely on *Realpolitik*. Although, the recommended process would likely result in far fewer covert actions, there is no reason to believe that the United States would be prevented from responding to serious threats. Kissinger's high-handed disproportionate manipulation of the Chilean political system would have been prohibited. But other types of covert action, carefully crafted and keyed to the interests they are intended to support, would still be possible. Moreover, they would likely receive greater political support, and thus have a greater likelihood of success, than some of the poorly thought out, unfocused programs that have occurred in the past. In sum, there is no necessary contradiction between a systematic, thoughtful process for managing covert action and a realistic appraisal of national interest.

CONCLUSION

Such an application of the just-war framework would not end controversy regarding covert action, nor prevent inappropriate or unethical actions. The claim for a conscious application of just-war guidelines is modest: it will help to make more rigorous Webster's common-sense criteria, and to improve the quality of decisions regarding one of the most controversial aspects of U.S. national security policy. Reforming the process along the lines suggested would signal that the United States is concerned—even in secret activities—with issues of right and wrong and not merely with power. It would promote openness and accountability, and underscore that we firmly reject the "repugnant philosophy" of the Doolittle Report.

QUESTIONS FOR FURTHER DISCUSSION

1. How does Barry relate "just-war theory" to the subject of CIA covert actions?
2. To what extent does Barry find covert actions morally acceptable for the United States?
3. What methods of covert action did the United States use against the Allende regime in Chile, and how effective were they?
4. What would be the consequences of prohibiting all forms of U.S. covert action? How about just certain kinds of covert action? Which would you prohibit and which would you keep? What criteria would you use to make these judgments?

ENDNOTES

1. "Report of the Special Study Group [Doolittle Committee] on the Covert Activities of the Central Intelligence Agency. September 30, 1954 [excerpts]" in William M. Leary, ed., *The Central Intelligence Agency, History and Documents* (University, Alabama: The University of Alabama Press, 1984), p. 144.
2. See James Turner Johnson and George Weigel, *Just War and the Gulf War* (Washington, D.C.: Ethics and Public Policy Center, 1991).
3. *Symposium on Moral and Legal Constraints on Low-Intensity Conflict*, Sponsored by the Office of the Assistant Secretary of Defense for Special Operations and Low Intensity Conflict, US. Naval War College, Newport, Rhode Island, April 9–10, 1992.
4. National Conference of Catholic Bishops, *The Challenge of Peace* (Washington, D.C.: U.S. Catholic Conference, 1983), pp. 25–29. (Hereafter, National Conference of Catholic Bishops, *The Challenge of Peace.*)
5. Thomas Aquinas, *Summa Theologica*, trans. Joseph Rickaby, S. J. (London: Burns and Gates, 1892), Question XL, Article I. (Hereafter, Aquinas, *Summa Theologica.*)

6. National Conference of Catholic Bishops, *The Challenge of Peace,* pp. 29–32.

7. Aquinas, *Summa Theologica,* Q. XLI, Art. I.

8. Paul Ramsey, *War and the Christian Conscience* (Durham, N.C.: Duke University Press, 1969), pp. 47–48.

9. The classic modern work on just-war theory is Michael Walzer, *Just and Unjust Wars* (New York: Basic Books, 1977).

10. Charles R. Beitz, "Recent International Thought," *International Journal,* Spring 1988, p. 190.

11. William E. Colby, "Public Policy, Secret Action," *Ethics and International Affairs,* 1989, p. 63. (Hereafter, Colby, "Public Policy, Secret Action.")

12. William Webster, address to the Eighth Circuit Judicial Conference, July 12, 1991. Mimeographed transcript of remarks made available by the Public Affairs Office of the Central Intelligence Agency.

13. See Donald Secrest, Gregory G. Brunk, and Howanl Tamashiro, "Moral Justification for Resort to War With Nicaragua: The Attitudes of Three American Elite Groups," *Western Political Quarterly,* September 1991, pp. 541–59.

14. Sissela Bok, *Secrets: On the Ethics of Concealment and Revelation* (New York: Pantheon Books, 1982), p. 191.

15. Charles R. Beitz, "Covert Intervention as a Moral Problem," *Ethics and International Affairs,* 1989, pp. 49–50.

16. John P. Langan, letter to the author dated May 28, 1992.

17. The following discussion is drawn primarily from documents of the Church Committee, which investigated CIA covert actions in the mid-1970s, as well as from memoirs of some of the participants and other government officials and commentators. (These include William Colby, Henry Kissinger, Cord Meyer, David Atlee Phillips, and Arthur Schlesinger.) A summary of the Church Committee's findings, and recommendations for reform, can be found in Gregory Treverton, *Covert Action: The Limits of Intervention in the Postwar World* (New York: Basic Books, 1987). A case study based on Treverton's research has been published by the Carnegie Council on Ethics and International Affairs: *Covert Intervention in Chile, 1970–73,* Carnegie Council on Ethics and International Affairs, 1990.

18. United State Senate, *Staff Report of the Select Committee to Study Government Operations with Respect to Intelligence Activities: Covert Action in Chile, 1963–73* (Washington D.C.: U.S. Government Printing Office, 1975), pp. 15–17.

19. *New York Times,* March 12, 1976.

20. Assessment dated September 7, 1970, declassified and quoted in the Church Committee report.

21. The U.S. decision process is described in detail in the Church Committee Report, *Alleged Assassination Attempts Involving Foreign Leaders,* as well as in Kissinger's memoirs and John Ranelagh, *The Agency: The Rise and Decline of the CIA* (New York: Simon and Schuster, 1986), pp. 514–20.

22. David Atlee Phillips, *The Night Watch* (New York: Ballantine Books, 1977), pp. 283–87.

23. Sissela Bok, *Lying: Moral Choice in Public and Private Life* (New York: Random House, 1978), p. 30.

24. See Alberto R. Coll, "Normative Prudence as a Tradition of Statecraft," *Ethics and International Affairs,* 1991, pp. 36–37.

25. *National Security Decision Directive (NSDD) 286,* partially declassified on December 15, 1987, *Intelligence Authorization Act, Fiscal Year 1991,* Title VI.

26. Joseph Boyle, "Natural Law and International Ethics," in Terry Nardin and David Mapel, eds., *Traditions of International Ethics* (Cambridge: Cambridge University Press, 1992), p. 115.

27. The author is indebted to Joel Rosenthal of the Carnegie Council on Ethics and International Affairs for this point. (Letter to the author dated May 12, 1992.)

28. Colby, "Public Policy, Secret Action," p. 63.

29. *Report of the Twentieth Century Fund Task Force on Covert Action and American Democracy* (New York: Twentieth Century Press, 1992), p. 8.

30. Loch K. Johnson, "On Drawing a Bright Line for Covert Operations," *American Journal of International Law,* April 1992, p. 286.

21. COVERT ACTION, PENTAGON STYLE

JENNIFER D. KIBBE

Since 1947, presidents have turned to the CIA for the conduct of covert actions. Moreover, the system of accountability set up to supervise this aggressive use of intelligence agencies has focused on that agency. This essay reminds readers that the role of the military has quietly grown in this domain, despite an ambiguous (if non-existent) statutory authority and loose oversight.

1. INTRODUCTION

Until September 11, 2001, covert action had long been the province of the Central Intelligence Agency (CIA). The attacks on the World Trade Center and the Pentagon, however, not only gave Washington a new enemy, but changed its conception of how best to fight that enemy, leading to a newfound emphasis on Special Operations Forces (SOF). Resources dedicated to SOF have increased significantly since 9/11, and even though they still account for only a small portion of the total military budget, SOF have become an increasingly important weapon in the U.S. national security arsenal. This, in turn, has raised significant questions about whether some of what SOF are doing is covert action and if so, whether there is appropriate congressional oversight of those operations.

The research field of military covert action is, in some ways, an extremely small one, in the sense that very few scholars have focused specifically on this issue. This is, perhaps, not surprising given the difficulty in researching a topic that is, in general, highly classified. There are, however, three different literatures that discuss at least some aspect of the issue. The overall topic of covert action is covered in the intelligence literature, although it focuses almost exclusively on the CIA's role in conducting it. The military literature discusses the nature and expansion of SOF although, as will be explained later, the Pentagon essentially defines the issue of military covert action away, claiming that only the CIA conducts covert action. As a result, the SOF literature must be read with a careful eye to precise

definitions and interpretations. The third relevant body of literature is the scholarship that has focused on both the U.S. and the international legal ramifications of conducting covert action. This chapter is an attempt to draw these disparate strands together while mapping the way forward for future research. After explaining those parts of U.S. law that pertain to military covert action, the chapter lays out exactly what SOF are and the various sources of confusion in analyzing them. Next, this chapter details the myriad ways in which SOF's size and authority have expanded since 9/11 and considers the different types of risks that are posed by that expansion. The chapter concludes with a discussion of the future directions that research in the field should take.

2. COVERT ACTION UNDER U.S. LAW

Covert action is defined in U.S. law as activity that is meant "to influence political, economic, or military conditions abroad, where it is intended that the role of the United States Government will not be apparent or acknowledged publicly" (Intelligence Authorization Act 1991; hereafter IAA). It is, therefore, an active instrument of foreign policy, as opposed to intelligence per se, which entails collecting and analyzing information for policymakers to use in conducting foreign policy. Although it is often used interchangeably with the term "clandestine," the two are legally distinct: "clandestine" refers to the tactical secrecy of the operation itself, while "covert" refers to the secrecy of its sponsor (Kibbe 2004, 104). Thus, a clandestine mission that is part of a declared war might be conducted in secret in order to increase its chances of success, but once it has taken place, the country sponsoring the mission would acknowledge having done so. On the other hand, a state might undertake an activity such as issuing propaganda, where the activity itself is quite public but the country's sponsorship of it remains hidden, thus rendering it a covert action.

Although covert action is most often associated with such high-profile and controversial actions as the disastrous Bay of Pigs operation or the U.S. overthrows of the regimes in Iran (1953) and Guatemala (1954), it comprises a wide range of activity, from propaganda and disinformation to political influence operations, economic destabilization, and paramilitary operations (L.K. Johnson 1989; Treverton 1987, 13–28).

According to the 1991 Intelligence Authorization Act, an outgrowth of the Iran-Contra scandal which is still the governing legislation on covert action, any department or agency of the United States Government that intends to undertake a covert mission must ensure that two requirements are met: 1) that the action be conducted pursuant to a written presidential finding that it is important for U.S. national security; and 2) that the congressional intelligence committees are notified of the action as soon as possible after the finding has been issued and before the operation begins, unless "extraordinary circumstances" exist, in which case the President must fully inform the committees "in a timely fashion" (IAA 1991; Kibbe 2007, 62).

The 1991 law also specified, however, a few exceptions to the basic definition of covert action. The law exempts both intelligence and traditional counterintelligence activities, but the most relevant exception for the current discussion is that concerning "traditional military activities or routine support to such activities" (IAA 1991). The interpretation of this phrase, which is not defined in the law itself, plays a central role in the debate over which actions taken by the military constitute covert action and thus require a presidential finding and congressional notification. Some discussion of the legislative intent underlying the term is presented in Kibbe (2004) and Meyer (2007),[1] but for the fullest understanding, one should also consult the Conference Committee's report (U.S. House of Representatives 1991; hereafter H.R.) and the Senate Intelligence Committee's report (U.S. Senate 1991).

In explaining their intent, the conferees distinguished between two time frames and set different standards for what constitutes traditional military activities in each period. During the period during or right before acknowledged hostilities (as in Iraq or Afghanistan, for example), anything the military does, as long as it is under the control of a military commander, is to be considered traditional military activity, even if U.S. sponsorship of it is not acknowledged (H.R.1991).

As for unacknowledged activities undertaken "well in advance of a possible or eventual U.S. military operation," the determination of whether or not they are traditional military activities depends "in most cases" upon whether they constitute "routine support" to such an operation (H.R. 1991). The conferees (referencing the Senate Intelligence Committee's report) considered "routine support" to be unilateral U.S. activities to provide or arrange for logistical or other support for U.S. military forces in the event of a military operation that is intended to be publicly acknowledged (even if that operation ends up not taking place). Examples cited by the Senate committee included caching communications equipment or weapons in an area where such a future military operation is to take place; acquiring property to support an aspect of such an operation; and obtaining currency or documentation for use in such an operation (U.S. Senate 1991). "Other-than-routine" activities that would constitute covert action if conducted on an unacknowledged basis include: recruiting or training foreign nationals to support a future U.S. military operation; efforts to influence foreign nationals to take certain actions during a future U.S. military operation; and efforts to influence and affect public opinion in the country concerned (U.S. Senate 1991).

This two-stage framework for defining the "traditional military activities" exception to covert action regulations raises several questions. First, it leaves unresolved the distinction between routine and non-routine support during the period "well in advance" of any acknowledged U.S. military presence. What if SOF conducts an unacknowledged operation that is unilateral but is not one of the three specific actions listed as examples of routine support? One can imagine a possible debate about whether the operation could be accurately interpreted as providing routine support.

A larger issue is the meaning of the word "anticipated" in terms of delineating the first time frame with the much lower bar for what constitutes traditional military activities. The conferees defined "anticipated" hostilities as those for which operational planning has already been approved. However, as Kibbe notes, at least some in the Pentagon have interpreted that as granting them the power to undertake activities "years in advance" of any overt U.S. military involvement (2004). This interpretation would seem to conflict with Congress's two-stage framework; "years in advance" clearly fits more accurately within its second time period, where the traditional military activities determination rests on whether or not it can be considered routine support.

Beyond the interpretation of the word "anticipated," the Bush administration advanced several other arguments to bolster its position that the increased activity by special operations forces since 9/11 falls under the rubric of traditional military activities. One popular formulation is that the current "war on terrorism" is just that—a war—and therefore any military action taken to prosecute it, unacknowledged or not, is not a covert action. To support this argument, many in the administration pointed to Senate Joint Resolution 23, which authorized the use of force in response to the attacks of September 11, 2001. That resolution authorizes the president: "to use all necessary and appropriate force against those nations, organizations, or persons he determines planned, authorized, committed, or aided the terrorist attacks that occurred on September 11, 2001, or harbored such organizations or persons, in order to prevent any future acts of international terrorism against the United States by such nations, organizations or persons" (U.S. Senate 2001). There is debate about just how broadly the resolution should be interpreted, but at least some legal experts contend that it grants the president virtually unlimited legal authority as long as he "determines" that a particular target has some connection to Al Qaeda (Kibbe 2004, 108).

Others in the Bush administration interpreted the situation even more broadly, contending that, as a result of the 9/11 attacks, any act undertaken as part of the "war on terror" is part of the self-defense of the United States and, thus, a traditional military activity that does not require a presidential finding or congressional notification. Some administration critics, however, took issue with the Bush administration's expansive interpretation of traditional military activities (Kibbe 2004, 108).

Whatever the reasoning used, the bottom line is that during the Bush administration, the Pentagon established the position that only the CIA conducts covert action, legally speaking. The military, by contrast, conducts what it calls "operational preparation of the battlefield"; in essence, traditional military activity. Hersh quotes a knowledgeable unnamed source as noting that "[t]he President signed an Executive Order after September 11 giving the Pentagon license to do things that it had never been able to do before without notifying Congress. The claim was that the military was 'preparing the battle space,' and by using that term they were able to circumvent congressional oversight. Everything is justified in terms of fighting the global war on terror" (Hersh 2008).

The Senate Intelligence Committee tried to clarify the parameters of military covert action by including language in the 2004 Intelligence Authorization Act explicitly declaring that all unacknowledged SOF activity in foreign countries where regular U.S. military forces are not already present is covert action. The new language, however, was strongly opposed by the Pentagon and both Armed Services Committees, on the grounds that it misconstrued or even ignored the traditional military activities exception and, in the end, no new restriction on special operations was enacted (Kibbe 2004, 107).

Since that time, the degree to which Congress has attempted to challenge the Pentagon on this issue is not publicly known (it is possible legislators have done so in classified settings). There have been some indications, however, that at least some members are uncomfortable with the Pentagon's increasing latitude in unacknowledged operations. In the spring of 2005, for example, Rep. David Obey (D-Wisc.), then the ranking minority member on the House Appropriations Committee, intended to offer an amendment cutting off all funding for national intelligence programs unless the president agreed to keep Congress fully informed about covert activities conducted by the military. He then announced that he had changed his mind because the White House had promised fuller cooperation. Obey later told Seymour Hersh that "the White House reneged on its promise to consult more fully with Congress" (Hersh 2008). At the time of this writing, it is still too soon to know where the Obama administration stands on the issues of military covert action and notification of Congress.

The irony in the debate about military covert action and whether it is skirting congressional oversight is that numerous scholars contend that that oversight is not particularly stringent in the first place (Ott 2003; McDonough, Rudman and Rundlet 2006; Walker 2006; Kibbe 2008; Snider 2008). Congressional oversight of intelligence is hampered by its split jurisdiction among the Intelligence, Armed Services and Appropriations Committees, partisanship on Capitol Hill, and Congress's inherently subservient position (to the executive) in terms of access to information.

In just one example of how the oversight of CIA covert action may not be the ideal standard to hold up as a model, the law provides that in "extraordinary circumstances," the president can meet his obligation to notify Congress of a covert action finding by notifying just the leadership of the House and Senate and the leadership of the two Intelligence Committees (the so-called Gang of Eight), instead of briefing the two committees in their entirety. These Gang of Eight briefings are governed by strict rules, including that no staff be present and that the attendees not take notes or disclose the information to anyone, including other members of the committees or legal counsel. They cannot even discuss the issue with other members of the Gang of Eight. In effect then, although those in the leadership may have the information, they have been effectively silenced. According to an aide to a member of the Gang of Eight, notification of a finding "is just that—notification, and not a sign-off on activities. Proper oversight is done by fully briefing the members of the intelligence committee" (Hersh 2008).

Nonetheless, intelligence scholars generally agree that, while still in need of improvement, Congress's oversight role is a critical one. Few suggest that any covert action is being conducted without at least some oversight from within the executive branch, but when policy officials have to face the added step of explaining such operations to members of Congress, the chances are that much greater that the appropriate questions about the potential risks involved will get asked.

3. SPECIAL ACCESS PROGRAMS

Besides the definition of covert action, which is covered under the law regulating intelligence, the other U.S. legal element that plays a role in the question of military covert action stems from the legislation governing the military. Established by Executive Order 12958 (Clinton 1995), special access programs (SAPs) are sensitive programs that impose "need-to-know and access controls beyond those normally provided for access to confidential, secret,

or top secret information" (U.S. Department of Defense 2008; hereafter DOD). According to the order, programs are only to be given this beyond-top-secret designation when an agency head determines that the vulnerability of or threat to specific information is great enough that normal classification procedures are inadequate (Clinton 1995). By law, the congressional defense committees (i.e., the House and Senate Appropriations and Armed Services Committees and Appropriations Defense Subcommittees) are to receive thirty days' notice of an SAP before it begins (Special access programs 2006). However, the Bush administration asserted that the president's right to classify information is a constitutional one that may not be limited by the Congress and, thus, reserved the right "especially in wartime" to immediately establish SAPs without notifying Congress (Kibbe 2007, 65–66).

The law specifying the reporting requirements for SAPs also states that the Secretary of Defense must submit an annual report to the defense committees listing a "brief description" of each program, including its "major milestones," its actual cost for each year it has been active and its estimated costs in the future (Special access programs 2006). One caveat, however, is that the SAP reporting process has been criticized for falling far short of effective oversight. According to military analyst William Arkin:

> A list of names gets sent forward with a one- or two-line description of what the program is, and there are literally a half dozen people within the entire U.S. Congress who have a high enough clearance to read that report. So, when you're talking about hundreds of programs, and then you're talking about layers of different types of special access programs, I think we can all agree they don't get very effective oversight.
>
> *Arkin 2005*

Further limiting the chances of effective congressional oversight, there are three categories of special access programs, one of which is a "waived SAP" meaning that the defense secretary can waive the reporting requirement for a program if he determines that inclusion of its information in the report to Congress "would adversely affect the national security" (DOD 2006b). In such cases, the secretary must provide the information to the chairman and ranking minority member of each of the defense committees (Special access programs 2006). The problem with this procedure, however, is the same as that of the provision whereby the administration can notify just the Gang of Eight in the case of covert actions deemed to be too sensitive to brief to the whole committees. Hersh provides a case study on how SAPs, protected from too many questions, can lead to a veritable Pandora's box in his account of how the program authorizing SOF units to coercively interrogate high-value detainees in Afghanistan morphed into the Abu Ghraib scandal in Iraq (Hersh 2004).

4. SPECIAL OPERATIONS FORCES

The debate about military covert action centers on Special Operations Forces (SOF). The importance of the definition of covert action, the traditional military activities exception, and SAPs becomes clear when viewed in conjunction with the considerable increase in SOF's size, budget, and responsibilities

since 9/11. First, though, it's important to clarify what SOF are. Special operations forces are elite forces that are considered "special" in two distinct ways: first, by using unique skills that regular forces do not have, and second, by performing more conventional missions at a high level of proficiency and in situations involving very high stakes or political sensitivity (Fitzsimmons 2003, 206–7). One of the difficulties inherent in discussions of military covert action is that descriptions of SOF's missions and structure include two cross-cutting dichotomies that can create confusion. First, SOF operations are often categorized in terms of whether they are direct (SOF working "directly against enemy targets themselves") or indirect (trying to achieve objectives by working with indigenous forces and populations) (Tucker and Lamb 2007, 153). Broadly speaking, SOF missions are categorized as shown in Table 21.1.

TABLE 21.1   DIRECT AND INDIRECT SPECIAL OPERATIONS FORCES (SOF) MISSIONS

Direct SOF Missions	
Counterterrorism	offensive measures taken to prevent, deter, preempt, and respond to terrorism (DOD 2008)
Counterproliferation	actions taken to defeat the threat and/or use of weapons of mass destruction against the United States (DOD 2008)
Direct Action	short duration strikes and other small-scale offensive actions which employ specialized military capabilities to seize, destroy, capture, exploit, recover, or damage designated targets (DOD 2008)
Special Reconnaissance	reconnaissance and surveillance actions conducted as special operations to collect or verify information of strategic or operational significance, employing military capabilities not normally found in conventional forces (DOD 2008)
Information Operations	actions taken to influence, disrupt, corrupt or usurp adversarial information, information systems, and decision making while protecting those of the United States (DOD 2008)
Indirect SOF Missions	
Unconventional Warfare	"a broad spectrum of military and paramilitary operations, normally of long duration, predominantly conducted through, with, or by indigenous or surrogate forces." Includes, but is not limited to, guerrilla warfare, subversion, sabotage and intelligence activities (DOD 2008)
Psychological Operations	planned operations to convey selected information and indicators to foreign audiences to influence their emotions, motives, objective reasoning, and ultimately the behavior of foreign governments, organizations, groups, and individuals (DOD 2008)
Foreign Internal Defense	"actions of a foreign government to curb subversion, lawlessness, and insurgency. SOF's primary contribution is to organize, train, advise, and assist host-nation military and paramilitary forces" (Tucker and Lamb 2007, xix)
Civil Affairs	activities involved in either establishing and conducting military government or civil administration until civilian authority or government can be restored; minimizing civilian interference with military operations; limiting the adverse impact of military operations on civilian populations and resources (Tucker and Lamb, xix)

While this distinction is useful as an overall guideline, it is important to understand that the line between the two categories is not impermeable. Note, for example, that the Pentagon's definition of unconventional warfare includes the language "predominantly conducted by, with, or through indigenous or surrogate forces," leaving open the possibility that U.S. personnel might, in some cases, conduct guerrilla warfare themselves (Tucker and Lamb 2007, 154).

A second, more informal distinction that is commonly made, however, is that between overt, unclassified, or "white" operations and/or forces, and classified or "black" operations and/or forces. Confusion results from the use by some of the term "black" to refer to both covert *and* clandestine missions, thus blurring the line drawn by the legal definition of covert action. Further muddying the issue is the fact that, while many associate black operations with direct missions such as covert raids designed to kill terrorists and white operations with such indirect missions as training foreign counterterrorist forces, in reality, the dividing lines between direct/indirect and black/white do not completely correspond. Thus, while many counterterrorist operations are conducted covertly, they could be conducted overtly, on an acknowledged basis as well. Similarly, indirect missions such as training foreign internal defense forces, for example, are usually conducted in uniform, but some training of foreign covert forces might well be done out of uniform on an unacknowledged basis. Compounding the issue further still, some of the SOF missions that can be conducted overtly can also be conducted by some elements of the conventional forces (Fitzsimmons 2003, 209–10).

A third source of confusion in terms of the definitions of SOF's roles and missions arises from the fact that particular units within SOF are associated with certain types of missions and are thus typically thought of as being either overt or covert. The units traditionally involved in white special operations include Army Special Forces (SF, or Green Berets), most Ranger units, most of the Navy SEALs, two Marine Special Operations Battalions, and numerous aviation, civil affairs, and psychological operations units.

The black operators, referred to as special mission units, fall under the Joint Special Operations Command (JSOC), and comprise the elite units of each service's special operations forces: 1st Special Forces Operational Detachment-Delta (Delta Force),

Naval Special Warfare Development Group (DEVGRU, or SEAL Team 6), the Air Force's 24th Special Tactics Squadron, the Army's 160th Special Operations Aviation Regiment and 75th Ranger Regiment, and the highly classified Intelligence Support Activity (ISA, known more recently as Gray Fox).

The problem is that although the JSOC units (which are not formally acknowledged by the Pentagon) are thought of as specializing in direct action, even that distinction is not iron-clad. Thus, for example, Gray Fox conducts both direct strike missions (covert) and intelligence missions, which could be either covert or merely clandestine (Smith 2007). Conversely, although regular Special Forces are known for their indirect foreign internal defense missions, they do train for (overt) direct action missions as well.

One final source of confusion is that JSOC's special mission units can operate independently, in coordination with the CIA (but under JSOC's direction) or on a CIA-directed operation. The distinction is important in terms of the law governing covert action (and the corresponding congressional reporting requirements), but the authority under which operations that become public knowledge have been conducted is often unclear in public accounts, making it hard to determine the exact contours of the problem without having classified access. What is clear is that in those situations where JSOC operates independently but in coordination with CIA (for example, CIA agents and local assets making contacts for the JSOC operatives), Congress only receives a partial picture of how the money it authorized for the CIA operation is being used (Hersh 2008).

It is easy to see, then, how confused discussions of SOF and the question of military covert action can get, particularly because many journalists, analysts, and possibly even some legislators are unaware of the overlapping categories and definitions and often use the terms inaccurately. When the question involves covert action, where the answer stems from a precise legal definition surrounded by gray area, using the same terms to mean different things at best only further adds to the problem and, at worst, creates opportunity for obfuscation.

5. THE EXPANSION OF SPECIAL OPERATIONS FORCES

Whatever terms are used to describe SOF, their expansion in size and responsibilities since 9/11 is undeniable (Scarborough 2004, 1–28; M. Johnson 2006; Smith 2007, 235–73). This growth is the result of a combination of factors, including the increased prominence of unconventional threats, their successful record in Afghanistan, and former Defense Secretary Donald Rumsfeld's commitment to transforming the military into a leaner, more agile organization capable of combating post–Cold War irregular threats (M. Johnson 2006, 273; Kibbe 2007, 60). The amount allocated to SOF has more than doubled since 2001, to a total budget of more than $7 billion (Lardner 2008). In addition, the 2006 Quadrennial Defense Review (QDR), the Pentagon's main planning document for the next four years, aimed to increase SOF personnel, which numbered 50,000 at the beginning of 2006, by 14,000 through 2011, at a cost of nearly $28 billion (DOD 2006c; Kibbe 2007, 60).

Beyond these tangible increases, however, Rumsfeld also made several institutional changes that had important ramifications for SOF's scope and authority. In addition to replacing those military leaders he deemed too tentative in enacting the changes he envisioned, Rumsfeld increased Special Operations Command (SOCOM)'s authority in January 2003 by making it a supported, as well as a supporting, command, meaning it could now plan and execute its own missions (if authorized by the secretary and, if necessary, the president), rather than serving solely in a support role for the regional commands. Several authors describe SOCOM's new status as freeing SOF from restrictions imposed by the regional commanders, enabling them to react immediately and conduct the terrorist "manhunts" Rumsfeld wanted (Hersh 2004; Scarborough 2004, 27; Smith 2007, 248).

Another significant change came in 2004 when President Bush issued a new Unified Command Plan, designating SOCOM as the lead military command in the war on terrorism. Other less dramatic but still significant moves in Rumsfeld's quest to elevate SOF in the military hierarchy included increasing JSOC's headquarters from a two-star to a three-star command, giving its commander more authority in his dealings with other military officers (Kibbe 2007, 61) and placing the deputy commander of SOCOM on the twelve-person Deputies Advisory Working Group, which was made a permanent part of the Defense Department's senior management structure in March 2006. As Stevenson notes, "no other combatant commander was so privileged" (Stevenson 2006, 39–40).

In addition to these structural changes, Rumsfeld continually fought for increased freedom for SOF, or more accurately JSOC, to pursue suspected terrorists. Although information regarding such highly classified plans is hard to come by for obvious reasons, there have been some notable reports of his success in this regard. According to Hersh, sometime after 9/11, Rumsfeld created a Special Access Program granting JSOC units blanket advance approval to kill or capture and, if possible, interrogate high value targets (the program that led, eventually, to Abu Ghraib; Hersh 2004).

In the spring of 2004, after a two-year turf war with the CIA and the State Department, Rumsfeld signed, with Bush's approval, a classified order granting SOF broad new authority to attack the Al Qaeda network anywhere in the world, as well as "a more sweeping mandate to conduct operations in countries not at war with the United States" (Schmitt and Mazzetti 2008; see also Hersh 2005). According to the *New York Times*, the order specified fifteen to twenty countries where Al Qaeda operatives were thought to be either operating or have sought sanctuary, including Syria, Pakistan, Yemen, Saudi Arabia and several other Persian Gulf States (although it expressly excluded Iran; Schmitt and Mazzetti 2008). Nearly a dozen SOF raids have reportedly been carried out since then in "Syria, Pakistan and elsewhere," some "in close coordination with" the CIA and some in support of CIA-directed operations. The order apparently requires varying levels of approval for different states, with Somalia, for example, needing only the approval of the defense secretary, but select other countries, including Pakistan and Syria, requiring presidential approval (Schmitt and Mazzetti 2008). Special operations forces' reach was reportedly expanded yet again in late 2006 as they were authorized to conduct cross-border operations from southern Iraq into Iran (the CIA would soon join them under the auspices of a presidential finding; Hersh 2008).

Another important step in the expansion of SOF's operational scope came in early 2006 with the signing of the National Military Strategic Plan for the War on Terrorism, which ordered the Defense Department "to undertake a broad campaign to find and attack or neutralize terrorist leaders, their havens, financial networks, methods of communication and ability to move around the globe" (Shanker 2006, 16). The new counterterrorist strategy was soon followed by a set of three operational plans implementing it. One of the plans set out "precisely how U.S. special operations troops would find, fix, and finish" terrorist leaders. The plan significantly expanded the role of special operations forces, placing them in embassies in a wide number of Middle Eastern capitals to gather intelligence and, where necessary, carry out covert action..." (Smith 2007, 266).

The question of SOF operating independently out of embassies triggered more of the bureaucratic infighting that had accompanied Rumsfeld's campaign to have SOF, and thus the Pentagon, lead the "war against terrorism" (Kibbe 2007, 70). A two-year review of the issue finally led to a presidential directive staking out at least rough agreement on each agency's "lanes in the road," and designating the National Counterterrorism Center (NCTC) as the authority responsible for ensuring that all parties lived up to it. Although the extent of the Pentagon's control over the "war on terrorism" is a continual issue, particularly for the CIA, the problem reportedly lessened in the post-Rumsfeld regime, mainly because of the long-established relationships among his successor, Robert Gates, Director of National Intelligence Mike McConnell, and CIA Director Michael Hayden (Starks 2007).

By late 2008, no in-depth analysis had yet been done regarding the extent to which Gates and other new key military leaders subscribe to Rumsfeld's vision of muscular SOF conducting unfettered counterterrorism raids around the world. Anecdotally, there have been conflicting indications. On the one hand, the new SOCOM commander, Adm. Eric Olson, made clear in May 2008 that he would not be exercising SOCOM's authority to conduct its own missions separate from the regional commands, saying he intended to focus instead on coordinating the military's counterterrorism operations around the world (Shanker 2008, 10). On the other hand, however, the Pentagon seems to have continued using JSOC just as aggressively in the nearly two years since Rumsfeld's departure. In early 2007, it was reported that a highly classified JSOC unit had conducted raids into Somalia from Ethiopia in an attempt to target Al Qaeda operatives fleeing the Ethiopian army's invasion (Gordon and Mazzetti 2007), and in July 2008, Bush authorized SOF to conduct raids into the highly sensitive Pakistani tribal areas (Schmitt and Mazzetti 2008).

Certainly there is no sign of any reversal of SOF's popularity in the future. As one SOF officer noted, "Everyone is infatuated with SOF... To do anything against SOF would be absolute sacrilege on both sides of the aisle" (Naylor 2006). Indeed, during the 2008 presidential campaign, both candidates promised to expand special operations forces. The question is, which parts of SOF will get the attention, the white or black units? There has been increasing discussion in the literature that Al Qaeda is more of a global insurgency than just a terrorist network and that, therefore, the fight against it is better conceived of as a global counterinsurgency than as a "war against terrorism" (Kilcullen 2005; Gompert and Gordon 2008; Roper 2008). Consequently, there has been an increased call for the Pentagon to shift its emphasis away from JSOC's "hunter-killer" teams and to focus more on the counterinsurgency tactics aimed at winning "hearts and minds" that are the trademark of the unclassified SOF units like the Green Berets (Kilcullen 2005; Naylor 2006; Tucker and Lamb 2007).

Some of this newfound enthusiasm for counterinsurgency has begun to show up in the military's doctrine and pronouncements, helped in no small part by the tactic's at least partial success in Iraq. One cannot assume, however, that that necessarily means the United States intends to deemphasize military covert action. First, as explained above, there is the fact that some indirect action can also be covert. Second, many of those who stress that the United States should be fighting a counterinsurgency campaign include covert direct action as one of its necessary components. As one of their five pillars of counterinsurgency, Morgenstein and Vickland, for example, call for the "*discriminate* use of force [emphasis in original] such as Special Operations Forces (SOF) hunting jihadists in Afghanistan and North Africa. Our SOF capabilities must be expanded to more effectively hunt down those we cannot convince to end their destructive crusade" (Morgenstein and Vickland 2008, 4).

A relevant case in point of the murkiness of what lies ahead, despite all the lip service being paid to indirect counterinsurgency measures, is the military's new Africa Command (AFRICOM), launched in October 2007. Africa Command was designed as a hybrid military command in the sense that it is to conduct a combination of stability operations, development, and humanitarian assistance, coordinating with the State Department and the U.S. Agency for International Development (USAID) on the latter two tasks. Many scholars, not to mention African states, have been skeptical of the Pentagon's stated intentions, however, pointing out that its previous operations in North and East Africa, although similarly couched in the terminology of counterinsurgency and development, have in practice included a healthy component of JSOC strikes aimed at eliminating individual terrorists (Berschinski 2007; Stevenson 2007).

6. RISKS

The unprecedented expansion in SOF's size, authority, and geographic range since 9/11 has brought with it a variety of risks. The first set of such risks are the international legal implications of unacknowledged operations conducted by the military. Under international law, using formal military personnel to conduct a covert military operation (in a country with which the United States is not at war) constitutes an act of war (Stone 2003, 11). While the same is true of covert action taken by the CIA, "most of the world has come to look at CIA *de facto* wars as a way of life because most powers benefit from their own CIA-equivalents operating in foreign countries" (Stone 2003, 12). The prospect of the U.S. military operating wherever it wants on a covert basis, however, is not likely to be a welcome development. "The world will rightly ask: Where does it stop? If the U.S. employs SOF to conduct deniable covert action, then is the next step a clandestine tomahawk missile strike, or maybe even a missile strike whose origin is manipulated to conceal U.S. fingerprints?" (Stone 2003, 12).

Moreover, there are additional legal ramifications of military covert operations for the individual personnel involved. The law of war is predicated upon the maintenance of a clear distinction between combatants and civilians, through the use of a uniform or distinctive insignia (Parks 2003, 508). Special operations forces conducting unacknowledged military missions constitute a clear violation of that principle. Under the Geneva Conventions, military personnel wearing civilian clothing and acting as spies and saboteurs are guilty of perfidy, an international law violation, and would be denied prisoner of war status and protection if captured (Parks 2003, 511–513; McAndrew 2006, 159).[2] Moreover, military personnel caught conducting covert operations could also be classified as unlawful combatants and lose their combatant immunity from prosecution for committing acts that would otherwise be criminal under domestic or international law (Stone 2003, 12; Yoo and Ho 2003, 221). In addition, U.S. policy, in the form of the Defense Department's Law of War Program, explicitly requires that "[m]embers of the DoD [Department of Defense] Components comply with the law of war during all armed conflicts, however such conflicts are characterized, and in all other military operations" (DOD 2006a).

It is important to note that this issue is not relevant in the event SOF are captured by members of Al Qaeda. As many have pointed out, Al Qaeda is not a party to and does not abide by the Geneva Conventions in any case (technically, captured SOF would be crime victims, or hostages; Dunlap 2002, 29; Yoo and Ho 2003, 116–19).[3] Rather, these risks come into play in those situations where U.S. military personnel are captured (by other government forces) while conducting covert operations in countries with which the United States is not formally at war, even when the target of those operations is some terrorist entity and not the country itself. Washington might well be able to sweep an incident under the official rug in the case of allies, as it has seemingly done in the case of the Italian attempt to prosecute CIA agents for the extraordinary rendition of an Egyptian terror suspect. One can imagine a very different outcome, however, if the country involved were Iran or North Korea.

Several sources point out that this highlights one of the fundamental differences between covert operations conducted by the CIA and those conducted by SOF. In the case of the former, operatives fully understand from the outset that they will be working covertly and that, should they be captured, they cannot expect any formal protection from either the United States government or international law. Military personnel, however, begin their service under a very different understanding: that if they follow all lawful orders, if they are captured, they will receive the protection of both the government and the Geneva Conventions. Moreover, military commanders cannot require SOF personnel to actively hide their military identity, and thus their status as lawful combatants, to their own detriment, which means the military may have problems conducting such missions effectively (Stone 2003, 13). While it is possible for members of SOF to voluntarily agree to forego those protections, this creates several additional problems. First, while those individuals may have agreed to a new "bargain" defining their service, it nonetheless sets the precedent to the outside world of members of the U.S. military acting covertly and runs the risk of lessening the protection afforded other, uniformed U.S. military personnel who are subsequently captured (Kibbe 2004,113).

Second, the methods used to solicit volunteers are "fraught with the dangers of undue influence, peer pressure, traditional military values...and, perhaps most important, [the lack of] informed consent" (Stone 2003, 13).

Beyond the possible contraventions of international law, unacknowledged military operations also risk damaging both the United States' image in world opinion and its relations with other states. As Smith points out, the U.N. Special Rapporteur on extrajudicial, summary or arbitrary executions has been highly critical of the U.S. Predator missile strikes against Al Qaeda militants in Yemen and Pakistan (2007, 266). It is unclear under whose aegis (CIA or SOF) these strikes have been conducted but, as explained earlier, what is distasteful to the rest of the world when the CIA does it will be even more damaging to Washington's standing when conducted covertly by the military. Furthermore, particularly in the case of military covert operations being discovered in countries with which the United States is not already at war, the state involved is likely to resent its sovereignty being infringed upon. At best, the state could become less willing to cooperate with U.S. policy wishes and, at worst, might try some sort of reprisal.

Another category of risks posed by SOF's rapid expansion are more logistical and bureaucratic in nature. One issue is whether it is even possible to expand SOF's ranks to the degree envisioned without undermining their very "specialness." Special operations forces are distinctive for being the most highly trained military personnel but, between the military's overall retention problems and the pressure to produce more SOF warriors quickly, many fear that some of their training will inevitably be degraded. Other problems stemming from SOF's expansion include other forces and agencies resenting SOF's new prominence and the problem of SOF and CIA operatives unknowingly interfering with each other in the field (Fitzsimmons 2003, 213; M. Johnson 2006, 287–88; Kibbe 2007, 71–2).

Finally, there is also the seemingly more mundane risk that covert operations conducted with little or no oversight can court criminal activity, a scenario that has played itself out in at least one particularly relevant case. In the early 1980s, the Reagan administration used the covert SOF Intelligence Support Activity (ISA) to help prosecute its war against Nicaragua's Contras with minimal oversight. By the middle of the decade, ISA's wings had been clipped and several senior officers were court-martialed for their roles in various arms deals and financial scandals, in what became known overall as the Yellow Fruit scandal, after the code name for one of ISA's front companies (Emerson 1988; Hersh 2005).

One of the dangers of expanding SOF's size, authority, and geographic reach so rapidly and significantly is that, when that expansion is combined with the legal gray areas in the definition of covert action, it becomes even easier to either hide military covert action from congressional oversight on purpose or for it to be overlooked by accident. Either way, the danger is that the above risks are not being given the appropriate consideration.

7. FUTURE RESEARCH DIRECTIONS

The preceding discussion points to some logical avenues for future research. First, there is an ongoing need for further clarification of what unacknowledged military operations have been conducted since 9/11, whatever they are called by the Pentagon. It is, obviously, not an easy task, given their classified nature and the military's reluctance to concede the possibility even exists. Given the risks involved in such operations, however, and the likelihood that they will continue in the near future, the issue is simply too important to leave unresolved until the relevant records are declassified.

In a related vein, another important avenue will be to follow the evolution of the Pentagon's counterterrorism-cum-counterinsurgency strategy as it is applied in key regions such as North and East Africa, Southeast Asia and the Middle East to see just what its implications are for military covert action. Africa Command will be a particularly interesting case study to watch as it unfolds. One interesting twist on the issue is, if in fact the military does intend to move significantly away from JSOC-style counterterrorist strikes, whether it will be able to effectively do so, or whether the culture Rumsfeld nurtured in the Pentagon and in some areas of SOF has already become too ingrained.

Another vital area for research is on the legislative side. There is an important need for thoughtful solutions to the problem of congressional oversight and its weakness in terms of both military and CIA covert action. September 11 changed America's national security landscape and the multi-faceted expansion of SOF is part of Washington's reaction to that change. Perhaps it is time for Congress to update the language in the covert action legislation to take

SOF's evolution into account. Finally, Congress is notoriously difficult to reform, so some attention should be paid to exploring not just the best solution to Congress's inefficacy problem but also to the most effective way to get members of Congress to implement that solution.

QUESTIONS FOR FUTHER DISCUSSION

1. How does the work of SOCOM resemble or differ from traditional CIA covert actions?
2. If you were an attorney for the Pentagon, how would you argue a case in favor of SOCOM operations that may be equivalent to traditional CIA covert actions?
3. Should the "findings" procedure apply to all agencies in the executive branch, not just the CIA?
4. Who should operate the Predator, the Reaper, and other UAVs: the military or the CIA?

ENDNOTES

1. Note that while much of the substance of Meyer's discussion of the legislation's intent is accurate, the committee reports cited are actually those from 1990, the year before the law was actually passed.
2. Protocol Additional to the Geneva Conventions of 12 August 1949, and Relating to the Protection of Victims of International Armed Conflicts, Dec. 12, 1977 (Protocol I), art. 37.
3. Although, as Yoo and Ho argue, the law of war does apply to the overall conflict with Al Qaeda, as it has been defined by the Bush administration (2003, 209–15).

REFERENCES

Arkin, W. 2005. Interview with Amy Goodman. *Democracy Now!* January 27.

Berschinski, R. G. 2007. *AFRICOM'S Dilemma: The "Global War on Terrorism," "Capacity Building," Humanitarianism, and the Future of U.S. Security Policy in Africa.* Strategic Studies Institute, U.S. Army War College.

Clinton, W. J. 1995. *Executive Order 12958: Classified National Security information* (as amended by George W. Bush, 2003).

Dunlap, Brig. Gen. C. J. 2002. International Law and Terrorism: Some "Qs and As" for Operators. *Army Lawyer* (Oct.–Nov.): 23–30.

Emerson, S. 1988. *Secret Warriors: Inside the Covert Operations of the Reagan Era.* New York: Putnam.

Fitzsimmons, M. 2003. The Importance of Being Special: Planning for the Future of US. Special Operations Forces. *Defense and Security Analysis* 19:203–18.

Gompert, D. C., and J. Gordon IV. 2008. *War by Other Means: Building Complete and Balanced Capabilities for Counterinsurgency.* Santa Monica, Calif.: RAND.

Gordon, M. R., and M. Mazzetti. 2007. U.S. Used Base in Ethiopia to Hunt Al Qaeda. *New York Times* (February 23): 1.

Hersh, S. M. 2004. The Gray Zone. *The New Yorker* (May 24). http://www.newyorker.com/archive/2004/05/24/040524fa_fact, accessed December 21, 2008.

———. 2005. The Coming Wars. *The New Yorker* (January 24–31). http://www.newyorker.com/archive/2005/01/24/050124fa_fact, accessed December 21, 2008.

———. 2008. Preparing the Battlefield. *The New Yorker* (July 7). http://www.newyorker.com/reporting/2oo8/07/07/080707fa_fact_hersh, accessed December 21, 2008.

"Intelligence Authorization Act, Fiscal Year 1991." P. L. 102–88, 105 Stat. 429 (1991), Section 602.

Johnson, L. K. 1989. *America's Secret Power: The CIA at Home and Abroad.* New York: Oxford University Press.

Johnson, M. 2006. The Growing Relevance of Special Operations Forces in U.S. Military Strategy. *Comparative Strategy* 25:273–96.

Kibbe, J. D. 2004. The Rise of the Shadow Warriors. *Foreign Affairs* 83:102–15.

———. 2007. Covert Action and the Pentagon. *Intelligence and National Security* 22:57–74.

———. 2008. Congressional Oversight of Intelligence: Why It's Not Working and How to Fix It. Presented at the Annual ISAC/ISSS Conference, Globalization and Security: American Foreign Policy and the New Administration.

Kilcullen, D. J. 2005. Countering Global Insurgency. *Journal of Strategic Studies* 28, no. 4:597–617.

Lardner, R, 2008. Commando Leaders Shift Away from Rumsfeld Strategy. *Associated Press* (May 10).

McAndrew, M. 2006. Wrangling in the Shadows: The Use of United States Special Forces in Covert Military Operations in the War on Terror. *Boston College International and Comparative Law Review* 29:153–64.

McDonough, D., M. Rudman, and P. Rundlet. 2006. *No Mere Oversight: Congressional Oversight of Intelligence Is Broken.* Center for American Progress.

Meyer, J. T. 2007. Supervising the Pentagon: Covert Action and Traditional Military Activities in the War on Terror. *Administrative Law Review* 59:463–78.

Morgenstein, J., and E. Vickland. 2008. The Global Counter Insurgency: America's New National Security and

Foreign Policy Paradigm. *Small Wars Journal* (February 18). http://smallwarsjournal.com/mag/2008/02/the-global-counter-insurgency.php, accessed December 21, 2008.

Naylor, S. D. 2006. More than Door-Kickers. *Armed Forces Journal* (March). http://www.armedforcesjournal .com/2006/03/1813956, accessed December 21, 2008.

Ott, M. C. 2003. Partisanship and the Decline of Intelligence Oversight. *International Journal of Intelligence and Counterintelligence* 16:69–94.

Parks, W. H. 2003. Special Forces' Wear of Non-Standard Uniforms. *Chicago Journal of International Law* 4:493–547.

Roper, D. S. 2008. Global Counterinsurgency: Strategic Clarity for the Long War. *Parameters* (Autumn): 92–108.

Scarborough, R. 2004. *Rumsfeld's War: The Untold Story of America's. Anti-Terrorist Commander.* Washington, D.C.: Regnery Publishing.

Schmitt, E., and M. Mazzetti. 2008. Secret Order Lets U.S. Raid Al Qaeda in Many Countries. *New York Times* (November 10): 1.

Shanker, T. 2006. Pentagon Hones Its Strategy Against Terrorism. *New York Times* (February 5): 16.

_____. 2008. Wider Antiterror Role for Elite Forces Rejected. *New York Times* (May 21): 10.

Smith, M. 2007. *Killer Elite.* New York: St. Martin's Press.

Snider, L. B. 2008. *The Agency and the Hill: CIA's Relationship with Congress, 1946–2004.* Washington, D.C.: Center for the Study of Intelligence, CIA.

Special access programs: congressional oversight. 10 U.S.C. 119 (2006). Available from: GPO Access, http://www .gpoaccess.gov/index.html, accessed July 22, 2009.

Starks, T. 2007. New Players, New Hope for Intelligence Comity. *CQ Weekly* (March 26): 880–81.

Stevenson, J. 2006. Demilitarizing the "War on Terror." *Survival* 48:37–54.

_____. 2007. The Somali Model? *The National Interest* (July/Aug.): 41–45.

Stone, Col. K. 2003. *All Necessnry Means—Employing CIA Operatives in a Warfighting Role alongside Special Operations Forces.* Strategy Research Project, U.S. Army War College.

Treverton, G. F. 1987. *Covert Action: The Limits of Intervention in the Postwar World.* New York: Basic Books.

Tucker, D., and C. J. Lamb. 2007. *United States Special Operations Forces.* New York: Columbia University Press.

U.S. Department of Defense. 2006a. *Directive No. 2311.01E: DOD Law of War Program,* May 9. http://www.fas.org/irp/doddir/dod/d2311_01e.pdf, accessed December 27, 2008.

_____. 2006b. *Directive No. 5205.07: Special Access Program (SAP) Policy,* January 5 (Incorporating Change 1, February 25, 2008). http://www.fas.org/irp/doddir/dod/d5205_07.pdf, accessed December 27, 2008.

_____. 2006c. *Quadrennial Defense Review Report,* http://www.defenselink.mil/pubs/pdfs/QDR20060203.pdf, accessed December 27, 2008.

_____. 2008. *Department of Defense Dictionary of Military and Associated Terms,* Joint Publication 1–02, April 12, 2001 (As Amended through October 17, 2008). http://dtic .mil/doctrine/jel/doddict/, accessed December 27, 2008.

U.S. House of Representatives. Permanent Select Committee on Intelligence. 1991. *Conference Report on Intelligence Authorization Act, Fiscal Year 1991.* 102nd Cong., H.Rept. 166.

U.S. Senate. Joint Resolution. 2001. *Authorization for Use of Military Force.* 107th Cong., 115 Stat. 224.

U.S. Senate. Select Committee on Intelligence. 1991. *Authorizing Appropriations for Fiscal Year 1991 for the Intelligence Activities of the U.S. Government.* 102nd Cong., S. Rept. 85.

Walker, M, B. 2006. Reforming Congressional Oversight of U.S. Intelligence. *International Journal of Intelligence and Counterintelligence* 19:702–20.

Yoo, J. C., and J. C. Ho. 2003. The Status of Terrorists. *Virginia Journal of International Law* 44:207–28.

Reprinted with permission from Jennifer D. Kibbe, "Covert Action, Pentagon Style," in Loch K. Johnson, ed, *The Oxford Handbook of National Security Intelligence* (New York: Oxford University Press, 2010): pp. 569–586.

22. ASSASSINATION AS AN INSTRUMENT OF AMERICAN FOREIGN POLICY

BRUCE D. BERKOWITZ

One of the more extreme and morally questionable forms of paramilitary covert action is the assassination plot against a foreign leader. This essay examines the use of this method from a legal, practical, and ethical perspective.

Soon after the September 11 terrorist attacks on New York and Washington, U.S. officials announced that they had evidence linking Osama bin Laden to the attacks. As Americans began to recover from their initial shock, many of them asked, "Why don't we just get rid of the guy?"

The terrorist tragedy reopened one of the most controversial issues in national security policy: assassination. Few topics raise more passion. Yet, despite the intense emotions assassination raises, assassination rarely gets the kind of dispassionate analysis that we routinely devote to other national security issues. That is what I will do here. When it comes to assassination, four questions are key: What is it? Is it legal? Does it work? And when, if ever, is assassination acceptable?

WHAT IS IT?

One reason assassination—or, for that matter, banning assassination—provokes so much disagreement is that people often use the term without a precise definition and thus are really arguing about different things. One needs to be clear. Depending on the definition, one can be arguing about activities that are really quite different.

For example, is killing during wartime assassination? Does assassination refer to killing people of high rank, or can anyone be the target of assassination? Does it matter if a member of the armed forces, a civilian government official, or a hired hand does the killing? Depending on the definition, killing a military leader during a bombing raid might be

"assassination" but killing a low-level civilian official with a sniper might not.

For what it is worth, the *Merriam-Webster Dictionary* defines *assassination* by referring to the verb *assassinate*, which is defined as "to injure or destroy unexpectedly and treacherously" or "murder by sudden or secret attack usually for impersonal reasons." In other words, assassination is murder—killing a person—using secrecy or surprise. Assassination stands in contrast to murder without surprise (e.g., a duel). Also, assassination is not murder for personal gain or vengeance; assassinations support the goals of a government, organization, group, or cause.

Although people associate assassinations with prominent people, strictly speaking, assassination knows no rank. Leaders are often the targets of state-sponsored assassination, but history shows that generals, common soldiers, big-time crime bosses, and low-level terrorists have all been targets, too. Also, it does not seem to matter how you kill the target. It does not matter if you use a bomb or a booby trap; as long as you target a particular person, it's assassination.

For our purposes, assume that assassination is "deliberately killing a particular person to achieve a military or political objective, using the element of surprise to gain an advantage." We can call such a killing "sanctioned assassination" when a government has someone carry out such an action—as opposed to, say, "simple assassination," killing by an individual acting on his own. Then the question is, should we allow the United States to sanction such activities? And, if we allow the government to sanction assassination, when and how should do it?

IS IT LEGAL?

You might be surprised to learn that there are no international laws banning assassination. The closest thing to a prohibition is the 1973 Convention on the Prevention and Punishment of Crimes Against Internationally Protected Persons, Including Diplomatic Agents. This treaty (which the United States signed) bans attacks against heads of state while they conduct formal functions, heads of government while they travel abroad, and diplomats while they perform their duties.

The Protected Persons Convention was intended to ensure that governments could function and negotiate even during war. Without it, countries might start a war (or get drawn into one) and then find themselves unable to stop because there was no leader at home to make the decision to do so and because their representatives were getting picked off on their way to cease-fire negotiations.

But other than these narrow cases, the Protected Persons Convention says nothing about prohibiting assassination. Even then it applies only to officials representing bona fide governments and "international organizations of an intergovernmental character." So presumably the convention shields the representatives of the United Nations, the World Trade Organization, the International Red Cross, and, probably, the PLO. It does not protect bosses of international crime syndicates or the heads of terrorist groups such as Al Qaeda.

Another treaty that some might construe as an assassination ban is the Hague Convention on the "laws and customs" of war. The Hague Convention states that "the right of belligerents to adopt means of injuring the enemy is not unlimited." (This was a bold statement in 1907, when the convention was signed).

The Hague Convention tried to draw a sharp line between combatants and noncombatants; combatants were entitled to the convention's protections but were also obliged to obey its rules. For example, the Hague Convention tried to distinguish combatants by requiring them to wear a "fixed distinctive emblem recognizable at a distance." Wear the emblem while fighting, and you are entitled to be treated as a POW if captured; fail to follow the dress code, and you might be hanged as a mere bandit.

Alas, maintaining this definition of a "combatant" proved a losing battle throughout the twentieth century. Guerrilla warfare transformed civilians into soldiers. Strategic bombing transformed civilians into targets. Headquarters staff, defense ministers, and civilian commanders in chief today are all more likely to wear suits than uniforms. Teenage paramilitary soldiers in Liberia are lucky to have a pair of Levis to go along with their AK-47s, let alone fatigues or insignia. That is why, practically speaking, a "combatant" today is anyone who is part of a military chain of command.

Yet the Hague Convention may be more interesting not for what it prohibits but for what it permits. The closest the convention comes to banning assassination is when it prohibits signatories from killing or wounding "treacherously individuals belonging to the hostile nation or army." But when it refers to "treachery," it is referring to fighting under false pretenses (e.g., flying the enemy's flag or wearing his uniform to lure him to death). The Hague Convention specifically permits "ruses of war." Snipers, land mines, deception, camouflage, and other sneaky tactics are okay. In fact, one might even argue that, since the convention prohibits *indiscriminate* killing, state-sanctioned assassination—the most precise and deliberate killing of all—during war is exactly what the treaty calls for.

The third international agreement that is relevant to assassination is the Charter of the United Nations, which allows countries to use military force in the name of self-defense. If a country can justify a war as "defensive," it can kill any person in the enemy's military chain of command that it can shoot, bomb, burn, or otherwise eliminate. And it can use whatever "ruses of war" it needs to get the job done. As a result, the main legal constraints on sanctioned assassination other than domestic law, which makes murder a crime in almost all countries, are rules that nations impose on themselves.

The U.S. government adopted such a ban in 1976, when President Ford—responding to the scandal that resulted when the press revealed CIA involvement in several assassinations—issued Executive Order 11905. This order prohibited what it called "political assassination" and essentially reaffirmed an often-overlooked ban that Director of Central Intelligence Richard Helms had adopted for the CIA four years earlier. Jimmy Carter reaffirmed the ban in 1978 with his own Executive Order 12036. Ronald Reagan went even further in 1981; his Executive

Order 12333 banned assassination in toto. This ban on assassination remains in effect today.

Even so, there has been a disconnect between our policy and practice. The United States has tried to kill foreign leaders on several occasions since 1976, usually as part of a larger military operation.

For example, in 1986, U.S. Air Force and Navy planes bombed Libya after a Libyan terrorist attack against a nightclub frequented by American soldiers in Berlin. One of the targets was Muammar Qaddafi's tent. During Desert Storm in 1991, we bombed Saddam Hussein's official residences and command bunkers. After the United States linked Osama bin Laden to terrorist bombings of U.S. embassies in Kenya and Tanzania in 1998, we launched a cruise missile attack at one of his bases in Afghanistan.

In each case, U.S. officials insisted that our forces were merely aiming at "command and control" nodes or at a building linked to military operations or terrorist activities. In each case, however, the same officials admitted off the record that they would not have been upset if Qaddafi, Saddam, or bin Laden had been killed in the process.

More recently, according to press reports, presidents have also approved so-called lethal covert operations—operations in which there is a good chance that an unfriendly foreign official might be killed. For example, the press reported a CIA-backed covert operation to topple Saddam in 1996 that probably would have killed him in the process, given the record of Iraqi leadership successions (no one has left office alive). After the September 11 terrorist strikes on New York and Washington, former Clinton officials leaked word to reporters that the CIA had trained Pakistani commandos in 1999 to snatch bin Laden. Given the record of such operations, bin Laden would likely not have survived.

In short, the unintended result of banning assassinations has been to make U.S. leaders perform verbal acrobatics to explain how they have tried to kill someone in a military operation without really trying to kill him. One has to wonder about the wisdom of any policy that allows officials to do something but requires them to deny that they are doing it. We would be better off simply doing away with the prohibition, at least as it applies to U.S. military operations.

DOES IT WORK?

The effectiveness of assassination has depended much on its objectives. Most (but not all) attempts to change the course of large-scale political and diplomatic trends have failed. Assassination has been more effective in achieving small, specific goals.

Indeed, past U.S. assassination attempts have had great difficulty in even achieving the minimal level of success: killing the intended target. According to the available information, *every* U.S. effort to kill a high-ranking official since World War II outside a full-scale war has failed. This record is so poor that it would be hard to find an instrument of national policy that has been less successful in achieving its objectives than assassination (although price controls or election reform may come in a close second).

According to the Church Committee investigations of the 1970s, the CIA supported assassins trying to kill Patrice Lumumba of the Congo in 1961 and repeatedly tried to assassinate Fidel Castro between 1961 and 1963. In addition, American officials were either privy to plots or encouraged coups that caused the death of a leader (Rafael Trujillo of the Dominican Republic in 1961, Ngo Dinh Diem of South Vietnam in 1963, General Rene Schneider of Chile in 1970, and, later, President Salvador Allende in 1973). And, as noted, in recent years the United States has tried to do away with Qaddafi, Saddam, and bin Laden.

What is notable about this record is that it is remarkably free of success. Castro, Qaddafi, Saddam, and (at least at this writing) bin Laden all survived. (As this is being written, U.S. forces are hunting bin Laden as part of the larger war against the Taliban in Afghanistan.) What is more, Qaddafi continued to support terrorism (e.g., the bombing of Pan Am flight 103). Saddam has managed to outlast the terms of two presidents who wanted to eliminate him (George Bush and Bill Clinton), while continuing to support terrorism—and developing weapons of mass destruction.

One might have predicted this dismal record just by considering why American leaders have resorted to the assassination option. More often than not, assassination is the option when nothing seems to work but officials think that they need to do *something*. When diplomacy is ineffective and war seems too costly, assassination becomes the fallback—but without anyone asking whether it will accomplish anything.

This seems to have been the thinking behind the reported U.S. covert operation to eliminate Saddam in the mid-1990s. Despite a series of provocations—an assassination attempt against former president George Bush, violence against Shi'ite Muslims and Kurds, and violations of U.N. inspection requirements—the Clinton administration was unwilling to wage a sustained, full-scale war against him. Diplomacy was also failing, as the United States was unable to hold together the coalition that won Desert Storm. Covert support to Saddam's opponents in the military was the alternative. It was an utter failure.

True, some other countries have been more successful in that they have killed their target. For example, after the terrorist attack on Israeli athletes in the 1972 Munich Olympics, Israeli special services tracked down and killed each of the Palestinian guerrillas who took part (they also killed an innocent Palestinian in a case of mistaken identity). In 1988 Israeli commandos killed Khalil Al-Wazir, a lieutenant of Yasser Arafat's, in a raid on PLO headquarters in Tunisia. More recently, Israel has killed specifically targeted Palestinian terrorist leaders— for example, Yechya Ayyash, who was killed with a booby-trapped cell phone.

Other countries have also attempted assassinations with some degree of tactical success. During the Cold War, the KGB was linked to several assassinations. Most recently, the Taliban regime in Afghanistan was suspected of being involved in the assassination of Ahmed Shah Massoud, the leader of the Northern Alliance opposition.

But even "successful" assassinations have often left the sponsor worse off, not better. The murder of Diem sucked the United States deeper into a misconceived policy. The assassination of Abraham Lincoln (carried out by a conspiracy some believe to have links to the Confederate secret service) resulted in Reconstruction. German retribution against Czech civilians after the 1942 assassination of Nazi prefect Reinhard Heydrich by British-sponsored resistance fighters was especially brutal. The 1948 assassination of Mohandas Gandhi by Hindu extremists led to violence that resulted in the partition of India.

In short, assassination has usually been unreliable in shaping large-scale political trends the way the perpetrators intended (though the assassination of Yitzhak Rabin by a Zionist extremist in 1995 may be the exception). When it accomplishes anything beyond simply killing the target, it is usually by depriving an enemy of the talents of some uniquely skilled individual. For example, in 1943 U.S. warplanes shot down an aircraft known to be carrying Admiral Isoroku Yamamoto—the architect of Japan's early victories in the Pacific. His loss hurt the Japanese war effort. The same could be said of the loss of Massoud to the Northern Alliance.

The problem is, picking off a talented individual is almost always harder than it looks. One paradox of modern warfare is that, although it is not that hard to kill many people, it can be very difficult to kill a particular person. One has to know exactly where the target will be at a precise moment. This is almost always hard, especially in wartime.

SHOULD WE DO IT, AND IF SO, HOW?

This is the most complex issue, of course. The morality of sanctioned assassination depends mainly on whether and when one can justify murder. Most religions and agnostic philosophies agree that individuals have the right to kill in self-defense when faced with immediate mortal danger. This principle is codified in American law. And, as we have seen, even international law seems to allow killing—even killing specific individuals—when it can be justified as armed self-defense.

Although most Americans do not like the idea of deliberate killing, they do not completely reject it, either. Most would agree that their government should be allowed to kill (or, more precisely, allow people to kill in its behalf) in at least two situations.

One situation is when a police officer must eliminate an immediate threat to public safety—for example, shooting an armed robber or apprehending a suspect who has proven dangerous in the past and who resists arrest. The other situation is when soldiers go to war to defend the country from attack. In addition, many—but not all—Americans believe that the government should be allowed to kill in the case of capital crimes.

It is probably not a coincidence that the U.S. Constitution also envisions these three—and only these three—situations in which the federal government might take a life: policing, going to war, and imposing capital punishment. Logically, then, assassination must fit into one of these three tracks. Assassination can be considered a police act, in which case it must follow the rules for protecting accused criminals. Or it can be considered a military act, in which case it must follow the rules that control how the United States wages war. Or it can be considered capital punishment, in which case it must follow the rules of due process.

Given this, when would we want to allow government to kill a particular foreign national? Clearly we should not use assassination as a form of de facto capital punishment. Unless the intended target presents a clear and immediate threat, there is always time to bring a suspect to justice, where we could guarantee due process. Similarly, although police should be able to protect themselves and others while making an arrest, we would not want police to pursue their targets with the expectation that they would routinely kill them.

The only time we should consider assassination is when we need to eliminate a clear, immediate, lethal threat from abroad. In other words, assassination is a military option. We need to understand it as such because the United States will face more situations in which it must decide whether it is willing, in effect, to go to war to kill a particular individual and how it will target specific individuals during wartime. Two factors make this scenario likely.

First, technology often makes it hard for one *not* to target specific people. Weapons are so accurate today that, when one programs their guidance systems, you aim not just for a neighborhood, or a building in the neighborhood, but for a particular *room* in a particular building. In effect, even bombing and long-range missile attacks have become analogous to sniping. You cannot always be sure you will hit your target—just as snipers often miss and sometimes hit the wrong target—but you still must aim at specific people.

Second, the nature of the threats we face today will likely require us to target specific individuals. Terrorist organizations today use modern communications to organize themselves as worldwide networks. These networks consist of small cells that can group and regroup as needed to prepare for a strike. This is how the bin Laden organization has operated. Seeing how successful these tactics have been, many armies will likely often adopt a similar approach. To defeat such networked organizations, our military forces will need to move quickly, find the critical cells in a network, and destroy them. This inevitably will mean identifying specific individuals and killing them—in other words, assassination.

But when we do so, we should be clear in our own minds that, when the United States tries to assassinate someone, we are going to war—with all the risks and costs that war brings. These include, for example, diplomatic consequences, the danger of escalation, the threat of retaliation against our own leaders, the threat of retaliation against American civilians, and so on.

Because assassination is an act of war, such activities should always be considered a military operation. American leaders need to resist the temptation to use intelligence organizations for this mission. Intelligence organizations are outside the military chain of command. Intelligence operatives are not expected to obey the rules of war and thus are not protected by those rules. At the same time, intelligence organizations are also not law enforcement organizations. In many situations, having intelligence organizations kill specific individuals looks too much like a death sentence without due process.

Indeed, there is reason to question whether intelligence organizations are even technically qualified for assassination. In every publicly known case in which the CIA has considered killing a foreign leader, the agency has outsourced the job. In most cases, it has recruited a foreign intelligence service or military officials with better access. In some of the attempts to kill Castro, the CIA recruited Mafia hit men. Even in the more recent reported cases of lethal covert actions, foreigners would have done the actual killing. It is hard to maintain control and quality when you subcontract assassination services—as the record shows.

The United States did not ask for the threats we currently face, and killing on behalf of the state will always be the most controversial, most distasteful policy issue of all. That is why we need to use blunt language and appreciate exactly what we are proposing. Sugarcoating the topic only hides the tough issues we need to decide as a country. But if we do need to target specific people for military attack, it is important that we get it right.

QUESTIONS FOR FUTHER DISCUSSION

1. What exactly is meant by the term assassination and has the CIA engaged in such activities?
2. What are the legal arguments for and against assassination plots?
3. Does assassination help a nation achieve its foreign policy goals?
4. What are the ethical arguments that surround this controversial topic?

23. EVALUATING COVERT ACTION

LOCH K. JOHNSON

Some intelligence operations are non-controversial and are minimally invasive with respect to another nation's sovereignty; others, such as assassination, strike at the very heart of sovereignty. Through the use of a "ladder of escalation," this essay attempts to array the severity of intelligence operations, among them mild and extraordinarily harsh covert actions.

INTRODUCTION

This analysis of covert operations, as conducted by Western intelligence services, explores the problem of assessing their effects on international order and comity. Despite a tendency of commentators to overlook this form of intervention, the topic is important; in contemporary global relations, covert acts of hostility between nations occur with a high rate of frequency.[1]

The study is organized into three sections. The first presents a "ladder of escalation" for covert operations, one based on a rising level of intrusion abroad as policy makers climb upward from low-risk to high-risk activities. The second section briefly surveys leading ethical, philosophical and practical issues involved in trying to evaluate the effects of secret intelligence activities. And the third section offers a set of guidelines for evaluating the propriety of proposed covert operations.

I. A LADDER OF ESCALATION FOR COVERT OPERATIONS

In 1965 strategist Herman Kahn of the Hudson Institute published an influential volume in which he offered a metaphor for understanding the coercive features of international affairs. Kahn referred to this methodological device as an "escalation-ladder metaphor," which he described as a "convenient list of the many options facing the strategist in a two-sided confrontation."[2] His ladder addressed primarily the overt manifestations of hostile acts carried out by one state against another, building from low-level expressions of enmity ("subcrisis

maneuvering," which included political, economic and diplomatic gestures, as well as—a step up—solemn and formal declarations of displeasure) and continuing ultimately to "spasm or insensate war"—Step 44, a full-scale nuclear exchange.

Similarly, covert operations can be arrayed for heuristic purposes according to their degree of intrusiveness abroad, from nonforcible to forcible intervention (with all the accompanying caveats Kahn advanced regarding the limitations of a ladder metaphor[3]). In a ladder of escalation for covert operations (displayed in Table 23.1), the underlying analytical dimension traveling upward is the extent to which most observers would view the options as increasingly serious violations of international law and national sovereignty, and, therefore, as intensified assaults on the international order (as contemporarily defined).

THE STEPS ON THE LADDER

THRESHOLD ONE: ROUTINE INTELLIGENCE OPERATIONS. At the lower end of the ladder for covert operations—Threshold One—are arrayed such relatively benign activities as routine sweeps of a nation's own embassy facilities overseas to detect possible electronic implantations, and the giving of instruction and security equipment to enhance the personal safety of friendly foreign leaders against threats to their lives (Rung-1 security measures). Also at this threshold is the assignment of intelligence officers to gather information from foreign officials in their normal daily rounds, say, at an embassy reception in Rome (a Rung-2 collection operation). At this

TABLE 23.1 A PARTIAL ESCALATION LADDER OF STRATEGIC INTELLIGENCE OPTIONS

Threshold Four

Extreme Options	38. Use of chemical-biological, other deadly agents (PM)
	37. Major secret wars (PM)
	36. Assassination plots (PM)
	35. Small-scale coups d'état (PM)
	34. Major economic dislocations; crop destruction (E)
	33. Environmental alterations (PM/E)
	32. Pinpointed retaliation against noncombatants (PM)
	31. Torture (POL/C)
	30. Hostage taking (POL/C)
	29. Major hostage-rescue attempts (PM)
	28. Theft of sophisticated weapons or materiel (PM)
	27. Sophisticated arms supplies (PM)

Threshold Three

High-Risk Options	26. Massive increases of funding in democracies (POL)
	25. Disinformation against democratic regimes (P)
	24. Disinformation against autocratic regimes (P)
	23. Small-scale hostage-rescue attempts (PM)
	22. Training of foreign military forces for war (PM)
	21. Limited arms supplies for offensive purposes (PM)
	20. Limited arms supplies for balancing purposes (PM)
	19. Economic disruption without loss of life (E)
	18. Large increases of funding in democracies (POL)
	17. Massive increases of funding in autocracies (POL)
	16. Large increases of funding in autocracies (POL)
	15. Sharing of sensitive intelligence (C)
	14. Embassy break-ins (C/CE)
	13. Truthful, contentious information in democracies (P)
	12. Truthful, contentious information in autocracies (P)
	11. High-level, intrusive political surveillance (C)
	10. High-level recruitment and penetrations (C/CE)

Threshold Two

Modest Intrusions	9. Low-level funding of friendly groups (POL)
	8. Truthful, benign information in democracies (P)
	7. Truthful, benign information in autocracies (P)
	6. Stand-off TECHINT against target nation (C)
	5. "Away" targeting of intelligence officer (C/CE)
	4. "Away" targeting for intelligence gathering (C)

Threshold One

Routine Operations	3. Sharing of low-level intelligence (C)
	2. Ordinary embassy-based observing and conversing (C)
	1. Passive security measures; protection of leaders (S)

Key: C = collection of intelligence
   S = security (a passive form of counterintelligence)
   CE = counterespionage (an active form of counterintelligence)
   P = covert propaganda (a form of covert action)
   POL = political covert action
   E = economic covert action
   PM = paramilitary covert action

Note: For definitions of the terms in the key, see L. JOHNSON, AMERICA'S SECRET POWER: THE CIA IN A DEMOCRATIC SOCIETY 17–21, 29–35, 76–77 (1989); and the glossary to SENATE SELECT COMM. TO STUDY GOVERNMENTAL OPERATIONS WITH RESPECT TO INTELLIGENCE ACTIVITIES, FINAL REPORT, S. REP. NO. 755, 94th Cong., 2d Sess., BK. 1, FOREIGN AND MILITARY INTELLIGENCE 614–96 (1976) (known as the Church Committee report).

threshold, too, low-level information is exchanged between friendly intelligence services by "intelligence liaison officers" (Rung 3)—a common arrangement in the West.

These activities represent little or no serious infringement upon a nation's sense of sovereignty and the noninterventionist norm; they are widely practiced, with minimal international repercussions.[4] The first rung (security measures) represents the least controversial of all the intelligence activities carried out between states, since every nation maintains some form of passive defense—most thrown up within the defending nation's own territories with no intrusion against another nation—a basic shield against attack.

THRESHOLD TWO: MODEST INTRUSIONS. With Threshold Two, one begins to escalate the degree of intrusiveness and, concomitantly, the risks involved in using the strategic intelligence option. This category could include attempts to recruit, say, a foreign ministry clerk in Geneva or elsewhere outside his or her homeland—in this sense, "away" (Rung 4, collection); recruitment attempts against a low-level Cuban intelligence officer, still *outside* the target nation (Cuba) but more risky than the previous rung because an intelligence officer—someone with access to the target nation's deepest secrets—becomes the specific object of recruitment (Rung 5, counterespionage); and the use of distant (or "stand-off") technical intelligence (TECHINT) surveillance against the target nation—high-altitude reconnaissance satellites, for instance (Rung 6, collection).

This category would also include the insertion of truthful covert propaganda material with uncontroversial themes (say, on the importance of preserving NATO) into foreign media outlets of nondemocratic regimes, as a means of reinforcing overt policy pronouncements (Rung 7, covert action); again propaganda, but targeted against democratic regimes with a free press (Rung 8, covert action); and the payment of modest sums to political, labor, intellectual and other organizations and individuals abroad favorably disposed toward one's foreign-policy objectives (Rung 9, covert action). All of these examples represent common and widely, if begrudgingly, accepted practices, even though they obviously infringe upon a nation's sovereign rights. Even violations of a nation's airspace by satellites and reconnaissance airplanes—TECHINT collection methods once considered highly provocative—are now largely accepted with existential resignation as part and parcel of international affairs in the modern Age of Surveillance.

Still, the lines of demarcation between acceptable and unacceptable intervention can be fuzzy and controversial. Texts on the subject published by the United Nations General Assembly have elicited divided views from members. One illustration comes from the Special Committee on Friendly Relations, established by the General Assembly. In 1967 it reported the opinion of some committee members that covert propaganda and the secret financing of political parties represented "acts of lesser gravity than those directed towards the violent overthrow of the host government."[5] Other Assembly representatives, however, rejected this perspective—especially those who wished to avoid legitimizing covert operations that (in their view) had harmed their nations in the past. As a result of this divided opinion, the special committee equivocated, neither supporting nor prohibiting covert propaganda and secret political funding. A perspicacious student of the committee's work has concluded: "the texts that the General Assembly approved represent compromise formulations that are open to multiple interpretations."[6]

THRESHOLD THREE: HIGH-RISK OPERATIONS. Threshold Three marks a still more significant series of steps toward dangerous covert activity that could trigger within the target nation a response damaging to international comity. Key features of this escalation zone include close-up, on-the-ground, direct operations against more sensitive targets (including activities within the target nation's own territory), as well as the use of methods and materiel that can lead to violence.

On Rung 10, for example, an intelligence service "pitches" (tries to recruit) a high-level potential defector inside the target nation, or attempts a high-level penetration into the opposition service—again on the adversary's own turf (counterespionage). On Rung 11, the aggressor undertakes intrusive surveillance operations (wiretaps, for instance) against prominent political leaders within their own country; or he may employ the "tradecraft"—that is, the strategic intelligence modus operandi—of TECHINT or HUMINT (human intelligence: spies) against the target nation's highest decision councils (a collection operation). If discovered, a serious diplomatic rift could likely result.

This third threshold also consists of more intense covert actions. With Rungs 12 and 13, propaganda operations remain truthful and in accord with the overt policy statements of the sponsoring nation; but now they pump into the media of nondemocratic and democratic regimes (respectively) more contentious themes—say, in the days before the end of the Cold War in 1989, by attributing the prowess of the West European peace movement to financial and propaganda support from Soviet intelligence agencies.

At Rung 14, the covert aggressor attempts a break-in (a "second-story" or "black-bag" job) against a target nation's embassy, either in a foreign capital or in the aggressor's own capital (collection and counterespionage)—operations considered extremely risky and requiring high-level approval when resorted to by the Government of the United States.[7] Rung 15 again involves the sharing of intelligence with other secret services; but, unlike Rung 3, in this case the information is highly sensitive, say, related to U.S. nuclear targeting plans, offered in an effort to gain greater attack coordination among NATO nations should war break out against the West (a U.S.-French example is presented in Table 23.2).

Rungs 16 and 17 reflect, first, a large and, then, a massive increase, respectively, in funding for covert political purposes in an autocratic nation—say, a rise in secret expenditures of $1 million, then $5 million in a poor country; or $10 million, and then $20 million in a more affluent one. These large amounts of money can have a significant effect on elections, particularly within a small, developing nation. It is these sizable sums that no doubt most concerned those members of the General Assembly special committee discussed earlier who opposed permissive language that would condone nonforcible covert influence in the domestic politics of other nations.[8]

Again, as with propaganda, a distinction is made between nondemocratic target nations on Rungs 16 and 17 and those which are democratic on Rung 18. Interference in the internal affairs of democracies is considered a more serious step—all the more so if the operation is designed to rig a free election, in contrast, say, to building up a political party between elections (though the distinctions here can become fine).

In a similar fashion, Damrosch argues that "a political system that denies basic political rights is in my view no longer a strictly internal affair."[9] The advancement of individual freedoms—particularly those according a citizen the right to make political choices—is central to Damrosch's normative analytic framework, and it is vital to the argument offered here as well. Tyrants who suppress human

rights and the political participation of their citizens undermine whatever claim they may have had to protection from outside influence based upon the noninterventionist norm, for the human rights norm is a powerful countervailing claimant. As Damrosch writes (with reference to the use of overt economic sanctions, although the argument applies equally well to the various covert operations discussed here): "a state does not violate the nonintervention norm (or any other international law rule) when it uses economic sanctions to induce a target state to hold free and fair elections or otherwise to enhance compliance with human rights principles of political participation."[10]

At Rung 19, the aggressor undertakes limited covert attacks against economic entities within the target nation. A power line is destroyed here, an oil storage depot contaminated there, perhaps labor strikes are encouraged inside the major cities—all carefully planned to remain within the limits of harassment operations, with a low probability that life will be lost.

At Rung 20, a nation resorts to paramilitary operations (arms supplies) to counter weapons already introduced into a territory by an adversary, say, a modest supply of unsophisticated—but still deadly—arms provided by the United States to a favored rebel faction (or factions) as a means of balancing the correlation of forces in a civil war. At Rung 21, the weapons are supplied to a friendly faction without prior intervention by an outside adversary; and Rung 22 involves the secret training of foreign armies or factions for combat (for an Israeli-SriLankan example, see Table 23.2). Rung 23 envisages a hostage rescue attempt that could involve loss of life, but one carefully designed to be small-scale so as to limit the potential for casualties (a Son Tay village raid in Vietnam, in contrast to the more ambitious Iranian rescue attempt during the Carter administration).[11]

At Rungs 24 and 25 (maintaining the distinction between nondemocratic and democratic regimes), propaganda activities take a decidedly nasty turn, involving deception and disinformation that run contrary to the aggressor nation's avowed public policies (say, falsely blaming an adversary for an assassination attempt against the pope, or falsifying documents to stain an adversary's reputation on an important matter[12]). Even propaganda operations against nations without free media are of concern here (albeit less so than against democracies), because of the "blow back" or "replay" phenomenon by which information directed toward adversaries abroad can find its way back home to deceive citizens in Western nations with free media.

At Rung 26, massive expenditures are dedicated to improving the political fortunes of friendly factions within a democratic regime (say, $20 million in a small democracy and $50 million or more in a larger one), in hopes of bringing them to power—tampering in a major way with electoral outcomes in free societies (political covert action). Attempts at covertly influencing truly democratic elections—those in which the rights of political dissent and opposition are honored—represent violations of the noninterventionist norm (and related rules of international law) and have no claim to legitimacy, in contrast to those operations directed against self-interested autocratic regimes.

THRESHOLD FOUR: EXTREME OPTIONS. With Threshold Four, a nation enters an especially dangerous and controversial realm of strategic intelligence. Here is where the lives of innocent people may be placed in extreme jeopardy. At Rung 27, the types of weapons provided are more potent than at earlier rungs. Rebellious factions inside the target nation (or within its foreign theater of war) are secretly provided with highly sophisticated weapons—say, Stinger and Blowpipe antiaircraft missiles—that enable them to take the offensive, causing a major escalation in the fighting (the 1988–1989 Afghanistan scenario in which the Central Intelligence Agency supplied anti-Communist rebels with such weapons). Rung 28 represents access to sophisticated weapons through theft, the most extreme case being the stealing of nuclear bombs (or materiel for making them, as Israeli intelligence has been accused of doing; see Table 23.2).

At Rung 29, a nation faces the prospect of extensive casualties, which would probably accompany a major effort to rescue hostages—what President Bush referred to in 1989 as "collateral damage" (that is, civilian deaths) in his public explanation of his rejection, for the time being, of this approach to freeing U.S. hostages held by terrorist groups in Lebanon.[13] At Rung 30, force is intended, carefully planned, and directed against specific individuals. Opposition intelligence personnel or foreign leaders are kidnaped ("arrested") for information (a collection operation), for instance, or for secret bargaining (political and paramilitary covert action). An illustration is the 1989 abduction by Israeli commandos of Sheik Abdul Karim Obeid, a leader of the Party of

God, a pro-Iranian faction in Lebanon believed to be holding three Israeli soldiers.

At Rung 31, hostages are tortured in a cruel attempt to coerce compliance in a hostage swap or some other deal (political covert action), or to obtain information (collection). At Rung 32, acts of brutality are directed against lower-level noncombatants in retaliation for hostile intelligence operations (counterespionage).[14] These two rungs would also encompass various gross violations of human rights.

Beginning with Rung 33, strategic intelligence activities escalate to include violence-laden economic covert actions, as well as paramilitary operations against targets of wider scope—often affecting sizable numbers of noncombatants in the civilian population. On Rung 33, the aggressor intelligence agency tries to bring about major environmental alterations, from the defoliation or burning of forests to the contamination of lakes and rivers, the creation of floods through the destruction of dams, and even operations (tried by the United States during its war in Vietnam) to control weather conditions through cloud seeding. At Rung 34, the aggressor attempts to wreak major economic dislocations within the target nation by counterfeiting currencies to fuel inflation and economic chaos, sabotaging industrial facilities, destroying crops through the introduction of agricultural parasites into the fields, or spreading hoof-and-mouth disease among livestock.

Rung 35 represents the level of the coup d'état, intimately involving the aggressor intelligence service in the overthrow of a foreign adversary—though with minimal intended bloodshed. Rung 36 is the level at which assassination plots are carried out against specific foreign officials, murder of the highest order. Finally, standing at the top of the escalation ladder are two forms of secret warfare that inevitably affect large numbers of combatants and noncombatants: the launching of protracted, full-blown covert warfare against an inimical regime, with the sponsoring, combat-ready intelligence officers guiding indigenous rebel armies—comparable in scope to the CIA's lengthy "secret" war in Laos during the 1960s (Rung 37); and the spreading of biological, chemical or other toxic substances to bring about widespread death in the target nation (Rung 38).[15]

WESTERN COVERT OPERATIONS IN COMPARATIVE PERSPECTIVE

The examples of intelligence operations presented in this section are drawn largely from American experience. The various official investigations into the U.S. intelligence community conducted in 1975–1976 and in 1987 provided a rich source of data on this nation's secret agencies and their activities since 1947. Further, the scholarly research on American intelligence, stimulated by the new data, is much more extensive than anything available on the secret services of other nations. Yet it must be emphasized that most developed nations in the West (and certainly the former Soviet Union in the East) have vigorously engaged in most of the operations found on the ladder of escalation presented above.[16] The public record on intelligence operations carried out by Western nations other than the United States is spare, because these nations have been more successful in concealing their "dark arts" from public scrutiny; nevertheless, Table 23.2 presents some illustrations from these other countries (as well as the United States) to underscore the point that covert intelligence operations are a widespread phenomenon in the Western world (not to mention the East, which is beyond the scope of this study).

The primary usefulness of the ladder metaphor resides in the opportunity it affords for a visual inspection of covert options, roughly organized according to the growing risk and degree of violence involved in their implementation (and, implicitly, the rising moral qualms and legal controversies that attend them). Ladder construction is an opening exercise in trying to accomplish the more difficult

TABLE 23.2   SOME REPORTED WESTERN INTELLIGENCE OPERATIONS SINCE 1945

Threshold	Nation	Reported Operation
Four	United States	Paramilitary action in Laos (1960s); assassination plots in Cuba and the Congo (1960s)
	United Kingdom	Paramilitary operations in Albania (1949), Iran (1953), and Oman (1960s)
	Chile	Assassination of Ambassador Letelier (1976)
	South Africa	Assassination plots in Zimbabwe (1980s)
	Israel	Assassination of PLO leader (1988), bombing of nuclear reactor storage sites in France (1979), paramilitary actions in Egypt (1950s), other assassination plots over the years, theft of uranium oxide (1968)
	France	*Rainbow Warrior* sinking (1985); sabotage and various assassination plots against leaders in Algeria and Egypt (1950s) and Libya (1980)
Three	Israel, United States	Covert weapons sales to Iran (1986)
	Israel	Training Sri Lanka security forces (1984)
	West Germany	Economic disruption in Guinea (1958)
	United States/France	Sharing of sensitive nuclear intelligence(1970s–)
	United Kingdom	Propaganda in the Middle East (1950s–1960s)
Two	United States	TECHINT surveillance worldwide
	France	Spying on U.S. officials in Paris (1964)
	United Kingdom	Worldwide intelligence collection
One	United States/United Kingdom	Sharing of low-level intelligence
	United States	Assisting security of Egyptian leaders (1978), worldwide U.S. embassy security

Sources (in order of the operations presented in the table).

Threshold Four: W. COLBY & P. FORBATH, HONORABLE MEN: MY LIFE IN THE CIA 191–202 (1978) (on Laos); S. REP. NO. 465, 94th Cong., 2d Sess. (1975) (on assassination plots); C. ANDREW, HER MAJESTY'S SECRET SERVICE 492–93 (1986) (on UK in Albania); J. RICHELSON, FOREIGN INTELLIGENCE ORGANIZATIONS 26 (1988) (on UK in Iran); Charters, *The Role of Intelligence Services in the Direction of Covert Paramilitary Operations*, in INTELLIGENCE: POLICY AND PROCESS 339 (A. Maurer, M. Tunstall & J. Keagle eds. 1985) (on UK in Oman); Lardner, *Pinochet Linked to Murder Cover-Up*, Wash. Post, Feb. 5, 1987, at A1, col. 5 (on Chile); Rule, *Trial in Zimbabwe Points to Pretoria*, N.Y. Times, June 18, 1988, at A3, col. 1 (on S. Africa); D. RAVIV & Y. MELMAN, EVERY SPY A PRINCE (1990); J. RICHELSON, *supra*, at 203, 205–10 (on Israel); B. & M.-T. DANIELSSON, POISONED REIGN: FRENCH NUCLEAR COLONIALISM IN THE PACIFIC (1986) (on *Rainbow Warrior*); J. RICHELSON, *supra*, at 163, 167 (on France).

Threshold Three: S. REP. NO. 216 & H. REP. NO. 433, 100th Cong., 1st Sess. 168(1987); W.COHEN & G. MITCHELL, MEN OF ZEAL 235 (1988); and J. RICHELSON, *supra*, at 204–05 (on Israeli arms sales to Iran); Raviv & Melman, *Killing of Wazir Ruthless and Efficient*, L.A. Times, Apr. 22, 1988, at Al, col. 1 (on Israel); J. RICHELSON, *supra*, at 204 (on Israel); *id.* at 167 (on W. Germany's involvement in this joint operation with other allied nations); Ullman, *The Covert French Connection*, FOREIGN POL'Y, Summer 1989, at 3 (on U.S.-French sharing); J. RICHELSON, *supra*, at 26 (on UK).

Threshold Two: J. BAMFORD, THE PUZZLE PALACE (1984); Kahn, *Big Ear or Big Brother?*, N.Y. Times, May 16, 1976, at 13 (on the U.S. TECHINT operations); J. RICHELSON, *supra*, at 160 (on France); J. RICHELSON & D. BALL, THE TIES THAT BIND: INTELLIGENCE COOPERATION BETWEEN THE UKUSA COUNTRIES (1985) (on UK espionage).

Threshold One: J. RICHELSON & D. BALL, *supra* (on U.S.-UK intelligence sharing); Hersh, *Congress is Accused of Laxity on C.I.A.'s Covert Activity*, N.Y. Times, June 1, 1978, at A1, col. 6 (on security equipment for Egypt); L. JOHNSON, AMERICA'S SECRET POWER: THE CIA IN A DEMOCRATIC SOCIETY 31–35 (1989) (on routine counterintelligence).

Note: Two points ought to be emphasized about this table. First, it is meant to be illustrative, not exhaustive, and simply to show that covert operations have been widely carried out by Western intelligence services. Second, while this study focuses on *Western* intelligence practices, the former Soviet Union and other non-Western nations have also engaged robustly in this entire range of covert operations. On this second point, see note 16 *supra*.

task of drawing a "bright line" separating acceptable strategic intelligence operations from those that may be rejected as unacceptable.

II. INFLUENCES ON THE USE OF COVERT OPERATIONS

What (if anything) is beyond the pale of acceptability in the spectrum of strategic intelligence operations outlined in Table 23.1? Can—should—a bright line be drawn, proscribing (at least for Western intelligence services) certain repugnant covert practices?

A considerable amount of printer's ink has been devoted to these important questions.[17] The issues are complex and good people part company in response.[18] As with most complicated social questions, where one stands regarding the usefulness and legitimacy of strategic intelligence options depends considerably upon one's earlier education, socialization, evolving political and international perspectives (weltanschauung or "operational codes") and peer group influences, not to mention global circumstances and media reporting, among other influences on the formation of foreign-policy beliefs.[19] Before attempting to answer the difficult bright-line question, it may be useful to consider in summary form some key variables that most analysts consider important in evaluating covert operations.

ETHICAL PERSPECTIVES

One's sense of proper morality in the conduct of international affairs will influence how one assesses the options presented in Table 23.1. "Do no evil, though the world shall perish," urged the eighteenth-century German philosopher Immanuel Kant. Taken to the extreme for strategic intelligence considerations, the Kantian school (the "deontologists," in philosophical jargon) would reject every rung on the ladder of escalation beyond the first. In this spirit, Secretary of State Henry L. Stimson is reported to have closed down his Department's cryptographic division in 1929 with the aphorism "Gentlemen do not read other people's mail" (a view he soon rejected as imprudent in an increasingly dangerous world).[20]

A former Under Secretary of State has suggested that the United States "ought to discourage the idea of fighting secret wars or even initiating most covert operations." He continues:

> When…we mine harbors in Nicaragua…we fuzz the difference between ourselves and the Soviet

Union. We act out of character….When we yield to what is, in my judgment, a childish temptation to fight the Russians on their own terms and in their own gutter, we make a major mistake and throw away one of our great assets.[21]

At the opposite ethical extreme is a point of view so nationalistic that virtually any use of secret intelligence agencies in defense of the nation-state becomes acceptable. The consequences of one's acts are more important, from this vantage point, than the intrinsic worthiness (or unworthiness) of the acts themselves. If the consequence is to help preserve the nation against a foreign threat, the act is justifiable. In light of the present anarchic and hostile world environment, a nation must defend itself in every possible way—including by using all the dark arts available through the secret services.

Arguing from this realist's viewpoint, a top-secret U.S. government report concluded in 1954: "We must learn to subvert, sabotage and destroy our enemies by more clear, more sophisticated and more effective methods than those used against us." The report went on to observe: "It may become necessary that the American people will be made acquainted with, understand and support this fundamentally repugnant philosophy."[22] In the next decade, Secretary of State Dean Rusk warned that the United States would have to "fight in the back alleys of the world."[23] More recently, a former CIA official questioned rhetorically: "Must the United States respond like a man in a barroom brawl who will fight only according to Marquis of Queensberry rules?"[24] (G. Gordon Liddy, a former CIA officer and Watergate conspirator, has put it even more colloquially on the campus lecture circuit: "The world isn't Beverly Hills; it's a bad neighborhood at 2:00 o'clock in the morning."[25])

In between the poles of Kantian and consequentialist morality lies a vast expanse of strategic intelligence options less pure in form than the two extremes of "Do no evil" and "Do anything" (and even the consequentialists cited above would no doubt disagree on how far a nation ought to march down the road of "anything goes"—certainly, Dean Rusk has a more refined sense of moral limits than G. Gordon Liddy). In making moral judgments about covert options in this middle ground, some analysts might blanch at the measures listed for Thresholds One and Two on the ladder of escalation; most, though, probably would not. Ethical debate can grow quite heated, however, over the more intrusive interventions against national sovereignty envisaged at Thresholds Three and Four.

Even those ethicists who generally prefer nonintervention are prepared, nonetheless, to acknowledge the existence of certain conditions in which the use of secret intelligence agencies abroad may be in order. Foremost among these conditions, for some analysts, is simple self-defense—a central stanchion in the traditional theory of the just war (though the term "self-defense" can be notoriously slippery).[26] High on the list, too, is the moral imperative to help people who face enslavement, wholesale brutality or genocide—covert intervention on humanitarian grounds.[27]

Others would add to this list the need to assist oppressed friends of Western democratic values (or, at least, anti-Communists) who ask for help—a considerable opening of the interventionist door.[28] Going a step further, some ethicists would defend the sovereign independence of any state, regardless of regime type; they prefer to honor, above all, the inviolability of national boundaries as a central postulate of contemporary international law (the main public defense of the U.S. insistence, supported by the United Nations in 1990, that Iraq remove its invasion force from neighboring Kuwait).[29] Some would use only the degree of force that was proportional to the perceived threat—another key postulate of just war theory.[30] Still others would eschew most unilateral actions, seeking greater moral legitimacy in multilateral intervention.[31] Practical considerations are also essential to some analysts: they argue that, to be acceptable, covert intervention must have a good chance of succeeding and should be in harmony with the overt policy positions of the sponsoring nation.[32]

While these propositions (like the wider literature they briefly summarize) are clouded in ambiguity, the spires of four fundamental conclusions poke through the mists. The first, as recently expressed by two intelligence officials, posits that "given the depravity of the world around us...free societies have no choice but to engage in intelligence activities if they are to remain free."[33] The underlying assumption here—one accepted by most contemporary scholars, government leaders and citizens—is an acceptance of the preeminence of the nation-state and the correctness of its defense. World order theorists have a different vision, perhaps ultimately a better one, in which global human needs gain ascendancy over state interests; but, for the present at least, their arguments remain quixotic.[34]

If one accepts the need for some intelligence activities, the next question becomes: which ones are acceptable? At this point, the second major ethical conclusion emerges, namely, that this determination depends morally upon the extent to which one is willing to accept loss of life—(collateral damage, in Pentagon language)—and the physical destruction of property as a part of one's covert intervention.[35] Here are the considerations that give one pause about Threshold Four and lend it the epithet "extreme."

A third major conclusion follows from the second: while agreement on the moral acceptability of low-threshold intelligence activities is widespread, the appropriateness of higher-threshold activities is a subject riven by dissension. As a former CIA director accurately states, "There are few absolutes in the ethics of covert action."[36] Experts and laymen alike are frequently of two minds on when, or even whether, covert violence ought to be part of a nation's foreign policy.

In light of this disagreement, the fourth conclusion—a procedural one that lies at the heart of this analysis—is that no single authority ought to make this important decision. Rather, in a free society—and on contentious issues in particular—decision by a group of elected officials is more appropriate (though, for sensitive intelligence matters, one small in size and whose deliberations are conducted in secrecy when the delicacy of international affairs so requires). The great moral issues of covert intervention warrant debate, even if confined to a more limited number of elected officials than normally participate in policy deliberations in Western democracies. These often far-reaching decisions stand to benefit significantly from the virtues of a candid dialogue between the branches: from the airing of different points of view and the pooling of experience and insight; in a word, from democracy.

Difficult ethical issues may not be resolved in any definitive fashion by a group decision process; but pooling the ethical judgments of leading officials has a better chance of arriving at a worthy outcome than entrusting the outcome to one or two individuals deciding alone. At any rate, this is the gamble that underpins constitutional democracy.

VIEW OF THE ENEMY

Just as ethical perspectives are important in determining the proper level of intrusiveness abroad, so, too, is one's perception of the adversary. For some, the adversary is so venal, intractable and dangerous—the devil incarnate—that the us-them relationship can only be zero-sum. Mixing realpolitik with Bible-belt morality, a chairman of the House Committee on Armed Services once referred to the U.S.-Soviet competition in the 1960s as "a battle between Jesus Christ and the hammer-and-sickle."[37] No room for reconciliation here; therefore, extreme intelligence options designed to subdue the Soviet Satan become acceptable, even attractive.

Others hold a more hopeful outlook toward the adversary as someone with whom one may deal, cautiously to be sure, but with a reasonable chance of a positive-sum outcome. As illustrated by President Ronald Reagan's transition from denouncing the Soviet Union as an "evil empire" to rejecting this characterization, attitudes regarding the enemy can change—and, presumably with them, the acceptability of harsh strategic intelligence options directed against the erstwhile foe. (This transformation can also operate in the reverse direction, as shown by President Jimmy Carter's switch to a harder line—and a raft of fresh covert actions—against the Soviets following their surprise invasion of Afghanistan in 1979.)[38]

TARGET REGIMES

The type of target regime is also significant, as the "democracy-autocracy" rungs on the ladder of escalation are meant to underscore. Some analysts believe that, in selecting strategic intelligence options, it makes a difference whether one has targeted free and open societies, on the one hand, or closed totalitarian and authoritarian regimes, on the other hand. In targeting the former, they argue, one ought to be more circumspect and less intrusive; as regards the latter, restraints can be fewer—especially against the totalitarian regimes, which (some maintain) represent a greater threat to Western civilization than authoritarian ones.[39]

Covert propaganda serves as an illustration. To interfere with the free press in a democracy (say, the London *Times*) is abhorrent to some, striking at a central root of Western values; yet, since *Pravda* and *Isvestiia*, for example, were widely considered as mere organs of the Soviet Communist Party (until recently), trying to influence their pronouncements was fair game.[40] (These distinctions regarding regimes lose much of their force, however, at Threshold Four where the dangers to innocents are magnified.)

LEADERSHIP PERSONALITY

Although political science as a discipline has been slow to recognize the importance of individual personalities as an influence on public affairs, selected writers from Aristotle to Harold Lasswell have underscored the analytic value of this approach to the study of government. Closely related to the questions of one's ethical perspective and perception of the enemy, discussed earlier, differing personality characteristics can lead policy makers toward divergent views on the efficacy and appropriateness of the various strategic intelligence options.

The Reagan administration's first Director of Central Intelligence (DCI), William J. Casey, by reputation a hard-core, zero-sum, anti-Communist "tough guy," was presumably more prepared to move up the ladder of escalation than, say, one of his predecessors, William E. Colby, who acknowledged some moral restraints on covert operations and harbored some sense of the possibilities for détente with the Soviet Union.[41] Certainly, the funding for covert action declined precipitously under Colby and rose sharply under Casey.[42] Although these budget trends occurred for several reasons extending far beyond simply the personalities of the DCIs in office, one speculates (hard data are elusive on most questions of personality) with some confidence that their individual make-up played a role—with Casey the fiery Cold War combatant and Colby the more restrained pragmatist.

IMMINENT THREAT

If information is the sine qua non of good decision making, time as a variable stands close by in importance. An assessment of intelligence options will depend on one's sense of imminent threat to the national security. If (to use an extreme scenario) a nation's leaders believed that a major city in their territory—perhaps the capital itself—were about to be vaporized by a nuclear bomb stolen by terrorists, they would no doubt use every means available to avoid this calamity. The means would presumably include even the assassination of the suspected terrorists, if the nation's leaders were persuaded that murder would prevent the greater number of deaths resulting from a nuclear explosion—a consequentialist's imperative. Given the luxury of more time (the normal circumstance), the ladder of escalation can be climbed more slowly and with greater deliberation.

SEVERITY OF THE THREAT

Relevant, too, as the above scenario implies, is the perceived severity of the threat. Terrorists armed with nuclear weapons demand a quick and highly intrusive response. In contrast, Greenpeace environmentalists in creaky, old sailing vessels protesting nuclear testing in the Pacific Ocean represent a much more modest threat to a nation's sovereignty, warranting only a low-rung covert response (if any at all). Certainly, the bombing in 1983 of the *Rainbow Warrior* in Auckland harbor by two French intelligence officers represents a response far out of proportion to the threat—however accidental the death of a Greenpeace photographer on board may have been. The bombing was also a provocative slap at New Zealand's sovereignty (not to mention the civil liberties of the owners and passengers of the ship). If the French had felt so threatened by the *Rainbow Warrior* (a "bucket of bolts," according to a New Zealand national security official), disabling the ship at sea with a low-charge explosive on the propeller shaft—or even tangled wire—would have been enough covert action to deter its further passage.[43]

Prevailing conditions of war or peace are necessary considerations, as well. If one nation is involved in an overt military conflict with another nation, whether or not formally declared, its leaders have presumably decided the threat to their national interests is sufficiently grave to warrant a major foreign-policy response. In these conditions—and especially in circumstances of a formally declared war—covert operations are likely to be stepped up. (The high point of covert-action budgeting by the United States in the postwar period coincides with the zenith of U.S. involvement in Vietnam, as the American Government funded expensive paramilitary operations in support of its overt fighting.[44]) Indeed, in a major overt war, assassination plots against the adversary's leaders and other extreme measures become standard fare—although even the rules of open warfare proscribe some activities, such as the use of chemical and biological agents against noncombatants. In times of overt warfare, then, while not all bets are off on moral restraint, a good many are when it comes to supportive strategic intelligence.[45]

SHORT-TERM AND LONG-TERM EFFECTS

Ideally, one would also like to know before judging the appropriateness of a covert operation what its effects will be on the future of the target nation, its people and their relationship toward the perpetrator of the covert operation. This is the most difficult task of all, for the seeds of time reveal to no mortal which grain will grow and which will not. While it may have seemed appropriate at the time for the CIA to encourage, covertly, rebellion among Hungarian and Ukrainian freedom fighters in the 1950s, the end result was disastrous for the erstwhile rebels.

Looking back at America's covert relationship with the Kurds, the Bay of Pigs invaders, the Meo tribesmen and others, one critic sees them as "so many causes and peoples briefly taken up by the CIA and then tossed aside like broken toys."[46] To what extent do Western (or non-Western) nations have a confident sense of the historical forces their covert operations may unleash? The answer is very little—especially over the long term. Clearly, the United States was unable to anticipate how despised the Shah of Iran would become within his own nation after the CIA (and British intelligence) helped him into power in 1953.

The inherent difficulty of predicting long-range historical outcomes has been exacerbated by the ignorance the United States has sometimes displayed about the circumstances within target nations. High-level ignorance of Fidel Castro's wide popularity in Cuba (a phenomenon well understood by CIA analysts) led U.S. officials to endorse the ill-fated Bay of Pigs paramilitary operation in 1961, which was advocated by the CIA's paramilitary specialists. Can-do covert-action bureaucrats displaced intelligence analysts from the decision process, leaving policy makers with the one-sided view that Castro could easily be toppled.[47]

While mistakes and misjudgments will continue to occur as long as human beings remain fallible, governments contemplating covert intervention ought at a minimum, as Charles Beitz has noted, "to know enough about the culture and values of the target society to make informed judgments about its welfare, and enough about its politics and history to calculate the likely consequences of the kinds of intervention contemplated."[48] This level of understanding requires greater attention by decision makers to the recommendations of intelligence analysts and outside academic experts (though the expertise of covert-action specialists is frequently valuable and ought to be weighed, too).

III. A BRIGHT LINE ON THE LADDER OF COVERT ESCALATION

Taking these considerations into account, where should one draw a bright line against excessive covert operations? As suggested earlier, this question defies a single easy answer by any one policy maker, whether president, prime minister or a ranking member of the legislative branch. Each important covert operation warrants inspection on a case-by-case basis, drawing upon the substantive knowledge and ethical wisdom of a small number of well-informed individuals: elected officials in the executive and legislative branches (and their top aides) who understand the theory and practice of strategic intelligence, who have studied the conditions in the target nation and its region, and, most important in a democracy, who are sensitive to the likely attitudes of the American public toward the proposed secret intervention.

THE IMPORTANCE OF PROCESS

This essay emphasizes the importance of a thorough decision-making process for covert operations. It advocates the involvement of elected officials with national security experience, assisted by well-trained intelligence and foreign-policy specialists who understand the possibilities—as well as the limitations and dangers—of using secret agencies in support of democratic values.

Who should stand within this "witting circle" of strategic intelligence decision makers? The model used in the United States at present approaches a good balance between secrecy and accountability. Important intelligence initiatives are first thoroughly scrutinized by intelligence professionals, then by top policy aides in the executive branch, followed by their principals (including, since December of 1974, formal presidential approval for covert actions), and, finally, by the House and Senate intelligence committees. In times of emergency, the number of legislative participants is limited to just the top eight leaders of Congress.[49]

Ambiguity and controversy continue to surround these procedures, especially over whether the congressional intelligence committees (or at least the top leaders of Congress) should be provided with prior notification of all important intelligence operations. Since passage of the 1980 Intelligence Oversight Act, which seemed to require prior notice (though the language contains some ambiguities), the White House has failed to honor this understanding in only a single known instance: the Iran-contra affair.[50]

Notwithstanding this significant breach, most officials in the intelligence community, the White House and the Congress have come to accept the new oversight as an appropriate means for deciding on strategic intelligence operations and at the same time trying to keep the secret services within the boundaries of American law and the prevailing sense of propriety. The great tragedy of the Iran-contra episode, critics stress, was the disdainful attitude of high officials toward this delicate balance. Some individuals in the Reagan administration evidently failed to understand the intelligence investigations of 1975 and the resulting bipartisan reforms; or, more likely, they understood, but rejected, the idea of legislative involvement in intelligence policy.[51] "Excluding Congress [during the Iran-contra operations] also excluded one more 'political scrub,'" concludes Gregory F. Treverton, "one more source of advice about what the range of American people would find acceptable."[52]

Why was Congress excluded? The administration's National Security Adviser, Vice Adm. John M. Poindexter, himself a key participant in approving the controversial operations, testified before Congress: "I didn't want any interference."[53] Nor, apparently, did the Director of the CIA. According to the testimony of Lt. Col. Oliver L. North (Poindexter's aide), CIA Director Casey sought the establishment of an entity "that was self-financing, independent of appropriated monies and capable of conducting activities similar to the ones that we had conducted [the Iran-contra operations]."[54] Casey's goal, continued North, was nothing less than an "off-the-shelf, self-sustaining, stand-alone" supersecret agency within the CIA, completely unaccountable to outside authorities. Moreover, executive and legislative investigators learned that the Iran-contra planners had even excluded the President, as a way of allowing the White House plausible "deniability."[55] In short, they excluded democracy.

The rejection of democratic procedures by National Security Council (NSC) staffers during the Iran-contra affair points to another critical element of strategic intelligence: the importance of personal integrity of those holding positions of public responsibility. As the Greeks well understood, the forms of government—the decision processes emphasized here—are but empty shells; they must be made to work by honest individuals who possess more than mere love for their country. They must also have a deep appreciation of the principles of democracy—a system of governing that, as a guard against the abuse of power, depends upon the kind of "interference" so disdained by Admiral Poindexter.[56] Ironically, military personnel are generally imbued with a strong sense of ethics and the importance of democratic procedure: above all, the idea, vital to constitutional government, of civilian supremacy in decision making. In the Iran-contra case, however, this socialization failed with respect to Poindexter and North.

Admiral Poindexter professes that he was simply the victim of a liberal attack aimed at the Reagan administration.[57] How widely this view is shared is unknown (although some Republicans on the congressional Iran-contra investigating committees seemed prepared in their "Minority Report" to exonerate the admiral and his staff[58]). To many critics, however, the affair went much deeper than partisan politics, striking at the foundations of constitutional government by undermining the appropriations process, as well as the sanctity of law and the established intelligence-reporting requirements. The judicial system found Poindexter and North guilty of various felony counts; and leading Republicans and Democrats, conservatives and liberals alike, spoke against the controversial operations of the NSC staff during hearings and investigations into the affair.[59]

Consequently, when one speaks of process as vital to the assessment of strategic intelligence options, one must in the same breath add a caveat: as always in discussions of legitimate government, officeholders are expected to honor the laws and respect the rights and opinions of those to whom, in a democracy, they owe their office, the people. In turn, the people in modern society are forced to rely chiefly upon their elected surrogates in both Congress and the White House to monitor and assess the wisdom of secret foreign-policy initiatives.

GUIDELINES FOR APPRAISING PROPOSED COVERT INTERVENTIONS

A case-by-case examination relying upon a small, bipartisan group of executive-legislative overseers is, then, the most sensible approach to evaluating the acceptability of covert operations (especially since ethical standards in a society can change). This review process, however, need not begin anew each time in a vacuum; some widely accepted standards can provide at least general guidance to the deliberations.

THRESHOLD FOUR. On the ladder of escalation presented in Table 23.1, most observers would probably agree that Western nations can shun altogether the highest rung—the use of chemical-biological agents and other toxic substances. The other extreme

options of Threshold Four (Rungs 27–37) should garner support in only the most extraordinary circumstances: when the survival of one's society is at stake (self-defense), or for humanitarian purposes when passivity might lead to enslavement, wholesale brutality or genocide within a heinous regime (see the following).

One perplexing scenario at Threshold Four arises when an indigenous, democratically inclined faction asks for covert assistance to overthrow an autocratic regime or to repel foreign intruders. In such instances, sophisticated arms supplies (Rung 27), small-scale coups (Rung 35) and eventually even major "secret" wars —"overt-covert" intervention (Rung 37)—may be indicated. First, however, the prudent policy maker will want to see whether the pro-democracy faction exhibits signs of legitimacy among the indigenous populace, whether it has a viable leadership and a credible organization—that is, some reasonable chance of succeeding, rather than simply raising false hopes—and, whether less-extreme responses might work instead. Among the less-extreme possibilities is Rung 17 or, better still whenever possible, open activity, including economic inducements and punishments, diplomatic negotiations, moral suasion and financial support.[60]

Above all, those who propose secret intervention must remember the risks of being drawn into a swampland of protracted and costly warfare, with no victory in sight—indeed, with the possible decimation of the supported faction. Again, the Kurds in the Middle East and the Meo tribesmen of Laos serve as painful reminders of this possibility, if policy makers will only bother to glance back over the ribbon of the past.

The temptation can be strong to move quickly toward the fourth threshold in an effort to rid the world of an evil dictator. The case of Panama's General Manuel Antonio Noriega may be used to illustrate the arguments. The United States finally chose to depose this autocrat in 1989 through an overt military operation; but, in retrospect, even some analysts who normally eschew clandestine interventions have wondered whether a covert action against Noriega might not have been the lesser of two evils. The appeal of a quick coup—or an assassination—in this and similar cases lies, partially, in the limited loss of life that may accompany a stealthier approach to foreign policy, in contrast to all the collateral damage that an open military invasion brings in its wake. Several hundred civilians were killed in the U.S. attack against Noriega; thousands perished in the attack against Saddam Hussein's armies in the Persian Gulf (1991).

The avoidance of deaths among innocent non-combatants, a central tenet of the just war tradition, is a principle enjoying widespread support; yet the promise of a quick coup or assassination (discussed later)—although such tactics may safeguard innocent civilians—can draw a nation all too readily into unsavory remedies for its international grievances. Better, in the judgment of this observer, to renounce these dark and slippery options in favor of open military action (if all the other overt options have failed)—even if the cost in human lives may sometimes prove to be higher than in a more narrowly conceived paramilitary operation. If intervention had to be open and highly visible, with the possibility of considerable loss of life (civilian and military), policy makers might be more inclined to think with extra care about the necessity of using force to influence the affairs of other nations.

More broadly, U.S. policy makers might well contemplate more seriously whether it is really the responsibility of this nation to rid the world of dictators. Does the United States have the resources—money, lives, will—for this mission? From the American point of view, was Noriega—as repugnant as he obviously is—the most dangerous or heinous threat for the U.S. military to target for attack (say, over the Colombian drug lords)? Was his forced extradition to the United States for trial as a drug dealer worth the lives of those killed, American and Panamanian, during the invasion?

If force is to be used against a dictator, a multilateral overt operation would be preferable to a U.S. paramilitary operation in all but a few extreme situations (examined in a moment); it bears emphasis, however, that overt intervention itself ought to be a matter of last resort, turned to only when U.S. interests are directly and obviously assailed. For the most part, the unfortunate, worldwide problem of dictatorial regimes must be combated through diplomacy, trade sanctions and moral suasion (using, among other things, the increasingly strong force of world media condemnation to turn tyrants into international pariahs). Above all, the United States must rely upon the indigenous population itself to rise up against a cruel master, just as the American colonists did in 1776 against difficult odds and, more recently, the courageous citizens of Eastern Europe and the Soviet Union. These democratic rebellions may then

warrant measured support, overt and covert, from external sources—especially where political rights have been suffocated.

Two important exceptions, mentioned earlier, may be stated to the overt-over-covert rule: the use of covert operations in self-defense against possible attack by weapons of mass annihilation, and for humanitarian purposes against autocrats with genocidal designs. First, if a dictator is reliably believed to be on the verge of obtaining a capacity to use chemical, biological or nuclear weapons against other nations or groups, this threat must be dealt with before it is too late. In 1981 Israel chose an overt military air strike to destroy an Iraqi nuclear reactor in Baghdad thought to be used for making nuclear bombs. In lieu of unilateral action of this kind, a limited paramilitary strike—ideally, multinational in character—may be indicated in the future against outlaw regimes that threaten a chemical-biological or nuclear offensive.

Ideally, the covert action would involve a small force acting under proper international (ideally, UN) authority and with the most exacting supervision. When diplomatic initiatives fail to curb the weapons appetite of outlaw regimes, this approach may serve as a better alternative—in the extreme case of chemical-biological or nuclear threats—than a full-scale military invasion, with all the loss of civilian lives that option usually entails.

The second exception, for which a similar response would be indicated, is the Hitler-like mass murderer. Leaders of this bent warrant arrest by a multinational paramilitary arm—again, ideally under UN authority and supervision—followed by a fair trial.

THRESHOLD THREE. The options of Threshold Three are similarly clouded by broad patches of gray. Again, the best approach is to tilt against their use unless the reasons for accepting them are compelling (based on the opinion, in the American case, of the President and the members of the intelligence committees) and never to accept an option that would violate the laws binding the sponsoring government. For Thresholds Three and Four, policy makers would do well to recall the prudent prescription tendered by John Quincy Adams in his inaugural address. America, in his view, should try to be "the friend of all the liberties in the world, [but] the guardian of only her own."

Thoughtful critics have long emphasized the wisdom of keeping the more extreme covert options in reserve for only the most pressing circumstances. Just when "absolutely essential," said soon-to-be Secretary of State Cyrus Vance in 1975 about covert action; only when they "truly affect our national security," seconded Clark Clifford, a drafter of the 1947 National Security Act and a former Secretary of Defense, also in 1975; just for "a grave, unforeseen threat," advised the Church Committee in 1976; and only when "conducted in an accountable manner and in accordance with law," concluded the majority report of the Iran-contra congressional investigative committees in 1988.[61]

THRESHOLDS ONE AND TWO. At the bottom end of the ladder, Thresholds One and Two will probably continue to be acceptable behavior (in this imperfect world) to most practitioners and observers. Perhaps even these options will be eliminated one day, when human beings overcome their petty hostilities toward one another and are willing to live in a world of respectful neighbors (comparable to the union of the United States since Reconstruction).

SPELLING OUT THE GUIDELINES. In characterizing strategic intelligence options, other metaphors in addition to the escalation ladder are suggestive, among them the practice of medicine. Like the physician, the managers of strategic intelligence should employ the least interventionist means possible to cure the illness, inflicting the least amount of violence on the patient.

The practice of law is suggestive, too. The strategic intelligence decision circle can be thought of as a "courtroom" within the confines of the executive and legislative branches. Here is where elected officials (the President, Vice President and intelligence committee members—or just the two executive officers and the top eight leaders of Congress in times of emergency) serve as a bipartisan standing jury, allowing an opportunity for devil's advocacy among top officials before decisions that may affect a nation's destiny are cast in concrete.[62]

The various thoughts and caveats surveyed in this analysis suggest a checklist of eleven guidelines for consideration by those responsible for deciding upon the merits of proposed covert operations:

1. Whenever possible, shun covert operations in favor of diplomatic resolution of international disputes.

2. Keep covert operations in harmony with publicly stated policy objectives.

3. Conduct only those covert operations which, if exposed, would not unduly embarrass the United States.

4. Consult with intelligence analysts and other experts, not just covert-action specialists, before proceeding.

5. Never bypass established decision procedures, including reporting requirements (which, except in times of acute emergency, ought to be prospective, not merely retrospective).

6. Never violate the laws of the United States (short of the rare Lincolnesque need to save the nation in a time of desperation).

7. Against fellow democracies eschew all but the most routine covert operations.

8. Even against nondemocratic regimes, remain at the lower, less-intrusive end of the escalation ladder, applying the just war rule of proportionality and rising upward only in despair.

9. Reject arrangements for information sharing or other intelligence activities with any nation practicing, or allowing within its territory, a consistent pattern of gross violations of internationally recognized human rights.

10. In almost all cases, reject secret wars, coups d'état and other extreme measures, for if America's interests are so jeopardized as to require major forceful intervention, properly authorized overt warfare—ideally, multinational in nature and at the invitation of a legitimate government or faction—is a more appropriate and honorable option.

11. In considering covert operations, always remember above all the importance to the United States of its longstanding tradition of fair play.

The first guideline may seem obvious enough. All too often, however, policy makers are tempted to try a silent "quick fix" through the use of secret agencies (the "quiet option"), rather than to employ trained diplomatic negotiators (who themselves may have to engage in secret discussions with adversaries, a much more time-honored and acceptable procedure than secret intelligence operations). A too-quick dismissal of the diplomatic approach in favor of a paramilitary hostage rescue attempt in Iran led Secretary of State Vance to resign from the Carter administration over Middle East policy.[63]

The second guideline, if followed by the Reagan administration, would have stopped it short of a secret sale of arms to Iran (another paramilitary operation) in sharp contradiction to America's overt policy of refusing to sell weapons to terrorist groups or their allies. Some thoughtful observers maintain that a two-track foreign policy may be necessary at times, with the open track going in one direction to fool adversaries and the secret track going in another direction toward a nation's true objectives. In time of war, deceptive operations are obviously useful and will always be employed in combat situations; but, short of open warfare or other situations of acute emergency, the existence of two diverging tracks leads only to a disjointed foreign policy and ought to be avoided. Seeking détente with the Soviet Union, for example, while carrying out aggressive covert actions against it (as occurred during key periods of the postwar era) rarely made sense.[64]

The third guideline would make policy makers think twice about secret alliances with particularly unsavory individuals, like General Noriega for intelligence collection, former Nazis for counterintelligence (Klaus Barbie for one), and organized crime figures for assassination plots.[65] This is not to say that the United States should deal only with angels (they are in short supply) but to suggest that, even in the pursuit of national objectives, some limits ought to be recognized. Americans have long recoiled from the crass philosophy that the end justifies the means.

The fourth guideline seeks to avoid the trap of "groupthink." Study after study of U.S. intelligence has revealed a tendency to drive lower- and middle-level officials (individuals with genuine country expertise)—especially analysts during times of crisis—from policy forums in favor of reliance on more action-oriented, covert-action specialists who may understand less about the history and culture of the target nation.[66] This tendency does not mean that policy makers should go to the other extreme and discount the views of covert-action experts; the best of those in the CIA's Operations Directorate have genuine country expertise and a prudent sense of what will work (the Bay of Pigs mistake notwithstanding). A key objective of these consultations with specialists should be to calculate, to the extent possible, the likely side effects (long- and short-term) of a covert intervention.

Guidelines 5 and 6 emphasize the importance of honoring the established decision process for covert operations. Here the purpose—so vital in a democracy—is to maintain both dialogue and

accountability, drawing upon the collective judgment of Congress and the President, touted earlier. (Recall that the "never" in guideline 6 falls short of denying the President the right to take those steps he or she considers necessary to save the nation, steps for which the President will later be held accountable.) Of the various prescriptions presented here, none is more central than this emphasis on process: *never bypass established decision procedures.*

The remaining guidelines, Nos. 7 through 11, underscore the special place of democratic values in the world's political evolution.[67] The seventh, for example, acknowledges the value that Americans place in the global fellowship of democracies. The nurturing of free societies—perhaps never more vital than now, as the quest for liberty shows new strength in once-captive nations—has done great harm when America's leaders order harsh covert operations against fellow democracies. This final set of guidelines recognizes that the higher rungs on the ladder of escalation are fraught with risk and clouded with ethical doubt. Indeed, in circumstances serious enough to warrant the consideration of covert options above Rung 23, the use of overt force backed by a formal declaration of war (or at least given legitimacy through the provisions of the War Powers Resolution) would be in order. As for the exceptions—when a renegade regime approaches chemical-biological or nuclear weapons sufficiency, and when a mass murderer conducts genocide within his society—a paramilitary operation (as described earlier) can be justified.

Among the more controversial, and questionable, options on the escalation ladder is the assassination plot. Almost always, it remains an unworthy, illegal and, for that matter, impractical approach to America's international problems.[68] Even if one places ethical considerations aside, assassination plots invite retaliation against U.S. leaders, who are highly vulnerable in our open society. Further, the execution of a foreign leader offers no assurance that the next-in-command will be any more favorably disposed toward the United States (say, if Raúl Castro replaced his brother Fidel). Such plots are also difficult to implement; certainly, Castro proved able to elude the many CIA attempts against his life.[69]

On this macabre subject, one can speculate on a range of possible scenarios. The Hitler scenario is usually the first to be raised. What if the United States, France or Britain had murdered Hitler before the war? What if his second-in-command would have followed a different path with regard to the Holocaust or to expanding the external war? And even if Hitler's assassination had brought about a retaliation against Franklin D. Roosevelt, would it still not have been worth trading two lives for the six million lost in the Holocaust?

The trouble with these and similar questions is that they are too speculative: the monstrous intentions of Adolf Hitler were less clear before the war (*Mein Kampf* notwithstanding) than they became later. Further, his underlings seem in retrospect to have been as mad as he—perhaps madder in some instances. Should it be U.S. policy to assassinate all who are, or might become, venal tyrants—and their immediate staff and relatives, too, just to be on the safe side? And is the matter of retaliation— the safety of our own leaders—unimportant? Even if the evidence is compelling that the prevention of genocide is at stake, better to arrest and try a monster of Hitler's proportions than to resort to assassination—though if he resists arrest by a legitimate force, death could be the immediate (if unintended) consequence.

In times of war, properly authorized by Congress, assassination takes on a different coloration. As a former CIA Director, Admiral Stansfield Turner, has put it:

> [Assassination] is tempting to me only in wartime. I would have approved assassinating Saddam Hussein after the 16th of January [1991, the date

when Congress gave its authority to use force against Hussein's armies as the U.S. President saw fit]. And that's exactly the reason: there's a big difference between a President—and, heaven help us, somebody below him—taking it on him- or herself to say, "Noriega ought to die," and the Congress of the United States and the public of the United States saying, "We're going to war with Panama, and Noriega is just as much a target as Joe Jones, Private First-Class." And if you happen to target Noriega specifically—and surely we targeted Saddam Hussein, [but] it didn't work—I think that's all right.[70]

The eleventh guideline stands as a reminder that Americans take pride in the difference between their country and autocratic regimes. This nation's reputation for fair play—often stained by CIA excesses— has distinguished American foreign policy from the approach of more brutal governments and has won respect and friendship for the United States in many parts of the world. In the interest of maintaining this vital difference between dictators and democracies, Roger Fisher (among others) has argued against using the coercive instruments of covert action. He urges, instead, greater reliance on "the most powerful weapons we have: idealism, morality, due process of law, and belief in the freedom to disagree, including the right of other countries to disagree with ours."[71]

In Table 23.3, instances of failed U.S. covert operations are presented to suggest how they might have

TABLE 23.3   FAILED U.S. OPERATIONS THAT MIGHT HAVE BEEN REJECTED OR MODIFIED THROUGH THE FILTER OF THE RECOMMENDED GUIDELINES

Guidelines	Ill-Begotten U.S. Secret Operations (Selected)[a]
1.	Iran rescue attempt (1980)
2.	Iran arms sale (1984)
3.	Funding of Christian Democratic Party in Italy (1979)
4.	Bay of Pigs (1961)
5.	Contra diversion (1985)
6.	Operation CHAOS (1967–1974)
7.	Anti-Allende operations in Chile (1963–1973)
8.	Escalation of covert actions in Nicaragua (1982–1987)
9.	Ties with Panama dictator Gen. Noriega (1975–1989)
10.	Anti-Diem activities in Vietnam (1963)
11.	Assassination plots in Cuba and the Congo (1960–1965)

[a] On these operations, see L. JOHNSON, AMERICA'S SECRET POWER: THE CIA IN A DEMOCRATIC SOCIETY (1989).

been avoided (or at least modified) by adherence to these eleven guidelines.

IV. CONCLUSION

Can the West truly compete in the present international arena without resorting to extreme covert operations, when its adversaries have often seemed prepared to carry out the most ruthless measures against the democracies? Thoughtful people disagree on this question. This observer is persuaded, however, that the democracies will win their ideological battle with the nondemocratic regimes mainly by virtue of their higher principles and more humane behavior, together with their greater economic prowess. The people of the world care most about food and shelter, clean air and pure water, the education of their children, and their rights to good health, political dissent, liberty, justice and happiness. The West has much to offer here.

As a leading member of the U.S. House Committee on Foreign Affairs has said, "The best way to promote our interests is to promote our ideals."[72] In contrast, brutality, coercion and violence—too often the specialties of nondemocratic regimes—are poor alternatives. Those who ply these wares have won no admiration, only fear—an inefficient means of achieving societal cohesion.

The excessive use of highly intrusive intelligence options has done much to discredit the West, making its secret services sometimes seem little different from that of its erstwhile enemy, the Soviet KGB.[73] By employing Western intelligence agencies mainly for low-intrusive collection operations, and by resorting to more aggressive operations—particularly covert actions—only with considered regard for the guidelines presented above, the West can reclaim the high esteem it enjoyed globally in the aftermath of the Second World War.

QUESTIONS FOR FURTHER DISCUSSION

1. What are the mildest forms of covert action? The most severe?
2. How can one evaluate the effectiveness of covert actions?
3. Is it possible to anticipate the long-term effects of a covert action, or can one only attempt to judge the short-term effects?
4. What have been America's most successful and unsuccessful covert actions?

ENDNOTES

1. On the frequency of U.S. covert operations since 1947, see L. JOHNSON, AMERICA'S SECRET POWER: THE CIA IN A DEMOCRATIC SOCIETY 103, fig. 6.1 (1989). A recent, purportedly comprehensive survey of security studies manages to ignore covert operations altogether, focusing instead on overt (especially forcible) forms of intervention. *See* Walt, *The Renaissance of Security Studies,* 35 INT'L SECURITY STUDS. 211 (1991). For a study sensitive to the question of nonforcible intervention (both overt and covert), see Damrosch, *Politics Across Borders: Nonintervention and Nonforcible Influence over Domestic Affairs,* 83 AJIL I (1989). As Damrosch notes: "Most of the scholarly literature on [foreign] intervention in [the] internal affairs [of other nations] has focused on forcible forms of influence." *Id.* at 3.
2. H. KAHN, ON ESCALATION: METAPHORS AND SCENARIOS 37 (1965).
3. *Id.* at 38.
4. On the nonintervention norm, see Damrosch, *supra* note 1, at 6–13.
5. *See* Report of the Special Committee on Principles of International Law concerning Friendly Relations and Co-operation among States, UN Doc. A/6799, at 161 (1967), *quoted in* Damrosch, *supra* note 1, at 10–11. On the use of covert propaganda and secret political financing, see L. JOHNSON, *supra* note 1, at 22–26; and G. TREVERTON, COVERT ACTION: THE LIMITS OF INTERVENTION IN THE POSTWAR WORLD (1987).
6. Damrosch, *supra* note 1, at 11.
7. On the advantages and risks of embassy break-ins, see the testimony of former Attorney General John Mitchell, in *Intelligence Activities: Hearings Before the Senate Select Comm. to Study Governmental Operations with Respect to Intelligence Activities,* 94th Cong., 1st Sess. (1975), Vol. 2, *Huston Plan,* at 123 (chaired by Sen. Frank Church, D., Idaho) [hereinafter *Church Comm. Hearings*]; Richard M. Nixon, response to Interrogatory No. 17, SENATE SELECT COMM. TO STUDY GOVERNMENTAL OPERATIONS WITH RESPECT TO INTELLIGENCE ACTIVITIES, FINAL REPORT, S. REP. NO. 755, 94th Cong., 2d Sess. (1976), BK. 4, SUPPLEMENTARY DETAILED STAFF REPORTS ON FOREIGN AND MILITARY INTELLIGENCE 157–58 [hereinafter CHURCH COMM. REPS.]; *id.,* BK. 1, FOREIGN AND MILITARY INTELLIGENCE 123; and author's interview with James J. Angleton, former CIA Chief of Counterintelligence, L. JOHNSON, *supra* note 1, at 297–98 n.5.
8. Damrosch, *supra* note 1, at 10–11.
9. *Id.* at 36.
10. *Id.* at 46.

11. On the Son Tay prison raid, designed to free U.S. POWs in Vietnam (unsuccessfully, since the prisoners had been evacuated by the North Vietnamese three weeks earlier—an unfortunate intelligence failure), see H. KISSINGER, WHITE HOUSE YEARS 282 (1979); and B. SCHEMMER, THE RAID (1976). On the aborted Iran rescue attempt, see Halperin & Halperin, *The Key West Key,* FOREIGN POL'Y, Winter 1983–84, at 114.

12. The Reagan administration evidently believed, and wanted to spread the word, that the assassination plot in 1984 against Pope John Paul II had been an operation by the Soviet secret service, the KGB, even though the U.S. intelligence community had no compelling evidence to this effect. See remarks by Donald Gregg, a former CIA officer on the NSC staff, in Johnson, *Making the Intelligence 'Cycle' Work,* 2 INT'L J. INTELLIGENCE & COUNTERINTELLIGENCE 17 (1986–87). On a CIA counterintelligence scheme to falsify and distribute copies of Soviet Premier Nikita Khrushchev's "secret speech" denouncing the Stalin era, see Hersh, *The Angleton Story,* N.Y. Times, June 25, 1978, §6 (Magazine), at 13.

13. President George Bush, White House press release, Washington, D.C. (Aug. 15, 1989).

14. A memorable illustration of Soviet practice in this regard was reported by Bob Woodward of the *Washington Post.* According to him (on the basis of interviews with then CIA Director William Casey), the KGB obtained the quick release of three Soviet hostages held by Hezbollah terrorists in Lebanon by seizing a relative of one of the Hezbollah leaders, castrating him, stuffing his testicles in his mouth, shooting him in the head, and dumping his body at a Hezbollah site with the warning that more of the same would occur if the hostages were further detained. B. WOODWARD, VEIL: THE SECRET WARS OF THE CIA, 1981–1987, at 416 (1987).

15. On the CIA's paramilitary operations in Laos, see W. COLBY & P. FORBATH, HONORABLE MEN: MY LIFE IN THE CIA 191–202 (1978); and V. MARCHETTI & J. MARKS, THE CIA AND THE CULT OF INTELLIGENCE 205–06 (1974).

16. *See, e.g.,* J. RICHELSON, SWORD AND SHIELD: THE SOVIET IINTELLIGENCE AND SECURITY APPARATUS (1986); COMPARING FOREIGN INTELLIGENCE: THE US, THE USSR, AND THE THIRD WORLD (R. Godson ed. 1988); and R. SHULTZ & R. GODSON, DEZINFORMATSIA: ACTIVE MEASURES IN SOVIET STRATEGY (1984).

17. See, for example, the series of lead articles in 3 ETHICS & INT'L AFF. (1989); Hulnick & Mattausch, *Ethics and Morality in United States Secret Intelligence,* 12 HARV. J. L. & PUB. POL'Y 509 (1989); J. NYE, ETHICS AND FOREIGN POLICY: AN OCCASIONAL PAPER (Aspen Institute Human Studies, No. 1, 1985); Godfrey, *Ethics and Intelligence,* 56 FOREIGN AFF. 624 (1978); Falk, *CIA Covert Action and International Law,* 12 SOCIETY 39 (1975); and Damrosch, *supra* note 1.

18. See the useful summary of these issues in M. J. Smith, *Ethics and Intervention,* 3 ETHICS & INT'L AFF. 1 (1989).

19. On the operational codes of foreign-policy leaders, see Johnson, *Operational Codes and the Prediction of Leadership Behavior,* in A PSYCHOLOGICAL EXAMINATION OF POLITICAL MAN 80 (M. Herman ed. 1977).

20. *Quoted in* V. MARCHETTI & J. MARKS, *supra* note 15, at 167.

21. *Should the CIA Fight Secret Wars?,* HARPER'S, September 1984, at 1, 37 (round-table discussion, remarks of George Ball).

22. *Quoted in* CHURCH COMM. REPS., *supra* note 7, BK. 1 at 9.

23. *Quoted in id.* at 9.

24. *Should the CIA Fight Secret Wars?, supra* note 21, at 44 (remarks of Ray Cline).

25. Liddy, Lecture at University of Georgia (May 4, 1986) (based on author's notes).

26. See, respectively, Beitz, *Covert Intervention as a Moral Problem,* 3 ETHICS & INT'L AFF. 48 (1989); and Colby, *Public Policy, Secret Action, id.* at 63, 69.

27. *See* M. WALZER, JUST AND UNJUST WARS (1977).

28. *See, e.g.,* Colby, *supra* note 26, at 69. Damrosch, *supra* note 1, at 37, writes: "the nonintervention norm must not become a vehicle for exalting the abstract entity of the state over the protection of individual rights and fundamental freedoms."

29. *See* Smith, *supra* note 18, at 21.

30. On proportionality, see Colby, *supra* note 26, at 65, 66.

31. See, respectively, Treverton, *Imposing a Standard: Covert Action and American Democracy,* 3 ETHICS & INT'L AFF. 27, 32 (1989); and Buultjens, *The Ethics of Excess and Indian Intervention in South Asia, id.* at 82.

32. *See* Treverton, *supra* note 31; and Colby, *supra* note 26.

33. Hulnick & Mattausch, *supra* note 17, at 522.

34. *See, e.g.,* R. JOHANSEN, THE NATIONAL INTEREST AND THE HUMAN INTEREST: AN ANALYSIS OF U.S. FOREIGN POLICY 386 (1980).

35. *See* Buultjens, *supra* note 31.

36. Colby, *supra* note 26, at 69.

37. Rep. L. Mendel Rivers (D., S.C.), *quoted in* McCarry, *Ol' Man Rivers,* ESQUIRE, October 1970, at 171.

38. On Reagan's move away from "evil empire" rhetoric toward more cordial relations with his Soviet counterpart, see the two-part series by Newhouse, *Annals of*

Diplomacy: The Abolitionist, NEW YORKER, Jan. 2 and 9, 1989, at 37 and 51, respectively (the President's first public rejection of the "evil empire" label occurred on May 31, 1988); on Carter's reaction to the Soviet invasion of Afghanistan, see his own account in J. CARTER, KEEPING FAITH 471–89 (1982).

39. *See* Kirkpatrick, *Dictators and Double Standards*, COMMENTARY, November 1979, at 34; and, with a far different conclusion, Damrosch, *supra* note 1.

40. *See* Johnson, *The CIA and the Media*, 1 INTELLIGENCE & NAT'L SECURITY 143 (1986).

41. For Colby on the decline of the Soviet ideological threat (several years before the *glasnost* era), see *Interview with William E. Colby*, U.S. NEWS & WORLD REP., July 3, 1978, at 37, 39. On Casey's aggressive approach to the use of strategic intelligence, see Alpern, *America's Secret Warriors*, NEWSWEEK, Oct. 10, 1983, at 38; and Morris, *William Casey's Past*, Atlanta Const., Aug. 31, 1987, at A11, col. 4. See also CIA Director Stansfield Turner's higher tolerance for the Marxist regime in Nicaragua than that expressed by his successor, William Casey: *From an Ex-CIA Chief: Stop the 'Covert' Operation in Nicaragua*, Wash. Post, Apr. 21, 1983, at C1, col. 2.

42. *See* Johnson, *Covert Action and Accountability: Decision-Making for America's Secret Foreign Policy*, 33 INT'L STUDS. Q. 81, 87 (1989).

43. Conversations with Air Marshal Sir Ewan Jamieson (in charge of New Zealand's counterintelligence at the time of the investigation into the *Rainbow Warrior* bombing), Conference on Military Strategy, Georgia Institute of Technology, Atlanta, Georgia (Aug. 24–26, 1989).

44. Johnson, *supra* note 42, at 87.

45. As one illustration of the distinction made in government circles between peacetime and wartime use of strategic intelligence, the reporting requirements of the Hughes-Ryan Act were considered null and void when the President was acting under the provisions of the War Powers Resolution (though this exemption was removed by legislators in 1980 with passage of the Intelligence Oversight Act, more formally known as the Accountability for Intelligence Activities Act, tit. V of Intelligence Authorization Act for Fiscal Year 1981, Pub. L. No. 96–450, §407(b)(I), 94 Stat. 1975, 1981 (1980), 50 U.S.C. §413 (1988) (amending National Security Act of 1947).

46. Mount, *Spook's Disease*, NAT'L REV., Mar. 7, 1980, at 300, 300.

47. *See* P. WYDEN, BAY OF PIGS: THE UNTOLD STORY (1979).

48. Beitz, *supra* note 26, at 49.

49. On this "Gang of Eight" leading legislators, see L. JOHNSON, *supra* note 1, at 222–29. The 1991 intelligence oversight amendments, tit. VI of Intelligence Authorization Act, Fiscal Year 1991, Pub. L. No. 102–88, 105 Stat. 429, 441 (adopted Aug. 14, 1991), continue this procedure. *Id.* at 443, §503(c)(2).

50. For the 1980 Intelligence Oversight Act, see *supra* note 45. On the strict adherence to this law before the Iran-contra violation, see H.R. REP. No. 705, 100th Cong., 2d Sess. 54 (1988). On the debate over prior notice, see L. JOHNSON, *supra* note 1, at 225–28. The 1991 Intelligence Oversight Authorization Act, *supra* note 49, permits the executive branch more leeway on reporting ("in a timely fashion"—though only in times of "extraordinary circumstances"; 105 Stat. at 443, §503(c)(2) and (3)).

51. *See, e.g., Elliott Abrams Is Guilty*, N.Y. Times, Oct. 11, 1991, at A14, cols. 1–2 (unsigned editorial, citing to this effect State Department official Elliott Abrams, convicted of lying to Congress about the illegal supply of weapons to the contras during the Iran-contra affair). For an argument against any serious legislative oversight of intelligence, see Seabury, *A Massacre Revisited*, 7 FOREIGN INTELLIGENCE LITERARY SCENE 1, 2 (1988).

52. Treverton, *supra* note 31, at 43.

53. For Poindexter's statement, see 8 *Hearings Before the Senate Select Comm. on Secret Military Assistance to Iran and the Nicaraguan Opposition and House Select Comm. to Investigate Covert Arms Transactions with Iran*, 100th Cong., 1st Sess. 159 (1987) (chaired by Sen. Daniel K. Inouye, D., Haw., and Rep. Lee H. Hamilton, D., Ind.) [hereinafter *Inouye-Hamilton Hearings*].

54. *Id.* at 240–41; *see also* REPORT OF THE CONGRESSIONAL COMMITTEES INVESTIGATING THE IRAN-CONTRA AFFAIR, S. REP. NO. 216 & H. REP. NO. 433, 100th Cong., 1st Sess. 333 (1987) [hereinafter INOUYE-HAMILTON REP.]. For an overview of the Iran-contra affair, see T. DRAPER, A VERY THIN LINE: THE IRAN-CONTRA AFFAIR (1991).

55. See, for example, Vice Admiral Poindexter's testimony, *Inouye-Hamilton Hearings*, *supra* note 53; INOUYE-HAMILTON REP., *supra* note 54, at 16, 339; and REPORT OF THE PRESIDENT'S SPECIAL REVIEW BOARD (1987) (Tower Commission report).

56. As Justice Brandeis put it in his famous dictum, "The doctrine of the separation of powers was adopted by the Convention of 1787, not to promote efficiency but to preclude the exercise of arbitrary power." Myers v. United States, 272 U.S. 52, 293 (1926).

57. Fund-raising letter to "Fellow American," signed by John M. Poindexter, Rear Admiral, USN (Ret.), and

reading in part: "I must now face the liberals' accusations surrounding the 'Iran-Contra affair.' And as I stand, one man, alone against the massive onslaught of liberal special interests who want to imprison me for serving my country, I must turn to you for help..." (undated, but received by the author in August 1989).

58. See INOUYE-HAMILTON REP., *supra* note 54, at 431–585 (Minority Report).

59. See W. COHEN & G. MITCHELL, MEN OF ZEAL (1988); and Drew, *Letter from Washington*, NEW YORKER, Mar. 30, 1987, at 111. The case against North was dismissed by a U.S. district court in 1991 after the Iran-contra independent prosecutor announced that he would abandon the prosecution because the immunity granted to North by Congress in 1987 (to gain his testimony in hearings) had created too great an obstacle. *See* Johnston, *Judge in Iran-Contra Trial Drops Case Against North after Prosecutor Gives Up*, N.Y. Times, Sept. 17, 1991, at A1, col. 6, A12, cols. 3–6.

60. *See* the Bush administration's $9 million request to Congress (September 21, 1989) for open support of the anti-Sandinista candidate in Nicaragua's approaching presidential election. Shepard, *Bush Seeks $9 million for Nicaraguan Opposing Ortega in Presidential Bid*, Atlanta J. & Const., Sept. 22, 1989, at A4, col. 1.

61. For the Vance and Clifford testimonies, see *Church Comm. Hearings, supra* note 7, Vol. 7, *Covert Action*, at 50–55. For the Church Committees' conclusion, see CHURCH COMM. REPS., *supra* note 7, BK. 1 at 159; for the Inouye-Hamilton Committees' conclusion, see INOUYE-HAMILTON REP., *supra* note 54, at 383.

62. The Chairman of the Senate Select Committee on Intelligence, David L. Boren (D., Okla.) has suggested that, in times of extraordinary circumstances, the executive branch should be allowed to report to just the Speaker and House Minority Leader and their Senate counterparts, a "Gang of Four." *See* Senator Boren's remarks, Association of Former Intelligence Officers (Mar. 28, 1988), *quoted in* the Association's newsletter. PERISCOPE, Spring 1988, at 8. This recommendation was also advanced in the "Minority Report" of the Inouye-Hamilton Committees, INOUYE-HAMILTON REP., *supra* note 54, at 585.

63. See the former Secretary's account in his memoirs, C. VANCE, HARD CHOICES: CRITICAL YEARS IN AMERICA'S FOREIGN POLICY 598–413 (1983).

64. *See* Johnson, *Strategic Intelligence: An American Perspective*, 3 INT'L J. INTELLIGENCE & COUNTERINTELLIGENCE 299, 323 (1990).

65. On U.S. intelligence ties with Noriega, see *Drugs, Law Enforcement and Foreign Policy: Hearings Before the Senate Subcomm. on Terrorism, Narcotics, and International Operations*, 100th Cong., 2d Sess. 234–43 (1989); on Barbie, see Saxon, *Klaus Barbie, Lyons Nazi Leader, Dies*, N.Y. Times, Sept. 26, 1991, at C19, col. 4; and on CIA ties with organized crime in the 1960s, see SENATE SELECT COMM. TO STUDY GOVERNMENTAL OPERATIONS WITH RESPECT TO INTELLIGENCE ACTIVITIES, ALLEGED ASSASSINATION PLOTS INVOLVING FOREIGN LEADERS: INTERIM REPORT, S. REP. NO. 465, 94th Cong., 1st Sess. (1975). On refusing intelligence cooperation with regimes engaged in human rights violations, see Farer, Low-Intensity Conflict and International Order: The Prospect for Consensus 63 (paper, U.S. Institute of Peace Project on Strengthening World Order and the United Nations Charter System against Secret Warfare and Low-Intensity Conflict, 1990).

66. On the phenomenon of banishing intelligence and other experts from high councils when key decisions are being made (and related policy-making pathologies), see I. JANIS, GROUPTHINK (2d ed. 1982); Jervis, *Intelligence and Foreign Policy*, 11 INT'L SECURITY 141 (1986–87); and Betts, *Analysis, War, and Decision: Why Intelligence Failures Are Inevitable*, 31 WORLD POL. 61 (1978).

67. On this theme, see Damrosch, *supra* note 1, esp. at 37–50; and Farer, *supra* note 65.

68. However, in the two exceptional cases mentioned in the preceding paragraph, if the regime leader is killed during the destruction of the chemical-biological and nuclear facilities (in the first instance), or during his arrest (in the second instance), this unintended result is defensible in light of the need to protect large civilian and innocent populations—a consequentialist verdict that in these situations seems compelling.

On the illegality of assassinations, see Exec. Order No., 12,333, signed by President Ronald Reagan on December 4, 1981, 1981 PUB. PAPERS (RONALD REAGAN) 1128. The order continued a prohibition against assassination initiated by President Gerald R. Ford, Exec. Order No. 11,905, February 18, 1976, 1976–77 PUB. PAPERS (GERALD R. FORD) 349. Since President Bush has never revoked the order, it remains in force. *See* Parks, *Memorandum of Law: Executive Order 12333 and Assassination*, ARMY LAW., December 1989, at 4. Pointing to Article 2(4) of the UN Charter, one authority maintains: "Assassination is unlawful killing, and would be prohibited by international law even if there were no executive order proscribing it." W. Hays Parks,

Chief, International Law Branch, International Affairs Division, Department of the Army, *id.*

69. S. Rep. No. 465, *supra* note 65.

70. Interview with the author, McLean, Virginia (May 1, 1991).

71. Fisher, *The Fatal Flaw in Our Spy System,* Boston Globe, Feb. 1, 1976, at A9, col. 4.

72. Remarks, Rep. Steven J. Solarz (D., N.Y.) (C-Span television broadcast, May 22, 1988).

73. For evidence on this point, see generally Beitz, *supra* note 26; L. Johnson, *supra* note 1; J. Prados, Presidents' Secret Wars: CIA and Pentagon Covert Operations Since World War II (1986); G. Treverton, *supra* note 5; and P. Wyden, *supra* note 47.

VII

COUNTERINTELLIGENCE

Polonius: "Your bait of falsehood takes this carp of truth..."
—SHAKESPEARE, *Hamlet*, 2.1.60

Although it was never directly mentioned in the National Security Act of 1947, America's secret agencies quickly adopted a second intelligence mission in support of their primary mission of intelligence collection and analysis: namely, the protection of America's secrets from espionage by hostile, and sometimes even friendly, foreign powers. This mission is known as *counterintelligence* (Church Committee 1976; Godson 1996; Johnson 1987; Zuehlke 1980). The purpose of counterintelligence (CI) is to uncover and thwart foreign intelligence operations directed against the United States, especially infiltration by foreign agents.

Defined more formally, counterintelligence is the

knowledge needed for the protection and preservation of the military, economic, and productive strength of the United States, including the security of the Government in domestic and foreign affairs against or from espionage, sabotage, and all other similar clandestine activities designed to weaken or destroy the United States. (Commission on Government Security 1957, 48–49)

Or in a more recent definition found in Executive Order 13470, signed in 2008 by President George W. Bush, counterintelligence is "information and activities to identify, receive, exploit, disrupt, or protect against espionage."

As Jennifer E. Sims puts it, "Counterintelligence is traditionally understood to include operations designed to block, disrupt, or destroy the intelligence operations of an adversary" (Sims and Gerber 2009, 21). Counterintelligence specialists wage nothing less than a secret war against antagonistic intelligence services and terrorist organizations—the latter task a subsidiary of CI known as *counterterrorism* (CT). As a CI expert noted in testimony before the Church Committee (1975a, 163): "In the absence of an effective U.S. counterintelligence program, [adversaries of democracy] function in what is largely a benign environment."

THE CONCERNS OF COUNTERINTELLIGENCE

Over the years, the United States has faced numerous adversaries, from British Redcoats and Barbary

Pirates in the early days to the Soviet Red Army and Al Qaeda terrorists in the modern era. In the midst of the Cold War, over 1,000 Soviet officials were on permanent assignment in the United States, according to FBI figures (Church Committee 1975a, 163). Among them, the FBI identified over 40 percent as members of the KGB or GRU, the Soviet civilian and military intelligence units. Estimates on the number of unidentified intelligence officers lurking in the United States raised this figure to over 60 percent of the Soviet "diplomatic" representation, and some defector sources have estimated that 70–80 percent of Soviet Embassy officials in Washington, D.C., and Soviets assigned to the United Nations in New York City had intelligence connections of one kind or another.

The opening of American deepwater ports to Russian ships in 1972 gave the Soviet intelligence services "virtually complete geographic access to the United States," a counterintelligence specialist testified before the Church Committee. In 1974, for example, over 200 Soviet ships with a total crew complement of 13,000 officers and men called at 40 deepwater ports in the United States. Various exchange groups provided additional opportunities for Soviet intelligence gathering within the United States. Some 4,000 Soviets entered the United States as commercial or exchange visitors on an annual basis during the latter decades of the Cold War, and the FBI identified over 100 intelligence officers among the approximately 400 Soviet students who attended American universities during this period as part of an East-West student exchange program. In addition, in the 1970s, the United States experienced a sharp increase in the number of Soviet immigrants to the United States, along with a rise in East-West commercial exchange visitors. Recently, the co-chair of a joint investigative committee on intelligence expressed shock at the FBI estimates on the number of suspected Al Qaeda terrorists and sympathizers who continued to move about inside the United States after the September 11, 2001, attacks (Pelosi 2002). Russian and Chinese spying inside the United States continues unabated, never mind that the Cold War ended in 1991 (Sims and Gerber 2009, 2–3).

Foreign intelligence agents have attempted to recruit U.S. executive branch personnel and Congressional staff members. They have also tried to steal secrets in America regarding weapons systems as well as commercial activities and strategies (Johnson 1989). The most elusive counterintelligence threat has been from "illegal" agents, who have no easily detectable contacts with their intelligence service. The problem of "illegals" is summarized by the FBI as follows:

> The illegal is a highly trained specialist in espionage tradecraft. He may be a [foreign] national and/or a professional intelligence officer dispatched to the United States under a false identity. Some illegals [may be] trained in the scientific and technical field to permit easy access to sensitive areas of employment.

> The detection of…illegals presents a most serious problem to the FBI. Once they enter the United States with either fraudulent or true documentation, their presence is obscured among the thousands of legitimate emigrés entering the United States annually. Relatively undetected, they are able to maintain contact with [their foreign masters] by means of secret writing, microdots, and open signals in conventional communications that are not susceptible to discovery through conventional investigative measures. (Church Committee 1976, 164)

The espionage activities of nations and terrorist cells against the territory of the United States, as well as its citizens, troops, diplomats, and interests abroad, are extensive and relentless, especially by the Soviet Union during the Cold War and today by an assortment of "rogue nations" and terrorist organizations—not to mention Russia, China, and even traditional America allies such as France. To combat these threats, America's counterintelligence officers have developed sophisticated investigative techniques to obtain information about adversaries (at home and abroad) and to guard the U.S. intelligence agencies. The task is difficult technically; moreover, the targeting of counterintelligence operations can raise sensitive legal and ethical questions at home. "U.S. counterintelligence programs, to be both effective and in line with traditional American freedoms," a CIA official told the Church Committee (1975a, 164),

> must [on the one hand] steer a middle course between blanket, illegal, frivolous and unsubstantiated inquiries into the private lives of U.S. citizens, and [on the other hand] excessive restrictions which will render the Government's counterintelligence arms impotent to protect the nation from foreign penetration and covert manipulation.

COUNTERINTELLIGENCE AS A PRODUCT: INFORMATION ABOUT "THE ENEMY"

Counterintelligence is both a product and an activity. The product is reliable information about all hostile foreign intelligence services and other threats, such as Al Qaeda cells within the United States. It is necessary to understand the organizational structure of the enemy, its key personnel, its methods of recruitment and training, and the details of specific operations. The efforts of intelligence services through the world to conceal such information from one another, through various security devices and elaborate deceptions, creates what former CIA Chief of Counterintelligence James Angleton (borrowing a line from the poet T. S. Eliot) referred to as a "wilderness of mirrors."

COUNTERINTELLIGENCE AS AN ACTIVITY: COUNTERESPIONAGE AND SECURITY

As an activity, CI consists of two matching halves: counterespionage and security. *Counterespionage* (CE) is the offensive, or aggressive, side of counterintelligence. It involves identifying specific adversaries and developing detailed knowledge about the operations they are planning or conducting. Counterespionage personnel must then attempt to block these operations by infiltrating the hostile service, an operation known as a "penetration," and by using sundry forms of manipulation. Ideally, as in jujitsu, the thrust of the hostile operation is turned back against the enemy.

Security is the passive, or defensive, side of counterintelligence. It entails putting in place static defenses against all hostile and concealed operations aimed at the United States, regardless of who might be attempting to carry them out. Security defenses include screening and clearance of personnel and establishment of programs to safeguard sensitive intelligence information—in a phrase, the administration of security controls. The objectives are to defend the personnel, installations, and operations against enemy intelligence services and terrorists.

Among the specific defensive devices used for information control by counterintelligence officers are security clearances (consisting of thorough inquiries into the backgrounds of job candidates), polygraphs, locking containers, security education, document accountability, censorship, camouflage, and codes. Grim-faced uniformed guards with German shepherds patrol the electrified fences at the CIA's headquarters, and, inside, polygraph experts administer tests of loyalty to all new recruits and, periodically for seasoned intelligence officers, cross-examine them on whether they have had any associations with foreigners. The polygraph has produced uneven results. Several traitors have been able to fool the machines, among them Aldrich H. Ames, a Russian recruit at the heart of the CIA (discovered in 1994 and now in prison for life). On occasion, though, polygraph sessions have uncovered treasonous behavior, and not long ago they even elicited a confession from a nervous would-be employee that he had murdered his wife and buried her body in his back yard.

Beyond armed guards and watchdogs, devices for physical security include fences, lighting, general systems, alarms, badges, and passes. The control of a specific area relies on curfews, checkpoints, and restricted zones. As a CIA counterintelligence officer has observed (Church Committee 1975a, 166), the security side of counterintelligence "is all that concerns perimeter defense, badges, knowing everything you have to know about your own people," while the counterespionage side "involves knowing all about foreign intelligence services—their people, their installations, their methods, and their operations—so that you have a completely different level of interest."

COUNTERINTELLIGENCE AS ORGANIZATION

At the CIA, the Office of Security is responsible for protecting that agency's personnel and installations, while counterespionage operations are largely the preserve of the Operations Directorate and its CI staff (which has personnel overseas using official or nonofficial cover). To combat terrorism more effectively, DCI William J. Casey established a Counterterrorism Center (CTC) in 1986. Despite its preponderance of CIA personnel, the center has 24 officers from a dozen other agencies, including the FBI and the Department of State (the two most important links); the Department of Defense; the Secret Service; the Department of Energy; the Bureau of Alcohol, Tobacco and Firearms; the Naval Investigative Service; the Federal Aviation Agency (another vital participant in this mission); the National Security Agency; the Immigration and Naturalization Service; and, most recently, the new Department of Homeland Security.

A senior officer in the center has remarked:

The whole concept behind the CTC was to bring elements from all four [CIA] Directorates together and put them under one single chain-of-command, so that we'd have all the necessary resources together to tackle the problem. In addition, we brought in these detailees from outside [the CIA], so that we'd have a very close relationship with the intelligence community. These people can pick up a secure [telephone] line and cut through the bureaucratic thickets that we normally face. (Johnson 2000, 177)

The 1993 bombing of the World Trade Center in New York City and the 1995 bombing of a federal building in Oklahoma City, as well as bombings at the U.S. embassies in Kenya and Tanzania in 1998, led Congress to fund expansively those agencies combating terrorism, including the CTC (even though it did not deal with U.S. domestic terrorism—exclusively the FBI's preserve, until the 9/11 attacks). After September 11, 2001, the steady funding for counterterrorism became a flood. Despite funding and sophisticated organizations, some forms of terrorism are nearly impossible to stop, such as a suicide attack carried out by an individual or a group prepared to die in the cause (as happened against Egyptian President Anwar Sadat in 1979, the U.S. Marine base in Lebanon in 1983, and the Israeli Embassy in Buenos Aires in 1992, and with the events of September 11, 2001).

In combating terrorism, the CTC has worked closely with the Nonproliferation Center (both located at the CIA), since each has a mandate to curb the use of dangerous weapons against mass populations. Both centers have concluded that a terrorist organization is more likely to use biological or chemical weapons against the United States, or a radioactive "dirty" bomb, rather than a fission or fusion nuclear device. The NPC concentrates on the supply side of the weapons problem, trying to stem the flow of weapons at the origins of production and distribution; the CTC focuses on the demand side, frustrating terrorist groups from acquiring weapons or weapons material (uranium, plutonium, or chemical-biological substances) in the first place.

The most important defense against terrorism is information about its likely occurrence, so that law enforcement officials can intercede before an attack takes place. To this end, the perfection of humint and other collection methods stands at the top of the CTC's priorities—especially the infiltration of terrorist organizations or the wooing of a defector from the enemy's camp. These are difficult tasks, as modern terrorist organizations are sophisticated, tightly controlled, and acutely aware of the CTC's aspirations.

In growing frustration over the failure of the CTC and the FBI to adequately share counterterrorism information with each other both before and after the 9/11 attacks on the United States, President George W. Bush established a new Terrorist Threat Integration Center (TTIC) in 2003. As the president said in his State of the Union Address that year, the purpose of the TTIC was "to merge and analyze all threat information in a single location." Continued the president: "In order to better protect our homeland, our intelligence agencies must coexist like they never had before." The TTIC incorporates the CIA and FBI counterterrorism units along with representatives involved in counterterrorism from throughout the government. The precise structure and mission of the TTIC remains foggy, however, and riven with bureaucratic bickering—much like the new Department of Homeland Security (with its obvious interest in counterintelligence matters). Among the confusions was how the TTIC would relate to the CIA's Counterterrorism Center, which has a comparable mission.

THE PENETRATION AND THE DOUBLE AGENT

Several kinds of operations exist within the rubric of counterespionage (the more aggressive side of counterintelligence). One, however, transcends all the others in importance: the *penetration*, or, in the common vernacular, the "mole." Since the primary goal of counterintelligence is to contain the intelligence services and saboteurs of the enemy, it is desirable to know his plans in advance and in as much detail as possible. This logical, but challenging, objective may be achieved through a high-level infiltration of an adversary's intelligence service or government, or of a terrorist cell. As DCI John McCone observed in 1963 during the Cold War, "Experience has shown penetration to be the most effective response to Soviet and Bloc [intelligence] services" (Church Committee 1975a, 167).

Furthermore, a well-placed infiltrator in a hostile intelligence or terrorist camp may be better able than anyone else to determine whether one's own service has been penetrated by an outsider. A former director of the Defense Intelligence Agency (DIA) has emphasized that the three principal programs used by the United States to meet, neutralize, and defeat hostile penetrations are penetrations of America's own, the security screening and clearance of personnel, and efforts to physically safeguard sensitive intelligence information (Carroll Report of 1964, cited by the Church Committee 1976, 167).

Methods of infiltrating the opposition service take several forms. Usually the most effective and desirable penetration is recruitment of an agent-in-place. He or she is already in the employment of an enemy intelligence service or a terrorist group. Ideally, the agent-in-place will be both highly placed and susceptible to recruitment by the United States. The prospective recruit—say, a Pakistani diplomat at the U.N. with suspected ties to remnants of the Taliban regime in Afghanistan (and, therefore, possible ties to Al Qaeda)—is approached and asked to work for "the government" of the United States (in fact, the CIA or the FBI). Various inducements may be used to entice the recruit. Money is the most popular bait since the Cold War, while during the Cold War foreigners—notably disaffected individuals inside the intelligence services of the Soviet Bloc—would sometimes spy for the United States purely out of a sense of anti-Communist ideology or disenchantment over the misdirection of communism by Joseph Stalin and other Soviet dictators. The importance of money as a trigger for treason in the post-Cold War era was recently illustrated in the United States. In 2003, Brian P. Regan, an intelligence analyst with access to spy satellite technology and a $100,000 credit card debt, was convicted of plotting to sell to Iraqi officials the coordinates of U.S. satellite targeting in the Persian Gulf region.

If recruitment is successful, an agent-in-place operation can be highly fruitful, since the agent is presumably already trusted within his or her organization and will have unquestioned access to key secret documents. Jack E. Dunlap, who worked at and spied on the National Security Agency in the 1960s, is a well-known example of a Soviet agent-in-place within the U.S. intelligence service during the Cold War. His handler was a Soviet Air Force attaché at the Soviet Embassy in Washington. A single penetration can be an intelligence goldmine, as were Kim Philby (inside MI6, British foreign intelligence), Aldrich H. Ames (CIA), Robert P. Hanssen (FBI) for the Soviet Union, and Col. Oleg Penkovsky (KGB) for the United States.

Another method of infiltration is the double agent. Double agents, however, are costly and time-consuming, and they are risky, because the loyalty of the agent remains a question mark, with double-crosses being commonplace. The running of double agents involves much pure drudgery with few dramatic results, as new information must be constantly and painstakingly checked against existing files. Moreover, passing credible documents back to the enemy to ensure the credibility of the double agent can be a major undertaking. The operations must appear plausible to the adversary, so—to make fake papers seem realistic—the genuine article must be provided now and again. In this process, classified documents must be cleared—typically a slow and contentious activity, since intelligence agencies are reluctant to release any classified information to an outsider. "This means letting a lot of good stuff go to the enemy, without much in return," complained a CIA counterintelligence officer to a Senate Committee (Church Committee 1976, 168).

To accomplish each of these tasks, hard work, careful planning, and considerable staff resources are necessary. The extraordinary staffing requirements of double-agent operations restricted the capacity of the British to run many of them during World War II—only approximately 150 for the entire period of the war and no more than about 25 at any one time—even though the task was eased significantly by the ability of the British to read German secret ciphers throughout most of the war (Masterman 972).

THE DEFECTOR

Almost as good as the agent-in-place, and less troublesome to manage than the double agent, is the "defector with knowledge." In this case the challenge consists of a skillful interrogation and validation of the defector's bona fides (as usual), but without the worrisome, ongoing requirement to provide the agent with a credible mix of false and genuine documents along with other logistical support. Although an agent-in-place is preferable because of the ongoing useful information he or she can provide, often an agent-in-place does not want to accept the risk of staying in place—especially in nations where the security is sophisticated and the execution of traitors swift and often painful. The agent's usual preference is to defect to safety in the United States. As a result, agents-in-place are harder to come by in tightly controlled totalitarian regimes with robust counterintelligence services of their own; defection is more likely. In contrast, agents-in-place are more easily recruited in the developing nations, where sophisticated security that might discover them is often lacking.

Defectors recruited overseas by the CIA are occasionally brought to the United States and resettled if they are considered highly important (that is, someone likely to provide valuable ongoing information or someone who has already provided vital information and now seeks exfiltration to avoid capture and execution in his or her own country). The FBI is notified and, after the CIA completes its interrogation, FBI counterintelligence officers may interrogate. Terrorists captured in the United States are normally interrogated first by the FBI, then by the CIA; the process is vice versa for terrorists captured abroad. Sometimes the bona fides of a defector remain in dispute for many years, as in the case of Yuri Nosenko, who defected from the U.S.S.R. soon after the assassination of President John F. Kennedy in 1963. The FBI viewed Nosenko as a legitimate defector; the CIA's chief of counterintelligence worried, however, that Nosenko was really a false defector, sent to the United States to sow disinformation.

THE DECEPTION OPERATION

The penetration (mole) or double agent is closely related to another important counterespionage method: the *deception operation*. Simply stated, the deception is an attempt to give the enemy a false impression about something, causing him to take action contrary to his own interests. Fooling the Germans into a believing that D-Day landings would occur in the Pas de Calais rather than in Normandy is a classic example of a successful deception operation during World War II.

Deception is related to penetration, because U.S. agents-in-place operating within foreign intelligence agencies or terrorist groups can serve as an excellent channel through which misleading information can flow to the enemy. So moles and double agents can serve as both collectors of intelligence and instruments of deception. In another illustration of an approach to deception, the CIA might allow a hostile foreign penetration into its own intelligence service and then carefully feed false information through him or her back to the enemy.

OTHER COUNTERINTELLIGENCE TECHNIQUES

Counterespionage operations also include surreptitious surveillance of various kinds (for instance, audio, mail, physical, and "optical"—that is, photography), as well as interrogation (sometimes keeping the subject incommunicado until his or her bona fides are verified). Part and parcel of the CE trade are decoding of secret messages sent by an adversary to a mole, trailing suspected agents, observing "dead drops" (the exchange of material, such as secret documents or instructions, between a spy and his handler), and photographing individuals entering opposition embassies or at other government locations. At the Arlington Cemetery funeral of CIA officer Richard Welch in 1975, Eastern European diplomats were discovered among the media corps snapping photographs of CIA officers (and their automobile license plates) who were attending the burial service. Since the focus of offensive counterintelligence is disruption of the enemy service, provocation can be an important element of counterespionage, too. This approach involves harassment of an adversary, such as publishing the names of his agents or sending a troublemaking false defector into his midst who is in reality an agent provocateur.

COUNTERINTELLIGENCE AND RESEARCH

Good research is critical to effective counterintelligence. It involves amassing encyclopedic knowledge on suspected foreign spies, including American citizens associated (wittingly or unwittingly) with hostile intelligence services or terrorist organizations. Such research can step over the line of protected civil liberties in the United States unless care is taken by the intelligence agencies to honor the law and the rights of citizens.

Counterintelligence officials also have a responsibility for preparing guidelines regarding interrogation of defectors. The matter of counterintelligence interrogation methods has been controversial, raising the question of what techniques should be permissible in a democracy. In 2003, the CIA captured in Pakistan Kahlid Sheikh Mohammed (known as KSM, for short, by U.S. counterintelligence officers), the suspected mastermind of the Pentagon and World Trade Center attacks two years earlier. Immediately, media accounts around the world (including in the United States) speculated that he might be mistreated—even tortured—by his CIA handlers. Officials within the CIA responded that no brutal force would be used, not the least because psychological pressure was considered more effective. Former CIA officers speculated that the Al Qaeda strategist would be subjected to sleep deprivation; if he cooperated, he would be given rewards, such as good food, rest, and a television. They conceded, though, that while there would be no stretching on the rack, the captured terrorist might be forced to sit or stand in awkward or painful positions for hours at time—"torture lite." Only subsequently did it come to light that KSM was waterboarded, a harsh form of interrogation that simulates the sense of drowning in water. It remains a matter of intense dispute whether this extreme counterintelligence method achieves results, but one conclusion is widely accepted: in the court of world opinion, torture harms America's reputation for fair play and ethical behavior (Johnson 2007c).

The line between acceptable and unacceptable interrogation techniques is not well defined and in the light of the savage 9/11 attacks is apt to be smudged by interrogators who may be angry about past attacks as well as concerned about the possibility of another sudden strike against the United States unless warning information is extracted quickly from the subject. "There was a before 9/11 and there was an after 9/11," Cofer Black, the head of the CIA's Counterterrorism Center, has said. "After 9/11, the gloves came off" (Harden 2003, A1). Abu Zubaydah, another top Al Qaeda leader captured in Pakistan after the September 11, 2001 attacks, was on painkillers because of a pistol shot to the groin; until he began to cooperate, interrogators held back his full medication. Reports suggest that other Al Qaeda suspects have been chained, naked and hooded, to the ceiling; routinely kicked to keep them awake; and shackled so tightly that blood flow is halted. Most alarming are charges that two Al Qaeda prisoners were killed during interrogation at a U.S. military base in Afghanistan, beaten to death with blunt instruments (Campbell 2003, 1). If the assertion is proved true, the interrogators would be subject to U.S. civil and military prosecutions. Those being interrogated can also be threatened with the prospect that they will be turned over to a government allied with the United States that is known to have a decidedly malevolent approach to interrogation and few, if any, laws on the subject (Egypt, for example).

Counterintelligence officials also study such subjects as use of proprietary companies by foreign intelligence services or terrorist cells, and the organization and methods of those who practice terrorism. Further, they analyze defector briefs and, if they suspect that internal classified documents have been compromised, they help ascertain who had access and what secrets might have been lost (the latter a process called "damage assessment").

COUNTERINTELLIGENCE AND LIAISON

Liaison among U.S. counterintelligence services, at home and abroad, is vital as well, as no single CI organization can do its job alone. The relationship among CI units is especially important for the United States, because counterintelligence—with all its intricacies and deceptions—requires close coordination among agencies and sharing of records; yet, traditionally, the American intelligence "community" has been organizationally fragmented. Thus, a liaison system to overcome these centrifugal forces is crucial. This need for coordination is especially important between CIA and FBI counterintelligence units, since the CIA has foreign jurisdiction and the FBI domestic, but they must jointly monitor the movements of foreign spies who travel in and out of these two jurisdictions. Sometimes this coordination has suffered spectacular failures. In 1970, for example, FBI Director J. Edgar Hoover terminated formal liaison with the CIA and all other CI units in the government because of a disagreement over how to handle a particular East European defector. Far more tragically, the FBI and the CIA proved unable to share information effectively about the whereabouts of Al Qaeda terrorists just prior to the attacks against the World Trade Center and the Pentagon in 2001, losing track of two known to be inside the United States weeks before the attacks.

Liaison with foreign intelligence services overseas can undergo strain, too. Each nation fears that the intelligence services of its allies have been infiltrated by hostile agents and, therefore, that the ally should not be given sensitive information. Nonetheless, cooperation does take place, since all intelligence services seek information and—with precautions—will take it where they can get it, if the information is useful.

COUNTERINTELLIGENCE AND ACCOUNTABILITY

The counterintelligence mission is among the most secretive of all intelligence activities—the heart of the onion. Its tight compartmentalization makes proper supervision a challenge for lawmakers and executive overseers. The most disquieting chapter in U.S. counterintelligence occurred during the 1960s when America's secret agencies began to spy at home, against the very people they had sworn to protect (Johnson 1985). In the midst of the Cold War, the CIA generated a data bank on 1.5 million U.S. citizens, almost all of whom were simply exercising their First Amendment rights to dissent against the war in Vietnam. Many had their mail intercepted and read, their telephones tapped, their day-to-day activities monitored. The NSA intercepted every cable sent overseas or received by Americans. The FBI carried out 500,000 investigations of so-called subversives (again, mainly Vietnam war dissenters, plus civil rights activists and even Klan members were added to the "enemies list"), without a single case ending in a court conviction.

During this period, FBI agents wrote anonymous letters meant to incite violence among African Americans. The Bureau's counterintelligence program, labeled "Cointelpro," involved not only spying on but harassing civil rights activists and Vietnam war dissidents, in an attempt to fray or break family and friendship ties. A campaign to wreck America's civil rights movement stood at the center of Cointelpro.

The overzealous pursuit of counterintelligence threatened the very foundations of American democracy, undermining basic U.S. laws and the constitutional right to free expression. Only when the CIA's transgressions leaked to the press in 1974, triggering a Congressional inquiry, did these illegal operations by the CIA, the FBI, the NSA, and military intelligence units come to a halt. Counterintelligence—so vital to the nation's security—had strayed, and Americans were again reminded of Madison's warning (etched on the walls of the Library of Congress) that "power, lodged as it must be in the hands of human beings, is ever liable to abuse." A democracy cannot remain free without having strong accountability over its counterintelligence corps. The proper balance between security and civil liberties was tested again after the 9/11 attacks, when the second Bush Administration initiated warrantless wiretaps against American citizens inside the United States and critics cried foul, perceiving this privacy intrusion as a violation of the Foreign Intelligence Surveillance Act of 1978.

THE READINGS

In the first selection in this part of the book, Paul Redmond brings his long experience in CIA counterintelligence (CI) to bear on the question of defending America's secrets. He examines several cases in which the CI defenses of the United States failed abysmally. Next, Stan A. Taylor and Daniel Snow review the motivations of 139 American traitors during the Cold War, as well as how they were unmasked. The authors found money to be the most prevalent motive for treason, although during the 1950s some Americans spied for the Soviet Union out of attraction to communist ideology. With respect to the post-Cold War era, Taylor and Snow note that treason continues and that materialism remains the primary motivation. As for improvements in capturing spies, the authors give considerable credit to the establishment of better electronic surveillance procedures in the United States as a result of the passage of the Foreign Intelligence Surveillance Act in 1978.

The third selection is drawn from a Senate Select Committee on Intelligence report on the discovery in 1995 of a Soviet/Russian mole in the CIA: Aldrich Hazen Ames, the most devastating counterintelligence failure in the history of the Agency. The damage caused by Ames' treachery, and how counterintelligence officials finally tracked him down, are the subjects of this fascinating, if disheartening, report.

In the final selection, Professor Robert Jervis raises important questions about correct approaches to CI and explores the problem of shielding the nation against foreign deception operations.

24. THE CHALLENGES OF COUNTERINTELLIGENCE

PAUL J. REDMOND

A former Chief of CIA Counterintelligence and one of the leading investigators in the hunt to find the Russian mole inside the CIA (Aldrich Ames) explores the difficulties of guarding America's secrets against the prying eyes of hostile intelligence services.

1. COUNTERINTELLIGENCE DEFINITIONS

Counterintelligence, known in the trade as "CI," is a complex, controversial subject that is hard to define. Only at the strategic level are there reasonably consistent definitions of counterintelligence. According to the current, official U.S. government definition: "Counterintelligence means information gathered and activities conducted to identify, deceive, exploit, disrupt or protect against espionage, other intelligence activities, sabotage or assassination conducted for or on behalf of foreign powers, organizations or persons or their agents, or international terrorist organizations or activities."[1] A former senior counterintelligence officer of the KGB's First Chief Directorate[2] defines CI as "special activities of security organizations authorized and directed by the government to protect the State and its citizens against espionage, sabotage and terrorism."[3]

The Russians also have an institutional definition for counterintelligence or *kontrrazvedka*—"State agencies granted special powers in the fight against the intelligence services (razvedka) of other states and the subversive activity of organizations and individuals used by those services. Counterintelligence is one of the instruments in the hands of the political authorities of the state" (Mitrokhin 2002).

As is the case with the Russians, a British definition of counterintelligence includes countersubversion—"...protection of national security against threats from espionage, terrorism and sabotage from the activities of foreign powers and from activities intended to overthrow or undermine parliamentary democracy by political industrial or violent means.[4]"

While these strategic definitions are mostly in agreement in that they mention espionage, sabotage, and terrorism, they encompass a wide diversity of activity, a variety of professional skills, and a range of tactical purposes and means. As a former national counterintelligence executive observed, "Across the profession, there are vast differences in understanding of what counterintelligence means, and how it is done, and even the basic terminology it employs" (Van Cleave 2008). CI means different things to different organizations and intelligence officers, and encompasses a wide continuum of activities from analysis of observed events through the aggressive operational activity of mounting deception operations, from conduct of espionage investigations to the intensely personal, clandestine activity of recruiting and securely managing human sources among the enemy—without simultaneously being deceived.

The U.S. military, which runs "offensive" counterintelligence operations against the enemy, places CI under the overall umbrella of "force protection."[5] The FBI, which is part of the U.S. Department of Justice and is the "lead" U.S. agency in the field, does engage in operational CI activity but it tends to emphasize CI as a law enforcement activity, counterespionage, or the identification and successful prosecution of spies.

The Central Intelligence Agency embraces under the rubric of counterintelligence a very wide variety of activities. They include the recruitment and management of sources within foreign intelligence services; "asset validation" to prevent the opposition from deceiving the U.S. intelligence community by running sources they actually control; the maintenance of good operational "tradecraft" to prevent the opposition from uncovering American intelligence-collection operations; analysis of the capabilities and intentions of the foreign intelligence opposition; and counterespionage operations with the FBI. To other national security or defense agencies not engaged in operational intelligence activities but rather consumers and analysts of intelligence information or custodians/producers of other sorts of national-security data, counterintelligence means primarily programs to prevent the enemy from stealing secrets. Agencies such as the United States Department of Homeland Security actually engaged in government operations have to design programs to protect not only sensitive technical programs and intelligence data but also to defend, at the tactical level, against terrorist organizations suborning employees to facilitate the infiltration of terrorists and/or weapons into the United States.

The end of the Cold War brought even more complications to the definition and conduct of counterintelligence by the United States. While U.S. intelligence agencies tried, with an almost complete lack of success, to run deception operations against the Warsaw Pact during the Cold War, counterintelligence meant mostly counterespionage against the efforts of the Soviet Union, its allies and, to a lesser degree, China to steal secrets. The break-up of the Soviet Union mostly eliminated the espionage activity by the states of Eastern Europe but Russia and China have remained counterintelligence threats. Moreover, a host of new ones have emerged including "non-State actors" such as terrorist organizations and the drug cartels. The post-9/11 era has further complicated matters by raising the bureaucratic and operational issues of the relationship between counterterrorism and counterintelligence, not to mention the perennial conundrum of defining and coping organizationally with the overlapping roles of counterintelligence and security. The intersection of the roles of CI and security leads, in turn, to the question of where the CI function should reside within an organization. Further confounding the definition of CI the advent of the "cyber" era has raised the issue of "cyber CI" and how a national defense entity protects itself against attacks on its databases, electronically controlled operations, and digital communications.

Even the basic terminology of CI is not universally shared. Different intelligence/security services within the same government use different words. The German Federal Intelligence Service (BND) uses the term "Gegenspionage" which, translated literally, means "the countering of espionage," but the internal security service, Federal Office for the Protection of the Constitution, BfV, uses the term "Spionageabwehr" which means "counter espionage."[6] In English, "counterintelligence" is even spelled differently: "counterintelligence," "counter intelligence" and "counter-intelligence."[7]

The various organizational positions and levels of status and influence within government agencies that the CI function occupies also reflect the complexity of the subject. Perhaps because of Russia's Byzantine cultural heritage and the conspiratorial roots of the Bolsheviks, the external part of KGB, the First Chief Directorate and its successor organization the SVR, places tremendous emphasis on CI. It maintains an entire organization, Directorate K, in Moscow. The SVR also has a CI career track and a CI section, referred to as Line KR, within each residency.[8] Except temporarily in the aftermath of spy scandals and major operational failures, the CIA historically has put less emphasis on CI. Although it has not established a separate CI operations officer track within the National Clandestine Service, it does have career CI officers at CIA Headquarters and some posted abroad. Perhaps most curiously, during the latter part of the Cold War, the head of CI in one European service also had as his duties legislative and public affairs.

This diversity of approach is also reflected in CI's relationship to the security function in various organizations. In the U.S. National Security Agency, the functions are fully merged in the Associate Directorate for Security and Counterintelligence. From the Edward Lee Howard spy case[9] the CIA learned the painful lesson that lack of internal communication can lead to disaster. In this instance, there had been no effective sharing of information among the Directorate of Operations, Office of Security, and Office of Medical Services. As a result, the CIA as an institution did not recognize Howard as a CI threat. At the CIA, counterintelligence and security are still separate organizations, but the interchangeability of personnel appears to make for effective cooperation.

In addition to the complexity of the subject, one other factor makes CI hard to discuss in public. It is probably the most arcane and certainly among the most secret, conspiratorial, and "sensitive" of intelligence activities. Thus, it is a very hard subject to describe to the "uncleared" reader in anything but the abstract. The following discussion of the multifarious aspects of CI endeavors to overcome this difficulty by describing situations and cases. In the interests of security and ease of getting publication clearance, some of these cases have been "sterilized," but the writer hopes they remain faithful to the lessons they reveal.

Regardless of the complexity of the subject, the diversity of the functions and activities it encompasses, and the "spooky" nature of the business, one basic rule must apply to counterintelligence: "all things in moderation." Because there was a belief that the Soviets had penetrated the CIA, during the 1960s and early 1970s CI reigned supreme, paralyzing operations against the Warsaw Pact by assuming that the KGB knew of and controlled all operations. During the tenure of DCI William Colby in the mid-1970s, there was a reaction to this mindset that destroyed CI at the CIA and led to spies in the Agency going undetected and the flowering of opposition-controlled cases. These two periods represent a typical sine wave of either too much or too little CI in the U.S. intelligence community. The waves oscillate in radical reaction to the previous peak, rarely staying in the moderate range required to deal rationally with the hard issues of counterintelligence.

2. THE VARIOUS ASPECTS OF COUNTERINTELLIGENCE

2.1 COUNTERINTELLIGENCE AS COUNTERESPIONAGE

"Catching spies," or counterespionage, which is the detection and neutralization of human spies, is probably the first thing that comes to mind when the general public thinks of "counterintelligence." It is also the easiest to describe since there are many well-documented, important spy cases. This is indeed a very important aspect of CI. During the Cold War, the Warsaw Pact and its allies such as Cuba had spectacular success in penetrating every U.S. government agency engaged in national security (except apparently the Coast Guard), most defense contractors, and the U.S. Congress. An informal historical review of Cold War spy cases shows that at any one time there were at least seven significant spies working for the enemy in the U.S. national security establishment.

During that tense era in international affairs, four spy cases alone could have given the Soviet Union a decisive advantage if war had broken out. The Walker spy case in the U.S. Navy[10] provided cryptographic key material and encryption equipment design data enabling the KGB to read over a million messages, which would have allowed the Russians virtually to neutralize the deterrence of the American submarine-based missile systems. The Clyde Conrad spy ring[11] provided the Soviets, via the Hungarian military intelligence service, the details of the U.S. Army's operational plans and communications in Western Europe, which could have provided the Warsaw Pact a decisive advantage in a ground war in Western Europe. Robert Hanssen, who worked for both the KGB and GRU[12] off and on for about twenty years before his arrest in 2001, passed the Soviets enough documentary data to neutralize U.S. efforts to continue a viable democratic government in time of a nuclear war. Aldrich Ames, an equally notorious spy who worked for the KGB for about nine years until he was arrested in 1994, compromised nearly all the CIA's human sources working against the Soviet Union in the mid-1980s.

These four spy cases capture the spectrum of ways in which espionage cases begin. The Ames case resides at the end of the spectrum that is hardest to pursue, empirical indications that there is a problem—secrets are getting to the opposition—but no clues as to how. In the mid-1980s, the KGB started, in a rather rapid-fire manner, to arrest CIA's Soviet sources. After a period of analysis, false trails, and inattention to the problem, a joint CIA-FBI examination of the very large number of officers aware of the compromised cases produced a small number of people on whom to concentrate. This process eventually focused on Ames, chronologically linking his operationally approved contacts with a Russian in the Washington embassy to financial transactions. When combined with some suggestive source reporting, this effort enabled the FBI to mount a very skillful investigation culminating in his arrest.

The Ames episode represents the extreme difficulty of pursuing a case when the only way to attack the problem is massive analysis of the people aware of the cases compromised. So-called knowledge ability or "bigot lists" are a farce in the U.S. government. Even in the rare cases where good records actually exist, they are almost useless because hundreds of employees can know about an operation. The FBI found in the mid-1980s they could not pursue the compromise of a Soviet source because about 250 people at one field office alone had knowledge of the operation (Bromwich 1997). On the other hand, non-American CI officers can have an easier time both in protecting their operations and investigating losses. Knowledgeable CI professionals in the U.S. government estimate that fewer than ten KGB officers knew the identities of Ames and Hanssen, and a former senior Greek intelligence officer recently stated to the media that only three of his colleagues knew the identity of Steven Lalas, a State Department communications officer who spied for the Greeks from 1977 to 1993.[13]

So-called lead information is helpful in starting and pursuing an espionage investigation in direct proportion to its specificity. Multiple CIA human sources in three different Warsaw Pact intelligence services provided information over many years that the Hungarian Military Intelligence Service had a very valuable source in the U.S. Army's V Corps in Germany. Through one human asset involved in the actual processing of the product but not knowledgeable about the source, the CIA was even able to inform the Army of specific documents passed and the disturbing fact that amendments to operational plans were occasionally reaching the Red Army Headquarters in Moscow before they were issued to U.S. forces. Eventually, after many years and a massive investigation based on a large accumulation of diverse lead material, plus some good luck, the Army was able to identify Clyde Conrad (and a net of associate spies) as the source. Conrad was subsequently arrested and successfully prosecuted by the Federal Republic of Germany. The CIA had multiple sources reporting on the case. However, because of excellent compartmentation within the Warsaw Pact intelligence services, no single source had more than a few small pieces of the puzzle. As a consequence this very damaging operation ran for many years before enough information accumulated to allow the U.S. Army investigators to focus on Conrad.

While "lead information" is much more valuable than a well-founded suspicion of a CI problem, the pursuit of leads can be extraordinarily difficult and fraught with the potential for mistakes. For years the CIA and FBI fruitlessly pursued lead information from the 1960s indicating that a CIA officer had volunteered to provide information on the Agency's operations in the USSR. Many years later during the course of the intensive research which led to the Aldrich Ames spy case, it became clear that this "old lead" from a Soviet intelligence source was his garbled version of a U.S.-controlled volunteer, a walk-in

to a Soviet installation in the United States. In the early 1980s, the CIA received from two separate, well-placed KGB officers similar information that a CIA "communicator" had an operational meeting with the KGB in a North African city during a particular time period. The Agency and the FBI chased that "lead" for years until it became clear, following his arrest, that John Walker was the person the Soviets met on that occasion. At that time, senior and middle-grade KGB officers apparently assumed all communicators worked for the CIA.

The Walker spy case illustrates how empirical data pointing to a CI problem and general lead information is not enough to unearth a spy. During the 1970s and early 1980s, Navy flag officers had expressed anger and extreme frustration that Soviet electronic collection ships seemed to appear regularly at just the right places and times to conduct intercept operations during U.S. naval maneuvers, particularly in the Mediterranean. This was an obvious indication that the Soviets somehow had insight into U.S. operational planning. During this period the CIA did disseminate one CI report from a Soviet intelligence officer who alleged that the USSR had achieved massive success in reading U.S. Navy communications. Even if these two straws in the wind had been considered together, which they probably were not, they did not provide a sufficient basis to attack the problem. The start of the case had to wait until the best kind of lead came along, the specific identification of a spy by a source or, as in this case, a "snitch." Walker's former wife, apparently drunk, called an FBI office to say her husband was a spy; the FBI acted on the lead and Walker was eventually arrested. Often the problem with pursuing snitch leads is persuading superiors to take them seriously, as happened in a case involving another KGB penetration of the U.S. Navy, when security authorities discounted the statement of a discontented wife that her husband was a spy and his espionage career thus ran four years longer than it should have.

Two other cases illustrate the supreme value of specific source information, the other end of the continuum from purely empirical indicators of a CI problem. Resourceful and persistent operational work by the FBI, with help from the CIA, led to source reporting unambiguously identifying Robert Hanssen as a spy (Risen 2003, A1). Likewise, the KGB defector Vitaliy Sergeyevich Yurchenko[14] provided enough specific information to enable the CIA within minutes to identify former employee Edward L. Howard as a KGB asset.

Other factors also play a role in starting espionage investigations. Through the security/polygraph process the CIA has identified individuals who had been directed to apply for employment by foreign intelligence services and most recently, apparently by terrorist organizations.[15] The espionage investigation of Jonathan Pollard[16] was started because of the alertness and CI consciousness of a fellow employee. While the KGB, with its massive resources, caught U.S. spies in the USSR through surveillance of CIA officers, only rarely have Western security services had similar success.

Defectors represent a special case as sources of spy leads. Historically, they have been gold mines for data in starting investigations; but once the excitement of their defection is over, they have told all that they know and attention toward them lags, they often start to make up stories. During the effort which led to Ames's identification as a spy, a defector from the then KGB's internal security component, the Second Chief Directorate (now FSB), concocted a story for his American handler about the recruitment of a CIA officer in Moscow. It turned out that he made up the story to retain the attention of the CIA and FBI. All espionage investigations should view all spy leads with skepticism, at least initially, and they should judge leads on Oscar Wilde's principle that "the truth is rarely pure and never simple."

Another maxim which applies to counterespionage and CI in general is "your CI capability is only as good as your records." Leads to spies are more often than not ambiguous and fragmentary. CI analysis has been described as trying to do a monocolor jigsaw puzzle with pieces fitting in multiple places or not at all, or more simply, the archaeological reconstruction of shards from a broken pot. Records in the form of formal data in storage or, as was the case in the two examples cited below, institutional memory, are invaluable in resolving leads. In the mid-1980s, a European service obtained from a source in a Warsaw Pact intelligence service the detailed description for a dead drop site that the source knew only had been cased and written up for an important spy. Investigation and surveillance of the site proved fruitless. Several years later, a CIA source in another country identified a spy who was connected to the dead drop site, thus reinforcing the evidence against the spy and resolving the original lead. The connection was made only because the intelligence officers involved happened to remember the original dead

drop data, not because there were organized holdings of such information.

Another case where institutional memory played a major role involved an informal discussion between a CIA officer and a senior member of a European service. The subject was lead information to KGB penetrations in the U.S. computer industry, where the principal spies had European and South Asian connections. The Western European officer noted the leads "sounded" similar to information acquired from a completely different source several years earlier. He went home and confirmed his suspicions from his service's rather good records and the CIA eventually found similar data residing in the proverbial shoe box under a desk. The connection of the data considerably expanded and refined the investigation. It is hoped that the advent of the cyber era and "link analysis" is now being used to correlate leads and identify spies more systematically. However, data processing and manipulation should not be viewed as a substitute for professional expertise gained by career CI professionals with years of experience. The two CIA officers who played the major role in identifying Aldrich Ames as a spy followed their instincts in focusing on him as a candidate and, using their vast knowledge and experience, were even able to accurately construct, from fragmentary data before his arrest, a significant part of his KGB meeting plan.

2.2 COUNTERINTELLIGENCE AS "ASSET VALIDATION"

The vetting of sources or "asset validation" usually, and too narrowly, is applied to human sources by American intelligence services. This counterintelligence function is at the very heart of all human collection operations and it should be applied also to technical collection and SIGINT operations.[17] It is critically important to determine to the degree possible that the source is not a fabricator or under opposition control. The disastrous CURVEBALL source, who reinforced the Bush administration's predisposition to believe Iraq had a weapons-of-mass-destruction program, is a classic example. He was a source of German intelligence that was dealing with the Pentagon's Defense Humint Service (DHS), and he was never properly vetted until after his data were used to support the invasion of Iraq. It is equally critical to determine, if possible, whether a source may be under the control of the opposition and thus used to provide disinformation or lure officers out onto the street for a contact, where they can be apprehended and noisily declared persona non grata.

During the Cold War, the Warsaw Pact and its allies enjoyed spectacular success in running controlled cases against the CIA. During much of the Cold War, *all* the "sources" the CIA was running against Cuba were controlled by its intelligence service. With a very small number of possible exceptions, the same parlous state of affairs existed in the operations against East Germany. The KGB, unlike most Western intelligence services, reflexively favored running controlled cases and mounted many "dangle" operations.[18] The same conspiratorial mindset that motivated the KGB to attempt many controlled operations led them, as a matter of course, not to trust their own sources. Thus they engaged intensively, one might say obsessively, in testing and validation. In the mid-1980s American CI officers were amazed to learn that a former U.S. military officer was still the subject of elaborate testing by the KGB about ten years after he started working for the Soviets and had been of enough value to meet personally with a KGB general and directorate chief.

It is clear that the Warsaw Pact's success in running cases against American intelligence was at least partly a function of American naïveté, lack of professionalism, and the refusal of officers to believe their case could be a fabricator or controlled by the opposition, particularly when promotions were involved. It must be emphasized, however, that asset validation is a very difficult task, particularly when the source is handled in a "denied area"[19] and there are few, if any, other sources of "collateral" information on which to rely for comparison. Most Western intelligence sources in denied areas are "met" only briefly for a very quick passage of information or are handled impersonally by dead drops or clandestine electronic communications. There is no regular opportunity for personal meetings and the type of systematic debriefing that can identify and pursue issues related to the source's validity. In the absence of any sources of its own within the opposition service to warn them, Western services running cases in denied areas have had to rely on the value of the intelligence provided, corroboration of its validity by other sources, if available, and the operational circumstances surrounding the case—particularly how it started.

This is a very complicated, difficult business. It is not a science. In one Warsaw Pact country in the 1970s, an individual purporting to be an officer of the internal security service volunteered by note to the CIA. He was handled impersonally by dead drop over many years and provided valuable information concerning his services plans to run controlled cases against the CIA and other operations against the U.S. embassy. He even warned of an impending ambush by the internal security service. Because he had been of established value, CIA CI officers were stunned to learn, at the end of the Cold War, that the case had been controlled from the beginning. It appears that his country's internal security service, taking the long view so alien to Western services, was trying to establish him as a contingency asset for a major disinformation operation in the future. It is noteworthy that the only doubts about the case were expressed by the initial case officer who picked up the first dead drop. He observed people in the area and expressed the view that they might have been surveillants. This case reinforces the informal maxim of some CI officers: "the answer (to the validity of the case) always resides in the first 10–15 pages of the file."

A source in another Eastern European country had been providing valuable, validated military R&D data for many years when his handling officer was ambushed by the security service when meeting the asset on the street in the capital. CI officers at the CIA assumed the source had been compromised because of a mistake on his or the Agency's part and only learned to their amazement after the Cold War that the case had been controlled all along. The Eastern European service had been running the case for years to have something "on the shelf" to use against the CIA, should the need arise. As the chief of the service said, he did not care that they were passing valuable information because it hurt only the Russians, not his own country.

Three other cases illustrate another aspect of how the validation of sources is not easy and a decision to declare a case controlled should not be made lightly. At the height of U.S.-Soviet tensions in the 1960s, an East European intelligence official living behind the iron curtain volunteered to American intelligence and started providing CI information on Warsaw Pact spies in the West. While the information appeared to have potential, CI officers began doubting his bona fides when he also began suggesting that Western intelligence officers travel into other Eastern European countries to recruit senior communist intelligence officers whom he believed to be disaffected. Given the Cold War atmosphere and the operational conditions then prevailing behind the iron curtain, such suggestions were ludicrous. Some CI officers, not unreasonably, concluded that he was a controlled case trying to lure the CIA into an operational fiasco in Eastern Europe. Nonetheless, the CIA and an allied service continued to run the case and he turned out to be the one of the most valuable sources of CI information in history. It became clear over time that the individual was mentally unstable and his outlandish operational suggestions were the result of his ignorance of life on the other side of the iron curtain and his assumption that Western services were as powerful as those in the Soviet Bloc.

The Soviet engineer who started volunteering by note during a period when timid management precluded the Agency from replying to his overtures is another example illustrating the need to persevere despite well-founded, in fact compelling, doubts. Because of the CIA's passivity over a considerable period of time, the engineer eventually out of frustration pounded on the trunk of the car of a U.S. diplomat who was filling his tank at one of the diplomatic gas stations in Moscow, an area very well covered by KGB surveillance, both static and mobile. The combination of this suicidal means of volunteering, plus the obscurity and initially incomprehensible nature of the data provided, logically led officers at the CIA to believe he was a controlled case, until knowledgeable engineers and experts in the DOD determined that his production was extraordinarily valuable. That case turned out to be the most significant run by the CIA against the USSR during the Cold War.

Another case involved risk taking. The CIA had been running a source in Europe who returned to Moscow with the expectation of being assigned to an office with access to a veritable gold mine of military information. After his return home, a source provided the CIA enough information to make it clear that the KGB had learned something of the operation but was apparently following an investigative avenue that probably would not lead quickly to this potentially superb source. He eventually signaled for a contact and CI officers had to calculate the odds on whether the KGB had found him and was setting the Agency up for an ambush. Based on a seat-of-the-pants assessment of known KGB investigative intentions, the likelihood of a huge payoff in intelligence product, plus a lot of hope, the CIA decided to make the contact. It came off without incident and produced a massive amount of very valuable intelligence.

The in-place source or defector who does not tell you all he knows, either to protect himself or to apply future leverage, is another challenge to asset validation. The most famous such case is Alexander Orlov, a senior Bolshevik intelligence officer, who defected in Canada in 1938 because he thought he was about to be assassinated as part of the Great Purge. He knew the identities of most of the important spies working for the Soviets in the West, including the high-level penetrations of the British government; but he did not reveal this information, having sent a message to Stalin via the head of Bolshevik intelligence saying that he would tell all if anything happened to himself or his family. The only effective way to get a full debriefing from a source inclined to hold back is to subject him to an officer with an in-depth, intimidating knowledge of the subject matter and good human-relations skills. When the principal CIA case officer handling Colonel Oleg Penkovskiy[20] first met him in a hotel room in London, he asked him whether so-and-so (by first name and patronymic) had issued him the dreary sack of a suit he was wearing. So-and-so was the apparatchik who issued civilian clothing to Soviet military intelligence officers traveling abroad. The intimate knowledge on the part of the CIA officer would have sufficiently impressed Penkovskiy and created enough rapport to minimize any inhibitions.

While it depends on disciplined attention to detail, great expertise, unbiased analysis, healthy skepticism, and sense of conspiracy, asset validation, like counterespionage, is not a science or a bureaucratic exercise. It is an art which is aided greatly by an experiential, intuitive understanding, in other words, "feel." One noteworthy case involved an engineer who volunteered in Moscow with plans for a new Soviet aircraft. The initial approach of this would-be source and data provided simply did not "feel" right to the CI officers examining it in Washington. There was simply something "off" about his "presentation." When overhead satellite coverage imaged an aircraft on a runway which resembled the volunteer's reporting, some CI officers asked "How much plywood and balsa wood did it take to build that fake?" The volunteer did turn out to be controlled. On the other side of the coin, similarly skeptical officers were on too many other occasions successfully fooled by the KGB, which resulted in the loss of operational techniques, noisy persona non grata declarations, and some successful disinformation operations.

The vetting of SIGINT information and sources, and the product of other technical collection operations, is one of the most difficult and perhaps the most controversial aspect of "asset validation." The SIGINT practitioners stand on the assertion, "SIGINT never lies." SIGINT is often based on cryptanalytic successes or major technical collection breakthroughs and it is almost impossible for intelligence officers to gain enough access to the operations to make independent judgments about the sources. SIGINT, as now practiced in the West, presents a fertile area for the opposition to engage in deception and disinformation operations.

3. COUNTERINTELLIGENCE AS DISINFORMATION OPERATIONS

The section above on source vetting described the difficulties of determining whether a human source is valid. This section looks at the issue from the other side: the purposes and techniques of running operations against the opposition, in order to control their activities, misinform them, trap them, or get them to reveal their operational techniques and capabilities. In the early 1920s, the State Political Directorate (OGPU) of the Soviet Union penetrated existing, anti-Communist organizations. Instead of eliminating them, it co-opted and expanded them into an organization that had the operational name, "The Trust." This control enabled the OGPU effectively to neutralize a large part of the opposition to the Bolsheviks.

During World War II deception and disinformation played a vital role in operations against Germany. Prior to the Normandy invasion in 1944, the British used apprehended Nazi spies, along with a massive disinformation campaign involving the creation of an entirely fictitious Allied army corps, to persuade the Germans that the invasion would be directed against the Pas de Calais, not Normandy. The success of this operation was, of course, founded on superb British CI operations, which identified and neutralized all Nazi sources in Great Britain, thus eliminating any sources still working for the Germans who could have cast doubt on the information provided by those under British control. The British were also greatly aided in this effort by excellent intelligence on German reactions to the deception campaign afforded by successful decryption of German military communications. Another spectacular World War II success involved an elegant, if macabre, operation in which the British arranged to have float ashore in Spain the perfectly documented corpse of an ostensibly drowned British officer carrying fake war plans. The corpse successfully misled the Germans into thinking the allies intended to invade Sardinia and Greece instead of Sicily. In this operation, the British illustrated their skill at disinformation, counterintelligence, and attention to detail, by using the corpse of an individual who had died of pneumonia, a cause of death that apparently displays pathological signs similar to drowning.[21]

After receiving data from Aldrich Ames on almost all CIA's human source operations against the USSR in 1985, the KGB, apparently under pressure from the Soviet leadership, quickly started arresting these sources, which ran the risk of alerting CIA to a CI problem and jeopardizing Ames. To mitigate this risk, the KGB CI Directorate conducted a number of disinformation operations to try to explain away the compromises of the American sources. In the summer of 1985, a KGB officer working for the CIA in Africa who was compromised by Ames went on home leave carrying operational directions to a dead drop containing a large number of rubles, which he planned to spend while on vacation. He did not return from home leave. Instead the CIA received information from a source in Europe that the officer had been arrested picking up the dead drop in Moscow. At about the same time, the CIA and FBI received essentially the same story about this compromise from another KGB source. After Ames was identified as a spy, it became clear that the KGB knew that both the sources were working for the Americans and, to protect Ames, used them as unwitting vehicles to misinform U.S. Intelligence before they found ways to lure the officers back to the USSR.

The United States intelligence community has not distinguished itself in running controlled sources against the opposition. While the U.S. military allegedly had success in running "perception management" operations against Iraq before operation Desert Storm, the American effort during the Cold War was consistently unsuccessful. The U.S. military policy is that "Offensive Counterintelligence Operations" (OFCO) are run to protect and enhance national security. The Defense Intelligence Agency subscribes to the following succinct objectives of double agent operations as summarized from the book, *The Double-Cross System* by Sir John C. Masterman. The objectives are: 1. Control the adversary's espionage system and by doing so, in effect make him work for you. 2. Identify, neutralize or suppress new agents and spies. 3. Obtain information on the personnel and methods of the adversary service. 4. Secure access to adversary codes and ciphers 5. Gain evidence of the adversary's intentions. 6. Influence the enemy's operational intentions. 7. Systematically deceive the enemy (Masterman 1972). Item 5 represents a very important example where "counter" intelligence can greatly assist "positive" intelligence. Considerable insight into an adversary's policies and intentions can be gained from knowing the thrust and focus of his intelligence-collection activities.

In its own operations and in cooperation with the military services, the FBI has sought to convince the opposition of a dangle's value in an effort to induce hostile intelligence services to handle the operation in the United States, which would give the Bureau very valuable information on how they operate in America. The CIA, with very rare exceptions, has not tried to run controlled operations; rather it has served merely to coordinate such operations run abroad by other agencies.

The lack of U.S. success in this area during the Cold War is at least partly attributable to the KGB's success in penetrating U.S. intelligence. Ames and Hanssen, complemented by other lesser-known sources in the military, provided the KGB with detailed information on the double-agent program, all the doctrine, the complete "play book" of operational techniques and many, if not all, the specific operations. The apparent success of deception operations against Iraq prior to Desert Storm bespeaks a salutary improvement in the U.S. CI posture, because it shows Saddam Hussein did not have the valuable sources within the U.S. intelligence establishment enjoyed by the KGB.

4. COUNTERINTELLIGENCE AS OPERATIONAL TRADECRAFT

In any organization engaged in intelligence collection, the imposition of the highest possible standards of operational security, or tradecraft, is a critical counterintelligence function, particularly in the intelligence services of Western democracies. Unless the discipline of good operational security is forcefully imposed on the average American case officer,[22] the default will be sloppy or non-existent tradecraft. Putative sources will be met in the dining room of a posh hotel literally next to the U.S. embassy. Operational failures will be explained away by the case officer's statement that he was using "semi-clandestine" tradecraft, and officers operating

in alias abroad will call home on cell phones. In the early twenty-first century the use of sloppy tradecraft presents the U.S. intelligence community with a daunting and critical challenge. An entire generation of new American case officers is getting its initial, formative, "on-the-street" experience in the war zone of Iraq, meeting sources with armed and sometimes armored military or paramilitary escorts or within fortress compounds. This sort of "tradecraft" bears no resemblance to the clandestine operational activities required to recruit and manage human sources elsewhere.

5. COUNTERINTELLIGENCE AS THE RECRUITMENT AND RUNNING OF CI SOURCES

The very best way to engage in counterintelligence activities is to have a valid source, or preferably sources, in the opposition service who can tell you what spies they have, or are trying to develop, in your government or defense industries; what technical, cyber, or disinformation operations they are running or plan to mount; and what they are doing to detect and negate your own intelligence-collection operations. The acquisition of such sources is a controversial subject. It is a fact that most of the productive counterintelligence sources acquired by the West during the Cold War were volunteers. Armchair media and academic experts advocate a passive approach, denigrating the use of resources to pursue actively the recruitment of foreign intelligence officers. This approach ignores a significant fact. Many of the volunteers acted only after, and probably as a result of, exposure to, and cultivation by, American intelligence officers. In addition, to get the most from a source requires cultural understanding and great substantive expertise, which cannot be learned from a file, book, movie, or television series, and can be gained only by close, long-term engagement with the opposition.

Unfortunately, the best example of an extraordinarily productive counterintelligence human source is FBI Special Agent Robert Hanssen, who volunteered to and worked for the KGB and GRU off and on for about twenty-one years. Over his spy career Hanssen informed the Soviets/Russians of human-source operations the CIA and KGB were running against the Soviet Union/Russia; some truly exquisite and productive technical and SIGINT collection operations; details of the double-agent program; and, of signal importance, full details of the FBI's counterintelligence program and operations against the Russians. This latter body of data gave the KGB/SVR an enormous advantage in acquiring and managing sources in the United States.

6. COUNTERINTELLIGENCE: DEVELOPING ISSUES AND CHALLENGES

Much of the material used above to describe the various aspects of counterintelligence is of Cold War vintage. Even though that body of historical data continues to shed light on the modalities of CI, several new factors and issues must be taken into account, not least the role of counterterrorism.

6.1 COUNTERINTELLIGENCE AND COUNTERTERRORISM

The practical goals of counterintelligence and counterterrorism (CT) are identical: the identification and neutralization of secret organizations engaged in secret operations to attack the United States and its allies. However, the difference in the nature of the threats has caused U.S. bureaucracies to separate the functions, particularly at the CIA and the FBI. Counterintelligence professionals thus face the challenge of ensuring that all the rules and standards of their discipline, such as operational security/tradecraft, asset validation, and counterespionage, are observed in the CT arena.

Since the Cold War never led to a military clash between the superpowers, the CI emphasis was on uncovering and neutralizing espionage, that is, on the stealing of secrets. The United States and some of its allies are now engaged in shooting wars and it must defend against sabotage and terrorist attacks both by state and "nonstate" entities. Therefore CI must work to protect not just secrets, but installations, operations, communications, and data storage as well as people. Today a hostile intelligence entity might be just as likely to be planning to kill or kidnap a U.S. official as to recruit him as a spy. Civilian CI officers should recognize the increasing relevance of the U.S. Department of Defense's concept of "force protection," which includes CI in a broad program of security disciplines to protect people, facilities, equipment, and operations.

6.2 COUNTERINTELLIGENCE: THE CYBER THREAT AND DENIGRATION OF COMPARTMENTATION

The so-called cyber threat has recently been described as the "new frontier" of counterintelligence. The cyber era has greatly complicated the work of counterintelligence officers. It is now much easier for an insider to steal vast amounts of national security information simply by downloading data onto devices such as thumb drives or to insert "malware" into networks to facilitate data exfiltration from remote platforms when plain hacking has been unable to penetrate the network.

There exists at the human, professional, and management levels a mutual disaffinity between CI officers and the "computer people." The former are mostly the proverbial "social science majors" who are not computer experts and who, by experience, think in terms of human spies. The latter, by technical training and experience, are motivated to create the smoothest flow of data to as many people as quickly as possible. The technical approach is best illustrated by Deputy Defense Secretary Paul Wolfowitz's statement that "the U.S. intelligence system needs to be adapted to the information age... we must emphasize speed of exchange and networking to push information out to people who need it, when they need it, wherever they are" (Inside the Pentagon 2002).

The complications for CI created by the onset of the computer age are being exacerbated by the post-9/11 conventional wisdom that failure "to connect the dots" led to that disaster. The 9/11 Commission Report emphasized the need to change the "mindset" in the intelligence community from "need to know" to "need to share" (Director of National Intelligence 2008, 6). The Director of National Intelligence, Vice Admiral J.M. McConnell (Ret.), and his Associate Director and Chief Information Officer Major General (Ret.) Dale Meyerosse, took the policy a step further by decreeing that "need to share" would become "responsibility to provide" (Director of National Intelligence 2008, 9). Regardless of the lip service paid to security and statements about "managing risk," this new policy will inevitably lead to a further breakdown in compartmentation, as more and more networks are interconnected, easing the work of spies and making the work of identifying and neutralizing them more difficult.

In addition to the understandable tendency of the computer people to speed the widest possible dissemination of data and the post-9/11 mindset to do away with "need to know," the American tendency to think mostly in terms of technical solutions comes into play in the issues facing counterintelligence. The National Counterintelligence Executive has recently emphasized that "…computer architecture and the soundness of electronic systems" are a key CI issue (Warrick and Johnson, 2008, A1A). Professional CI officers thus face three major challenges. One is to remind management that people are always involved, whether as an insider spy or as an opposition intelligence officer attacking U.S.-national-security organizations through electronic means. The second challenge is that CI professionals must learn enough about data processing and networks to communicate and work effectively with information management officers. Only with this basic knowledge can CI officers force a rational balance between information flow and dissemination and the need to find technical ways sensibly to restrict data and to establish techniques and procedures quickly to identify the inevitable hostile activity within and among networks. This issue presents intelligence officers with the third challenge: to inculcate CI awareness into the professional culture of information-technology professionals, who alone have the expertise to design the necessary policies and systems.

6.3 COUNTERINTELLIGENCE: LAW ENFORCEMENT AND NATIONAL SECURITY

Another dysfunction similar to that between CI officers and computer experts exists between CI officers and law enforcement. Counterintelligence officials are intent on protecting national security by identifying and neutralizing threats posed by hostile intelligence entities. Law enforcement officers at the U.S. Department of Justice (DOJ) are almost exclusively focused on making successful prosecutions, with the result that once the arrest of a spy is imminent or has taken place, CI considerations are not allowed to come into play. For instance, in one recent case, DOJ prosecutors included in the charging documents all of the considerable body of data known to have been passed to the opposition by the spy in order to intimidate him into accepting a plea agreement. While that ploy succeeded, CI officers were greatly hampered doing a damage assessment because the spy and his lawyer quickly figured out precisely what the government knew and refused, despite the terms of a plea agreement, to expand on its knowledge.

In another instance, CI officers gained personal access to a foreign intelligence officer who had been handling a minor spy in the United States. That officer, in effect, volunteered to help the CI officers but

the government chose to go ahead with an arrest and well-publicized prosecution, which eliminated any chance the officer would help U.S. authorities identify other spies the foreign intelligence service was running against the United States. Another incident involved a technical collection operation uncovered by outstanding CI work. Law enforcement officers at the management level would not even consider using the still-secret discovery for a possible disinformation operation. Rather, they insisted on a public announcement of the find and a noisy expulsion of a foreign intelligence office. American CI professionals face the challenge of stimulating discussion at the National Security Council level to determine whether national security issues can be given equal importance to prosecutorial considerations in such cases.

QUESTIONS FOR DISCUSSION

1. What means are used to protect a nation's secrets against adversarial intelligence services?
2. Which of the several counterintelligence approaches is most desirable to uncover moles within one's own intelligence services?
3. Does counterintelligence pose risks to a nation's civil liberties?
4. How would you evaluate torture, extraordinary rendition, and warrantless wiretaps as methods to enhance counterintelligence effectiveness?

ENDNOTES

1. Executive Order 12333, Sec. 3.5, as amended on July 31, 2008.
2. The First Chief Directorate was the foreign intelligence arm of the Soviet KGB, and is now named the SVR.
3. Colonel General Oleg Danilovich Kalugin, former Chief of Directorate K (Counterintelligence) of the KGB First Chief Directorate, October 2008.
4. British Security Service Act of 1989.
5. Defined as "[p]reventive measures taken to mitigate hostile actions against Department of Defense Personnel (to include family members), resources, facilities, and critical 'information." Joint Publication 1–02, Department of Defense Dictionary of Military and Associated Terms, a 0073, amended through October 17, 2008.
6. Dr. Dirk Doerrenberg, former Director of Counterintelligence for the BfV, December 2008.
7. The terms counterintelligence and CI will be used interchangeably in this chapter.

8. The Russian intelligence representation abroad, the equivalent of a CIA "station" is called a "residency."

9. Howard, a former CIA case officer, was identified in 1985 as spying for the KGB, and escaped to the USSR where he subsequently died.

10. John Walker, a U.S. Navy Communicator, started working for the KGB in 1968 and along with his brother, son, and a friend spied for the Soviets for about seventeen years.

11. Conrad, a retired U.S. Army Sergeant, was arrested in 1988 as part of a spy net in the U.S. Army, which by that time had existed for seventeen years.

12. The GRU is the Russian military intelligence service.

13. Statement by retired General Nikolaos Gryllakis, former head of Greek security. Undated translation/transcription of Greek television show, "Fakeli" (files).

14. Vitaliy Sergeyevich Yurchenko, a senior KGB counterintelligence officer, defected to the CIA in Rome in August 1985 and redefected to the USSR three months later.

15. The prospect of a polygraph examination has also deterred existing spies from applying to CIA for employment or accepting an assignment there.

16. Jonathan Pollard, a U.S. Navy civilian intelligence analyst, was arrested in 1985 for spying for Israel.

17. SIGINT or signals intelligence is one of the many examples of "int" terminology including MASINT, IMINT, and HUMINT imposed on the U.S. government by the Department of Defense. Some civilian, professional intelligence officers prefer "human espionage" to HUMINT.

18. "Dangle" is the term of art for an individual controlled by a CI service who is put in the way of a hostile service, making himself as attractive as possible in the hope the service will take him on as an agent, a "double agent." The American media, displaying their usual ignorance of the intelligence business, have taken to describing spies such as Aldrich Ames and Robert Hanssen as "double agents," apparently because they were employees of intelligence organizations. They should be labeled spies or penetrations.

19. "Denied area" is an intelligence term of art describing an extremely hostile operational environment with heavy surveillance.

20. Penkovskiy was a Soviet military intelligence officer who worked for the United States and Great Britain from 1960 lo 1962.

21. This operation is described in the 1956 movie, *The Man Who Never Was.*

22. The term "case officer" has been used to designate the operations officer who manages a human source or, in a broader sense, the officer in charge of a technical collection project. Under the influence of Washington-based personnel professionals, this title apparently has been replaced by the bureaucratic term "core collector."

REFERENCES

Bromwich, M. R. 1997. *Office of the Inspector General Department of Justice Report, A Review of the FBI's Performance in Uncovering the Espionage Activities of Aldrich Hazen Ames.* Unclassified Executive Summary (April 21).

Director of National Intelligence. 2008. *United States Intelligence Community Information Sharing Strategy* (February 22).

Inside the Pentagon. 2002. *Deputy Defense Secretary Backs New Approach to Processing Intelligence* (September 26).

Masterman, J. C. 1972. *The Double-Cross System in the War of 1939 to 1945.* New Haven, Conn.: Yale University Press, 1972.

Mitrokhin, V. I., ed. 2002. *KGB Lexicon, The Soviet Intelligence Officer's Handbook.* London: Frank Cass.

Risen, J. 2003. "Jailing in Russia Is a Reminder that Spy Wars Still Smolder," *New York Times* (June 16): A1.

Van Cleave, M. 2008. "Meeting Twenty-First Century Security Challenges 2008 The NCIX and the National Counterintelligence Mission: What Has Worked, What Has Not and Why." *Washington Post* (April 3): A1.

Warrick, J., and C. Johnson, 2008. "Chinese Spy 'Slept' in U.S. for Decades." *Washington Post* (April 3): A1.

Reprinted with permission from Paul Redmond "The Challenges of Counterintelligence," in Loch K. Johnson, ed., *The Oxford Handbook of National Security Intelligence* (New York: Oxford University Press, 2010: 537–554).

25. COLD WAR SPIES: WHY THEY SPIED AND HOW THEY GOT CAUGHT

STAN A. TAYLOR AND DANIEL SNOW

Why do some people commit treason against their own country? Taylor and Snow examine this question and find that the answer is simple enough: for money. They note, too, that the United States has become somewhat more effective in catching American traitors, as a result of improvements in electronic surveillance procedures.

The purpose of this study is to ask why certain Americans decided to betray their country and how it is that they were caught. While the general intelligence literature has grown rapidly, not much has been written about traitors as a class or group.[1] Several books have been written about Soviet citizens who have betrayed their government, particularly about those who have defected to the West.[2] And a fair amount has been written about specific Americans who have betrayed their government, particularly the famous cases.[3] But beyond the well known cases, often little exists except one or two short newspaper articles on specific traitors. And as a *category*, very little has been written about Americans who have betrayed their government and revealed classified information to other states.[4]

For this research, we created a database consisting of 139 Americans who have been *officially* charged with spying against their government. We have attempted to include all who either began their treason or were caught during or immediately after the Cold War.[5] To the best of our knowledge, this is a fairly complete list. Obviously, undetected traitors are not included and we have also left out moles or penetration agents—foreign agents who have entered America legally or illegally and have attempted to penetrate national security organizations—unless they acquired US citizenship and were caught. We have relied solely on public information and realize that this may not present the entire picture. But more information is publicly available than is generally realized. We collected information about 40 variables associated with each case. These variables included: date of birth, date of arrest, personal habits (gambling, drinking, and drug habits), sexual preferences, how they were recruited, and a range of other variables....[6]

WHY THEY SPIED

MODELS OF ESPIONAGE

Some scholars have developed highly sophisticated models which, they believe, explain espionage.[7] These models consider various psychological attributes, situational factors, and behavioral chains, coupled with insight from several academic disciplines. Others adopt rather simple models.[8] Nearly all such attempts to explain espionage, however, focus on two areas: factors associated with the individual and factors associated with the situation. No single explanation adequately explains treason nor any other human action. Even the most treasonous of individuals must have access to classified information before it can be pilfered. And only a small percentage of those who do have access to classified information (fewer than .001 percent) ever commit treason.[9]

Our research suggests that nearly all motivations can be grouped into four categories—money, ideology, ingratiation, and disgruntlement. Of these four, money and disgruntlement appear to be growing in importance and ideology and ingratiation appear to be waning (see Figure 25.1)[10]. We also consider a few additional, and probably idiosyncratic, variables

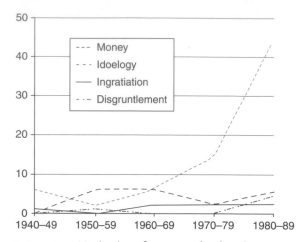

FIGURE 25.1 Motivations for treason by decade.

which we believe cannot be overlooked, especially when combined with other motives.

MONEY

Money appears to be the most prevalent motive for betrayal in recent American history. William Webster, when he was Director of Central Intelligence (DCI), told a reporter that he had not known of a traitor since 1986 who had been motivated by anything beyond money.[11] "It was a truism of the 1980s that ideology was out; materialism was in."[12]

Our data reveal that financial gain has been the primary motivation in 55.4 percent of all cases of Cold War espionage, by far the single most prevalent motive. This counts those whose intent was to get money even though they may have been arrested before any money changed hands. When linked with secondary factors (disgruntlement, ideology, etc.) money was the motive in 62.6 percent of the 139 cases. Seventy-one percent of enlisted personnel were motivated *solely* by money. Until military pay raises in the early 1980s, pay for low ranking military personnel was traditionally meager and many of our cases turned to espionage merely to pay outstanding debts or to allow them to live more stylishly.[13] Rather than turn to family, friends, or banks for loans, they turned to the KGB or related services.

It is difficult to know precisely how much money was involved in each case. Unless the foreign intelligence services revealed how much they paid, or unless the captured spy kept careful records of his or her payments, many dollar amounts are estimates. From what is known, it appears that 17 were paid between $10,000 and $100,000, seven were paid between $100,000 and $1,000,000, and four were paid over $1,000,000.[14] The recent American traitor Aldrich Ames typifies this financial motive. Ames related that he "felt a great deal of financial pressure" and that it was stress from this pressure that led him to conceive "a scam to get money from the KGB."[15] The scam got out of hand and Ames continued to betray his country. His reports to the KGB cost at least ten human lives, compromised scores of intelligence operations, and earned him at least $1,397,300.[16] Ames' vulnerability to monetary temptation is revealed in the crass "Publisher's Clearinghouse"-like document given him by his Russian handlers. This piece of paper tallied the money and prizes available to him for his continuing service....

The prevalence of avarice in these cases is remarkable. Thomas Patrick Cavanagh was sentenced to life imprisonment on 23 May 1985 for his involvement in espionage. Cavanagh was an engineer for Northrop Corporation who was working on what was called "quiet" radar techniques. Facing serious financial crises, he contacted what he thought was a KGB agent and offered him information for $25,000. As was often the case in our research, the "KGB agent" was an FBI undercover agent and Cavanagh was arrested. His explanation is typical of many of those who were trying to get into the espionage business for monetary gain. Cavanagh matter-of-factly suggested that since he did not know how to rob a bank, he instead offered classified documents to a foreign country. "There was this piece of paper. I thought it might be worth $25,000. I took the avenue of least resistance. I didn't have the foggiest idea of how to rob a bank."[17]

William Bell was arrested in 1981 for providing classified information about sensitive technologies being developed at Hughes Aircraft to Polish intelligence. After being arrested, Bell was asked if he supported or had sympathies for the Polish government. "No" he replied, "Mr Zacharski [his Polish handler] had found a fool who needed money. I had a weak spot. He took advantage of me."[18]

The prevalence of financial motivation may reflect increasing materialism and greed, but it also says something about recruitment techniques. All intelligence officers are taught to involve money as quickly as possible when dealing with potential or actual assets. When money is exchanged and a receipt is signed, the semblance of a contract is created. A reporting relationship based on ideology, revenge, or other motives is not entirely under the control of the case officer and is less stable.

IDEOLOGY

Conventional wisdom suggests that while most Soviet citizens betrayed their country for ideological reasons, Americans have done so solely for money. As with most conventional wisdom, this generalization is not entirely true. In fact, all traitors, regardless of national origin, have reacted to somewhat similar changing social circumstances. Many early traitors in the West appeared to be motivated by ideological considerations—at least to the degree that anyone acts on single motivation. In Britain, all of the members of the Cambridge ring (Philby, Burgess, Maclean, Blunt, and Cairncross) were attracted to communism early in life. In the United States, the Rosenbergs, Klaus Fuchs, Alger Hiss, and Lauchlin Curry, as well as the much later Larry Wu-Tai Chin, had all been at one time members of the Communist Party.[19]

But after the famous atomic spies cases in the early 1950s, the number of Americans who spied for ideological reasons dropped dramatically. And those that do appear are not the typical cases of communist sympathizers. Several international events seem to be responsible for this trend—revelations about the horrors of Stalin were verified in the 1950s and Soviet violence in Hungary and other Eastern European countries did much to disabuse ideological communists in the West of the purity of the Soviet version of Marxism.

Ultimately, it appears, capitalist materialism prevailed over Marxist materialism—when historical and dialectical materialism failed, avarice was always ready to step in. On both sides of the Iron Curtain, money came to replace beliefs as a motive for betrayal. While Oleg Penkovsky risked his life in the late 1950s and early 1960s to betray what he believed was an evil political system, Victor Belenko, who flew his MiG-25 from the Soviet Union to Hokkaido in 1976, was more anxious to escape his dreary family life and line his pockets with large sums of money.[20]

In about 23.7 percent of 139 cases, we find ideology to be a primary motive. Even in these cases, other motives were apparent. For example, the Chinese-American, Larry Wu-Tai Chin, who joined the Communist Party in China in 1942 seems to illustrate the allure of money more than the allure of ideology. Chin may have begun as an agent-in-place

for the Chinese communists, but the longer he lived in the West, the more he continued his espionage in order to maintain his rather opulent life style.

Jonathan Jay Pollard and Anne Henderson-Pollard also illustrate this shading of motives. The Pollards originally contacted Israeli military personnel and agreed to pass information Jonathan would obtain from the US Navy. Pollard's Zionist sympathies seem to have prompted his original betrayal, but, as with Chin, before long Pollard was attracted to the $30,000 per year he was promised by his Israeli contacts.

But over the last 15 years, ideology has almost disappeared as a motive. Only six individuals appear to have entered into espionage for ideological reasons since 1980, five of whom appear to have been motivated *solely* by ideological considerations. Thomas Dolce (who actually began spying in late 1979) wanted to support the white-dominated South African government; Glenn Souther developed Marxist leanings while in college; Jeffrey Carney spied for East Germany, essentially because of his anti-American feelings; Michael Moore wanted to defect to the USSR while serving as an American seaman in the Philippines; Frederick Hamilton's desire to end the perennial border dispute between Peru and Ecuador led him to give US electronic intercepts to Ecuadorian officials; and Robert Kim, a naturalized US citizen born in South Korea, appears to have been a mole. In fact, Hamilton appears to be the only *purely* ideologically motivated traitor to enter into espionage since 1984, and he was motivated by a commitment to peace rather than to a Cold War ideology.

INGRATIATION

Ingratiation becomes a motive when information is betrayed to foreign sources in order to fulfill friendship or love obligations or in order to make favorable impressions on someone whose approval is desired. In our database, ingratiation figured as the primary motive in eight, or 5.8 percent, of the cases. This is not enough cases to allow broad conclusions, but it does appear that ingratiation is declining as a motive. Ingratiation, especially sexually motivated ingratiation, may be a relic of the Cold War.

The use of same- or opposite-sex "honey traps" to attract and, if necessary, blackmail potential traitors has been a favorite theme of novelists and scriptwriters, but has been little understood and vastly overrated by them. In our database, there are only four cases of betrayal brought on by blackmail and they are spread over many years—1951, 1960, 1970, and 1984. Ingratiation's effectiveness may be judged by the handful of spies who were motivated by it. Though there is no publicly-available evidence to support it, we believe that if we had a record of every KGB, or related service, attempt to attract a potential traitor through some variety of friendship, the list would be much longer than it is in our database which counts only those who succumbed and were caught.

The case of the only FBI agent ever arrested for treason illustrates this motive. Richard Miller was recruited by the FBI in 1963 and served in New York, Puerto Rico, Florida, and California. In 1981 he was given a counterintelligence position in the Los Angeles FBI office. His past performance had been far from stellar and he had been suspended twice for weighing more than FBI guidelines allowed. Moreover, his marriage was disintegrating. After a series of extra-marital affairs, in May 1984 Miller met Svedana Ogorodnikov, who described herself to Miller as a KGB major. Miller became emotionally and sexually involved with her. Miller was arrested on 2 October 1984 and, after three separate trials, was convicted of espionage. Miller argued throughout the trials that he was trying to ingratiate himself with Ogorodnikov for counterintelligence purposes, but two different judges and even a member of Miller's family believed that the KGB had capitalized on Miller's emotional needs and compromised his career through seduction.[21]

Ingratiation's decline probably results from several developments. One is the end of the Cold War. Clearly, if Soviet and East European secret service defectors are to be believed, various forms of seduction were part of the KGB espionage arsenal.[22] One prominent Soviet defector suggested that compromise and coercion based on various levels and types of friendship were techniques in which KGB officers were well-trained.[23] Moreover, seductions and sexual affairs now can have graver medical consequences than they did for much of the Cold War. Also, the instability of the international system and the fast pace of technological developments make long-term spy operations less useful. Effective and efficient intelligence operations today require short-time success and do not allow long-term development of relationships. Finally, the role of sex in espionage has always attracted more attention than it merited. American secret services have found that happy and well-adjusted family men and women make better agents than those who are sexually promiscuous, emotionally impaired, and susceptible to blackmail.[24]

DISGRUNTLEMENT

Like money, disgruntlement is a motive of growing importance. By disgruntlement we refer to the sense of personal dissatisfaction that stems from feelings of being overlooked, overworked, and underappreciated. No cases of disgruntlement occurred in the 1940s, and virtually none occurred in the 1950s. However, as the military and defense industry grew, the likelihood of disgruntled employees taking revenge against their employers by betraying secrets also grew. Disgruntlement has grown in importance in the last five years.[25] Disgruntlement was the primary motive in 2.9 percent of our 139 cases. People entrusted by their government with classified information are given a unique ability to exact revenge on that government if it offends them.

If we consider those who, though not completely disgruntled, were not entirely "gruntled" (to borrow from Oscar Wilde), then disgruntlement becomes a more prevalent motive. Disgruntlement comes from a variety of sources. Often, disgruntled because of low pay, individuals have attempted to supplement their income through selling information. We classified these cases as motivated by disgruntlement rather than by greed. In other cases, dissatisfaction with their treatment would lead individuals to treason. The case of Daniel Walter Richardson illustrates the latter point. Richardson was described in reports as a mediocre soldier, and in August 1987 was demoted from tank instructor to tool room manager for his chronic tardiness. Shortly after, he called the Soviet embassy in Washington and offered to sell them defense information. The FBI intercepted this call and, posing as the KGB, was able to stage a meeting with Richardson. At this meeting, Richardson turned over a training manual and circuitry from an M-1 tank. Richardson illustrates disgruntlement leading to a desire for revenge and followed by an attempt to sell secrets for money.

Other cases illustrate this pattern. Allen John Davies left the Air Force in 1984 as a result of poor job performance. Two years later he tried to get revenge by attempting to sell classified information to Soviet agents. A disgruntled ex-CIA employee, Edwin G. Moore, followed a similar path. Unhappy about his failure to be promoted in the CIA, Moore collected ten boxes of classified documents and attempted to sell them to Soviet diplomats in Washington.

There is an interesting parallel between disgruntlement as a motive for espionage and disgruntlement as a motive for leaking classified or confidential information. Leaking is virtually a national pastime in Washington. Hardly a week passes without some public revelation of information that was meant to be confidential or private. Every president since Eisenhower has complained about the debilitating and discouraging effects of leaking. One in-depth study of several cases of unauthorized leaks revealed that disgruntlement and revenge are the primary motives of such leaking.[26]

OTHER FACTORS

Other factors account for the remaining 12.2 percent of our cases. As with more common motives, when combined with other motives these miscellaneous factors figure in a larger percentage of espionage cases. But as a sole or primary motivation, they are rare. Some, however, deserve comment.

One under-appreciated motive is fantasy. We were surprised by the number of spies who appear to have developed an addiction to the mystique of espionage. We call this the "James Mitty" syndrome because it combines the allure of a James Bond lifestyle with a Walter Mitty sense of fantasy.

Two cases illustrate this motivation. William Kampiles was a young man who was so attracted to the life of espionage that he sought a position with the CIA's Directorate of Administration in March 1977 and was assigned to cable. When he did not get selected as a case officer in the Directorate of Operations, he concocted a plan through which he thought he could prove to his bosses that he had all of the skills necessary to be a case officer. Seeing a classified document left lying on a filing cabinet one night, he stole it, fled to Greece, and eventually sold it to the Soviet Embassy.[27] His logic was that as soon as he was hired by the KGB, he could confess to the CIA and become a double agent.

Jeffery Loring Pickering was convicted of espionage in 1983 and was described as a person who fantasized about espionage. Even in the many cases where money, disgruntlement, or ideology was the primary motive, we were surprised to notice the large number of cases where an obsession with excitement and intrigue, or a fascination with spying, blended and shaded with other motives.

Though closely related to disgruntlement, a desire to bolster one's ego or self-importance also played a role in some cases. For example, Samuel

Loring Morison was hired as an analyst for the Navy Intelligence Support Center (NISC) in 1974. Described by his peers as an "oddball genius" and an "eccentric patrician," Morison considered himself to be above many of the rules that governed the handling of sensitive information. In 1978, two years after he was hired by the NISC, Morison became involved with Jane's Defense Weekly as a part-time editor. Morison regularly pushed the security limits until, in 1984, he provided Jane's with three secret US satellite-photos of a Soviet submarine under construction. Jane's published the pictures, revealing some of the resolution capabilities of the ultrasecret KH-11 spy satellite. Morison's principle motivation for doing this was to impress his higher-ups at Jane's.

Kinship was a factor in several cases. In the famous Walker case, John Walker involved both his brother and his son. Kinship even played a factor in the demise of the Walker ring—it was his former wife who reported John's spying to the FBI. The Pollard case involved kinship ties, Edward Howard's escape required his wife's complicity, and Aldrich Ames' wife was also convicted of spying.

In summary, people enter into treason for a variety of reasons and any attempt to classify risks oversimplification since every human being is unique and no human act is ever motivated by a single factor. However, the cases in our database suggest that avarice, disgruntlement (including job dissatisfaction, desires to harm to one's employer and alienation), ideology, and ingratiation explain the

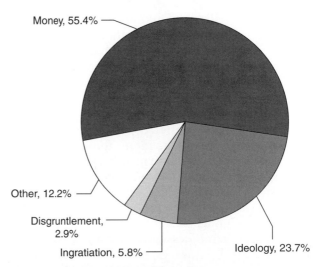

FIGURE 25.2 Motivations for treason.

overwhelming number of cases of treason (see Figure 25.2, p. 311). The next question, however, is how they are caught.

HOW THEY GOT CAUGHT

Many counterintelligence methods are closely guarded. But one can imagine that they are somewhat similar to crime detection methods. Known foreign intelligence service officers in the United States are kept under close surveillance and embassies and other buildings, particularly those of hostile states, are monitored. It is widely suspected that telephone calls and correspondence with certain embassies and individuals might also be monitored. But until 1978, one of the most frequently used law enforcement techniques for detecting criminal behavior was not available to the intelligence community. That technique was electronic surveillance.

FOREIGN INTELLIGENCE SURVEILLANCE ACT

In order to address that problem, Congress passed the Foreign Intelligence Surveillance Act (FISA) in 1978. This act established warrant-like procedures to authorize electronic surveillance of foreign powers and their agents.[28] The effect of FISA on the detection and conviction of American traitors has been overlooked by intelligence scholars. The authors of the most thorough study yet published, for example, conclude that they "cannot determine" why the government was more successful in the 1980s than it had been earlier in catching espionage attempts.[29] Our data suggest that FISA played a major role in this development.

From the end of World War II up to 1978, many changes were made to the procedures governing electronic surveillance for domestic criminal purposes. But the procedures for authorizing the collection of electronic surveillance for national security purposes remained the same—presidential authorization. Although presidents believed they had extremely broad powers to authorize warrantless electronic surveillance for national security purposes, that practice suffered from two significant problems. First, there were many abuses. Presidents and other senior government officials could order electronic surveillance and place entities of foreign governments located in the United States or their agents, as well as US persons suspected of spying for these entities, under the most intrusive of electronic surveillance techniques without court issued warrants. These techniques, especially when conducted against US persons, exceeded the "unreasonable

search and seizure" and "probable cause" requirements of the Fourth Amendment. But, as long as national security was invoked, senior government officials were willing to overlook constitutional niceties and condone this questionable behavior.

Second—and from a counterintelligence point of view, perhaps more serious—the evidence obtained through arguably illegal monitoring techniques was often rejected by American courts.[30] Thus, many who engaged in treason against the United States found evidence against them either rejected by courts or found decisions against them overturned by higher courts. Aware of this latter fate, the Federal Bureau of Investigation (FBI) became reluctant to use evidence obtained in this manner in courts.

> A series of lower court decisions between 1971 and 1977 accepted the Executive's argument that warrantless national security-related electronic surveillance could lawfully be authorized by the President or...the Attorney General.... In several cases, however, surveillances were found to be unlawful when courts retrospectively disagreed with the judgments of Executive officials as to whether national security, rather than law enforcement, objectives were being served by warrantless electronic surveillance.[31]

Moreover, the government became reluctant to seek normal surveillance warrants through open court procedures for three reasons. First, to do so might result in unwanted "publicity about the secret information and [establish] the fact of its loss."[32] To convince a regular court to issue a warrant required publicly proving the significance of that information, a task which often could not be done without revealing other classified information relating to it. Second, purchased secret information is often viewed suspiciously by the government that buys it. That government does not know whether it is false information made up just to make a sale, misinformation given purposely to mislead it, or valuable secret information which might enhance its national security. Corroboratory information revealed in an open warrant procedure tends to confirm the veracity and importance of the purloined information. And, third, and perhaps most importantly, to reveal enough information to obtain a warrant in an open court might compromise the sources and methods through which the information was obtained.

FISA changed all of this. It created a special court procedure that is "consistent with the 'reasonable search' requirement of the Fourth Amendment."[33] Under FISA, the Department of Justice was not bound by the traditional "probable cause" standard required to obtain warrants in normal criminal cases. Yet, at the same time, it was bound by specified procedures which protected civil liberties by banning electronic surveillance of Americans merely on the order of a government official under a loosely defined national security standard.

> [FISA] established comprehensive legal standards and procedures for the use of electronic surveillance to collect foreign intelligence and counterintelligence within the United States. The Act provided the first legislative authorization for wiretapping and other forms of electronic surveillance for intelligence purposes against foreign powers and foreign agents in this country. It created the Foreign Intelligence Surveillance Court comprised of seven federal district judges, to review and approve surveillances capable of monitoring United States persons who are in the United States.[34]

In general, FISA has been supported both by law enforcement agencies as well as by most civil libertarians. Evidence obtained under FISA has been accepted in courts as long as it satisfied the foreign intelligence and counterintelligence requirements of the act and as long as the procedural requirements of the act were met. Perhaps the most thorough constitutional justification of FISA can be found in *United States v. Duggan* (743 F.2d 59[2d Cir. 1984]) where both Fourth and Fifth Amendment challenges to this kind of electronic surveillance were addressed by the court.[35]

FISA allows the government to obtain a court order authorizing electronic surveillance, but to do so in a non-public setting which protects national security information and intelligence methods from foreign scrutiny. The problems of the earlier warrant procedure were overcome while at the same time American citizens were assured that their government could not "spy" on them capriciously.

RECORD OF FISA

The record of FISA is good and may say more about the increase in successful espionage prosecution in recent years than other explanations. For example, "between 1965 and 1974, an average of 177 warrantless national security surveillances were approved annually by the Attorney General."[36] The FISA Court, by contrast, approved an annual average of 530 surveillances between 1980 and 1994 (see Table 25.1).

TABLE 25.1 FOREIGN INTELLIGENCE SURVEILLANCE ACT COURT-SURVEILLANCE ORDERS ISSUED

Year	FISA Orders Issued
1979 (partial year)	207
1980 (first full year)	319
1981	431
1982	475
1983	583
1984	635
1985	587
1986	573
1987	512
1988	534
1989	546
1990	598
1991	593
1992	484
1993	511
1994	575

Source: United States Senate Select Committee on Intelligence and Administrative Office of the US Court System.

Given the length of time necessary to put together a solid court case for treason, the surge of espionage cases in 1984 and 1985 may be attributable to the impact of the FISA court. It is also obvious why 1984 is often referred to as "The Year of the Spy" and the 1980s as "The Decade of the Spy." In the Ames case, for example, the FBI was searching for a penetration agent in the CIA as early as 1987. After dropping the investigation in 1989, they began again in 1991 and identified Ames as the traitor in March 1993, but did not arrest him until February 1994. Even after learning that Ames was the long sought KGB agent-in-place, it took nearly a year to complete the evidence necessary for a trial.[37]

Until all of the classified information relating to the detection and arrest of each case is made public, it is difficult to document the precise contribution of the FISA legislation. But the raw numbers do suggest that FISA made a significant difference in the government's ability to detect and prosecute traitors. Clearly, the Carter administration's decision to prosecute espionage more vigorously also contributed to the higher arrests in the mid-1980s, but that new vigor would not have been possible without FISA.

Excluding those who defected and were not caught, from 1945 to 1977, 23 percent of the detected spies were caught during their first attempt at espionage, suggesting that many continued their espionage for longer periods of time. From 1978 to date, however, 38 percent have been caught in their first foray into espionage. This probably reflects not only increasing skills on the part of counterintelligence agents, but also the role of FISA in making electronic surveillance more available and usable in court.

PHYSICAL SEARCHES

To make matters even worse for traitors, Congress recently adopted legislation creating FISA-like procedures covering physical searches, a category that was explicitly left out of the 1978 FISA Act. In 1980, then Attorney-General Benjamin Civiletti asked that requests for national security-related physical search authorizations also be considered under FISA. A few physical search authorizations were actually approved by the FISA court even though the original legislation was specifically limited to electronic surveillance. Several earlier attempts to include physical searches under the FISA procedures failed.

In 1981, however, the Reagan administration convinced the USA court that it had no authority to approve applications for physical searches. It is somewhat ironic that "the only government request that the FISA Court has ever rejected was done at the insistence of the Executive Branch itself."[38]

Following Aldrich Ames's arrest in 1994, however, both public opinion and the mood of Congress changed regarding physical searches. Physical searches are now under the FISA procedures and the government can obtain court orders authorizing access to phone records, banking information, and other personal data by following the procedural requirements of FISA.[39] Prior to this change, it was easier to tap a telephone than to obtain telephone records.

FAULTY TRADECRAFT

In any discussion of why spies are caught, one often overlooked motive deserves mention. After reading as much data as was available about our 129 cases, we are amazed at the poor level of tradecraft, even abject stupidity, displayed in many cases. This is especially apparent among one-time-sellers, but even among those with some understanding of tradecraft, foolish blunders played a significant role in their eventual detection. One worries, in fact,

that an especially acute spy with good tradecraft might be very difficult to catch. But even spies with some tradecraft skills (Walker, Howard, and Ames, for example) made foolish mistakes, perhaps stemming from feelings of overconfidence, which often betrayed them. Since 1976, at least 16 of the spies in our database telephoned or walked into the Soviet Embassy and asked if they would like to buy some secrets. In every case the FBI, who had intercepted the calls, met these would-be spies, bought what they had to offer, and then arrested them. In one case, the budding traitor threw a package of classified material with a note in it asking for money over the wall of the Soviet Embassy. The Soviets thought it was a bomb and called the Washington fire department who came and collected the material. Aldrich Ames, one of the most recent traitors, paid $540,000 cash for a home while earning a $62,000-a-year salary. Robert Haguewood walked into a bar and started talking to a stranger on an adjacent stool about his desire to sell classified information to the Soviets. The man was an off-duty policeman. Time and time again, these spies would engage in activities that any thinking person would avoid.

INTELLIGENCE AFTER THE COLD WAR

Some have wondered whether clandestine intelligence gathering and counterintelligence activities are needed in the post-Cold War world. Senator Daniel Patrick Moynihan, former member of the Senate Intelligence Committee, has introduced legislation that would assign most of the CIA's current functions to State, Defense, and other government departments and change the focus of most intelligence gathering operations to open sources.[40] Less draconian is the proposal of former CIA director Stansfield Turner, who has proposed significant shifts in priorities in the US intelligence community. Admiral Turner believes that economic intelligence ought to be the primary goal of the intelligence community, and that it should reorganize its efforts to reflect that new priority.[41]

Others, however, might remind us of Lord Palmerston's adage, first expressed in the House of Commons in 1848, that there are no eternal enemies and there are no eternal friends, there are only eternal interests. If that is the case, then all states will continue to gather information about other states, and all states will try to protect against that collection. Even without the Soviet challenge, intelligence gathering will continue and counterintelligence efforts will still be necessary. In fact, the collection of both open- and denied-source information may be more important now than it was during the Cold War.

Stanley Hoffmann once said that as the "physics of power declines, the psychology of power rises."[42] That is, as the material elements of power become less capable of shaping and determining events, then perceptions and images become more important. And as perceptions and images become more important, then what Joseph Nye calls "soft power" becomes more important.[43] With the end of the Cold War, the eggs of power—particularly nuclear weapons—have become relatively less important. But that merely forces attention to the hens that make that power possible—the economies and social and political developments of other states.

This logic suggests that all nations will continue to collect clandestine intelligence information and that all nations will need to protect against that activity through counterintelligence efforts. What has changed is the nature of the intelligence desired. Strategic intelligence—information about abilities and intentions of hostile or potentially hostile states—is still important. But information about general social, economic, and political conditions of states has become perhaps even more significant. What used to be called non-strategic intelligence may be the new strategic intelligence.[44] In the information age, information, indeed, may be the principle commodity of international relations.

The recent case of Aldrich Ames, who may be the most damaging traitor in all American history, suggests two conclusions. First, treason is still possible, even after the Cold War. Ames began his treason in 1991, and continued to sell classified information to non-Communist Russia even after the Soviet Union collapsed in 1989. He was identified as a Russian asset in March 1993, but not arrested until February 1994.[45] His activities were celebrated in Moscow, but will be condemned in the United States for years to come.[46] Within the last 15 years, we know of attempts by France, Israel, Japan, Germany, and South Korea to gather denied information about the United States.

Second, while some isolated cases of ideologically motivated treason may still be found, most recent treason has been motivated by cupidity and avarice. Knowing how difficult it is to change institutional directions, one can only speculate whether the profile of traitors that existed during the years that James Angleton headed the CIA's counterintelligence efforts made it more or less difficult to identify non-ideological traitors. Angleton headed counterintelligence efforts over the very two decades during which our data suggest ideology was declining and other motives were becoming more important. Clearly, current counterintelligence profiles must pay more attention to the kinds of motivations we have discussed.[47] As a thoughtful reviewer of an earlier version of this article suggested, it may have been difficult for the CIA to find people like Ames when it was searching for people like Philby.

QUESTIONS FOR FURTHER DISCUSSION

1. What are the primary motivations that lead people to spy against their own nation? How would you describe what these individuals have in common, if anything?
2. How have these motivations changed over time, and why?
3. How has the United States caught those engaged in treason?
4. How can one balance the needs of counterintelligence and security, on the one hand, and civil liberties, on the other hand? Has the Foreign Intelligence Surveillance Act achieved this balance when it comes to wiretaps?

ENDNOTES

1. The prolific writer Rebecca West published one of the early and interesting books on treason. In her *The Meaning of Treason* (NY: Viking 1946) and *The New Meaning of Treason* (ibid. 1964), West discusses some specific British traitors during World War II. Her Epilogue in both volumes is a good introduction to the concept of ideological treason. See also Chapman Pincher, *Traitors* (London: Penguin 1988) for a more lengthy discussion of treason.

2. See e.g. Gordon Brook-Shepherd, *The Storm Petrels: The First Soviet Defectors, 1928–1938* (London: Weidenfeld 1977) and the same author's *The Storm Birds: Soviet Postwar Defectors* (NY: Harcourt Brace Jovanovich 1989). The best bibliography for both first- and second-hand accounts of Soviet defectors and Western agents-in-place is Raymond G. Rocca and John J. Dziak, *Bibliography on Soviet Intelligence and Security Services* (Boulder, CO: Westview 1985).

3. See e.g. John Barron, *Breaking the Ring: The Bizarre Case of the Walker Family Spy Ring* (Boston: Houghton Mifflin 1987), Wolf Blitzer, *Territory of Lies: The Exclusive Story of Jonathan Jay Pollard* (NY: Harper & Row 1989),

and Robert Lindsey, *The Falcon and the Snowman* (NY: Simon & Schuster 1979).

4. Of the recent books, Theodore R. Sarbin *et al.* (eds.) *Citizen Espionage: Studies in Trust and Betrayal* (Westport, CT. Praeger 1994) is, by far, the best generally available trade book. The Defense Personnel Security Research Center, created by the Dept. of Defense in the wake of several security breaches in 1984 and 1985 and located at Monterey, California, has published several reports, primarily for use within the defense community. See, for example, Susan Wood and Martin F. Wiskoff, *Americans Who Spied Against Their Country Since World War II* (Monterey, CA: Def. Pers. Security Res. Center). See also, Thomas B. Allen and Norman Polmar, *Merchants of Treason* (NY: Delacourt 1988), Ronald Kessler, *Spy vs. Spy: Stalking Soviet Spies in America* (NY: Scribner's 1988), Pincher, *Traitors* (note 1), and Robert J. Lamphere and Tom Shachtman, *The FBI-KGB War: A Special Agent's Story* (NY: Random House 1986). Most of these works are somewhat anecdotal and earlier works consider only a few cases.

5. Several deified databases obviously exist; however, we have had access to none of them. By far the best and most thorough analysis of espionage cases is Wood and Wiskoff, *Americans Who Spied* (note 4). Their database was created from unclassified information; however, their study was conducted under government contract and they had cooperative personnel at all of the intelligence agencies with whom they dealt. Their database included cases through 1990, while ours includes cases through 1996. As a contracted study, their report was not as widely distributed as it should have been. But any student of treason should obtain it. No research on American traitors would be possible were it not for the valuable contributions made by the Defense Personnel Security Research Center and the Dept. of Defense Security Institute. The latter's *Recent Espionage Cases* is the only data available on some spies. Our rather narrow definition of traitor as an American citizen who was charged with treason caused us to omit several early ideological spies whose prosecution was considered too sensitive by the government. For example, we have not included William Weisband, an NSA spy, because he was charged only with failing to report to a grand jury even though he was a known spy. We have not included cases of economic espionage in our database unless the traitor was charged by the government under espionage acts. We did not include the case of two Connecticut company executives who

sold carbon-carbon technologies and equipment to Indian defense-related organizations. They were convicted of violating export laws, but were not charged with espionage. Similar cases are discussed in Peter Schweizer, *Friendly Spies: How America's Allies Are Using Industrial Espionage to Steal Our Secrets* (NY: Adantic Monthly Press 1993).

6. On 11 July 1995 the National Security Agency released communications relating to the Rosenberg case which could not have been made public at the time without compromising sensitive collection techniques. See David Kahn, "VENONA Messages and Atomic Bomb Espionage," in *World Intelligence Review* (formerly *Foreign Intelligence Literary Scene*) 14/2 (1995) p.1 and Lamphere and Shachtman, *FBI-KGB War* (note 4).

7. See e.g. the excellent article by Carson Eoyand, "Models of Espionage," in Sarbin, *Citizen Espionage* (note 4) Ch. 4.

8. See e.g. the MICE model (motivation, ideology, compromise or coercion and ego) first described by KGB defector Stanislav Levchenko, *On The Wrong Side: My Life in the KGB* (Washington, DC: Pergamon-Brassey's 1988).

9. Herbig accepts the figure of 3 million Americans holding security clearances in the 1980s. See Katherine L. Herbig, "A History of Recent American Espionage," in Sarbin, *Citizen Espionage* (note 4) p. 45. Approximately 30 were charged with espionage during the same time period.

10. Joseph P. Parker and Martin F. Wiskoff, *Temperament Constructs Related to Betrayal of Trust* (Monterey, CA: Def. Pers. Security Res. Center 1991) p. 50.

11. "US Finds it Difficult to Catch Spies Who Sell Out For Cash, Not Ideology," *Wall Street Journal,* 30 June 1986, p. 26, quoted in Sarbin, *Citizen Espionage* (note 4) p. 51.

12. Herbig, "A History of Recent American Espionage" (note 9) p. 51.

13. See ibid. p. 53.

14. Wood and Wiskoff, *Americans Who Spied* (note 4) p.55.

15. The quotation is from an FBI transcript interview with Ames and is reported in US Congress, Senate, Select Committee on Intelligence, *An Assessment of the Aldrich H. Ames Espionage Case and Its Implications for U.S. Intelligence,* S. Rpt. 103–90, 103d Cong., 2d sess. (Washington, DC: 1994) p. 11.

16. See US Senate, *An Assessment of the Aldrich H. Ames Case* (note 15) p. 39. *U.S. News & World Report,* 6 March, 1995, p. 50, claims Ames' revelations could have resulted in 30 deaths.

17. *The San Francisco Examiner,* 21 June 1987, p. l. Also cited in Herbig (note 9) p. 54.

18. United States, Senate, Select Committee on Intelligence, *Meeting the Espionage Challenge: A Review of United States Counterintelligence and Security Programs,* Report 99–522, 98th Cong., 2d sess. (Washington, DC, 1986), p. 118.

19. For many of the insights in this section, I am indebted to Herbig (note 9).

20. John Barron, *MIG Pilot: Lt. Victor Belenko's Final Escape* (NY: Reader's Digest Press 1980) is the most complete account of Belenko's delivery of the Soviet Foxbat jet fighter into Western hands.

21. Most of the information on Richard Miller is taken from articles in the *Los Angeles Times* by William Overend published on 24 Oct. 1985, 7 Nov. 1985 and 15 July 1986. Mr. James McQuivey also interviewed Miller's son Paul in 1991 and used that interview in a class case study of Miller that is in the authors' possession.

22. "The use of sex to lure and entrap potential agents is known to be a technique of Soviet and bloc intelligence services," according to George C. Constantinides, *Intelligence and Espionage: An Analytical Bibliography* (Boulder, CO: Westview 1983) p. 292. But Constantinides rightly discredits David Lewis' *Sexpionage: The Exploitation of Sex by Soviet Intelligence* (NY: Harcourt Brace 1976) for being based on "a potpourri of fact, rumor, and speculation," p. 292.

23. Levchenko, *On the Wrong Side* (note 8).

24. Joseph P. Parker and Martin F. Wiskoff, *Temperament Constructs Related to Betrayal of Trust* (Monterey, CA: 1991), pp. 32–35.

25. Herbig (note 9) p. 50.

26. See Martin Linsky, *How the Press Affects Federal Policymaking: Six Case Studies* (NY: Norton 1986).

27. Kampiles sold for $3,000 a technical manual for the KH-11, an overhead reconnaissance satellite, a highly classified US secret. This satellite, the capabilities of which were unknown to the Soviets, provided real-time photographs in high resolution. Had Kampiles known the significance of his information, he could have sold the manual at a considerably higher price.

28. Public Law 95-511. This legislation passed Congress as S. 1566. Electronic surveillance refers to wire taps, television monitoring, hidden microphones, electronic tracing devices, and other electronic means to gather evidence. S. 1566 did not address the question of physical searches.

29. Wood and Wiskoff, *Americans Who Spied* (note 4) pp. A12 and A13.

30. Americo R. Cinquegrana, "FISA: A Reformist Success Story," in *Foreign Intelligence Literary Scene* 8/6 (1989) p. 2.

31. Ibid. p. 2.

32. Herbig (note 9) p. 64. The case of William Weisband, mentioned in note 5 above, illustrates this principle. Had Weisband been caught after passage of FISA, prosecution would have been possible.

33. US Senate, *Foreign Intelligence Surveillance Act of 1978,* Report No. 95–701, 95th Cong., 2d sess. (Washington, DC: 1978) p. 9.

34. US Senate, *The Foreign Intelligence Surveillance Act of 1978: The First Five Years,* Report 98–660, 98th Cong., 2d sess. (Washington DC 1984) p. l.

35. FISA has survived unscathed over 20 challenges in various court cases. See, for example, *United States v. Fahey,* 540 F. Supp. 1306, 1314 (E.D.N.Y. 1982), *United States v. Megahey,* No. 83–1313, 2d cir. 8 Aug. 1984, and *United States v. Belfied,* 692 F. 2d 141 (D.C. Cir. 1982). These and other cases are discussed in United States Senate, Foreign Intelligence Surveillance Act (note 34).

36. Cinquegrana, "FISA" (note 30).

37. US Senate, *Assessment of the Aldrich H. Ames Case* (note 15).

38. Cinquegrana (note 30) p. 12.

39. This is contained in Section 303 of S. 2056. See, United States, Senate, Select Committee on Intelligence, *The Counterintelligence and Security Enhancements Act of 1994,* Report 103–296, 103d Cong. 2d sess. (Washington, DC 1994) p. 8.

40. Moynihan explained the rationale for his legislation on Public Television's *MacNeil/Leher News Hour* on 13 Feb. 1995: The text of this discussion is available on Lexis/Nexis, 15 Feb. 1995.

41. Stansfield Turner, "Intelligence for a New World Order," *Foreign Affairs* 70 (Fall 1991), pp. 151–152.

42. Stanley Hoffmann, "Perceptions, Reality, and the Franco-American Conflict," in John C. Farrell and Asa P. Smith (eds.), *Image and Reality in World Politics* (NY: Columbia UP 1967) p. 58.

43. Joseph S. Nye, Jr., "Soft Power," *Foreign Policy* No. 80 (Fall 1990), pp. 153–171.

44. In 1976 and 1977, the Senate Intelligence Committee, on the urging of then member Senator Adlai Stephenson, III, undertook a lengthy study of so-called non-strategic intelligence—general information about the social, economic, and political conditions within the Soviet Union. In the wake of criticism of the intelligence community for its failure to see more clearly the pending collapse of the Soviet Union in 1989, the

strategic importance of general social, economic, and political information now seems more apparent.

45. Literally hundreds of newspsaper and magazine articles have been written about the Ames case. Undoubtedly, scores of books will follow, not to mention TV mini-series and movies. But the best brief official record is found in United States Senate, *An Assessment of the Aldrich H. Ames Espionage Case* (note 15).

46. It appears his KGB managers even sent him photographs of the "beautiful land" on which his country house (dacha) would be located when he had to end his treason. See "The Cold War's Last Spy," U.S. *News and World Report,* 6 March 1995, p. 59.

47. Angleton continues to have supporters and detractors. Perhaps the most objective review of the literature about Angleton can be found in "Of Moles and Molehunters: A Review of Counterintelligence Literature, 1977–92" written by Cleveland C. Cram and published as an intelligence monograph by the CIA's Center for the Study of Intelligence in 1993.

From Stan A. Taylor and Daniel Snow, "Cold War Spies: Why They Spied and How They Got Caught," *Intelligence and National Security* 12 (April 1997): 101–125. Reprinted by permission of the publisher (Taylor & Francis Ltd, http://www.informaworld.com).

26. TREACHERY INSIDE THE CIA

SENATE SELECT COMMITTEE ON INTELLIGENCE

In 1994, the U.S. Senate Select Committee on Intelligence (SSCI) conducted an investigation into one of America's most damaging counterintelligence failures: the treachery of Aldrich H. Ames inside the Central Intelligence Agency. This chapter provides a look at the Committee's findings.

In the end, regardless of what the Committee may recommend or what Congress may enact, fundamental change will come only if the Director of Central Intelligence, supervisors at all levels, and the employees of the CIA bring it about. The Committee intends to monitor the Agency's progress in this regard, but the leadership must come from within.

The Committee undertook its inquiry not for the purpose of assessing individual blame—which is the exclusive responsibility of the Executive branch—but rather to learn what had gone wrong and to evaluate the institutional lessons to be learned from the Ames case. Nevertheless, the Committee believes that the recent actions taken by the Director of Central Intelligence, R. James Woolsey, against past and current CIA officials implicated in the Ames case warrant comment.

On March 10 of this year, Director Woolsey appeared before the Committee in closed session to outline his interim responses to the Ames case. One area for reform which was cited by the Director was "management accountability." According to the Director: "[T]o my mind, this is very much at the heart of the entire matter." The Committee strongly shares this view.

Despite the CIA Inspector General's recommendation that 23 current and former CIA officials be held accountable for the Agency's failure to prevent and detect Ames' espionage activities, Director Woolsey chose only to issue letters of reprimand to 11 individuals—7 retired and 4 current Agency employees. None of the individuals cited by the Inspector General was fired, demoted, suspended or even reassigned as a result of this case. In response to what was arguably the greatest managerial breakdown in the CIA's history, the disciplinary actions taken by the Director do not, in the collective experience and judgment of the Committee, constitute adequate "management accountability."

All Committee Members believe that the Director's disciplinary actions in this case are seriously inadequate and disproportionate to the magnitude of the problems identified in the Inspector General's report. It is clear, given the immense national security interests at stake, that there was "gross negligence"—both individually and institutionally—in creating and perpetuating the environment in which Ames was able to carry out his espionage activities for nine years without detection.

The Committee is concerned about the message that Director Woolsey's mild disciplinary actions will send to the overwhelming majority of CIA employees who are dedicated, conscientious, patriotic, and hard-working professionals, many of whom are exposed daily to risk and hardship. For the current employees who were faulted by the Inspector General for their role in the Ames case to remain in their grades and positions falls far short of the level of accountability expected by the Committee. Indeed, in the wake of the Director's decision, many professionals within the Intelligence Community have contacted the Committee to register the same sentiment.

As this report documents, the failures evident in the Ames case were numerous and egregious. While it might be argued that the majority of individuals cited by the Inspector General were guilty of acts of omission rather than commission, the seriousness of these omissions cannot be overstated. The failures of the individuals cited by the Inspector General led to the loss of virtually all of CIA's intelligence assets targeted against the Soviet Union at the height of the Cold War. Ten of these agents were executed. The inability of the CIA to get to the bottom of these losses in a timely way was itself a significant management failure.

If there is not a higher standard of accountability established by DCIs, then a repeat of the Ames tragedy becomes all the more likely. Management accountability within the Intelligence Community should be no less than the highest levels found elsewhere in the Executive branch. Director Woolsey's actions do not meet this standard.

Having noted in strong terms the magnitude of CIA's failures, the Committee would be remiss not to point out what went right. A traitor, responsible for heinous acts of espionage, was identified and convicted. He has been imprisoned for life. In the end, this was accomplished by the work of a small group of CIA and FBI personnel who took part in what became a long and arduous inquiry—for some, lasting almost nine years. At least one member of this group appears to have pushed from the very beginning to get to the bottom of the 1985 compromises. It was his impetus that eventually put the investigation back on track in 1991. Over time, the scope and pace of the investigation had taken many twists and turns, some caused by the KGB and some by internal factors beyond the control of the investigators themselves. The commentary which follows is not intended to diminish in any way what was ultimately accomplished by this dedicated group of investigators and analysts.

Finally, the Committee notes that its recommendations are based upon the situation that pertained through early 1994. Director Woolsey has promulgated some new policies since then and has announced his intention to institute still others. While the Committee believes in general that stronger measures are needed, it is too early to pass judgment on the Director's recent actions.

THE FAILURE TO "FIX" PAST COUNTERINTELLIGENCE PROBLEMS

The counterintelligence function at the CIA is weak and inherently flawed. Despite repeated internal and external reports which have recognized a long-standing cultural problem with the counterintelligence function, CIA managers have, judging from the Ames case, failed to fix it.

In particular, the Committee was struck by the number of internal and external studies undertaken after 1985—which became known as the "Year of the Spy" following the exposure of spies John Walker, Ronald Pelton, Edward Lee Howard, and Jonathan Pollard—which pointed out the systemic and deeply-rooted problems in the CIA's conduct of counterintelligence.

As summarized by the recent report of the CIA Inspector General, these internal and external reports over the years focused on common themes:

> That a counterintelligence career was held in low esteem at the CIA and did not attract high caliber officers. This was, in part, because officers gained promotions by agent recruitments, not by analyzing problems in recruitment operations;

> That there was an ambiguous division of responsibility for counterintelligence among CIA offices;

> That counterintelligence information was not being shared properly among CIA components; and

> That CIA was reluctant to share counterintelligence information fully and in a timely manner with the FBI. (IG Report, pp. 16–22)

The poor state of counterintelligence at the CIA in the mid-1980s can be explained in part by the reaction to the so-called "Angleton era." James Angleton had been the head of the Counterintelligence Staff of the CIA from 1954 until 1974 (when he was involuntarily retired by DCI William Colby). He became convinced that the KGB had penetrated the CIA. Accordingly, Angleton was suspicious of virtually every Soviet agent who was recruited by the CIA and suspicious of every CIA officer responsible for such recruitment. On occasion, his suspicions led to CIA officers being fired without adequate justification.

While several of the officers who had been unjustly fired were later compensated, the counterintelligence function was effectively undermined by the negative reaction to Angleton's relentless pursuit of spies, particularly within the Soviet-East European (SE) Division of the Directorate of Operations, which had the principal responsibility for recruiting Soviet agents for the CIA.

In addition, there appears to have been an excessive focus within the Directorate on the recruitment of intelligence sources to the exclusion of counterintelligence concerns. Few officers wanted to go into counterintelligence because promotions and recognition came from successful recruitments, not from questioning, or identifying problems with, ongoing operations. Further, there was an image of a "corporate elite" constructed among these officers which led them to dismiss too readily the possibility of a spy among them.

By all accounts, these attitudes were prevalent within the Directorate of Operations at the time Ames sabotaged the Agency's Soviet operations in the summer of 1985, and they greatly contributed to management's failure to focus upon the CIA employees who had had access to the compromised cases (as explained in detail below).

The CIA made some efforts to address these shortcomings after "the Year of the Spy." In 1988, the head of the counterintelligence staff was made an "Associate Deputy Director" in the Directorate of Operations, and was double-hatted as the head of a new Counterintelligence Center (CIC). The CIA and FBI also signed a new Memorandum of Understanding (MOU) in 1988, which provided, at least on paper, for improved sharing of information in counterintelligence cases.

But these new bureaucratic "trappings" for the counterintelligence function did not overcome the fundamental problems which continued to be cited in reports issued in the 1990s. Despite the formation of a "lead office" for counterintelligence and the 1988 MOU with the FBI, the sharing of counterintelligence information between CIA components and with the FBI continued to be a serious problem, as was clearly evident in the Ames case.

In conclusion, the Committee finds that, despite repeated internal and external reports which recognized a longstanding cultural problem in the counterintelligence function, the CIA failed to implement adequate solutions. Indeed, the Committee believes the fundamental problems persist.

RECOMMENDATION NO. 1: The Director of Central Intelligence should revise the CIA's strategy for carrying out the counterintelligence function. The Director should institute measures to improve the effectiveness of counterintelligence to include (a) establishing as a requirement for promotion among officers of the Directorate of Operations, service in a counterintelligence or counterintelligence-related position during their careers; (2) establishing incentives for service in a counterintelligence position; (3) instituting effective and comprehensive counterintelligence training for all officers of the Directorate of Operations and for appropriate officers assigned elsewhere in the

CIA; and (4) ensuring adequate access to ongoing foreign intelligence operations by those charged with the counterintelligence function. The Committee will make this a "special interest area" for purposes of oversight until it is satisfied the weaknesses noted above have been adequately addressed.

THE FAILURE TO DEAL WITH SUITABILITY PROBLEMS

As the Ames case all too clearly demonstrates, the CIA Directorate of Operations is too willing to dismiss, deny, or ignore suitability problems demonstrated by its officers.

From the outset of his career at the CIA, Ames demonstrated serious suitability problems which, over the years, should have led his supervisors to reassess his continued employment. These problems included drunkenness, disregard for security regulations, and sloppiness towards administrative requirements. In the years immediately before he began to commit espionage and during the rest of his career, his supervisors were aware of his personal and professional deficiencies, but did not make his problems part of his official record, nor act effectively to correct them. Despite his recognized unsuitability, there is little evidence that his assignments, activities, or access to sensitive information were in any way limited as a result.

Prior to Ames's assignment to the counterintelligence staff of the SE Division in 1983, his supervisor in Mexico City sent a message to CIA headquarters recommending that Ames be counseled for alcohol abuse when he returned. While Ames's supervisor recognized a chronic problem, the message to headquarters apparently stemmed from an incident which occurred at an official reception at the U.S. Embassy where Ames was drunk and became involved in a loud argument with a Cuban official. On another occasion, Ames was involved in a traffic accident in Mexico City and was so drunk he could not answer police questions nor recognize the U.S. Embassy officer sent to help him. In fact, based upon recent interviews with his colleagues, Ames was notorious for long, alcoholic lunches, often slurring his speech when he returned to the office. None of this behavior prompted any serious effort to correct the problem while Ames was overseas, or when he later returned to CIA headquarters.

In April 1983, when CIA headquarters asked Ames's supervisors in Mexico City whether Ames qualified for a staff position in another Latin

American country, they recommended against it, citing his alcohol problem, his failure to do financial accountings, and his generally poor performance. Nevertheless, six months later, when a former supervisor of Ames requested him to fill a position in the SE Division at headquarters—the most sensitive element of the Directorate of Operations—there is no indication that Ames' alcohol problem or poor performance were ever noted. Indeed, Ames was placed in a position which provided him access to the identities of virtually all of the Soviet intelligence officers by the CIA without his new supervisors being aware of the problems he had had in Mexico City.

The alcohol abuse counseling that Ames ultimately did receive upon his return to headquarters amounted to one conversation with a counselor, who, according to Ames, told him that his case was not a serious one when compared to many others in the Directorate of Operations.

In 1983, during the assignment in Mexico City, Ames also began an extra-marital relationship with a Colombian national, Rosario Casas Dupuy (hereinafter "Rosario"), herself a recruited asset of the CIA. Over time, the seriousness of their relationship became apparent to several of Ames's colleagues, but this never led to any action by Ames's supervisors, despite the fact that CIA regulations prohibit sexual relationships with recruited assets and require that reports of "close and continuing" relationships with foreign nationals be submitted by employees. Despite the security implications of this relationship, the violation of Agency regulations was ignored.

In fact, Ames did not file an official report concerning his relationship with Rosario until April 1984, four months after she came to the United States to live with him. Indeed, it appears that until their marriage in August 1985, Ames (still married to his first wife) and Rosario continued to live together, without any perceptible concern being registered by the CIA. While the counterintelligence staff recommended in February 1985, that in view of the anticipated marriage, Ames be moved to a less sensitive position, nothing changed. Ames continued in the same position.

While his alcohol problem abated during this assignment to the SE Division—at least as a matter of attracting official attention—it resurfaced during his assignment in Rome. He was known among colleagues for his long, alcoholic lunches, for sleeping at his desk, for often slurred speech, and generally as a marginal performer. On one occasion, after an

Embassy reception, he was so drunk that he passed out on a street and awakened in a hospital. While his supervisor was unhappy, this incident did not become part of Ames' record, nor does it appear that this episode led to counseling or any serious reevaluation of Ames' fitness for continued service. Indeed, the same supervisor extended Ames' tour in Rome for a third year.

Over his career, Ames repeatedly demonstrated carelessness and disdain for security requirements. In 1975, while on his way to meet a CIA source in New York, Ames left a briefcase of classified materials identifying the source on a subway train. Although the briefcase was ultimately recovered, it might well have compromised the source's relationship with the CIA. In the fall of 1984, he brought Rosario to CIA housing where CIA undercover officers were staying, in violation of security regulations. In August 1985, he took her to the safe house where the Soviet defector Yurchenko was being debriefed, again in violation of security procedures. In Rome, he was known to prepare classified reports at home. During his assignments at CIA headquarters between 1989 and 1994, he was occasionally found in other CIA offices where he had no reason to be, and with materials he had no reason to have.

He was equally negligent throughout his career in complying with the administrative requirements imposed on officers of the Directorate of Operations, such as submitting financial accountings for the cases he was handling.

Despite these and other incidents, Ames never received a single official reprimand during his 31-year career at the CIA. Indeed, most of the incidents and shortcomings which have come to light since Ames was arrested were never made a matter of official record. Once on board, his fitness to serve in the Directorate of Operations was never reevaluated.

The Committee appreciates that intelligence officers of the Directorate of Operations are often placed in jobs and situations with stresses and strains that far exceed those of the average government employee. But these positions also demand self-control and personal discipline. Particularly in overseas assignments, it may be impossible to separate an intelligence officer's private life from his or her public, official one. A single misstep can prove his undoing or that of other officers.

It is the Committee's perception, which the Ames case confirms, that the Directorate of Operations has been far too willing to dismiss or ignore flagrant examples of personal misconduct among its officers. Excessive drinking and extra-marital relationships with sources have all too often been seen as part of the job, rather than as indicators of problems. Security concerns are too often dismissed as the bureaucratic whining of small-minded administrators. All too often an officer who has been through training, gone through the polygraph examination, and had an overseas assignment, is accepted as a "member of the club," whose fitness for assignments, promotions, and continued service becomes immune from challenge.

Director Woolsey, in a recent speech, said that the "culture" of the directorate must be changed. The Committee shares that view. Such change will not come solely by changing regulations or personnel. It will come only when supervisors at every level of the directorate take seriously their responsibilities as managers. Personal misconduct should be documented. Officers who do not meet acceptable standards of personal behavior should not be assigned to sensitive positions nor qualify for supervisory positions. Personal shortcomings should be factored into consideration of promotions and bonus awards. While officers with personal problems should be given an opportunity, as well as appropriate assistance, to rehabilitate themselves, failing that, their employment with the directorate, if not with the Agency itself, should be terminated.

RECOMMENDATION NO. 2: The Director of Central Intelligence should ensure that where evidence of suitability problems comes to the attention of supervisors, it is made a matter of official record and factored into the consideration of assignments, promotions, and bonus awards; that efforts are made to counsel and provide assistance to the employee where indicated, and, if the problem persists over time, the employment of the individual is terminated. The Committee will make this a "special interest area" for purposes of oversight until it is satisfied these policies have been instituted and are being observed within the Directorate of Operations.

RECOMMENDATION NO. 3: The Director of Central Intelligence should, in particular, take prompt and effective action to deal with what appears to be a widespread problem of alcohol abuse by ensuring that CIA employees experiencing such problems are identified and are put into effective counseling and/or treatment. During this period, these employees should be suspended from their duties until they have demonstrated to a qualified professional their

fitness to return to service. Should their problems continue, their employment should be terminated.

RECOMMENDATION NO. 4: The Director of Central Intelligence should institute, consistent with existing legal authority, an "up or out" policy for employees of the CIA, similar to that of the Foreign Service, without waiting for the report required by section 305 of the Intelligence Authorization Act for Fiscal Year 1995, pertaining to the Intelligence Community as a whole. Chronically poor performance should be grounds for dismissal from the Agency. If the Director decides not to institute such a policy and does not provide a persuasive rationale to the Committee for his decision, the Congress should enact legislation requiring such a policy during the next Congress.

RECOMMENDATION NO. 5: The Director of Central Intelligence should review and revise the performance appraisal reporting system of the CIA, to include a review of the factors upon which employees are rated and the grading system which now exists, to institute a system which reflects more accurately job performance. Where supervisors are concerned, their rating should include an assessment of how well they have supervised the performance and development of their subordinates.

THE FAILURE TO COORDINATE EMPLOYEES' OPERATIONAL ACTIVITIES

The Ames case provides a striking example of CIA supervisors failing to critically evaluate the contacts of an operations officer—with known personal shortcomings and in an extremely sensitive position—with Soviet officials in 1984 and 1985. Further, the fact that Ames virtually ceased submitting reports of such contacts, in violation of standard Agency procedures, never became known to his SE Division supervisors or made part of his official record.

In 1984, while occupying a position within the SE Division which gave him access to the identities of Soviet agents working with the CIA and FBI, Ames, with the approval of his immediate supervisor, began making contacts with Soviet Embassy officials in Washington, D.C. According to testimony received by the Committee, it was not infrequent that Directorate of Operations Officers at CIA headquarters were asked to "help out" other CIA elements that had responsibility for establishing relationships and maintaining contacts with foreign individuals located in the Washington area.

The Committee has been advised that Ames's senior supervisors in the SE Division were unaware that he was having these meetings and would have disallowed them had they known.

In any event, to permit a person in Ames's position, and someone with the personal and professional shortcomings already noted, to meet alone with Soviet Embassy officials substantially increased the risk of the disaster that eventually occurred. It provided Ames with an opportunity that he otherwise may not have had, or may have had difficulty in contriving on his own.

After June 1985, after his espionage activities had begun, Ames repeatedly failed to submit reports of his contacts with Soviet officials. While his failure prompted complaints from the FBI, the CIA element that Ames was supporting failed to bring this to the attention of his supervisors in the SE Division, nor was it reflected in his official record. Again, had Ames' SE Division supervisors been aware of his failure to file these reports, it may have alerted them to a possible problem. Since the advancement of Directorate of Operations officers depends upon their official reporting, the failure to file such reports should have suggested something was amiss.

A similar failure occurred during his assignment in Rome. While his supervisor was aware that he was meeting alone with Soviet officials in Rome (one of whom was Ames' KGB contact), Ames explained his failure to file reports of such meetings on the basis that he had obtained little worthwhile information. This apparently was enough to satisfy the supervisor.

RECOMMENDATION NO. 6: The Director of Central Intelligence should revise the policies and procedures governing the operational activities of CIA officers to ensure that these activities are better supervised, controlled, coordinated, and documented.

THE FAILURE TO APPLY A STRUCTURED METHODOLOGY TO THE INVESTIGATION OF INTELLIGENCE COMPROMISES

The most puzzling deficiency in the Ames case was the failure, in the wake of the 1985–86 compromises, to aggressively investigate the possibility that CIA had been penetrated by a KGB spy.

Certainly by the fall of 1986, the CIA was aware that it had suffered a disaster of unprecedented proportions which was not explained by the defection of Edward Lee Howard. Within a matter of months, virtually its entire stable of Soviet agents had been imprisoned or executed. In the days of the Cold War, Soviet operations represented the Agency's principal *raison d'etre*. There were no operations which had greater importance to its mission. The CIA was left virtually to start from scratch, uncertain whether new operations would meet the same fate as its old ones.

To be sure, these compromises involved extremely sensitive agents. There was a need for discretion in terms of how the matter was handled. But this does not explain or excuse the Agency's tentative, tepid response. Initially, some CIA officers could not believe that the KGB would "roll up" all of CIA's sources at once if the KGB had a source in the CIA who was still in place. Taking some comfort that new operations appeared to be surviving, some believed the problem had gone away. But this in no way explains the seeming lack of urgency to get to the bottom of what had gone so drastically wrong.

The obvious place to begin would have been with the CIA employees who had had access to the information which had been compromised. At least one official in the SE Division made a strong plea to his supervisors at the time that they needed to "investigate it, not study it." But this did not happen. The CIA task force created in October 1986, undertook what was largely an analytical review of the compromised cases. The task force did oversee an Office of Security review of personnel who had served in Moscow, but no broader examination was made of all CIA officers who had had access to the compromised cases. No systematic effort was made to identify and investigate problem employees and their activities, as was eventually done in 1991–92.

Later, the CIA came to suspect that the KGB was running ploys against them, purposely suggesting reasons for the compromises other than a penetration of the CIA itself. Even then, however, any sense of urgency was lacking. CIA analysts waited for things to happen, for more information to surface. They continued to analyze and conjecture. There was no clear sense of purpose, no clear methodology, and no clear sense of what was required to get to the bottom of the compromises.

In a related counterintelligence investigation of a report suggesting that the KGB may have recruited a source in a particular office in the CIA, a CIA investigator conducted a systematic investigation of over 90 employees who were assigned to that office. The inquiry took more than year. But investigators did not conduct the same type of inquiry of the CIA employees who had had access to the information that was actually compromised in 1985 until 1991–1992.

The FBI was officially brought into the case in October 1986, when the CIA learned that two sources recruited by the FBI had been compromised. But the two agencies worked their investigations separately, despite the likelihood that the compromises were caused by the same source (whether it be human or technical).

While the FBI and CIA task forces regularly exchanged information on the compromises and on the progress of their respective analyses, they never performed a systematic assessment, together, of the CIA employees who had had access to the compromised information, until mid-1991.

Why CIA management during the 1986–1991 period did not attach more importance or urgency to getting to the bottom of the 1985 compromises is incomprehensible to the Committee. While CIA Director William Casey and Deputy Director for Operations (DDO) Clair George, who were in office at the time the compromises occurred, reportedly regarded them as "a huge problem," the Agency's response was to create a 4-person team to analyze the problem. No one believed there was a basis for bringing in investigators from the FBI at this juncture, apparently because CIA was unable to pin responsibility on a particular CIA employee.

While Casey and George became deeply enmeshed in the Iran-contra scandal in the fall of 1986 and spring of 1987, this circumstance does not explain, in the view of the Committee, why a problem so close to the heart of the CIA's mission was not given more attention by senior management. Indeed, once Casey and George departed the scene, it does not appear that their successors—either as DCI or as DDO—gave the inquiry any particular emphasis or priority. DCI William Webster, his deputy Robert M. Gates, and the new DDO Richard Stolz were briefed on the compromises in 1988, but did not delve deeply into either the nature of the problem (which was now several years old) or what the Agency was doing to resolve it.

Due to the extraordinary sensitivity of this inquiry, there was only one junior investigator from the Office of Security assigned to the case from 1985 until 1991. He was responsible for investigating all counterintelligence leads and reports coming in which involved CIA employees. After he began to develop information regarding Ames' unexplained affluence in the fall of 1989, he was diverted from

this investigation for a nine-month period, first for training and then to handle other leads. There was no one else assigned to pick up the Ames leads. Nor was consideration given to having the FBI pick up the leads, despite the fact that the information now focused upon a particular CIA employee within the United States.

While the Committee believes that the investigator in question made a good faith effort to work the leads he was given, he was essentially self-trained and, because of the compartmented nature of the investigation, was given very little help and guidance. Overworked and overloaded, he did not use all of the investigative techniques he might have utilized to get at Ames' financial situation. Indeed, the statutory authority invoked by the CIA in 1992 to obtain access to Ames' bank records was available to the Agency in 1989. Had this authority been utilized at the time information was received concerning Ames's unexplained affluence, it might well have led to his detection at a much earlier stage. The investigator also apparently made no effort to develop information regarding Ames's unexplained affluence during his assignment in Rome. Efforts to verify the financial condition of Ames's in-laws in Bogota were shoddy and ineffective, producing inaccurate information which supported rather than exposed Ames's contrived explanation.

The Committee does not think it fair to hold the investigator assigned to the case solely responsible for these failures. CIA managers simply failed to assign enough investigators to such an important task and failed to provide them with sufficient legal and administrative support to ensure that all appropriate avenues would be explored and all appropriate investigative authorities utilized. Since the professional investigative expertise of the FBI was effectively spurned during this period, insufficient resources and expertise were brought to bear on the case.

The Committee believes that those in charge of the CIA during the 1986–1991 period—Director William Casey, Acting Director and later Deputy Director Robert Gates, Director William Webster, and Deputy Director and later Acting Director Richard Kerr—must ultimately bear the responsibility for the lack of an adequate investigative response to the 1985 compromises. Whatever they may have personally understood the situation to be, they were in charge. It was their responsibility to find out what was being done to resolve the 1985 compromises. Based upon the information available to the Committee, they failed to do so.

Their failure is especially disheartening when one realizes that the information developed in August 1992, which finally focused the investigation on Ames—correlating his bank deposits in 1985 and 1986 with his meetings with Soviet officials—was available to investigators since 1986. Unfortunately, no one asked for it, even when alerted to Ames's unexplained affluence in October 1989.

Although the 1985–86 compromises represented a unique situation for the CIA, the Ames case demonstrates the lack of a clear *modus operandi* for dealing with situations where intelligence sources are known to have been compromised.

RECOMMENDATION NO. 7: The Director of Central Intelligence should establish procedures for dealing with intelligence compromises. At a minimum, these procedures should entail a systematic analysis of all employees with access to the relevant information and, if suspects are identified, provide an investigative methodology to determine whether there is evidence of unexplained affluence, unreported travel, unreported contacts, or other indicators of possible espionage. This type of systematic analysis should begin when a known compromise occurs, not after CIA has eliminated the possibility of a technical penetration, or after CIA has narrowed the range of possible suspects to one or two employees. Analysis and investigation should be undertaken on the basis of access and opportunity, and should not be delayed waiting for evidence on culpability.

RECOMMENDATION NO. 8: Pursuant to section 811 of the Intelligence Authorization Act for Fiscal Year 1995, the FBI should be notified immediately of any case where it is learned that an intelligence source has been compromised to a foreign government, regardless of whether the CIA believes at the time that there is a basis for an FBI counterintelligence or criminal investigation of a particular employee or employees. The CIA should also coordinate with the FBI subsequent investigative actions involving employees potentially involved in the case in order not to prejudice later criminal or counterintelligence activities of the FBI and in order to benefit from the investigative assistance and expertise of the FBI.

RECOMMENDATION NO. 9: The Director of Central Intelligence should require that all employees assigned as counterintelligence investigators have appropriate training, experience, and supervision which ensures, at a minimum, such investigators will be familiar with, and know how to utilize, the investigative authorities available to the CIA and the FBI.

RECOMMENDATION NO. 10: CIA management must ensure that adequate analytical and investigative resources are assigned to counterintelligence cases, and that other kinds of staff assistance (e.g., legal support, administrative support) are made available. In turn, those involved in these cases must ensure that their needs are communicated to their supervisors. The Inspector General of the CIA should periodically assess the counterintelligence cases of the CIA to ensure that adequate resources are being afforded to particular cases.

RECOMMENDATION NO. 11: The status of significant counterintelligence investigations must be regularly briefed to senior Agency officials, including the Director of Central Intelligence. Such briefings should include an explanation of the resources and expertise being brought to bear upon a particular case.

THE FAILURE TO EXPEDITE THE INQUIRY AFTER 1991

The period after the CIA and FBI decided to join forces in June 1991—compared with the period between 1985 and 1991—was relatively intense and focused. For the first time, investigators conducted a systematic review of the CIA employees who had had access to the compromised information, and there was an intensive, productive effort to link Ames and other priority suspects to the compromises.

Yet even during this phase, the investigation took an inordinate amount of time and was plagued by past inefficiencies. The joint investigative unit still had only four people (two from each agency); and there was still a lone CIA investigator working with them. While members of the joint investigative unit did obtain support from the CIA Office of Security and the FBI Washington Metropolitan Field Office, they were still but a few people carrying an extraordinarily demanding workload.

In August 1991, the joint investigative unit developed a list of 29 CIA employees for priority scrutiny. Ames was at the top of the list.

Yet the first letters to go out to financial institutions requesting access to Ames's financial records did not go out until June 1992, almost 10 months later.

In August 1992, when investigators correlated the records of Ames's bank deposits with what was known about Ames's 1985 meetings at the Soviet Embassy, the joint investigative unit suspected they had their man. When they learned in October of Ames's Swiss bank accounts, their suspicions were confirmed.

But according to the Inspector General's report, this crucial information was not presented to FBI headquarters until January 1993. It was explained to the Committee that the joint investigative unit was looking at possible suspects in addition to Ames. But this still does not explain why significant information pertaining to Ames was not passed contemporaneously to the FBI, particularly given the presence of two FBI agents on the joint investigative unit.

On the basis of the work of the joint investigative unit—which culminated in the March 1993 Skylight/playactor report—the FBI assembled an investigative team and tasked the team members to acquaint themselves with the facts. The FBI began an intensive investigation of Ames shortly thereafter. The Committee was advised in the course of its investigation that FBI headquarters had determined that the earlier information developed on Ames by the joint investigative unit did not meet the standards for an intensive FBI investigation. The Committee believes, however, that there was ample evidence by October 1992, to reasonably suggest that Ames was acting in 1985 (and thereafter) as an agent of the Soviet Union. The FBI's hesitation resulted in a six-month delay before the FBI began to apply the full array of its investigative capabilities against Ames. Once applied, they produced impressive results. Indeed, the FBI investigative team from the Washington Metropolitan Field Office, together with the CIA, did a superb job in bringing the investigation to a successful conclusion.

RECOMMENDATION NO. 12: The Director of the FBI should ensure that adequate resources are applied to counterintelligence cases involving the CIA and other federal agencies, and that FBI headquarters is apprised immediately of significant case developments which could form the basis for the FBI's opening an intensive counterintelligence investigation.

RECOMMENDATION NO. 13: The Attorney General and the Director of the FBI should review the FBI's

guidelines for the conduct of counterintelligence investigations to determine whether clearer guidance is needed in determining whether a subject of a counterintelligence inquiry is acting as an agent of a foreign power.

FAILURE TO RESTRICT THE ASSIGNMENTS AND ACCESS TO SUSPECTS IN COUNTERINTELLIGENCE CASES

The Ames case reveals glaring weaknesses in the CIA's procedures for dealing with the career assignments of employees who are under suspicion for compromising intelligence operations. The CIA failed to restrict Ames's assignments and access even after information surfaced in 1989 which indicated Ames was a possible counterintelligence problem.

In September 1989, after a poor tour in Rome, which was known to the managers in the SE Division, his SE superiors allowed Ames to return to the SE Division and assigned him to the office supporting to all Soviet and East European operations in Europe, a position affording him broad access to sensitive information. He remained assigned to the SE Division until August 1990. During this period, investigators learned about Ames's unexplained affluence and developed information regarding several large bank deposits and a particularly large currency exchange. Yet none of this appears to have had any bearing on Ames's continued assignment or access during this period.

In fact, at the end of this assignment, notwithstanding his own poor performance record (he was then ranked 3rd from the bottom among 200 officers in his rating group), Ames was appointed to serve on a promotion board for mid-level CIA operations officers. This assignment gave him access to the personnel records of an entire class of mid-level CIA operations officers.

In October 1990, SE Division managers reassigned Ames to the Counterintelligence Center (CIC) because he had performed poorly and they wanted him out of the Division. Apparently, supervisors in the CIC knew Ames was a poor performer and were aware that questions had been raised about his unexplained affluence. Yet they believed they could manage the problem. After his arrest, these officials recognized that Ames' position had given him access to data which identified virtually every double agent operation controlled by the

United States. It is unclear how or why this access was permitted. It is clear that despite the security concerns raised about Ames, his CIC supervisors did not ascertain or evaluate the extent of his access at the time.

In April 1991, while Ames was assigned to the CIC, the Office of Security carried out an updated background investigation of Ames. The results of this investigation were evaluated and shared with the investigator assigned to the special task force. Reflecting interviews with his co-workers in Rome and his Arlington, Virginia neighbors, the investigation produced information that Ames had frequent contacts in Rome with Soviet and East European officials not fully explained by his work requirements, frequently violated security regulations by leaving his safe open and doing classified work at home, and lived far beyond his CIA salary in both Rome and Arlington. (One of those interviewed went so far as to say that he would not be surprised if Ames were a spy.)

Inexplicably, the CIA security officer who reviewed the investigative report evaluated it as "raising no CI concerns" and the task force investigator assigned to the case did not regard the report as providing any new information. Ames retained his security clearance and his job in the Counterintelligence Center, and no further action was taken to follow-up on the information developed in this report. Indeed, the special task force members viewed the investigative report, together with the favorable results of the April 1991 polygraph, as giving Ames "a clean bill of health."

In September 1991, despite having been "booted out" of the SE Division a year earlier, and despite the special task force inquiry then underway, Ames was allowed to return to the SE Division to conduct a special study of the KGB. While the study itself did not call for particularly sensitive access, Ames once again was given access to the personnel and records of the SE Division.

In December 1991, he was assigned to the Counternarcotics Center (CNC) where he remained until his arrest in 1994. This apparently was the first assignment made on the basis of the security concerns about Ames. But due to the sensitivity of the investigation into the 1985–86 compromises, CNC senior managers were not told of the investigation or the suspicions about Ames until the beginning of the FBI's intensive investigation in 1993. Even then, there was little or no effort made to evaluate and control the extent of Ames'

access to classified information. Indeed, investigators later learned that Ames had computer access to a vast range of classified information that did not pertain to counternarcotics. Moreover, when a computer upgrade was installed in November 1993, it provided Ames with the capability to "download" vast quantities of information onto computer discs which he could take out of the building. Fortunately, Ames was arrested before he was able to pass these discs to his KGB handlers. But the fact that he was provided this capability at all at a time when his arrest was imminent is indicative of the CIA's lack of attention to this security problem.

RECOMMENDATION NO. 14: The Director of Central Intelligence should establish procedures to inform current and prospective supervisors about employees under suspicion in counterintelligence cases. While the need to protect the secrecy of the investigation is essential, as well as the need to protect the employees themselves from unfair personnel actions, the assignment of employees under suspicion without frank consultations at the supervisory level increases the likelihood of serious compromises and leads to conflict between CIA elements.

RECOMMENDATION NO. 15: The Director of Central Intelligence should issue procedures to require, in any case in which an employee is under suspicion for espionage or related activities, that a systematic evaluation be made of the employee's access to classified information, and that appropriate and timely actions be taken to limit such access. While care must obviously be taken to ensure that such actions do not tip off the employee that he or she is under suspicion, the failure to evaluate the access of an employee in these circumstances may eventually result in damage that might have been prevented.

RECOMMENDATION NO. 16: The Director of Central Intelligence should establish more stringent criteria for CIA employees serving on promotion and assignment boards, which, among other things, prevent the appointment to such panels of employees with poor performance records or records of suitability problems.

DEFICIENCIES IN SECURITY PROCEDURES

The Ames case demonstrated numerous deficiencies in the CIA's use of the polygraph, its control over classified documents and materials, and its coordination of security and counter-intelligence functions.

THE POLYGRAPH

Ames was able to pass polygraph examinations in 1986 and 1991 with relative ease. Although deeply involved in espionage activities, he was able to answer questions such as whether he worked for a foreign intelligence service, or had contacts with foreign nationals which he failed to report, without showing signs of deception.

The CIA Inspector General's report faults the 1986 examination, finding that the examiner was "too chummy" with Ames. When Ames showed a slight reaction to a question asking whether he had ever been "pitched," i.e., asked to work for a foreign intelligence service, the examiner appeared to readily accept his explanation that he was concerned about being "pitched" in his upcoming assignment in Rome.

The 1991 polygraph examination, according to the Inspector General's report, was deficient in that the examiners (there were two separate sessions) were not sufficiently familiar with the existing information on Ames' unexplained affluence, or with the information developed in the April 1991 background investigation of Ames. The examination was also deficient in that the investigator assigned to the special task force had not participated directly in the examination process, and there had been no prior planning in terms of how the CIA would handle the situation if Ames suddenly made damaging admissions.

According to Ames's debriefings, he did not take drugs or use any particular technique to pass the polygraph examinations. Acting on the advice of the KGB, he tried only to be cooperative and stay as calm as he could. Since he was acquainted with how polygraph examinations were conducted, he also was able to manipulate the process to prevent a "problem" from arising.

If Ames's account is true, it seems to indicate problems beyond those cited by the Inspector General's report, i.e. that examiners should be better informed and prepared. Indeed, it suggests that the CIA's reliance on the results of polygraph examinations needs to be far more circumspect than in the past.

RECOMMENDATION NO. 17: The Director of Central Intelligence should tighten polygraph procedures to make the polygraph more useful. Such procedures should include random examinations instead of exams at regular intervals, with little or no prior notice, and variations in the polygraph technique. These procedures should also ensure that polygraph examinations involving employees under suspicion are carefully planned and constructed, and that appropriate prior notification is made to the Federal Bureau of Investigation if such cases have potential criminal implications. In addition, the Director should review the policies applicable to the training, supervision, and performance appraisal of polygraph examiners to ensure that polygraph examinations are conducted in a professional manner and produce optimum results.

RECOMMENDATION NO. 18: The Director of Central Intelligence should institute a fundamental reevaluation of the polygraph as a part of CIA's security program. As the Ames case demonstrates, the polygraph cannot be relied upon with certainty to detect deception. This necessarily puts far more reliance on other aspects of the security process, e.g., background investigations, supervisory reporting, psychological testing, financial reporting, etc. The DCI's review should also include a reevaluation of the use of inconclusive polygraph test results. Even where the polygraph does indicate deception, such information is often useless unless damaging admissions are also obtained from the subject. The Committee believes that if an employee with access to particularly sensitive information does not make such admissions but continues to show deception to relevant questions after adequate testing, there should be additional investigation of the issues in question to attempt to resolve them. Should such investigation fail to do so, the CIA should have the latitude, without prejudice to the employee, to reassign him or her to less sensitive duties.

CONTROL OF CLASSIFIED DOCUMENTS AND MATERIALS

The Ames case also demonstrated gaps in the control of sensitive classified information. Ames was able—without detection—to walk out of CIA headquarters and the U.S. Embassy in Rome with bags and envelopes stuffed with classified documents and materials. Many of the classified documents he passed to his KGB handlers were copies of documents that were not under any system of accountability. Ames did not even have to make copies of them. In his last job in the Counter narcotics Center at the CIA, Ames was able to "download" a variety of classified documents onto computer discs and then simply remove them to his home. When he attended a conference in Turkey in 1993, he brought a lap-top computer to do work in his hotel room. This apparently raised no security concern among those familiar with the incident. He was also able to visit offices he had no reason to be in, and gain access to information he had no business seeing.

In the late 1970s, the CIA instituted a policy calling for random and unannounced spot-checks of personnel leaving Agency compounds. But the policy was discontinued soon thereafter due to the inconvenience caused to those subject to such searches.

Ames recounted later that his KGB handlers were amazed at his ability to gain access to sensitive operations and take large bundles of classified information out of CIA offices without arousing suspicion, a sad commentary on the laxness of security at the CIA.

RECOMMENDATION NO. 19: The Director of Central Intelligence should reinstate the policy making persons leaving CIA facilities subject to random searches of their person and possessions, and require that such searches be conducted unannounced and periodically at selected locations. Such searches should be conducted frequently enough to serve as a deterrent without unduly hampering the operation of the facilities involved.

RECOMMENDATION NO. 20: The Director of Central Intelligence should institute computer security measures to prevent employees from being able to "download" classified information onto computer diskettes and removing them from CIA facilities. In addition, existing policies for the introduction, accountability, dissemination, removal, and destruction of all forms of electronic media should be reevaluated. The ability of the CIA's security managers to "audit" specific computer-related functions in order to detect and monitor the actions of suspected offenders should be upgraded.

RECOMMENDATION NO. 21: The Director of Central Intelligence should institute a policy requiring employees to report to their supervisor any instance in which a CIA employee attempts to obtain classified information which the CIA employee has no apparent reason to know. In turn, supervisors should be required to report to the CIA Counterintelligence

Center any such case where a plausible explanation for such a request cannot be ascertained by the supervisor.

RECOMMENDATION NO. 22: The Director of Central Intelligence should institute new policies to improve the control of classified documents and materials within the CIA. In particular, the Directorate of Operations should undertake an immediate and comprehensive review of its practices and procedures for compartmenting information relating to clandestine operations to ensure that only those officers who absolutely need access can obtain such information. Further, the Directorate should establish and maintain a detailed, automated record of the access granted to each of its employees.

COORDINATION OF SECURITY AND COUNTERINTELLIGENCE

The Ames case demonstrated a serious division between security and counterintelligence activities in the CIA. Even though an investigator from the Office of Security (OS) participated in the investigation of the 1985–86 compromises under the auspices of the Counterintelligence Center (CIC), he failed to coordinate properly with OS with respect to Ames' 1991 polygraph examination. OS had initiated a background investigation of Ames in March 1991, but went ahead with the polygraph in April without the benefit of the background investigation. As it turned out, the background investigation provided significant information about Ames that was largely ignored by the investigator assigned to the CIC in light of Ames's passing the polygraph examination.

Citing senior security officials, the Inspector General's report noted there had always been a "fault line" in communications between the CIC and its predecessors, and the OS. The CIC had not always shared information regarding its counterintelligence investigations and had failed to make use of OS's investigative expertise. Indeed, the search to find the cause of the 1985 compromises might have moved more quickly from analysis to investigation if there had been better coordination between security and counterintelligence.

The Inspector General's report also found "a gradual degradation" of the resources and authority given the security function since 1985, concluding that "this degradation has adversely affected the Agency's ability to prevent and deter activities such as those engaged in by Ames...." The

Committee shares the view that this decline has been too great, too precipitous. The Committee had recommended an increase in personnel security funding for the CIA and other agencies for Fiscal Year 1995, but was unable to sustain its initiative due to the lack of interest shown by the agencies involved.

Responding to the continuing problem of CIA offices failing to share pertinent information on CIA personnel with one another, Director Woolsey recently created a new Office of Personnel Security that combines elements of the old Office of Personnel, the Office of Medical Services, and the Office of Security. While this consolidation may facilitate the sharing of information regarding suitability problems, it may also hamper the exchange of counterintelligence information from the CIC and may further dilute the security function, particularly the expertise of security investigators.

The Committee believes that the personnel security function should be preserved with a separate office. Routine monitoring of Agency employees from a security perspective remains an important function and one that must be accomplished without carrying a presumption that persons are under suspicion. An effective personnel security program would deter potential traitors, limit the burden on counterintelligence investigators and result in faster, more effective counterintelligence investigations.

RECOMMENDATION NO. 23: The Director of Central Intelligence should reexamine the decision to combine the Office of Security with the other elements of the CIA's new personnel center, and should ensure sufficient funding is provided to the personnel security function in Fiscal Year 1995 and in future years. The Director should also clarify the relationship between security and counterintelligence, specifying their respective functions and providing for effective coordination and cooperation between them.

FAILURE TO ADVISE THE OVERSIGHT COMMITTEES

The CIA failed to notify the congressional oversight committees in any meaningful way of the compromises of 1985–1986, as required by applicable law.

Indeed, in the hearings held annually on counterintelligence matters and in numerous staff briefings on the subject from 1985 until 1994, the massive compromises of 1985–86 were never once mentioned by representatives of the CIA or the FBI.

Based upon the recollections of individuals, there were two occasions when the 1985–86 compromises were alluded to in discussions with Members or staff of the Senate Select Committee on Intelligence (SSCI). The first mention came during a staff visit to Moscow in December 1988. The second occurred in 1992 during a visit to Moscow by two Members of the Committee. But on each occasion, the information provided was fragmentary and anecdotal and did not specifically address what was being done by the CIA about the problem. Informal staff efforts to follow-up on each of these conversations were put off by the CIA.

The Committee strongly believes that both the CIA and the FBI had an obligation to advise the oversight committees at the time of the 1985–86 compromises. Section 502 of the National Security Act of 1947 specifically requires intelligence agencies to report to the oversight committees "any significant intelligence failure." The compromises of 1985–86 resulted in a virtual collapse of CIA's Soviet operations at the height of the Cold War. According to the SE Division officers memorandum of November, 1986, the evidence was at that point "overwhelming" and clearly indicated a problem of disastrous proportions. The oversight committees were responsible for funding the activities of the Directorate of Operations. They should have been formally notified pursuant to section 502 of the National Security Act of 1947.

THE NEED FOR CONTINUED FOLLOW-UP

Many of the problems identified by the Committee are deep-seated and pervasive, and will not be solved easily or quickly. Yet these problems are too important and too integral to the functioning of an agency with important national security responsibilities not to merit continuing and intensive scrutiny by both CIA managers and the congressional oversight committees.

While the Committee intends to make the CIA's response to this report an area of "special oversight interest" in the years ahead, the Committee also directs the Inspector General of the CIA to provide the Committee, through the Director of Central Intelligence, with a report no later than September 1, 1995, and annually thereafter, on the CIA's progress in responding to the recommendations contained in this report and to the continuing counterintelligence and security challenges that the CIA faces.

QUESTIONS FOR FURTHER DISCUSSION

1. What was Aldrich Ames' motivation for spying against the United States from inside the CIA?

2. How was he apprehended? Why did it take so long?

3. Do you think other instances of treason could happen inside the government today? What are the best approaches to prevent this from happening again?

4. Why has counterintelligence often been the neglected stepchild among intelligence activities?

Reprinted from "An Assessment of the Aldrich H. Ames Espionage Case and Its Implications for U.S. Intelligence," *Staff Report*, Select Committee on Intelligence, U.S. Senate, 103d Cong., 2d. Sess. (November 1, 1994), pp. 53–72.

27. COUNTERINTELLIGENCE, PERCEPTION, AND DECEPTION

ROBERT JERVIS

Drawing on a line of poetry by T.S. Eliot, a former Chief of CIA Counterintelligence (James J. Angleton) often referred to counterintelligence as a "wilderness of mirrors." The metaphor was meant to underscore the dizzying task of trying to determine the bona fides of a defector, or whether an operation by an adversary is real or is a deceptive trick—the essence of the counterintelligence challenge. This essay highlights some of the twists and turns that inevitably occur while defending a nation against hostile intelligence activities.

If intelligence is the neglected child of international politics, counterintelligence is the more neglected—and more misunderstood—stepchild. To most Americans, even experts and scholars, it seems dull because it smacks of police work; excessively defensive because it can only protect, rather than advance, our interests; and unsavory because it calls for mistrust of, if not spying on, members of our own government and society. There is some validity to this impression but also much wrong with it, as explained in other chapters in this volume. In any case, these concerns do not make the subject less important, and they may obscure its broader significance.[1]

COUNTERINTELLIGENCE AND THE NATURE OF THE REGIME

One reason for its neglect is that counterintelligence fits uncomfortably within most democracies. Almost by definition, democracies thrive in and foster open societies. The free flow of people and information, widespread discussion, and high levels of trust are greatly valued by these systems and necessary for their functioning. The citizens in a democracy can accept the idea that some information must be withheld from them in order to keep it from adversaries, but there are sharp limits to the forms and the extent of secrecy that can be tolerated. Moreover, it is hard for democracies to function when people mistrust one another, when government officials have to wonder whether every inquiry from citizens or colleagues might be designed to elicit information to be passed on to enemies, and when information and proposed courses of action have to be immediately scrutinized for the possibility that they are of alien design. In an immigrant country like the United States, the idea that newcomers, even from hostile countries, might be spies is particularly corrosive. If the American project is successful, those who come here will become loyal citizens; the very possibility that they will not indicates not only deep personal flaws on their part, but the failure of the American ideal. In the United Kingdom class plays a role similar to Americanism. One reason why the British were slow to develop a system of security clearances, and to investigate the suspicious behavior of people who turned out to be devastatingly effective spies for the Soviet Union, was the sense that those with the proper social credentials could be trusted.

These problems do not arise in dictatorships, many of which are built on betrayal and suspicion. Dictators must foster personal loyalty, but they also must be wary that even their closest associates might turn on them. The idea that others might be spies is second nature to people in these regimes and, indeed, is often useful as a means of internal control. Joseph Stalin's Soviet Union was extreme in its employment of fear and purges, but the basic phenomenon is part of the DNA of dictatorial regimes.[2] These tend toward paranoia, but we should remember that even paranoids have enemies—the fact that the only way to change a dictatorship is through stealth and deception means that nothing can be beyond suspicion. The fact that paranoia comes naturally to most dictatorships does not mean that it is without a heavy price. Although paranoia does not in itself undermine the founding principles of the regime, its operation may well weaken it. Even the most autocratic rulers need loyal supporters; a government without a modicum of trust cannot function; constant purges may enable the dictator to survive and have many of his policies carried out, but they can destroy important instruments of state power. To take only the most obvious example, one reason for the poor performance of the Soviet armed forces in the wake of the German attack in June 1941 was that Stalin had removed most of his best officers in the preceding years.

INTELLIGENCE, PERCEPTION, AND DECEPTION

If the purpose of foreign policy is to advance the national interest (however interpreted), the purpose of intelligence is to provide an understanding of the world on which foreign policy can be based and to support instruments to influence and possibly deceive others. Readers of my previous work will not be surprised to see that I put perception and deception at the center of international politics, and they are surely central to intelligence and counterintelligence. It is tempting to believe that good policy requires a good understanding of the environment, but this is not always the case. The British decision to fight on after the fall of France in 1940 was based at least in part on a picture of the world that was wildly off the mark.[3] As in everyday life, misunderstandings between nations may result in not only comedy, but also success for one actor or the other, and sometimes even mutually beneficial outcomes. This is, however hardly a formula for the long run. It is also true that despite their constantly saying how much they seek accurate information and analysis, national leaders often find intelligence unwelcome because it tends to increase uncertainty or contradict existing policy.[4] But even the most closed-minded decision maker eventually needs to understand the world in which he or she is operating. Even when they scorn the formal intelligence apparatus, as Richard Nixon did when he

famously referred to "those clowns out at Langley,"[5] their perceptions are essential to their behavior, and these can rarely be formed on the basis of first-hand experience.

Deception is central as well. Although self-deception plays a large role in the making of foreign policy because people adjust their perceptions to avoid doubts and remorse, this psychological dynamic will largely be put aside here.[6] More central to intelligence and, especially, counterintelligence, is that actors need both to be on guard against being deceived and often to deceive others. Indeed, the knowledge that deception is possible strongly affects the interpretation of all incoming information and the uses to which it is put. Counterintelligence and deception are closely intertwined. Most obviously, the state must fear that the other side is using its agents to convey a false picture. The other side of this coin is that the state can use the other's intelligence service in order to propagate its own deceptions, as I will discuss further below.

A WILDERNESS OF MIRRORS

International politics is characterized and complicated by the fear that things are not what they seem, that apparently solid intelligence is built on sand, and that trusted information is misleading. States often want others to accept a certain picture of the world and an image of themselves that will further their interests. This picture may indeed be an accurate one, but it also may not be, which means that perceivers always must be wary.

This is nowhere more true than in counterintelligence. The state is trying to see whether the adversary (assuming only one for the sake of exposition) is spying on it while simultaneously trying to see whether its own spies are secure and loyal. (We can make parallel analyses of other forms of intelligence, most obviously involving signals and codes.) Since by definition it is very hard to detect a good spy and at least as hard to tell whether one of your spies has been "turned" and is now feeding you false information and betraying secrets to the adversary, a heightened and indeed hypersensitive readiness to perceive deception comes with the territory. But the inevitable cost of this stance will sometimes be to see plots that do not exist, to discount accurate information, to disregard if not jail loyal informants, and to induce a great deal of paranoia within one's government if not country. Because each side knows that the other is trying to play with its senses and prey on its vulnerabilities, counterintelligence inevitably leads one into what James Angleton, the famous (or notorious) Central Intelligence Agency (CIA) chief of counterintelligence, called a wilderness of mirrors.[7]

If the best spy is someone you would never be likely to suspect, then your adversary will try to recruit such a person or have her cultivate the appropriate appearance. This means that the very appearance of being above suspicion should incite suspicion. Of course if the other side understands this, it might recruit people with shady backgrounds because their very unreliability makes you believe that they are less likely to be spies. While this is an exaggeration to a point of caricature, I think that it is good caricature, which means that the features it presents are important and recognizable. The basic point is that in this world it is far from clear what can be trusted, and since both sides are playing the game, indications of trustworthiness are subject to manipulation. The result is that there are no firm guidelines and that anyone who is confident that she has her bearing is lost.

The effects and the disequilibrium this situation creates are best illustrated by the opportunities and dilemmas posed when a member of the adversary's intelligence service offers to provide information or to defect. The obvious question is whether the person is genuine or remains an agent of the adversary; it is equally obvious that there will rarely be a clear answer. Either an unwarranted acceptance or an unwarranted rejection will have high costs. Furthermore, many kinds of evidence have the paradoxical qualities noted above. If everything seems in order, a skeptic will note that this is just what would be expected from a well-prepared enemy agent; gaps or inconsistencies in his story that at first glance seem to indicate that he is a plant could point in the opposite direction because it is unlikely that the adversary would commit such obvious errors. So it is not surprising that offers to provide information often trigger much agonizing by the recipients; many sincere offers are rebuffed,[8] and battles can rage for years about whether the source is genuine or an enemy agent. The most obvious and controversial case is that of Yuri Nosenko, the KGB officer who defected in 1964, bringing with him the story that the Soviets had no ongoing connection with Lee Harvey Oswald and President John F. Kennedy's assassination.[9] Given the high stakes and the inherent ambiguities, these kinds of questions

cannot be readily answered and become the center of acrimonious debates.

Indeed, they spill over into arguments about the fundamental integrity of the state's intelligence and counterintelligence systems, debates that can rarely be settled and that exact a high cost. Thus the Nosenko affair gave added urgency to the search for a high-level Soviet agent or mole. For years, Angleton scrutinized CIA, casting doubt on many officials and forcing some out until Director of Central Intelligence (DCI) William Colby decided that Angleton was doing enormous damage and had to be dismissed. Indeed if Colby was correct (and the consensus—which of course could be wrong—is that he was), then by delaying the acceptance of Nosenko's information, displacing valuable officers, and sowing enormous distrust within the organization, Angleton did more damage than most Soviet agents could have. Similarly, some in the United Kingdom believed that the head of MI5, Sir Roger Hollis, was a Soviet mole, and the attempt to show this greatly weakened the organization.

Colby felt that the United States had erred on the side of being too suspicious and rejecting valuable sources: "I never thought that the object of CIA was to protect itself against the KGB. The object of CIA is to get into the Kremlin."[10] Unfortunately, though, CIA could not "get into the Kremlin" if it were penetrated, because the mole would expose our spies, as Aldrich Ames did. These situations make it very hard to know what is sensible. We have to recognize that the most loyal person can indeed turn out to be a spy and the suspicious volunteer from the other side may indeed be a good source. This creates an atmosphere that is hard to cope with. One may not be able to be a good counterintelligence officer without being somewhat paranoid, and the job itself encourages paranoia. Colleagues who thought Angleton had come close to losing his mind by the end of his career may have been right, and perhaps he had overlearned a lesson from the experience early in his career when he worked with Kim Philby, the rising star in British intelligence who turned out to be a Soviet agent. DCI Richard Helms said, "If [Angleton] overdid it, maybe he did, but that's a difficulty inherent in the job."[11] How can one maintain one's balance in an area where almost anything could be true, where appearances are designed to be deceiving, and in which familiar signposts may have been twisted to point in the wrong direction?

NOT TAKING DECEPTION
SERIOUSLY ENOUGH

One reaction to this difficult environment is to downplay if not ignore the danger of deception. For many years before and during World War II American authorities refused to take Soviet espionage seriously; this was not a uniquely American failing, as the British were at least as negligent. Although the revelation of the World War II spies led to more careful security checks and a sensitivity to the danger of penetration by Soviet agents, the United States paid relatively little attention to Soviet deception, despite the fact that the Soviets were clearly devoting great efforts to this task. I was surprised by this when I became a consultant to CIA in 1978. My sense is that American intelligence analysts, and probably those in other countries as well, resist taking deception as seriously as they should because doing so would make their already-difficult task even more trying. They work with fragmentary and contradictory information, and if on top of this they had to consider the chance that much of what they were seeing was designed by the other side for this purpose, they could end up paralyzed. The possibility that some parts of the adversary's government are misinformed or are deceiving other parts (as was true in Iraq) is also likely to be ignored, because it too can undercut the validity of what would otherwise be very valuable intelligence.

DECEPTION COMES AT A COST

Another reason for both paranoia and the opposite willingness to accept information from questionable sources is that in order to mount a successful deception campaign, one often must provide the adversary with some valid information of value. One way an agent establishes his bona fides is by providing information that an imposter could not know and that the state would not want revealed to the adversary. For those running a double agent, designing such information is a crucial task. It requires not only knowing the other side's perceptual predispositions in order to understand what information will be seen as accurate, but also difficult choices about what can be divulged that will be seen as valuable enough to be enticing without doing much harm to the state.[12] This "feed" (or "chickenfeed" as it is also called) obviously requires delicate judgments. These are easier to reach the more the state knows about what the adversary knows—or thinks—about the state. Sometimes information can be given up

because the state knows that the adversary already knows it (although it is important that the adversary not know that the state knows it). Information that is unknown but about to come out through other sources also can be good feed, and similarly useful is information that is unknown but that cannot be acted on with sufficient speed to harm the state. Furthermore, good feed does not have to be correct, but only seen as correct (or even plausible) by the other side. Even information that is later shown to have been wrong may be usefully employed if the agent can later explain why things did not turn out as he thought they would. Thus an agent who falsely reported that a state was soon going to take a certain action can explain away the fact that it did not do so by pointing to changes in circumstances or personnel that led the decision to be revoked. Of course the adversary is almost always sensitive to the danger that it is being fed, but the judgments it has to make are extremely difficult.

How much the state is willing to give up depends in part on the importance of the deception being designed. The famous case of the Double Cross system in which the British ran the entire German spy network in the United Kingdom throughout World War II involved a willingness to reveal significant information because the ultimate prize of deceiving the Germans about the location of the D-Day invasion was of the utmost importance. Perceivers who understand this then face the added complication that the very value of the information they are getting may indicate, not that the agent is a trustworthy source, but that she is part of a scam of enormous proportions. Perhaps the best prescription would then be to trust the information on all but the most important question. But this would be extremely difficult to do and requires knowing what the state considers to be the vital question for which it is hoarding its capability.

In light of what I said earlier about the necessary paranoia of counterintelligence, one might wonder how these deception efforts could ever succeed. That they can is explained not only by the knowledge that rejecting all reports would be folly, but also by the fact that a service develops a great political, bureaucratic, and psychological stake in its agents. It is very hard for an organization that owes its power—if not its very existence—to its prowess in developing spies to see that they have been turned and that the agency itself is now an instrument of the adversary. The very fact that other agencies within the government try to discredit these agents gives the organization that is running them added reason to stand up for them. Furthermore, it is hard for the individuals most involved to recognize that they may be being made fools of, and in many cases the agency becomes the defender of its agents and overlooks what in retrospect were glaring clues to their true nature.[13] As a Soviet intelligence officer told a nervous double agent he was running, "You'll have no problem. They *want* to believe you."[14]

TO USE OR DESTROY THE OTHER'S INTELLIGENCE?

The example of Angleton reminds us that a state may employ counterintelligence to cripple the adversary's intelligence service by turning its own counterintelligence against it. The advantages of doing so are obvious: If the state can use the other's counterintelligence to convince the leaders it has moles, the adversary's intelligence will be discredited and shunted aside, and in effect the state will have developed a protective shield. Even if the adversary service has good information about the state, it will not be believed, and so the service will be rendered harmless.

Dictatorial regimes make easier targets than do democracies because of their heightened paranoia. Adversary services have only to play into this, not generate it. Furthermore, intelligence in dictatorships is almost always fragmented, convoluted, and politicized. To bring unpleasant news to the leader's attention is to risk not just one's career, but one's life. So it is no surprise that dictatorships tend to be ill-informed.[15] Much important information did not reach Adolf Hitler in part because his underlings feared him, but the most striking example of a dictator's refusal to believe bad news was Stalin's inability to accept the overwhelming evidence that Hitler was about to attack in the spring of 1941.[16] Fearing that the British and perhaps Hitler's subordinates were trying to provoke him, Stalin assumed that his spies who correctly reported German plans were in fact double agents and dismissed (and then killed) his intelligence chief who kept calling these reports to his attention.[17] The Germans sought to discredit the Soviet intelligence services, and Stalin's misguided faith in his own policy and his enormous suspicions of his own government apparatus made their job much easier.

The possibility of this tactic presents two dilemmas, one for the state sending messages and the other for the perceiver. The perceiver's difficulty is that there is no easy answer to the question of how much paranoia is enough; as we have just seen, too much can disable intelligence, but even paranoids have enemies and there are real reasons for counterintelligence officials to be on guard against penetration and to view officers, agents, and information with suspicion. States have been badly harmed both by being too vigilant and by not being vigilant enough.

The sender's dilemma is that there can be advantages to both using and weakening the adversary's service. It may seem obvious that the state should try to degrade and discredit the adversary's intelligence system and so render it blind. But this is not necessarily to the state's benefit. In many cases and in many ways the adversary's intelligence may be of value to the state. As I noted at the start, the state wants to project a desired image (sometimes deceptive and sometimes not). This requires a sensitive and respected perceiving apparatus. An adversary that is blind will not be able to gather the information the state is trying to keep from it, but neither will it be able to read the messages the state is trying to send. Of course there are lots of channels for delivering these messages, but a well-functioning intelligence service has the major advantages of being considered reliable by those it serves and having direct access to them. Many signals—either figurative or literal—can be picked up only by an intelligence service, and many messages are much more credible if it is believed that the state is trying to keep them secret.

The adversary's having a good intelligence system is no panacea, of course, and it can miss a great deal. Thus Richard Nixon's elaborate plan to frighten the Soviets into assisting the United States in Vietnam by putting strategic forces on alert in the fall of 1969 failed because Soviet intelligence did not detect the American activities until they were almost completed, and at that point it misinterpreted them.[18] Furthermore, in some cases the state can send credible messages that do not depend on intelligence channels, as when it makes moves that are plain for all to see, even if their meaning can remain subject to debate.

Nevertheless, in many cases the adversary's service is the most important channel by which the state is able to project a desired image. On occasion, the intelligence service can be used as a back channel for communication. This may have the advantage of permitting conversations and feelers that can be disavowed if it becomes necessary because either side can claim that its representatives were speaking without authorization. Indeed, at times the state will mistakenly believe that the agent was speaking officially when in fact this was not the case. Thus at the time, and for years later, it was believed that the Soviet intelligence agent Aleksandr Feklisov's conversations with John Scali during the Cuban Missile Crisis conveyed Soviet positions. Although what he proposed was close to the solution arrived at, we now know that he was acting on his own. Another advantage of using intelligence channels is that the messages are more likely to be kept secret, not only from other countries and the general public, but from wide sections of the government. Of course there is a cost to this, as the history of the Nixon administration shows, but the advantages are not trivial. Third and relatedly, because they are so secret and unusual, messages passed by intelligence agents are often taken especially seriously. This does not guarantee they will be believed, but at least they will receive high-level attention.

Perhaps the most interesting role of the adversary's service is in a double cross: manipulating an adversary's intelligence through double agents or allowing the tapping of communications channels that the targeted state has under countersurveillance. Here the adversary believes that it has a direct pipeline into important and highly credible information. It thinks it is getting the best possible data on the state's capabilities and is figuratively if not literally overhearing the state's leaders talking about what they plan to do. This seems like pure gold, and of course it can be. The Soviet spies in the United States and the United Kingdom in the 1940s produced information of great value (as we will see below, however, this did not always harm the West). Similarly, well-placed military officers in the USSR and Eastern Europe like Oleg Penkovsky and Ryczard Kuklinski provided the United States with invaluable information on Soviet capabilities, thinking, and war plans. But as counterintelligence is well aware, if these sources are in fact being controlled by the adversary, they can do enormous harm. The classic case is of course the Double Cross system mentioned earlier. By controlling the German spy ring in the United Kingdom, the British were able to mislead the Germans as to the location of the D-Day invasion. Indeed, the credibility of the sources was so high that they were believed when soon after D-Day they reported that the Normandy landings were a feint and the main crossing would be at Calais. It is hard to overstate the importance of Hitler's error: Had he known that the landings were coming at Normandy or had he released his reserve divisions as soon as the Allied troops hit the beaches, he could have pushed the invaders into the sea.

Somewhat simpler and more complex forms of using the adversary's intelligence are also possible. A (relatively) simple method is just to release a message in a way or through channels that you know will take it to the adversary, although the adversary does not know that you know this. For example, during the Berlin Crisis, Secretary of State Dean Rusk apparently urged that certain war plans be transmitted to West Germany because he knew that German poor security meant that they would soon find their way into Soviet hands and that this would bolster the credibility of American threats.[19] More complicated, and even more risky, is the "double bluff," in which true information is released through a channel that the state knows that the adversary believes is being used for deception in the expectation that it will be interpreted as being misleading.[20] What is crucial and difficult is that the state must be one step ahead of the adversary in its knowledge of what is believed.

The previous examples involve the state's manipulation of the other side's intelligence. But sometimes the state can benefit from spies it has *not* discovered. These too can be highly credible sources of information, and sometimes it is in the state's interest to have its secrets conveyed to the adversary. For example, if the state is planning to stand firm in a confrontation, it usually wants the other side to know this, and for this purpose a spy at the highest levels will be extraordinarily useful. In other cases when the state is acting out of fear of the adversary and does not itself harbor aggressive intentions, it may also want this known but be unable to convincingly show this through normal diplomatic channels and behavior. It is not far-fetched to argue that Philby, the great Soviet spy, served the West as well as Stalin extraordinarily well by his great access to the American establishment in the dangerous years of 1949–1951. What he was hearing was that the United States would forcibly resist further Soviet incursions but that it did not plan offensive actions of its own. If this is what was conveyed to Moscow and believed, this would have both restrained Stalin from pressing harder and reassured him that he did not need to act preventively to forestall Western aggression. Philby may then have influenced history, and he could do so only because of the strength of the Soviet intelligence system and the failure of Western counterintelligence.

In closing I want to return to the crucial nature of perceptions and their links to deception. To have their desired impact, messages have to be interpreted in a way that the sender intends. This is far from automatic. People's perceptions are strongly driven by their needs and expectations, which are difficult for senders to comprehend, let alone manipulate. Attempts to project images, accurate or not, will work only if the receiver is receptive. One might think that the appropriate way to design a deception plan is to first decide what you want to do and then to develop ways of convincing the adversary that you are going to do something else. In fact, this is not likely to work. The adversary will interpret the evidence in light of what he expects you to do, and it will be very difficult to change his mind. So you have to first know what he expects you to do, and then plan to do something different and develop a deception plan that will reinforce what he already believes. The Allied deception plan would not have convinced Hitler that the invasion would take place at Calais and/or Norway if Hitler had not believed this for reasons of his own. This returns us to the close links between intelligence and counterintelligence. Attempts to use the adversary's intelligence system to convey a desired message require a good understanding of how the adversary sees the world. Counterintelligence, then, is much more than passive defense and can fulfill its potential only in close coordination with other instruments.

QUESTIONS FOR FURTHER DISCUSSION

1. Explain the meaning of the phrase "deception operation."
2. What is the best remedy against deception and other ruses played by foreign intelligence services against a nation's homeland?
3. Why do you think that the FBI and the CIA sometimes disagree on the bona fides of defectors?
4. Is paranoia a useful or harmful characteristic for a counterintelligence officer?

ENDNOTES

1. See William Odom, *Fixing Intelligence* (New Haven: Yale University Press, 2003). As Odom makes clear and as many of the essays in this volume stress, counterintelligence is not, or not only, about catching spies. It is intelligence about other countries' intelligence. Like intelligence, it is about gathering and analyzing information, and what is done with the information varies according to the circumstances. Preventing the penetration of one's own society and government is only the most obvious response. The alternatives and their resulting complications are much deeper.
2. For the argument that tyrants are different from normal people, see Stephen Rosen, *War and Human Nature* (Cambridge: Harvard University Press, 2005), chapter 5.
3. David Reynolds, "Churchill and the British 'Decision' to Fight on in 1940: Right Policy, Wrong Reasons," in *Diplomacy and Intelligence During the Second World War*, ed. Richard Langhorne (New York: Cambridge University Press, 1985), 147–67.
4. I have discussed this further in the concluding chapter of my forthcoming book, *The Politics and Psychology of Intelligence and Intelligence Failure* (Ithaca, NY: Cornell University Press, forthcoming).
5. Quoted in Rhodri Jeffreys-Jones, *The CIA and American Democracy,* 2nd ed. (New Haven: Yale University Press, 1998), 177.
6. For further discussion see Robert Jervis, "Understanding Beliefs," *Political Psychology* 27 (October 2006): 641–64.
7. David Martin, *Wilderness of Mirrors* (New York: Harper & Row, 1980).
8. For one example, see Barry Royden, "Tolkachev, A Worthy Successor to Penkovsky," *Studies in Intelligence* 47, no. 3 (2003): 5–34.
9. For the latest in a long stream of books about the case, see Tennent Bagley, *Spy Wars* (New Haven: Yale University Press, 2007).
10. "Reflections of DCIs Colby and Helms on the CIA's 'Time of Troubles,'" *Studies in Intelligence* 51 (Summer 2007): 19.
11. Quoted in Martin, *Wilderness of Mirrors,* 206.
12. This means that deception planners have to know what their own state is planning to do: "It is impossible, or at any rate highly dangerous, to tell a lie until you know what the truth is going to be." M. D. Foot, "Conditions Making for Success and Failure of Deception and Denial: Democratic Regimes," in *Strategic Denial and Deception: The Twenty-first Century Challenge,* ed. Roy Godson and James Wirtz (New Brunswick, NJ: Transaction, 2002), 120.
13. In fact, in some cases the agent does not have "a true nature," or at least a true loyalty, and may be providing both accurate and inaccurate information to both sides.
14. Quoted in Bagley, *Spy Wars,* 274.
15. Ralph White, "Why Aggressors Lose," *Political Psychology* 11 (June 1990): 227–42.

16. Zachary Shore, *What Hitler Knew: The Battle for Information in Nazi Foreign Policy* (New York: Oxford University Press, 2003).

17. David Murphy, *What Stalin Knew: The Enigma of Barbarossa* (New Haven: Yale University Press, 2005); for a different version see Geoffrey Roberts, *Stalin's Wars* (New Haven: Yale University Press, 2006), 61–81.

18. William Burr and Jeffery Kimball, "Nixon's Secret Nuclear Alert: Vietnam War Diplomacy and the Joint Chiefs of Staff Readiness Test, October 1969," *Cold War History* 3 (January 2003): 113–56.

19. Marc Trachtenberg, *A Constructed Peace: The Making of the European Settlement, 1945–1963* (Princeton: Princeton University Press, 1999), 295n39.

20. Robert Jervis, *The Logic of Images in International Relations*, 2nd ed. (New York: Columbia University Press, 1989); Thaddeus Holt, *The Deceivers: Allied Military Deception in the Second World War* (New York: Scribner, 2004).

ACCOUNTABILITY AND CIVIL LIBERTIES

Hamlet: "Come, come, and sit you
down, you shall not budge,
You go not till I set you up a glass
Where you may see the inmost part of you."
—SHAKESPEARE, *Hamlet*, 3.4.17–20

Virtually every nation in the world has a secret intelligence apparatus, whether just a few agents in key foreign capitals (if the nation is poor) or a vast network of humans and machines for spying around the world (if the nation is affluent). By collecting information from abroad and by engaging in the companion activities of counterintelligence and covert action, an intelligence establishment can help provide a shield against external threats—what the first President George Bush, a former Director of Central Intelligence (DCI), liked to call the nation's "first line of defense."

THE SPECIAL CASE OF INTELLIGENCE

In most nations, intelligence agencies are treated as exceptions from the rest of government. They are cloaked in secrecy, allowed exceptional access to policymakers, and given leeway to get the job done—even if that means breaking laws overseas (almost always the case) and engaging in unsavory activities that would be deemed inappropriate for other government agencies. From the beginning, the United States embraced this laissez-faire philosophy for intelligence activities, even as its leaders sought to "bind down" the rest of the government "with the chains of the Constitution" (as Thomas Jefferson expressed the theory of checks and balances in his draft of the Kentucky Resolutions in 1798). The Founders well understood the dangers from abroad to the new Republic and were willing to grant broad discretionary powers to America's intelligence officers as they endeavored to protect the nation from foreign threats.

As the United States matured and its intelligence service expanded in the aftermath of World War II, this hands-off philosophy continued. The Cold War against the communist world required a strong and flexible intelligence shield; in the nuclear age, a nation might not survive another surprise attack like the one that shook the nation at Pearl Harbor. A top secret study group reported to the Eisenhower Administration in 1954 that

> we are facing an implacable enemy whose avowed objective is world domination by whatever means and at whatever cost. There are no rules in such a game. Acceptable norms of human conduct do not apply. We must develop effective espionage and counterespionage services. We must learn to subvert, sabotage and we must destroy our enemies by more clear, more sophisticated and more effective methods than those used against us. (Church Committee 1976, 9)

In light of these hostile conditions, the CIA and its fellow agencies would have to be set loose to fight the communists. If the United States were to win this ideological battle, often fought "in the back alleys of the world" (as Secretary of State Dean Rusk often described this hidden side of the Cold War), America's intelligence agencies would have to be as tough and as effective as anything the Soviet Union could field.

This is not to say the CIA was without supervision, even in this warlike climate (however "cold"). Most of its activities were approved by the White House and were reported, in broad outline at least, to small oversight subcommittees in the House and Senate. The approvals were highly discretionary, however, allowing DCIs broad scope to fill in the details in this struggle against communism; and reporting to Congress was usually sketchy, perfunctory, and frequently rebuffed. "No, no, my boy, don't tell me," a leading Senator overseer, John Stennis (D, Mississippi), told DCI James R. Schlesinger in 1973 when he tried to provide a full accounting of the CIA's operations abroad. "Just go ahead and do it, but I don't want to know!" (Johnson 2000, 202).

Model democracy or not, the United States would follow the practice of other nations—democracies and dictatorships alike—in placing the secret agencies outside the normal framework of governmental supervision. If Americans were to be secure, a hostile world demanded no less.

AN ABRUPT CHANGE OF PHILOSOPHY

In 1975, this philosophy of intelligence exceptionalism changed dramatically, a rare occurrence in this or any other government. The shift resulted not

from any sudden sea change in world affairs; that would not happen until the dissolution of the Soviet Empire in 1991. Rather, the stimulus arose from revelations at home regarding alleged abuses of power by the CIA (Johnson 1980, 1985, 1989; Smist 1994). Looking into charges of malfeasance published by the *New York Times*, government investigators uncovered a startling number of transgressions during this season of inquiry known as the "Year of Intelligence" (or what many intelligence officers recall more ruefully as the "Intelligence Wars").

The horrors that emerged from the investigations included assassination plots against foreign leaders; illegal mail openings, wiretaps, and interception of international cable traffic; intelligence files on over a million American citizens; improper drug experiments and unlawful sequestering of dangerous chemicals and biological materials; a master spy plan to conduct surveillance against Vietnam war dissenters in the United States; intelligence infiltration into a wide range of groups in American society, from universities to religious and media organizations; incitement of violence against African American groups; and covert actions abroad aimed not just at autocracies but at democratically elected regimes as well.

The effects of this breathtaking catalog of secret government excesses were profound. From then on, America's support for a muscular, unbound intelligence capability would have to compete with another value long central to the rest of America's government: liberty—safeguarding the American people against the power of their own government, not only foreign governments. Beginning in 1975, the nation's leaders undertook an unprecedented experiment to balance security and liberty with respect to its secret agencies. In contrast, most other democracies continued to shelter their intelligence services under a special status outside the purview of parliamentary overseers.

THE EXPERIMENT IN ACCOUNTABILITY UNFOLDS

In the United States, reformers shed the traditional exceptionalism bestowed on intelligence in favor of a new kind of experiment in an intelligence partnership between the legislative and executive branches. America's intelligence agencies could be subjected to the norms of rigorous accountability, a hallmark of constitutional government (Currie 1998; Snider 1997). This era of enhanced supervision, following

30 years of benign neglect by Congress, began with the establishment of three new oversight panels: a Senate Select Committee on Intelligence (SSCI, in 1976), a White House Intelligence Oversight Board (IOB, 1976), and a House Permanent Select Committee on Intelligence (HPSCI, 1977).

The Congressional committees have authority to hold hearings on intelligence matters, whether routine or in response to charges of impropriety; to scrutinize annual budgets line by line; to inspect intelligence facilities at home and abroad; to draft intelligence legislation; and, in the Senate, to conduct confirmation hearings on nominations for the office of DCI and other top intelligence managers. On behalf of the president, the IOB carries out special inquiries into allegations of abuse.

The thoroughness with which these groups pursue their duties depends on how much media attention is focused on claims of wrongdoing, as well as on the philosophy of members toward the concept of intelligence accountability (for some, an oxymoron). Among the members of these three panels, a few have expressed the view that intelligence should return to its status as a special case, with only the lightest supervision from Capitol Hill. They join the chorus of antireformers inside and outside the government who look on the new oversight as an exercise in "micromanagement"—too many legislative fingers clumsily probing into delicate intelligence operations that require quickness, skill, and secrecy for success.

Barry Goldwater (R, Arizona) provides an example of the antireformist view. Ironically having risen to the chairmanship of the Senate Intelligence Committee, whose creation he opposed, the Senator opined in 1982: "When it comes to covert operations, it would be best if they [the CIA's leaders] didn't have to tell us anything." The antireformers complain, too, that legislators cannot be trusted with the nation's secrets; loquacious by nature, politicians will invariably babble—perhaps inadvertently, or even on purpose if they oppose a secret operation (a "leak item veto"). Senator Goldwater viewed his own legislative chamber as a place with "more leaks than the men's room at AnhauserBusch" (Johnson 1996, 52).

In rebuttal, pro-reformers are quick to recite the litany of abuses uncovered in 1975 that led to new oversight in the first place. They echo James Madison's warnings about the corrupting nature of power and the need to have "ambition counteract ambition" (*Federalist Paper* No. 51), pitting one branch of government against another. They dismiss the micromanagement criticism, noting that—despite the tightened supervision—secret operations have moved swiftly forward when necessary. They argue, too, that leaks from Capitol Hill (as opposed to the executive branch) have been few and insignificant.

The very existence of this debate over intelligence reform raises eyebrows in most countries. Leaders overseas, even in fellow democracies, find it difficult to understand why the United States would intentionally seek to handicap its intelligence agencies—just as they failed to understand why Americans insisted on pursuing the Watergate investigation in 1974, at the expense of discrediting their own government and driving an incumbent president from office in shame.

Even at home, the experiment has hardly been a smooth evolution toward some golden means of accountability agreed on by everyone. On the contrary, it has been characterized by fits and starts. Among the enduring features have been an executive order prohibiting assassination plots against foreign leaders (1976); a Foreign Intelligence Surveillance Act (1978), which establishes judicial safeguards against overzealous wiretaps for purposes of national security; strict reporting requirements, which force the secret agencies to keep Congressional overseers informed of intelligence operations and the discovery of abuse inside their high walls; persistent questioning by lawmakers and staff that requires intelligence managers to explain and defend their budgets and programs; and expectations on Capitol Hill that intelligence reports will be shared with the Congressional intelligence committees on the same footing as executive officials.

More contentious has been the question of when the intelligence agencies should inform Congress about their operations, especially controversial covert actions designed to manipulate foreign governments. Should the reports come before or after these operations are launched? After demanding "prior notification" in a 1980 statute, lawmakers retreated somewhat (under pressure from President George H. W. Bush in 1991) to the current prescription of prior reporting in most cases but with an escape hatch for the president of a couple of days delay in times of emergency. Any delay, though, must be fully explained to the two oversight committees at the time the report is sent to Congress. This strikes most people as a sensible compromise and is a good illustration of the constructive debate on intelligence between the legislative and executive branches of government that has gone on since 1975.

BALANCING LIBERTY AND SECURITY: AN UNFINISHED STORY

The current equilibrium between liberty and security in the intelligence domain has failed to satisfy everyone. On the reform side, some have called for the abolition of the CIA, particularly in light of its failure to predict the U.S.S.R.'s disintegration in 1991 (although it did better in tracking the Soviet decline, especially the economic dimension, than is usually acknowledged). On the antireform side, the criticism of legislative micromanagement continues, with commentators advocating a repeal of the assassination prohibition; the unprecedented use of the Peace Corps as a cover for CIA officers abroad; the adoption of media, academic, and clerical credentials by intelligence officers; and more aggressive participation in coups d'état against regimes deemed unfriendly to the United States—all activities deemed inappropriate by reformers in 1975 (Johnson 2002). A central goal of the antireformers remains dismantlement of the three oversight panels, removing what they see as undue constraints on the intelligence agencies.

Even those not on the extremes of this debate have raised troubling questions about the success of the experiment. At times the secret agencies have simply ignored Congress and the IOB, as if the new oversight rules were so much flotsam in the wake of the ship of state as it plows through the turbulent seas of international affairs. During the Iran-*contra* affair of the Reagan Administration (a full decade into the new oversight), the staff of the National Security Council (NSC) bypassed Congress to raise secret funds for its covert actions in Nicaragua from foreign potentates and private citizens within the United States, making a mockery of Congress' power of the purse and, therefore, of constitutional government. Officers of the CIA and the NSC staff also lied to legislative investigators about their involvement in the affair. When the less-than-forthright nature of his testimony became clear, one high-ranking CIA officer proffered this gloss: he had been "technically correct, if specifically evasive." This is not exactly the sort of comity the new spirit of intelligence partnership and accountability was meant to engender.

More recently, the CIA failed to inform legislative overseers of its ties to Col. Julio Roberto Alpirez

in Guatemala, an unsavory agent charged with murder. Further, the National Reconnaissance Office (NRO) misled legislators about major cost overruns in its new headquarters buildings, as well as the NRO's improper accumulation of unspent appropriated funds. Although less serious than the blow struck against democratic procedures by the Iran-*contra* affair, neither of these cases did anything to nurture the bonds of trust and cooperation between the branches that are so vital for accountability to succeed.

While the intelligence agencies have occasionally transgressed against both the spirit and the letter of the law behind the new oversight, Congress, too, has been far from perfect in meeting its responsibilities. Some members and staff have been dedicated overseers, trying to make the balance between liberty and security succeed. They have pored over intelligence budgets and asked probing questions of intelligence officials during open and closed hearings. Others, though, have been distracted, perhaps less interested in the subject, facing a tough reelection bid, or simply true believers in the pre-1975 philosophy of laissez-faire for the secret agencies. Keeping the balance has required the devotion of at least a few individuals willing to dedicate the necessary time to maintain the eternal vigilance that is the price of liberty, and usually there have been a few lawmakers so disposed—but not many. Particularly important have been the attitudes of the chairs of the House and Senate intelligence committees, and that has been a mixed record: Some have been dynamic overseers while others have been rather passive.

A QUALIFIED SUCCESS

With the major exception of Iran-*contra*—an appalling lapse in accountability from which, presumably, the nation has learned some lessons—the watchdogs on the oversight panels have been sufficient in number and commitment to make the experiment a qualified success, unless one believes that secret agencies ought to be abolished or, at the opposite extreme, that they should be given the broad leeway they once enjoyed. Although the current state of intelligence accountability is still imperfect and subject to ongoing debate and adjustment (like democracy itself), most government officials and observers agree that it represents a workable balance between the two important values of security and liberty.

Certainly most people who have closely examined the subject value the contribution made by secret agencies to America's security. During the Cold War, the eyes and ears of these agencies helped keep a third world war at bay by providing a reasonably clear understanding of Soviet military capabilities and activities. Indeed, the modern espionage capabilities of both superpowers greatly reduced anxieties and the likelihood of hair-trigger responses on either side of the Iron Curtain. Moreover, no one wants to see a return to the abuses of power by the secret agencies that were revealed to the American people by the Church Committee during the Year of Intelligence.

Close followers of intelligence issues also understand that the key to a stronger U.S. intelligence capability lies not in upsetting the current oversight arrangements that were so carefully hammered out on the anvil of experience by bipartisan majorities over the years since 1975. Rather, improved performance will require organizational and attitudinal changes within the executive branch. The needed reforms include, above all, further strengthening of the DCI's authority over community-wide budgets and appointments. Otherwise, the intelligence "community" will remain a collection of tribal fiefdoms with little interest in working together and sharing information.

Even more important to the success of American intelligence will be a willingness on behalf of policymakers to clarify their precise intelligence needs to the secret agencies in a timely fashion, then listen with an open mind to the findings of these agencies. This seemingly simple and obvious requirement has, nonetheless, become the Achilles heel of American intelligence—especially the problem of listening. All too often policymakers have shunted aside accurate intelligence that failed to conform with their preconceptions or ideological preferences or, worse still, have exaggerated the intelligence they have received in order to bolster their policy arguments. This charge has been made by critics of the administrations of President George W. Bush and U.K. Prime Minister Tony Blair with respect to the possible existence of weapons of mass destruction in Iraq in 2003. Both are said to have hyped the threat to gain public support for a military invasion.

AN IMMUTABLE PRINCIPLE FOR DEMOCRACIES

A free government must maintain security from foreign and internal threats or it will not survive, but it must have liberty at home as well. A true democracy depends on both. In his memoir, former DCI Robert M. Gates (1996) writes,

> …some awfully crazy schemes might well have been approved had everyone present [in the White House] not known and expected hard questions, debate, and criticism from the Hill. And when, on a few occasions, Congress was kept in the dark, and such schemes did proceed, it was nearly always to the lasting regret of the presidents involved. (p. 559)

Here is another reminder of the necessity for checks on the use of executive power—especially secret executive power. Accountability is a tenet of free government that remains as valid today as it did when it animated the thinking of the Founders and the writing of the American Constitution over 200 years ago.

THE READINGS

In the first selection, Gregory F. Treverton spells out the importance of bringing the intelligence agencies into the normal framework of American government, facing the rigors of accountability just like the more open agencies have always experienced. He refers to the new intelligence oversight as an "uncompleted experiment" and notes that the new procedures, though certainly an improvement on the overlook approach of an earlier era, are still "no guarantee against stupid presidential decisions" (such as the Iran-*contra* affair).

Frederick P. Hitz, an attorney and former CIA Inspector General, offers a rather different view, as the title of his article suggests: "Unleashing the Rogue Elephant: September 11 and Letting the CIA Be the CIA." In 1975, Senator Frank Church, who had just learned about the CIA's involvement in assassination plots against foreign leaders, accused the Agency on a national television news show of behaving like a rogue elephant on a rampage. Hitz seeks fewer restraints on the intelligence agencies so they can combat terrorism more energetically, though he is quick to add that "it is equally important that these changes not throw the CIA back into the pre-1974 era of limited Congressional oversight and little executive branch accountability that led to earlier excesses." The debate over where to draw the line between security and liberty is ongoing, with Hitz seeking to place it a little more toward the security side.

In the next piece, a legal counsel in the CIA, Frederic F. Manget, examines the role of the third branch of government in intelligence matters: the judiciary. He reports that the federal courts have not been shy to assert their authority over the intelligence agencies when individual rights may have been jeopardized by intelligence operations. In such cases, judges routinely require intelligence officials to visit the courthouse and explain their activities—another safeguard for liberty envisioned by the Founders when they created the judicial branch of government.

In the following selection, Loch K. Johnson offers a history of the Church Committee investigation in 1975, which opened a Pandora's box of intelligence threats to civil liberties in the United States. The safeguards against future intelligence abuse established by the committee "have endured," Johnson argues, "and, on most occasions, they have brought greater sobriety to the conduct of intelligence operations at home and abroad. Someone beyond the walls of the secret agencies is now steadily watching their activities; would-be violators of the public trust know they might be caught—a vital check on abuse." Johnson's study of intelligence abuses uncovered in the mid-1970s is a reminder of how the darkest stain on the U.S. intelligence ledger came about as a result of the fear of communism that gripped the nation during the Cold War.

Fear has frequently been the reason the government has tilted, from time to time, too far toward security at the expense of liberty: the fear of the Japanese that led President Franklin D. Roosevelt to authorize the internment of Japanese American citizens during World War II; the fear of communists that produced the witch hunts of the House Un-American Activities Committee and, later, of Senator Joseph McCarthy; the fear of student dissent that led to CIA spying at home during the Vietnam war; the fear of civil rights activists that inspired the FBI's Cointelpro; and the fear of terrorism that could now lead to the trampling of civil liberties for Arab Americans and other minorities in the search for Al Qaeda supporters inside the United States. Of course, Japanese sabotage was a legitimate concern during the World War II, just as communism was during the Cold War. Moreover, some students broke the law during the Vietnam war era, even robbing banks and murdering bank guards to support their radical activities. But there are lawful ways to deal with criminal acts without resorting to mass internments, Congressional hearings guided less by evidence than innuendo, illegal surveillance, secret harassment of citizens, and jailing of terrorist suspects without legal counsel or formal charges. The goal is to maintain security while preserving democracy, not by turning a democracy into a totalitarian state.

Finally, this part ends with a series of viewpoints on the use of the National Security Agency for warrantless wiretapping in the United States—a controversial issue during the confirmation hearings for CIA Director Gen. Michael V. Hayden, who served as NSA Director at the time the wiretaps were initiated by the George W. Bush Administration. These perspectives were written originally for a Yale University School of Law "debate" on the matter in 2006.

28. INTELLIGENCE: WELCOME TO THE AMERICAN GOVERNMENT

GREGORY F. TREVERTON

For most of America's history, intelligence agencies were treated differently from the rest of the government. Their operations were considered too sensitive for normal procedures. Yet when the intelligence agencies were accused in 1974 of abusing their powers by engaging in spying at home, reformers argued that the time had come to bring the dark side of government more into the sunlight of stricter accountability. Treverton examines the merits of viewing intelligence organizations as a regular part of America's government, as subject to constitutional safeguards as any other department or agency.

Congress was deeply engaged in intelligence at the beginning of the Republic: in 1775 the Second Continental Congress set in motion covert operations to secure French supplies for Washington's army. The next year Thomas Paine, the first congressional "leaker," was dismissed for disclosing information from the Committee of Secret Correspondence. For the next century and a half, however, the congressional role lapsed. A disengaged America had little need for foreign intelligence, and for the first thirty years after World War II the preeminence of the president and the imminence of the cold war induced Congress to leave intelligence to the executive, for better or worse.

Events of the 1970s changed that. Since then, the role of Congress in intelligence matters has increased dramatically, and the intelligence community has become like the rest of the government. In the intelligence agencies' relations with Congress, especially, they are coming to resemble the Agriculture or Commerce departments. The House and Senate Intelligence committees have become, like other committees on Capitol Hill, the patrons as well as the overseers of "their" government agencies.

Intelligence officials are finding, as have other members of the executive branch before them, that congressional patrons who control purse strings are also tempted to tell them how to run their business. For their part, members of Congress find secret oversight politically awkward. In the words of Republican Senator William Cohen, then vice-chairman of the Senate Intelligence Committee: "It's not exactly a Faustian bargain, ... But if we wish to have access, we are bound."[1]

The paradox of secret oversight by the branch of government meant to be characterized by open debate is sharpest in the realm of covert action. There, intelligence officials are tempted to see their congressional overseers as potential leakers, while the overseers fear being misled or deceived or becoming responsible, in secret, for covert actions they cannot easily stop even if they oppose them.

Yet the oversight process has not worked badly even for covert action; ironically, the recent Iran-contra debacle is testimony to that judgment even as it also testifies to the limits whereby process can impose wisdom on the making of American public policy. This grappling over secret *operations* gets the headlines; as a vexing constitutional question, it merits them.

However, covert action is only a small part of oversight, and despite the publicity accorded it, the balance between executive and Congress in the making of foreign policy is probably more affected by a related change: Congress now receives virtually the same intelligence *analysis* as the executive. One senior Central Intelligence Agency (CIA) official described the agency as "involuntarily poised equidistant between the executive and legislative branches."[2] Asking whether intelligence agencies can serve both masters is shorthand for a wider question about the implications of intelligence joining an American government in which the fault lines sometimes divide along the executive-legislative gap but often cut across it.

"PLAUSIBLE DENIAL" AND THE "BUDDY SYSTEM"

Since its first serious investigations of intelligence in the mid-1970s, Congress has become steadily more involved in secret operations. Its most recent investigations into the Iran-contra affair, however, testify to the continuing puzzles, constitutional and procedural. These questions run through all of foreign affairs but are sharper in the realm of intelligence.

The investigations in the mid-1970s began very much in the shadow of Watergate; the press was full of intimations that intelligence agencies had acted outside the law, beyond the ken of Congress and the control even of presidents. Democratic Senator Frank Church, the chairman of the Senate investigating committee, likened the CIA to a "rogue elephant on the rampage."[3] In the event, the committees did not find much evidence of rogue elephants in the CIA or other agencies involved in foreign intelligence, like the National Security Agency or the Defense Intelligence Agency.[4]

Yet the committees did find a troubling looseness in the control of covert action. Part of the problem was CIA abuse of so-called plausible denial, a practice intended to protect the American government, a practice also abused by Oliver North and John Poindexter during the arms sales to Iran in the 1980s. A second part of the problem was a kind of "buddy system" in which oversight consisted of informal conversations between the director of central intelligence (DCI) and a few senior members of Congress. Neither plausible denial nor the buddy system emerged because the CIA had broken free of its political masters. Rather, they emerged because that was how successive administrations and Congress had wanted it.

In 1975, testifying before the Senate committee—often called the "Church committee" after its chairman—about charges that the CIA had tried to kill Fidel Castro, former DCI Richard Helms was vivid in describing plausible denial and almost plaintive in drawing its implications:

It was made abundantly clear...to everybody involved in the operation that the desire was to get rid of the Castro regime and to get rid of Castro...the point was that no limitations were put on this injunction...one...grows up in [the]

tradition of the time and I think that any of us would have found it very difficult to discuss assassinations with a President of the U.S. I just think we all had the feeling that we're hired out to keep those things out of the Oval Office.[5]

If he had ever thought he would later have to testify before Congress about what he had done, Helms reflected, he would have made sure that his orders were clear and in writing.

By their own testimony, not a single member of the National Security Council (NSC) outside the CIA knew of, much less authorized, those plots.[6] Even inside the CIA, officials spoke with each other about these operations only in riddles. And if they spoke of them at all with those outside the CIA charged with approving covert operations, they did so indirectly or in circumlocutions. Thus, in 1975 the Church committee spent hours trying to unravel whether terse references in documents to "disappear" or "direct positive action" or "neutralize" referred to assassination. It could not be sure. And that was precisely the point of plausible denial. Those CIA officials who spoke in circumlocutions could feel they had done their duty as they understood it. Their political superiors could understand what they would, ask for more information if they desired, but also forebear from asking. If things went awry, they could, if they chose, disclaim knowledge and do so more or less honestly.

These effects of plausible denial are extreme in the instance of the Cuban assassination plots, but similar effects ran through covert actions of the 1950s and 1960s. Dean Rusk, who served Presidents Kennedy and Johnson as secretary of state, observed that he routinely knew little of CIA operations: "I never saw a budget of the CIA, for example."[7] Of thousands of covert action projects between 1949 and 1968, only some 600 received consideration outside the CIA by the National Security Council body then charged with reviewing covert operations.

For its part, the American Congress was more interested in making sure the CIA had what it needed in the fight against communism than in overseeing its operations. The fate of several congressional initiatives for improving oversight that came to naught in these early years is eloquent testimony to the mood of the time and the temper of Congress. In early 1955 Democratic Senator Mike Mansfield, later chairman of the Foreign Relations Committee, introduced a resolution calling for a joint oversight committee. The resolution had thirty-five cosponsors. It also had the strong opposition not only of the executive but also of the "club" of senior senators. In hearings on the resolution, Mansfield elicited the following comment from Senator Leverett Saltonstall, the ranking Republican on the Armed Services Committee:

> It is not a question of reluctance on the part of the CIA officials to speak to us. Instead, it is a question of our reluctance, if you will, to seek information and knowledge on subjects which I personally, as a Member of Congress and as a citizen, would rather not have, unless I believed it to be my responsibility to have it because it might involve the lives of American citizens.[8]

In April 1956 the resolution was voted down, 59–27, with a half dozen cosponsors voting against it.

The debate did, however, result in the creation of formal CIA subcommittees in both Armed Services committees. Yet the buddy system remained largely unchanged. Allen Dulles, the near legend, was DCI until the Bay of Pigs fiasco in 1961; relaxed and candid with senior members, he had their absolute trust. In the Senate Armed Services Committee, Senator Richard Russell appointed to the formal subcommittee those senators with whom he had been meeting informally on CIA matters—Saltonstall and Harry Byrd. Later he added Lyndon Johnson and Styles Bridges. When, in 1957, the Appropriations Committee formed a subcommittee for the CIA, its members were Russell, Byrd, and Bridges. They both authorized and appropriated, often at the same meeting. Most CIA business continued to be conducted as before—by Dulles and Russell, meeting informally.

THE CLIMATE CHANGES

The Bay of Pigs marked the end of an era for the CIA. It was a stunning defeat for an agency known only for success. Dulles and his deputy, Richard Bissell, were eased out of their jobs. Yet neither executive procedures for, nor congressional oversight of, intelligence changed all that much.

A decade later, with the big expansion in covert action in Asia as the war in Vietnam heated up, the executive branch undertook somewhat more formal procedures. For instance, the NSC body charged with reviewing covert action (after 1970 called the 40 committee) considered operations in Chile on 23 separate occasions between March 1970 and October 1973, the period surrounding the presidency of Salvador Allende. Still, in numbers, most covert action projects continued not to be approved by anyone outside the CIA. By the early 1970s only about a fourth of all covert actions came before the NSC review body.[9]

During the 1960s more committees of Congress were receiving more information from the CIA than in the early days; however, about clandestine operations the CIA did not often volunteer information and Congress did not often ask. The role of Congress had not moved from receiving information to overseeing operations. In 1961 after the Bay of Pigs, and again in 1966, Democratic Senator Eugene McCarthy attempted unsuccessfully to revive the idea of a CIA oversight committee.

Watergate and Chile, coming on the heels of the war in Vietnam, changed all that. So did the passing of a congressional generation and the enacting of internal reforms that dispersed authority away from committee chairmen. The buddy system, smooth and private, had depended on a handful of congressional barons. Thus, as a former CIA director of congressional liaison put it, "When Chairmen Russell, [Carl] Hayden, [Mendel] Rivers, and [Carl] Vinson retired between 1965 and 1971, CIA's congressional constituency retired with them."[10] Or as William Colby, the DCI at the time of the first congressional investigations, later recalled:

> There had been a time when the joint hearing held by the Senate's intelligence subcommittees would have been deemed sufficient [to end the matter]. Senators with the seniority and clout of [John] McClellan and [John] Stennis then could easily have squelched any demands for further action on the part of their junior colleagues. But this was no longer the case.[11]

Congress's disinclination to ask about secret operations was the first change. Neither reticence nor deference were hallmarks of the congressional class of 1974, elected as Watergate played out on the nation's television screens. Congress passed the Hughes-Ryan act of 1974, the operative paragraph of which reads:

> No funds appropriated under the authority of this or another Act may be expended by or on behalf of the [CIA] for operations in foreign countries, other than activities intended solely for obtaining necessary intelligence, unless and until the President finds that each such operation is important to the national security of the United States and reports, in a timely fashion, a description and

scope of such operation to the appropriate committees of the Congress.[12]

From the verb "finds" came the noun "finding"—a written document bearing the president's signature. As was often the case, Congress sought to change the pattern of executive action not by making specific decisions but rather by changing the process by which decisions were made. The Hughes-Ryan act was intended to end the abuse of plausible denial displayed in the Cuban assassination plots, which seemed to have confused procedures within the executive—and deluded Congress—more than it protected anyone.

Hughes-Ryan required the president to put his name and his reputation on the line. It was meant to ensure that there would be no future wrangles such as those over assassinations. Covert actions, wise or stupid, would reflect presidential decision; there would be no doubt that someone was in charge. It also meant that members of Congress would find it harder to assert that they had been kept in the dark. Less often could they speechify in professed ignorance of covert action. The "appropriate committees" now became six: the Intelligence subcommittees of Armed Services and Appropriations in both houses plus the Foreign Affairs and Foreign Relations committees.

TENDING THE "GOVERNMENT'S" SECRETS

A year later Congress established the Church Committee and a parallel investigating committee in the House, chaired by New York Democrat Otis Pike. Those committees, the Church Committee in particular, represented an innovation in constitutional relations between the executive and Congress.[13] At the heart of the wrangling between the committees and the Ford administration over access to classified documents lay a constitutional issue: were those secret documents, written and classified by the CIA or State, the property of the executive only? Or were they the "government's" documents, to which Congress should have access on terms decided by it and which could be declassified by its decision as well as that of the executive? Popular usage mirrors ambiguity about what constitutes "the government," particularly in foreign affairs. Constitutionally, Congress is a coequal branch of the government, yet people often speak of "the government" more narrowly to refer to a particular administration in power.

The committees did not resolve the question of who controlled documents. In the nature of the system, they could not. But Congress and the executive did move a long way toward the view that even in matters of clandestine operations. Congress has its own right to the "government's" secret documents and that it bears the responsibility that goes with that right.

The Ford administration was a grudging partner in adjusting the constitutional bargain. A few in the administration, Colby foremost among them, believed the changes were fundamentally correct; others felt that, given the public mood, the administration simply had no choice. The administration had something of a dual approach to the Church Committee. At one level, that of executive prerogatives in foreign affairs, it was opposed to the investigation and its results. It held, thus, that publication of an interim report on assassinations was not only wrong but also a mistake that would harm the reputation of the United States. At another level, however, it was prepared to work with the committee, particularly to protect intelligence sources and methods. In that regard the administration and the committee shared an interest; the committee had no reason to want to endanger intelligence methods or agents' lives. In the case of the assassination report, the issue boiled down to whether the committee would publish the names of some thirty-three CIA officers. The administration argued that publishing the names would tarnish reputations and might, in one or two instances, endanger the individuals in question. Colby even took the issue to district court.

In the end, the committee and the administration reached a sensible compromise. The committee agreed to delete the names of twenty of the officers, required for neither the substance nor the credibility of the report. The remaining names were left in. Most were those of senior officers and were already in the public domain. The committee felt, moreover, that senior officials should be held publicly accountable for their actions. Like most compromises, it pleased neither side fully but was one with which both could live.[14]

In seeking to establish its position, the Church committee was assiduous about leaks. Not a single secret worth mention got out.[15] The same could not be said of the Pike Committee, whose entire final report leaked into the press in 1976 after the fall House had voted not to release it until the president certified that it did not contain information that would harm U.S. intelligence activities.[16]

When the House, like the Senate, later decided to establish a permanent intelligence committee, the Pike Committee experience, which had created acrimony not only between the committee and the administration but within the House as well, was much on the House's collective mind. As one sophisticated former staffer observed: "The message from the House was clear: no more fiascos. The new...committee would have to stay in line; the honor of the House was at stake."[17]

The House did not agree to a permanent committee until 1977, a year after the Senate. The vote was closer—227–171 in the House, compared with 75–22 in the Senate; and the House committee was granted less autonomy and control over classified information. For instance, the Senate committee was authorized to disclose classified information over the president's objection, while in the House that right rested with the full body. The House committee was also smaller and more partisan—13 members, nine of them Democrats, in a House of 435, compared with 15, eight Democrats, in a Senate of 100. The House Democrats were chosen by the Speaker, not the majority caucus, evidence of a desire to retain control. By contrast, the Senate committee, following the relatively bipartisan approach of the Church Committee, made the ranking minority member the vice-chairman, a unique arrangement in Congress.

Initially, the two congressional investigations resulted only in two new permanent oversight committees, increasing the number of congressional overseers of intelligence from six committees to eight, albeit ones with more access to information. Yet the institutional legacy of permanent select committees in each house of Congress has turned out to be an important one. The committees established the principle of rotating memberships, limiting tenures to six years in the House and eight in the Senate, to broaden their representation within Congress, thus guarding against a recurrence of the buddy system in image or in fact.

Reflecting their different lineages, the Senate committee was initially more self-confident in its approach to oversight. A cadre of members and staff from the Church committee moved to the new permanent committee, while the House started afresh, staffed mostly by ex-intelligence officials. Over time, however, the House staff, though smaller and divided along partisan lines, acquired the reputation of being more professional, especially in those aspects of oversight that seldom find their way into headlines—budgets, collection systems, and intelligence products.

Over time, too, the committees were stamped by the styles and personalities of their chairmen as well as by the character of their parent bodies. The House committee was chaired in the 1980s by Edward Boland and Lee Hamilton, members of experience and stature in the legislature by comparison with their counterparts on the Senate side, Republican David Durenberger and Democrat Patrick Leahy. The Republican ascendance to control of the Senate in 1980 not only brought new young senators to control of the committee, but also shifted the focal point for congressional scrutiny of secret operations to the House. And it frayed cooperation between the two committees.

By the latter half of the 1980s, with the Democrats again in control of the Senate, the Senate committee reflected its parent body in being less partisan than the House. Its Democrats were mostly moderates, senators like David Boren, Sam Nunn, and Ernest Hollings, who had few counterparts on the House committee. Some of those moderate Democrats, especially southerners, were attracted to the Intelligence Committee as a way to become active in foreign affairs without acquiring the liberal taint of the Foreign Relations Committee.

The Carter administration, disinclined from the start to resort to covert action, found its intelligence relations with Congress easy. It first pressed the House to establish a permanent intelligence committee, then cooperated with Congress in passing the Intelligence Oversight Act of 1980, the most important law in the realm of covert action. The act cut back the executive's reporting requirements for covert action to the two Intelligence committees; eight committees were too unwieldy for both executive and Congress, and virtually invited executive charges of being "too leaky." At the same time, however, the act charged the two committees with informing other relevant committees, especially Foreign Affairs, Foreign Relations, and the two Appropriations committees. It also made clear that Congress wanted to be notified of all covert actions, not just those carried out by the CIA; secret executive recourse to other agencies, in particular the military, was denied.

Congress also tiptoed toward prior notification of covert action; the "timely fashion" of the Hughes-Ryan act, which allowed notification after the fact (within twenty-four hours came to be the understanding), became "fully and currently informed," including "any significant anticipated intelligence activity" in the 1980 act. Yet notifying Congress still was not a "condition precedent to the initiation" of covert action. And the act gave the president another escape hatch, for in emergencies he was permitted to limit notice to eight members—the chairmen and ranking minority members of the Intelligence committees, the Speaker and minority leader of the House, and the majority and minority leaders of the Senate—the "gang of eight" or the "eight wise men," depending on the describer's inclinations.

THE "COVERT" WAR IN CENTRAL AMERICA

The tussle between executive and Congress, which had been restrained when operators and overseers shared the view that the covert instrument should be used sparingly, grew more passionate with the surge of covert actions in the 1980s. The Reagan administration came into office determined to make covert assistance to "freedom fighters" around the world a key element of its global pressure on the Soviet Union. Strikingly, in light of what came later, Reagan's executive order 12333 gave the CIA full responsibility for covert actions except in time of war or by specific presidential instruction.[18]

With the new administration, however, attitudes changed more than directives or procedures. One congressional staffer referred to men like NSC staffer Lieutenant Colonel Oliver North as "field grades," people eager for action, long on energy, but short on political savvy. William Miller, the staff director of both the Church committee and the first permanent Senate Intelligence Committee, observed that the CIA and its sister agencies were led in the late 1970s by people who had been through the experience of investigation and reform. They were "so immersed in the constitutional questions that they could recite chapter and verse. Questions of law and balance occurred naturally to them." By contrast, the Reagan leadership was dominated by "advocates, people who were always trying to get around the roadblocks, who were looking for a way to get it done."[19]

In Central America, the long reign of the Somoza family in Nicaragua had come to an end in 1979, bringing to power the regime's armed opponents, the Sandinista National Liberation Front, in uneasy partnership with a range of civilian opposition groups. Early in its tenure, the Reagan administration charged that the Sandinistas were becoming a base for Cuban and Soviet subversion in the region and, specifically, that they were shipping arms to guerrilla opponents of the U.S.-supported

government of El Salvador. At first, the Sandinistas were confronted primarily by remnants of Somoza's hated National Guard who had found sanctuary in Honduras, but over time several of the Sandinistas' original allies fell out with the government. One of them opened a new anti-Sandinista front operating out of Costa Rica.

Congressional opposition to the administration's course in Nicaragua grew in direct proportion to the breakdown in congressional-executive relations. The administration sought to unite the Sandinistas' armed opponents—dubbed the contras—and to support them. Yet the purpose of that covert support seemed a moving target, which suggested to Congress either confusion or deception. In November 1981 President Reagan signed National Security Council Decision Directive 17 proposing to build a force of contras to interdict arms shipments from Nicaragua to the rebels in El Salvador. However, the directive, when turned into a finding, contained language—"engage in paramilitary…operations in Nicaragua, and elsewhere"— that seemed to permit almost anything.[20] The congressional Intelligence committees first made clear in their classified reports on the CIA budget that they opposed covert efforts to overthrow the Sandinista government or Nicaragua. Then, at the end of 1982, they put that language, as the Boland amendment, publicly into the appropriations bill. Named for Edward P. Boland, then chairman of the House Intelligence Committee it stipulated that no money could be used "for the purpose of overthrowing the Government of Nicaragua or provoking a military exchange between Nicaragua and Honduras."[21]

The aims of America's covert intervention remained in dispute while the war intensified, especially as the CIA opened a second front in Costa Rica. In response, Boland and the House shifted their focus from appropriations to authorization, proposing not to limit covert action in Nicaragua but to end it. The House voted to do so in July 1983. However, the Senate Intelligence committee, with the Republicans in the majority, was prepared to approve more money if the administration would be precise about its objectives. The administration "thoroughly scrubbed" a new finding, which was signed in September 1983.[22]

In October the House again voted to end the contra program but at year's end the House-Senate conference compromised, accepting the revised presidential finding, which expanded the American aim from halting arms flows from Nicaragua to pressuring the Sandinistas to negotiate with their neighbors. However Congress capped funding at $24 million, enough for one year's operations, thus requiring the administration to return to Congress before the end of the fiscal year if it wanted the program to continue.[23]

Any limited American objective seemed less plausible after revelations early the next year that the CIA itself had mined Nicaraguan harbors. The mining, a new phase in the covert war, was itself an act of war and one that threatened the shipping of both American allies and the Soviet Union. The operation was approved by the president in the winter, probably in December 1983.[24] The Sandinistas protested on January 3, 1984, that the contras were laying mines in Nicaraguan harbors, and the rebel leaders, who plainly had no capacity to lay mines on their own, finally learned their lines and announced on January 8 that they would do so.

On January 31, 1984, DCI William Casey met with the House Intelligence Committee and mentioned the mining, though the meeting was primarily about releasing further funds for the overall contra project. The House committee apparently did not share its information with its Senate colleagues, although the CIA may have briefed several members of the Senate committee and its staff. The Senate, however, was pushing toward its February recess, and the administration twice asked for a delay so that Secretary of State George Shultz could also attend. As a result, a full briefing of the Senate committee was delayed, and many, perhaps most, members remained unaware of the operation, especially of the direct CIA role in it.

Casey first met with the full Senate Intelligence committee on March 8, for over an hour, but this meeting too dealt primarily with authorizing the release of funds, over which the Intelligence committee was fighting a jurisdictional battle with Appropriations. Only one sentence dealt with the mining, and it, like the rest of the briefing, was delivered in Casey's inimitable mumble.[25] Many on the committee did not learn of the mining until a month later, and then almost by accident.

Casey nodded toward the letter of the law with his brief reference, but the episode angered even Senator Barry Goldwater, the Republican committee chairman and a man not known for his opposition to covert action. He had not understood the reference. When he learned about the mining operation, once the committee staff received a full briefing on April 2,

he was furious. His letter to Casey, which leaked into the press, was notable for its unsenatorial prose as well as for its displeasure: "It gets down to one, little, simple phrase: I am pissed off!"[26] In the wake of this episode, the Senate committee moved toward the House's position, and Congress cut off further covert assistance with a second Boland amendment enacted into law in October 1984, thus rejecting the president's request for $21 million more.

By the end of 1984 the House of Representatives had voted three times against paramilitary aid, only to have the operation rescued by House-Senate conferences. Yet despite these losses, the Reagan administration was succeeding in framing the debate on its own ground. Americans' deep ambivalence—their fears of U.S. involvement competed with their distaste for the Sandinistas—left covert support standing as a "middle option," cheap in money and American blood, and hard for members of Congress, even Democrats, to vote against lest they be branded "soft on communism" by a popular president.

In early 1985 President Reagan again asked for aid to the contras, this time for $14 million. The House again voted down the aid after a sharp debate. However, when Sandinista leader Daniel Ortega unwisely journeyed to Moscow just after the vote, those Democrats who had voted against covert aid looked soft and foolish. They responded by enacting economic sanctions, largely symbolic, against Nicaragua. In August 1985 Congress compromised on $27 million in "nonmilitary" aid to the contras; this was not to be administered by the CIA, and the agency was barred from direct contact with the contras or assistance in their training. Congress did not restore CIA funding for this purpose until October 1986.

This off-again, on-again funding, deeply frustrating to those in the Reagan administration most committed to the contras, bred circumventions of the congressional restrictions—efforts suspected in press accounts as early as the spring of 1985. The second Boland amendment applied to the CIA, the Defense Department, and "any other agency or entity involved in intelligence."[27] Some in the administration felt it did not prevent the NSC staff or other officials from seeking aid from other sources. By early 1984, as the $24 million ran out, the president directed the NSC staff, in the words of national security adviser Robert McFarlane, "to keep the contras together 'body and soul.'" Casey and other officials began to approach governments ranging from Israel to Brunei to Saudi Arabia and quietly canvassed private sources in the United States, South Korea, Taiwan, and Latin America. That private support totaled some $34 million during the period of the aid cutoff.[28]

By May 1984, when the congressional appropriation ran out, Oliver North, the NSC staff's deputy director for political-military affairs, had become coordinator of the private support, dubbed "the Enterprise" by those involved. In October when Congress barred any CIA involvement, the agency issued a "cease and desist" order to its stations. Nevertheless, about a dozen CIA officers remained involved in North's operation, apparently construing his role to signify White House authorization. By the fall of 1985, North was overseeing the shipping of privately purchased arms to the contras and the construction of a secret airfield in Costa Rica. North, who also called his operation "Project Democracy," relied on a network of conservative organizations and ex-military men, one of whom, retired general Richard V. Secord, was also a key conduit for arms sales to Iran.

In the fall of 1986 a Beirut newspaper published a bizarre account of a secret mission to Iran the previous May by former national security adviser McFarlane. The account, which first seemed another piece of partisan Middle East nonsense, turned out to be true. McFarlane's delivery of U.S. weapons to Iran was part of a sequence running back to August 1985. The first two shipments had been made by Israel, through middlemen, with U.S. approval and assurance that depleted Israeli stocks would be replenished. The operation, also managed day to day by North, was so closely held that even the CIA was at first cut out, though Casey himself was central. Critical meetings were held with no analytic papers prepared beforehand and no record of decisions kept afterward.

North sought and received CIA help in November 1985 when, in a comedy of errors, Secord could not get one shipment through Portugal to Israel. When he heard of the CIA involvement, John McMahon, the agency's deputy director, angrily barred any further CIA involvement without a presidential finding. The next month the president signed one finding to provide retroactive approval for the shipments; the new national security adviser, Admiral John Poindexter, destroyed that finding a year later because, he later testified, it would have been embarrassing to the president.[29]

The president approved another finding on January 17, 1986, "to establish contact with moderate elements within and outside the Government of Iran by providing these elements with arms, equipment and related materiel." However, the accompanying background paper, prepared by North, was explicit about the link to getting U.S. hostages out of Lebanon:

> This approach...may well be our *only* way to achieve the release of the Americans held in Beirut....If all of the hostages are not released after the first shipment of 1,000 weapons, further transfers would cease.[30]

In February, American arms were first shipped directly from the United States by the CIA to Israel for transfer to Iran. Three other shipments were made, the last in late October. In all, some 2,000 TOW antitank weapons, as well as other weapons and spare parts were sold to Iran. Three U.S. hostages were released, but three more were taken during the course of the operation.

The strange tale became more bizarre when it was revealed that the profits of the Iranian arms sales had been diverted to support the Nicaraguan contras. The arms had been sold to Iran for nearly $16 million more than the CIA had paid the Pentagon for them. In a scheme masterminded by North, the profits were then laundered through Swiss bank accounts, to be drawn on by the contras. When the scheme was revealed, North was fired, and his boss, Poindexter resigned.

The story unfolded first through an executive investigating panel, named by the president in December 1986 and chaired by former Senator John Tower. Then Congress began a joint Senate-House investigation in January 1987, which treated the nation to the spectacle of public testimony by the central figures, most notably Oliver North, through the hot summer of 1987. The focus of both investigations was narrowly the diversion of profits from the Iran arms sales to the contras: had the president authorized or known of it? This charge remained unproven. The investigations, however, did what Congress had been unable, in part unwilling, to do before—unravel the trail of private support for the contras.

The narrow initial focus broadened further through the criminal trials of McFarlane, North, and Poindexter. McFarlane, distraught to the point of breakdown by what had been done, pleaded guilty to lying to Congress. North, the loyal soldier to the end, asserted his innocence; he was found guilty of destroying documents and other charges but not of deceiving Congress. North's light sentence reflected the discrediting of what had been the administration's primary defense, one accepted by the Tower panel: that the wrongdoing was the result of a small cabal centered on North. North plainly was central, but just as plainly the circle of those involved was wider than the administration wanted to acknowledge.

SOURCES OF TENSION: EXTERNAL AND INTERNAL

The sources of tension in the intelligence role of Congress are displayed in this history. They are both external and internal to Congress. The houses of Congress not only share a distrust of the executive, no matter which party is in power, but they are also jealous of each other. The two Intelligence committees do not automatically share information, as is apparent in the case of the mining of Nicaragua's harbors. Working together is all the harder if, as in this case, there is both disagreement on the merits and partisan division: Democrats controlled the House, Republicans the Senate from 1980 until 1986. In December 1985, during the time CIA assistance was cut off, the Intelligence committees did approve some money for "communications" and "advice" to the contras, subject to conditions negotiated with the committees. There then ensued an exchange of letters suggesting that the two chairmen were uncertain—or disagreed—over what was permitted and what was proscribed.[31]

Moreover, despite their authority, the Intelligence committees do not monopolize oversight of covert operations. Because covert actions are foreign policy, the Foreign Affairs and Foreign Relations committees have an interest in their authorization; because they cost money, the Appropriations committees have their stakes. The tracks of both sets of jurisdictional battles are visible in the Nicaraguan episode.

However, the sharper tensions arise between Congress and the executive. Even with good will in both branches, congressional overseers have to get deeply into the details of ongoing operations, which is hard for them and uncomfortable for covert operators in the executive branch. Critical details can fall between the cracks: it may be that Senate committee members, like Goldwater, simply were not paying attention when Casey mumbled about the mining. Even their staffs are hard-pressed to keep up with the details of forty-odd covert actions. As one staffer close to the process put it: "How can you know which

detail will jump up and bite you? Things move fast. How long did the mining take from beginning to end? A few weeks."[32]

For members, oversight remains something of an unnatural act. They are not hard to interest in intelligence; the lure of secrecy and the mystique of covert operations are a powerful tug on their attentions. At the beginning of the One-hundredth Congress in 1987, 60 members of the House signed up for four openings on the Intelligence Committee. Given rotating memberships, chairs can come quickly; Republican Senator Dave Durenberger became chairman of the Senate committee after only six years. Still, the assignment is one among many, whatever its fascination. Members have little political reason to become involved, still less to take responsibility for particular operations. Politicians' temptation to use their special access to information on morning talk shows competes uneasily with the disciplines of committee membership. Sometimes the special access is, in political terms, more a burden than an asset; as Senator Daniel K. Inouye, the first chairman of the permanent Senate Intelligence Committee, observed, in words not much different from Saltonstall's thirty years before: "How would you like to know a very, very high official of a certain government was on our payroll?"[33]

On balance, members have resolved the contest between responsibility and self-promotion or credit taken in favor of the former. The temptations of the latter are always there, and the dividing line is fine, but the penalties for being seen to traverse it are high: recent incidents demonstrate both these points. In early 1987 Senator Patrick Leahy, the chairman of the Senate Intelligence Committee, was forced to resign his chairmanship after leaking an unclassified but not yet released version of the committee's Iran-contra report. His action was unwise, but by the standard applied to Leahy, the executive branch would be depopulated. In 1988 House Speaker Jim Wright told a reporter that he had "received clear testimony from CIA people that they have deliberately done things to provoke an overreaction on the part of the Government in Nicaragua."[34] He was not the first to characterize American policy in that way, he later denied he had leaked secret testimony, and the incident was later overshadowed by his other ethical problems. But at the time, invoking the CIA as the source was enough to earn him a storm of criticism.

Iran-contra provides most graphic testimony to the tensions in the congressional role when the committees confront a determined president, especially if they themselves are of divided mind. Administrations, especially one as committed to covert operations as the Reagan administration, are bound to want the flexibility of broad, general findings that give the CIA room to adapt to changing circumstances. Congress is almost equally bound to be wary of signing a blank check, particularly when the administration is committed. McGeorge Bundy, who ran the NSC review committee for the Kennedy and Johnson administrations, emphasized by understatement in 1975 the difficulty reviewers outside the CIA confront:

> I think it has happened that an operation is presented in one way to a committee…and executed in a way that is different from what the committee thought it had authorized.[35]

Norman Mineta, a charter member of the House Intelligence Committee, put his frustration more colorfully in speaking of the executive: "They treat us like mushrooms. Keep us in the dark and feed us a lot of manure."[36]

At more than one point in the Iran-contra affair, administration officials deceived Congress. The January 1986 arms sales finding was explicit: do not tell Congress. The congressional overseers did not find out about the operation until the following autumn—not "fully and currently informed" by anyone's definition. Earlier, the Intelligence committees responded to press accounts that the ban on aid to the contras was being circumvented. In August 1985, for instance, the House asked the administration about North's activities. The response drafted by McFarlane and North and signed by the former, said that at no time did I or any member of the National Security Council staff violate the letter or spirit of the restrictions.[37]

That is outright deception, even granting some ambiguity in the wording of the ban. Did the wording mean no administration official could seek other sources of aid? If so, how could Congress enforce the ban? Its means were limited, as they are in more normal cases. Even if the committees are united in their opposition to an operation, they cannot easily stop it, for if the administration is determined to proceed it can fund the operation for a year from the CIA Contingency Reserve.[38] Congress has in two cases resorted to public legislation banning covert action—the Boland amendments and the 1976 Clark-Tunney amendment on Angola. These were signs that it did not trust the administration, or its designated overseers of covert action, or both.

In the instance of aid to the contras, however, Congress's will was also limited. In part, it was reluctant to take on a popular president even on a controversial issue. The reluctance is customary in relations between the executive and Congress, even if the president is less popular than Reagan; unless the president is plainly out of step with the American people, members of Congress do not like to confront the presidency. The House Intelligence Committee, like its parent body, was sharply divided over aid to the contras; in later votes, whichever side captured a group of thirty-odd swing votes, mostly Democratic and mostly conservative southerners, carried the day. The Senate although wavering, probably had a consistent majority favoring aid in principle.

In those circumstances, it is perhaps less surprising that the committees were halfhearted in inquiring into violations of the ban that their later, retrospective investigations framed the issues narrowly or that Congress breathed an audible sigh of relief that Reagan had left the presidency by the time new revelations during the trials of his former aides might have raised questions of impeachment.

LIMITS TO THE SYSTEM

Aid to the contras was as divisive within the Intelligence committees as it was in the nation, but almost every other covert action has elicited a near consensus, even within the House committee. The congressional overseers have been informed of the covert action and recorded their views; presidents cannot lightly ignore those views, especially if they are held by senior committee members in both parties. Lest the president miss the point, the committees can take a formal vote to underscore their view. More than once, apparently, such votes have induced a president to rescind approval of an operation.[39]

In other cases the committees have said, in the words of one staff member, "Hey, do you know how risky that is?"[40] Hearing an affirmative response, they have let the program go ahead despite their doubts. They did so in the case of Angola, letting the administration resume covert aid to Jonas Savimbi's UNITA (Union for the Total Independence of Angola, in its Portuguese acronym) in 1986 to the tune of some $15 million a year; they did so in that case despite the fact that Lee Hamilton, the House Intelligence committee chairman, took his personal opposition to the House floor.

The Reagan administration wanted to make use of covert action much more frequently than did its predecessor, and the oversight committees, reflecting the mood of Congress and probably of the American people as well, assented to that expansion of covert action. The centerpiece of the Reagan program was aid to the resistance in Afghanistan, begun under the Carter administration, which came to total more than a half billion dollars a year by 1986. Indeed, Congress was if anything ahead of the executive, appropriating unrequested additional money for the resistance in 1983 and pressing the administration to deliver more sophisticated weaponry.

In a sense the system "worked" even in the instance of arms sales to Iran. In deciding to sell, the president pursued a policy that was opposed by his secretaries of state and defense and about which he was afraid to inform the congressional oversight committees. Those should have been warning signals aplenty that the policy was unwise.

If presidents are determined to do something stupid, they will find someone, somewhere, to do it.

In seeking to circumvent the requirements of process, the president, it appears, also set himself up for deception. It was he who was not told when the Iran and contra operations crossed. Keeping Congress in the dark also encouraged looseness within the executive, just as it did a quarter century earlier in the CIA's attempted assassinations of Fidel Castro. North and Poindexter mistakenly construed plausible denial after their own fashion, much the same as Helms and his colleagues had, keeping their president ignorant in order to protect him. Although convinced the president would approve the use of proceeds from the Iranian arms sales for the contras as an "implementation" of his policy, Poindexter "made a very deliberate decision not to ask the President" so that he could "insulate [him] from the decision and provide some future deniability."[41]

When the president's closest advisers become the operators, the president loses them as a source of detached judgment on the operations. They become advocates; not protectors of the president (even if he does not quite realize his need for protection). So it was with McFarlane and Poindexter; once committed, they had reason to overlook the warning signals thrown up by the process. Excluding Congress also excluded one more "political scrub," one more source of advice about what most Americans would find acceptable.

In circumventing the ban on aid to the contras, the Reagan administration's approach to Congress was more one of contempt than of exclusion. An isolated act or two of aiding the contras would have been a close call, given the ambiguity of the ban. But close congressional votes do not excuse establishing "the Enterprise." Poindexter and North were explicit in their later testimony before Congress: "I simply did not want any outside interference," and "I didn't want to tell Congress anything," they said, respectively.[42]

"The Enterprise" is the most troubling piece of the entire story, one the congressional investigations paused over far too briefly. It was an attempt to escape congressional oversight entirely, to construct a CIA outside the American government. As North put it: "Director Casey had in mind…an overseas entity that was…self-financing, independent of appropriated monies."[43] The idea was dangerous, but the price the administration eventually paid for it was high. If covert actions are to be undertaken, they should be done by the agency of government constructed to do them—the Central Intelligence Agency. It has both the expertise and the accountability.

INFORMATION AND THE BALANCE OF POWER

Disputes over secret operations between Congress and the executive have grabbed the headlines, yet the day-to-day balance of power between the two branches has been more affected by the sharply increased availability of intelligence analysis to Congress. This latter change has coincided with the tug-of-war over operations and so has been obscured by it. However, Congress now receives nearly every intelligence item the executive does. In this way, too, the intelligence agencies are coming to have a more customary relationship with Congress, but one that is more awkward for them than for the Agriculture or Commerce departments.

Intelligence agencies, the CIA in particular, were conceived as servants of their executive masters. It bears remembering that *the* intelligence issue in the early postwar period was not operations; rather it was avoiding another Pearl Harbor. That problem was what to do about fragmented intelligence that could neither sort out signals of warning from surrounding "noise" nor make the warning persuasive to senior officials of government. This problem, along with the balkanized way the separate armed services had fought World War II, begat the National Security Council. It also begat the sequence of efforts to coordinate

American intelligence, beginning with the Central Intelligence Group in 1946.

Congress was a promoter of these changes but essentially a bystander to them. As in other areas of government, it used laws to shape processes in the executive branch. Long after it had tried to centralize and formalize the intelligence process in the executive, it left its own oversight of intelligence and its role in receiving intelligence information informal and fragmented. Changing congressional attitudes toward operations both coincided with and produced an altered view of intelligence products. If Congress was to know about and judge covert operations, it was logical to assess them in light of the intelligence premises on which they were based.

Some numbers suggest the extent of the change over the past decade. Virtually everything the CIA produces goes to the two Intelligence committees, and most also goes to the Foreign Affairs, Foreign Relations, Armed Services, and Appropriations committees. All eight committees receive the CIA "newspaper," the National Intelligence Daily (NID). The CIA alone sends some 5,000 reports to Congress each year and conducts over a thousand oral briefings.[44] By contrast, CIA records show only twenty-two briefings to Congress (on topics other than covert action) about Chile in the decade 1964–74.[45] Overall, the CIA gave perhaps a hundred briefings a year to Congress in the mid-1970s.[46]

What is true of CIA analyses is also the case in varying degrees for the products of other intelligence agencies. Just as the Intelligence committees get a biweekly list of new CIA publications, they receive indexes from the Defense Intelligence Agency (DIA), along with the DIA daily summary.[47] The National Security Agency provides weekly summaries of signals intelligence. Committee staffers can get access to "raw" intelligence, like defense attache or CIA agent reports, by special request, although in the most sensitive cases these must be made by the committee chairman to the DCI. People move in both directions from committee staffs to intelligence community analyst jobs, and occasionally committee staffers get friendly calls from intelligence community analysts suggesting that they ask for a particular item.

The change is marked enough without overstating it. Because intelligence is available on Capitol Hill does not mean it is read. Congress is an oral culture, while written products are the intelligence analyst's predilection. If they read, members of Congress, like their counterparts in the executive,

will turn to the *New York Times* and *Washington Post* before they pick up the NID. The committees, especially the Intelligence committees, are tightly compartmented in their handling of classified material, which means that getting access to some intelligence is at least a bother. And since knowledge is power and access prestige, Hill staffers who receive intelligence may hold it, not share it.

The people within the intelligence community who conduct the briefings or write the reports are analysts, not operators. They are more professorial than conspiratorial in temperament. They work for the CIA's Directorate of Intelligence, not its Directorate of Operations, and they tell their neighbors openly that they work for the CIA or for the State Department's Bureau of Intelligence and Research or the Pentagon's DIA.

They get much of their information about foreign governments the same way academics do, through reading periodicals or transcripts of media monitored openly by the Foreign Broadcast Information Service. In addition they have access to two sets of secret sources—diplomatic cables sent by State Department officers abroad and raw intelligence, such as agent reports produced by the CIA's Directorate of Operations or foreign communications monitored secretly by the National Security Agency.

The change is dramatic for these analysts, many of whom had never dealt with Congress before a decade ago and all of whom have been steeped in a professional culture that separates intelligence from policy lest the former be biased or politicized through contact with the latter. When the subject is technical and, preferably, out of the limelight, briefing Congress is a welcome chance to educate another set of consumers. Yet the analysts recognize that members of Congress, like executive officials, seldom are disinterested consumers of information. They seek it as leverage, often to be used against the executive that is the analysts' ostensible master. If the subject is politically hot, like Central America in the 1980s, the experience is painful, the sense of being manipulated keen.

CONGRESS AS LEVER OR ALLY?

Sometimes Congress listens to intelligence analysis when the executive will not. In such cases, benefits and risks are two sides of the same coin. In June 1987, Representative Duncan Hunter smashed a Toshiba radio-cassette player on the steps of the Capitol. The purpose of his stunt was attention: Toshiba and a Norwegian firm had deliberately sold the Soviet Union milling equipment that would make Soviet submarines quieter, hence harder to track. Hunter charged that the $17 million sale might "cost the West $30 billion to regain the superiority we lost."[48] The Toshiba bashing was the culmination of a series of events in which the CIA's Technology Transfer Assessment Center (TTAC) had, in effect, hawked its analyses around Washington.

The story began not with TTAC but with a disaffected Japanese employee who took the story of the Toshiba sale to COCOM, the Paris-based export control organization comprising the NATO allies and Japan. Staffers at COCOM, however, accepted Toshiba's word that it had sold only permitted technology. The employee then took his story to the U.S. embassy in Tokyo, which put him in touch with TTAC. The first stop for TTAC was the State Department, which made a diplomatic "demarche" to Japan. Like most such demarches, it was, however, brushed off for want of hard information. Moreover, the State Department looked askance at TTAC: TTAC's desire to control the issue left its colleagues at State's Bureau of Intelligence and Research feeling cut out, and policy officials at State were nervous about the repercussions of the issue on relations with two allies. Yet the tradition of CIA independence, plus TTAC's control of the issue, made it difficult for State to influence what TTAC said.

The next stop was the Defense Department, where Undersecretary Fred Iklé, a willing listener, agreed to take the issue up in his forthcoming trip to Japan. For Iklé the issue was one among several, not primary, and his trip produced little more than the demarche. But Iklé's office, briefed by TTAC and now with a better case in hand, in turn briefed Senator Jake Gam, a kindred hard-liner on technology transfer. At about the same time, December 1986, mention of this "major technology transfer" appeared in classified written briefings to the two Intelligence committees. Word was spreading.

Within two months the issue was public. First it went again to COCOM, where this time TTAC briefed representatives of the fifteen member nations. As Japan and Norway responded, Washington buzzed with rumors of a big new case. In late February the House Armed Services seapower subcommittee was briefed on the issue, and the next month, at hearings on the omnibus trade bill, Iklé's deputy, Richard Perle, referred obliquely to an export control violation he "could go into in a classified hearing." A

week later the conservative *Washington Times* broke the story, quoting unnamed officials "outside the government."

From then on, TTAC did not lack audiences; it had more than it wanted. Members of Congress outbid each other in proposals for retaliating against the wrongdoers, especially Toshiba, for Norway had acted to defuse the issue by admitting guilt and working with the United States. In the end, the weight of other interests at play in U.S.-Japanese relations began to be felt, and congressional leaders cooperated with the executive in enacting sanctions against Toshiba that, while sounding tough, were relatively mild.

The kind of interaction with Congress reflected in the Toshiba affair was uncharted water. On one hand, Guy DuBois, the principal TTAC analyst, sought to hold to the traditional line between intelligence and policy: "Once you state a position, how that position affects policy . . . is not your business."[49] On the other hand, DCI Casey had given TTAC a mandate that was more than providing information; it was to be a player in a quasi-prosecutorial process. In that sense, its information was to be nearly self-implementing: if it could prove guilt then that would frame the response. Congress was not the principal prosecutor, but telling it was a way to make sure someone paid attention.

The Toshiba case coincided with William Webster's arrival as DCI, replacing the late William Casey; plainly, Webster's main mission was repairing relations with Congress after Iran-contra. "To Webster," the TTAC analyst recalled, "Congress has an insatiable appetite and to the extent we can, we satisfy it." Moreover, "if a Congressman finds out that you decided not to be completely forthcoming," the credibility of the CIA could be damaged. The CIA's role, however, was not simply responding to congressional requests: "If they ask a stupid question, tell them it's stupid, then tell them what the smart question is and answer it."

It is still rare for Congress to be the lead consumer of intelligence. Most of the time Congress's effect is indirect. Since Congress will also know what the executive knows, executive officials are prudent to pay attention to intelligence lest they be skewered by Congress for the failure. Consider the contrast between the fall of the shah of Iran in 1978 and the departure from the Philippines of President Ferdinand Marcos in 1986.[50] The experience with the shah had taught policy officials in both the executive and Congress not to dismiss unwelcome news about Marcos, nor to assume, as they had about the shah, that Marcos knew his politics better than Washington did. That the Philippine opposition—moderate, Catholic, and U.S.-educated—was both much more accessible to intelligence collection and much more acceptable than Iran's mullahs made the lesson easier to learn.

The Philippine crisis moved more slowly than the Iranian, beginning in earnest with the assassination of opposition leader Benigno Aquino on the airport tarmac in Manila as he returned from the United States in August 1983. The intelligence community concluded that if Marcos had not ordered the assassination, it almost certainly had been done on his behalf. From then on the Philippines was on the congressional agenda almost as much as it was on that of the executive. The contrast with Iran could hardly be sharper; a 1979 House Intelligence committee postmortem on the Iran case contains not a single reference to Congress.[51]

The State Department worried about Congress in the instance of Toshiba, but in the instance of the Philippines the East Asia "mafia" in the executive—including State, Defense, and the NSC—welcomed congressional pressure as a way to persuade *their bosses*, not least the president, that Marcos might have to go. An August 1985 Senate Intelligence Committee report concluded that "the Marcos government is unlikely to pursue the changes necessary to stop the economic hemorrhaging, to slow or halt the insurgency or to heal the major lesions that are infecting the political process."[52] Later in the year, the links between Congress and the executive were tightened when one Senate Foreign Relations Committee staffer moved to the intelligence community to be national intelligence officer for East Asia and the Pacific.

Another Senate Foreign Relations Committee staff member described the interaction:

> The people in the State Department were using us, the Foreign Relations Committee, to get their point across in the White House. They were delighted when [Chairman Richard] Lugar decided to write a letter, not to Marcos but to the President of the United States. In other words, we laid it right on the President; We shifted our focus from the President of the Philippines to the President of the United States.

In November 1985, Marcos called a snap election for February 1986. The opposition managed to unite to name Aquino's widow, Corazon, as its presidential candidate. In December 1985 the intelligence community was still predicting a narrow Marcos victory, but by January 1986 it labeled the election too close to call, and on the eve of the vote it actually predicted an Aquino victory while also betting that Marcos would fix the results if need be. On January 30 President Reagan announced a bipartisan mission of U.S. election observers, cochaired by Lugar.

The effect of Congress's access to intelligence was most evident in the crunch. Most of the U.S. observers witnessed fraud by the ruling party, but as late as February 11, as votes trickled in, Reagan commented that the United States was concerned about both violence and "the possibility of fraud, although it could have been that all of that was occurring on both sides," a quote that so pleased Marcos that he had it shown over and over on Philippine television.[53]

At this point, the intelligence community was told, in effect, to put up or shut up. It responded with convincing proof of massive fraud by Marcos's party. Thus the administration had to act in the knowledge that Congress would soon have the same proof. Its options—to ride out the storm with Marcos, for instance—were correspondingly constrained. By February 15 the White House had dropped the "fraud on both sides" line, and on the 17th Lugar called for Marcos to resign.

Judgments about whether the sharing of intelligence with Congress creates more consensus or less, let alone whether it produces wiser policy or more foolish, are hard to make and inevitably subjective. In retrospect, if the departure of Marcos is regarded as a success, the fact that Congress knew what the executive did seems to have contributed to that success. Unwise options were foreclosed, and senior officials, especially the president, had to see the election as it was, not as they might wish it to be: Congress was watching. At the end, sharing intelligence about what Marcos had done in stealing votes made a compelling case and was enough to produce consensus.

In the case of Nicaragua, however, if shared intelligence produced a more enlightened debate, it surely did not produce consensus. This issue, like so many others, turned not on what the Sandinistas did but what their actions meant, implied, or portended. On those latter questions, even good intelligence assessments are seldom convincing. Officials in the executive and Congress disagreed, unsurprisingly, despite looking at the same data and reading the same analyses of it.

So far, there is little evidence of analysts cutting their cloth to suit congressional consumers. However, it may simply be that the congressional role is new. A cynic would say that analysts always hedged their bets, and critics would argue that analysts feel the most formidable pressures to change assessments from their bosses in the executive branch. Analysts did not soften the news in the Philippines even though it was unwelcome to some in the administration; nor did TTAC hold back in the Toshiba case because the State Department did not much like its assessment (and Congress liked it too much). In the heat of the debate over Nicaragua, the House Intelligence Committee, while generally praising intelligence community performance, certainly did not feel it had been pandered to—quite the contrary.[54]

THE SPECIAL CASE OF VERIFICATION

The more direct role of intelligence agencies in the political process is especially apparent in battles over arms control verification. Since the Senate must ratify treaties, verification is plainly an issue for Congress. Treaty supporters and opponents, as well as those who seek a way out by voting against the treaty without being labeled against arms control, all use verification as an argument. In the process they seek, understandably, to push decisions about what is finally a political issue—whether existing monitoring arrangements provide for adequate verification—onto the technical intelligence agencies, which in turn want, again understandably, to confine their role to describing those monitoring arrangements.

Verification was not an issue during the debate over SALT I in 1972, but charges of Soviet violations of that treaty, as well as the much more ambitious aims of SALT II, raised the issue five years later. Accordingly, in 1977 the Senate Foreign Relations Committee asked the Intelligence Committee for a thorough review of monitoring capabilities. The report was relatively sanguine. It appeared verification would not, after all, be a stumbling block in the ratification debate.[55]

Then, in March 1979 the United States lost access to monitoring facilities in Iran. Verification returned to the agenda, especially for the fence sitters, prominent among whom was Senator John Glenn, who said he could not support the treaty until the lost capabilities were replaced. The Intelligence Committee's final report, released on the eve of the floor debate, distinguished between the treaty's numerical limits and many of its qualitative constraints that could be monitored with high confidence, and several qualitative limits for which confidence was relatively low.[56]

Opponents zeroed in on the low-confidence provisions, while supporters pointed to the committee judgment that the treaty itself would enhance America's ability to monitor the treaty limits. The ratification vote boded to be a close-run thing, due largely to verification issues, but the whole debate was rendered moot by the Soviet invasion of Afghanistan. President Carter withdrew the treaty from Senate consideration.

In 1988 the Senate Intelligence Committee's unanimous judgment was decisive in removing verification as an issue in the discussion over the Intermediate Nuclear Forces (INF) treaty.[57] The treaty itself both embodied the most elaborate verification arrangements ever negotiated and simplified verification by eliminating weapons systems entirely, not merely reducing them in number. In its report approving the INF treaty, the committee explicitly opened the debate on a future strategic arms treaty by observing that strategic reductions would be far more demanding to monitor than those in the INF treaty.

The committee report also sought to protect the intelligence community by noting that verification is not simple, nor does it alone settle whether a treaty is desirable; a bad treaty that can be verified is still a bad treaty. It also distinguished carefully between monitoring and verification—the former an intelligence community responsibility, the latter a judgment by the executive of whether Soviet behavior as reported by the community is compatible with the treaty.[58]

CLIENTS AND PATRONS

Yet another sign that the intelligence community has joined the American government is that the institutional relations that have grown up between intelligence agencies and their congressional overseers have come to resemble those between domestic agencies and their congressional committees. Although the committees can be sharply critical of their agencies—witness covert actions or particular "intelligence failures"—in general the interests of the overseers and those overseen run parallel. The creation of the two intelligence oversight committees was thus the best thing that ever happened to the intelligence community, even if the heat of specific disputes sometimes has obscured that fact for intelligence officials.

The committees and their staffs have created a pool of people knowledgeable about intelligence and able to serve as advocates throughout the two chambers. By the time both new committees had been formed, in 1977, only 3 percent of House and 20 percent of Senate incumbents had served on the then-existing oversight subcommittees of Appropriations and Armed Services. Ten years later the percentages were 8 and 43. Over the period between 1980, when the Intelligence committees became the budget authorizers for intelligence, and 1986, the CIA budget more than doubled, growing faster than the defense budget. The total budget for the intelligence community nearly tripled, reaching close to $20 billion.[59]

Indeed, the committees have been accused of becoming as much protectors of the intelligence community as overseers—a risk that runs through all relations between Congress and executive agencies. It is true that the base of knowledge among members and staff does build understanding. The difference between the congressional investigations of intelligence in the mid-1970s and the Iran-contra panel was, for better or worse, striking: the latter was narrow, disciplined, and, Oliver North excepted, boring, with no visible sentiment for ending covert operations, much less for dismantling the CIA.

The bulk of the increase in the intelligence budget has gone for expensive satellites and other technical collection systems, where the role of Congress and the link to arms control have been central. The fall of the shah underscored the need for better human intelligence and analysis, and the closing of the Iranian monitoring sites showed just how fragile U.S. technical collection could be. As members of the Intelligence committees came to know what U.S. intelligence can do, they naturally became sympathetic to what more it could do with more money. That was particularly the case in monitoring arms control, for if judgments about verification are subjective, those about monitoring are less so: if existing systems provide 50 percent confidence in monitoring some aspect of Soviet weaponry, the argument that an additional system would increase the confidence to 80 percent can be relatively straightforward.

For example, in its report on the INF treaty, the Senate Intelligence Committee prefaced its positive judgment about verification with this statement on behalf of new technical collection systems needed to verify a future strategic arms treaty: "The Committee feels that this potential gap between intelligence capabilities and intelligence requirements must be appreciated by Members of the Senate."[60] As is typical of the multifaceted relations between committees and agencies, the committee apparently had in mind not only systems the intelligence community eagerly sought, but also ones about which it had doubts.

Other cases of congressional involvement, departures in the realm of intelligence, also look more familiar in the domestic sweep of executive-congressional relations. A good example is counterintelligence. Early in the Reagan administration the breaking wave of spy scandals elicited a number of dramatic proposals from political officials in and around the White House. Most of these ideas were judged excessive or unwise by career counterintelligence professionals; the Senate Intelligence Committee came to share that judgment, and careerists and Congress cooperated in beating back the proposals.

Later in the administration, concern remained high, fed by evidence that the new U.S. embassy in Moscow was riddled with eavesdropping devices. By then, cooler heads had come to the fore in the White House, and the Senate committee now sided with them about counterintelligence even as Congress and the White House were at loggerheads over aid to the contras.[61] The committee became a player in the administration debate, siding with those who proposed to take strong measures (the FBI and part of the CIA) against those who worried that Soviet retaliation could hinder America's ability to run foreign policy (State and the CIA's espionage managers). Liberals on the committee were persuaded to the FBI view both because they came to believe the administration was not doing enough and because they wanted to demonstrate that their attitude toward the intelligence agencies was not purely negative, that they could say "yes" as well as "no."

Joining the government means pluses and minuses for the intelligence community that are familiar from the experience of domestic agencies. For instance, for most of its history the CIA was better at understanding foreign governments than its own. One congressional staffer described Clair George, the CIA director of congressional affairs during the contra affair and a career clandestine service officer, as a man convinced that "Washington was a foreign country and he was the station chief in hostile terrain, mounting operations against the

Congress."[62] Joining the American government provides both sympathetic guides to and experience in reconnoitering that terrain.

The negative side is also familiar: the more "your" congressional committees know, the more able they are to help you, but also the more they are tempted to tell you how to do your business. The Intelligence committees have been voracious requirers of reports even if, like other committees, they receive more than they can digest. Like other committees, they have also been tempted to "micromanage"; the line between oversight and management can blur, especially perhaps if the subject to be managed is exciting.

To be sure, micromanagement is relative, and the intelligence budget is not subject to anything like the intrusions of, say, the Armed Services committees into the defense budget. The CIA, for instance, has all training lumped under a single budget line item. Still, the CIA is coming to look like other agencies of government, for good and ill. Simple aging has made it more bureaucratic in any case, but congressional oversight has abetted that tendency. Projects conceived one year do not get approved until the next. Even minor operations require major paperwork. And despite renewed fondness for covert action on the part of American administrations, CIA officers retain an anxious eye on their political masters outside the executive; no one wants to be a subject of the next congressional investigation. The CIA is becoming more cautious; its officers want authorization in writing. On balance, the caution is a benefit, but it has come at some cost to the entrepreneurial spirit of the CIA.

OPEN QUESTIONS

The process of intelligence becoming a more ordinary part of the government is an uncompleted experiment. It is not, however, reversible. It was inevitable that the intelligence community would come to resemble the rest of the government as the conditions that spawned it as an exception changed: the waning of the deepest fears of the cold war, the loss after the Bay of Pigs of the CIA's image of mastery, the tarnishing of the presidency by Watergate, and the rise of investigative journalism. Perhaps the most important changes are internal to Congress, for intelligence oversight had been the quintessential working of the congressional club. When age removed those few committee chairmen from Congress, and reform meant that they would not

be replaced, intelligence's relation to Congress was bound to change.

In 1954 when news of the covert operation to overthrow Guatemala's President Jacobo Arbenz leaked out, it was the leak that was discredited, not the operation. In *Time's* overheated prose, the revelations were "masterminded in Moscow and designed to divert the attention…from Guatemala as the Western Hemisphere's Red problem child."[63] Not so three decades later, not even if the initial leak was in Beirut in Arabic.

The government that intelligence has joined is a divided one, its divisions institutionalized. The executive-legislative division is the most obvious but not always the most important. In areas like agriculture or commerce, for instance, it is taken for granted that, whether particular observers like it or not, executive agencies and congressional committees serve essentially the same domestic constituencies. Those agencies and committees then contend within their respective arenas against representatives of other constituencies.

Intelligence analysis, by contrast, represents no conventional domestic interest groups. It is a source of advice about foreign countries. Offering advice within a single branch is political enough. Whether the intelligence community can sustain its credibility in offering advice across two branches, often in sharp contention remains to be seen. Congress may come to feel it wants its own intelligence analysts, as it came into another area of advice, the budget, to feel it required its own budgeteers, the Congressional Budget Office. A Congressional Intelligence Office does not seem imminent, however. It would ensue, if it did only from a bitter conflict between the executive and Congress. Nor is there a stream of congressional action whose shape and deadlines would argue for an in-house intelligence service comparable to the one that exists for the budget.

Yet it is instructive, and perhaps a little fearsome, to contemplate, now that Congress and intelligence analysts are acquainted, just how perfect they are for each other. The lives of foreign policy officials in the executive are dominated by their in-boxes; for them, analysis is a nuisance unless they can be sure it will support their predilections. Moreover, when assistant secretaries average not much more than a year in tenure, neither they nor intelligence analysts have much incentive, or much opportunity, to take the measure of each other.

By contrast, members of Congress, and still more their staffs are not so driven by their in-boxes.

Their quest to signify means a hunt for information and for issues, just what intelligence analysts have to offer. And career paths in Congress and intelligence fit together neatly, most members are, in effect, elected for life if they choose and the tenures of their senior staffers are much longer than those of assistant secretaries.

Arrangements linking Congress to intelligence analysis are portentous but will change only gradually, for the most part out of the spotlight and out of the headlines. The focal point of conflict between the two branches will remain covert operations. There, in the nature of both constitutional and political reality, the conflict cannot be resolved, for it runs to the heart of foreign policy: balancing the responsibility of Congress with the primacy of the president.

The 1988 debate over when Congress would be notified of covert actions is illustrative of that fact. On its face the debate seemed almost trivial: both sides agreed that normally the president should inform the committees of a covert action in advance if possible, within a day or so of its start; and so the debate was over whether the forty-eight-hour requirement would be binding or not. Both sides cited examples to suit their preferences: proponents of a mandatory requirement cited arms sales to Iran, opponents, an offer by Canada during the Carter administration to help in smuggling U.S. hostages out of Iran but only if the U.S. Congress were not notified.[64]

Like most debates about intelligence, the argument was about not only the powers of the president but also about where to strike the balance between expediency and accountability. Over the past two decades the balance has moved toward accountability, and in one sense the Iran-contra affair can be seen as confirmation that the evolution has worked tolerably well. Yet there can be no full resolution to the dilemma, for secret operations inescapably raise the trade-off between democratic, thus open, process and effective, hence secret, foreign policy.

Observers fearful that increased congressional involvement poses a risk to secrecy have proposed combining the separate House and Senate committees into one joint intelligence committee. The idea of a joint committee, however, is misdirected. While a single committee might give the president less justification for excluding Congress as "too leaky," Congress has not been leaky, certainly not by comparison with the executive.

The disadvantage of having two committees is the risk of miscommunication: witness the mining of the Nicaraguan harbors. Yet given the institutional jealousies of the two houses, the advantages of two committees—their different personalities, different priorities, and a greater claim to credibility in their respective houses—outweigh that risk. Moreover, the greatest risk to oversight is that the overseers will become co-opted. So it was by all accounts with an earlier joint committee, the Joint Atomic Energy Committee. Having two points of oversight, and even a certain amount of competition between them, reduces the chance that the overseers will become only the patrons of those they oversee.

Congress neither desires nor is able to approve every covert action in advance. Apart from constitutional questions, the process is simply too slow: Congress's instruments are blunt. One way to increase congressional control over controversial operations would be to require the Intelligence committees to approve any withdrawal from the CIA Contingency Reserve. That would be uncomfortable for the committees in that it would put them more directly on the line in the eyes of their congressional colleagues, but it would at least spare them the discomfort of having to choose between silent opposition to an operation and public exposure of it.

When administrations feel secrecy is at a premium, they can resort to informing only the "gang of eight," a procedure that had been used only once by mid-1988.[65] Had relations between Casey and the committees been better, the Reagan administration might have done so in the instance of Iranian arms sales. That would not necessarily have resulted in wiser policy, for it is conceivable that the gang of eight would have been seduced down the path from geostrategic interests to releasing hostages just as the president was. But the subsequent debate would then have been about the wisdom of the policy, not about whether Congress was deceived.

In the future, major covert actions will be overt, as was aid to the contras or to the resistance in Afghanistan. The controversy over them will spill into public, even if they are not propelled there by the executive. If some options are thereby foreclosed, at least the choices will be openly debated. Administrations will have to make evident how those covert programs support coherent public policies. And because major covert actions will not remain secret, presidents will be well advised, before the fact, to ask themselves whether the covert action could bear the test of disclosure: would it still seem sensible once it were public?

The views of congressional overseers will give the president a good indication of what the public would think if it knew of the operation. If the administration is out of step with what the public will accept, as in the case of arms sales to Iran, it may learn that in advance, rather than being punished by Congress after the fact. If the public is divided or confused, as with aid to the contras, the administration probably can have its way. This process is about the best we can do. It is, as Iran-contra testifies, no guarantee against stupid presidential decisions or the resulting public scandals.

QUESTIONS FOR FURTHER DISCUSSION

1. What does Treverton mean when he writes: "Welcome to the American Government"?
2. What have been the main sources of tension between Congress and the executive branch over intelligence activities?
3. How optimistic is Treverton—and are you—about the chances of successful Congressional accountability for intelligence operations?
4. Have lawmakers become too meddlesome when it comes to sensitive intelligence activities, or have they provided a valuable safeguard against the abuse of secret power?

ENDNOTES

1. Quoted in Susan F. Rasky, "Walking a Tightrope on Intelligence Issues," *New York Times,* October II, 1988, p. A26.
2. Quoted in "Taking Toshiba Public," Case C15–88–858.0, Harvard University, Kennedy School of Government, 1988, p. 5.
3. At a press conference at the Capitol, July 19, 1975, quoted in Gregory F. Treverton, *Covert Action: The Limits of Intervention in the Postwar World* (Basic Books, 1987), p. 5.
4. The committees did find some rogue elephants in domestic intelligence activities, especially those of the Federal Bureau of Investigation.
5. *Alleged Assassination Plots Involving Foreign Leaders,* An Interim Report of the Senate Select Committee to Study Governmental Operations with Respect to Intelligence Activities, S. Rept. 94–465, 94 Cong. 1 sess. (Government Printing Office, 1975), p. 149. (Hereafter cited as *Assassination Report.*)
6. See *Assassination Report,* p. 108ff.
7. Richard B. Russell Library Oral History No. 86, taped by Hughes Gates, February 22, 1977, University of Georgia, Athens, Georgia, cited in Loch K. Johnson, *America's Secret Power: The CIA in a Democratic Society* (Oxford University Press, 1989), p. 108.
8. Quoted in "History of the Central Intelligence Agency," in *Supplementary Detailed Staff Reports on Foreign and Military Intelligence,* bk. 4, *Final Report,* S. Rept. 94–755, Senate Select Committee to Study Governmental Operations with Respect to Intelligence Activities, 94 Cong. 2 sess. (GPO, 1976), p. 54.
9. *Covert Action in Chile, 1963–1973,* Committee Print, Senate Select Committee to Study Governmental Operations with Respect to Intelligence Activities, 94 Cong. 1 sess. (GPO, 1975), pp. 41–42.
10. David Gries, "The CIA and Congress: Uneasy Partners," *Studies in Intelligence* (September 1987), p. 77. This is an unclassified article in a CIA journal. In the original, "Vinson" is rendered "Vincent," a typographical error that is, perhaps, inadvertent testimony to just how foreign the Congress was to the CIA.
11. William Colby and Peter Forbath, *Honorable Men: My Life in the CIA* (Simon and Schuster, 1978), pp. 402–03.
12. Officially, Foreign Assistance Act of 1974, sec. 32 (88 Stat. 1804).
13. For an intriguing account of the Senate Select Committee, see Loch K. Johnson, *A Season of Inquiry: The Senate Intelligence Investigation* (University Press of Kentucky, 1985).
14. For instance, Colby regards the outcome as "not unreasonable." See Colby and Forbath, *Honorable Men,* p. 429.
15. The Church committee was more often the victim of leaks than the perpetrator. See Johnson, *Season of Inquiry,* pp. 206–07.
16. It was published by the *Village Voice* as "The CIA Report the President Doesn't Want You to Read," February 16 and 23, 1976.
17. Loch Johnson, "The U.S. Congress and the CIA: Monitoring the Dark Side of Government," *Legislative Studies Quarterly,* vol. 5 (November 1980), pp. 491–92.
18. The order was printed in *New York Times,* December 5, 1981, pp. 18–19.
19. Interview, January 16, 1986.
20. This account is drawn primarily from the subsequent congressional investigation, *Report of the Congressional Committees Investigating the Iran-Contra Affair with Supplemental, Minority, and Additional Views,* H. Rept. 100–400, S. Rept. 100–216, 100 Cong. 1 sess. (GPO, 1987) (hereafter cited as *Iran-Contra Affair*); and from the earlier *Report of the President's Special Review Board*

(known as the Tower commission after its chairman, former Senator John Tower) (GPO, 1987). (Hereafter cited as *Tower Commission*.) The NSC documents are quoted in *Washington Post*, March 10, 1982.

21. *Report of the Select Committee on Intelligence, U.S. Senate, Jan 1, 1983 to Dec. 31, 1984*, S. Rept. 98–665, 98 Cong. 2 sess. (GPO, 1984), pp. 4–5. (Hereafter *Intelligence Report*.)

22. The phrase is Oliver North's, quoted in *Iran-Contra Affair*, p 3.

23. 23 The House-Senate conference report spoke of Nicaragua "providing military support (including arms, training, and logistical, command and control, and communications facilities) to groups seeking to overthrow the Government of El Salvador." See *Intelligence Report*, pp. 6–7.

24. See Stephen Kinzer, "Nicaraguan Says No Mines Are Left in Nation's Ports," *New York Times*, April 13, 1084, p. A1; Philip Taubman, "How Congress Was Informed of Mining of Nicaragua Ports," *New York Times*, April 16, 1984, p. A1; and Bernard Gwenzman, "C.I.A. Now Asserts It Put Off Session with Senate Unit," *New York Times*, April 17, 1984, p. A1. See also the account in *Intelligence Report*, p. 4ff.

25. Interviews with Intelligence Committee staff members, January 1987.

26. The letter was dated April 9; see Joanne Omang and Don Oberdorfer, "Senate Votes, 84–12, to Condemn Mining of Nicaraguan Ports," *Washington Post*, April 11, 1984, p. A16.

27. *Iran-Contra Affair*, p. 41.

28. The quote and the estimate are both from *Iran-Contra Affair*, pp. 37 and 4, respectively.

29. *Iran-Contra Affair*, p. 7.

30. The finding is printed in *Tower Commission*, pp. B60, B66 (emphasis in the original).

31. *Tower Commission*, p. III-22.

32. Interview, January 9, 1986.

33. As quoted in "Overseeing of C.I.A. by Congress Has Produced Decade of Support," *New York Times*, July 7, 1986, p. A10.

34. Quoted in Susan F. Rasky, "Walking a Tightrope," *New York Times*, October 11, 1988, p. A26.

35. Quoted in Johnson, *America's Secret Power*, p. 125.

36. Quoted in Martin Tolchin, "Of C.I.A. Games and Disputed Rules," *New York Times*, May 14, 1984, p. A12.

37. *Iran-Contra Affair*, p. 123.

38. Interview with CIA officials, August 1986 and January 1987.

39. One reported instance was an operation in Suriname in early 1983. See Philip Taubman, "Are U.S. Covert Activities Best Policy on Nicaragua?" *New York Times*, June 15, 1983, p. A1.

40. Interview, January 9, 1987.

41. Testimony before the Iran-Congress investigation, quoted in *Iran-Contra Affair*, p. 271.

42. *Iran-Contra Affair*, p. 19.

43. *Iran-Contra Affair*, p. 333.

44. Robert M. Gates, "The CIA and American Foreign Policy," *Foreign Affairs*, vol. 66 (Winter 1987–88), p. 224; and Gries, "The CIA and Congress," p. 78.

45. *Coven Action in Chile*, p. 49.

46. "Taking Toshiba Public," p. 5.

47. The information in this paragraph derives from interviews with congressional staffers conducted principally in September 1988.

48. "Taking Toshiba Public," p. 1.

49. This and subsequent quotes from DuBois are from "Taking Toshiba Public."

50. The source for this account is W. E. Kline, "The Fall of Marcos," Case C16–88-868.0, Harvard University, Kennedy School of Government, 1988.

51. See *Iran: Evaluation of U.S. Intelligence Performance Prior to November 1978*, Committee Print, Subcommittee on Evaluation of the House Permanent Select Committee on Intelligence, 96 Cong. 1 sess. (GPO, 1979).

52. This and the following quote are from "The Fall of Marcos," pp. 18–19.

53. "The Fall of Marcos," p. 20.

54. See *U.S. Intelligence Performance on Central America: Achievements and Selected Instances of Concern*, Committee Print, Subcommittee on Oversight and Evaluation of the House Permanent Select Committee on Intelligence, 97 Cong. 2 sess. (GPO, 1982).

55. See Stephen J. Flanagan, "The Domestic Politics of SALT II: Implications for the Foreign Policy Process," in John Spinier and Joseph Nogee, eds., *Congress, the Presidency and American Foreign Policy* (Pergamon Press, 1981), pp. 63–64.

56. *Principal Findings on the Capabilities of the U.S. to Monitor the SALT II Treaty*, Committee Print, Senate Select Committee on Intelligence, 96 Cong. 1 sess. (GPO, 1979).

57. *The INF Treaty Monitoring and Verification Capabilities*, S. Rept. 100–318, Senate Select Committee on Intelligence, 100 Cong. 2 sess. (GPO, 1988).

58. *INF Treaty*, S. Rept. 100–318, p. 5.

59. Numbers of members and the CIA budget are from Gries, "The CIA and Congress," p. 78. The total

intelligence community budget is an estimate, compiled from interviews and published sources.

60. *INF Treaty*, S. Rept. 100–318, p. 3.

61. See, for instance, *Meeting the Espionage Challenge: A Review of United States Counterintelligence and Security Program*, S. Rept. 99–522, Senate Select Committee on Intelligence, 99 Cong. 2 sess. (GPO, 1986).

62. Interview, January 18, 1987.

63. *Time*, February 8, 1954, p. 36.

64. *Intelligence Oversight Act. of 1988*, H. Rept. 100–705, 100 Cong. 2 sess. (GPO, 1988), pt. 1, pp. 56–57. See also Dick Cheney, "Covert Operations: Who's in Charge," *Wall Street Journal*, May 3, 1988. However, a subsequent investigation by the Senate Intelligence Committee left doubt that the Canadian example actually happened.

65. *Intelligence Oversight Act of 1988*, H. Rept. 100–705, p. 11.

From Treverton, Gregory F., "Intelligence: Welcome to the American Government," in Thomas E. Mann, ed., *A Question of Balance: The President, the Congress, and Foreign Policy.* pp. 70–108. © 1990, The Brookings Institution. Reprinted with permission.

29. UNLEASHING THE ROGUE ELEPHANT: SEPTEMBER 11 AND LETTING THE CIA BE THE CIA

FREDERICK P. HITZ

The year 1975 was a watershed in the history of U.S. intelligence. That year the secret agencies were subjected to three serious inquiries into their activities, in response to newspaper allegations that they had engaged in illegal activities—most notably, spying at home. Called a "rogue elephant" by one of the leading investigators, the CIA found itself facing new restrictions and reporting requirements, as lawmakers attempted to leash the Agency. Over the next 25 years, intelligence reformers and anti-reformers debated the proper level of supervision, in hopes of maintaining accountability without stifling the effectiveness of intelligence officers. Hitz argues that the leash on the CIA is too tight and suggests ways to improve intelligence effectiveness without eroding civil liberties.

Media outlets have argued that the United States has had an "intelligence failure," decrying the intelligence community for failing to warn the American people of the September 11 attacks on the World Trade Center in New York and on the Pentagon in Virginia. In addition, there is constant clamor that the Central Intelligence Agency (CIA) has been unwisely stifled since the Church Committee hearings of 1975–76[1] and the resultant executive orders of Presidents Ford, Carter, and Reagan that sought to govern the conduct of intelligence activities.[2] There is a cry to unleash the CIA from its perceived legal and policy restrictions and permit it to fight the terrorist threat facing the United States on terms that will succeed against this pernicious force. Some of this impetus comes from a rash of recent studies such as the report of the bipartisan National Commission on Terrorism (NCT), which urged the Director of Central Intelligence (DCI) to modify the current guidelines restricting the recruitment of agents with spotty human rights records, when applied to terrorist informants, with the assertion that "one cannot prowl the back streets of states where terrorist incidents occur and recruit only nice people."[3]

Have the CIA and other intelligence community entities been unwisely constrained in their abilities to pursue the terrorist target by outmoded policies dating from the Cold War? This article will examine four potential modifications to such policies. One possible change is to loosen restraints on the CIA in the recruitment of so-called "dirty assets." A second is to grant domestic law enforcement powers to the CIA to better pursue the terrorist target. Third, the government could repeal the prohibition in Executive Order 12,333 of assassination in peacetime. Finally, impediments could be removed that currently prevent the use of agents in special categories such as journalists, clerics, and academics, if the need is great and cooperation is voluntary. Each possibility will be addressed in turn.

The theme underlying this analysis will be one of balancing. Our need to gather better intelligence about threats posed to the United States and the international community by transnational terrorist groups must be weighed against the constraints imposed by current United States law and practice, the U.S. Constitution, and our status as a constitutional democracy.

I. RECRUITMENT OF "DIRTY ASSETS"

To some degree, the argument over the use of unsavory assets is misleading. By definition, spies are liars, law-breakers, and traitors. They may not be violating U.S. law in supplying CIA spymasters with intelligence information about their own country's defenses or political decision-making, but they are surely violating the laws of the country that they are betraying. John Le Carre wrote with much accuracy when he crafted Alee Leamas' reply to his girlfriend's complaint about using a villain as an agent of East German intelligence:

> What do you think spies are: priests, saints and martyrs? They're a squalid procession of vain fools, traitors too, yes; pansies, sadists and drunkards, people who play cowboys and Indians to brighten their rotten lives. Do you think they sit like monks in London, balancing the rights and wrongs?[4]

Guidelines were established in 1995 that directed CIA case officers in the field to balance human rights and other criminal violations committed by their agents against the positive intelligence supplied or likely to be supplied by these agents. The unintended intersection of several different global and domestic developments after the 1991 collapse of the Soviet Union has prompted confusion over these guidelines and their implementation.

At the end of the Cold War, the then-Deputy Director of Operations (DDO) at the CIA, Richard Stolz, observed that the Directorate probably had more reporting agents on its payroll than it needed to deal with the new post-Soviet world. Always sensitive to the accusation from the ranks that the quantity of spy recruitments counted more than the quality, Mr. Stolz sought to reverse this perception by instituting an asset validation system. Under this asset validation system, pursuant to agreed principles relating to the value and number of intelligence reports produced by a given spy, the Directorate of Operations (DO) could trim its roster of non-reporting or marginally-reporting agents. Mr. Stolz retired before he could evaluate the results of his validation system, so the Inspector General (IG) of the CIA made it the subject of one of his periodic inspections of the Directorate of Operations in 1994. The Office of Inspector General (OIG) concluded in its 1994 inspection report that the Directorate had made a substantial start at validating its agent base

and eliminating marginal producers in some offices, but there had not been complete buy-in by other offices. Thus, it was recommended that the DCI lend his support to the effort.[5]

At about the same time, the *New York Times* reported that an agent on the CIA's payroll in Guatemala had been involved in the murder of an American citizen inn-keeper and the husband of an American citizen.[6] Even though subsequent investigations by the CIA, OIG and the President's Intelligence Oversight Board both concluded that neither CIA employees nor Guatemalan Colonel Julio Alpirez had been involved in the murders of the two Americans, the reports found that CIA headquarters and the U.S. Congress had been inadequately informed about human rights violations by agents in Guatemala. The CIA had on its payroll several agents whose human rights records were notoriously poor, and they were not producing much positive intelligence information on drug trafficking or other post-Cold War targets to justify their salary or retention.[7] Out of these reports, and the disciplinary measures taken by DCI John Deutch pursuant to them, came the infamous 1995 guidelines concerning the recruitment of foreign intelligence assets with egregious human rights records. The CIA Office of General Counsel drafted a regulation requiring headquarters' involvement in the recruitment or retention of spies with unsatisfactory human rights records or a record of substantial criminal violations.[8] Although originally intended as a "sanity check" for field agents to enable them to advocate the retention of a spy with dirty hands who nonetheless had ample potential to aid U.S. intelligence collection, the regulation became an invitation to do nothing in an allegedly risk-averse CIA culture. Because spy runners had more on their plates overseas than they could possibly accomplish, it has apparently become easier not to seek a waiver (which in some instances had to go to the DCI for approval) and let the relationship with the malefactor expire.

In any event, that is history. Congress urged the CIA to alter the "dirty hands" guidelines to encourage risk-taking in the recruitment of assets knowledgeable about terrorism after September 11.[9] The DCI has responded by eliminating the requirement of a DCI waiver in the recruitment or retention of dirty assets, leaving that to a dialogue between the field agent and the DDO. Importantly, however, the Agency has retained the requirement of an audit trail in these cases in recognition of a need for some explanation to headquarters why a dirty asset ought to be on the payroll. Left untouched is § 1.7(a) of E.O. 12,333 requiring senior officials of the intelligence community to

> [r]eport to the Attorney General possible violations of federal criminal laws by employees and of specified criminal laws by any other person as provided in procedures agreed upon by the Attorney General and the head of the department or agency concerned, in a manner consistent with the protection of intelligence sources and methods, as specified in those procedures.[10]

Presumably this would still cover knowledge by an American spy runner of an agent's involvement in the death of an American citizen or a U.S. person (an alien legally residing in the United States).

II. GRANTING DOMESTIC LAW ENFORCEMENT POWERS TO THE CIA

When the CIA was created in 1947 out of the elements of the wartime Office of Strategic Services (OSS), it was statutorily prohibited from having "police, subpoena, law-enforcement powers, or internal security functions."[11] This was due to President Truman's aversion to creating an American gestapo and some fancy footwork by Federal Bureau of Investigation head J. Edgar Hoover, who was determined to keep the fledgling CIA on a short leash if he could not accrue overseas intelligence powers for his own organization.[12]

For the first two decades of the CIA's existence, the prohibition on the exercise of domestic law enforcement powers was not controversial. The CIA's mission was clearly overseas, countering the spread of Stalinist Communism first in Europe, then in the Far East, and soon all over the globe. It concentrated on clandestine reporting and analysis of political and economic events overseas for the President and his senior policymakers. Congress had little oversight or interest in means used to achieve what was universally considered laudable ends. Lawmakers encouraged the CIA in covert action projects designed to roll back the sweep of Communism, and otherwise remained largely supportive, from a distance, of the Agency's overseas mission.

The Vietnam War and the presidential terms of Lyndon Johnson and Richard Nixon saw a breakdown in the consensus of support for the CIA in Congress and the American public. Part of this breakdown was caused by revelations in *Ramparts* magazine, Seymour Hersh's articles for the *New York Times*, and Congressional hearings conducted by Senator Frank Church (D-Idaho) and Congressman Otis Pike (D-N.Y.) beginning in 1974. These three sources of information indicated the CIA had become substantially involved in domestic activity during its short history.[13] Revealed for the first time to the American public was the CIA's involvement with the National Student Association, the establishment of proprietary domestic foundations to support anti-Communist activity abroad, and an operation aptly named CHAOS designed to infiltrate American student organizations opposed to the Vietnam War to determine if there were foreign links. It was out of this pungent stew that the current system of congressional oversight for the intelligence agencies was ladled. Congressional initiatives reinforced the presidential executive orders mentioned earlier. The new congressional oversight committees, the House Permanent Select Committee on Intelligence (HPSCI) and the Senate Select Committee on Intelligence (SSCI), made it clear in the Intelligence Authorization Act for Fiscal Year 1981 that they wanted to be kept "fully and currently informed of all intelligence activities" by the intelligence agencies.[14] Congress's purposes also included conformity by the CIA with the statutory ban on domestic law enforcement activities.

The principal force pulling the CIA into the domestic arena prior to the end of the Cold War was its shared jurisdiction with the FBI in counterintelligence matters involving U.S. citizens and U.S. persons. The FBI clearly has primacy in counterintelligence investigations conducted within the borders of the United States, but the responsibility is shared for suspected CIA spies like Aldrich Ames. Furthermore, many domestic cases have overseas connections that are often the province of the CIA to investigate. Advances in technological surveillance in recent years have complicated matters further, blurring the lines between that which is clearly domestic and foreign, when information from both domains can easily be intercepted by both organizations.

The U.S. Constitution's Fourth Amendment prohibition against "unreasonable searches and seizures"[15] extends to counterintelligence cases involving U.S. citizens and U.S. persons. When, however, the U.S. government proposes to conduct surveillance of an individual suspected of being the "agent of a foreign power," it can do so without presenting itself to an Article III court or magistrate, under the terms of the Foreign Intelligence Surveillance Act (FISA) of 1978.[16] Instead, the government can go to the special FISA court and obtain a warrant as long as "the primary purpose" for the surveillance is "to obtain foreign intelligence information."[17] If the government believes that there is enough evidence to support a possible criminal prosecution, as it did in the Ames investigation, then the government must go to an Article III court or magistrate to obtain criminal warrants before proceeding with the surveillance.[18] (The government never obtained Article III judicial warrants in the Ames case. Although Mr. Ames's attorney intended to challenge this in court, the case never went to trial.)

Since the end of the Cold War, however, the CIA's mission has changed radically. The principal targets of intelligence concern are no longer just political and economic developments abroad that impinge on American national interests, but terrorism, the proliferation of weapons of mass destruction, and drug-trafficking, all of which have domestic law enforcement ramifications. Well before September 11, the CIA sat alongside colleagues from domestic law enforcement agencies (such as the FBI, the Drug Enforcement Administration (DEA), Customs, and the Bureau of Alcohol, Tobacco and Firearms (ATF) of the Treasury Department) in DCI Centers dealing with counterterrorism, counternarcotics, and counterintelligence issues. Today, the movement of people, money, and illegal goods can proceed seamlessly from country to country, including the United States—a negative byproduct of globalization. Any distinction between the requirements of domestic law enforcement and foreign intelligence gathering are becoming hopelessly blurred in these new world disorders of terrorism and proliferation.

Arguably, the United States has just taken a major step in resolving the ancient question of "should spies be cops?" in the affirmative with passage of the USA PATRIOT Act.[19] Along with the creation of an Office of Homeland Security, this Act represents a decision on the part of the President and the Congress that the nation expects its defenders to be proactive in the struggle against terrorism of all kinds. Instead of merely responding to threats and criminal acts after they happen, the USA PATRIOT Act seeks to create the basis for prevention. Unquestionably,

the gathering and analysis of foreign intelligence is intended to play a prominent role in this mix, and a greater involvement of the intelligence community and CIA in domestic law enforcement proceedings is inevitable.

Let us quickly examine several of the legal changes in the USA PATRIOT Act and their consequences for the intelligence community. Section 203 of the Act amends Rule 6(e)(3)(c) of the Federal Rules of Criminal Procedure to permit disclosure of grand jury information when the matters involve "foreign intelligence and counterintelligence."[20] Such disclosures can be made

> to any Federal law enforcement, intelligence, protective, immigration, national defense, or national security official in order to assist the official receiving that information in the performance of his official duties.[21]

Although these disclosures may be used by the recipient "only as necessary in the conduct of that person's official duties,"[22] this represents a major departure from the traditional legal principle of grand jury secrecy. Although this provision is bound to be tested in the courts, grand jury secrecy has never been absolute; if the executive branch establishes some safeguards in the use of grand jury material, section 203 may pass constitutional muster given the enormity of the threat posed to American citizens by international terrorist attacks.

Less clear is what happens to the line separating the CIA from domestic law enforcement when it is sitting at the elbow of the FBI and the Immigration and Naturalization Service, trying to help make a criminal case against a U.S. person based upon a seamless chain of evidence provided by foreign sources and domestic informants.

Section 504 of the Act amends the FISA to permit consultation between intelligence officials conducting FISA-approved surveillance efforts and law enforcement officials.[23] The matters to be consulted upon must pertain to terrorist threats, but there is opportunity for definitional creep as the pressure for preventive action in this area of concern intensifies.

Finally, section 218 of the Act further amends the FISA to change the standard with which the FISA court will grant authority to conduct foreign intelligence surveillance.[24] Instead of the "primary purpose" test, section 218 amends the certification by the government to require only that foreign intelligence be "a significant purpose" for the FISA surveillance or physical search.[25] This change allows the scope of permitted national security surveillance to creep close to the boundaries of Fourth Amendment limitations. The fact that the domestic legal authority prohibition continues to haunt these determinations also means that the executive branch will have to exercise great care to specify guidelines for the application of these significant statutory changes.

My view is that the CIA should squarely address the inconsistencies that its new foreign intelligence mission is creating and seek legislative clarification and amendment of the prohibition against domestic law enforcement powers. It is better to seek an alteration of its 1947 charter to account for the new realities of its role in combating terrorism, proliferation of weapons of mass destruction, and drug-trafficking. This route of caution and clarification is preferable to being forced to change as a consequence of judicial action, which will understandably focus more on the rights of Americans than the difficulty of the anti-terrorist mission.

III. REPEALING THE PROHIBITION OF ASSASSINATION

No issue has generated more heat and produced less light than the feckless debate as to whether the provisions in Executive Order 12,333 prohibiting direct and indirect participation in assassination by the U.S. Government and its employees should be rescinded.[26]

Previously, presidents contemplating a military response to an attack on Americans have successfully argued that their powers under the U.S. Constitution as Commander in Chief and executor of the nations laws[27] gave them ample authority to strike back at the attackers, even if the strike was likely to kill the head of state or commander who may have authorized the attack. President Ronald Reagan's bombing of Muammar Qaddafi's compound in Libya in 1986—after the United States recovered signal intercepts implicating Libyan intelligence officers in the bombing of a Berlin discotheque in which several U.S. soldiers were killed—might have been justified as death incident to a military action had Qaddafi died in the strike. Likewise, President Bill Clinton's response to terrorist attacks on the U.S embassies in Dar-es-Salaam and Nairobi in 1998, in which a pharmaceutical factory in Sudan and a terrorist training camp in Afghanistan were destroyed by U.S. cruise missiles (the latter strike having been directed at the supposed perpetrator, Osama bin Laden), could also have been justified as death incident to military action.

There is little doubt in the wake of the September 11 attacks and the Joint Resolution of Congress of September 14 authorizing the use of force[28] that the efforts of the United States to capture or destroy Osama bin Laden and the Al Qaeda network will be governed by the Joint Resolution, the constitutional authorities of the President, and the laws of war, rather than Executive Order 12,333's provisions prohibiting assassination.

What activity then *is* affected by these executive order provisions? The answer would appear to be political assassinations occurring in peacetime. For that reason, it is worth reviewing the final report of the Church Committee in 1975, which first gave rise to the prohibitions of peacetime political assassinations.[29] Church concluded that the "cold-blooded, targeted, intentional killing of an individual foreign leader has no place in the foreign policy of the U.S."[30] The Church Report documented involvement by the U.S. Government in assassination plots against five foreign leaders during the 50s, 60s, and early 70s, four of whom died violently at the hands of others.[31] In fact, no foreign leader was assassinated by U.S. operatives, but it was not for want of trying. Indeed, the failures came about largely as a consequence of a lack of developed competence in this line of work by the CIA. The first conclusion one draws from this record is that the CIA did not relish the task of assassination planning. It was not what intelligence officers signed up to do, and they were not very good at it.[32]

Second, what happens if the plot is successful? Who would succeed Saddam Hussein if we assassinated him? Might any new leader be worse than the assassinated one? Although it was not the result of assassination, when President Arbenz decamped from Guatemala in 1954 as a consequence of U.S. sponsored covert action, the United States became the de facto guarantor of his incompetent successor, Castillo Armas. Guatemala, in effect, became a ward of the United States for the next forty-five years because the United States had chosen to intervene to replace an elected leader. So much for plausible deniability.

Third, if the United States starts down the road of political assassination for its own foreign policy goals, what will stop other nations from targeting our leaders for assassination? What does it say about our respect for the law of nations and our own adherence to the rule of law?[33] I agree with the Church Committee's conclusion that "[i]t may be ourselves that we injure most if we adopt tactics 'more ruthless than the enemy.'"[34] Short of war, the Committee noted, "assassination is incompatible with American principles, international order, and morality."[35]

Fourth, there is little evidence that retaliating against terrorists by assassinating their leaders is an effective deterrent to future terrorist acts. Assassination appears to beget assassination, if we are guided by the example of the Israelis. Assassination has been no more successful in the struggles between the IRA and the Protestant majority in Northern Ireland, or those of the Basque separatists in Northern Spain.

Finally, if the U.S. chooses to embark upon a course of political assassination in peacetime to nip a potential future Hitler in the bud, who makes the judgment that any given leader is another Hitler? Who exercises control, and what audit trail will exist to establish accountability for the decision?

I would like to see the answers to these questions before the executive order banning assassinations is lifted, especially since there appears to be ample authority in the hands of the President to pursue the September 11 attackers under both the Joint Resolution of Congress of September 14 and the U.S. Constitution.

IV. PROHIBITION ON RECRUITMENT OF JOURNALISTS, CLERICS, AND ACADEMICS

As controversial and unproductive as lifting the ban on peacetime assassinations would be, the removal of the barriers against the intelligence community's use of journalists, clerics, and academics would be equally controversial but, unlike assassinations, could be productive.

Use of so-called "angel" assets, including Peace Corps and USAID workers, by the CIA fell into disfavor at the same time that the Church and Pike committees were holding hearings on the CIA's behavior and Seymour Hersh was writing exposes on the CIA's "family jewels" in the *New York Times*. The *Times* editorialized in 1996 that from the Agency's creation in 1947 until the Church and Pike Committee investigations in 1975, about fifty journalists were paid by CIA for their services at various times.[36] In addition, foreign correspondents and CIA station chiefs often swapped information informally, and many other journalists were used as "unwitting sources" of

intelligence information.[37] At the time of the investigations, there were eleven CIA officers working under journalistic cover provided by fifteen news organizations.[38]

As a result of the controversy engendered by the revelations of Agency use of journalistic cover, then DCI George H. W. Bush issued regulations in 1976 limiting the CIA's use of the clergy and the media.[39] The regulations provided that the CIA would not enter into any paid or contractual relationships with full or part-time U.S.-accredited journalists or any similar clandestine relationships with clergymen or missionaries."[40] The regulations did not prohibit, however, the gathering of information "volunteered" by journalists or clergy, or the use of journalistic or clerical cover.[41]

One year later, in recognition of the "special status afforded the press under the Constitution," then-DCI Stansfield Turner promulgated stricter regulations prohibiting "any relationship" with full or part-time U.S.-accredited journalists, as well as non-journalist staff employees of the print media, without the express approval of their senior management.[42] The 1977 regulations also prohibited the use of any U.S. media organization as cover for Agency employees or activities.[43] Like the 1976 regulations, the Turner policy permitted voluntarily supplied information from journalists. Unlike the Bush regulations, however, the new policy established a small loophole allowing the DCI to make exceptions to the stated prohibitions in the event of an emergency.[44]

This two-sentence loophole remained buried for nearly twenty years until the Council on Foreign Relations presented its report on intelligence reform at the end of the Cold War. It included a suggestion that the CIA rethink its policy on non-official cover and reconsider the use of journalistic cover.[45] In response, then-DCI John Deutch made the disclosure, startling to many, that the CIA had in fact used the loophole on several occasions since the regulations were enacted.[46]

The firestorm that ensued in Congress led to the insertion in the Intelligence Authorization Act of FY 1997 of section 309, which declares it to be the "policy" of the United States that the intelligence community may not use a U.S.-accredited correspondent of a U.S. news media organization for intelligence purposes unless the President or the DCI signs a waiver that such use is "necessary to address the overriding national security interest of the United States."[47] Voluntary cooperation by a journalist is still permitted as long as it is in writing.[48] Unstated is any congressional position on journalistic cover.

In the aftermath of September 11, the President and Congress are obliged to raise again the issue of the use of "angel" assets and the cover they might provide. As observers call for greater flexibility and creativity from the intelligence community, especially in the recruitment and deployment of nonofficial cover human sources of intelligence, it seems arbitrary and absurd to rule out any potential method of getting close to Al Qaeda and other anti-American terrorist networks. To be sure, consideration of the privileged position certain professions occupy under the U.S. Constitution should continue to carry weight, but the waiver provision set forth in section 309 provides a sensible solution to a tough problem. Under section 309, the waiver and finding procedure is sufficiently cumbersome and weighty that it is unlikely to be invoked on a casual basis, and the requirement that a proposed waiver must go to the HPSCI and the SSCI insures a measure of accountability. Furthermore, it contemplates that the individuals involved in the intelligence gathering activity will only do so on a voluntary basis. I would broaden the section 309 test to all of the "angel" asset categories: clerics, academics, and Peace Corps and USAID workers.

From this, it is clear that some changes in the laws and rules governing intelligence activities are necessary for the intelligence community to be successful in its struggle to prevent international terrorist acts, especially those directed at Americans. By the same token, it is equally important that these changes not throw the CIA back into the pre-1974 era of limited congressional oversight and little executive branch accountability that led to earlier excesses. The terrorist threat need not become an excuse for abusing the rights of Americans. If the failure to warn of the September 11 attacks indeed constitutes a massive "intelligence failure"[49] these changes alone will not save the day for the CIA and the intelligence community. A greater understanding of the cultures and circumstances in the Near East and South Asia that produced Osama bin Laden and Al Qaeda will be of far greater importance in sharpening human source intelligence operations against terrorism and fundamentalist Islam than changing the rules under which the intelligence community operates. To accomplish this mission successfully, U.S. intelligence will have to do it the old fashioned way. It will have to learn the languages, spend time on the ground, get its hands dirty, and listen to chatter in the bazaar.[50]

QUESTIONS FOR FURTHER DISCUSSION

1. What does Hitz mean when he uses the phrase "rogue elephant"? Is the CIA a rogue elephant? Has it been? Could it be?
2. Evaluate Hitz's argument about repealing the executive order that currently prohibits assassination plots by the CIA against foreign heads of state.
3. Should journalists, clerics, and scholars be used by the CIA for intelligence purposes? If so, under what conditions and guidelines?
4. How would you contrast Senator Church's views with those of Mr. Hitz?

ENDNOTES

1. The hearings were conducted by Senator Frank Church (D-Idaho) after revelations by the CIA and in the media of CIA violations of rights of American citizens, etc. *See* SELECT COMM. TO STUDY GOVERNMENTAL OPERATIONS WITH RESPECT TO INTELLIGENCE ACTIVITIES, ALLEGED ASSASSINATION PLOTS INVOLVING FOREIGN LEADERS, S. REP. NO. 94–465 (1975).
2. President Ford promulgated Executive Order (E.O.) 11,905, which was followed by E.O. 12,306 under President Reagan. *See* Exec. Order No. 11,905, 41 Fed. Reg. 7703 (Feb. 18,1976); Exec. Order No. 12,306, 46 Fed. Reg. 29,693 (June 1, 1981). These orders were superseded by E.O. 12,333, which was promulgated by President Reagan and is still in effect *See* Exec. Order 12,333, 46 Fed. Reg. 59,941 (Dec. 4, 1981).
3. Vernon Loeb, *Panel Advocates Easing CIA Rules on Informants: Agency Disputes Commission Finding*, WASH. POST, June 6, 2000, at A25.
4. John Le Carre, THE SPY WHO CAME IN FROM THE COLD 246 (1963).
5. The IG report on the asset validation system remains classified.
6. See Tim Weiner, *Guatemalan Agent of C.I. A. Tied to Killing of American*, NY TIMES, March 22, 1995, at Al; *see also* Tim Weiner, *Shadowy Alliance—A Special Report; in Guatemala's Dark Heart, CIA Lent Succor to Death*, NY TIMES, April 2, 1995, at Al.
7. *See* INVESTIGATIONS STAFF, OFFICE OF INSPECTOR GENERAL, CENTRAL INTELLIGENCE AGENCY, REPORT NO. 95–0024-IG, REPORT OF

INVESTIGATION: GUATEMALA 2 (1995); INTELLIGENCE OVERSIGHT BOARD, REPORT ON THE GUATEMALAN REVIEW 4 (1996).

8. See Walter Pincus, *CIA Steps Up "Scrub Down" of Agents: Agency May Weigh Rights Violations Against Value of Information,* WASH. POST, July 28, 1995, at A25.

9. *See* Intelligence Authorization Act for Fiscal Year 2002, Pub. L. No. 107–108, 115 Stat. 1394 (2001).

10. Exec. Order No. 12,333, *supra* note 1, at 59,945.

11. National Security Act of 1947 § 102a, 50 U.S.C. § 403 (1994).

12. *See* Christopher Andrew, FOR THE PRESIDENT'S EYES ONLY 156 (1995).

13. *See id.* at 405.

14. §501(a), Pub. L. No. 66–450, 94 Stat. 1975, 1981 (1980) (codified as amended at 50U.S.C. 413 (1994)).

15. U.S.CONST. amend. IV.

16. 50 U.S.C. § 1805 (1994).

17. 50 U.S.C. §§ 1804(a)(7)(B), 1823(a)(7)(B); United States v. Duggan, 743 F.2d59, 77 (2d Cir. 1984); *see also* United States v. Nicholson. 955 F. Supp. 588, 591 (E.D. Va. 1997) (holding that a FISA physical search was "constitutionally indistinguishable from the FISA-authorized electronic surveillance unanimously upheld by federal courts"); United States v. Bin Laden, 126 F. Supp 2d 264, 285 (S.D.N.Y. 2000).

18. *See* United States v. Truong Dinh Hung, 629 F.2d 908, 915–16 (4th Cir. 1980), *cert. denied,* 454 U.S. 1144 (1982).

19. Uniting and Strengthening America by Providing Appropriate Tools Required to Intercept and Obstruct Terrorism Act (USA PATRIOT Act) of 2001, Pub. L. No. 107–56, 115 Stat. 272 (2001).

20. USA PATRIOT Act § 203(a)(l)(i), 115 Stat. at 279; *see generally* Sara Sun Beale & James E. Felman, *The Consequences of Enlisting Federal Grand Juries in the War on Terrorism: Assessing the USA PATRIOT Act's Changes to Grand Jury Secrecy,* 25 HARV. J.L. & PUB. POLY 699 (2002).

21. *Id.*

22. § 203(a)(l)(ii), 115 Stat. at 279.

23. § 504, 115 Stat. at 364–65.

24. §218, 115 Stat. at 291.

25. *Id.*

26. *See* Exec. Order 12,333, *supra* note 2, at 59, 592.

27. See U.S. CONST, art. II, §§ 2–3.

28. Joint Resolution to Authorize the Use of United States Armed Forces Against Those Responsible for the Recent Attacks Launched Against the United States, Pub. L. No. 107–40, 115 Stat, 224 (2001).

29. See SELECT COMM. TO STUDY GOVERNMENTAL OPERATIONS WITH RESPECT TO INTELLIGENCE ACTIVITIES, *supra* note 1.

30. *Id.* at 6.

31. See *id.* at 4.

32. *See* John Ranelagh, THE AGENCY: THE RISE AND DECLINE OP THE CIA 336 (1986).

33. *See* SELECT COMM. TO STUDY GOVERNMENTAL OPERATIONS WITH RESPECT TO INTELLIGENCE ACTIVITIES, *supra* note 1, at 258, 282.

34. *Id.* at 259.

35. *Id.* at l.

36. See, Editorial, *No Press Cards for Spies,* N.Y. TIMES, Mar. 18, 1996, at A14.

37. *See id.*

38. "Assets" are generally defined as sources that provide information to intelligence agencies as part of a salaried relationship that is based on gifts, reimbursement of expenses, or regular financial payments. There may or may not be an element of control. "Cover" is the use of employment, name, or facilities of any non-official U.S. organization to provide an identity for CIA employees or activities.

39. See *The CIA and the Media: Hearings Before the Subcomm. on Oversight of the House Permanent Select Comm. on Intelligence,* 95m Cong; 331–32 (1978). For a list of the ways in which intelligence agencies cooperate with journalists, see Lt. Col. Geoffrey B. Demarest, *Espionage in International Law,* 24 DENV. J. INTL. L. & POLY 321, 345 (1996).

40. See *The CIA and the Media: Hearings Before the Subcomm. on Oversight of the House Permanent Select Comm. on Intelligence, supra* note 39.

41. *See id.*

42. See *id.* at 333.

43. *See id.*

44. *See id.* at 334.

45. See COUNCIL ON FOREIGN RELATIONS, MAKING INTELLIGENCE SMARTER: THE FUTURE OF U.S. INTELLIGENCE (1996).

46. Former DCI Turner admitted to approving the use of journalists three times but asserted that on at least one occasion the permission was not used. *See* Walter Pincus, *Turner: CIA Nearly Used a Journalist in Teheran.* WASH. POST., Mar. 1, 1996, at A15. Deutch stated that he had not used the loophole at all during his tenure. *See* 142 CONG. REC. 12,153 (1996) (letter from DCI John Deutch).

47. Intelligence Authorization Act for Fiscal Year 1997 § 309, Pub.L. No. l04–293, 110 Stat. 3461, 3467 (codified at 50 U.S.C. 403–7 (Supp. 1997)).

48. *See id.*
49. I continue to believe that it is rather a "failure of intellect" as Harlan Ullman argued skillfully last October. Harlan Ullman, *Intellect Over Intelligence.* FIN. TIMES, Oct. 19, 2001, at 17.

50. The author has written an op-ed piece on this subject. *See* Frederick P. Hitz, Editorial, *Not Just a Lack of Intelligence, a Lack of Skills,* WASH. POST, Oct. 21, 2001, at B3.

30. INTELLIGENCE AND THE RISE OF JUDICIAL ACCOUNTABILITY

FREDERIC F. MANGET

Throughout most of the history of U.S. intelligence, the secret agencies were different from the rest of the government in an important way: they had little to no oversight exercised over them by entities outside their walls. This was especially true when it came to congressional and judicial accountability. In the mid-1970s, Congress changed this through the establishment of permanent oversight committees in both of its chambers. At the same time, President Gerald R. Ford established an Intelligence Oversight Board in the Office of the Presidency. As Frederic Manget points out in this piece, now the judicial branch of government has also gotten into the intelligence act.

1. INTRODUCTION

Intelligence and law enforcement occupy different worlds, but they are parallel worlds that have common dimensions. The differences are legion. Missions, cultures, tools, histories, authorities, restrictions, and resources, not to mention theory and practice, are so often incompatible that wise and experienced managers of the two worlds have often thrown their hands skyward and told their troops, "Just muddle through!"

On closer examination, however, there are enough similarities or at least points of congruity that hope for a grand unified field theory continues to exist. For example, ask any major Western intelligence service or national police force what their significant missions are and each would answer: Stop terrorists. Catch spies. Block narcotics trafficking. Smash weapons smuggling. At the highest levels of government-policy execution, intelligence and law enforcement may be viewed as different aspects of national power (among others) to be applied to problems or threats to national interests. There may be two mules pulling that load, but they should be heading in roughly the same direction and held in tentative harmony by the harness and the mule driver...

Law enforcement seeks to subject those violating criminal laws to justice. Prosecutions establish a description of a past criminal act in a trial proceeding and judges and juries impose judgment. Evidence for and against a defendant is the end use of law enforcement information. An accused person is entitled to protections and rules of process based on the basic compact between the people and the government, such as the Constitution of the United States. Law enforcement must engender enough evidence to prove guilt beyond a reasonable doubt, and the accused are presumed to be innocent. Openness, transparency, and fairness are the essential hallmarks of the Western notion of criminal justice.

Detectives and intelligence officers may both collect and analyze information, but they are different. Detectives try to meet specific and long-established legal standards of probable cause, beyond a reasonable doubt, or preponderance of the evidence. Intelligence does not provide evidence or proof, and it is hardly ever certain. It deals with threat-based national security imperatives and foreign entities that take countermeasures and build denial and deception operations into a wilderness of mirrors. (Lowenthal 4–7)

Intelligence looks at the world as it finds it, in order to provide estimates of what is happening and what will happen to policymakers so that their decisions will be better informed. Intelligence seeks a best guess of what reality may be. Protection of secret sources and methods is a fundamental aspect of intelligence, and the discovery of the prosecution's information required by criminal proceedings is anathema. There is always reasonable doubt. Corroboration is the best hope for a piece of intelligence information, not proof. The violation of other nations' espionage laws is the heart of human intelligence activities. Treason, betrayal, compromise, deception, seduction, double-dealing, and theft are tools of the trade (Baker 36–40).

2. FROM MANY, ONE

The post–World War II experience in the United States, however, has been the convergence of the two worlds. America's experiment with centralized, all-source, independent, and civilian intelligence began in 1947 with the creation of the Central Intelligence Agency. It was a creature of public statutory law, the National Security Act of 1947, enacted by a democratic process and subject to the historical American preference for checks and balances in government. The act specifically prohibited CIA from having law enforcement powers or internal security functions.

That prohibition remains unchanged in the National Security Act today (section 403–4a(d)(1)). It reflects the deep uneasiness surrounding the creation of the CIA based upon fears that a unified intelligence and police force would tend toward abuses associated with Nazi Germany and the Soviet Union's centralized security and espionage apparatuses. It also stemmed from the resistance of the powerful and long-established federal law enforcement agency, the Federal Bureau of Investigation, with its own mission, political support, history, and culture. (Riebling)

There were many aspects of this policy of separation of intelligence and law enforcement. The CIA could not arrest anyone or issue subpoenas. The CIA could not conduct electronic surveillance inside the United States (EO12333 section 2.4(a)). Intelligence community agencies could not collect foreign intelligence by acquiring information concerning the domestic activities of U. S. persons. Representatives of intelligence-community agencies could not joint or otherwise participate in any organizations within the United States without disclosing their intelligence affiliation, except according to procedures approved by the attorney general. (Civiletti 13–15)

On the other hand, the FBI could not conduct espionage overseas. It had to coordinate in advance with the CIA its intelligence-related activities and contacts with foreign liaison and security services. Foreign intelligence information that resulted from grand jury proceedings could not be shared with the intelligence community. Prosecutors could not pass to non-law enforcement officials any foreign intelligence information resulting from criminal wiretap surveillance. The separation was reflected in the organization of the FBI, the CIA, and the Department of Justice and was referred to in shorthand as the "wall" (Hulnick 1997, 269).

Even from this beginning, however, the wall developed a number of one-way and two-way mirrors. Although the CIA had no law enforcement powers, it could support law enforcement activities. This became settled in intelligence law, both in executive orders (EO 12333 section 2.6) and statute (National Security Act section 403–5a). In 1997 a specific and explicit law enforcement authority for the intelligence community was added to the National Security Act. Upon the request of a law enforcement agency, elements of the intelligence community may collect information outside the United States about individuals who are not United States persons, even if the law enforcement agency intends to use the information collected for purposes of a law enforcement investigation.

Other parts of the National Security Act were added that required that other federal agencies disclose to the Director of Central Intelligence foreign intelligence acquired in the course of a criminal investigation (National Security Act section 403–5b(a)(1)). Law enforcement agencies were later authorized by statute to share with the intelligence community any foreign intelligence information that was formerly withheld under the prohibition on disclosing information from a grand-jury proceeding. (Collins 1261) Intelligence agencies were also allowed to obtain access to electronic, wire, or oral interception information that had been generated by a criminal investigation authorized under Title III of the U.S. criminal code (PATRIOT Act).

The FBI's overseas activities also expanded. The Department of Justice opined in 1989 that the FBI has the authority to override customary or other international law in its extraterritorial law enforcement activities. The FBI could investigate and arrest fugitives in another state without the consent of the host government (OLC Opinion 195). Supreme Court cases contributed to this trend. One held that an extradition treaty was not the exclusive means by which the United States could take custody of a suspect in a foreign country in which he had been apprehended by persons acting on behalf of the United States without regard to the treaty's provisions (*U.S. v. Alvarez-Machain* 1992, 655).

Another held that the Fourth Amendment requirement that government searches be "reasonable" does not apply to the search and seizure of property in a foreign country owned by a nonresident alien who has no significant voluntary connection with the United States (*U.S. v. Verdugo-Urquidez* 1990, 259). In addition, the Ames spy case in the mid-1990s led to a reorganization of U.S. counterintelligence lanes in the road between the FBI and the intelligence community. A new statutory provision required intelligence agencies to immediately advise the FBI of any information indicating that classified information may have been disclosed in an unauthorized manner to a foreign power or agent of a foreign power, which is a potential crime under several U.S. laws (IAA FY 95 section 402a). It also required prior coordination and consultation between the agencies for any further actions they might take. In the mid-1990s, the FBI vigorously expanded the mission of the legal attaches attached to U.S. embassies to enhance cooperation with foreign law enforcement agencies, many of whom also had internal security and intelligence functions as well.

Much of this convergence of worlds occurred because of the convergence of targets. Both intelligence agencies and law enforcement agencies were directed to bring their rapidly overlapping methods to bear on the same individuals, organizations, and activities. The crime of espionage always had both a foreign intelligence and a criminal law aspect, leading to overlapping FBI and CIA counterintelligence activities that created a history of both friction and effective joint spy-catching. The Intelligence Identities Protection Act was specifically added to the U.S. criminal code to address a gap in the espionage and related crimes that seem to allow publication of the true identities of U.S. intelligence officers serving under cover. In the 1970s, the U.S. created and expanded a number of other extraterritorial crimes. Violations of U.S. domestic criminal law could now be committed outside the territory of the United States by foreign nationals. These included aircraft hijacking and piracy, weapons proliferation (notably chemical and biological weapons), international narcotics trafficking, and organized crime. The U.S. later added terrorism and related crimes and borderless offences such as the cybercrimes of computer hacking and sabotage.

This resulted in a critical need to reconcile the intelligence imperative for secrecy with law enforcement's requirement for fair trials. As a result, the U.S. amended the procedures by which information is introduced into criminal trial processes. The Classified Information Procedures Act (C1PA) was enacted in 1980 to address the problem of greymail. Greymail is the risk that a defendant will publicly disclose classified information that could damage national security interests of the United States. Prior to the passage of CIPA, when criminal procedure rules required that the defendant have access to classified materials, the government had to make an uninformed guess as to what would ultimately be disclosed in the trial and how much damage would occur. CIPA is meant to mitigate that uncertainty while keeping the essence of those basic criminal processes required by long-held notions of a fair trial in an adversarial judicial system.

CIPA is procedural rather than substantive, and thus does not affect the outcome of whether classified information must be disclosed to the defendant or used in a public proceeding. It does, however, limit the threat of ambush that dogged prosecutors in earlier cases. CIPA requires notice of what classified information the defense intends to use. It allows for the court to hear in camera (in chambers, not in a public courtroom) and ex parte (only one party—the government—is present) presentations in order to review classified information and determine if it must be disclosed in order to ensure a fair trial or otherwise meet criminal due process, discovery, and evidentiary requirements. It also allows the government to propose unclassified substitutions for classified information that would give the defendant the same ability to put on a defense as would the use of the original classified information. The court also has the ability under CIPA to fashion sanctions, including dismissal, in cases where the government refuses to disclose the classified information at issue.

The government can use CIPA procedures to get evidentiary rulings from the court on the classified information in advance of public hearings or trials. Once those evidentiary rulings are made, the government then can assess the risk of proceeding with the prosecution and any resulting damage to intelligence interests that might occur. The defendant still has the substantive rights to demand discovery and proof, but the government can make a more rational and informed decision. Intelligence officers cannot act with one eye looking over their shoulder at a theoretical future prosecution of someone, somewhere, for some crime that might threaten some intelligence source or method, to be determined at some future time. All of the criminal procedure requirements that are second nature to law enforcement agents—Miranda warnings, search warrants, chain of custody integrity—would seriously hamper intelligence collection (Fredman 1998).

CIPA processes have been challenged by numerous defendants on the grounds that they violate fair-trial notions of due process under the Constitution, but the law is settled that CIPA successfully—if slowly and painfully—holds both Constitutional law enforcement rules and intelligence equities in a reasonable and lawful balance.

Issues related to surveillance also led to another area in which law enforcement and intelligence community components had to develop statutory rules of engagement to reconcile different needs. In 1978 the Foreign Intelligence Surveillance Act (FISA) was enacted to establish a court to hear government applications for orders authorizing electronic surveillance (and later, unconsented physical searches) directed at foreign powers and agents of foreign powers, rather than potential criminals or criminal evidence.

Searches by the U.S. government are constrained by the Fourth Amendment of the Constitution, which requires that searches be reasonable and in most cases authorized by a judicial search warrant. (Hall) The issue that arose was whether information gathered as foreign intelligence could be used as evidence by law enforcement authorities to convict a criminal defendant. FISA required robust secrecy and entirely ex parte hearings and application procedures, a rarity in criminal proceedings.

For many years, the legal reasoning in a seminal espionage case controlled the approach of the U.S. government in counterintelligence activities (U.S. vs. Truong 1980). In the 1970s, U.S government counterintelligence uncovered a U.S. Information Agency employee (Humphrey) who was giving classified diplomatic information to a Vietnamese citizen (Truong) who then passed it to North Vietnamese officials who were negotiating with U.S. representatives in Paris. The FBI, using a national security rationale rather than a criminal standard under Title III, bugged Truong's apartment and tapped his phone over the course of a number of months. At some point in the foreign counterintelligence surveillance, prosecutors from the Department of

Justice began to take an active part in directing the surveillance.

When the issue arose of whether the incriminating evidence surfaced by the surveillance could be admitted in evidence in the criminal case against Humphrey and Truong, the court opined that so long as the primary purpose of the surveillance was collection of information relating to activities of a foreign power, the resulting information could be used in the criminal case. But at some point during the surveillance of Truong, the primary purpose changed and became collection of information to support a prosecution. The court noted that the involvement of the law enforcement officers determined the shift in the primary purpose of the collection, and thus information collected under foreign intelligence rules could not be used for criminal trial purposes after the change of primary purpose. The "primary purpose" test was adopted by a number of other federal circuits in cases where issues of surveillance arose, and it was the basis of relationships between law enforcement and intelligence agencies and their rules of engagement, lanes in the road, and tribal encounters for over twenty years.

The wall finally came tumbling down in 2002. The Foreign Intelligence Surveillance Court of Review (the appellate court for decisions made by the Foreign Intelligence Surveillance Court, or FISC, which authorizes FISA searches and surveillance), convened for the first time in history to hear an appeal brought by the U.S. government from a FISC surveillance order imposing a number of restrictions on the government based upon the wall and the primary purpose test. The FISC opinion stated that it could approve FISA surveillance applications only if the government's objective is not primarily directed toward criminal prosecution of the foreign agents for their foreign intelligence activity.

The Court of Review did not agree. It said that at some point in the 1980s ("…the exact moment is shrouded in historical mist") the Department of Justice applied the pre-FISA Truong analysis to FISA without justification (In re Sealed Case 2002). There is now no need to find a primary purpose of either national security intelligence collection or acquisition of information about a crime in order to pass any wall established by FISA. The end of the wall is reflected in every major recent review of U.S. intelligence policy and organization, which all call for increased information sharing, unity of command and control, and removal of barriers to joint and complementary action among elements of the U.S. government.

This convergence of law enforcement and intelligence missions and activities has not reconciled the underlying bases for each sphere of activity, however. For example, foreign intelligence surveillance differs markedly from that in criminal investigations. In the criminal context, the Fourth Amendment reasonableness requirement usually requires a showing of probable cause and a warrant. But that is not universal. The central requirement is one of reasonableness. The probable cause standard is peculiarly related to criminal investigations and is often unsuited to determining reasonableness of other searches (*Board of Education v. Earls* 2002, 828). The Supreme Court has repeatedly opined that in situations involving "special needs" that go beyond a routine interest in law enforcement, a warrant is not required. The Court has found no warrant requirement in circumstances in which the government faces an increased need to be able to react swiftly and flexibly or when there are at stake interests in public safety beyond the interests in ordinary law enforcement, such as response to an emergency beyond the need for general crime control (In re Sealed Case 2002, 745–46).

Foreign intelligence collection, especially related to a threat to public safety, has many of the characteristics of a special need. The executive branch of the U.S. government has consistently taken the position that foreign intelligence collection is far removed from ordinary criminal law enforcement. Methodology and rules for criminal searches are "…inconsistent with the collection of foreign intelligence and would unduly frustrate the President in carrying out his foreign intelligence responsibilities … (W)e believe that the warrant clause of the Fourth Amendment is inapplicable to such (foreign intelligence) searches" (Gorelick 1994, 63).

There are thus significant distinctions between searches undertaken for ordinary law enforcement purposes and those done for intelligence purposes (Howell 145–147) (Kris).

Foreign intelligence surveillance may be undertaken without probable cause to believe that a crime has been committed. The surveillance may be of considerable duration and scope. Its purpose is to gather information about the intentions and capabilities of foreign governments or organizations, rather than to obtain admissible evidence of a crime. Yet, foreign intelligence gained through a wiretap may be used as evidence in a criminal

prosecution. The Department of Justice has ongoing concerns that the increasing blur between law enforcement and intelligence activities will lead to the avoidance of criminal law protections by disguising a criminal investigation as an intelligence operation, where less stringent restraints apply to the government.

Counterintelligence in particular raises many of the difficult issues. Only a small percentage of all counterintelligence cases can be considered for successful prosecutions. Investigations of foreign intelligence agents are seldom conducted from the outset as they would be if eventual prosecution were expected. Many counterintelligence professionals believe that prosecutions should never be brought against hostile foreign agents because it would only result in their replacement by other unknown agents whose activities would not come to the attention of the U.S. counterintelligence community.

The convergence of targets and especially the need to meet international terrorist threats caused a recent reorganization of the intelligence and law enforcement communities. The Department of Homeland Security created in 2002 has components that are deeply rooted in law enforcement and policing authorities, such as customs, border patrol, and immigration. Yet it also has several components that are part of the intelligence community, including an office of intelligence analysis and even part of the Coast Guard. The FBI has created a new National Security Service from its former counterintelligence and counterterrorism elements, all under an executive assistant director reporting to the new Director of National Intelligence (DNI). The Department of Justice has a new National Security Division that combines the intelligence policy (the Office of Intelligence Policy Review), counterespionage, and counterterrorism components of the Department under a new Assistant Attorney General for national security. In 2002, the Counterintelligence Enhancement Act called for the creation of the National Counterintelligence Executive (NCIX) to be the head of U.S. counterintelligence and develop government-wide counterintelligence policies and plans. The NCIX is now under the new DNI, created by the Intelligence Reform and Terrorism Prevention Act of 2004 (IRTPA). New DNI centers such as the National Counterterrorism Center (NCTC), which often replicated previous DCI centers, were created to bring together, or "fuse," intelligence, law enforcement, and related efforts directed at joint targets. The organizational hallmark of these centers was widespread and rapid sharing of information and personnel.

This convergence should not mask the fundamental differences between the two worlds, however. The United States continues to be wary of combining the powers and authorities of intelligence and law enforcement regimes. (Thompson 6) Intelligence activities require secrecy, swiftness, and latitude for success. Law enforcement activities require openness, painstaking and often slow diligence, and strict adherence to complicated legal rules of engagement for success. The authorities and restrictions for each activity have been tailored to meet the unique characteristics of each and maintain an acceptable level of checks and balances by maintaining the real differences between the two areas. For example, in 1991 rules for authorizing and conducting covert actions, and notifying Congress of such actions, were codified and added as Title V of the National Security Act of 1947, as amended. The general definition of covert action had several exceptions, one of which was "traditional law enforcement activities" or support to them.

The legislative history of Title V contains descriptions of traditional law enforcement activities, which include those conducted by the FBI to apprehend, or otherwise cooperate with foreign law enforcement authorities to apprehend those who have violated U.S. laws or the laws of other nations. It also includes activities of other U.S. government agencies (such as DEA) that assist other countries, with their consent, in the destruction or interdiction of narcotics supplies or products in those countries. "Routine support" is specifically described as not a "backdoor instrument of covert action" (Senate Report No. 102–85, 47–48).

This distinction is important because if an action of the U.S. government falls within the definition of "covert action," then a number of requirements must be met to lawfully authorize it, all of which would be unreasonably burdensome for law enforcement goals to be efficiently met. It is a clear indication that for many purposes, the differences between intelligence and law enforcement should be maintained and the policy of the United States is to separate the two.

An additional and still-current wall between intelligence and law enforcement is the restriction on direct involvement by the military in domestic law enforcement. Most of the agencies in the intelligence community are located within the Department of Defense (DOD). Since the immediate aftermath of the Civil War, the DOD has been largely prohibited from participating in civilian law enforcement by *posse comitatus* statutes, with the recent exception of the authority to assist law enforcement counternarcotics activities. But military personnel may still not be involved in the arrest and detention of suspects (Doyle 1995).

There is current interest in reviving proposals to create an agency whose operations would overlap in the middle between intelligence and law enforcement. Commentators have raised the British domestic security service MI-5 as a possible model. It would carry out an intelligence function separate from the law enforcement mission now owned by the FBI and the Department of Homeland Security. It would be directed toward collection and analysis of intelligence related to threats within the United States, and to the disruption and prevention of such threats, whether domestic, foreign, or international in nature. Reconciling a domestic intelligence service with traditional foreign intelligence and domestic law enforcement, and ensuring that civil-liberties interests are not unduly affected in an area where American public is wary, would be highly challenging.

Other issues arose as the world shrank, as well. These issues included oversight by different sets of congressional committees with varying agendas. Judiciary, intelligence, and defense committees are separate and different areas of responsibility. Even though there is some effort to have sufficient "crossover" membership on all concerned committees, there is still significant overlap, underlap, and opacity, all enveloped by the fog of legislation.

Coordination of intelligence and law enforcement activities is a perennial if not a daily issue. In the late 1980s, there were investigations into two international banks, the Bank of Credit and Commerce International (BCCI) and Banca Nazionale del Lavoro (BNL) who were alleged to have laundered money for criminal enterprises. The investigations revealed that the CIA had acquired information about possible crimes committed by the banks but had not made the information available to the Justice Department. Most observers concluded that there was no effort by the CIA to protect either of the banks or hide the information from the Justice Department, but congressional committees recommended that procedures be established to ensure that relevant information about international criminal activity collected by the intelligence community would be made available to law enforcement, while still protecting intelligence sources and methods (Snider et al. 1994).

As a result of the bank scandals, the Joint Task Force on Intelligence and Law Enforcement was established in 1993. It was comprised of senior attorneys from CIA and the Justice Department, and it made a number of recommendations to improve information sharing, coordination, and the management of data searches and retrieval. One was the creation of a Joint Intelligence-Law Enforcement Working Group (JICLE) which began operations in 1994. Although JICLE has faded into the bureaucratic graveyard, it is an example of the continuing efforts to bridge the gap between intelligence and law enforcement operations by establishing methods to keep channels of communication open and operating.

3. WE DON'T NEED NO STINKIN' BADGES

When intelligence activities relate to collection of information, they are governed by rules significantly different than those that apply to law enforcement activities targeting the exact same information. Intelligence information comes into the criminal process in two major ways. One is when intelligence collection results in information that may be useful for the prosecution in developing its case in chief. Law enforcement agencies routinely receive a great deal of information in disseminated intelligence reports that is for lead purposes only and remains classified and under the general control of the originating intelligence agency. Law enforcement agencies may use it to develop their own independently acquired information, but not as evidence to be introduced in a public court proceeding. If the lead-purpose information is important enough for the prosecutors to want to use it as evidence, then the clash of civilizations and cultures is joined.

Most intelligence information is fragmentary, nebulous, riddled with alternative meanings, and related to "proximate reality," rather than truth. It is an incomplete mosaic at best. If it were not, it would be news or history, not intelligence. Concepts such as the general ban on hearsay testimony or the best evidence rule, which are central trial procedure concepts in the United States, cannot be reconciled with the intelligence concepts of compartmentation, need to know, and protection of sources and methods so that they will continue to generate intelligence. Chain of custody issues and search warrants are not part of intelligence tradecraft. "Beyond a reasonable doubt" is a concept alien to intelligence collection or analysis.

Intelligence information also enters the criminal justice system because of the prosecution's efforts to comply with discovery rules requiring the disclosure to the defense of certain types of information. Federal discovery obligations apply not only to law enforcement agencies but also to other government agencies that are aligned with the prosecution. Alignment occurs when another agency becomes an active participant in the investigation or prosecution of a particular case. Alignment is significant in counterterrorist and weapons-proliferation cases because of the extensive cooperation between intelligence and law enforcement agencies in those areas.

The most important discovery rules are the constitutional requirements of the *Brady* and *Giglio* cases, Federal Rule of Criminal Procedure (FRCrP) 16, and the Jencks Act. *Brady* requires the government to disclose to the defendant any evidence that is material to the guilt or punishment of the accused (*Brady v. Maryland* 1963). *Giglio* requires the same discovery for evidence material to the impeachment of a government witness (*Giglio v.* U.S. 1972). FRCrP 16 obligates the government to disclose any relevant written or recorded statement of the defendant within the custody or control of the government, and any documents or tangible objects that are material to the defense, belong to the defendant, or are intended for use in the government's case in chief. The Jencks Act requires the government to disclose any statements of government witnesses within its possession that relate to the witnesses' testimony.

Prosecutors generally conduct a prudential search of intelligence community files prior to indictment because they have objective, articulable factors justifying the conclusion that the files probably contain classified information that may have an impact upon the government's decision whether to seek an indictment, and what crimes and defendants should actually be charged. The prudential search includes a search for Brady and other information that would be the subject of the government's post-indictment discovery obligations.

Intelligence agency files must be reviewed in a particular criminal case based on several factors. The first is whether the intelligence agency has been an active participant in the investigation or prosecution of a case. If so, alignment generally results and the agency's files are subject to the same requirements of search and disclosure as the files of the prosecuting attorney or lead agency (usually the

FBI). If the defendant makes an explicit request that certain files be searched, and there is a non-trivial prospect that the examination of those files will yield material exculpatory information, then courts usually also require a file review.

In addition, if prosecutors acquire information that suggests the defendant may have had, or as part of his defense at trial will assert that he has had, contacts with an intelligence agency, then some limited review by the affected agency is almost always done. In such cases, a positive defense of acting pursuant to public authority under FRCrP 12.3 may be implicated. Such a defense is based upon the notion that if a defendant thought he was acting under a lawful and authorized directive by the government, he would not have the required mental state of knowingly violating a criminal law. In those circumstances, determining the existence and extent of any contact between a defendant and an intelligence agency becomes important to the prosecution's case.

If the prosecution is required by these discovery rules to examine the voluminous holdings of the intelligence community, it is a serious drain on law enforcement and prosecution resources. If the prosecution is required by these discovery rules to disclose intelligence information to the defendants, their attorneys, clerks, secretaries, experts, and other defense team personnel, then the risk to the sources of the information expands greatly. And if these process rules allow the defendants to disclose the information in open court in order to have a fair chance to put on their defenses, then the damage is no longer potential but actual. CIPA allows the government to calculate and understand in advance the risk of going forward with a prosecution, but it does not change the fundamental rules of criminal process.

A typical CIPA case involves classified information surfacing either from the defendant's own knowledge or from discovery obligations of the U.S. government to allow defense counsel to search or use such information. The court usually convenes a pretrial conference to attempt to resolve as many issues as possible. It then enters a protective order requiring appropriate security procedures and limited access to the classified information, including in some cases even prohibiting defense counsel from discussing some matters with the defendants themselves. The defense is required to notify the government under section 5 of CIPA of what classified information the defense intends to disclose.

The government then attempts to challenge disclosure of the classified information based upon the regular procedural objections to evidence (everything from not material to hearsay). The government then tries to minimize damage by proposing unclassified summaries or substitutions for any classified information that the court rules may be disclosed by the defense. There is a provision for an interlocutory (pre-verdict) appeal of court rulings, and a range of sanctions the court can use if the government does not allow the defense to disclose the classified information. CIPA has been in effect for almost thirty years, without significant amendment, and the general view of the U.S. government is that it has achieved its purpose.

Individuals in custody also create immediate conflicts between intelligence and law enforcement. The criminal law system in Anglo-American jurisdictions (among others) wants those in jeopardy of criminal penalties to have a level playing field. Fundamental notions of what is fair include those explicitly set out in the Constitution: the Fifth Amendment right against self-incrimination, and the Sixth Amendment right to legal counsel. Assuming the U.S. government has lawful grounds for incarcerating individuals other than to try them on criminal charges (such as holding enemy prisoners of war), application of such basic elements of criminal law would raise tremendous barriers to acquiring information about future threats. The Miranda warning of the right to remain silent and to have an attorney appointed and paid for by the state would end almost any conceivable intelligence interrogation.

The status of detainees of the U.S. government in military custody at Guantanamo Bay and other locations overseas has created an epic clash over how the U.S. criminal system should treat them. As this is written, the first of the military-commission proceedings are beginning. The U.S. Supreme Court has held that the detainees have a right to petition federal civilian courts for writs of habeas corpus to challenge their detentions. Habeas corpus is a long-time staple of the criminal law system that allows convicted federal prisoners another venue to allege they are being wrongfully held, other than a strict appellate review. Use of the military criminal law system under either the Uniform Code of Military Justice (UCMJ) or the laws of war does not reconcile the fundamentally different ends of intelligence and law enforcement. The UCMJ largely follows the civilian Federal Rules of Criminal Procedure, including a version of CIPA.

The Supreme Court has also opined that Common Article 3 of the Geneva Conventions apply to such detainees (*Hamdan v. Rumsfeld* 2006). Article 3 states that prisoners of war may not be forced to provide any information except name, rank, and serial number. They may be asked for and even volunteer more information, but no physical or mental torture or any other form of coercion may be inflicted on prisoners of war to secure from them information of any kind whatever. Prisoners of war who refuse to answer may not be threatened, insulted, or exposed to unpleasant or disadvantageous treatment of any kind. They also cannot be denied regular visits from the Red Cross and packages from home (FM 27–10 para. 93).

Other issues arise when intelligence agencies provide direct assistance to law enforcement organizations. The circumstances under which a defendant is rendered to a court of competent jurisdiction may become litigated if the defense raises the *Toscanino* exception to the *Ker-Frisbie* doctrine. The *Ker-Frisbie* doctrine (based on two seminal cases) holds that a trial court will not bar a trial based upon the conditions under which the defendant is brought before the court *(Ker v. Illinois* 1886; *Frisbie v. Collins* 1952). Even if the defendant is taken into custody and transported before the court in some manner that is arguably unlawful, the court will not dismiss the case so long as the defendant can expect a fair trial before that particular court. *Toscanino* was a Second Circuit decision that created an exception to the *Ker-Frisbie* doctrine (U.S. *v. Toscanino* 1974). The court in *Toscanino* said that if the conduct of government agents who rendered the defendant to the court's jurisdiction was so outrageous as to shock the conscience of the court, then the court would at least hear defense motions to dismiss based upon those conditions.

If an intelligence agency supplies resources of equipment, personnel, or technical assistance for a clandestine exfiltration or delivery of a prisoner, then it is possible that the conditions of the operation could be litigated. Disclosure of intelligence sources, methods, and sensitive operational activities would be likely to be an issue in such litigation. There has not been much historical success in raising the *Toscanino* defense, but it has been raised.

Press reporting has also described renditions of individuals by the U.S. government to a number of foreign jurisdictions, where the individuals then become subject to those other nations' law enforcement systems. The renditions are described as clandestine and do not involve formal extradition procedures that are a staple of many treaties involving public law enforcement jurisdictional proceedings. Press reports also describe claims by a number of individuals that they were delivered to law enforcement authorities who tortured or otherwise abused them. It is not difficult to imagine the difficulties in avoiding such circumstances or defending against spurious claims if secret intelligence resources are involved in such transport.

4. GO DIRECTLY TO JAIL. DO NOT PASS GO. DO NOT COLLECT $200.

Enforcement of criminal laws is also a significant limitation on the ability of the intelligence establishment to conduct particular activities. There is no comprehensive and universal legal principle that exempts intelligence agencies from substantive criminal prohibitions. Intelligence activities that might implicate a U.S. criminal statute have to be reviewed one by one.

Intelligence agencies have special authorities that allow them to lawfully conduct activities that could be unlawful if conducted by other federal agencies or private individuals or organizations. Much of the authority granted to intelligence agencies is based upon the need for secrecy and the fact that most intelligence activities are directed at foreign governments, organizations, and individuals. International law principles and treaties relating to extradition of criminal suspects have established long-held norms about how to treat those accused of espionage and related crimes. Such crimes have at their base clandestine actions by national governments that are recognized and accepted by customary international law and formal conventions. Accordingly, such crimes are deemed "political" crimes and are not subject to extradition agreements.

A related concept is that of diplomatic immunity, in which certain diplomats are beyond the reach of the criminal laws of any nation except their own. The only sanction in such instances is not a law enforcement penalty, but rather the diplomatic one of expulsion from the territory of the host nation (the declaration of the status of persona non grata). Intelligence officers with diplomatic immunity thus do not have a get-out-of-jail-free card issued by the law enforcement authorities, but they do have a free ticket home.

This latitude for action based upon special authorities is limited when a specific criminal prohibition applies. For example, in the current executive order that is a presidential charter for the U.S. intelligence community, there is a section that states: "*Consistency With Other Laws.* Nothing in this Order shall be construed to authorize any activity in violation of the Constitution or statutes of the United States." Further, the intelligence authorization acts passed (until recently) on a near-annual basis contained similar language.

The National Security Act uses similar language to limit the use of covert action (National Security Act Title V). It establishes by statute the authority of the president to use clandestine means to influence political, economic, or military conditions abroad, where it is intended that the role of the U. S. government will not be apparent or acknowledged publicly. The definition of covert action specifically excludes traditional law enforcement activities. In order to authorize a covert action, the president must issue a finding that meets certain requirements in the act. The act states, however: "A finding may not authorize any action that would violate the Constitution or any statute of the United States."

This limit on intelligence activities created a grey area in which government officials thrash around trying to reconcile law enforcement requirements with intelligence authorities. Some U.S. criminal statutes are so broadly worded that a specific exemption has been explicitly included to prevent otherwise authorized intelligence activities from being at least arguably covered by the prohibitions. For example, under Title 18 of the U.S. criminal code, it is a crime to intercept electronic communications. Since intercepting electronic communications is the basic function of signals intelligence (SIGINT), a large portion of the intelligence community would be affected. Accordingly, the drafters exempted from the definition of the crime electronic surveillance within the United States that is covered by FISA, as well as the acquisition of foreign intelligence information from international or foreign communications (18 U.S.C. sections 2511(2)(e)-(f) (2005)).

Cybercrime, in the form of fraud and related actions in connection with unauthorized access or damage to computer systems, also contains a specific intelligence and law enforcement exemption (18 U.S.C. section 1030(f)(2005)). Other statutes are broadly worded but not extraterritorial in application. Activities conducted abroad that do not involve U.S. persons or property or have a sufficient nexus with the territory of the United States may not be crimes.

Other criminal laws, however, are in fact clearly intended to apply to the activities of the U.S. government. For example, if possession of a biological or chemical weapon does not fall within the exceptions in the criminal statutes implementing the Biological and Chemical Weapons Conventions (relating to the purpose of the possession), intelligence agencies would be violating the law (18 U.S.C. sections 175(c), 229F(7) (2005)). The federal crime of torture specifically refers to persons "acting under the color of law," meaning those acting on behalf of an official governmental entity. Torture is an extraterritorial federal crime and may not be authorized by any federal intelligence, military, or law enforcement official (18 U.S.C. sections 2340–2340A (2005)).

Unclear language in some criminal statutes and different circumstances that have expanded the reach of others create problems for intelligence agencies and their employees. In some statutes there is neither a specific exemption for otherwise authorized intelligence activities nor a clear intent to extend the criminal law to cover such activities. Wire and mail fraud statutes state that "whoever" obtains money or property by means of false representations and uses the mail, telephone, radio, or television to do so will be committing a federal crime (18 U.S.C. sections 1341, 1343 (2005)). There is no specific exclusion for otherwise lawful and authorized intelligence activities. "Whoever" seems all-inclusive. If defrauding includes acquiring secrets of foreign persons and organizations by subterfuge or deceit, intelligence activities might be arguably included. In light of intelligence needed by the U.S. national security policymakers, that would be absurd.

Another example is the crime related to provision of support to terrorists or terrorist groups. It applies to, "whoever knowingly provides material support or resources to a foreign terrorist organization, or attempts or conspires to do so" (Antiterrorism and Effective Death Penalty Act section 303). There is no intelligence exception in the text of the statute. There is no discussion of intelligence activities in the legislative history and no explicit expression of congressional intent to include or exclude intelligence activities from the definition of the crime.

On its face, that language would prohibit an intelligence agency and its employees from providing money or equipment to assist a human asset in establishing his bona fides in order to penetrate a terrorist organization. Precluding the federal government itself from taking steps to fight international terrorism defies both logic and the statutory purposes expressed in legislative report language. Providing material support to a terrorist organization in order to penetrate and defeat it brings the intelligence world—where all is not as it seems in many circumstances—into conflict with a law enforcement system that is premised upon constitutional and common law requirements of clarity, proof beyond a reasonable doubt, fairness, and lines between right and wrong.

Other examples demonstrate the difficulty of using a law enforcement system to impose limits on foreign intelligence activities. Intelligence agencies deploy officers and assets in the field under various types of cover. Cover protects their personal safety and their affiliation with the United States government. It requires ruses, deception, false-flag persona, and misrepresentation. In the U.S. criminal code, however, "(w)hoever falsely and willfully represents himself to be a citizen of the United States shall be fined under this title or imprisoned not more than three years, or both." Such an act is a felony. There is no exception for intelligence activities. According to the strict statutory language, a non-U.S. citizen working for the CIA cannot say that he is a U.S. citizen to anyone who is a potential intelligence source.

In these circumstances, principles of statutory interpretation of criminal laws are the only way to reconcile statutory intent with statutory language. The most significant principle stems from the *Nardone* case, which states that criminal laws of general applicability should not be interpreted to apply to actions of the government as sovereign unless there is specific language to that effect (*Nardone v. U.S.* 1937, 384). Other rules of interpretation also require looking to the reasons for enactment of the statute and the purpose to be gained by it, and construing the statute in the manner which is consistent with such purpose. A statute should not be read literally where such a reading is contrary to its purposes.

The difficulty with reliance on such rules is that *Nardone* is not universal in its reach and each set of circumstances requires examination of the specific facts involved. Advance review by legal counsel for intelligence agencies can help insulate intelligence officers from exposure. Intelligence agency employees proceed at their own peril when they carry out operations over the objections of agency counsel that are based upon potential criminal liability. Yet in grey areas, employees could be subject to criminal investigations for actions taken under the stress,

danger, and critical time pressures experienced in the field. A criminal investigation has highly serious effects upon individuals and organizations, even if no charges or other sanctions are ever brought after years go by.

Subjecting intelligence activities to advance legal review for potential criminal activities and producing legal opinions in coordination with the appropriate criminal law enforcement elements of the Department of Justice is burdensome, slow, and inefficient. The Department of Justice dislikes and resists formal declinations of prosecution. Intelligence activities that raise such a risk are simply avoided.

The use of "dirty" assets also creates the same dangers. Sources of certain intelligence information may be individuals who have committed crimes even though their actions took place completely overseas. This can occur in areas such as terrorism, narcotics trafficking, and weapons proliferation. Law enforcement wants to convict them or use them to convict others. Intelligence wants to use them to collect information that will remain secret. This conflict is ancient, as illustrated by the famous Biblical passage describing Joshua's battle at Jericho. Joshua sent two men to spy on Jericho, and Rahab the "harlot" hid them, lied to Jericho authorities, and deceived all around her in assisting the Israelites. Continuing to use human assets to collect intelligence after information surfaces tying them to a crime significantly increases the likelihood that a successful criminal case cannot be brought against them without seriously risking intelligence equities. In such a case it is very difficult to serve both intelligence and criminal interests.

Concerns with criminal statutes also led to the passage of Title XI of the National Security Act. It creates a statutory-interpretation presumption that domestic U.S. laws implementing international treaties and conventions would not make unlawful otherwise lawful and authorized intelligence activities, absent express statutory language to the contrary. Title XI recognizes that it would be exceedingly difficult for the Departments of State and Justice to ensure that every new transnational criminal convention and its implementing legislation contain a specific exemption for intelligence activities. Trying to address issues of espionage, covert action, and other unacknowledged national state activities in an international convention would be close to impossible. Public discussion necessary to adopt such agreements would be very damaging to the clandestine activities that the agreements sought to protect. As a result, it was imperative to craft this rule of statutory interpretation to make congressional intent manifest when it otherwise was silent.

Secrecy has not shielded intelligence agencies from scrutiny under criminal law standards, either. All components of the U.S. intelligence community are required by executive order and presidential direction to report possible violations of federal, criminal laws by employees, and certain specified federal criminal laws by any other persons, according to procedures developed between the attorney general and the intelligence organization involved.

In 1982, the then-serving attorney general and director of central intelligence promulgated such procedures for CIA. They require the CIA's General Counsel (currently a Senate-confirmed, presidential appointment) to report to the Criminal Division of the Department of Justice and the FBI any information that an Agency employee may have violated any federal crime, and any information that any person may have committed any of a list of serious federal offenses such as those involving intentional infliction or threat of death or serious physical harm, espionage, or perjury or false statements. Crimes reporting under those procedures is extensive. In addition, in the late 1980s Congress created a statutory Inspector General for CIA. The Inspector General's duties include investigating possible violations of federal criminal laws that involve programs or operations of CIA, and reporting any such information to the attorney general.

Law enforcement can be a profound deterrent to intelligence activities, either advertently or inadvertently. Criminal law can bar actions of even the President of the United States. It is unlikely that government employees will be found guilty of a crime if they are carrying out in good faith what is otherwise a lawful activity, since they would not have the *mens rea*, or guilty mind, necessary for a crime to be proven. Nevertheless, the threat of a criminal investigation itself can be a punishing and debilitating experience for both the individuals and their agencies, often lasting years in duration.

Intelligence issues also create problems for prosecutions when they arise in almost any part of a criminal case. This is especially notable in prosecutions in two areas of high interest and significance to both law enforcement and intelligence agencies. Espionage prosecutions by their nature involve someone who has had access to classified national security information. Such defendants already have

knowledge about the government's case against them without any discovery or chance for the government to minimize the risk of disclosure of sensitive information through the CIPA process. The case in chief will almost always involve a high risk that other sensitive information will have to be revealed to achieve a conviction, thus multiplying in ways difficult to evaluate the damage already caused by the defendant.

This significant additional hurdle for the prosecution also arises when an employee of the intelligence community is charged with crimes other than espionage. Typically these charges involve either some type of violation of anti-corruption ethics laws or more often, violations of perjury laws or prohibitions of false statements to Congress or others (such as inspector generals) investigating some aspect of intelligence activities. The problem is multiplied when independent counsel prosecutors operate without the usual check on prosecutorial discretion that operates when the executive branch agencies decide on whether the damage of going forward with a prosecution greatly outweighs the likelihood of achieving a significant conviction for a major crime. This dilemma arose most notably during the existence of the statutory independent counsel created to minimize possible conflicts of interest arising when the Department of Justice prosecutes senior U.S. government officials (such as the Iran-Contra prosecutions). The statute creating the independent counsel was not renewed by Congress after it expired, but the appointment of quasi-independent special counsels by the attorney general continues.

Terrorism cases raise an additional problem for the prosecution. Terrorist acts and the activities of terrorist organizations have at their base a violent attack on the United States or its citizens and their property anywhere in the world. The national security and intelligence elements of the U.S. government expend enormous efforts to prevent such attacks. Law enforcement contributes to that preemption in a number of significant ways, but fundamentally law enforcement actions are geared toward capturing those committing crimes in the past and amassing evidence to prove their guilt beyond a reasonable doubt. If a potential terrorist has not yet committed a terrorist act, the prevention role of the intelligence community prevails and the retribution role of the law enforcement community has to stand to the side, often to its future detriment in criminal trials.

In addition, the special authorities of the intelligence community have given rise to a number of instances in which defendants assert the "CIA defense." It is a variation of the defense of public authority, in which a defendant essentially argues that if he in fact did the acts as charged by the prosecution, he was authorized to do so by the government itself (FRCrP 12; U.S. *v. Rosenthal* 1986, 1235–1237; *Smith v.* U.S. 1984, 432) Because the intelligence community operates in secrecy and in fact is lawfully authorized to do certain activities that would be criminal violations if conducted by private entities, the CIA defense can be a significant weakness in a prosecution. If allowed under the rules of criminal procedure, a defendant may demand much more discovery from the intelligence community, including testimony by intelligence officials, and thus expand the greymail danger. It may also raise doubts in the minds of jurors who have the generally widespread exposure of the public to Hollywood notions of the CIA and other intelligence agencies having roving bands of desperados with licenses to kill, all being directed by sinister conspirators to hide the aliens in New Mexico at all costs.

5. THE WORLD IS FLAT, EXCEPT WHEN IT IS ROUND

The post–World War II expansion of international law enforcement is creating new challenges and problems for intelligence services. Increasingly, some nations are advocating universal jurisdiction, in which certain of their criminal laws may be applied to individuals with no connection to the country seeking to try them. Jurisdiction generally has been restricted to the territory of a particular nation or to its citizens. Universal jurisdiction would allow a national of Kenya to be tried in Belgium for certain crimes (such as crimes against humanity or genocide) committed against Kenyans in Kenya. Other principles of international law have also expanded the ability of a state to prosecute conduct that occurs outside its territory (the protective principle, the objective territorial principle, the national principle, and especially the passive personality principle, which allows a state to prosecute someone for crimes against nationals of that state; U.S. *v. Bin Laden* 2000).

Demands for war-crimes trials have also led to the creation of international institutions under the purview of the United Nations or the NATO Alliance.

A number of international criminal tribunals were created to deal with charges against individuals in the former Yugoslavia, Rwanda, and Sierra Leone, for example. The International Criminal Court (ICC) was also established by international convention as an ongoing venue for such charges to be heard.

The trial of two alleged Libyan intelligence operatives for the destruction of Pan Am Flight 103 over Scotland was a hybrid legal proceeding demonstrating the high cost of international joint ventures involving both law enforcement and intelligence. The trial was held at The Hague, but the law applied was Scots law and the court was composed of Scots judges. There was an extensive and costly trial, which involved the first time in history that a CIA officer testified in a foreign criminal proceeding. The split verdict left many participants unsatisfied with the result and the resources it took to translate a vast, multinational intelligence and law enforcement effort to identify those responsible for the terrorist act into a judicial proceeding bound by rules of fairness, individual rights, and certainties needed for convictions.

The problems associated with intelligence and law enforcement under domestic criminal statutes and systems is multiplied exponentially when foreign nations attempt joint prosecutions under notions of international criminal laws that are often vague and enforced in widely varying ways (e.g., „crimes against humanity," or "genocide.") Intelligence information is very likely to become an issue in such situations as the executive agencies of the involved governments direct collection and analysis against potential defendants who are also targets of intense foreign and defense policy interest. By agreement with the prosecutors, such agencies establish procedures for the tribunal proceedings minimizing exposure of intelligence sources and methods. The sources and methods may be at risk because information in the case could reveal highly sensitive information ranging from direct evidence of criminal acts and intent (SIGINT intercepts of conversations of defendants discussing the alleged crimes) to the location of wanted individuals sought by police departments (unmanned aerial vehicle electro-optical imagery of cars or houses where such individuals might be located). Exposure of such information to foreign nationals involved in the prosecution or defense of war crimes would significantly increase the risk of any participating nation's intelligence secrets being exposed. At best, international law is imprecise, uncertain, and dependent upon actions of foreign nations and foreign courts. Criminal law enforcement, by contrast, requires precision, clarity, and predictability if it is to have political legitimacy.

6. CONCLUSION: TOMORROW IS ANOTHER DAY

At the end of the day, the most pressing issues in the intersection of intelligence and law enforcement will probably involve a balance between the parts of the two worlds that are irreconcilable. In certain areas, intelligence equities should and will prevail, and in other areas law enforcement will be the prime actor. In the grey area where the two imperatives overlap, mission managers will have to further their own goals while devoting reasonable efforts to avoid impeding the other's mission.

The most pressing issue is the creation of a domestic intelligence organization separate from law enforcement and foreign intelligence establishments. It is driven by the most dangerous threat facing the United States: nuclear weapons in the hands of suicidal terrorists such as al-Qaida, who would use them. The authorities, rules of engagement, restrictions, safeguards, oversight, and resources for such an intelligence organization would have to be established in a balance of national security interests with privacy and other civil liberties.

A second issue is the extent to which traditional notions of due process in the United States' law enforcement system hamper or otherwise significantly restrict the intelligence community in its primary roles of producing foreign intelligence and supporting military operations. The right to remain silent does not apply to a suicide bomber bent on destroying a city (Posner 2006).

Another issue relates to the appropriate use of the armed forces. Restrictions on military involvement with domestic civilian law enforcement or even military operations against an enemy inside the United States may be out of date.

In addition, military law enforcement (including military commissions and the enforcement of the laws of war) differs from civilian law enforcement. The current effort to try non-state actors and unlawful combatants detained by the United States in the war on terrorism by military commissions has led to litigation and confusion in heroic proportions, and that is not over yet (Hamdan).

A further issue is the extent to which technical means of conducting surveillance have advanced to such a degree that they intrude on Americans' long-held notions of the acceptable boundary between government scrutiny and citizens' privacy. Reasonable expectations of privacy that grew out of many years of uncomplicated police work enforcing domestic criminal laws may not be appropriate for the effective prevention of unidentified foreign terrorists. The recent debate regarding amendments to FISA underscored the deep wariness many Americans have about any extension of foreign intelligence collection by intrusive means inside the United States or outside the United States when the target of the collection is a U.S. person.

These issues are part of a seamless web and each issue affects the others, for the most part. What is clear is that immediate post–World War II notions of the differences between one side of the border of the United States and the other do not fit the world as we find it. Where, in fact, is cyberspace?

The divide between national security and law enforcement is, "…carved deeply into the topography of American government" (Carter et al. 1998, 82). Intelligence and law enforcement will continue to co-exist more or less peacefully, but there are continuing issues that probably have no better solution than the professionals of both worlds, and their policy making masters, act in well-informed and well-intentioned ways to support and deconflict their activities and missions. The different cultures and narratives of each community are significant and important (Best). They affect the view that each has of the other and of themselves. That affects the ability of managers to manage them, overseers to watch them, and ultimately the ability of the U.S. government to succeed in their areas of operation.

As one commentator noted, FBI officers are from Mars, from Fordham, from the football team, from the Boy and Girl Scouts, from off the street. CIA officers are from Venus, from Yale, from the tennis team, from the front row in class where they always raise their hands, from a book-lined study, from academe (Gorman 2003).

Muddling through is part of the job.

QUESTIONS FOR FURTHER DISCUSSION

1. Do you think there is a proper role for the judicial branch in the supervision of intelligence activities?

2. Which organization do you think provides the best safeguards against the misuse of secret power by the CIA and other intelligence agencies: the National Security Council, the Office of the DNI, the Congress, the courts, or the media?
3. What kinds of intelligence activities are covered by the FISA Court?
4. What are some reasons why the court system may not provide a strong check on the executive branch when it comes to intelligence operations?

REFERENCES

Antiterrorism and Effective Death Penalty Act, Pub. L. No. 104–132, no Stat. 1214.

Authority of the Federal Bureau of Investigation to Override Customary or Other International Law in the Course of Extraterritorial Law Enforcement Activities, 13 Op. Ofc. Legal Counsel 195 (1989).

Board of Education v. Earls. 536 U.S. 822 (2002).

Commission on Intelligence Capabilities of the U.S. Regarding Weapons of Mass Destruction (WMD Commission). 2005. *Report to the President.*

Commission on Roles and Capabilities of the U.S. Intelligence Community (Aspin-Brown Commission). 1996. *Preparing for the 21st Century: An Appraisal of U.S. Intelligence.*

Baker, S. A. 1994–95. Should Spies Be Cops? *Foreign Policy* 97 (Winter): 36.

Best, R. A., Jr. 2001. *Intelligence and Law Enforcement: Countering Transnational Threats to the U.S.* Washington, D.C.: Congressional Research Service.

Brady v. Maryland, 373 U.S. 83 (1963).

Carter, A., J. Deutch, and P. Zelikow. 1998. Catastrophic Terrorism: Tackling the New Danger. *Foreign Affairs* (November–December).

Civiletti, B. R. 1983. Intelligence Gathering and the Law. *Studies In Intelligence.* Center for the Study of Intelligence 27, no. 2 (Summer): 13.

Classified Information Procedures Act, as amended, 18 U.S.C.A. app. 3 sections 1–16.

Collins, J. M. 2002. *And the Walls Came Tumbling Down: Sharing Grand Jury Information with the Intelligence Community under the USA PATRIOT Act*, 39 American Criminal Law Review 1261.

Doyle, C. 1995. *The Posse Comitatus Act & Related Matters: The Use of the Military to Execute Civilian Law*, Congressional Research Service Report 95–964 S (September 12).

Executive Order 12333. (EO 12333).

Federal Rules of Criminal Procedure. (FRCrP).

Foreign Intelligence Surveillance Act, as amended. (FISA).

Fredman, J. 1998. Intelligence Agencies, Law Enforcement, and the Prosecution Team. *Yale Legal and Policy Review* 16:331.

Frisbie v. Collins, 342 U.S. 519 (1952).

Funk, W. *Electronic Surveillance of Terrorism: The Intelligence/ Law Enforcement Dilemma—A History*, 11 Lewis & Clark L. Rev. 1099 (2007).

Giglio v. United States, 405 U.S. 150 (1972).

Gorelick, J. S. 1994. *Amending the Foreign Intelligence Surveillance Act: Hearings Before the House Permanent Select Comm. on Intelligence*, 103d Cong, 2d Sess., 62.

Gorman, S. 2003. FBI, CIA Remain Worlds Apart. *National Journal* (August 1).

Hall, J. W. 2000. Search and Seizure. 3rd ed., section 36.7.

Hamdan v. Rumsfeld, 126 S. Ct. 2749 (2006).

Hamdi v. Rumsfeld, 542 U.S. 507 (2004).

Howell, B. A., and D. J. Lesemann. 2007. Symposium, *Protecting the Nation at the Expense of Individuals? Defining the Scope of U.S. Executive Power at Home and Abroad in Times of Crisis: FISA's Fruits in Criminal Cases: An Opportunity for Improved Accountability*, 12 UCLA Journal of International Law & Foreign Affairs 145 (2007).

Hulnick, A. S. 1997. Intelligence and Law Enforcement. *International Journal of Intelligence and Counterintelligence* 10 (Fall): 269.

In re Scaled Case No. 02–001, 310 F.3d 717 (FISA Ct. Rev. 2002).

Intelligence Authorization Act for Fiscal Year 1995, 50 U.S.C. section 402a (2005).

Johnson, L. K., and J. J. Wirtz. 2008. *Intelligence and National Security: The Secret World of Spies.* 2nd ed. New York: Oxford University Press.

Ker v. Illinois, 119 U.S. 436 (1886).

Kris, D. S., and J. D. Wilson. *National Security Investigations & Prosecutions* §§ 2.9–2.15 [2008 loose-leaf].

Lowenthal, M. M. 2006. *Intelligence: From Secrets to Policy.* 3rd ed. Washington D.C.: CQ Press.

Manget, F. F. 2006. Intelligence and the Criminal Law System. *Stanford Law and Policy Review* 17:415.

Nardone v. United States, 302 U.S. 379 (1937).

National Commission on Terrorist Attacks upon the U.S. 2004. *9/11 Commission Report.*

National Security Act of 1947, as amended.

Posner, R. A. 2006. *Not a Suicide Pact: The Constitution in a Time of National Emergency.* New York: Oxford University Press.

Riebling, M. 2002. *Wedge: The Secret War between the FBI and the CIA.* New York: Touchstone.

Senate Select Committee on Intelligence and House Permanent Select Committee on Intelligence, Joint

Inquiry Into Intelligence Community Activities Before and After the Terrorist Attacks of September 11, 2001, Senate Report No. 107–351, House Report No. 107–792 (2d Sess. 2002).

Smith v. United States, 592 F. Supp. 424 (E.D. Va. 1984).

Snider, L. B., E. Rindskopf, and J. Coleman. 1994. *Relating Intelligence and Law Enforcement: Problems and Prospects*. Washington: Consortium for the Study of Intelligence.

Thompson, B. G. 2006. *The National Counterterrorism Center: Foreign and Domestic Intelligence Fusion and the Potential Threat to Privacy*, 6 PGH *Journal of Technology Law and Policy*, 6.

United States v. Alvarez-Machain, 504 U.S. 655 (1992).

United States v. Bin Laden, 92 F. Supp. 2d 189 (S.D.N.Y. 2000).

United States v. Rosenthal, 793 F.2d 1214 (11th Cir. 1986).

United States v. Toscanino, 500 F.2d 267 (2d Cir. 1974), *reh'g denied*, 504 F.2d 1380 (2d Cir. 1974).

United States v. Truong, 629 F.2d 908 (4th Cir. 1980), cert, denied, 454 U.S. 1144 (1982).

United States v. Verdugo-Urquidez, 494 U.S. 259 (1990).

U.S. Department of Army, Field Manual 27–10, The Law of Land Warfare (1956). (FM 27–10).

USA PATRIOT Act (United and Strengthening America by Providing Appropriate Tools Required to Intercept and Obstruct Terrorism Act of 2001). Pub. L. No. 107–56, 115 Stat. 272.

From Frederic F. Manget, "Intelligence and the Rise of Judicial Intervention" in Loch K. Johnson, ed., *Handbook of Intelligence Studies* (New York: Routledge, 2007), pp. 329–342. Reproduced by permission of Taylor and Francis Books UK.

31. CONGRESSIONAL SUPERVISION OF AMERICA'S SECRET AGENCIES: THE EXPERIENCE AND LEGACY OF THE CHURCH COMMITTEE

LOCH K. JOHNSON

A former assistant to Senator Frank Church, who led the Senate inquiry into alleged CIA abuses of power in 1975, Johnson reviews the experiences of that investigation and gauges the contribution made by the Church Committee to the search for a proper balance between security against America's enemies and the civil liberties of its own citizens.

KEEPING AN EYE ON THE HIDDEN SIDE OF GOVERNMENT

For purposes of gathering and interpreting information from around the world, the United States created thirteen major agencies during the Cold War, known collectively as the "intelligence community" and led by a Director of Central Intelligence (DCI). Seven of the agencies have a predominantly military mission and are within the jurisdiction of the Defense Department (among them, the National Security Agency or NSA, which gathers signals intelligence); five are associated with civilian departments, such as the Federal Bureau of Investigation (FBI) within the Justice Department; and one, the Central Intelligence Agency (CIA), stands alone as an independent entity answerable directly to the president (Lowenthal 1992; Richelson 1999). Together, these agencies comprise the largest cluster of information-gathering organizations in American history, and rivalled in world history only by the intelligence apparatus of the Soviet Union during the Cold War and Russia today.

Concealed from public scrutiny, America's intelligence agencies pose a major challenge to the idea of government accountability in a democratic society (Ransom 1970, 1975; Johnson 1986). This essay examines the failure of legislative supervisors to hold the intelligence community in check during the Cold War, leading to a significant erosion of civil liberties in the United States. It explores as well the prerequisites necessary to lessen the probability of the further abuse of power by the secret agencies.

A CONCEPTUAL FRAMEWORK

An extensive literature exists on the subject of congressional control over administrative agencies, commonly referred to as legislative oversight (e.g., Aberbach 1990; Ogul 1976; Scher 1963). As Spence notes (1997), positive theorists and quantitative empiricists have pointed to the capacity of lawmakers to shape the environment of agency decision making in such a way as to align bureaucrats toward the goals of oversight committees on Capitol Hill. For instance, Calvert, McCubbins, and Weingast (1989), as well as McCubbins et al. (1989), maintain that executive agencies are essentially "hard-wired" at their statutory inception to honor legislative intentions (*ex ante* control). Moreover, they posit, lawmakers have potent sanctions that may be used to punish rogue bureaucratic behavior, notably the power of the purse to reduce funding for recalcitrant agencies (*ex post* control).

Theorists emphasize as well that organized interest groups provide an added safeguard to assist lawmakers in thwarting errant bureaucrats who fail to uphold original legislative mandates. Lobbyists set off "fire alarms" to alert members of Congress when agencies have violated expected norms (McCubbins and Schwartz 1984). Media reporting on agency activities can serve a similar function. Moreover, lawmakers and their staff can engage in "police patrolling," that is, a more active and direct monitoring of agency activities through persistent hearings and less formal dialogues with agency personnel.

Yet, in contrast to these roseate theories on the efficacy of legislative oversight, a more extensive body of research that stretches over four decades of scholarly reporting offers quite a different impression. From this point of view, lawmakers have engaged in oversight only sporadically and half-heartedly (Bibby 1968; Ransom, 1970, 1977; Dodd and Schott 1979, 170–184; Johnson 1994). This failure of accountability has stemmed chiefly from a lack of motivation among members of Congress to immerse themselves in oversight activities, such as hearings and detailed budget reviews. For lawmakers, greater political advantage lies in the passage of legislation, where credit-claiming—vital to re-election—is more visible to constituents (Mayhew 1986).

Further, representatives have often been reluctant to become involved in (and, thus, responsible for) controversial agency decisions; better to keep a distance from potential trouble (Walden 1970). Information asymmetries have contributed as well to the failure of oversight, giving agencies room to maneuver as lawmakers remain unaware of informal rules, internal memoranda, and private deals struck inside the vast domains of the executive departments (Spence 1997, 200).

THE SPECIAL CASE OF INTELLIGENCE

With respect to the intelligence agencies, the limited relevance of the safeguards heralded by the positivists and quantitative empiricists is manifest. In the first place, the statutory rules established for the secret agencies by the National Security Act of 1947 (50 U.S.C. 401) are broadly worded and often ambiguous. In one clause, for instance, this statute grants the CIA with authority to "perform such other functions and duties related to intelligence affecting the national security as the President or the National Security Council may direct …"—not exactly a tight legislative leash.

As for the appointment power, it is true that lawmakers have closely examined the credentials of some DCI nominees, rejecting a handful over the years in hotly debated hearings (as with the donnybrook over the failed nomination of Anthony Lake during the Clinton Administration). Yet, the Office of DCI is notoriously weak. The DCI is head of the CIA, but exercises only marginal control over the dozen other agencies in the community. Their separate chiefs have extensive discretionary authority and are seldom subjected to the kind of legislative scrutiny directed toward DCI nominations (Johnson 2000).

Fire alarms set off by lobbyists or by media reporters are unreliable, too. Few interest groups exist in this policy domain, and those that do (the Boeing corporation, for instance, which manufactures surveillance satellites) are rarely able to discuss whatever grievances they may have in public, given the classified nature of their work. And as Dana Priest, the *Washington Post's* correspondent with an intelligence beat, has remarked (2003), the "high walls" of the intelligence agencies make it very difficult to report on intelligence activities. These walls are important to protect the nation's secrets from foreign spies; however, they have the effect, too, of isolating the intelligence agencies from the normal processes of legislative accountability envisioned in the Constitution (Article I), the *Federalist Papers* (e.g., No. 51), and various Supreme Court opinions (among the most famous, Justice Brandeis's comments in *Myers v. U.S.*, 272 U.S. 52 [1926]).

Police patrolling by Congress itself has been minimal, resulting from the lack of motivation by lawmakers in all policy domains, alluded to earlier. Specifically with respect to intelligence, members of Congress made it clear during the early stages of the Cold War that they were content to rely on the intelligence professionals to take care of business, with limited congressional supervision. The House and the Senate maintained small oversight subcommittees on the Armed Services and Appropriations Committees, but they met only infrequently and the questioning was typically brief if not perfunctory. One of the overseers, Leverett Saltonstall (D, Massachusetts), said on the floor of the Senate in 1956 that he was hesitant to "obtain information which I personally would rather not have, unless it was essential for me as a member of Congress to have it. …"(Holt 1995, 211).

Intelligence enjoyed a special dispensation since the days of the American Revolution (Knott 1996). The sense was that secret operations were too sensitive to be treated as normal government activities. The intelligence agencies would have to be kept apart; whether fighting Barbary pirates in the early days or communists during the Cold War, the nation would have to rely on the good intentions and sound judgment of its spymasters and professional intelligence officers.

The results of this "hands off" approach to intelligence supervision are probed here, using the methodologies of archival research, interviews with government officials, and participant observation as a scholar-in-residence on Capitol Hill. Lord Acton's venerable aphorism provides a working hypothesis: "Power corrupts and absolute power corrupts absolutely." To which he might have added, "especially secret power."

AN AWAKENING

In 1974, a pivotal year in American politics, the nation had just withdrawn from the war in Vietnam and the ensuing Watergate scandal produced the first ever resignation of a president, Richard M. Nixon. It was a time of great turmoil and the confidence of Americans in their institutions of government began to plummet. Coming on top of these jarring experiences, the *New York Times* accused the CIA of spying at home.

In December, the newspaper's allegations produced a firestorm of public outrage (Colby 1978). Congressional offices received thousands of letters from citizens across the country. "Watergate might only be a prelude" to an even deeper assault on democracy, worried a constituent from Minnesota—a common theme in these mailings (Mondale 1975). A feeling of anger and dismay spread through the Congress. "To whom are the intelligence agencies responsible?" the fiery orator John Pastore (D, Rhode Island) demanded to know as he introduced a resolution calling for an investigation. On January 21, 1975, senators voted overwhelmingly in support of the resolution (Johnson 1986). The House launched its own inquiry as well, and, not to be left behind, so did the White House under the leadership of President Gerald R. Ford (Smist 1994). If the Orwellian charges were true, something had to be done.

The formal name of the investigative panel created by the Senate was the "Special Select Committee to Investigate Intelligence Activities," known less formally as the "Select Committee on Intelligence" or simply the Church Committee after its chairman, Frank Church (D, Idaho), with whom I served as a special assistant during the 16-month inquiry. A veteran of the Senate (elected at age 32, almost two decades earlier) and an expert on foreign affairs, Church was drawn chiefly to the accusation in the *Times* that dealt with CIA excesses overseas. Most of the others on the eleven-member panel were more

concerned about the charges of domestic spying, particularly the next ranking Democrat Walter F. Mondale (Minnesota). Church asked him to lead a special subcommittee looking into this aspect of the Committee's investigation. The four additional Democrats on the Committee were Philip Hart of Michigan, Walter "Dee" Huddleston of Kentucky, Robert Morgan of North Carolina, and Gary Hart of Colorado. The Republican members included John Tower of Texas, Howard Baker of Tennessee, Barry Goldwater of Arizona, Charles Mathias of Maryland, and Richard Schweiker of Pennsylvania.

The charges of intelligence abuse came as a shock to lawmakers. This is not to say that they were unaware of problems that had cropped up in the intelligence community from time to time. Earlier reports had surfaced that the FBI kept extensive data banks on U.S. citizens, for example, and rumors were rife in the nation's Capitol about the personal files kept by Bureau Director J. Edgar Hoover on government officials, used to "encourage" their support of his programs and budgets (Ungar 1975). Yet, despite occasional revelations about intelligence improprieties (and dismay over the CIA's disastrous Bay of Pigs operation in 1961), no efforts toward reform had managed to gain the support of a majority in either chamber of Congress. Certainly none of the members of Congress serving in 1974 had ever suggested that America's secret agencies might be engaged in widespread spying against the very people they had sworn to protect (although in 1947 a few of their predecessors had expressed fears about this possibility when Congress passed the CIA's founding statute).

The paths of spies and lawmakers had seldom crossed. The FBI enjoyed the most frequent presence on Capitol Hill, having learned early the skills of legislative lobbying. Its officers came across as dedicated, hardworking public servants engaged in catching bank robbers, white-collar criminals, and Soviet spies. The drumbeat message from the Bureau was straightforward: its legitimate law enforcement and counterintelligence duties helped keep thugs, terrorists, and foreign agents at bay and deserved the approbation of the American people (Kessler 2003).

Moreover, lawmakers comforted themselves in the thought that both chambers had intelligence oversight subcommittees within the jurisdictions of the Armed Services and Appropriations Committees. These panels were supposed to monitor the nation's intelligence activities on behalf of the Congress, freeing the vast majority of lawmakers from concern—and culpability (Barrett 1998). Hence, when the allegations of abuse came to light in 1974, the public and their representatives in Washington were taken aback.

MANDATE FOR REFORM

The scope of the Church Committee investigation was staggering. The Senate Watergate Committee had taken over a year to examine just that single event; during the next eight months, Congress expected the Church Committee to probe a multitude of alleged intelligence abuses that had taken place over the past quarter century. Members of the Committee would eventually have to seek an additional eight-month extension to complete their work. As the Committee started up, it confronted one frustration after another, for the executive branch did its best to slow the pace of the inquiry. Compliance with the Committee's documents request would take time, the White House argued; the Committee would have to be patient. It seemed like the same old stonewalling that had plagued the Senate during its Watergate inquiry.

Slowly, however, the Church Committee managed to uncover revealing documents during the summer of 1975 and, at last, was prepared to hold public hearings in September. The initial focus was a master spy plan prepared for President Nixon by a young White House aide from Indiana by the name of Tom Charles Huston. Despite laws to the contrary (not to mention the first amendment to the Constitution), the so-called Huston Plan recommended using the nation's secret agencies to spy on Vietnam War dissenters. Huston and the intelligence chiefs who signed onto the Plan, including DCI Richard Helms and FBI Director Hoover, portrayed the United States as a nation under siege by student radicals. The document revealed, as Mondale observed during the hearings (U.S. Senate 1975), an "enormous, unrestricted paranoid fear about the American people."

The executive branch had concluded, wrongly, that the youthful dissenters were agents of Moscow. As a result, the United States would have to move outside the framework of the Constitution and the law; the legal system had become too confining in the struggle against the Soviet Union, itself unrestrained by a Bill of Rights. The enemy was sinister and lawless, so, the United States would have to become that way, too. Fire would have to be fought

with fire. Yet, as Huston conceded in testimony before the Committee (U.S. Senate 1975), his spy plan raised the risk that the secret agencies would "move from the kid with a bomb to the kid with a picket sign, and from the kid with the picket sign to the kid with the bumper sticker of the opposing candidate. And you just keep going down the line."

The Committee's chief counsel, Frederick A.O. Schwarz, Jr. (grandson of the toy manufacturer) saw this chilling declension as the most important insight to emerge from the inquiry. "Government," he concluded (Schwarz 2000), "is going—inevitably and necessarily, I submit—to keep on going down that line, once it departs from suspected violation of the law as the only legitimate ground to investigate Americans."

The Huston Plan was just the first of many jolts to the Committee as it opened a Pandora's box of wrongdoing. One abuse after another came tumbling out as lawmakers and staff investigators shined a light into the hidden recesses of government (U.S. Senate 1976). Looking over the shoulder of the Church Committee, the American public discovered:

- The FBI had created files on over 1 million Americans and carried out over 500,000 investigations of "subversives" from 1960–74, without a single court conviction.
- NSA computers had monitored every cable sent overseas, or received from overseas, by Americans from 1947–75.
- The Internal Revenue Service had allowed tax information to be misused by intelligence agencies for political purposes.
- FBI agents had conducted a campaign to incite violence among African-Americans.
- An FBI counterintelligence program ("Cointelpro") had harassed civil rights activists and Vietnam war dissidents, in an attempt to fray and often break apart family and friendship ties.

COINTELPRO

Senators on the Church Committee found Cointelpro deeply troubling. With its spying at home (Operation CHAOS), the CIA had also acted in a manner inconsistent with American laws and values; but Cointelpro stunned lawmakers, for it went beyond even domestic spying. Internal Bureau documents revealed that from 1956 to 1971 the FBI had carried out smear campaigns against individuals and groups across the country, simply because they had expressed opposition to the war in Vietnam, criticized the slow pace of the civil rights movement, or (quite the opposite) advocated racial segregation. The attacks were directed against people in all walks of life and of various political persuasions; the expansive hatred of the Bureau's leaders embraced black leaders and white supremacists alike, with critics of the war in Vietnam thrown in for good measure. As Mondale recalled, "no meeting was too small, no group too insignificant" to escape the FBI's attention (2000).

Among the thousands of Cointelpro victims was Dr. Anatol Rapoport, a gifted social scientist at the University of Michigan. He attracted the Bureau's attention because of his criticism of the war in Indochina and his "suspicious" origins (he had been born in Russia shortly before his parents immigrated to America early in the twentieth century). The FBI's agent in charge for the Ann Arbor area, responding to top secret directives from Bureau headquarters, set out to "neutralize" Professor Rapoport—a term used by the FBI to mean the harassment of an individual as a means for curbing his or her dissent. The Bureau mailed anonymous letters to senior administrators at the University, as well as to prominent citizens in Ann Arbor and throughout the state, claiming without a shred of evidence that Rapoport was, if not a communist, then at least an apologist for communism and a troublemaker. The letters were typically signed "a concerned citizen" or "a concerned taxpayer."

The Bureau also placed informants in Rapoport's classrooms to report on his "subversive" activities. He was to be embarrassed, discredited, and spied upon in whatever imaginative ways the FBI's special agent could devise. These pressures, whose underlying source Rapoport never comprehended (Rapoport 1975), eventually led him to resign from the University of Michigan and take up a faculty post at the University of Toronto. The FBI had won. Although he remained a critic of the war in Vietnam, Cointelpro had damaged Rapoport's career, drained him emotionally, strained his family and professional ties, and drove him from this country.

White supremacists also failed to fit into Hoover's Procrustean bed of conformity. The FBI sent another of its poisonous letters, this time written in Southern slang, to a wife of a Ku Klux Klan member, intimating that her husband was having an affair with another woman. The Klan, the women's liberation movement, socialists, the New Left, antiwar and civil

right activists—all became enemies of the Republic whom the Bureau set out secretly to destroy (U.S. Senate 1976). In the Twin Cities, an FBI *agent provocateur* encouraged striking taxi drivers to construct a bomb for use in their battle against local teamsters; in California, a Bureau office boasted in a memorandum back to headquarters:

> Shootings, beatings, and a high degree of unrest continues to prevail in the ghetto area of southeast San Diego. Although no specific counterintelligence action can be credited with contributing to this overall situation, it is felt that a substantial amount of the unrest is directly attributable to this program.

One day in the middle of the Committee's inquiry, a staff aide came across Hoover's "Personal & Confidential" files at FBI Headquarters in Washington, D.C. (Gittenstein 2000). Most of the files had been destroyed by the Director's assistant, Johnny Moore, who started burning the papers in reverse alphabetical order after Hoover died. Moore had gotten to "C" before being discovered and stopped by Bureau officials. In "B" was a file labeled "Black Bag Jobs." It contained documents that proved Hoover had wiretapped Dr. Martin Luther King, Jr., the famed civil rights leader, without the benefit of a court order. When the Church Committee investigator presented lawmakers with this and related papers, even the more sceptical among them began to realize: "My god, Hoover really did these things!"

Soft-spoken, bearded Philip Hart was one of the most influential members of the Committee (one of the Senate's three office buildings is now named after him). His struggle with cancer prevented him from attending most Committee meetings, but he found the strength to come to the opening hearing on the FBI. Hundreds of people filled the ornate Senate Caucus Room, site of famous investigations into the sinking of the Titanic, the Pearl Harbor attack, Joseph McCarthy's witch-hunt, and the recent Watergate scandal. With his frail body bent over the Committee bench, Hart listened intently to testimony from witnesses about Cointelpro. When it came time for him to speak, the cavernous hall fell silent as reporters and tourists strained to hear his weakened voice. He recalled that he had been sceptical when his own family of political activists had complained about how the FBI was trying to discredit opposition to the war in Vietnam. With his words cracking in emotion, Hart conceded that they had been right all along; he had been wrong to defend the Bureau. Not a soul stirred in the Caucus Room as he continued:

> As a result of my superior wisdom in high office, I assured them they are on pot—it just wasn't true. [The FBI] wouldn't do it. What you have described is a series of illegal actions intended to deny certain citizens their first amendment rights, just like my children said.

It was the most poignant moment in the Committee's inquiry.

TARGETING REVEREND KING

Nor were lawmakers apt to forget other key FBI documents unearthed by the Committee. The most shocking to the Committee's members was an anonymous letter written by the Bureau, accompanied by a tape recording. As King travelled around the country, FBI agents had followed him and placed listening devices in his hotel room, recording compromising romantic liaisons. The Bureau then mailed the letter and tape to King in 1964, 34 days before he was to receive the Nobel Prize for Peace. In a ploy interpreted as an attempt by the FBI to push King into taking his own life, the letter read (U.S. Senate 1976):

> King, there is only one thing left for you to do. You know what it is. You have just 34 days in which to do it. (The exact number has been selected for a specific reason.) It has a definite practical significance. You are done. There is but one way out for you. You better take it before your filthy, abnormal fraudulent self is bared to the nation.

A month later, the Bureau sent a copy of the tape recordings to Mrs. King, who joined her husband in denouncing the blackmail attempt.

The goal of wrecking the civil rights movement stood at the heart of Cointelpro and the efforts to ruin Rev. King were relentless. All the elements of the Bureau's dark side came together as it directed its full surveillance powers against him. In tandem with the blackmail attempt, the Bureau initiated whispering campaigns to undermine the moral authority of the civil rights leader, and sent anonymous letters to newspapers that questioned his patriotism. The purpose, according to an FBI document, was to knock King "off his pedestal" (U.S. Senate 1976). Like Professor Rapoport, he would be "neutralized." Hoover pressured his subordinates to either rewrite

their field reports on King, falsely labelling him the pawn of a Soviet agent—or else lose their jobs.

In 1964, the FBI bugged King's hotel suite at the Democratic National Convention, along with rooms occupied by delegates of the Mississippi Freedom Democratic Party, using this information to disrupt civil rights activists at the convention. Further, the Bureau blocked King from receiving honorary degrees, tried unsuccessfully to keep him from meeting with the Pope, planted an attractive female *agent provocateur* on his staff, and supplied friendly reporters with a stream of prurient stories about his private life (U.S. Senate 1976).

The Bureau continued to harass King until his final days. Committee investigators assigned to examine the case brooded darkly about the possibility of a Bureau set up to end the life of the civil rights leader. They wondered if, on a fateful trip to Memphis, King might have been "encouraged" by FBI media leaks to abandon plans to stay in a white-owned hotel and move instead to the less secure, black-owned Lorraine Hotel. The Committee never found any evidence to support this theory, but close associates of the slain civil rights leader continue to harbor suspicions about FBI and local law enforcement complicity in King's assassination (Pepper 2003). Andrew Young, for example, points to the quick removal of potential evidence from the murder scene, even the cutting down of bushes across the street from the Lorraine near the area where the fatal shots were fired (Young 2000). After King's death, when lawmakers began to consider whether his birthday should be made a national holiday, the FBI developed plans to brief selected members of Congress on how to stop the proposal.

During hearings into the King case, Senator Mondale asked the Committee's chief counsel, Schwarz: "Was there any evidence at any time that [the FBI] was suspicious that [Dr. King] was about to or had committed a crime?" The answer was "no." Mondale asked further: "Was he ever charged with fomenting violence? Did he ever participate in violence?" Again the answer was "no." Mondale considered King the nation's greatest civil rights hero, an apostle of non-violence at a time in American history when there were tremendous pressures to use violence. King was a man of the cloth, acting from a deep sense of conviction—only to be treated by the FBI as a common criminal. "There is nothing in this case that distinguishes that particular action from what the KGB does with dissenters in that country [the U.S.S.R.]," he said in disgust during a Committee hearing (U.S. Senate 1976). He concluded: "I think it is a road map to the destruction of American democracy."

Schwarz remembers being "shocked" by the attacks on King:

> Here was a peaceful civil rights leader whom I admired as much as anybody in our history, and the FBI was trying to get him to commit suicide. The bureau called the Southern Christian Leadership Conference a black hate organization. The words were all upside down. (2000)

When the Attorney General in the Ford Administration, Edward H. Levi, former dean of the law school at the University of Chicago, came before the Church Committee, Mondale—who had evolved into the Committee's leading interrogator on matters of domestic intelligence—asked him what he intended to do about cleaning up the FBI mess. The AG's answers were far from what Committee members, most of whom had gone to law school and two of whom (Mondale and Morgan) had served as state attorneys general, expected to hear from the nation's chief law enforcement officer and a noted constitutional scholar. Levi sought unprecedented authority for the Bureau to act against a group or individual, before a crime was committed—the same slippery slope that had led to Cointelpro in the first place. He seemed to have forgotten that the job of the FBI was to focus on actual or suspected violations of the law, not just the expression of ideas. Levi had assumed the role of the Bureau's protector, while Mondale had taken on the role of the Committee's leading defender of civil liberties. A collision was inevitable.

Mondale suggested to the AG that his guidelines were "vaguely defined" and that, if they were not strengthened and codified into law, they "would be swept away as quickly as a sand castle is overrun by a hurricane" (U.S. Senate 1976). The temperature in the Senate Caucus Room rose as the two men confronted each other across the green-baize hearing table. When Levi resorted to an evasive answer, Mondale stared at him and said, "Well, I think that kind of arrogance is why we have trouble between the executive and the legislative branch." Levi replied, "I apologize to Senator Mondale if I appeared arrogant. I thought that someone else was appearing arrogant, but I apologize."

Mondale had put the AG on notice: the Committee was not going to be a push over; it would strenuously defend the liberties of American citizens. Despite this public confrontation, Mondale and Levi soon met privately and placed behind them any bad feelings, agreeing to work together in the crafting of FBI guidelines that would be acceptable both to the Committee and to the Justice Department. It was an important turning point in the investigation that led to constructive negotiations between the branches over proper guidelines for Bureau activities.

A WIDENING GYRE OF ABUSE

As the investigation unfolded, the Church Committee discovered just how far the violations of public trust had extended to the CIA and military intelligence units as well. For instance:

- The CIA had opened the mail to and from selected American citizens, which generated 1.5 million names stored in the Agency's computer bank (Operation CHAOS). No one was immune, not Leonard Bernstein, not John Steinbeck, not Arthur Burns; even Richard Nixon had made the CIA's "watch list."
- Army intelligence units had conducted investigations against 100,000 U.S. citizens during the Vietnam war era.
- The CIA had engaged in drug experiments against unsuspecting subjects, two of whom had died from side effects.
- The CIA had manipulated elections even in democratic regimes like Chile.
- The CIA had infiltrated religious, media, and academic organizations inside the United States.
- The CIA had plotted failed assassination attempts against Fidel Castro of Cuba and Patrice Lumumba, among other foreign leaders.

The CIA's assassination plots and drug experiments were as unacceptable to the Church Committee as the FBI's Cointelpro operations had been. The CIA had even resorted to the recruitment of mafia mobsters to assist in the plots against Castro.

In Joseph Conrad's *Heart of Darkness*, the protagonist Marlow discovers in the jungles of central Africa the savagery that had befallen upon his once civilized companion, Mr. Kurtz. Isolated in a primitive setting, Kurtz had succumbed to a steady moral deterioration. In the last hours of his life, he peered into his own soul and, confronting the decay, cried out in despair: "The horror! The horror!" The allegory suited the secret agencies. Removed from the rest of democratic society, they had descended into a primordial underworld, using methods deemed necessary to combat foreign enemies, then turning these dark arts against citizens at home whose only crime had been to express beliefs that the White House or the intelligence chiefs found objectionable. In this crusade, the secret agencies had adopted some of the tactics of the repressive regimes they opposed. To argue that the United States had to abandon liberty in the name of security was to say that the nation had to become more like its enemies in order to protect itself from them—a pernicious doctrine that the Committee rejected out of hand.

How could the intelligence community have strayed so far from its rightful duties and into this heart of darkness? The answer stemmed in part from the paranoia engendered by the Cold War, even though—as acknowledged by William Sullivan (1975), the top FBI agent in charge of Cointelpro—there were not enough communists in the United States to carry the smallest precinct in New Hampshire, let alone take over the country. Sullivan told the Committee that the secret agencies had been caught up in an anti-communist tide that swept aside safeguards against the misuse of power (just as, today, a war against global terrorism in the wake of the 9/11 attacks against the United States holds the danger of eroding civil liberties at home, especially for law-abiding Arab-Americans). As Sullivan recalled, during the FBI's operations against Rev. King,

> No holds were barred. We have used [similar] techniques against Soviet agents. [The same methods were] brought home against any organization against which we were targeted. We did not differentiate. This is a rough, tough business. (U.S. Senate 1976)

He added that never once had he heard a discussion about the legality or constitutionality of any aspect of the FBI's internal security program. His explanation: "We were just naturally pragmatic."

During the Committee's public hearings on the NSA and its interception of cables sent to and from U.S. citizens (Operation SHAMROCK), a revealing exchange took place between Senator Mondale and the NSA's deputy director, Benson Buffham (U.S. Senate 1975):

MONDALE: Were you concerned about its legality?
BUFFHAM: Legality?
MONDALE: Whether it was legal.
BUFFHAM: In what sense? Whether that would have been a legal thing to do?

MONDALE: Yes.
BUFFHAM: That particular aspect didn't enter into the discussion.
MONDALE: I was asking you if you were concerned about whether that would be legal and proper.
BUFFHAM: We didn't consider it at the time, no.

It was a response echoed by other agency representatives during the hearings. One of the Committee members asked Clark Clifford, who had helped to draft the charter for the CIA in 1947 and served as secretary of defense during the Johnson Administration, about constitutional protections against abuses. He replied, "Well, that was a different time when we could afford that."

Criticism of the intelligence agencies was widely considered unpatriotic. They had to be given broad discretionary powers if they were to be successful in subduing America's adversaries at home and abroad. As a consequence, the secret agencies took on the features of a political police, growing increasingly autonomous, insulated, and aggressive. As William W. Keller has written (1989, 154), the intelligence community became "a state within the state, which would not be bound by the constraints of the constitutional order."

Responsibility for the abuses did not fall on the intelligence community alone. Presidents of both parties used the secret agencies to spy on political adversaries. Lawmakers were derelict, as well, for permitting the growth of an inadequately supervised security state. Intelligence scholar Harry Howe Ransom has drawn the proper conclusion (1984, 21): the Congress had become "a sleeping watchdog." James R. Schlesinger, DCI in 1973, remembers his initial briefing to the small Senate oversight subcommittee of that day (1993). As he began his briefing, John Stennis (D, Mississippi) interrupted the DCI: "No, no my boy, don't tell me. Just go ahead and do it, but I don't want to know."

William Sullivan of the FBI testified about another influence that contributed to the lawlessness that gripped the intelligence agencies (U.S. Senate 1976). "During World War Two, we had grown up topsy-turvy," he said, "when legal matters were secondary to achieving victory against the Nazis. This mentality carried over easily into the new war against the communists." During the course of its inquiry, the Committee came across a telling top secret document that had been prepared for President Dwight D. Eisenhower (U.S. Senate 1976, 9). A key passage advised that in the war against communism:

...hitherto acceptable norms of human conduct do not apply. If the U.S. is to survive, long-standing American concepts of "fair play" must be reconsidered...we must learn to subvert, sabotage, and destroy our enemies by more clear, more sophisticated and more effective methods than those used against us.

The underlying philosophy reminded Schwarz (2000), the Committee counsel, of Macbeth's words: inevitably, the invention returns home "to plague the inventor."

The FBI's skillful lobbying of lawmakers further warded off serious oversight. So did its clever promotion of a favorable public relations image, as with the television show *The FBI Story*, which starred the dashing actor Efrem Zimbalist, Jr. The FBI censored the program's scripts and CBS beamed the program into millions of living rooms each week during the 1960s. Self-promotion helped the Bureau gain remarkable popularity and independence, free from congressional probes and detailed laws to guide its activities (Ungar 1975).

Hannah Arendt's ever lingering "banality of evil" (1973) entered the picture, too. When asked by the Committee how he could have brought himself to participate in the Cointelpro operations, William Sullivan replied (U.S. Senate 1976):

I was so inured and accustomed to any damn thing I was told to do, I just carried it out and kept my resentment to myself. I was married and trying to buy a house with a big mortgage and raise a family.

The Church Committee came to the conclusion that the overwhelming majority of the men and women in the nation's intelligence agencies had consistently carried out their assignments with integrity and devotion to the law and constitutional principles. Some had given their lives in the defense of liberty. America owed its freedom in part to their dedication in the struggle against those who wish to harm the United States. Yet some intelligence officers had clearly overstepped the boundaries of law and propriety, and the Committee felt impelled to adopt measures that would help protect citizens against future abuses.

STEPS TOWARD REFORM

The initial congressional response to the CIA's domestic spying was to pass the Hughes-Ryan Act on December 31, 1974 (22 U.S.C. 2422). This statute, which marks the beginning of the new era of intelligence accountability, required the president to review and authorize (in a "finding") every important CIA covert action, then report to Congress on those he had approved. Prior to the Hughes-Ryan law, pinning down responsibility for covert action was, observed Mondale during the Church Committee inquiry, "like nailing jello to a wall." With this statute in place, there would be no more plausible denial; no more vanishing paper trails. It was the first attempt since the creation of the CIA to place meaningful limits on its activities.

The Congress then began its formal investigations, with probes by the Church Committee in the Senate and the Pike Committee in the House (led by Otis Pike, D, New York, and concentrating on the quality of intelligence reporting, as opposed to the Church Committee focus on charges of abuse). Along with the inquiry conducted by the White House (the Rockefeller Commission, led by Vice President Nelson Rockefeller), the congressional committees did much to educate the American people on the importance of more meaningful intelligence supervision.

In May 1976, the Church Committee presented 96 proposals for reform of domestic intelligence alone, many of which were adopted by the Congress. The most significant, affecting both domestic and foreign intelligence, was the creation of a permanent Senate Select Committee on Intelligence (SSCI). As Mondale noted at the time (1976), "If there is one lesson that our Committee felt above all must be learned from our study of the abuses which have been reported, it has been the crucial necessity of establishing a system of congressional oversight." The Senate had put into place a potentially effective standing committee, equipped with a large and experienced professional staff, devoted to monitoring the secret agencies day-by-day and reviewing their programs and budgets with a fine-tooth comb.

The creation of an intelligence oversight committee in the Senate was not an easy task, opposed as it was by the White House, the intelligence agencies, and even a few members of the Church Committee on the Republican side (Tower, Goldwater, and Baker). In floor debate on the proposal, Church and Mondale stressed the necessity of providing the new committee with annual budget authorization, realizing that without the power of the purse as leverage over the intelligence community no form of accountability would succeed. Opponents introduced a number of weakening amendments; but, one-by-one, they were defeated and on May 19, 1976, by a vote of 72 to 18, the Senate created the new intelligence oversight committee. It was a remarkable achievement. Institutional inertia normally carries the day in the Congress, yet the Church Committee had been able to bring about a major power shift. Responsibility for supervision of the intelligence agencies would be largely removed from the jurisdiction of the Armed Services Committee and given the closer attention it warranted.

Not to be left behind, President Ford set up an Intelligence Oversight Board (IOB) in the White House in 1976, and (also by executive order in the same year) he prohibited further assassination plots against foreign leaders. In 1977, the House established an intelligence oversight committee of its own, patterned after the Senate model and designated the House Permanent Select Committee on Intelligence (HPSCI).

Many of the reforms advanced by the Church Committee and eventually adopted were of a technical nature, dealing with FBI investigative methods and how they should be employed without violating the civil liberties of American citizens. Others were broader, including the recommendation that the CIA clarify and sharply limit its ties to U.S. journalists. The Committee proposed a single eight-year term limit on the directorship of the FBI; no more imperial czars like Hoover, who served an incredible forty-eight years in that capacity. The Congress eventually settled on a ten-year term. The Committee recommended as well that the Office of Professional Responsibility (OPR), established in reaction to the Watergate scandal, be given legal status, thereby providing it firmer footing to probe allegations of abuse inside the intelligence agencies. During the Carter Administration, the President bestowed upon Vice President Walter Mondale extensive responsibilities over intelligence issues, especially with respect to the FBI and domestic intelligence matters. In turn, Mondale and the new AG, Griffin Bell of Georgia, relied upon OPR to oversee intelligence activities (Mondale 2000; Bell 1982). The attorneys in OPR were expected to investigate fully any allegations of intelligence misconduct, reporting their findings and conclusions to the Vice President and the AG.

Since the Carter years OPR has been less actively involved in intelligence oversight, as its responsibilities broadened to investigate charges of misconduct across the policy board. Its attorneys are expected as well as to represent the government in litigation and to provide legal advice to the AG, which places OPR

in a "precarious position in the Justice Department because it threatens the prerogatives of the prosecuting divisions. ..." (Elliff 1979). Contributing to OPR's demise as a vigorous intelligence overseer has been the fact that no president and or vice president since the Carter years have been as focused on questions of intelligence accountability as were Jimmy Carter and Walter Mondale. The creation of an inspector general at the Department of Justice has further diminished the influence of OPR. Nevertheless, the Office has played a useful mediating role at times between the FBI and the prosecuting divisions in the Justice Department (Elliff 1979, 169); and it has conducted some important investigations into charges of wrongdoing in the Department, including an inquiry into alleged financial improprieties by FBI Director William Sessions during the Reagan Administration (Kessler 2002, 277–283).

The Church Committee also proposed that all non-consensual electronic surveillance, mail-opening, and unauthorized entries be conducted only with the authority of a judicial warrant, instead of allowing the White House and the intelligence agencies to use such invasive tools at their own discretion. Further, the Committee stressed that the threshold for FBI investigations should be sufficiently high to ensure that only groups with a record of violence would be targeted for intelligence gathering; and the Committee took a strong stand, in addition, against the conduct of intelligence operations inside the United States by the CIA or any other foreign-oriented component of the intelligence community. In 1978, as urged by the Church Committee, Congress passed the Foreign Intelligence Surveillance Act (FISA; 50 U.S.C. 1801–1811), which provided for a special FISA court to review wiretap requests. The third branch of government, too, was now firmly in the business of intelligence oversight.

THE LEGACY OF THE CHURCH COMMITTEE

Soon after the investigation, historian Henry Steele Commager observed (1976, 32) that the indifference of the intelligence agencies to constitutional restraint was "perhaps the most threatening of all the evidence that [emerged] from the findings of the Church Committee." The inquiry was able to focus citizen awareness on this threat, creating a foundation of public support indispensable for the reform measures subsequently adopted by Congress and the executive branch. Legislators laid out the facts for the American people—a difficult and important duty in itself—about the extent of lawlessness that had overtaken the secret agencies. The Committee was unable to plumb to the depths of every intelligence abuse; it did not have time enough. Rather it laid out key findings that pointed to a pattern of wrongdoing, without trying to probe every specific allegation. This public airing proved thorough enough to bring about a sea change in attitudes throughout the intelligence community.

The Committee's central conclusion was clear and important: the law works. In every case where the secret agencies had violated the law, the Committee demonstrated how U.S. security objectives could have been achieved through legal means. As the Committee emphasized, security and liberty were compatible values in a democracy; it was possible to defend the nation without becoming a police state. Thoughtful intelligence officers began to understand how the unlawful activities of their agencies had actually interfered with the nation's legitimate intelligence and counterintelligence duties.

The Committee made it clear as well that the principle of accountability was valid even with respect to the hidden side of government—indeed, there most especially. The Senate and House intelligence oversight committees would now stand guard as watchmen to America's civil liberties, replacing the small and ineffectual subcommittees that the nation had relied upon before, only to see fail. Today as the nation's spymasters plan their secret operations, they must take into account the likely reactions of two full committees of elected representatives. This new relationship has strengthened the intelligence community by better defining its limits and responsibilities, and by tying the secret agencies closer to the values and beliefs of the American people and their surrogates in Congress. The resulting higher level of professionalism among the intelligence agencies has helped to restore public confidence and respect in their activities, a primary objective of the Church Committee.

The Committee conveyed to the American people that the Senate would stand up for their constitutional rights. "'We can't slide back into the days of J. Edgar Hoover'—that was the message delivered by the Committee through its promulgation of guidelines and recommendations," recalls John Elliff, the Committee's top staff aide for the FBI side of the inquiry (2000). William E. Colby, DCI during the investigation, wrote afterward that the Church Committee had shed light on the boundaries "within which [the intelligence community]

should, and should not, operate" (1976, 11). The current DCI, George Tenet, himself a former SSCI staff director, has similarly stated that the new oversight procedures represent "...our most vital and direct link to the American people—a source of strength that separates us from all other countries of the world" (1997).

DISCUSSION AND CONCLUSION

The importance of establishing intelligence oversight committees in the Senate and the House cannot be overemphasized. The protection of freedom requires daily attention; someone has to be continuously on guard. That "someone" in the world of intelligence now includes two permanent, well-staffed committees that concentrate exclusively on intelligence activities, not (as earlier) small, feckless subcommittees that occasionally reviewed the nation's secret operations as an adjunct to their principal duties. Robert M. Gates, a career intelligence officer and DCI under the first President Bush, has come to this conclusion about the new era of intelligence oversight (1997, 559):

> ...some awfully crazy schemes might well have been approved had everyone present not known and expected hard questions, debate, and criticism from the Hill. And when, on a few occasions, Congress was kept in the dark, and such schemes did proceed, it was nearly always to the lasting regret of the presidents involved.

Here was the most vital result of the Church Committee's work: the establishment of safeguards to ensure that lawmakers are able to provide a check against abuses by the secret, not just the more open, agencies of government. This is not to say that the Church Committee created a fool-proof system of intelligence accountability. The Iran-*contra* affair of 1986–87 served as a reminder that even robust legislative safeguards are no guarantee against the misuse of power by determined conspirators in the executive branch (Cohen and Mitchell 1988). That scandal led to a further tightening of oversight procedures, however, including the creation of a CIA Office of Inspector General directly answerable to Congress (Kaiser 1994; Currie 1998).

The best assurance against future abuse lies, as the ancient philosophers realized, in the selection of individuals of the highest integrity for positions of power. Then, lawmakers and their staff on the oversight committees must maintain close watch over intelligence budgets and programs, posing detailed questions in hearings and probing fearlessly into any activities that seem untoward. Outside the executive branch, only Congress has the authority to insist on access to intelligence documents and testimony; if elected representatives lapse into complacency, the secret agencies will again drift toward autonomy and the arrogance that isolation breeds.

Even now there are signs that some have failed to learn this lesson of American democracy. A senior official in the Association of Retired Intelligence Officers opined in the wake of Iran-*contra* that those who had lied to legislators during that affair were right to have done so, since sensitive intelligence operations are none of Congress's business (cited in Turner 1991). In 1994, Senate overseers learned that the National Reconnaissance Office (NRO, a component of the intelligence community that builds and manages spy satellites) had run up $159 million in cost overruns for the construction of its new headquarters in Virginia, without properly informing lawmakers (*New York Times* 1994); and, in 1995, the CIA failed to report, as required by law, on its questionable ties to a suspected murderer in the Guatemalan military (*New York Times* 1996). Just in the past two years, DCI Tenet resisted a probe by lawmakers on a special Senate-House Joint Committee of Intelligence into the failure of the intelligence community to warn the nation of the 9/11 attacks (see, e.g., Lewis 2002). The second Bush White House has stonewalled efforts by a commission to further investigate this subject and related weaknesses in U.S. security (Johnson 2003).

This backsliding emphasizes the need for renewed attention to the question of intelligence accountability. Still, these episodes notwithstanding, the safeguards set up by the Church Committee and the Ford Administration in 1976 have endured and, on most occasions, they have brought greater sobriety to the conduct of intelligence operations at home and abroad. Someone beyond the walls of the secret agencies is now steadily watching their activities; would be violators of the public trust know they might be caught—a vital check on abuse.

This nation must have strong and effective intelligence agencies; America's security depends on it. Yet that power has to remain within the framework of the Constitution, not relegated to some dark outside realm. This is all the more true in an age where the methods of spying are far more sophisticated than in the era of J. Edgar Hoover. Breaches of faith will occur again; such is the nature of the human condition. It is imperative, however, that responsible

officials remain ever vigilant in their protection of lawful political activities, ensuring that citizens do not become the target of secret intimidation by the intelligence community. The constitutional right to free expression must remain the lynchpin of American democracy.

With the safeguards established in 1976, citizens of the United States are far less likely to suffer abuse at the hands of the secret agencies than during the earlier years of benign neglect. The effectiveness of the safeguards will continue to depend on the resolve of lawmakers to carry out their duties of accountability with fresh resolve, with a willingness to engage in day-to-day "police patrolling," and with a determination to preserve liberty at home even in the face of global terrorism.

QUESTIONS FOR FURTHER DISCUSSION

1. What triggered the Church Committee investigation in 1975?
2. What were the strengths and weaknesses of the Church Committee inquiry?
3. How has intelligence in the United States changed as a result of the Church Committee's probe?
4. What do you make of the argument that the Church Committee weakened American intelligence and made the nation vulnerable to the intelligence mistakes that were made in 2001 (9/11) and 2003 (Iraq)?

REFERENCES

Aberbach, Joel D. 1990. *Keeping a Watchful Eye: The Politics of Congressional Oversight*. Washington, D.C.: The Brookings Institution.

Arendt, Hannah. 1973. *The Origins of Totalitarianism*. New York: Harcourt.

Barrett, David M. 1998. Glimpses of a Hidden History: Sen. Richard Russell, Congress and Early Oversight of the CIA. *International Journal of Intelligence and Counterintelligence* 11 (3): 271–99.

Bell, Griffin B., with Ronald J. Astrow. 1982. *Taking Care of the Law*. New York: Morrow.

Bibby, John F. 1968. Congress' Neglected Function. In *The Republican Papers*, edited by Melvin R. Laird, 477–488. New York: Anchor.

Calvert, Randall, Mathew D. McCubbins, and Barry R. Weingast. 1989. A Theory of Political Control and Agency Discretion. *American Journal of Political Science* 33 (3): 588–611.

Cohen, William S., and George J. Mitchell. 1988. *Men of Zeal: A Candid Inside Story of the Iran-Contra Hearings*. New York: Viking.

Colby, William E. 1976. After Investigating U.S. Intelligence. *New York Times*, February 26.

———. with Peter Forbath. 1978. *Honorable Men*. New York: Simon and Schuster.

Commager, Henry Steele. 1976. *Intelligence: The Constitution Betrayed*. New York Review of Books, September 30.

Currie, James. 1998. Iran-Contra and Congressional Oversight of the CIA. *International Journal of Intelligence and Counterintelligence* 11 (2): 185–210.

Dodd, Lawrence, and Richard Schott. 1979. *Congress and the Administrative State*. New York: Wiley.

Elliff, John T. 1979. *The Reform of FBI Intelligence Operations*. Princeton: Princeton University Press.

———. 2000. Author's telephone interview: April 14.

Gates, Robert M. 1997. *From the Shadows*. New York: Simon and Schuster.

Gittenstein, Mark. 2000. Author's telephone interview: April 14.

Holt, Pat M. 1995. *Secret Intelligence and Public Policy*. Washington, D.C.: CQ Press.

Johnson, Loch K. 1986. *A Season of Inquiry*. Lexington: University Press of Kentucky.

———. 1994. Playing Ball with the CIA: Congress Supervises Strategic Intelligence. In *Congress, the Executive, and the Making of American Foreign Policy*, edited by Paul E. Peterson, 49–73. Norman: University of Oklahoma Press.

———. 2000. *Bombs, Bugs, Drugs, and Thugs: Intelligence and America's Quest for Security*. New York: New York University Press.

———. 2003. Author's interviews with members and staff of the Kean Commission, Washington, D.C.: January–March.

Kaiser, Frederick M. 1994. Impact and Implications of the Iran-contra Affair on Congressional Oversight of Covert Action. *International Journal of Intelligence and Counterintelligence* 7 (2): 205–234.

Keller, William W. 1989. *Liberals and J. Edgar Hoover: Rise and Fall of a Domestic Intelligence State*. Princeton: Princeton University Press.

Kessler, Ronald. 2003. *The Bureau: The Secret History of the FBI*. New York: St. Martin's.

Knott, Stephen F. 1996. *Secret and Sanctioned: Covert Operations and the American Presidency*. New York: Oxford University Press.

Lewis, Neil. 2002. Senator Insists C.I.A. Is Harboring Iraq Reports. *New York Times*, October 4.

Lowenthal, Mark. 1992. *U.S. Intelligence: Evolution and Anatomy*, 2nd edition. Washington, D.C.: Center for Strategic and International Studies.

Mayhew, David. 1986. *The Electoral Connection*. New Haven: Yale University Press.

McCubbins, Mathew D., and Thomas Schwartz. 1984. Congressional Oversight Overlooked: Police Patrols and Fire Alarms. *American Journal of Political Science* 28 (1): 165–179.

———. Roger G. Noll, and Barry R. Weingast. 1989. Structure and Process, Politics and Policy: Administrative Arrangements and the Political Control of Agencies. *Virginia Law Review* 75 (3): 431–482.

Mondale, Walter F. 1975. Personal archives. (Church Committee), Minneapolis.

———. 1976. Personal archives (Church Committee), Minneapolis.

———. 2000. Author's interview, Minneapolis: February 17. *New York Times*. 1994. Unsigned editorial, May 19.

———. 1996. Unsigned editorial, August 18.

Ogul, Morris S. 1976. *Congress Oversees the Bureaucracy: Studies in Legislative Supervision*. Pittsburgh: University of Pittsburgh Press.

Pepper, William F. 2003. *An Act of State*. Verso, London.

Priest, Dana. 2003. Remarks, Panel on Congress, Intelligence and Secrecy During War, Woodrow Wilson Center, May 9, Washington, D.C.

Ransom, Harry Howe. 1970. *The Intelligence Establishment*. Cambridge: Harvard University Press.

———. 1975. Secret Intelligence Agencies and Congress. *Society* 123(2): 33–38.

———. 1977. Congress and the Intelligence Agencies. In *Congress Against the President*, edited by Harvey C. Mansfield, 153–166. New York: Praeger.

———. 1984. CIA Accountability: Congress As Temperamental Watchdog. Paper, American Political Science Association Annual Convention, September 1, Washington, D.C.

Rapoport, Anatole. 1975. Author's interview, Toronto: September 21.

Richelson, Jeffrey T. 1999. *The U.S. Intelligence Community*, 4th edition. Boulder; Westview Press.

Scher, Seymour. 1963. Conditions for Legislative Control. *Journal of Politics* 25 (3): 526–551.

Schlesinger, James R. 1994. Author's interview, Washington, D.C.: June 16.

Schwarz, Frederick A. O., Jr. 2000. Author's interview, New York City: April 27.

Smist, Frank, Jr. 1994. *Congress Oversees the United States Intelligence Community*, 2nd ed. Knoxville: University of Tennessee Press.

Spence, David. 1997. Agency Policy Making and Political Control: Modeling Away the Delegation Problem. *Journal of Public Administration Research and* Theory 7 (2): 199–219.

Sullivan, William. 1975. Author's interview, Boston: September 21.

Tenet, George. 1997. Remarks, Panel on Does America Need the CIA? Gerald R. Ford Library, November 19, Ann Arbor, Michigan.

Turner, Stansfield. 1991. Purge the C.I.A. of K.G.B. Types. *New York Times*, October 2.

Ungar, Sanford. 1975. *FBI.* Boston: Atlantic Monthly Press.

U.S. Congress. 1987. Report on the Iran-*Contra* Affair. *Senate Select Committee on Secret Military Assistance to Iran and the Nicaragua Opposition and House Select Committee to Investigate Covert Arms Transactions with Iran.* S. Rept. 100–216 and H. Rept 100–433, November.

U.S. Senate. 1975. Hearings. *Select Committee to Study Governmental Operations with Respect to Intelligence Activities* (Church Committee), 94th Cong., 2d. Sess., September–December.

———. 1976. Final Report. *Select Committee to Study Governmental Operations with Respect to Intelligence Activities* (Church Committee). S. Rept. 94–755, 95th Cong., 1st. Sess., May.

Walden, Jerrold L. 1970. The C.I.A.: A Study in the Arrogation of Administrative Power. *George Washington Law Review* 39 (3): 66–101.

Young, Andrew. 2000. Author's interview, Minneapolis: June 6.

32. WARRANTLESS WIRETAPS

YALE UNIVERSITY SCHOOL OF LAW SYMPOSIUM (ALAN DERSHOWITZ, SENATOR CONRAD BURNS, JOHN J. DONOHUE, DAVID B. RIVKIN, JR., DAKOTA RUDESILL, STEPHEN A. VADEN, AND LOCH K. JOHNSON)

In 2005, the New York Times revealed the existence of a warrantless wiretapping program adopted by the second Bush Administration in the struggle against global terrorism. Opponents of the program argued that it violated the Foreign Intelligence Surveillance Act (FISA) of 1978, which set in place a formal legal requirement for all wiretaps and other surveillance used by the federal government for intelligence-gathering purposes. Supporters countered with the argument that in times of emergency, as currently faced by the United States, bypassing FISA had become necessary for the nation's security. Yale University's School of Law assembled some experts to discuss the pros and cons of these arguments, and their conclusions are presented in this selection.

A STICK WITH TWO ENDS

ALAN DERSHOWITZ

Civil libertarians shouldn't be afraid of technology. First, there is no way to stop it. Second, there is almost always a way of using technology to enhance civil liberties. Third, civil liberties always require the striking of an appropriate balance between freedom and security. Technology is, to paraphrase Dostoyevsky, a stick with two ends.

The recent disclosure of a massive data "mining" program being conducted by the NSA raises the most profound concerns about how to strike the appropriate balance. Surely it does not require that we ignore or discard a significant breakthrough in our ability to catch the bad guys before they blow us up. We should figure out a way of cabining this useful technology within the rule of law. This is a daunting task, because the technology does not fit neatly into our existing constitutional structure.

The Fourth Amendment reads as follows:

The right of the people to be secure in their persons, houses, papers, and effects, against unreasonable searches and seizures, shall not be violated, and no Warrants shall issue, but upon probable cause, supported by Oath or affirmation, and particularly describing the place to be searched, and the persons or things to be seized.

Plainly, its language and history presuppose retail intrusions on individuals based on particularized probable cause or reasonableness. It was written for the technology of a time in which eavesdropping, mail openings and general searches were the feared intrusions. When electronic wiretapping was developed, the Supreme Court held that wiretaps must be conducted pursuant to search warrants and that the warrants must be based on probable cause. Moreover, the intrusion must be subjected to what is called a "minimization" requirement, under which only those portions of a conversation which are relevant to criminal conduct can appropriately be monitored. In 1978 Congress enacted the Foreign Intelligence Surveillance Act (FISA) to regulate the government's collection of "foreign intelligence" information in furtherance of U.S. counterintelligence. FISA has been broadened since 1978, but it still requires a showing—in advance if possible and after-the-fact if necessary—of particularized cause against individuals. It also requires careful recordkeeping that permits subsequent oversight and accountability. Although the FISA court has only rarely denied requests for national security wiretaps, the very existence of this court and the requirement of sworn justification serves as a check on the improper use of the powerful and intrusive technologies that are permitted in national security cases.

But what the National Security Agency is now doing is a far cry from retail intrusions based on individualized probable cause. According to the *New York Times*, the Bush Administration decided to bypass the FISA warrant process in order to "monitor the international telephone calls and international e-mail messages of hundreds, perhaps thousands, of people inside the United States without warrants over the past three years." The so-called "special collection program" is reported to have expanded in scope so quickly that, at any given time, around 500 Americans' phone and e-mail communications are being recorded. Surveillance of communications between "foreign powers" and "U.S. persons" used to be conducted by the FBI and based on individualized suspicion. The Administration now appears to be focused on the NSA-directed "data mining" of massive amounts of computer-recorded conversations and correspondences. This change is part of a general shift in priorities from after-the-crime deterrence to before-the-terrorism preemption.

The major problems with the NSA program are that we don't know what we don't know and that there is no accountability or external check on what is being done. We were made aware of the program by a *New York Times* report that acknowledged that it was withholding some information. There is almost certainly some additional information that the *Times* did not succeed in learning. Moreover, there may be other technologies and actions that are currently in use of which we're simply unaware.

Although we are assured by the administration that the NSA program is targeting only terrorists and those who talk to or work with them, we have no way of knowing that this is always the case. Remember that Richard Nixon tried to use the excuse of national security to spy on his political opponents. Nor was Nixon alone. Even the Kennedy administration authorized the bugging of Martin Luther King's hotel rooms. And the current administration has taken the position that classified national security information can be leaked in order to discredit a political opponent.

At the very least, the FISA law should be amended to require sworn justifications for the monitoring of any conversation or communication involving a citizen or permanent resident. It should also require precise recordkeeping, Congressional oversight and periodic public disclosure of the kind of general information that does not endanger national security but that does provide a basis for cost-benefit

analysis. Finally, it should define the criteria for different levels of intrusion.

Some have wondered why I have been less of an absolutist about certain rights than other civil libertarians following the attacks of 9/11. There are several reasons. First, I eschew all absolutism, even with regard to civil liberties and human rights. As I have written elsewhere, I do not believe rights come from God, nature or any other external source. Rights are not "out there" waiting to be discovered. They are human inventions that grow out of human experiences. In a word, rights come from wrongs—from a recognition of past human mistakes or evils and a determination not to repeat them. Second, among the greatest threats to civil liberties is terrorism itself. Were the United States to become victim to another large scale, mass casualty terrorist attack—especially one involving biological, chemical or nuclear weapons—the first casualty would likely be civil liberties. It is therefore in the interest of civil libertarians to encourage lawful, smart, proportional and moral technologies and actions that hold promise of reducing the likelihood of terrorist attacks, so long as these technologies and steps are consistent with essential liberties.

I agree with Benjamin Franklin's oft quoted, but largely misunderstood, dictum: "They that can give up essential liberty to obtain a little temporary safety deserve neither liberty nor safety." The key words, often deemphasized by those who invoke Franklin, are "essential liberty" and "a little temporary safety." Some liberties are more essential than others. Freedom of expression and dissent, for example, may be more essential to democracy than freedom to bear arms or to refuse to disclose one's identity when entering a public building. All liberty is a matter of degree, as is all safety. The essence of a democracy is to strike the appropriate balance, rather than to set up a clash of absolutes. This balance requires an assessment of the kind and degree of intrusions on liberty as well as assessment of the kind, degree, likelihood, and proximity of the danger sought to be prevented. It also requires a consideration of alternative means of reducing the feared danger. The feel of freedom should never be lost. Nor should the right to dissent ever be diminished.

Applying these criteria to the NSA program leads me to express the cautious conclusion that we should continue to employ and develop sophisticated technologies to secure information that could help us preempt terrorist attacks, but that we must take steps to construct a jurisprudence, grounded in the values of the Fourth Amendment, that strikes the appropriate balance between liberty and security. We have barely begun this daunting task.

TERRORISM SURVEILLANCE CRITICAL (WITH OVERSIGHT)

SENATOR CONRAD BURNS

All Americans should be outraged that the existence of the Terrorism Surveillance program was irresponsibly leaked to the *New York Times*. There's a reason our efforts in the Global War on Terror are classified—we cannot afford to advertise to terrorists our sources and methods. I believe the leak of this program is a direct threat to our national security and must be thoroughly investigated and prosecuted to the fullest extent.

First, this leak of national security information has made us vulnerable as a nation. Gathered intelligence indicates that Osama bin Laden stopped using satellite phones once he learned that we were listening to his communications. CIA Director Porter Goss, in a recent *Washington Post* editorial, called the leak "one of the most egregious examples of an unauthorized criminal disclosure of classified national defense information in recent years." As Goss said, "the bin Laden phone went silent" and now that the NSA Terrorist Surveillance program has been leaked, this tool is measurably less useful than before its exposure.

Second, I believe, from what I know right now, this program is absolutely critical to our national security, entirely reasonable, and must not be interrupted. In any war, collecting intelligence regarding your enemy's operations is necessary and, as such, is consistent with our efforts in both World Wars. I've been in many intelligence and defense briefings in my 18 years in the Senate, and the threat we face today is unlike any other in the history of the world. We must use all of the available technological advances that we possess in our arsenal.

Third, I agree with the President that if anyone inside America is communicating with an al Qaeda agent or suspected foreign terrorist, we have a responsibility to use that information to protect Americans. This program is not neighbors spying on neighbors. One party to the call must be outside the U.S. and one party must be a suspected terrorist. No exceptions.

I believe these are points all Americans and the Congress can agree on.

The Foreign Intelligence Surveillance Act (FISA) was not intended for the 21st century methods and tactics used by our terrorist enemies. Every president since Carter has utilized statutory authority and affirmative court decisions to operate outside FISA's jurisdiction. In a *Chicago Tribune* editorial, John Schmidt, a former Associate Attorney General under President Clinton, said "Bush's authorization (of) NSA electronic surveillance into phone calls and emails is consistent with court decisions and positions of the Justice Department under prior presidents."

In 2002, the FISA court ruled in the case of *U.S. v. Truong* that a federal "court, as did all other courts to have decided the issue, held that the President did have inherent authority to conduct warrantless searches to obtain foreign intelligence information." Indeed, the 4th Circuit Court of Appeals, in hearing the Truong case, decided "we agree that the Executive Branch need not always obtain a warrant for foreign intelligence surveillance." Going further, the 4th Circuit Court said, the "needs of the Executive are so compelling in foreign intelligence that a uniform warrant requirement would 'unduly frustrate' the President in carrying out his foreign affairs responsibility," and "the Executive (branch) possesses unparalleled expertise to make the decision to conduct foreign intelligence surveillance" while "the Judiciary is largely inexperienced" in this area.

Beyond the legal questions, I believe the program does require oversight, and its current level of oversight is not adequate. As co-equal branches of government, the Constitution tasks Congress with oversight of the Executive branch as a check on executive power. Limited briefings to the so-called Gang of Eight are not what the Framers of the Constitution had in mind. That said, the members of the Gang of Eight, if they had serious reservations about the legal basis for the program, needed to have acted in the course of at least 12 briefings, rather than objecting now. As members of Congress, we have an obligation to represent our constituency, but more importantly to preserve, protect, and defend the country, and that includes the Constitution. We each have power here in Washington to effect change, and when we feel we need to do so, we must.

Ultimately, the legal basis for the program may rest with the courts. Senate Judiciary Committee Chairman Arlen Specter (R-PA) has suggested the entire program be taken to the FISA Court so its legal status may be decided once and for all.

I believe the President acted in the best interests of the country when he authorized the use of this program in the wake of 9/11. Five and a half years later the threat remains and the leak of this program comes at a time when we need to be at our strongest in protecting America.

SECURITY, DEMOCRACY AND RESTRAINT

JOHN J. DONOHUE

The revelation of the NSA's domestic spying program raises a host of legal and policy questions. On its face, the program would seem to run afoul of the 1978 Foreign Intelligence Surveillance Act (FISA), and the Bush Administration's puzzling and contradictory statements on this legal issue have not been reassuring. First, given the explicit prohibitions of the 1978 Act, the Administration's allusions to pre-FISA precedents for Presidential spying are inapposite. Second, the claims that Congress implicitly authorized such behavior as part of the grant of authority to pursue military action in Afghanistan and/or Iraq seem hollow in light of the Administration's assertion that the President had the constitutional authority to engage in this type of domestic surveillance even in the face of a direct legislative ban. Third, in the aftermath of 9/11, the Administration asked for—and received—various amendments to FISA, which raises the question of why a further FISA amendment to cover the NSA program was not sought. Finally, the President's explicit prepared statement in April 2004 that "When we're talking about chasing down terrorists, we're talking about getting a court order before we do so" raises legitimate questions about whether the Administration has been caught misleading the public and skirting the law.

Is there a benign explanation for the Administration's conduct? Two questions exist. First, does the spying program advance the legitimate interests of the nation by reducing the risk of terrorist attacks within the United States? While we now know that the Bush Administration did not adequately heed clear signs about Bin Laden's intentions to attack within the United States and the specific warnings about terrorist use of planes, we do have a record of almost four and one-half years without a subsequent terrorist attack. It is hard to know whether the NSA surveillance campaign played any role in resisting further attack, but there is at least some possibility that it has.

Second, even if the program is helpful, is there a justification for failing to seek Congressional authority or to at least consult with the appropriate Congressional committees? Perhaps extreme secrecy would be needed in this case, since any effort to overturn the law (or share information with Congress?) would tip off the enemy to the need to avoid electronic surveillance. But, Bin Laden knew years ago that his cell phone conversations were tapped by the United States, so one assumes that our enemies probably knew or expected that they were being tapped in communicating with individuals in the U.S. itself. Given that the argument for extreme secrecy is uncertain and the Administration's behavior in the wake of the revelations raises concerns about its consciousness of guilt, the dangers of the Administration's course of conduct become more troubling. The loyal opposition will necessarily worry that unlawful snooping—most ominously against political opponents—could result from such unchecked assertions of Presidential power. The Administration's conduct in numerous other instances—from the release of the name of an undercover CIA operative under circumstances suggesting an attempt to punish a political adversary to the array of errors and misstatements leading up to the war in Iraq—buttresses the concern that the Administration pursues its agendas without feeling the need to be candid with the American people.

One factor might count in the Administration's favor on the question of whether its actions and secrecy were justified—the decision of the *New York Times* not to reveal the program when it learned of it a year ago. Apparently, the Administration made its case to the *New York Times* that legitimate national security interests would be jeopardized if the program were revealed, and the *Times* accepted those representations. Unfortunately, the power of this arguably independent endorsement of the Administration's position has been somewhat undercut by the *Times'* admitted gullibility and/or culpability in erroneously pumping up the pre-war stories about Iraqi weapons of mass destruction at the behest of the White House. The *New York Times* may also have some explaining to do.

Now that the NSA program has been revealed, any cost to national security has presumably been paid, and the highest priority would seem to be to resolve how the nation's interests in security and democratic decision-making can both be appropriately protected. Given the allegations and evidence about prisoner abuse and torture, the need for the country to address openly the appropriate limits on the pursuit of national security is evident. It is worth remembering that many aggressive acts unilaterally taken by the U.S. in furtherance of short-term national security objectives have ended up imposing larger long-term costs. For example, Ronald Reagan's championing and arming of Bin Laden and the other Afghan "freedom fighters" as they battled the Soviet Union looks far more questionable today than it did back in the 1980s. The same can be said of the CIA's overthrow of the Mossadegh regime in Iran in 1953 that has had such unhappy long-term results. One suspects that a sober assessment of the full array of aggressive, unilateral U.S. foreign policy initiatives over the last half century might well reveal that actions that initially looked appealing to zealous executive-branch officials commonly produced scant benefits and large costs.

MUCH ADO ABOUT

DAVID B. RIVKIN, JR.

The frenzy surrounding the NSA surveillance program is nothing short of remarkable. The legal and constitutional case supporting the President's actions is quite compelling, and even his harshest critics concede its policy value. Meanwhile, there is absolutely no evidence that the program has been abused or politicized in any way; if impropriety existed, the very same critics, who saw fit to leak information about the surveillance effort to the *New York Times*, would have promptly disclosed this evidence. Thus, the criticisms, even when stripped of partisanship and a hefty dose of anti-Bush sentiment, regrettably manifest a broad underlying problem that is plaguing our political and legal discourse—a veritable hostility towards all discretionary exercise of presidential power. This tendency is particularly dangerous at a time of a "long war" against a dangerous and determined Islamist adversary, when the need for such uniquely presidential policy attributes (e.g., speed and unity of design) is all the more palpable.

For a lawyer like myself, whose practice encompasses administrative law, the critics' efforts to portray the 1978 Foreign Intelligence Surveillance Act (FISA) as a regulatory straitjacket, that allegedly renders unlawful the NSA surveillance program,

border on laughable. To begin with, FISA, far from being a comprehensive regulatory edifice, applies only to four specific surveillance scenarios. Indeed, since FISA applies to electronic surveillance, carried out for "foreign intelligence purposes," and the NSA surveillance program focuses exclusively on gathering military intelligence about parties who are waging war against us, it is not even clear that FISA is at all relevant—foreign intelligence is not the same as military intelligence.

Meanwhile, howls of outrage greet the Administration's assertion that the September 2001 congressional Authorization to Use Military Force ("AUMF") provided additional blessing for the Executive's collection of battlefield intelligence. But exactly the same argument—that the AUMF authorized the President to use all traditional aspects of war prosecution—was embraced by the Supreme Court in the Hamdi case. (In that case, the Administration foes argued that the AUMF, because it did not expressly refer to detention of enemy combatants, could not have overridden the so-called Non-Detention Act, which barred the incarceration of U.S. citizens without trial.) Collecting intelligence on one's enemy is certainly every bit as traditional an aspect of waging war as detaining captured enemy combatants. To emphasize, a perfectly plausible and defensible construction of the existing statutory authorities fully vindicates the President's surveillance program and does not require us to reach the constitutional issues.

But what about the Constitution? The politicians and journalists would have you believe that it is unprecedented for the Executive to invade the privacy of Americans without a warrant. Yet, even a cursory reading of the 4th Amendment suggests that searches and seizures can be undertaken without a judicial imprimatur, so long as they are reasonable. In a world where the government deploys random sobriety checkpoints to apprehend drunken motorists, where U.S. citizens returning to the United States are randomly searched by custom agents, and airline travelers are randomly selected for intrusive body searches—all of which clearly invade one's privacy and bodily autonomy and do so without a shred of probable cause—the notion that it is not reasonable to invade the privacy of some Americans' telephone conversations in order to prevent attacks in which thousands of Americans would be killed is self-evidently absurd.

To suggest that all of the intercept activities must be conducted pursuant to a warrant is not only impractical, given the need for urgent action, but also betrays a further fundamental misunderstanding of the Fourth Amendment. While the Executive can constitutionally carry out a "reasonable" search that infringes on personal privacy, a warrant cannot be granted by a court absent "probable cause." Applying the higher probable cause standard would mean the NSA could only surveil the conversations of full-fledged al Qaeda agents, leaving invaluable conversations among al Qaeda sympathizers unmonitored.

The broader problem with the critics is that discretionary presidential action lies at the heart of executive power. To suggest that the President can act only with judicial blessing would vitiate his key constitutional attributes. The Framers, who placed much importance on executive independence and went to great lengths to ensure that the Executive would not be dominated by the Legislature, would have been horrified by current efforts to make him the ward of the courts. This is not to suggest that we should not be concerned about abuses of executive power, which have certainly occurred in the past. However, the proper way to deal with such abuses is through political accountability, with both Congress and the American people vigilant over the President's actions. In a world of endemic leaks, this is not a particularly difficult undertaking. Presented with the evidence of wrongdoing, Congress can cut off funds for NSA surveillance and even impeach the President. The American people can punish him and his party at the polls. But accountability for abusing power is very different than preventing the legitimate use of power.

DOMESTIC SURVEILLANCE AND DISTRUST

DAKOTA RUDESILL

The debate about warrantless surveillance of Americans by the NSA is not about whether Al Qaeda is a threat, nor whether we need to keep an ear to Osama's agents. Everyone agrees it is, and we should.

Nor is the debate about whether the NSA's precise (still classified) method of surveillance should be employed. If it is legal or can be made legal, it may well have merit.

The big question is not even whether this particular administration (which benefits from the service of countless able and honorable Americans) should be

trusted to search our bytes without explicit authorization or robust oversight by Congress, and without the warrant requirements of the Fourth Amendment and the Foreign Intelligence Surveillance Act.

Rather, the real issue is whether we should largely shelve a notion long at the core of American political thought: profound skepticism of government, especially when it acts in the name of national security.

FISA, and indeed our republic itself, are products of informed distrust. If we still agree with Hamilton that humanity is "ambitious [and] vindictive" and with Madison that government is "but the greatest of all reflections of human nature," then we ought not accept arguments that boil down to "just trust us." Weakening institutional checks leaves us little choice but to depend on the good intentions of the president's men rather than the rule of law.

The FISA law of 1978 struck a careful balance between the equally necessary but inherently conflicting imperatives of security and liberty: allowing surveillance while preventing a repeat of the wiretapping abuses of prior presidents via a warrant requirement and congressional oversight. Similarly, the Constitution created an Executive strong enough to protect the country, but sufficiently limited by co-equal Judicial and Legislative branches to prevent the kind of abuses of military power to which the British army subjected the Colonies.

The Constitution's separated, diffused, but in practical terms *shared* power regarding national security adds up to institutionalized skepticism. In contrast, the Administration seeks unitary, concentrated, exclusive power for the Executive—the kind of aggregation the Framers knew imperiled liberty.

The current Executive claims that it, without going to court, may decide whether its own electronic searches in the United States are legal under the Fourth Amendment. President Bush has cited "multiple safeguards to protect civil liberties" now in place within the Executive. Yet the Administration's own "unitary Executive" theory accords the president all Executive authority. How, then, do subordinates check a misguided president?

How would Congress? The Constitution explicitly grants the legislature not only sole appropriations power, but authority to make "all Laws which shall be necessary and proper" for "all...Powers vested" in the federal government, including "the Government and Regulation" of the Armed

Forces. Remarkably, the Justice Department alleges that any law limiting presidential power to order warrantless military foreign intelligence surveillance in the United States of suspected terrorists would be *unconstitutional*—that is, not just challenged but *trumped* by the president's inherent wartime authority. This cannot be reconciled with the Constitution's purpose and plain text, which embody shared power.

Furthermore, when Congress's senior "Gang of Eight" was briefed about the NSA program in 2003, the Administration reportedly stipulated that they consult with no one else—not even the intelligence committee's legal and technical experts with top level clearances who would draft any classified annex to an intelligence bill that would authorize, regulate, or de-fund the program. The Administration thus blocked Congress from acting regarding programs within its comprehensive legislative authority, executing a sort of pre-emptive veto.

Meanwhile, its public legal arguments add up to a post-enactment veto power. Consider: if the president's inherent constitutional authority, plus the generally worded post-9/11 Authorization for the Use of Military Force, gives him authority to wiretap in contravention of the plain text—indeed, the entire point—of a highly specific statute like FISA, where does his authority end? How many other laws passed by Congress and signed by prior presidents can Bush and his successors invalidate at will? What congressional powers remain intact regarding national security beyond appropriations, declaring war, ratifying treaties, and confirming nominations? Do even these?

If judicial and congressional institutional skepticism of state power in wartime is circumscribed so dramatically, we will get a system dominated by an Executive the people have fewer ways to check—and therefore little choice but to trust—between presidential plebiscites.

If ever there were a time for such unipolar government in America (and I doubt it), this is not it. We are witnessing tremendous expansion in the volume and searchability of personal electronic information. Major decisions about the balance between security and liberty are about to be made.

Executive dominance would mean that just one branch of government would be making most of the decisions. That would not reflect the Constitution's vision of shared national security power. Getting the liberty/security balance right in the electronic age will not be easy, but Congress must not abandon

this challenge to the bona fides of any Executive—for Congress's own sake, and for ours.

PRE-9/11 POLITICIANS IN A POST-9/11 WORLD

STEPHEN A. VADEN

How soon some of our elected leaders choose to forget! It was only 4½ years ago, following the attacks of 9/11, that the members of the U.S. Congress stood on the steps of the Capitol and sang *God Bless America.* Hands joined, they vowed to take any and all steps necessary to attack terrorist camps sheltering those responsible for the destruction of the World Trade Center and the attack on the Pentagon while adapting America's intelligence capabilities to ensure such attacks never occurred again.

Fast forward to today and Democratic Party Chairman Howard Dean, heading into the midterm election, vowed as a campaign pledge that should his party take control of one or both houses of Congress, Democrats will grind the normal business of government to a halt to engage in endless hearings to investigate "the most corrupt administration since Warren Harding." Adding a bipartisan spirit, Judiciary Committee Chairman Arlen Specter summoned Attorney General Alberto Gonzales to answer a long series of accusatory questions.

This blast of Beltway huffing and puffing came about because President Bush had the audacity to determine that individuals located inside the U.S. calling persons overseas with suspected terrorist connections do not have a reasonable expectation of privacy.

Four years ago, we were all in agreement—the "wall" separating domestic and foreign intelligence gathering had to be breached. The wall had produced fatal consequences. Fearful of running afoul of then-in-place FISA guidelines, FBI agents refused to request a search warrant that would allow them to investigate the contents of Al Qaeda terrorist Zacarias Moussaoui's computer hard drive. Thus, a computer belonging to a man now suspected of being the "twentieth hijacker" sat in a Minneapolis FBI office unexamined from August 16, 2001, until after the attacks. As the 9/11 Commission concluded, absent the "wall," FBI agents would have discovered files full of flight simulation programs and information on dispersing aerial pesticides.

We will never know whether the FBI could have followed the leads Moussaoui's computer would have provided to disrupt 9/11. A Washington which fetishized bureaucratic obstacles and believed that a fantastical wall separating the CIA from the FBI could also separate America from its enemies overseas never gave its top counterterrorist agents the chance. If the rhetoric of today's political discourse is to be believed, America looks set to make the same mistake all over again, rebuilding the obsolescent wall it just so recently razed.

Unfortunately, Congress only is engaged in doing what it does best: evading responsibility and passing the buck to the other two branches of government. Many of the proposed "solutions" to the "problem" of terrorist surveillance involve expanding the jurisdiction of the unelected and therefore unaccountable FISA court judges. Congress would like nothing more than to be able to continue its disturbing pattern of making ill-conceived public attacks on highly important and useful intelligence programs while washing its hands of its oversight responsibilities entirely. Congress must not be allowed to repeat the mistakes of the past and shirk its constitutional duties; the only thing worse than a preening politician in a suit is a pseudo-politician in a robe.

The Bush Administration's failure to force Congress to play its role in protecting America from terrorist attacks, not the Administration's institution of the NSA program, is the most troubling aspect of the current debate. Rather than bearing all the burden and blame itself, the Bush Administration should actively involve Congress in the management of our intelligence programs. President Bush has asserted without rejoinder that the Administration reviews the status of the NSA program every 45 days. Nothing stands in the way of the President's sending a subordinate to brief the House and Senate Intelligence Committees, or subcommittees thereof, on the status of the program at that same interval.

Such meetings would necessarily be subject to the strictest secrecy requirements. Members of the committees would be free at these meetings to raise objections and demand accommodations to any concerns about privacy or any other supposed rights violations occurring. However, the key difference would be that in this formalized consultative process, congressmen's words would actually stand a chance of having an effect, unlike the unthinking comments bandied about on *Meet the Press*. As classified minutes of these meetings would also be kept, advice that resulted in

damaging limitations to our intelligence gathering capabilities (or, in the worst case scenario, allowing terrorists to exploit the resulting vulnerability to attack) could be traced back to its originator in an ensuing investigation. Then, the American public could render its verdict at the next election as to whether the intelligence capabilities sacrificed were indeed worth it.

What would keep members of Congress from using the classified briefings to continue their demagogic ways? One need only compare the measured reaction to the revelation of the NSA program of Group of Eight member and California Democratic Congresswoman Jane Harman to the vitriolic partisan response of House Minority Leader Nancy Pelosi to see the difference a little actual responsibility can make. Surveillance is not the problem. Political rhetoric stripped of common sense and accountability is.

NSA SPYING ERODES RULE OF LAW

LOCH K. JOHNSON

The Bush administration finds itself embroiled in controversy over whether its program of NSA spying, a highly classified operation leaked to the public in December 2004, is necessary and lawful in the struggle against terrorism. The cause of the furor is the President's authorization by secret executive order to allow the NSA to eavesdrop on Americans without first acquiring a warrant. Critics maintain that this right violates the intent of the Foreign Intelligence Surveillance Act.

The FISA statute stemmed from the findings of the Church Committee in 1975–76, a panel of inquiry into alleged domestic spying, led by Senator Frank Church (D, Idaho). The Committee discovered that the FBI had carried out 500,000 investigations into so-called subversives from 1960 to 1974 without a single court conviction; the CIA had engaged in extensive mail-openings inside the U.S. (Operation Chaos); and Army intelligence units had conducted clandestine inquiries against 100,000 U.S. citizens opposed to the war in Vietnam.

The NSA took part in this widespread assault against freedom and privacy at home. Its "Operation Shamrock" monitored every cable sent overseas or received by Americans from 1947 to 1975, and its "Operation Minaret" swept in the telephone conversations of an additional 1,680 citizens. The effects of such spying, as Senator Walter Mondale

(D, Minnesota) noted in public hearings, was to "discourage political dissent in this country." None of these NSA wiretaps went through a judicial review. When Mondale asked the NSA deputy director whether he was concerned about the program's legality, the official replied with a look of embarrassment: "That particular aspect didn't enter into the discussions."

In light of these abuses, Congress worked with both Presidents Ford and Carter to craft reforms that would protect the civil liberties of Americans against improper uses of the intelligence agencies. The FISA law took aim directly at the problem of warrantless wiretaps by the NSA. No longer could presidents or their aides decide by themselves who in this nation would be subjected to electronic surveillance. Henceforth, an impartial court comprised of experienced judges would decide the merits of an administration's request for a national security wiretap.

The FISA Court has worked well over the years, although some critics have assailed it for too easily approving warrant requests—indeed, all but five of over 17,000 requests since its inception. But the Court is not just a rubber stamp. Administrations have been careful to seek warrants only when the case is strong and that is why the approval rate is high. If the requests of the current administration for wiretaps are as urgent as President George W. Bush has asserted, the Court would no doubt have granted approval.

The Administration has drawn upon three major arguments to defend its bypassing of FISA procedures. First, DOJ attorneys maintain that the President has an inherent constitutional authority to wiretap under the commander in chief clause. Yet many legal scholars have called into question that point of view. Justice Jackson's famous opinion in the Youngstown case concluded that a president's power is "at its lowest ebb" when in conflict with the "expressed or implied will of Congress." The FISA law was an express and specific effort by lawmakers to curtail warrantless wiretaps.

Second, the administration claims that in the wake of the 9/11 attacks Congress provided the president with "authorization for use of military force"—a blank check in the war against global terrorism. That authorization, though, said nothing about electronic surveillance of American citizens; rather it was intended to give the president authority to carry out military retaliation against Al Qaeda

terrorists in Afghanistan and their host, the Taliban regime.

Finally, the administration argues that the warrant procedures in the 1978 law are slow and cumbersome, as well as out-of-date in the light of new technology; in the struggle against terrorists, the U.S. must be nimble and fast moving. The FISA law, however, is agile. Warrants can be obtained in hours or even minutes; moreover, in times of crisis, the executive branch is permitted leeway to conduct wiretaps immediately for as long as 72 hours, applying for a warrant at the end of that period. If the law needs updating, the proper remedy is to amend it, rather than undermining the rule of law by using a secret executive order to waive the FISA statute.

The Senate Judiciary Committee, which has held one hearing on the surveillance program, will need a strong backbone—and probably subpoenas—to find out about its full dimensions. It may turn out that, contrary to preliminary media reports, the NSA program has merit and should be continued; but Congress and the FISA Court have an obligation to review the program. Then, if necessary, lawmakers can seek an amendment to the FISA law to improve its effectiveness.

The U.S. must defeat Al Qaeda and its affiliated terrorist organizations, but at the same time we have to keep civil liberties intact. Excessive executive branch discretion is a slippery slope, as revealed by the Church Committee. It found that America's secret agencies began by focusing on legitimate national security threats, only to be drawn into political surveillance. Tom Charles Huston, the architect of Nixon's domestic spy plan to monitor anti-Vietnam War activists, conceded to Church Committee investigators: "The risk was that you would get people who would be susceptible to political considerations as opposed to national security considerations, or would construe political considerations to be national security considerations—to move from the kid with a bomb to the kid with a picket sign, and from the kid with the picket sign to the kid with the bumper sticker of the opposing candidate. And you just keep going down the line." This danger is why a judicial check on national security wiretapping is essential.

QUESTIONS FOR FURTHER DISCUSSION

1. Contrast the argument of President George W. Bush in favor of warrantless wiretapping in

some circumstances with those of his critics who oppose this approach.

2. To what extent does this controversy over wiretapping by the National Security Agency (NSA) echo the concerns of reformers on the Church Committee in 1975?

3. Why does David Rivkin think that the controversy is "much ado about nothing"?

4. Is it possible to have effective oversight with respect to the NSA without revealing its modus operandi to America's enemies?

From Symposium (Alan Dershowitz, Senator Conrad Burns, John J. Donohue, David B. Rivkin, Jr., Dakota Rudesill, Stephen A. Vaden, Loch K. Johnson) from Yale Law School's *Opening Argument*, Yale University School of Law 1 (February 2006): pp. 1–8. Reprinted with permission.

IX

INTELLIGENCE ACTIVITIES IN THE AFTERMATH OF THE 9/11 AND WMD INTELLIGENCE FAILURES

Polonius: "Hath there been such a time, I'd fain
   know that,
That I have positively said 'tis so,
When it proved otherwise?"
King: "Not that I know."

—SHAKESPEARE, *Hamlet*, 2.2.153–155

The September 11, 2001, terrorist attacks on the World Trade Center and the Pentagon and the failure of the U.S. intelligence agencies and key allied governments to assess accurately the status of Iraq's programs to develop weapons of mass destruction (WMD) on the eve of the Second Gulf War were transformational events for the U.S. intelligence community. Both events are widely considered to be intelligence failures, but more recent explanations of what went wrong are beginning to emerge. The history of these events highlights how the limits of intelligence collection and analysis, politics, and the interaction between intelligence professionals and policymakers led, in the 9/11 instance, to lethargy in the face of an acute threat posed by Islamic fundamentalists. In the WMD example, in contrast, the intelligence and policy communities displayed

a strong interest and examined the available data at length. The 9/11 case suggests that the U.S. government fell victim to a fundamental intelligence mistake, failing to respond to valid threat indicators prior to the terrorist attacks. The government then made quite a different error in the WMD case, reaching the conclusion that Iraq was in the process of restarting its prohibited weapons program.

THE SEPTEMBER 11 ATTACKS

When the Islamic terrorist organization Al Qaeda used civilian airliners to attack the World Trade Center and the Pentagon, many observers believed that the U.S. intelligence community had obviously failed to generate the warnings needed to stop the terrorist group before it could strike. Because of the devastating effects of the attacks, many assumed that the intelligence mistakes leading up to 9/11 were complete and total. In fact, though, the intelligence community had been tracking Islamic fundamentalists for years and had generated a steady stream of estimates about the possibility of terrorist attacks directed against U.S. forces and interests overseas, as well as against the American homeland itself. The intelligence community recognized that Al Qaeda had emerged from the remnants of U.S.-supported *mujahideen* fighters, who had successfully battled Soviet forces occupying Afghanistan. The community also recognized that, in the aftermath of the Soviet defeat, some of these "holy warriors" had gravitated toward Osama bin Laden, a Saudi financier who had built a reputation as a construction expert in Afghanistan. Bin Laden's motivations and rhetoric have changed over time, but initially his anger seemed to have been directed toward what he believed was a corrupt Wahabi regime in Saudi Arabia. The American military presence in the Persian Gulf and Saudi Arabia, necessitated by the need to pressure Baghdad to end its WMD programs following the first Gulf War, only fueled Bin Laden's hatred toward the Saudi Royal Family and the United States. Emboldened by its victory over the Soviets, Al Qaeda did not shy away from directly attacking the remaining superpower, the United States.

By the mid-1990s, the CIA had identified Bin Laden not only as an advocate of violence but also as someone who was willing to organize and direct attacks against U.S. interests. By 1998, he had become increasingly public about his intentions, issuing a *fatwa* and holding press conferences in which he called for attacks against Americans. In August 1998, Al Qaeda attacked U.S. embassies in Nairobi in Kenya and Dar es Salaam in Tanzania. In 2000, after a failed attempt to attack the USS *The Sulivans*, his followers launched a suicide attack against the USS *Cole*, moored in the Gulf of Aden off the coast of Yemen. This attack produced 50 American casualties and nearly sank the ship. Bin Laden talked openly about his ambitions, which were codified in an insightful article published by *Foreign Affairs* (Rashid 1999).

As the threats posed by Al Qaeda became realities, U.S. officials were confronted, too, with a series of warnings that the United States was not prepared or organized to meet the challenge of international terrorism. Findings from no less than 11 major commissions and studies addressed the topic of intelligence reform. Several of these studies offered recommendations to improve coordination between the FBI and the rest of the intelligence community. Reform was needed to eliminate the wall that separated U.S. law enforcement officers from intelligence officials, a division that made it difficult to respond to terrorist networks that crossed domestic and international boundaries. A report issued in 2000 by the National Commission on Terrorism, for example, proposed clarifying the FBI's authority to investigate terrorist groups; allowing the CIA access to Bureau informants linked to terrorist organizations; placing terrorism high on the agendas of officials at the CIA, FBI, and NSA; and establishing new procedures for the quick dissemination of terrorist information to national security officials (Hart-Rudman 2001). Few of these recommendations, however, were acted upon. When Al Qaeda operatives infiltrated the United States prior to September 11, 2001, they effectively exploited the seam running between the intelligence community and domestic law enforcement agencies.

U.S. officials and organizations were slow to respond to the emerging threat posed by Al Qaeda, as well as to warnings that the U.S. government was poorly organized to meet the threat posed by transnational terrorist networks. Long accustomed to dealing with the menace of a Warsaw Pact conventional assault across what was then the inter-German border, or the prospect of a strategic nuclear exchange with the Soviet Union, officials and organizations were late in understanding the rising menace of international terrorism and how it was beginning to exploit the communication and transportation networks made possible by the information revolution and globalization. Mass casualty terrorism was recognized as a possibility, but policymakers and scholars alike debated whether such extreme violence would actually be carried out by terrorist organizations, or even whether nonstate actors were capable of creating high-casualty events. Most observers concluded that the 1993 attack on the World Trade Center by Islamic fundamentalists and the 1996 Aum Shinrikyo sarin attack on the Tokyo subway were failures. Some analysts also argued that launching a mass-casualty incident could easily rebound to the detriment of a terrorist organization, mobilizing governments and publics alike to undertake increasingly harsh and effective measures to eradicate the masterminds of terrorism and their supporters.

By the time President Bill Clinton left office, intelligence analysts had developed an increasingly alarming picture of Al Qaeda's international reach and ambitions to wreak havoc on the United States. Rocked by scandal and afflicted by chronic hand wringing—Attorney General Janet Reno repeatedly warned that Al Qaeda might retaliate if attacked—the Clinton Administration failed to translate its growing recognition of the threat into effective action. When President George W. Bush arrived in Washington to begin his term of office, his staff (with its own foreign policy agenda) seemed slow to recognize the looming threat. Here Al Qaeda might have enjoyed a lucky break: Preparations for the 9/11 attacks roughly corresponded to the change of administrations in Washington, a time when the effectiveness of the U.S. government is reduced. Al Qaeda was able to capitalize on the fact that a new team was in the White House, busy moving in and holding its first meetings. The threat of transnational terrorism was rising to the top of the Bush Administration's agenda by the late summer of 2001, but by then it was too late.

THE IRAQ WMD ESTIMATE

In the aftermath of the 9/11 attacks, debate about the possibility of mass-casualty terrorism was laid to rest and a new threat came into sharp focus: WMD terrorism. All eyes focused on Iraq and the possibility that Saddam Hussein's regime had restarted its program to develop nuclear weapons following the ejection of U.N. Special Commission (UNSCOM) inspectors in the late 1990s. Many feared that the interests of Saddam and Al Qaeda might coincide, leading to an alliance of convenience that could make Bin Laden's often-stated interest in WMD a reality. With this nightmarish, if somewhat far-fetched, scenario in the background, the Bush Administration apparently made the political decision that the risk of living with an Iraq armed with WMD outweighed the risk of taking direct action to bring about regime change in Iraq. Support for this decision was provided by the October 2002 Iraqi Weapons of Mass Destruction National Intelligence Estimate (NIE). Although the judgments of this NIE were heavily qualified (the estimate went into some detail about the limitations of its conclusions and the data used in reaching them), it was seen by most policymakers within the U.S. government as evidence that Saddam had again embarked on the path of obtaining nuclear weapons. Subsequent findings now suggest that the 2002 NIE was off the mark. No significant WMD programs were uncovered following the American and British invasion of Iraq in March 2003 that began

the Second Gulf War and drove Saddam's Ba'athist regime from power. But by the time the weaknesses of the 2002 NIE were clear, the die had been cast.

The origins of the intelligence community's overestimate of Iraq's WMD capability probably can be found in its underestimation of Iraq's nuclear capabilities that became apparent following the First Gulf War (1990–91). Information obtained by U.S. forces in the immediate aftermath of that war, data gleaned from UNSCOM inspections, and the revelations of Hussein Kamil (Saddam's son-in-law, who for a time defected to the West) settled first-order questions about the suspected Iraqi WMD program: Saddam seemed to be interested in all types of WMD. With justification, the intelligence community concluded that information available to it before the First Gulf War really was just the tip of the iceberg and, at least until the mid-1990s, more data became available that painted an increasingly vivid picture of Iraq's previous WMD efforts. What emerged was a policy-intelligence consensus about Iraq's WMD: Saddam Hussein would do everything in his power to obtain mass-casualty weapons, and the full extent of Iraq's WMD program was being concealed by the regime. New data generally confirmed worst-case estimates of Iraq's WMD capability. This estimate and the baseline data used to assess Iraq's WMD programs did not significantly change beliefs inside the Bush Administration and most agencies in the intelligence community until the aftermath of the Second Gulf War, although U.N. weapons inspectors and a few elements inside the U.S. intelligence community raised doubts before the U.S.-led invasion in 2003.

A turning point for most analysts in the American intelligence community came with the ejection of UNSCOM inspectors in the late 1990s. Analysts concluded that the Iraqi regime, no longer hamstrung by the threat of detection by UNSCOM, would be able to restart its WMD programs and, given Saddam's objectives, probably *would* restart its WMD programs. What analysts failed to realize, however, was that the Iraqi regime had been subjected to nearly a decade of international sanctions, UNSCOM inspections, continuous overflights, and concerted preventive attacks (the First Gulf War and Operation Desert Fox) intended to destroy, disrupt, and dissuade further efforts to produce, store, train with, or equip a large-scale WMD arsenal. These actions had a profound effect on the ability and will of the Iraqi regime to continue its WMD programs. Nevertheless, Saddam Hussein and his henchmen continued to create suspicion that nefarious activities might be taking place beyond the view of the prying eyes of the U.S. and allied intelligence agencies. Without a true "net assessment" to evaluate the full effect of international policies against Iraq—and there is no agency in the U.S. government that evaluates the overall success of U.S. foreign and defense policy—developments in Iraq tended to be judged with an eye toward Iraq's past capabilities, which were based on data gathered in the early 1990s and reflected the status of Iraq's programs in the 1980s.

If Western analysts were going to accurately assess the changing nature of Iraq's WMD program and current capabilities, they needed to step outside this policy-intelligence consensus about Iraqi behavior (a problem similar to the one faced by Israeli analysts prior to the Yom Kippur War in 1973). This type of assessment is extraordinarily difficult, because analysts would have to abandon their own policy-analytical-historical context to evaluate available information in a detached way. The U.S. intelligence community failed to undertake this reassessment of Iraq's weapons policies and capabilities; no one in the government of the United States attempted to reassess the underlying assumptions behind the Iraq estimate of October 2002. No one realized that the policy-intelligence consensus was no longer falsifiable, because most of the positive—as well as the negative—evidence, quite possibly manipulated by Iraqi denial and deception operations, suggested the presence of a clandestine Iraqi nuclear program. If matters look cut-and-dried to intelligence analysts, suspicions should have been raised that results might have been a little *too* cut-and-dried. This did not occur, however, in terms or the Iraq NIE. Indeed, there were no "intelligence dissenters" to that document—individuals who objected to the consensus and tried to make their opinions known. No one inside the U.S. government stepped forward effectively to object to the data, analysis, or conclusions contained in the Iraq NIE—although behind the scenes some officials in the Department of State intelligence service (Intelligence and Research, or INR), in the Energy Department intelligence unit, and in Air Force Intelligence did raise objections, without success. By and large, the NIE was considered to be rather ho-hum.

THE READINGS

The readings in this section examine these two intelligence-policy failures. The first selection is excerpted from the 9/11 Commission Report. Chaired by Thomas H. Kean and Lee H. Hamilton, the commission produced a document that offers a riveting account of the events leading up to the September 11 tragedy. The report should be read in its entirety by everyone, but especially by students who were too young in 2001 to absorb the full shock of the events of that dark day. The sections of the Commission Report that we present here contain its recommendations for overcoming the organizational weaknesses of the U.S. government revealed on 9/11. They also highlight the global threat posed by the rise of transnational terrorist networks and outline a national strategy to meet that threat. The report also offers reforms needed to make effective defense, homeland security, and intelligence a reality.

The second reading, written by Amy Zegart, confronts the problem of organizational and management failures in the intelligence community as major explanations for the 9/11 and Iraqi WMD intelligence failures. Her work is known for its criticism of the government for not reforming its institutions adequately to protect the nation—what she refers to as "adaptation failure." She laments the outcome of reform efforts in 2004, which "left the secretary of defense with greater power, the director of national intelligence with little, and the Intelligence Community even more disjointed."

In the third article in this part of the book, co-editor James Wirtz looks at recent U.S. intelligence failures through a counterintelligence lens. He examines how denial and deception operations by foreign adversaries have added to the odds that America intelligence officers may lack a proper understanding of world events.

Next a prominent CIA intelligence analyst, Paul Pillar, puts the Iraqi WMD issue under a microscope. He finds deeply troubling instances of the misuse of intelligence, including the cardinal sin: the politicization of information by policy officials to suit their own political objectives. He offers a set of sensible reforms that, if adopted, would improve the way in which intelligence is treated in Washington, D.C.

Finally, James Burch examines intelligence in various democracies and assesses whether the establishment of a domestic intelligence agency in the United States is viable for meeting the asymmetric threats of the twenty-first century.

33. 9/11 INTELLIGENCE FAILURE

KEAN COMMISSION

The 9/11 Commission, chaired by former New Jersey Republican Governor Thomas H. Kean and former Representative Lee H. Hamilton (D, Indiana), produced an influential account of the events surrounding the September 11, 2001, Al Qaeda attacks on the World Trade Center and the Pentagon. The report achieved best-selling status and remains a valuable research document on global terrorism. Our selection from the report identifies the nature of the terrorist threat facing the United States, the organizational reforms needed to meet this challenge, and national strategies that the commissioners believed should be adopted to keep terrorism at bay.

WHAT TO DO? A GLOBAL STRATEGY (REFLECTING ON A GENERATIONAL CHALLENGE)

Three years after 9/11, Americans are still thinking and talking about how to protect our nation in this new era. The national debate continues.

Countering terrorism has become, beyond any doubt, the top national security priority for the United States. This shift has occurred with the full support of the Congress, both major political parties, the media, and the American people.

The nation has committed enormous resources to national security and to countering terrorism. Between fiscal year 2001, the last budget adopted before 9/11, and the present fiscal year 2004, total federal spending on defense (including expenditures on both Iraq and Afghanistan), homeland security, and international affairs rose more than 50 percent, from $354 billion to about $547 billion. The United States has not experienced such a rapid surge in national security spending since the Korean War.[1]

This pattern has occurred before in American history. The United States faces a sudden crisis and summons a tremendous exertion of national energy. Then, as that surge transforms the landscape, comes a time for reflection and revaluation. Some programs and even agencies are discarded; others are invented or redesigned. Private firms and engaged citizens redefine their relationships with government, working through the processes of the American republic.

Now is the time for that reflection and reevaluation. The United States should consider *what to do*—the shape and objectives of a strategy. Americans should also consider *how to do it*—organizing their government in a different way.

DEFINING THE THREAT

In the post-9/11 world, threats are defined more by the fault lines within societies than by the territorial boundaries between them. From terrorism to global disease or environmental degradation, the challenges have become transnational rather than international. That is the defining quality of world politics in the twenty-first century.

National security used to be considered by studying foreign frontiers, weighing opposing groups of states, and measuring industrial might. To be dangerous, an enemy had to muster large armies. Threats emerged slowly, often visibly, as weapons were forged, armies conscripted, and units trained and moved into place. Because large states were more powerful, they also had more to lose. They could be deterred.

Now threats can emerge quickly. An organization like al Qaeda, headquartered in a country on the other side of the earth, in a region so poor that electricity or telephones were scarce, could nonetheless scheme to wield weapons of unprecedented destructive power in the largest cities of the United States.

In this sense, 9/11 has taught us that terrorism against American interests "over there" should be regarded just as we regard terrorism against America "over here." In this same sense, the American homeland is the planet.

But the enemy is not just "terrorism," some generic evil.[2] This vagueness blurs the strategy. The catastrophic threat at this moment in history is more specific. It is the threat posed by *Islamist* terrorism—especially the al Qaeda network, its affiliates, and its ideology.[3]

Usama Bin Ladin and other Islamist terrorist leaders draw on a long tradition of extreme intolerance within one stream of Islam (a minority tradition), from at least Ibn Taimiyyah, through the founders of Wahhabism, through the Muslim Brotherhood, to Sayyid Qutb. That stream is motivated by religion and does not distinguish politics from religion, thus distorting both. It is further fed by grievances stressed by Bin Ladin and widely felt throughout the Muslim world—against the U.S. military presence in the Middle East, policies perceived as anti-Arab and anti-Muslim, and support of Israel. Bin Ladin and Islamist terrorists mean exactly what they say: to them America is the font of all evil, the "head of the snake," and it must be converted or destroyed.

It is not a position with which Americans can bargain or negotiate. With it there is no common ground—not even respect for life—on which to begin a dialogue. It can only be destroyed or utterly isolated.

Because the Muslim world has fallen behind the West politically, economically, and militarily for the past three centuries, and because few tolerant or secular Muslim democracies provide alternative models for the future, Bin Ladin's message finds receptive ears. It has attracted active support from thousands of disaffected young Muslims and resonates powerfully with a far larger number who do not actively support his methods. The resentment of America and the West is deep, even among leaders of relatively successful Muslim states.[4]

Tolerance, the rule of law, political and economic openness, the extension of greater opportunities to women—these cures must come from within Muslim societies themselves. The United States must support such developments.

But this process is likely to be measured in decades, not years. It is a process that will be violently opposed by Islamist terrorist organizations, both inside Muslim countries and in attacks on the United States and other Western nations. The United States finds itself caught up in a clash *within* a civilization. That clash arises from particular conditions in the Muslim world, conditions that spill over into expatriate Muslim communities in non-Muslim countries.

Our enemy is twofold: al Qaeda, a stateless network of terrorists that struck us on 9/11; and a radical ideological movement in the Islamic world, inspired in part by al Qaeda, which has spawned terrorist groups and violence across the globe. The first enemy is weakened, but continues to pose a grave threat. The second enemy is gathering, and will menace Americans and American interests long after Usama Bin Ladin and his cohorts are killed or captured. Thus our strategy must match our means to two ends: dismantling the al Qaeda network and prevailing in the longer term over the ideology that gives rise to Islamist terrorism.

Islam is not the enemy. It is not synonymous with terror. Nor does Islam teach terror. America and its friends oppose a perversion of Islam, not the great world faith itself. Lives guided by religious faith, including literal beliefs in holy scriptures, are common to every religion, and represent no threat to us.

Other religions have experienced violent internal struggles. With so many diverse adherents, every major religion will spawn violent zealots. Yet understanding and tolerance among people of different faiths can and must prevail.

The present transnational danger is Islamist terrorism. What is needed is a broad political-military strategy that rests on a firm tripod of policies to

- attack terrorists and their organizations;
- prevent the continued growth of Islamist terrorism; and
- protect against and prepare for terrorist attacks.

More Than a War on Terrorism

Terrorism is a tactic used by individuals and organizations to kill and destroy. Our efforts should be directed at those individuals and organizations.

Calling this struggle a war accurately describes the use of American and allied armed forces to find and destroy terrorist groups and their allies in the field, notably in Afghanistan. The language of war also evokes the mobilization for a national effort. Yet the strategy should be balanced.

The first phase of our post-9/11 efforts rightly included military action to topple the Taliban and pursue al Qaeda. This work continues. But long-term success demands the use of all elements of national power: diplomacy, intelligence, covert action, law enforcement, economic policy, foreign aid, public diplomacy, and homeland defense. If we favor one tool while neglecting others, we leave ourselves vulnerable and weaken our national effort.

Certainly the strategy should include offensive operations to counter terrorism. Terrorists should no longer find safe haven where their organizations can grow and flourish. America's strategy should be a coalition strategy, that includes Muslim nations as partners in its development and implementation.

Our effort should be accompanied by a preventive strategy that is as much, or more, political as it is military. The strategy must focus clearly on the Arab and Muslim world, in all its variety.

Our strategy should also include defenses. America can be attacked in many ways and has many vulnerabilities. No defenses are perfect. But risks must be calculated; hard choices must be made about allocating resources. Responsibilities for America's defense should be clearly defined. Planning does make a difference, identifying where a little money might have a large effect. Defenses also complicate the plans of attackers, increasing their risks of discovery and failure. Finally, the nation must prepare to deal with attacks that are not stopped.

Measuring Success

What should Americans expect from their government in the struggle against Islamist terrorism? The goals seem unlimited: Defeat terrorism anywhere in the world. But Americans have also been told to expect the worst: An attack is probably coming; it may be terrible.

With such benchmarks, the justifications for action and spending seem limitless. Goals are good. Yet effective public policies also need concrete objectives. Agencies need to be able to measure success.

These measurements do not need to be quantitative: government cannot measure success in the ways that private firms can. But the targets should be specific enough so that reasonable observers—in the White House, the Congress, the media, or the general public—can judge whether or not the objectives have been attained.

Vague goals match an amorphous picture of the enemy. Al Qaeda and its affiliates are popularly described as being all over the world, adaptable, resilient, needing little higher-level organization, and capable of anything. The American people are thus given the picture of an omnipotent, unslayable hydra of destruction. This image lowers expectations for government effectiveness.

It should not lower them too far. Our report shows a determined and capable group of plotters. Yet the group was fragile, dependent on a few key personalities, and occasionally left vulnerable by the marginal, unstable people often attracted to such causes. The enemy made mistakes—like Khalid al Mihdhar's unauthorized departure from the United States that required him to enter the country again in July 2001, or the selection of Zacarias Moussaoui as a participant and Ramzi Binalshibh's transfer of money to him. The U.S. government was not able to capitalize on those mistakes in time to prevent 9/11.

We do not believe it is possible to defeat all terrorist attacks against Americans, every time and everywhere. A president should tell the American people:

- No president can promise that a catastrophic attack like that of 9/11 will not happen again. History has shown that even the most vigilant and expert agencies cannot always prevent determined, suicidal attackers from reaching a target.
- But the American people are entitled to expect their government to do its very best. They should expect that officials will have realistic objectives, clear guidance, and effective organization. They are entitled to see some standards for performance so they can judge, with the help of their elected representatives, whether the objectives are being met.

ATTACK TERRORISTS AND THEIR ORGANIZATIONS

The U.S. government, joined by other governments around the world, is working through intelligence, law enforcement, military, financial, and diplomatic channels to identify, disrupt, capture, or kill individual terrorists. This effort was going on before 9/11 and it continues on a vastly enlarged scale. But to catch terrorists, a U.S. or foreign agency needs to be able to find and reach them.

No Sanctuaries

The 9/11 attack was a complex international operation, the product of years of planning. Bombings like those in Bali in 2003 or Madrid in 2004, while able to take hundreds of lives, can be mounted locally. Their requirements are far more modest in size and complexity. They are more difficult to thwart. But the U.S. government must build the capacities to prevent a 9/11-scale plot from succeeding, and those capabilities will help greatly to cope with lesser but still devastating attacks.

A complex international terrorist operation aimed at launching a catastrophic attack cannot be mounted by just anyone in any place. Such operations appear to require

- time, space, and ability to perform competent planning and staff work;
- a command structure able to make necessary decisions and possessing the authority and contacts to assemble needed people, money, and materials;
- opportunity and space to recruit, train, and select operatives with the needed skills and dedication, providing the time and structure required to socialize them into the terrorist cause, judge their trustworthiness, and hone their skills;
- a logistics network able to securely manage the travel of operatives, move money, and transport resources (like explosives) where they need to go;
- access, in the case of certain weapons, to the special materials needed for a nuclear, chemical, radiological, or biological attack;
- reliable communications between coordinators and operatives; and
- opportunity to test the workability of the plan.

Many details…illustrate the direct and indirect value of the Afghan sanctuary to al Qaeda in preparing the 9/11 attack and other operations. The organization cemented personal ties among veteran jihadists working together there for years. It had the operational space to gather and sift recruits, indoctrinating them in isolated, desert camps. It built up logistical networks, running through Pakistan and the United Arab Emirates.

Al Qaeda also exploited relatively lax internal security environments in Western countries, especially Germany. It considered the environment in the United States so hospitable that the 9/11 operatives used America as their staging area for further training and exercises—traveling into, out of, and around the country and complacently using their real names with little fear of capture.

To find sanctuary, terrorist organizations have fled to some of the least governed, most lawless places in the world. The intelligence community has prepared a world map that highlights possible terrorist havens, using no secret intelligence—just indicating areas that combine rugged terrain, weak governance, room to hide or receive supplies, and low population density with a town or city near enough to allow necessary interaction with the outside world. Large areas scattered around the world meet these criteria.[5]

In talking with American and foreign government officials and military officers on the front lines fighting terrorists today, we asked them: If you were a terrorist leader today, where would you locate your base? Some of the same places come up again and again on their lists:

- western Pakistan and the Pakistan-Afghanistan border region
- southern or western Afghanistan
- the Arabian Peninsula, especially Saudi Arabia and Yemen, and the nearby Horn of Africa, including Somalia and extending southwest into Kenya
- Southeast Asia, from Thailand to the southern Philippines to Indonesia
- West Africa, including Nigeria and Mali
- European cities with expatriate Muslim communities, especially cities in central and eastern Europe where security forces and border controls are less effective

In the twentieth century, strategists focused on the world's great industrial heartlands. In the twenty-first, the focus is in the opposite direction, toward remote regions and failing states. The United States has had to find ways to extend its reach, straining the limits of its influence.

Every policy decision we make needs to be seen through this lens. If, for example, Iraq becomes a failed state, it will go to the top of the list of places that are breeding grounds for attacks against Americans at home. Similarly, if we are paying insufficient attention to Afghanistan, the rule of the Taliban or warlords and narcotraffickers may reemerge and its countryside could once again offer refuge to al Qaeda, or its successor.

RECOMMENDATION: The U.S. government must identify and prioritize actual or potential terrorist sanctuaries. For each, it should have a realistic strategy to keep possible terrorists insecure and on the run, using all elements of national power. We should reach out, listen to, and work with other countries that can help.

We offer three illustrations that are particularly applicable today, in 2004: Pakistan, Afghanistan, and Saudi Arabia.

Pakistan

Pakistan's endemic poverty, widespread corruption, and often ineffective government create opportunities for Islamist recruitment. Poor education is a particular concern. Millions of families, especially those with little money, send their children to religious schools, or madrassahs. Many of these schools are the only opportunity available for an education, but some have been used as incubators for violent extremism. According to Karachi's police commander, there are 859 madrassahs teaching more than 200,000 youngsters in his city alone.[6]

It is hard to overstate the importance of Pakistan in the struggle against Islamist terrorism. Within Pakistan's borders are 150 million Muslims, scores of al Qaeda terrorists, many Taliban fighters, and—perhaps—Usama Bin Ladin. Pakistan possesses nuclear weapons and has come frighteningly close to war with nuclear-armed India over the disputed territory of Kashmir. A political battle among anti-American Islamic fundamentalists, the Pakistani military, and more moderate mainstream political forces has already spilled over into violence, and there have been repeated recent attempts to kill Pakistan's president, Pervez Musharraf.

In recent years, the United States has had three basic problems in its relationship with Pakistan:

- On terrorism, Pakistan helped nurture the Taliban. The Pakistani army and intelligence services, especially below the top ranks, have long been ambivalent about confronting Islamist extremists. Many in the government have sympathized with or provided support to the extremists. Musharraf agreed that Bin Ladin was bad. But before 9/11, preserving good relations with the Taliban took precedence.
- On proliferation, Musharraf has repeatedly said that Pakistan does not barter with its nuclear technology. But proliferation concerns have been long-standing and very serious. Most recently, the Pakistani government has claimed not to have known that one of its nuclear weapons developers, a national figure, was leading the most dangerous nuclear smuggling ring ever disclosed.
- Finally, Pakistan has made little progress toward the return of democratic rule at the national

level, although that turbulent process does continue to function at the provincial level and the Pakistani press remains relatively free.

Immediately after 9/11, confronted by the United States with a stark choice, Pakistan made a strategic decision. Its government stood aside and allowed the U.S.-led coalition to destroy the Taliban regime. In other ways, Pakistan actively assisted: its authorities arrested more than 500 al Qaeda operatives and Taliban members, and Pakistani forces played a leading part in tracking down KSM, Abu Zubaydah, and other key al Qaeda figures.[7]

In the following two years, the Pakistani government tried to walk the fence, helping against al Qaeda while seeking to avoid a larger confrontation with Taliban remnants and other Islamic extremists. When al Qaeda and its Pakistani allies repeatedly tried to assassinate Musharraf, almost succeeding, the battle came home.

The country's vast unpoliced regions make Pakistan attractive to extremists seeking refuge and recruits and also provide a base for operations against coalition forces in Afghanistan. Almost all the 9/11 attackers traveled the north-south nexus of Kandahar–Quetta–Karachi. The Baluchistan region of Pakistan (KSM's ethnic home) and the sprawling city of Karachi remain centers of Islamist extremism where the U.S. and Pakistani security and intelligence presence has been weak. The U.S. consulate in Karachi is a makeshift fortress, reflecting the gravity of the surrounding threat.[8]

During the winter of 2003–2004, Musharraf made another strategic decision. He ordered the Pakistani army into the frontier provinces of northwest Pakistan along the Afghan border, where Bin Ladin and Ayman al Zawahiri have reportedly taken refuge. The army is confronting groups of al Qaeda fighters and their local allies in very difficult terrain. On the other side of the frontier, U.S. forces in Afghanistan have found it challenging to organize effective joint operations, given Pakistan's limited capabilities and reluctance to permit U.S. military operations on its soil. Yet in 2004, it is clear that the Pakistani government is trying harder than ever before in the battle against Islamist terrorists.[9]

Acknowledging these problems and Musharraf's own part in the story, we believe that Musharraf's government represents the best hope for stability in Pakistan and Afghanistan.

- In an extraordinary public essay asking how Muslims can "drag ourselves out of the pit we find ourselves in, to raise ourselves up," Musharraf has called for a strategy of "enlightened moderation." The Muslim world, he said, should shun militancy and extremism; the West—and the United States in particular—should seek to resolve disputes with justice and help better the Muslim world.[10]

- Having dome close to war in 2002 and 2003, Pakistan and India have recently made significant progress in peacefully discussing their long-standing differences. The United States has been and should remain a key supporter of that process.

- The constant refrain of Pakistanis is that the United States long treated them as allies of convenience. As the United States makes fresh commitments now, it should make promises it is prepared to keep, for years to come.

RECOMMENDATION: If Musharraf stands for enlightened moderation in a fight for his life and for the life of his country, the United States should be willing to make hard choices too, and make the difficult long-term commitment to the future of Pakistan. Sustaining the current scale of aid to Pakistan, the United States should support Pakistan's government in its struggle against extremists with a comprehensive effort that extends from military aid to support for better education, so long as Pakistan's leaders remain willing to make difficult choices of their own.

Afghanistan

Afghanistan was the incubator for al Qaeda and for the 9/11 attacks. In the fall of 2001, the U.S.-led international coalition and its Afghan allies toppled the Taliban and ended the regime's protection of al Qaeda. Notable progress has been made. International cooperation has been strong, with a clear UN mandate and a NATO-led peacekeeping force (the International Security Assistance Force, or ISAF). More than 10,000 American soldiers are deployed today in Afghanistan, joined by soldiers from NATO allies and Muslim states. A central government has been established in Kabul, with a democratic constitution, new currency, and a new army. Most Afghans enjoy greater freedom, women and girls are emerging from subjugation, and 3 million children have returned to school. For the first time in many years, Afghans have reason to hope.[11]

But grave challenges remain. Taliban and al Qaeda fighters have regrouped in the south and

southeast. Warlords control much of the country beyond Kabul, and the land is awash in weapons. Economic development remains a distant hope. The narcotics trade—long a massive sector of the Afghan economy—is again booming. Even the most hardened aid workers refuse to operate in many regions, and some warn that Afghanistan is near the brink of chaos.[12]

Battered Afghanistan has a chance. Elections are being prepared. It is revealing that in June 2004, Taliban fighters resorted to slaughtering 16 Afghans on a bus, apparently for no reason other than their boldness in carrying an unprecedented Afghan weapon: a voter registration card.

Afghanistan's president, Hamid Karzai, is brave and committed. He is trying to build genuinely national institutions that can overcome the tradition of allocating powers among ethnic communities. Yet even if his efforts are successful and elections bring a democratic government to Afghanistan, the United States faces some difficult choices.

After paying relatively little attention to rebuilding Afghanistan during the military campaign, U.S. policies changed noticeably during 2003. Greater consideration of the political dimension and congressional support for a substantial package of assistance signaled a longer-term commitment to Afghanistan's future. One Afghan regional official plaintively told us the country finally has a good government. He begged the United States to keep its promise and not abandon Afghanistan again, as it had in the 1990s. Another Afghan leader noted that if the United States leaves, "we will lose all that we have gained."[13]

Most difficult is to define the security mission in Afghanistan. There is continuing political controversy about whether military operations in Iraq have had any effect on the scale of America's commitment to the future of Afghanistan. The United States has largely stayed out of the central government's struggles with dissident warlords and it has largely avoided confronting the related problem of narcotraficking.[14]

RECOMMENDATION: The President and the Congress deserve praise for their efforts in Afghanistan so far. Now the United States and the international community should make a long-term commitment to a secure and stable Afghanistan, in order to give the government a reasonable opportunity to improve the life of the Afghan people. Afghanistan must not again become a sanctuary for international crime and terrorism. The United States and the international community should help the Afghan government extend its authority over the country, with a strategy and nation-by-nation commitments to achieve their objectives.

- This is an ambitious recommendation. It would mean a redoubled effort to secure the country, disarm militias, and curtail the age of warlord rule. But the United States and NATO have already committed themselves to the future of this region—wisely, as the 9/11 story shows—and failed half-measures could be worse than useless.
- NATO in particular has made Afghanistan a test of the Alliance's ability to adapt to current security challenges of the future. NATO must pass this test. Currently, the United States and the international community envision enough support so that the central government can build a truly national army and extend essential infrastructure and minimum public services to major towns and regions. The effort relies in part on foreign civil-military teams, arranged under various national flags. The institutional commitments of NATO and the United Nations to these enterprises are weak. NATO member states are not following through; some of the other states around the world that have pledged assistance to Afghanistan are not fulfilling their pledges.
- The U.S. presence in Afghanistan is overwhelmingly oriented toward military and security work. The State Department presence is woefully understaffed, and the military mission is narrowly focused on al Qaeda and Taliban remnants in the south and southeast. The U.S. government can do its part if the international community decides on a joint effort to restore the rule of law and contain rampant crime and narcotics trafficking in this crossroads of Central Asia.[15]

We heard again and again that the money for assistance is allocated so rigidly that, on the ground, one U.S. agency often cannot improvise or pitch in to help another agency, even in small ways when a few thousand dollars could make a great difference.

The U.S. government should allocate money so that lower-level officials have more flexibility to get the job done across agency lines, adjusting to the circumstances they find in the field. This should include discretionary funds for expenditures by military units that often encounter opportunities to help the local population.

Saudi Arabia

Saudi Arabia has been a problematic ally in combating Islamic extremism. At the level of high policy, Saudi Arabia's leaders cooperated with American diplomatic initiatives aimed at the Taliban or Pakistan before 9/11. At the same time, Saudi Arabia's society was a place where al Qaeda raised money directly from individuals and through charities. It was the society that produced 15 of the 19 hijackers.

The Kingdom is one of the world's most religiously conservative societies, and its identity is closely bound to its religious links, especially its position as the guardian of Islam's two holiest sites. Charitable giving, or *zakat*, is one of the five pillars of Islam. It is broader and more pervasive than Western ideas of charity—functioning also as a form of income tax, educational assistance, foreign aid, and a source of political influence. The Western notion of the separation of civic and religious duty does not exist in Islamic cultures. Funding charitable works is an integral function of the governments in the Islamic world. It is so ingrained in Islamic culture that in Saudi Arabia, for example, a department within the Saudi Ministry of Finance and National Economy collects zakat directly, much as the U.S. Internal Revenue Service collects payroll withholding tax. Closely tied to zakat is the dedication of the government to propagating the Islamic faith, particularly the Wahhabi sect that flourishes in Saudi Arabia.

Traditionally, throughout the Muslim world, there is no formal oversight mechanism for donations. As Saudi wealth increased, the amounts contributed by individuals and the state grew dramatically. Substantial sums went to finance Islamic charities of every kind.

While Saudi domestic charities are regulated by the Ministry of Labor and Social Welfare, charities and international relief agencies, such as the World Assembly of Muslim Youth (WAMY), are currently regulated by the Ministry of Islamic Affairs. This ministry uses zakat and government funds to spread Wahhabi beliefs throughout the world, including in mosques and schools. Often these schools provide the only education available; even in affluent countries, Saudi-funded Wahhabi schools are often the only Islamic schools. Some Wahhabi-funded organizations have been exploited by extremists to further their goal of violent jihad against non-Muslims. One such organization has been the al Haramain Islamic Foundation; the assets of some branch offices have been frozen by the U.S. and Saudi governments.

Until 9/11, few Saudis would have considered government oversight of charitable donations necessary; many would have perceived it as interference in the exercise of their faith. At the same time, the government's ability to finance most state expenditures with energy revenues has delayed the need for a modern income tax system. As a result, there have been strong religious, cultural, and administrative barriers to monitoring charitable spending. That appears to be changing, however, now that the goal of violent jihad also extends to overthrowing Sunni governments (such as the House of Saud) that are not living up to the ideals of the Islamist extremists.[16]

The leaders of the United States and the rulers of Saudi Arabia have long had friendly relations, rooted in fundamentally common interests against the Soviet Union during the Cold War, in American hopes that Saudi oil supplies would stabilize the supply and price of oil in world markets, and in Saudi hopes that America could help protect the Kingdom against foreign threats.

In 1990, the Kingdom hosted U.S. armed forces before the first U.S.-led war against Iraq. American soldiers and airmen have given their lives to help protect Saudi Arabia. The Saudi government has difficulty acknowledging this. American military bases remained there until 2003, as part of an international commitment to contain Iraq.

For many years, leaders on both sides preferred to keep their ties quiet and behind the scenes. As a result, neither the U.S. nor the Saudi people appreciated all the dimensions of the bilateral relationship, including the Saudi role in U.S. strategies to promote the Middle East peace process. In each country, political figures find it difficult to publicly defend good relations with the other.

Today, mutual recriminations flow. Many Americans see Saudi Arabia as an enemy, not as an embattled ally. They perceive an autocratic government that oppresses women, dominated by a wealthy and indolent elite. Saudi contacts with American politicians are frequently invoked as accusations in partisan political arguments. Americans are often appalled by the intolerance, anti-Semitism, and anti-American arguments taught in schools and preached in mosques.

Saudis are angry too. Many educated Saudis who were sympathetic to America now perceive the United States as an unfriendly state. One Saudi reformer noted to us that the demonization of Saudi Arabia in the U.S. media gives ammunition to radicals, who accuse reformers of being U.S. lackeys. Tens of thousands of Saudis who once regularly traveled to (and often had homes in) the United States now go elsewhere.[17]

Among Saudis, the United States is seen as aligned with Israel in its conflict with the Palestinians, with whom Saudis ardently sympathize. Although Saudi Arabia's cooperation against terrorism improved to some extent after the September 11 attacks, significant problems remained. Many in the Kingdom initially reacted with disbelief and denial. In the following months, as the truth became clear, some leading Saudis quietly acknowledged the problem but still did not see their own regime as threatened, and thus often did not respond promptly to U.S. requests for help. Though Saddam Hussein was widely detested, many Saudis are sympathetic to the anti-U.S. insurgents in Iraq, although majorities also condemn jihadist attacks in the Kingdom.[18]

As in Pakistan, Yemen, and other countries, attitudes changed when the terrorism came home. Cooperation had already become significant, but after the bombings in Riyadh on May 12, 2003, it improved much more. The Kingdom openly discussed the problem of radicalism, criticized the terrorists as religiously deviant, reduced official support for religious activity overseas, closed suspect charitable foundations, and publicized arrests—very public moves for a government that has preferred to keep internal problems quiet.

The Kingdom of Saudi Arabia is now locked in mortal combat with al Qaeda. Saudi police are regularly being killed in shootouts with terrorists. In June 2004, the Saudi ambassador to the United States called publicly—in the Saudi press—for his government to wage a jihad of its own against the terrorists. "We must all, as a state and as a people, recognize the truth about these criminals," he declared, "[i]f we do not declare a general mobilization—we will lose this war on terrorism."[19]

Saudi Arabia is a troubled country. Although regarded as very wealthy, in fact per capita income has dropped from $28,000 at its height to the present level of about $8,000. Social and religious traditions complicate adjustment to modern economic activity and limit employment opportunities for young Saudis. Women find their education and employment sharply limited.

President Clinton offered us a perceptive analysis of Saudi Arabia, contending that fundamentally friendly rulers have been constrained by their desire to preserve the status quo. He, like others, made the case for pragmatic reform instead. He hopes the rulers will envision what they want their Kingdom to become in 10 or 20 years, and start a process in which their friends can help them change.[20]

There are signs that Saudi Arabia's royal family is trying to build a consensus for political reform, though uncertain about how fast and how far to go. Crown Prince Abdullah wants the Kingdom to join the World Trade Organization to accelerate economic liberalization. He has embraced the *Arab Human Development Report*, which was highly critical of the Arab world's political, economic, and social failings and called for greater economic and political reform.[21]

Cooperation with Saudi Arabia against Islamist terrorism is very much in the U.S. interest. Such cooperation can exist for a time largely in secret, as it does now, but it cannot grow and thrive there. Nor, on either side, can friendship be unconditional.

RECOMMENDATION: The problems in the U.S. Saudi relationship must be confronted, openly. The United States and Saudi Arabia must determine if they can build a relationship that political leaders on both sides are prepared to publicly defend—a relationship about more than oil. It should include a shared commitment to political and economic reform, as Saudis make common cause with the outside world. It should include a shared interest in greater tolerance and cultural respect, translating into a commitment to fight the violent extremists who foment hatred.

PREVENT THE CONTINUED GROWTH OF ISLAMIST TERRORISM

In October 2003, reflecting on progress after two years of waging the global war on terrorism, Defense Secretary Donald Rumsfeld asked his advisers: "Are we capturing, killing or deterring and dissuading more terrorists every day than the madrassas and the radical clerics are recruiting, training and deploying against us? Does the US need to fashion a broad, integrated plan to stop the next generation of terrorists? The US is putting relatively little effort into a long-range plan, but we are putting a great deal of effort into trying to stop terrorists. The cost-benefit ratio is against us! Our cost is billions against the terrorists' costs of millions."[22]

These are the right questions. Our answer is that we need short-term action on a long-range strategy, one that invigorates our foreign policy with the attention that the President and Congress have given to the military and intelligence parts of the conflict against Islamist terrorism.

Engage the Struggle of Ideas

The United States is heavily engaged in the Muslim world and will be for many years to come. This American engagement is resented. Polls in 2002 found that among America's friends, like Egypt—the recipient of more U.S. aid for the past 20 years than any other Muslim country—only 15 percent of the population had a favorable opinion of the United States. In Saudi Arabia the number was 12 percent. And two-thirds of those surveyed in 2003 in countries from Indonesia to Turkey (a NATO ally) were very or somewhat fearful that the United States may attack them.[23]

Support for the United States has plummeted. Polls taken in Islamic countries after 9/11 suggested that many or most people thought the United States was doing the right thing in its fight against terrorism; few people saw popular support for al Qaeda; half of those surveyed said that ordinary people had a favorable view of the United States. By 2003, polls showed that "the bottom has fallen out of support for America in most of the Muslim world. Negative views of the U.S. among Muslims, which had been largely limited to countries in the Middle East, have spread....Since last summer, favorable ratings for the U.S. have fallen from 61% to 15% in Indonesia and from 71% to 38% among Muslims in Nigeria."[24]

Many of these views are at best uninformed about the United States and, at worst, informed by cartoonish stereotypes, the coarse expression of a fashionable "Occidentalism" among intellectuals who caricature U.S. values and policies. Local newspapers and the few influential satellite broadcasters—like al Jazeera—often reinforce the jihadist theme that portrays the United States as anti-Muslim.[25]

The small percentage of Muslims who are fully committed to Usama Bin Ladin's version of Islam are impervious to persuasion. It is among the large majority of Arabs and Muslims that we must encourage reform, freedom, democracy, and opportunity, even though our own promotion of these messages is limited in its effectiveness simply because we are its carriers. Muslims themselves will have to reflect upon such basic issues as the concept of jihad, the position of women, and the place of non-Muslim minorities. The United States can promote moderation, but cannot ensure its ascendancy. Only Muslims can do this.

The setting is difficult. The combined gross domestic product of the 22 countries in the Arab League is less than the GDP of Spain. Forty percent of adult Arabs are illiterate, two-thirds of them women. One-third of the broader Middle East lives on less than two dollars a day. Less than 2 percent of the population has access to the Internet. The majority of older Arab youths have expressed a desire to emigrate to other countries, particularly those in Europe.[26]

In short, the United States has to help defeat an ideology, not just a group of people, and we must do so under difficult circumstances. How can the United States and its friends help moderate Muslims combat the extremist ideas?

RECOMMENDATION: The U.S. government must define what the message is, what it stands for. We should offer an example of moral leadership in the world, committed to treat people humanely, abide by the rule of law, and be generous and caring to our neighbors. America and Muslim friends can agree on respect for human dignity and opportunity. To Muslim parents, terrorists like Bin Ladin have nothing to offer their children but visions of violence and death. America and its friends have a crucial advantage—we can offer these parents a vision that might give their children a better future. If we heed the views of thoughtful leaders in the Arab and Muslim world, a moderate consensus can be found.

That vision of the future should stress life over death: individual educational and economic opportunity. This vision includes widespread political participation and contempt for indiscriminate violence. It includes respect for the rule of law, openness in discussing differences, and tolerance for opposing points of view.

RECOMMENDATION: Where Muslim governments, even those who are friends, do not respect these principles, the United States must stand for a better future. One of the lessons of the long Cold War was that short-term gains in cooperating with the most repressive and brutal governments were too often outweighed by long-term setbacks for America's stature and interests.

American foreign policy is part of the message. America's policy choices have consequences. Right or wrong, it is simply a fact that American policy regarding the Israeli-Palestinian conflict and American actions in Iraq are dominant staples of popular commentary across the Arab and Muslim world. That does not mean U.S. choices have been wrong. It means those choices must be integrated with America's message of opportunity to the Arab and Muslim world. Neither Israel nor the new Iraq will be safer if worldwide Islamist terrorism grows stronger.

The United States must do more to communicate its message. Reflecting on Bin Ladin's success in reaching Muslim audiences, Richard Holbrooke wondered, "How can a man in a cave outcommunicate the world's leading communications society?" Deputy Secretary of State Richard Armitage worried to us that Americans have been "exporting our fears and our anger," not our vision of opportunity and hope.[27]

RECOMMENDATION: Just as we did in the Cold War, we need to defend our ideals abroad vigorously. America does stand up for its values. The United States defended, and still defends, Muslims against tyrants and criminals in Somalia, Bosnia, Kosovo, Afghanistan, and Iraq. If the United States does not act aggressively to define itself in the Islamic world, the extremists will gladly do the job for us.

- Recognizing that Arab and Muslim audiences rely on satellite television and radio, the government has begun some promising initiatives in television and radio broadcasting to the Arab world, Iran, and Afghanistan. These efforts are beginning to reach large audiences. The Broadcasting Board of Governors has asked for much larger resources. It should get them.
- The United States should rebuild the scholarship, exchange, and library programs that reach out to young people and offer them knowledge and hope. Where such assistance is provided, it should be identified as coming from the citizens of the United States.

An Agenda of Opportunity

The United States and its friends can stress educational and economic opportunity. The United Nations has rightly equated "literacy as freedom."

- The international community is moving toward setting a concrete goal—to cut the Middle East region's illiteracy rate in half by 2010, targeting women and girls and supporting programs for adult literacy.
- Unglamorous help is needed to support the basics, such as textbooks that translate more of the world's knowledge into local languages and

libraries to house such materials. Education about the outside world, or other cultures, is weak.

- More vocational education is needed, too, in trades and business skills. The Middle East can also benefit from some of the programs to bridge the digital divide and increase Internet access that have already been developed for other regions of the world.

Education that teaches tolerance, the dignity and value of each individual, and respect for different beliefs is a key element in any global strategy to eliminate Islamist terrorism.

RECOMMENDATION: The U.S. government should offer to join with other nations in generously supporting a new International Youth Opportunity Fund. Funds will be spent directly for building and operating primary and secondary schools in those Muslim states that commit to sensibly investing their own money in public education.

Economic openness is essential. Terrorism is not caused by poverty. Indeed, many terrorists come from relatively well-off families. Yet when people lose hope, when societies break down, when countries fragment, the breeding grounds for terrorism are created. Backward economic policies and repressive political regimes slip into societies that are without hope, where ambition and passions have no constructive outlet.

The policies that support economic development and reform also have political implications. Economic and political liberties tend to be linked. Commerce, especially international commerce, requires ongoing cooperation and compromise, the exchange of ideas across cultures, and the peaceful resolution of differences through negotiation or the rule of law. Economic growth expands the middle class, a constituency for further reform. Successful economies rely on vibrant private sectors, which have an interest in curbing indiscriminate government power. Those who develop the practice of controlling their own economic destiny soon desire a voice in their communities and political societies.

The U.S. government has announced the goal of working toward a Middle East Free Trade Area, or MEFTA, by 2013. The United States has been seeking comprehensive free trade agreements (FTAs) with the Middle Eastern nations most firmly on the path to reform. The U.S.-Israeli FTA was enacted in 1985, and Congress implemented an FTA with Jordan in 2001. Both agreements have expanded trade and investment, thereby supporting domestic economic reform. In 2004, new FTAs were signed with Morocco and Bahrain, and are awaiting congressional approval. These models are drawing the interest of their neighbors. Muslim countries can become full participants in the rules-based global trading system, as the United States considers lowering its trade barriers with the poorest Arab nations.

RECOMMENDATION: A comprehensive U.S. strategy to counter terrorism should include economic policies that encourage development, more open societies, and opportunities for people to improve the lives of their families and to enhance prospects for their children's future.

Turning a National Strategy Into a Coalition Strategy

Practically every aspect of U.S. counterterrorism strategy relies on international cooperation. Since 9/11, these contacts concerning military, law enforcement, intelligence, travel and customs, and financial matters have expanded so dramatically, and often in an ad hoc way, that it is difficult to track these efforts, much less integrate them.

RECOMMENDATION: The United States should engage other nations in developing a comprehensive coalition strategy against Islamist terrorism. There are several multilateral institutions in which such issues should be addressed. But the most important policies should be discussed and coordinated in a flexible contact group of leading coalition governments. This is a good place, for example, to develop joint strategies for targeting terrorist travel, or for hammering out a common strategy for the places where terrorists may be finding sanctuary.

Presently the Muslim and Arab states meet with each other, in organizations such as the Islamic Conference and the Arab League. The Western states meet with each other in organizations such as NATO and the Group of Eight summit of leading industrial nations. A recent G-8 summit initiative to begin a dialogue about reform may be a start toward finding a place where leading Muslim states can discuss—and be seen to discuss—critical policy issues with the leading Western powers committed to the future of the Arab and Muslim world.

These new international efforts can create durable habits of visible cooperation, as states willing to step up to their responsibilities join together in constructive efforts to direct assistance and coordinate action.

Coalition warfare also requires coalition policies on what to do with enemy captives. Allegations that the United States abused prisoners in its custody make it harder to build the diplomatic, political, and military alliances the government will need. The United States should work with friends to develop mutually agreed-on principles for the detention and humane treatment of captured international terrorists who are not being held under a particular country's criminal laws. Countries such as Britain, Australia, and Muslim friends, are committed to fighting terrorists. America should be able to reconcile its views on how to balance humanity and security with our nation's commitment to these same goals.

The United States and some of its allies do not accept the application of full Geneva Convention treatment of prisoners of war to captured terrorists. Those Conventions establish a minimum set of standards for prisoners in internal conflicts. Since the international struggle against Islamist terrorism is not internal, those provisions do not formally apply, but they are commonly accepted as basic standards for humane treatment.

RECOMMENDATION: The United States should engage its friends to develop a common coalition approach toward the detention and humane treatment of captured terrorists. New principles might draw upon Article 3 of the Geneva Conventions on the law of armed conflict. That article was specifically designed for those cases in which the usual laws of war did not apply. Its minimum standards are generally accepted throughout the world as customary international law.

Proliferation of Weapons of Mass Destruction

The greatest danger of another catastrophic attack in the United States will materialize if the world's most dangerous terrorists acquire the world's most dangerous weapons.... [A]l Qaeda has tried to acquire or make nuclear weapons for at least ten years.... [O]fficials worriedly discuss[ed], in 1998, reports that Bin Ladin's associates thought their leader was intent on carrying out a "Hiroshima."

These ambitions continue. In the public portion of his February 2004 worldwide threat assessment to Congress, DCI Tenet noted that Bin Ladin considered the acquisition of weapons of mass destruction to be a "religious obligation." He warned that al Qaeda "continues to pursue its strategic goal of obtaining a nuclear capability." Tenet added that

"more than two dozen other terrorist groups are pursuing CBRN [chemical, biological, radiological, and nuclear] materials."[28]

A nuclear bomb can be built with a relatively small amount of nuclear material. A trained nuclear engineer with an amount of highly enriched uranium or plutonium about the size of a grapefruit or an orange, together with commercially available material, could fashion a nuclear device that would fit in a van like the one Ramzi Yousef parked in the garage of the World Trade Center in 1993. Such a bomb would level Lower Manhattan.[29]

The coalition strategies we have discussed to combat Islamist terrorism should therefore be combined with a parallel, vital effort to prevent and counter the proliferation of weapons of mass destruction (WMD). We recommend several initiatives in this area.

STRENGTHEN COUNTERPROLIFERATION EFFORTS. While efforts to shut down Libya's illegal nuclear program have been generally successful, Pakistan's illicit trade and the nuclear smuggling networks of Pakistani scientist A. Q. Khan have revealed that the spread of nuclear weapons is a problem of global dimensions. Attempts to deal with Iran's nuclear program are still underway. Therefore, the United States should work with the international community to develop laws and an international legal regime with universal jurisdiction to enable the capture, interdiction, and prosecution of such smugglers by any state in the world where they do not disclose their activities.

EXPAND THE PROLIFERATION SECURITY INITIATIVE. In May 2003, the Bush administration announced the Proliferation Security Initiative (PSI): nations in a willing partnership combining their national capabilities to use military, economic, and diplomatic tools to interdict threatening shipments of WMD and missile-related technology.

The PSI can be more effective if it uses intelligence and planning resources of the NATO alliance. Moreover, PSI membership should be open to non-NATO countries. Russia and China should be encouraged to participate.

SUPPORT THE COOPERATIVE THREAT REDUCTION PROGRAM. Outside experts are deeply worried about the U.S. government's commitment and approach to securing the weapons and highly dangerous materials still scattered in Russia and other countries of the Soviet Union. The government's main instrument in this area, the Cooperative Threat Reduction Program (usually referred to as "Nunn-Lugar," after the senators who sponsored the legislation in 1991), is now in need of expansion, improvement, and resources. The U.S. government has recently redoubled its international commitments to support this program, and we recommend that the United States do all it can, if Russia and other countries will do their part. The government should weigh the value of this investment against the catastrophic cost America would face should such weapons find their way to the terrorists who are so anxious to acquire them.

RECOMMENDATION: Our report shows that al Qaeda has tried to acquire or make weapons of mass destruction for at least ten years. There is no doubt the United States would be a prime target. Preventing the proliferation of these weapons warrants a maximum effort—by strengthening counterproliferation efforts, expanding the proliferation Security Initiative, and supporting the Cooperative Threat Reduction program.

Targeting Terrorist Money

The general public sees attacks on terrorist finance as a way to "starve the terrorists of money." So, initially, did the U.S. government. After 9/11, the United States took aggressive actions to designate terrorist financiers and freeze their money, in the United States and through resolutions of the United Nations. These actions appeared to have little effect and, when confronted by legal challenges, the United States and the United Nations were often forced to unfreeze assets.

The difficulty, understood later, was that even if the intelligence community might "link" someone to a terrorist group through acquaintances or communications, the task of tracing the money from that individual to the terrorist group, or otherwise showing complicity, was far more difficult. It was harder still to do so without disclosing secrets.

These early missteps made other countries unwilling to freeze assets or otherwise act merely on the basis of a U.S. action. Multilateral freezing mechanisms now require waiting periods before being put into effect, eliminating the element of surprise and thus virtually ensuring that little money is actually frozen. Worldwide asset freezes have not been adequately enforced and have been easily circumvented, often within weeks, by simple methods.

But trying to starve the terrorists of money is like trying to catch one kind of fish by draining the ocean. A better strategy has evolved since those early months, as the government learned more about how al Qaeda raises, moves, and spends money.

RECOMMENDATION: Vigorous efforts to track terrorist financing must remain front and center in U.S. counterterrorism efforts. The government has recognized that information about terrorist money helps us to understand their networks, search them out, and disrupt their operations. Intelligence and law enforcement have targeted the relatively small number of financial facilitators—individuals al Qaeda relied on for their ability to raise and deliver money—at the core of al Qaeda's revenue stream. These efforts have worked. The death or capture of several important facilitators has decreased the amount of money available to al Qaeda and has increased its costs and difficulty in raising and moving that money. Captures have additionally provided a windfall of intelligence that can be used to continue the cycle of disruption.

The U.S. financial community and some international financial institutions have generally provided law enforcement and intelligence agencies with extraordinary cooperation, particularly in supplying information to support quickly developing investigations. Obvious vulnerabilities in the U.S. financial system have been corrected. The United States has been less successful in persuading other countries to adopt financial regulations that would permit the tracing of financial transactions.

Public designation of terrorist financiers and organizations is still part of the fight, but it is not the primary weapon. Designations are instead a form of diplomacy, as governments join together to identify named individuals and groups as terrorists. They also prevent open fundraising. Some charities that have been identified as likely avenues for terrorist financing have seen their donations diminish and their activities come under more scrutiny, and others have been put out of business, although controlling overseas branches of Gulf-area charities remains a challenge. The Saudi crackdown after the May 2003 terrorist attacks in Riyadh has apparently reduced the funds available to al Qaeda—perhaps drastically—but it is too soon to know if this reduction will last.

Though progress apparently has been made, terrorists have shown considerable creativity in their methods of moving money. If al Qaeda is replaced by smaller, decentralized terrorist groups, the premise behind the government's efforts—that terrorists need a financial support network—may become outdated. Moreover, some terrorist operations do not rely on outside sources of money and may now be self-funding, either through legitimate employment or low-level criminal activity.[30]

PROTECT AGAINST AND PREPARE FOR TERRORIST ATTACKS

In the nearly three years since 9/11, Americans have become better protected against terrorist attack. Some of the changes are due to government action, such as new precautions to protect aircraft. A portion can be attributed to the sheer scale of spending and effort. Publicity and the vigilance of ordinary Americans also make a difference.

But the President and other officials acknowledge that although Americans may be safer, they are not safe. Our report shows that the terrorists analyze defenses. They plan accordingly.

Defenses cannot achieve perfect safety. They make targets harder to attack successfully, and they deter attacks by making capture more likely. Just increasing the attacker's odds of failure may make the difference between a plan attempted, or a plan discarded. The enemy also may have to develop more elaborate plans, thereby increasing the danger of exposure or defeat.

Protective measures also prepare for the attacks that may get through, containing the damage and saving lives.

TERRORIST TRAVEL

More than 500 million people annually cross U.S. borders at legal entry points, about 330 million of them noncitizens. Another 500,000 or more enter illegally without inspection across America's thousands of miles of land borders or remain in the country past the expiration of their permitted stay. The challenge for national security in an age of terrorism is to prevent the very few people who may pose overwhelming risks from entering or remaining in the United States undetected.[31]

In the decade before September 11, 2001, border security—encompassing travel, entry, and immigration—was not seen as a national security matter. Public figures voiced concern about the "war on drugs," the right level and kind of immigration, problems along the southwest border, migration crises originating in the Caribbean and elsewhere, or

the growing criminal traffic in humans. The immigration system as a whole was widely viewed as increasingly dysfunctional and badly in need of reform. In national security circles, however, only smuggling of weapons of mass destruction carried weight, not the entry of terrorists who might use such weapons or the presence of associated foreign born terrorists.

For terrorists, travel documents are as important as weapons. Terrorists must travel clandestinely to meet, train, plan, case targets, and gain access to attack. To them, international travel presents great danger, because they must surface to pass through regulated channels, present themselves to border security officials, or attempt to circumvent inspection points.

In their travels, terrorists use evasive methods, such as altered and counterfeit passports and visas, specific travel methods and routes, liaisons with corrupt government officials, human smuggling networks, supportive travel agencies, and immigration and identity fraud. These can sometimes be detected.

Before 9/11, no agency of the U.S. government systematically analyzed terrorists' travel strategies. Had they done so, they could have discovered the ways in which the terrorist predecessors to al Qaeda had been systematically but detectably exploiting weaknesses in our border security since the early 1990s.

We found that as many as 15 of the 19 hijackers were potentially vulnerable to interception by border authorities. Analyzing their characteristic travel documents and travel patterns could have allowed authorities to intercept 4 to 15 hijackers and more effective use of information available in U.S. government databases could have identified up to 3 hijackers.[32]

Looking back, we can also see that the routine operations of our immigration laws—that is, aspects of those laws not specifically aimed at protecting against terrorism—inevitably shaped al Qaeda's planning and opportunities. Because they were deemed not to be hona fide tourists or students as they claimed, five conspirators that we know of tried to get visas and failed, and one was denied entry by an inspector. We also found that had the immigration system set a higher bar for determining whether individuals are who or what they claim to be—and ensuring routine consequences for violations—it could potentially have excluded, removed, or come into further contact with several hijackers who did not appear to meet the terms for admitting short-term visitors.[33]

Our investigation showed that two systemic weaknesses came together in our border system's inability to contribute to an effective defense against the 9/11 attacks: a lack of well-developed counterterrorism measures as a part of border security and an immigration system not able to deliver on its basic commitments, much less support counterterrorism. These weaknesses have been reduced but are far from being overcome.

RECOMMENDATION: Targeting travel is at least as powerful a weapon against terrorists as targeting their money. The United States should combine terrorist travel intelligence, operations, and law enforcement in a strategy to intercept terrorists, find terrorist travel facilitators, and constrain terrorist mobility.

Since 9/11, significant improvements have been made to create an integrated watchlist that makes terrorist name information available to border and law enforcement authorities. However, in the already difficult process of merging border agencies in the new Department of Homeland Security—"changing the engine while flying" as one official put it[34]—new insights into terrorist travel have not yet been integrated into the front lines of border security.

The small terrorist travel intelligence collection and analysis program currently in place has produced disproportionately useful results. It should be expanded. Since officials at the borders encounter travelers and their documents first and investigate travel facilitators, they must work closely with intelligence officials.

Internationally and in the United States, constraining terrorist travel should become a vital part of counterterrorism strategy. Better technology and training to detect terrorist travel documents are the most important immediate steps to reduce America's vulnerability to clandestine entry. Every stage of our border and immigration system should have as a part of its operations the detection of terrorist indicators on travel documents. Information systems able to authenticate travel documents and detect potential terrorist indicators should be used at consulates, at primary border inspection lines, in immigration services offices, and in intelligence and enforcement units. All frontline personnel should receive some training. Dedicated specialists and ongoing linkages with the intelligence community are also required. The Homeland Security Department's Directorate of

Information Analysis and Infrastructure Protection should receive more resources to accomplish its mission as the bridge between the frontline border agencies and the rest of the government counterterrorism community.

A BIOMETRIC SCREENING SYSTEM

When people travel internationally, they usually move through defined channels, or portals. They may seek to acquire a passport. They may apply for a visa. They stop at ticket counters, gates, and exit controls at airports and seaports. Upon arrival, they pass through inspection points. They may transit to another gate to get on an airplane. Once inside the country, they may seek another form of identification and try to enter a government or private facility. They may seek to change immigration status in order to remain.

Each of these checkpoints or portals is a screening—a chance to establish that people are who they say they are and are seeking access for their stated purpose, to intercept identifiable suspects, and to take effective action.

The job of protection is shared among these many defined checkpoints. By taking advantage of them all, we need not depend on any one point in the system to do the whole job. The challenge is to see the common problem across agencies and functions and develop a conceptual framework—an architecture—for an effective screening system.[35]

Throughout government, and indeed in private enterprise, agencies and firms at these portals confront recurring judgments that balance security, efficiency, and civil liberties. These problems should be addressed systemically, not in an ad hoc, fragmented way. For example:

What information is an individual required to present and in what form? A fundamental problem, now beginning to be addressed, is the lack of standardized information in "feeder" documents used in identifying individuals. Biometric identifiers that measure unique physical characteristics, such as facial features, fingerprints, or iris scans, and reduce them to digitized, numerical statements called algorithms, are just beginning to be used. Travel history, however, is still recorded in passports with entry-exit stamps called cachets, which al Qaeda has trained its operatives to forge and use to conceal their terrorist activities.

How will the individual and the information be checked? There are many databases just in the United States—for terrorist, criminal, and immigration history, as well as financial information, for instance. Each is set up for different purposes and stores different kinds of data, under varying rules of access. Nor is access always guaranteed. Acquiring information held by foreign governments may require painstaking negotiations, and records that are not yet digitized are difficult to search or analyze. The development of terrorist indicators has hardly begun, and behavioral cues remain important.

Who will screen individuals, and what will they be trained to do? A wide range of border, immigration, and law enforcement officials encounter visitors and immigrants and they are given little training in terrorist travel intelligence. Fraudulent travel documents, for instance, are usually returned to travelers who are denied entry without further examination for terrorist trademarks, investigation as to their source, or legal process.

What are the consequences of finding a suspicious indicator, and who will take action? One risk is that responses may be ineffective or produce no further information. Four of the 9/11 attackers were pulled into secondary border inspection, but then admitted. More than half of the 19 hijackers were flagged by the Federal Aviation Administration's profiling system when they arrived for their flights, but the consequence was that bags, not people, were checked. Competing risks include "false positives," or the danger that rules may be applied with insufficient training or judgment. Overreactions can impose high costs too—on individuals, our economy, and our beliefs about justice.

- A special note on the importance of trusting subjective judgment: One potential hijacker was turned back by an immigration inspector as he tried to enter the United States. The inspector relied on intuitive experience to ask questions more than he relied on any objective factor that could be detected by "scores" or a machine. Good people who have worked in such jobs for a long time understand this phenomenon well. Other evidence we obtained confirmed the importance of letting experienced gate agents or security screeners ask questions and use their judgment. This is not an invitation to arbitrary exclusions. But any effective system has to grant some scope, perhaps in a little extra inspection or one more check, to the instincts and discretion of well trained human beings.

RECOMMENDATION: The U.S. border security system should be integrated into a larger network of screening points that includes our transportation system and access to vital facilities, such as nuclear reactors. The President should direct the Department of Homeland Security to lead the effort to design a comprehensive screening system, addressing common problems and setting common standards with systemwide goals in mind. Extending those standards among other governments could dramatically strengthen America and the world's collective ability to intercept individuals who pose catastrophic threats.

We advocate a system for screening, not categorical profiling. A screening system looks for particular, identifiable suspects or indicators of risk. It does not involve guesswork about who might be dangerous. It requires frontline border officials who have the tools and resources to establish that people are who they say they are, intercept identifiable suspects, and disrupt terrorist operations.

THE U.S. BORDER SCREENING SYSTEM

The border and immigration system of the United States must remain a visible manifestation of our belief in freedom, democracy, global economic growth, and the rule of law, yet serve equally well as a vital element of counterterrorism. Integrating terrorist travel information in the ways we have described is the most immediate need. But the underlying system must also be sound.

Since September 11, the United States has built the first phase of a biometric screening program, called US VISIT (the United States Visitor and Immigrant Status Indicator Technology program). It takes two biometric identifiers—digital photographs and prints of two index fingers—from travelers. False identities are used by terrorists to avoid being detected on a watchlist. These biometric identifiers make such evasions far more difficult.

So far, however, only visitors who acquire visas to travel to the United States are covered. While visitors from "visa waiver" countries will be added to the program, beginning this year, covered travelers will still constitute only about 12 percent of all noncitizens crossing U.S. borders. Moreover, exit data are not uniformly collected and entry data are not fully automated. It is not clear the system can be installed before 2010, but even this timetable may be too slow, given the possible security dangers.[36]

- Americans should not be exempt from carrying biometric passports or otherwise enabling their identities to be securely verified when they enter the United States; nor should Canadians or Mexicans. Currently U.S. persons are exempt from carrying passports when returning from Canada, Mexico, and the Caribbean. The current system enables non-U.S. citizens to gain entry by showing minimal identification. The 9/11 experience shows that terrorists study and exploit America's vulnerabilities.
- To balance this measure, programs to speed known travelers should be a higher priority, permitting inspectors to focus on greater risks. The daily commuter should not be subject to the same measures as first-time travelers. An individual should be able to preenroll, with his or her identity verified in passage. Updates of database information and other checks can ensure ongoing reliability. The solution, requiring more research and development, is likely to combine radio frequency technology with biometric identifiers.[37]
- The current patchwork of border screening systems, including several frequent traveler programs, should be consolidated with the US VISIT system to enable the development of an integrated system, which in turn can become part of the wider screening plan we suggest.
- The program allowing individuals to travel from foreign countries through the United States to a third country, without having to obtain a U.S. visa, has been suspended. Because "transit without visa" can be exploited by terrorists to enter the United States, the program should not be reinstated unless and until transit passage areas can be fully secured to prevent passengers from illegally exiting the airport.

Inspectors adjudicating entries of the 9/11 hijackers lacked adequate information and knowledge of the rules. All points in the border system—from consular offices to immigration services offices—will need appropriate electronic access to an individual's file. Scattered units at Homeland Security and the State Department perform screening and data mining: instead, a government-wide team of border and transportation officials should be working together. A modern border and immigration system should combine a biometric entry-exit system with accessible files on visitors and immigrants, along with intelligence on indicators of terrorist travel.

Our border screening system should check people efficiently and welcome friends. Admitting large numbers of students, scholars, businesspeople, and tourists fuels our economy, cultural vitality, and political reach. There is evidence that the present system is disrupting travel to the United States. Overall, visa applications in 2003 were down over 32 percent since 2001. In the Middle East, they declined about 46 percent. Training and the design of security measures should be continuously adjusted.[38]

RECOMMENDATION: The Department of Homeland Security, properly supported by the Congress, should complete, as quickly as possible, a biometric entry-exit screening system, including a single system for speeding qualified travelers. It should be integrated with the system that provides benefits to foreigners seeking to stay in the United States. Linking biometric passports to good data systems and decisionmaking is a fundamental goal. No one can hide his or her debt by acquiring a credit card with a slightly different name. Yet today, a terrorist can defeat the link to electronic records by tossing away an old passport and slightly altering the name in the new one.

Completion of the entry-exit system is a major and expensive challenge. Biometrics have been introduced into an antiquated computer environment. Replacement of these systems and improved biometric systems will be required. Nonetheless, funding and completing a biometrics-based entry-exit system is an essential investment in our national security.

Exchanging terrorist information with other countries, consistent with privacy requirements, along with listings of lost and stolen passports, will have immediate security benefits. We should move toward real-time verification of passports with issuing authorities. The further away from our borders that screening occurs, the more security benefits we gain. At least some screening should occur before a passenger departs on a flight destined for the United States. We should also work with other countries to ensure effective inspection regimes at all airports.[39]

The international community arrives at international standards for the design of passports through the International Civil Aviation Organization (ICAO). The global standard for identification is a digital photograph; fingerprints are optional. We must work with others to improve passport standards and provide foreign assistance to countries that need help in making the transition.[40]

RECOMMENDATION: The U.S. government cannot meet its own obligations to the American people to prevent the entry of terrorists without a major effort to collaborate with other governments. We should do more to exchange terrorist information with trusted allies, and raise U.S. and global border security standards for travel and border crossing over the medium and long term through extensive international cooperation.

IMMIGRATION LAW AND ENFORCEMENT

Our borders and immigration system, including law enforcement, ought to send a message of welcome, tolerance, and justice to members of immigrant communities in the United States and in their countries of origin. We should reach out to immigrant communities. Good immigration services are one way of doing so that is valuable in every way—including intelligence.

It is elemental to border security to know who is coming into the country. Today more than 9 million people are in the United States outside the legal immigration system. We must also be able to monitor and respond to entrances between our ports of entry, working with Canada and Mexico as much as possible.

There is a growing role for state and local law enforcement agencies. They need more training and work with federal agencies so that they can cooperate more effectively with those federal authorities in identifying terrorist suspects.

All but one of the 9/11 hijackers acquired some form of U.S. identification document, some by fraud. Acquisition of these forms of identification would have assisted them in boarding commercial flights, renting cars, and other necessary activities.

RECOMMENDATION: Secure identification should begin in the United States. The federal government should set standards for the issuance of birth certificates and sources of identification, such as driver's licenses. Fraud in identification documents is no longer just a problem of theft. At many entry points to vulnerable facilities, including gates for boarding aircraft, sources of identification are the last opportunity to ensure that people are who they say they are and to check whether they are terrorists.[41]

STRATEGIES FOR AVIATION AND TRANSPORTATION SECURITY

The U.S. transportation system is vast and, in an open society, impossible to secure completely against terrorist attacks. There are hundreds of commercial airports, thousands of planes, and tens of thousands of daily flights carrying more than half a billion passengers a year. Millions of containers are imported annually through more than 300 sea and river ports served by more than 3,700 cargo and passenger terminals. About 6,000 agencies provide transit services through buses, subways, ferries, and light-rail service to about 14 million Americans each weekday.[42]

In November 2001, Congress passed and the President signed the Aviation and Transportation Security Act. This act created the Transportation Security Administration (TSA), which is now part of the Homeland Security Department. In November 2002, both the Homeland Security Act and the Maritime Transportation Security Act followed. These laws required the development of strategic plans to describe how the new department and TSA would provide security for critical parts of the U.S. transportation sector.

Over 90 percent of the nations $5.3 billion annual investment in the TSA goes to aviation—to fight the last war. The money has been spent mainly to meet congressional mandates to federalize the security checkpoint screeners and to deploy existing security methods and technologies at airports. The current efforts do not yet reflect a forward-looking strategic plan systematically analyzing assets, risks, costs, and benefits. Lacking such a plan, we are not convinced that our transportation security resources are being allocated to the greatest risks in a cost-effective way.

- Major vulnerabilities still exist in cargo and general aviation security. These, together with inadequate screening and access controls, continue to present aviation security challenges.
- While commercial aviation remains a possible target, terrorists may turn their attention to other modes. Opportunities to do harm are as great, or greater, in maritime or surface transportation. Initiatives to secure shipping containers have just begun. Surface transportation systems such as railroads and mass transit remain hard to protect because they are so accessible and extensive.

Despite congressional deadlines, the TSA has developed neither an integrated strategic plan for the transportation sector nor specific plans for the various modes—air, sea, and ground.

RECOMMENDATION: Hard choices must be made in allocating limited resources. The U.S. government should identify and evaluate the transportation assets that need to be protected, set risk-based priorities for defending them, select the most practical and cost-effective ways of doing so, and then develop a plan, budget, and funding to implement the effort. The plan should assign roles and missions to the relevant authorities (federal, state, regional, and local) and to private stakeholders. In measuring effectiveness, perfection is unattainable. But terrorists should perceive that potential targets are defended. They may be deterred by a significant chance of failure.

Congress should set a specific date for the completion of these plans and hold the Department of Homeland Security and TSA accountable for achieving them.

The most powerful investments may be for improvements in technologies with applications across the transportation modes, such as scanning technologies designed to screen containers that can be transported by plane, ship, truck, or rail. Though such technologies are becoming available now, widespread deployment is still years away.

In the meantime, the best protective measures may be to combine improved methods of identifying and tracking the high-risk containers, operators, and facilities that require added scrutiny with further efforts to integrate intelligence analysis, effective procedures for transmitting threat information to transportation authorities, and vigilance by transportation authorities and the public.

A LAYERED SECURITY SYSTEMS

No single security measure is foolproof. Accordingly, the TSA must have multiple layers of security in place to defeat the more plausible and dangerous forms of attack against public transportation.

- The plan must take into consideration the full array of possible enemy tactics, such as use of insiders, suicide terrorism, or standoff attack. Each, layer must be effective in its own right. Each must be supported by other layers that are redundant and coordinated.
- The TSA should be able to identify for Congress the array of potential terrorist attacks, the layers of security in place, and the reliability provided by each layer. TSA must develop a plan as described above to improve weak individual layers and the effectiveness of the layered systems it deploys.

On 9/11, the 19 hijackers were screened by a computer-assisted screening system called CAPPS. More than half were identified for further inspection, which applied only to their checked luggage.

Under current practices, air carriers enforce government orders to stop certain known and suspected terrorists from boarding commercial flights and to apply secondary screening procedures to others. The "no-fly" and "automatic selectee" lists include only those individuals who the U.S. government believes pose a direct threat of attacking aviation.

Because air carriers implement the program, concerns about sharing intelligence information with private firms and foreign countries keep the U.S. government from listing all terrorist and terrorist suspects who should be included. The TSA has planned to take over this function when it deploys a new screening system to take the place of CAPPS. The deployment of this system has been delayed because of claims it may violate civil liberties.

RECOMMENDATION: Improved use of "no-fly" and "automatic selectee" lists should not be delayed while the argument about a successor to CAPPS continues. This screening function should be performed by the TSA, and it should utilize the larger set of watchlists maintained by the federal government. Air carriers should be required to supply the information needed to test and implement this new system.

CAPPS is still part of the screening process, still profiling passengers, with the consequences of selection now including personal searches of the individual and carry-on bags. The TSA is dealing with the kind of screening issues that are being encountered by other agencies. As we mentioned earlier, these screening issues need to be elevated for high-level attention and addressed promptly by the government. Working through these problems can help clear the way for the TSA's screening improvements and would help many other agencies too.

The next layer is the screening checkpoint itself. As the screening system tries to stop dangerous people, the checkpoint needs to be able to find dangerous items. Two reforms are needed soon: (1) screening people for explosives, not just their carry-on bags, and (2) improving screener performance.

RECOMMENDATION: The TSA and the Congress must give priority attention to improving the ability of screening checkpoints to detect explosives on passengers. As a start, each individual selected for special screening should be screened for explosives. Further, the TSA should conduct a human factors study, a method often used in the private sector, to understand problems in screener performance and set attainable objectives for individual screeners and for the checkpoints where screening takes place.

Concerns also remain regarding the screening and transport of checked bags and cargo. More attention and resources should be directed to reducing or mitigating the threat posed by explosives in vessels' cargo holds. The TSA should expedite the installation of advanced (in-line) baggage-screening equipment. Because the aviation industry will derive substantial benefits from this deployment, it should pay a fair share of the costs. The TSA should require that every passenger aircraft carrying cargo must deploy at least one hardened container to carry any suspect cargo. TSA also needs to intensify its efforts to identify, track, and appropriately screen potentially dangerous cargo in both the aviation and maritime sectors.

THE PROTECTION OF CIVIL LIBERTIES

Many at our recommendations call for the government to increase its presence in our lives—for example, by creating standards for the issuance of forms of identification, by better securing our borders, by sharing information gathered by many different agencies. We also recommend the consolidation of authority over the now far-flung entities constituting the intelligence community. The Patriot Act vests substantial powers in our federal government. We have seen the government use the immigration laws as a tool in its counterterrorism effort. Even without the changes we recommend, the American public has vested enormous authority in the U.S. government.

At our first public hearing on March 31, 2003, we noted the need for balance as our government responds to the real and ongoing threat of terrorist attacks. The terrorists have used our open society against us. In wartime, government calls for greater powers, and then the need for those powers recedes after the war ends. This struggle will go on. Therefore, while protecting our homeland, Americans should be mindful of threats to vital personal and civil liberties. This balancing is no easy task, but we must constantly strive to keep it right.

This shift of power and authority to the government calls for an enhanced system of checks and balances to protect the precious liberties that are vital to our way of life. We therefore make three recommendations.

First, to open up the sharing of information across so many agencies and with the private sector,

the President should take responsibility for determining what information can be shared by which agencies and under what conditions. Protection of privacy rights should be one key element of this determination.

RECOMMENDATION: As the President determines the guidelines for information sharing among government agencies and by those agencies with the private sector, he should safeguard the privacy of individuals about whom information is shared.

Second, Congress responded, in the immediate aftermath of 9/11, with the Patriot Act, which vested substantial new powers in the investigative agencies of the government. Some of the most controversial provisions of the Patriot Act are to "sunset" at the end of 2005. Many of the act's provisions are relatively noncontroversial, updating America's surveillance laws to reflect technological developments in a digital age. Some executive actions that have been criticized are unrelated to the Patriot Act. The provisions in the act that facilitate the sharing of information among intelligence agencies and between law enforcement and intelligence appear, on balance, to be beneficial. Because of concerns regarding the shifting balance of power to the government, we think that a full and informed debate on the Patriot Act would be healthy.

RECOMMENDATION: The burden of proof for retaining a particular governmental power should be on the executive, to explain (a) that the power actually materially enhances security and (b) that there is adequate supervision of the executive's use of the powers to ensure protection of civil liberties. If the power is granted, there must be adequate guidelines and oversight to properly confine its use.

Third, during the course of our inquiry, we were told that there is no office within the government whose job it is to look across the government at the actions we are taking to protect ourselves to ensure that liberty concerns are appropriately considered. If, as we recommend, there is substantial change in the way we collect and share intelligence, there should be a voice within the executive branch for those concerns. Many agencies have privacy offices, albeit of limited scope. The Intelligence Oversight Board of the President's Foreign Intelligence Advisory Board has, in the past, had the job of overseeing certain activities of the intelligence community.

RECOMMENDATION: At this time of increased and consolidated government authority, there should be a board within the executive branch to oversee adherence to the guidelines we recommend and the commitment the government makes to defend our civil liberties.

We must find ways of reconciling security with liberty, since the success of one helps protect the other. The choice between security and liberty is a false choice, as nothing is more likely to endanger America's liberties than the success of a terrorist attack at home. Our history has shown us that insecurity threatens liberty. Yet, if our liberties are curtailed, we lose the values that we are struggling to defend.

SETTING PRIORITIES FOR NATIONAL PREPAREDNESS

Before 9/11, no executive department had, as its first priority, the job of defending America from domestic attack. That changed with the 2002 creation of the Department of Homeland Security. This department now has the lead responsibility for problems that feature so prominently in the 9/11 story, such as protecting borders, securing transportation and other parts of our critical infrastructure, organizing emergency assistance, and working with the private sector to assess vulnerabilities.

Throughout the government, nothing has been harder for officials—executive or legislative—than to set priorities, making hard choices in allocating limited resources. These difficulties have certainly afflicted the Department of Homeland Security, hamstrung by its many congressional overseers. In delivering assistance to state and local governments, we heard—especially in New York—about imbalances in the allocation of money. The argument concentrates on two questions.

First, how much money should be set aside for criteria not directly related to risk? Currently a major portion of the billions of dollars appropriated for state and local assistance is allocated so that each state gets a certain amount, or an allocation based on its population—wherever they live.

RECOMMENDATION: Homeland security assistance should be based strictly on an assessment of risks and vulnerabilities. Now, in 2004, Washington, D.C., and New York City are certainly at the top of any such list. We understand the contention that every state and city needs to have some minimum infrastructure for emergency response. But federal homeland security assistance should not remain a program for general revenue sharing. It should supplement state and local resources based

on the risks or vulnerabilities that merit additional support. Congress should not use this money as a pork barrel.

The second question is, Can useful criteria to measure risk and vulnerability be developed that assess all the many variables? The allocation of funds should be based on an assessment of threats and vulnerabilities. That assessment should consider such factors as population, population density, vulnerability, and the presence of critical infrastructure within each state. In addition, the federal government should require each state receiving federal emergency preparedness funds to provide an analysis based on the same criteria to justify the distribution of funds in that state.

In a free-for-all over money, it is understandable that representatives will work to protect the interests of their home states or districts. But this issue is too important for politics as usual to prevail. Resources must be allocated according to vulnerabilities. We recommend that a panel of security experts be convened to develop written benchmarks for evaluating community needs. We further recommend that federal homeland security funds be allocated in accordance with those benchmarks, and that states be required to abide by those benchmarks in disbursing the federal funds. The benchmarks will be imperfect and subjective; they will continually evolve. But hard choices must be made. Those who would allocate money on a different basis should then defend their view of the national interest.

COMMAND, CONTROL, AND COMMUNICATIONS

The attack on 9/11 demonstrated that even the most robust emergency response capabilities can be overwhelmed if an attack is large enough. Teamwork, collaboration, and cooperation at an incident site are critical to a successful response. Key decision-makers who are represented at the incident command level help to ensure an effective response, the efficient use of resources, and responder safety. Regular joint training at all levels is, moreover, essential to ensuring close coordination during an actual incident.

RECOMMENDATION: Emergency response agencies nationwide should adopt the Incident Command System (ICS). When multiple agencies or multiple jurisdictions are involved, they should adopt a unified command. Both are proven frameworks for emergency response. We strongly support the decision that federal homeland security funding will be contingent, as of October 1, 2004, upon the adoption and regular use of ICS and unified command procedures. In the future, the Department of Homeland Security should consider making funding contingent on aggressive and realistic training in accordance with ICS and unified command procedures.

The attacks of September 11, 2001 overwhelmed the response capacity of most of the local jurisdictions where the hijacked airliners crashed. While many jurisdictions have established mutual aid compacts, a serious obstacle to multi-jurisdictional response has been the lack of indemnification for mutual-aid responders in areas such as the National Capital Region.

Public safety organizations, chief administrative officers, state emergency management agencies, and the Department of Homeland Security should develop a regional focus within the emergency responder community and promote multi-jurisdictional mutual assistance compacts. Where such compacts already exist, training in accordance with their terms should be required. Congress should pass legislation to remedy the long-standing indemnification and liability impediments to the provision of public safety mutual aid in the National Capital Region and where applicable throughout the nation.

The inability to communicate was a critical element at the World Trade Center, Pentagon, and Somerset County, Pennsylvania, crash sites, where multiple agencies and multiple jurisdictions responded. The occurrence of this problem at three very different sites is strong evidence that compatible and adequate communications among public safety organizations at the local, state, and federal levels remains an important problem.

RECOMMENDATION: Congress should support pending legislation which provides for the expedited and increased assignment of radio spectrum for public safety purposes. Furthermore, high-risk urban areas such as New York City and Washington, D.C., should establish signal corps units to ensure communications connectivity between and among civilian authorities, local first responders, and the National Guard. Federal funding of such units should be given high priority by Congress.

PRIVATE-SECTOR PREPAREDNESS

The mandate of the Department of Homeland Security does not end with government; the department is also responsible for working with the private sector to ensure preparedness. This is entirely appropriate, for the private sector controls 85 percent of the critical infrastructure in the nation. Indeed, unless a terrorist's target is a military or other secure government facility, the "first" first responders will almost certainly be civilians. Homeland security and national preparedness therefore often begins with the private sector.

Preparedness in the private sector and public sector for rescue, restart, and recovery of operations should include (1) a plan for evacuation, (2) adequate communications capabilities, and (3) a plan for continuity of operations. As we examined the emergency response to 9/11, witness after witness told us that despite 9/11, the private sector remains largely unprepared for a terrorist attack. We were also advised that the lack of a widely embraced private-sector preparedness standard was a principal contributing factor to this lack of preparedness.

We responded by asking the American National Standards Institute (ANSI) to develop a consensus on a "National Standard for Preparedness" for the private sector. ANSI convened safety, security, and business continuity experts from a wide range of industries and associations, as well as from federal, state, and local government stakeholders, to consider the need for standards for private sector emergency preparedness and business continuity.

The result of these sessions was ANSI's recommendation that the Commission endorse a voluntary National Preparedness Standard. Based on the existing American National Standard on Disaster/Emergency Management and Business Continuity Programs (NFPA 1600), the proposed National Preparedness Standard establishes a common set of criteria and terminology for preparedness, disaster management, emergency management, and business continuity programs. The experience of the private sector in the World Trade Center emergency demonstrated the need for these standards.

RECOMMENDATION: We endorse the American National Standards Institute's recommended standard for private preparedness. We were encouraged by Secretary Tom Ridge's praise of the standard, and urge the Department of Homeland Security to promote its adoption. We also encourage the insurance and credit-rating industries to look closely at a company's compliance with the ANSI standard in assessing its insurability and creditworthiness. We believe that compliance with the standard should define the standard of care owed by a company to its employees and the public for legal purposes. Private-sector preparedness is not a luxury; it is a cost of doing business in the post-9/11 world. It is ignored at a tremendous potential cost in lives, money, and national security.

HOW TO DO IT? A DIFFERENT WAY OF ORGANIZING THE GOVERNMENT

As presently configured, the national security institutions of the U.S. government are still the institutions constructed to win the Cold War. The United States confronts a very different world today. Instead of facing a few very dangerous adversaries, the United States confronts a number of less visible challenges that surpass the boundaries of traditional nation-states and call for quick, imaginative, and agile responses.

The men and women of the World War II generation rose to the challenges of the 1940s and 1950s. They restructured the government so that it could protect the country. That is now the job of the generation that experienced 9/11. Those attacks showed, emphatically, that ways of doing business rooted in a different era are just not good enough. Americans should not settle for incremental, ad hoc adjustments to a system designed generations ago for a world that no longer exists.

We recommend significant changes in the organization of the government. We know that the quality of the people is more important than the quality of the wiring diagrams. Some of the saddest aspects of the 9/11 story are the outstanding efforts of so many individual officials straining, often without success, against the boundaries of the possible. Good people can overcome bad structures. They should not have to.

The United States has the resources and the people. The government should combine them more effectively, achieving unity of effort. We offer five major recommendations to do that:

- unifying strategic intelligence and operational planning against Islamist terrorists across the foreign-domestic divide with a National Counterterrorism Center;
- unifying the intelligence community with a new National Intelligence Director;
- unifying the many participants in the counterterrorism effort and their knowledge in a

network-based information-sharing system that transcends traditional governmental boundaries;
- unifying and strengthening congressional oversight to improve quality and accountability; and
- strengthening the FBI and homeland defenders.

UNITY OF EFFORT ACROSS THE FOREIGN-DOMESTIC DIVIDE

Joint Action

Much of the public commentary about the 9/11 attacks has dealt with "lost opportunities."...These are often characterized as problems of "watchlisting," of "information sharing," or of "connecting the dots."...[T]hese labels are too narrow. They describe the symptoms, not the disease.

In each of our examples, no one was firmly in charge of managing the case and able to draw relevant intelligence from anywhere in the government, assign responsibilities across the agencies (foreign or domestic), track progress, and quickly bring obstacles up to the level where they could be resolved. Responsibility and accountability were diffuse.

The agencies cooperated, some of the time. But even such cooperation as there was is not the same thing as joint action. When agencies cooperate, one defines the problem and seeks help with it. When they act jointly, the problem and options for action are defined differently from the start. Individuals from different backgrounds come together in analyzing a case and planning how to manage it.

In our hearings we regularly asked witnesses: Who is the quarterback? The other players are in their positions, doing their jobs. But who is calling the play that assigns roles to help them execute as a team?

Since 9/11, those issues have not been resolved. In some ways joint work has gotten better, and in some ways worse. The effort of fighting terrorism has flooded over many of the usual agency boundaries because of its sheer quantity and energy. Attitudes have changed. Officials are keenly conscious of trying to avoid the mistakes of 9/11. They try to share information. They circulate—even to the President—practically every reported threat, however dubious.

Partly because of all this effort, the challenge of coordinating it has multiplied. Before 9/11, the CIA was plainly the lead agency confronting al Qaeda. The FBI played a very secondary role. The engagement of the departments of Defense and State was more episodic.

- Today the CIA is still central. But the FBI is much more active, along with other parts of the Justice Department.
- The Defense Department effort is now enormous. Three of its unified commands, each headed by a four-star general, have counterterrorism as a primary mission: Special Operations Command, Central Command (both headquartered in Florida), and Northern Command (headquartered in Colorado).
- A new Department of Homeland Security combines formidable resources in border and transportation security, along with analysis of domestic vulnerability and other tasks.
- The State Department has the lead on many of the foreign policy tasks....
- At the White House, the National Security Council (NSC) now is joined by a parallel presidential advisory structure, the Homeland Security Council.

So far we have mentioned two reasons for joint action—the virtue of joint planning and the advantage of having someone in charge to ensure a unified effort. There is a third: the simple shortage of experts with sufficient skills. The limited pool of critical experts—for example, skilled counterterrorism analysts and linguists—is being depleted. Expanding these capabilities will require not just money, but time.

Primary responsibility for terrorism analysis has been assigned to the Terrorist Threat Integration Center (TTIC), created in 2003, based at the CIA headquarters but staffed with representatives of many agencies, reporting directly to the Director of Central Intelligence. Yet the CIA houses another intelligence "fusion" center: the Counterterrorist Center that played such a key role before 9/11. A third major analytic unit is at Defense, in the Defense Intelligence Agency. A fourth, concentrating more on homeland vulnerabilities, is at the Department of Homeland Security. The FBI is in the process of building the analytic capability it has long lacked, and it also has the Terrorist Screening Center.[43]

The U.S. government cannot afford so much duplication of effort. There are not enough experienced experts to go around. The duplication also places extra demands on already hard-pressed

single-source national technical intelligence collectors like the National Security Agency.

COMBINING JOINT INTELLIGENCE AND JOINT ACTION

A "smart" government would *integrate* all sources of information to see the enemy as a whole. Integrated all-source analysis should also inform and shape strategies to collect more intelligence. Yet the Terrorist Threat Integration Center, while it has primary responsibility for terrorism analysis, is formally proscribed from having any oversight or operational authority and is not part of any operational entity, other than reporting to the director of central intelligence.[44]

The government now tries to handle the problem of joint management, informed by analysis of intelligence from all sources, in two ways.

- First, agencies with lead responsibility for certain problems have constructed their own interagency entities and task forces in order to get cooperation. The Counterterrorist Center at CIA, for example, recruits liaison officers from throughout the intelligence community. The military's Central Command has its own interagency center, recruiting liaison officers from all the agencies from which it might need help. The FBI has Joint Terrorism Task Forces in 84 locations to coordinate the activities of other agencies when action may be required.
- Second, the problem of joint operational planning is often passed to the White House, where the NSC staff tries to play this role. The national security staff at the White House (both NSC and new Homeland Security Council staff) has already become 50 percent larger since 9/11. But our impression, after talking to serving officials, is that even this enlarged staff is consumed by meetings on day-to-day issues, sifting each day's threat information and trying to coordinate everyday operations.

Even as it crowds into every square inch of available office space, the NSC staff is still not sized or funded to be an executive agency.... [S]ome...problems...arose in the 1980s when a White House staff, constitutionally insulated from the usual mechanisms of oversight, became involved in direct operations. During the 1990s Richard Clarke occasionally tried to exercise such authority, sometimes successfully, but often causing friction.

Yet a subtler and more serious danger is that as the NSC staff is consumed by these day-to-day tasks, it has less capacity to find the time and detachment needed to advise a president on larger policy issues. That means less time to work on major new initiatives, help with legislative management to steer needed bills through Congress, and track the design and implementation of the strategic plans for regions, countries, and issues....

Much of the job of operational coordination remains with the agencies, especially the CIA. There DCI Tenet and his chief aides ran interagency meetings nearly every day to coordinate much of the government's day-to-day work. The DCI insisted he did not make policy and only oversaw its implementation. In the struggle against terrorism these distinctions seem increasingly artificial. Also, as the DCI becomes a lead coordinator of the government's operations, it becomes harder to play all the position's other roles, including that of analyst in chief.

The problem is nearly intractable because of the way the government is currently structured. Lines of operational authority run to the expanding executive departments, and they are guarded for understandable reasons; the DCI commands the CIA's personnel overseas; the secretary of defense will not yield to others in conveying commands to military forces; the Justice Department will not give up the responsibility of deciding whether to seek arrest warrants. But the result is that each agency or department needs its own intelligence apparatus to support the performance of its duties. It is hard to "break down stovepipes" when there are so many stoves that are legally and politically entitled to have cast-iron pipes of their own.

Recalling the Goldwater-Nichols legislation of 1986, Secretary Rumsfeld reminded us that to achieve better joint capability, each of the armed services had to "give up some of their turf and authorities and prerogatives." Today, he said, the executive branch is "stove-piped much like the four services were nearly 20 years ago." He wondered if it might be appropriate to ask agencies to "give up some of their existing turf and authority in exchange for a stronger, faster, more efficient government wide joint effort."[45] Privately, other key officials have made the same point to us.

We therefore propose a new institution: a civilian-led unified joint command for counterterrorism.

It should combine strategic intelligence and joint operational planning.

In the Pentagon's Joint Staff, which serves the chairman of the Joint Chiefs of Staff, intelligence is handled by the J-2 directorate, operational planning by J-3, and overall policy by J-5. Our concept combines the J-2 and J-3 functions (intelligence and operational planning) in one agency, keeping overall policy coordination where it belongs, in the National Security Council.

RECOMMENDATION: We recommend the establishment of a National Counterterrorism Center (NCTC), built on the foundation of the existing Terrorist Threat Integration Center (TTIC). Breaking the older mold of national government organization, this NCTC should be a center for joint operational planning and joint intelligence, staffed by personnel from the various agencies. The head of the NCTC should have authority to evaluate the performance of the people assigned to the Center.

- Such a joint center should be developed in the same spirit that guided the military's creation of unified joint commands, or the shaping of earlier national agencies like the National Reconnaissance Office, which was formed to organize the work of the CIA and several defense agencies in space.

  NCTC—Intelligence. The NCTC should lead strategic analysis, pooling all-source intelligence, foreign and domestic, about transnational terrorist organizations with global reach. It should develop *net* assessments (comparing enemy capabilities and intentions against U.S. defenses and countermeasures). It should also provide warning. It should do this work by drawing on the efforts of the CIA, FBI, Homeland Security, and other departments and agencies. It should task collection requirements both inside and outside the United States.

- The intelligence function (J-2) should build on the existing TTIC structure and remain distinct, as a national intelligence center, within, the NCTC. As the government's principal knowledge bank on Islamist terrorism, with the main responsibility for strategic analysis and net assessment, it should absorb a significant portion of the analytical talent now residing in the CIA's Counterterrorist Center and the DIA's Joint Intelligence Task Force—Combatting Terrorism (JITF-CT).

  NCTC—Operations. The NCTC should perform joint planning. The plans would assign operational responsibilities to lead agencies, such as State, the CIA, the FBI, Defense and its combatant commands, Homeland Security, and other agencies. The NCTC should not direct the actual execution of these operations, leaving that job to the agencies. The NCTC would then track implementation; it would look across the foreign-domestic divide and across agency boundaries, updating plans to follow through on cases.[46]

• The joint operational planning function (J-3) will be new to the TTIC structure. The NCTC can draw on analogous work now being done in the CIA and every other involved department of the government, as well as reaching out to knowledgeable officials in state and local agencies throughout the United States.

• The NCTC should not be a policymaking body. Its operations and planning should follow the policy direction of the president and the National Security Council.

   NCTC—Authorities. The head of the NCTC should be appointed by the president, and should be equivalent in rank to a deputy head of a cabinet department. The head of the NCTC would report to the national intelligence director, an office whose creation we recommend below, placed in the Executive Office of the President. The head of the NCTC would thus also report indirectly to the president. This official's nomination should be confirmed by the Senate and he or she should testify to the Congress, as is the case now with other statutory presidential offices, like the U.S. trade representative.

• To avoid the fate of other entities with great nominal authority and little real power, the head of the NCTC must have the right to concur in the choices of personnel to lead the operating entities of the departments and agencies focused on counterterrorism, specifically including the head of the Counterterrorist Center, the head of the FBI's Counterterrorism Division, the commanders of the Defense Department's Special Operations Command and Northern Command, and the State Department's coordinator for counterterrorism.[47] The head of the NCTC should also work with the director of the Office of Management and Budget in developing the president's counterterrorism budget.

• There are precedents for surrendering authority for joint planning while preserving an agency's operational control. In the international context, NATO commanders may get line authority over forces assigned by other nations. In U.S. unified commands, commanders plan operations that may involve units belonging to one of the services. In each case, procedures are worked out, formal and informal, to define the limits of the joint commander's authority.

The most serious disadvantage of the NCTC is the reverse of its greatest virtue. The struggle against Islamist terrorism is so important that any clear-cut centralization of authority to manage and be accountable for it may concentrate too much power in one place. The proposed NCTC would be given the authority of planning the activities of other agencies. Law or executive order must define the scope of such line authority.

The NCTC would not eliminate interagency policy disputes. These would still go to the National Security Council. To improve coordination at the

---

BOX 33.1

Consider this hypothetical case. The NSA discovers that a suspected terrorist is traveling to Bangkok and Kuala Lumpur. The NCTC should draw on joint intelligence resources, including its own NSA counterterrorism experts, to analyze the identities and possible destinations of these individuals. Informed by this analysis, the NCTC would then organize and plan the management of the case, drawing on the talents and differing kinds of experience among the several agency representatives assigned to it—assigning tasks to the CIA overseas, to Homeland Security watching entry points into the United States, and to the FBI. If military assistance might be needed, the Special Operations Command could be asked to develop an appropriate concept for such an operation. The NCTC would be accountable for tracking the progress of the case, ensuring that the plan evolved with it, and integrating the information into a warning. The NCTC would be responsible for being sure that intelligence gathered from the activities in the field became part of the government's institutional memory about Islamist terrorist personalities, organizations, and possible means of attack.

   In each case the involved agency would make its own senior managers aware of what it was being asked to do. If those agency heads objected, and the issue could not easily be resolved, then the disagreement about roles and missions could be brought before the National Security Council and the president.

White House, we believe the existing Homeland Security Council should soon be merged into a single National Security Council. The creation of the NCTC should help the NSC staff concentrate on its core duties of assisting the president and supporting interdepartmental policymaking.

We recognize that this is a new and difficult idea precisely because the authorities we recommend for the NCTC really would, as Secretary Rumsfeld foresaw, ask strong agencies to "give up some of their turf and authority in exchange for a stronger, faster, more efficient government wide joint effort." Countering transnational Islamist terrorism will test whether the U.S. government can fashion more flexible models of management needed to deal with the twenty-first-century world.

An argument against change is that the nation is at war, and cannot afford to reorganize in midstream. But some of the main innovations of the 1940s and 1950s, including the creation of the Joint Chiefs of Staff and even the construction of the Pentagon itself, were undertaken in the midst of war. Surely the country cannot wait until the struggle against Islamist terrorism is over.

"Surprise, when it happens to a government, is likely to be a complicated, diffuse, bureaucratic thing. It includes neglect of responsibility, but also responsibility so poorly defined or so ambiguously delegated that action gets lost."[48] That comment was made more than 40 years ago, about Pearl Harbor. We hope another commission, writing in the future about another attack, does not again find this quotation to be so apt.

UNITY OF EFFORT IN THE INTELLIGENCE COMMUNITY

In our first section, we concentrated on counterterrorism, discussing how to combine the analysis of information from all sources of intelligence with the joint planning of operations that draw on that analysis. In this section, we step back from looking just at the counterterrorism problem. We reflect on whether the government is organized adequately to direct resources and build the intelligence capabilities it will need not just for countering terrorism, but for the broader range of national security challenges in the decades ahead.

The Need for a Change

During the Cold War, intelligence agencies did not depend on seamless integration to track and count the thousands of military targets—such as tanks and missiles—fielded by the Soviet Union and other adversary states. Each agency concentrated on its specialized mission, acquiring its own information and then sharing it via formal, finished reports. The Department of Defense had given birth to and dominated the main agencies for technical collection of intelligence. Resources were shifted at an incremental pace, coping with challenges that arose over years, even decades.

[T]he resulting organization of the intelligence community…is outlined [in Box 33.2].

The need to restructure the intelligence community grows out of six problems that have become apparent before and after 9/11:

- *Structural barriers to performing joint intelligence work.* National intelligence is still organized around the collection disciplines of the home agencies, not the joint mission. The importance of integrated, all-source analysis cannot be overstated. Without it, it is not possible to "connect the dots." No one component holds all the relevant information.

- By contrast, in organizing national defense, the Goldwater-Nichols legislation of 1986 created joint commands for operations in the field, the Unified Command Plan. The services—the Army, Navy, Air Force, and Marine Corps—organize, train, and equip their people and units to perform their missions. Then they assign personnel and units to the joint combatant commander, like the commanding general of the Central Command (CENTCOM). The Goldwater-Nichols Act required officers to serve tours outside their service in order to win promotion. The culture of the Defense Department was transformed, its collective mind-set moved from service-specific to "joint," and its operations became more integrated.[49]

- *Lack of common standards and practices across the foreign-domestic divide.* The leadership of the intelligence community should be able to pool information gathered overseas with information gathered in the United States, holding the work—wherever it is done—to a common standard of quality in how it is collected, processed (e.g., translated), reported, shared, and analyzed. A common set of personnel standards for intelligence can create a group of professionals better able to operate in joint activities, transcending their own service-specific mind-sets.

BOX 33.2   MEMBERS OF THE U.S. INTELLIGENCE COMMUNITY

- Office of the Director of Central Intelligence, which includes the Office of the Deputy Director of Central Intelligence for Community Management, the Community Management Staff, the Terrorism Threat Integration Center, the National Intelligence Council, and other community offices.
- The Central Intelligence Agency (CIA), which performs human source collection, all-source analysis, and advanced science and technology

National Intelligence Agencies

- National Security Agency (NSA), which performs signals collection and analysis
- National Geospatial–Intelligence Agency (NGA), which performs imagery collection and analysis
- National Reconnaissance Office (NRO), which develops, acquires, and launches space systems for intelligence collection

- Other national reconnaissance programs

Departmental Intelligence Agencies

- Defense Intelligence Agency (DIA) of the Department of Defense
- Intelligence entities of the Army, Navy, Air Force, and Marines
- Bureau of Intelligence and Research (INR) of the Department of State
- Office of Terrorism and Finance Intelligence of the Department of Treasury
- Office of Intelligence and the Counterterrorism and Counterintelligence Divisions of the Federal Bureau of Investigation of the Department of Justice
- Office of Intelligence of the Department of Energy
- Directorate of Information Analysis and Infrastructure Protection (IAIP) and Directorate of Coast Guard Intelligence of the Department of Homeland Security.

- *Divided management of national intelligence capabilities.* While the CIA was once "central" to our national intelligence capabilities, following the end of the Cold War it has been less able to influence the use of the nation's imagery and signals intelligence capabilities in three national agencies housed within the Department of Defense: the National Security Agency, the National Geospatial-Intelligence Agency, and the National Reconnaissance Office. One of the lessons learned from the 1991 Gulf War was the value of national intelligence systems (satellites in particular) in precision warfare. Since that war, the department has appropriately drawn these agencies into its transformation of the military. Helping to orchestrate this transformation is the under secretary of defense for intelligence, a position established by Congress after 9/11. An unintended consequence of these developments has been the far greater demand made by Defense on technical systems, leaving the DCI less able to influence how these technical resources are allocated and used.
- *Weak capacity to set priorities and move resources.* The agencies are mainly organized around what they collect or the way they collect it. But the priorities for collection are national. As the DCI makes hard choices about moving resources, he or she must have the power to reach across agencies and reallocate effort.
- *Too many jobs.* The DCI now has at least three jobs. He is expected to run a particular agency,

the CIA. He is expected to manage the loose confederation of agencies that is the intelligence community. He is expected to be the analyst in chief for the government, sifting evidence and directly briefing the President as his principal intelligence adviser. No recent DCI has been able to do all three effectively. Usually what loses out is management of the intelligence community, a difficult task even in the best case because the DCI's current authorities are weak. With so much to do, the DCI often has not used even the authority he has.
- *Too complex and secret.* Over the decades, the agencies and the rules surrounding the intelligence community have accumulated to a depth that practically defies public comprehension. There are now 15 agencies or parts of agencies in the intelligence community. The community and the DCI's authorities have become arcane matters, understood only by initiates after long study. Even the most basic information about how much money is actually allocated to or within the intelligence community and most of its key components is shrouded from public view.

The current DCI is responsible for community performance but lacks the three authorities critical for any agency head or chief executive officer: (1) control over purse strings, (2) the ability to hire or fire senior managers, and (3) the ability to set standards for the information infrastructure and personnel.[50]

The only budget power of the DCI over agencies other than the CIA lies in coordinating the budget requests of the various intelligence agencies into a single program for submission to Congress. The overall funding request of the 15 intelligence entities in this program is then presented to the president and Congress in 15 separate volumes.

When Congress passes an appropriations bill to allocate money to intelligence agencies, most of their funding is hidden in the Defense Department in order to keep intelligence spending secret. Therefore, although the House and Senate Intelligence committees are the authorizing committees for funding of the intelligence community, the final budget review is handled in the Defense Subcommittee of the Appropriations committees. Those committees have no subcommittees just for intelligence, and only a few members and staff review the requests.

The appropriations for the CIA and the national intelligence agencies—NSA, NGA, and NRO—are then given to the secretary of defense. The secretary transfers the CIA's money to the DCI but disburses the national agencies' money directly. Money for the FBI's national security components falls within the appropriations for Commerce, Justice, and State and goes to the attorney general.[51]

In addition, the DCI lacks hire-and-fire authority over most of the intelligence community's senior managers. For the national intelligence agencies housed in the Defense Department, the secretary of defense must seek the DCI's concurrence regarding the nomination of these directors, who are presidentially appointed. But the secretary may submit recommendations to the president without receiving this concurrence. The DCI cannot fire these officials. The DCI has even less influence over the head of the FBI's national security component, who is appointed by the attorney general in consultation with the DCI.[52]

COMBINING JOINT WORK WITH STRONGER MANAGEMENT

We have received recommendations on the topic of intelligence reform from many sources. Other commissions have been over this same ground. Thoughtful bills have been introduced, most recently a bill by the chairman of the House Intelligence Committee Porter Goss (R-Fla.), and another by the ranking minority member, Jane Harman (D-Calif.). In the Senate, Senators Bob Graham (D-Fla.) and Dianne Feinstein (D-Calif.) have introduced reform proposals as well. Past efforts have foundered, because the president did not support them; because the DCI, the secretary of defense, or both opposed them; and because some proposals lacked merit. We have tried to take stock of these experiences, and borrow from strong elements in many of the ideas that have already been developed by others.

RECOMMENDATION: The current position of Director of Central Intelligence should be replaced by a National Intelligence Director with two main areas of responsibility: (1) to oversee national intelligence centers on specific subjects of interest across the U.S. government and (2) to manage the national intelligence program and oversee the agencies that contribute to it.

First, the National Intelligence Director should oversee *national intelligence centers* to provide all source analysis and plan intelligence operations for the whole government on major problems.

- One such problem is counterterrorism. In this case, we believe that the center should be the intelligence entity (formerly TTIC) inside the National Counterterrorism Center we have proposed. It would sit there alongside the operations management unit we described earlier, with both making up the NCTC, in the Executive Office of the President. Other national intelligence centers—for instance, on counterproliferation, crime and narcotics, and China—would be housed in whatever department or agency is best suited for them.
- The National Intelligence Director would retain the present DCI's role as the principal intelligence adviser to the president. We hope the president will come to look directly to the directors of the national intelligence centers to provide all-source analysis in their areas of responsibility, balancing the advice of these intelligence chiefs against the contrasting viewpoints that may be offered by department heads at State, Defense, Homeland Security, Justice, and other agencies.

Second, the National Intelligence Director should manage the national intelligence program and oversee the component agencies of the intelligence community. (See Figure 33.1.)[53]

- The National Intelligence Director would submit a unified budget for national intelligence

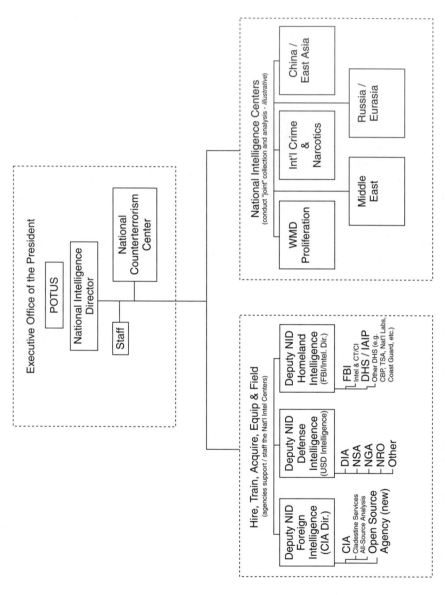

FIGURE 33.1 Unity of effort in managing intelligence.

Executive Office of the President

POTUS

National Intelligence Director

Staff

National Counterterrorism Center

National Intelligence Centers
(conduct "joint" collection and analysis - *illustrative*)

WMD Proliferation

Int'l Crime & Narcotics

China / East Asia

Middle East

Russia / Eurasia

Hire, Train, Acquire, Equip & Field
(agencies support / staff the Nat'l Intel Centers)

Deputy NID Foreign Intelligence (CIA Dir.)

CIA
Cladestine Services
All-Source Analysis
Open Source Agency (new)

Deputy NID Defense Intelligence (USD Intelligence)

DIA
NSA
NGA
NRO
Other

Deputy NID Homeland Intelligence (FBI/Intel. Dir.)

FBI
Intel & CT/CI
DHS / IAIP
Other DHS (e.g. CBP, TSA, Nat'l Labs, Coast Guard, etc.)

that reflects priorities chosen by the National Security Council, an appropriate balance among the varieties of technical and human intelligence collection, and analysis. He or she would receive an appropriation for national intelligence and apportion the funds to the appropriate agencies, in line with that budget, and with authority to reprogram funds among the national intelligence agencies to meet any new priority (as counterterrorism was in the 1990s). The National Intelligence Director should approve and submit nominations to the president of the individuals who would lead the CIA, DIA, FBI Intelligence Office, NSA, NGA, NRO, Information Analysis and Infrastructure Protection Directorate of the Department of Homeland Security, and other national intelligence capabilities.[54]

- The National Intelligence Director would manage this national effort with the help of three deputies, each of whom would also hold a key position in one of the component agencies.[55]
  - Foreign intelligence (the head of the CIA).
  - Defense intelligence (the under secretary of defense for intelligence).[56]
  - Homeland intelligence (the FBI's executive assistant director for intelligence or the under secretary of homeland security for information analysis and infrastructure protection).

    Other agencies in the intelligence community would coordinate their work within each of these three areas, largely staying housed in the same departments or agencies that support them now.

Returning to the analogy of the Defense Department's organization, these three deputies—like the leaders of the Army, Navy, Air Force, or Marines—would have the job of acquiring the systems, training the people, and executing the operations planned by the national intelligence centers.

And, just as the combatant commanders also report to the secretary of defense, the directors of the national intelligence centers—e.g., for counterproliferation, crime and narcotics, and the rest—also would report to the National Intelligence Director.

- The Defense Department's military intelligence programs—the joint military intelligence program (JMIP) and the tactical intelligence and

related activities program (TIARA)—would remain part of that department's responsibility.

- The National Intelligence Director would set personnel policies to establish standards for education and training and facilitate assignments at the national intelligence centers and across agency lines. The National Intelligence Director also would set information sharing and information technology policies to maximize data sharing, as well as policies to protect the security of information.
- Too many agencies now have an opportunity to say no to change. The National Intelligence Director should participate in an NSC executive committee that can resolve differences in priorities among the agencies and bring the major disputes to the president for decision.

The National Intelligence Director should be located in the Executive Office of the President. This official, who would be confirmed by the Senate and would testify before Congress, would have a relatively small staff of several hundred people, taking the place of the existing community management offices housed at the CIA.

In managing the whole community, the National Intelligence Director is still providing a service function. With the partial exception of his or her responsibilities for overseeing the NCTC, the National Intelligence Director should support the consumers of national intelligence—the president and policymaking advisers such as the secretaries of state, defense, and homeland security and the attorney general.

We are wary of too easily equating government management problems with those of the private sector. But we have noticed that some very large private firms rely on a powerful CEO who has significant control over how money is spent and can hire or fire leaders of the major divisions, assisted by a relatively modest staff, while leaving responsibility for execution in the operating divisions.

There are disadvantages to separating the position of National Intelligence Director from the job of heading the CIA. For example, the National Intelligence Director will not head a major agency of his or her own and may have a weaker base of support. But we believe that these disadvantages are outweighed by several other considerations:

- The National Intelligence Director must be able to directly oversee intelligence collection inside the United States. Yet law and custom has counseled against giving such a plain domestic role to the head of the CIA.

- The CIA will be one among several claimants for funds in setting national priorities. The National Intelligence Director should not be both one of the advocates and the judge of them all.
- Covert operations tend to be highly tactical, requiring close attention. The National Intelligence Director should rely on the relevant joint mission center to oversee these details, helping to coordinate closely with the White House. The CIA will be able to concentrate on building the capabilities to carry out such operations and on providing the personnel who will be directing and executing such operations in the field.
- Rebuilding the analytic and human intelligence collection capabilities of the CIA should be a full-time effort, and the director of the CIA should focus on extending its comparative advantages.

RECOMMENDATION: The CIA Director should emphasize (a) rebuilding the CIA's analytic capabilities; (b) transforming the clandestine service by building its human intelligence capabilities; (c) developing a stronger language program, with high standards and sufficient financial incentives; (d) renewing emphasis on recruiting diversity among operations officers so they can blend more easily in foreign cities; (e) ensuring a seamless relationship between human source collection and signals collection at the operational level; and (f) stressing a better balance between unilateral and liaison operations.

The CIA should retain responsibility for the direction and execution of clandestine and covert operations, as assigned by the relevant national intelligence center and authorized by the National Intelligence Director and the president. This would include propaganda, renditions, and nonmilitary disruption. We believe, however, that one important area of responsibility should change.

RECOMMENDATION: Lead responsibility for directing and executing paramilitary operations, whether clandestine or covert, should shift to the Defense Department. There it should be consolidated with the capabilities for training, direction, and execution of such operations already being developed in the Special Operations Command.

- Before 9/11, the CIA did not invest in developing a robust capability to conduct paramilitary operations with U.S. personnel. It relied on proxies instead, organized by CIA operatives without the requisite military training. The results were unsatisfactory.
- Whether the price is measured in either money or people, the United States cannot afford to build two separate capabilities for carrying out secret military operations, secretly operating standoff missiles, and secretly training foreign military or paramilitary forces. The United States should concentrate responsibility and necessary legal authorities in one entity.
- The post-9/11 Afghanistan precedent of using joint CIA-military teams for covert and clandestine operations was a good one. We believe this proposal to be consistent with it. Each agency would concentrate on its comparative advantages in building capabilities for joint missions. The operation itself would be planned in common.
- The CIA has a reputation for agility in operations. The military has a reputation for being methodical and cumbersome. We do not know if these stereotypes match current reality; they may also be one more symptom of the civil-military misunderstandings.... It is a problem to be resolved in policy guidance and agency management, not in the creation of redundant, overlapping capabilities and authorities in such sensitive work. The CIA's experts should be integrated into the military's training, exercises, and planning. To quote a CIA official now serving in the field: "One fight, one team."

RECOMMENDATION: **Finally, to combat the secrecy and complexity we have described, the overall amounts of money being appropriated for national intelligence and to its component agencies should no longer be kept secret. Congress should pass a separate appropriations act for intelligence, defending the broad allocation of how these tens of billions of dollars have been assigned among the varieties of intelligence work.**

The specifics of the intelligence appropriation would remain classified, as they are today. Opponents of declassification argue that America's enemies could learn about intelligence capabilities by tracking the top-line appropriations figure. Yet the top-line figure by itself provides little insight into U.S. intelligence sources and methods. The U.S. government readily provides copious information about spending on its military forces, including military intelligence. The intelligence community should not be subject to that much disclosure. But when even aggregate categorical numbers remain hidden, it is hard to judge priorities and foster accountability.

UNITY OF EFFORT IN SHARING INFORMATION

Information Sharing

We have already stressed the importance of intelligence analysis that can draw on all relevant sources of information. The biggest impediment to all-source analysis—to a greater likelihood of connecting the dots—is the human or systemic resistance to sharing information.

The U.S. government has access to a vast amount of information. When databases not usually thought of as "intelligence," such as customs or immigration information, are included, the storehouse is immense. But the U.S. government has a weak system for processing and using what it has. In interviews around the government, official after official urged us to call attention to frustrations with the unglamorous "back office" side of government operations.

In the 9/11 story, for example, we sometimes see examples of information that could be accessed—like the undistributed NSA information that would have helped identify Nawaf al Hazmi in January 2000. But someone had to ask for it. In that case, no one did. Or…the information is distributed, but in a compartmented channel. Or the information is available, and someone does ask, but it cannot be shared.

What all these stories have in common is a system that requires a demonstrated "need to know" before sharing. This approach assumes it is possible to know, in advance, who will need to use the information. Such a system implicitly assumes that the risk of inadvertent disclosure outweighs the benefits of wider sharing. Those Cold War assumptions are no longer appropriate. The culture of agencies feeling they own the information they gathered at taxpayer expense must be replaced by a culture in which the agencies instead feel they have a duty to the information—to repay the taxpayers' investment by making that information available.

Each intelligence agency has its own security practices, outgrowths of the Cold War. We certainly understand the reason for these practices. Counterintelligence concerns are still real, even if

the old Soviet enemy has been replaced by other spies.

But the security concerns need to be weighed against the costs. Current security requirements nurture over classification and excessive compartmentation of information among agencies. Each agency's incentive structure opposes sharing, with risks (criminal, civil, and internal administrative sanctions) but few rewards for sharing information. No one has to pay the long-term costs of overclassifying information, though these costs—even in literal financial terms—are substantial. There are no punishments for *not* sharing information. Agencies uphold a "need-to-know" culture of information protection rather than promoting a "need-to-share" culture of integration.[57]

RECOMMENDATION: Information procedures should provide incentives for sharing, to restore a better balance between security and shared knowledge.

Intelligence gathered about transnational terrorism should be processed, turned into reports, and distributed according to the same quality standards, whether it is collected in Pakistan or in Texas.

The logical objection is that sources and methods may vary greatly in different locations. We therefore propose that when a report is first created, its data be separated from the sources and methods by which they are obtained. The report should begin with the information in its most shareable, but still meaningful, form. Therefore the maximum number of recipients can access some form of that information. If knowledge of further details becomes important, any user can query further, with access granted or denied according to the rules set for the network—and with queries leaving an audit trail in order to determine who accessed the information. But the questions may not come at all unless experts at the "edge" of the network can readily discover the clues that prompt to them.[58]

We propose that information be shared horizontally, across new networks that transcend individual agencies.

- The current system is structured on an old mainframe, or hub-and-spoke, concept. In this older approach, each agency has its own database. Agency users send information to the database and then can retrieve it from the database.
- A decentralized network model, the concept behind much of the information revolution, shares data horizontally too. Agencies would still

have their own databases, but those databases would be searchable across agency lines. In this system, secrets are protected through the design of the network and an "information rights management" approach that controls access to the data, not access to the whole network. An outstanding conceptual framework for this kind of "trusted information network" has been developed by a task force of leading professionals in national security, information technology, and law assembled by the Markle Foundation. Its report has been widely discussed throughout the U.S. government, but has not yet been converted into action.[59]

RECOMMENDATION: The president should lead the government-wide effort to bring the major national security institutions into the information revolution. He should coordinate the resolution of the legal, policy, and technical issues across agencies to create a "trusted information network."

- No one agency can do it alone. Well-meaning agency officials are under tremendous pressure to update their systems. Alone, they may only be able to modernize the stovepipes, not replace them.
- Only presidential leadership can develop government-wide concepts and standards. Currently, no one is doing this job. Backed by the Office of Management and Budget, a new National Intelligence Director empowered to set common standards for information use throughout the community, and a secretary of homeland security who helps extend the system to public agencies and relevant private-sector databases, a government-wide initiative can succeed.
- White House leadership is also needed because the policy and legal issues are harder than the technical ones. The necessary technology already exists. What does not are the rules for acquiring, accessing, sharing, and using the vast stores of public and private data that may be available. When information sharing works, it is a powerful tool. Therefore the sharing and uses of information must be guided by a set of practical policy guidelines that simultaneously empower and constrain officials, telling them clearly what is and is not permitted.

"This is government acting in new ways, to face new threats," the most recent Markle report explains. "And while such change is necessary,

it must be accomplished while engendering the people's trust that privacy and other civil liberties are being protected, that businesses are not being unduly burdened with requests for extraneous or useless information, that taxpayer money is being well spent, and that, ultimately, the network will be effective in protecting our security." The authors add: "Leadership is emerging from all levels of government and from many places in the private sector. What is needed now is a plan to accelerate these efforts, and public debate and consensus on the goals."[60]

UNITY OF EFFORT IN THE CONGRESS

Strengthen Congressional Oversight of Intelligence and Homeland Security

Of all our recommendations, strengthening congressional oversight may be among the most difficult and important. So long as oversight is governed by current congressional rules and resolutions, we believe the American people will not get the security they want and need. The United States needs a strong, stable, and capable congressional committee structure to give America's national intelligence agencies oversight, support, and leadership.

Few things are more difficult to change in Washington than congressional committee jurisdiction and prerogatives. To a member, these assignments are almost as important as the map of his or her congressional district. The American people may have to insist that these changes occur, or they may well not happen. Having interviewed numerous members of Congress from both parties, as well as congressional staff members, we found that dissatisfaction with congressional oversight remains widespread.

The future challenges of America's intelligence agencies are daunting. They include the need to develop leading-edge technologies that give our policymakers and warfighters a decisive edge in any conflict where the interests of the United States are vital. Not only does good intelligence win wars, but the best intelligence enables us to prevent them from happening altogether.

Under the terms of existing rules and resolutions the House and Senate intelligence committees lack the power, influence, and sustained capability to meet this challenge. While few members of Congress have the broad knowledge of intelligence activities or the know-how about the technologies employed, all members need to feel assured that good oversight is happening. When their unfamiliarity with the subject is combined with the need to preserve security, a mandate emerges for substantial change.

Tinkering with the existing structure is not sufficient. Either Congress should create a joint committee for intelligence, using the Joint Atomic Energy Committee as its model, or it should create House and Senate committees with combined authorizing and appropriations powers.

Whichever of these two forms are chosen, the goal should be a structure—codified by resolution with powers expressly granted and carefully limited—allowing a relatively small group of members of Congress, given time and reason to master the subject and the agencies, to conduct oversight of the intelligence establishment and be clearly accountable for their work. The staff of this committee should be nonpartisan and work for the entire committee and not for individual members.

The other reforms we have suggested—for a National Counterterrorism Center and a National Intelligence Director—will not work if congressional oversight does not change too. Unity of effort in executive management can be lost if it is fractured by divided congressional oversight.

RECOMMENDATION: Congressional oversight for intelligence—and counterterrorism—is now dysfunctional. Congress should address this problem. We have considered various alternatives: A joint committee on the old model of the Joint Committee on Atomic Energy is one. A single committee in each house of Congress, combining authorizing and appropriating authorities, is another.

- The new committee or committees should conduct continuing studies of the activities of the intelligence agencies and report problems relating to the development and use of intelligence to all members of the House and Senate.
- We have already recommended that the total level of funding for intelligence be made public, and that the national intelligence program be appropriated to the National Intelligence Director, not to the secretary of defense.[61]
- We also recommend that the intelligence committee should have a subcommittee specifically dedicated to oversight, freed from the consuming responsibility of working on the budget.
- The resolution creating the new intelligence committee structure should grant subpoena authority to the committee or committees. The majority party's representation on this committee should never exceed the minority's representation by more than one.
- Four of the members appointed to this committee or committees should be a member who also serves on each of the following additional committees: Armed Services, Judiciary, Foreign Affairs, and the Defense Appropriations subcommittee. In this way the other major congressional interests can be brought together in the new committee's work.
- Members should serve indefinitely on the intelligence committees, without set terms, thereby letting them accumulate expertise.
- The committees should be smaller—perhaps seven or nine members in each house—so that each member feels a greater sense of responsibility, and accountability, for the quality of the committee's work.

The leaders of the Department of Homeland Security now appear before 88 committees and subcommittees of Congress. One expert witness (not a member of the administration) told us that this is perhaps the single largest obstacle impeding the department's successful development. The one attempt to consolidate such committee authority, the House Select Committee on Homeland Security, may be eliminated. The Senate does not have even this.

Congress needs to establish for the Department of Homeland Security the kind of clear authority and responsibility that exist to enable the Justice Department to deal with crime and the Defense Department to deal with threats to national security. Through not more than one authorizing committee and one appropriating subcommittee in each house, Congress should be able to ask the secretary of homeland security whether he or she has the resources to provide reasonable security against major terrorist acts within the United States and to hold the secretary accountable for the department's performance.

RECOMMENDATION: Congress should create a single, principal point of oversight and review for homeland security. Congressional leaders are best able to judge what committee should have jurisdiction over this department and its duties. But we believe that Congress does have the obligation to choose one in the House and one in the Senate, and that this committee should be a permanent standing committee with a nonpartisan staff.

Improve the Transitions Between Administrations

In…the transition of 2000–2001,…the new administration did not have its deputy cabinet officers in place until the spring of 2001, and the critical subcabinet officials were not confirmed until the summer—if then. In other words, the new administration—like others before it—did not have its team on the job until at least six months after it took office.

RECOMMENDATION: Since a catastrophic attack could occur with little or no notice, we should minimize as much as possible the disruption of national security policymaking during the change of administrations by accelerating the process for national security appointments. We think the process could be improved significantly so transitions can work more effectively and allow new officials to assume their new responsibilities as quickly as possible.

- Before the election, candidates should submit the names of selected members of their prospective transition teams to the FBI so that, if necessary, those team members can obtain security clearances immediately after the election is over.
- A president-elect should submit lists of possible candidates for national security positions to begin obtaining security clearances immediately after the election, so that their background investigations can be complete before January 20.
- A single federal agency should be responsible for providing and maintaining security clearances, ensuring uniform standards—including uniform security questionnaires and financial report requirements, and maintaining a single database. This agency can also be responsible for administering polygraph tests on behalf of organizations that require them.
- A president-elect should submit the nominations of the entire new national security team, through the level of under secretary of cabinet departments, not later than January 20. The Senate, in return, should adopt special rules requiring hearings and votes to confirm or reject national security nominees within 30 days of their submission. The Senate should not require confirmation of such executive appointees below Executive Level 3.
- The outgoing administration should provide the president-elect, as soon as possible after election day, with a classified, compartmented list

that catalogues specific, operational threats to national security; major military or covert operations; and pending decisions on the possible use of force. Such a document could provide both notice and a checklist, inviting a president-elect to inquire and learn more.

ORGANIZING AMERICA'S DEFENSES IN THE UNITED STATES

The Future Role of the FBI

We have considered proposals for a new agency dedicated to intelligence collection in the United States. Some call this a proposal for an "American MI-5," although the analogy is weak—the actual British Security Service is a relatively small worldwide agency that combines duties assigned in the U.S. government to the Terrorist Threat Integration Center, the CIA, the FBI, and the Department of Homeland Security.

The concern about the FBI is that it has long favored its criminal justice mission over its national security mission. Part of the reason for this is the demand around the country for FBI help on criminal matters. The FBI was criticized, rightly, for the overzealous domestic intelligence investigations disclosed during the 1970s. The pendulum swung away from those types of investigations during the 1980s and 1990s, though the FBI maintained an active counterintelligence function and was the lead agency for the investigation of foreign terrorist groups operating inside the United States.

We do not recommend the creation of a new domestic intelligence agency. It is not needed if our other recommendations are adopted—to establish a strong national intelligence center, part of the NCTC, that will oversee counterterrorism intelligence work, foreign and domestic, and to create a National Intelligence Director who can set and enforce standards for the collection, processing, and reporting of information.

Under the structures we recommend, the FBI's role is focused, but still vital. The FBI does need to be able to direct its thousands of agents and other employees to collect intelligence in America's cities and towns—interviewing informants, conducting surveillance and searches, tracking individuals, working collaboratively with local authorities, and doing so with meticulous attention to detail and compliance with the law. The FBI's job in the streets of the United States would thus be a domestic equivalent, operating under the U.S. Constitution and quite different laws and rules, to the job of the CIA's operations officers abroad.

Creating a new domestic intelligence agency has other drawbacks.

- The FBI is accustomed to carrying out sensitive intelligence collection operations in compliance with the law. If a new domestic intelligence agency were outside of the Department of Justice, the process of legal oversight—never easy—could become even more difficult. Abuses of civil liberties could create a backlash that would impair the collection of needed intelligence.
- Creating a new domestic intelligence agency would divert attention of the officials most responsible for current counterterrorism efforts while the threat remains high. Putting a new player into the mix of federal agencies with counterterrorism responsibilities would exacerbate existing information-sharing problems.
- A new domestic intelligence agency would need to acquire assets and personnel. The FBI already has 28,000 employees; 56 field offices, 400 satellite offices, and 47 legal attaché offices; a laboratory, operations center, and training facility; an existing network of informants, cooperating defendants, and other sources; and relationships with state and local law enforcement, the CIA, and foreign intelligence and law enforcement agencies.
- Counterterrorism investigations in the United States very quickly become matters that involve violations of criminal law and possible law enforcement action. Because the FBI can have agents working criminal matters and agents working intelligence investigations concerning the same international terrorism target, the full range of investigative tools against a suspected terrorist can be considered within one agency. The removal of "the wall" that existed before 9/11 between intelligence and law enforcement has opened up new opportunities for cooperative action within the FBI.
- Counterterrorism investigations often overlap or are cued by other criminal investigations, such as money laundering or the smuggling of contraband. In the field, the close connection to criminal work has many benefits.

Our recommendation to leave counterterrorism intelligence collection in the United States with the FBI still depends on an assessment that the FBI—if it makes an all-out effort to institutionalize change—can do the job.... [W]e have been impressed by the determination that agents display in tracking down details, patiently going the extra mile and working the extra month, to put facts in the place of speculation. In our report we have shown how agents in Phoenix, Minneapolis, and New York displayed initiative in pressing their investigations.

FBI agents and analysts in the field need to have sustained support and dedicated resources to become stronger intelligence officers. They need to be rewarded for acquiring informants and for gathering and disseminating information differently and more broadly than usual in a traditional criminal investigation. FBI employees need to report and analyze what they have learned in ways the Bureau has never done before.

Under Director Robert Mueller, the Bureau has made significant progress in improving its intelligence capabilities. It now has an Office of Intelligence, overseen by the top tier of FBI management. Field intelligence groups have been created in all field offices to put FBI priorities and the emphasis on intelligence into practice. Advances have been made in improving the Bureau's information technology systems and in increasing connectivity and information sharing with intelligence community agencies.

Director Mueller has also recognized that the FBI's reforms are far from complete. He has outlined a number of areas where added measures may be necessary. Specifically, he has recognized that the FBI needs to recruit from a broader pool of candidates, that agents and analysts working on national security matters require specialized training, and that agents should specialize within programs after obtaining a generalist foundation. The FBI is developing career tracks for agents to specialize in counterterrorism/counterintelligence, cyber crimes, criminal investigations, or intelligence. It is establishing a program for certifying agents as intelligence officers, a certification that will be a prerequisite for promotion to the senior ranks of the Bureau. New training programs have been instituted for intelligence-related subjects.

The Director of the FBI has proposed creating an Intelligence Directorate as a further refinement of the FBI intelligence program. This directorate would include units for intelligence planning and policy and for the direction of analysts and linguists.

We want to ensure that the Bureau's shift to a preventive counterterrorism posture is more fully institutionalized so that it survives beyond Director Mueller's tenure. We have found that in the past the

Bureau has announced its willingness to reform and restructure itself to address transnational security threats, but has fallen short—failing to effect the necessary institutional and cultural changes organization-wide. We want to ensure that this does not happen again. Despite having found acceptance of the Director's clear message that counterterrorism is now the FBI's top priority, two years after 9/11 we also found gaps between some of the announced reforms and the reality in the field. We are concerned that management in the field offices still can allocate people and resources to local concerns that diverge from the national security mission. This system could revert to a focus on lower-priority criminal justice cases over national security requirements.

RECOMMENDATION: A specialized and integrated national security workforce should be established at the FBI consisting of agents, analysts, linguists, and surveillance specialists who are recruited, trained, rewarded, and retained to ensure the development of an institutional culture imbued with a deep expertise in intelligence and national security.

- The president, by executive order or directive, should direct the FBI to develop this intelligence cadre.
- Recognizing that cross-fertilization between the criminal justice and national security disciplines is vital to the success of both missions, all new agents should receive basic training in both areas. Furthermore, new agents should begin their careers with meaningful assignments in both areas.
- Agents and analysts should then specialize in one of these disciplines and have the option to work such matters for their entire career with the Bureau. Certain advanced training courses and assignments to other intelligence agencies should be required to advance within the national security discipline.
- In the interest of cross-fertilization, all senior FBI managers, including those working on law enforcement matters, should be certified intelligence officers.
- The FBI should fully implement a recruiting, hiring, and selection process for agents and analysts that enhances its ability to target and attract individuals with educational and professional backgrounds in intelligence, international relations, language, technology, and other relevant skills.

- The FBI should institute the integration of analysts, agents, linguists, and surveillance personnel in the field so that a dedicated team approach is brought to bear on national security intelligence operations.
- Each field office should have an official at the field office's deputy level for national security matters. This individual would have management oversight and ensure that the national priorities are carried out in the field.
- The FBI should align its budget structure according to its four main programs—intelligence, counterterrorism and counterintelligence, criminal, and criminal justice services—to ensure better transparency on program costs, management of resources, and protection of the intelligence program.[62]
- The FBI should report regularly to Congress in its semiannual program reviews designed to identify whether each field office is appropriately addressing FBI and national program priorities.
- The FBI should report regularly to Congress in detail on the qualifications, status, and roles of analysts in the field and at headquarters. Congress should ensure that analysts are afforded training and career opportunities on a par with those offered analysts in other intelligence community agencies.
- The Congress should make sure funding is available to accelerate the expansion of secure facilities in FBI field offices so as to increase their ability to use secure email systems and classified intelligence product exchanges. The Congress should monitor whether the FBI's information-sharing principles are implemented in practice.

The FBI is just a small fraction of the national law enforcement community in the United States, a community comprised mainly of state and local agencies. The network designed for sharing information, and the work of the FBI through local Joint Terrorism Task Forces, should build a reciprocal relationship, in which state and local agents understand what information they are looking for and, in return, receive some of the information being developed about what is happening, or may happen, in their communities. In this relationship, the Department of Homeland Security also will play an important part.

The Homeland Security Act of 2002 gave the under secretary for information analysis and infrastructure protection broad responsibilities. In practice, this directorate has the job to map "terrorist threats to the homeland against our assessed vulnerabilities in order to drive our efforts to protect against terrorist threats."[63] These capabilities are still embryonic. The directorate has not yet developed the capacity to perform one of its assigned jobs, which is to assimilate and analyze information from Homeland Security's own component agencies, such as the Coast Guard, Secret Service, Transportation Security Administration, Immigration and Customs Enforcement, and Customs and Border Protection. The secretary of homeland security must ensure that these components work with the Information Analysis and Infrastructure Protection Directorate so that this office can perform its mission.[64]

Homeland Defense

At several points in our inquiry, we asked, "Who is responsible for defending us at home?" Our national defense at home is the responsibility, first, of the Department of Defense and, second, of the Department of Homeland Security. They must have clear delineations of responsibility and authority.

We found that NORAD, which had been given the responsibility for defending U.S. airspace, had construed that mission to focus on threats coming from outside America's borders. It did not adjust its focus even though the intelligence community had gathered intelligence on the possibility that terrorists might turn to hijacking and even use of planes as missiles. We have been assured that NORAD has now embraced the full mission. Northern Command has been established to assume responsibility for the defense of the domestic United States.

RECOMMENDATION: The Department of Defense and its oversight committees should regularly assess the adequacy of Northern Command's strategies and planning to defend the United States against military threats to the homeland.

The Department of Homeland Security was established to consolidate all of the domestic agencies responsible for securing America's borders and national infrastructure, most of which is in private hands. It should identify those elements of our transportation, energy, communications, financial, and other institutions that need to be protected,

develop plans to protect that infrastructure, and exercise the mechanisms to enhance preparedness. This means going well beyond the preexisting jobs of the agencies that have been brought together inside the department.

RECOMMENDATION: The Department of Homeland Security and its oversight committees should regularly assess the types of threats the country faces to determine (a) the adequacy of the government's plans—and the progress against those plans—to protect America's critical infrastructure and (b) the readiness of the government to respond to the threats that the United States might face.

We look forward to a national debate on the merits of what we have recommended, and we will participate vigorously in that debate.

QUESTIONS FOR FURTHER DISCUSSION

1. How is the threat posed by Al Qaeda different from the threats posed by nation-states?
2. Do you think the recommendations proposed by the commissioners represent an effective response to the challenge posed by weapons of mass destruction in the hands of terrorists?
3. What do you think will be the main challenges faced by the National Counterintelligence Center in trying to coordinate an effective federal government response to transnational terrorist networks?
4. Why did the commissioners conclude that the U.S. intelligence community was badly organized to combat international and domestic terrorism?

ENDNOTES

1. For spending totals, see David Baumann "Accounting for the Deficit," *National Journal*, June 12, 2004, p. 1852 (combining categories for defense discretionary, homeland security, and international affairs).
2. White House press release, "National Strategy for Combating Terrorism," Feb. 2003 (online at <www.whitehouse.gov/news/releases/2003/02/20030214-7.html>).
3. "Islamist terrorism is an immediate derivative of *Islamism.* This term distinguishes itself from *Islamic* by the fact that the latter refers to a religion and culture in existence over a millennium, whereas the first is a political/religious phenomenon linked to the great events of the 20th century. Furthermore Islamists define themselves as 'Islamiyyoun/Islamists'

precisely to differentiate themselves from 'Muslimun/ Muslims.'...Islamism is defined as an Islamic militant, anti-democratic movement, bearing a holistic vision of Islam whose final aim is the restoration of the caliphate." Mehdi Mozaffari, "Bin Laden and Islamist Terrorism," *Militaert Tidsskrift*, vol. 131 (Mar. 2002), p. 1 (online at <www.mirkflem.pup.blueyonder.co.uk/pdf/ islamistterrorism.pdf>). The Islamist movement, born about 1940, is a product of the modern world, influenced by Marxist-Leninist concepts about revolutionary organization. "Islamists consider Islam to be as much a religion as an 'ideology,' a neologism which they introduced and which remains anathema to the ularnas (the elerical scholars)." Olivier Roy, *The Failure of Political Islam*, trans. Carol Volk (Harvard Univ. Press, 1994), p. 3. Facing political limits by the end of the 1990s, the extremist wing of the Islamist movement "rejected the democratic references invoked by the moderates; and as a result, raw terrorism in its most spectacular and destructive form became its main option for reviving armed struggle in the new millennium." Gilles Kepel, *Jihad: The Trail of Political Islam*, trans. Anthony Roberts (Harvard Univ. Press, 2002), p. 14.

4. Opening the Islamic Conference of Muslim leaders from around the world on October 16, 2003, then Malaysian prime minister Mahathir Mohamad said: "Today we, the whole Muslim ummah [community of believers] are treated with contempt and dishonour. Our religion is denigrated. Our holy places desecrated. Our countries are occupied. Our people are starved and killed. None of our countries are truly independent. We are under pressure to conform to our oppressors' wishes about how we should behave, how we should govern our lands, how we should think even." He added: "There is a feeling of hopelessness among the Muslim countries and their people. They feel that they can do nothing right. They believe that things can only get worse. The Muslims will forever be oppressed and dominated by the Europeans and Jews." The prime minister's argument was that the Muslims should gather their assets, not striking back blindly, but instead planning a thoughtful, long-term strategy to defeat their worldwide enemies, which he argued were controlled by the Jews. "But today the Jews rule the world by proxy. They get others to fight and die for them." Speech at the Opening of the Tenth Session of the Islamic Summit Conference, Oct. 16, 2003 (online at <www.oicsummit2003. org.my/speech_03.php>).

5. CIA map, "Possible Remote Havens for Terrorist and Other Illicit Activity," May 2003.

6. For the numbers, see Tariq interview (Oct. 20, 2003).

7. For Pakistan playing a key role in apprehending 500 terrorists, see Richard Armitage testimony, Mar. 23, 2004.

8. For Pakistan's unpoliced areas, see Tasneem Noorani interview (Oct. 27, 2003).

9. Pakistanis and Afghanis interviews (Oct. 2003); DOD Special Operations Command and Central Command briefings (Sept. 15–16, 2004); U.S. intelligence official interview (July 9, 2004).

10. Pervez Musharraf, "A Plea for Enlightened Moderation: Muslims Must Raise Themselves Up Through Individual Achievement and Socioeconomic Emancipation," *Washington Post*, June 1, 2004, p. A23.

11. For a review of ISAF's role, see NATO report, "NATO in Afghanistan," updated July 9, 2004 (online at <www.nato.int/issues/afghanistan>).

12. United States Institute of Peace report, "Establishing the Rule of Law in Afghanistan," Mar. 2004, pp. 1–3 (online at <www.usip.org/pubs/specialreports/srll7.html>).

13. For the change, see Lakhdar Brahimi interview (Oct. 24, 2003); U.S. officials in Afghanistan interview (Oct. 2003). For the request that the United States remain, see Kandahar province local leaders interview (Oct. 21, 2003). For the effect of the United States leaving, see Karim Khalili interview (Oct. 23, 2003).

14. Some have criticized the Bush administration for neglecting Afghanistan because of Iraq. Others, including General Franks, say that the size of the U.S. military commitment in Afghanistan has not been compromised by the commitments in Iraq. We have not investigated the issue and cannot offer a judgment on it.

15. Even if the U.S. forces, stretched thin, are reluctant to take on this role, "a limited, but extremely useful, change in the military mandate would involve intelligence sharing with civilian law enforcement and a willingness to take action against drug warehouses and heroin laboratories." United States Institute of Peace report, "Establishing the Rule of Law in Afghanistan," Mar. 2004, p. 17.

16. For barriers to Saudi monitoring of charities, see, e.g., Robert Jordan interview (Jan. 14, 2004); David Aufhauser interview (Feb. 12, 2004).

17. For the Saudi reformer's view, see Members of *majles al-shura* interview (Oct. 14, 2003).

18. Neil MacFarquhar, "Saudis Support a Jihad in Iraq, Not Back Home," *New York Times*, Apr. 23, 2004, p. Al.

19. Prince Bandar Bin Sultan, "A Diplomat's Call for War," *Washington Post*, June 6, 2004, p. B4 (translation of original in *Al-Watan*, June 2, 2004).

20. President Clinton meeting (Apr. 8, 2004).

21. For Jordan's initiatives, see testimony of William Burns before the Subcommittee on the Middle East and Central Asia of the House International Relations Committee, Mar. 19, 2003 (online at <www.house.gov /international_ jrelations/108/burn0319.htm>). For the report, see United Nations Development Programme report, *Arab Human Development Report 2003: Building a Knowledge Society* (United Nations, 2003) (online at <www.miftah.org/Doc/Reports/Englishcomplete2003.pdf>).

22. DOD memo, Rumsfeld to Myers, Wolfowitz, Pace, and Feith, "Global War on Terrorism," Oct. 16, 2003 (online at <www.usatoday.com/news/washington/executive/rumsfeld-memo.htm>).

23. For the statistics, see James Zogby, *What Arabs Think: Values, Beliefs, and Concerns* (Zogby International, 2002). For fear of a U.S. attack, see Pew Global Attitudes Project report, *Views of a Changing World: June 2003* (Pew Research Center for the People and the Press, 2003), p. 2. In our interviews, current and former U.S. officials dealing with the Middle East corroborated these findings.

24. For polling soon after 9/11, see Pew Research Center for the People and the Press report, "America Admired, Yet Its New Vulnerability Seen as Good Thing, Say Opinion Leaders; Little Support for Expanding War on Terrorism" (online at <http://peoplepress.org/reports/print.php3?ReportID=145>). For the quotation, see Pew Global Attitudes Project report, "War With Iraq Further Divides Global Publics But World Embraces Democratic Values and Free Markets," June 3, 2003 (online at <www.pewtrusts.com/ideas/ideas_item.cfm?content_item_id=l645&content_type_id=7>).

25. For the Occidentalist "creed of Islamist revolutionaries," see, e.g., Avishai Margalit and Ian Buruma, *Occidentalism: The West in the Eyes of Its Enemies* (Penguin Press, 2004).

26. We draw these statistics, significantly, from the U.S. government's working paper circulated in April 2004 to G-8 "sherpas" in preparation for the 2004 G-8 summit. The paper was leaked and published in *Al-Hayat.* "U.S. Working Paper for G-8 Sherpas," *Al-Hayat,* Feb. 13, 2004 (online at <http://english.daralhayat.com/Spec/02-2004/Article-20040213-ac40bdaf-c0a8-01ed004e-5e7ac897d678/story.html>).

27. Richard Holbrooke, "Get the Message Out," *Washington Post,* Oct. 28, 2001, p. B7; Richard Armitage interview Jan. 12, 2004.

28. Testimony of George Tenet, "The Worldwide Threat 2004; Challenges in a Changing Global Context,"

before the Senate Select Committee on Intelligence, Feb. 24, 2004.

29. U.S. Department of Energy Advisory Board. report, "A Report Card on the Department of Energy's Nonproliferation Programs with Russia," Jan. 10, 2001, p. vi.

30. For terrorists being self-funded, see United Nations report, "Second Report of the [UN] Monitoring Group, Pursuant to Security Council Resolution 1390," Sept. 19, 2002, p. 13.

31. For legal entry, see White House report. Office of Homeland Security, "The National Strategy for Homeland Security," July 2002, p. 20 (online at <www.whitehouse.gov/homeland/book/index.html>). For illegal entry, see Chicago Council on Foreign Relations task force report, *Keeping the Promise: Immigration Proposals From the Heartland* (Chicago Council on Foreign Relations, 2004), p. 28.

32. The names of at least three of the hijackers (Nawaf al Hazmi, Salem al Hazmi, and Khalid al Mihdhar) were in information systems of the intelligence community and thus potentially could have been watchlisted. Had they been watchlisted, the connections to terrorism could have been exposed at the time they applied for a visa or at the port of entry. The names of at least three of the hijackers (Nawaf al Hazmi, Salem al Hazmi, and Khalid al Mihdhar), were in information systems of the intelligence community and thus potentially could have been watchlisted. Had they been watchlisted, their terrorist affiliations could have been exposed either at the time they applied for a visa or at the port of entry. Two of the hijackers (Satain al Suqami and Abdul Aziz al Omari) presented passports manipulated in a fraudulent manner that has subsequently been associated with al Qaeda. Based on our review of their visa and travel histories, we believe it possible that as many as eleven additional hijackers (Wail al Shehri, Waleed al Shehri, Mohand al Shehri, Hani Hanjour, Majed Moqed, Nawaf al Hazmi, Hamza al Ghamdi, Ahmed al Ghamdi, Saeed al Ghamdi, Ahmed al Nami, and Ahmad al Haznawi) held passports containing these same fraudulent features, but their passports have not been found so we cannot be sure. Khalid al Mihdhar and Salem al Hazmi presented passports with a suspicious indicator of Islamic extremism. There is reason to believe that the passports of three other hijackers (Nawaf al Hazmi, Ahmed al Nami, and Ahmad al Haznawi) issued in the same Saudi passport office may have contained this same indicator; however, their passports have not been found, so we cannot he sure.

33. Khallad Bin Attash, Ramzi Binalshibh, Zakariya Essabar, Ali Abdul Aziz Ali, and Saeed al Ghamdi (not the individual by the same name who became a hijacker) tried to get visas and failed. Kahtani was unable to prove his admissibility and withdrew his application for admission after an immigration inspector remained unpersuaded that he was a tourist. All the hijackers whose visa applications we reviewed arguably could have been denied visas because their applications were not filled out completely. Had State visa officials routinely had a practice of acquiring more information in such cases, they likely would have found more grounds for denial. For example, three hijackers made statements on their visa applications that could have been proved false by U.S. government records (Hani Hanjour, Saeed al Ghamdi, and Khalid al Mihdhar), and many lied about their employment or educational status. Two hijackers could have been denied admission at the port of entry based on violations of immigration rules governing terms of admission—Mohamed Atta overstayed his tourist visa and then failed to present a proper vocational school visa when he entered in January 2001; Ziad Jarrah attended school in June 2000 without properly adjusting his immigration status, an action that violated his immigration status and rendered him inadmissible on each of his six subsequent reentries into the United States between June 2000 and August 5, 2001. There were possible grounds to deny entry to a third hijacker (Marwan al Shehhi). One hijacker violated his immigration status by failing to enroll as a student after entry (Hani Hanjour); two hijackers overstayed their terms of admission by four and eight months respectively (Satam al Suqami and Nawaf al Hazmi). Atta and Shehhi attended a flight school (Huffman Aviation) that the Justice Department's Inspector General concluded should not have been certified to accept foreign students, see DOJ Inspector General's report, "The INS' Contacts with Two September 11 Terrorists: A Review of the INS's Admissions of Atta and Shehhi, its Processing of their Change of Status Applications, and its Efforts to Track Foreign Students in the United States," May 20, 2002.
34. John Gordon interview (May 13, 2004).
35. For a description of a layering approach, see Stephen Flynn, *America the Vulnerable: How the U.S. Has Failed to Secure the Homeland and Protect Its People From Terrorism* (HarperCollins, 2004), p. 69.
36. The logical and timely rollout of such a program is hampered by an astonishingly long list of congressional mandates. The system originated in the Illegal Immigration Reform and Immigrant Responsibility Act of 1996 and applied to all non-U.S. citizens who enter or exit the United States at any port of entry. Pub. L. No. 104–208, 110 Stat. 3009 (1996), § 110. The Data Management Improvement Act of 2000 altered this mandate by incorporating a requirement for a searchable centralized database, limiting the government's ability to require new data from certain travelers and setting a series of implementation deadlines. Pub. L. No. 106–215, 114 Stat. 337 (2000), § 2(a). The USA PATRIOT Act mandated that the Attorney General and Secretary of State "particularly focus" on having the entry-exit system include biometrics and tamper-resistant travel documents readable at all ports of entry. Pub. L. No. 107–56, 115 Stat. 272 (2001), § 1008(a). In the Enhanced Border Security and Visa Entry Reform Act, Congress directed that, not later than October 26, 2004, the attorney general and the secretary of state issue to all non-U.S. citizens only machine-readable, tamper-resistant visas and other travel and entry documents that use biometric identifiers and install equipment at all U.S. ports of entry to allow biometric authentication of such documents. Pub. L. No. 107–173, 116 Stat. 543 (2002), § 303(b). The Act also required that increased security still facilitate the free flow of commerce and travel. Ibid. § 102(a)(l)(C). The administration has requested a delay of two years for the requirement of tamper-proof passports. Testimony of Thomas Ridge before the House Judiciary Committee, Apr. 21, 2004 (online at <www.dhs.gov/dhspublic/display?theme=45&content=3498&print=true>). Program planners have set a goal of collecting information, confirming identity, providing information about foreign nationals throughout the entire immigration system, and ultimately enabling each point in the system to assess the lawfulness of travel and any security risks.
37. There are at least three registered traveler programs underway, at different points in the system, designed and run by two different agencies in the Department of Homeland Security (outside the U.S.VISIT system), which must ultimately be the basis for access to the United States.
38. For the statistics, see DOS report, "Workload Statistics by Post Regions for All Visa Classes," June 18, 2004. One post-9/11 screening process, known as Condor, has conducted over 130,000 extra name-checks. DOS letter, Karl Hofmann to the Commission, Apr. 5, 2004. The checks have caused significant delays in some cases but have never resulted in visas being denied on terrorism grounds. For a discussion of

visa delays, see General Accounting Office report, "Border Security: Improvements Needed to Reduce Time Taken to Adjudicate Visas for Science Students and Scholars," Feb. 2004. We do not know all the reasons why visa applications have dropped so significantly. Several factors beyond the visa process itself include the National Security Entry-Exit Registration System, which requires additional screening processes for certain groups from Arab and Muslim countries; the Iraq war; and perhaps cyclical economic factors. For the cost to the United States of visa backlogs, see National Foreign Trade Council report, "Visa Backlog Costs U.S. Exporters More Than $30 Billion Since 2002, New Study Finds," June 2, 2004 (online at <www.nftc.org/newsflash/newsflash .asp?Mode=View&article id=1686&Category=All>).

39. These issues are on the G-8 agenda. White House press release, "G-8 Secure and Facilitated Travel Initiative (SAFTI)," June 9, 2004 (online at <www.whitehouse .gov/news/releases/2004/06/20040609-51.html>). Lax passport issuance standards are among the vulnerabilities exploited by terrorists, possibly including two of the 9/11 hijackers. Three models exist for strengthened prescreening: (1) better screening by airlines, such as the use of improved document authentication technology; (2) posting of border agents or inspectors in foreign airports to work cooperatively with foreign counterparts; and (3) establishing a full preinspection regime, such as now exists for travel to the United States from Canada and Ireland. All three models should be pursued, in addition to electronic prescreening.

40. Among the more important problems to address is that of varying transliterations of the same name. For example, the current lack of a single convention for transliterating Arabic names enabled the 19 hijackers to vary the spelling of their names to defeat name-based watchlist systems and confuse any potential efforts to locate them. While the gradual introduction of biometric identifiers will help, that process will take years, and a name match will always be useful. The ICAO should discuss the adoption of a standard requiring a digital code for all names that need to be translated into the Roman alphabet, ensuring one common spelling for all countries.

41. On achieving more reliable identification, see Markle Foundation task force report, *Creating a Trusted Information Network for Homeland Security* (Markle Foundation, 2003), p. 72 (online at <www.markle.org>).

42. General Accounting Office report, *Mass Transit: Federal Action Could Help Transit Agencies Address Security*

Challenges, GAO-03-263, Dec. 2002 (online at <www .gao.gov/new.items/d03263.pdf>).

43. The Bush administration clarified the respective missions of the different intelligence analysis centers in a letter sent by Secretary Ridge, DCI Tenet, FBI Director Mueller, and TTIC Director Brennan to Senators Susan Collins and Carl Levin on April 13, 2004. The letter did not mention any element of the Department of Defense. It stated that the DCI would define what analytical resources he would transfer from the CTC to TTIC no later than June 1, 2004. DCI Tenet subsequently told us that he decided that TTIC would have primary responsibility for terrorism analysis but that the CIA and the Defense Intelligence Agency would grow their own analysts. TTIC will have tasking authority over terrorism analysts in other intelligence agencies, although there will need to be a board to supervise deconfliction. George Tenet interview (July 2, 2004). We have not received any details regarding this plan.

44. "TTIC has no operational authority. However, TTIC has the authority to task collection and analysis from Intelligence Community agencies, the FBI, and DHS through tasking mechanisms we will create. The analytic work conducted at TTIC creates products that inform each of TTIC's partner elements, as well as other Federal departments and agencies as appropriate." Letter from Ridge and others to Collins and Levin, Apr. 13, 2004.

45. Donald Rumsfeld prepared statement, Mar, 23, 2004, p. 20.

46. In this conception, the NCTC should plan actions, assigning responsibilities for operational direction and execution to other agencies. It would be built on TTIC and would be supported by the intelligence community as TTIC is now. Whichever route is chosen, the scarce analytical resources now dispersed among TTIC, the Defense Intelligence Agency's Joint Interagency Task Force—Combatting Terrorism (JITF-CT), and the DCI's Counterterrorist Center (CTC) should be concentrated more effectively than they are now.

The DCI's Counterterrorist Center would become a CIA unit, to handle the direction and execution of tasks assigned to the CIA. It could have detailees from other agencies, as it does now, to perform this operational mission. It would yield much of the broader, strategic analytic duties and personnel to the NCTC. The CTC would rely on the restructured CIA (discussed in the next section) to organize, train, and equip its personnel.

Similarly, the FBI's Counterterrorism Division would remain, as now, the operational arm of the

Bureau to combat terrorism. As it does now, it would work with other agencies in carrying out these missions, retaining the JITF structure now in place. The Counterterrorism Division would rely on the FBI's Office of Intelligence to train and equip its personnel, helping to process and report the information gathered in the field.

The Defense Department's unified commands—SOCOM, NORTHCOM, and CENTCOM—would be the joint operational centers taking on DOD tasks. Much of the excellent analytical talent that has been assembled in the Defense Intelligence Agency's JITFCT should merge into the planned NCTC.

The Department of Homeland Security's Directorate for Information Analysis and Infrastructure Protection should retain its core duties, but the NCTC should have the ultimate responsibility for producing net assessments that utilize Homeland Security's analysis of domestic vulnerabilities and integrate all source analysis of foreign intelligence about the terrorist enemy.

The State Department's counterterrorism office would be a critical participant in the NCTC's work, taking the lead in directing the execution of the counterterrorism foreign policy mission.

The proposed National Counterterrorism Center should offer one-stop shopping to agencies with counterterrorism and homeland security responsibilities. That is, it should be an authoritative reference base on the transnational terrorist organizations: their people, goals, strategies, capabilities, networks of contacts and support, the context in which they operate, and their characteristic habits across the life cycle of operations—recruitment, reconnaissance, target selection, logistics, and travel. For example, this Center would offer an integrated depiction of groups like al Qaeda or Hezbollah worldwide, overseas, and in the United States.

The NCTC will not eliminate the need for the executive departments to have their own analytic units. But it would enable agency-based analytic units to become smaller and more efficient. In particular, it would make it possible for these agency-based analytic units to concentrate on analysis that is tailored to their agency's specific responsibilities.

A useful analogy is in military intelligence. There, the Defense Intelligence Agency and the service production agencies (like the Army's National Ground Intelligence Center) are the institutional memory and reference source for enemy order of battle, enemy organization, and enemy equipment. Yet the Joint Staff and all the theater commands still have their own J-2s. They draw on the information they need, tailoring and applying it to their operational needs. As they learn more from their tactical operations, they pass intelligence of enduring value back up to the Defense Intelligence Agency and the services so it can be evaluated, form part of the institutional memory, and help guide future collection.

In our proposal, that reservoir of institutional memory about terrorist organizations would function for the government as a whole, and would be in the NCTC.

47. The head of the NCTC would thus help coordinate the operational side of these agencies, like the FBI's Counterterrorism Division. The intelligence side of these agencies, such as the FBI's Office of Intelligence, would be overseen by the National Intelligence Director we recommend later in this chapter.

48. The quotation goes on: "It includes gaps in intelligence, but also intelligence that, like a string of pearls too precious to wear, is too sensitive to give to those who need it. It includes the alarm that fails to work, but also the alarm that has gone off so often it has been disconnected. It includes the unalert watchman, but also the one who knows he'll be chewed out by his superior if he gets higher authority out of bed. It includes the contingencies that occur to no one, but also those that everyone assumes somebody else is taking care of. It includes straightforward procrastination, but also decisions protracted by internal disagreement. It includes, in addition, the inability of individual human beings to rise to the occasion until they are sure it is the occasion—which is usually too late.... Finally, as at Pearl Harbor, surprise may include some measure of genuine novelty introduced by the enemy, and some sheer bad luck." Thomas Schelling, foreword to Roberta Wohlstetter, *Pearl Harbor: Warning and Decision* (Stanford Univ. Press, 1962), p. viii.

49. For the Goldwater-Nichols Act, see Pub. L. No. 99-433,100 Stat. 992 (1986). For a general discussion of the act, see Gordon Lederman, *Reorganizing the Joint Chiefs of Staff: The Goldwater-Nichols Act of 1986* (Greenwood, 1999); James Locher, *Victory on the Potomac: The Goldwater-Nichols Act Unifies the Pentagon* (Texas A&M Univ. Press, 2003).

50. For a history of the DCI's authority over the intelligence community, see CIA report, Michael Warner ed., *Central Intelligence; Origin and Evolution* (CIA Center for the Study of Intelligence, 2001). For the Director's view of his community authorities, see DCI directive, "Director of Central Intelligence Directive 1/1: The

Authorities and Responsibilities of the Director of Central Intelligence as Head of the U.S. Intelligence Community," Nov. 19, 1998.

51. As Norman Augustine, former chairman of Lockheed Martin Corporation, writes regarding power in the government, "As in business, cash is king. If you are not in charge of your budget, you are not king." Norman Augustine, *Managing to Survive in Washington: A Beginner's Guide to High-Level Management in Government* (Center for Strategic and International Studies, 2000), p. 20.

52. For the DCI and the secretary of defense, see 50 U.S.C. § 403–6(a). If the director does not concur with the secretary's choice, then the secretary is required to notify the president of the director's nonconcurrence. Ibid. For the DCI and the attorney general, see 50 U.S.C. § 403–6(b)(3).

53. The new program would replace the existing National Foreign Intelligence Program.

54. Some smaller parts of the current intelligence community, such as the State Department's intelligence bureau and the Energy Department's intelligence entity, should not be funded out of the national intelligence program and should be the responsibility of their home departments.

55. The head of the NCTC should have the rank of a deputy national intelligence director, e.g., Executive Level II, but would have a different title.

56. If the organization of defense intelligence remains as it is now, the appropriate official would be the under secretary of defense for intelligence. If defense intelligence is reorganized to elevate the responsibilities of the director of the DIA, then that person might be the appropriate official.

57. For the information technology architecture, see Ruth David interview (June 10, 2003). For the necessity of moving from need-to-know to need-to-share, see James Steinberg testimony, Oct. 14, 2003. The Director still has no strategy for removing information-sharing barriers and—more than two years since 9/11—has only appointed a working group on the subject. George Tenet prepared statement, Mar. 24, 2004, p. 37.

58. The intelligence community currently makes information shareable by creating "tearline" reports, with the nonshareable information at the top and then, below the "tearline," the portion that recipients are told they can share. This proposal reverses that concept. All reports are created as tearline data, with the shareable information at the top and with added details accessible on a system that requires permissions or authentication.

59. See Markle Foundation Task Force report, *Creating a Trusted Information Network for Homeland Security* (Markle Foundation, 2003); Markle Foundation Task Force report, *Protecting America's Freedom in the Information Age* (Markle Foundation, 2002) (both online at <www.markle.org>).

60. Markle Foundation Task Force report, *Creating a Trusted Information Network*, p. 12. The pressing need for such guidelines was also spotlighted by the Technology and Privacy Advisory Committee appointed by Secretary Rumsfeld to advise the Department of Defense on the privacy implications of its Terrorism Information Awareness Program. Technology and Privacy Advisory Committee report, *Safeguarding Privacy in the Fight Against Terrorism* (2004) (online at <www.sainc.com/tapac/TAPAC_Report_Final_5-1004.pdf>). We take no position on the particular recommendations offered in that report, but it raises issues that pertain to the government as a whole—not just to the Department of Defense.

61. This change should eliminate the need in the Senate for the current procedure of sequential referral of the annual authorization bill for the national foreign intelligence program. In that process, the Senate Armed Services Committee reviews the bill passed by the Senate Select Committee on Intelligence before the bill is brought before the full Senate for consideration.

62. This recommendation, and measures to assist the Bureau in developing its intelligence cadre, are included in the report accompanying the Commerce, Justice and State Appropriations Act for Fiscal Year 2005, passed by the House of Representatives on July 7, 2004. H.R. Rep. No. 108–576, 108th Cong., 2d sess. (2004), p. 22.

63. Letter from Ridge and others to Collins and Levin, Apr. 13, 2004.

64. For the directorate's current capability, see Patrick Hughes interview (Apr. 2, 2004).

Reprinted from The 9/11 Commission (the Kean Commission), *Final Report of the National Commission on Terrorist Attacks Upon the United States* (New York: Norton, July 2004): 361–428.

34. SPYING BLIND

AMY B. ZEGART

Government activities take place in an organizational setting. Professor Zegart is an expert on organizational behavior and she applies this public administration approach to the study of intelligence agencies. She rebukes officials for their failure to embrace reform proposals that would help correct the deep-seated flaws in the institutional design of U.S. intelligence.

What's needed for the fix is known. But is it accepted? Not generally. And is it well on the way to getting implemented? Not at all. Can we say we're really on the way to remedying the problems that got us into the deep shit we're in? The answer is no. But we have to. There is no other way.

—*Former senior intelligence official*[1]

History suggests that transformative change rarely occurs during ordinary times. Instead, dramatic departures from the past often require a large external shock—a tragedy, catastrophic failure, scandal, or focusing event that challenges conventional wisdom and exposes the dangers of the status quo. Examples abound. The Civil War led to ratification of the Thirteenth, Fourteenth, and Fifteenth Amendments of the U.S. Constitution. The Great Depression produced Roosevelt's New Deal. World War II gave rise to the CIA, the United Nations, and the Marshall Plan. The Cuban missile crisis of 1962 ushered in an era of détente between the United States and the Soviet Union. By this reasoning, the adaptation failure of U.S. intelligence agencies before 9/11 may not be surprising. But adaptation failure after 9/11 is. If ever we would expect to find a catalyst for major change, the worst terrorist attack in U.S. history should be it. As one senior government official remarked, "You can talk about how we missed watchlisting two guys, that information sharing wasn't what it should have been, that there were cultural differences between the FBI and CIA. But find me a time when the world went to war without a galvanizing event."[2]

Yet nearly six years after 9/11, the Intelligence Community's most serious deficiencies remain. In this chapter, I examine the missed opportunities to overhaul the U.S. Intelligence Community since the attacks, the current state of intelligence capabilities, and prospects for the future. Such assessments are always incomplete. Only a rearview mirror in a distant future will reveal how many plots al Qaeda hatched, how many were stopped, and what U.S. capabilities, policies, and actions made a difference. And that's to say nothing of what new enemies may emerge. As one former intelligence official ruefully noted, "By the time we master the al Qaeda problem, will al Qaeda be the problem?"[3] International politics is rife with uncertainty.

Nevertheless, two things are already clear: 9/11 was not enough to jolt U.S. intelligence agencies out of their Cold War past, and future adaptation—to terrorism or any other threat—is unlikely. The nature of organizations, rational self-interest, and the fragmented federal government make intelligence agencies exceptionally impervious to reform, even after catastrophic failure. Adaptation is not impossible, but it is close.

ADAPTATION FAILURE SINCE 9/11

There have been two rounds of opportunities to transform U.S. intelligence agencies since 9/11. The first lasted a little more than a year. Between the attacks and December 2002, Congress and the president passed the USA PATRIOT Act, created the Department of Homeland Security, and the Congressional Intelligence Committees launched their Joint Inquiry of 9/11. What policymakers did not do was tackle intelligence overhaul. In the nation's darkest hour, when prospects for intelligence reform were brightest, elected officials chose to place their energies elsewhere. As we shall see, this was no accident; incentives and institutional fragmentation created strong pressures for President Bush and congressional leaders to avoid rather than confront the Intelligence Community's worst problems.

Round two began in July 2004, when the convergence of an extraordinary set of circumstances thrust intelligence reform back onto the political agenda. Again, a sudden turn of events raised the possibility of dramatic change. And again, it was not enough. Although Congress attempted to pass a major restructuring of the Intelligence Community, the 2004 reform bill was obstructed by the same forces that had thwarted reform for decades: bureaucratic resistance, tepid presidential support, and opposition from key congressional committee chairmen who stood to lose and had the power to resist. The Intelligence Reform and Terrorism Prevention Act of 2004 started with high hopes but ended up producing only modest changes.

ROUND ONE: AVOIDING REFORM, 2001 TO 2002

On the evening of September 11, 2001, with smoke still billowing from the Pentagon, congressional leaders gathered on the Capitol steps. Standing shoulder to shoulder, Democrats and Republicans expressed a newfound bipartisanship and a determination to fight terrorism. They then burst into a spontaneous chorus of "God Bless America." Several days later, the *New York Times* wrote that Washington was experiencing a "disaster-driven level of bipartisan civility not seen here in decades."[4] The moment seemed ripe for a major transformation of U.S. intelligence agencies.

Nobody seized the opportunity. Inside Congress, the House and Senate Intelligence Committees decided to investigate the terrorist attacks before considering reform legislation.[5] After twelve expert reports and hundreds of recommendations urging extensive intelligence reforms during the previous ten years, Congress's intelligence watchdog committees announced that they needed to study the issues more. Meanwhile, the White House spent the first forty-five days after 9/11 pressing for the USA PATRIOT Act,

which granted the FBI and other law enforcement agencies a number of authorities that had been proposed and scuttled in previous years.[6] In the aftermath of tragedy, both the White House and Congress settled for a quick fix. "The administration wanted to look like they were doing something…but there was no effort to connect the contributing factors of 9/11 and what the PATRIOT Act would solve,"[7] noted one congressional staffer. Others agreed. "Everyone wants to do something," said one former FBI official. "It's human dynamics. Logic and common sense are not a part of the formula."[8] Six weeks after 9/11, the new law sailed through Congress with astonishing speed and little debate. Only a single senator, Russ Feingold (D-WI), voted against it.[9] As the FBI official noted, "If you're a member of Congress, following a tragedy like 9/11, are you going to vote against the PATRIOT Act?"[10] (emphasis his).

In the following year, the president and Congress missed three more chances to reform the U.S. Intelligence Community. The first came in November 2001, when General Brent Scowcroft delivered a classified report to the White House urging radical overhaul.[11] Scowcroft was no ordinary messenger. He had served as national security advisor to two presidents (Gerald Ford and George H. W. Bush), was considered one of the best informed and most well respected foreign policy officials in Washington, and had recently been appointed chairman of the President's Foreign Intelligence Advisory Board. Scowcroft's report, moreover, had been requested by President Bush himself in May 2001, four months before September 11, as an independent, comprehensive review of U.S. intelligence capabilities.[12] Now, eight weeks after the attacks, Scowcroft turned in his recommendations. They were bold. He urged stripping the three largest defense intelligence agencies from the Pentagon—the National Reconnaissance Office, which builds and runs spy satellites; the National Security Agency, which intercepts signals communications; and the National Imagery and Mapping Agency, which handles imagery and mapping[13]—and placing them directly under the control of the director of cental intelligence.[14] The idea was to give the director of central intelligence real power "to direct" the entire Intelligence Community, "not plead and cajole," said one former official familiar with the report.[15]

Pentagon reaction was swift and lethal: Secretary of Defense Donald Rumsfeld hated the idea.[16] As one former intelligence official paraphrased, "Rumsfeld says 'No fucking way.' He tells Scowcroft to put it into the wastepaper basket."[17] The proposal quickly died.

The next opportunity came in June 2002, when President Bush proposed the creation of a Department of Homeland Security. The move signaled a major policy reversal for the president, who had initially preferred integrating homeland security efforts in a small White House office rather than creating a massive new cabinet department. But with pressure mounting on Capitol Hill to do more, with congressional midterm elections just months away, and with Senator Joe Lieberman's democratic homeland security department bill gaining momentum in Congress, the president had to act fast. On June 6, he abruptly announced a proposal to merge twenty-two different agencies, including the Coast Guard, Customs Service, Immigration and Naturalization Service, Federal Emergency Management Agency (FEMA) and the recently created Transportation Security Administration, into a new homeland security department. "Employees of this new agency," the president announced in a nationally televised address, "will come to work every morning knowing their most important job is to protect their fellow citizens."[18] It would be the largest government reorganization since the 1940s.

Once more, intelligence reform was not a major part of the plan. The overriding purpose of the Homeland Security Department was identifying and protecting critical U.S. targets from terrorist attack, improving emergency response to disasters, and integrating border patrol functions, not revamping the U.S. intelligence system. Although the president's proposal included an intelligence division within the new department, its role was limited and its capabilities weak. The Homeland Security Department's Information Analysis and Infrastructure Protection (IAIP) division was an analysis shop only, charged with analyzing foreign and domestic terrorism threat reporting and assessing U.S. vulnerabilities. It had no power to collect intelligence. It had no tasking authority over other agencies. And it had no ability to knock bureaucratic heads together. Rather than integrating the CIA, FBI, and other intelligence agencies, IAIP was beholden to them for information.[19] Moreover, it was housed outside the DCI's control and inside a behemoth new department whose consolidation was expected to take years.[20] With twenty-two human resource service centers,[21] more than eighty different financial management

applications,[22] and 170,000 employees whose jobs ranged from inspecting plants to distributing hurricane relief supplies, the Department of Homeland Security was not likely to produce crack intelligence analysis any time soon. Many feared, in the words of one counterterrorism official, that DHS "[wouldn't] know its ass from its elbow."[23]

Even without intelligence reform in the mix, the homeland security bill proved contentious. By the summer of 2002, business as usual was already returning to Washington. Agencies targeted for absorption in the new department, as well as the congressional committees that oversaw them, began slicing and dicing the president's proposal to protect their own pieces. Secretary of Health and Human Services Tommy G. Thompson launched a campaign behind the scenes to keep units rather than cede them to DHS. "Make sure this doesn't happen!" he told one of his deputies.[24] In Congress, turf trumped party loyalty; Republican-led committees in the House picked apart virtually every aspect of the president's bill. The Judiciary Committee voted against moving the Secret Service to the new department, and also voted to split the Immigration and Naturalization Service in half, moving only part of it to DHS. The Transportation and Infrastructure Committee voted to keep FEMA and the Coast Guard out entirely. The Ways and Means Committee agreed to let the Customs Service move only if the Treasury Department retained management authority over it. In addition, a bitter partisan feud erupted, with Democrats pressing to extend federal employment protections to homeland security workers and Republicans blasting them during an election season for being soft on national security. In the end, it took extensive lobbying (including an unprecedented joint visit to Congress by the administration's top four cabinet officers, Secretary of State Colin Powell, Defense Secretary Donald Rumsfeld, Attorney General John Ashcroft, and Treasury Secretary Paul O'Neill), some bitter wrangling, and the help of the Republican leadership in Congress—which established a special nine-member panel to write the House bill and stacked it with administration supporters who overruled committee votes—to secure passage of the Homeland Security Act of 2002.[25]

No sooner had the ink dried than the president circumvented DHS's new intelligence directorate. On January 28, 2003, just days after swearing in Tom Ridge as the first Secretary of Homeland Security, Bush announced the creation of a new Terrorist Threat Integration Center (TTIC) in his

State of the Union address. TTIC ("T-TIC") would report directly to the director of central intelligence and would be responsible for terrorism threat analysis, the same functions that had been assigned to the Homeland Security Department's Information Analysis and Infrastructure Protection Directorate. Ridge was stunned. His deputies were furious. "It was as if the White House created us and then set out to marginalize us," one later recalled.[26] Confusion was rampant. Senators Susan Collins (R-ME) and Joseph Lieberman (D-CT), the chair and ranking members of the Senate Homeland Security and Governmental Affairs Committee, quickly held hearings[27] where they demanded "critically important information about the structure of the Terrorist Threat Integration Center, and how it and other key agencies would share responsibility for the collection, analysis, and dissemination of terrorism-related intelligence."[28] Nearly a year later, little had been settled. "The very fact of TTIC's creation," noted a Markle Foundation expert task force in December 2003, "has caused confusion within the federal government and among state and local governments about the respective roles of TTIC and the DHS."[29]

In short, fourteen months after September 11, the president and Congress passed a major homeland security bill which failed to remedy any of the organizational shortcomings in U.S. intelligence that had left the United States so vulnerable to terrorist attack. The Homeland Security Act of 2002 did not integrate the Intelligence Community, improve human intelligence, change agency incentives and cultures to enhance information sharing, reform the FBI, or match intelligence resources against priorities. What's more, before any ribbons were cut, DHS's intelligence directorate was stripped of its primary function. The Homeland Security Department's Information Analysis and Infrastructure Protection directorate was weak by design and undermined before it ever began.

The fourth and final opportunity for intelligence reform occurred in December 2002, when the Congressional Joint Inquiry issued its final report about the September 11 attacks. The report's nineteen recommendations included establishing a powerful new director of national intelligence, revamping the intelligence priority process, and considering whether a new domestic intelligence agency should replace the FBI. But by then, the momentum for reform was gone. As former Bush Deputy Homeland Security Advisor Richard Falkenrath

observed, the report's recommendations "were ignored."[30] Intelligence reform went nowhere for the next year and a half.

THE LIMITS OF CATASTROPHE

In each of these four episodes, crisis was not enough. During the first year after 9/11, lawmakers went 0 for 4 on intelligence reform. These failures were not for lack of information or urgency. Days after the attacks, as the president and Congress rushed to draft the USA PATRIOT Act, reports were already surfacing about more far-reaching problems in the Federal Bureau of Investigation.[31] In November, at the very moment Defense Secretary Donald Rumsfeld was trashing Scowcroft's sweeping intelligence reform plan behind closed doors, even the *New York Times* editorial page was calling for "radical change."[32] And throughout the fall of 2002 as Bush administration officials lobbied for a new Department of Homeland Security, the House and Senate Intelligence Committees' Joint Inquiry released staggering details about the Intelligence Community's failures leading up to the 9/11 attacks.[33] "[T]he Community made mistakes prior to September 11 and the problems that led to those mistakes need to be addressed and to be fixed," declared Joint Inquiry Staff Director Eleanor Hill.[34] But problems weren't fixed. Intelligence deficiencies were everywhere in the headlines but nowhere on the political agenda.

This was more than a case of bad luck or timing. A track record that poor with tragedy so recent and reforms so urgently needed suggests something more systematic at work. Closer examination reveals that the same enduring realities that prevented adaptation before 9/11 stymied adaptation afterward.

In the weeks following the attacks, elected officials faced strong pressure to do something. But they responded to this pressure in ways that maximized electoral returns and minimized political costs. For the House and Senate Intelligence Committees, this meant investigating what went wrong rather than pushing massive legislative overhaul. Studying the problem had the advantage of demonstrating fast action and resolve without triggering opposition and almost certain defeat by the Congressional Armed Services Committees. As one congressional intelligence staffer bitterly complained in the spring of 2002, "we suck at getting things done.... We're a subcommittee of armed services. They swallow our bills."[35]

The same logic explains why 9/11 prompted the president and Congress to pass the PATRIOT Act instead of instituting more sweeping changes to the FBI and the rest of the Intelligence Community. Throwing together old proposals to enhance the FBI's legal authorities was far easier than mandating new and far-reaching changes inside the bureau. Increasing investigatory powers was an FBI crowd pleaser. Demanding that agents do their jobs in fundamentally different ways was quite another matter. The PATRIOT Act made improvements and headlines without making tough choices or raising the hackles of the FBI. From the perspective of executive branch officials and members of Congress, the new law was an ideal response to 9/11. From a national security perspective, it was a squandered opportunity to do more.

Rational self-interest and structural fragmentation also led the president to dismiss reform recommendations from the very intelligence study he had requested. When General Scowcroft submitted his intelligence restructuring plan in November 2001, Secretary of Defense Rumsfeld vehemently opposed it and the president quickly scrapped it. This should not be surprising. Turf-conscious Defense Department officials had been rejecting the same types of reforms for years, and for years presidents had capitulated to their demands, concluding that intelligence reform was not worth the fight. The post-9/11 period was no different. If anything, the costs of intelligence reform may have been even higher: With the onset of military operations in Afghanistan, the president could ill-afford to pick a fight with the Pentagon and its supporters on Capitol Hill.

It should also come as no surprise that when pressure finally forced the president to reorganize the government, he took the path of least resistance. For months, Bush had opposed the creation of a new homeland security department, changing his mind only when it appeared that a democratic bill might pass Congress without his support. Including intelligence reform would have made a difficult government reorganization bill impossible. As it was, the president had to fight hard to win.

Instead, like so many presidents before him, Bush settled for a lower cost approach to intelligence reform: using his unilateral powers of office to mitigate a handful of problems where the odds of success were high and the opposition weak. From September 2001 to August 2004, the president studiously avoided getting embroiled with the Defense Department, opting instead to direct more minor changes through executive orders and announcements. The most significant of these were an executive order tasking the U.S. attorney general with improving coordination of terrorist tracking efforts—an initiative that was still floundering four years later—and the establishment of TTIC.[36] From the president's vantage point, such changes were far more attractive than the alternatives. The Terrorist Threat Integration Center, for example, could be stood up overnight with staff from existing agencies. It could report directly to the director of central intelligence rather than another cabinet official. It required no approval from congressional committees or their powerful chairmen. It posed no serious threat to the Pentagon. And it usurped the power of the one department incapable of fighting back—the Department of Homeland Security, which had not yet opened for business. Like his predecessors, President Bush calculated the costs and benefits of his alternatives. He chose intelligence solutions that were easy and quick instead of difficult and permanent. Catastrophic failure was not enough to alter incentives and institutional realities.

ROUND TWO: THE REFORM THAT WASN'T, 2004

Intelligence reform appeared all but dead until July 2004, when three factors suddenly converged: Director of Central Intelligence George Tenet resigned; the Senate Intelligence Committee issued a scathing report criticizing prewar intelligence assessments of Iraq's weapons of mass destruction,[37] and the 9/11 Commission released its final report.

Together, these three events temporarily suspended the enduring realities that normally impede legislative reform. While bureaucrats ordinarily fiercely oppose such changes, Tenet's resignation removed the Intelligence Community's staunchest and most public defender. During the summer and fall of 2004, as the 9/11 Commission and 9/11 families' groups took aim at U.S. intelligence agencies, there was no public face to defend them. At the same time, the Senate Intelligence Committees Iraq report momentarily shifted the electoral incentives for members of Congress. During ordinary times, most legislators have little reason to champion intelligence reform, while lawmakers serving on the Armed Services Committees have every reason to block it. But the Senate report was released in the middle of a national election campaign with a tight presidential race, and it linked intelligence failures to an issue that was then gripping the nation: whether legislators had voted to authorize the war in Iraq based on flawed intelligence.[38] Questions about intelligence failures and the Iraq War dogged congressional candidates on the campaign trail everywhere from New York to Nebraska. Intelligence reform was no longer about abstract organizational charts, but about how to avoid making mistakes that were costing American soldiers their lives.

Finally, the 9/11 Commission and the 9/11 families' organizations served as powerful interest groups, lobbying lawmakers and using public media to press their reform agenda. Between July 22, when the commission released its final report, and December 10, 2004, two days after Congress passed the Intelligence Reform and Terrorism Prevention Act, the commission and the families received more national television news coverage than the war in Iraq.[39] These were the first intelligence reform interest groups in U.S. history, and they were powerful forces for change. In interviews, several officials involved in post-9/11 intelligence reform efforts said that the families and the commission were crucial. "It was the kind of ultimate pressure," said one.[40]

Even with all of these advantages, however, the intelligence reform bill was nearly derailed and ultimately diluted by the same forces that had defeated similar efforts for years: vigorous opposition from the Defense Department and prodefense lawmakers on the Congressional Armed Services Committees, and tepid support by the president. Rational incentives and structural fragmentation once again led to disappointment. The 2004 Intelligence Reform and Terrorism Prevention Act produced only modest changes.

THE PENTAGON: "TRASHING EVERYTHING"

In the fall of 2004, just like the 1992 and 1996 reform episodes, Defense Department officials savaged legislative proposals to create a powerful new director of national intelligence and streamline the Intelligence Community—two of the principal recommendations of the 9/11 Commission—because these changes threatened to undermine Pentagon control over defense intelligence agencies and the lion's share of the intelligence budget. According to Republican Representative Christopher Shays

(R-CT), Secretary of Defense Donald Rumsfeld "just trashed everything about the national intelligence director," in private meetings on Capitol Hill.[41] Other lawmakers from both parties issued similar assessments. One Democrat described Rumsfeld as someone who "was not at all enthusiastic about intelligence reform."[42] Another Republican angrily noted, "the Pentagon for months was working behind the scenes to derail the bill."[43]

The Pentagon's public campaign was equally damaging. Representative Jane Harman (D-CA), the ranking Democrat of the House Intelligence Committee and one of the chief architects of the 2004 reform bill, later remarked, "No one missed the big fights when we were doing the intel reform law with the Pentagon. If any of you missed it, I'm not sure what planet you were on."[44] One key salvo came on October 21, when General Richard Myers, chairman of the Joint Chiefs of Staff, delivered a bombshell letter to House Armed Services Committee Chairman Duncan Hunter (R-CA). In the letter, Myers opposed giving the proposed director of national intelligence strong budgetary authorities over intelligence agencies housed in the Pentagon, arguing that only a Pentagon-controlled budget would ensure sufficient "support to the warfighters."[45] It was a move taken right out of the Defense Department's intelligence reform opposition playbook. In 1992 and 1996, when intelligence reform bills started gathering momentum in Congress, senior defense officials used similar arguments in similar letters sent to Congressional Armed Services Committee chairmen. Both times, the letters helped deliver death blows to the bills.[46]

Although supporting the warfighter proved to be an effective public relations argument, it was a red herring: in reality, nothing in the proposed reforms threatened to disrupt the military chain of command. The real threat was to Pentagon dominance over intelligence collection agencies, a dominance that had over time gutted the Intelligence Community's ability to produce strategic intelligence that anticipated threats and sought to keep warfighters off the battlefield in the first place. Senator Pat Roberts (R-KS), chairman of the Senate Intelligence Committee, drove the point home on national television. Appearing on the November 21, 2004 edition of *Fox News Sunday*, Roberts declared, "I want to point something out. You know, I'm a former Marine. There are no ex-Marines. I am a former Marine, all right? I serve on the Armed Services Committee."

His voice grew louder and his tone more angry as he continued: "No bill that I have seen...had anything to do with doing any harm to tactical intelligence in regards to that warfighter in the field.... There is no reason, if we do intelligence reform, that these agencies we are talking about, these so-called combat support agencies, will not continue to support the warfighter. Nobody is against that."[47]

Despite such rebuttals, intelligence reform still made little headway. As in earlier efforts, Pentagon opposition in 2004 had powerful allies on the House and Senate Armed Services Committees and other prodefense lawmakers who feared diminishing their own jurisdictions if intelligence reform succeeded. Opposition from House Armed Services Committee Chairman Duncan Hunter (R-CA) and House Judiciary Chairman James Sensenbrenner (R-WI) grew so strong that on November 20, House Speaker Dennis Hastert (R-IL) pulled the intelligence reform bill from floor consideration. Senator Susan Collins (R-ME), one of the champions of intelligence reform, called November 20 "the weakest moment" in the 2004 reform battle.[48]

THE PRESIDENT: "GET THIS THING OFF OUR BACKS."

The 2004 intelligence reform bill also drew lukewarm public support from the president. "The president was not engaged," declared one democratic lawmaker. "For a long time the White House was in denial about the failure."[49] In press reports and interviews, officials and staffers in both parties agreed.[50] As one former Republican official put it, "The president...did absolutely nothing to stop Defense Department lobbying and did not engage after that time.... It was less the White House feeling the compulsion to do something. It was, 'Get this thing off our backs.'"[51] Here, too, rational self-interest was to blame. President George W. Bush, like all presidents since Harry Truman, knew that successful intelligence reform required battling, and defeating, his own Department of Defense. Former Senator Gary Hart (D-CO) described the persistence of presidential reluctance this way:

> Imagine the president sitting in the room with a secretary of defense, Harry. The director of central intelligence says, "Mr. President, I cannot do my job unless I have authority over the entire range of intelligence." That's going to require Secretary of Defense. Harry down the table there to give up his intelligence agencies. I'm asking you to introduce

legislation to get this to happen." Harry down the table is going to say, "Mr. President, if you do that, you'll destroy the Pentagon." That's just the kind of conversation that goes on.[52]

Congress ultimately passed the Intelligence Reform and Terrorism Prevention Act in December 2004, which created a new director of national intelligence and National Counterterrorism Center, among other changes. However, Pentagon opposition forced lawmakers to weaken substantially the new intelligence chief's legal authorities over two vital levers: control over budgets and personnel across the Intelligence Community. As one former official put it, "the language is fuzzy on both.... You're right back to cajoling, wheedling, trying to get cooperation."[53]

A LACK OF PROGRESS REPORT

Six years after the World Trade Center and Pentagon attacks, the U.S. Intelligence Community's worst problems endure. Although legislative, executive, and internal agency initiatives have made many changes to U.S. intelligence agencies, most have created halting progress. Some have made matters worse. None could be declared successes yet. In March 2005, three and a half years after 9/11, the Commission on the Intelligence Capabilities of the United States regarding Weapons of Mass Destruction (the Silberman-Robb Commission) released a report about another intelligence failure: analysis of Iraqi weapons of mass destruction in the run-up to the 2003 Iraq War. The commission found that the Intelligence Community was "dead wrong in almost all of its pre-war judgments."[54] The commission also found the causes of failure to be systemic. Despite the "laudable steps" taken to improve U.S. intelligence agencies, the commission noted that, "we believe that many within those agencies do not accept the conclusion that...the Community needs fundamental change if it is to confront the threats of the 21st century." The commission pointedly noted that time and time again, others had targeted the "same fundamental failings," without success. "The Intelligence Community is a closed world," the commission noted, "and many insiders admitted to us that *it has an almost perfect record of resisting external recommendations*" (emphasis theirs).[55]

WHO'S IN CHARGE?

The 9/11 Commission found that before September 11, "the intelligence community's confederated structure left open the question of who really was in charge of the entire U.S. intelligence effort."[56] This is still the case today, despite the creation of the director of national intelligence with the passage of the Intelligence Reform and Terrorism Prevention Act of 2004. Indeed, instead of enhancing coordination and centralization, the 2004 legislation has triggered a scramble for turf that has left the secretary of defense with greater power, the director of national intelligence with little, and the Intelligence Community even more disjointed. Many intelligence experts and officials believe that John Negroponte, who became the first director of national intelligence in April 2005, succeeded only in adding yet another bureaucratic layer to an already fragmented system.[57] When Negroponte abruptly announced his resignation in January 2007, his staff had already ballooned to 1,500 people, prompting outcries from members of Congress. "I don't see the leadership," noted Senator Dianne Feinstein (D-CA) in a Senate Intelligence Committee hearing. "What I see…is the growth of a bureaucracy over there. And…it concerns me very much."[58]

Since 9/11, Pentagon dominance has grown rather than diminished. Details of Defense Department intelligence programs are classified, but public reports suggest an ever-widening expansion of units and activities that often duplicate existing capabilities in other agencies and are not well overseen by either the DNI or Congress. In 2002, the Defense Department quietly and successfully lobbied Congress to pass legislation consolidating Pentagon intelligence activities under a new position, undersecretary of defense for intelligence. In the words of former senior intelligence official John Gannon, the move added "more heft to what already was the IC's thousand pound gorilla."[59] The undersecretary of defense, Stephen Cambone, who served until 2007, dramatically increased the number of clandestine teams conducting secret counterterrorism operations and collecting information abroad—activities that had traditionally been performed by the CIA.[60] He also expanded Pentagon intelligence activities at home, transforming a small unit called the Counterintelligence Field Activity (CIFA)—which was created in 2002 to protect U.S. military installations from terrorist attack—into a sprawling agency with a 1,000-member staff, nine directorates, and wide-ranging responsibilities that include conducting terrorism investigations of Americans inside the United States.[61] By 2005, CIFA had the authority to give orders to approximately 4,000 Army, Air

Force, and Navy investigators in the United States, in addition to its own staff, making its counterterrorism investigatory ranks equal to the FBI's.[62] One former senior defense intelligence official described CIFA's evolution this way: "They started with force protection from terrorists, but when you go down that road, you soon are into everything…where terrorists get their money, who they see, who they deal with."[63]

None of these activities came at the behest of Director Negroponte. Instead, from 2005 to 2007, the nation's first director of national intelligence labored unsuccessfully to exercise the powers he had on paper. For example, although the intelligence reform act gave the DNI power to transfer personnel across different agencies—a measure deemed critical for integrating the Community—within months of the new law, Secretary Rumsfeld issued a Defense Department directive that required Pentagon "concurrence" for any personnel transfers affecting defense intelligence agencies.[64] In October 2006, Representative Jane Harman (D-CA) blasted Secretary of Defense Rumsfeld, calling him "the best bureaucratic infighter in the history of America," and complained that "finding a way to outsmart" Rumsfeld on intelligence reform was "a high art" that had "not been mastered."[65]

Other agencies have resisted central management from the director of national intelligence as well. Between 2005 and 2006, a bureaucratic food fight erupted over the division of staffing and responsibilities between the CIA's Counterterrorist Center and the DNI's new National Counterterrorism Center. According to one DNI official, during the summer of 2005, even when DNI staffers requested additional parking at CIA headquarters, the CIA turned them down. "Nothing's changed," complained the official. "CIA still thinks they're in charge. They don't get that we *own* those parking spaces."[66]

In interviews, intelligence officials from a variety of agencies expressed grave concerns about the DNI's ability to forge the Intelligence Community into a coherent whole.[67] "The DNI," one noted, "is turning out to be nothing more than another layer on top of sixteen organizations."[68] Another issued an even more negative assessment. "The American public has been sold a bill of goods," he said. "When the next attack happens, an awful lot of people will say, 'How could this happen? We created a DNI.'"[69] Even the DNI's creators share these concerns. In February 2006, Senator Susan Collins (R-ME), one of the chief architects of the 2004 intelligence reform bill, noted, "Director Negroponte has battles to fight within the bureaucracy, and particularly with the Department of Defense. DOD is refusing to recognize that the director of national intelligence is in charge of the intelligence community."[70] In April 2006, the House Intelligence Committee warned that the DNI was heading down the path toward becoming "another layer of large, unintended and unnecessary bureaucracy."[71] Committee Chairman Peter Hoekstra (R-MI) described the report as a "shot across the bow."[72] Ranking member Jane Harman (D-CA), another key player in the creation of the DNI, was even more critical. "The concept behind intelligence reform," she said on national television, "was to create a unified command structure…not a bureaucracy. We've said that Mr. Negroponte should stop calling himself ambassador. He's a director. In order to change cultures, you have to lead. You have to make some people mad at you. You have to send new signals."[73]

Instead of sending new signals, however, Negroponte resigned nine months later, leaving the top two DNI posts vacant at the same time. His departure led many to worry that turnover would further bog down the slow pace of reform. "I am deeply troubled by the timing of this announcement and the void of leadership at the top of our Intelligence Community," said Senate Intelligence Committee Chairman Jay Rockefeller (D-WV). "The leadership of the Intelligence Community is too important."[74] By March 2007, the Intelligence Community was in the full throes of leadership transition, with a new secretary of defense, a new undersecretary of defense for intelligence, a new director of national intelligence, a vacant deputy DNI slot, and a CIA leadership team that had been in place less than a year.

Information sharing and analysis, two critical shortcomings raised in the wake of 9/11, have not improved much and in some cases have gotten worse. In 2003, President Bush established the Terrorist Threat Integration Center to provide a hub for analyzing terrorism-related intelligence across the Community. TTIC confused the lines of authority at first, until the 2004 intelligence reform bill expanded the agency's mission and renamed it the National Counterterrorism Center (NCTC). Today, NCTC is widely considered to be one of most successful improvements in U.S. intelligence. Different agency officials now sit in the same room and draft collective analytic reports about terrorism. The Center also has developed a classified counterterrorism Web site, NCTC Online, which provides synthesized terrorism intelligence to policymakers, analysts, and a number of other consumers across the U.S. government.[75]

All that sounds good. Now consider this: Because NCTC's analysts have varying levels of security clearances and come from different agencies, they still see different pieces of information.[76] Most U.S. intelligence agencies have no experience conducting all-source analysis, so the personnel they assign to NCTC are learning on the job. As one senior government official put it, "Eleven organizations sent people to NCTC. Only two of them sent people who knew what they were doing."[77] Officials still resist sharing information with colleagues assigned from other agencies even when the rules allow it.[78] Fusing intelligence is done by humans, not computers; information is stored on nearly thirty separate, incompatible information networks. To access them all, NCTC analysts must use more than a half dozen different computers stacked underneath their desks. "It's a little scary," noted Senator Mike DeWine (R-OH) in a May 2006 Senate Intelligence Committee hearing. "[I]t's like we have duct-taped our systems together. Surely we can do better than this."[79]

This is the shining example. Information sharing in other parts of the Intelligence Community is far more problematic. In 2005 the Silberman-Robb Commission wrote that, "No shortcoming of the Intelligence Community has received more attention since the September 11 attacks than the failure to share information." Yet, despite "literally dozens" of Intelligence Community information sharing initiatives, including executive guidelines and statutory requirements, the commission found that only "minor advances" had been made.[80] The commission urged that the new director of national intelligence make improving the Community's information management system a top priority.[81]

The president quickly responded, appointing a career intelligence official named John Russack to develop a Community-wide information sharing system in June 2005. But Russack was initially given only a two-person staff to do the job.[82] He left seven months later. In December 2005, the 9/11 Commission's Public Discourse Project issued a report card assessing implementation of its recommendations. Information sharing efforts received a D.[83] In July 2006, another expert task force, this time from the Markle Foundation, concluded that improvements had been made, but found "turf wars and unclear lines of authority," officials who "still cling" to old ways of doing business, and a diminishing sense of commitment and determination to improve information sharing.[84] "[A]lmost five years since the terrorist attacks of September 11," the report concluded, "systematic, trusted information sharing remains more of an aspiration than a reality."[85] In January 2007, the Intelligence Community's chief information officer, Major General Dale Meyerrose, offered a similarly discouraging progress report. "The policy that's in place took three years to write, four years to coordinate, and we've not touched it in five," he told the Senate Intelligence Committee. Although Meyerrose noted that his office had been working hard to improve information sharing for over a year and that he expected to produce a series of proposals soon, he underscored that "most of the sharing issues we face are cultural and process rather than technology."[86]

Strategic analysis has not fared any better. In March 2005, the Silberman-Robb Commission found that the pressure to respond to current events was still driving out big picture thinking. "The Intelligence Community we have today is buried beneath an avalanche of demands for 'current intelligence,'" the commission noted.[87] While it found the "pressing need" to meet the tactical demands of military and other requirements necessary, the commission made clear that inattention to strategic analysis posed grave long-term consequences.[88] "Across the board," the commission wrote, "the Intelligence Community knows disturbingly little about the nuclear programs of many of the world's most dangerous actors. In some cases, it knows less now than it did five or ten years ago."[89]

A year later, strategic intelligence again topped the list of unresolved problems. At his May 2006 confirmation hearings to become CIA director, General Michael Hayden singled out rebuilding strategic intelligence as one of the agency's greatest challenges and his top priorities. "We must set aside talent and energy to look at the long view and not just be chasing our version of the current news cycle," Hayden declared, or else the United States would "be endlessly surprised." Hayden bluntly told the committee that doing so would not be easy because of the natural pressures to put current demands ahead of long-term needs. "I actually think it might be worse now than it has been historically," he said, noting that the twenty-four-hour news cycle as well as the operations tempo in Afghanistan, Iraq, and the war on terror have

"suck[ed] energy into doing something into the here and now."[90] Outside the hearings, other intelligence officials echoed the theme. John McLaughlin, who served as the CIA's deputy director and then acting director, complained in May 2006 that the demand for instant information had made CIA analysts "the Wikipedia of Washington."[91] Carl W. Ford, Jr., a veteran intelligence official who served in both the CIA and State Department, was even more critical: "We haven't done strategic analysis for so long that most of our analysts don't know how to do it anymore," he told a reporter. Without "fundamental changes" in analysis, Ford noted, "we will continue to turn out the $40 billion pile of fluff we have become famous for."[92]

HUMAN INTELLIGENCE

The CIA's human intelligence capabilities have also made little progress since September 11. The reason: to date, the agency's approach to improving human intelligence has focused primarily on increasing the number of spies rather than improving quality or dramatically increasing nontraditional recruitment models to penetrate terrorist groups. In November 2004, the president issued a memorandum that directed the CIA to expand its spy ranks by 50 percent.[93] The agency responded, tripling the number of trained clandestine case officers from 2001 to 2006.[94] But to many intelligence veterans, this was precisely the wrong approach: success requires fewer and better spies operating differently, not more of the same.[95] "The conditions of looking for human intelligence are so different from the Cold War that just more money and more people doesn't guarantee you anything," said former CIA bin Ladin Unit Chief Michael Scheuer.[96] In interviews, several other clandestine case officers agreed. Here's how one CIA veteran described the problem:

> The core element to our business is access. In the Cold War, we wanted to recruit against bureaucracies, and so we were on the diplomatic circuit, we were out there, and that gave us access. We need access, somehow, we need to figure out how do you get access to people that are not on the diplomatic circuit. That's the enemy, that's where they are, that's their battlefield, that's their environment. We need to be in that environment. And we're not going to get there if we sit in the green zone in Baghdad....The whole terrain has shifted, and we still, we haven't shifted with it, except to say, "we want to get back to basics."[97]

"If we were really serious about this," said another, "we would have said the NOC (nonofficial cover) is our primary model of how case officers are deployed. And the exception will be somebody sitting inside an embassy, writing telegrams. But we have never, ever even come close to that position. We have never even contemplated that."[98] John MacGaffin, a thirty-one-year veteran of the CIA's clandestine service, put it more bluntly: "Fifty percent more gets you to 'Stupid.' You'll get 50 percent more of what you've got now."[99]

THE FBI

The FBI has attempted the most ambitious changes, with perhaps the most disappointing results. Since 2001, the bureau has made counterterrorism its top priority; hired roughly 1,000 new special agents;[100] doubled its analyst corps;[101] created Field Intelligence Groups to integrate law enforcement and intelligence operations in the field offices; begun training some special agents alongside CIA clandestine case officers to enhance the bureau's human intelligence capabilities;[102] consolidated intelligence, counterterrorism, and counterintelligence functions into a single National Security Branch run by a senior FBI official; and undertaken a massive technology modernization campaign.[103] Interviews with several FBI officials in 2006 and 2007 emphasized the same theme: the FBI is trying to transform itself. As one special agent put it, "We get it. We get it. We really do."[104]

Nevertheless, old law enforcement priorities and attitudes have been slow to change.[105] In 2005, forty-seven of the fifty-six field office heads still came from the Criminal Division.[106] Until 2007, newly hired special agents still received more time for vacation than counterterrorism training.[107] And analysts were still being given secretarial tasks. A 2005 Justice Department survey of more than 800 FBI analysts (two-thirds of the total employed by the FBI at the time)[108] found that on average, analysts were spending only half their time actually doing analysis.[109] Other duties commonly included answering phones, escorting visitors, and collecting the trash.[110] In personal interviews, one FBI analyst who had previous experience as a translator and analyst in another intelligence agency recalled having to spend a week watching repair workers so that FBI office security would not be compromised. One said he was required to work nights and weekends operating the switchboard and escorting the

cleaning crew. Another told Justice Department officials that, "A lot of my job doesn't require a college education."[111] Twenty-seven percent of analysts surveyed said that the FBI's special agents—who dominate the bureau—"rarely" or "never" understood what capabilities they had or what functions they were supposed to be performing.[112] Field interviews by the Congressional Research Service and others confirmed the persistence of the old cops-and-robbers culture. As one special agent-in-charge put it, the special agents, not analysts, "will always be the center of the universe."[113]

Changing this law enforcement culture has proven particularly vexing.[114] In May 2006, one FBI official was caught short when asked by a reporter whether FBI agents really wanted to work in the bureau's new National Security Branch, which is the heart of the FBI's counterterrorism, counterintelligence, and intelligence activities. "Not really," the official admitted. "[Agents] say to me, 'Hey, I joined up to arrest people.'"[115] Another FBI official put it this way. "We are working for a better corporate sense of how we employ our resources. We are trying to turn ourselves into an organization that is intelligence driven which has historically been operations driven...[but] it's a huge evolutionary process.... It's like shifting the direction of an aircraft carrier in mid-stream....Every day it's a battle."[116] Even FBI Director Robert Mueller admitted that one of the bureau's most important continuing challenges is ensuring that "the persons who do not wear the badge and the gun have the equal respect" of others in the FBI. "We're developing that," Mueller noted in January 2007, but added, "We're not where we need to be."[117] In March 2007, the bureau's own Web site still classified FBI employees as either special agents or "professional support staff"—a term that lumped analysts together with secretaries, auto mechanics, janitors, and all other bureau employees.[118]

According to FBI officials, 2006 marked the beginning of a radical transformation in how FBI field offices used intelligence analysis.[119] Dubbed "domain awareness," the new initiative no longer held field office heads responsible for pursuing specific cases. Instead, the special agents-in-charge [SACs] of all fifty-six U.S. field offices were evaluated based on how well they understood the threats to their geographic jurisdictions, how well they identified information gaps surrounding key issues, and how well they devised programs to fill them. "This has been really over the last year a very dramatic shift in how we're approaching problems," noted FBI intelligence directorate chief Wayne Murphy in 2007. He added:

> If a year ago, I asked an SAC to define for me how they understood a particular problem, the way they defined their understanding was framed in terms of how many cases they had. What we've worked to do, and I think successfully, is to create a methodological approach to say you can't say you understand a problem if you define it by what you already know about it. You understand a problem if you have indices to understand it, you've investigated whether it's just smoke or whether there's really a fire there, and you've taken steps to close those knowledge gaps.[120]

As the above description suggests, the domain awareness initiative requires a better understanding of and respect for intelligence analysis. Importantly, however, FBI analysts remain only notional partners in this effort; bureau rules still mandate that senior positions in the field, including the top spot in every U.S. field office, be staffed by FBI special agents—or in the words of one bureau official, the people who "carry guns and risk their lives."[121] These rules mean that analysts must still do battle from below, convincing their special agent superiors that chasing information has as much value as chasing suspects. As one analyst put it, despite progress in domain awareness, "outreach to our own agency" remains an ongoing frustration.[122] John Gannon, a respected senior intelligence official who spent twenty-four years working with the FBI in various positions—including the CIA's analytic branch chief, chairman of the National Intelligence Council, and staff director of the House Homeland Security Committee—offered a more pessimistic assessment. "If you go to the Defense Intelligence [Agency or] if you're CIA," he told the Senate Intelligence Committee in January 2007, "you have analytic structures where any analyst who is working in those organizations can look right up the chain of command to the director, and it is all analytic managers who are reviewing the process and applying rigor to what is done. And ultimately, that analytic system can challenge the agent culture." But, he quickly added, "I don't think that can ever happen out of the FBI system as it is."[123]

Efforts to improve the bureau's antiquated technology systems have been even more feckless. In February 2005, Director Mueller announced he was scrapping the bureau's Trilogy technology modernization program—at the cost of nearly $200

million—because it did not work.[124] A new system, named Sentinel, is now underway. It is expected to cost an additional $425 million and will not be fully operational until 2009. In May 2006, four and a half years after 9/11, the Justice Department's Inspector General testified that, "the FBI still does not have a modern, effective case management records system."[125] Director Mueller himself called the technology modernization program his "greatest frustration." Reflecting on the bureau's continued technology weaknesses in early 2007, he noted:

> I would love to be able to go out and get a contractor and say, "okay, come in and fix it." Part of the problem is that you have to change your business practices, as well. We've probably had the same business practices in place for ninety-eight years of our existence. And one of the things you do *not* want to do is just tell the technologists to go ahead and change it without changing your business practices. We're in that process. If there's one area of impatience that I have, it's that area [emphasis his].[126]

These and other developments have led to a series of increasingly dire prognoses. In March 2005, the Silberman-Robb Commission noted with concern that the FBI's transformation into an intelligence organization "is still in doubt."[127] In December 2005, the 9/11 Commission issued more alarming warnings. "Reforms are at risk from inertia and complacency," the commission declared in its report card. "[T]hey must be accelerated or they will fail."[128] And in May 2006, John Gannon issued this stark assessment to the Senate Judiciary Committee:

> The salient fact is that, approaching five years after 9/11, we still do not have a domestic intelligence service that can collect effectively against the terrorist threat to the homeland or provide authoritative analysis of that threat. It is not enough to say that these things take time. It could not be clearer from the Intelligence Community's experience over the past 25 years that it is extraordinarily difficult to blend the families of intelligence and law enforcement, and that the Bureau's organizational bias toward the latter for deep-seated historic reasons—is powerful and persistent.[129]

Although Gannon had argued for some time that the FBI was the right agency to develop a domestic intelligence capability after 9/11, by the spring of 2006 he had given up. "[W]atching the FBI struggle with its new national intelligence mandate and recalling earlier interagency 'culture wars' in my career," Gannon declared, "I have changed my mind. I now doubt that the FBI, on its present course, can get there from here."[130]

MAKING HEADLINES MORE THAN PROGRESS

Instead, it is fair to say that U.S. intelligence agencies since 9/11 have made more headlines than progress. The CIA has been an agency in turmoil. In September 2004, former House Intelligence Committee Chairman Porter Goss succeeded George Tenet as CIA Director.[131] His twenty-month tenure was steeped in controversy. Several senior agency officials quit in protest over Goss's weak management and fierce personality clashes with Goss's management team, who were viewed as overly partisan. Then, in May 2006, Goss announced his surprise resignation amidst revelations that one of his closest aides, Kyle "Dusty" Foggo, was under investigation in a corruption probe linked to former Congressman Randy "Duke" Cunningham (R-CA). It was a scandal made for the movies, with press reports that Foggo had attended poker parties with prostitutes in—of all places—the Watergate Hotel.

News headlines throughout 2005, 2006, and 2007 were also full of revelations about the Intelligence Community's secret activities and the ensuing political furor over their legality and publication. In November 2005, the *Washington Post* reported the existence of a top secret system of foreign CIA prisons or "black sites" that were being used to hold and interrogate some of the most important al Qaeda detainees.[132] One month later, the *New York Times* revealed that the National Security Agency had been wiretapping phone calls between parties in the United States and foreign countries, including American citizens suspected of al Qaeda connections—all without court warrants.[133] The NSA wiretapping program ignited a political firestorm about the program's legality, the security risks of revealing it, and whether White House, Justice Department, and intelligence officials had properly briefed members of Congress. Then in May 2006, *USA Today* reported that the National Security Agency had also secretly collected the domestic telephone records of millions of Americans and was mining the data to find clues of terrorist threats.[134] When General Michael Hayden appeared before the Senate Intelligence Committee for his CIA director confirmation hearings on May 18, scandal, not reform, was the main topic of conversation. As Committee Chairman Pat Roberts (R-KS) noted at the opening of the hearing, "the public debate in regard to your nomination has been dominated not by your record as a manager or your qualifications, the needs of the CIA, its strengths and its weaknesses and its future, but rather the debate is focused almost entirely on the presidentially authorized activities of another agency."[135] Finally, in March 2007 a Justice Department inspector general report found that the FBI had improperly used provisions of the PATRIOT Act to gather telephone, bank, and other information about American citizens. Bipartisan outrage erupted on Capitol Hill, with Democratic committee chairmen vowing to hold more hearings.[136]

ADAPTATION IN PERSPECTIVE

Some will argue that the assessment above is unduly harsh. The overwhelming consensus in Washington is that while much work remains, U.S. intelligence agencies are making progress. Scores of officials whose names are not known and whose work goes unheralded have dedicated their professional careers to one goal: getting the right information into the right hands to protect American lives. The steady refrain is that talented officials are working hard, and that we are safer now than before. As one FBI official remarked, "What bugs me the most is that the public believes the FBI is not an organization with truly dedicated people who want to make a difference. They are not here to make a lot of money. They do it for very altruistic reasons. The public often loses sight of that."[137]

Yes, tremendous effort has been expended, individuals have made extraordinary sacrifices, and improvements have been made. But some perspective is in order. Effort often does not translate into performance. And progress is not the same as success. The question is not whether the CIA and FBI are better equipped than they were on September 10, 2001—certainly a low standard. Nor is it whether the CIA and FBI have smart and dedicated officials; they always have. The question is whether these two agencies, and the rest of the U.S. Intelligence Community, have adapted to the point where they now stand a reasonable chance of preventing the next catastrophe. The evidence is not encouraging.

It is often said that change takes time. But it is now sixteen years since the end of the Cold War and the U.S. Intelligence Community is still struggling to develop the rudimentary building blocks to combat terrorism. History is filled with examples where more was accomplished in far less time. Twelve years after the Soviet Union stunned the world by launching Sputnik, the first satellite, the United States landed a man on the moon and won the space race. In 1945, just four years after Japan's surprise attack decimated much of the Pacific fleet at Pearl Harbor, the United States had built a fighting force that had crossed two oceans and defeated both Germany and Japan.[138] Within two years of the end of World War II, American leaders had helped create the United Nations and launched the Marshall Plan to rebuild Europe. And in 1787, it took less than one hundred working days to draft the U.S. Constitution.[139]

Yet here we are. Although al Qaeda has not attacked the U.S. homeland since 9/11, there is little evidence to suggest that effective intelligence is the reason. As one Congressional Intelligence Committee lawmaker noted in the fall of 2005, "We still stink at collecting. We still stink at analysis... all the problems we set out to correct are still there."[140]

CONCLUSION

This chapter's argument can be summed up in two words: Organization matters. The structures, cultures, and incentives of U.S. intelligence agencies critically influence what they do and how well they do it. Structures create capabilities and jurisdictions, determining who performs which tasks by what authority at what level of competence. Culture has an invisible but powerful hold, coloring how intelligence officials view the world and their role in it. Incentives unavoidably give greater weight to certain issues, jobs, and interests, encouraging some activities more than others. Individual leadership also plays a vital role in the policy process. Too often, however, discussion of foreign policy success and failure treats individuals as the only important factors, ignoring the powerful organizational forces in the background. Although organization alone cannot guarantee good policy outcomes, it can significantly affect what gets done, and how well. At the dawn of the Cold War, Senator Henry M. "Scoop" Jackson (D-WA) underscored the importance of getting the organizational basics right, noting, "Organization by itself cannot assure a strategy for victory in the cold war. But good organization can help, and poor organization can hurt."[141] Decades later, the 9/11 Commission, the Silberman-Robb Commission, and the House and Senate Intelligence Committees all confronted a radically different enemy but came to the same conclusion.

Criticizing U.S. intelligence agencies is nothing new. As early as 1948, the *New York Times* castigated a newly created CIA as "one of the weakest links in our national security."[142] The stakes, however, have never been higher. The spread of weapons of mass destruction, the information revolution, and the rise of transnational terrorist networks have changed the old rules and realities of international relations. For the first time in history, great power does not bring security. It is now the weak who threaten the strong. And it is intelligence, not military might, which provides the first and last line of defense. The United States' ability to protect itself hinges on whether U.S. intelligence agencies built for a different enemy at a different time can adapt. Many obstacles stand in the way. The crux of the problem lies in the enduring realities of American politics, and success requires finding ways to overcome them.

QUESTIONS FOR FURTHER DISCUSSION

1. How have institutional matters affected the performance of America's secret agencies?
2. Is it likely that institutional reforms in the Intelligence Community prior to the 9/11 attacks would have prevented this disaster?
3. How would you go about improving the relationship between the FBI and the CIA, both with quite different bureaucratic cultures?
4. Do you share Professor Zegart's pessimism about the intelligence reforms of 2004? How could the Intelligence Reform and Terrorism Prevention Act of 2004 be amended to achieve the outcomes she desires?

ENDNOTES

1. Interview, November 2006.
2. Interview, March 2007.
3. Interview, February 2006.
4. Adam Clymer, "A Nation Challenged: The Political Parties; Disaster Forges a Spirit of Cooperation in a Usually Contentious Congress," *New York Times*, September 20, 2001, p. B3.
5. Interviews with four congressional staffers, April 2002 and October 2005.
6. The PATRIOT Act included three provisions that President Clinton had tried, but failed, to pass in the mid-1990s: "roving wiretaps," which enabled the FBI to obtain a single court warrant for multiple telephone and communications devices used by a single terrorism suspect rather than requiring separate court orders for each device; expanded FBI access to telephone and

other records in terrorism cases; and lower restrictions governing the FBI's use of "pen registers" or "trap and trace" devices to monitor the identities of those sending and receiving communication in terrorism cases. For a discussion of the statutory changes President Clinton sought but never won, see President William Clinton, "President's Statement on Antiterrorism Bill Signing," April 24, 1996, Clinton Materials Project (National Archives). http://clinton6.nara.gov/1996/04/1996–04-24-president-statement-on-antiterrorism-bill-signing.html (accessed February 3, 2006); *Congress and the Nation*, vol. IX (1993–96) (Washington, DC: Congressional Quarterly Press), pp. 727–33. For an analysis of the provisions of the PATRIOT Act, see Charles Doyle, "The USA Patriot Act: A Legal Analysis," *Congressional Research Service Report RL 31377*, April 15, 2002.

7. Interview, October 2005.

8. Interview, July 2006.

9. In the House, 357 representatives voted in favor of the PATRIOT Act, while 66 voted against it.

10. Interview, July 2006.

11. Walter Pincus, "Rumsfeld Casts Doubt On Intelligence Reform: Changes Suggested by Presidential Panel," *Washington Post*, April 9, 2002, p. A17; interview with former government official, November 2005. This report was the first of two classified reviews of U.S. intelligence led by Scowcroft.

12. Walter Pincus, "Rumsfeld Casts Doubt On Intelligence Reform: Changes Suggested by Presidential Panel," *Washington Post*, April 9, 2002, p. A17.

13. In 2003 the National Imagery and Mapping Agency was renamed the National Geospatial-Intelligence Agency.

14. Walter Pincus, "Rumsfeld Casts Doubts On Intelligence Reform: Changes Suggested by Presidential Panel," Washington Post, April 9, 2002, p. A17.

15. Interview, November 2005.

16. Spencer Ackerman, "Small Changes," *New Republic*, December 13, 2004, p. 12; interview with former government official, October 2005; interview with former government official, November 2005.

17. Spencer Ackerman, "Small Change," *New Republic*, December 13, 2004, p. 12.

18. "Remarks by the President in Address to the Nation," June 6, 2002, Office of the Press Secretary, the White House, available at http://www.whitehouse.gov/news/releases/2002/06/20020606-8.html (accessed July 18, 2006).

19. President George W. Bush, "A Bill to Establish a Department of Homeland Security," submitted to Congress June 18, 2002, available at http://www.whitehouse.gov/news/releases/2002/06/20020618-5.html (accessed July 19, 2006).

20. See fox example, Government Accountability Office, *Department of Homeland Security: A Comprehensive and Sustained Approach Needed to Achieve Management Integration*, GAO 05-139, March 16, 2005.

21. Amelia Gruber, "Squeezing Services," *Government Executive Magazine*, March 1, 2005, available at http://www.govexec.com/features/0305-01/0305-01sls4.htm (accessed July 18, 2006).

22. Todd Datz, "From the Ground Up," *CSO Magazine*, March 1, 2004.

23. Quoted in Michael Crowley, "Bush's Disastrous Homeland Security Department," *New Republic*, March 15, 2004, p. 17.

24. Susan B. Glasser and Michael Grunwald, "Department's Mission was Undermined from Start," *Washington Post*, December 22, 2005, p. A01.

25. *The Homeland Security Act of 2002*: Public Law 107–296, 107th Cong., 2nd sess., November 25, 2002.

26. Quoted in Susan B. Glasser and Michael Grunwald, "Department's Mission was Undermined from Start," *Washington Post*, December 22, 2005, p. A01.

27. "Consolidating Intelligence Analysis: A Review of the President's Proposal to Create a Terrorist Threat Integration Center," Senate Committee on Homeland Security and Governmental Affairs, 108th Cong., 1st sess., February 14, 2003 and February 26, 2003.

28. Press release, "Senator Collins Receives Answers on Terrorist Threat Integration Center: Satisfied with Response, but Concerned by Its Delay," April 20, 2004, Senate Committee on Homeland Security and Governmental Affairs.

29. Task Force on National Security in the Information Age, Markle Foundation, *Creating a Trusted Network for Homeland Security: Second Report of the Markle Foundation Task Force*, December 2003, p. 3.

30. Richard A. Falkenrath, "The 9/11 Commission Report: A Review Essay," *International Security* 29, 3 (Winter 2004–05): 172.

31. Joby Warrick, Joe Stephens, Mary Pat Flaherty, and James V. Grimaldi "FBI Agents Ill-Equipped to Predict Terror Acts," *Washington Post*, September 24, 2001, p. A01.

32. Editorial, "The Spy Puzzle," *New York Times*, November 4, 2001, p. 12.

33. These were: "Joint Inquiry Staff Statement, Part I," HPSCI and SSCI hearing, 107th Cong., 2nd sess., September 18, 2002; "The Intelligence Community's Knowledge of the September 11 Hijackers Prior

to September 11, 2001," 107th Cong., 2nd sess., September 20, 2002; "The FBI's Handling of the Phoenix Electronic Communication and Investigation of Zacarias Moussaoui Prior to September 11, 2001," HPSCI and SSCI hearing, 107th Cong., 2nd sess., September 24, 2002; "Counterterrorism Information Sharing with Other Federal Agencies and with State and Local Governments and the Private Sector," HPSCI and SSCI hearing, 107th Cong., 2nd sess., October 1, 2002; "Joint Inquiry Staff Statement: Proposals for Reform within the Intelligence Community," HPSCI and SSCI hearing, 107th Cong., 2nd sess., October 3, 2002; "Joint Inquiry Staff Statement: Hearing on the Intelligence Community's Response to Past Terrorist Attacks Against the United States from February 1993 to September 2001," HPSCI and SSCI heating, 107th Cong., 2nd sess., October 8, 2002; "Joint Inquiry Staff Statement," HPSCI and SSCI hearing, 107th Cong., 2nd sess., October 17, 2002. The staff statements were submitted in open hearings which also featured testimony by senior government officials, key intelligence personnel, and outside experts.

34. Eleanor Hill, "Joint Inquiry Staff Statement, Part I," HPSCI and SSCI hearing, 107th Cong., 2nd sess., September 18, 2002.

35. Interview, April 2002.

36. TTIC later became the National Counterterrorism Center.

37. Senate Select Committee on Intelligence, *US. Intelligence Community's Prewar Intelligence Assessments on Iraq*, 108th Cong., 2nd sess., July 9, 2004.

38. Senate Select Committee on Intelligence, *U.S. Intelligence Community's Prewar Intelligence Assessments on Iraq*, 108th Cong., 2nd sess., July 9, 2004.

39. Analysis from based on full text LexisNexis searches of ABC, CBS, NBC, CNN, Fox News, MSNBC, CNBC, and *The News Hour with Jim Lehrer* between July 22, 2004 and December 10, 2004.

40. Interview, November 2005.

41. Quote in Philip Shenon and Douglas Jehl "House Proposal Puts Less Power in New Spy Post," *New York Times*, September 25, 2004, p. Al.

42. Interview, October 2005.

43. Interview, October 2005. See also comments made by Representative Jane Harman and Senator Pat Roberts, *Fox News Sunday*, November 21, 2004.

44. Representative Jane Harman, Intelligence Reauthotization News conference with members of the House Permanent Select Committee on Intelligence, March 30, 2006. Harman went on to say that she believed the law had overcome Pentagon objections and provided adequate statutory budget authority to the DNI, but needed more vigorous leadership to be effective.

45. Myera's letter can be found in Intelligence Reform and Terrorism Prevention Act of 2004 Conference Report, *Congressional Record* S11939–S12010, appendix. Available at www.fas.org/irp/congress/2004_cr/sl20804.html (accessed February 22, 2006).

46. Letter from Richard Cheney to Senator Les Aspin, March 17, 1992, available at http://www.fas.org/irp/congress/1992_cr/cheney1992.pdf (accessed February 16, 2006); letter from Deputy Secretary of Defense John White to Senate Armed Services Committee Chairman Strom Thurmond (R-SC), April 29, 1996, described in Walter Pincus, "Panels Continue Impasse on Intelligence," *Washington Post*, June 7, 1996, p. A21.

47. Pat Roberts, *Fox News Sunday*, November 21, 2004.

48. Quoted in Walter Pincus, "Intelligence Bill Clears Congress," *Washington Post*, December 9, 2004, p. A4.

49. Interview, October 2005.

50. Interviews with four officials, October 2005 and November 2005. See also Mary Curtius, "Intelligence Reform Looks Like a Lame Duck for Now," *Los Angeles Times*, November 12, 2004, p. A24; Charles Babington and Mike Allen, "White House View of Stalled Bill in Doubt," *Washington Post*, November 24, 2004, p. A4; Michael Isikoff and Bleanor Clift, "Intel Reform: Did Bush Push. Hard?" *Newsweek*, December 6, 2004, p. 6; Julie Hirschfield Davis, "Intelligence Reform in Limbo," *Baltimore Sun*, November 23, 2004, p. 1A; Elisabeth Bumiller and Philip Shenon, "Bush Urged to Get Pentagon In Step on Intelligence Bill," *New York Times*, November 23, 2004, p. A20.

51. Interview, November 2005.

52. Interview, May 2004.

53. Interview, November 2005.

54. Letter from the Honorable Laurence H. Silbmeran and The Honorable Charles S. Robb to the president, March 31, 2005, reprinted in *Silberman-Robb Commission Report*, preface.

55. *Silbeman-Robb Commission Report*, p. 6.

56. *9/11 Commission Report*, p. 93.

57. Walter Pincus, "Some Lawmakers Doubt DNI Has Taken Intelligence Reigns," *Washington Post*, February 2, 2006, p. A09; interview with Congressional Intelligence Committee member, October 2005; interview with former CIA official, February 2006. See also Richard A. Posner, *Countering Terrorism* (Oxford: Rowman & Littlefield, 2006); Scott Shane, "In New Job, Spymaster Draws Bipartisan Criticism," *New York Times*, April 20, 2006, p. A1; John Lehman, "Are We Any Safer?" *Proceedings of the U.S. Naval Institute*, September 2006.

58. Senate Select Committee on Intelligence, "Progress Made on Intelligence Reform" 110th Cong., 1st sess., January 23, 2007.

59. John Gannon, written testimony submitted to the Senate Judiciary Committee, hearing on FBI oversight, 109th Cong., 2nd, sess., May 2, 2006.

60. Eric Schmitt, "Clash Foreseen Between CIA and Pentagon," *New York Times*, May 10, 2006, p. A1.

61. Barton Gellman and Dafna Linzer, "Pushing the Limits of Wartime Powers," *Washington Post*, December 18, 2005, p. A01.

62. Walter Pincus, "Pentagon's Intelligence Authority Widens; Fact Sheet Details Secretive Agency's Growth from Focus on Policy to Counterterrorism," *Washington Post*, December 19, 2005, p. A10.

63. Quote in Walter Pincus, "Pentagon's Intelligence Authority Widens; Fact Sheet Details Secretive Agency's Growth from Focus on Policy to Counterterrorism," *Washington Post*, December 19, 2005, p. A10.

64. Eric Schmitt, "Clash Foreseen between CIA and Pentagon," *New York Times*, May 10, 2006, p. A1.

65. Jane Harman, Remarks at the Second Annual Rand/Terrorism Early Warning Group Conference, Santa Monica, CA, October 19, 2006. Secretary Rumsfeld announced his resignation on November 8, one day after Democrats regained control of both the House and Senate in the 2006 midterm elections.

66. Interview, July 2005.

67. Interviews with six current and former intelligence officials, October 2005, November 2005, and February 2006.

68. Interview, May, 2006.

69. Interview, February 2006.

70. Quote in Scott Shane, "Year into Revamped Spying, Troubles and Some Progress," *New York Times*, February 28, 2006, p. A12.

71. House Permanent Select Committee on Intelligence, Intelligence Authorization Act for Fiscal Year 2007, 109th Cong., 2nd sess., April 6, 2006, Report 109–411.

72. Quote from *Fox News Sunday*, April 23, 2006.

73. Ibid.

74. Press release, office of Senator Jay Rockefeller, January 4, 2007, available online at http://www.senate.gov/rockefeller/news/2007/pr010407a.html (accessed March 9, 2007).

75. Admiral John Scott Redd, Director, National Counterterrorism Center, "Statement for the Record," Senate Foreign Relations Committee hearing, 109th Cong., 2nd sess., June 13, 2006.

76. Michael Isikoff and Daniel Klaidman, "Look Who's Not Talking—Still," *Newsweek*, April 4, 2005, p. 30.

77. Interview, March 2007.

78. Michael Isikoff and Daniel Klaidman, "Look Who's Not Talking—Still," *Newsweek*, April 4, 2005, p. 30.

79. Senator Mike DeWine, Hearing on the Nomination of General Michael Hayden to be the director of CIA, SSCL, 109th Cong 2nd sess., May 18,2006. See also comments on NCTC by former Acting CIA Director John McLaughlin, Council on Foreign Relations Meeting, "Intelligence Support to the Military," Washington, DC, April 4, 2006; Helen Fessenden, "The Limits of Intelligence Reform," *Foreign Affairs* 84, 6 (November–December 2005), pp. 106–20.

80. *Silberman-Robb Commission Report*, p. 320.

81. Ibid. pp. 320–21. Information sharing with state and local agencies is worse. See Richard Falkenrath, "Prepared Statement of Testimony before the Senate Committee on. Homeland Security and Governmental Affairs," 109th Cong., 2nd sess., September 12, 2006.

82. Shane Harris and Greta Wodele, "Bureaucracy Hinders 9/11 Commission. Recommendations," *National Journal*, January 13, 2006.

83. *Final Report on 9/11 Commission Recommendations*, 9/11 Public Discourse Project, December 5, 2005, available at www.9-11.pdp.org (accessed December 5, 2005), p. 3.

84. Zoe Baird and James Barksdale, chairmen, Markle Foundation Task Force on National Security in the Information Age, *Mobilizing Information to Prevent Terrorism: Accelerating Development of a Trusted Information Sharing Environment*, July 2006, p. 7.

85. Ibid., p. 1.

86. Testimony of Major General Dale Meyerrose, associate director of National Intelligence and chief information officer, Senate Select Committee on Intelligence, "Progress Made on Intelligence Reform," 110th Cong., 1st sess., January 23, 2007.

87. *Silberman-Robb Commission Report*, p. 5.

88. Ibid.

89. Ibid.

90. Testimony of Michael Hayden, Senate Select Committee on Intelligence, "Hearing on the Confirmation of General Michael B. Hayden to become Director of the Central Intelligence Agency," 109th Cong., 2nd sess., May 18, 2006.

91. Quoted in Tim Weiner, "Langley, We Have a Problem," *New York Times*, May 14, 2006, Week in Review, section 4, p. 1.

92. Quoted in Tim Weiner, "Langley, We Have a Problem," *New York Times*, May 14, 2006, Week in Review, section 4, p. 1.

93. Office of the Press Secretary, the White House, "Memorandum for the Director of Central Intelligence," November 23, 2004, available at www.wlhitehouse.gov/news/releases/2004/11/print/20041123–5.html (accessed February 8, 2006). See also hearing of the House Select Committee on Homeland Security, Subcommittee on Intelligence, Information Sharing, and Terrorism Risk Assessment, 109th Cong., 2nd sess., May 10, 2006; U.S. Government Accountability Office, "Information Sharing: The Federal Government Needs to Establish Policies and Processes for Sharing Terrorism-Related and Sensitive but Unclassified Information," GAO-06-385, March 17, 2006.

94. Mark Mazzetti, "CIA Making Rapid Strides for Regrowth," *New York Times*, May 17, 2006, p. A1.

95. Interviews with four former clandestine officials, December 2004 and June 2005; interview with member of Congressional Intelligence Committee, October 2005; Siobhan Gorman, "Fewer Better Spies Key to Intelligence Reform, Former Official Says," *National Journal*, March 18, 2005.

96. Quoted in Siobhan Gorman, "Fewer Better Spies Key to Intelligence Reform, Former Official Says," *National Journal*, March 18, 2005.

97. Interview, December 2004.

98. Interview, December 2004.

99. Quoted in Siobhan Gorman, "Fewer Better Spies Key to Intelligence Reform, Former Official Says," *National Journal*, March 18, 2005.

100. Federal Bureau of Investigation, "The FBI Workforce by the Numbers," www.fib.gov/page2/aug04/workforce082504.htm (accessed February 10, 2006).

101. Testimony of Director Robert Mueller, House Appropriations Subcommittee on Science, State, Justice and Commerce and Related Agencies, 109th Cong., 1st sess., September 14, 2005.

102. Interview with FBI official October 2006; interview with former CIA official, November 2006.

103. The National Security Branch was created in September 2005. For more see the FBI's Web site at http://www.fbi.gov/hq/nsb/nsb_faq.htm (accessed July 25, 2006).

104. Interview, October 2006. Six other current FBI officials expressed similar views in interviews conducted during the fall of 2006.

105. Chitra Ragavan, "Fixing the FBI," *U.S. News and World Report*, March 28, 2005, pp. 19–30; *Silberman-Robb Commission Report*, pp. 451–57; hearing of the House Appropriations Subcommittee on Science,

State, Justice and Commerce and Related Agencies, 109th Cong., 1st sess., September 14, 2005.

106. *Silberman-Robb Commission Report*, p. 453.

107. In early 2007, the bureau added three more weeks of national security training to its eighteen-week new agent training program. Interview with senior law enforcement official, March 2007; testimony of John S. Pistole, deputy director of the FBI, Senate Select Committee on Intelligence, "Intelligence Reform," 110th Cong., 1st sess., January 23, 2007.

108. Office of the Inspector General, Audit Division, U.S. Department of Justice, *The Federal Bureau of Investigation's Efforts to Hire, Train, and Retain Intelligence Analysts*, Audit Report 05–20, May 2005, p. 116.

109. Ibid., p. 64.

110. Ibid., pp. x–xi, *Silberman-Robb Commission Report*, p. 455; hearing of the House Appropriations Subcommittee on Science, State, Justice and Commerce and Related Agencies, 109th Cong., 1st sess., September 14, 2005; testimony of Glenn A. Fine, Inspector General, U.S. Department of Justice, Senate Judiciary Committee hearing, "FBI Oversight," 109th Cong., 2nd sess., May 2, 2006.

111. Office of the Inspector General, Audit Division, U.S. Department of Justice, *The Federal Bureau of Investigation's Efforts to Hire, Train, and Retain Intelligence Analysts*, Audit Report 05–20, May 2005, p. 86.

112. Ibid., p. xi.

113. Quote in testimony by Todd Masse, House Appropriations Subcommittee on Science, State, Justice and Commerce and Related Agencies, 109th Cong., 1st sess., September 14, 2005.

114. For an excellent discussion of the differences between law enforcement and intelligence cultures, see Richard A, Posner, *Countering Terrorism* (Oxford: Rowman & Littlefield, 2006), chapter 5.

115. Quoted in Jeff Stein, "FBI Under the Gun," *CQ Weekly*, May 1, 2006, p. 1152.

116. Interview, October 2006.

117. Interview, January 2007.

118. Available at http://www.fbi.gov/aboutus/faqs/faqsone.htm (accessed March 8, 2007).

119. Interview with Robert Mueller, January 2007; interview with Wayne Murphy, February 2007; interview with two FBI special agents, October 2006.

120. Interview, February 2007.

121. Interview, October 2006.

122. Interview, October 2006.

123. Testimony before the Senate Select Committee on Intelligence, "Intelligence Reform," 110th Cong., 1st sess., January 25, 2007.

124. U.S. Department of Justice, "The Federal Bureau of Investigation's Management of the Trilogy Information Technology Modernization Project," pp. 27–30; Senate Appropriations Subcommitee on Commerce, Justice, and State, the Judiciary, and Related Agencies, "FBI Information Technology Modernization," hearing, 109th Cong., 1st sess., February 3, 2005; Jonathan Krim, "FBT Rejects Its New Case File Software: Database Project Has Cost Nearly $170 Million," *The Washington Post*, January 14, 2005, p. A05.

125. Glenn A. Fine, Inspector General, United States Department of Justice, testimony before the Senate Judiciary Committee, "FBI Oversight," 109th Cong., 2nd sess., May 2, 2006.

126. Interview, January 2007.

127. *Silberman-Robb Commission Report*, p. 454.

128. *Final Report on 9/11 Commission Recommendations*, 9/11 Public Discourse Project, December 5, 2005, available at www.9–11.pdp.org (accessed December 5, 2005), p. 3.

129. John Gannon, written testimony submitted to the Senate Judiciary Committee, hearing on "FBI Oversight," 109th Cong., 2nd. sess., May 2, 2006.

130. Ibid.

131. Goss was effectively demoted three months later when Congress passed the Intelligence Reform and Terrorism Prevention Act, which established the director of national intelligence.

132. Dana Priest, "CIA Holds Terror Suspects in Secret Prisons," *Washington Post*, November 2, 2005, p. A1.

133. James Risen and Eric Lichtblau, "Bush Lets U.S. Spy on Callers without Courts," *New York Times*, December 16, 2005, p. A1.

134. Leslie Cauley, "NSA has Massive Database of Americans' Phone Calls," *USA Today*, May 11, 2006, p, 1A. Note: significant details of this original report were subsequently recanted, although the program was verified by additional sources in other reports. See Frank Ahrens and Howard Kurtz, "USA Today Takes Back Some of NSA Phone-Records Report," *Washington Post*, July 1, 2006, p. A02. The call records do not include contents of the conversations.

135. Senator Pat Roberts, hearing on the nomination of General Michael Hayden to be director of the CIA, Senate Select Committee on Intelligence, 109th Cong., 2nd. sess., May 18, 2006.

136. Quoted in David Stout, "F.B.I. Head Admits Mistakes in Use of Security Act," *New York Times*, March 10, 2007, p. A1.

137. Interview, October 2006.

138. The Silberman-Robb Commission first made this comparison, p. 452.

139. National Archives, "Constitution of the United States: Questions and Answers," http://www.archives.gov/national-archives-experience/charters/constitution_q_and_a.html (accessed July 25, 2006).

140. Interview, October 2005.

141. Henry M. Jackson, "How Shall We Forge a Strategy for Survival?" Address before the National War College (April 16, 1959), in Karl F. Inderfurth and Loch K. Johnson, eds., *Decisions of the Highest Order: Perspectives on the National Security Council* (Pacific Grove, CA: Brooks/Cole, 1988), pp. 78–81.

142. Hanson W. Baldwin, "Intelligence—I; One of the Weakest Links in Our Security, Survey Shows—Omissions, Duplications," *New York Times*, July 20, 1948, p. 6.

35. HIDING IN PLAIN SIGHT: DENIAL, DECEPTION, AND THE NON-STATE ACTOR

JAMES J. WIRTZ

Professor Wirtz explores the relationship between failures of intelligence analysis and the counter-intelligence problem of guarding against denial and deception operations by foreign adversaries.

Carl von Clausewitz, the famous military philosopher, never put much stock in denial and deception. "Denial," in this case, refers to practices that are intended to prevent accurate information from reaching opponents. "Deception," on the other hand, involves deliberate activities that are intended to provide opponents with misleading information, causing them to perceive reality according to the deceiver's intentions. For Clausewitz, most attempts to deceive opponents were usually not worth the effort. In his day and age, such tactics were often too costly, and had the effect of diverting resources that were crucial to the main military attack.[1] While much has changed since this Prussian philosopher offered his commentary on early nineteenth century European warfare, today it remains a matter of debate as to whether the information revolution has enhanced or has limited the prospects for contemporary denial and deception.[2]

Among military historians and those who study security and intelligence affairs, there exists virtually unanimous agreement that the information revolution has empowered individuals at the expense of governments and bureaucracies, giving everyday people the communication, organizational, and analytical capabilities that were only possessed by national governments a few short decades ago. But there is less recognition of a new recent twist in the practice of denial and deception. Given that information about global events has become ubiquitous, it is becoming difficult for states, despite their enormous resources, to hide significant developments from the outside world. At the same time, it is becoming increasingly easy for individuals or small groups with limited resources and nefarious intentions simply to "hide in plain sight" from law enforcement and intelligence agencies. In other words, it might be possible that the information revolution has empowered the individual vis-à-vis the state when it comes to denial and deception, giving terrorists and criminal organizations new abilities to blend in with civil society. The practice of denial and deception has thus become the crucial enabler for contemporary terrorist cells, especially those operating within major urban areas.

To explore this important facet of denial and deception, this article will briefly describe what is meant by the terms "denial" and "deception" and why each term is important to both world politics and military combat. This article will then explain how terrorist cells and criminal organizations use denial and deception, while at the same time discussing the ways in which such organizations can be hampered in their use of such techniques. (For example, because terrorist organizations or spontaneous cells have limited resources, they tend to practice denial rather than deception when it comes to preventing their detection by state authorities.) The article will then briefly explore new ways in which the information revolution might, in the end, aid governments and other traditional state actors by making it increasingly difficult for terrorists to "hide in plain sight."

DENIAL AND DECEPTION

Denial and deception are activities that work together to misdirect or mislead opponents about a deceiver's presence, activities, or intentions. They create the possibility that one's whole diplomatic or strategic outlook might be based on false assumptions or incomplete assessments of reality, and that these erroneous assessments are the product of a sustained campaign carried out by one's opponents. If the developing situation is a bit too simple, or if potentially threatening events seem to be unfolding in a particularly benign way, or if innocent explanations for unusual events seem to clutter reports from the field, or even highly classified intelligence estimates, then prudent policymakers and intelligence analysts should begin to suspect that they are falling victim to denial and deception. When it comes to denial and deception, policymakers and analysts alike should operate on the principle of *caveat emptor*.

Denial is based on secrecy and a keen awareness of the signatures—observable phenomena related to planning, preparing, and undertaking an operation—that can tip off an opponent about what is actually about to happen. When these signatures are denied to an opponent—as they largely were by Japan in the weeks leading up to Pearl Harbor—the "noise" of innocuous events or alternative erroneous explanations can drown out the accurate "signals" that would otherwise indicate that an event is about to transpire.[3] In other words, opponents cannot determine what is about to transpire because they do not possess the information needed to develop an accurate and timely estimate of what is happening. Of course, efforts at denial vary in quality.[4] Nevertheless, denial is a common practice in international relations and military operations. Governments and militaries rarely make public their fundamental objectives, or even their own estimates of their strengths and weaknesses, in a political or military contest. Denial is a constant when it comes to diplomacy and strategy: policymakers, strategists, and intelligence analysts can safely assume that their opponent is withholding information.[5]

Deception can take a myriad of forms and is limited only by the creativity and guile of the deception planner. Bogus stories published by legitimate media outlets, fake documents and plans, and false electronic signals or communications have all been used to give an opponent an inaccurate sense of what is about to transpire. In contrast to denial, which generally requires only security or self-awareness when it comes to the "signatures" (observable electronic, seismic, social, or biometric

evidence) generated by various activities, deception can be costly because it can require the expenditure of resources to create a convincing false front. For example, the Battle for Khe Sanh, which distracted U.S. commanders from the looming threat posed by the Viet Cong to the cities of South Vietnam on the eve of the 1968 Tet Offensive, involved several divisions of the People's Army of Vietnam. In this case, deception involved activities that were so costly to the communist war effort that observers still debate which action was, in fact, the main avenue of attack and which initiative was the effort at deception.[6]

Efforts at denial and deception rely on several factors for their success. Practitioners of denial and deception need accurate information not only about the way their opponents collect and analyze information, but also about their opponent's beliefs, plans, and expectations. In other words, denial and deception require good intelligence about the opponent. Without this information, it might be impossible to control the flow of information to the opponent or provide information that will be perceived as credible or compelling. Technical virtuosity also plays a part in denial and deception, in the sense that the deceiver must employ artistry to attract the target's attention to the misleading information without raising suspicion. Denial and deception work because they play off an opponent's need for information, while heightening the opponent's sensitivity to the information that the deceiver intends to provide, which often includes a message that the opponent also happens to want to hear. According to Donald Daniel, "denial plays against an adversary's eagerness while deception plays to it. That is, while the denier conceals information from the opponent, the deceiver happily provides him with false clues."[7] The opponent is desperate to learn about the deceiver's intentions, but the opponent has to discover the planted information "naturally" if the deception is to take a firm hold within their intelligence community.

Although the practice of denial and deception in theory sounds highly demanding, in practice it can work splendidly, especially if the deceiver can channel the flow of information in a way that supports the target's preferred conception of reality. In the early 1970s, for example, Israeli officials based their defense policy on three assumptions that came to be described as "the concept": Egypt would be at the center of any Arab coalition against

Israel, Egypt would not launch a significant attack without a strong prospect of victory, and, unless Egypt destroyed the Israeli Air Force, an Arab victory would not be possible. Israeli officials also believed that their intelligence agencies would provide a "war warning," which would allow them to mobilize their reserves or even launch a preemptive attack—actions that would produce an Arab defeat. The "concept" held sway, despite some unusually compelling contradictory evidence and an Egyptian denial and deception campaign that was itself amateurish.[8] Even though Israel was equipped with an enormous amount of intelligence that should have raised flags—including actual Syrian and Egyptian war plans, reconnaissance photographs showing unprecedented force deployments along the Suez Canal and Golan Heights, a warning from a credible and trusted spy from the inner circle of Egyptian government, information that Soviet personnel and dependents were hightailing it out of Cairo and Damascus, and signals intelligence suggesting that their opponents were about to strike—the Israelis never managed to act as if they were about to be hit by an all-out Arab assault. As a result, the outbreak of the 1973 Yom Kippur War was marked by one of the greatest intelligence-command failures in military history. Despite the availability of accurate, detailed, and compelling indications of what was about to transpire, Israeli analysts and officials could not overcome their existing conception of reality in order to act in time to head off disaster.[9]

The practice of denial and deception is effective because it addresses the expectations of the target. Conventional wisdom, based on estimates made by Barton Whaley nearly forty years ago, continues to support the notion that denial and deception are effective about ninety percent of the time it is attempted.[10] Once the deceiver understands the target's biases, it is very difficult for the target to escape the trap. In fact, John Ferris, a leading historian of twentieth century intelligence, has noted that only four qualities allow the target to escape effective denial and deception: "superior power and initiative; intelligence of outstanding quality or else so poor that it cannot pick up misleading signals, [and] an inability or unwillingness to act on any knowledge, true or false."[11] Ironically, two of the qualities identified by Ferris can be characterized as sheer incompetence, while superior performance is often in short supply. Given the fact that most governments fall somewhere in the middle of this range of

capabilities, it is not surprising that efforts at denial and deception are often effective.

HIDING IN PLAIN SIGHT

Most of the literature, history, and practice of denial and deception involve state actors or military organizations that possess the resources required to (1) deny an opponent accurate information about their true intentions and (2) create a second misleading "image" that largely conforms to the expectations of the opponent. This is no small task. It requires a large team of analysts and operatives, as well as an effort to deny the opponent accurate information and signatures related to one's true intentions. It also requires an understanding of the preferences and expectations of the target, and an effective way to transmit information to the opponent in an attractive and compelling manner. Traditional denial and deception uses denial to set the stage for deception. In other words, denial is used to whet the target's appetite for information, while deception schemes are used to satisfy the need for information with stories that fit the needs of the deceiver. For many non-state actors—terror cells or even super-empowered individuals who would like to use violence to achieve their own political objectives—engaging in traditional denial and deception activities will likely be beyond their capabilities. They simply lack the resources to generate and then offer an alternative reality to feed to the target. Yet, other forms of denial and deception are not beyond their reach—especially if they reverse the traditional balance between denial and deception.

Unlike states of large military formations, small terrorist cells or individuals face a less daunting challenge when it comes to denial. In contrast to an armored corps moving across the desert, for example, a terrorist cell does not generate a dust, heat, electromagnetic, or radar signature that can be detected from hundreds of miles away. The signature created by a terrorist group preparing to launch an attack is relatively weak and diffuse, making it difficult to detect against the noise generated by the normal everyday activities of the communities in its midst. The challenge is more daunting for deception, however, because small cells lack the human or material resources needed to undertake significant deception activities.[12] They cannot launch duplicate, redundant efforts to mislead opponents. Furthermore, increasing the size of their organizations or the scope of their operations is unlikely to improve their prospects for success because it tends to increase the risk of detection. The more people involved in an operation, the greater the risk that someone will go to the police, speak to untrustworthy third parties, or risk detection or arrest following some minor run-in with local law enforcement.

Because of their weakness vis-à-vis the state, terrorist cells or individuals must incorporate denial as a fundamental principle of their operations.[13] Terrorists rely on denial for their very existence. It becomes a strategic asset for terrorists because without it, they cannot hope to exist, especially given the large asymmetry between their resources and the resources of local law enforcement and the state. Denial involves the tightest operational security, coupled with a rudimentary strategy of deception. For terrorists, "deception" involves maintaining a normal routine to the greatest extent possible as a cover for the nefarious plans and operations undertaken by the cell. This technique can be referred to as "hiding in plain sight." In fact, deception is based on an understanding of what the target of deception believes to be normal, and the degree to which the target of deception can assimilate anomalies before responding. Deception is therefore not based on feeding the target erroneous information, but on making one's actions comply with the expectations of the target.

Terrorists who hide in plain sight use their normalcy to appeal to the widely shared belief that what appears to be normal actually *is* normal in its entirety. In other words, because the image they present to the outside world fails to match a pre-existing notion of what (or who) constitutes a "threat," terrorists are largely left alone, despite some anomalies in their behavior. Writing about the cell that bombed the World Trade Center in 1993, Bell notes, "no one in authority noticed the zealous sermons in the obscure storefront mosques or imagined that the wars of the Middle East might come to Manhattan. This lack of official concern persisted despite the visibility of militant Islam: the kidnappings and bombs of Beirut, the warnings in Algeria and Egypt and the threats of violence directed against the U.S. Homeland." Although analysts and a few local authorities knew about Sheikh Omar Abdel Rahman and the message he was delivering to his followers, no one took the blind cleric seriously. "His cover," according to Bell, "was that no American authority could imagine him as dangerous. He appeared to be an itinerant migrant who preached in seedy rented rooms."[14]

The persistent blindness of U.S. elected officials, law enforcement personnel, and intelligence analysts about the true nature of the al-Qaeda threat allowed members of the group to hide in plain sight in the months leading up to September 11, 2001.[15] Despite the fact that Osama bin-Laden made little effort to hide his ambition of attacking U.S. citizens and interests wherever he could find them, or that al-Qaeda had established a track record of attacking U.S. interests across the Middle East and Africa, or that various law enforcement officials and intelligence analysts were sounding alarms about specific events, the terror cells in the United States operated virtually unimpeded prior to the September 11 tragedy. Given this track record, it is hard to escape the conclusion that a little denial can go a long way, especially in the information age.

TOWARD COUNTERDECEPTION

Unlike most observers, Barton Whaley has expressed optimism about the possibility of counterdeception, the effort to detect and defeat the denial and deception strategies used by terrorist cells. He has devised a theory of counterdeception that is particularly well suited to detecting those who are hiding in plain sight. While counterdeceprion is relatively simple in theory, it is more difficult to put into practice. But counterdeception sometimes does occur and could be more common in the future, especially if law enforcement officers, intelligence analysts, and elected officials recognize the principles behind the effort to detect individuals who are hiding in plain sight.

Counterdeception is based on the idea that every type of human endeavor has a large but knowable set of characteristics that must be present if it is true to form. Imitations of real activity, or "false fronts," will lack certain key characteristics, or will have extraneous characteristics added to a specific endeavor. The detection of these anomalies is the key element in discovering denial and deception because, according to Whaley, "every real thing is always, necessarily, completely congruent with all its characteristics."[16] Moreover, not all anomalies have to be detected before an analyst can uncover denial and deception. The detection of one anomaly is enough to raise the possibility that something is fundamentally amiss.[17] Whaley is not alone in offering what amounts to a scientific method for uncovering denial and deception. Richards Heuer has developed a similar technique—an "analysis of competing hypotheses"—to validate the theoretical assumptions underlying intelligence estimates.[18] Heuer suggests that analysts can overcome cognitive biases and organizational preferences by comparing competing hypotheses and rejecting explanations that fail to account for key elements in a developing situation. Anomalies are evidence that something is amiss; they are the Achilles heels of deception planners.

Two factors, however, complicate this simple observation about what is needed to detect denial and deception. The first is the problem of measurement error. In other words, not every observation of reality is accurate, and errors can be read as either false positives or false negatives. No simple solution is available to overcome the problem of measurement error, in the sense that it is difficult to define and detect significant social anomalies in the first place. An analytical or political decision must be made to assess what sort of thresholds should be used to trigger further investigation once an anomaly is detected. The second problem involves the decision to respond to an anomaly, which again is a matter of political or analytical judgment. As Bell notes, some officials recognized that Sheikh Omar Abdel Rahman and his followers did not appear to be typical residents of Jersey City, but this awareness was not translated into effective action. The decision to respond to anomalies might be made on the basis of the principles of risk management: anomalies involving certain type of groups or certain types of targets might be selected for additional investigation by police officers or intelligence analysts. In that sense, the detection of anomalies might not be the end of an investigation, but a signal to refocus information collection and analytical efforts.

The information revolution makes it easier to hide in plain sight by facilitating the movement of ideas, people, and resources across international boundaries because the movement of outsiders, as well as ideas and resources, are now an everyday occurrence. But the information revolution also might provide law enforcement officials and intelligence analysts with additional information needed to separate legitimate actors from those just masquerading as average people. Everyday life is increasingly digitized as people make full use of the services and resources made possible by the information revolution. This activity leaves a digital record in a myriad of unexpected ways and places. Templates and algorithms already exist that can detect anomalies in normal activities, such as the loss or theft of credit cards, unauthorized entry into secure facilities, or even increasingly routine airline baggage delays. There is no reason to subject anyone to this level of scrutiny on a daily basis, but it might be possible to explore the digital reality behind individuals or groups that somehow manage to attract the attention of intelligence and law enforcement officials. The requirement to fashion a convincing "electronic history" might be beyond the ability of small groups or terrorist cells. The absence of this history—living off the grid—in some settings might be cause for suspicion itself. In fact, the U.S. intelligence community already has recognized the difficulty in manufacturing a credible electronic history to match the cover story supplied to its own clandestine operatives.[19]

CONCLUSION

Admittedly, if taken to their logical conclusions, the ideas presented here are downright Orwellian. But this is not a call to monitor people everywhere in real time to make sure that their "digital" lives roughly correspond to some template based on their geographic location, employment and family history, or their socioeconomic status. Instead, the article offers a tool that law enforcement can use to evaluate terrorist suspects quickly. It describes why terrorists need to hide in plain sight while undertaking their operations, and how their modus operandi differs from the more traditional practice of denial and deception. It also identifies a critical weakness in their tradecraft that might be beyond their ability to remedy quickly with available resources. In other words, once individuals come to the attention of law enforcement officials in the course of some investigation, their electronic bona fides could be matched against their stories. Anomalies would not be evidence of guilt, but prudence would suggest that they might require further investigation.

Recent history has shown that terror cells have lived quietly in the United States, trying to give the appearance of normalcy until they can carry out their attacks. History also has shown that law enforcement and intelligence officials have not performed well in responding to anomalous behavior. Armed with rudimentary tradecraft, the September 11 hijackers were able to hide in plain sight while only attracting a modest amount of attention. They did reasonably well mimicking the behavior of average college students, who often lack visible means of support and have been known to spend more time lounging about or in bars than studying. But when cell members showed interest in learning how to take off and fly, but not land, commercial airliners, they were not acting as "normal" student pilots. At that point they had blown their cover. The September 11 hijackers never tipped their hand in terms of their plans, but they did fail to preserve their image as run-of-the-mill student pilots. The detection of anomalies might not be the final solution when it comes to discovering denial and deception or detecting terrorists, but it is a good place to start.

QUESTIONS FOR FURTHER DISCUSSION

1. How serious a challenge is the use of denial and deception by a nation's adversaries?
2. What steps can be taken to cope with this challenge?
3. What "tool" does Dr. Wirtz advance to make the United States less vulnerable to denial and deception?
4. What are the implications of counterdeception activities for a nation's concerns about civil liberties?

ENDNOTES

1. Because deception requires significant forces to be convincing, by definition it implies that these forces will not be available to support the main attack. Clausewitz judged that efforts beyond simple operational security—the attempt to minimize the opponent's ability to gather information about plans, troop movements, or the combat readiness of various units—were probably not worth the effort. Denial and deception might pay some dividends, but in all likelihood, these benefits would be modest compared to the resources required to create an effective diversion. Luttwak, Edward N. *Strategy: The Logic of War and Peace.* Cambridge: Harvard University Press, 1987. 9–10.
2. Handel, Michael. *Masters of War.* London: Frank Cass, 1996. 131.
3. Wohlstetter, Roberta. *Pearl Harbor: Warning and Decision.* Stanford: Stanford University Press, 1962.
4. U.S. intelligence analysts, for example, became suspicious when they discovered large hatched ships involved in the Baltic lumber trade slowly moving from Soviet ports to Cuba in the late summer of 1962. The fact that these ships were riding high in the water and were being unloaded at night further raised the possibility that they were delivering something other than wood to Cuban ports. The fact that the ships' cargo was

not visible to U.S. intelligence analysts did little to allay their suspicions about what the Soviets were up to in Cuba.

5. Bruce, James B. "Denial and Deception in the 21st Century: Adaptation Implications for Western Intelligence." *Defense Intelligence Journal* 15 no.2 (2006): 13–27.
6. Wirtz, James J. "Deception and the Tet Offensive." *The Journal of Strategic Studies* 13 no. 2 (1990): 82–98.
7. Daniel, Donald C.F. "Denial and Deception." In *Transforming U.S. Intelligence,* edited by Jennifer E. Sims and Burton Gerber, 134–146. Washington, D.C.: Georgetown University Press, 2005.
8. Israeli intelligence determined that the "exercise" that the Egyptians apparently intended to use as a cover for their mobilization was, in fact, not taking place.
9. Bar-Joseph, Uri. *The Watchman Fell Asleep: The Surprise of the Yom Kippur War and its Sources.* Albany, NY: State University of New York Press, 2005.
10. Whaley, Barton. "Stratagem: Deception and Surprise in War." Rand Corporation, 1969.
11. Ferris, John. "'FORTITUDE' in Context: The Evolution of British Military Deception in Two World War, 1914–1945." In *Paradoxes of Strategic Intelligence: Essays in Honor of Micahel I. Handel,* edited by Richard K. Betts and Thomas G. Mahnken, 117–165. London: Frank Cass, 2003.
12. According to J. Bowyer Bell, "Organizations and movements, defined by...recognized and legitimate [governments] as illicit, must seek cover to operate....denial is so vital that it becomes a strategic necessity...." Bell, J. Bowyer. "Conditions Making for Success and Failure of Denial and Deception: Nonstate and Illicit Actors." In *Strategic Denial and Deception: The Twenty-First Century Challenge,* edited by Roy Godson & James J. Wirtz, 129–166. New Brunswick: Transaction Publishers, 2002.
13. Ibid., 147.
14. Ibid.
15. Rashid, Ahmed. "The Taliban: Exporting Extremism." *Foreign Affairs* 78 no. 6 (1999): 22–35. See also *The 9/11 Commission Report: Final Report of the National Commission on Terrorist Attacks Upon the United States* by National Commission on Terrorist Attacks. New York: W.W.Norton & Company, 2004.
16. Whaley, Barton, and Jeffrey Busby. "Detecting Deception: Practice, Practitioners, and Theory." In *Strategic Denial and Deception: The Twenty-First Century Challenge,* edited by Roy Godson and James J. Wirtz, 181–221. New Brunswick: Transaction Publishers, 2002.

17. Ibid.
18. Heuer, Richard J. *Psychology of Intelligence Analysis.* Washington, D.C.: Government Printing Office, 1999.
19. According to Jose Rodriguez, the outgoing head of the U.S. National Clandestine Service, the widespread availability of public, real estate, and corporate data bases has made creating convincing cover stories for clandestine agents "hard as nails," see Richard Willing "How U.S. Spies are Recruited, Trained is Morphing," *USA Today* October, 1, 2007, p. 10A.

36. INTELLIGENCE, POLICY, AND THE WAR IN IRAQ

PAUL R. PILLAR

The purpose of intelligence is to provide decision-makers with reliable, timely, actionable information that might illuminate the policy choices before them. That entire raison d'etat is destroyed when the decision-makers (or intelligence officers) twist the information to suit policy needs (or career advancement opportunities)—the "politicization" of intelligence that is taboo, but all too often a reality. Former CIA analyst Paul Pillar traces the unfortunate emergence of the politicization phenomenon during the build-up to the invasion of Iraq in 2003.

A DYSFUNCTIONAL RELATIONSHIP

The most serious problem with U.S. intelligence today is that its relationship with the policy-making process is broken and badly needs repair. In the wake of the Iraq war, it has become clear that official intelligence analysis was not relied on in making even the most significant national security decisions, that intelligence was misused publicly to justify decisions already made, that damaging ill will developed between policymakers and intelligence officers, and that the intelligence community's own work was politicized. As the national intelligence officer responsible for the Middle East from 2000 to 2005, I witnessed all of these disturbing developments.

Public discussion of prewar intelligence on Iraq has focused on the errors made in assessing Saddam Hussein's unconventional weapons programs. A commission chaired by Judge Laurence Silberman and former Senator Charles Robb usefully documented the intelligence community's mistakes in a solid and comprehensive report released in March 2005. Corrections were indeed in order, and the intelligence community has begun to make them.

At the same time, an acrimonious and highly partisan debate broke out over whether the Bush administration manipulated and misused intelligence in making its case for war. The administration defended itself by pointing out that it was not alone in its view that Saddam had weapons of mass destruction (WMD) and active weapons programs, however mistaken that view may have been.

In this regard, the Bush administration was quite right: its perception of Saddam's weapons capacities was shared by the Clinton administration, congressional Democrats, and most other Western governments and intelligence services. But in making this defense, the White House also inadvertently pointed out the real problem: intelligence on Iraqi weapons programs did not drive its decision to go to war. A view broadly held in the United States and even more so overseas was that deterrence of Iraq was working, that Saddam was being kept "in his box," and that the best way to deal with the weapons problem was through an aggressive inspections program to supplement the sanctions already in place. That the administration arrived at so different a policy solution indicates that its decision to topple Saddam was driven by other factors—namely, the desire to shake up the sclerotic power structures of the Middle East and hasten the spread of more liberal politics and economics in the region.

If the entire body of official intelligence analysis on Iraq had a policy implication, it was to avoid war—or, if war was going to be launched, to prepare for a messy aftermath. What is most remarkable about prewar U.S. intelligence on Iraq is not that it got things wrong and thereby misled policymakers; it is that it played so small a role in one of the most important U.S. policy decisions in recent decades.

A MODEL UPENDED

The proper relationship between intelligence gathering and policymaking sharply separates the two functions. The intelligence community collects information, evaluates its credibility, and combines it with other information to help make sense of situations abroad that could affect U.S. interests. Intelligence officers decide which topics should get their limited collection and analytic resources according to both their own judgments and the concerns of policymakers. Policymakers thus influence which topics intelligence agencies address but not the conclusions that they reach. The intelligence community, meanwhile, limits its judgments to what is happening or what might happen overseas, avoiding policy judgments about what the United States should do in response.

In practice, this distinction is often blurred, especially because analytic projections may have policy implications even if they are not explicitly stated. But the distinction is still important. National security abounds with problems that are clearer than the solutions to them; the case of Iraq is hardly a unique example of how similar perceptions of a threat can lead people to recommend very different policy responses. Accordingly, it is critical that the intelligence community not advocate policy, especially not openly. If it does, it loses the most important basis for its credibility and its claims to objectivity. When intelligence analysts critique one another's work, they use the phrase "policy prescriptive" as a pejorative, and rightly so.

The Bush administration's use of intelligence on Iraq did not just blur this distinction; it turned the entire model upside down. The administration used intelligence not to inform decision-making, but to justify a decision already made. It went to war without requesting—and evidently without being influenced by—any strategic-level intelligence assessments on any aspect of Iraq. (The military made extensive use of intelligence in its war planning, although much of it was of a more tactical nature.) Congress, not the administration, asked for the now-infamous October 2002 National Intelligence Estimate (NIE) on Iraq's unconventional weapons programs, although few members of Congress actually read it. (According to several congressional aides responsible for safeguarding the classified material, no more than six senators and only a handful of House members got beyond the five-page executive summary.) As the

national intelligence officer for the Middle East, I was in charge of coordinating all of the intelligence community's assessments regarding Iraq; the first request I received from any administration policymaker for any such assessment was not until a year into the war.

Official intelligence on Iraqi weapons programs was flawed, but even with its flaws, it was not what led to the war. On the issue that mattered most, the intelligence community judged that Iraq probably was several years away from developing a nuclear weapon. The October 2002 NIE also judged that Saddam was unlikely to use WMD against the United States unless his regime was placed in mortal danger.

Before the war, on its own initiative, the intelligence community considered the principal challenges that any post-invasion authority in Iraq would be likely to face. It presented a picture of a political culture that would not provide fertile ground for democracy and foretold a long, difficult, and turbulent transition. It projected that a Marshall Plan-type effort would be required to restore the Iraqi economy, despite Iraq's abundant oil resources. It forecast that in a deeply divided Iraqi society, with Sunnis resentful over the loss of their dominant position and Shiites seeking power commensurate with their majority status, there was a significant chance that the groups would engage in violent conflict unless an occupying power prevented it. And it anticipated that a foreign occupying force would itself be the target of resentment and attacks—including by guerrilla warfare—unless it established security and put Iraq on the road to prosperity in the first few weeks or months after the fall of Saddam.

In addition, the intelligence community offered its assessment of the likely regional repercussions of ousting Saddam. It argued that any value Iraq might have as a democratic exemplar would be minimal and would depend on the stability of a new Iraqi government and the extent to which democracy in Iraq was seen as developing from within rather than being imposed by an outside power. More likely, war and occupation would boost political Islam and increase sympathy for terrorists' objectives—and Iraq would become a magnet for extremists from elsewhere in the Middle East.

STANDARD DEVIATIONS

The Bush administration deviated from the professional standard not only in using policy to drive intelligence, but also in aggressively using intelligence to win public support for its decision to go to war. This meant selectively adducing data—"cherry-picking"—rather than using the intelligence community's own analytic judgments. In fact, key portions of the administration's case explicitly rejected those judgments. In an August 2002 speech, for example, Vice President Dick Cheney observed that "intelligence is an uncertain business" and noted how intelligence analysts had underestimated how close Iraq had been to developing a nuclear weapon before the 1991 Persian Gulf War. His conclusion—at odds with that of the intelligence community—was that "many of us are convinced that Saddam will acquire nuclear weapons fairly soon."

In the upside-down relationship between intelligence and policy that prevailed in the case of Iraq, the administration selected pieces of raw intelligence to use in its public case for war, leaving the intelligence community to register varying degrees of private protest when such use started to go beyond what analysts deemed credible or reasonable. The best-known example was the assertion by President George W. Bush in his 2003 State of the Union address that Iraq was purchasing uranium ore in Africa. U.S. intelligence analysts had questioned the credibility of the report making this claim, had kept it out of their own unclassified products, and had advised the White House not to use it publicly. But the administration put the claim into the speech anyway, referring to it as information from British sources in order to make the point without explicitly vouching for the intelligence.

The reexamination of prewar public statements is a necessary part of understanding the process that led to the Iraq war. But a narrow focus on rhetorical details tends to overlook more fundamental problems in the intelligence-policy relationship. Any time policymakers, rather than intelligence agencies, take the lead in selecting which bits of raw intelligence to present, there is—regardless of the issue—a bias. The resulting public statements ostensibly reflect intelligence, but they do not reflect intelligence analysis, which is an essential part of determining what the pieces of raw reporting mean. The policymaker acts with an eye not to what is indicative of a larger pattern or underlying truth, but to what supports his case.

Another problem is that on Iraq, the intelligence community was pulled over the line into policy advocacy—not so much by what it said as by its conspicuous role in the administration's

public case for war. This was especially true when the intelligence community was made highly visible (with the director of central intelligence literally in the camera frame) in an intelligence-laden presentation by Secretary of State Colin Powell to the UN Security Council a month before the war began. It was also true in the fall of 2002, when, at the administration's behest, the intelligence community published a white paper on Iraq's WMD programs—but without including any of the community's judgments about the likelihood of those weapons being used.

But the greatest discrepancy between the administration's public statements and the intelligence community's judgments concerned not WMD (there was indeed a broad consensus that such programs existed), but the relationship between Saddam and al Qaeda. The enormous attention devoted to this subject did not reflect any judgment by intelligence officials that there was or was likely to be anything like the "alliance" the administration said existed. The reason the connection got so much attention was that the administration wanted to hitch the Iraq expedition to the "war on terror" and the threat the American public feared most, thereby capitalizing on the country's militant post-9/11 mood.

The issue of possible ties between Saddam and al Qaeda was especially prone to the selective use of raw intelligence to make a public case for war. In the shadowy world of international terrorism, almost anyone can be "linked" to almost anyone else if enough effort is made to find evidence of casual contacts, the mentioning of names in the same breath, or indications of common travels or experiences. Even the most minimal and circumstantial data can be adduced as evidence of a "relationship," ignoring the important question of whether a given regime actually supports a given terrorist group and the fact that relationships can be competitive or distrustful rather than cooperative.

The intelligence community never offered any analysis that supported the notion of an alliance between Saddam and al Qaeda. Yet it was drawn into a public effort to support that notion. To be fair, Secretary Powell's presentation at the UN never explicitly asserted that there was a cooperative relationship between Saddam and al Qaeda. But the presentation was clearly meant to create the impression that one existed. To the extent that the intelligence community was a party to such efforts, it crossed the line into policy advocacy—and did so in a way that fostered public misconceptions contrary to the intelligence community's own judgments.

VARIETIES OF POLITICIZATION

In its report on prewar intelligence concerning Iraqi WMD, the Senate Select Committee on Intelligence said it found no evidence that analysts had altered or shaped their judgments in response to political pressure. The Silberman-Robb commission reached the same conclusion, although it conceded that analysts worked in an "environment" affected by "intense" policymaker interest. But the method of investigation used by the panels—essentially, asking analysts whether their arms had been twisted—would have caught only the crudest attempts at politicization. Such attempts are rare and, when they do occur (as with former Undersecretary of State John Bolton's attempts to get the intelligence community to sign on to his judgments about Cuba and Syria), are almost always unsuccessful. Moreover, it is unlikely that analysts would ever acknowledge that their own judgments have been politicized, since that would be far more damning than admitting more mundane types of analytic error.

The actual politicization of intelligence occurs subtly and can take many forms. Context is all-important. Well before March 2003, intelligence analysts and their managers knew that the United States was heading for war with Iraq. It was clear that the Bush administration would frown on or ignore analysis that called into question a decision to go to war and welcome analysis that supported such a decision. Intelligence analysts—for whom attention, especially favorable attention, from policymakers is a measure of success—felt a strong wind consistently blowing in one direction. The desire to bend with such a wind is natural and strong, even if unconscious.

On the issue of Iraqi WMD, dozens of analysts throughout the intelligence community were making many judgments on many different issues based on fragmentary and ambiguous evidence. The differences between sound intelligence analysis (bearing in mind the gaps in information) and the flawed analysis that actually was produced had to do mainly with matters of caveat, nuance, and word choice. The opportunities for bias were numerous. It may not be possible to point to one key instance of such bending or to measure the cumulative effect of such pressure. But the effect was probably significant.

A clearer form of politicization is the inconsistent review of analysis: reports that conform to policy preferences have an easier time making it through the gauntlet of coordination and approval than ones that do not. (Every piece of intelligence analysis reflects not only the judgments of the analysts most directly involved in writing it, but also the concurrence of those who cover related topics and the review, editing, and remanding of it by several levels of supervisors, from branch chiefs to senior executives.) The Silberman-Robb commission noted such inconsistencies in the Iraq case but chalked it up to bad management. The commission failed to address exactly why managers were inconsistent: they wanted to avoid the unpleasantness of laying unwelcome analysis on a policymaker's desk.

Another form of politicization with a similar cause is the sugarcoating of what otherwise would be an unpalatable message. Even the mostly prescient analysis about the problems likely to be encountered in postwar Iraq included some observations that served as sugar, added in the hope that policymakers would not throw the report directly into the burn bag, but damaging the clarity of the analysis in the process.

But the principal way that the intelligence community's work on Iraq was politicized concerned the specific questions to which the community devoted its energies. As any competent pollster can attest, how a question is framed helps determine the answer. In the case of Iraq, there was also the matter of sheer quantity of output—not just what the intelligence community said, but how many times it said it. On any given subject, the intelligence community faces what is in effect a field of rocks, and it lacks the resources to turn over every one to see what threats to national security may lurk underneath. In an unpoliticized environment, intelligence officers decide which rocks to turn over based on past patterns and their own judgments. But when policymakers repeatedly urge the intelligence community to turn over only certain rocks, the process becomes biased. The community responds by concentrating its resources on those rocks, eventually producing a body of reporting and analysis that, thanks to quantity and emphasis, leaves the impression that what lies under those same rocks is a bigger part of the problem than it really is.

That is what happened when the Bush administration repeatedly called on the intelligence community to uncover more material that would contribute to the case for war. The Bush team approached the community again and again and pushed it to look harder at the supposed Saddam-al Qaeda relationship—calling on analysts not only to turn over additional Iraqi rocks, but also to turn over ones already examined and to scratch the dirt to see if there might be something there after all. The result was an intelligence output that—because the question being investigated was never put in context—obscured rather than enhanced understanding of al Qaeda's actual sources of strength and support.

This process represented a radical departure from the textbook model of the relationship between intelligence and policy, in which an intelligence service responds to policymaker interest in certain subjects (such as "security threats from Iraq" or "al Qaeda's supporters") and explores them in whatever direction the evidence leads. The process did not involve intelligence work designed to find dangers not yet discovered or to inform decisions not yet made. Instead, it involved research to find evidence in support of a specific line of argument that Saddam was cooperating with al Qaeda—which in turn was being used to justify a specific policy decision.

One possible consequence of such politicization is policymaker self-deception. A policymaker can easily forget that he is hearing so much about a particular angle in briefings because he and his fellow policymakers have urged the intelligence community to focus on it. A more certain consequence is the skewed application of the intelligence community's resources. Feeding the administration's voracious appetite for material on the Saddam-al Qaeda link consumed an enormous amount of time and attention at multiple levels, from rank-and-file counterterrorism analysts to the most senior intelligence officials. It is fair to ask how much other counterterrorism work was left undone as a result.

The issue became even more time-consuming as the conflict between intelligence officials and policymakers escalated into a battle, with the intelligence community struggling to maintain its objectivity even as policymakers pressed the Saddam-al Qaeda connection. The administration's rejection of the intelligence community's judgments became especially clear with the formation of a special Pentagon unit, the Policy Counterterrorism Evaluation Group. The unit, which reported to Undersecretary of Defense Douglas Feith, was dedicated to finding every possible link between Saddam and al Qaeda, and its briefings accused the intelligence community

of faulty analysis for failing to see the supposed alliance.

For the most part, the intelligence community's own substantive judgments do not appear to have been compromised. (A possible important exception was the construing of an ambiguous, and ultimately recanted, statement from a detainee as indicating that Saddam's Iraq provided jihadists with chemical or biological training.) But although the charge of faulty analysis was never directly conveyed to the intelligence community itself, enough of the charges leaked out to create a public perception of rancor between the administration and the intelligence community, which in turn encouraged some administration supporters to charge intelligence officers (including me) with trying to sabotage the president's policies. This poisonous atmosphere reinforced the disinclination within the intelligence community to challenge the consensus view about Iraqi WMD programs; any such challenge would have served merely to reaffirm the presumptions of the accusers.

PARTIAL REPAIRS

Although the Iraq war has provided a particularly stark illustration of the problems in the intelligence-policy relationship, such problems are not confined to this one issue or this specific administration. Four decades ago, the misuse of intelligence about an ambiguous encounter in the Gulf of Tonkin figured prominently in the Johnson administration's justification for escalating the military effort in Vietnam. Over a century ago, the possible misinterpretation of an explosion on a U.S. warship in Havana harbor helped set off the chain of events that led to a war of choice against Spain. The Iraq case needs further examination and reflection on its own. But public discussion of how to foster a better relationship between intelligence officials and policymakers and how to ensure better use of intelligence on future issues is also necessary.

Intelligence affects the nation's interests through its effect on policy. No matter how much the process of intelligence gathering itself is fixed, the changes will do no good if the role of intelligence in the policymaking process is not also addressed. Unfortunately, there is no single clear fix to the sort of problem that arose in the case of Iraq. The current ill will may not be reparable, and the perception of the intelligence community on the part of some policymakers—that Langley is enemy territory—unlikely to change. But a few steps, based on the recognition that the intelligence-policy relationship is indeed broken, could reduce the likelihood that such a breakdown will recur.

On this point, the United States should emulate the United Kingdom, where discussion of this issue has been more forthright, by declaring once and for all that its intelligence services should not be part of public advocacy of policies still under debate. In the United Kingdom, Prime Minister Tony Blair accepted a commission of inquiry's conclusions that intelligence and policy had been improperly comingled in such exercises as the publication of the "dodgy dossier," the British counterpart to the United States' Iraqi WMD white paper, and that in the future there should be a clear delineation between intelligence and policy. An American declaration should take the form of a congressional resolution and be seconded by a statement from the White House. Although it would not have legal force, such a statement would discourage future administrations from attempting to pull the intelligence community into policy advocacy. It would also give some leverage to intelligence officers in resisting any such future attempts.

A more effective way of identifying and exposing improprieties in the relationship is also needed. The CIA has a "politicization ombudsman," but his informally defined functions mostly involve serving as a sympathetic ear for analysts disturbed by evidence of politicization and then summarizing what he hears for senior agency officials. The intelligence oversight committees in Congress have an important role, but the heightened partisanship that has bedeviled so much other work on Capitol Hill has had an especially inhibiting effect in this area. A promised effort by the Senate Intelligence Committee to examine the Bush administrations use of intelligence on Iraq got stuck in the partisan mud. The House committee has not even attempted to address the subject.

The legislative branch is the appropriate place for monitoring the intelligence-policy relationship. But the oversight should be conducted by a nonpartisan office modeled on the Government Accountability Office (GAO) and the Congressional Budget Office (CBO). Such an office would have a staff, smaller than that of the GAO or the CBO, of officers experienced in intelligence and with the necessary clearances and access to examine questions about both the politicization of classified intelligence work and the public use of intelligence. As with the GAO, this office could conduct inquiries at the request of members of Congress. It would make its results public as much as possible, consistent with security requirements, and it would avoid duplicating the many other functions of intelligence oversight, which would remain the responsibility of the House and Senate intelligence committees.

Beyond these steps, there is the more difficult issue of what place the intelligence community should occupy within the executive branch. The reorganization that created the Office of the Director of National Intelligence (DNI) is barely a year old, and yet another reorganization at this time would compound the disruption. But the flaws in the narrowly conceived and hastily considered reorganization legislation of December 2004—such as ambiguities in the DNI's authority—will make it necessary to reopen the issues it addressed. Any new legislation should also tackle something the 2004 legislation did not: the problem of having the leaders of the intelligence community, which is supposed to produce objective and unvarnished analysis, serve at the pleasure of the president.

The organizational issue is also difficult because of a dilemma that intelligence officers have long discussed and debated among themselves: that although distance from policymakers may be needed for objectivity, closeness is needed for influence. For most of the past quarter century, intelligence officials have striven for greater closeness, in a perpetual quest for policymakers' ears. The lesson of the Iraq episode, however, is that the supposed dilemma has been incorrectly conceived. Closeness in this case did not buy influence, even on momentous issues of war and peace; it bought only the disadvantages of politicization.

The intelligence community should be repositioned to reflect the fact that influence and relevance flow not just from face time in the Oval Office, but also from credibility with Congress and, most of all, with the American public. The community needs to remain in the executive branch but be given greater independence and a greater ability to communicate with those other constituencies (fettered only by security considerations, rather than by policy agendas). An appropriate model is the Federal Reserve, which is structured as a quasi-autonomous body overseen by a board of governors with long fixed terms.

These measures would reduce both the politicization of the intelligence community's own work and the public misuse of intelligence by policymakers. It would not directly affect how much attention policymakers give to intelligence, which they would continue to be entitled to ignore. But the greater likelihood of being called to public account for discrepancies between a case for a certain policy and an intelligence judgment would have the indirect effect of forcing policymakers to pay more attention to those judgments in the first place.

These changes alone will not fix the intelligence-policy relationship. But if Congress and the American people are serious about "fixing intelligence," they should not just do what is easy and politically convenient. At stake are the soundness of U.S. foreign-policy making and the right of Americans to know the basis for decisions taken in the name of their security.

QUESTIONS FOR FURTHER DISCUSSION

1. What is "broken" about the intelligence-policy-making process, according to Pillar?
2. What are the "varieties of politicization"?
3. What is your critique of Pillar's suggestions for reform?
4. What options does an intelligence analyst have if he or she thinks intelligence is being misused by a policymaker?

37. INTELLIGENCE AND HOMELAND SECURITY

JAMES BURCH

Homeland security expert James Burch takes a look at intelligence organizations in democratic regimes, comparing America's intelligence reforms with efforts to improve intelligence activities in fellow open societies. He focuses on the potential value of a domestic intelligence agency in the United States.

OVERVIEW

The safest place in the world for a terrorist to be is inside the United States....As long as terrorists don't do something that trips them up against our laws, they can do pretty much all they want.
—*Brent Scowcroft, former National Security Advisor*[1]

Several paradigms were altered on 9/11. The U.S. intelligence community, largely focused on state actors, now faced the threat posed by elusive terrorists. The community also had to address the asymmetry posed by the terrorists' use of unconventional and relatively unsophisticated methods to inflict loss of life and damage—a more complex intelligence task. Lastly, due to terrorist disregard for national borders, laws, and transnational financing, the United States had to change its concept of foreign versus domestic intelligence.[2]

The area of domestic intelligence raises several issues. First, law enforcement and intelligence operate in different worlds—one seeks to prosecute, the other to gather information.[3] Second, with the development of multiple state fusion centers and the creation of additional organizations focused on intelligence, there is a corresponding increase in bureaucratization. This adds to the challenge of sharing information. Lastly and perhaps most importantly, there are issues concerning the protection of civil liberties and effective oversight.

The challenge in developing a viable domestic intelligence capability for the United States centers on how to organize these capabilities optimally within the larger U.S. intelligence framework, how

to ensure streamlined information sharing between foreign intelligence and the multitude of law enforcement agencies, and how best to implement oversight mechanisms to protect civil liberties and ensure accountability of intelligence operations. *Organizational mechanisms*, *information sharing*, and *oversight* are the three critical components to instituting an effective domestic intelligence capability.

One of the proposed constructs to meet these organizational and information sharing challenges is to create a domestic intelligence agency. The United States is unique among Western or highly industrialized countries in that it does not possess one. This paper examines the feasibility, suitability, and acceptability of instituting a domestic intelligence agency in the United States from the viewpoint of organization, information sharing, and oversight. It will assess the domestic intelligence organizations of three countries that possess liberal democratic institutions—the United Kingdom's Military Intelligence 5 (MI5), the Australian Security Intelligence Organisation (ASIO), and India's Intelligence Bureau (IB)—to determine their relative effectiveness in countering terrorism, identify their strengths and shortfalls, and determine applicable policy recommendations for the United States.

Specific criteria are used to establish a measure of assessment for a domestic intelligence agency. In this case, the criteria are derived from the Geneva Centre for the Democratic Control of Armed Forces (DCAF), which partners with countries to promote governance and determine recommendations that promote government reform. Examples of some criteria are the subordination of intelligence to national laws, effective coordination, and oversight.

Examining countries with similar democratic institutions, threats, and (in the case of Australia and India) geographic scope will result in identifying key factors for instituting an effective domestic intelligence capability for the United States. This examination will also determine whether current intelligence reform policies are targeting perceived intelligence shortfalls and offer additional recommendations. It will also determine whether the establishment of a domestic intelligence agency is feasible, acceptable, and suitable to meeting the asymmetric threats of the 21st century.

INTRODUCTION

Al Qaeda conducted a devastating strike on 9/11 by using airliners as weapon of mass destruction (WMD). In terms of scale, it incurred a relatively small cost to create billions of dollars' worth of damage.[4] The psychological impact was also devastating and prompted a massive response and reorganization of the U.S. government to combat this threat.[5] Part of this reorganization was a close examination of the Federal Bureau of Investigation (FBI). A Congressional inquiry into 9/11 revealed several FBI shortcomings:

- "The FBI's decentralized structure and inadequate information technology made the Bureau unable to correlate the knowledge possessed by its components. The FBI did not gather intelligence from all its many cases nation-wide to produce an overall assessment of al Qaeda's presence in the United States."
- "Many FBI field offices had not made counterterrorism a top priority and they knew little about al Qaeda before September 11."
- The FBI also did not inform policymakers of the extent of terrorist activity in the United States. "Although the FBI conducted many investigations, these pieces were not fitted into a larger picture."[6]

These findings highlighted a domestic intelligence gap and, as a result, have led to several larger governmental initiatives and internal FBI reforms. Another organizational alternative is to create a domestic intelligence agency to focus solely on domestic intelligence and collection. Supporters of a domestic intelligence agency have proposed this alternative as the best method to address the domestic intelligence gap effectively. In attempting to address this gap, however, there are additional issues. First, there are opposing viewpoints as to whether the domestic intelligence apparatus should remain within and tied to the FBI versus establishing it as an independent entity. Second, the creation of another bureaucracy raises concerns about the effectiveness of information sharing. Third, an increased focus on domestic intelligence leads to concerns about civil liberties and oversight. Examining the domestic intelligence structures of the United Kingdom, Australia, and India in terms of these three issues can assist in determining the applicability of those structures and offer implementation considerations for the United States.

Advocates for a separate domestic intelligence agency point to several advantages. The first is a symbolic one: the creation of such an agency would emphasize the government's commitment to preventing another catastrophic attack.[7] As Mark Lowenthal states, "several issues spill over into the domestic realm—economies, narcotics, crime, and terrorism—thus curtailing the activities of much of the intelligence community…"[8] A domestic intelligence agency would also focus directly on these domestic-foreign terrorism nexus' issues and afford greater precision to developing and categorizing the domestic threat. Creating an agency strictly focused on this mission could more directly address the domestic intelligence gap as compared to the higher organizational and bureaucratic changes that have been implemented since 9/11. Second, there is inherent competition between law enforcement and intelligence for resources and focus. Harry Ransom highlighted this competitive tension when referring to CIA intelligence and operations: "The ill advised marriage of intelligence collection-analysis-estimates with covert action has further complicated role theory."[9] Advocates for a domestic intelligence agency argue that the FBI's intelligence function will always take a secondary role to its law enforcement responsibilities due to the focus on "making cases" and the preponderance of the FBI's leadership coming from law enforcement.[10] Combining two missions that operate in different worlds and possess different challenges under one organization contributes to operational ineffectiveness.

Lastly, it is much easier to recruit, perform undercover work, and take advantage of the loyal Muslim base in the United States.[11] As one FBI official noted before a Congressional inquiry, "foreign governments often knew more about radical Islamist activity in the United States than did the U.S. Government because they saw this activity as a threat to their own existence."[12] The development of a domestic intelligence baseline to categorize the terrorist threat in terms of cells, planning efforts, and underlying support networks would directly support investigatory efforts. For the advocates, a renewed focus by a domestic intelligence agency dedicated to developing these intelligence resources in the United States would directly support prevention efforts.

Despite the advantages, there is also considerable opposition. Opponents counter that the addition of another organization adds another layer of bureaucracy, making it harder to overcome the already-obscured relationship between law enforcement and intelligence.[13] Creating another agency, while having the merit of focusing on intelligence issues, does not address the larger problem of information sharing outside of its organization.[14] As Eric Taylor states, "added bureaucracies will only cause agile terrorist groups glee as they outmaneuver sluggish government attempts to counter them."[15]

There is also the potential abuse of civil liberties and danger of politicization. U.S. intelligence agencies historically have had limited roles in internal security.[16] Letting an organization pursue an aggressive domestic intelligence agenda could lead to the domestic spying abuses similar to those of the 1950s and 1960s.[17] The potential for such abuse will also increase the scrutiny of the executive branch, which could lead to a backlash similar to the Church and Pike Committee recommendations.[18] There is also the danger of politicization. As Ransom asserts, "... politicization is inherent in the production of intelligence because information is crucial to gaining and preserving political power."[19] A domestic intelligence agency has the unique potential of becoming politicized. As Ransom further states, the CIA was insulated from partisan politics from 1947 to 1967 because, "a foreign policy consensus prevailed, secrecy normally expected by an intelligence agency was maintained and congressional knowledge and monitoring of intelligence operations was very limited."[20] Those sets of circumstances do not exist today.

The arguments for developing a domestic intelligence agency center on its prevention activities, the organization's unity of purpose, and the recruitment of intelligence sources. The reasons for not implementing are the additional layers of bureaucracy that do not facilitate information sharing, the potential abuse of civil rights, and the danger of politicization. The challenge and key task is to determine how to organize domestic intelligence efforts, how to facilitate information sharing, and how to protect against potential abuses in the U.S.

Democracies, by their nature, are faced with a conflicting dilemma regarding terrorism. As Benjamin Netanyahu, the former Prime Minister of Israel, states:

> The governments of free societies charged with fighting a rising tide of terrorism are thus faced with a democratic dilemma: If they do not fight terrorism with the means available to them, they endanger their citizenry; if they do, they appear to endanger the very freedoms which they are charged to protect.[21]

This dilemma lies at the center of the public debate. Richard A. Posner, a noted jurist, identifies two issues. The first is where to draw the line between security and liberty; the second is which controls are necessary to prevent any law enforcement or intelligence agency from crossing the line leading to potential civil rights abuses.[22] As Posner further notes, public safety and personal liberty are both constitutional values.

The challenge is to devise a system that balances law enforcement and intelligence equities, allows for information sharing, and ensures effective oversight and accountability of intelligence activities. The Geneva Centre for the Democratic Control of Armed Forces (DCAF) offers some benchmarks:

- Domestic intelligence and collection are subject to national laws.
- The separation of foreign and domestic intelligence requires an effective coordination of collection.
- Coordination is performed by an executive branch entity.
- Joint assessments are undertaken ideally by an independent body.
- Executive, legislative, and judicial branches exercise oversight.[23]

Examining the United Kingdom's Military Intelligence 5 (MI5), the Australian Security Intelligence Organisation (ASIO), and the Indian Intelligence Bureau (IB) in terms of these benchmarks can offer ideas and insight into implementation challenges for improving homeland security intelligence in the United States. Each of the countries is similar in that they possess democratic institutions. Australia and India are more similar to the United States in that both possess a federalist-type structure with the sharing of power between the federal government and state or provincial institutions. This distinction is considerably less in the United Kingdom. Additionally, India—the world's largest democracy—can be compared more readily with the United States in terms of the scope of domestic intelligence challenges. Other specific intelligence similarities and challenges include:

- The refocus of the British, Australian, and Indian intelligence on transnational terrorism and internal security issues since 9/11.
- The reorganization of the British, Australian, and Indian intelligence communities through creation of special task forces and assessment bodies focused on terrorism.
- The passage of strong anti-terror legislation and the subsequent debate over internal security and civil liberties.

There are, however, significant differences. The United Kingdom, Australia, and India possess parliamentary systems where the power of the executive is divided between the head of state and head of government. The head of government, in this case the prime minister, is also reliant on the support of the legislative branch or parliament. This support is expressed through a vote of confidence or no confidence. The distinction and separation between the executive and legislative branches of government is much clearer in the United States. Other differences include those of language and culture within India versus the United States, the United Kingdom, and Australia. The ethnic differences in India have resulted in significant and recurring sectarian violence since its independence in 1947. The United Kingdom has also faced a similar issue with regard to the Irish Republican Army (IRA). Simply put, a relationship exists between countries with significant internal stability problems and the nature of the oversight mechanisms they possess. Specific differences include:

- The United Kingdom is much smaller geographically than the United States. Additionally, the United Kingdom and Australia are island nations with fewer border control and security issues than the United States or India.
- Indian geography—its scale and proximity to terrorist safe havens in Afghanistan, Iran, Pakistan, and the Kashmir—coupled with its much larger

population and significant Muslim minority leads to greater internal security issues beyond the scale of the United Kingdom, Australia, and the United States.

Considering the similarities and differences, there is value in assessing the effectiveness of the United Kingdom's MI5, Australia's ASIO, and India's IB. The applicability of their practices will be assessed by using the DCAF's benchmarks and utilizing the following criteria:

- *Feasible*: Task can be accomplished with forces and resources.
- *Suitable*: Will mission be accomplished if tasks are carried out successfully?
- *Acceptable*: Results are politically supportable.[24]

THE UNITED KINGDOM'S SECURITY SERVICE BRANCH—MILITARY INTELLIGENCE 5 (MI5)

We're always trying to improve our intelligence gathering but these groups operate in an immensely secretive way, it is very, very difficult often to track down exactly what they're doing....
—*Tony Blair, Prime Minister of the United Kingdom*[25]

ORGANIZATION

The MI5, also known as the Security Service, is the United Kingdom's domestic intelligence agency. It is responsible for responding to a wide range of security threats that include terrorism, counterintelligence, weapons of mass destruction, and organized crimes. MI5 falls under the Home Ministry, which has no precise U.S. equivalent.[26] The Security Service is one of three tier-one intelligence organizations. The Secret Intelligence Service, or MI6, focuses on foreign intelligence and the Government Communications Headquarters (GCHQ) is responsible for communications intercept and code breaking efforts.[27]

MI5 is chartered to conduct domestic surveillance operations against a wide variety of targets, but it does not possess independent arrest powers.[28] The philosophy behind this organizational relationship is to force MI5 to work hand-in-hand with the various fifty-six police forces in the United Kingdom, particularly the Metropolitan and provincial Special Branches (SB).[29] As Peter Chalk states, "The Special Branch structure is the primary instrument through which intelligence is translated into operational activity and prosecutions."[30]

Despite the terrorist attacks in London (2005), the MI5 can point to credible successes. Former Director of MI5 Dame Eliza Manningham-Buller has stated that MI5 is tracking approximately 200 radical groups and over 1,600 individuals who are actively supporting or linked to terrorist activities focused on the United Kingdom—whether domestically or in foreign areas.[31] Given MI5's size, the scope of these numbers would suggest a high degree of coordination, precision, and fidelity between Britain's foreign intelligence community, its assessment bodies, and law enforcement entities.[32]

STRATEGIC OUTLOOK

The United Kingdom has a history of combating terrorists, particularly in its long struggle against the IRA. As a result, MI5 has an established tradition of conducting domestic intelligence operations to include electronic surveillance, recruitment, and infiltration of terrorist groups. It also has a well established working relationship with law enforcement.

The events of 9/11 fundamentally shifted the focus of the United Kingdom's intelligence apparatus. Islamic terrorism is now identified as the number one threat.[33] MI5's intelligence functions are part of a greater government counterterrorism strategy known as CONTEST. The overarching aim of this strategy is to reduce the risk of terrorism through pursuit of four strategic approaches or lines of operation: *prevent, pursue, protect,* and *prepare.*[34] Intelligence gathering and disrupting terrorist activities are identified as two integral components under pursuit activities. MI5 performs a unique service to support these two lines of operation.[35]

INFORMATION SHARING

MI5 serves as an assessment agency as well as a collection entity. Its analysis directly supports the United Kingdom's Joint Intelligence Committee (JIC), which serves as the government's focal point for intelligence prioritization and assessment.[36] The JIC also provides regular assessments to ministers and other senior officials.[37] The establishment of the Joint Terrorism Analysis Centre (JTAC) in June 2003 (under the supervision of MI5) brings analysts from the respective intelligence agencies under one umbrella to facilitate the sharing of intelligence and breaking down of cross-agency barriers.[38] Underneath the JTAC structure, the various Special Branches have pooled their resources to develop Regional Intelligence Cells that share

responsibilities and support further information sharing.[39]

Although the United Kingdom has a highly-evolved intelligence structure with a long tradition of conducting domestic intelligence, there have been several instances of information-sharing shortfalls. MI5 has been criticized for not providing warning of the Bali attacks in October 2002, the Mombasa attack in November 2002, and failing to pass specific intelligence regarding the shoe bomber, Richard Reid.[40]

The development of a strategic intelligence architecture and information sharing policies is a relevant issue for the United States. Information sharing remains a problematic issue despite the United Kingdom's well-established intelligence mechanisms, clearly defined missions and roles, and assessment organs. An examination of the U.S. intelligence architecture and information sharing practices—a key 9/11 shortfall—is critical and uniquely relevant particularly given the numerous changes, reorganizations, and reforms within the U.S. intelligence community. An assessment of these changes is necessary particularly as the events of 9/11 move further into the past.

OVERSIGHT

The authority of Britain's Cabinet structure from a majority in the House of Commons affords the Prime Minister greater latitude on national security and intelligence matters.[41] Although the *Security Service Act of 1989* codified MI5's rules, missions, and functions, the intelligence and security services were largely exempt from the scrutiny of Parliament and the public until the passing of the *Intelligence Services Act of 1994.*[42] As a result of this legislation, Parliament's Intelligence and Security Committee (ISC) now reviews the budget, administration, and policy of all three intelligence agencies.[43] Its legislative oversight function, however, is much more limited than the U.S. congressional committee system.[44]

Executive oversight is also exercised by the ISC, which consists of nine members of parliament from various political parties. The ISC reports directly to the prime minister and is charged with producing an annual report on intelligence activities.[45] This committee operates within Britain's "ring of secrecy," which is bounded by the *Official Secrets Act.*[46] The *Official Secrets Act* allows the British government to exercise, in effect, prior restraint with respect to any disclosure of information that can be deemed harmful to the national interest.[47] Although the ISC is chartered with exercising oversight, its members are appointed by and answer directly to the prime minister—creating the potential for a conflict of interest. Additionally, despite the oversight mechanisms, MI5 continues to remain essentially a self-tasking organization requiring no separate approval before initiating a new operation.[48] There have also been instances of politicization, particularly during the 1980s when MI5 conducted counter-subversive operations against leftwing politicians and organizations whom Prime Minister Margaret Thatcher termed, "the Enemy Within."[49]

CONCLUSION

MI5's strengths lie in its ability to operate under a well-defined executive structure that utilizes an independent intelligence assessment umbrella and operates under a well-understood set of laws. The organization also has a long history of performing its internal security and domestic intelligence functions. The United Kingdom also possesses several highly-evolved mechanisms to coordinate the sharing of intelligence. Despite this structure, there have been several instances where MI5 did not share its intelligence. Effective intelligence sharing remains an issue. Although there are existing oversight mechanisms, the structure of the United Kingdom's oversight organs also inhibits significant legislative oversight of the intelligence process. Utilizing the DCAF benchmarks listed in Figure 37.1, the United Kingdom's strengths lie in its strong executive coordination and independent assessment process. Its

domestic intelligence agency also operates under a well-defined set of national laws, although the effectiveness of information sharing remains an issue. Lastly, given the United Kingdom's oversight structure and MI5's past abuses, the oversight and accountability mechanisms that balance civil liberties versus public safety remain a potential area of concern. An assessment of information-sharing practices and oversight procedures—given the numerous changes within the U.S. intelligence community and the recent FBI controversy on the handling and accountability of National Security Letters—is of particular relevance for the United States.

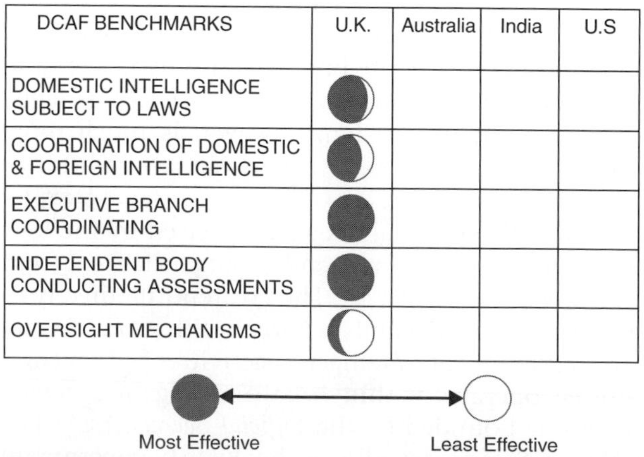

THE AUSTRALIAN SECURITY INTELLIGENCE ORGANISATION (ASIO)

> In the difficult fight against the new menace of international terrorism, there is nothing more crucial than timely and accurate intelligence.
> —*John Howard, Australian Prime Minister*[50]

ORGANIZATION

The Australian Security Intelligence Organisation (ASIO) serves as Australia's domestic intelligence organization. Similar to MI5, it is chartered to address a wide variety of threats.[51] ASIO works closely with the Australian Protective Service (APS), with both agencies falling under Australia's Attorney General.[52] ASIO is also one of three tier-one intelligence organizations. The Australian Secret Intelligence Service (ASIS) functions as the foreign intelligence entity while the Defence Signals Directorate (DSD) is focused on signals intelligence.[53]

Heavily influenced by the British philosophy of separating domestic intelligence and law enforcement powers, ASIO does not have independent arrest powers.[54] As such, ASIO must work closely with police entities particularly the APS—roughly equivalent to the FBI or the Royal Canadian Mounted Police (RCMP). The primary venue for APS-ASIO interaction is through the National Threat Assessment Centre, which serves as the focal point for collaboration with federal organizations and state police forces.[55]

STRATEGIC OUTLOOK

Australia does not have a long history of combating terrorists. It has not been plagued by an internal threat (like the United Kingdom by the IRA)

DCAF BENCHMARKS	U.K.	Australia	India	U.S
DOMESTIC INTELLIGENCE SUBJECT TO LAWS	◑			
COORDINATION OF DOMESTIC & FOREIGN INTELLIGENCE	◑			
EXECUTIVE BRANCH COORDINATING	●			
INDEPENDENT BODY CONDUCTING ASSESSMENTS	●			
OVERSIGHT MECHANISMS	◔			

● Most Effective ←——————→ ○ Least Effective

FIGURE 37.1 DCAF Benchmarks versus the U.K.

or India's numerous internal security issues due to its linguistic and ethnic differences. Additionally, Australia has been largely isolated by the nature of its geography. As a whole, Australia has typically viewed its strategic threats in a foreign context and has prized international cooperation with its allies to deal with its security issues.

Despite its lack of internal threats, the Australian government has taken a serious and very thorough approach to internal security. It went through significant security preparations for the Sydney 2000 Olympic Games, which also highlighted the value of international cooperation.[56] The Australian government now recognizes Islamic terrorism as its highest threat priority and has committed significant resources to counterterrorism as a result of the 9/11 attacks and al Qaeda statements that identify Australia as a target.[57] ASIO's intelligence function operates as part of the government's four-pronged counterterrorism approach: *prevention, preparedness, response,* and *recovery.* Improving intelligence capacity, increasing the effectiveness of information sharing, seeking better detection capabilities, and improving law enforcement coordination are the overarching themes under prevention and preparedness.[58]

Despite the lack of a historical internal security threat or Australia's priority as a target for a terrorist attack, the ASIO can point to some success in categorizing and tracking domestic terrorist threats. Similar to the MI5, ASIO also has the reputation for thoroughness and developing precise intelligence. On November 18, 2005, Australian authorities foiled the activities of two terrorist cells. ASIO and Australian law enforcement agencies were able to prevent an attack possibly aimed at critical infrastructure as a result of an eighteen-month long investigation into individuals with possible linkages to al Qaeda and radical Kashmiri groups.[59]

INFORMATION SHARING

Like MI5, ASIO also serves as an analytic assessment agency. The Office of National Assessment (ONA) serves as Australia's premier strategic assessment organization. ONA, ASIO, ASIS, and DSD also enjoy close access to the prime minister's office.[60] The National Intelligence Group (NIG), which resides under ASIO, collates intelligence from multiple sources and disseminates products to governmental and law enforcement officials through Joint Intelligence Groups.[61] Executive coordination of domestic intelligence and other matters is accomplished through the National Security Committee of Cabinet (NSC) and the Secretaries' Committee on National Security (SCoNS). The NSC consists of senior policy makers while the SCoNS consists of department secretaries who, like those in the United Kingdom, are professional bureaucrats.[62]

Although Australia's intelligence system is modeled on the United Kingdom's, with domestic intelligence having to work closely with law enforcement entities, there have also been corresponding shortfalls in information sharing. ASIO's performance was also criticized for disregarding threat assessments from regional analysts regarding the Bali attack in 2002—an area directly under ASIO's concern.[63] Like the United Kingdom, Australia has a highly defined intelligence community; however, its track record on information sharing is an issue. Despite Australian and British similarities and the ability of their domestic intelligence agencies to possibly develop greater precision in categorizing the domestic threat, their information sharing problems remain a relevant issue for the United States.

OVERSIGHT

ASIO's statutory responsibilities are outlined in the *ASIO Act of 1979.* Although Australia is similar to the United Kingdom, there is a greater distinction between executive and legislative oversight roles. The *Intelligence Services Act of 2001* expanded the role of the Parliamentary Joint Committee on Intelligence and Security in overseeing Australia's intelligence apparatus.[64] The committee can initiate investigations or respond to requests from the Attorney General.[65] Australia's executive oversight is also more robust. The Inspector General of Intelligence and Security (IGIS) is an independent officer appointed by the Governor-General and located within the prime minister's office. This unique arrangement allows the IGIS to assist the government and parliament in oversight matters, but allows the office to act independently. The IGIS also enjoys total access to all intelligence and possesses the power of independent inquiry.[66] This oversight also includes access to case files, warrant powers, and financial records.

Although not a method of oversight, the Australian government also has an aggressive public outreach program. The federal government has established National Security Public Information Guidelines for all agencies engaged in national security issues to promote the public's understanding of the missions and threat. A National Security Public Information Campaign also seeks to encourage public vigilance. Security information is pushed via a variety of media to inform the Australian public of the government's efforts against terrorism and to create a safer environment.[67] These efforts directly support ASIO's efforts in engaging communities to derive community-based information conduits to support its assessments. This is in stark contrast to MI5's historical outlook regarding public engagement, which took the major step of instituting a public website only after 9/11.[68] Despite these strong oversight mechanisms, ASIO has also been criticized for heavy-handed and intrusive tactics in the past against leftwing groups.[69]

CONCLUSION

ASIO's strength, like MI5, lies in its ability to operate under a well-defined structure and an independent assessment umbrella. ASIO also has a long history in internal security and domestic intelligence. Despite possessing a highly-evolved information sharing structure, there have also been corresponding shortfalls in ASIO's information sharing performance. Lastly, Australia has robust executive and legislative oversight mechanisms, which although not possessing a perfect track record, are effective in overseeing the country's intelligence process. An examination of Australian oversight mechanisms and public outreach programs may offer some areas for improvement in the United States. When compared to the DCAF benchmarks in Figure 37.2, Australia's top strengths lie in its strong laws governing domestic

intelligence, the ability of the executive body to coordinate intelligence, and its independent assessment capability. Similar to the United Kingdom, it also has faced some information sharing shortfalls and although it possesses a better-defined executive and legislative oversight process, there have been instances of past abuse.

THE INDIAN INTELLIGENCE BUREAU (IB)

> We are fully on board as far as the global war against terror is concerned. We will cooperate with everybody, bilaterally, regionally, at the global level, in the fight against terror.
> —*Manmohan Singh, Prime Minister of India*[70]

ORGANIZATION

The Intelligence Bureau (IB) functions as India's internal security agency.[71] One of the longest-functioning intelligence agencies, its roots can be traced back to the Imperial Intelligence Bureau, which served British interests in India.[72] It is chartered with a wide range of responsibilities spanning from combating terrorists and the separatist efforts of *Naxalists* (Indian Maoists) to critical infrastructure protection—particularly aviation security.[73] The IB falls under India's Ministry of Home Affairs although the Director of the IB can report to the Prime Minister on intelligence issues.[74] Unlike the United Kingdom and Australia, which possess separate foreign espionage and signals intelligence organizations, India's Research and Analysis Wing (RAW) oversees all of India's foreign intelligence.[75] Similar to MI5 and ASIO, the IB does not have independent arrest powers and must rely on federal and state law enforcement elements.

India has been hard-pressed to reform its intelligence apparatus. Following the eleven-week skirmish in 1999 with Pakistan, the Group of Ministers (GoM) initiated a major study of India's security and intelligence. This study, headed by former RAW director Girish Saxena, submitted numerous recommendations to streamline the intelligence process.[76] The Saxena Committee performed the first major review of Indian national security and intelligence since its independence in 1947.[77] For the IB, these initiatives included the development of an independent signals intelligence capability, an expansion of the IB's field presence by bolstering its Subsidiary Intelligence Bureaus (SIB) at the state level, implementation of Inter-State Intelligence Support Teams, development

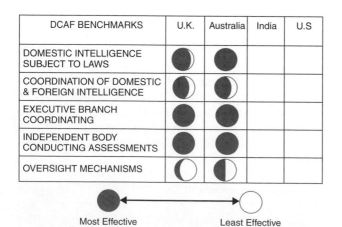

DCAF BENCHMARKS	U.K.	Australia	India	U.S
DOMESTIC INTELLIGENCE SUBJECT TO LAWS	●	●		
COORDINATION OF DOMESTIC & FOREIGN INTELLIGENCE	◗	◗		
EXECUTIVE BRANCH COORDINATING	●	●		
INDEPENDENT BODY CONDUCTING ASSESSMENTS	●	●		
OVERSIGHT MECHANISMS	○	◐		

● Most Effective ←→ ○ Least Effective

FIGURE 37.2 DCAF Benchmarks versus the U.K.-Australia.

of Joint Task Forces for Intelligence (JTFIs), and a Multi Agency Centre (MAC) to electronically collate and database related intelligence.[78]

Despite its promise, most of the reforms have not been implemented—due largely to bureaucratic infighting. The Ministry of Home Affairs and the Ministry of Finance have disapproved the key elements recommended by the committee.[79] The development of the IB's signals intelligence capability has been stalled. The Finance Ministry has disapproved the IB's request for computer trained personnel to develop and maintain the MAC. Funding for the JTFIs and associated training has also been cut. This bureaucratic confrontation is attributable to the long-standing infighting between the Indian Administrative Service officers who dominate the Home ministry and the Indian Police Service officers who constitute the majority of the IB.[80] The inability of the Indian government to institute meaningful intelligence reforms, establish clear organizational mission roles and responsibilities, and manage the competitive tensions between different bureaucracies is of critical importance given the similarities of the U.S. intelligence community and its efforts to reform itself, institute organizational change, and establish a strategic approach to combating terrorism in a post-9/11 environment.

STRATEGIC OUTLOOK

India has faced many internal security problems since establishing its independence in 1947. Consisting of a multitude of ethnicities, languages, and particularly due to the partition of India and Pakistan, India has faced numerous acts of sectarian violence. In 1999, the hijacking of Indian Airlines flight 814 prompted calls for stronger anti-terrorism legislation. The subsequent events of 9/11 affected the Indian government's perception of the al Qaeda threat and provided an opportunity for parliamentarians to enact stronger legislation that addressed transnational terrorism and financing issues.[81] In 2002, the legislature, led by the nationalist Bharatiya Janata Party, passed *The Prevention of Terrorism Act (POTA)*—a strong anti-terror legislation similar to the United States, the United Kingdom, and Australia.[82] The legislation came under severe criticism and was later repealed in 2004 with the entrance of a new government under the opposing Congress party.[83] The July 2006 terrorist attacks in Mumbai have renewed the demands for more stringent anti-terrorism legislation.

Although the Indian government has recognized the threat posed by al Qaeda through its proximity to the Indian subcontinent, the government has been unable to articulate precisely its approach to combating terrorism. A key shortfall in the *POTA* legislation was that it lacked any linkage to a wider counterterrorism strategy and approach. As Swati Pandey states:

> For a counterterrorism law, lawmakers should consider the state's police capabilities, the legal system, and the political leanings of its population to make sure that the law will be successful. If these means are sufficient, then the goals of the law can be reached.[84]

The absence of political buy-in, unclear linkages between the legislation's intent and the actual capabilities of security forces, and poor existing oversight mechanisms result in a mismatch between the strategic vision and actual practice. The Indian government's approach has been erratic with limited consensus between political parties. These inconsistencies stem from India's longer-term inadequacy in managing national security. As B. Raman asserts, this is due to three factors:

> The absence of long-term thinking and planning are due to preoccupation with day-to-day crisis management and short-term compulsions, the inhibition of fresh thinking and a coordinated approach to national security issues due to the undue influence of narrow departmental mindsets, and the absence of a watchdog set-up, uninfluenced by departmental loyalties, to monitor the implementation of the national security decisions and remove bottlenecks.[85]

Given this framework and unlike MI5 and ASIO, the role of the IB is less clear. The IB clearly has many domestic intelligence functions. Conversely, unclear strategic guidance, obscured responsibilities, bureaucratic infighting, and extremely limited oversight mechanisms severely hamper its ability to execute its mission. The Indian shortfalls of translating strategic intent into coherent intelligence reform and community management are of paramount—*indeed critical*—importance for the United States as it attempts to redefine its intelligence apparatus in a post 9/11 environment.

INFORMATION SHARING

The challenges faced by the IB are also a reflection of the Indian national security apparatus. The Saxena Committee recommended the implementation of an Intelligence Coordination Group (ICG) and Technology Coordination Group (TCG) to work closely with the National Security Council Secretariat (NSCS) and the Joint Intelligence Committee (JIC).[86] These groups were intended to focus on resource allocation, annual reviews, national estimates, and executive oversight.[87]

Bureaucratic infighting has also plagued the information sharing and assessment process. The National Security Council (NSC), revived as part of the committee's recommendations, has been ineffective in orchestrating the various agencies towards a single purpose.[88] The NSC is rarely convened and does not have a dedicated staff structure to support this process.[89] Senior officials also state that there is little to no coordination between the IB, RAW, and the newly formed Defence Intelligence Agency (DIA).[90]

Although India's organizational structures are similar to the United Kingdom and Australia, they are not as developed or resourced. Bureaucratic infighting and the lack of strong executive direction have limited the IB's effectiveness. There is also an inherent instability in India's organizational approaches and processes to managing national security and intelligence functions.[91] Despite its responsibility for domestic intelligence, the IB has not been given the requisite tools to perform various responsibilities. As Praveen Swami, an Indian journalist noted for his coverage of Indian national security issues commented, "The head of the U.S.' Federal Bureau of Investigation can authorize the cash down purchase of millions of dollars of equipment, while the Director of India's Intelligence Bureau cannot authorize the purchase of a new desktop computer for his secretary."[92]

OVERSIGHT

The Saxena Committee also attempted to address oversight issues by defining India's different intelligence agency's missions and roles and to ensure executive oversight via the NSCS.[93] The inability to implement these reforms, particularly at the executive and assessment level, has resulted in little progress. Additionally abuse of the *Official Secrets Act of 1923* prohibits national security issues from coming into the forefront of public debate.[94] As Sarath Ramkumar notes, "Top-level political appointees quickly become vigilant in seeking to preserve three main bureaucratic prerogatives of secrecy: control over preservation, control over custody and control over access."[95]

In the absence of a wider public debate, India's parliamentary members rarely discuss or understand the wider implications of India's intelligence issues.[96] In fact, the IB and the RAW are not formally accountable to the parliament.[97] The lack of an effective oversight structure leads to India's legislature being removed from the process. The Standing Committee on Home Affairs has received briefings on the IB's activities, but few of its members have a background in intelligence or are sufficiently staffed to exercise effective oversight.[98] Ramkumar offers the following insightful assessment of India's intelligence community:

> Intelligence agencies are not islands that exist outside executive control. The usefulness and the quality of intelligence is only as good as the government of the day requires. Any serious reforms in the field of intelligence need an understanding of the precise role of intelligence agencies in serving the nation's national security interest.[99]

The lack of executive and legislative oversight mechanisms has resulted in the politicization of the IB. Most of the bureau's focus has been on political surveillance and election-related information gathering in support of the ruling party.[100] As one member of the National Security Advisory Board commented recently, "How can we expect the IB to function if a large part of its resources is directed at serving the ruling political party of the day?"[101]

Although the United Kingdom and Australia have suffered from oversight shortfalls, the Indian shortcomings in this area have hampered greater intelligence reforms. Understanding the linkage between implementing reform and oversight, given the challenge faced by the Indian government, is of unique importance for the United States. Improving the effectiveness of intelligence oversight—an identified 9/11 recommendation—serves to link the intent and vision of national strategy to the implementation of intelligence reforms.[102]

CONCLUSION

The IB has not been given the necessary tools and resources to fulfill its mission. Although the IB has a long history of performing its internal security function, the majority of its focus has been on political surveillance. Despite sound recommendations and higher-level organizational initiatives, bureaucratic infighting and petty competition have inhibited translating these initiatives into meaningful activities. Lastly, despite possessing definitive intelligence

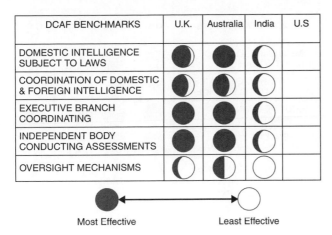

DCAF BENCHMARKS	U.K.	Australia	India	U.S
DOMESTIC INTELLIGENCE SUBJECT TO LAWS	◐	●	◑	
COORDINATION OF DOMESTIC & FOREIGN INTELLIGENCE	◑	◐	◑	
EXECUTIVE BRANCH COORDINATING	●	●	◑	
INDEPENDENT BODY CONDUCTING ASSESSMENTS	●	●	◑	
OVERSIGHT MECHANISMS	○	◐	○	

Most Effective ← → Least Effective

FIGURE 37.3 DCAF Benchmarks versus the U.K.-Australia-India.

organizations and mandated assessment entities, the lack of strong executive direction and bipartisanship, weak legislative oversight, organizational instability, and ineffective resourcing have resulted in a listless national security and intelligence apparatus. These limitations, when compared to the DCAF benchmarks in Figure 37.3, display a marginal effectiveness. India's intelligence apparatus does not operate under a well-defined set of laws and coordination between intelligence agencies remains an endemic problem. Its independent assessment capability has not been properly resourced and bureaucratic infighting greatly inhibits the ability of the executive to coordinate and direct intelligence efforts. Lastly, India's almost total lack of executive and legislative oversight severely limits accountability and the ability to reform the system.

DOMESTIC INTELLIGENCE AGENCY: APPLICATION FOR THE UNITED STATES?

Proponents of a domestic intelligence agency highlight the importance of prevention, yet domestic intelligence agencies focused solely on information gathering and developing sources have not been proven to be more effective in preventing terrorist attacks. They may have a greater ability to develop better and more precise intelligence assessments on the nature of the domestic threat. The bombings in London (2005) and Mumbai (2006), however, highlight the point that not all attacks can be prevented. Additionally, the metrics for how many attacks have been prevented and where these agencies can cite unreported successes is absent due to their classified nature. By examining the United Kingdom,

Australia, and India, it is evident that the challenges of coordinating intelligence, sharing information, and implementing oversight mechanisms are problematic and relevant issues for their domestic intelligence agencies.

ORGANIZATION

For the United States, intelligence coordination and assessment were highlighted as significant shortfalls after 9/11. Although the United States does not have an assessment apparatus as highly centralized and evolved as the United Kingdom or Australia, it has been recognized as a shortfall and steps have been taken to address this issue. The major change was the creation of the Department of Homeland Security with an intelligence charter. The U.S. government also adopted measures to implement intelligence coordination and improve identified shortfalls through the creation of the Director for National Intelligence (DNI), the National Counter Terrorism Center (NCTC), and revamping the FBI's intelligence capability.[103] Calls for further FBI reforms have continued. As a result of further findings, the FBI consolidated many of its intelligence functions under the creation of the National Security Servicer.[104] Despite the creation of these new agencies and initiatives, the effectiveness of these organizations to implement and institutionalize intelligence reforms, manage resources, and develop strategic assessments as envisioned in the national strategy is questionable, particularly since these initiatives have occured within a relatively short period of nearly six years after 9/11 and given similar Indian attempts over the last decade.

INFORMATION SHARING

As with the United Kingdom, Australia, and India, information sharing is a significant issue for the United States. This is recognized as a core issue in the *National Intelligence Strategy for the United States.*[105] Further measures have been taken to address this issue by creating the NCTC, instituting the DHS, reforming the FBI's headquarters, implementing Field Intelligence Groups (FIGs), and developing state intelligence fusion centers. The domestic intelligence challenge in the United States is similar to India's in terms of organization and the scope of the problem. Despite higher-level initiatives, the FBI continues to have a "law enforcement" mindset, is experiencing similar problems with implementing its information sharing technology, and is faced with coordinating with multiple state and local efforts.[106] The DHS has also been faced with similar bureaucratic hurdles. Additionally, there is no clear linkage or relationship between the NCTC and the numerous state and local fusion centers that have been created since 9/11.[107] As a result, the level of integration remains questionable. Despite the plethora of executive findings and directives, there are still significant bureaucratic hurdles and infighting to sharing information.

OVERSIGHT

Intelligence oversight remains an issue for the United States. Controversies such as the National Security Agency's (NSA) electronic surveillance and the Department of Defense's Counter Intelligence Field Activities (CIFA) monitoring of U.S. persons, the intelligence activities in Guantanamo, and the handling of National Security Letters remain at the forefront of the political debate. Intelligence initiatives have been undertaken since 9/11, but most of these efforts—particularly with regard to domestic intelligence—have received significant criticism due to ineffective implementation efforts and a lack of bipartisan buy-in. While oversight issues are also challenges for MI5, ASIO, and the IB, Australia seems to have a highly developed, resourced, and aggressive executive and legislative oversight component. A closer examination of Australia's oversight practices and mechanisms could yield practical lessons for the United States. Additionally, the United States needs to streamline and improve its legislative oversight process—a key recommendation of the 9/11 Commission—to ensure proper safeguards for civil liberties and accountability of intelligence operations.[108] Progress in this area has been tepid.

CONCLUSION

When compared to the DCAF benchmarks in Figure 37.4, the United States possesses a well-defined set of laws operating under a strong executive mechanism. These strengths are offset, however, by a weaker executive and legislative oversight process. Although U.S. oversight mechanisms limit the statutory ability of the FBI and other agencies to conduct domestic intelligence, there are still oversight shortfalls in terms of staffing, resources, and legislative access. As seen in the Indian case, limited oversight can also lead to poor implementation of intelligence initiatives. Although there have been numerous fact-finding commissions, such as the 9/11, the

DCAF BENCHMARKS	U.K.	Australia	India	U.S
DOMESTIC INTELLIGENCE SUBJECT TO LAWS	●	●	◐	●
COORDINATION OF DOMESTIC & FOREIGN INTELLIGENCE	◐	◐	○	◐
EXECUTIVE BRANCH COORDINATING	●	●	○	●
INDEPENDENT BODY CONDUCTING ASSESSMENTS	●	●	○	◐
OVERSIGHT MECHANISMS	◐	◐	○	◐

● Most Effective ⟷ ○ Least Effective

FIGURE 37.4   DCAF Benchmarks versus U.K.-Australia-India-U.S.

Commission on *Intelligence Capabilities of the United States regarding Weapons of Mass Destruction*, and the numerous panels prior to 9/11, there has not been a strategic and bipartisan approach to overseeing and tracking the implementation and effectiveness of these reforms. Lastly, although steps have been taken to institutionalize the NCTC's independent assessment capability and fuse domestic and foreign intelligence, it is uncertain whether these steps are translating into positive action, whether they are truly combining with the efforts of the DHS or regional, state, or large metropolitan fusion centers, or whether an additional layer of bureaucracy has been added to an already heavily bureaucratized intelligence apparatus.

SUMMARY

Although domestic intelligence agencies possess several shortfalls in not being able to prevent terrorist attacks and have corresponding information-sharing shortfalls and oversight issues, these shortfalls do not address the entire scope of the problem. While domestic intelligence agencies may not be able to prevent all terrorist attacks, are they more successful in preventing most attacks? Do effective domestic intelligence agencies, solely focused on intelligence gathering and unencumbered by law enforcement responsibilities, possess a better ability to focus and develop precise intelligence? Without access to classified sources or performance measures, most literature would suggest that domestic intelligence agencies are more effective in developing intelligence through the penetration of terrorist cells and collation of other intelligence data.[109]

Additionally, the combination of law enforcement and intelligence functions under the FBI and the Attorney General, acting as the federal government's chief legal officer, has also led to civil rights abuses. Opponents to the creation of a domestic intelligence agency fail to recognize that the argument for separating domestic intelligence from law enforcement functions was precisely the reason for limiting the West German government's ability to exercise arbitrary power when it was reconstituted as a nation in the 1950s.[110] In other words, the German domestic intelligence apparatus was consciously separated from law enforcement responsibilities to prevent an abuse of power. Balancing civil rights and public safety remains a problematic issue for democracies whether they possess a domestic intelligence agency or not. Despite the arguments posed by the advocates for and opponents of having a domestic intelligence agency for the United States, an examination of MI5, ASIO, and the IB have shown that domestic intelligence agencies are not necessarily the solution to the domestic intelligence gap. They may possess a greater ability to better categorize threats and operate unencumbered by complicated and competing mission roles within one agency. In terms of the feasibility, suitability, and acceptability of implementing this organizational construct for the United States, it is *feasible* to develop a U.S. domestic intelligence agency if the resources and executive direction are applied to instituting this capability. The critical *feasibility* issue, however, is whether the United States can translate strategic guidance and direction into meaningful change, reform, and capability that mitigate the domestic intelligence gap—whether under a domestic intelligence agency or some other organizational construct. This is the clear lesson from India's attempt to reform the IB and institute larger intelligence reforms.

Suitability (whether the mission will be accomplished if the tasks are carried out successfully) is also contingent on the ability to translate strategic intent into meaningful change. The 9/11 Commission did not see a need to create a domestic intelligence agency *unless their other recommendations were not adopted*—to create an effective NCTC and Director of National Intelligence (DNI).[111] The effectiveness of the DNI to implement reform was questionable when 96 percent of the FBI's intelligence function fell *outside* of the DNI's purview.[112] Continued FBI reform attempts, as evidenced by reorganization

efforts in 1998, 1999, 2000, and 2001, are indicative of organizational instability or resistance to change.[113] Organizational instability and resistance to change can also be applied to NSA. Additionally, the obstacles to creating a unified DHS are another indication of bureaucratic intransigence. The implementation of a strategic vision into reality is clearly a challenge that India has had to face. These shortfalls and others would indicate that current tasks and reforms are not being effectively implemented.

Like the United States, the United Kingdom, Australia, and India have been unable to prevent terrorist attacks. In the absence of definitively demonstrating that domestic intelligence agencies are better positioned to prevent most attacks, the single largest obstacle to implementing this organizational construct in the United States is cultural. Given the history and structure of the United States, it is probably still not *acceptable* to have a domestic intelligence agency. Although the political supportability was stronger after 9/11, most Americans do not like to feel that they are being spied upon by their government or neighbors.[114] Additionally, as Kate Martin points out, "Nothing in the pre-September 11 law prevented the CIA from informing the FBI that the suspected terrorists had entered the United States, and nothing would have prevented the FBI from pursuing them."[115] The issue lies in the practical interpretation of these regulations. It was the inability to effectively put these regulations into practice that led to information-sharing shortfalls prior to 9/11. It is also the inability to effectively implement the post 9/11 regulations and intelligence initiatives through a bipartisan approach—such as the NSA monitoring program—that creates continued foreign-domestic information sharing gaps.

The central issue is not whether to have a combined law enforcement and intelligence organization versus a sole domestic intelligence agency. The issue is effective *organizational reform, information sharing,* and *oversight.*[116] Effective organizational change, information sharing, and oversight are not necessarily achieved through high-level organizational repositioning, implementing common information data systems, or passing new regulations for managing intelligence operations and reform. The absence of a significant terrorist attack in the United States since 9/11 is also not a good indicator that the intelligence apparatus is operating more efficiently. The creation of additional bureaucracies, an increased centralization of intelligence functions that inhibits the analysis of opposing alternatives, and the inability of the U.S. Congress to reform its oversight process may have actually led to greater drawbacks rather than progress. Although the United States has developed strategies and applied significant resources to address its weaker areas—such as the creation of the DNI to oversee the intelligence community, the NCTC to integrate domestic-foreign intelligence and develop assessments, and the professionalization of the DHS and the FBI's intelligence functions—there remains a level of uncertainty whether these initiatives have resulted in greater progress and meaningful transformation. This uncertainty continues to place the United States at risk. To address these information sharing and oversight uncertainties, the following actions are recommended:

- Assess the ability of the DNI to exercise leadership and management over the intelligence community in terms of controlling resources, implementing cross-organizational information sharing initiatives, and effecting reform consistent with the *National Intelligence Strategy for the United States*. This is a clear lesson learned from similar Indian attempts to reform its intelligence community since the 1999 GoM findings.
- Capitalizing on the British and Australian strengths in developing strategic assessments and categorizing domestic threats, conduct an end-to-end organizational review of NCTC to analyze its performance compared to its stated mission, particularly its ability to support its domestic intelligence assessment within a *national* and not strictly federal context.
- Given the identified information-sharing shortfalls with countries possessing domestic intelligence agencies, conduct a review of information sharing and knowledge management policies to assess the applicability of current policies versus actual practice, most notably providing warning and the sharing of raw and unevaluated intelligence between organizations.[117]
- Review the FBI's and DHS's intelligence reform initiatives in terms of professionalization, information sharing, strategic focus, and resource allocation to determine if there is a continued law enforcement versus intelligence mindset, as evidenced by Indian bureaucratic infighting.
- Drawing from Australian strengths, reevaluate executive and congressional oversight mechanisms and reforms to identify duplicative

functions, staffing, resources, and the ability to link strategic intent to implementation of intelligence reforms.

Merely implementing a U.S. domestic intelligence agency will not prevent further terrorist attacks. Although the domestic intelligence agencies of the United Kingdom, Australia, and to a lesser extent, India, have had their successes, they have also suffered the same shortcomings of the United States in terms of information sharing and oversight. Additionally, there have been numerous organizational changes and attempts at reform since 9/11. Only an in-depth appraisal of the DNI and NCTC's performance, the ability of intelligence and law enforcement organizations to share information, the FBI's progress at reforming itself, the implementation of the DHS as an organization with a domestic intelligence function, and the ability to provide effective oversight will determine whether the intelligence shortfalls identified in the congressional inquiry into the attacks on 9/11 have been addressed.[118]

QUESTIONS FOR FURTHER DISCUSSION

1. In what ways have domestic intelligence organizations and activities evolved recently in the United States?
2. How does Burch deal with the question of oversight for domestic intelligence operations?
3. What is Burch's view of domestic intelligence effectiveness in other lands?
4. What vulnerabilities do you think the United States continues to face in its homeland defenses? Would you be willing to see taxes rise if the money were spent toward improving homeland security against another 9/11 attack? What could be done to help ensure that the monies would not be misspent on pork barrel projects?

ENDNOTES

1. U.S. Congress, House, Permanent Select Committee on Intelligence and Senate Select Committee on Intelligence, *Report of the Joint Inquiry into the Terrorist Attacks of September 11, 2001*, 107th Congress, 2nd Session, December 2002, S. Rept. No. 107–531, H. Rept. No. 107–792, 244. http://www.fas.org/irp/congress/2002_rpt/911rept.pdf.
2. National Commission on Terrorist Attacks upon the United States, *The 9/11 Commission Report* (New York: W.W. Norton & Company, 2004), 353. The inability

to manage and fuse foreign and domestic intelligence information was identified as a key shortfall.

3. Gregory F. Treverton, "Intelligence, Law Enforcement, and Homeland Security," *The Century Foundation* (January 8, 2002): I. http://www.tef.org/Publications/HomelandSecurity/treverton-intelligence.pdf.

4. National Commission on Terrorist Attacks, *The 9/11 Commission Report*, 172. The estimate for al Qaeda's monetary cost to plan and execute the 9/11 attacks ranges from $400,000 to $500,000.

5. U.S. Congress, Senate, *Homeland Security Act of 2002*, Public Law 107–296, sec. 101 (2002), 13; http://fli.fiudlaw.com/ news.findlaw.com/hdocs/docs/terrorism/hsa2002.pdf. Section 101 established the Department of Homeland Security and reorganized several preexisting government agencies under it.

6. Permanent Select Committee on Intelligence, *Report of the Joint Inquiry*, 245.

7. Paul R. Pillar, "Intelligence," in *Attacking Terrorism: Elements of a Grand Strategy* (Washington, DC: Georgetown University Press, 2004), 134.

8. Mark W. Lowenthal, *Intelligence: From Secrets to Policy*, 3rd ed (Washington, DC: CQ Press, 2006), 234.

9. Harry Howe Ransom, "The Politicization of Intelligence," in *Strategic Intelligence: Windows Into a Secret World*, ed. Loch K. Johnson and James J. Wirtz (Los Angeles, CA: Roxbury Publishing Company, 2004), 175.

10. Harvey Rishikof, "The Role of the Federal Bureau of Investigation in National Security," in *Intelligence and National Security Strategist: Enduring Issues and Challenges*, ed. Roger Z. George and Robert D. Kline (New York: Rowan & Littlefield Publishers, Inc., 2006), 126: The Marlke Foundation, *Protecting America's Freedom in the Information Age: A Report of the Morkle Foundation Task Force* (October 2002), 21. http://www.markle.org/downloadahle_assets/nstf_full.pdf.

11. Michael Massing, "A War on Terrorism is Futile," in *Are Efforts to Reduce Terrorism Successful?*, ed. Lauri S. Friedman (New Haven, CT: Greenhaven Press, 2005), 25.

12. Permanent Select Commmittee on Intelligence, *Report of the Joint Inquiry*, 245.

13. Larry M. Wortzel, "Americans Do Not Need a New Domestic Spy Agency to Improve Intelligence and Homeland Security," *The Heritage Foundation*, no. 818 (January 10, 2003): 2. http://www.heritage.org/Rescarch/HomelandDefense/loader.cfm?url=/commonspot/security/getfile.cfm&PageID=34700.

14. Erie R. Taylor, "The Department of Homeland Security May Make Americans Less Safe," in *Homeland Security*, ed. James D. Torr (New Haven, CT: Greenhaven Press, 2004), 64.

15. Ibid., 61.

16. Frederic R. Manget, "Another System of Oversight: Intelligence and the Rise of Judicial Intervention," in *Strategic Intelligence: Windows Into a Secret World*, ed. Loch K. Johnson and James J. Wirtz (Los Angeles, CA: Roxbury Publishing Company, 2004), 408.

17. B. Raman, *Intelligence: Past, Present, and Future* (New Delhi, India: Lancer Publishers & Distributors, 2002), 6.

18. Manget, "Another System of Oversight," 408; Rishikof, "The Role of the Federal Bureau of Investigation in National Security," 126.

19. Ransom, "The Politicization of Intelligence," 171.

20. Ibid., 175.

21. Benjamin Netanyahu, *Fighting Terrorism: How Democracies Can Defeat the International Terrorist Network* (New York: Farrar, Straus and Giroux, 1995), 30.

22. Richard A. Posner, *Remaking Domestic Intelligence* (Palo Alto, CA: Hoover Institution Press, 2005), 73.

23. Geneva Centre for Democratic Control of Armed Forces, "Intelligence Services and Democracy," no. 13, Geneva Centre for the Democratic Control of Armed Forces (DCAF) (April 2002): 3–13, http://www.dcaf.ch/_docs/WP13.pdf.

24. Department of Defense, *Joint Staff Officer's Guide* (Washington, DC: GPO, 2000), 4-87, G-75.

25. Tony Blair, "BBC Breakfast with Frost Interview," interview by Sir David Frost, *British Broadcasting Corporation (BBC)* (30 September 2001); http://news.bbc.co.uk/1/hi/programmes/breakfast_with_frost/1571541.stm.

26. Lowenthal, *Intelligence: From Secrets to Policy*, 291.

27. Frank Gregory, "Intelligence led Counter-terrorism: A Brief Analysis of the UK Domestic Intelligence System's Response to 9/11 and the Implications of the London Bombings of 7 July 2005," *Real Instituto Elcano de Estudios Internacionoles y Estraegeicos*, no. 94 (7 December 2005), 3; http://www.realinstitutoelcano.org/analisis/78l/Gregory781-v.pdf.

28. U.S. Congress, Senate, *Catching Terrorists: The British System versus the U.S. System*, Hearing Before a Subcommittee of the Committee on Appropriations, 109th Congress, and Session (September 14, 2006), 23; http://frwchgate.access.gpo.gov/cgi-bin/getdoc.cgi?dbname=109_senate_hearings&docid=f:30707.pdf.

29. Todd Masse, *Domestic Intelligence in the United Kingdom: Applicability of the MI5 Model to the United States* (Washington DC: The Library of Congress, 19 May 2003), 6; http://www.fas.org/irp/crs/RL31920.pdf.

30. Peter Chalk and William Rosenau, *Confronting the Enemy Within: Security Intelligence, The Police, and Counterterrorism in Four Democracies* (Santa Monica, CA: RAND Corporation, 2004), 12. http://www.rand.org/pubs/monographs/2004/RAND_MG100.pdf.

31. Jane's Intelligence Digest, *Britain: Intelligence versus Terrorism* (London: Jane's Information Group, 2006), 1.

32. According to MI5, the Security Service currently employs approximately 2,800 persons. The organization as a whole has experienced targeted growth since 9/11. See MI5's website at www.mi5.gov.uk.

33. Her Majesty's Government, *Countering International Terrorism: the United Kingdom's Strategy*, CM6888 (July 2006), 16; http://www.mi5. gov.uk/files/pdf/ct_strategy.pdf.

34. Ibid., 2.

35. Ibid., 16.

36. U.S. Congress, Senate, *Catching Terrorists: The British System versus the U.S. System*, 22.

37. Chalk and Rosenau, *Confronting the Enemy Within*, 10.

38. Paul Tumelty, "An In-Depth Look at the London Bombers," *Terrorism Monitor* 3, no. 15 (July 28, 2005): 4; http://jamestown.org/terrorism/news/uploads/ter_003_015.pdf.

39. Gregory, "Intelligence led Counter-terrorism," 3.

40. Jim Dempsey, "Domestic Intelligence Agencies: The Mixed Record of the UK's MI5," *Center for Democracy and Technology* (27 January 2003), 2; http://www.cdt.org/security/usapatriot/030127mi5.pdf.

41. Masse, Domestic *Intelligence in the United Kingdom*, 6.

42. Chalk and Rosenau, *Confronting the Enemy Within*, 31; Gregory, "Intelligence led Counter-terrorism," 3.

43. U.S. Congress, Senate, *Catching Terrorists; The British System versus the U.S. System*, 28.

44. Lowenthal, *Intelligence: From Secrets to Policy*, 292–293.

45. Chalk and Rosenau, *Confronting the Enemy Within*, 14–15.

46. U.S. Congress, Senate, *Catching Terrorists: The British System versus the U.S. System*, 28.

47. Masse, *Domestic Intelligence in the United Kingdom*, 9. The doctrine of prior restraint was deemed unconstitutional in the United States in *New York Times v. United States (1971)*.

48. Chalk and Rosenau, *Confronting the Enemy Within*, 51, 53.

49. Ibid., 14.

50. John Howard, "Prime Minister's Address to the Nation," *Prime Minister of Australia News Room* (March 20, 2003), http://www.pm.gov.au/news/speeches/speech79.html.

51. Inspector-General of Intelligence and Security, annual report 2005–2006, 25 September 2006, File Reference 2005/125, 22 http://www.igis.gov.au/annuals/05-06/pdf/IGIS_AR_2005-06.pdf.

52. Nicholas Grono, "Australia's Response to Terrorism," *Studies in Intelligence*, 48, no. 1 (2004): 28; http://www.cia.gov/csi/studies/vol48no1/articleo3.html.

53. Australian Government, *Protecting Australia Against Terrorism 2006: Australia's National Counterterrorism Policies and Arrangements* (2006), 40–4l; http://www.dpmc.gov.au/publications/protecting_australia_2006/docs/paat_2006.pdf.

54. Director-General of Security, *ASIO Report to Parliament* 2005–2006, September 2006, Reference no. eAl004090, viii, 42; http://www.asio.gov.au/Publications/comp.htm. Under Australia's *ASIO Legislation Amendment Act 2006*, ASIO possesses special warrant powers to initiate questioning and detention for particular circumstances under the review of the Attorney General.

55. Australian Government, *Protecting Australia Against Terrorism 2006*, 40.

56. Grono, "Australia's Response to Terrorism," 27.

57. Australian Government, *Protecting Australia Against Terrorism 2006*, 8.

58. Ibid., 13.

59. Mark Thomson, *Jane's Terrorism & Security Monitor* (London: Jane's Information Group, 2006), 1.

60. Inspector-General of Intelligence and Security, *Annual Report* 2005–2006, 52.

61. Director-General of Security, *ASIO Report to Parliament* 2005–2006, 51.

62. Australian Government, *Protecting Australia Against Terrorism 2006*, 16.

63. Chalk and Rosenau, *Confronting the Enemy Within*, 49.

64. Australian Government, *Protecting Australia Against Terrorism 2006*, 42.

65. Chalk and Rosenau, *Confronting the Enemy Within*, 40.

66. Australian Government, *Protecting Australia Against Terrorism 2006*, 41–42.

67. Ibid., 24.

68. Gregoty, "Intelligence led Counter-terrorism,"4.

69. Chalk and Rosenau, *Confronting the Enemy Within*, 50.

70. Manmoham Singh, "Interview of Prime Minister Dr. Manmohan Singh," interview by Charlie Rose, *Charlie Rose Show* (21 September 2004), http://www.indianembassy.org/pm/pin_charlie_rose_sep_21_04.html.

71. Jane's Intelligence Digest, *Jane's Sentinel Security Assessment: South Asia-India: Security and Foreign Forces* (London: Jane's Information Group, 2006), 29.

72. Maloy Krishna Dhar, *Open Secrets: India's Intelligence Unveiled* (New Delhi, India: Manas Publications, 2005), 11.

73. Ministry of Home Affairs, *Annual Report* 2006-07 (Government of India: 2007), 28, 31–32; http://mha.nic.in/Annual-Reports/ar0607_Eng.pdf.

74. Sarath Ramkumar, "Intelligence Agencies: Need for Greater Attention by the Government," *Institute of Peace & Conflict Studies*, no. 579 (17 September 2001): 1; http://www.ipcs.org/newKashmirLevel2.jsp?action=showView&kValue=909&subCatID=null&mod=null.

75. Jane's Intelligence Digest, *Jane's Sentinel Security Assessment: South Asia—India: Security and Foreign Forces*, 28.

76. Rahul Bedi, "Indian intelligence gathering undermined by budget cuts," *Jane's Intelligence Review* (1 July 2004): 2.

77. Praveen Swami, "Handicapped Intelligence," *Frontline* 21, no. 14 (July 2004): 1; http//www.hinduonnet.com/fline/fl2114/stories/20040716001204900.htm.

78. Rahul Bedi, "Indian Security Shake Up," *Jane's Intelligence Review,* (4 May 2001): 2; Praveen Swami, "A New Intelligence Organisation," *Frontline* 19, no. 6 (March 2002): 2; http://www.hinduonnet.com/fline/fl1906/19061240.htm.

79. Praveen Swami, "Bureaucrats Kill Critical Intelligence Reforms," *The Hindu* (June 18, 2004): 1; http://www.hinduonnet.com/thehindu/2004/06/18/stories/2004061805171100.htm.

80. Bedi, "Indian intelligence gathering undermined by budget cuts," 2; Praveen Swami, "Stalled reforms," *Frontline* 20, no. 9 (April/May 2003): 5; http://www.hinduonnet.com/fline/fl2009/stories/20030509002108700.htm.

81. Swati Pandey, *Law and Counterterrorism: The Prevention of Terrorism Act in a Strategic Dimension*, Institute of Peace & Conflict Studies Research Papers (April 2004), 4; http://www.ipcs.org/IRP04.pdf.

82. Government of India, Parliament, *Prevention of Terrorism Act, 2002* (March 28, 2002), Bill No. 5-C of 2002; http://rajyasabha.nic.in/bills-ls-rs/5-c-2002.pdf.

83. Jane's Intelligence Digest, Jane's *Sentinel Security Assessment: South Asia—India: Security And Foreign Forces*, 39; Pandey, *Law and Counterterrorism*, 5. Pandey highlighted the use of the *POTA* legislation to target political opponents.

84. Pandey, *Law and Counterterrorism*, 9. See pages 9–12 for the importance of linking law to national strategy.

85. Raman, *Intelligence: Past, Present, and Future*, 358–359.

86. Saikat Datta, "There Are No Secrets Here," *New Delhi Outlook* (19 November 2006): 1; http://www.outlookindia.com. The Joint Intelligence Committee had merged with National Security Council Secretariat in 1998, but was reformed into its own separate entity.

87. Bhashyam Kasturi, "The Intelligence Secret," *Institute of Peace & Conflict Studies*, no. 589 (27 September 2001): 1; http://www.ipcs.org/newKashmirLevel2.jsp?action=showView&kValue=899&subCatID=null&mod=null; Bedi, "Failures prompt India to reform intelligence service," *Jane's Intelligence Review* (23 May 2001): 3.

88. Dhar, 15.

89. Bedi, "Failures prompt India to reform intelligence service," 7.

90. George Iype, "Why intelligence fails, and terrorists suceeed," *Rediff* (20 July 2006): 1; http://www.rediff.com/news/2006/jul/20george.htm.

91. U.S. Congress, Senate, *Catching Terrorists: The British System versus the U.S. System*, 23–24. Stability in organizational relationships and intelligence sharing processes is touted as a significant strength of the British system where these functions have been allowed to mature over time.

92. Swami, "Bureaucrats kill critical intelligence reforms," 2.

93. Kasturi, "The Intelligence Secret," 1.

94. Sarath Ramkumar, "Revamping of Intelligence Apparatus," *Institute of Peace & Conflict Studies*, no. 328 (22 February 2000): 1; http://www.ipcs.org/newKashmirLevel2.jsp?action=showView&kValue=641&subCatID=null&mod=null.

95. Ramkumar, "Intelligence Agencies: Need for greater attention by the government," 1.

96. Swami, "Handicapped Intelligence," 4.

97. Dhar, *Open Secrets: India's Intelligence Unveiled*, 83.

98. Swami, "Stalled reforms," 4.

99. Sarath Ramkumar, "KRC: Government's Success, but Intelligence Failure," *Institute for Peace & Conflict Studies*, no. 392 (30 July 2000): 2; http://www.ipcs.org/newKashmirLevel2.jsp?action=showView&kValue=1036&subCatID=null&mod=null.

100. Bedi, "India's security shake up," 2.

101. Saikat Datta, "War Below the Radar," *New Delhi Outlook* (31 July 2006): 1; http://www.outlookindia.com.

102. National Commission on Terrorist Attacks, *The 9/11 Commission Report*, 395.

103. U.S. Congress, Senate, *Intelligence Reform and Terrorism Prevention Act of 2004*. Public Law 108–458 (Washington DC: GPO, December 17, 2004), 3644; http://frwebgate.access.gpo.gov/cgi-bin/getdoc.cgi?dbname=l08_cong_public_laws&docid=f:pub1458.108.pdf.

Section 101(a) established the Office of the DNI. The act also codified the NCTC. Congressional Research Service, *FBI Intelligence Reform Since September 11, 2001: Issues and Options for Congress* (Washington DC: The Library of Congress, August 4, 2004), 5-6; http://www.fas.org/irp/crs/RL32336.pdf.

104. Commission on the Intelligence Capabilities of the United States Regarding Weapons of Mass Destruction, *Report to the President of the United States* (Washington DC: GPO, March 31, 2005), 30; http://www.wmd.gov/report/wmd_report.pdf. The report specifically called for the consolidation of the FBI's counterterrorism and counterintelligence function under the Directorate of Intelligence. It also identified several other shortfalls with the FBI's progress in transforming its organizational culture and intelligence reforms. See Chapter 10 of the report for further details.

105. Office of the Director of National Intelligence, *The National Intelligence Strategy of the United States: Transformation through Integration and Innovation* (Washington, DC: GPO, October 2005), 1. The strategy highlights the necessity of integrating foreign and domestic intelligence efforts to eliminate the traditional gap in U.S. national security efforts.

106. Dhar, *Open Secrets: India's Intelligence Unveiled*, 13–14, 84–85. Dhar highlights these challenges for the Intelligence Bureau.

107. U.S. Congress, House, Committee on Homeland Security, *Statement of Kenneth Bouche, Colonel, Illinois State Police Regarding a Hearing on "State and Local Fusion Centers and the Role of DHS"* (September 7, 2006), 4; http://www. fas.org/irp/congress/2006_hr/090706bouche.pdf.

108. National Commission on Terrorist Attacks, *The 9/11 Commission Report*, 419.

109. The Markle Foundation, *Protecting America's Freedom in the Information Age*, 107.

110. U.S. Congress, Senate, *Catching Terrorists: The British System versus the U.S. System*, 37.

111. National Commission on Terrorist Attacks, *The 9/11 Commission Report*, 423.

112. Commission on the Intelligence Capabilities of the United States Regarding Weapons of Mass Destruction, 459. The DNI is chartered to exercise greater oversight since the creation of the National Security Service.

113. Posner, *Remaking Domestic Intelligence*, 37.

114. Pillar, "Intelligence," 134.

115. Kate Martin, "Domestic Intelligence and Civil Liberties," *SAIS Review* 24, no. 1 (Winter-Spring 2004): 12.

116. National Commission on Terrorist Attacks, *The 9/11 Commission Report*, 423.

117. Netanyahu, *Fighting Terrorism*, 138. Netanyahu highlights the sharing of basic, or raw, data versus the sharing of intelligence warning. He highlights the fact that basic data are often not shared between intelligence agencies of the same government due to the need to protect the information's source or from outright organizational jealousy.

118. Permanent Select Committee on Intelligence, *Report of the Joint Inquiry into the Terrorist Attacks of September 11, 2001*. This study identified many of the foreign-domestic intelligence sharing shortfalls, the inability of the intelligence community to provide assessments, and particularly the FBI's shortfalls in intelligence.

Reprinted with permission from James Burch, "A Domestic Intelligence Agency for the United States? A Comparative Analysis of Domestic Intelligence Agencies and Their Implications for Homeland Security," *Homeland Security Affairs* 3 (June 2007); pp. 1–16.

X

INTELLIGENCE IN OTHER LANDS

Hamlet: "…For every man hath business and desire
Such as it is…"

—SHAKESPEARE, *Hamlet*, 1.5.130–131

Although most states, nonstate actors, and even corporations have organizations that collect, analyze, and disseminate information, intelligence organizations are not all cut from the same mold. They often undertake different missions, have different capabilities, and are subjected to different types of public or governmental oversight. The U.S. intelligence community is not a typical national intelligence organization. It specializes in technical intelligence collection (e.g., electronic and photographic space surveillance), and it takes a "social science" approach to intelligence analysis. It is also governed by a strict normative and legal code of conduct that is supposed to distance intelligence work from domestic politics.

The United States also is a relative newcomer when it comes to running large intelligence organizations, although at moments of crisis the nation has usually found a way to recruit spies and organize their "take" to meet military and diplomatic needs. Other great powers—France, Great Britain, China, Russia—have long maintained competent and sometimes quite extensive intelligence organizations and operations. Additionally, smaller states—Israel and

interwar Poland, for example—have developed highly capable intelligence organizations to offset powerful and threatening neighbors. In fact, it was Polish intelligence that gave the Allies in World War II their greatest asset. Polish mathematicians reproduced a German code machine, known as "Enigma," and using outmoded code "keys" supplied to them by French intelligence were able to read encoded Nazi radio traffic. The intelligence produced by Enigma, known as "Ultra," was closely guarded and highly valued by the Allies because it literally gave them the capability to read Nazi war plans before they were received by frontline commanders.

CLASSIFICATION AND COMPARISON OF ORGANIZATIONS

There is no commonly accepted scheme for separating intelligence agencies into categories, but scholars have used several variables to facilitate the comparative study of intelligence organizations. First, scholars classify national intelligence organization in terms of whether they perform covert actions, paramilitary operations, espionage, technical collection, military intelligence, political intelligence, or internal security and surveillance. They are also interested in determining which of these operations tends to dominate a state's approach to intelligence and who or which agency actually runs the overall intelligence operation. Sometimes states maintain separate organizations to undertake each intelligence function, and sometimes several or all functions are lumped together in a single organization. National priorities and resource constraints can also limit the scope of intelligence activities: Few states have the capability to launch reconnaissance satellites to observe their opponents from space or to monitor events in more than a few areas of special interest. Additionally, culture, history, and tradition shape intelligence organizations and national outlooks about the proper role of intelligence organizations in foreign, defense, and domestic policy.

Second, scholars often use an important distinguishing characteristic to classify national intelligence and security organizations. They look to see whether a division of responsibility exists between monitoring external threats and domestic security and surveillance. States that maintain this distinction between external and domestic activities have a greater likelihood of having professional intelligence organizations that are responsive to the rule of law and oversight by other government institutions and elected officials. By contrast, when domestic and external intelligence and security activities are undertaken by a single organization, most scholars believe that it is likely that intelligence will simply be used as an instrument of state terror to keep a ruling party, clique, or dictator in power. John Dziak (1988) has called this second type of intelligence institution the "counterintelligence state."

The counterintelligence state forms when the distinction between legitimate government and intelligence infrastructure vanishes and the resources of the state come to serve the interests of the ruling elite, which include intelligence functionaries. The counterintelligence state maintains a large intelligence-security force that is responsible for identifying and responding to both domestic and international threats to the regime. Left to its own devices, it often identifies broad and arbitrary domestic and foreign threats, placing virtually everyone not in the intelligence-security force under suspicion. These threats, in turn, justify calls for constant vigilance and the maintenance of a large surveillance and enforcement apparatus. The intelligence-security force is never accountable to the public. Instead, it

protects the privileges of the members of the regime and security apparatus itself (Waller 1994). In the counterintelligence state, all political and social dissent is identified as a threat to national security and a crime against the state.

In the past, counterintelligence states have been linked to the influence of the "dead hand of ideology" on state security organizations. In other words, ideology itself predetermines domestic and international threats to the state or regime; the nature, source, or severity of the threats to the nation is not something open to discussion or analysis under these circumstances. Steven David (1999), however, has developed a theory of "omnibalancing" that can also account for the rise of the counterintelligence state. David stands traditional realist notions of security on their head by suggesting that for many states, internal threats—not the military threat posed by other states—preoccupy national leaders. In these situations, political dissidents, rival ethnic or religious factions, or state institutions themselves (such as the military) pose the greatest threat to regime survival. The intelligence-security force thus becomes the premier government institution; senior intelligence officials often find themselves at the top of the ruling regime.

Third, scholars are interested in the degree to which intelligence organizations exist as independent institutions within a government and the degree to which they are held accountable by other bodies for their activities and performance. The counterintelligence state represents an extreme situation when intelligence work, national policy, and what amounts to "oversight" are fused into a single entity. Intelligence organizations, however, are subjected to different amounts of scrutiny and enjoy varying degrees of autonomy. Some intelligence agencies face judicial or legislative oversight that requires detailed and highly classified information about their activities. Others are subjected to less public oversight: Intelligence managers might simply have to offer general reports to some executive authority. Of related interest is the degree to which intelligence work emerges as a recognized profession within a state and the history and culture that shapes the way intelligence organizations operate.

Fourth, intelligence institutions vary in terms of the degree to which they conduct scientific and technical intelligence. Some maintain highly effective programs to reverse-engineer captured weapons or other items of military or industrial significance. Some intelligence organizations focus on economic espionage—gathering corporate secrets, product designs, and research results—to support domestic enterprises. Not all intelligence organizations apply traditional social science methodology in intelligence analysis. Some rely on espionage alone or on commercially or publicly available information to gain insights into their opponent's motivations and behavior. The *Komitet Gosudarstvennoy Bezopasnosti* (KGB), for example, maintained a minimum analytic capability and relied on espionage for insights into current events. The KGB often delivered this raw intelligence directly to senior Soviet officials. This lack of analytical capability sometimes led to bizarre activities. In the weeks leading up to the Cuban Missile Crisis, Soviet agents fanned out across Washington trying to pick up bits of information about the Kennedy Administration's response to the Soviet decision to deploy long-range nuclear-armed missiles to Cuba. It was unlikely, however, that officials would be discussing Soviet missile deployments to Cuba—especially if the missiles remained, as the Soviets intended, hidden from the prying eyes of U S. reconnaissance capabilities. It is difficult to accept, but one of the world's largest intelligence organizations relied on overheard loose talk in D.C. bars and bistros as its primary mode of "analysis."

Fifth, scholars often classify intelligence organizations in terms of their collaborative activities—that is, the nature and intensity of their relationships with foreign intelligence agencies. Most intelligence organizations maintain formal and informal contacts with friendly and even rival intelligence agencies. These channels are used to backstop normal diplomatic communications by providing secure methods of transmitting sensitive information, to conform to or explain formal and public diplomatic positions, or to communicate when normal diplomatic relations have been severed. Among allied governments, collaboration among intelligence agencies can be highly extensive, and in some instances—such as the war on terrorism—it is actually crucial to success. Governments often decide to share classified information, and intelligence professionals are usually charged with delivering these materials. Sometimes personnel in friendly intelligence agencies cannot resist the opportunity to exploit existing lines of communication to penetrate other intelligence organizations. For instance, in the mid-1980s, Israeli intelligence officers used Jonathan Pollard, a U.S. intelligence analyst who volunteered to spy for Israel, to obtain classified U.S. information that was not granted through formal intelligence channels.

SOME EXAMPLES OF FOREIGN INTELLIGENCE SERVICES

More information is publicly available about the U.S. intelligence community than about all other national intelligence agencies combined. It is difficult to say exactly what accounts for this state of affairs, but it can probably be attributed to American attitudes toward intelligence and government. Americans generally dislike secret organizations and secret government, while at the same time they are fascinated by the technical accomplishments and rumors of daring spies and covert operations undertaken by the intelligence community. All intelligence communities, however, are influenced by the specific history, culture, and legal setting in which they evolve. The three intelligence communities briefly described here—British, French, and Russian—are different, but each attempts to maintain internal security, foreign intelligence, and covert operations.

GREAT BRITAIN

The responsibility for intelligence oversight in Great Britain resides with the Cabinet (which represents the dominant party or coalition in Parliament). The prime minister is responsible for all of the country's intelligence agencies and chairs the Ministerial Committee on Intelligence Services. A Parliamentary Intelligence and Security Committee provides additional intelligence oversight and reports to the prime minister about once a year. The difference between external and internal intelligence operations in Great Britain is less distinct than it is in the United States, although in the aftermath of September 11 the separation of foreign and domestic intelligence operations within the United States is also beginning to break down. The British government, unlike the U.S. government, can exercise prior restraint when it comes to publication of articles that reveal classified information. In other words, the British government can take legal action to stop "leaks" before they make it into the press. British and U.S. intelligence services routinely share classified information.

There are three major organizations within the British intelligence community. MI5, also known as the Security Service, is primarily responsible for domestic security and surveillance. Its activities are directed against criminals, espionage, and terrorists. MI6, also known as the Secret Intelligence Service, collects and analyzes information about external threats. The British government also maintains a service similar to the U.S. National Security Agency, called the GCHQ (Government Communication Headquarters), which collects and analyzes signals intelligence.

FRANCE

Although intelligence oversight in Great Britain resembles the system in the United States to the extent that both the executive and legislative branches of government monitor events within the intelligence community, oversight procedures in France are weak and ill-defined. In the aftermath of the 1995 *Rainbow Warrior* incident, when French intelligence operatives blew up a Greenpeace vessel, killing one crew member, there was a renewed interest in intelligence oversight. A *Comité Interministerielle de Renseignement* (the Interministry Committee on Intelligence) was formed. Made up mainly of civil servants, its goal is primarily to collate intelligence analysis rather than "control" intelligence operations. There also is a parliamentary committee intended to provide some oversight, but in a strong presidential system, parliamentary committees are relatively benign. Part of the intelligence community reports to the Defense Ministry, while other parts report to the Minister of the Interior.

The French intelligence community consists of several organizations. The DSGE (*Direction Generate de la Securite Exteriure*, or General Directorate for External Security) is responsible for producing strategic estimates to support the foreign ministry, humint, sigint, clandestine operations, and economic espionage. The DSGE reports to the Defense Ministry. The DRM *(Directoire du Renseignement Militaire*, or Directorate of Military Intelligence) is responsible for supporting the French military. It also is responsible for technical intelligence and for conducting imagery analysis. The DPSD (*Directorire de la Protection et e la Securite de la Defense*, or Directorate for Defense Protection and Security) is responsible for observing the French military, with an eye toward monitoring its political reliability. In addition, French presidents sometimes form their own ad hoc or "private" intelligence cells to deal with especially sensitive issues.

RUSSIA

In the early 1990s, the KGB was divided into several agencies. The Federal Security Service (FSB—*Federal'naya Sluzba Besnopasnoti*) is responsible for domestic security and for counterintelligence. The Foreign Intelligence Service *(SVR—Sluzhba Vneshnei Razvedki)* is responsible for economic espionage, for humint, and for maintaining contacts with other foreign intelligence agencies. The SVR works with foreign intelligence organizations on halting black market trade in weapons of mass destruction and precursor materials, conducting the war on terrorism, stopping the drug trade, and combating organized crime and money laundering. The SVR also serves as a liaison with the intelligence services of several former Soviet republics, including Azerbaijan and Belarus. The Federal Border Service (FPS—*Federal'naya Pogranichnaya Sluzhba)* conducts security operations, intelligence gathering, and counterintelligence along Russia's borders. It also focuses on counter-drug operations to stop the movement of illicit drugs into and through Russia. In addition to these major intelligence services, about eight other agencies supply paramilitary, police, and special operations units to supplement intelligence and security operations.

The Soviet Union was the quintessential counterintelligence state, the merger of intelligence, security, and policymaking bodies that inspired John Dziak to coin the term in the 1980s. Given this history, it is not surprising that intelligence oversight has barely taken hold inside the emerging Russian democracy. According to Mark Kramer, the large Russian intelligence community is only partially accountable to elected officials:

> Most observers inside and outside Russia agree that democratic control of the intelligence/security complex is tenuous at best and, in some cases, nonexistent. Russia's intelligence and security forces enjoy extraordinary powers both formal and informal to act on their own. Although greater democratic oversight will not necessarily ensure that Russia's intelligence and security agencies are used for purposes conducive to democracy, the lack of democratic control all but guarantees that grave abuses will occur. (Kramer 2002, 1)

The path toward democratic oversight of intelligence services is even less clear-cut in other former Soviet Republics. Kramer (2002) notes that intelligence organizations have been used for partisan political purposes in Ukraine, Belarus, Georgia, Armenia, Azerbaijan, Central Asia, and Moldova.

THE READINGS

In the selections that follow, our authors provide insights into the history, culture, and capabilities of the national intelligence communities they survey. Alexander Orlov, a former Soviet intelligence officer, provides a look into the Soviet intelligence community. The Soviets took a dim view of open-source intelligence, intelligence analysis, and even the process of fusion—combining information from a variety of sources to create "all-source" intelligence. Instead, they operated on the idea that real intelligence was based on obtaining access to other nation's secrets. They also tried to play an active role misdirecting the finished intelligence produced by competing intelligence organizations. Orlov's description of Soviet intelligence highlights the role of national and bureaucratic culture in shaping the practice of intelligence.

The final selection, by Percy Cradock, offers a nuanced assessment of the performance of the British intelligence community in the second half of the twentieth century. Intelligence professionals may help make history; but, Cradock notes, the march of events and the resulting record of intelligence failures and successes also shape intelligence organizations.

38. THE SOVIET INTELLIGENCE COMMUNITY

ALEXANDER ORLOV

Soviet intelligence activities focused on espionage, tradecraft, and covert operations. More than anything else, secrets stolen or obtained by clandestine agents were most prized by the Soviets. Notice how this former Soviet insider takes a dim view of open-source intelligence and analysis. For the Soviets, real intelligence was based on stealing other people's secrets.

Like the Western intelligence services, the Russians get information about foreign states from two principal sources, from secret informants and undercover agents and from legitimate sources such as military and scientific journals, published reference material, and records of parliamentary debates. But the Russians regard as true intelligence (razvedka) only the first type of information, that procured by undercover agents and secret informants in defiance of the laws of the foreign country in which they operate. Information obtained from legitimate sources and publications they consider mere research data. In the eyes of Russian officers it takes a real man to do the creative and highly dangerous work of underground intelligence on foreign soil, while the digging up of research data in the safety of the home office or library can be left to women or young lieutenants just beginning their careers. The Western intelligence services, on the other hand, treat both types of information as intelligence, often with a much higher regard for research than for undercover work.

FUNDAMENTAL DOCTRINE

It is in these variant attitudes toward the two types of information that the difference between Soviet and Western intelligence doctrine begins to emerge. The difference is not just a theoretical one; in practice it affects every phase of intelligence activity from operational planning and choice of strategy to evaluation of the reliability of information procured and its importance to policy makers.

Both Soviet and Western intelligence services strive to learn the secret intentions, capabilities, and strategic plans of other states, but they don't go about it in the same way. The Russians believe that such important secrets can and should be procured directly from the classified files in offices of the government in question and from informants among its civil servants. When the Russians suspect that another country is trying to form a coalition directed against the Soviet Union, they don't seek information about it in newspaper editorials, panel discussions, or historical precedents, although all these sources may shed some light on the matter; they set out to steal the secret diplomatic correspondence between the conspiring states or to recruit an informant on the staff of the negotiators if they don't have one there already. When the Russians want to know the number of bombers in the air force of a potential adversary, they get the figure, not by doing library research on the productive capability of airplane plants or assembling educated guesses and rumors, but by asking their secret informers within the foreign air force or war ministry and by stealing the desired information from government files.

The Americans, on the other hand, and to a certain extent the British, prefer to rely more heavily on legitimately accessible documents. The American intelligence agencies are said to monitor as many as five million words daily—the equivalent of 50 books of average length—from foreign radio broadcasts alone. From enormous quantities of open material like this, analysts derive a lot of information about foreign countries, their economies and finance, their industries, agriculture, and trade, their population and social trends, their educational and political systems, the structure of their governments, their leaders' past lives and present views, etc. Drawing on that colossal warehouse of encyclopedic data, intelligence officers write reports and compose national estimates of foreign countries for the benefit of policy makers.

Admiral Ellis Zacharias, Deputy Chief of Naval Intelligence in the last war, wrote that in the Navy 95% of peacetime intelligence was procured from legitimately accessible sources, another 4% from semi-open sources, and only 1% through secret agents. Another authority on American intelligence, Gen. William J. Donovan, who headed the Office of Strategic Services during the war, expressed the same predilection for "open sources" by saying that intelligence is not the "mysterious, even sinister" thing people think it is, but more a matter of "pulling together myriad facts, making a pattern of them, and drawing inferences from that pattern." This predilection for open sources lies at the core of the American doctrine of intelligence.

But how can intelligence officers pick out from the vast amount of encyclopedic data that flows in to them the key developments for their purposes? One of the chiefs of American intelligence, a distinguished professor and noted scholar, had this to say on the subject:

> How can surveillance [of the world scene] assure itself of spotting…the really unusual? How can it be sure of putting the finger on the three things per week out of the thousands it observes and the millions that happen which are really of potential import? The answer is…procure the services of wise men—and wise in the subject—and *pray that their mysterious inner selves are of the kind which produce hypotheses of national importance.*

In the Russian view, such an approach is but one step removed from mysticism and metaphysics. What if the "mysterious inner selves" of the researchers and analysts fail to produce the right hypotheses? How safe is it, in general, to rely on hypotheses in matters of such profound complexity as world politics, where nothing is stable and enemies of yesterday become today's friends and fight together against their former allies? A hypothesis may be wisdom itself, yet turn out to be utterly wrong. Not only intelligence officers but statesmen of the highest caliber have time and again been proved wrong in acting on undeniably wise hypotheses.

In 1940–41 Stalin based his strategy on the calculation that Hitler would not attack the Soviet Union. He knew that it was not in Germany's interests to get into a two-front war, and he thought that Hitler understood this too. In the spring of 1941 the British Joint Intelligence Committee also estimated that Hitler would not be so foolish as to add the powerful Soviet Union to his formidable enemies in the West. But these logical hypotheses went up in all-too-real smoke on 22 June that year.

Stalin, who was his own intelligence boss and liked to take a personal part in the cloak-and-dagger business, warned his intelligence chiefs time and again to keep away from hypotheses and "equations with many unknowns" and concentrate instead on acquiring well-placed informants and access to the secret vaults of foreign governments. He used to say, "An intelligence hypothesis may become your hobby horse on which you will ride straight into a self-made trap." He called it "dangerous guesswork." In 1932 he had ordered that our quarterly intelligence surveys of foreign countries no longer be sent him. Although based on secret data, these surveys were interspersed with unsubstantiated hypotheses and subjective views; they corresponded roughly to the national estimates which the American intelligence agencies produce for the National Security Council. After that the NKVD sent him the cream of raw intelligence only—summaries of important documents stolen from other governments and reports from exceptionally valuable secret informants like foreign ambassadors and general staff officers.

During his periodic conferences with the chiefs of the intelligence services Stalin would often interject: "Don't tell me what you think, give me the facts and the source." But sometimes he would violate his own rule and ask one or another intelligence chief for an opinion. Such was the case during a joint conference which Stalin and Voroshilov had in the summer of 1936 with the chiefs of the NKVD and the Red Army intelligence Department. Stalin asked Artouzov, deputy chief of military intelligence, "With whom would Poland side in a war between Germany, Italy, and Japan on the one side and Russia, France, and England on the other?" Without hesitation Artouzov answered: "Poland will always be with France and England." "You are a jackass," retorted Stalin. "If Poland didn't side with Germany against us, she would be crushed by the German mechanized divisions on their way to the Soviet Union and would not live to see another day, whereas if she allied herself with Germany she could hope to expand if things went well, and if things went badly she might still get a negotiated settlement." Artouzov did not live to see his illogical prediction come true; he was shot in the great purge, in 1937.

In the Soviet Union research on publicly accessible materials is conducted by the Academy of Sciences, the universities, the scientific journals, and the Ministries of Foreign Affairs, Industry, Trade, Finance, and Statistics. The NKVD based its work 100% on secret sources and undercover agents. The Main Intelligence Department of the Army did study some legitimately accessible sources, but only those dealing with military matters, such as foreign military and scientific journals, army and navy manuals, military textbooks, topographic explorations, and anything printed anywhere about the armed forces of the world. But even in army intelligence the main efforts, at least 80% Jof the total, were concentrated on building and operating networks of secret informants and on the procurement of secret documents.

Had the Soviet intelligence agencies put their main efforts and resources into building up encyclopedias of world-wide information from overt sources and on processing and analyzing that enormous amount of incoming raw material, they would have never been able to acquire the secrets of the manufacture of the atomic and hydrogen bombs or the blueprints of the American nuclear-powered submarines or to infiltrate the key departments of the American, British, and European governments. Important state secrets and especially clues to the intentions and plans of potential enemies cannot be found in libraries or encyclopedias, but only where they are kept under lock and key. The task of intelligence services is to acquire the keys and deliver the secrets to their governments, thus providing them with the foreknowledge and orientation needed for the making of decisions.

When General Douglas MacArthur, who had been blamed for not having foreseen certain developments in the Korean War, was asked by the Senate investigating committee in 1951 to explain why the North Korean invasion caught the Americans by surprise, he gave a classic reply from which many an intelligence chief could take his cue. He said:

> I don't see how it would have been humanly possible for any man or group of men to predict such an attack as that...*There is nothing, no means or methods, except the accidental spy methods—if you can get somebody to betray the enemy's highest circles, that can get such information as that.* It is guarded with a secrecy that you cannot overestimate.

Thus, under the fire of the investigation, General MacArthur, who was not an expert in intelligence, arrived with excellent logic at an idea which touches the very heart of the intelligence problem. "There is nothing, no means or methods, except...spy methods...that can get such information as that." This is the essence of the Soviet doctrine of intelligence.

POLITICAL INTELLIGENCE

While The Main Intelligence Department (GRU) of the Soviet Ministry of Defense does only military intelligence, the Foreign Directorate of the Committee of State Security (KGB), successor to the NKVD, is actively engaged in at least seven lines of intelligence and related work, not counting sabotage and guerrilla warfare.

The first line, which is considered the most important, is the so-called diplomatic intelligence, the purpose of which is to keep the Soviet government informed of the secret deals between the governments of capitalistic countries and of the true intentions and contemplated moves of each of these governments toward the Soviet Union. This information is to be procured from primary sources within the secret councils of the foreign governments. The principal sources are the following: foreign diplomats, including ambassadors; the staffs of foreign ministries, including code clerks, secretaries, etc.; private secretaries to members of the cabinet; members of parliaments; and ambitious politicians seeking financial aid and left wing support. The life history of such officials is studied beginning with their school years, and their character traits, weaknesses and vices, and intimate lives and friendships are analyzed with the purpose of finding the Achilles' heel of each and securing the right approach to him through the right person, say a former classmate, intimate friend, or relative.

These well-prepared approaches have often paid off. Some politicians have been lured into the Soviet network by promises that the Soviet Union would use its secret levers of influence in their countries to further their political fortunes. Such promises have often been accompanied by "subsidies," ostensibly to promote goodwill toward Russia but in reality a bribe. A number of high officials have succumbed to outright offers of money. Others, especially those who in their youth had belonged to Fabian and other idealistic circles, were influenced by humanitarian arguments and persuaded that they must help the Soviet Union stop the march of fascism. Considerable success was achieved among foreign diplomats tinted with homosexual perversions; it is no secret that the biggest concentration of homosexuals can be found in the diplomatic services of Western countries. Those of these who agreed to work for the Russian network were instructed to approach other homosexual members of the diplomatic corps, a strategy which was remarkably successful. Even when those approached declined the offer to collaborate, they would not denounce the recruiter to the authorities. Soviet intelligence officers were amazed at the mutual consideration and true loyalty which prevailed among homosexuals.

It is usually supposed easier to lure into the Soviet network a code clerk or secretary than a diplomat or statesman; a man in an important government position is expected to know better than to take the road of treachery, and he has much more to lose if caught doing so. The experience of Soviet intelligence has in many instances, however, not borne out this view. Honesty and loyalty may often be more deeply ingrained in simple and humble people than in men of high position. A man who took bribes when he was a patrolman does not turn honest when he becomes the chief of police; the only thing that changes is the size of the bribe. Weakness of character, inability to withstand temptation, light-mindedness, wishful thinking, and bad judgment are also traits that accompany a man to the highest rungs of his career.

The consensus of Soviet intelligence chiefs has been that departmental and private secretaries in a foreign ministry are often more valuable as sources of information than an ambassador, because a well-placed secretary can supply documentary data on a wider scale, covering the policies of the foreign government toward a number of countries. An ambassador is considered a much bigger prize, however, because he can be used not only as a source of information but also as a competent consultant for the Russian Foreign Office and even as an agent who can influence to a certain extent the foreign policy of his government.

The second line of Soviet intelligence activity is to procure data on the military posture of Western and other countries, the quality and strength of their armies, navies, and air forces, their degree of mechanization, mobility, fire power, technological advancement, and modernization, and the productive capacity of the armament industries and the mobilization plans of the big powers. Soviet intelligence watches with a jealous eye every new invention in the field of arms and tries to steal it while it is still in the blueprint stage or on the drawing board so that Soviet inventors and engineers can be the first to apply it. With the advent of the nuclear and rocketry age, which has completely revolutionized the material base, strategy, and very concept of warfare, Soviet intelligence strains all its efforts to obtain immediate information on the progress being made by the leading Western countries in these advanced fields and to gauge the striking and retaliatory power of the Western world.

As we have said, the KGB does not look for this information in public documents. Neither is it interested in monitoring foreign radio transmissions and distilling from them crumbs of random information. It procures the military secrets of foreign governments from the classified files of the general staffs of those countries, from the secret reports of foreign defense ministries, from military research laboratories and proving grounds, and so it knows that what it gets represents, even if incompletely, the true facts on which Soviet policy makers can confidently base their decisions.

In wartime, military intelligence becomes the principal function of every branch of the Intelligence Directorate of the KGB. The main task of its field posts, its underground *residenturas* abroad, is then to inform the Soviet government by radio and other means about the war plans of the enemy, his troop concentrations and movements, the size of his uncommitted reserves in men and materiel, and the extent of the damage inflicted on the enemy by the air forces of the Soviet Union and its allies. Diplomatic intelligence concentrates the efforts of its informants and secret agents on watching the relations among the governments of the enemy coalition, with special emphasis on frictions among them. The residenturas must keep a sharp eye also on Russia's allies in the war, immediately signaling to the Soviet government if an ally puts out peace feelers and is gravitating toward a separate peace with the enemy. It may be recalled that during World War II the Kremlin sounded an alarm when it intercepted rumors that British representatives were about to meet in Franco's Spain with emissaries of Hitler. During the worst days of the last war, when Russia's defenses were crumbling and the Western allies were slow in opening a second front, there were moments when the Western leaders were jittery at the thought that Stalin might try to save what was left of the country by making a separate peace with Germany.

While the residenturas abroad keep the government informed of the enemy's grand strategy and his capabilities and vulnerabilities, day-to-day tactical or combat intelligence is taken care of by the intelligence sections of the Soviet armed forces and by the special detachments (Osoby Otdel) of the KGB attached to all army units down to the regimental level. It is their duty to supply the Soviet commander with data on the size, disposition, and fighting strength of the enemy force with which the troops under his command will soon be locked in battle. The standard sources of military intelligence are supplemented by material obtained in raids the KGB guerrilla detachments make on enemy headquarters, by ground and aerial photo reconnaissance, and by the interrogation of prisoners, refugees, and spies who pose as refugees.

ECONOMIC WARFARE

The third line of Soviet intelligence is called economic intelligence, which contrary to what might be supposed has little to do with studying the economy of foreign countries. It was created for the purposes of exercising State control over Soviet export and import operations and of protecting Soviet foreign trade from the pressures and abuses of international cartels and other organizations of monopolistic capital.

In the 1930's, for instance, the Division of Economic Intelligence discovered that the biggest electric concerns of the world had entered into a "gentlemen's agreement" according to which they would not compete with each other in their dealings with Soviet Russia and would overcharge her on purchases up to 75% over current world prices. I myself saw a letter signed by the vice president of General Electric Co. addressed to the presidents of the German AEG and the Swiss Brown Bovery Co. which contained a list of prices made up especially for the Soviet Union 60 to 75% higher than the regular market prices. General Electric tried to justify this extortion by pointing out that Russia's credit standing was "not too good." The gentlemen's agreement was finally broken up by the Soviet government, but not before Soviet trade had suffered losses totaling tens of millions of dollars.

PLANTS

The fourth line of Soviet intelligence is misinformation. The Soviet government is interested not only in obtaining information about the policies and impending moves of other countries but also in misinforming and misleading the foreign governments concerning its own position and intentions. But whereas in procuring secret information from abroad the intelligence officer is given free rein to steal whatever he considers valuable, the task of misinforming the outer world about the Soviet Union cannot be left to the discretion of the individual officer or even of the intelligence service as a whole. What false information or rumors should be deviously placed within earshot of some foreign government is a question of high policy, since the purpose is to induce this government to do what the Kremlin wants it to do, perhaps to bluff it into inaction or into making a concession. In this area, therefore, Soviet intelligence cannot act without specific directives as to the substance of the misinformation and the way it should be planted.

When in the 1930's, for instance, the Soviet government wanted to obtain a mutual defense treaty with France in order to counteract the growing menace of Hitler's Germany, Soviet intelligence was given instructions to introduce into French General Staff channels certain pages from a German army report which showed that Germany was planning to occupy the Rhineland at the beginning of 1936 and invade France within eighteen months after that. Similarly, at about this same time, an effort was made to shake England out of her complacency by slipping into British intelligence channels (through a German double agent) inflated figures concerning German aircraft production; these created quite a stir in the highest councils of the British government. Here the task of the misinformation desk of the NKVD had been to fabricate ostensible photocopies of the German documents with such skill that they would seem genuine even to trained military experts.

During the Spanish civil war, in which a Russian tank brigade fought against the forces of General Franco and Russian pilots flew the newest and best Soviet fighter planes (I-15 and 1–16) and medium bombers (CB) against the German air squadrons supporting him, the misinformation desk was ordered to introduce into German military intelligence channels the information that these Soviet planes were not of the latest design, that Russia had in her arsenal thousands of planes of second and third succeeding generations possessing much greater speed and higher ceiling. In August 1937 German experts had examined and tested two Soviet I-16 fighters when they landed by mistake on an enemy air strip in the Madrid sector, and they had been amazed at the quality and performance of the planes, which in some respects surpassed German fighters. Now the false information that the Russians had on the production line still better and more modern models served Stalin's evident aim of impressing upon Hitler that the Soviet Union was better armed than he thought and that it would be wiser for Germany to have Russia as a partner than as an opponent.

PENETRATION

The fifth line of Soviet intelligence is infiltration into the security agencies and intelligence services of foreign countries. This activity holds a special challenge and a peculiar fascination for Soviet intelligence officers. Although they regard foreign intelligence officers as mercenary spies (while thinking of themselves as devoted revolutionaries carrying out dangerous assignments for the Party), the Soviet officers do have a feeling of kinship with them and react to an encounter with one of them with the same thrill and curiosity that enemy fighter pilots feel on sighting each other across a space of sky. Their hostile attitude toward their foreign counterparts becomes sincerely friendly the moment the latter begin to cooperate as informants.

The principal aims pursued in infiltrating foreign security agencies are the following: to find out what these agencies know about Soviet intelligence operations in the country in question; to determine whether they have succeeded in planting counterspies in the Soviet network or in recruiting anyone connected with the residentura; to learn in good time of any intended arrests of network personnel; and to use their facilities to check up on persons in whom the Soviet residentura happens to be interested. The penetration of foreign *intelligence* services is done to find out whether they have succeeded in creating a spy network in Soviet Russia, and if so who these spies are, what secret information they have transmitted, and what lines of communication they use.

In some of the Western countries, furthermore, the intelligence services have access to the confidential papers of other departments of the government, including defense and foreign affairs. This practice is justified on the ground that it helps them evaluate the information from their own secret sources abroad and render more accurate estimates of the intentions and capabilities of other countries. Whatever the merits of this argument, the NKVD was quick to take advantage of the resulting convenient concentration in one place of secret documents from several government departments; it instructed its residenturas abroad to try to procure from the intelligence services not only their own information but also that which they receive from other government departments, for example military attache reports and the political analyses and estimates of ambassadors.

Although the intelligence services of different capitalistic countries do not always have harmonious relations with one another, thanks to national rivalry and personal jealousies, they do cooperate with one another to a certain extent in combating Soviet espionage and subversion. Some of them exchange information in this field, forwarding to each other photographs of known or suspected Soviet spies. Soviet acquisition of this correspondence reveals what they know about Russian intelligence activities and may sometimes warn of an impending exposure and arrest of an agent. In my time, however, the secret information procured from foreign intelligence services rarely gave us cause for alarm. Much of it was incompetent and out of date. As a rule the strength of the Soviet armed forces was ridiculously belittled. The reports on Soviet espionage activities were based more on hindsight than foresight, and they frequently contained outright fantasies concocted by unscrupulous doubles and falsifiers. But though much of the information collected by the foreign intelligence services about Russia was found to be worthless, it was by no means worthless to Soviet intelligence to know about this.

It is generally said that knowledge of two things is indispensable to the charting of foreign policy in a time of crisis—the real power of one's own country and the power of the potential enemy. But to these a third must be added: one must also know what image one's own power creates in the eyes of the adversary. This is very important, because however distorted that image, it is what he is going to act upon. By infiltrating the intelligence services of foreign countries Soviet intelligence can learn and report to policy makers how each country assesses the capabilities and deficiencies of the Soviet Union. It is then up to the policy makers to figure out what mistakes the potential enemy will be likely to make when the chips are down as a result of the distortions in his view of the Soviet Union as a world power.

The infiltration of a foreign intelligence service is a much more hazardous operation than the acquisition of informants in other government departments, because the foreign intelligence officers are wise to such practices and may maneuver the recruiting officer into a trap or grab him outright before he can get away. The KGB therefore advises its residenturas not to rush things but to approach and cultivate first a friend or relative of the target officer and use him as a go-between. Then ʾbe actual recruiting and all meetings until the recruited officer has proved his sincerity (by turning over important information) should take place on territory outside the jurisdiction of the target country.

The safest way to infiltrate a foreign intelligence service without fear of being trapped is to transplant a completely reliable agent into that organization, for example to induce an old and trusted informant in some other branch of the government to seek employment with the intelligence service. Sometimes it may be necessary for him first to cultivate socially for this purpose a senior officer of the intelligence service. Agents planted in a foreign intelligence service can be used not only to procure secret information but also as a channel through which misinformation about the Soviet Union and other countries can be introduced.

The intelligence and security services of none of the big world powers have escaped infiltration by Soviet agents. Gen. Walter Bedell Smith, as head of the CIA, was aware of Soviet successes in this field, and in September 1953 he expressed his apprehension in the following words: "I believe the communists are so adroit and adept that they have infiltrated practically every security agency of the government."

POLITICAL ACTION

The sixth line of Soviet intelligence is to influence the decisions of foreign governments through secret agents occupying important positions within them. In the last two decades there have been quite a few instances in which highly placed Soviet secret agents were able to tip the scales of policy in favor of the Soviet Union. Some of these agents started out as junior diplomats in the foreign offices of the West and climbed with the help of their socially prominent families to high government positions. Others were already mature politicians and statesmen when they were seduced by money and other base considerations. One of the leading members of Mussolini's cabinet and the Fascist Grand Council succumbed

to an offer of money and agreed to collaborate with Soviet Russia.

A leading member of the parliament of a mid-European country, who was not thought to be a friend of the Soviet Union, would meet secretly with the Soviet ambassador and take his instructions concerning the position he should assume in certain matters affecting Soviet interests. In another European country an inspector of the national secret police, who had become a Soviet informant, reported the police had documentary proof that an influential member of the cabinet was a partner in a big narcotics ring and owned, together with a famous racketeer, a luxury brothel a few blocks away from the presidential palace in the center of the capital. This minister was so powerful in the councils of the government, as well as in the underworld, that the head of the secret police was afraid to tangle with him. Moscow ordered the residentura to steal all the incriminating documents, and photographs of them were shown to the minister at the Soviet embassy, as a "friendly gesture," by the soviet ambassador himself, who happened to be a former chief of the Foreign Department of the OGPU, i.e. of Soviet intelligence. The friendly gesture was well understood, and it inaugurated a period of close collaboration between the minister and Soviet intelligence. His task was not merely to provide information but to influence the policies of his government as directed by the Soviet Foreign Commissariat.

Another type of KGB political action is to pave the way in ticklish international matters for later negotiations between the Soviet Foreign Office and other governments. If exploratory talks conducted, directly or through go-betweens, by Soviet intelligence agents with representatives of a foreign government produce results satisfactory to both sides, the official diplomats of both countries can then take over. If not, the Kremlin remains free to disclaim any knowledge of them. A Russian intelligence officer by the name of Ostrovsky who had secretly negotiated the establishment of diplomatic relations with Roumania became the first Soviet ambassador to that country.

Another activity along this line consists of clandestine attempts to induce leaders of a political opposition to stage a coup d'etat and take over the government. The inducement would be a promise of political and financial support and, if the state happened to border on Soviet territory, military aid as well. In 1937, for instance, one of the chiefs of intelligence was commissioned by Stalin personally to enter into secret negotiations with former Roumanian Minister of Foreign Affairs Titulesku, who lived at that time in Menton, on the Franco-Italian border, and persuade him to overthrow the reactionary regime of Prime Minister Maniu. Stalin offered financial and military aid against a promise by Titulesku that upon assumption of power he would sign a mutual assistance pact with the Soviet Union.

INDUSTRIAL INTELLIGENCE

Although intelligence activity is as old as society, this seventh line of Soviet operation is something new, first begun in 1929. Its purpose was to assist in the industrialization of the Soviet Union by stealing production secrets—new inventions, secret technological processes, etc.—from the advanced countries of Europe and America. Soviet intelligence organizations abroad began to recruit engineers, scientists, and inventors working in the laboratories and plants of the big industrial concerns of the world.

At this time the Soviet Union, besides buying big quantities of machinery and even whole plants from the industrial companies of the West, negotiated with them for the purchase of patents and the know-how for production processes. A number of such purchases were made and foreign engineers came to instruct the Russians in the application of the new methods. But often, when the price demanded by foreign concerns for their "technical aid" was too high—it always ran into many millions of dollars—the head of the Soviet government would challenge the Foreign Department of the NKVD to steal the secrets in question from them. The response to these challenges was invariably enthusiastic, and after a number of them had been successfully met the new Division for Industrial Intelligence was created within the NKVD Foreign Department.

Sometimes the theft of all the necessary formulas, blueprints, and instructions would still not enable Soviet engineers and inventors to construct a complicated mechanism or duplicate a production process. They would need the human component, the special skill or engineering know-how. In such cases officers of the Division for Industrial Intelligence would, with offers of additional rewards, persuade the appropriate foreign engineers to make a secret trip to Russia to instruct the Russian engineers or supervise the laboratory experiments on the spot. Precautions were taken to insure that the traveler's passport should not bear

any border stamps or other traces of his visit to the Soviet Union: the engineer would travel with his own passport only to the capital of an adjacent country, where he would turn it over for safekeeping to the local Soviet agent and get from him a false one on which he would proceed to Russia; then on the return trip he would turn this in and pick up the genuine passport where he had left it. The fees paid by the Russians for such trips ran sometimes as high as ten thousand dollars for a few days, but the savings realized amounted to millions of dollars. The following is a typical such operation.

A WORM TURNS

In view of the fact that the Soviet government was spending huge sums of money on industrial diamonds needed for the expanding oil industry, metallurgy, and various geological projects, it was naturally interested in an offer made by the German Krupp concern to supply newly invented artificial diamonds almost as hard and good as natural ones. The new product was named "vidi" from the German *wie Diamant*, "like diamond." The Commissariat of Heavy Industry bought some of the vidi, tested them in drilling operations, and was amazed at their high quality. It decided to buy the patent from Krupp and have German engineers build a plant to produce them in the Soviet Union.

Soon a delegation of German experts headed by two Krupp directors arrived in Moscow. Knowing how badly the Russians needed industrial diamonds for the five-year plan, they demanded a staggering price for this technical aid. When the deal was being discussed at the Politburo Stalin turned to the head of the NKVD and said: "The bastards want too much money. Try to steal it from them. Show what the NKVD can do!" This challenge was taken up eagerly, and one of the chiefs of the Foreign Department was charged with the operation.

The first step was to find out the location of the vidi factory and the names of the inventor and the engineers in charge of production. This task was assigned to a German agent, scientist Dr. B. In the Berlin Technische Hochschule, with which he was associated, Dr. B. looked up all the available treatises on achieving hard metal alloys and then approached a noted professor who had written some of them. From him he learned that a Krupp inventor had succeeded in attaining the hardest alloy known and that this was being produced in a plant on the outskirts of Berlin.

Dr. B. now went to the site of the plant and dropped in at a beer hall frequented by its technical personnel. After visiting the place a few times, he engaged some of the technicians in conversation. He represented himself as a scientist who was writing a book on hard metal alloys. "Oh, then you are working with our Cornelius," said one technician. Dr. B. said no, but he had known a Professor Cornelius. "No," said the technician, "he is not a professor, he is only a foreman in our plant, but he is a man who could teach the professors how to make industrial diamonds."

Through an inspector of the Berlin Polizei Presidium, another secret Soviet informant, the Russian residentura obtained information on Cornelius, including his home address, and the next day Dr. B. rang the doorbell there. He was admitted by Cornelius' wife, who told him that her husband had not yet returned from the plant. This Dr. B. knew; he had come early on purpose, hoping to learn something about Cornelius from his wife. He told her that he was a Doctor of Science and was writing a treatise on hard metal alloys and that his colleagues at the Technische Hochschule advised him to see Herr Cornelius, who might be helpful to him. He added that if Herr Cornelius was really an expert in that field and if he was willing to contribute to the research he might earn some money on the side.

Frau Cornelius, flattered that a scientist from the famous Technische Hochschule should come to seek advice from her husband and stimulated by the prospect of earning extra money, began to praise her husband's abilities and high reputation at the plant. She said that the engineer who had invented the process for producing artificial diamonds had trusted only her husband, because he alone knew how to handle the specially built electric oven, and now that the inventor had fallen out with Krupp and quit, her husband was practically in charge of the whole thing. He could demand from Krupp any salary he wanted, and they would have to give it to him; but he was not that kind of man. For him devotion to the company came first.

When Cornelius returned home Dr. B. restated the purpose of his visit and, in order to underscore his purely scientific interest in the matter and allay any possible suspicion, invited him to his personal room at the Technische Hochschule for the following Saturday. On Saturday, after a talk at the Hochschule, he took him for dinner to his luxurious ten room flat in the eight-story apartment house

which he had inherited from his father. He had seen at once that Cornelius was too illiterate technologically to be able to explain in scientific terms the secrets of production, even if he wanted to. He was only a foreman trained by the inventor to operate the oven. What Dr. B. wanted was to find out the name of the inventor, his whereabouts, and the history of his break with the Krupp concern. After an excellent dinner and a few glasses of brandy, Cornelius enjoyed telling the story to his genial host.

The inventor's name was Worm. When he saw what fabulous prices Krupp was getting for the industrial diamonds which he had created and which cost the company so little, he decided to build secretly a plant of his own and realize some of these profits for himself. He borrowed money from the bank, rented a little shop, made an oven like the one he had constructed for Krupp, installed the minimum equipment needed, and made a few profitable sales of vidi to foreign customers. With the proceeds of these he was able to pay off part of the loan, and it looked as though he was on the way to becoming a rich man. But at this point the Krupp concern learned about his disloyal competition and swooped down on him with all the fury of an industrial giant. He was summarily fired. Customers were warned that if they bought a single ounce of vidi from him Krupp would never sell them anything. The bank suddenly became rigid and demanded prompt repayment. In spite of his talents as an engineer and inventor Worm could not find work. All doors were politely but firmly closed in his face.

Dr. B. hurried to see Herr Worm. Here too, he contrived to ring the doorbell when the man was not at home; he had found that women are more talkative than men, especially when they have an opportunity to do a bit of advertising for their husbands. Frau Worm was overjoyed that someone was interesting himself in her husband. The Krupps were brutes, she said; they ruled the country. Her husband was a martyr. They had driven him to desperation. All his savings had gone into the enterprise, and it was ruined with one blow.

Dr. B. listened to her story with unfeigned sympathy. He said he had an interesting proposition for her husband which might get him out of his difficulties. From that moment he became her trusted friend, the man who was going to save her husband from strangulation by the Krupps. He left his telephone number for Worm to call.

The next day they met at the Technische Hochschule and from there went to Dr. B.'s apartment.

Dr. B. suggested that in order to escape from the Krupp stranglehold Worm would have to offer his talents to a foreign concern. He said he knew a big Scandinavian company which might be interested in acquiring the secret process of vidi production and entering the field in competition with Krupp; he would check. A few days later he informed Worm that the company was definitely interested; it had authorized him to advance the inventor up to ten thousand German marks. He asked Worm to submit a description of the vidi production process and furnish data on equipment needed, cost, etc.

For the time being, Dr. B. declined to name the company. This did not necessarily look suspicious, because as a go between he was entitled to a commission and would need to protect his own interests. But Worm got a strange hunch. "I want to warn you," he said, "that if my invention is needed for the Russians I will have nothing to do with them!" Dr. B., taken aback, hastened to reassure him that it was a Scandinavian concern all right. It turned out that Worm was a fanatical Nazi and Russian-hater.

Something had to be done to overcome that burning hatred if Worm was to be maneuvered into giving his vidi invention to Russia. While he was writing up his process Dr. B. would supplement the advance, giving him another thousand marks every week or so, which delighted Frau Worm. He also had the Worms several times for dinner at his home. When Frau Worm wanted to buy things which she had been denying to herself for long, but her husband kept too wary an eye on his dwindling advances, Dr. B. sensed this and immediately came to her assistance. He privately gave her money for herself with the understanding that she would repay it when her husband struck it rich; he was convinced that a prosperous future was just around the corner for them.

Worm's description of his process was sent to Moscow. After a close study, the Russian engineers declared that without the personal guidance of the inventor they would have trouble constructing and operating the special oven required; it was supposed to make several thousand revolutions a minute under an enormously high temperature. Moscow wanted to have the inventor at any cost. Now the friendship Dr. B. had cultivated with Frau Worm paid off. She cajoled her husband and wrangled with him for a whole week arid at last brought him to the realization that they had no choice, that this was their last and only chance.

The Soviet trade delegation in Berlin signed an official two-year contract with Worm, under which he received a flat sum in German currency, a monthly allowance in marks for his wife—who preferred to remain in Germany—and a salary for himself in Russian rubles. He was entitled to a suite in a first-class Moscow hotel with restaurant and other services and to a chauffeured automobile and two vacations in Germany per year at Russia's expense. He took with him to Moscow a German engineer by the name of Mente who had been his assistant at the Krupp plant.

Worm's letters to his wife breathed hatred toward everything Russian. He contracted rheumatic fever during his stay and returned to Germany a broken and embittered man. But he had fulfilled his contract with the Soviets to the letter, turning over to them his cherished brainchild, the priceless vidi process.

QUESTIONS FOR FURTHER DISCUSSION

1. Are there situations when access to an opponent's classified communications will not provide insights into future events?
2. Did the Soviets have any faith in intelligence analysis?
3. Who did the Soviets believe were the best people to target in their quest for classified information?
4. Has the information revolution made it easier to disseminate misinformation?

From Alexander Orlov, "The Theory and Practice of Soviet Intelligence," *Studies in Intelligence* Vol. 7 (Spring 1963): pp. 45–65.

39. THE BRITISH EXPERIENCE WITH INTELLIGENCE

PERCY CRADOCK

In this essay, Cradock assesses the performance of British Intelligence since World War II. Weaved into this assessment is a description of the limits of intelligence and a discussion of how the changing national fortunes of Great Britain in the second half of the twentieth century transformed the role of intelligence in the formulation of foreign policy. Cradock concludes that British intelligence passed the ultimate test: it outperformed its competitors.

In judging the performance of any intelligence organization we need first to come to a realistic understanding of the limits to intelligence. There is too often an exaggerated idea of what it can achieve and a corresponding readiness to criticize anything short of omniscience. It is commonly assumed that the outside world is knowable and that it is the function of the intelligence officer to know it, and know it in advance. Inability to do so is a fault and results in what is called an intelligence failure. This view, in extreme form, would have it that foreign state secrets are out there and attainable. They are arcane admittedly, a set of sibylline books, and expensive or dangerous to acquire; but they are intelligible, given the key. The pages can then be read and their content passed to the policy-makers.

To recognize how far this is from the reality of foreign affairs, needs only a moment's reflection. International dealings, even confined to the present tense, are infinitely variable, an amalgam of the fears, ambitions, collusions and contentions of the great cast of states that make up the international community. Little that happens is thoroughly foreordained and planned. Miscalculations abound. Governments are commonly acted upon rather than acting. The "events, dear boy, events" of Harold Macmillan's celebrated remark crowd in upon them.

If this is the present, the future is even more contingent and uncertain. Some facts about other states may be established with reasonable accuracy: their economic resources, the number of their tanks, aircraft and missiles, even perhaps the intangibles, such as organization and morale. Such facts are necessary, but in themselves insufficient. They are what one eminent American analyst called the "secrets," hidden but knowable, as opposed to the "mysteries," by their nature impenetrable. But it is on this second, much more elusive, category that a view has to be formed if intelligence estimates are to do their work; on the thinking that drives policy, above all, on the intentions of governments. These are the true *arcana imperii*; and, short of some extraordinary stroke of luck, or genius, they are likely to remain obscure. Intelligence targets are commonly closed societies; and even where this is not so, the foreign leaders themselves often do not see their way clearly, or determine it long in advance, and in most cases still prefer to keep their cards hidden.

To attempt a reading here calls for qualities very different from those needed in the earlier, factual stages of enquiry: a capacity, based on a careful study of culture, history and practice, to enter into the mind of a foreign leader and speculate in a relatively informed way on his likely reactions in certain situations. Such predictive assessment goes well beyond pure analysis: the "hard intelligence" to hand is usually fragmentary or ambiguous; this is much more a work of imaginative transference and, as such, highly fallible.

With time and study it is usually possible to construct a working model of the other side which will serve as a guide to likely behaviour. But this too is not without its risks. The analyst readily becomes attached to his creation, to his picture of Stalin, or Mao or Saddam, and prone to reject any new or awkward reports which do not fit his assumptions. We all become attached to our own views. But in the end these are only hypotheses; and what seem rules built on careful observation and induction can easily be overridden in special cases. So, in the Cuban crisis of 1962, the hitherto sound principle that the Russians would not expose their strategic missiles outside Soviet territory proved highly misleading.

Given such conditions, all that we can do, while seeking by all means available to read a foreign state's intentions, is to accept that in the last resort intelligence is an attempt to know the unknowable and scale down our expectations accordingly.

This recognition has been made harder by one historical fact, the extraordinary success of Allied intelligence against the Axis in the Second World War. This has set all successors an impossible standard. In that irrecoverable golden age of Western intelligence, Sigint ensured that the enemy's military dispositions and often his strategic intentions were laid out before Allied leaders as on an illuminated screen. But there was nothing remotely similar in the post-war era. There were successes against Third World targets, but, although James Bamford states that Soviet military communications were readable for a while after the war, the West did not have access to Soviet communications which would have revealed strategic thinking.[1] There was never again going to be anything like the intercepted Japanese telegram of 12 June 1941, reporting Hitler's determination to have done with Russian communism and enabling the JIC Chairman to bring his committee to a confident prediction of an early full-scale German assault on the Soviet Union. By contrast, the JIC and CIA analysts of the next generation found themselves excluded from knowledge of the other side's councils and reduced to picking up fragments from outside the fortress, by studying Soviet externals, the leaders' statements and Russian behaviour in Turkey and Iran, and thereby slowly constructing a plausible sketch of their adversary.

Memories of the wartime achievement have bedevilled judgements of intelligence performance, by policy-makers and media alike, ever since, raising unreal expectations. But, in fairness, it is only the second-best, post-1945 standards, not those of Ultra or Magic, that can be applied to the Joint Intelligence Committee's work in the period under review.

As we have seen, the Committee successfully discharged its main post-war task of identifying the chief threat to British interests and predicting the form Soviet policies could be expected to take. The work was helped by the insights of the embassy in Moscow and, above all, by Soviet conduct in Eastern and South-Eastern Europe, in Iran and, finally, in Germany. The full portrait took time, up to 1947–8 when the vital ideological element was added, but it was to the life and immensely influential in shaping the course of British and Allied policy in the early post-war years.

The Committee was surprised by the speed of Soviet atomic development but correct in identifying Soviet strategic caution, perhaps the most important single judgement of the period. In the first major postwar crisis, the Berlin blockade, though the Committee gave no formal warning, there was widespread expectation of pressure on the city, and precise details of the Russian plans for strangulation were probably not a practical target.

In the Korean War, there was at first a shortage of intelligence in London because of policy differences with the Americans, though it must be said that even if US assessments had been available, they would probably have been misleading. For various reasons both allies were in the dark. On the issue of Chinese involvement, the Committee came close to the truth at several points but in the end failed to predict large-scale intervention. The Chiefs of Staff, however, working on the basis of JIC material, gave ample notice, to the Cabinet and to Washington, of the impending danger. The JIC was correct in seeing China as a largely independent actor, not just a Soviet puppet, the US view, and supported the Chiefs and the government in their ultimately successful efforts to bring United States strategy down to earth.

Suez was a policy rather than an intelligence failure. In the nature of things, the Committee's warnings made little impact, but they read well in retrospect: Nasser's determination to make the Canal work; his ability to do so; Soviet caution; the dangers of even coincidence (let alone collusion) with Israel; the overriding need for a short, sharp victory if there was to be a military campaign; the unpleasant consequences if that were not achieved; the risks to Nuri's regime in Iraq. What they failed to point out was the illusory nature of military victory in Egypt, even if that could be brought about, and the resilience and independence of Arab nationalism. In this and the undue emphasis on military rather than political and economic responses to the problems of the area the Committee was a creature of its time.

In the second Berlin crisis, the Committee accurately predicted the division of the city to meet the refugee efflux and Khrushchev's permission to Ulbricht to erect this new barrier. It took two years of high tension for the permission to be given: as often with strategic estimates, the outcome was foreseen but not the precise timing; and, on the policy side, despite the warning on the books, no contingency planning was undertaken. When eventually the Wall went up the East Germans achieved tactical surprise. The Allies were preparing for more dangerous situations, involving their own troops, and were nonplussed.

On Sino-Soviet relations, the JIC, like the CIA, was alive to the signs of dispute between the two communist giants and to the immense implications of such a rift. The problem here was getting the policymakers to pay attention. The British policy paper of 1960, postponing a Sino-Soviet split until a Russian conversion to democracy, was perhaps an extreme case, but illustrated well the reluctance of many Western politicians and advisers to believe that the Soviet and the Chinese governments could ever do anything so opposed to their best interests as to fall out (their best interests, of course, being defined in Western terms).

In the case of Cuba and Vietnam, the Committee, like Britain, was relegated to the sidelines. The Cuban crisis was sudden, and fast: the real emergency was over in a week; and the JIC had to make do with items of cold intelligence passed on by the CIA after the decisions had been taken on them. Vietnam was a slow tragedy and there was ample time to comment on its unfolding. The Committee identified many of the coming dangers but could not get beyond the role of a Greek chorus, bewailing events it might foresee but which it had no power to change. At the policy level, the picture was the same, the British Prime Minister seeking a larger role, but rebuffed, gently in the case of Cuba, brutally in the case of Vietnam.

In the smaller, purely British operations of Kuwait and Indonesian confrontation, there was plentiful intelligence, both strategic and tactical, and policy was well served and effective. In the case of Rhodesia, there was little surprise about the unilateral declaration of independence and the errors lay on the policy-making side, chiefly in the wishful thinking on the effect of sanctions. Finally, we return to East-West crises with Czechoslovakia in 1968, where, admittedly, there was uncertainty, even in the Kremlin, until the last moment, but which in the end cannot be reckoned an intelligence, or policy, success. The failure probably lay in a misreading of the nature of Russian control in Eastern Europe and an underrating of the part pure violence played in the Soviet empire.

Given the perplexities and obscurities of the situation in each instance, this was a creditable performance. Where the JIC went wrong was usually in attributing rational motivation to the other side, most strikingly in the case of China in the Korean War. What I have called "the rational assumption" often appears in studies on intelligence as "mirror imaging" and is rightly condemned. But mirror imaging is usually the cruder form of the failing, the reasoning, "We would not do this, therefore they will not." Such thinking commits the serious error of disregarding the "otherness" of all foreign governments and the way in which what to us looks illogical or excessive may not be so in a foreign environment. So, in the Yom Kippur War of 1973, what Kissinger called "the notion of starting an unwinnable war to restore self-respect" had a strength for Sadat that the West, and Israel, failed to appreciate. So Russians and Chinese in their schism had very different ideas of what constituted their best interests from those entertained in Western capitals. And Mao's priorities for China in 1950 had a native consistency which only close acquaintance with him and his background could have disclosed.

At the same time, the analyst has a defence. In order to communicate with colleagues, ministers and allies he must follow rational procedures and modes of expression. Rationality is after all the condition of intelligent discourse; without it the world becomes arbitrary and unfathomable, my hunch against yours. It must also be assumed that the foreign leader—be it Stalin, Mao or Nasser—is doing the best for his country, as he sees it. The trap is in the last four words and in the tendency to set too narrow and domestic a standard, to overlook the differing views of rationality that can prevail in other political systems and cultures, and to forget the amount of emotion and unreason that can enter the most serious decisions. In the end the only safeguard is understanding of the other side and a consequent feel for their likely behaviour.

It is sometimes said that the Committee produced too varnished and unified judgements and gave the policy-maker no indication of the other interpretations that might be placed on the same facts. In Washington, by contrast, there were always a number of estimates to choose from. With limited resources Britain had to operate on a narrower front. Dissenting views were allowed in the Committee's papers, though differences were rarely deep and the permission was scarcely, if ever, invoked. But there were obvious dangers in offering a plurality of views or falling back into the old pre-war individualism. And failure to give a clear guide to ministers could be seen as an abdication of responsibility: the JIC had access to superior information; it owed them a judgement. And, provided the approach to that judgement was transparent, provided the agreed facts, the possible interpretations and the reasons for preferring one to another were clearly set out, the policymaker was able to follow the line of argument but in the end, if he felt strongly, free to diverge and come to another conclusion.

There was also a risk that the Committee, as an interdepartmental group, would produce only safe, uncontentious views and reflect only a low-level Whitehall consensus. Committees are by nature often dull and the JIC must have been often humdrum. Churchill, though a great man for unifying intelligence, shrank from the logical conclusion and did not think highly of the committee approach to truth. Writing of the prelude to the German invasion of Russia in 1941, he said, "I had not been content with this form of collective wisdom and preferred to see the originals myself…thus forming my own opinion sometimes at much earlier dates."[2]

It is true that in specific instances gifted individuals could, and did, outperform the JIC. Whether over a period the track record would have been so much better is less certain. The Committee itself would probably have forecast the German invasion of Russia as early as February 1941 if Cavendish-Bentinck had not had to carry the military with him. In any case the structure of government in Whitehall, the need to bring maximum expertise to bear on each issue, and the concern to escape pre-war disarray ruled out any other approach. A price had to be paid for coordinated intelligence and the record shows that it was worth paying.

Ideally, intelligence and policy should be close but distinct. Too distinct and assessments become an in-growing, self-regarding activity, producing little or no work of interest to the decision-makers. The French lord in Shakespeare's *Henry V* who on the eve of Agincourt measures the exact distance between the English and the French tents, a matter of supreme indifference to the French leaders, is an early exponent of worthy but irrelevant research and he has had many descendants. The analyst needs to

be close enough to ministers to know the questions troubling them and he must not fight shy of tackling the major issues. In its earliest days the JIC had to pronounce on life-and-death matters: invasion of Britain or not; a German invasion of Russia or not; and so on; and modern practitioners must maintain the same level of courage, or presumption.

Too close a link and policy begins to play back on estimates, producing the answers the policymakers would like, as happened with Soviet intelligence. The analysts become courtiers, whereas their proper function is to report their findings, almost always unpalatable, without fear or favour.

The best arrangement is intelligence and policy in separate but adjoining rooms, with communicating doors and thin partition walls, as in cheap hotels.

But however well connected the analysts are, the transition from intelligence to policy is often an uncertain one. Policy conclusions are commonly inherent in estimates; but the decisions lie with ministers: they have the privilege of interpreting the facts differently or ignoring them altogether. At this stage the situation and its likely development are no longer the sole considerations; other factors, party politics, economic interests, public opinion, personal convictions and vanities, enter the equation and can prove decisive. It is also in the nature of government, with its day-to-day pressures and concern with immediate issues, that strategic warnings are not always acted upon. Cruder stimuli are usually required. The predictions are rarely categorical: coming events are described at best as "probable" or, more usually, "on balance likely." Departments are unwilling to embark on contingency planning except for the plainest threats. They lack the resources and the danger may not materialize. When Sir Alec Douglas-Home, Commonwealth Secretary at the time of Suez, was many years later asked why ministers had disregarded the warnings that the venture would go wrong, he said, "A warning is a different thing from it happening. You often get warnings of this sort and then the results are different."[3] Suez was an extreme case of ministerial blindness; but there is something in Home's answer: governments may be alive to a possibility without taking the remedial action the historian would like to have seen.

With the rare exception, such as the exhortation to rearmament during the Korean War, the Committee sedulously avoided policy recommendations. Its concern was with the first part of

Cabinet papers, namely, what is the problem and how is it likely to develop? But the Joint Intelligence Organization was never a separate entity like the CIA; its staff were mainly seconded, not permanent; and the Committee members themselves met only for a limited time each week. Their connections with departments and policy remained close. This was particularly true in the case of the Chairman, who was also the senior Foreign Office official responsible for defence and security policy. In practice the JIC always stood in a close relationship, not only with the Chiefs of Staff, but also with senior ministers. How close depended in part on ministerial tastes and in part on the urgency of the international situation. It was inseparable from policy in the early Cold War years, in the assessment of the Soviet threat which prompted such responses as the Atlantic Alliance and the Marshall Plan. The Berlin blockade, the alarms of the Korean War and the fear of similar proxy attacks in Europe again made its assessments highly relevant and the policy arguments with the Americans over Korea were barely concealed behind the intelligence exchanges with Washington. Bevin's Cabinet papers and correspondence with Attlee over foreign policy show strong signs of JIC and Chiefs of Staff influence.

Over Suez, by contrast, there was a gulf between intelligence and policy, to the country's great cost. There was probably also a less intimate link with policy than in the past over the second Berlin crisis in 1958–61. Macmillan acted as his own Foreign Minister and evolved a highly individual approach to East–West relations. He put specific questions to the JIC, as over French progress toward nuclear weapons, and had JIC assessments on the UK deterrent as background to the decisions over Blue Streak and Polaris; but the policy style and structure were very much his own.

In 1964, as Harold Wilson takes over, we have the Cabinet Secretary, Burke Trend, telling him of the practice hitherto of submitting JIC papers and offering two examples, on North Vietnamese intentions and capabilities, and on the possible scale and nature of an attack on the UK in the event of a major war in the next four years. He asks whether he should proceed along these lines and is told "Yes."4 Copies also go to the Foreign Secretary, the Commonwealth Secretary, the Defence Secretary and, in the case of the paper on a possible attack on the UK, the Home Secretary. We can also assume that the regular weekly survey of intelligence is sent round to the same addresses. But again, with exceptions, as in the

case of estimates on Rhodesia, Wilson is probably not an avid reader of intelligence. His later obsession with the subject took a different form.

In fact, as we move into the 1960s there is an impression that the JIC assessments become less central to British foreign policy. There are a number of reasons. First, after Cuba the East–West confrontation becomes rather less acute. The Berlin blockade and the Korean War were direct challenges, occupying the centre of the stage. In the next decades, though the long-term threat persists, there are more international agreements regulating East–West competition. There is more caution, more time for the constructive work of diplomacy, most of it lying outside the Committee's remit.

The second reason is that Britain itself becomes less central in world affairs. Its power declines, not only in relation to the Soviet Union but also, even more critical, in relation to the United States. Beginning with the Eisenhower–Khrushchev meeting at Camp David in 1959, the Americans and the Russians develop the habit of meeting à *deux* to discuss East–West issues. Kennedy meets Khrushchev in Vienna in June 1961, Lyndon Johnson meets Kosygin at Glassboro in 1967. Britain is no longer needed as auxiliary or intermediary. The signing of the Partial Test Ban Treaty in August 1963 is the last time Britain occupies her old place at the top table.

The effect of superpower bilateralism is intensified by continuing British economic decline and the enforced retreat in 1968 from a worldwide to a predominantly European role. It is true of course that Britain is financially embarrassed throughout the period of this study. In Attlee's and Bevin's day the sudden withdrawal of Lend-Lease and the onerous American loan left little doubt about the true situation. But Britain was then one of the Big Three, a victorious power, with large and highly trained armed forces, vast tracts of territory still under its control and a sharp industrial advantage over other European economies. At the time of the Korean War US testimony shows how essential an element Britain was in American decision-making. By the late 1960s this situation has changed: the armies have melted away, the empire has been dismantled, but the economic troubles persist and intensify.

The decline brings an increasing element of pretence and posturing into British policy, an attempt to make up for declining material assets by manipulating the symbols of power, nuclear status, the special relationship, diplomatic finesse, the outer forms rather than the substance. The charade reflects a disturbing unwillingness to come to terms with the realities of Britain's new position. Macmillan, as a born showman, is rather better at the game than Wilson and in any case is luckier in having to face less acute economic pressures. The decreasing relevance of Britain is painfully demonstrated in Wilson's unsuccessful attempts to mediate over Vietnam.

But there is not only a decline in power; there is also a growing uncertainty of direction, the realzation by British governments that, with the success of European economic integration, the American alliance and the Commonwealth are no longer in themselves a sufficient basis for policy. The policy papers make the new dilemmas clear. A study in 1958 by a committee of Permanent Secretaries, entitled "The Position of the United Kingdom in World Affairs," is traditional in its priorities. Defeating Russian and Chinese efforts to dominate the world and preserving and strengthening the cohesion of the Commonwealth come first. Europe is well down the list: "We aim to strengthen our ties with Europe and are seeking to negotiate a European Free Trade Area. We support the North Atlantic Alliance as the bulwark against Soviet encroachment in Europe."[5]

But in 1960 there is a big change. The "Future Policy Study, 1960–70," provides the background to Macmillan's strategy in the 1960s. It is written by a Foreign Office team under Sir Patrick Dean (still JIC Chairman) and submitted to the Prime Minister via a steering committee chaired by Sir Norman Brook, the Cabinet Secretary. It recognizes the importance of the EEC, foreseeing it as "one of the three giants," along with the United States and the Soviet Union, by the year 1970, and acknowledges that it would seriously weaken Britain's own standing in the Commonwealth and the Atlantic Alliance, and the cohesion of the Alliance itself, if Britain found itself excluded from Europe; moreover that, as a relatively small economic power, the country would risk serious damage if it failed to establish a satisfactory association with the EEC. In its key section, entitled "The Balance between Our Friends," the paper enunciates as a basic rule of British policy that "we must never allow ourselves to be put in a position where we would have to make a final choice between the United States and Europe."[6]

In this new policy language we encounter in early form the persistent British belief that America or Europe involved an exclusive choice. It was in many ways a false dichotomy. It was not how the United States saw it: consistent American advice was

that British influence in Washington would depend on British influence in Europe. But it was the fear of successive British governments that Europe meant sacrifice, a fear reinforced by the fact that the approach to Europe had to be made at the same time as decisions on the future of the British deterrent which underlined the critical importance of the American link. In such a situation the principle of "no final choice" had its attractions. But it could only too readily become an excuse for putting off any thorough analysis of the future courses open to the country, a principle of evasion and indecision. Indeed it could be argued that Britain has remained in this state of suspended judgement on Europe ever since those days.

Britain's situation in the late 1960s, which was at the same time the source of its uncertainty and illusion, was eloquently defined by someone who was pre-eminently in a position to know, Sir Con O'Neil, the government's chief official negotiator with Europe, in a lecture delivered in 1972:

> Britain's experience had been different, or seemed different; and for a long time we misinterpreted it. The world still seemed our oyster, though in fact we lacked the power to open it. We had escaped defeat and occupation; we had been spared the collapse of our society and institutions. But we had not escaped exhaustion and diminution, the common lot of our European neighbours.[7]

Against this background of diminution and uncertainty, the influence of the Committee was bound to decline. But it retained its hold on the primary concern of any government, national security. So long as the Soviet Union posed the main threat to Western Europe its views would be certain to command attention. And so long as the outside world remained dangerous and unpredictable— sadly a permanent condition of international life— the Committee could never be disregarded. Middle East wars, oil crises, terrorist plots would provide a steady *raison d'être*. Moreover by then the post-Cold War security agenda was already beginning to appear in its assessments. The first papers on "The development of nuclear weapons by fifth countries" come in 1960; and the first intelligence from Northern Ireland of impending trouble from the IRA begins to arrive as early as December 1965.[8]

The Committee has also to be seen as an important element in US–UK relations. Britain was fortunate in being able to act on the outside world not only directly but also, on occasion, through the most powerful of proxies, the United States. As will have become apparent, this study is almost as much about United States as about British estimates and policy. From the Second World War on there was a continuous intimate dialogue between the two governments about world affairs. All British governments sought as a cardinal objective to exert maximum influence in Washington. In Macmillan's definition of 1957 the British deterrent itself became largely an agent of influence. One very effective means of exercising this persuasion was the production of highly regarded intelligence estimates and their regular exchange with US counterparts. Fortunately, for most of the time the two sides agreed on the problem and the response. Where they differed always presented the most delicate choices for London between narrower British interests and the demands of solidarity with Washington. For better or worse, US–UK relations were always the key strand of British foreign policy.

As we look back over these first twenty to twenty-five years of the post-war era, the record of the JIC shows it as an important part of central government, intimately involved in the main crises of the period and exerting a powerful influence on foreign policy in Britain and even, to some extent, in America. It looks on the world coolly and realistically, with few illusions; the pretences and evasions are there, but they belong to the realm of policy. It has to its credit a number of accurate or enlightened forecasts of coming events, though like any body required to read the future, it has its share of mistakes. Its main merit, however, may lie less in individual assessments of greater or lesser accuracy than in the fact of its existence as a responsible and increasingly influential organization bringing together at manageable and less than Cabinet level the chief sources of knowledge on international affairs and engaging them in a continuous and forward-looking discussion and evaluation of the evolving scene. Thereby it contributed substantially to the ideal of efficient and prescient policy-making. Despite the best intentions, government is usually a hand-to-mouth affair. The Committee made it less so.

At a more basic level the achievement consists simply in the coordination of intelligence, giving Britain a critical advantage over competitors. In his memoirs in 1956 President Truman reflected that "if there had been something like co-ordination of information in the government it would have been more difficult, if not impossible, for the Japanese to succeed in the sneak attack on Pearl Harbor."[9] The same lack of co-ordination bedevilled American intelligence four years later in the Korean War and was similarly lamented in later inquests.

A final example. At the end of the Second World War the JIC conducted a study on "Why Germany lost the War?" The resulting paper gave as one of the reasons the fragmented state of German intelligence:

> Within the Abwehr [the principal German intelligence service] there was little or no centralised evaluation of intelligence, which was in itself nearly always derived from personal sources…reports were often rejected on internal grounds by the service ministries, who lacked the means of assessing the reliability of the information which they received.

In addition to the internal weakness of the Abwehr, the salient weakness of German Intelligence, and one of its main causes of failure, was the absence of any inter-service staff for the co-ordination and appreciation of intelligence. Both Keitel and Jodl have stated that no organisation comparable with the allied joint intelligence machinery was ever formed. Operational intelligence was supplied by each of the service ministries and by the Abwehr direct to the planning staff of OKW [the supreme command of the armed forces] where it was inadequately coordinated.[10]

This tells the whole story. Britain was very fortunate that, in those desperate days and for many years afterwards, in London such matters were distinctly better managed.

QUESTIONS FOR FURTHER DISCUSSION

1. Can good intelligence salvage bad policy?
2. Is there a correlation between national strength and status and the relevance of intelligence to policymakers?
3. Can intelligence help compensate for a lack of military or economic resources?
4. Are policy prescriptions inherent in the conclusions of intelligence estimates?

ENDNOTES

1. James Bamford, *Body of Secrets: How America's NSA and Britain's GCHQ Eavesdrop on the World* (London, Century, 2001).
2. Churchill on committee work, quoted in R.V. Jones, *Most Secret War* (London, Hamish Hamilton, 1978).
3. Hennessy, *The Prime Minister*, p. 236.

4. PRO PREM 13/8, Minute by Sir Burke Trend, 24 October 1964.

5. PRO PREM 11/2321, of 5 June 1958, "The Position of the United Kingdom in World Affairs."

6. PRO CAB 129/100, FP (60) 1, "Study of Future Policy, 1960–1970," 24 February 1960.

7. Sir Con O'Neil, Stamp Memorial Lecture, 1972, quoted in David Hannay (ed.), *Britain's Entry into the European Community* (London, Frank Cass, 2000), p. xxii, Sir Con O'Neil's Report on the Negotiations of 1970–2.

8. Peter Rose, *How the Troubles Came to Northern Ireland* (London, Macmillan, 2000), p. 18.

9. Harry S. Truman, *Memoirs, Vol. 2: Years of Trial and Hope 1946–1953* (London, Hodder & Stoughton, 1956), p. 56.

10. 10. PRO CAB 81/132, JIC (46) 33 of 20 October 1946.

EPILOGUE
THE FUTURE OF INTELLIGENCE

Ghost: "Adieu, adieu, adieu, remember me."
—SHAKESPEARE, *Hamlet*, 1.5.92

Although there are examples of espionage, counterintelligence, denial and deception, and intelligence fusion throughout all of recorded history, the practice and understanding of intelligence is not static. Intelligence is shaped by the times. Technology, strategic culture, societal trends, economics, politics, and a sense of necessity influence the practice of intelligence and attitudes toward intelligence practitioners. New capabilities have been integrated into intelligence efforts over time. The emergence of radio communications led to the birth of Signals Intelligence, aircraft and earth-orbiting satellites to Photographic Intelligence, and radar and various other electronic devices led to Measurement and Signatures Intelligence. Intelligence operatives always seem willing to incorporate the latest technology, or to exploit whatever social movement or fad that comes along, in order to gain entry into some target, or to gain insight into what the opponent is planning.

Despite this willingness to incorporate new technology and tradecraft, intelligence organizations are based on a legacy system. As bureaucracies, they organize people and things in a way that reflects the technological and social setting of the 19th century. They are intended to concentrate knowledge and control into the hands of a few people at the top of the organizational hierarchy. Reforms generally involve increasing the span of organizational control when it comes to channeling the flow of analysis and information to the top of the bureaucracy. New organizations—the Central Intelligence Agency or the Office of the Director of National Intelligence—are created to link disparate parts of the government together so that more sources of information can be incorporated into ever more comprehensive analysis. This traditional way of doing business, however, is currently under siege. The information revolution is empowering outsiders vis-à-vis government, and individual analysts vis-à-vis the collective efforts of the intelligence community, making it possible, indeed, imperative, to change organizational structures to capitalize on these emerging social and technological trends. The information revolution is in the process of transforming the way the intelligence community is organized and the way intelligence analysts go about their business.

The information revolution is transforming intelligence processes. Not only are policymakers, analysts, and scholars confronted with a torrent of data, information and analysis, they must cope with virtual realities often described as "cyberspace." Advances in communication and computer technologies are creating new collective workspaces, creating opportunities for collaboration that were considered fanciful in the 1980s. The barriers between intelligence practitioner and scholar are breaking down as both exploit these new technologies—a fact reflected in the intelligence community's efforts to tap sources of expertise outside of government. The information revolution also is lowering the barriers between foreign and domestic intelligence activities and the way local, state, and national law enforcement and intelligence agencies conduct their business.

To illustrate the challenges facing intelligence organizations today, this epilogue explores three emerging issues that will influence the future study and practice of intelligence: homeland security; collective intelligence; and the broad application of intelligence and warning methodologies to mitigate risk. All of these topics illustrate how theory and practice are merging as scholars and practitioners respond to the threats and opportunities created by globalization and the information revolution.

INTELLIGENCE AND HOMELAND SECURITY

Officials recognized the general problem posed by the rise of transnational terrorist networks, one of the externalities created by globalization, before the September 11, 2001 Al-Qaeda attacks against the World Trade Center and the Pentagon (Zegart 2007). In December 2000, for example, the National Intelligence Council reported that foreign threats were beginning to emerge as local problems. Threats that emerged in states with "poor governance" were spilling across national boundaries in the form of "diverse, free-wheeling, transnational networks." The Council predicted that as a result, "terrorist tactics will become increasingly sophisticated and designed to achieve mass casualties" (National Intelligence Council, 2000, 50). Globalization was blurring traditional distinctions between foreign enemies and domestic problems created by criminals, gang activity, local protest movements or mentally unbalanced individuals. The U.S. intelligence community recognized the asymmetric threats posed by non-state actors, but it was not prepared in terms of organization, processes, or legal standing to meet these threats.

Operatives in these new transnational actors, however, found a way to capitalize on the structural weaknesses that are inherent in the U.S. government, especially the boundaries that exist between domestic law enforcement agencies and the externally focused intelligence community. The result was 9/11. Information and analysis still does not flow easily in this "intra-governmental" setting, making it difficult to coordinate actions against even well understood threats. For instance, intelligence agencies are only marginally constrained by legal restrictions as they track targets of interest in foreign lands. By contrast, domestic law enforcement agencies must possess a reasonable criminal predicate before they can track individuals within the United States. Law enforcement can throw caution to the winds, but operations that fail to meet strict legal standards are unlikely to produce evidence that can be used in a criminal prosecution. Legal constraints can thus slow or prevent the flow of information between law enforcement and the intelligence community.

The intelligence community's focus on prediction, warning, and interdiction also stands in contrast to law enforcement's goal of investigating crime and bringing perpetrators to justice. Linking national intelligence organizations to state, local, and federal law enforcement agencies is not just a matter of overcoming bureaucratic rice bowls or eliminating stove piping. It involves coordinating activities of agencies that face different constraints and embrace different objectives to achieve a common goal, that is, to prevent the next terrorist attack (Markle Foundation 2002).

Intelligence for homeland security also is undertaken in a multidisciplinary setting. Law enforcement organizations, firefighters, emergency medical service personnel, public health officials can all be involved in assessing and responding to a single event. In other words, officials have to be sensitive to the different paradigms employed by these disparate organizations in order to foster real cooperation across disciplinary boundaries.

If the information revolution is enabling transnational networks to bridge the divide between domestic and international settings, the same technologies are being employed to bridge the gaps between state, local, and federal agencies. Along with these new technologies, new operating procedures and philosophies are slowly emerging to animate the process of gathering, fusing, analyzing, and disseminating intelligence across disparate jurisdictions and agencies. Nevertheless, there is much work to be done when it comes to producing and disseminating intelligence for homeland security. There are no best practices, for example, when it comes to telling police on the beat about "what to look for" when it comes to intelligence collection. There also is little agreement on what types of information—finished intelligence, warnings, raw intelligence about incidents in nearby jurisdictions—that should be moved to individuals in the field. Scores of state, metropolitan, and regional intelligence "fusion" and command centers are emerging across the Untied States to move information and analysis to officials. But in the absence of unified homeland security intelligence doctrine, each of these entities is devising competing answers to the problems of how best to provide intelligence to local communities (Masse, O'Neil, and Rollins 2007).

A fundamental question facing those interested in homeland security still involves the definition of exactly what is meant by homeland security intelligence (Masse 2006). Today, intelligence officials, first responders, and law enforcement personnel are slowly moving away from a focus on "terrorism" when it comes to intelligence; instead, they are shifting to an "all hazard" approach that can better respond to the everyday demands they face in their jurisdictions. Although some worry that this orientation could mark a general decline in interest in the issue of homeland security, this approach could provide dual benefits. First, it recognizes the fact that most jurisdictions spend most of their time and resources dealing with "mundane" activities—organized crime, gang activity, drug problems, and traditional hazards (such as chemical spills, power outages, fires, floods). Second, it would encourage intelligence organizations and law enforcement to maintain a high degree of situational awareness. The ability to distinguish normal hazards from terrorist incidents can greatly mitigate unnecessary damage to society, allowing officials to respond appropriately to natural disasters, nefarious activity, or hoaxes. An all-hazard approach also might be the best way to fulfill the counterterrorism mission, because it raises the possibility of detecting novel efforts to create mayhem. Ultimately, an all-hazard approach to intelligence recognizes political reality. Most problems faced by local communities have little to do with transnational terror networks. If intelligence is going to succeed, it must "piggy-back" on efforts to address local problems, for example, gang activity.

COLLECTIVE INTELLIGENCE

Collective intelligence is a new phenomenon produced by the information revolution. It reflects the cyber-assisted melding of human consciousness into a collective awareness of global knowledge, or at least that is the best way to summarize the myriad of emerging possibilities and threats created as more people and more information gain access to the Internet (Malone 2008). Collective intelligence will emerge as more scientists, scholars, officials, and average citizens use the Internet to contact each other to pursue mutual objectives, discover commercial, technical or social research opportunities,

or to debate matters of local and global public policy (Brown and Isaacs 2008). Some observers believe that collective intelligence will morph into a form of global consciousness, as political, scientific or social questions are debated on the World Wide Web. Identity, knowledge, and reality, or at least a common conception of reality, will be mediated by search engines combing through the collective contents of the Web. Others prefer to use the metaphor "global brain" to describe the "collectively intelligent network that is formed by the people of this planet together with the computers, knowledge bases and communication links that connect them together" (Heylighen 2008). The information revolution has already transformed society; collective intelligence is an optimist way of thinking about the possibilities created by emerging communication and computer technologies.

Scholars and practitioners face two issues when confronting the concept of collective intelligence. The first is practical. Theorists and managers need to devise ways to incorporate new technologies and practices into existing institutions and bureaucracies. If new technologies make it possible for individuals to access databases, conduct analysis, and communicate information and plans for action to colleagues and fellow travelers across the world, how can analysts and intelligence officials be empowered to take the same sorts of actions in a setting hamstrung by regulations, classification, and bureaucratic constraints? The issue they face is to find ways to integrate analytical and action networks into what are relatively hierarchical organizations. Analysts have to have access to these new forms of "artificial intelligence" because advanced search engines and other analytical tools can actually find information related to a topic of interest, regardless of whether or not the analyst knows about the information in the first place.

The second issue raised by the notion of collective intelligence is the possibility that the intelligence community's comparative advantage over other types of state and non-state actors could be waning. Proponents of what is known in the literature as "open-source intelligence" often describe the information revolution as a boon to humanity, empowering people to become masters of their own destiny when it comes to local, regional or even international issues (Steele 2002). Open-source advocates note that intelligence agencies were slow to capitalize on the information revolution because it called into question their *raison d'etre*: maintaining superior situational awareness through the use of classified data and communication channels (Steele 2001). Nevertheless, as more groups and individuals are equipped with state of the art computational and communication systems, they can combine local knowledge with virtually the same resources available to the intelligence community to conduct data mining, high quality analysis, or intelligence preparation of the battlefield.

The fact that other empowered networks or even individuals are helping to populate this collective intelligence expands the operating environment for traditional intelligence agencies. Not only do they have to monitor social, political, or military events in some distant land, they also have to monitor activities underway in cyberspace. State agencies ignore developments in cyberspace at their own peril, because it can help define reality on the ground and enable all sorts of nefarious activities. Some observers of collective intelligence even believe that cyberspace itself is already defining reality by serving as a source of information for people who are not eyewitnesses to some unfolding event. The "electronic community," which is controlled by no one, already seems to be a place that people turn for information, opinion, and analysis (Rheingold 2008).

INDICATIONS AND WARNING VS. SPECIFIC EVENT PREDICTION

When it comes to intelligence analysis, both scholars and practitioners focus their attention on what is best characterized as "specific event prediction": the need to provide policymakers with timely warning of an impending attack, natural disaster, or some other sort of critical development. Sometimes, analysts "get it right" and provide senior officers with timely and accurate warning. For example, U.S. Naval Intelligence provided such an accurate prediction of Japanese plans that it was largely responsible for the U.S. victory at the Battle of Midway. "Strategic surprise," "surprise attack" or "intelligence failure," however, are the terms used to describe when analysts fail to provide specific event prediction, and explaining these sorts of failure are one of the central issues in the field of intelligence studies.

Specific event prediction is challenging. In fact it is so challenging, that the conventional wisdom suggests that intelligence failures are inevitable for the simple reason that the exact nature of the next intelligence challenge is unknown, making it difficult to tailor current reforms to meet future exigencies

(Betts 1977). As a result, practitioners and analysts have turned to indications and warning (I&W) methodologies as a new way to respond to emerging threats, especially those posed by non-state actors. Drawn from the literature on risk assessment and management and influenced by the traditional use of indications and warning methodologies to estimate the likelihood of military conflict, an I&W approach can provide a way to detect anomalies, to refocus intelligence collection efforts, and to change the alert status of security forces and procedures.

Indications and warning methodology is based on devising a series of indicators that highlight a change of status of an opponent's forces, especially the move from normal "peacetime" operations to a wartime or attack posture. Guided by strategic analysis, which identifies likely risks and productive collection targets, I&W analysts monitor the external environment for expected signs of attack, suspicious behavior, or anomalous situations (Davis 2007). During the Cold War, when attack indicators focused on major military formations, I&W analysts relied on national technical means (NTM) to spot changes in the operational posture of major military units. Today, I&W often involves subtler targets, individuals, or clandestine cells that are undertaking criminal activities or terrorism. Because these clandestine cells often "hide in plain sight" while undertaking their nefarious activities, I&W methodologies provide a useful way to detect anomalies that suggest that something is amiss. This might sound impossibly difficult when it comes to tracking the behavior of individuals or small groups, but U.S. law enforcement personnel did notice prior to the September 11, 2001, terror attacks that certain pilots were interested in flying, but not landing, airliners (Wirtz 2008).

Once anomalies are detected, analysts can refocus collection efforts to develop a better understanding of the target under consideration. In terms of homeland security, I&W analysis can be used to focus the efforts of law enforcement personnel who can investigate abnormal patterns of activity. Indeed any method that permits investigators to concentrate their efforts on potentially important targets would be superior to random surveillance or blanket security measures. A cursory effort might be all that is necessary to determine whether some anomaly is completely innocent or should be the subject of a sustained surveillance effort.

An indications and warning methodology also can do much to improve security because it can provide policymakers with a justification for raising, or reducing, security precautions in light of suspected threats or changes in the potential activities of opponents. Since people cannot remain at high levels of alert indefinitely, intelligence is critical to all security measures involving human operators. Warning is literally the message to security personnel that "today" is the day they need to be on the *qui vive*. The capture of an al Qaeda operative on the way to bomb Los Angeles International Airport in 1999, for instance, can be attributed to effective action taken in response to a general alert, not a specific warning about a unique event or the identification of an individual suspect (Perrow 2005). Changing alert levels and procedures themselves can create a mission kill when it comes to the activities of small cells. Because they have to minimize their operational and logistical signatures to reduce the possibility of detection, a change in security could send them back to the drawing board, forcing them to optimize their operations to meet new conditions.

CONCLUSION

Globalization and the information revolution are raising new challenges for the intelligence community, challenges that will occupy scholars and practitioners for years to come. Traditional defenses against foreign threats are becoming increasingly ineffective as the information revolution is making it easier for both state and non-state actors to cross national boundaries. The information revolution also is empowering individuals and national and international networks at the expense of state actors and traditional bureaucracies.

These trends have changed the nature of the intelligence "target" and the domain of knowledge and practice relevant to the production of finished intelligence, espionage, and the management of secret organizations in society. The scope and complexity of the threat environment is increasing: intelligence for homeland security now must cover foreign and domestic threats while integrating data and analysis generated by a variety of organizations and disciplines. Today, there is no consensus on how to fuse this data and provide it to first responders, no doctrine to integrate multiple disciplines and organizations, and no agreement on how to improve situational awareness while preserving civil liberties.

The information revolution has altered intelligence production, and how new technologies and best practices can be integrated into existing organizations. Artificial intelligence is becoming a reality and some observers believe that these technologies will eventually coalesce into a global form of collective intelligence. While this global transformation is taking place, intelligence managers and analysts struggle to keep pace with these emerging information technologies and systems and to devise ways to best integrate them into the production of finished intelligence.

The future intelligence enterprise will become increasingly concerned with the coordination of disparate organizations into a collective endeavor. Scholars and practitioners will become increasingly interested in devising ways to empower people to better serve national purposes and the international effort to achieve security. We hope that those of you serious enough about intelligence to have read this work will take up the challenge.

U.S. INTELLIGENCE LEADERSHIP, 1947–2010

DIRECTORS, NATIONAL INTELLIGENCE

2005–2007 John D. Negroponte
2007–2009 J. M. ("Mike") McConnell
2009– Dennis C. Blair

DIRECTORS, CENTRAL INTELLIGENCE

1947–1950 Rear Adm. Roscoe H. Hillenkoetter
1950–1953 Gen. Walter Bedell Smith
1953–1961 Allen W. Dulles
1961–1965 John A. McCone
1965–1966 Vice Adm. William F. Raborn, Jr.
1966–1973 Richard Helms
1973 James R. Schlesinger
1973–1976 William E. Colby
1976–1977 George H. W. Bush
1977–1981 Adm. Stansfield Turner
1981–1987 William J. Casey
1987–1991 William H. Webster
1991–1993 Robert M. Gates
1993–1995 R. James Woolsey
1995–1997 John M. Deutch
1997–2004 George J. Tenet
2004–2005 Porter J. Goss

CHAIRS, SENATE SELECT COMMITTEE ON INTELLIGENCE

1976–1977 Daniel K. Inouye, Democrat, Hawaii
1977–1981 Birch Bayh, Democrat, Indiana
1981–1985 Barry Goldwater, Republican, Arizona
1985–1987 David Durenberger, Republican, Minnesota
1987–1993 David L. Boren, Democrat, Oklahoma
1993–1995 Dennis DeConcini, Democrat, Arizona
1995–1997 Arlen Specter, Republican, Pennsylvania
1997–2001 Richard C. Shelby, Republican, Alabama
2001–2003 Bob Graham, Democrat, Florida
2003–2006 Pat Roberts, Republican, Kansas
2006–2009 John D. Rockefeller IV, Democrat, West Virginia
2009– Diane Feinstein, Democrat, California

CHAIRS, HOUSE PERMANENT SELECT COMMITTEE ON INTELLIGENCE

1977–1985 Edward P. Boland, Democrat, Massachusetts
1985–1987 Lee H. Hamilton, Democrat, Indiana
1987–1989 Louis Stokes, Democrat, Ohio
1989–1991 Anthony C. Beilenson, Democrat, California
1991–1993 Dave McCurdy, Democrat, Oklahoma
1993–1995 Dan Glickman, Democrat, Kansas
1995–1997 Larry Combest, Republican, Texas
1997–2004 Porter J. Goss, Republican, Florida
2004–2006 Peter Hoekstra, Republican, Michigan
2007– Silvestre Reyes, Democrat, Texas

THE ORGANIZATION OF THE U.S. INTELLIGENCE COMMUNITY

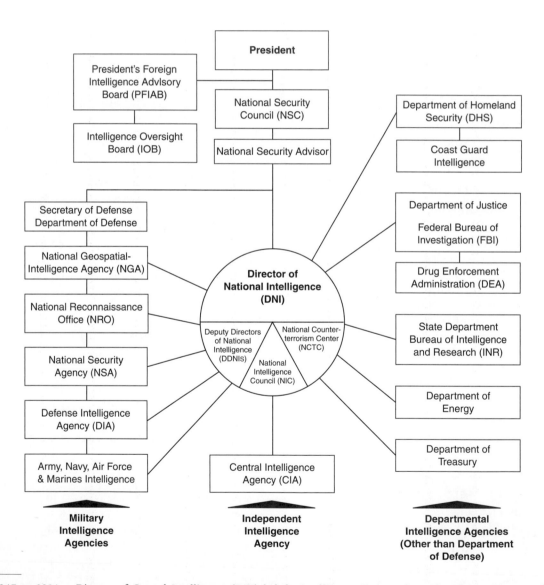

*From 1947 to 2004, a Director of Central Intelligence (DCI) led the Intelligence Community, rather than a Director of National Intelligence. The Coast Guard became a part of the IC in 2001, the Department of Homeland Security in 2003, and the Drug Enforcement Administration in 2006.

INTELLIGENCE WEBSITES

This listing draws in part on helpful suggestions from Professor Frank Smist and the late John Macartney.

GENERAL

- http://www.columbia.edu/cu/lweb/indiv/lehman/guides/intell.html>
- http://www.loyola.edu/dept/politics/intel.html.

NATIONAL SECURITY ACT OF 1947

- http://www.intelligence.gov/0-natsecact_1947.shtml>

DIRECTOR OF NATIONAL INTELLIGENCE

- http://www.odni.gov

CENTER FOR THE STUDY OF INTELLIGENCE

- https://www.cia.gov/csi/

INTELLIGENCE AGENCIES

- https://www.cia.gov
- http://www.fbi.gov
- http://www.state.gov
- http://www.defenselink.mil
- http://www.usdoj.gov
- http://www.nsa.gov

NATIONAL SECURITY ARCHIVE

- http://www.gwu.edu/~nsarchiv/

CONGRESSIONAL OVERSIGHT COMMITTEES

- http://www.senate.gov
- http://intelligence.house.gov
- http://www.gpoaccess.gov/congress/house/permintel/index.html

ASSOCIATION OF FORMER INTELLIGENCE OFFICERS

- http://www.afio.com

NATIONAL MILITARY INTELLIGENCE ASSOCIATION

- http://www.nmia.org

FEDERATION OF AMERICAN SCIENTISTS

- http://www.fas.org

COUNTERINTELLIGENCE

- http://www.ncix.gov
- http://www.fbi.gov/hq/ci/cointell.htm

INTELLIGENCE REPORTS

- http://www.gpoaccess.gov/int/report.html (Aspin-Brown Commission, 1996)
- http://www.gpo.gov/congress/house/intel/ic21/ic21_toc.html (HPSCI Staff Report, 1996)
- http://www.fas.org/irp/congress/1998_cr/s980731-rumsfeld.htm (Rumsfeld Commission, 1998)

- http://www.fas.org/irp/cia/product/jeremiah .html (Jeremiah Report on Indian nuclear tests, 1998)
- https://www.cia.gov/csi/books/shermankent/ toc.html (commentary on famed CIA analyst Sherman Kent)
- http://www.dni.gov/nic/foia_vietnam_content .html (Vietnam documents)
- https://www.cia.gov/csi/books/princeton/ index.html (Soviet NIEs)

- http://www.fas.org/irp/congress/2004_rpt/h10- 558.pdf (HPSCI Report on Humint)
- http://www.hanford.gov/oci/maindocs/ci_r_ docs/amescase.pdf (SSCI Report on Ames)
- http://govinfo.library.unt.edu/nssg/Reports/ reports.htm (Hart-Rudman Commission, 2001)
- http://www.faqs.org/docs/911/911Report.html (Kean Commission, 2004)
- http://www.wmd.gov/report/ (Silberman-Robb Commission, 2005)

SELECT BIBLIOGRAPHY

Aid, Matthew M. 2009. *The Secret Sentry.* New York: Bloomsbury Press.

Aldrich, Richard J. 2002. *The Hidden Hand: Britain, America, and Cold War Secret Intelligence.* Woodstock, NY: Overlook Press, 2002.

Anderson, Jack. 1973. "How the CIA Snooped Inside Russia," *Washington Post* (December 10): B17.

Andrew, Christopher. 1995. *For the President's Eyes Only: Secret Intelligence and the American Presidency From Washington to Bush.* New York: HarperCollins.

Aspin-Brown Commission. 1996. *Preparing for the 21st Century: An Appraisal of U.S. Intelligence.* Report of the Commission on the Roles and Capabilities of the United States Intelligence Community. Washington, DC: Government Printing Office.

Bamford, James. 1984. *The Puzzle Palace.* Boston: Houghton Mifflin.

Bar-Joseph, Uri. 2005. *The Watchman Fell Asleep: The Surprise of Yom Kippur and its Sources.* Albany: State University of New York Press.

Berkowitz, Bruce, and Allen Goodman. 2000. *Best Truth: Intelligence in the Information Age.* New Haven, CT: Yale University Press.

Betts, Richard. 1978. "Analysis, War and Decision: Why Intelligence Failures are Inevitable," *World Politics* 31(1): 61–89.

———. Richard K. 2002. "Fixing Intelligence," *Foreign Affairs* 81 (January–February): 43–59.

Bissell, Richard M., Jr., with Jonathan E. Lewis and Frances T. Rudlo. 1996. *Reflections of a Cold War.* New Haven, CT: Yale University Press.

Born, Hans, Loch K. Johnson, and Ian Leigh. 2005. *Who's Watching the Spies? Establishing Intelligence Service Accountability.* Washington, DC: Potomac Books.

Brown, Juanita, and David Isaacs. 2008. "The World Café: Awakening Collective Intelligence and Committed Action," in Mark Tovey (ed.), *Collective Intelligence: Creating a Prosperous World at Peace.* Oakton, VA: Earth Intelligence Network: 47–53.

Brugioni, Dino A. 1969. "The Unidentifieds," *Studies in Intelligence* (Summer): 1–20.

Burrows, William E. 1986. *Deep Black: Space Espionage and National Security.* New York: Random House.

Campbell, Duncan. 2003. "Afghan Prisoners Beaten to Death," *The Guardian* (March 7): 1.

Central Intelligence Agency. 1983. *Fact Book on Intelligence.*

Church Committee (Select Committee to Study Governmental Operations with Respect to Intelligence Activities). 1975a. Declassified CIA memorandum, Committee files, U.S. Senate, 94th Cong., 2d Sess.

———. 1975b. "Alleged Assassination Plots Involving Foreign Leaders," *Interim Report.* S. Rept. No. 94–465. Washington, DC: U.S. Government Printing Office.

———. 1976. *Final Report, Sen. Rept. No. 94–755*, vol. 1. Washington, DC: U.S. Government Printing Office.

Cirincione, Joseph. 2000. "Assessing the Assessment: The 1999 National Intelligence Estimate of the Ballistic Missile Threat," *Nonproliferation Review* 7 (Spring): 125–137.

Cohen, William S., and George J. Mitchell. 1988. *Men of Zeal: A Candid Inside Story of the Iran-Contra Hearings.* New York: Viking.

Colby, William E., and Peter Forbath. 1978. *Honorable Men: My Life in the CIA.* New York: Simon & Schuster.

Commission on Government Security, Report. 1957. Washington, DC: U.S. Government Printing Office.

Currie, James. 1998. "Iran-Contra and Congressional Oversight of the CIA," *International Journal of Intelligence and Counterintelligence* 11 (Summer): 185–210.

Davis, Jack. 2007. "Strategic Warning: Intelligence Support in a World of Uncertainty and Surprise," in Loch K. Johnson (ed.), *Handbook of Intelligence Studies.* London: Routledge: 173–188.

Diamond, John. 2008. *The CIA and the Culture of Failure.* Stanford, CA: Stanford University Press.

Gates, Robert M. 1996. *From the Shadows.* New York: Simon & Schuster.

Godson, Roy S. 1996. *Dirty Tricks or Trump Cards: U.S. Covert Action and Counterintelligence.* Washington, DC: Brassey's, 1996.

Graham, Bob, with Jeff Nussbaum. 2004. *Intelligence Matters.* New York: Random House.

Halpern, Samuel, and Hayden B. Peake, "Did Angleton Jail Nosenko?" *International Journal of Intelligence and Counterintelligence* 3 (Winter): 451–464.

Handel, Michael. 1977. "The Yom Kippur War and the Inevitability of Surprise," *International Studies Quarterly* 21, 3:461–501.

Harden, Toby. 2003. "CIA 'Pressure' on Al Qaeda Chief," *Washington Post* (March 6): A1.

Hart-Rudman Report. 2001. Commission on National Security/21st Century. Washington, DC.

Hastedt Glenn. 1986. "The Constitutional Control of Intelligence," *Intelligence and National Security* 1 (May): 255–271.

Hennessy, Peter. 2003. *The Secret State: Whitehall and the Cold War.* London: Penguin.

Heuer, Richard J., Jr. 1999. *Psychology of Intelligence Analysis.* Washington, DC: Center for the Study of Intelligence.

———. 1981. "Strategic Deception and Counterdeception," *International Studies Quarterly* 25 (June): 294–327.

Heylighen, Francis. 2008. "The Emergence of a Global Brain," in Mark Tovey (ed.), *Collective Intelligence: Creating a Prosperous World at Peace.* Oakton, VA: Earth Intelligence Network: 305–314.

Hitz, Frederick P. 2004. *The Great Game: The Myth and Reality of Espionage.* New York: Knopf.

Hughes, R. Gerald, Peter Jackson, and Len Scott, eds. 2008. *Exploring Intelligence Archives.* New York: Routledge.

Hulnick, Arthur S. 1986. "The Intelligence Producer-Policy Consumer Linkage: A Theoretical Approach," *Intelligence and National Security* 1 (May): 212–233.

———. 1999. *Fixing the Spy Machine: Preparing American Intelligence for the Twenty-First Century.* Westport, CT: Praeger.

Jackson, William R. 1990. "Congressional Oversight of Intelligence: Search for a Framework," *Intelligence and National Security* 5 (July): 113–137.

Jeffreys-Jones, Rhodri. 1989. *The CIA and American Democracy.* New Haven, CT: Yale University Press.

Jervis, Robert. 1986–87. "Intelligence and Foreign Policy," *International Security* 11 (Winter): 141–161.

Johnson, Loch K. 1980. "The U.S. Congress and the CIA: Monitoring the Dark Side of Government," *Legislative Studies Quarterly* 5 (November): 477–99.

———. 1985. A *Season Inquiry: The Senate Intelligence Investigation.* Lexington: University Press of Kentucky.

———. 1989. *America's Secret-Power: The CIA in a Democratic Society.* New York: Oxford University Press.

———. 1996. *Secret Agencies: U.S. Intelligence in a Hostile World.* New Haven, CT: Yale University Press.

———. 2000. *Bombs, Bugs, Drugs, and Thugs: Intelligence and America's Quest for Security*, p. 177. New York: New York University Press.

———. 2001. "The CIA's Weakest Link," *Washington Monthly* 33 (July/August): 9–14.

———. 2004. "The Aspin-Brown Intelligence Inquiry: Behind the Closed Doors of a Blue Ribbon Commission," *Studies in Intelligence* 48 (Winter), pp. 1–20.

———. 2007. *Seven Sins of American Foreign Policy.* New York: Longman.

———, (ed.). 2007a. *Strategic Intelligence,* 5 Vols. Westport, CT: Praeger.

———, (ed.). 2007b. *Handbook of Intelligence Studies.* London: Routledge.

———. 2007c. "Educing Information: Interrogation: Science and Art, *Studies in Intelligence* 51 (December): 43–46.

———. 2007d. "An Introduction to the Intelligence Studies Literature," in Loch K. Johnson (ed.), *Strategic Intelligence: Understanding the Hidden Side of Government.* Westport, CT: Praeger: 1–20.

Johnson, Paul. 1997. "No Cloak and Dagger Required: Intelligence Support to U.N. Peacekeeping," *Intelligence and National Security* 12 (October): 102–112.

Johnson, William R. 1987. *Thwarting Enemies at Home and Abroad: How to Be a Counterintelligence Office.* Bethesda, MD: Stone Trail Press.

Kaiser, Frederick M. 1992. "Congress and the Intelligence Community: Taking the Road Less Traveled," in Roger H. Davidson (ed.), *The Postreform Congress.* New York: St. Martin's Press: 279–300.

Kam, Ephraim. 1988. *Surprise Attack.* Cambridge: Harvard University Press.

Kent, Sherman. 1949. *Strategic Intelligence for American World Policy.* Princeton: Princeton University Press.

Kerr, Richard, Thomas Wolfe, Rebecca Donegan, and Aris Pappas. 2008. "Intelligence Collection and Analysis on Iraq: Issues for the U.S. Intelligence Community," in James P. Pfiffner and Mark Phythian (eds.), *Intelligence and National Security Policymaking on Iraq: British and American Perspectives.* Manchester, UK: Manchester University Press: 151–161.

Knott, Stephen F. 1996. *Secret and Sanctioned: Covert Operations and the American Presidency.* New York: Oxford University Press.

Kramer, Mark. 2002. "Oversight of Russian's Intelligence and Security Agencies: The Need for and Prospects of Democratic Control," PONARS Policy Memo 281, <http://www.csis.org/ruseura/ponars/policymemos/pm_0281.pdf>.

Lowenthal, Mark M. 2005. *U.S. Intelligence: Evolution and Anatomy,* 3rd ed. Westport, CT: Praeger.

———. 2008. *Intelligence: From Secrets to Policy.* Washington, DC: CQ Press.

———. 2009. *Intelligence: From Secrets to Policy,* 4th ed. Washington, DC: CQ Press.

Malone, Thomas W. 2008. "What is Collective Intelligence and What will We Do About It?," in Mark Tovey (ed.), *Collective Intelligence: Creating a Prosperous World at Peace.* Oakton, VA: Earth Intelligence Network: 1–4.

Markle Foundation. 2002. *Protecting America's Freedom in the Information Age.* New York: Markle Foundation.

Masse, Todd. 2006. *Homeland Security Intelligence: Perceptions, Statutory Definitions, and Approaches.* CRS Report for Congress. Order Code RL33616.

Masse, Todd, Siobhan O'Neil, and John Rollins. 2007. *Fusion Centers: Issues and Options for Congress.* CRS Report for Congress. Order Code RL34070.

Masterman, Sir John. 1972. *Double Cross System of the War of 1939–45.* New Haven, CT: Yale University Press.

May, Ernest R. 1992. "Intelligence: Backing Into the Future," *Foreign Affairs* 71 (Summer): 63–72.

Medina, Carmen A. 2008. "The New Analysis," in Roger Z. George and James B. Bruce (eds.), *Analyzing Intelligence: Origins, Obstacles, and Innovations.* Washington, DC: Georgetown University Press: 238–248.

Millis, John. 1998. Speech, Central Intelligence Retiree's Association, Langley, Virginia.

National Intelligence Council. 2000. *Global Trends 2015: A Dialogue About the Future with Nongovernmental Experts.* Washington, DC: Central Intelligence Agency.

Naylor, Sean. 2003. "The Lessons of Anaconda," *New York Times* (March 2): A13.

9/11 Commission. 2004. *Report.* New York: Norton.

Odom, William. 2003. *Fixing Intelligence.* New Haven, CT: Yale University Press.

Omsted, Kathryn. 1996. *Challenging the Secret Government: The Post-Watergate Investigations of the CIA and FBI.* Chapel Hill: University of North Carolina Press.

———. 2002. *Red Spy Queen: A Biography of Elizabeth Bentley.* Chapel Hill: University of North Carolina Press.

Pelosi, Nancy (D, California). 2002. Remarks to Loch K. Johnson, Athens, Georgia (November 26).

Perrow, Charles. 2005. Organizational or Executive Failures? *Contemporary Sociology* 34(2): 99–107.

Pfiffner, James P., and Mark Phythian (eds.). 2008. *Intelligence and National Security Policymaking on Iraq.* Manchester, U.K.: Manchester University Press.

Powers, Thomas. 1979. *The Man Who Kept the Secrets: Richard Helms and the CIA.* New York: Knopf.

Prados, John. 1986. *Presidents' Secret Wars: CIA and Pentagon Covert Operations Since World War II.* New York: Dial.

Ransom, Harry Howe. 1970. *The Intelligence Establishment.* Cambridge, MA: Harvard University Press.

Rashid, A. 1999. "The Taliban: Exporting Extremism," *Foreign Affairs* 78: 22–35.

Richelson, Jeffrey. 1999. *The U.S. Intelligence Community,* 4th ed. Cambridge, MA: Ballinger.

Rockefeller Commission. 1975. *Report.* Washington, DC: Government Printing Office.

Schelling, Thomas C. 1962. "Preface" to Roberta Wohlstetter, *Pearl Harbor: Warning and Decision.* Stanford, CA: Stanford University Press.

Schwarz, Frederick A. O., Jr. 1987. "Recalling Major Lessons of the Church Committee," *New York Times* (July 20): A25.

Scoville, Herbert. 1976. "Is Espionage Necessary for Our Security?" *Foreign Affairs* 54 (April): 482–495.

Senate Select Committee on Secret Military Assistance to Iran and the Nicaraguan Opposition and House Select Committee to Investigate Covert Arms Transactions with Iran. 1987. *Hearings and Final Report.* Washington, DC: Government Printing Office.

Shulsky, Abram N., and Gary J. Schmitt. 1993. *Silent Warfare: Understanding the World of Intelligence,* 2nd rev. ed. Washington, DC: Brassey's.

Sims, Jennifer E., and Burton Gerber (eds.). 2005. *Transforming U.S. Intelligence.* Washington, DC: Georgetown University Press.

———. 2009. *Vaults, Mirrors, and Masks: Rediscovering U.S. Counterintelligence.* Washington, DC: Georgetown University Press.

Smist, Frank J., Jr. 1994. *Congress Oversees the United States Intelligence Community,* 2nd ed. Knoxville: University of Tennessee Press.

Snider, L. Britt. 1997. *Sharing Secrets With Lawmakers: Congress as a User of Intelligence.* Washington, DC: Central Intelligence Agency, Center for the Study of Intelligence.

Steele, Robert D. 1999. "Relevant Information and All Source Analysis: The Emerging Revolution," *American Intelligence Journal* 19: 23–30.

———. 2001. *On Intelligence: Spies and Secrecy in an Open World.* Washington, DC: OSS International Press.

———. 2002. *The New Craft of Intelligence: Personal, Public & Political—Citizen's Action Handbook for Fighting Terrorism, Genocide, Disease, Toxic Bombs & Corruption.* Washington, DC: OSS Press.

Theoharis, Athan G. 1978. *Spying on Americans: Political Surveillance From Hoover to the Huston Plan.* Philadelphia: Temple University Press.

———. (ed.). 2006. *The Central Intelligence Agency: Security Under Scrutiny.* Westport, CT: Greenwood Press.

Treverton, Gregory F. 1987. *Covert Action: The Limits of Intervention in the Postwar World.* New York: Basic Books.

———. 2001. *Reshaping National Intelligence for an Age of Information.* New York: Cambridge University Press.

Troy, Thomas F. 1991–92. "The 'Correct' Definition of Intelligence," *International Journal of Intelligence and Counterintelligence* 5 (Winter): 433–454.

Turner, Michael A. 2005. *Why Secret Intelligence Fails.* Washington, DC: Potomac Books.

Turner, Stansfield. 1985. *Secrecy and Democracy: The CIA in Transition.* Boston: Houghton Mifflin.

———. 2005. *Burn Before Reading.* New York: Hyperion.

Usowski, Peter S. 1988. "John McCone and the Cuban Missile Crisis: A Persistent Approach to the Intelligence-Policy Relationship," *International Journal of Intelligence and Counterintelligence* 2 (Winter): 547–576.

Waller, Michael J. 1994. *Secret Empire: The KGB in Russia Today.* Boulder, CO: Westview.

Weiner, Tim. 2007. *Legacy of Ashes: The History of the CIA.* New York: Doubleday.

Westerfield, H. Bradford. 1995. *Inside CIA's Private World: Declassified Articles From the Agency's Internal Journal, 1995–1992.* New Haven, CT: Yale University Press.

Wicker, Tom, et al. 1966. "CIA Operations: A Plot Scuttled." *New York Times,* April 25: A1.

Wirtz, James J. 1989. The Intelligence Paradigm. *Intelligence and National Security* 4(4): 829–837.

———. 1998. "Organizing for Crisis Intelligence: Lessons from the Cuban Missile Crisis," in James G. Blight and David A. Welch (eds.), *Intelligence and the Cuban Missile Crisis.* London: Frank Cass.

———. 1991. *Intelligence Failure in War: The American Military and the Tet Offensive.* Ithaca, NY: Cornell University Press.

———. 2008. Hiding in Plain Sight: Denial, Deception, and the Non-State Actor. *The SAIS Review of International Affairs* 28(1): 55–63.

Wise, David. 1976. *The American Police State: The Government Against the People.* New York: Random House.

Wohlstetter, Roberta. 1962. *Pearl Harbor: Warning and Decision.* Stanford: Stanford University Press.

Woolsey, R. James. 1993. Testimony, *Hearings,* U.S. Senate Select Committee on Intelligence, 103rd Cong., 2nd Sess.: March 6.

Zegart, Amy B. 2007. *Spying Blind: The CIA, the FBI, and the Origins of 9/11.* Princeton, NJ: Princeton University Press.

Zuehlke, Arthur A. 1980. In Roy S. Godson (ed.), *Intelligence Requirements for the 1980s: Counterintelligence.* Washington, DC: National Strategy Information Center.

NAME INDEX

SUBJECT INDEX